■ THE RESOURCE FOR THE INDEPENDENT TRAVELER

"The guides are aimed not only at young budget travelers but at the indepedent traveler; a sort of streetwise cookbook for traveling alone."

—*The New York Times*

"Unbeatable; good sight-seeing advice; up-to-date info on restaurants, hotels, and inns; a commitment to money-saving travel; and a wry style that brightens nearly every page."

—*The Washington Post*

"Lighthearted and sophisticated, informative and fun to read. [Let's Go] helps the novice traveler navigate like a knowledgeable old hand."

—*Atlanta Journal-Constitution*

"A world-wise traveling companion—always ready with friendly advice and helpful hints, all sprinkled with a bit of wit."

—*The Philadelphia Inquirer*

■ THE BEST TRAVEL BARGAINS IN YOUR PRICE RANGE

"All the dirt, dirt cheap."

—*People*

"Anything you need to know about budget traveling is detailed in this book."

—*The Chicago Sun-Times*

"Let's Go follows the creed that you don't have to toss your life's savings to the wind to travel—unless you want to."

—*The Salt Lake Tribune*

■ REAL ADVICE FOR REAL EXPERIENCES

"The writers seem to have experienced every rooster-packed bus and lunar-surfaced mattress about which they write."

—*The New York Times*

"A guide should tell you what to expect from a destination. Here Let's Go shines."

—*The Chicago Tribune*

"[Let's Go's] devoted updaters really walk the walk (and thumb the ride, and trek the trail). Learn how to fish, haggle, find work—anywhere."

—*Food & Wine*

LET'S GO PUBLICATIONS

TRAVEL GUIDES

Alaska 1st edition **NEW TITLE**
Australia 2004
Austria & Switzerland 2004
Brazil 1st edition **NEW TITLE**
Britain & Ireland 2004
California 2004
Central America 8th edition
Chile 1st edition
China 4th edition
Costa Rica 1st edition
Eastern Europe 2004
Egypt 2nd edition
Europe 2004
France 2004
Germany 2004
Greece 2004
Hawaii 2004
India & Nepal 8th edition
Ireland 2004
Israel 4th edition
Italy 2004
Japan 1st edition **NEW TITLE**
Mexico 20th edition
Middle East 4th edition
New Zealand 6th edition
Pacific Northwest 1st edition **NEW TITLE**
Peru, Ecuador & Bolivia 3rd edition
Puerto Rico 1st edition **NEW TITLE**
South Africa 5th edition
Southeast Asia 8th edition
Southwest USA 3rd edition
Spain & Portugal 2004
Thailand 1st edition
Turkey 5th edition
USA 2004
Western Europe 2004

CITY GUIDES

Amsterdam 3rd edition
Barcelona 3rd edition
Boston 4th edition
London 2004
New York City 2004
Paris 2004
Rome 12th edition
San Francisco 4th edition
Washington, D.C. 13th edition

MAP GUIDES

Amsterdam
Berlin
Boston
Chicago
Dublin
Florence
Hong Kong
London
Los Angeles
Madrid
New Orleans
New York City
Paris
Prague
Rome
San Francisco
Seattle
Sydney
Venice
Washington, D.C.

COMING SOON:

Road Trip USA

GREECE 2004

Joel August Steinhaus Editor
Christina Zaroulis Associate Editor

Research-Writers
Deirdre Foley-Mendelssohn
Alexa H. Hirschfeld
Alex Ioannidis
Allison Melia
Stuart Robinson
Previn Warren

Serena Tan Map Editor
Emma Nothmann Managing Editor

St. Martin's Press New York

HELPING LET'S GO If you want to share your discoveries, suggestions, or corrections, please drop us a line. We read every piece of correspondence, whether a postcard, a 10-page email, or a coconut. **Address mail to:**

Let's Go: Greece
67 Mount Auburn Street
Cambridge, MA 02138
USA

Visit Let's Go at **http://www.letsgo.com,** or send email to:

feedback@letsgo.com
Subject: "Let's Go: Greece"

In addition to the invaluable travel advice our readers share with us, many are kind enough to offer their services as researchers or editors. Unfortunately, our charter enables us to employ only currently enrolled Harvard students.

Distributed outside the USA and Canada by Macmillan.

ISBN: 0-312-31987-8

First edition
10 9 8 7 6 5 4 3 2 1

Let's Go: Greece is written by Let's Go Publications, 67 Mount Auburn Street, Cambridge, MA 02138, USA.

CONTENTS

CRETE **564**

APPENDIX **618**

MAPS

HOW TO USE THIS BOOK

COVERAGE LAYOUT. Your travels begin in Athens, capital, transportation hub, and host of the 2004 Olympic Games. From there coverage circles the Peloponnese, moves north through the mainland, and then heads to the islands beginning with those closest to Athens and spiraling outward, concluding with Crete.

TRANSPORTATION INFORMATION. For making connections between destinations, most information is given under the departure city. Parentheticals usually provide the trip duration followed by departure time and frequency, then the price.

NON-COVERAGE SECTIONS. Before departing flip to **Discover Greece** (the first chapter) to find regional highlights and Suggested Itineraries (p. 4) to help plan your trip. The **Essentials** (p. 33) section contains all necessary practical and logistical information. Get psyched by reading up on Greece's history and culture in **Life and Times** (p. 8). Along your way, the **Appendix** (p. 618) should come quite handy, lending a laundry list of Greek language, pronunciation, and terminology help as well as other quick reference materials. If you're thinking about making a more extended sojourn and want other options, look in **Alternatives to Tourism** (p. 68). For patrons of the Olympic Games, find information in the special and exclusive **2004 Summer Olympic Games** (p. 128) section.

SCHOLARLY ARTICLES. Find our five essays written by various contributors with distinct connections to the country. President of the ATHENS 2004 Organizing Committee, Gianna Angelopoulos-Daskalaki, gives her insights about the upcoming Summer Games. They appear at the end of the following chapters: **Life and Times, Athens, Peloponnese, Central Greece,** and **Northern Greece.**

PRICE RANGES AND RANKINGS. Our researchers list establishments in order of value and quality from best to worst. Our absolute favorites are denoted by the Let's Go thumbs-up (☒). Since the best value does not always mean the cheapest price, we have incorporated a system of price ranges in the guide. The table below lists how prices fall within each bracket.

GREECE	❶	❷	❸	❹	❺
ACCOMM.	under €10	€10-20	€20-35	€35-70	above €70
FOOD	under €3	€3-8	€8-15	€15-25	above €25

PHONE CODES AND TELEPHONE NUMBERS. Phone numbers in text are preceded by the ☎ icon. Since Greek telephone numbers now require the local code regardless of the region you're calling from, all local codes are incorporated into the telephone numbers in the text.

LANGUAGE AND OTHER QUIRKS. Greek characters are given for establishments that do not have a printed English transliteration. Transliterations give syllabic pronunciation with the stressed syllable all capitalized. For a guide to the Greek alphabet and pronunciation, consult the **Appendix** (p. 618).

A NOTE TO OUR READERS The information for this book was gathered by *Let's Go* researchers from May through August of 2003. Each listing is based on one researcher's opinion, formed during his or her visit at a particular time. Those traveling at other times may have different experiences since prices, dates, hours, and conditions are always subject to change. You are urged to check the facts presented in this book beforehand to avoid inconvenience and surprises.

RESEARCHER-WRITERS

Deirdre Foley-Mendelssohn *Crete and the Cyclades*

After researching for *Let's Go: Germany*, Deirdre set sail for the radiant southern Aegean. With a smile on her face and a song in her heart, Deirdre baked under Apollo's orb with more grace than the lapping shore and more optimism than the 2004 Olympic Committee. A student of language, Deirdre sent us to Crete on the wings of her words. Our beauty from Santa Cruz warded off overtures from toed and hooved animals alike to return sparkling prose and über-reliable info.

Alexa H. Hirschfeld *Athens and the Cyclades*

Alexa set up camp in Athens's Pangrati to capture the big city and to check out Olympic venues or, rather, construction. Although this New Yorker's maternal half hails from Northeast Aegean Chios, she has bumped around Cycladic Paros every summer since she was a *mikroula*. This Classics scholar has a number of ancient and modern languages under her belt—including Modern Greek. Weaving her way through the Knossos-like labyrinth that is Athens, she pieced together a cohesive treasure map to the city.

Alex Ioannidis *Central and Northern Greece*

In a perpetual state of hurry, Alex blazed through the mainland, criss-crossing the landscape to the more remote reaches of the country. Scientist by day, this Greek-speaking Baltimore native hiked his way into the true heart of the country. With an incisive eye, Alex sliced open the living veneer of Greek society and culture, giving us a thorough historical context for his travels. Neither inhibitions nor border guards could contain him, as he ventured into Albania and Turkey to complete his travel experience.

Allison Melia *Peloponnese, Saronic Gulf, Central Greece, the Sporades and Evia, and the Cyclades*

After editing *Let's Go: Turkey* and *Let's Go: Hawaii*, Allison yearned to see how the other half lives. With a natural knack for research and a travel-savvy wit, she enjoyed a yin-yang route of highs and lows, beaches and mountains, *fortes* and *pianos*, finding herself enigmatically caught in a power-play of lust for Greece. She found not only the hidden secrets but also the most popular places, giving travelers as dichotomous an experience as she had.

Stuart Robinson *Peloponnese and Ionian Islands*

With the Pollux to his Castor researching in the US, Stu departed on an aerial-style Odyssey of Herculaen proportions. After cultivating his masculine side, this hero confronted a fierce canine beast and resisted the wiles of the Sirens at Corfu's Pink Palace along the way. Though he found no cyclops, our well-traveled philosopher from L.A. proved the archetypal Researcher-Writer. When Stu was finished with her, Greece breathed a bittersweet sigh of relief. If Stu were an Olympic event, he would be the long jump.

Previn Warren *The Dodecanese and Northeast Aegean Islands*

Armed with board shorts, sunglasses, and often a pen, towering Previn, a recently published author, hit his island route to find beaches and the occasional ferry connection. Interested by the social study that is island culture and its tempermental ATMs, our rolling stone pitched and yawned through the waters beside the Turkish coast. A veritable Trojan Horse, hiding his cover and a few euros in his pocket, Previn left Greece reeling.

CONTRIBUTING WRITERS

Gianna Angelopoulos-Daskalaki is the president of the ATHENS 2004 Organizing Committee. She was appointed to her current position in 2000.

Thomas FitzGerald, Th.D., is an Orthodox priest and Professor of Church History and Historical Theology at Holy Cross Greek Orthodox School of Theology in Brookline, MA. Among his published works are *The Orthodox Church* and *Happy in The Lord: The Beatitudes for Everyday. The Ecumenical Movement* is due for 2004 publication.

Eleni N. Gage, a former Researcher-Writer and Editor of *Let's Go: Greece and Turkey 1995*, is the author of *North of Ithaka*, a travel memoir about Northern Greece to be published by the Free Press in Spring 2004.

Gregory A. Maniatis is the founder of *Odyssey Magazine*, the leading international magazine about Greece and Greeks around the world. He has also contributed to *New York Magazine*, the *Independent*, the *Washington Monthly*, Time-Life Books, and other publications.

Nicholas Papandreou is a writer living in Greece. He is the author of two novels, *A Crowded Heart* (Picador) and *Kleptomnemon: The Thief of Memories.* He is currently an advisor to the Ministry of the Aegean, where a major effort is underway to preserve the architectural integrity of the area. His articles and columns appear in weekly and monthly newspapers and magazines throughout Greece.

ACKNOWLEDGMENTS

Team GCE thanks our rockin' RWs who made it so easy, Serena for mappin', prod for making us look good, Rebecca for putting us in the big show, and the Biggie pod for great times. A special thank you to Emma, who had the only other pair of eyes to read this cover-to-cover as many times as our own did. We have been unbelievably lucky to have you.

Joel lifts his glass to Z, for making me feel so lucky, for trusting me, and for giving herself fully and completely to this book; and to Emma for giving me the chance, investing herself, and supporting me no matter what. Shout outs to: Rob in the 770, Bubber, Bone, Lionel, Bob Cobb, Thomas, my boys in Clav 10, roomies at 7 stories of love, HGC, Jesse for letting me play bass on one of his songs, Hard GI, Scrobins, Tom for runs, 18 Ellery, CK and TK for woking bok choy, B-Rab, Anne and Tim, Jasper, Winthrop F, awesome blossoms, the Royals, High Heat, and Stu for a knock-out job. To the memory of Auntie Tillie. Love to: G&P, B&B, Dan, Mike (not on the rug, man), and Michelle, of 419 fame, who saw me through it all. Finally, enternal gratitude to Mom and Dad for everything to which ink can do no justice.

Christina bows down to Snoop, a sensational brain, editor, icon, partner in crime, and—by far most importantly—buddy. Then there's fair Emma, who reinvented the role of ME, thrice editing every piece of our little baby. I cannot thank her enough. Much love to: My fam (pups and cats included), the epicenter of my life; Katya, my in-Cambridge gal-pal; Jen, my short-term but much-appreciated roommate; tenants of Caldwell Alley for all the good times; Poppy, for being remarkable at 90+ and giving me an in into the Greek world. Thank you: Mrs. Angelopoulos-Daskalaki, Dr. FitzGerald, and (for sure) CYA. An enthusiastic *yeia mas* to the Hellenic Republic, who has captivated me for years, served as my home for months, and kept me on my toes for a summer.

Serena sends thanks out to Jarek for being with me, across the Atlantic with its treacherous sea monsters.

Editor
Joel August Steinhaus
Associate Editor
Christina Zaroulis
Managing Editor
Emma Nothmann
Map Editor
Serena Tan
Typesetter
Thomas Bechtold

Publishing Director
Julie A. Stephens
Editor-in-Chief
Jeffrey Dubner
Production Manager
Dusty Lewis
Cartography Manager
Nathaniel Brooks
Design Manager
Caleb Beyers
Editorial Managers
Lauren Bonner, Ariel Fox,
Matthew K. Hudson, Emma Nothmann,
Joanna Shawn Brigid O'Leary,
Sarah Robinson
Financial Manager
Suzanne Siu
Marketing & Publicity Managers
Megan Brumagim, Nitin Shah
Personnel Manager
Jesse Reid Andrews
Researcher Manager
Jennifer O'Brien
Web Manager
Jesse Tov
Web Content Director
Abigail Burger
Production Associates
Thomas Bechtold, Jeffrey Hoffman Yip
IT Directors
Travis Good, E. Peyton Sherwood
Financial Assistant
R. Kirkie Maswoswe
Associate Web Manager
Robert Dubbin
Office Coordinators
Abigail Burger, Angelina L. Fryer,
Liz Glynn

Director of Advertising Sales
Daniel Ramsey
Senior Advertising Associates
Sara Barnett, Daniella Boston
Advertising Artwork Editor
Julia Davidson , Sandy Liu

President
Abhishek Gupta
General Manager
Robert B. Rombauer
Assistant General Manager
Anne E. Chisholm

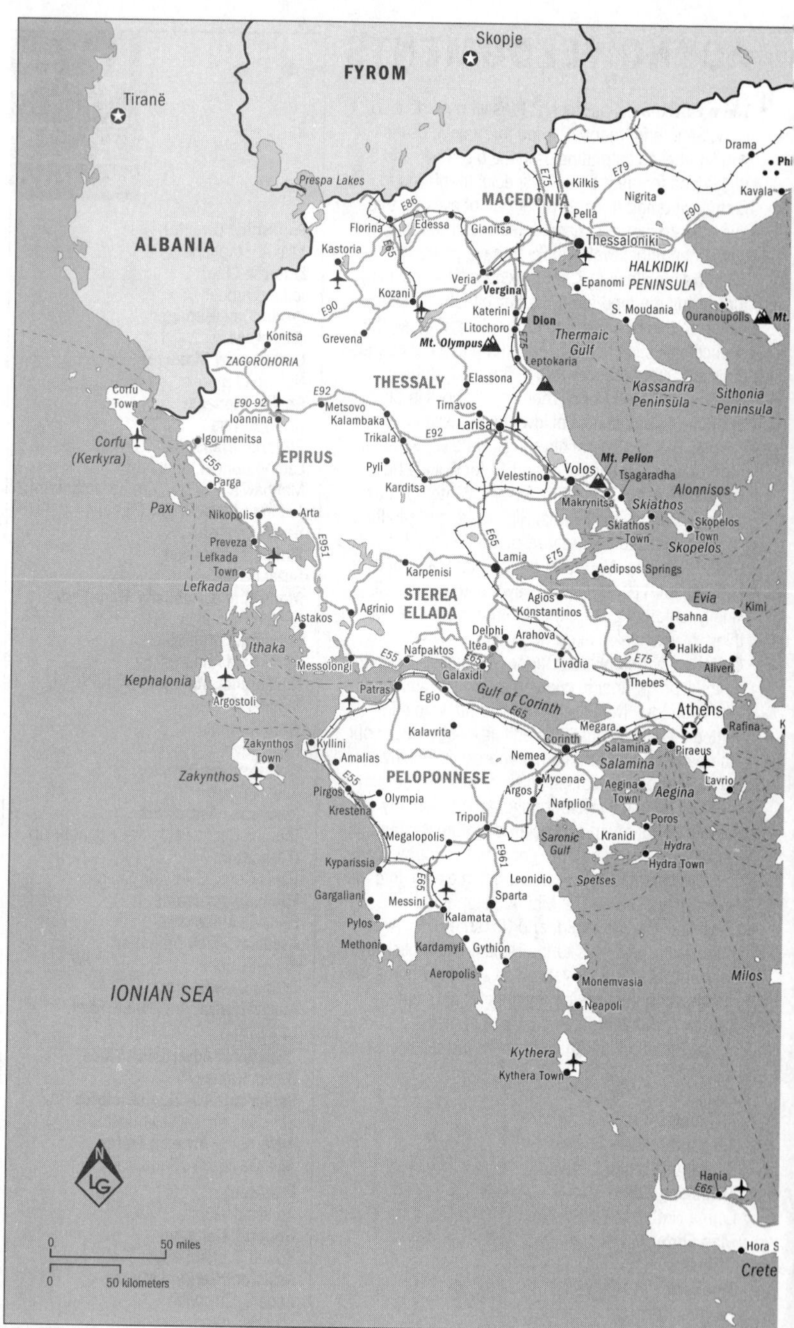

Skopje
FYROM
Tiranë
ALBANIA
Prespa Lakes
MACEDONIA
Drama
Kilkis
Nigrita
Kavala
Pella
Florina
Edessa
Gianitsa
Thessaloniki
Kastoria
HALKIDIKI
PENINSULA
Veria
Vergina
Epanomi
Kozani
Katerini
Dion
S. Moudania
Ouranoupolis
Litochoro
Thermaic
Gulf
Konitsa
Grevena
Mt. Olympus
ZAGOROHORIA
Leptokaria
THESSALY
Elassona
Kassandra
Peninsula
Sithonia
Peninsula
Corfu
Town
Metsovo
Tirnavos
Ioannina
Kalambaka
Larisa
Corfu
(Kerkyra)
Igoumenitsa
Trikala
EPIRUS
Mt. Pelion
Pyli
Velestino
Volos
Tsagaradha
Parga
Karditsa
Makrynitsa
Alonnisos
Skiathos
Paxi
Nikopolis
Arta
Skiathos
Town
Skopelos
Town
Skopelos
Preveza
Lefkada
Town
Lamia
Karpenisi
Aedipsos Springs
Lefkada
STEREA
ELLADA
Agios
Konstantinos
Evia
Kimi
Agrinio
Astakos
Psahna
Delphi
Arahova
Itea
Halkida
Ithaka
Nafpaktos
Livadia
Aliveri
Messolongi
Galaxidi
Thebes
Kephalonia
Patras
Egio
Gulf of Corinth
Athens
Argostoli
Rafina
Kalavrita
Megara
Zakynthos
Town
Kyllini
Corinth
Salamina
Piraeus
Nemea
Salamina
Amalias
Zakynthos
PELOPONNESE
Mycenae
Lavrio
Aegina
Town
Aegina
Pirgos
Olympia
Argos
Nafplion
Krestena
Tripoli
Poros
Saronic
Gulf
Kranidi
Megalopolis
Hydra
Hydra Town
Kyparissia
Leonidio
Spetses
Gargaliani
Messini
Sparta
Kalamata
Pylos
Methoni
Kardamyli
Gythion
Aeropolis
Monemvasia
Milos
IONIAN SEA
Neapoli
Kythera
Kythera Town
Hania
Hora S
Crete
N
LG
0
50 miles
0
50 kilometers

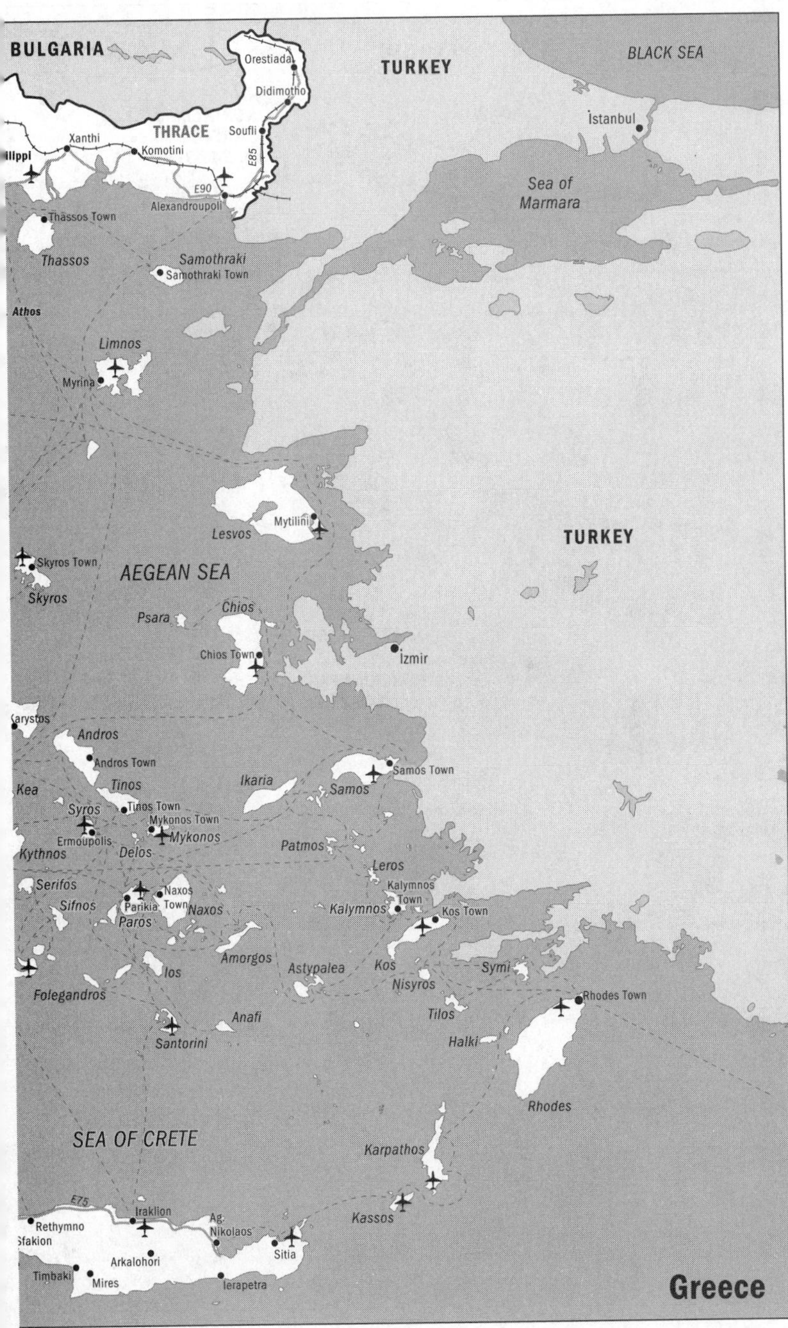
BULGARIA
TURKEY
BLACK SEA
Orestiada
Didimotho
THRACE
Soufli
İstanbul
Xanthi
Komotini
E85
E90
Alexandroupoli
Sea of Marmara
Thassos Town
Thassos
Samothraki
Samothraki Town
Athos
Limnos
Myrina
Mytilini
Lesvos
TURKEY
Skyros Town
AEGEAN SEA
Skyros
Chios
Psara
Chios Town
İzmir
Karystos
Andros
Andros Town
Samos Town
Ikaria
Samos
Kea
Tinos
Syros
Tinos Town
Mykonos Town
Ermoupolis
Mykonos
Kythnos
Delos
Patmos
Leros
Serifos
Kalymnos Town
Naxos Town
Sifnos
Parikia
Naxos
Kalymnos
Kos Town
Paros
Amorgos
Astypalea
Kos
Symi
Ios
Nisyros
Folegandros
Rhodes Town
Anafi
Tilos
Santorini
Halki
Rhodes
SEA OF CRETE
Karpathos
E75
Iraklion
Kassos
Rethymno
Ag. Nikolaos
Sfakion
Sitia
Arkalohori
Timbaki
Mires
Ierapetra
Greece

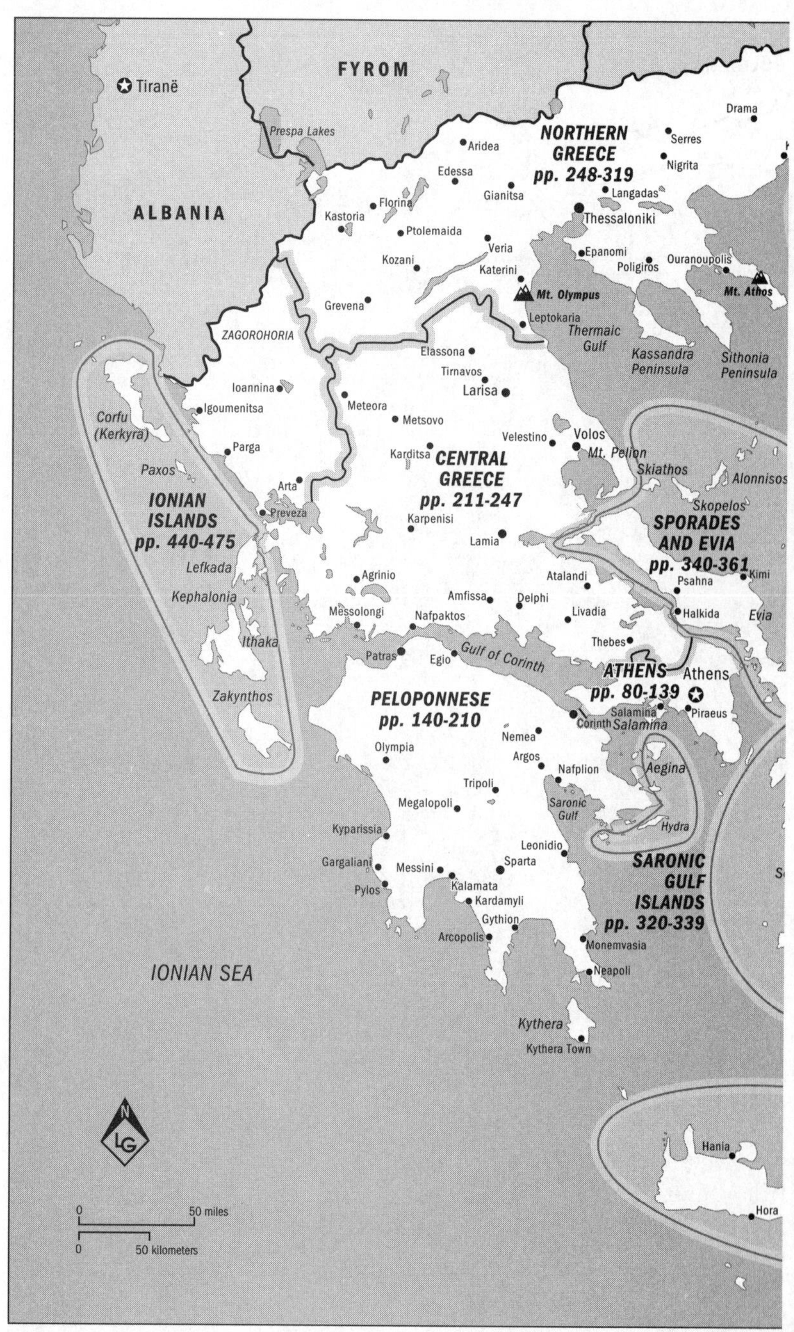
FYROM
Tiranë
ALBANIA
Prespa Lakes
NORTHERN GREECE pp. 248-319
Drama
Serres
Nigrita
Aridea
Edessa
Gianitsa
Langadas
Florina
Kastoria
Thessaloniki
Ptolemaida
Veria
Epanomi
Kozani
Katerini
Poligiros
Ouranoupolis
Mt. Olympus
Mt. Athos
Grevena
Leptokaria
Thermaic Gulf
Kassandra Peninsula
Sithonia Peninsula
ZAGOROHORIA
Elassona
Tirnavos
Larisa
Ioannina
Igoumenitsa
Meteora
Metsovo
Corfu (Kerkyra)
Velestino
Volos
Mt. Pelion
Parga
Karditsa
CENTRAL GREECE pp. 211-247
Paxos
Skiathos
Alonnisos
Arta
IONIAN ISLANDS pp. 440-475
Preveza
Skopelos
SPORADES AND EVIA pp. 340-361
Karpenisi
Lamia
Lefkada
Agrinio
Atalandi
Kimi
Psahna
Kephalonia
Amfissa
Delphi
Messolongi
Nafpaktos
Livadia
Halkida
Evia
Ithaka
Thebes
Patras
Egio
Gulf of Corinth
ATHENS pp. 80-139
Athens
Zakynthos
PELOPONNESE pp. 140-210
Salamina
Piraeus
Corinth
Salamina
Nemea
Olympia
Argos
Nafplion
Aegina
Tripoli
Megalopoli
Saronic Gulf
Hydra
Kyparissia
Leonidio
Gargaliani
Messini
Sparta
SARONIC GULF ISLANDS pp. 320-339
Pylos
Kalamata
Kardamyli
Gythion
Arcopolis
Monemvasia
IONIAN SEA
Neapoli
Kythera
Kythera Town
N
LG
Hania
0
50 miles
0
50 kilometers
Hora

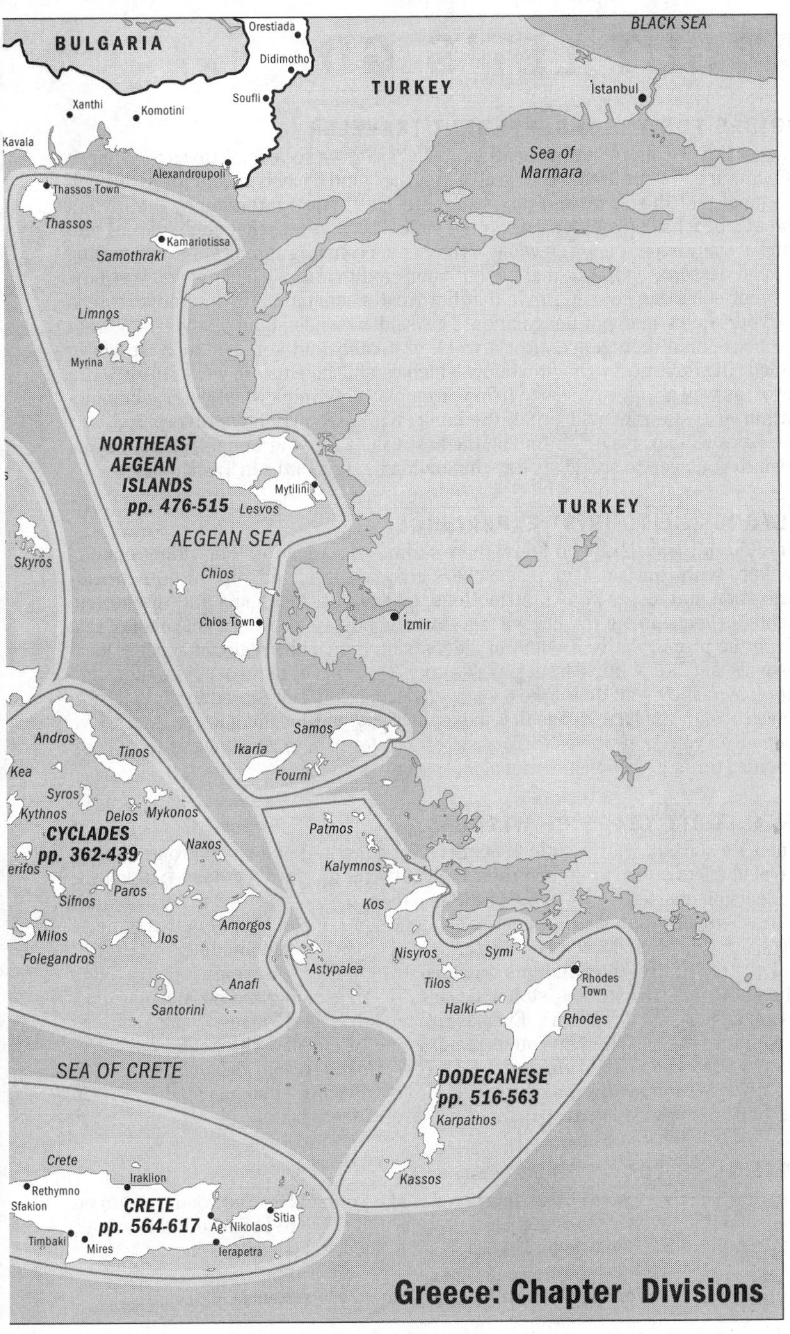
BULGARIA
TURKEY
BLACK SEA
Orestiada
Didimotho
Soufli
Istanbul
Xanthi
Komotini
Kavala
Alexandroupoli
Sea of Marmara
Thassos Town
Thassos
Kamariotissa
Samothraki
Limnos
Myrina
NORTHEAST AEGEAN ISLANDS pp. 476-515
Mytilini
Lesvos
AEGEAN SEA
TURKEY
Skyros
Chios
Chios Town
İzmir
Samos
Andros
Tinos
Ikaria
Kea
Fourni
Syros
Kythnos
Delos
Mykonos
CYCLADES pp. 362-439
Naxos
Patmos
Kalymnos
Paros
Sifnos
Kos
Amorgos
Milos
Ios
Folegandros
Nisyros
Symi
Astypalea
Tilos
Rhodes Town
Anafi
Halki
Rhodes
Santorini
SEA OF CRETE
DODECANESE pp. 516-563
Karpathos
Crete
Iraklion
Kassos
Rethymno
Sfakion
CRETE pp. 564-617
Sitia
Ag. Nikolaos
Timbaki
Mires
Ierapetra
Greece: Chapter Divisions

ABOUT LET'S GO

GUIDES FOR THE INDEPENDENT TRAVELER

Budget travel is more than a vacation. At *Let's Go,* we see every trip as the chance of a lifetime. If your dream is to grab a knapsack and a machete and forge through the jungles of Brazil, we can take you there. Or, if you'd rather enjoy the Riviera sun at a beachside cafe, we'll set you a table. If you know what you're doing, you can have any experience you want—whether it's camping among lions or sampling Tuscan desserts—without maxing out your credit card. We'll show you just how far your coins can go, and prove that the greatest limitation on your adventure is not your wallet, but your imagination. That said, we understand that you may want the occasional indulgence after a week of hostels and kebab stands, so we've added "Big Splurges" to let you know which establishments are worth those extra euros, as well as price ranges to help you quickly determine whether an accommodation or restaurant will break the bank. While we may have diversified, our emphasis will always be on finding the best values for your budget, giving you all the info you need to spend six days in London or six months in Tasmania.

BEYOND THE TOURIST EXPERIENCE

We write for travelers who know there's more to a vacation than riding double-deckers with tourists. Our researchers give you the heads-up on both world-renowned and lesser-known attractions, on the best local eats and the hottest nightclub beats. In our travels, we talk to everybody; we provide a snapshot of real life in the places you visit with our sidebars on topics like regional cuisine, local festivals, and hot political issues. We've opened our pages to respected writers and scholars to show you their take on a given destination, and turned to lifelong residents to learn the little things that make their city worth calling home. And we've even given you Alternatives to Tourism—ideas for how to give back to local communities through responsible travel and volunteering.

OVER FORTY YEARS OF WISDOM

When we started, way back in 1960, Let's Go consisted of a small group of well-traveled friends who compiled their budget travel tips into a 20-page packet for students on charter flights to Europe. Since then, we've expanded to suit all kinds of travelers, now publishing guides to six continents, including our newest guides: *Let's Go: Japan* and *Let's Go: Brazil.* Our guides are still annually researched and written entirely by students on shoe-string budgets, adventurous travelers who know that train strikes, stolen luggage, food poisoning, and marriage proposals are all part of a day's work. Even as you read this, work on next year's editions is well underway. Whether you're reading one of our new titles, like *Let's Go: Puerto Rico* or *Let's Go Adventure Guide: Alaska,* or our original best-seller, *Let's Go: Europe,* you'll find the same spirit of adventure that has made *Let's Go* the guide of choice for travelers the world over since 1960.

GETTING IN TOUCH

The best discoveries are often those you make yourself; on the road, when you find something worth sharing, please drop us a line. We're Let's Go Publications, 67 Mt. Auburn St., Cambridge, MA 02138, USA (feedback@letsgo.com).

For more info, visit our website: www.letsgo.com.

DISCOVER GREECE

A land where sacred monasteries are mountainside fixtures, 3hr. sea-side siestas are standard issue, and circle dancing and drinking until daybreak is a summer rite: Greece's treasures are impossibly varied. Renaissance men long before their time, the ancient Greeks sprung to prominence with their philosophical, literary, artistic, and athletic mastery. Millennia later, schoolkids still dream of Hercules and the Medusa; when those kids grow up, they hanker after Greece's island beaches, free-flowing booze, and the gorgeous natural landscape, which was once the playground of a pantheon of gods. The all-encompassing Greek lifestyle is a frustrating and delicious mix of high speed and sun-inspired lounging, as old men hold lively debates in town plateias, young kids zoom on mopeds around the clock, and unpredictable schedules force a go-with-the-flow take on life.

FACTS AND FIGURES

OFFICIAL NAME Hellenic Republic

POPULATION 10,623,835

CAPITAL Athens

LENGTH OF COASTLINE PER GREEK CITIZEN 1.3m

TOTAL AREA OF GREEK BEACHES 30,000 sq. km

DRINK OF CHOICE Ouzo

PERCENTAGE OF ISLANDS UNINHABITED 88%

RATIO OF FOREIGNERS TO LOCALS 9 tourists to every 10 Greeks

NUMBER OF CALORIES IN THE AVERAGE SOUVLAKI 528

WHEN TO GO

June through August is **high season** in Greece. Bar-studded beaches set the scene for revelry and Dionysian indulgence, as the 100° sun blazes over ancient cities and modern-day sun-worshippers alike. Hotels, domatia, and sights are, like the nightlife, in full swing. If the crowds or frantic pace of summer travel grate on you, consider visiting during May, early June, or September, when gorgeous weather smiles on thinner crowds. Avid hikers can take advantage of the mellower weather to traverse the unsullied expanses of Northern and Central Greece. In ski areas, winter brings another high season: you can hit the slopes at Mt. Parnassos (p. 213), Mt. Pelion (p. 234), or Metsovo (p. 263). The **low season** generally brings cheaper lodgings and food prices, but many sights and accommodations have shorter hours or close altogether. At this time of year, Greece hibernates, resting from summertime farming, fishing, and tourism. Ferries, buses, and trains run considerably less frequently, and life is quieter. For a temperature chart, see **Climate,** p. 618. For a list of Greek festivals, see **Festivals,** p. 30.

THINGS TO DO

Mountain chains, bougainvillea-speckled islands, silver-green olive groves, and the stark contrast of ochre land against the azure Aegean comprise the Greek landscape, the refuge of mythological beasts. This varied land of isolated villages, jas-

TOP TEN LIST

TOP TEN NATURAL WONDERS OF GREECE

hough Greeks have done all sorts of ool things—making pretty spiffy buildings even in ancient times—Greece itself has a lot to offer. *Let's Go* lists some highlights below.

. Balos (p. 572) on Crete offers **beaches** of utter seclusion while he volcanic black sands of Santorini (p. 414) are truly distinct.

. Watch out for Nisyros's active **volcano** (p. 560); it might loose its cool.

. Proud Lesvos flaunts one of the world's two **petrified forests** (p. 93).

. The blue caves (p. 469) of Zakynthos and the Pirgos Dirou (p. 99) of Mani offer distincitve fun with spelunking.

. Greece has the right to brag about its **gorges**—Samaria (p. 573) is Europe's longest and Vikos (p. 267) Europe's steepest.

. Nothing's better than a hot tub—except for **thermal baths,** like hose at Thermoplyae and Loutraki (p. 146).

. Greece has not one but two valleys overwhelmed with **butterflies**—omn Rhodes (p. 516) and Paros (p. 394).

. Chios's majestic **trees** (p. 487) aren't just evergreen eye-candy, hey support the island economy.

. The **sea turtles** of Zakynthos (p. 469) and Crete (p. 564) might be endangered, but they're really cute and magnificent to observe (from a distance).

0. While ascetics ponder God at he monasteries built into the rock **mountains** of Meteora (p. 244), Mt. Olympus (p. 289) actually accommodates gods—the hellinisic kind.

mine-scented islands, and majestic ruins satisfies even the pickiest visitor with its infinite diversions. Don't be afraid to plot out your own route: the famous Greek hospitality will make you feel welcome wherever you go. For more on regional bests, check out the **Highlights of the Region** boxes that begin each chapter.

THE ROAD TO RUIN(S)

As the birthplace of drama, democracy, and western philosophy, Greece's long history has left a wealth of sites in its impressive wake. The mother of all ruins, the **Acropolis** (p. 107), still presides over modern Athens. The gigantic, perfectly proportioned columns of the **Parthenon,** combined with the sun's beating rays and the brilliant gleam of white marble, conjures up the same awe inspired in millennia of worshippers and pilgrims. A voyage through the **Peloponnese** will transport you back to the era of nymphs, satyrs, and gods in disguise. Take a lap around the well-preserved stadium on the way to the original Olympic fields at **Ancient Olympia** (p. 175), peer into Agamemnon's tomb at **Mycenae** (p. 148), or experience catharsis after watching the performance of an ancient tragedy in the magnificent theater at **Epidavros** (p. 159). Byzantine times stand still at the extensive city-site of **Mystras** (p. 198), the former locus of Constantinople's rule in the Peloponnese. On the mainland, get to "know thyself" at the ancient **Oracle of Delphi** (p. 217). Chase after the floating island of **Delos,** birthplace of Apollo and Artemis, for a peek at the Temple of Apollo and an island-wide archaeological site (p. 376). More archaeological sites include: Heinrich Schliemann's reconstruction of the Minoan palace at **Knossos** (p. 591); an untarnished Minoan site at **Phaistos** (p. 597); Santorini's **Akrotiri,** a city frozen in time by a volcanic eruption (p. 420); one-time cult capital **Paleopolis** on Samothraki (p. 508); and the dual ruins of **Pella** and **Vergina** in Northern Greece, frequented by Philip II and his son Alexander the Great (p. 285). From Rhodes, you can reach the remnants of three of the seven wonders of the ancient world by daytrip. The **Colossus of Rhodes** leaves no trace today, though you can contemplate what its giant leg span must have been (p. 516).

ISLANDS IN THE SUN

In Greece's summertime schedule, beach-side days melt through spectacular sunsets into starry, disco-filled nights, in a continuum of hedonistic delight. Roll out of bed and onto the beach around noon; nap in the late afternoon after strenuous sunbathing; head for a harborside dinner at 11pm; throw back after-dinner drinks, catch a movie, or hit the clubs until 5am, all under the stars; watch the sun rise over the ocean; and hit the hay before another sun-drenched day. It's nearly impossible to resist the allure of Greek sun and sea. The islands have long been a sun-worshipper's paradise, from Apollo's followers to disciples of Coppertone. As soon as you sail from Athens to the **Saronic Gulf Islands** (p. 320), the roasting Greek sun will bronze your (entire) body and release your inhibitions. A favorite of international vacationers, **Skiathos** in the Sporades harbors the piney Biotrope of Koukounaries beach and magical Lalaria (p. 340). In the Aegean Sea, **Santorini's** black-sand beaches soak up the sun's hot rays and stay warm long after the stunning sunsets over the Sea of Crete (p. 414) have faded. Swim below sea caves once ransacked by pirates on the coast of **Skyros** (p. 352) or bask on the Lesvian shore, where beaches stretch out for miles from Sappho's home of **Skala Eressou** (p. 502). Stumble out of all those superfluous clothes at **Mykonos's** wild, nude Super Paradise beach (p. 371). If your eyes get tired of all those bare backsides, seek solace on a secluded strip of sand. The much-beloved haunt of booze-loving backpackers, **Corfu** is ringed by fabulous beaches on all sides, in addition to hosting that legendary party haven, the Pink Palace (p. 440). Snorkel, water-ski, or just loaf in the sun on **Ios** (p. 407) and **Naxos** (p. 382). Perfect your tan around **Paleohora** in Crete (p. 575) or at castle-crowned Haraki beach on **Rhodes** (p. 516).

TAKE A HIKE

LET'S GO PICKS

WILDEST LIFE: Cower before the predatory **raptors** of Dadia National Reserve (p. 318). Pad quietly through a **Valley of the Butterflies** on either Paros (p. 394) or Rhodes (p. 529). Tread softly on the beach homes of endangered **sea turtles** on Zakynthos (p. 469) or Crete (p. 564).

BEST BEACHES: The famous **black and red sand beaches** of Santorini (p. 414) satisfy those bored with golden pebbles. Brave the winding cliffside road to **Balos** (p. 572) and uncover a Cretan paradise.

BEST CASTLES: Check out the famous Phaistos disc and sit in the throne room of the **Palace of Phaistos** on Crete (p. 597). Get medieval with the **Knights of St. John** in their castle on Kos (p. 530).

MOST SPIRITUAL EXPERIENCE: Seek self-reflection on **Mt. Athos** (p. 303). Embrace your carnal instincts at the **Pink Palace,** Corfu (p. 451).

WILDEST PARTIES: Visit **Pierro's,** the first gay bar in Greece, on wild Mykonos (p. 371). Welcome to **The Jungle,** one of many places to get drunk on Ios (p. 407).

MOST GUT-WRENCHING RIDES: Hold on tight if you take the ride from tiny Diakofto to tinier **Kalavrita** (p. 168) on the rattling and rolling rack-railway. Imagine the fear in the eyes of those who were hauled up via rope as you take the easy way up (climbing the stairs) to the monasteries of **Meteora** (p. 244).

BEST PLACE TO CATCH FIREFLIES: The luminescent critters light up the forests of **Monodendri** (p. 266).

BEST PLACES TO FLEX: Take a lap around the **stadium** at Ancient Olympia (p. 175), and imagine the laurel wreath on your head. Or check out the modern **Olympic Games** in Athens (p. 128).

BEST PLACES TO HIDE: Not even your father will find you in the **Kamares Cave** (p. 595) where Rhea hid Zeus from Chronos. Watch out for stalactites in the **Pirgos Dirou Caves** of Mani (p. 199). The **blue caves** (p. 469) of Zakynthos have an aptly named deep glow. The tiny **coves of Symi** (p. 554) can shield you from your problems beach-style.

Tear yourself away from the fun in the sun to find an equally invigorating wilderness experience. Bust out your walking stick or rev up your engines. Hiking or motorbiking—or a combination of the two—lets you cruise between rural villages independent of constantly changing bus schedules. On foot, you'll cross through foothills draped with olive groves, passing mountain goats and wildflowers along the way. Drowsy **Dimitsana** (p. 181) and cobblestoned **Stemnitsa** (p. 183) distinguish themselves from the tourist bustle of the rest of the Peloponnese. In the Ionian Sea, Odysseus's kingdom of

Ithaka (p. 458) is an untapped hiker's paradise, where the Cave of the Nymphs—the hiding place for Odysseus's treasure and the conclusion of an enthralling hike—will seduce you. Northern **Thassos** (p. 511) is full of secluded ruins, superior hikes, and village-to-village strolls. Rural **Alonnisos** (p. 348), a largely uninhabited Sporadic island, is criss-crossed by trails and moped-friendly roads, and hugged by beaches ideal for refueling after a fatiguing hike. Outlying islands are protected as part of the National Marine Park and make for pleasant daytrips. The traditional Greek villages of the **Zagorohoria** (p. 266) and their surrounding wilderness make walking an adventure. Neighboring **Vikos Gorge** (p. 267), the world's steepest canyon, challenges hikers with a 6hr. trek. You can explore more gorgeous gorges on Crete: the **Samaria Gorge** (p. 573), Europe's longest, and the quieter **Valley of Death** (p. 617) plunge you below eagles' nests and trees clinging to the steep canyon sides. Eighty percent of the Greek landscape is mountainous, to the delight of climbers. Clamber to the abode of the gods at **Mt. Olympus** (p. 289), ascending over 2900 steep, stunning meters to one of its eight peaks. During the summer, Dionysus's old watering hole, **Mt. Parnassos,** makes a great hiking and mountain-biking trip (p. 213); in winter, skiers storm the 2400m slopes. The trails around **Zaros** in Crete wind up to mountainside sanctuaries and to Zeus's childhood hiding place, **Kamares Cave** (p. 596).

SUGGESTED ITINERARIES

RUINS, RAMBLES, AND RELICS (1-2 WEEKS)

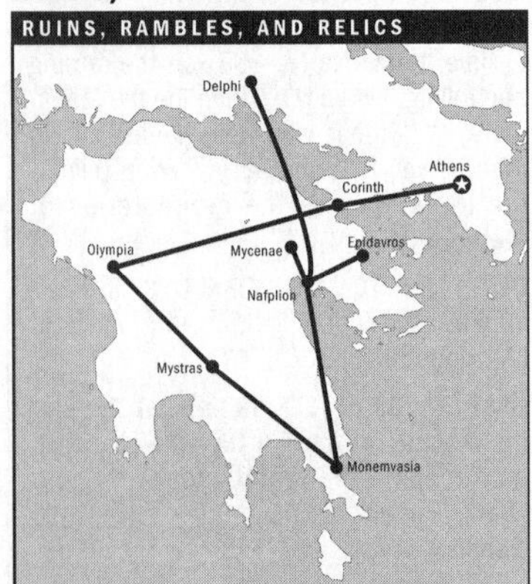

Put down that well-worn copy of the *Odyssey:* it's time to see the real deal. Arrive in **Athens** (p. 80) and charge straight to the gleaming **Acropolis,** which still looms over the city (p. 107), and the neighboring **Agora.** Escape the hot sun and lose yourself in the rooms and rooms of ancient treasure and statuary at the **National Archaeological Museum** (p. 114). Then head out from the capital to **Ancient Corinth,** whose fountain once quenched Pegasus's thirst (p. 144). Send up a cheer in the stadium at **Ancient Olympia,** and wonder at the life-like perfection of the Hermes of Praxiteles. Clamber over the Byzantine wonderland of **Mystras,** a maze-like ruined city (p. 144), and to the otherworldly pedestrian and donkey-only city of **Monemvasia** (p. 140). Watch the setting sun color Venetian **Nafplion** (p. 154), then stroll the waterfront in the evening. On the way back to Athens, visit **Mycenae** and walk beneath the Lion's Gate (p. 148), then exult in the perfect acoustics of the theater at **Epidavros** (p. 159). End your journey with a pilgrimage to **Delphi,** the ancient oracle that still retains its mystic aura (p. 217).

POST-EURAIL PARTY (1 WEEK)

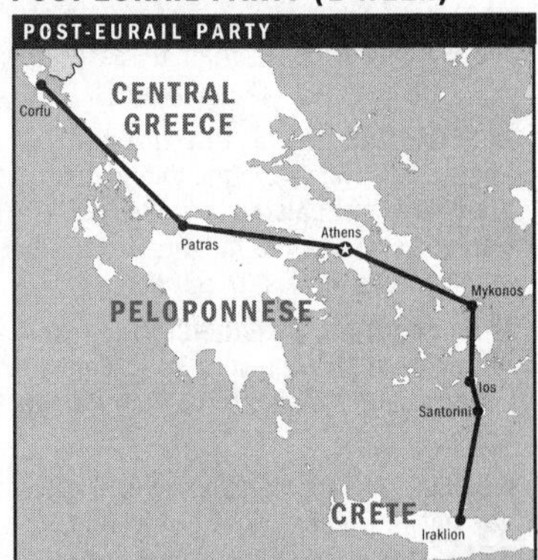

Finish up a Eurail trip by taking the ferry from Brindisi, Italy to **Corfu** (p. 440), home to gorgeous beaches and the infamous Pink Palace. Continue on via Patras to **Athens,** where you can catch an eyeful of the Acropolis before heading out to the islands (p. 80). As soon as you get off the ferry to

Mykonos, start shedding those inhibitions: nude beaches abound, and nightlife sizzles (p. 371). When you've warmed up for a day, move on to **Ios,** an isle of pure bacchic hedonism (p. 407). Recuperate from the damage on the black sand beaches of **Santorini** (p. 414), then test out the tawny sand outside **Iraklion,** on Crete (p. 585).

OLYMPIC ADVENTURE (1-2 WEEKS)

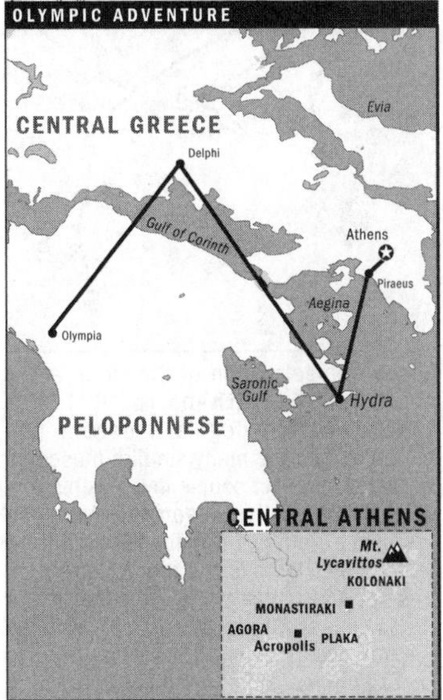

If you're going to Greece for the **Olympic Games** (p. 128), save some time between your venue-hopping for a little Hellenic exploration. Although you won't have much time to escape the crowded streets of **Athens** (p. 80), that doesn't mean that you can't enjoy the country. Begin with a morning trek to the top of the brilliant **Acropolis** (p. 107); from up there, even Olympic Athens seems peaceful. Stroll back down to the base of the hill for an amble around the **Agora** (p. 111), the heart of ancient Athens. **Plaka** (p. 95) at midday is a great place to break up a day of athletic events; its narrow streets provide much needed shade and quiet. Keep your eyes peeled for VIPs while strolling in the chic neighborhood of **Kolonaki**. After window shopping on its boutique-lined roads, have a cooling coffee frappé in the square in late afternoon. Then head for the top of rocky **Mt. Lycavittos** (p. 100) for a brilliant red sunset over the city. When the crowds and heat get to be too much, catch the Metro to **Piraeus**, hop aboard the next ferry to the nearby but charming **Saronic Gulf Islands** (p. 320), and unwind. Little **Hydra** (p. 331) may be the perfect stop for the traffic-weary: no cars are allowed on the island. Back on the mainland, find a day or two for a trip to the site of the great Oracle of Apollo, **Delphi** (p. 216), or a pilgrimage to where it all began, **Olympia** (p. 172).

HIKER'S DELIGHT (2 WEEKS)

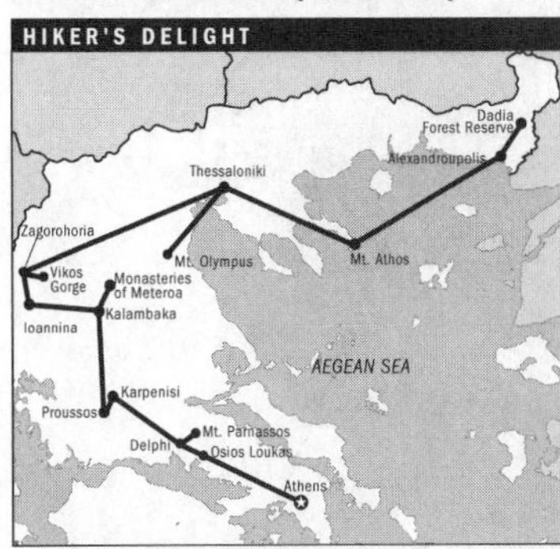

Set off from **Athens** (p. 80) to trek through undertouristed mainland Greece, home of cliffside Byzantine monasteries, cobblestoned traditional villages, and the splendor of Greece's mountainous landscapes. First set out toward **Mt. Parnassos**, where winter skiing cedes to hikers in the summer. Check out the nearby monastery of **Osios Loukas** (p. 215), which dates to the 10th century. Next, head toward **Karpenisi,** the capital of the mountainous Evritania region (p. 222). Either hit some of the higher peaks in the area or strike out among the tiny villages of the neighborhood; **Proussos,** with its spectacular cliffside monastery, is a highlight (p. 226). Avoid the traditional means of ascent to the **Monasteries of Meteora**—a terrifying, free-swinging rope—and save your prayers to give thanks for the fabulous view (p. 244). Pass through Ioannina on the way to the **Zagorohoria** villages, eminently hikeable and extremely friendly (p. 266). Save a day for the **Vikos Gorge** (p. 267), the steepest on earth. For the greatest hike of them all head straight to the home of the gods on **Mt. Olympus** (p. 289). Men have the opportunity, with the proper forms, to trek around a different sort of mountain: between the monasteries of **Mt. Athos** (p. 303). Follow the road toward **Alexandroupoli** (p. 316)

and finish your adventures in the **Dadia Forest Reserve** (p. 318), near the Turkish border among this coveted breeding ground for endangered raptors.

ISLAND ESCAPE (2 WEEKS)

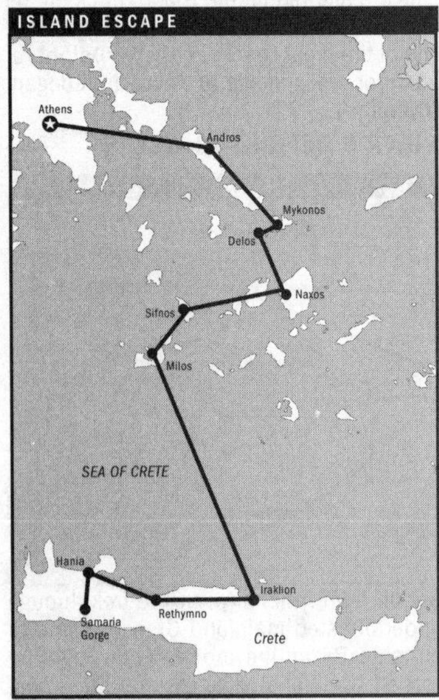

For a slower, more relaxed trip, leave from Athens for **Andros,** a beach-lovers' paradise surrounded by small Neoclassical towns (p. 362). Don't miss the sunsets; you certainly won't miss the crowds that jam other beach islands. Shake off your sloth at one of the crazed clubs of **Mykonos** (p. 371), and do penance for the previous night's debauchery during a daytrip to the sacred isle of **Delos,** the birthplace of Apollo and Artemis (p. 376). Next stop is **Naxos,** to snorkel among caves, sea urchins, and crystalline sand. Enjoy the moderate quiet of **Sifnos** (p. 428) with its authentically Greek atmosphere and unbelievable physical beauty. Check out the amazing beaches of **Milos** (p. 424) before heading south to **Crete** (p. 564). Start in **Iraklion** (p. 585) visiting the sites of Knossos and Phaistos, without neglecting Zeus's hide-out, the Kamares Cave. Then head west stopping in **Rethymno** (p. 578) and onto **Hania** (p. 565), where you can hike the **Samaria Gorge,** Europe's longest, or discover the tranquility of hard-to-reach **Balos.**

GREEK TO ME (3 WEEKS)

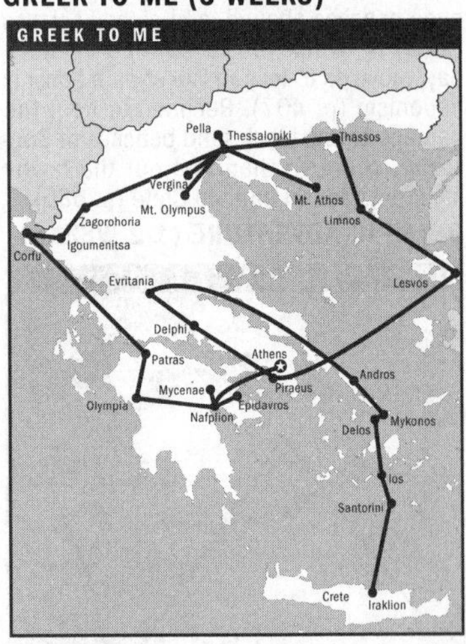

To see a large portion of Greece in a few weeks, start in **Athens** (p. 80); the National Archaeological Museum, the Acropolis, and the many smaller museums provide a refresher course in Greek history. Move on to **Nafplion**, a gorgeous Venetian city and a perfect base for exploring the neighboring sights of the theater of **Epidavros** (p. 159), the alleged abode of the Atreus clan at **Mycenae** (p. 148), and the original Olympic field at sacred **Olympia** (p. 172). Head to Patras to catch the ferry to **Corfu** (p. 440), an island that mixes overdevelopment with untouched wilderness. Cross back to the mainland at Igoumenitsa on your way to the **Zagorohoria** (p. 266), a district of petite towns that stick to traditional folkways. The Byzantine sights of **Thessaloniki** beckon (p. 271), with fabulous mosaics and the awesome archaeological sites of **Vergina** (p. 285) and **Pella** (p. 286), a quick jaunt away. The industrious will set out for **Mt. Olympus** (p. 289), to grapple with the gods' abode. Men who plan ahead and collect the proper approvals and forms may visit **Mt. Athos,** the ultratraditional monastic community jutting out of Halkidiki (p. 275). Recline for a few days on the shores of **Thassos** just offshore (p. 508), then loop down to **Limnos** (p. 505) off the Turkish coast. Let a ferry carry you to the widely varied landscapes of **Lesvos** (p. 493), Sappho's home and the birthplace of Nobel laureate Odysseus Elytis, before you sail back to **Piraeus**, Athens's modern port. From there, make a quick trip to the sacred oracle of **Delphi** (p. 216), then move on to **Evritania** (p. 222), a hilly rural district on the mainland. Hop the ferry to **Andros** (p. 362), a relaxing rural paradise that invites long hikes. Get freaky on **Mykonos** (p. 371); pay for the sins incurred with a daytrip to the sacred isle of **Delos,** birthplace of Apollo and Artemis (p. 376). Party naked on **Ios** (p. 407), then snooze on the black sand beaches of **Santorini** (p. 414); the picturesque white cliffside buildings are postcard-perfect. Finish your excursion on **Crete,** exploring the ruins of Knossos and Phaistos just outside of **Iraklion** (p. 585).

LIFE AND TIMES

The entire world has shared in the intellectual, literary, artistic, and religious majesty of Greece, a land so small for having achieved so much. Among rocky fields, dusty olive groves, and windswept cliffs, the Greeks have flourished for millennia against all odds. The country's unique position at the crossroads of Europe and Asia has defined its times. The relics of Crete's Minoan civilization reveal Egyptian and Babylonian influence, while, in the bushy beards and long black robes of Orthodox priests, the mores of the Eastern Roman Empire have survived through the Byzantine Era to the present time. Four hundred years under the Ottoman Turks left a spice in Greek food, an Eastern twang in its *bouzouki* music, and an occasional skyline of minarets. Greece declared independence in 1821 and now struggles to maintain the glory of Classical Athens and the splendor of Imperial Byzantium in a post-industrial nation governed by a reborn democracy.

HISTORY AND POLITICS

ANCIENT GREECE (3000 BC TO AD 324)

With its pervasive influence on Western language, philosophy, and literature, ancient Greece has long transfixed the world. Greek culture grew from agricultural and fishing communities; the coastal Aegean fostered prosperity with its access to the ocean and its nearby olive trees, grapes, forests, and fertile land. Walled towns, constructed around a central high point, or **acropolis,** protected seaside settlements. Immigrants and traders from Anatolia, the Levant, and Egypt added a dash of global chic to the ancient Greek world.

EARLY GREEK CIVILIZATION

THE BRONZE AGE. The discovery of metalworking kicked off a rapid expansion of Greek influence. Peering over the shoulders of their eastern neighbors, Greeks learned bronze toolmaking and weaponry. Three Aegean cultures measured their power and greatness with bronze: the mainland's Mycenaean, Crete's Minoan, and the islands' Cycladic. Island civilization flourished early on as the **Cycladic** culture infused a Middle Eastern influence with a strong geometric element in its architecture. By 2000 BC, the **Minoans** (named for the Minotaur's step-dad) busily constructed palaces at Knossos (p. 591), Malia (p. 601), and Phaistos (p. 597) as centers of government, religion, and trade; a strong fleet made the Minoans the lords of the Aegean. Around 1500 BC, however, a mysterious **cataclysm**—hypothesized tidal waves, volcano eruptions, alien invasions, etc.—wiped out the Minoans.

THROUGH THE TROJAN WAR. The mainland **Mycenaeans** (a.k.a. Achaeans or Hellenes—named both for a tribe in Thessaly and for Helen of Troy), overtook the Aegean after the Minoans faded. Based in Mycenae and Tyrins, they built citadels surrounded by "Cyclopean" walls—so called because later Greeks thought only a Cyclops could lift such massive stones. Mycenaean rule extended throughout the southern mainland, Crete, and the Cyclades and Dodecanese as far as Cyprus, where archaeologists have uncovered remnants of Mycenaean culture. The Mycenaeans' language, **Linear A,** has been a mystery as great as the cause of the Minoans' demise. Linear B, developed from the Minoan Linear A, has puzzled generations of linguists—recently this tongue action has proven to be proto-Greek.

The Mycenaeans attacked Troy in Asia Minor around 1250 BC, igniting the most mythologized, obsessed-over, and written-about war in history. Perhaps the greatest histories of the **Trojan War,** Homer's **Iliad** and **Odyssey,** compiled the oral lore of the war into two epic poems around 850 BC (during the subsequent Dorian Era).

DORIAN BREAK-UP AND THE POLIS

DORIAN INVASION. Bronze Age Aegean civilizations met an abrupt end in the 12th century BC, when invading **Dorians** burst in from the Balkan highlands to the north. The invasion scattered the Mycenaeans in a **diaspora** that relocated Greeks to Asia Minor (where Homer may have lived) and to the Black Sea. A **dark age** of rule by the decidedly un-dainty Dorians followed. But it wasn't all bad under Dorian rule: the Greek language and alphabet settled into a single, national language, accompanied by an increasingly cohesive national identity. Tribal divisions, however, still prevented a centralized government like the Mycenaeans'. Industry, agriculture, and trade passed into the hands of hundreds of small, independent villages of self-sufficient farmers. Their political independence and Dorian destruction of "high" civilization paved the path to the city-state and Classical splendor.

RISE OF THE CITY-STATE. After the Dorian invasions, the *polis*, or city-state, rose as the major Greek political structure. A typical *polis* encompassed the city proper and the surrounding hinterland, which provided food and wood. Within the town, the acropolis (a fortified citadel atop the city's highest point and often a religious center bedecked with **temples**) and the **agora** (the marketplace and center of commercial and social life) marked the two major cultural landmarks. Within the agora thinkers waxed philosophical, and traders hawked their wares amid the **stoas,** open-air paths lined with columns. Outside the city center, amphitheaters and stadiums hosted political and religious gatherings as well as athletic games.

By the 9th century BC, many city-states caught the imperialism bug and began to expand and colonize overseas, spreading their military influence and culture throughout the Mediterranean. Colonization had benefits, as city-states became increasingly prosperous and formed economic, religious, and military ties among themselves. Religion and sports united in the **Olympic Games** (p. 128), where the athletic fields of Olympia hosted politically charged competitions between states. Through similar transnational events, the residents of city-states began to feel more Greek, and less Athenian or Spartan. By 700 BC the inhabitants of Greece called themselves **Hellenes.** This new identity created a contrast between Greeks and foreigners, whom the Hellenes called **barbaroi (barbarians),** after the sound of foreigners' language, thought to sound like a savage "bar bar bar."

Starting in 495 BC, barbarian invasions—from the eastern **Persians** under Darius and his son Xerxes as well as the empire of **Carthage** to the southwest in North Africa—threatened the Greek city-states. During the **Persian Wars** (490-477 BC), Athens and Sparta led the defense of Greece. The Greeks overcame overwhelming odds to defeat the mighty Persians in legendary battles at Marathon, Salamis, and Plataea. In Sicily and southern Italy (then called **Magna Graecia**—wider Greece), the western Mediterranean city-states fended off Carthaginian assaults and saved western Greece from foreign rule. The Hellenic victories ushered in a period of prosperity with flourishing artistic, commercial, and political success.

CLASSICAL GREECE (500-400 BC). With the end of the Persian Wars, Athens rose to prominence as the wealthiest and most influential *polis*. Equipped with a strong navy (built for use in the Persian Wars upon the advice of famed

IN RECENT NEWS

FYROMESE FIGHT

Travelers eager for a fiery lecture should innocently, but not softly, muse on the ethnic origin of Alexander the Great. Though no evidence proves the Macedonians spoke a Greek derivative, the Greeks have gone to great lengths to show that the Macedonia of Alexander was thoroughly Hellenized.

The historical sensitivity stems from the recent independence of FYROM (The Former Yugoslav Republic of Macedonia). Calling themselves Macedonia and flaunting Philip's 16-pointed Macedonian sun on their flag, FYROM shocked Greece with claims to "Greater Macedonia," including the Greek state of that name. Though outsiders often view Greek anxiety over losing their portion of Macedonia, which includes Thessaloniki, as absurd, such fears are not historically groundless. The area was bitterly contested in the Balkan Wars and occupied during both World Wars.

This conflict has often taken a historical dimension. As when Bulgarian occupiers systematically destroyed the mosaics of Phillipi to erase traces of the region's Greek heritage, the recent conflict with FYROM channeled much Greek funding into preserving the archeological sites of Philip II's Macedon. Though Greek-FYROM relations have normalized, tourists can still reap the peaceful fruits of this "historical" battle. From the beautiful artifacts of Philip II's tomb at Vergina, to the charming walkways of Macedonian sacred city

statesman and general **Themistokles**), Athens made waves in the Mediterranean and established itself as the powerful head of the **Delian League,** an organization of city-states formed in name to defend against Persian aggression but in effect acting as an Athenian empire. Athens prospered, fostering the art, literature, philosophy, and government (including **democracy**) that echo throughout Western culture.

The proverbial yin to Athens's yang, Sparta rivaled the great democracy, heading a similar collection of city-states on the mainland known as the **Peloponnesian League.** Commercial and democratic Athens prided itself on its cultural achievements, while antithetical Sparta with its oligarchic agroculture valued stoic military training above all else. Spartan men spent their lives from ages seven to 60 in military training, conquest, or defense; women trained to become fit mothers and proper models for their military sons. The competition between Athens and Sparta culminated in the violent **Peloponnesian War** (431-404 BC), sparked in part by rapid Athenian expansion under **Pericles.** The war ended in defeat for Athens, as Spartan soldiers captured the city and established their trademark oligarchy. During this period the Greek *polis* system began to rot; the historian **Thucydides,** our best source on the Peloponnesian War, identified the problem as a *stasis*—the Greeks lost internal unity, while subject city-states chafed under Athenian dominion.

MACEDONIAN RULE

With Athens, a leader among the Greek cities, so weakened, the period after the Peloponnesian War witnessed a gradual devolution of city-state power. Sparta and later Thebes tried to lead and maintain a unified Greek alliance but ultimately succumbed to Persian political influence. A new force in **Macedonia** soon capitalized on the weakness of the rest of Greece, seizing control. **King Philip** with his improved **phalanx** conquered the Greek city-states in 338 BC at the Battle of Chaeronea and bound them into a union subject to his monarchy.

After Philip's assassination in 336 BC, his 20-year-old son **Alexander,** once a student of Aristotle's, took the throne. Alexander ruled Greece with an iron fist—in 335 BC he mercilessly razed Thebes—and consolidated control of his father's empire. In control of Greece, he turned his ambitions for expansion eastward, toward an epithet for the ages. By the time of his sudden death at 33, he ruled Egypt and the entire Persian Empire, having spread Greek culture and language throughout the eastern Mediterranean—truly deserving the name Alexander the Great. During the Hellenistic Era that followed, literary and artistic forms diffused throughout the former empire, and Classical learning reached faraway realms.

The Macedonian empire quickly crumbled after the death of Alexander in 323 BC, leaving three powers in its wake: the **Antigonids** in Macedonia, the **Seleucids** in Asia Minor, Syria, and Persia, and the **Ptolemies** in Egypt. The dissolution of Alexander's imperial stronghold restored a measure of independence to the Greek city-states. Three Greek powers ruled during the 3rd century BC: the Peloponnesian **Achaean Confederacy,** the Delphi-based **Aetolian Confederacy,** and the city-state of Sparta. However, Greek self-rule would not last; by 27 BC the upstart Roman Empire had conquered Greece and incorporated it into the province of **Achaea.**

MAGNA GRAECIA TO MAGNA ROMA

Greek self-rule was short-lived. In the 3rd century BC, **Rome** made alliances with Greek cities and began expanding its empire into Greek territory. Ruling Greece was particularly satisfying for the Romans, who had once been subject to Greek power, and who admired and wished to adopt Greek culture. Roman influence filled the power vacuum left by Alexander, as the Romans defeated the Seleucids of Asia Minor and conquered Macedonia in the **First and Second Macedonian Wars.** At the end of the second in 197 BC, Greeks gained a nominal "independence," but Rome treated Greece as a satellite, not a free state. Greek cities began to support their former enemies against Rome and the Achaean Confederacy openly rebelled in 146 BC. In response Rome flexed its muscles, destroying Corinth and loading Greece with oppressive restrictions. Rome had no consistent policy toward its Greek province. The Roman Emperor Hadrian ran public works programs and a fair government, but Emperor Sulla destroyed the economy and even massacred the population. Even as Roman legions took over Greek land, Hellenic culture seeped into Roman society; Greek slaves often tutored Roman children, Greek sculpture was brought to Roman homes, and Roman architects imitated Greek styles. Adopting what they admired, the Romans created a **Greco-Roman culture** that spread Greek influence to the farthest reaches of the Roman Empire.

BYZANTINE ERA (AD 324-1453)

Unlike other lands ruined by the Roman Empire's fall, Greece emerged into a period of cultural rebirth, prosperity, and power stretching from the Balkans through Greece to Asia Minor and Egypt, the lands soon referred to as **Byzantium.**

ROMAN EMPIRE: EAST SIDE

As Rome slowly declined, the empire split into lop-sided halves: a stronger eastern half (centered in Anatolia, the Levant, and Greece) and a weakened western half based in Rome. The unusual political arrangement ended in a scramble for power, won by **Constantine** in AD 312. Legend holds that before his decisive victory at the Milvian Bridge, Constantine saw a vision of a cross of light in the sun, bearing the fiery inscription, "In Hoc Signo, Vinces" (In this sign, conquer). The great leader interpreted this as a sign from the Christian God and had the cross painted on his troops' shields. Constantine soon legalized Christianity within his empire, and founded **Constantinople** (modern Istanbul) in 324, giving the empire a new Christian capital, built over ancient Byzantium. While barbarian invaders overran the Roman half (Western Europe), this eastern empire, today known as the Byzantine Empire, became a center of learning, trade, and influence unrivaled in its time.

NETTLESOME NEIGHBORS

During the 6th century, **Emperor Justinian's** battles against the Sassanians of Persia and the western Vandals (who had sacked Rome) overstretched the empire's strength. Justinian's successes came in domestic politics as he codified Roman laws and undertook massive building projects such as the awe-inspiring church of **Agia Sophia,** an architectural masterpiece that still stands in Istanbul. However the empire's power waned under the force of constant raids by Slavs, Mongols, and Avars. In many areas of the mainland and Peloponnese, barbarian conquests wiped out Greek culture entirely, and the Greek language and script only returned after later missions from Constantinople.

WIDENING THE EAST-WEST DIVIDE

Ensuing Arab conquests and the challenge of Islam helped bring the empire closer together, as did the religious movement **iconoclasm**—icon-smashing. Greek Christians came to believe that iconography (a visual representation of God) violated the **Second Commandment,** which demands that the faithful make no graven image of God. They interpreted their defeats in battle as punishment for this violation. By the early 700s, Church doctrine demanded that all images be demolished—a policy whose enforcement depended on the Greeks' performance in war. Eventually iconoclasm itself was smashed in 843—to the benefit of latter-day art historians.

Non-Christian conquerors created the **Byzantine Commonwealth,** which further divided Constantinople from Rome and the West. The crowning of **Charlemagne** as Holy Roman Emperor in 800 finalized the split between West and East. The bitter **Great Schism** of 1054 caused a mutual excommunication between the Orthodox and Roman Catholic Churches—each church declared the other a false church.

THE CURSE OF CRUSADERS

Even as they protected themselves from invaders, the Byzantine Greeks continued to spread **Christianity.** Missionaries reached out into the Slavic kingdoms and Russia, sowing the seeds of Orthodox Christianity throughout Eastern Europe. In 1071 the Byzantines lost control of eastern Anatolia to the Selçuk Turks; Greek monasteries in the Aegean and Black Sea areas transformed into armed fortresses to ward off Turkish pirates. From 1200 to 1400, the Byzantine Empire was plagued by Norman and Venetian crusaders, who conquered and looted Constantinople in 1204 and imposed western Catholic culture upon the city. Despite strong leaders, Byzantium needed to ally with Latin, Slavic, and even Turkish rulers through marriage in order to survive. Finally the once indomitable Byzantine Empire was reduced to only Constantinople and its environs. On May 29, 1453 (a day still considered cursed by Greeks), the Ottomans at last overran the much-reduced city.

OTTOMAN OCCUPATION (1453-1829)

As soon as the Turkish captors moved in, they gave Constantine's capital the undignified name, **Istanbul,** corrupting the Greek *steen poli* (to the city). The city again became the seat of an empire. For centuries the **Ottoman Empire** prospered, though eventually its diverse regions grew apart and the empire weakened. The Muslim Turkish rulers treated their Greek subjects as a **millet**—a separate community ruled by its own religious leaders. Greeks paid the *cizye*, a head tax dictated by Islamic law, but could otherwise worship freely as they chose. The Orthodox Church became the moderator of culture and tradition and the foundation of Greek autonomy. Though Greeks could choose to integrate into Ottoman society, anti-Turk nationalist sentiments began to build. Encouraged to revolt by Orthodox leaders, Greeks began to chafe in the 400 year pressure cooker of Turkish rule. By the 19th century, they were pushing for complete independence from the empire.

THE GREAT IDEA (1821-1900)

GREEK NATIONALIST REVOLT

On March 25, 1821, Bishop Germanos of Patras raised a Greek flag at the monastery of Agia Lavra, sparking an empire-wide rebellion. Middle-class rebels hoped that the Orthodox Russian czar and Greek peasants would join the revolt; when they didn't, the rebels met a crushing defeat. Disorganized but impassioned guerrillas in the Peloponnese and islands waged sporadic war on the Turkish government for the next decade. Under the leadership of rebel heroes Botsaris, Koundouritis, Miaoulis, Mavrokordatos, and Ypsilanti, the Greeks slowly chipped away at Ottoman control. Finally, in 1829, with great support from European powers, Greece won independence. Russia, Britain, and France wanted a free Greece but also sought to restrict its power. The narrow borders of the new Greece included only a fraction of the six million Greeks living under Ottoman rule. For the next century, Greek politics centered around achieving the *Megali Idea*—the **Great Idea:** freeing Constantinople from the Turks and uniting all Greeks, even those in Asia Minor, into one sovereign state. Although Greece gained much territory over the next century, including the great city of **Salonica** (Thessaloniki) in Macedonia and the island of **Crete,** it never realized these ambitious goals.

POST-REVOLUTION POLITICS

After the War of Independence, joy soon dissolved into disappointment. Puny and poor, the new Greek state was divided by the agrarian problem that plagued it for the rest of the century: landowners clung to their traditional privileges, while peasants demanded land redistribution, which had motivated them to fight.

The first president, **Ioannis Kapodistrias,** was elected in 1827, and made an earnest—if autocratic—attempt to create a strong government. His assassination in 1831 thwarted plans to establish a democratic government and prompted intervention into Greek politics. The European powers declared Greece a **monarchy,** handing the crown to the young German **Prince Otto** in 1833. Often called an "insensitive" ruler, Otto was a rich, powerful teenager who angered Greeks by handing out high-ranking positions to his German cronies. He moved the capital from its provisional site in Nafplion to **Athens,** and in 1843 created a parliamentary system. Though he embraced the *Megali Idea*—and consequently made friends in his new country—his support for Austria in opposing Italian unification led to an upsurge in latent resentments against the leadership. In 1862, the Athens garrison staged a coup, ousting Otto from power. The British stepped in and installed Danish prince, **George I,** as king. George's rule brought stability and a new constitution in 1864, which downplayed the king's power, emphasizing the importance of the elected prime minister. Land distribution, however, remained unsolved.

TWENTIETH CENTURY

EXPAND AND CONTRACT

In 1920 Prime Minister **Eleftherios Venizelos,** immortalized in street names throughout modern Greece, wrangled new Greek territory in the aftermath of the Balkan Wars and World War I. Savvy Balkan alliances nearly doubled Greece's territory. Defying King Constantine's request for neutrality, Venizelos set up an Allied revolutionary government in Thessaloniki. After World War I, Venizelos discovered Greece would not be receiving land in Asia Minor so in 1919 he ordered an outright invasion of Turkey. However the young Turkish general (and de facto leader of the country) Mustafa Kemal, later known as **Atatürk,** crushed the invasion. As the Greek army retreated, the Turkish forces ordered the slaughter of Greek citizens all along the Turkish coast. The 1923 **Treaty of Lausanne** enacted a massive **population exchange** that sent a million Greeks living in Asia Minor to live in Greece and sent 400,000 Turkish Muslims from Greece to Turkey. This exchange concluded the *Megali Idea* but kicked off a series of economic problems for Greece.

THE SECOND WORLD WAR

Political turmoil rocked the 1930s, as Greeks lived through brief intervals of democracy amid a succession of monarchies interspersed with military rule. King George II lost power by a series of coups that reinstated a democracy; Venizelos, the former Prime Minister, headed the new government for five years, though royalists eventually forced his exile. The extreme nationalist **General Metaxas** succeeded him as Prime Minister in a fixed election, as George II regained the throne in 1936. Metaxas inaugurated an oppressive military state, yet his leadership during the early stages of World War II earned him lasting respect. Most notably Metaxas rejected Mussolini's request that Italy occupy Greece during World War II with a resounding "Οχι!" (No!). Although the nation defeated the Italian forces, Greece eventually fell to Germany in 1941 and endured four years of bloody and brutal Axis occupation. The communist-led resistance received broad popular support, though many resistance fighters received aid from the Western powers, which were eager to prevent a communist Greece.

CIVIL WAR AND RECONSTRUCTION

The Civil War, a devastating time marked by purges and starvation, broke out in 1944. With economic support supplied by the US under the auspices of the **Truman Doctrine,** the anti-communist coalition government eventually defeated the Soviet-backed Democratic Army in 1949. The US also instituted the **Certificate of Political Reliability,** which lasted until 1962 and required citizens to pledge anti-communist sympathies so that power remained out of Communist hands. Keeping a visible hand in Greek politics, the US helped place General Papagos, **Constantine Karamanlis,** and the right-wing Greek Rally Party in power. When Karamanlis resigned after the assassination of a communist official in 1963, left-wing **George Papandreou** came to power, to America's chagrin. The respite from right-wing power was short-lived; the army staged a coup on April 21, 1967, which resulted in **military junta** rule for seven years. Making use of torture, censorship, and arbitrary arrest to repress Communist forces, the junta enjoyed official US support and investment at the height of the Cold War. The junta fell in 1973 after the government helped provoke a **Turkish invasion of Cyprus** and a nationwide **student uprising.** Former president Karamanlis returned to take power in 1975, instituting parliamentary elections and organizing a referendum on the form of government. Monarchy was defeated by a two-thirds vote and a new constitution was drawn up in 1975, calling for parliamentary government with a ceremonial president appointed by the legislature—the system still in use today.

TODAY

TOWARD EUROPE

Under the guidance of party founder **Andreas Papandreou,** the leftist Panhellenic Socialist Movement (PASOK) won landslide electoral victories in 1981 and 1985. Appealing to voters with the simple slogan *"Allaghi"* (Change), Prime Minister Papandreou promised a radical break with the past. In office he steered Greece into the European Economic Community (EEC) and pioneered the passage of women's rights legislation, though many of his policies were anti-Western: he spoke against

NATO and maintained friendships with Libyan strongman Mohammar Qaddafi and the leader of the Palestinian Liberation Organization Yasser Arafat. When a scandal involving the chair of the Bank of Crete implicated government officials in 1989, Papandreou lost control of Parliament. After three general elections in the space of 10 months, **Constantine Mitsotakis** of the New Democracy Party (*Nea Demokratia*, or ND) became Prime Minister by a slim majority.

AUGMENTATION AND AUSTERITY

Attempting to solve Greece's economic and diplomatic problems and align the country with mainstream European politics, Mitsotakis imposed an **austerity program** that limited wage increases and authorized the sale of state enterprises. This policy became tremendously unpopular when it threatened thousands of public sector jobs, and, in 1993, a resurgent Papandreou defeated Mitsotakis in an emergency election. Two years later, poor health forced Papandreou to leave his post.

Fellow socialist **Costas Simitis** took control of the party and has since pursued aggressive economic reforms, privatizing banks and companies despite the opposition of perpetually striking labor unions. The ruling PASOK party has also made strides in international relations by being more NATO-friendly and opening talks with Turkey. The administration has slashed Greece's budget deficit, brought inflation down, and cut the national debt in an attempt to meet the qualifying standards for entry into the **European Monetary Union (EMU).** Simitis, who slimly eked out reelection in the 2000 election over ND challenger **Costas Karamanlis,** was instrumental in helping Greece's successful bid to enter the EMU in January 2001.

THE KKE

The Greek Communist Party, or KKE, is the third-strongest political party in Greece, but still far behind New Democracy and PASOK. Looking askance at NATO, the West, and US influence, KKE members cringe at American cultural dominance. Be prepared for a lot of angry graffiti, equating Americans with Nazis and the US President with Hitler. Noisy Western patriots will probably meet with no more than angry glances or verbal harassment, but it's a good idea to lie low.

GREECE AND TURKEY: BREAKING THE ICE

One of Simitis's continuing projects is normalizing relations with nearby Turkey. The two nations have been on less-than-friendly terms in the past (p. 13), but, in

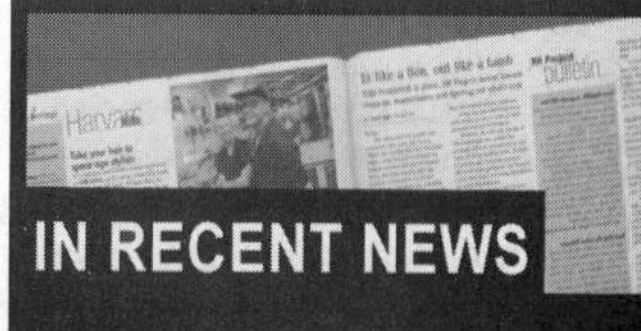

IN RECENT NEWS

NOVEMBER 17

The events of September 11 2001 combined with approaching Olympic Games on their home soil got the Athenian government rolling in 2002 to make its first arrest of suspects of the November 17 (N17) terrorist group in July of that year. The breakthrough came shortly after a failed bombing attempt in Piraeus on June 29, 2002. Most significantly, the alleged head honcho Alexandros Giotopoulos (often spelled Yotopoulos), was arrested July 17, 2002 on the island of Lipsi where he was spending holiday with his family.

The anti-Western terrorist organization, opposed to Greek membership in NATO and the EU, borrows its name from the date of the 1973 student uprising in protest to the junta regime. Although the group has occasionally targeted international politicians—the most recent assassination was of a British government worker, Stephen Saunders, in June 2000—the primary targets of the group are Greek public figures. Since 1975, N17 has claimed responsibility for 23 deaths.

In the fall of 2003, when *Let's Go Greece 2004* went to press, trials were being held of alleged group members. Alleged assasin Savvas Xeros, an icon-painter and child of an Orthodox priest, and, of course Giotopoulos, who denies any involvement with the group, are the prime characters to follow in the N17 hearings. Security concerns surrounding N17 remain high, particularly since September 6 when two bombs went off in the court complex where the trials are being held.

great part through mutual displays of support after both countries suffered devastating earthquakes in 1999, they have recently begun to earn each other's trust. In January 2001 Foreign Minister **George Papandreou**—widely considered a future prime minister candidate—traveled to Turkey, the first such visit in 37 years. There he signed cooperation agreements concerning tourism, the environment, the protection of investments, and terrorism. Talks have even begun concerning the fiery issue of Cyprus, which is divided into Turkish and Greek Cypriot states.

PEOPLE

DEMOGRAPHICS

THE MANY...

About **10.6 million** people live in Greece. The population is 98% ethnically Greek and 98% Greek Orthodox (p. 17), but the extremely homogeneous population is overshadowed by the large number of foreign visitors who travel in Greece.

...AND THE FEW

Both the government, which does not recognize official ethnic divisions, and the Greek people generally deny any overt racism. But there is a growing concern about widespread prejudice toward a rapidly expanding refugee and migrant population. Roughly 400,000 ethnic **Albanians,** most in Northern Greece, make up the country's largest minority population; recently, reports of violence perpetrated by the Greek border patrol against illegal Albanian immigrants have cropped up. The **Gypsies,** or **Roma,** make up another significant minority group; they have remained on the fringes of Greek society for centuries and are now concentrated in Athens and Thessaloniki. Plagued by poor health, low literacy rates, and extensive poverty, the Roma population is typically viewed by Greeks as one of the country's largest social problems. The most populous religious minority group is made up of over 130,000 Slavic and Turkish **Muslims** in Thrace who remain separated from the Greeks in both language and culture. **Jewish** communities were present in Greece since the first century AD, but the majority of the Jewish population was deported to concentration camps during the Nazi occupation of World War II (p. 14). Only about 4500 Jews live in Greece at present. Other official minorities include the **Vlachs** and the **Sarakatsanis,** both groups of nomadic shepherds descended from Latin speakers who settled in Greece. The region of Macedonia has some 60,000 **Slavs** still unrecognized by the Greek government as a minority.

LANGUAGE

THE MODERN TONGUE

The Greek language (Ελληνικα, eh-lee-nee-KAH) is much more than a medium for communication. Greeks use it carefully and treat it adoringly. It is a link to their cherished past and a key to continued Greek independence in the future. Because barely 12 million people speak it around the world, each and every speaker of Greek is essential to the continuation of the language. For that reason passing the language through the generations is often portrayed as a solemn duty.

To the non-Greek speaker, the intricate levels of nuance, idiom, irony, and poetry imbued in the language can present a seemingly impenetrable wall to understanding. Indeed, Greek is one of the most difficult languages for English speakers to learn fluently. With complex conjugations for verbs and strict declensions for adjectives and nouns, Greek will bring back bad memories of high school classics class. Although mastering Greek is a truly daunting task, learning enough to order a meal, send a postcard, and get to the airport is surprisingly easy. While the Greek language is obsessively phonetic, a cursory knowledge of the **alphabet** (p. 620) does not always help with the many double consonants, double vowels, and *tonos* (syllabic stresses), which are not always phonetically consistent. Making matters easier though, all multisyllabic Greek words come with handy accents, which mark the syllable to be emphasized. Sentences are usually simple and sentence structure is very similar to English. Greeks tend to speak quickly, so listen carefully for important, recognizable nouns and you may well get the point. If all else fails, resort to signals and gestures. Greeks constantly use their hands and their bodies when they talk, and body language is often as useful as a dictionary.

With a little work, any tourist to Greece should be able to get by easily. Don't be embarrassed to practice your Greek in front of native speakers. Greeks are famously welcoming of foreigners who try their hands at the language, although they may not be able to repress the occasional giggle when, instead of ordering another bottle of wine, for example, you ask for their hand in marriage. Of course almost all Greeks—and certainly anyone working in the tourist industry—will understand English, but try to learn a little Greek.

RELIGION

ANCIENT GODS

Greek myths bubble with spicy, titillating **scandal** as they explain the origins of our natural phenomena. The adventures of the gods and their long-suffering mortal counterparts have inspired artists, writers, and psychoanalysts. Greek mythology connects human events with a divine order and ties history to the gods. Moreover, mythology and literature are inextricably intertwined. From epic poems we learn of the Greek gods and their habits, and the characters of early literature become almost as much a part of mythology as the gods themselves. **Homer's** semi-divine heroes project mythic shadows of Mycenaean kings and military leaders.

Greek religion evolved alongside this mythic history. Worship in the Greek pantheon centered around praying and leaving offerings to gods whose all-too-human exploits were chronicled by the Greeks. Religious sects lacked any overarching unity or mutual exclusivity. Worship revolved around specific locations, temples, and rites. People were free to worship whomever they chose (and to develop patron gods—and enemy gods). Greek religion was thus a changeable and multifaceted creature. Though individual rites and ceremonies were preset, overall religious practices could change drastically through the centuries.

Rituals of communion with the gods were often as scandalous as the myths that inspired them: extreme chemical **intoxication** and large-scale **orgies** were legitimate routes to a state of religious ecstasy. The Greek gods behaved very much like humans who could never die—they lacked strong morals and got into lots of silly arguments without fear of any real retribution.

The Greeks by no means thought their gods were lightweights to be trifled with, however: mythology is full of ugly examples of what happens to those who challenge gods. Humans were often unwilling participants in religious myths. The talented weaver **Arachne** was turned into a spider (hence the word "arachnid") because she dared to compete with Athena. **Tantalus** was condemned to stand in a pool in Hades, forever tormented by hunger and thirst with oh-so-tantalizing food and water just beyond his grasp. **King Minos,** poor fool, didn't make a sacrifice on time, so Poseidon gave Minos's wife **Pasiphaë** an insatiable lust for a bull. Pasiphaë then bore a baby, a cannibal bull-boy, the **Minotaur.**

GREEK GOD	ROMAN NAME	JOB DESCRIPTION
Zeus	Jupiter	King of gods; law maker; kept order with efficient thunderbolt.
Hera	Juno	Queen of Olympus; goddess of women and marriage; Zeus's sister and wife.
Ares	Mars	God of war and the spirit of battle; represented the gruesome aspects of fighting.
Hephæstus	Vulcan	Fire god; divine smith and patron of all craftsman; Aphrodite's homely husband.
Demeter	Ceres	Goddess of the Earth and fertility.
Aphrodite	Venus	Love goddess; mom and boss; of Eros (Cupid); noted philanderer.
Athena	Minerva	Goddess of wisdom and craft; Athens's protectress; born from Zeus's head.
Hades	Pluto	God of the Underworld; Zeus's brother; Motto: Always room for one more.
Poseidon	Neptune	God of the sea and of water; brother of Zeus.
Apollo	Apollo	Sun god; patron of music, song, and poetry; python-slayer; Artemis's twin.
Artemis	Diana	Goddess of the hunt, the moon, wild animals, vegetation, chastity, and childbirth.
Dionysus	Bacchus	God of wine, fertility, revelry, and all things in between.
Hermes	Mercury	Messenger god; presided over animals, commerce, shrewdness, and persuasion; patron god of travelers.

THE ORTHODOX CHURCH

Christianity in Greece dates from the first century AD. The **Apostle Paul** and other missionaries first spread the Christian faith and established Christian communities in a number of cities in Greece and Asia Minor. Five of Paul's epistles (letters), eventually forming part of the **New Testament,** were addressed to these new Christian communities. By the 4th century, the Christians had escaped persecution and the Church was well established throughout the Mediterranean. Since the Greek peninsula and islands as well as all the Balkans were within the Roman-Byzantine Empire until the 15th century, the Churches there were part of Eastern Christianity, centered at the **Patriarchate of Constantinople (Istanbul).** A member of the family of Orthodox Churches, the Church of Greece received autocephalous status in 1850. The Church of Crete, the dioceses of some other Greek islands, and the dioceses in Northern Greece remain a part of the Patriarchate of Constantinople. The Church of Cyprus has been autocephalous since the 4th century.

Today's Orthodox Church of Greece is the preeminent religious body in the country. Over 90% of the population, gathered in over 7000 **parishes** divided among about 80 **dioceses,** is baptized. There are hundreds of monastic communities. With other Orthodox Churches throughout the world, the Church of Greece centers its teachings upon Jesus and his Gospel. Orthodox Christianity affirms a loving God who entered into this life in the person of Jesus. Honored as Lord and Savior, Christ revealed the one God as Father, Son, and Holy Spirit: the Holy Trinity. The Church celebrates this faith in its worship, especially in the Holy Eucharist known as the **Divine Liturgy.** The Sacraments and other blessings also bear witness to the presence and actions of God. The faith of the Church is expressed in its scripture and tradition, which includes icons, prayers, and the **Ecumenical Councils.** Because of their religious example, the saints are greatly honored.

OTHER RELIGIOUS TRADITIONS

While the Orthodox Christian faith is preeminent in Greek society, the Greek Constitution guarantees freedom of religion and repudiates proselytism. There are a small number of Armenian Orthodox and Roman Catholic communities. Some Muslim communities exist, predominantly in Northern Greece. Before World War II, there was a thriving Jewish population in Thessaloniki, though only a few organized Jewish communities now remain.

FOOD AND DRINK

Recent medical studies have highlighted the Greek diet as a good model for **healthy** eating; its reliance on unsaturated olive oil and vegetables has prevented high rates of heart disease despite the fairly sedentary lifestyle of the populace. Unfortunately the prevalence of cheap and greasy foods has caused some recent health concerns in Greece. Penny-pinching carnivores will thank Zeus for lamb, chicken, or beef **souvlaki** and hot-off-the-spit **gyros**—pronounced "yee-RO"—stuffed into a pita. Vegetarians can also eat their fill on the cheap. **Toast** (τοστ) refers to a panini-like grilled sandwich not to be confused with plain, square bread out of the toaster. **Tzatziki**, a garlicky cucumber yogurt dip served with bread is a good way to start off a meal (or ripen your breath enough to ward off any overly amorous overtures). Try the feta-piled **horiatiki** (a.k.a. Greek salad), savory pastries like **tiropita** (a phyllo pastry full of feta) and **spanakopita** (spinach-phyllo-feta pastry), and the fresh fruits and vegetables found at markets and vendor stands in most cities. Bottles of **spring water** are dirt cheap so there's no excuse not to keep hydrated.

Liquid refreshment typically involves a few basic options, including the strong, sweet sludge that is **Greek coffee** or the frothy, iced coffee **frappés** that take an edge off the heat in the summer. Potent **raki** and **tsipouro,** moonshine born from the remnants of wine-making, are especially popular on the mainland and Crete. **Ouzo,** a powerful, licorice-flavored Greek spirit sure to earn your respect, is served with **mezedes,** which are snacks consisting of octopus, cheese, and sausage tidbits.

Breakfast, served only in the early morning, is generally constituted of a simple piece of toast with *marmelada* or a pastry. **Lunch,** a hearty and leisurely meal, can begin as early as noon but is more likely eaten sometime between 2 and 5pm. After a few hours' nap, it's time to eat again. **Dinner,** a drawn-out, relaxed affair is served late, sometime between 10pm and midnight—then party all night or head home for another nap. A Greek restaurant is known as a **taverna** or **estiatorio;** a grille is a **psistaria.** Many restaurants don't offer printed menus. Waiters will ask you if you want salad, appetizers, or the works, so be careful not to wind up with mountains of food; Greek portions tend to be large. Restaurants often put bread and water on the table as a matter of course; an added charge for the bread and sometimes the water might or might not be listed on the menu. You will rarely see ice or butter; many restaurants won't have them. Service is always included in the check, but it is customary to leave some coins as an extra tip.

ON THE MENU

ARE YOU PREPARED?

Menu's in Greek tavernas are noto-riously deceptive. Their thick page may be covered with over 100 dishes but when it comes time to order, point-ing to an item on the menu is greeted with the refrain "DTHEN EE-neh EH-tee-mo" or "it is not prepared." You very well might try to order four or five items before you actually arrive at one that is attainable on that day. Rather than getting frustrated, you should take the unavailability of menu items as an encouraging sign that you have discov-ered an authentic taverna with fresh homestyle cuisine.

Greeks enjoy slow oven-cooked and stewed dishes like *yemista* (peppers, tomotoes, or other stuffable vegetable filled with rice and beef), *yiouvets* (lamb or chicken cooked slowly in orzo with a tomato sauce), and the ubiqui-tous moussaka (eggplant casserole). Pasta and vegetables infused with their sauce's flavor and tender lamb pieces which melt in your mouth are the hallmark of these dishes.

Such characteristics, however demand extended cooking times to be added to often already lengthy preparation times. For this reason a traditional taverna will carefully pre-pare its 4-5 dishes du jour in the morning. These "EH-tee-mo" or pre-pared dishes will be put on display under glass at the back of the res-taurant and are available for almost immediate consumption. Those offended by such prefabrication should bear in mind that many of the dishes are actually enhanced by maturing in their juices. The meals are prepared—are you?

CUSTOMS AND ETIQUETTE

Greek hospitality is legendary. From your first days in the country, you may be invited to drop by a stranger's home for coffee, share a meal at a local taverna, or attend an engagement party or baptism. The invitations are genuine; it's impossible to spend any length of time in the country and not have some friendly interaction with locals. Greet new acquaintances (along with shopkeepers and waiters) with *kalimera* (good morning) or *kalispera* (good evening). Personal questions aren't considered rude in Greece, and pointed inquires can be a bit disconcerting. Expect to be asked about family, career, salary, and other information by people you've just met. Returning questions in kind is expected and appreciated.

FOOD AND DRINK

As a general rule, when offered food or drink, take it—it's almost always considered rude to refuse. Coffee is usually offered upon arriving at someone's home. Wine drinkers should be aware that glasses are filled only halfway and constantly replenished; it's considered bad manners to empty your glass. When eating dinner at a restaurant, the bill is usually paid by the host rather than split amongst the diners. Never offer money in return for an invitation to dine in someone's home. A small gift, such as toys for the host's children, is a welcome token of gratitude.

PHOTOGRAPHY

Take signs forbidding photography seriously. Never photograph anything having to do with the military. Even if photography isn't specifically forbidden in a particular church or monastery, it remains amazingly rude and offensive.

ART AND ARCHITECTURE

The ancient Greeks prized aesthetics above all else, as their virtually flawless, carefully crafted works affirm. Greeks didn't produce art just to admire its beauty. Ancient works of art served religious or practical functions: decorative pottery was a hot export item, used for storing (and chugging) wine, while sculptures represented gods in temples or served as offerings and monuments to the dead. Architecture developed through the construction of temples, commercial buildings, and stadiums for performance of religious plays and for governmental gatherings. The mythological scenes painted on vases and in frescoes expressed religious values, political propaganda, or even made sexual jokes.

Greek art grew around the belief that "man is the measure of all things." The living human form became artists' favorite subject after years of dabbling with abstract and stylized geometrical shapes. Meanwhile Greek temples incorporated light and space as integral parts of the place of worship. It is impossible to overestimate how much Western culture owes to the architectural and artistic achievements of the ancient Greeks—Augustus Caesar, Michelangelo, Jacques-Louis David, Thomas Jefferson, Constantine Brancusi, and even Salvador Dalí found inspiration in Greek works. Contemporary artists still learn from 2500-year old Greek masterpieces, though many exist only as fragments.

ROOTS

CYCLADIC/MINOAN PERIOD (3000-1100 BC)

The Bronze Age Cycladic civilizations produced a minimalist style of sculpture, mostly small marble statuettes. These miniature pieces gracefully simplified the human form; a nude goddess, arms folded straight across her body, is a typical figure. Many of these enigmatic idols dazzle visitors to the **Goulandris Museum of Cycladic and Ancient Greek Art** in Athens (p. 115).

The Minoans of Crete also created scores of miniature votive statuettes, like the two earthenware **snake goddesses,** decorated with opaque colored glazes, which reside in Iraklion's **Archaeological Museum** (p. 589). It was Minoan **architecture,** however, that brought them glory, as Cycladic cultures took their cue from Minoan palaces like **Knossos** (p. 591). The palaces were cities unto themselves and their labyrinthine complexity echoed the complicated administrative and religious roles of Minoan priest-kings. The palaces' massive pillars, ceremonial stairways, and decorative stucco show Near Eastern aesthetic and structural influence, which arrived via commercial contact with Egypt and Mesopotamia.

Minoan artists used plaster to sculpt bull-leaping ceremonies, gardens, and jumping dolphins in vibrantly painted and lifelike frescoes. Though a little dusty, several Minoan **frescoes** were preserved in the ash of a volcanic eruption that destroyed much of Thira (modern Santorini) near 1500 BC and can be seen at the **National Archaeological Museum** in Athens (p. 114). Similar fresco paintings, restored by Sir Arthur Evans, can be seen at Knossos or in Iraklion's **Archaeological Museum** (p. 589). A versatile bunch, the Minoans were also renowned throughout the Aegean for their multicolored **Kamares-style pottery,** which consisted of red and white ornamentation on a dark background. Kamares-style designs included curvy abstract patterns and stylized ocean and plant motifs.

MYCENAEAN PERIOD (1600-1100 BC)

The architecture of the mainland Mycenaean culture developed in response to the Cretan Minoans. The Mycenaeans' palaces at Mycenae, Tiryns, and Pylos (p. 191) followed a more symmetrical design than earlier architecture and centered around the *megaron*, a Near East-inspired reception room. Decorative frescoes revamped the fanciful Minoan model according to Mycenaean warrior taste.

Trailblazers in their own right, the Mycenaeans were the first Europeans to produce sculpted monuments, as in the **royal tombs** and triangular **Lion's Gate** sculpture at Mycenae (p. 151). Dated to the 13th century BC, the Lion's Gate is the earliest monumental sculpture known. By 1500 BC Mycenaean royal graves had evolved into **tholos,** beehive-shaped stone structures covered in packed earth. The relief work on these tombs shows Minoan influence, whereas the large-scale masonry is distinctly Mycenaean.

GEOMETRIC PERIOD (1100-700 BC)

A new ceramics-based art evolved out of the collapse of Mycenaean civilization and the Dark Age that followed. There to pick up the pieces were the Athenians, who stood at the center of the new movement. Their pottery of the **Proto-Geometric Period** (1100-900 BC) was decorated with Mycenaean-inspired spirals, arcs, wavy lines, and concentric circles. These patterns became more intricate in the **Geometric Period,** when artists covered pottery and clay figurines with geometric motifs that resembled woven baskets. Identically posed stick-figure humans and grazing animals began to appear among the continuous, patterned bands and tight rows of thick black lines. Near Eastern contact with Greece showed up again in Syrian and Phoenician floral and animal designs. At this time Corinth joined Athens as a major ceramics center. Architects of the Geometric Period focused on the development of one-room temples with columned porches. These temples were essentially regarded as the houses of the gods or goddesses they honored, and each **oikos** (house) came complete with a sculpture of its inhabitant.

ARCHAIC PERIOD (700-480 BC)

During the Archaic Period, Greek art and architecture morphed from the stylization of earlier times to the curving, human realism of the Classical Period. Sculptors and vase painters produced abstract images of the human form, and architects fine-tuned building and proportion in construction. They perfected structures such as the acropolis, agora, amphitheater, and gymnasium.

The Doric and Ionic orders—whose columns have lined many an art history student's nightmares—departed along their own paths during these years. The **Doric order** breathed new life into the former design of a one-room *cella* (a temple's inner sanctum) and its surrounding area with new columns and classy marble. Around the 6th century BC, the Greek colonies along the coast of Asia Minor branched off into the exotic **Ionic order.** The curlicued Ionic columns contrasted with the austere Doric order in the slender, fluted bodies of each column, often topped with twin volutes (scrolled spiral uppers). Ornate Ionic temples boasted forests of columns: the Temple of Hera at Samos (p. 485) sported 134.

In the beginning of the 5th century BC, sculpture turned toward realistic depiction, reaching its height soon afterward in the Classical Period. The relaxed posture of the free-standing **Kritios Boy** (490 BC), now in Athens's **Acropolis Museum** (p. 110), broke the stiff, symmetrical mold of its archaic model (see kouros below) with an individualized personality: the Kritios Boy's weight is shifted onto one leg and his hips and torso tilt as naturally as the Earth on its axis. As sculptors focused on realism, two-dimensional art remained firmly abstract. Athenian **vase painters** depicted humans using Corinth's **black figure technique,** drawing black silhouettes with carved features. Human figures appeared in the half-profile of Egyptian art: moving figures' chests faced forward, and each person stared straight out with both eyes. The figures conveyed emotion with gestures rather than facial expression, and most pulled their hair in grief or flailed their limbs in joy.

While architects were fussing over columns, early Archaic sculptors began to craft large-scale figures called **kouroi.** Each *kouros* was a naked, idealized young man, symmetrically posed, with one leg forward, hands clenched at his sides, smiling goofily under stylized curls. The *kouroi* stood in temples as offerings to deities or as memorials to fallen warriors. An early example dedicated to Poseidon at Sounion (c. 590 BC) now stands in the **National Archaeological Museum** in Athens (p. 114). In the 6th century BC, a new obsession with the natural human form led to more lifelike *kouroi*. The female equivalent of the *kouros*, the *kore*, posed in the latest fashions instead of in her birthday suit; sculptors focused on the drape of a *kore*'s clothing, suggesting the female form through folds and hemlines.

CLASSICAL PERIOD (480-323 BC)

The arts flourished during the Classical Period, as Athens reached the peak of its political and economic power under Pericles and his successors (p. 9). Perfecting Doric architecture and dabbling in the Ionic style, Classical temples were more spacious and fluid than the stocky temples of the Archaic Period. The peerless Athenian **Acropolis** (p. 107), built during this period, embodied "classic" for the entire Classical world; its star attraction, the **Parthenon,** shows the fullness of the Greek obsession with perfect proportions. *Everything* on the Parthenon—from its floor space to the friezes above the columns—is in a four-to-nine ratio.

Sculptors mastered the natural representation of the human form during the Classical Period. The milestone sculptures of the **Temple of Zeus** at Olympia (p. 175) exhibit a meticulous attention to detail. Indeed the personal Classical style fully broke from formulaic Archaic sculpture. Notable sculptures from the Classical Period include the **Charioteer** (470 BC) at Delphi (p. 219) and the **Poseidon** (465 BC), now in the **National Archaeological Museum** (p. 114).

By the middle of the 5th century BC, Classical sculptors had loosened the stylized stiffness of the early Archaic Period, favoring a detailed realism that still lacked facial expression. Sculptors pursued a universal perfection of the human form, suppressing the imperfections that make people unique. This impersonal, idealized **severe style** embodied the idealization of Plato's forms and the athletic heroism that Pindar praised in his Olympic odes. It remained in vogue through the start of the 4th century BC. Classical potters swooned over the **red figure technique** that had been gaining steam since 540 BC. Red figure vase painting featured a black painted background, allowing the naturally reddish clay to show through as the drawn figures. Vase-makers then painted on details with a fine brush. Inspired by the new-found realism in sculpture, anonymous early Classical masters—one known as the **Berlin Painter,** another as the **Kleophrades Painter**—lent their subjects an unparalleled level of psychological depth.

HELLENISTIC PERIOD (323-46 BC)

After the death of Alexander the Great, a new Hellenistic Period rose out of the ashes of Classical Greece. Eastern Greeks made architecture a flamboyant affair. Pushing aside the simpler Doric and Ionic styles, they whipped up ornate, flower-topped **Corinthian-style columns.** Hellenistic architects worked on a monumental scale, building complexes of temples, *stoas* (colonnaded walkways), and palaces. Astoundingly precise **acoustics** graced the enormous amphitheaters at **Argos** (p. 151) and **Epidavros** (p. 159); a coin dropped on stage is audible in the most distant seat in the theaters—even 2200 years after their construction.

Hellenistic sculpture exuded passion, displaying all the technical mastery and twice the emotion of Classical works. Artists tested the aesthetic value of ugliness, sculpting the grotesque figure of **Laocoön** as snakes writhe around him, dragging him to death; only a Roman copy of the Hellenistic original survives. With the arrival of the **Roman empire** in Greece, the Hellenistic style shifted to suit Roman tastes. Greek artists created works for Romans in Italy and for the old Hellenistic kingdoms of the east. Architects built mostly Christian churches; even the Parthenon was temporarily converted to a church, though it was (fortunately) left unaltered in its structure. Under the Romans Greek art and architecture spread throughout the empire, but its innovative glory had passed.

BYZANTINE AND OTTOMAN (AD 324-1829)

The art and architecture in Greece under Byzantine and Ottoman rule belonged more to these imperial cultures than to native Greek culture. Byzantine artistry developed within a set of religious conventions that limited creative experimentation but still created magnificent mosaics, iconography, and church architecture. Early Byzantine churches make apparent their roots in Roman Christianity; based on the Roman basilica layout, the Byzantine versions were long buildings with a semicircular apse at one end and windows lining a wooden ceiling (forming a clerestory). An outer courtyard lined with columns stood on a church's western side; on the eastern side, people entered the vestibule through two doors. These doors opened onto the *naos*, the church proper. Inside a central nave reached from the church's inner door to the choir rows and was separated from two side aisles by arched colonnades. The floor and lower parts of the walls were usually covered in **marble** and the upper parts reserved for **mosaics** and often **frescoes.**

Byzantine artists transformed almost any flat surface they found into art, illuminating manuscripts, carving ivory panels, embossing bronze doors, and covering *cloisonée* enamels with jewels. The dazzling mosaics and **icons** of Byzantine churches showed the greatest of Byzantine talent: artists underwent years of spiritual and technical training before gaining permission to portray sacred subjects. Byzantine icons aimed for religious authenticity, intended to transmit the spiritual power of the subject. Each figure stared out with a soul-searing gaze, adding to the power of the images; a determined frontal pose against a gold background in the church's dim light created the illusion of the figure floating between the wall and the viewer. In Byzantine mosaics a unique

ALBANIA
FYROM
PELLA
Ruins of the Macedonian city once home to Philip II and his son, Alexander the Great.
Phillippi
Amphibolis
MACEDONIA
Vergina
Thessaloniki
TO BRINDISI, ANCONA
DODONI
The site of Zeus's oak-tree oracle.
GREECE
Dion
Olynthos
Mt. Athos
Thermaic Gulf
Mount Olympus
THESSALY
Perama Cave
Meteora
Ioannina
Krannon
EPIRUS
Acheron
Nekromentio
Volos
SPORADES
Nikopolis
IONIAN
DELPHI
One of the most important sources of wisdom in the ancient world.
Aktion
Evia
Thermon
Eretria
Levadia
ISLANDS
Gulf of Corinth
Osios Loukas
Plataiai
Athens
PELOPONNESE
Corinth
Isthmia
Ancient Corinth
Naos Poseidonos
Nemea
Aegina
Olympia
Tiryns
Temple of Aphaia
Mantinia
Epidavros
OLYMPIA
Argos
Asini
The temples, training grounds, and stadium of the first Olympic Games.
Troizen
SARONIC GULF ISLANDS
Vassae
Tegea
Saronic Gulf
N
LG
Mystras
Nestor's Palace
Ancient Messini
Sparta
MYCENAE
Legendary home to Agamemnon and the Atreus clan of classical tragedy.
Ionian Sea
Monemvasia
MEDITERRANEAN SEA
Byzantine Sights
Ancient Ruins
Falasarna
0 50 miles
0 50 kilometers

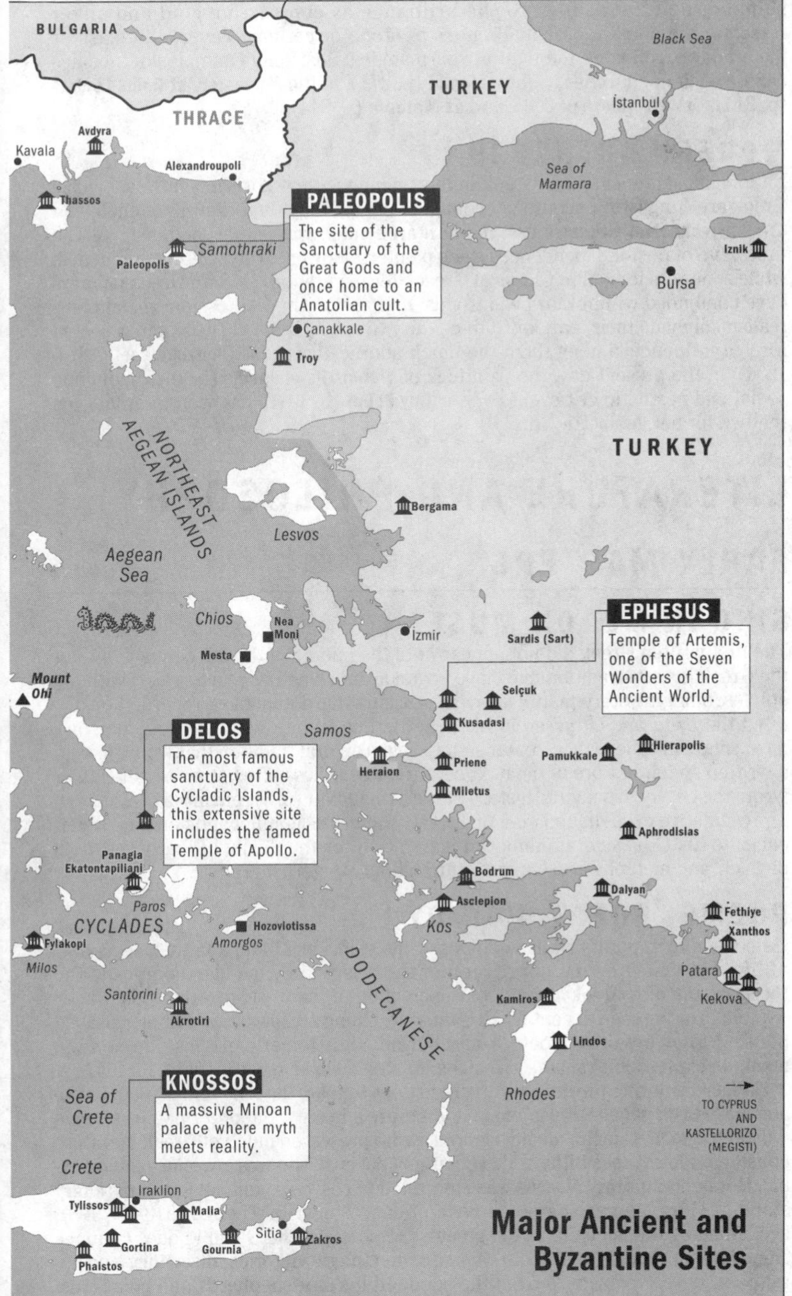
BULGARIA
THRACE
TURKEY
Black Sea
İstanbul
Sea of Marmara
Kavala
Avdyra
Alexandroupoli
Thassos
PALEOPOLIS
The site of the Sanctuary of the Great Gods and once home to an Anatolian cult.
Samothraki
Paleopolis
Iznik
Bursa
Çanakkale
Troy
NORTHEAST AEGEAN ISLANDS
TURKEY
Bergama
Lesvos
Aegean Sea
Chios
Nea Moni
Mesta
İzmir
Sardis (Sart)
EPHESUS
Temple of Artemis, one of the Seven Wonders of the Ancient World.
Mount Ohi
Selçuk
Kusadasi
DELOS
The most famous sanctuary of the Cycladic Islands, this extensive site includes the famed Temple of Apollo.
Samos
Heraion
Priene
Miletus
Pamukkale
Hierapolis
Aphrodisias
Panagia Ekatontapiliani
Paros
CYCLADES
Hozoviotissa
Amorgos
Fylakopi
Milos
Bodrum
Asclepion
Kos
Dalyan
Fethiye
Xanthos
Patara
Kekova
DODECANESE
Santorini
Akrotiri
Kamiros
Lindos
Rhodes
TO CYPRUS AND KASTELLORIZO (MEGISTI)
KNOSSOS
A massive Minoan palace where myth meets reality.
Sea of Crete
Crete
Iraklion
Tylissos
Malia
Sitia
Zakros
Gortina
Gournia
Phaistos
Major Ancient and Byzantine Sites

shimmering effect added to the brilliance as contrasting gold and silver **tesserae,** the constituent small cubes of stone or ceramic covered in glass or metallic foil, reflected the light at sharp angles. Sparkling examples of mosaics can be seen in churches in **Thessaloniki** (p. 271), at the **Monastery of Osios Loukas** (p. 215), on **Mt. Athos** (p. 303), and at **Meteora** (p. 244).

MODERN ART (1829-)

Nationalist sentiment after Greek independence led the government to subsidize Greek art. King Otto encouraged young artists to study their craft in Munich, and the **Polytechneion,** Greece's first modern art school, was established in 1838. The first wave of post-independence Greek painters showed strong German influence, while sculptors looked to Classical Greece for inspiration. Modern Greek painters have contended within European trends: Impressionism, Expressionism, and Surrealism all made their mark on 19th-century Greek artists. Other painters rejected foreign influence, among them the much adored **Theophilos Chatzimichael** (1873-1934). In the present day, the paintings of **Yiannis Psychopedis** (b. 1945) combine social and aesthetic criticism. Painter **Opy Zouni** (b. 1941) has won international renown for her geometric art.

LITERATURE AND PHILOSOPHY

EARLY MASTERS

SING IN ME, OH MUSE

The first written Greek did not appear until the middle of the 8th century BC, but the Greek literary tradition may have begun as much as 150 years earlier, with the epic-crooning mystery man **Homer.** The original bard may have recorded or dictated the *Iliad* and *Odyssey* in his own lifetime (if he was indeed one person); most scholars believe that Homer simply began an oral tradition that would lead to a written epic literature in the next century. Regardless of whether or not Homer wrote the poetry, his mythic history of the Trojan War (p. 8) remains a classic text, representative of such fundamental literary themes as conflict and heroism. References to his *Odyssey,* an immortal inspiration for the theme of journeys—both physical and metaphysical—appear throughout Western literature.

POEMS, POETS, POETRY

Homer's contemporary **Hesiod** composed the **Works and Days,** a farmer's-eye view of life that lamented the oppression of the aristocracy; he also composed the **Theogony,** the first Greek account of the creation of the world and the gods' wacky exploits. During the 7th century BC, anti-everything **Archilochus** of Paros inscribed the first known written poetry—anti-heroic, anti-Homeric elegies. In one fragment, he expresses no shame at tossing his shield aside in battle to run for his life.

On Lesvos during the 6th century, lyric poet **Sappho,** the lone female poet of the ancient world, sang of love, lovin', and nature's beauty. Sappho's poems survive only in fragments, as the medieval monks who preserved much of Greek literature considered her verses filthy and evil, largely because she was a woman and bisexual. Her contemporary **Alcaeus** was embroiled in Lesvos's political feuds; his angry stance colors his very personal lyric poems. **Pindar** of Thebes (518-438 BC), acclaimed by the ancients as the greatest of poets, wrote Olympic odes commissioned by sports-nut nobles to commemorate athletic victories. **Theocritus,** a pastoral poet, portrayed scenes from the subdued lives of shepherds and goatherds.

Roman poet **Horace** later revived the Greek model, taking its images and meters (the *sapphic* and *alcaic*), and looking to latter-day Greek poet **Callimachus** as his master. Callimachus (305-240 BC), living in Alexandria, wrote elegies in Hellenistic Greek about the origins of rites and customs; only fragments of his work survive. Callimachus's influence shaped the Alexandrian revival in Rome, where poet **Catullus** took up his slogan **mega biblion, mega kakon**—big book, big bore.

STORY BECOMES HISTORY

Herodotus—geographer, anthropologist, and the so-called "Father of History"—wrote up the epic battles and personalities of the Persian Wars in his monumental (and rather sensationalist) *Histories*. His incredibly detailed account of the wars must have come from interviews with elderly men with sharp memories, as the Persian Wars took place during Herodotus's childhood. **Thucydides** immortalized the Peloponnesian Wars, chronicling Athens's conflict with Sparta; he took the opportunity to examine the effects of war on nations and people while he was at it.

SCIENCE AND PHILOSOPHY

The philosophical-scientific writings of the ancient Greeks awed even the practically minded Romans. Other civilizations sought religious answers to the big questions, but the scattered Greek pantheon gave no easy answers, and philosophical reasoning took over instead. The first philosopher, according to Hellenic tradition, was the 6th century BC thinker **Thales of Miletus;** as none of his writings have survived, we'll have to take their word for it. Thales believed that the universe had an ordered structure and that everything moved toward a predetermined end. This **teleology,** or end-oriented worldview, contributed to every major Greek philosophy. **Pythagoras,** a math whiz, came up with theorems that still make regular appearances in high school math homework.

Early philosophical works, surviving on fragments of papyrus and in the reports of later writers, paved the road for **Socrates** (469-399 BC). A poor, ugly convict, Socrates described himself as a gadfly nipping at the ass of the horse that was Classical Athens. He brought philosophy down from the stars and into the muddy stalls of the *agora*, where he spent his days picking over the morals and beliefs of anyone who would stop for a chat. His impersonal style of asking questions is still called the Socratic Method. All the while he insisted on his own superior wisdom because he was aware of his own total ignorance. His radical lifestyle and constant questioning eventually angered influential Athenians, and he was sentenced to death for corrupting the youth. Socrates died by drinking hemlock in 399 BC.

Plato (428-348 BC) and **Aristotle** (384-322 BC) mused about the cosmos—heavenly bodies were divine, as their circular shapes embodied perfection. The ancient Greek **universe** centered around the earth; spherical planets traveled in circular orbits. Aristotle observed spontaneous events: his science had no need for pesky experimental proof, since experiments were unnatural, fake constructions—not spontaneous and real. In the same century, **Euclid** wrote *The Elements*, the source of geometry even to the present and one of the most widely translated works ever. **Archimedes** stole the show by creating complex mathematical formulas with circles and cylinders and by inventing the **Archimedes screw,** a device to move water.

Greeks experimented in **medicine** as well. In the 5th century BC, before he became famous for his oath, **Hippocrates** suggested that disease might not be the result of divine punishment but rather of natural causes. Combined speculation and observation yielded the idea of **four humors** flowing through the body (yellow bile, black bile, phlegm, and blood); an imbalance caused illness. Research at the museum in **Alexandria,** Egypt, in the 3rd century BC pushed medical knowledge further. Work on animal brains, hearts, and organs inspired **Galen of Pergamum** to try dissection. A pioneer in the queasy art of human dissection, Galen's work expanded knowledge about the human anatomy. Under Roman rule, Greek natural science wilted. The Romans were impressed by the vast body of knowledge the Greeks had acquired, but they were confused by the concept of "knowledge for knowledge's sake." Science should be a means to a useful and practical end, thought the hard-nosed Latins. During the Middle Ages, the advancements in European medical knowledge evaporated entirely. Luckily Greek scientists had written about their findings, and we can still read them today.

BYZANTINE LITERATURE

The genre of pseudo-historical romance took Greece by storm in the first century AD, along with personal love poems like *Erotopaegnia (Love Games)* and erotic novels. The era of the romance novel also produced the most read work of literature ever: the Greek-language **New Testament** of the Bible. After Emperor Constantine converted to Christianity in 338 (p. 11), most literature was written by monastery-bound theologians or court historians. **Plutarch,** writing around AD 100, constructed biographies of famous Greeks and Romans in *Parallel Lives*. In the 6th century, **Procopius,** one of Emperor Justinian's generals, reported on all aspects of his boss's reign. He wrote two conventional tracts for publication, *On the Wars* and *On the Buildings*, and left behind a **Secret History**—an insider's account of the **deviant debauchery** common in the court of Justinian and his wife Theodora. **Photios** (820-893), twice appointed Patriarch of Constantinople, admired the "pagan" works of Homer and encouraged their study. This avid reader was a writer as well; his massive *Biblioteca* chronicled Greek works in over 270 articles.

MODERN LITERATURE

Greek independence in 1821 (p. 13) gave rise to the **Ionian School** of modern literature, which dealt with the political and personal issues of the Greek revolution. **Dionysios Solomos** (1798-1857)—whose *Hymn to Liberty* became the Greek national anthem—is still referred to as the National Poet. Twentieth-century poets would infuse their own odes with Modernism, alternately denouncing and celebrating nationalism and politics. Winner of a 1979 Nobel Prize in Literature, **Odysseas Elytis** (1911-96) looked at politics in a different light and incorporated French Surrealism in an effort toward national redemption.

The many novels of **Nikos Kazantzakis** (1883-1957), perhaps the best known modern Greek author, include *Odyssey* (1958), a modern sequel to the Homeric epic, *Report to Greco* (1965), *Zorba the Greek* (1946), and *The Last Temptation of Christ* (1951); the last two made successful films. *Freedom or Death* (1956), his homage to Greek revolts against the Ottomans on his home Crete, analyzes the Greek-Turkish conflict and explores the concept of masculinity.

THE PERFORMING ARTS

THEATER

Born in the 5th century BC from a tradition of **goat songs** *(tragodoi)* dedicated to the god Dionysus, the plebeian roots of Greek drama are worlds away from our view of theater as high art. Greek drama began as a religious rite in which all attendants were both performers in the chorus and audience members. Individual acting began when, at a public competition of masked choruses in Dionysus's honor, young **Thespis** stepped out of the crowd to become Athens's first actor—hence, "thespian." By adding a second actor and other characters, **Aeschylus** (525-456 BC) composed the plays *Prometheus Bound* and the *Oresteia*, a trilogy about Agamemnon's ruinous return home from the Trojan War. **Sophocles** (496-406 BC) followed, creating the cathartic *Oedipus* trilogy, which details the ruinous tale of Oedipus, a man who becomes king by killing his father and marrying his mother. **Euripides** (485-406 BC), Sophocles's contemporary, added *Medea* and the *Bacchae* to the tradition. **Aristophanes** (450-385 BC) tossed aside the tragic medium, and wrote *The Clouds*, *Lysistrata*, and *The Frogs* in bawdy, slapstick "Old Comedy" form; Aristophanes's swipes at Socrates helped to bring about the philosopher's execution. **Menander,** creator of "New Comedy," wrote sunnier works.

Modern Greek theater labors in the shadow of its classical predecessor. A few contemporary playwrights such as **Iakovos Kambanellis** (b. 1922) and **Demitris Kehadis** (b. 1933) have wooed audiences with portrayals of 20th-century Greek life. Classical Greek theater survives as an important influence, as a body of work read and studied, and as a living, performed art. In Greece the Athens Festival (p. 106), held from June to September, features Classical drama at the ancient Theater of Herod Atticus, as well as concerts, opera, choruses, ballet, and modern dance. At the **Epidavros Theater Festival** (p. 159), even a language barrier won't detract from the ominous chorus that, in Aeschylus's time, made "boys die of fright and women have miscarriages." Tickets and programs for the festivals are available two weeks in advance at the Athens Festival Box Office, Stadiou 4, inside the arcade; this office also sells tickets to many smaller theaters and festivals, including those at Philippi, Thassos, and Dodoni.

MUSIC

Greeks have made music since the Bronze Age and early musical instruments from this period have been found on Crete. Although they had no system of musical notation before the 5th century BC, they devised a theory of harmonics. It was necessary for early poets to remember musical formulas, since poems were sung or chanted—partially to help poets remember endless epics. The musical choruses of religious rites naturally became part of evolving drama and music remained essential to Classical theater. Folk music and dances flourished in the Byzantine Era. Dances from southern Greece were often tragic or funereal; northern dances celebrated war and the harvest. Cretans danced in religious and burial rites. Today these regional distinctions have blurred. In many areas it's common to see a wide circle of locals and tourists, hands joined, dancing. The group leader flashes footwork, twirling in circles while winding around a handkerchief. Some dancers throw backward somersaults. The dance steps for the followers are comfortably repetitive. Don't hesitate to join in—stamp your feet and enjoy yourself.

Much of Greek lyric song is poetic. A new musical style emerged from Turkey's western coast in the late 19th century and unsettled these classical notions. Gritty, urban **rembetika** used traditional Greek instruments to sing about the ugly side of modern life, focusing on drugs, prison, and alienation. Convicts sang *rembetika* laments about smoking hashish and life on the run. During the population exchange with Turkey in the 1920s (p. 13), it emerged as the cry of the underclass, as newly transplanted refugees living in urban shantytowns embraced its sorrowful expressiveness. After decades of increasingly inauthentic performances, interest in traditional *rembetika* has resurfaced, and musicians strumming *bouzouki* (a traditional Greek instrument similar to a mandolin) can be found in several clubs. Trendier venues offer a playlist saturated with Western music—American hits of the 70s and 80s taint the idyllic Greek air all summer long. Popular local band **Pyx Lax** is gaining an international following. **Anna Vissi,** a native of Cyprus, has been called the Greek Madonna as she continues to light up the Greek pop charts in her mid-40s. **Despina Vandi** has more a Britney Spears flavor to her music but has a similarly sizeable following.

HOLIDAYS & FESTIVALS

Greece celebrates a host of religious and political holidays throughout the year. Dates for 2004 include the following:

DATE	NAME & LOCATION	DESCRIPTION
January 1	Feast of St. Basil/New Year's Day	Carrying on a Byzantine tradition, Greeks cut a New Year's sweet bread *(vassilopita)* baked with a lucky coin inside.
January 6	Epiphany	The Eastern Church's celebration of Jesus's baptism.
February 2	Carnival	Three weeks of feasting and dancing precede Lenten fasting. Patras, Skyros, and Kephalonia host the best celebrations.
February 23	Clean Monday	Start of Lent, the 4-week period of fasting before Easter.
March 25	Greek Independence Day/ Feast of the Annunciation	Commemorates the 1821 struggle against the Ottoman Empire and celebrates the Immaculate Conception.
April 11	Easter	The single holiest day in the Greek calendar celebrates Jesus's resurrection from the dead.
April 23	St. George's Day	Rowdy festivals in Limnos and Hania honor the dragon-slaying knight.
May 1	Labor Day	A celebration of workers and a communist demonstration.
May 20	Ascension	Commemorates Jesus's ascension into heaven. Celebrated 40 days after Easter with different rituals in each region.
May 30	Pentecost	The day of the Holy Spirit, celebrated 50 days after Easter.
August 15	Feast of the Assumption of the Virgin Mary	A celebration throughout Greece, particularly on Tinos, that honors Mary's ascent into heaven.
September 8	The Virgin Mary's Birthday	To celebrate Mary's birthday; some villages finance a feast by auctioning off the honor of carrying the Virgin's icon.
October 26	Feast of St. Demetrius	Celebrated enthusiastically in Thessaloniki. The feast coincides with the opening of a new stock of wine.
October 28	Ohi Day	Commemorates Metaxas's cry of "Οχι!" (No!) to Mussolini's demand to occupy Greece.
December 25	Christmas	Greeks celebrate both Christmas Eve and Christmas Day. Children make the rounds singing *kalanda* (carols).

ADDITIONAL RESOURCES

GENERAL HISTORY

John Boardman. *Oxford History of Classical Art* (Oxford University Press). A must-read guide, detailing the history of Greek and Roman aesthetic innovation.

Paul Cartledge. *Cambridge Illustrated History of Ancient Greece* (Cambridge University Press). A well-written, comprehensive commentary on all aspects of Ancient Greece.

Richard Clogg. *A Concise History of Greece* (Cambridge University Press). A well organized account of Modern Greek history, detailing the nineteenth and twentieth centuries as they unfolded in Greece.

MYTHOLOGY

Thomas Bulfinch. *The Age of Fable* from *Bulfinch's Mythology* (Modern Library). *The* authority on Greek mythology.

Joseph Campbell. *The Hero with a Thousand Faces* (Princeton University Press). Part of the inspiration for George Lucas's *Star Wars*, Campbell's analysis of myth draws parallels between myth and the journey of life. He postulates that there is a single archetypical mythic hero who reflects man's search for identity.

FICTION AND NON-FICTION

Aristophanes. *Lysistrata*. Athenian women go on a sex strike in an attempt to force their husbands to end the Peloponnesian War. Try Jeffrey Henderson's translation.

Wilis Barnstone. *Sappho and the Greek Lyric Poets* (Penguin). An excellent translation of works by Lesvos's favorite literary daughter.

Louis De Bernieres. *Corelli's Mandolin* (Vintage). An emotional novel about star-crossed lovers—a Kephalonian woman and an Italian officer stationed on the island during WWII.

John Fowles. *The Magus* (Dell). A story of mystery and manipulation inspired by Fowles's years as a teacher on the island of Spetses.

FILM

Mediterraneo (1991). Eight soldiers find themselves stranded on an anonymous Greek island during World War II in this Italian comedy.

Z (1969). Directed by Costa-Gavras, the thinly veiled depiction of a conspiracy to assassinate a liberal Greek politician won the Academy Award for Best Foreign Film.

Zorba The Greek (1964). An exuberant, sentimental film based on the novel by Nikos Kazantzakis. The most well-known movie about Greece (and rightfully so).

TRAVEL BOOKS

Henry Miller. *Colossus of Marousi* (Norton). Zealous account of Miller's travels in Greece at the start of World War II.

Patricia Storace. *Dinner with Persephone* (Vintage Books). With dry humor and gorgeous detail, the American poet meditates on her travel in Greece in the early 1990s.

Lawrence Durrell. *Prospero's Cell* and *Reflections on a Marine Venus* (Marlowe & Co). Both books relate to the author's years spent on the island of Corfu (p. 440).

Patrick Leigh Fermor. *The Mani* (Viking). Fermor, known for rallying Cretan resistance in World War II, writes an account of his adventures in the Mani in the 1950s.

Willard Manus. *This Way to Paradise: Dancing on the Tables* (Lycabettus Press). The hilarious memoirs of an American expat living in pre-tourist Rhodes.

The Greeks are everywhere: 1.5 million in America, over a half million in Germany, at least that many in the former USSR, and hundreds of thousands in Canada, South Africa, Asia, and Australia. All told, five million self-described Greeks live outside Greece. Melbourne, Toronto, New York, and Chicago all describe themselves as the "biggest Greek city outside Greece."

A disproportionate number of famed Greeks are from the diaspora. Aristotle Onassis (Turkey), Maria Callas (New York), and Spain's Queen Sophia come to mind, as do the poet Constantine Cavafy (Egypt), film director Costa Gavras (France), and actress Jennifer Aniston (California). George Stephanopoulos and Michael Dukakis (both Massachusetts) trail-blazed for the legions of Greek-Americans in politics. Pete Sampras and hockey star Chris Chelios are two of many sports world stars. Nicholas Negroponte (UK), founder of the Media Lab at MIT, is one of the diaspora pioneers in academia.

But in leaving their home, Greeks always looked back—nostalgia, after all, is a Greek word. Rather than fade into their adopted cultures, they maintained arriktoi desmoi—unbreakable bonds—with their heritage. The very idea of modern Greece was imported by diaspora Greeks. Before the 1821 Revolution, most Ottoman subjects in the Greek peninsula were uneducated peasants. The Western-educated diaspora taught these Greeks about their history, explaining that they were the inheritors of ancient Greece.

The independence movement began in Paris and Vienna, where the first Greek newspapers and books were published in the 18th century. It was in Paris, too, where Adamantios Korais revived the classical Greek language; his synthetic version of it, katharevousa, remained Greece's official tongue until the 1970s. In London, Alexandros Mavrokordatos used his connections to finance the revolt against the Ottomans. In Odessa on the Black Sea in 1814, Greek merchants founded the society Filiki Etairia, which became the revolution's nexus.

During the following decades, diaspora Greeks built the country's most prestigious schools, the National Library, the Archaeological Museum, the University of Athens, the Athens Observatory, and much of the infrastructure. This tradition of using hard-won earnings from abroad to finance good works at home continues: Until the 1990s, diaspora remittances were Greece's largest source of foreign currency.

The diaspora elite's role in the Revolution was so profound that it sparked conflict with native Greeks—who, having suffered the Ottoman yoke, felt they had a greater claim to the new nation. But the historical vision of a Greece rooted in antiquity and Byzantium ultimately prevailed, expanding the notion of Greekness. Said one rousing orator in 1844 in the Greek parliament: "The Kingdom of Greece is not Greece. It constitutes only one part, the smallest and poorest. A Greek is not only a man who lives within the Kingdom, but also one who lives in Ioannina, Serrai, Adrianople, Constantinople, Smyrna, Trebizond, Crete and in any land associated with Greek history and the Greek race."

This notion of "cultural Greekness" was translated into the Great Idea, which guided Greek foreign policy for almost a century and sought to unite Greece with the capital of Byzantium, Constantinople (now Istanbul), and the Asia Minor coast. That dream ended in 1922, when Kemal Ataturk, the founder of Turkey, led an assault on Smyrna that killed tens of thousands of Greeks. The following year, the Treaty of Lausanne sent over 1 million Greeks from Asia Minor, their home for over 3,000 years, to Greece, a homeland they had never known. A similar fate befell the 100,000 Greeks in Egypt, driven out by Nasser's 1952 revolution. The most recent flood of ethnic immigration came in the 1990s, when hundreds of thousands of Greeks liberated from communist rule in Albania and the former USSR made their way home.

Today's diaspora communities are largely the product of two great waves of economic emigration from Greece: the first at the turn of the 20th century, the second after World War II. The Greek-American community has grown vastly in size, influence, and economic might—they constitute the most prosperous ethnic group in the US. Similar success stories can be told of the communities in Australia, Canada, and in 70 other countries around the world.

Gregory A. Maniatis is the founder of Odyssey Magazine, *the leading international magazine about Greece and Greeks around the world. He has also contributed to* New York Magazine, *the* Independent, *the* Washington Monthly, Time-Life Books, *and other publications.*

ESSENTIALS

FACTS FOR THE TRAVELER

ENTRANCE REQUIREMENTS

Passport (p. 35). Required for citizens of Australia, Canada, Ireland, New Zealand, the UK, and the US.

Visa (p. 35). Required for citizens of South Africa.

Work Permit (p. 35). Required for all EU citizens planning to work in Greece for more than 90 days and all other foreigners planning to work in Greece for any length of time.

Driving Permit (p. 61). Required for all those planning to drive.

EMBASSIES AND CONSULATES

GREECE CONSULAR SERVICES ABROAD

Australia Embassy: 9 Turrana St., Yarralumla, **Canberra,** ACT 2600 (☎02 6273 3011; fax 6273 2620). **Consulates:** 366 King William St., 1st Fl., **Adelaide,** SA 5000 (☎08 8211 8066; fax 8211 8820); Stanhill House, 34 Queens Rd., **Melbourne,** VIC 3004 (☎03 866 4524; fax 866 4933); 16 St. George's Terr., **Perth,** WA 6000 (☎08 9325 6608; fax 9325 2940); 15 Castlereagh St., Level 20, **Sydney,** NSW 2000 (☎02 9221 2388; fax 9221 1423).

Canada Embassy: 80 MacLaren St., **Ottawa,** ON K2P 0K6 (☎613-238-6271; www.greekembassy.ca). **Consulates:** 1170 Place du Frère André, Suite 300, **Montreal,** QC H3B 3C6 (☎514-875-2119; www.grconsulatemtl.net); 365 Bloor St. E Suite 1800, **Toronto,** ON M4W 3L4 (☎416-515-0133; www.grconsulate.com); 500-688 West Hastings St., **Vancouver,** BC V6B 1P1 (☎604-681-1381; fax 681-6656).

Ireland Embassy: 1 Upper Pembroke St., Dublin 2 (☎1 676 7254; fax 1 661 8892).

New Zealand Embassy: 5-7 Willeston St., 10th Fl., Box 24066, Wellington (☎04 473 7775; fax 473 7441).

South Africa Embassy: 1003 Church St., Hatfield, **Arcadia-Pretoria** 0028 (☎12 437 3523; fax 434 313). **Consulates:** 71 Victoria Embankment, Suite 1101, Victoria Maine Bldg., **Durban** 4000; 11 Wellington Road, 3rd Fl., Parktown, **Johannesburg** 2193 (☎11 484 1794).

UK Embassy: 1a Holland Park, London W113TP (☎020 7229 3850; www.greekembassy.org.uk). **Consulate:** 1a Holland Park, London W113TP (☎020 7221 6467; fax 7243 3202).

US Embassy: 2221 Massachusetts Ave., NW, **Washington, D.C.** 20008 (☎202-939-1300; www.greekembassy.org). **Consulates:** Tower Place, Suite 1670, 3340 Peachtree Rd., NE, **Atlanta,** GA 30326 (☎404-261-3313; atlanta@greekembassy.org); 86 Beacon St., **Boston,** MA 02108-3304 (☎617-523-0100; www.greekembassy.org/boston); 650 North St. Clair St., **Chicago,** IL 60611 (☎312-335-3915; www.greekembassy.org/chicago); 520 Post Oak Blvd., Suite 310, **Houston,** TX 77027 (☎713-840-7522; www.greekembassy.org/houston); 12424 Wilshire Blvd., Suite 800, **Los Angeles,** CA 90025 (☎310-826-5555; www.greekembassy.org/losangeles); World Trade Center, 2 Canal St., Suite 2318, **New Orleans,** LA 70130 (☎504-523-1167;

www.greekembassy.org/neworleans); 69 East 79th St., **New York,** NY 10021 (☎212-988-5500; www.greekembassy.org/newyork); 2441 Gough St., **San Francisco,** CA 94123 (☎415-775-2102; www.greekembassy.org/sanfrancisco); 2211 Massachusetts Ave. NW, **Washington, D.C.** 20008 (☎202-939-1318; www.greekembassy.org/dc).

CONSULAR SERVICES IN GREECE

A full listing of embassies is available at the Athens tourist office (p. 87). Embassies are generally open in the morning. All embassies, unless noted, are in **Athens.**

Australia: D. Soutsou and Tsoha 37, 115 21 (☎210 645 0404; www.auseb.gr). Open M-F 8:30am-12:30pm.

Canada: Ioannou Genadiou 4, 115 21 (☎210 727 3400; www.dfait-maeci.gc.ca/canadaeuropa/greece). Open M-F 8:30am-12:30pm. **Consulate:** Tsimiski 17, **Thessaloniki** 546 24 (☎231 025 6350; fax 231 025 6351).

European Community: Vas. Sofias 2 (☎210 727 2100; fax 210 724 4620). Open M-F 9am-5pm.

Ireland: Vas. Konstantinou 7, 106 74 (☎210 723 2771; fax 210 729 3383). Open M-F 9am-4pm.

South Africa: Kifissias 60, 151 25 (☎210 610 6645; www.southafrica.gr). Open M-F 8am-4pm.

UK: Ploutarchou 1, 106 75 (☎210 727 2600; www.british-embassy.gr). Open M-F 8am-3pm.

US: Vas. Sofias 91, 101 60 (☎210 721 2951; fax 210 645 6282; www.usembassy.gr). Open M-F 8:30am-5pm, visa service 8:30-noon. **Consulate:** Tsimiski 43, 7th Fl., **Thessaloniki** 546 23 (☎231 024 2905; www.usconsulate.gr).

TOURIST OFFICES

Tourist info in Greece is available in English 24hr. at ☎171.

Start early when trying to contact tourist offices—like most things Greek, they run on their own relaxed schedule. Polite persistence coupled with genuine excitement and interest works wonders. Two national organizations oversee tourism: the **Greek National Tourist Organization (GNTO),** known as the **EOT** in Greece, and the **tourist police.** The GNTO can supply general information about sights and accommodations throughout the country. (For additional info and offices abroad, see www.gnto.gr.) The main office is in Athens at Tsochas 7 (☎210 870 7000; info@gnto.gr). Another office is located at El. Venizelos Airport (☎210 354 5101, 210 353 0445). Tourist police deal with local issues: finding a room or bus schedules. Offices have long hours and the staff are often quite willing to help, though English may be limited. In smaller towns, travel agencies will be more helpful (and more likely to exist) than tourist offices; feel free to stop in and ask for advice. *Let's Go* lists tourist organizations in the **Practical Information** sections.

Australia and New Zealand: Level 3, 51 Pitt St., Sydney, NSW 2000 (☎02 9241 1663; fax 9235 2174; hto@tpg.com.au).

Canada: 91 Scollard St., 2nd Fl., **Toronto,** ON M5R 1G4 (☎416-968-2220; fax 968-6533; grnto.tor@sympatico.ca); 1170 Place du Frére André, Suite 300, **Montréal,** QC H3B 3C6 (☎514-871-1535; fax 871-1498; gntomtl@aei.ca).

UK and Ireland: 4 Conduit St., London W1S 2DJ (☎207 795 9300; www.tourist-offices.org.uk).

US: Head Office, Olympic Tower, 645 Fifth Ave., 9th Fl., New York, NY 10022 (☎212-421-5777; www.greektourism.com).

DOCUMENTS AND FORMALITIES

PASSPORTS

REQUIREMENTS. Citizens of Australia, Canada, Ireland, New Zealand, South Africa, the UK, and the US need valid passports to enter Greece and to re-enter their home countries. All except citizens of South Africa can apply for a passport at any post office, passport office, or court of law. Those of South Africa can apply for a passport at any Home Affairs office. File new or renewal applications well in advance of departure, but most offices do offer rush services for a very steep fee.

ONE EUROPE. The European Union (EU), with political, legal, and economic institutions spans 15 member states: Austria, Belgium, Denmark, Finland, France, Germany, Greece, Ireland, Italy, Luxembourg, The Netherlands, Portugal, Spain, Sweden, and the UK. By May 2004, 10 new members will join the EU: Cyprus, the Czech Republic, Estonia, Hungary, Latvia, Lithuania, Malta, Poland, Slovakia, and Slovenia. In 1999 the EU established **freedom of movement** across 15 countries–the entire EU minus Ireland and the UK, but plus Iceland and Norway. This means that border controls between these countries have been abolished and visa policies harmonized. While you're still required to carry a passport (or government-issued ID card for EU citizens) when crossing an internal border, once admitted into one country, you're free to travel to all participating states. The only times you'll see a border guard within the EU are traveling between the British Isles and the Continent. For more important travel consequences of the EU, see **The Euro** (p. 37) and **Customs in the EU** (p. 36).

PASSPORT MAINTENACE. Be sure to photocopy your passport, as well as your visas, traveler's check serial numbers, and any other important documents. Carry one set of copies in a safe place, apart from the originals, and leave another set at home. If you lose your passport, immediately notify the local police and the nearest embassy or consulate of your home government. To expedite its replacement, you will need to know all information previously recorded and show ID and proof of citizenship. Embassies in Athens can supply you with a replacement in as little as 2hr. Any visas stamped in your old passport will be irretrievably lost.

VISAS, INVITATIONS, AND WORK PERMITS

VISAS. As of August 2003, citizens of South Africa need a visa in addition to a valid passport for entrance to Greece; citizens of Australia, Canada, Ireland, New Zealand, the UK, and the US do not need visas. Visas cost US$45-60 and allow you to spend three months in Greece. Visas can be purchased at all Greek embassies and consulates in foreign countries. US citizens can take advantage of the **Center for International Business and Travel** (**CIBT;** ☎800-925-2428), which secures visas for travel to almost all countries for a service charge. Double-check on entrance requirements at the nearest Greek embassy or consulate (see **Embassies and Consulates Abroad,** p. 33) for updated info before departure.

WORK AND STUDY PERMITS. Admission as a visitor does not include the right to work, which is authorized only by a work permit. Entering Greece to study requires a special visa. (See **Alternatives to Tourism: Working,** p. 76.)

IDENTIFICATION

Always carry two forms of identification on your person, including at least one photo ID; a passport and a driver's license or birth certificate is usually adequate. Never carry all of your IDs together; split them up in case of theft or loss.

TEACHER, STUDENT, AND YOUTH IDENTIFICATION. The **International Student Identity Card (ISIC),** the most widely accepted form of student ID, provides discounts on some sights, accommodations, food, and transportation; access to 24hr. emergency helpline (North America ☎877-370-ISIC, elsewhere US collect +1 715-345-0505); and insurance benefits for US cardholders. Discounts include 15% off flights on Aegean Airlines, 25-30% off rentals with some major agencies, and free or reduced entry into National Archaeological Sites and Museums. Applicants must be students of a secondary or post-secondary school and must be at least 12 years old. Because of the proliferation of fake ISICs, some services (particularly airlines) require additional proof of student identity. The **International Teacher Identity Card (ITIC)** offers teachers the same insurance coverage and similar but limited discounts. For travelers who are under 26 years old but not students, the **International Youth Travel Card (IYTC)** offers many similar benefits as the ISIC. The **International Student Exchange ID Card (ISE)** also provides discounts, medical benefits, and the ability to purchase student airfares. Each of these identity cards costs US$22 or equivalent. ISICs and ITICs are valid for roughly six months; IYTCs are valid for one year. Many student travel agencies (p. 52) issue the cards; or for more information, contact the **International Student Travel Confederation (ISTC),** Herengracht 479, 1017 BS Amsterdam, The Netherlands (☎+31 20 421 28 00; www.istc.org).

CUSTOMS

Upon entering Greece you must declare certain items from abroad and pay a duty on the value of those articles if they exceed the allowance established by Greece's customs service. Note that goods and gifts purchased at duty-free shops abroad are not exempt from duty or sales tax; "duty-free" merely means that you need not pay a tax in the country of purchase. Duty-free allowances were abolished for travel between EU member states on July 1, 1999 but still exist for those arriving from outside the EU. Upon returning home you must likewise declare all articles acquired abroad and pay a duty on the value of articles in excess of your home country's allowance. In order to expedite your return, make a list of any valuables brought from home and register them with customs before traveling abroad and be sure to keep receipts for all goods acquired abroad.

CUSTOMS IN THE EU. As well as freedom of movement of people within the EU (p. 35), travelers in EU member states can also take advantage of the freedom of movement of goods. This means that there are no customs controls at internal EU borders (i.e., you can take the blue customs channel at the airport), and travelers are free to transport whatever legal substances they like as long as it is for their own personal (non-commercial) use—up to 800 cigarettes, 10L of spirits, 90L of wine (60L of sparkling wine), and 110L of beer. Duty-free allowances were abolished on July 1, 1999 for travel between EU member states, but travelers between the EU and the rest of the world still get a duty-free allowance when passing through customs.

MONEY

CURRENCY AND EXCHANGE

This chart is based on August 2003 rates between euros (€) and Australian dollars (AUS$); Canadian dollars (CDN$); Irish pounds (IR£); New Zealand dollars (NZ$); South African rands (ZAR); British pounds (UK£); and US dollars (US$).

EURO (€)		
	AUS$1 = €0.57	€1 = AUS$1.75
	CDN$1 = €0.63	€1 = CDN$1.59
	IR£1 = €1.42	€1 = IR£0.71
	NZ$1 = €0.51	€1 = NZ$1.96
	ZAR1 = €0.12	€1 = ZAR8.26
	US$1 = €0.88	€1 = US$1.14
	UK£1 = €1.42	€1 = UK£0.71

It's generally cheaper to convert money in Greece than at home. While currency exchange will probably be available in your arrival airport, it's wise to bring enough foreign currency to last for your first 24 to 72hr. When changing money, try to go only to a bank (τραπεζα, TRAH-peh-za) with at most a 5% margin between buy and sell prices. You lose money with every transaction, so **convert large sums.**

If you use traveler's checks or bills, carry some in small denominations for times when you are forced to exchange money at disadvantageous rates but bring a range of denominations since charges may be levied per check cashed. Store your money in a variety of forms; ideally at any given time, you will be carrying some cash, some traveler's checks, and an ATM and/or credit card.

THE EURO. The official currency of 12 members of the EU is now the euro. The currency has some important—and positive—consequences for travelers hitting more than one euro-zone country. First, money-changers across the euro-zone are obliged to exchange money at the official, fixed rate (see below), and at no commission (though they may still charge a small service fee). Second, euro-denominated traveler's checks allow you to pay for goods and services across the euro-zone, again at the official rate and commission-free.

TRAVELER'S CHECKS

Traveler's checks are a safe means of carrying funds. Check issuers provide refunds if the checks are lost or stolen and many provide additional services, such as toll-free refund hotlines abroad, emergency message services, and stolen credit card assistance. American Express and Visa are the most widely recognized brands. Most banks will exchange checks but often hit you with poor rates of exchange. When purchasing checks, ask about toll-free refund hotlines and the location of refund centers; always carry emergency cash.

American Express: Cheques available at select banks, at all AmEx offices, and online (www.americanexpress.com; US delivery only). American Express cardholders can also purchase cheques by phone (☎888-269-6669). AAA (p. 61) offers commission-free cheques to its members. Available in Australian, British, Canadian, European, Japanese, and US currencies. *Cheques for Two* can be signed by either of 2 people traveling together. For purchase locations or more information contact AmEx's service centers: in Australia ☎800 68 80 22; the UK 0800 587 6023; the US and Canada 800-221-7282; New Zealand 0508 555 358; elsewhere US collect +1 801-964-6665.

Visa: Checks available at banks worldwide. For nearest office location, call a service center: In the UK ☎0800 51 58 84; US 800-227-6811; elsewhere UK collect +44 020 7937 8091. Checks available in British, Canadian, European, Japanese, and US currencies.

Travelex/Thomas Cook In the UK ☎0800 62 21 01; in the US and Canada 800-287-7362; elsewhere UK collect +44 1733 31 89 50.

ESSENTIALS

CREDIT, DEBIT, AND ATM CARDS

Where accepted, credit cards often offer superior exchange rates—up to 5% better than the retail rate used by banks and currency exchange establishments. Credit cards may also offer services such as insurance or emergency help; sometimes they are required to reserve hotel rooms or rental cars. **MasterCard** (a.k.a. **EuroCard** or **Access**) and **Visa** are widely welcomed in Greece. **American Express** cards are often accepted; they work at some ATMs and at AmEx offices and major airports.

GETTING CASH. Banks in Greece and their ATM withdrawal rates:
Alpha Bank 1%
Bank of Piraeus €3.52 flat
National Bank of Greece €1.50+.05%
Agricultural Bank of Greece €1.50 flat
Merchants Bank €1.50+1% for European bank users, €2.50+1% for others
EuroBank €1.50 flat

ATM and debit cards are common in Greece. Depending on your home bank's system, you can probably access your bank account from abroad. ATMs get the same exchange rate as credit cards, but there is often a limit on the amount you can withdraw per day (around US$500). There is also typically a surcharge of US$5-10 per withdrawal. The two major international money networks are **Cirrus** (to locate ATMs, US ☎800-424-7787; www.mastercard.com) and **Visa/PLUS** (to locate ATMs US ☎800-843-7587; www.visa.com). Most ATMs charge a transaction fee.

PIN NUMBERS & ATMS. To use an ATM in Europe, you must have a four-digit **Personal Identification Number (PIN).** If your PIN is longer than four digits, talk to your bank. Credit cards don't usually come with PINs, so if you intend to hit up ATMs in Greece with a credit card, call the company to request one. People with alphabetic, rather than numeric, PINs may also be thrown off by the lack of letters on European cash machines. The following gives the corresponding numbers to use: 1=QZ; 2=ABC; 3=DEF; 4=GHI; 5=JKL; 6=MNO; 7=PRS; 8=TUV; and 9=WXY. Note that if you punch the wrong code into the machine three times, it will swallow your card for good.

GETTING MONEY FROM HOME

If you run out of money while traveling, the easiest and cheapest solution is to have someone back home make a deposit to your credit card or ATM card. Failing that, consider one of the following options.

WIRING MONEY. A **bank money transfer** means asking a bank back home to wire money to a bank in Greece. This is the cheapest way to transfer cash but it's also the slowest, usually taking several days or more. Note that some banks only issue local currency, with potentially poor exchange rates. Money transfer services like **Western Union** are faster and more convenient than bank transfers—but also much pricier. Western Union has many locations worldwide and can transfer money in as little as 15min. To find one, visit www.westernunion.com, or call from: Australia ☎800 501 500; Canada 800-235-0000; Greece 210 927 1010; New Zealand 800 27 0000; South Africa 0860 100031; the UK 0800 83 38 33; the US 800-325-6000. Money transfer services are also available at **American Express.**

US STATE DEPARTMENT (US CITIZENS ONLY). In dire emergencies only, the US State Department will forward money within hours to the nearest consular office, which will then disburse it according to instructions for a US$15 fee. If you wish to use this service, you must contact the Overseas Citizens Service division of the US State Department (☎202-647-5225; nights, Sundays, and holidays ☎202-647-4000).

COSTS

A bare-bones day in Greece (camping or sleeping in hostels/guest houses, buying food at supermarkets) would cost about €25-35; a slightly more comfortable day (sleeping in hostels/guesthouses and the occasional budget hotel, eating one meal a day at a restaurant, going out at night) would run €35-45. Don't forget to factor in emergency reserve funds (at least US$200) when planning how much money you'll need.

TIPPING AND BARGAINING

TIPPING. Greek law stipulates that restaurant and cafe prices include a 13% gratuity surcharge. It is common to round up your check to the nearest euro. You do not need to leave a tip unless you want to show your appreciation for a particularly good server (around 5% over your total). Similar rules apply to taxi rides.

BARGAINING. Bargaining skills probably won't get you as far as they would have even five years ago, but you can try your luck with them when appropriate. Paying the asked price for street wares might leave the seller marveling at your naïveté, while bargaining at the shop of a master craftsman will be seen as rude and disrespectful. For informal venues, the price tends to be more flexible. If unclear whether bargaining is appropriate in a situation, hang back and watch someone else buy. Merchants with any pride in their wares will refuse to sell to someone who has offended them in the negotiations. **Domatia** (p. 44) prices rise in summer and fall in the winter (unless you're visiting a mountain town known for winter activities). It is likely you will have success bargaining in domatia and other small **hotels.** If your **taxi** trip won't be metered or ticketed—though in general you should be seeking out metered rides—bargain before you get going.

TAXES

Greece imposes a value added tax (VAT), which is included in the market price, around 18% for most items (but, for example, 4% on books). Non-EU citizens can usually get a VAT refund of 18% on VAT items, but filing for one is an annoying process; even at Venizelos International Airport, it is hard to pinpoint a person to address the issue of VAT refunds. Still, if you have spent a considerable amount of money and are determined to get your refund, contact **Global Refund** (☎210 957 7091, 957 7092, or 957 7093), which supplies tax-free shopping in many Venizelos Airport shops. Keep in mind there are some restrictions on VAT refunds.

SAFETY AND SECURITY

PERSONAL SAFETY

EXPLORING. Solo travelers may feel like they stand out among Greeks, who don't usually travel alone. Westerners may also feel uncomfortable around pro-KKE, anti-American, and anti-Western graffiti (see **The KKE,** p. 15). If you encounter anti-

Western sentiment, just avoid conflict and walk away. To avoid unwanted attention, blend in as much as possible. Respecting local customs (sometimes dressing more conservatively) may placate would-be hecklers. Familiarize yourself with the area before setting out and carry yourself with confidence. Check maps indoors, not on the street. When traveling alone, tell someone at home your itinerary and never admit that you're by yourself. When walking at night, avoid dark alleyways. If you feel uncomfortable, leave as quickly and directly as you can.

SELF DEFENSE. There is no sure-fire way to avoid all threatening situations you might encounter while traveling but a good self-defense course will give you concrete ways to react to unwanted advances. **Impact, Prepare, and Model Mugging** can refer you to local courses in the US (☎800-345-5425; www.impactsafety.org). Workshops (2-3hr.) start at US$50; full courses (20hr.) run US$350-500.

DRIVING. If you use a **car,** learn Greek driving signals. If your car breaks down, wait for police to assist you. For long drives in desolate areas, invest in a cellular phone and a roadside assistance program (p. 61). **Sleeping in your car** is one of the most dangerous, often illegal, ways to get rest. For info on **hitchhiking,** see p. 62.

TERRORISM. The 2004 Olympics in Athens have forced Greece's government to focus on effectively combatting terrorism. Having pledged after September 11, 2001 to disband the high-profile, anti-NATO, anti-US **November 17 (N17) group** (see **November 17,** p. 15), officials arrested its alleged mastermind, Alexandros Giotopoulos, on July 17, 2002. Hearings against him and other N17 members began in March 2003. In 28 years N17 has claimed responsibility for 23 deaths, including the assassination of British Defense attaché Stephen Saunders on June 8, 2000. Tourists have rarely been targeted by Greek terrorist groups but should be aware of their existence and of potential terrorist threats surrounding the Olympics.

FINANCIAL SECURITY

PROTECTING YOUR VALUABLES. There are a few steps you can take to minimize the financial risk associated with traveling. First, **bring as little with you as possible.** Second, buy a few combination **padlocks** to secure your belongings either in your pack or in a hostel or train station locker. Third, **carry as little cash as possible.** Keep your traveler's checks and ATM/credit cards in a **money belt**—not a "fanny pack"—along with your passport and ID cards. Fourth, **keep a small cash reserve separate from your primary stash.** This should be about US$50 (US$ or euros are best) sewn into or stored in the depths of your pack, along with your traveler's check numbers and important photocopies.

CON ARTISTS AND PICKPOCKETS. In large cities **con artists** often work in groups and children are among the most effective. Beware of certain classics: sob stories that require money or mustard spilled/saliva spit onto your shoulder to distract you while they snatch your bag. **Never let your passport and your bags out of your sight. Pickpockets** are pervasive in urban areas, especially on public transportation such as on the Athens Metro. Also be alert in telephone booths. If you must say your calling card number, do so quietly; if you punch it in, make sure no one can look over your shoulder. Female travelers in particular should beware of one known trick: a female beggar, holding what appears to be a baby, approaches. The woman appears as if she will simply ask for money until she tosses the baby at the traveler, causing the traveler to drop her purse or bags. The beggar runs off with the bounty while the tricked tourist realizes the "baby" was a bundle of blankets.

ACCOMMODATIONS AND TRANSPORTATION. Never leave your belongings unattended; crime can occur anywhere. Be particularly careful on **buses** and **trains;** horror stories abound about determined thieves who wait for travelers to fall asleep.

Carry your backpack in front of you where you can see it. When traveling with others, sleep in alternate shifts. When alone use good judgement in selecting a train compartment: never stay in an empty one and use a lock to secure your pack to the luggage rack. Try to sleep on top bunks with your luggage stored above you (if not in bed with you), and keep important documents and other valuables on your person. If traveling by **car,** don't leave valuables in it while you are away.

DRUGS AND ALCOHOL

When you're in Greece, you're subject to its laws, so get to know them before leaving. If you carry **prescription drugs,** have a copy of the prescriptions themselves and a note from a doctor available, especially at border crossings. Keep all medication with you in your carry-on luggage. Authorities are particularly vigilant at the Turkish and Albanian borders.

HEALTH

BEFORE YOU GO

In your passport write the names of any people you wish to be contacted in case of a medical emergency and list any allergies or medical conditions. Matching a prescription to a foreign equivalent is not always easy, safe, or possible, so carry up-to-date, legible prescriptions or a statement from your doctor stating the medication's trade name, manufacturer, chemical name, and dosage. Names of important drugs in Greek tend to mimic their English names (i.e., Greek doctors and pharmacists recognize the words antibiotic, penicillin, acetominophen, etc.).

IMMUNIZATIONS AND PRECAUTIONS

Travelers should make sure that the following vaccines are up to date: **MMR** (for measles, mumps, and rubella); **DTaP** or **Td** (for diptheria, tetanus, and pertussis); **OPV** (for polio); **HbCV** (for haemophilus influenza B); and **HBV** (for B). For advice on immunizations and prophylaxis, consult the CDC (see below) in the US or the equivalent in your home country and check with a doctor for guidance.

USEFUL ORGANIZATIONS AND PUBLICATIONS

The US **Centers for Disease Control and Prevention** (**CDC;** ☎877-FYI-TRIP; toll-free fax 888-232-3299; www.cdc.gov/travel) maintains an international travelers' hotline and an informative website. The CDC's comprehensive booklet *Health Information for International Travel,* an annual rundown of disease, immunization, and general health advice, is free online or US$30 via the Public Health Foundation (☎877-252-1200). Consult the appropriate government agency of your home country for consular information sheets on health, entry requirements, **travel advisories,** and other issues for various countries. For quick information on health and other travel warnings, US citizens should call the **Overseas Citizens Services** (☎202-647-5225; 5pm-8:15am 202-647-4000), or contact a passport agency, embassy, or consulate abroad. For information on medical evacuation services and travel insurance firms, see the US government's website at http://travel.state.gov/medical.html or the **British Foreign and Commonwealth Office** (www.fco.gov.uk). For general health info, contact the **American Red Cross** (☎800-564-1234; www.redcross.org).

MEDICAL ASSISTANCE ON THE ROAD

All travelers from the EU receive free health care in Greece with the presentation of an **E111 form.** A doctor can be found on every inhabited island and in every town; emergency treatment is available to travelers of all nationalities in public hospitals. While Greece offers outstanding medical training, the healthcare system is vastly underfunded. Public hospitals are overcrowded; in some locations, their hygiene may not be the best. Private hospitals generally provide better care and heavier bills; to use them you will need good **health insurance.** If your regular policy does not cover travel abroad, you may wish to buy additional coverage (p. 52).

Pharmacies (φαρμακια, far-mah-KEE-ah), labeled by green or red crosses, are on every street corner. In most towns and cities, at least one pharmacy is open at all hours—most post listings of available 24hr. pharmacies in their windows. If you are concerned about obtaining medical assistance while traveling, you may wish to employ special support services. The *MedPass* from **GlobalCare, Inc.,** 6875 Shiloh Rd. East, Alpharetta, GA 30005, USA (☎800-860-1111; fax 678-341-1800; www.globalems.com), provides 24hr. international medical assistance, support, and medical evacuation resources. The **International Association for Medical Assistance to Travelers (IAMAT;** US ☎716-754-4883, Canada 519-836-0102; www.cybermall.co.nz/NZ/IAMAT) has free membership, lists English-speaking doctors worldwide, and offers detailed info on immunization requirements and sanitation.

Those with medical conditions (such as diabetes, allergies to antibiotics, epilepsy, or heart conditions) may want to obtain a **Medic Alert** membership (first year US$35, annually thereafter US$20), which includes a stainless steel ID tag, among other benefits, like a 24hr. collect-call number. Contact the Medic Alert Foundation, 2323 Colorado Ave, Turlock, CA 95382, USA (☎888-633-4298; outside US 209-668-3333; www.medicalert.org).

ONCE IN GREECE

ENVIRONMENTAL HAZARDS

Heat exhaustion and dehydration: Heat exhaustion leads to nausea, excessive thirst, headaches, and dizziness. Avoid it by drinking plenty of fluids, eating salty foods (e.g. crackers), and abstaining from dehydrating beverages (e.g., alcohol and caffeine).

Sunburn: If you get sunburned, drink more fluids than usual. Severe sunburns can lead to sun poisoning, a condition that affects the entire body, causing fever, chills, nausea, and vomiting. Sun poisoning should always be treated by a doctor.

High altitude: If traveling to mountainous regions of Greece, allow your body a couple of days to adjust to less oxygen before exerting yourself. Note that alcohol is more potent and UV rays are stronger at elevation.

FOOD- AND WATER-BORNE DISEASES

In Greece the tap water is fairly safe. Still bottled water is inexpensive and widely available, so drink it if you can and in rural areas where the water supply might be suspect. Always wash your hands before eating; your bowels will thank you. **Traveler's diarrhea** results from drinking untreated water or eating uncooked foods. Symptoms include nausea, bloating, and urgency. Try quick-energy, non-sugary foods to keep your strength up. Over-the-counter anti-diarrheals (e.g., Imodium) may counteract the problems. The most dangerous side effect is dehydration; drink water with a little sugar or honey and a pinch of salt, try decaffeinated soft drinks, or eat salted crackers. If you develop a fever or your symptoms don't go away after 4-5 days, consult a doctor. Consult a doctor immediately for children.

OTHER INFECTIOUS DISEASES

Rabies: Transmitted through the saliva of infected animals; fatal if untreated. By the time symptoms (thirst and muscle spasms) appear, the disease is in its terminal stage. If you are bitten, wash the wound thoroughly, seek immediate medical care, and try to have the animal located. A rabies vaccine, which consists of 3 shots given over a 21-day period, is available but is only semi-effective.

Hepatitis B: A viral infection of the liver transmitted via bodily fluids or needle-sharing. Symptoms, which may not surface until years after infection, include jaundice, loss of appetite, fever, and joint pain. A 3-shot vaccination sequence is recommended for health-care workers, sexually-active travelers, and anyone planning to seek medical treatment abroad; it must begin 6 months before traveling.

Hepatitis C: Similar to Hepatitis B, but the mode of transmission differs. IV drug users, those with occupational exposure to blood, hemodialysis patients, and recipients of blood transfusions are at the highest risk; the disease is also spread through sex and sharing items like razors and toothbrushes that may have traces of blood on them.

AIDS, HIV, AND STDS

For detailed information on Acquired Immune Deficiency Syndrome (AIDS) in Greece, call the US Centers for Disease Control's 24hr. hotline (☎800-342-2437) or contact the Joint United Nations Programme on HIV/AIDS (UNAIDS), 20, Ave. Appia, CH-1211 Geneva 27, Switzerland (☎+41 22 791 3666; fax 22 791 4187). Greece does not require HIV tests for tourists or visa-carriers. Some Sexually Transmitted Diseases (STDs) are easier to catch than HIV and can be deadly. Hepatitis B and C (p. 42) can also be transmitted sexually. Though condoms, available throughout Greece, may protect you from some STDs, oral or even tactile contact can lead to transmission. Bring reliable contraception with you.

WOMEN'S HEALTH

Women traveling in unsanitary conditions are vulnerable to **urinary tract** and **bladder infections,** common and uncomfortable bacterial conditions that cause a burning sensation and painful (often frequent) urination. Over-the-counter medicines can sometimes alleviate symptoms, but if they persist, see a doctor. **Vaginal yeast infections** may flare up in Greece, which is often exceedingly hot and sometimes humid. Wearing loosely fitting trousers or a skirt and cotton underwear will help, as will over-the-counter remedies like Monostat or Gynelotrimin. Bring supplies with you if you are prone to infection, as they may be difficult to find on the road. And, since **tampons** and **pads** are sometimes hard to find, bring supplies with you.

PACKING

LUGGAGE. If you plan to cover most of your itinerary by foot, a sturdy **frame backpack** is unbeatable. (For the basics on buying a pack, see p. 47.) Toting a **suitcase** or **trunk** is fine if you plan to live in one or two cities and explore from there but not a great idea if you plan to move around frequently. In addition to your main piece of luggage, a **daypack** (a small backpack or courier bag) is useful.

CLOTHING. If you are in Greece at the height of summer, you'll need little other than **comfortable shoes,** a few changes of **light clothes,** and a **warm jacket** or wool sweater. When Greece gets chilly in the winter months, rains come frequently so bring a **rain jacket. Flip-flops** are crucial for grubby hostel showers. To visit monasteries or churches, men will need a lightweight pair of pants and women will need a long skirt; both will need clothes that cover the shoulders. If you plan on taking ferries or hiking, you'll want a wool sweater and a windproof jacket.

SLEEPSACK. Some hostels require that you either provide your own linen or rent sheets. Save cash by making your own sleepsack: fold a full-size sheet in half the long way, then sew it closed along the long side and one of the short sides.

CONVERTERS AND ADAPTERS. In Greece, electricity is 220V AC, enough to fry any 110V North American appliance. **Americans** and **Canadians** should buy an **adapter** (which changes the shape of the plug) and a **converter** (which changes the voltage; US$20). Don't make the mistake of using only an adapter (unless appliance instructions explicitly state otherwise). **New Zealanders** and **South Africans** (who both use 220V at home) as well as **Australians** (who use 240/250V) won't need a converter but will need a set of adapters to use anything electrical. For more on all things adaptable, check out http://kropla.com/electric.htm.

FIRST-AID KIT. For a basic first-aid kit, pack: bandages, pain reliever, antibiotic cream, a thermometer, a Swiss Army knife, tweezers, moleskin, decongestant, motion-sickness remedy, diarrhea or upset-stomach medication (Pepto Bismol or Imodium), an antihistamine, sunscreen, insect repellent, burn ointment, and a syringe for emergencies (get an explanatory letter from your doctor).

FILM. Greeks tend to do an excellent job with developing film (about €7.50 for a roll of 24 color exposures). However, film and processing can be expensive, so you might consider bringing along film for your entire trip and developing it at home. Despite disclaimers airport security X-rays *can* fog film. Always pack film in your carry-on luggage since higher-intensity X-rays are used on checked luggage.

IMPORTANT DOCUMENTS. Don't forget your passport, traveler's checks, ATM and/or credit cards, adequate ID, and photocopies of them all (p. 35).

ACCOMMODATIONS

DOMATIA (ROOMS TO LET)

Private homes all over Greece put up signs offering domatia (rooms to let). Domatia are perhaps the ideal budget accommodations; they are cheap and allow you to stay in a Greek home and absorb some local culture. At more popular destinations, proprietors with rooms to let will greet your boat or bus, a practice which is theoretically illegal but common. Always negotiate with domatia owners before settling on a price. Before you accept a portside offer, have a set destination in mind and look for people whose domatia are in the area you want. Many rooms offered at the port or bus stop are inexpensive; since the proprietors are in direct competition with the other domatia owners, good deals abound. Make owners pinpoint the location of their houses to make sure that "10min. away" means 10min. on foot. Don't pay until you've seen the room.

While domatia may be run like small hotels in tourist towns, domatia in out of the way places can provide warm offers of coffee at night and friendly conversation. Prices are quite variable depending on region and season. You can expect to pay about €15-20 for a single (€30 for a double) in the more remote areas of Northern and Central Greece and €15-25 for a single (€35-45 for a double) on heavily traveled islands. Never pay more for domatia than you would for a hotel in town, and remember domatia owners can often be bargained down, especially when the house is not full. If in doubt, ask the tourist police: they may set you up with a room and conduct the negotiations themselves. Most private rooms operate only in high season and are the best option for those arriving without reservations.

A HOSTELER'S BILL OF RIGHTS There are certain standard features that we do not include in our hostel listings. Unless we state otherwise, you can expect that every hostel has no lockout, no curfew, a kitchen, free hot showers, some system of secure luggage storage, and no key deposit.

HOSTELS

Hostels are not as prevalent in Greece as they are throughout the rest of Europe. Those that exist (usually in the most popular tourist destinations) are almost never affiliated with an international hosteling organization. Thus a hosteling membership won't do you much good. In Greece a bed in a hostel will average €9; you can expect showers and sheets. Hostels are not regulated so don't be surprised if some are less than clean or don't offer sheets and towels.

BOOKING HOSTELS ONLINE. One of the cheapest and easiest ways to ensure a bed for a night is by reserving online. Our website features the **Hostelworld** booking engine; access it at **www.letsgo.com/resources/accommodations.** Hostelworld offers bargain accommodations everywhere from Argentina to Zimbabwe with no added commission.

Some Greek hostels offer private rooms for families and couples. They sometimes have kitchens and utensils for your use, bike or moped rentals, storage areas, and laundry facilities. Some hostels have a maximum stay of five days. Greek **youth hostels** generally have fewer restrictions than those farther north in Europe. Many are open year-round and few have early curfews (some curfews, however, are strictly enforced—you may be left in the streets if you come back too late). In summer they usually stay open from 6-10am and 1pm-midnight (shorter hours in winter). It's advisable to book in advance in the summer at some of the more popular hostels in Athens, Santorini, Crete, or Nafplion.

HOTELS

The government oversees the construction and (seemingly random) classification of most hotels. Proprietors are permitted to charge 10% extra for stays of less than three nights, and 20% extra overall from July until September 15. Most D- and E-class hotels start at €15 for singles and €25 for doubles. A hotel with no singles may still put you in a room by yourself. More information is available from the **Hellenic Chamber of Hotels,** Stadiou 24, Athens 105 64 (☎210 331 0022 or 331 0023; fax 210 322 5449; grhotels@otenet.gr). If a hotel owner solicits you, offering to drive you, make sure you establish the location on a map; it may be miles away.

Late at night, in the low season, or in a large town, it's a buyer's market and bargaining is appropriate. As a security deposit, hotels often ask for your passport and return it when you leave. Don't give it to them—suggest that they take down your passport number or offer to pay up front. You can often leave your luggage in the reception area during the afternoon, even if check-out was earlier. Sleazy hotel owners may offer you only their most expensive rooms, compel you to buy breakfast, squeeze three people into a hostel-size triple and charge each for a single, or quote a price for a room that includes breakfast and private shower and then charge extra for both. Don't pay until you've seen the room. If a room seems unreasonably expensive, stress that you don't want luxuries and they may give you a cheaper option. If you think you've been exploited, threaten to file a report with the tourist police. The threat alone often resolves "misunderstandings."

CAMPING AND THE OUTDOORS

Camping in Greece provides refuge from the regulations of hostels and the monotony of hotel rooms—not to mention saving you a lot of money. The Greek National Tourist Organization (GNTO; p. 34) is primarily responsible for campgrounds; most official GNTO campgrounds have drinking water, lavatories, and electricity. Many campgrounds rent tents. Ask at the local tourist offices for more information on the **Hellenic Touring Club,** which runs a number of campgrounds, especially in Northern Greece. Greece also has many private campgrounds, which may include pools, mini-markets, and tavernas. Prices depend on the facilities; you'll probably pay €4-6 per person and around €3 per tent.

An excellent general resource for travelers planning on spending time in the outdoors is the **Great Outdoor Recreation Pages** (www.gorp.com). A variety of publishing companies offer hiking guidebooks to meet the needs of novices or experts.

WILDERNESS SAFETY

Stay warm, stay dry, and stay hydrated. The vast majority of life-threatening wilderness situations can be avoided with this advice. Prepare yourself, however, by always packing raingear, a hat and mittens, a first-aid kit, a reflector, a whistle, high energy food, and extra water for any hike. Dress in wool or warm layers of synthetic materials designed for the outdoors; never rely on cotton for warmth, as it is useless when wet. Check **weather forecasts** and pay attention to the skies when hiking. Whenever possible, let someone know when and where you are going hiking, and try to hike with others; do not attempt a hike beyond your ability. See **Health,** p. 41, for information about outdoor ailments and basic medical concerns.

CAMPING AND HIKING EQUIPMENT

WHAT TO BUY...

Good camping equipment is both sturdy and light. Camping equipment is generally more expensive in Australia, New Zealand, and the UK than in North America.

Sleeping Bag: Most sleeping bags are rated by season ("summer" means 30-40°F at night; "4-season" or "winter" often means below 0°F). They are made either of **down** (warmer and lighter, but more expensive, and miserable when wet; US$250-300) or of **synthetic** material (heavier, more durable, and warmer when wet; US$70-210). **Sleeping bag pads** include foam pads (US$10-30), air mattresses (US$15-50), and Therm-A-Rest self-inflating pads (US$45-120). Bring a **stuff sack** for dry storage of your bag.

Tent: The best tents are free-standing (with their own frames and suspension systems), set up quickly, and only require staking in high winds. Low-profile dome tents are the best all-around. Good 2-person tents start at US$90, 4-person at US$300. Seal the seams of your tent with waterproofer, and make sure it has a rain fly.

Backpack: Internal-frame packs mold better to your back, keep a lower center of gravity, and flex adequately to allow you to hike difficult trails. **External-frame packs** are more comfortable for long hikes over even terrain, as they keep weight higher and distribute it more evenly. Any serious backpacking requires a pack of at least 4000 in^3 (16,000cc), plus 500 in^3 for sleeping bags in internal-frame packs. Sturdy backpacks cost anywhere from US$125-420—this is one area in which it doesn't pay to economize. Either buy a **waterproof backpack cover,** or store all of your belongings in plastic bags.

Boots: Be sure to wear hiking boots with good **ankle support.** They should fit snugly and comfortably over 1-2 pairs of wool socks and thin liner socks. Break in boots over several weeks before you go in order to spare yourself painful and debilitating blisters.

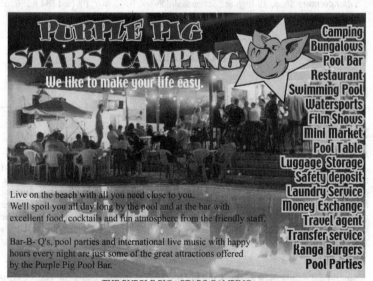

Other Necessities: Synthetic layers, like those made of polypropylene, and a **pile jacket** will keep you warm even when wet. A **"space blanket"** will help you to retain your body heat and doubles as a groundcloth (US$5-15). Plastic **water bottles** are virtually shatter- and leak-proof. Bring **water-purification tablets** for when you can't boil water. Although most campgrounds provide campfire sites, you may want to bring a small **grill** of your own. For most organized campgrounds in Europe, you'll need a **camp stove** (classic Colemans start at US$45) and a propane-filled **fuel bottle** to operate it.

...AND WHERE TO BUY IT

The mail-order/online companies listed below offer lower prices than many retail stores, but a visit to a local camping or outdoors store will give you a good sense of the look and weight of certain items.

Campmor, 28 Parkway, P.O. Box 700, Upper Saddle River, NJ 07458, USA (US ☎888-226-7667; www.campmor.com).

Discount Camping, 880 Main North Rd., Pooraka, South Australia 5095, Australia (☎08 8262 3399; fax 8260 6240; www.discountcamping.com.au).

Eastern Mountain Sports (EMS), 1 Vose Farm Rd., Peterborough, NH 03458, US (☎888-463-6367; www.ems.com).

L.L. Bean, Freeport, ME 04033 (US and Canada ☎800-441-5713; UK ☎0800 891 297; www.llbean.com).

Mountain Designs, 51 Bishop St., Kelvin Grove, Queensland 4059, Australia (☎07 3856 2344; fax 3856 0366; www.mountaindesigns.com).

Recreational Equipment, Inc. (REI), Sumner, WA 98352, US (US and Canada ☎800-426-4840; elsewhere 253-891-2500; www.rei.com).

YHA Adventure Shop, 19 High St., Staines, Middlesex, TW18 4QY, UK (☎1784 458625; fax 1784 464573; www.yhaadventure.com).

KEEPING IN TOUCH

BY MAIL

SENDING MAIL FROM GREECE

Airmail is the best way to send mail home from Greece. Write "airmail" or "par avion" on the front. **Aerogrammes,** printed sheets that fold into envelopes and travel via airmail, are available at post offices. Most post offices will charge exorbitant fees or simply refuse to send aerogrammes with enclosures. **Surface mail** is by far the cheapest and slowest way to send mail. It takes one to three months to cross the Atlantic and two to four to cross the Pacific—good for items you won't need to see for a while, such as souvenirs or other articles you've acquired that are weighing down your pack. These are standard rates for mail from Greece to:

Australia, Canada, New Zealand and the US: Allow 7-10 days for regular airmail. Postcards/aerogrammes cost €0.65. Letters up to 20g cost €0.95; 0.5kg packages €5.50.

Ireland and the UK: Allow 3-4 days for regular airmail. Postcards/aerogrammes cost €0.65. Letters up to 20g cost €0.90; packages of 0.5kg €4.80.

SENDING MAIL TO GREECE

Mark envelopes "air mail" and "par avion" or your letter or postcard will never arrive. In addition to the standard postage system whose rates are listed below, **Federal Express** (Australia ☎ 13 26 10, Canada and US 800-247-4747, New Zealand 0800 73 33 39, UK 0800 12 38 00; www.fedex.com) handles express mail services from most home countries to Greece.

Australia: Allow 7-10 days for airmail to Greece. Postcards and letters up to 20g cost AUS$1; packages up to 0.5kg AUS$14, up to 2kg AUS$50. EMS can get a letter to Greece in 3 days for AUS$27. Find rates at www1.auspost.com.au/pac.

Canada: Allow 7 days for airmail to Greece. Postcards and letters up to 30g cost CDN$1.25; packages up to 0.5kg CDN$10, up to 2kg CDN$35.55. Find rates at www.canadapost.ca/personal/rates/int/default-e.asp.

Ireland: Allow 7 days for airmail to Greece. Postcards and letters up to 25g cost €0.44; packages up to 2kg €7.80. Find rates at www.letterpost.ie.

New Zealand: Allow 7-10 days for airmail to Greece. Postcards NZ$1.50. Letters up to 200g cost NZ$2; small parcels up to 0.5kg NZ$17.23, up to 2kg NZ$55.25. Find rates at www.nzpost.co.nz/nzpost/inrates.

UK: Allow 7 days for airmail to Greece. Letters up to 20g cost UK£0.38; packages up to 0.5kg UK£2.78, up to 2kg UK£9.72. Find rates at www.royalmail.co.uk/calculator.

US: Allow 7 days for airmail to Greece. Postcards/aerogrammes cost US$0.70; letters under 1 oz. US$0.80. Packages under 1 lb. cost US$14; larger packages cost a variable amount (around US$15). Global Express Mail takes 2-3 days and costs US$26. Find rates at http://ircalc.usps.gov.

RECEIVING MAIL IN GREECE

There are several ways to arrange pick-up of letters sent to you by friends and relatives while you are abroad. Mail can be sent via **Poste Restante** (General Delivery) to almost any city or town in Greece with a post office and it is generally reliable. Address *Poste Restante* letters like so:

Zorba THE GREEK
Hania Post Office
Hania, Greece 73100
POSTE RESTANTE

The mail will go to a special desk in the central post office, unless you specify a post office by street address or postal code. It's best to use the largest post office, since mail may be sent there regardless. It is usually safer and quicker, though more expensive, to send mail express or registered. Bring your passport (or other photo ID) for pick-up; rarely there is a small fee. If the clerks insist that there is nothing for you, have them check under your first name as well. *Let's Go* lists post offices in the **Practical Information** section for each city and most towns.

American Express travel offices throughout the world offer a free **Client Letter Service** (mail held up to 30 days and forwarded upon request) for cardholders who contact them in advance. Address the letter in the same way shown above. Some offices will offer these services to non-cardholders (especially AmEx Traveler's Cheque holders), but call ahead to make sure. *Let's Go* lists AmEx office locations for large cities in **Practical Information** sections; for a free list, call ☎ 800-528-4800.

ESSENTIALS

BY TELEPHONE

CALLING HOME FROM GREECE

A **calling card** is probably your cheapest bet. You can frequently call collect without possessing a company's calling card by dialing their access number and following the instructions. **To call home with a calling card,** contact the operator for your service provider in Greece by dialing the appropriate toll-free access number.

COMPANY	TO OBTAIN A CARD, DIAL:	TO CALL ABROAD, DIAL:
AT&T (US)	800-222-0300	00 800 13 11
British Telecom Direct	0800 345 144	00 800 44 11
Canada Direct	800-668-6878	00 800 16 11
Ireland Direct	+353 1 661 4808	155 11 74
MCI (US)	800-444-3333	00 800 12 11
Sprint (US)	800-877-4646	00 800 14 11

All pay phones in Greece are card-operated, and you will need to purchase a card to operate the phone, even if you are going to use your own calling card to place the call (see **Calling Within Greece,** below). Although convenient, in-room hotel calls invariably include an arbitrary, sky-high surcharge (as much as US$10).

Let's Go has recently partnered with ekit.com to provide a calling card that offers a number of services, including email and voice messaging. Before purchasing any calling card, always be sure to compare rates with other cards, and to make sure it serves your needs (a local phonecard is generally better for local calls, for instance). For more information, visit www.letsgo.ekit.com.

A good option is to place international phone calls using prepaid phone cards from Greece's national phone service, known as the **OTE.** They are readily available at the widespread street kiosks (περιπτερο, peh-REE-pteh-ro) and at the OTE in denominations of €3, €6, €12, and €24. The time is measured in minutes or talk units. A €3 card will buy you 100 units, roughly equal to 5-10min. of international speaking time. (See **Placing International Calls,** below, for directions on how to place a direct international call.) Placing a collect call through an international operator is a more expensive option but may be necessary in case of emergency.

PLACING INTERNATIONAL CALLS. To call Greece from home or to call home from Greece, dial:

1. The **international dialing prefix.** To dial out of out of **Greece,** the **Republic of Ireland, New Zealand,** or the **UK,** dial 00; **Australia,** 0011; **Canada** or the **US,** 011; **South Africa,** 09.
2. The **country code** of the country you want to call. To call **Greece,** dial 30; **Australia,** 61; **Canada** or the **US,** 1; the **Republic of Ireland,** 353; **New Zealand,** 64; **South Africa,** 27; the **UK,** 44.
3. The **city/area code.** *Let's Go* lists the city/area codes for cities and towns in Greece opposite the city or town name, next to a ☎. If the first digit is a zero (e.g., 020 for London), omit the zero when calling from abroad.
4. The **local number.**

CALLING WITHIN GREECE

The only way to call within the country is to use a **prepaid OTE phone card** available at kiosks and OTEs. A €3 card will buy you 100 units, roughly 30min. of local calling within Greece or 5-10min. long-distance within Greece. There are local OTE offices in most towns and cardphones are often clustered outside.

CELL PHONES IN EUROPE. Cell phones are an increasingly popular option for travelers calling within Europe. Unlike North America, virtually all areas of Europe receive excellent coverage, and the widespread use of the **Global System for Mobiles (GSM)** allows one phone to function in multiple countries. A small chip called a **Subscriber Identity Module Card (SIM or "smart card")** can be purchased from carriers in each European country to provide a local number for any GSM phone. However, some companies lock their phones to prevent switches to competitor carriers, so inquire about using the phone in other countries before buying it. Phones in Europe generally cost around US$100 and run on prepaid minutes, purchased at many locations. Often incoming calls are free. For more info about GSM phones, go to www.vodafone.com, www.orange.co.uk, www.roadpost.com, www.cellular-abroad.com, www.t-mobile.com, or www.planetomni.com.

TIME DIFFERENCES

Greece is 2hr. ahead of Greenwich Mean Time (GMT); 7hr. ahead of New York; 10hr. ahead of Vancouver and San Francisco; 8hr. behind Syndney; 9hr. behind Auckland (NZ); and in the same timezone as Johannesburg. Greece observes **daylight savings time.**

4AM	7AM	NOON	2PM	8PM	10PM
Seattle San Francisco Los Angeles	Toronto New York Ottawa	London (GMT)	**Athens** Istanbul Nicosia	Hong Kong Manila Singapore	Sydney Canberra Melbourne

BY EMAIL AND INTERNET

Internet becomes more accessible each year in Greece. In all big cities, in most small cities and large towns, and on most touristed islands, you can find Internet access. Expect to pay between €3-6 per hour. Though in some places it's possible to forge a remote link with your home server, in most cases this is a much slower (and therefore more expensive) option than taking advantage of free **web-based email accounts** (e.g., www.hotmail.com and www.yahoo.com). Travelers with laptops can call an Internet service provider via a **modem.** Long-distance phone cards specifically intended for such calls can defray normally high phone charges; check with your long-distance phone provider to see if it offers this option. **Internet** access is listed in **Practical Information** sections. For lists of cybercafes in Greece, check out http://dmoz.org/Computers/Internet/Cybercafes/Greece/.

GETTING TO GREECE

BY PLANE

When it comes to airfare, a little effort can save you a bundle. If your plans are flexible enough to deal with the restrictions, courier fares are the cheapest. Tickets bought from consolidators and standby seating are also good deals, but last-minute specials, airfare wars, and charter flights often beat even these fares.

AIRFARES

Airfares to Greece peak between June and September and around holidays. The cheapest time to travel is between November and late March. Midweek (M-Th morning) round-trip flights run US$40-50 cheaper than weekend flights, but they are generally more crowded. Not fixing a return date ("open return") or arriving in and departing from different cities ("open-jaw") can be pricier than round-trip flights. Flights between Greece's large cities will tend to be cheaper.

BUDGET AND STUDENT TRAVEL AGENCIES

While knowledgeable agents specializing in flights to Greece can make your life easy and help you save, they may not spend the time to find you the lowest possible fare—they get paid on commission. Travelers holding **ISICs** or **IYTCs** (p. 36) qualify for big discounts from student travel agencies.

USIT: 19-21 Aston Quay, Dublin 2 (☎01 602 1600; www.usitworld.com). Ireland's leading student/budget travel agency has 22 offices throughout Northern Ireland and the Republic of Ireland.

CTS Travel: 30 Rathbone Pl., London W1T 1GQ, UK (☎0207 290 0630; www.ctstravel.co.uk). A British student travel agent with offices in 39 countries including the US, Empire State Building, 350 Fifth Ave., Suite 7813, New York, NY 10118 (☎877-287-6665; www.ctstravelusa.com).

STA Travel: 7890 S. Hardy Dr., Ste. 110, Tempe AZ 85284, USA (24hr. reservations and info ☎800-781-4040; www.sta-travel.com). A student and youth travel organization with over 150 offices worldwide (check their website for a complete listing). Ticket booking, travel insurance, railpasses, and more. In the UK, walk-in office 11 Goodge St., London W1T 2PF (☎0207 436 7779). In New Zealand, Shop 2B, 182 Queen St., Auckland (☎09 309 0458). In Australia, 366 Lygon St., Carlton Vic 3053 (☎03 9349 4344).

Travel CUTS (Canadian Universities Travel Services): 187 College St., Toronto, ON M5T 1P7 (☎416-979-2406; fax 979-8167; www.travelcuts.com). Offices across Canada and the US. In the UK, 295-A Regent St., London W1B 2H9 (☎0207 255 2191).

Wasteels: Skoubogade 6, 1158 Copenhagen K. (☎3314-4633; fax 7630-0865; www.wasteels.com). A huge chain with 180 locations across Europe. Sells Wasteels BIJ tickets discounted 30-45% off regular fare and 2nd-class international point-to-point train tickets with unlimited stopovers for those under 26 (sold only in Europe).

FLIGHT PLANNING ON THE INTERNET.

Many airline sites offer special last-minute deals on the Web. **www.greece-flights.com** specializes in discount fares; **www.easyjet.com** lists cheap London-Athens flights. Other sites do the legwork and compile the deals for you—try www.bestfares.com, www.flights.com, www.lowestfare.com, www.onetravel.com, and www.travelzoo.com. **StudentUniverse** (www.studentuniverse.com), **STA** (www.sta-travel.com) and **Orbitz.com** provide quotes on student tickets, while **Expedia** (www.expedia.com) and **Travelocity** (www.travelocity.com) offer full travel services. **Priceline** (www.priceline.com) allows you to specify a price but obligates you to buy any ticket that meets or beats it; be prepared for antisocial hours and odd routes. **Skyauction** (www.skyauction.com) allows you to bid on both last-minute and advance-purchase tickets.

COMMERCIAL AIRLINES

The commercial airlines' lowest regular offer is the **APEX** (Advance Purchase Excursion) fare, which provides confirmed reservations and allows "open-jaw" tickets. Generally, reservations must be made seven to 21 days ahead of departure, with seven- to 14-day minimum-stay and up to 90-day maximum-stay restrictions. These fares carry hefty cancellation and change penalties (fees rise in summer). Book high season APEX fares early; by May you will have a hard time getting your desired departure date. Use **Microsoft Expedia** (msn.expedia.com) or **Travelocity** (www.travelocity.com) to get an idea of the lowest published fares, then use the resources outlined here to try and beat those fares. Low season fares should be appreciably cheaper than the high season (June to Sept.) ones listed here.

TRAVELING FROM NORTH AMERICA

Basic round-trip fares to Athens range from roughly US$500-900. Standard commercial carriers like Delta and United will probably offer the most convenient flights, but they may not be the cheapest, unless you manage to grab a special promotion or airfare war ticket. You will probably find one of the following "discount" airlines a better deal, if any of their limited departure points is convenient for you.

Icelandair: ☎800-223-5500; www.icelandair.com. Stopovers in Iceland for no extra cost on most transatlantic flights. For last-minute offers, subscribe to their email.

Finnair: ☎800-950-5000; www.us.finnair.com. Cheap round-trips from San Francisco, New York, and Toronto to Helsinki; connections throughout Europe.

TRAVELING FROM THE UK AND IRELAND

Because of the many carriers flying from the UK to the continent, *Let's Go* only includes discount airlines or those with cheap specials here. The **Air Travel Advisory Bureau** in London (☎0207 636 5000; www.atab.co.uk) provides referrals to travel agencies and consolidators that offer discounted airfares out of the UK.

easyJet: UK ☎0870 600 00 00; www.easyjet.com. London to Athens (UK£47-136).

KLM: UK ☎0870 507 40 74; www.klmuk.com. Cheap round-trip tickets from London and elsewhere to Athens and other European cities.

TRAVELING FROM AUSTRALIA AND NEW ZEALAND

Singapore Air: Australia ☎13 10 11, New Zealand 0800 808 909; www.singaporeair.com. Flies from Auckland, Sydney, Melbourne, and Perth to Athens.

Thai Airways: Australia ☎1300 65 19 60, New Zealand 09 377 02 68; www.thaiair.com. Flies from Auckland, Sydney, and Melbourne to Athens.

TRAVELING FROM SOUTH AFRICA

Air France: ☎011 770 16 01; www.airfrance.com/za. Flies from Johannesburg to Paris; connections throughout Europe.

British Airways: ☎0860 011 747; www.british-airways.com/regional/sa. Flies from Cape Town and Johannesburg to the UK; connections throughout Europe.

Lufthansa: ☎0861 842 538; www.lufthansa.co.za. Flies from Cape Town, Durban, and Johannesburg to Germany, with connections to Athens and elsewhere.

AIR COURIER FLIGHTS

Those who travel light should consider courier flights. Most flights are round-trip only, with fixed-length stays (usually one week) and a limit of one ticket per issue. They often fly only out of major gateway cities, generally in North America. Super-discounted fares are common for "last-minute" flights (three to 14 days ahead).

International Association of Air Travel Couriers (IAATC), P.O. Box 980, Keystone Heights, FL 32656, USA (☎352-475-1584; fax 475-5326; www.courier.org). From 9 North American cities to Western European cities. 1-year membership US$45.

Global Courier Travel, P.O. Box 3051, Nederland, CO 80466, USA (www.globalcouriertravel.com). Searchable online database. 6 departure points in the US and Canada to Athens. Lifetime membership US$40, 2 people US$55

STANDBY FLIGHTS

Traveling standby requires flexibility in arrival and departure dates and cities. Companies dealing in standby flights sell vouchers rather than tickets and the promise to get you to (or near) your destination within a certain window of time (typically 1-5 days). Carefully read agreements with any company offering standby flights as tricky fine print can leave you in a lurch. To check on a company's service record in the US, call the **Better Business Bureau** (☎212-533-6200).

TICKET CONSOLIDATORS

Ticket consolidators, or **"bucket shops,"** buy unsold tickets in bulk from commercial airlines and sell them at discounted rates. The best place to look is the travel section of any major newspaper; many bucket shops have ads. Call quickly; availability is often extremely limited. Not all bucket shops are reliable, so insist on a receipt that gives full details of restrictions, refunds, and tickets, and pay by credit card (in spite of the 2-5% fee) so you can stop payment if you never receive your tickets. For more info, see www.travel-library.com/air-travel/consolidators.html.

TRAVELING FROM THE US AND CANADA

Travel Avenue (☎800-333-3335; www.travelavenue.com) finds the best published fares, then uses several consolidators to attempt to beat those fares. Other consolidators worth trying are **Pennsylvania Travel** (☎877-251-6866; www.patravel.com); **Rebel** (☎800-227-3235; www.rebeltours.com); **Cheap Tickets** (☎800-377-1000; www.cheaptickets.com). Online consolidators include the **Internet Travel Network** (www.itn.com); **Flights.com** (www.flights.com); **TravelHUB** (www.travelhub.com). These are just suggestions; *Let's Go* does not endorse any of these agencies. Be cautious and research companies before you give your credit card number.

CHARTER FLIGHTS

Charters are flights contracted by a tour operator with an airline to fly extra passengers during peak season. They fly less frequently than major airlines, make refunds particularly difficult, and are almost always fully booked. Schedules and itineraries may also change or be cancelled at the last moment, and check-in, boarding, and baggage claim are much slower. However, they can also be cheaper. **Discount clubs** and **fare brokers** offer members savings on last-minute charter and tour deals. Study contracts closely; you don't want to end up with an unwanted overnight layover. **Travelers Advantage** (US ☎877-259-2691; www.travelersadvantage.com; US$60 annual fee) specializes in European travel and tour packages.

BY FERRY, TRAIN, OR BUS

BY FERRY. Ferry travel is a popular way to get to and travel within Greece; ports can be reached from a seemingly unlimited number of points and finding a boat agency to facilitate your trip should not be difficult. Be warned that **ferries run on irregular schedules.** A few websites, like **www.ferries.gr,** have tried to keep updated schedules online but are often incomplete. You should try to take a look at a schedule as close to your departure date as possible; you can usually find one at a tourist office or posted at the dock. That said, you should also make reservations and **check in at least 2hr. in advance;** late boarders may find their seats gone. If you sleep on deck, bring warm clothes and a sleeping bag. Bicycles travel free, but motorcycles will have an extra charge. Bring food to avoid high prices on board.

The major ports of departure from Italy to Greece are Ancona and Brindisi, in the southeast. Bari, Otranto, and Venice also have a few connections. For Greece-Italy schedules, see Patras (p. 160), Kephalonia (p. 462), Corfu (p. 442), or Igoumenitsa (p. 250). Deck passage from Patras to Brindisi (17hr.) runs €30-35, including port tax. Patras travel agency **Manolopoulos,** Othonos Amalias 35 (☎2610 223 621), can provide information on ferries to Italy. Ferries also run from Greece to various Turkish ports. (See **Turkey Essentials,** p. 626.)

BY BUS. There are almost no buses running directly from any European city to Greece. **Busabout,** 258 Vauxhall Bridge Rd., London SW1V 1BS (☎0207 950 1661; www.busabout.com), is one of the very few European bus lines that services Greece. Transporting travelers to Italian cities on their own buses, they arrange ferry transport from Italian ports to Greece.

BY TRAIN. A number of international train routes connect Greece via Thessaloniki to most European cities. **Eurail** passes are valid in Greece, and may be a useful purchase if you plan to visit one of the 17 other European countries in which they are valid. Fifteen-day youth passes (aged 25 and under) cost US$414 (adults US$588). Eurail passes are available through travel agents, student travel agencies like STA and Council (p. 52), and **Rail Europe,** 500 Mamaroneck Ave., Harrison, NY 10528, USA (US ☎888-382-7245, Canada 800-361-7245, UK 08705 848 848; www.raileurope.com). Unfortunately, the Greek rail system is one of Europe's most antiquated and least efficient—for example, a trip from Vienna to Athens takes at least 3 days. For specific routes, see the **OSE** website (www.osenet.gr).

GETTING AROUND GREECE

BY FERRY AND HYDROFOIL

Widespread but unpredictable, cheap but slow, ferries may form the backbone of your adventures in Greek travel. Be prepared to arrive at the dock 1-2hr. before departure for a decent seat, though a 5min.-early or a 3hr.-late departure are both real (perhaps scary) possibilities. Bring a **windbreaker** if you feel inclined to wander the deck when at sea. For short distances, indoor seats fill up quickly.

MAKING SENSE OF FERRIES. The key to making good use of ferries is understanding ferry routes and planning your trip accordingly. Most ferries, rather than shuffling back and forth between two destinations, trace a four- or five-port route. Most ferry companies will allow you to buy your round-trip ticket **"split,"** meaning that you can ride the Piraeus-Syros-Tinos-Mykonos ferry from Piraeus to Syros, get off, get back on when the same ferry passes Syros several days later, proceed to Tinos, and so on. Remember that geographic proximity is no guarantee that you'll be able to get to one island from another. Also note that there is very little service from the Cyclades to the Dodecanese. Understanding ferry routes will also help you make sense of discrepancies in ticket prices (going to Hydra from Athens via Poros and Aegina is more expensive than simply going via Poros) and travel times. **Ferry schedules,** available for the region from the ferry companies or posted at the port police, are published weekly and give the departure times, routes, and names of each departing ferry. As particular ferries, even within companies, vary widely in quality, local travelers pay close attention to the names. Ask around or check on the web (www.ferries.gr) for tips, ferry schedules, and prices.

DOLPHIN RIDES. Flying Dolphins go twice as fast, look twice as cool, but cost twice as much. If you have cash to spare and want to minimize travel time, these crafts provide extensive, standardized, and sanitized transport between islands; offices and services are listed in the **Transportation** sections of all cities and towns. Keep in mind traveling by Dolphin is like traveling by seaborne airplane: passengers are assigned seats and required to stay in the climate-controlled cabin for the duration of the trip, which may be less than ideal for the easily seasick. There's also something somewhat unfortunate about sailing the Aegean in a craft that won't let you get salt on your fingers and wind in your hair.

BY BUS

Spending time in Greece most likely means spending time on the bus. Service is extensive and fares are cheap. On major highways buses tend to be more modern and efficient than in the mountainous areas of the Peloponnese or

Northern Greece. The **OSE** (see **By Train,** p. 57) offers limited bus service from a few cities. Unless you're sticking close to train routes, **KTEL** bus service should be sufficient. Always check with an official source about scheduled departures. Posted schedules are often outdated and all services are curtailed significantly on Saturday and Sunday; bus schedules on major holidays run according to Sunday schedules. The English-language weekly newspaper *Athens News* prints Athens bus schedules, and like almost everything else, they are available online (www.ktel.org). Try to arrive at least 10min. ahead of time, as Greek buses have a habit of leaving early. In major cities KTEL bus lines may have different stations for different destinations, and schedules generally refer to **endpoints** ("the bus leaves Kalloni at three and arrives in Mytilini at four") with no mention of the numerous stops in between. In villages a cafe or *zaccharoplasteio* (sweet shop) often serves as the bus station and you must ask the proprietor for a schedule.

ALL ABOARD! Ask the **conductor** before entering the bus whether it's going to your destination (the signs on the front are often misleading), and ask to be warned when you get there. If stowing bags underneath, make sure they're in the compartment for your destination (conductors take great pride in packing the bus for easy unloading, and may refuse to open the "final destination" compartment at the "halfway" stop). If the bus passes your stop, stand up and yell "**STAH-see**" (στασŋ). On the road stand near a sign (reading στασŋ) to pick up an intercity bus. KTEL buses are **green** or occasionally **orange,** while intercity buses are usually **blue.** For long-distance rides, **buy your ticket beforehand** in the office (if you don't, you may have to stand for the entire journey). For shorter trips, pay the conductor after you have boarded; reasonably close change is expected.

BY PLANE OR TRAIN

BY PLANE. In Greece, **Olympic Airways** can be found in **Athens** (☎2801 11 44444), in **Thessaloniki** (☎2310 368 666), and in many cities. The Olympic Airways website (www.olympic-airways.gr) lists information for every office around the globe. For flight information within Greece, check regional **Practical Information** listings of airports, destinations, and prices, or get an Olympic Airways brochure at any Olympic office. In recent years, Olympic's domestic service has increased appreciably; from Athens a 1hr. flight (US$75-125) can get you to most islands. Even in low season, remote destinations are serviced several times weekly, while more developed areas can have several flights per day. Try to reserve tickets one week in advance.

BY TRAIN. Although trains are cheap, they run less frequently, get pretty gritty, and are relatively slow. You may come across a new, air-conditioned, intercity train, which is a different entity altogether; although they are slightly more expensive and rare, they are worth the price. **Eurail** passes are valid on Greek trains. OSE (www.osenet.gr) connects Athens to major Greek cities (like Thessaloniki and Volos). Lines do not go to the west coast, and they are rarely useful for remote areas or archaeological sites. Bring food and a water bottle, because the on-board cafe is pricey. Lock your compartment and keep valuables on your person.

BY CAR

Cars are functional in Greece, a country where public transportation is generally nonexistent after 7pm. Ferries will take you island-hopping if you pay a transport fee for the car. Drivers must be comfortable with a standard transmission, winding mountain roads, notoriously reckless drivers (especially in Athens), and the Greek alphabet—signs in Greek appear roughly 100m before the transliterated versions. Driving can be a cheaper alternative to trains and buses for groups of travelers, and is especially useful for exploring remote villages in northern Greece.

RENTING

Agencies may quote low daily rates that exclude the 18% VAT and **Collision Damage Waiver (CDW)** insurance. Note some places quote low rates and then hit you with hidden charges, such as exorbitant refueling bills if you come back with less than a full tank, 100km per day minimum mileage, or up to €300 drop-off or special charge. Most companies won't let you drive the car outside Greece. Foreign drivers are required to have an **International Driving Permit** and an **International Insurance Certificate** to drive in Greece (see below).

RENTAL AGENCIES. You can generally make reservations before you leave by calling major international offices in your home country. However, occasionally the price and availability information they give doesn't jive with what the local offices in your country will tell you. Try checking with both numbers to make sure you get the best price and accurate information. Local desk numbers are included in the **Practical Information** of most town listings; for home-country numbers, call your toll-free directory.

To rent a car from most establishments in Greece, you need to be at least 21 years old. Some agencies require renters to be 23 or 25. Policies and prices vary from agency to agency. Small local operations occasionally rent to people under 21 but be sure to ask about the insurance coverage and deductible—and always check the fine print. Rental agencies in Greece include:

Auto Europe, 39 Commercial St., P.O. Box 7006, Portland, ME 04112, USA (Canada and US ☎888-223-5555 or 207-842-2000; www.autoeurope.com).

Avis (Australia ☎800 22 55 33, Canada and US 800-331-1084, New Zealand 0800 65 51 11, UK 08705 900 500; www.avis.gr).

Europe by Car, 1 Rockefeller Plaza, New York, NY 10020, USA (US ☎800-223-1516 or 212-581-3040; fax 246-1458; info@europebycar.com; www.europebycar.com).

Europcar, 145 av. Malekoff, 75016 Paris (☎01 45 00 08 06; Canada ☎800-227-7368; US 800-227-3876; www.europcar.com).

Hertz (Australia ☎9698 2555, Canada 800-263-0600, UK 08705 996 699, US 800-654-3001; www.hertz.gr).

COSTS AND INSURANCE. Rental car prices start at around €35 per day. Expect to pay more for larger cars. **Standard transmission** is really your only option when renting cars in Greece. Most rental packages offer unlimited kilometers. Return the car with a full tank of petrol to avoid high fuel charges at the end. Be sure to ask whether the price includes **insurance** against theft and collision. Remember that if you are driving a conventional vehicle on an **unpaved road** in a rental car, you are almost never covered by insurance; ask about this before leaving the rental agency. Beware that cars rented on an **American Express** or **Visa/MasterCard Gold** or **Platinum** credit cards in Greece might *not* carry the automatic insurance that they would in some other countries; check with your credit card company. Insurance plans almost always come with an **excess** (or deductible) of around €300. This means you pay for all damages up to that sum, unless they are the fault of another vehicle. The excess you will be quoted applies to collisions with other vehicles; collisions with non-vehicles, such as trees, ("single-vehicle collisions") will cost you even more. The excess can often be reduced or waived entirely if you pay an additional charge, around €15 per day. National car rental chains often allow **one-way rentals,** picking up in one city and dropping off in another. There is usually a minimum hire period and sometimes a hefty drop-off charge.

ON THE ROAD. City centers, especially that of Athens, tend to get hit hard with traffic. Speed limits often go unposted and are utterly ignored. **Petrol (gasoline)** prices vary but average about €0.80 per liter in Athens.The greatest threat when driving in Greece is reckless drivers. Also be careful on windy mountain roads.

CAR ASSISTANCE. The **Automobile and Touring Club of Greece (ELPA),** Messogion 395, Athens 11527 (☎210 606 8800; www.elpa.gr), provides assistance and offers reciprocal membership to foreign auto club members. They also have 24hr. emergency road assistance (☎104) and an information line (☎174 in Athens, 210 606 8838 elsewhere in Greece; open M-F 7am-3pm).

DRIVING PRECAUTIONS. When traveling in the summer, bring substantial amounts of water (a suggested 5L of **water** per person per day) for drinking and for the radiator. For long drives to unpopulated areas, register with police before beginning the trek, and again upon arrival at the destination. When traveling for long distances, make sure tires are in good repair and have enough air, and get good maps. A **compass** and a **car manual** can also be very useful. You should always carry a **spare tire** and **jack, jumper cables, extra oil, flares, a torch (flashlight),** and **heavy blankets** (in case your car breaks down at night or in the winter). If you don't know how to **change a tire,** learn before heading out, especially if you are planning on traveling in deserted areas. Blowouts on dirt roads are exceedingly common. If you do have a breakdown, **stay with your car;** if you wander off, there's less likelihood trackers will find you.

DRIVING PERMITS AND CAR INSURANCE

INTERNATIONAL DRIVING PERMIT (IDP). If you plan to drive a car while in Greece, you are legally required to have an International Driving Permit (IDP). Although Greek proprietors may ignore the law, get one if you know you plan on driving. Your IDP, valid for one year, must be issued in your own country before you depart; AAA affiliates cannot issue IDPs valid in their own country. You must be 18 years or older to receive the IDP. A valid driver's license from your home country must always accompany the IDP.

CAR INSURANCE. Most credit cards cover standard insurance. If you rent, lease, or borrow a car, you will need a **green card,** or **International Insurance Certificate,** to certify that you have liability insurance and that it applies abroad. Green cards can be obtained at car rental agencies, car dealers (for those leasing cars), some travel agents, and some border crossings. Rental agencies may require you to purchase theft insurance in areas that they consider to have a high risk of auto theft. Contact the automobile association in your country for information on obtaining an International Driving Permit and car insurance.

BY MOPED

UNSAFE AT ANY SPEED. A word of caution: most tourist related accidents occur on mopeds. Regardless of your experience driving a moped or motorcycle, winding, poorly maintained roads and reckless drivers make using a moped hazardous. Always wear a helmet and never ride with a backpack.

Motorbiking is a popular way of touring Greece's winding roads. Although renting wheels is the best and most cost efficient way to assert your independence from unreliable public transportation, you should be aware that they can be uncomfortable for long distances, dangerous in the rain, and unpredictable on rough roads. On many islands navigable roads suddenly turn into tiny trails that must be walked. Furthermore, moped (μηχανακι, mee-xah-NAH-kee) rental shop owners often loosen the front brakes on the bikes to discourage riders from using them (relying on the front brakes makes accidents more likely), so use the back brakes. If you've never driven a moped before, a cliffside road is not the place to learn.

RENTING. Shops renting mopeds are everywhere and most require only some sort of driver's license (a Greek license or International Driving Permit is not necessary). Bike quality, speed of service in case of breakdown, and prices for longer periods vary drastically, but you should expect to pay at least €10 per day for a 50cc scooter, the cheapest bike with the power to tackle steep mountain roads. More powerful bikes cost 20-30% more and usually require a Greek motorcycle license. Many agencies will request your passport as a deposit, but it's wiser just to settle up in advance; if they have your passport and you have an accident or mechanical failure, they may refuse to return it until you pay for repairs. Ask before renting if the price quote includes tax, insurance, and a full tank of gas, or you may pay a few unexpected euros. Information on local moped rentals is in the **Practical Information** section for individual cities and towns.

BY THUMB

Let's Go strongly urges you to consider the risks before choosing to hitchhike. Safety-minded hitchers avoid getting in the back of a two-door car and never let go of their backpacks. If they feel threatened, they insist on being let off, regardless of where they are. They may also act as if they are going to open the car door or vomit on the upholstery to get a driver to stop. Experienced hitchers pick a spot outside of built-up areas, where drivers can stop, return to the road without causing an accident, and they have time to inspect potential passengers as they approach. Women should not hitch in Greece. Greeks are not eager to pick up foreigners and foreign cars are often filled with other travelers. Sparsely populated areas have little or no traffic—those who hitchhike risk being stuck for hours. Hitchhikers write their destination on a sign in both Greek and English. Successful hitchers travel light and stack belongings visibly.

SPECIFIC CONCERNS

WOMEN TRAVELERS

Women exploring on their own face some additional safety concerns. Consider staying in hostels which offer single rooms that lock from the inside or in religious organizations with rooms for women only. Stick to centrally located accommodations and avoid solitary late-night treks or metro rides. Always carry extra money for a phone call, bus, or taxi. **Hitchhiking** is never safe for lone women—even for two women traveling together. Look as if you know where you're going and approach older women or couples for directions if you're lost or uncomfortable. Generally the less you look like a tourist, the better off you'll be. Wearing a conspicuous **wedding band** may help prevent unwanted overtures. In **cities,** you may be harassed no matter how you act or what you look like. Your best answer to verbal harassment is no answer at all; feigning deafness, sitting motionless, and staring straight ahead at nothing in particular will do a world of good that reactions usually don't achieve. The extremely persistent can sometimes be dissuaded by a firm, loud, and very public "Go away!" (FEE-ghe!). Remember the word for police: ah-stee-no-MEE-a (αστυνομια). Memorize the emergency numbers in places you visit. **Older Greek women** can help you if you get into a bind; they're sharp, wise, fearless, and your best allies if you need information, advice, or a respite from persistent amorous attempts by local men. Consider preparing for your trip with a self-defense course, which will both prepare you for a potential attack and raise your level of awareness of your surroundings (see **Self Defense,** p. 40). Also be sure you are aware of the health concerns that women face when traveling (p. 43).

TRAVELING ALONE

Traveling alone has many benefits, including independence and greater interaction with locals. Contrarily, solo travelers are more vulnerable to harassment and street theft. Try not to stand out as a tourist, look confident, and be especially careful in deserted or very crowded areas. If questioned, never admit that you are traveling alone. Maintain regular contact with someone at home who knows your itinerary. For more tips, pick up *Traveling Solo* by Eleanor Berman (Globe Pequot Press; US$17) or subscribe to **Connecting: Solo Travel Network,** 689 Park Road, Unit 6, Gibsons, BC V0N 1V7, Canada (☎604-886-9099; www.cstn.org; membership US$35). **Travel Companion Exchange,** P.O. Box 833, Amityville, NY 11701, USA (☎631-454-0880, or US 800-392-1256; www.whytravelalone.com; US$48), will link solo travelers with companions with similar travel habits and interests. To link up with a tour group, try **Contiki Holidays** (888-CONTIKI; www.contiki.com), which offers a variety of packages for 18- to 35-year-olds. Tours include accommodations, transportation, guided sightseeing and some meals; most average about $65 per day.

OLDER TRAVELERS

Senior citizens are eligible for a wide range of discounts on transportation, museums, movies, theaters, concerts, restaurants, and accommodations. If you don't see a senior citizen price listed, ask, and you may be delightfully surprised. The books *No Problem! Worldwise Tips for Mature Adventurers*, by Janice Kenyon (Orca Book Publishers; US$16) and *Unbelievably Good Deals and Great Adventures That You Absolutely Can't Get Unless You're Over 50*, by Joan Rattner Heilman (NTC/Contemporary Publishing; US$13) are both excellent resources. For more information, contact one of the following organizations:

ElderTreks, 597 Markham St., Toronto, ON M6G 2L7 (☎800-741-7956; www.eldertreks.com). Adventure travel programs for the 50+ traveler in Europe.

Elderhostel, 11 Ave. de Lafayette, Boston, MA 02111, USA (☎877-426-8056; www.elderhostel.org). Organizes 1- to 4-week "educational adventures" in Greece on varied subjects for those 55+.

The Mature Traveler, P.O. Box 15791, Sacramento, CA 95852, USA (☎800-460-6676; www.thematuretraveler.com). Deals, discounts, and travel packages for the 50+ traveler. Subscription $30.

Walking the World, P.O. Box 1186, Fort Collins, CO 80522, USA (☎800-340-9255; www.walkingtheworld.com). Organizes trips for 50+ travelers to Europe.

BISEXUAL, GAY & LESBIAN TRAVELERS

Though legal in Greece since 1951, homosexuality is still socially frowned upon, especially in more conservative villages, and gays are not legally protected from discrimination. Athens and Thessaloniki offer a slew of gay bars, clubs, and hotels. The islands of **Hydra, Lesvos, Rhodes, Ios,** and **Mykonos** (arguably the most gay-friendly destination in Europe) offer gay and lesbian resorts, hotels, bars, and clubs. Listed below are contact organizations, mail-order bookstores, and publishers that offer materials addressing some specific concerns. **Out and About** (www.planetout.com) offers a bi-weekly newsletter addressing travel concerns and a comprehensive site addressing gay travel concerns.

Gay's the Word, 66 Marchmont St., London WC1N 1AB, UK (☎+44 20 7278 7654; www.gaystheword.co.uk). The largest gay and lesbian bookshop in the UK, with both fiction and non-fiction titles. Mail-order service available.

Giovanni's Room, 1145 Pine St., Philadelphia, PA 19107, USA (☎215-923-2960; www.queerbooks.com). An international lesbian/feminist and gay bookstore with mail-order service (carries many of the publications listed below).

International Lesbian and Gay Association (ILGA), 81 rue Marché-au-Charbon, B-1000 Brussels, Belgium (☎+32 2 502 2471; www.ilga.org). Provides political information, such as homosexuality laws of individual countries.

TRAVELERS WITH DISABILITIES

Greece is only slowly beginning to respond to the needs of travelers with disabilities. The most renowned sights—even the Acropolis—are not wheelchair-accessible. Some hotels, train stations, and airports have installed facilities for the disabled, as have some cruise ships that sail to the islands. Special air transportation is available aboard Olympic Airways to many of the larger islands. Those with disabilities should inform airlines and hotels of disabilities when making reservations; time may be needed to prepare special accommodations. **Guide dog owners** should inquire as to the quarantine policies of each destination. While **rail** is probably the best form of travel for disabled travelers in Europe, the railway systems of Greece and its neighboring countries have limited resources for wheelchair accessibility. For those who wish to rent cars, some major **car rental** agencies (Hertz, Avis, and National) offer hand-controlled vehicles.

For a variety of books and other publications containing information for travelers with disabilities, contact **Mobility International USA (MIUSA),** P.O. Box 10767, Eugene, OR 97440, USA (☎541-343-1248; www.miusa.org). One advocacy group, the **Society for Accessible Travel and Hospitality (SATH),** 347 Fifth Ave., #610, New York, NY 10016, USA (☎212-447-7284; www.sath.org), publishes the magazine *Open World* (US$18, free for members) and online travel information. **Directions Unlimited,** 123 Green Ln., Bedford Hills, NY 10507, USA (☎800-533-5343), books individual and group vacations for the physically disabled.

MINORITY TRAVELERS

Greeks stare, point, whisper, and gossip as a daily pastime. The first thing to notice is that they're not just staring at *you*. Even the larger cities in Greece retain the aura of a small village, where everyone and everything is gossip material. While Greeks tend to hold stereotypes about every group of people imaginable, they place a great value on **individualism;** you may be asked (out of curiosity, not maliciousness) all manner of questions or referred to continually as "the [insert your nationality here]," "the [insert religion here]," or simply "the foreigner" (XEH-nos). If you deal with individual Greeks for any period of time, they'll treat you as you seem to be (honest, trustworthy, friendly). Still, Greek stereotypes remain global enough to be almost laughable. Greece presents two strong and entirely different views about foreigners, and travelers should expect to encounter both. On the one hand, the Greek tradition of **hospitality** (fee-lo-xeh-NEE-a) is unmatched in the Mediterranean. Greeks consider it almost a sacred duty to help travelers, loading them with homemade food and advice. On the other hand, it's important to remember Greece's historical position as the crossroads of empire: most European nations have at one time or another invaded, burned, betrayed, or colonized part of Greece, forging an intense "us-versus-them," Greek-underdog mentality. If you're not obviously Greek, everyone will want to know who you are. **Minority travelers** will have more trouble blending in and will have to deal with more stares, questions, and comments. While such curiosity may seem in-your-face and invasive, think of its roots: 3000 years of experience have taught Greeks to beware of foreigners—who could be spies, fugitives, or gods—even when they bear gifts. Once their curiosity is satisfied, they'll take pleasure in showing you around.

TRAVELERS WITH CHILDREN

Be sure that your child carries some sort of ID in case of an emergency. Greeks adore children and traveling with little ones will probably allow you friendly reception in their country. Many Greek museums and archaeological sites allow children under 18 in for free. When deciding where to stay with children, call ahead to make sure the hotels and pensions allow children; some hotels and domatia have large rooms for families and roll-away beds for children. If you rent a car, make sure the rental company provides a car seat for younger children. Children under two generally fly for 10% of the adult airfare on international flights (this does not include a seat). International fares are usually discounted 25% for children from two to 11. For more information consult one of the following books: *Backpacking with Babies and Small Children*, by Goldie Silverman (US$10); *Gutsy Mamas: Travel Tips and Wisdom for Mothers on the Road*, by Marybeth Bond (US$8); *How to take Great Trips with Your Kids*, by Sanford and Jane Portnoy (US$10); *Trouble Free Travel with Children*, by Vicki Lansky (US$9).

DIETARY CONCERNS

Greek meals are traditionally organized as follows: bread and butter or olive oil, followed by vegetable or seafood appetizers, then a meat or fish dish, followed by fresh fruit. **Vegetarians** (but not vegans—as it is virtually impossible to avoid all animal products in Greek food) can make do if they don't mind occasionally making a meal of appetizers—green beans (φασολακια, fah-so-LAH-kia), the omnipresent Greek salad (χοριατικη, ho-ree-ah-tee-KEE), spinach-phyllo-feta pastry (σπανοκοπιτα, spa-no-KO-pee-ta), boiled greens (χορτα, hor-TAH), fresh bread, and wine. In smaller towns many seemingly vegetarian entrees (like the myriad stuffed vegetables) can contain meat, especially in agricultural areas; **ask before you order.** Incidentally, **Lent** is an especially good time for vegetarians and vegans to visit Greece, when meat and meat stock disappear from many dishes. There are almost no Greek vegetarians though, so if questioned your best bet is to argue weather ("It's so hot I only want vegetables") or allergies ("I'm allergic to pork and beef"), as opposed to some kind of ideology. For **allergies,** the same rule applies: ask before you order, especially at local tavernas that simply serve whatever they have cooking. The travel section of the Vegetarian Resource Group (www.vrg.org/travel) has a comprehensive list of organizations and websites that are geared toward helping vegetarians and vegans traveling abroad. The website www.vegdining.com has an excellent database of vegetarian and vegan restaurants worldwide. For more information visit your local bookstore or health food store and consult *The Vegetarian Traveler: Where to Stay if You're Vegetarian*, by Jed and Susan Civic (Larson Publications; US$16).

Travelers who keep **kosher** should contact synagogues in larger Greek cities where they still exist for information on kosher restaurants. Your own synagogue or college Hillel should have access to lists of Jewish institutions across the nation. If you are strict in your observance, you may have to prepare your own food on the road. A good resource is the *Jewish Travel Guide*, edited by Michael Zaidner (Vallentine Mitchell; US$17).

OTHER RESOURCES

TRAVEL PUBLISHERS AND BOOKSTORES

Hunter Publishing, 470 W. Broadway, Fl. 2, South Boston, MA 02127, USA (☎617-269-0700; www.hunterpublishing.com), has an extensive catalogue of travel guides and diving and adventure travel books.

Rand McNally, P.O. Box 7600, Chicago, IL 60680, USA (☎847-329-8100; www.randmcnally.com), publishes road atlases.

Bon Voyage!, 2069 W. Bullard Ave., Fresno, CA 93711, USA (☎800-995-9716, outside US 559-447-8441; www.bon-voyage-travel.com). They specialize in Europe but have titles pertaining to other regions as well. Free newsletter.

Travel Books and Language Center, Inc., 4437 Wisconsin Ave. NW, Washington, D.C. 20016, USA (☎800-220-2665; www.bookweb.org/bookstore/travelbks/). Over 60,000 titles from around the world.

WORLD WIDE WEB

Almost every aspect of budget travel is accessible via the web. Within 10min. online, you can make a reservation at a hostel, get advice on travel hotspots from other travelers who have just returned from Greece, or find out exactly how much a train from Athens to Ioannina costs. Listed here are some budget travel sites to start off your surfing; other relevant websites are listed throughout the book.

WWW.LETSGO.COM We are proud to announce that our new website now features the full online content of all of our guides. In addition, trial versions of all nine Let's Go City Guides are now available for download on Palm OS™ PDAs. As always, our website also has photos and streaming video, online ordering of all our titles, info about our books, a travel forum buzzing with stories and tips, a newsletter, and links that will help you find everything you ever wanted to know about Greece.

THE ART OF BUDGET TRAVEL

How to See the World: www.artoftravel.com. A compendium of great travel tips, from cheap flights to self defense to interacting with local culture.

Rec. Travel Library: www.travel-library.com. A fantastic set of links for general information and personal travelogues.

Lycos: http://cityguide.lycos.com. General introductions to cities and regions throughout Greece, accompanied by links to applicable histories, news, and local tourism sites.

Backpacker's Ultimate Guide: www.bugeurope.com. Tips on packing, transportation, and where to go. Also tons of country-specific travel information.

Backpack Europe: www.backpackeurope.com. Helpful tips, a bulletin board, and links.

INFORMATION ON GREECE

CIA World Factbook: www.odci.gov/cia/publications/factbook/index.html. Tons of vital statistics on Greece's geography, government, economy, and people.

Foreign Language for Travelers: www.travlang.com. Brush up on your Greek.

MyTravelGuide: www.mytravelguide.com. Country overviews, with everything from history to transportation.

Geographia: www.geographia.com. Highlights, culture, and people of Greece.

Atevo Travel: www.atevo.com/guides/destinations. Detailed introductions, travel tips, and suggested itineraries.

World Travel Guide: www.travel-guides.com/navigate/world.asp. Helpful practical info.

GENERAL TRAVEL SITES

Air Traveler's Handbook: www.cs.cmu.edu/afs/cs/user/mkant/Public/Travel/airfare.html. Help finding cheap airfare.

Shoestring Travel: www.stratpub.com. An e-zine focusing on budget travel.

Eurotrip: www.eurotrip.com. Information and reviews on budget hostels, as well as info on traveling alone.

GREECE-SPECIFIC SITES

The Internet Guide to Greece: www.gogreece.com. Features maps, references, discussions, and extensive listings of Greek businesses, schools, news sources, and sports.

Athens 2004 Olympic Games: www.athens2004.com. The official site of the 2004 Games. This comprehensive site offers all you need to know about venues, transportation, event schedules, and tourism related to the Games—as well as information on the 2004 Paralympic Games.

Phantis: www.phantis.com. A Greek-specific search engine that accommodates regional queries and contains links to Greek city sites.

Kathimerini: www.ekathimerini.com. The online version of a reliable Greek newspaper, translated into English on a daily basis.

Hellenic Federation of Mountaineering and Climbing: www.climbing.org.gr. Learn about great hikes in Greece.

United Hellas: www.united-hellas.com. A would-be database of all things Greek, from small businesses and folk art sources to places to buy a boat.

Greek Ferries: www.ferries.gr. Claims to maintain a complete and updated list of ferry schedules over all the Greek islands.

The Ministry of Culture: www.culture.gr. Events, history, "cultural maps of Greece," and other frills.

ALTERNATIVES TO TOURISM

In 2002 nearly 700 million trips were made, projected to be up to a billion by 2010 (a lot more than the 1.7 million when Let's Go started in 1961). The dramatic rise in tourism has increased the interdependence of the economy, environment, and culture of many destinations—and the tourists they host. For example, Greece receives over 14 million visitors per year; tourism accounts for 8% of the country's GDP and 10% of the Greek workforce is employed in the tourism sector.

Two rising trends in sustainable travel are ecotourism and community-based tourism. **Ecotourism** focuses on the conservation of natural habitats and using them to build up the economy without exploitation or overdevelopment. **Community-based tourism** aims to channel tourist euros into the local economy by emphasizing tours and cultural programs that are run by members of the host community and that often benefit disadvantaged groups. Increased traffic on the seas as well as tourism on the coasts has put a strain on the marine ecology, endangering populations of marine wildlife. Burgeoning tourism within small communities can lead to major problems for local populations. For example, the insular and isolated village of Olimpos (p. 550) on the Dodecanesian island of Karpathos has increasingly begun to pander to large groups of foreign visitors, as locals clamber to produce traditional wares for competitive tourist peddling. The 2004 Summer Olympic Games will have a much broader, yet similar, impact on the entire country and local population. The country will need help both during and after the Games.

Those looking to **volunteer** in the efforts to resolve these issues have many options. They can participate in projects from modern Olympic management to preserving the remnants of the Games' antiquarian predecessors, now archaeological sites, as well as helping with a slew of other issues, either on an infrequent basis or as the main component of a trip. In this chapter, we recommend organizations that can help you find the opportunities that best suit your interests, whether you're looking to pitch in for a day or a year.

There are any number of other ways that visitors can integrate themselves with the communities they visit. Studying at a college or language program is one option. For those interested in archaeology, marine biology, the Classics, and/or simply teaching English, Greece provides many opportunities to get involved. Many travelers also structure their trips by the work that they can do along the way—either odd jobs as they go, or full-time stints in cities where they plan to stay for some time. The Summer Olympics have generated many work opportunities especially from now until the conclusion of the Games (p. 128). Foreigners have also found employment working as boathands on yachts or at various establishments hit hard by the massive influx of summer tourists.

GIVING BACK. To read more on specific organizations working to better their communities, look for our **Giving Back** features p. 351 and p. 497.

For more on volunteering, studying, and working in Greece and beyond, consult Let's Go's alternatives to tourism website, **www.beyondtourism.com**.

A NEW PHILOSOPHY OF TRAVEL

We at Let's Go have watched the growth of the 'ignorant tourist' stereotype with dismay, knowing that the majority of travelers care passionately about the state of the communities and environments they explore—but also knowing that even conscientious tourists can inadvertently damage natural wonders, rich cultures, and impoverished communities. We believe the philosophy of **sustainable travel** is among the most important travel tips we could impart to our readers, to help guide fellow backpackers and on-the-road philanthropists. By staying aware of the needs and troubles of local communities, today's travelers can be a powerful force in preserving and restoring this fragile world.

Working against the negative consequences of irresponsible tourism is much simpler than it might seem; it is often self-awareness, rather than self-sacrifice, that makes the biggest difference. Simply by trying to spend responsibly and conserve local resources, all travelers can positively impact the places they visit. Let's Go has partnered with **BEST (Business Enterprises for Sustainable Travel,** an affiliate of the Conference Board; see www.sustainabletravel.org), which recognizes businesses that operate based on the principles of sustainable travel. Below, they provide advice on how ordinary visitors can practice this philosophy in their daily travels, no matter where they are.

TIPS FOR CIVIC TRAVEL: HOW TO MAKE A DIFFERENCE

Travel by train when feasible. Rail travel requires only half the energy per passenger mile that planes do. On average, each of the 40,000 daily domestic air flights releases more than 1700 pounds of greenhouse gas emissions.

Use public mass transportation whenever possible; outside of cities, take advantage of group taxis or vans. Bicycles are an attractive way of seeing a community first-hand. And enjoy walking–purchase good maps of your destination and ask about on-foot touring opportunities.

When renting a car, ask whether fuel-efficient vehicles are available. Honda and Toyota produce cars that use hybrid engines powered by electricity and gasoline, thus reducing emissions of carbon dioxide. Ford Motor Company plans to introduce a hybrid fuel model by the end of 2004.

Reduce, reuse, recycle–use electronic tickets, recycle papers and bottles wherever possible, and avoid using containers made of styrofoam. Refillable water bottles and rechargeable batteries both efficiently conserve expendable resources.

Be thoughtful in your purchases. Take care not to buy souvenir objects made from trees in old-growth or endangered forests, such as teak, or items made from endangered species, like ivory or tortoise jewelry. Ask whether products are made from renewable resources.

Buy from local enterprises, such as casual street vendors. In developing countries and low-income neighborhoods, many people depend on the "informal economy" to make a living.

Be on-the-road-philanthropists. If you are inspired by the natural environment of a destination or enriched by its culture, join in preserving their integrity by making a charitable contribution to a local organization.

Spread the word. Upon your return home, tell friends and colleagues about places to visit that will benefit greatly from their tourist dollars, and reward sustainable enterprises by recommending their services. Travelers can not only introduce friends to particular vendors but also to local causes and charities that they might choose to support when they travel.

VOLUNTEERING

Though Greece is considered wealthy by international standards, there is no shortage of aid organizations to benefit the very real issues the region does face. From preserving storied remnants of the past to ensuring the survival of wildlife populations for the future, Greece has plenty of opportunities to satisfy a vast range of interests. Volunteering can be one of the most fulfilling experiences you have in life, especially if you combine it with the thrill of traveling in a new place. Most people who volunteer in Greece do so on a short-term basis, at organizations that make use of drop-in or once-a-week volunteers. These can be found in virtually every city and are referenced both in this section and in our town and city write-ups themselves. Short-term social services in Greece range from geriatric assistance, medical care, and work with refugees to wildlife and environmental conservation. The best way to find opportunities that match your interests and schedule may be to search online; most programs have at least contact information and at most detailed descriptions and instructions on the Internet. More intensive volunteer services may charge you a fee to participate. These costs can be surprisingly hefty (although they frequently cover airfare and most, if not all, living expenses). Most people choose to go through a parent organization that takes care of logistical details and frequently provides a group environment and support system. There are two main types of organizations—religious and non-sectarian—although there are rarely restrictions on participation for either.

2004 SUMMER OLYMPIC GAMES

This summer the Olympics return to their birthplace and to the first venue of the modern Games as we know them today. Approximately 16,000 athletes, 20,000 journalists, and seven million spectators will descend on Greece in August 2004—and you could be the one showing them to the stadium. The Athens 2004 Organizing Committee estimates that a total of 60,000 volunteers are necessary to carry out the Olympic and Paralympic Games, and the volunteer program offers the opportunity to see the world's most prestigious athletic competition from the inside. Positions are largely short term (5-10 days) but volunteers will be needed for various jobs from May through September. The Greek government is calling for local volunteers in order to rally much-needed support for the Games, and Cyprus has promised to sign up 5000 of its own citizens. However, foreign volunteers will have to play a large part. Anyone who will be 18 years old by December 31, 2004 is welcome to apply. Online applications can be filled out and submitted at www.athens2004.com. Send completed forms to Volunteers Division ATHENS 2004, Iolkou 8 and Filikis Eterias str., GR-142 34, Nea Ionia, Athens, Greece. Candidates will be interviewed and those selected will be required to attend a training program. Placements are available at competition and non-competition venues and knowledge of foreign languages is strongly desired.

A word to the wise: potential volunteers should secure their accommodations as early as possible, as Athens has already expressed concern about the inevitable housing crunch during the Games. For more information and mail-in applications, call ☎210 200 4000 or email volunteers@athens2004.com.

WILDLIFE CONSERVATION

SEA TURTLES

Archelon Sea Turtle Protection Society, Solomou 57, GR-104 32, Athens (☎/fax 210 523 1342; www.archelon.gr). Non-profit group devoted to studying and protecting sea turtles on the beaches of Zakynthos, Crete, and the Peloponnese. Opportunities for seasonal field work and year-round work at the rehabilitation center. €70/US$65 participation fee includes lodgings for work at the center. Field volunteers are accommodated at private campgrounds but must provide their own camping equipment.

The Mediterranean Association to Save the Sea Turtles (MEDASSET), Likavitou 1, GR-106 72, Athens (☎210 361 3572; www.euroturtle.org/medasset), asseses the condition of the endangered Mediterranean green turtle through research projects and fieldwork. Sites of interest include Zakynthos and Kephalonia but extend as far as Cypriot and Egyptian turtle nesting grounds.

Earth, Sea and Sky Ionian Nature Conservation, P.O. Box 308, Lincoln, England LN4 2GQ (www.earthseasky.org). Based on the island of Zakynthos, promotes awareness on sustainable tourism and conservation. Although particularly concerned with issues of the sea turtle, organizes a variety of volunteer programs and green activities.

OTHER FAUNA

Hellenic Ornithological Society, Vas. Irakleiou 24, GR-106 82, Athens (☎/fax 210 822 7937; www.ornithologiki.gr/en/enmain.htm) and Kastritsiou 8, GR-546 23, Thessaloniki (☎2310 244245; fax 2310 256774), organizes volunteer events to protect endangered species of birds. Also seeks volunteers to help with office work and educational presentations.

Lesbian Wildlife Hospital, O. Christofa I Chatzigianni, GR-811 02, Agia Paraskevi, Lesvos (☎225 303 2006; www.wildlifeonlesvos.org), provides medical aid for needy wildlife.

World Wildlife Federation Greece (WWF), Fillelinon 26, GR-105 58 Athens (☎210 331 4893; www.wwf.gr). This international organization's Greek branch can help you locate Greek volunteering opportunities.

SOCIAL WELFARE

Bridges of Friendship, Menekratous 14, GR-116 36 Athens (instphil@hol.gr). This NGO devoted to voluntary service and issues of homelessness accepts many volunteers to run its programs.

Centre for Battered Women and Children–Greek Care Volos, Alexandras 189, Gambeti, Volos (☎24210 25 489 and 24210 25 256), offers protection for abused women and their children.

Centre for Inspirational Living, Antimahou 7, Athens (☎210 725 7617; fax 210 724 0425), is an organization that works with AIDS/HIV patients and runs educational programs about AIDS/HIV for the general public.

Centre for the Support of Children and Families, Yiatrakou 12, Metaxourgeio (☎210 522 1149; fax 210 996 6956), is affiliated with the EU umbrella organization Street Children Network and works to integrate Roma street children into the state school system and Roma women into Greek society.

Cultural Centres of Greek Council for Refugees, Lykavitou 1, Athens (gcr1@gcr.gr), is an initiative of the **Hellenic Red Cross** (www.recross.gr) that works with the children of refugees and asylum seekers and their families to integrate them into Greek society.

The Drom Network for Roma Social Rights, Iona Dragoumi 57, Thessaloniki (☎2310 287 186), works against the social exclusion of the Roma people. Supports Roma children through primary school and provides social, medical, and legal support to the larger Roma community.

Korydalos Prison, Lykavitou 1, Athens (☎210 360 4678; fax 210 362 9842; hrc@netmode.ntua.gr), is an initiative of the Hellenic Red Cross (see above) that works with prisoners with mental disabilities and with juvenile delinquents to improve their prison conditions and to provide support and entertainment.

Medical Rehabilitation Centre for Torture Victims, Lycabettous 9, GR-106 72 Athens (http://virtuals.compulink.gr/mrct), has encouraged medical specialists and other volunteers to aid their cause since their 1989 establishment.

Proposal and Movement for an Alternative Way of Life, Aghiou Georgiou 104, Patras (☎2610 623 290; fax 2610 623 290; protasi@pat.forthnet.gr), works to provide alternatives to drugs for local youth and to educate the public about narcotics use.

OTHER OPPORTUNITIES

The American Farm School, Office of the Trustees and Greek Summer, 1133 Broadway, Suite 1625, New York, NY 10010, USA (☎212-463-8434; www.afs.edu.gr). For 100 years, this nonprofit organization has been committed to serving rural Greece. 6-week summer program for high school students on the Zannas Dairy Farm near Thessaloniki. US$3300.

Conservation Volunteers Greece, Omirou 15, GR-145 62, Kifisia (☎210 623 1120; fax 010 801 1489; cvgpeep@otenet.gr). Volunteers aged 18-30 participate in 1- to 3-week community programs in remote areas of Greece. Projects range from reforestation to preserving archaeological sites. Accommodations provided.

Elderhostel, Inc., 11 Avenue de Lafayette, Boston, MA 92111-1746, USA (☎877-426-8056; www.elderhostel.org), sends volunteers age 55 and over around the world to work in construction, research, teaching, and many other projects. Costs average US$100 per day plus airfare.

Service Civil International Voluntary Service (SCI-IVS), SCI USA, 3213 W. Wheeler St., Seattle, WA 98199, USA (☎/fax 206-350-6585; www.sci-ivs.org), arranges placement in work camps in Greece for those 18+. Registration fee US$65-125

Volunteers for Peace, 1034 Tiffany Rd., Belmont., VT 05730, USA (☎802-259-2759; www.vfp.org), arranges placement in work camps in Greece. Membership required for registration. Membership US$20. Programs US$200 for 2-3 weeks.

Council on International Educational Exchange (CIEE), 633 3rd Ave., 20th floor, New York, NY 10017-6706, USA (☎800-407-8839; www.ciee.org/study), lists volunteer programs in Greece.

Global Volunteers, 375 East Little Canada Rd., St. Paul, MN 55109, USA (☎800-487-1074; www.globalvolunteers.org/1main/greece/volunteer_in_greece.htm), organizes short service programs near Rethymno on Crete. 1- and 2-week programs US$2000-3000.

STUDYING ABROAD

Study abroad programs range from basic language and culture courses to college-level classes, often for credit. Research all you can before making a decision—determine costs and duration, as well as what kind of students participate in the program and what sort of accommodations are provided. In programs that have large groups of students who speak the same language, there is a trade-off. You may feel more comfortable in the community, but you will not have the same opportunity to practice a foreign language or to befriend other international students. Traditionally Greek college students live in apartments as opposed to dorms so you will be hard-pressed to experience dorm life studying abroad in Greece. A more likely scenario is that the study abroad program will place you, along with other students in the program, in an apartment. If you choose to live with a Greek family, there is the potential to build life-long friendships with locals and to experience day-to-day life in more depth. Keep in mind, however, that conditions can vary greatly from family to family and from region to region.

UNIVERSITIES

Some American schools still require students to pay for credits obtained elsewhere. Most university-level study abroad programs are meant as language and culture enrichment opportunities and therefore are conducted in Greek. Still many programs do offer classes in English and beginner- and lower-level language courses. Those relatively fluent in Greek, on the other hand, may find it cheaper to enroll directly in a university, although getting college credit may be more difficult. A good resource for finding programs that cater to your particular interests is www.studyabroad.com, which has links to various semester abroad programs based on a variety of criteria, including desired location and focus of study. The following is a list of organizations that can help place students in university programs abroad or have their own branch in Greece.

STUDENT VISAS

Citizens of Australia, Canada, the EU, New Zealand, and the US are all automatically allowed a 3-month stay in Greece, though they are not eligible for employment during that time; South Africans must apply for a visa. Apply for visa extensions at least 20 days prior to the 3-month expiration date. If you plan to **study** in Greece for longer than 3 months, a student visa is necessary. You must first obtain admission into an academic or language program in Greece. Then as long as you can prove financial support, you need to apply to your embassy for a student visa for however long you want to study (US$5 for 90-day visa). A tourist visa cannot be changed into a student visa while in Greece, so obtain one well before you leave.

AMERICAN PROGRAMS

Arcadia University for Education Abroad, 450 S. Easton Rd., Glenside, PA 19038, USA (☎866-927-2234; www.arcadia.edu/cea), operates programs in Greece. Costs range from $2550 (summer) to $16,300 (full-year).

International Association for the Exchange of Students for Technical Experience (IAESTE), 10400 Little Patuxent Pkwy. Suite 250, Columbia, MD 21044-3519, USA (☎410-997-2200; www.aipt.org). 8- to 12-week programs in Greece for college students who have completed 2 years of technical study. US$25 application fee.

AHA International, 741 SW Lincoln St., Portland, Oregon 97201-3178, USA (☎800-654-2051; www.aha-intl.org). 12-week terms in the fall and spring. Costs start at US$6448.

New York University in Athens, 19 University Place, Room 510c, New York, NY 10003, USA (☎212-998-3990; www.nyu.edu/studyabroad/athens). Undergraduate and graduate level classes in the heart of Athens. Luxurious accommodations at the Park Hotel. Excluding housing, undergraduate US$3480; graduate US$574 per credit.

SUNY Brockport, Office of International Education, SUNY Brockport, 350 New Campus Dr., Brockport, NY 14420, USA (☎716-395-2119 or 1-800-298-SUNY; fax 716-637-3218; www.brockport.edu/study_abroad), offers a 2-3 week summer Mythological Study Tour in Greece. Program visits ancient sites and relates ancient myths to Greek life. Basic program starts at $2165, with some additional costs.

Odyssey in Athens, P.O. Box 5666, Portsmouth, NH 03802, USA (☎/fax 603-431-4999; www.odysseyinathens.org), offers fall and spring semesters at the University of Indianapolis Athens branch. Provides students with residential hall housing in Plaka. Also organizes summer study programs. Semester US$7600; full-year US$14,330; summer program $2200.

University of Laverne, Athens (www.laverne.edu.gr). This small liberal arts university offers fall and spring study abroad. Houses students in furnished apartments near the US Embassy. 2-month summer study program also available. Half-year US$7100, shorter term US$5900; summer US$2700.

PROGRAMS IN GREECE

Several different types of programs are available for studying abroad in Greece: studying directly at a Greek university, studying through an international program, or going to a language school. Most of these programs are located in Greece's most traveled areas, especially in Athens, on Crete, and throughout the Cyclades. In addition aspiring archaeologists have a unique opportunity to work on current digs while studying abroad in Greece. Programs vary tremendously in expense, academic quality, living conditions, degree of contact with local students, and exposure to local culture and languages.

College Year in Athens, P.O. Box 390890, Cambridge, MA 02139, USA (US ☎617-868-8200; Greece ☎210 756 0749; www.cyathens.org), runs semester-long, full-year, and summer programs for undergraduates (usually juniors), which include travel as well as classroom instruction (all in English). The program has 2 tracks, 1 in Ancient Greek civilization and 1 in East Mediterranean area studies. Scholarships available. Students housed in apartments in the posh Kolonaki district. Also offers various summer programs, including intensive Modern Greek instruction on Paros and a 3-week archaeology program on Santorini.

American College of Thessaloniki (ACT), P.O. Box 21021, GR-555 10 Pylea, Thessaloniki (☎2310 398 398 or 398 239; www.anatolia.edu.gr), offers the opportunity to study in Greece in a predominately Greek student environment. Foreign students choose to enroll either for a term abroad or as an exchange student. Study abroad student fee US$6145; exchange student US$2845.

Deree College, Gravias 6, GR-153 42 Agia Paraskevi, Athens (☎210 600 9800; www.acg.gr). Part of the American College of Greece. Bachelor's degrees granted in a wide variety of subjects; classes taught in English. Open to students of all international backgrounds, including many Greek students.

LANGUAGE SCHOOLS

Unlike American universities, language schools are frequently independently run international or local organizations or divisions of foreign universities that rarely offer college credit. Language schools are a good alternative to university study if you desire a deeper focus on the language or a slightly less rigorous courseload. These programs are also good for younger high school students that might not feel comfortable with older students in a university program.

Omilo, Tsaldari 13, GR-151 22 Marousi (☎210 612 2896; www.omilo.com). Languages courses for 5 different levels offered in 5 distinctive Greek locations. 2-week course €450-500; 3-week €650.

Greek House (Hellenic Estia), Georganta 11 (☎210 808 5185; www.greekhouse.gr). Combined language instruction and cultural activities on Andros. 3-week €1000-1100.

Kentro Ellinikou Politsmou (Hellenic Culture Center), Tilemahou 14, GR-114 72 Athens (☎210 360 3379 for Athens; 227 506 1140 for Ikaria; www.hcc.gr). Seminars in Modern Greek language in Athens and on the Northeast Aegean island Ikaria. Prices begin at €880.

Hellenic Language School, National Registration Center for Study Abroad, P.O. Box 1395, Milwaukee, WI 53201, USA (☎414-278-0631; fax 414-271-884; study@nrcsa.com). Branches in Athens, Thessaloniki, and Chania, Crete. Classes follow immersion method. 2-week courses begin at US$1272; 4-week US$2454.

Languages Abroad, Box 502, 99 Avenue Rd., Toronto, Ontario M5R 2G5, Canada (US and Canada ☎800-219-9924; elsewhere 1 416 925 2112; www.languagesabroad.com). Modern Greek study in Athens. Accommodations, meals, insurance, and other services available for additional fee. 3-week course US$900; 4-week US$1090.

School of Modern Greek Language at the Aristotle University of Thessaloniki, Thessaloniki 541 24 (☎310 997 5712 or 997 5716; www.auth.gr/smg). Year-long courses and summer/winter intensive programs offered. Limited scholarships available. Consult website for reduced fee eligibility. Oct.-May courses start at €600; intensives at €220.

ART STUDY

Aegean Center for the Fine Arts, Paros 844 00 (☎228 402 3287; www.aegeancenter.org), offers 13-week spring session on the island of Paros and 14-week fall session with time spent in Italian facility in Tuscany and Paros facility. Singing, painting, drawing, photography, sculpture, printmaking, literature, creative writing, and art history classes. Studio apartment housing in Greece; villa accommodations in Italy. University credit available. Financial aid available. Fall term €8000; spring term €7000.

Art School of the Aegean, P.O. Box 1375, Sarasota, FL 34230-1375, USA (☎941-351-5597; www.artschool-aegean.com), offers 2- to 3-week summer programs in painting and ceramics for applicants 18+. From US$1700.

Island Center for the Arts, GR-370 03 Skopelos (www.islandcenter.org), runs painting and photography classes from the art-inspiring island of Skopelos. Offers university credit. 2-week course US$2195.

Dellatolas Marble Sculpture Studio, Spitalia, GR-842 00 Tinos (☎/fax 02830 23664, www.tinosmarble.com). Classes run May-Oct. 2-week course US$800.

Cycladic School, Ano Meria, GR-840 11 Folegandros (☎22860410137; fax 22860 41 472). 6-12 day classes feature drawing and painting instruction (p. 414).

OTHER INSTRUCTION

The Glorious Greek Kitchen (☎210 653 6800; 697 784 7833; www.cuisineinternational.com). Cooking classes are held on Ikaria where instructor Diane Kochilas recently opened a restaurant. 6-day class including island excursions US$1700.

Athens Institute of Sailing, Alimos Marina (US ☎877-369-1269; UK 0870 169 2907; Greece 210 931 7081; www.sailingcoursesingreece.com), provides a plethora of basic or intermediate sailing and yachting classes run out of an Athens marina. Taught in English. 4-weekend course US$600; 1-week course US$1500.

Dora Stratou Dance, Scholiou 8 GR-105 58 (☎210 324 4395; www.grdance.org), offers folk dance and culture classes. 1-week workshop €110.

Ionian Village, St. Basil Rd. 83, Garrison, New York 10524, USA (☎646-519-6190; www.ionianvillage.org), offers teens and young adults, up to the age of 30, religious, cultural, and artistic instruction. All of its 3 programs include travel, but programs are based at resort-like facility west of Patras. Because Ionian Village is under the direction of the Greek Orthodox Archdiocese of America (i.e. the Greek church), most participants are Greek Orthodox Christian or of Greek origin. Full registration US$2950-3175.

ARCHAEOLOGICAL DIGS

Students interested in classics and archaeology are most often those who find their way to Greece for study abroad. **Archaeologic Institute of America,** 656 Beacon St., Boston, MA 02215-2006, USA (☎617-353-9361; www.archaeological.org), puts out the *Archaeological Fieldwork Opportunities Bulletin*

(US$19.95), which lists field sites in Greece. This must be purchased from the David Brown Book Co., P.O. Box 511, Oakville, CT 06779 (☎860-945-9329; www.oxbowbooks.com). **Hellenic Ministry of Culture** (www.culture.gr) maintains a complete list of archaeological sites in Greece. Below is a limited list of organizations that can help you in your mission to find an archaeological dig in which to participate.

American School of Classical Studies (ASCSA), Souidias 54, Athens 10676 (☎210 72 36 313; www.ascsa.org), offers a variety of archaeological and Classical studies programs to undergraduates, graduate students, and Ph.D. candidates. Visit the website to find a list of publications and links to other archaeological programs.

German Archaeological Institute, Fidiou 1, GR-106 78 Athens (☎210 330 7400; www.dainst.org). Ever since Heinrich Schliemann started digging up Greece in the late 19th century, Germans have dominated the Greek archaeological scene. The Institute currently runs 6 projects in Greece.

British School in Athens, O. Souidhias 52, GR-106 76 Athens (☎210 721 0974 or 210 729 2146; UK office ☎207 862 8732; www.bsa.gla.ac.uk), conducts fieldwork annually; courses for undergraduates, postgraduates, and teachers also available.

Canadian Archaeological Institute in Athens, Dion. Aiginitou 7, GR-115 28 Athens, (☎210 722 3201; http://caia-icaa.gr), focuses archaeological fieldwork on 9 Greek sites. Research ongoing at 2 sites in Arcadia and Macedonia.

Irish Institute of Hellenic Studies in Athens (IIHSA), Pyrtaneiou 12, GR-105 56 Athens (☎210 324 1447; www.ucc.ie/iihsa), runs 2 current projects with more to come.

WORKING

Work opportunities tend to fall into two categories. Some travelers want long-term jobs that allow them to get to know another part of the world as a member of the community, while other travelers seek out short-term jobs to finance the next leg of their travels. Those who can teach English will find many job openings in Greece, and in some sectors (like agricultural work) permit-less workers are rarely bothered by authorities. Students can check with their universities' foreign language departments, which may have connections to jobs abroad. Friends in Greece can expedite work permits or arrange work-for-accommodations swaps.

Many popular youth hostels have bulletin boards with a variety of both long- and short-term employment opportunities. **City News** (http://athens.citynews.com/Employment.html) is a good resource listing updated opportunities for work in Athens. EU citizens will have a much easier time finding work and will generally make better pay than those from outside the EU. An interesting opportunity is **Trekking Hellas,** Fillelinon 7 GR-105 57, which employs numerous young travelers every year to guide others on various expeditions, including hiking trips and river treks, throughout Greece. (☎210 331 0323; www.trekking.gr. Salary €65 per day and up. Applicants must be at least 18 and be fluent in 3 languages, one of which must be Greek. Applications include physical tests and written examinations.)

WORK PERMITS

For **legal employment** in Greece, you must first get a work permit from a pre-arranged employer. Permits are available at the Ministry of Labor, Pireos 40, Athens 104 37.

LONG-TERM WORK

If you're planning to spend a substantial amount of time (more than three months) working in Greece, search for a job well in advance. International placement agencies are often the easiest way to find employment abroad, especially for teaching English. **Internships,** usually for college students, are a good way to segue into working abroad, although they are often unpaid or poorly paid (many say the experience, however, is well worth it). Be wary of advertisements or companies that claim the ability to get you a job abroad for a fee; often the same listings are available online or in newspapers—or even out of date. The following organizations, however, are reputable. **AIESEC International,** 127 W 26th St., Floor 10, New York, NY 10001, USA, offers paid internships in business and technology fields in over 80 countries, including Greece. (☎212-757-4062; www.aiesec.org.) **Council Exchanges,** 52 Poland St., London W1F 7AB, UK, charges a US$300-475 fee for arranging short-term working authorizations (generally valid for 3-6 months) and provides extensive information on different job opportunities in Greece. (UK ☎44 020 7478 2000; US 888-268-6245; www.councilexchanges.org.)

TEACHING ENGLISH

Teaching jobs abroad are rarely well paid, although some elite private American schools pay somewhat competitive salaries. Volunteering as a teacher in lieu of getting paid is also a popular option; even in those cases, teachers often get some sort of a daily stipend to help with living expenses. In almost all cases, you must have at least a bachelor's degree to be a full-fledged teacher, although college undergraduates can often get summer positions teaching or tutoring. Those who wish to teach English in Greece should have a university degree (preferably in English literature or history) and a solid command of English. To obtain a teaching license, you must present your diploma and your passport translated into Greek; contact the **Hellenic Ministry of Education,** Mitropoleos 15, Athens 10185. (☎210 323 1656; www.ypepth.gr.) Greek schools rarely require teachers to have a **Teaching English as a Foreign Language (TEFL)** certificate but certified teachers often find higher paying jobs. Native English speakers working in private schools are most often hired for English immersion classrooms where no Greek is spoken. Placement agencies or university fellowship programs are the best resources for finding teaching jobs in Greece. The alternative is to make contacts directly with schools or just to try your luck once you get there. If you are going to try the latter, the best time of the year is several weeks before the start of the school year in September. The following organizations are helpful in placing teachers in Greece.

International Schools Services (ISS), 15 Roszel Rd., Box 5910, Princeton, NJ 08543-5910, USA (☎609-452-0990; www.iss.edu), recruits teachers and administrators for American and English schools in Greece. All instruction in English. Candidates should have experience teaching or with international affairs; 2-year commitment expected.

Office of Overseas Schools, US Department of State, Room H328, SA-1, Washington, D.C. 20522, USA (☎202-261-8200; fax 261-8224; OverseasSchools@state.gov; www.state.gov/www/about_state/schools), keeps a comprehensive list of schools abroad and agencies that arrange placement for Americans to teach abroad.

GoAbroad.com, 8 East First Avenue, Suite 102, Denver, Colorado 80203, USA (☎720-570-1702; www.goabroad.com and www.teachabroad.com), has useful listings for various teaching opportunities in a number of countries including Greece in its "Teach Abroad" section.

AU PAIR WORK

Au pairs are typically women, aged 18-27, who work as live-in nannies, caring for children and doing light housework in foreign countries in exchange for room, board, and a small spending allowance or stipend. Most former au pairs speak favorably of their experience and of how it allowed them to experience the country without the high expenses of traveling. Drawbacks, however, often include long hours of constantly being on duty and the somewhat mediocre pay. Au pairs in Greece generally work 30-45 hours a week, including a few evenings for €45-70 per week, depending on the number of children, duties, and qualifications. Much of the au pair experience depends on the family you're placed with. The agencies below are a good starting point for looking for employment as an au pair.

Accord Cultural Exchange, 750 La Playa, San Francisco, CA 94121, USA (☎415-386-6203; www.cognitext.com/accord).

Au Pair in Europe, P.O. Box 68056, Blakely Postal Outlet, Hamilton, Ontario L8M 3M7, Canada (☎905-545-6305; fax 905-544-4121; www.princeent.com).

Athenian Nanny Agency, P.O. Box 51181, Kifisia T.K., 145.10 Athens (☎/fax 301 808 1005; mskinti@groovy.gr).

Childcare International, Ltd., Trafalgar House, Grenville Pl., London NW7 3SA, England (☎+44 020 8906 3116; fax 8906 3461; www.childint.co.uk).

Luck Locketts & Vanessa Bancroft Nanny and Domestic Agency, 400 Beacon Rd., Wibsey, Bradford, West Yorkshire BD6 3DJ, England (☎/fax 212 74 402 822; www.lucylocketts.com), places au pairs and experienced nannies in Greece.

SHORT-TERM WORK

Traveling for long periods of time can get expensive, so many travelers try their hand at odd jobs for a few weeks to make some extra cash to carry them through another month or two. For citizens of Greece and of EU countries, getting a job in Greece is relatively simple. For all others, finding work in Greece can be difficult. Job opportunities are scarce and the government tries to restrict employment to citizens and visitors from the EU. If your parents were born in an EU country, you may be able to claim dual citizenship or at least the right to a work permit.

Arrive in the spring and early summer to search for **hotel jobs** (bartending, cleaning, etc.). Most night spots offer meager pay but don't require much paperwork. Check the bulletin boards of hostels and the classified ads of local newspapers, such as the *Athens News*. Another popular option is to work several hours a day at a hostel in exchange for free or discounted room and/or board. Most often these short-term jobs are found by word of mouth or simply by talking to the owner of a hostel or restaurant. Many places, especially due to the high turnover in the tourism industry, are always eager for help, even if its only temporary. *Let's Go* lists temporary jobs like these wherever possible; look in the **Practical Information** sections of larger cities, or check out the list below for some of the available short-term jobs in popular destinations.

The 2004 Summer Olympic and Paralympic Games (www.athens2004.com) have a number of job openings remaining from May-Sept. 2004. (See **Volunteering,** p. 70)

Cafe Extrablatt, Alex. Svolou 46, Thessaloniki (☎2310 256 900), next to the youth hostel. Good Greek needed. Contact manager upon arrival. Pay negotiable. (p. 275)

Milos Beach Bar and Cafe (☎26710 83 188 from May-Oct.; in winter 26710 83 231) Skala, Kephalonia. Hires waitstaff, bartenders, and chefs for tourist season; summer hiring in Feb.-Apr. Call in advance and ask for Joya Grouzi. (p. 463)

Melissani Restaurant and Snack Bar (☎26740 22 395) in Sami, Kephalonia. This large beach bar is one of a few in the Ionian Islands that considers foreign job applicants. Call in advance. (p. 467)

The Pink Palace (☎26610 53 103; www.thepinkpalace.com) Agios Gordios, Corfu. Hires hotel staff, nightclub staff, and DJs. Send a letter of introduction, a resume, and a photo to Dr. George. Minimum 2-month commitment required. (p. 444)

FURTHER READING ON ALTERNATIVES TO TOURISM

Alternatives to the Peace Corps: Directory of Third World and U.S. Volunteer Opportunities, Joan Powell. Food First Books, 2000 (US$10).

How to Get a Job in Europe, Sanborn and Matherly. Surrey Books, 1999 ($US22).

How to Live Your Dream of Volunteering Oversees, Collins, DeZerega, and Heckscher. Penguin Books, 2002 (US$17).

International Directory of Voluntary Work, Whetter and Pybus. Peterson's Guides and Vacation Work, 2000 (US$16).

International Jobs, Kocher and Segal. Perseus Books, 1999 (US$18).

Overseas Summer Jobs 2002, Collier and Woodworth. Peterson's Guides and Vacation Work, 2002 (US$18).

Work Abroad: The Complete Guide to Finding a Job Overseas, Hubbs, Griffith, and Nolting. Transitions Abroad Publishing, 2000 ($16).

Work Your Way Around the World, Susan Griffith. Worldview Publishing Services, 2001 (US$18).

Invest Yourself: The Catalogue of Volunteer Opportunities, published by the Commission on Voluntary Service and Action (☎718-638-8487).

ATHENS Αθηνα

Greece has quickly become one of the world's top 15 destinations. Its capital city of Athens, however, has consistently been bypassed for the beaches, seaside lounge chairs, and sun of the islands. The striking coexistence of past and present in Athens have until now, only offered the opportunity for comparison—and after comparison, visitors have always ended up handing it to the past. The shadow of the Acropolis has loomed over Plaka's modern developments for many years and the legacy it recalls has weighed heavily on the descendants of its original builders—a permanent reminder of what their metropolis and civilization once were but no longer are. In the past few years, however, Greece has been changing, and the summer of 2004 promises to be a pivotal climax. Modern Greece, with Athens as its centerpiece, will be given the chance to break from the past, while maintaining a distinct pride in its ancient heritage evaluated in a new light. Besides ridding the capital's throughfares of cardboard, the 2004 Olympic Games will leave behind modern landmarks proudly standing amidst the city's ancient ones—landmarks with lasting functional purpose.

HIGHLIGHTS OF ATHENS

CATWALK past chic outdoor cafes in Kolonaki (p. 106), then shake it at the hotspot seaside clubs of Glyfada (p. 118).

LOSE YOURSELF amid ancient relics at the National Archaeological Museum (p. 114).

AMBLE through the medieval alleyways of Plaka (p. 95).

MAKE A PILGRIMAGE to Athena's Parthenon on the Acropolis (p. 108).

HAGGLE with wily merchants at the Varnakia flea market in Omonia (p. 91).

CATCH THE SPECTACLE of the 2004 Olympic Marathon that will follow the ancient route forged by Phidippides 2500 years ago (p. 134).

HISTORY

Athens's mythological history began when the Olympian gods jockeyed for the position of the Attic city's patron and namesake. They decided that whoever gave it the best gift would earn the city. **Poseidon** struck the Acropolis with his trident and sea water gushed forth from a well, but it was **Athena's** wiser gift, an olive tree, that won the city's lasting admiration and worship. Rising to political power as early as the 16th century BC, Athens was united as a *polis* (city-state) by the hero **Theseus** (a.k.a. Minotaur-slayer). By the 8th century, it had become the focal point of artistic endeavor in Greece and, in fact, in the entire Western world; initial fame for geometric pottery foreshadowed a bright future. Two centuries later, law-giver **Solon** ended the servitude of native citizens, restored rights to some slaves, and established democratic codification of the laws. After victories over the Persians at Marathon and Salamis in the 5th century BC, Athens experienced a **Golden Age** (under Pericles's democracy), the era that produced not only the Parthenon but also the masterpieces of Aeschylus, Sophocles, Euripides, and Aristophanes. These 70 years would go down in history as the very seed of inspiration from which Western mores, culture, aesthetics, laws, and philosophy sprouted.

Pericles's Athens fell apart during the bloody, drawn-out **Peloponnesian War** (431-404 BC) against Sparta. Political power shifted north under Philip of Macedon and his son **Alexander the Great,** but Athens remained a cultural center throughout the

5th and 4th centuries BC. In this period the city produced the philosophers **Socrates, Plato,** and **Aristotle** and the orator **Demosthenes.** By the 2nd century, the **Roman Empire** ruled the city. In 324 Emperor Constantine moved the capital of the Roman Empire to Byzantium, forsaking Athens. Though Athens remained the center of Greek education, its dominance (and buildings) lapsed into ruin when the emperor Justinian banned the teaching of philosophy in 529.

Around 1000 Byzantine emperor **Basil II** visited Athens. After praying to the Virgin Mary in the Parthenon, Basil ordered craftsmen to restore Athens to its former glory. The city was reborn again as it was on several occasions after that under successive conquerors—the Franks in 1205, the Catalans in 1311, the Accajioli merchant family in 1387, and the **Ottomans** (who ruled for 400 years) in 1456. The victory of the Greek independence movement in 1821 ushered in a new era of extensive renovation and restoration, as well as the awakening of a nationalistic spirit. Modern Athens's plateias, wide boulevards, and National Garden follow the plan of architects hired by Greece's first king, the German prince Otto (p. 13).

In the past century, Athens's population and commercial output have skyrocketed. The 1923 **Treaty of Lausanne** and **population exchange** (p. 14) with Turkey brought an influx of ethnic Greeks who had long been living in Asia Minor. The city swelled and has continued to do so with rural workers' flocking to the industrial and centralized urban atmosphere. In the past 100 years, the city's population has exploded from 169 families to almost half of Greece's 11 million residents. Preparations for the 2004 Olympic Games have fueled another age of urban renewal in Athens; the transit authority fought the sinister *"nefos"* (smog) tooth and nail by banning cars from historic Plaka and by further restricting drivers' access to downtown areas. Athens also gutted its underground, unearthing a wealth of fascinating relics from days past, while building a fancy, new public transportation system. The city no longer suffers from a confounding urban layout—the product of thousands of years of turnover. The spanking new Elephtherios Venizelos Airport, which lies to the city's southeast, has been consistently rated among the world's best airports ever since its 2001 opening.

INTERCITY TRANSPORTATION

Flights: El. Venizelou (☎210 353 0000, www.aia.gr), Greece's new international airport, operates as 1 massive yet easily navigable terminal. Arrivals are on the ground floor, departures on the 2nd. The new **Suburban Rail,** expected to be finished by summer 2004 for the Olympic Games, will run along the middle of the new Attiki Odos highway and serve the international airport from the city center in 30min. Since it will be connected efficiently with the 2 new stations, Neratziotissa, being developed on green line 1, and Doukissis Plakentias, on blue line 3, the most central stations will be, respectively, Omonia and Syndagma. 4 **bus** lines run to and from El. Venizelou from Athens, Piraeus, and Rafina. To get from **Pl. Syndagma** in the Athens city center to the airport take the **E95** (40min.; every 20min., 24hr; €2.90). Pick it up on Amalias, to the right of the top right corner of Pl. Syndagma. To get from the **Ethniki Amyna** subway station, take the **E94** (every 10min., 7:30am-11:35pm; €2.90; wait by the subway exit). From **Piraeus,** take the **E96** (every 20-40min., 24hr.; €2.90; in Pl. Karaiskaki on the waterfront, on busy Akti Tzelepi, across from Phillipis Travel). From **Rafina,** the bus (€3) leaves every 30min. from the stop midway up the ramp from the waterfront. Buses deposit you at one of the 4 departure entrances. Buses wait outside the 5 arrivals exits; walk out of the terminal and look for your bus number or enter the taxi queue. A **taxi** from El. Venizelos to Pl. Syndagma should cost €18-25 altogether depending on whether you are traveling before midnight or midnight-5am. This includes an extra €0.30 charge for each piece of luggage over 10kg and a €1.18 surcharge from the airport. Watch drivers carefully; they often rig the meters. Drivers may be unwilling to pick up travelers laden with luggage.

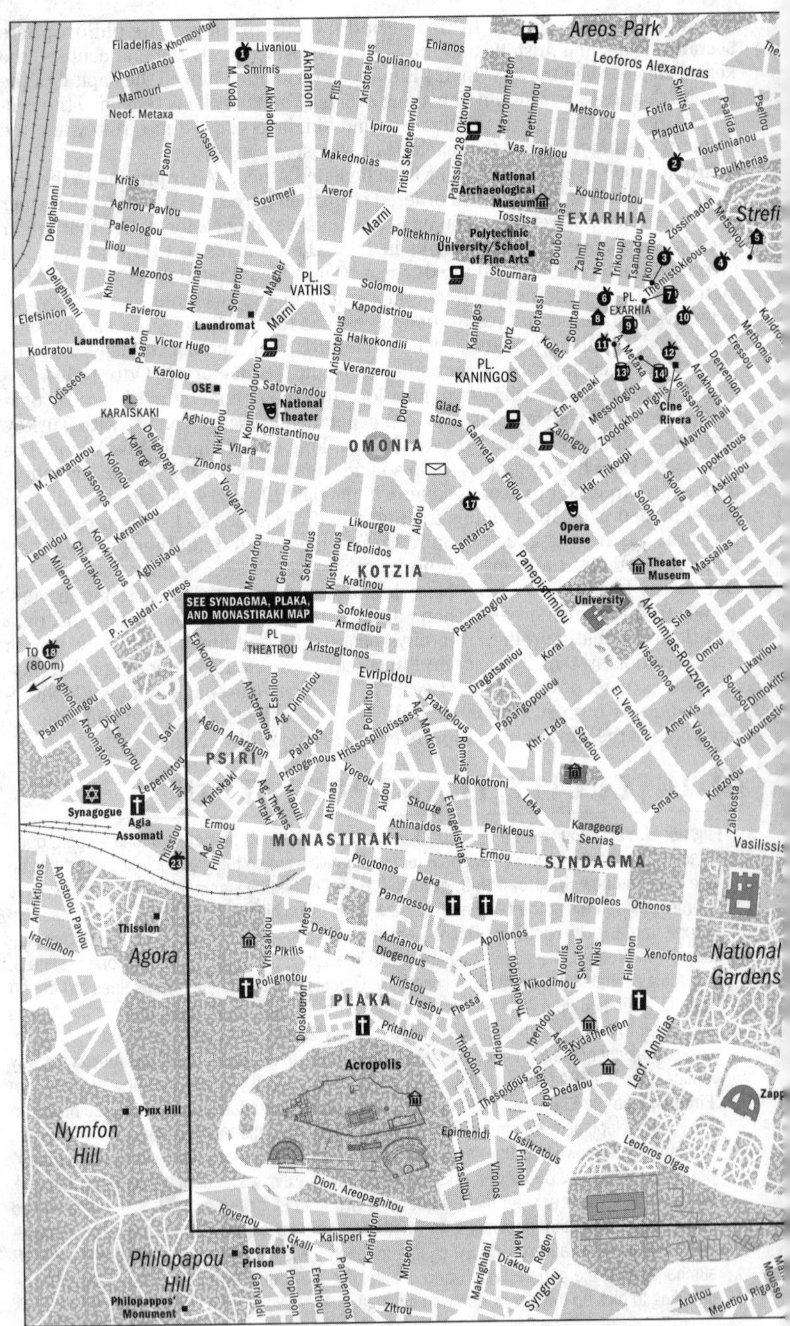

Areos Park
Leoforos Alexandras
Filadelfias
Khormovitou
Khomatianou
Mamouri
Neof. Metaxa
Livaniou
Smirnis
M. Voda
Alkiviadou
Akharnon
Filis
Aristotelous
Ioulianou
Enianos
Patission-28 Oktovriou
Mavrommateon
Rethimnou
Metsovou
Skilitsi
Fotifa
Psalida
Psellou
Plapduta
Ioustinianou
Poulkherias
Ipirou
Vas. Irakliou
Makednoias
Tritis Skeptemvriou
Liossion
Psaron
Kritis
Aghrou Pavlou
Paleologou
Iliou
Delighianni
Sourmeli
Averof
Marni
National Archaeological Museum
Tossitsa
Kountouriotou
EXARHIA
Bouboulinas
Zossimadon
Metsovou
Strefi
Politekhniou
Polytechnic University/School of Fine Arts
Stournara
Zaimi
Notara
Trikoupi
Tsamadou
Ikonomou
Themistokleous
Mezonos
Khiou
Akominatou
Sonierou
Magher
PL. VATHIS
Solomou
PL. EXARHIA
Kalidromiou
Methonis
Eressou
Elefsinion
Favierou
Laundromat
Kapodistriou
Botassi
Soultani
Kodratou
Victor Hugo
Halkokondili
Kaningos
Tzortz
Koleti
Dervenion
Karolou
Veranzerou
PL. KANINGOS
Em. Benaki
Messologiou
Arakhovis
Odisseos
OSE
Satovriandou
National Theater
Dorou
Zoodokhou Pighis
Velissariou
Cine Rivera
Mavromihali
PL. KARAISKAKI
Aghiou Konstantinou
Koumoundourou
Nikiforou
Glad-stonos
Ganveta
Zalongou
Vilara
OMONIA
Ippokratous
M. Alexandrou
Kalergi
Delighorghi
Zinonos
Har. Trikoupi
Kolonou
Iassonos
Voulgari
Fidiou
Skoufa
Asklipiou
Didotou
Solonos
Keramikou
Likourgou
Aidou
Opera House
Santaroza
Leonidou
Kolokinthous
Menandrou
Geraniou
Sokratous
Klisthenous
Efpolidou
Panepistimiou
Milerou
Ghiatrakou
Aghisilaou
KOTZIA
Theater Museum
Massalias
Kratinou
P. Tsaldari - Pireos
SEE SYNDAGMA, PLAKA, AND MONASTIRAKI MAP
Sofokleous
University
Armodiou
Pesmazoglou
Akadimias-Rouzvelt
Sina
Epikorou
PL THEATROU
Aristogitonos
Korai
Vissarionos
Omrou
Likavitou
TO 18 (800m)
Evripidou
Dragatsaniou
Aghion
Eshilou
Ag. Dimitriou
Polikitou
Praxitelous
Papargopoulou
El. Venizelou
Amerikis
Soutsou
Dimokritou
Psaromilingou
Dipilou
Aristofanous
Protogenous
Hrissospiliotissas
Ag. Markou
Romvis
Khr. Lada
Stadiou
Valaoritou
Voukourestiou
Arsomaton
Leokoriou
Sari
Agion Anargiron
Palados
PSIRI
Voreou
Kolokotroni
Karitsi
Lepeniotou
Ivis
Kariskaki
Ag. Thekias
Ag. Pitaki
Miaouli
Athinas
Aidou
Skouze
Evangelistrias
Leka
Kriezotou
Smats
Zalokosta
Synagogue
Agia Assomati
Ermou
Athinaidos
Perikleous
Karageorgi Servias
Vasilissis
Thissiou
Ag. Filipou
MONASTIRAKI
Ermou
SYNDAGMA
Ploutonos
Amfiktionos
Apostolou Pavlou
Deka
Pandrossou
Mitropoleos
Othonos
Thission
Iraclidhon
Agora
Areos
Vrissakiou
Dexipou
Pikilis
Adrianou
Diogenous
Apollonos
Filellinon
Xenofontos
National Gardens
Polignotou
Kiristou
Voulis
Skoufou
Nikis
Nikodimou
PLAKA
Lissiou
Flessa
Thoukididou
Dioskouron
Pritaniou
Iperidou
Kydatheneon
Asteriou
Leof. Amalias
Acropolis
Tripodon
Adrianou
Geronda
Dedalou
Thespidous
Zapp
Pynx Hill
Nymfon Hill
Epimenidi
Lissikratous
Frinhou
Leoforos Olgas
Thrassilou
Vironos
Dion. Areopaghitou
Rovertou
Kalisperi
Gkalli
Philopapou Hill
Socrates's Prison
Propileon
Erekhtiou
Garivaldi
Parthenonos
Kariatidon
Mitseon
Makrighiani
Makri
Diakou
Rogon
Syngrou
Philopappos' Monument
Zitrou
Arditou
Meletiou Riga
Mousso

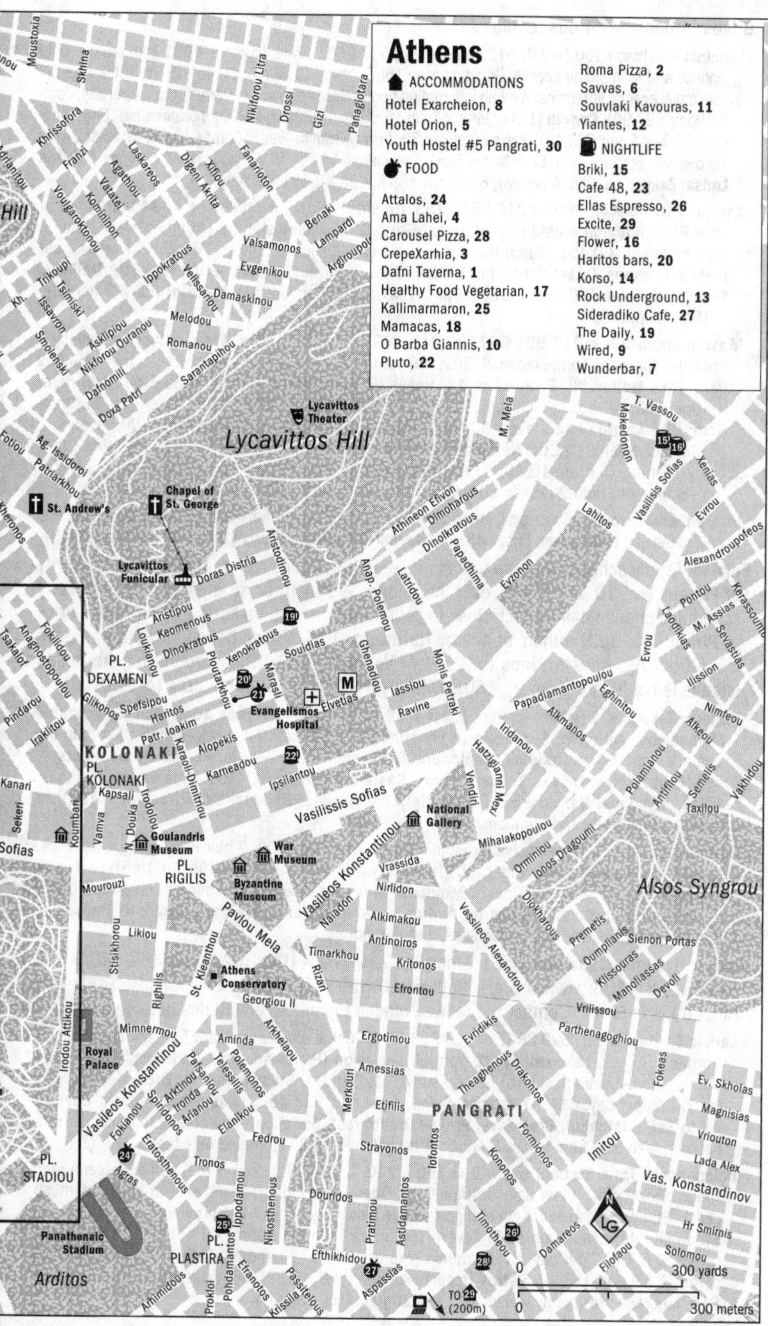

Athens
ACCOMMODATIONS
Hotel Exarcheion, 8
Hotel Orion, 5
Youth Hostel #5 Pangrati, 30
FOOD
Attalos, 24
Ama Lahei, 4
Carousel Pizza, 28
CrepeXarhia, 3
Dafni Taverna, 1
Healthy Food Vegetarian, 17
Kallimarmaron, 25
Mamacas, 18
O Barba Giannis, 10
Pluto, 22
Roma Pizza, 2
Savvas, 6
Souvlaki Kavouras, 11
Yiantes, 12
NIGHTLIFE
Briki, 15
Cafe 48, 23
Ellas Espresso, 26
Excite, 29
Flower, 16
Haritos bars, 20
Korso, 14
Rock Underground, 13
Sideradiko Cafe, 27
The Daily, 19
Wired, 9
Wunderbar, 7
Lycavittos Hill
Lycavittos Theater
Chapel of St. George
St. Andrew's
Lycavittos Funicular
PL. DEXAMENI
KOLONAKI
PL. KOLONAKI
Evangelismos Hospital
National Gallery
Goulandris Museum
War Museum
PL. RIGILIS
Byzantine Museum
Athens Conservatory
Royal Palace
Alsos Syngrou
PANGRATI
PL. STADIOU
Panathenaic Stadium
PL. PLASTIRA
Arditos
Vasilissis Sofias
Vasileos Konstantinou
Vasileos Alexandrou
Pavlou Mela
Vas. Konstandinov
Imitou
TO 30 (200m)
0 300 yards
0 300 meters

ATHENS

Buses: Athens has 4 bus terminals.

Terminal A: Kifissou 100 (☎210 512 4910 or 210 513 2601). Take blue bus **#051** from the corner of Zinonos and Menandrou near Pl. Omonia (every 15min., 5am-11:30pm; €0.45). Don't mistake the private travel agency at Terminal A for an information booth. Buses depart for: **Corfu** (10hr.; 4 per day, 7am-8:30pm; €27.90); **Corinth** (1½hr.; every 45min., 5:50am-10:30pm; €5.70); **Igoumenitsa** (8hr.; 5 per day, 6:30am-9pm; €28.45); **Patras** (regular: 3hr.; every 30min., 6am-10pm; €12.25; express: 2½hr.; 10 per day, 6:15am-7pm, Su 8:30am-7pm); **Thessaloniki** (6hr.; 11 per day, 7am-11:45pm; €28) via **Larisa; Zakynthos** (6hr.; 4 per day, 6:30am-4:45pm; €21.40, includes ferry).

Terminal B: Liossion 260 (☎210 831 7153, except Sa-Su). Take blue bus **#024** from Amalias near Pl. Syndagma outside the National Gardens or Panepistimiou (45min.; every 20min., 5am-midnight; €0.45). Watch the numbers on street signs–Liossion 260 is near several car mechanic shops. Buses depart for: **Delphi** (3hr.; 6 per day, 7:30am-8pm; €10.20); **Halkida,** Evia (1¼hr.; every 30min., 5:30am-9pm, 9:45, 10:30pm; €4.50); **Katerini** (6hr.; 3 per day, 9:45am-10pm; €24.70).

Mavromateon 29: ☎210 821 0872 or 210 823 0179. In Exarhia. Walk farther up Patission from the National Archaeological Museum, turn right on Enianos. It's on the corner of Areos Park. Take **trolley #2, 5, 9, 11** or **18.** Buses to: **Agia Marina** (2½hr; M-Sa 5 per day, 6am-4:30pm; €3.40) from which ferries depart for **Evia; Grammatiko** (2¼hr.; every hr., 5:30am-8pm; €3); **Lavrio** (1¾hr.; every 30min., 5:45am-9:30pm; €3.30); **Marathon** (2hr.; every hr., 5:30am-12:30am; €2.50); **Nea Makri** (1¼hr.; every hr., 5:45am-6:45pm; €2); **Rafina** (1hr.; every 30min., 5:30am-10:30pm; €1.60); **Sounion** (2hr.; every hr., 6:30am-4pm; €4.30). Tickets are sold from 2 stands 50m apart.

Pl. Eleftherias: From Pl. Syndagma, go west on Ermou, turn right on Athinas, turn left on Evripidou, and walk to the end of the street. Buses **#812** to **Daphni** and **836** to **Eleusis** (10min., 5am-11pm; €0.45).

Ferries: Check schedules at the tourist office, in the *Athens News,* with the Port Authority of Piraeus (☎210 422 6000), over the phone (☎1440), or at any travel agency. Ferry schedules change daily; check close to your departure and be flexible. Most ferries dock at **Piraeus** (p. 122), others at nearby **Rafina** (p. 125). Those headed for the Sporades leave from **Ag. Konstantinos** (p. 229) or **Volos** (p. 230). Those bound for the Ionian Islands leave from **Patras** (p. 160), **Kyllini** (p. 170), and **Igoumenitsa** (p. 250).

Piraeus: Take **Line 1** (green) on the subway south to its end, or take **bus #040** from Filellinon and Mitropoleos right off **Pl. Syndagma** (every 15min.). To basically all Greek islands other than the Sporades and Ionian: **Iraklion, Hania,** and **Rethymno,** Crete. Also to: **Aegina, Poros, Spetses,** and **Hydra; Chios, Lesvos, Lemnos, Leros, Kastelorizo, Patmos,** and **Astypalea; Ios, Kithnos, Milos, Mykonos, Naxos, Paros, Santorini,** and **Serifos; Rhodes.** See **Piraeus** (p. 122) for prices, frequencies, and durations.

Rafina: From Athens, buses leave for Rafina from Mavromateon 29, 2 blocks up along Areos Park, or a 15min. walk from Pl. Syndagma. (1hr.; every 30min., 5:40am-10:30pm; €1.65). Ferries to: **Marmari** on Evia, **Andros, Tinos, Mykonos, Paros** and **Naxos.** High-speed **catamarans** (often known as **Flying Dolphins**) sail to: **Andros, Mykonos, Paros, Naxos, Syros,** and **Tinos.** See **Rafina** (p. 125) for prices, frequencies, and durations.

Trains: Hellenic Railways (OSE), Sina 6 (☎210 362 4402, 362 4403, 362 4404, 362 4405, 362 4406; www.ose.gr). Call ☎210 529 7777 for reservations; ☎1440 lists timetables in Greek. Contact the railway offices to confirm schedules before your trip.

Larisis Station: ☎210 529 8837 or 210 823 7741. Ticket office open daily 5am-midnight. Serves Northern Greece. Take **trolley #1** from El. Venizelou (Panepistimiou) in Pl. Syndagma (every 10min., 5am-midnight; €0.45) or take subway to Sepolia. Trains depart for **Thessaloniki** (regular: 7hr., 5 per day, €14.10; express: 5½hr., 6 per day, €33-45 depending upon time of day). To get to **Sofia, Istanbul, Bratislava, Prague, Bucharest, Budapest,** and other international destinations, take train from Larisis Station to Thessaloniki (p. 271) and change there.

Peloponnese Train Station: ☎210 513 1601, 210 529 8739 for buses to Albania, Bulgaria, and Turkey. Ticket office open daily 5:45am-9pm. Open 24hr. From Diligani, easiest entry is through Larisis Station; exit to your right and go over the footbridge. From El. Venizelou (Panepistimiou) in Syndagma, take blue bus **#057** (every 15min., 5:30am-11:30pm; €0.45). Serves **Kalamata** (express: 6½hr., 3 per day, €7); **Nafplion** (express: 3½hr., 2 per day, €4.80); **Olympia** (express: 5½hr., 2 per day, €4.40); **Patras** (regular: 4¼hr., 2 per day, €5.30; express: 3½hr., 6 per day; €10. **Luggage storage** available (€1.60-3.20 per piece per day).

ATHENS

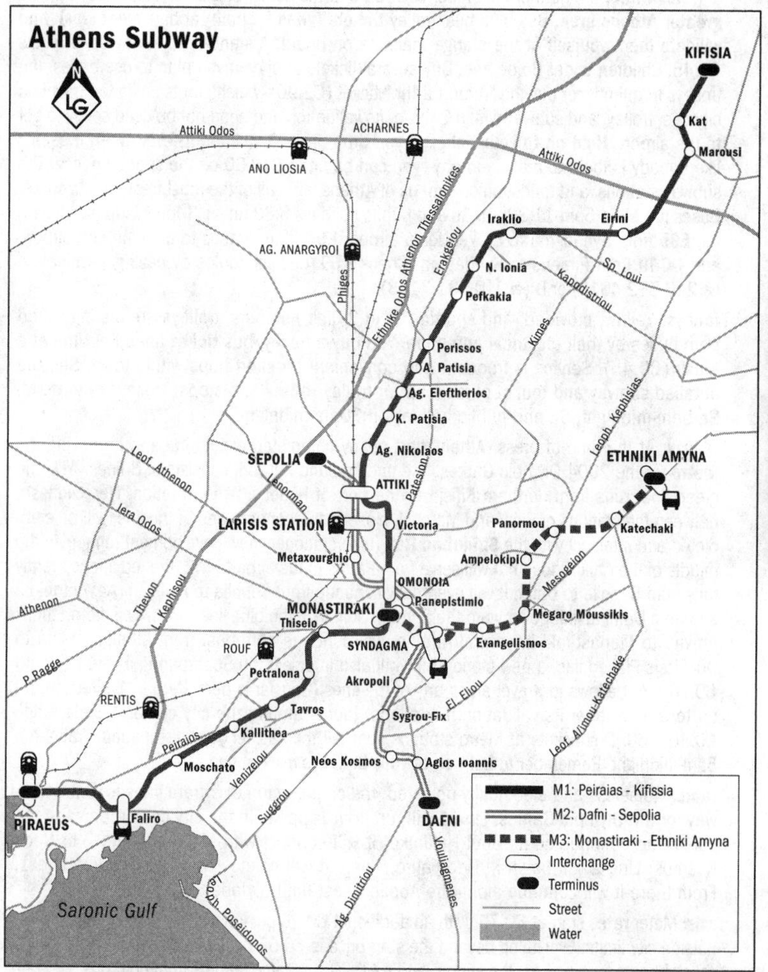

Luggage Storage: Pacific Ltd. (☎210 353 0160; www.pacifictravel.gr), in El. Venizelos Airport's arrivals terminal across from the large cafe, stores baggage. Open 24hr. Main branch at Nikis 26 (☎210 324 1007) in **Syndagma.** €2 per day, €30 per month. Open M-Sa 8am-9pm, Su 8am-2pm. Many **hotels** have free or inexpensive luggage storage.

LOCAL TRANSPORTATION

Buses: KTEL (ΚΤΕΛ) buses, the **yellow** ones, which leave from Terminals A and B, Mavromateon 29 and Pl. Eleftherias and travel all over the Attican peninsula, are punctual, so be on time. Buy KTEL bus tickets on board. The other buses you see more often around Athens and its suburbs are **blue,** many of them stretched out into double buses and designated by 3-digit numbers. Both are good for travel throughout the city and ideal for daytrips to **Daphni**

and **Kesariani,** the northern suburbs, **Glyfada** and the coast, and other destinations in the **greater Athens area.** Buy blue bus/trolley **tickets** (good for both) at any street **kiosk** and validate them yourself at the orange machine on board. A standard one-way ticket costs €0.45. Children under 6 ride free. Buy several tickets at once if you plan to use buses and trolleys frequently, or buy the "Airport 24hr." ticket (€2.90), which grants unlimited travel on city bus, trolley, and subway within 24hr. of its validation and need not be used solely to get to the airport. **Hold on to your ticket:** if you drop or don't validate it—even when it seems like nobody is there to make you pay—you can be fined €18-30 on the spot by police. The subway stations' and tourist office's maps of Athens label all of the most frequented **routes.** Buses run M-Sa 5am-11:30pm, Su and public holidays 5:30am-11:30pm. 24hr. service on the **E95** from Syndagma to El. Venizelou airport, **E96** from Piraeus to El. Venizelou airport, and **#040** from Piraeus to Syndagma. Check KTEL bus schedules by calling Terminals A (☎210 512 4910) or B (☎210 831 7153).

Trolleys: Yellow, crowded, and sporting 1- or 2-digit numbers, trolleys are distinguished from buses by their electrical antennae. You buy a trolley/bus **ticket** ahead of time at a **kiosk** (€0.45). Service is frequent and convenient for short hops within town. See the detailed subway and tourist office map for trolley **routes** and stops. Trolleys operate M-Sa 5am-midnight, Su and public holidays 5:30am-midnight.

Subway: At the time of press, Athens had nearly completed expanding and improving the **Metro** for the 2004 Olympic Games. The underground network consists of 3 lines. **M1,** the green line, runs from northern Kifisia to the port of Piraeus. A new station, Neratziotissa, between the stations of Eirini and Marousi, close to the northern end of the line, will be completed and intersect with the **Suburban Rail** (a revolutionary new development running in the middle of the Attiki Odos, that will serve from Patras to the airport.) **M2,** the red line, currently runs from Sepolia to Dafni. It will eventually continue from Sepolia to Peristeri (Ag. Antonios) and from Dafni to Ilioupoli toward the Saronic Gulf. **M3,** the blue line, which runs from Ethniki Amyna to Monastiraki in central Athens, will continue northeast from Ethniki Amyna to Doukissis Plakendias, a new station that will also intersect the Suburban Rail. The standard €0.70 ticket allows for travel along any of the lines (transfer is permitted) in 1 direction, for up to 90min. after its validation. For shorter jaunts around the city center, tickets range €0.30-0.60. Buy tickets at Metro stations; just tell the cashier your destination. Trains run 5am-midnight. Remember to **hold on to your ticket** to avoid a fine.

Trams: Noiseless and electrically-powered, the construction of 2 tram lines is well underway for the Olympic Games. Line 1 will run from Zappeio, in the city center, down to the coast and continue south until Helliniko. It will connect with Metro red line 2 in Neos Kosmos. Line 2 will begin in Neo Faliro, where it will connect with Metro green line 1. From there it will continue along the Apollo Coast until Glyfada Sq.

Taxis: Meter **rates** start at €0.75, with an additional €0.26 per km within city limits and €0.50 outside city limits. Everything beyond the start price is €0.50 per km midnight-5am. There's a €2 surcharge for trips from the airport, and a €0.70 surcharge for trips from port, bus, and railway terminals; add €0.29 extra for each piece of luggage over 10kg. Pay what the meter shows rounded up to the next €0.20 as a **tip.** Hail your taxi by shouting your destination—not the street address, but the area (e.g. "Pangrati"). The driver will pick you up if he feels like heading that way. Get in the cab and tell the driver the exact address or site. Many drivers don't speak English, so write your destination down (in Greek if possible); include the area of the city, since streets in different parts of the city may share the same name. It's common to ride with other passengers going in the same direction. For an extra €1.30 or €2.20 for pick-up by appointment, call a radio taxi: **Ikaros** (☎210 515 2800); **Ermis** (☎210 411 5200); **Kosmos** (☎1300). Get a full list in the *Athens News*.

Car Rental: Try the places on **Syngrou.** €35-50 for a small car with 100km mileage (including tax and insurance); about €200-350 per week. Student discounts up to 50%. Prices rise in summer.

PRACTICAL INFORMATION

TOURIST AND FINANCIAL SERVICES

Tourist Office: Tsoha 7 (info booth ☎210 870 7181, main desk 210 870 7000; www.gnto.grr), off Vas. Sofias in **Ambelokipi,** above Kolonaki. Take Metro **line 3** (blue) and get off at **Ambelokipi.** Open M-F 9am-3:30pm. Offers brochures on travel throughout Greece and an indispensable Athens map (same one offered in larger Metro stations). For bus, train, and ferry schedules and prices; lists of museums, embassies, and banks, you are best off visiting their website. Going straight to a travel agent (see below) is generally quicker and easier in order to schedule specific plans.

Travel Agencies: STA Travel, Voulis 43 (☎210 321 1188; statravel@robissa.gr). Open M-F 9:30am-5pm, Sa 9:30am-1:30pm. **Consolas Travel,** Aiolou 100 (☎210 325 4931; consolas@hol.gr), on the 4th fl. above the post office. Open M-F 8am-6pm. **Adrianos Travel, Ltd.,** Pandrossou 28 (☎210 323 1015; www.adrianostravel.gr), near Mitropoli Cathedral in Plaka, on the 2nd fl. Open M-F 9am-5pm, Sa 9am-1pm.

Banks: National Bank of Greece, Karageorgi Servias 2 (☎210 334 0500), in Pl. Syndagma. Open M-Th 8am-2:30pm, F 8am-2pm; open for **currency exchange** only M-Th 3:15-5:05pm, F 2:45-5:05pm, Sa 9am-2:50pm, Su 9am-12:50pm. AmEx, the post office, some hotels, and other banks (list available at tourist office) offer currency exchange. Commissions of about 5%. 24hr. currency exchange at the airport, but commissions there may be exorbitant.

American Express: Ermou 7 (☎210 322 3380), 1.5 blocks from Pl. Syndagma, between Nikis and Voulis on your left. This air-conditioned office specializing in retail travel cashes traveler's checks commission-free, exchanges money for small commissions, and provides travel services for AmEx cardholders. Open M-F 8:30am-4:30pm.

LOCAL SERVICES

International Bookstores: Around Syndagma, there are 2 **Eleftheroudakis Book Stores,** Panepistimiou 17 (☎210 325 8440) and Nikis 20 (☎210 322 9388), with 8 floors. A browser's delight, with classical and recent literature in Greek, English, French, and German. Open M-F 9am-9pm, Sa 9am-3pm. MC/V. **Pantelides Books,** Amerikis 9 (☎210 362 9763), in the basement of the arcade, overflows with variety in English. Open M, W 9am-4pm; Tu, Th-F 9am-8pm; Sa 9am-3pm. **Compendium Bookshop,** Nikis 28 (☎210 322 1248), has popular new and used books, large fiction and poetry sections, poetry readings in winter, and a children's book room. Open M-W 8:30am-4:30pm; Tu, Th-F 4-8:30pm; Sa 9:30am-3:30pm. **Zoodochou Pigis,** off of Akademias in Omonia, is lined with bookstores (because of the nearby university). Offers old books, new books, foreign books, magazines, and newspapers.

Libraries: The **British Council Library,** Pl. Kolonaki 17 (☎210 367 1300 or 210 363 3211), features books on English literature and language. Open Sept.-May M-F 9:30am-1:30pm, also open Tu-W 5:30-8pm; June-Aug. M-F 8:30am-3pm. **Hellenic American Union Library,** Massalias 22 (☎210 368 0000), on the 4th fl. of the Hellenic American Union behind the Panepistimio, has a wide variety of English books on Greece. Open M, Th 10am-5pm, Tu 10am-8pm, W 10am-6pm, F 10am-4pm. **American Embassy Library** (☎210 363 8114; www.usembassy.gr) gives free information over the phone and answers questions regarding the United States that can't easily be found elsewhere in Athens (from general information to addresses and phone numbers). Open M-F 9am-5pm. Open to the public only by appointment.

Laundromats: Most *plintirias* (launderers) have signs reading "Laundry." Be sure to specify that you don't mind mixing colors or you'll end up paying for several loads. At **Angelou Geront 10,** in Plaka, a kind Greek grandmother will wash, dry, and fold your laundry for €8. Open M-Sa

8am-4pm, Su 9am-2pm. Syndagma has **National,** a laundromat and dry cleaners, at Apollonos 17 (☎210 323 2226). Wash and dry €4.50 per kg. Open M-Th 4:30-8:30pm, F 8am-8pm. **Zenith,** Apollonos 12 and Pentelis 1 (☎210 323 8533), offers wash and dry (€4.40 per kg). Open M, W 8am-4pm; Tu, Th-F 8am-8pm. Launder 1 load for €9 near the train stations at **Psaron 9** (☎210 522 2856). Open M-F 8am-8pm, Sa 8am-5pm, Su 8am-2pm.

TAXI SMART Some drivers tinker with their meters, while others may not turn on the meter at all, taking you somewhere and then charging an exorbitant fee. Ask the cost of the fare in advance, and if you don't see the meter running, yell "Meter!" Also, if you ask for a hotel, the taxi driver may have another one in mind—a hotel that has paid him a commission to bring you there. Be firm about where you're going; don't trust a driver who says your hotel is closed.

ATHENS

EMERGENCY AND COMMUNICATIONS

Telephone Number Information: ☎131.

Emergencies: Police ☎100 or 133. **Ambulance** ☎166. **Doctors** ☎105 from Athens or 210 646 7811; line available 2pm-7am. **Poison control** ☎210 779 3777. **Fire** ☎199. **AIDS Help Line** ☎210 722 2222. *Athens News* lists emergency hospitals, but if you call an ambulance, they will know exactly where to take you at any given time. Free emergency health care for tourists.

Tourist Police: Dimitrakopoulou 77 (☎171). Great for information, assistance, and emergencies. English spoken. Open 24hr.

Pharmacies: Marked by a **green cross** hanging over the street. They're everywhere. About 1 every 4 blocks is open 24hr.; they rotate. Any pharmacy in a neighborhood, once it closes, will list on its door the nearest ones that are open 24hr.; you can also check "Useful Information" in *Athens News,* listing the day's emergency pharmacies.

Hospitals: Emergency hospitals/clinics on duty can be reached at ☎106. **KAT,** Nikis 2 (☎210 801 4411), is located between Marousi and Kifisia. **Geniko Kratiko Nosokomio (Y. Gennimatas; Public State Hospital),** Mesogion 154 (☎210 720 1211). **Ygeia,** Erithrou Stavrou 4 (☎210 682 7904), is a private hospital in Marousi. A state hospital, **Aeginitio,** Vas. Sofias 72 (☎210 722 0811) and Vas. Sofias 80 (☎210 777 0501), is closer to Athens's center. Near Kolonaki is the public hospital **Evangelismos,** Ypsilantou 45-47 (☎210 720 1000).

Post Offices: For customer service inquiries call the Greek National Post Office (ΕΛΤΑ; ELTA) at ☎800 11 82 000.

Syndagma branch (☎210 324 5970), on the corner of Mitropoleos, carries stamps, **exchanges currency,** and will hold **Poste Restante** items. **Postal code:** 10300.

Omonia branch, Aiolou 100 (☎210 321 6022, 321 6023, or 321 6024). Machine distributes stamps 24hr. (bring credit card). Holds **Poste Restante** and accepts parcels up to 2kg sent abroad. Open M-F 7:30am-8pm, Sa 7:30am-2pm. **Postal code:** 10200.

Exarhia branch, at the corner of Zaimi and K. Deligiani. **Exchanges currency** and accepts **Poste Restante.** Open M-F 7:30am-2pm. **Postal code:** 10022.

Acropolis/Plaka branch (☎210 921 8076) also **exchanges currency** and accepts **Poste Restante;** sends packages up to 2kg abroad. Open M-F 7:30am-2pm. **Postal code:** 11702.

Shipping: To send packages abroad, try parcel post available at the Syndagma ELTA branches of **Mitropoleos 60** (☎210 324 2489; open M-F 7:30am-7:30pm) and **Nikis 33** (open M-F 7:30am-2pm; MC/V), which also hold packages. **Postal code:** 10033.

Internet Access: Athens teems with Internet cafes. Expect to pay €3-6 per hr.

Arcade Internet Cafe, Stadiou 5 (☎210 324 8105; sofos1@ath.forthnet.gr), just up Stadiou from the plateia in **Syndagma,** set in a shopping center about 15m from the main throughfare. Owner is friendly and PC-proficient. Complimentary coffee. €3 per hr., €0.50 for every additional 10min., €1 min. Open M-Sa 9am-11pm, Su 11-8pm.

easyInternetCafe, Filellinon 2 (☎210 331 3034), in **Syndagma,** on the 2nd fl. above the Everest fast-food eatery, directly across from the plateia. 40 high-speed, flat-screen computers. Purchase "credit" from the automatic machine by the entrance. Since rates depend on the number of customers present at a given time, they range €0.80-3 per hr.

Rendez-Vous Cafe, Voulis 18 (☎210 322 3158; cafemeeting@hotmail.com), in **Syndagma.** Sip coffee or snack on freshly made sweets like white chocolate chip cookies (€0.40) while computing. €3.70 per hr., €1 min.; 10% off for students with ISIC. Open M-Sa 8am-9pm.

Skynet Internet Access, Apollonos 10 and Voulis 30 (☎210 322 7551; www.skynet.gr), in **Syndagma.** Provides Word, Access, Excel, Powerpoint, typing services, color printers, quick connection, scanners, and CD burners. €4.40 per hr., €1.47 min. Open M-F 9am-8:30pm, Sa 9am-3pm.

Bits'n Bytes Internet, Kapnikareas 19 (☎210 382 2545 or 210 330 6590; www.bnb.gr), in **Plaka.** This mother of new-age Internet cafes has fast connections in a spacious, air-conditioned, black light-lit joint. Midnight-9am €1.50 per hr., 9am-midnight €2.50 per hr. Vending machines sell coffee, hot chocolate, juice (€1), and sandwiches (€1-2). Open daily 24hr.

Internet World, Pandrossou 29 (☎210 331 6056; www.internet-greece.com), in **Plaka,** has kind and helpful management. €4 per hr. Open 10am-11pm.

Plaka Internet World, Pandrossou 29 (☎210 331 6056; www.internet-greece.gr), in **Plaka,** on the 4th fl. Large screens, fast connection, A/C, and a balcony where you can enjoy cold sodas and a great Acropolis view. €4 per hr. Open daily 10am-10pm.

Internet Cafe, Stournari 49 (☎210 383 8808; www.intergraphics.gr), in **Omonia.** Go to the 8th fl., get your ticket, then walk down to the computers on the 7th fl. Gaze at the city below while checking email (€2 per hr.) amid crowds of Athenian students. Open M-F 9am-9:30pm, Sa 10am-2pm.

Moc@fe Internet Cafe, Marni 49 (☎210 522 7717), near Pl. Karaiskaki in **Omonia.** This cornerside cafe serves up coffee and beer. €3 per hr., €1 min. (gets you 20min.). Every evening in Aug. free coffee or soda every hr. during Happy Hour. Open M-Sa 9am-2am, Su 9am-10pm.

Bits'n Bytes Internet, Akademias 78, between Em. Benaki and Zoodochou Pigis, in **Exharia.**

Deligrece Internet Cafe, Akadamias 87 (☎210 330 1895), in **Exharia.** A relaxing place to hang out in central Athens independent of its Internet access (€2.35 per hr.), Deligrece has satellite TV and cheap espresso (€2). Open daily 8:30am-midnight.

Quicknet Cafe, Glathstonos 4 (☎210 380 3771), just off of Patission, in **Exharia.** Extremely fancy with large new PCs with flat screens, fast connections, air-conditioning, and comfortable swivel chairs. €2.50 per hr., €1.50 min. Cappuccino €1.50.

Carousel Pizza Cybercafe, Eftihidou 32 (☎210 756 4305), on 2nd fl. between Pl. Plastira and Pl. Pangratiou, closer to Pl. Plastira, in **Pangrati.** Wood-oven baked pizza after 6pm (€4.50). €4 per hr., €3 for students. Open daily 10:30am-midnight.

IN RECENT NEWS

CANINE CALAMITY

After a 1990s buying spree for "fearsome guard dogs" to protect against the influx of refugees flooding Greece from unstable Balkan neighbors, local anxieties soon receded, and unwanted pets were released into the streets. Athens's stray canine population was estimated to be over 3000 and counting in 2001, at which point the animals had reportedly become so accustomed to life in the metropolis's center that the furry quadrupeds could be seen standing patiently at cross walks, waiting for the lights to turn green.

On the eve of the Olympic Games, the city has been consumed by much more than just spirited debates about what must be done to control this problem. A nasty incident of rogue poisonings on New Year's Day 2003, after which over 60 canine carcasses were found strewn about a city park, caused a split among both the citizenry and Parliament. Some, believing Olympic conspirators planned the extermination in preparation for their precious Games, banded together in demonstrations of unprecedented size through the National Gardens to the Parliament building.

On June 26, 2003, however, the Athens 2004 Committee announced a stray animals initiative. The heroic three-stage plan requires collecting stray animals, vaccinating and neutering them, and then realeasing the healthier beasts back into the city streets from which they came. The Committee insists there will be no euthanasia for these pups.

Lobby Internet Cafe, Imittou 113 (☎210 701 4607), near Pl. Pangratiou, in **Pangrati.** Primarily a cafe with a few computers and a printer (€0.25 per page) in the front. €4 per hr., €2 min. Open daily 9:30am-1am.

OTE: Patission 85 (☎210 821 4449 or 210 823 7040), Athinas 45 (☎210 321 6699), or Stadiou 15. Offers phonebooks for most European and Anglophone countries. Overseas collect calls can only be made at Patission location. For information on **overseas calls,** dial ☎161 from any land-line phone; for **directory assistance** in and outside of Athens, dial ☎131. Most phone booths in the city operate by **telephone cards** (€3, €6, €12, or €24) available at OTE offices, kiosks, and tourist shops. Push the "i" button on the phones for English instructions. For rate and general OTE info, call ☎134 (English spoken); for a domestic English-speaking operator, call ☎151. Open M-F 8am-2pm.

ORIENTATION

Athenian geography mystifies newcomers and natives alike. When you're trying to figure out the city, check out the detailed **free maps** available at the tourist office (p. 87): the city map includes bus, trolley, and subway routes. *Now in Athens* magazine has a more detailed street plan. If you lose your bearings, ask for directions back to well-lit **Syndagma.** The **Acropolis** provides a reference point, as does **Mt. Lycavittos.** Athenian streets often have multiple spellings or names, so check the map again before you panic about being lost. Several English-language **publications** can help you navigate Athens. The weekly publication *Athens News* gives addresses, hours, and phone numbers for weekly happenings, as well as listings, news, and ferry information (€1).

Athens and its suburbs occupy seven hills in southwestern Attica. **Syndagma,** the central plateia, is encircled by the other major neighborhoods. Clockwise, they are: **Plaka, Monastiraki, Psiri, Omonia, Exarhia, Kolonaki,** and **Pangrati.** A 30min. car, bus, or taxi ride south—keep in mind traffic conditions vary greatly in Athens—takes you to the seaside suburb of **Glyfada. Piraeus,** the primary port, lies to the southwest of central Athens. In a wider clockwise circle, **Kifisia** and **Marousi** outlie Athens to the north; the port of **Rafina** to the northeast; **Lavrio** to the southeast; and the coastal getaway of **Vouliagmeni** closer to Athens to the southeast. The new airport, **Eleftherios Venizelos,** is on the road to Lavrio.

SYNDAGMA. Pl. Syndagma (Συνταγμα, sin-TAHG-mah), also known as Constitution Square, stands at the center of Athens. The **Greek Parliament** (Βουλη, VOO-lee) occupies a pale yellow Neoclassical building on a large plateia uphill from the actual Syndagma plateia, on the edge of the **National Gardens** (Ο Εθνηκος Κυπος, OH eth-nee-KOS KEE-pos), once the royal gardens of Greece's Germanic monarchs, which lie at the center of the city. The main post office, American Express office, transportation terminals, and a number of travel agencies and banks cluster around the Syndagma plateia, along the horseshoe shaped by the streets of **Othonos, Filellinon,** and **Georgiou A.** The main entrance to the subway is located on the fourth side, just across from Parliament and from the commemorative **Tomb of the Unknown Soldier,** in front of Parliament on Amalias. Airport buses stop uphill from it, along Amalias to the right (facing Parliament) and across the street. Budget-friendly travel offices, restaurants, and hotels line the portion of **Filellinon** that extends uphill from the square, as well as **Nikis** and **Voulis,** parallel throughfares behind Filellinon. **Mitropoleos, Ermou,** and **Karageorgis Servias** (which becomes **Pericleus**, then **Athinados**) all begin here, perpendicular to Filellinon, and head on toward Monastiraki and Psiri. These areas also cater to travelers on a budget. They have a wealth of cafes and clothing shops interspersed with old churches. The plateia itself buzzes around the clock; car and moped traffic mingles perilously with pedestrians. People-watchers find this the best venue for spying on lounging kids, tourists, executives hailing cabs, blank-eyed drug addicts sharing sidewalks with street musicians, and brightly clad panhandlers begging for coins.

PLAKA. The corner of Syndagma where **Filellinon** meets **Othonos** points directly toward Plaka (Πλακα), the hill leading up to the Acropolis, once the center of the Old City and today home to most visitors staying in Athens. Pulsating with wanderers both night and day, Plaka is never easily navigable because it lacks one cohesive center—instead its motion flows through such long, narrow arteries as **Kydathenaon, Adrianou,** and **Nikodimou.** These, along with a multitude of their narrow offshoots and colorful, energetic intersections, undergo a regular transformation from mid-morning to dusk. Bustling and disorienting by morning, Plaka becomes the perfect place to linger over a coffee and observe the hum of Athenian life after the sun goes down. Bounded by the plateia of the **Cathedral Mitropolis,** as well as the city's two largest ancient monuments—the **Temple of Olympian Zeus** (p. 112) and the **Acropolis** (p. 107)—the neighborhood also contains the only medieval buildings to survive the double-edged shovel of archaeologists and the recent frantic building. Many of the city's cheap hotels and tourist eateries are here, as are legions of *kamakia* ("octopus spearers") who cat-call to passing women. Harassment is usually only verbal and an effort to impress friends.

MONASTIRAKI. Monastiraki (Μοναστηρακι; Little Monastery) has a frenetic flea market, home to vendors of rugs, furniture, leather, *bouzoukia*, and all varieties of souvenirs. Farther away from Plaka, along the border of the Acropolis, this area is contained between the outer walls of the ancient **Agora** and the boulevard of **Ermou.** Its main plateia, which shares its name, has a large Metro station; it is located just off Ermou, trickling outward, along the streets of **Mitropoleos, Pandrossou,** and **Ifestou,** among others. Here it's worth testing your bargaining skills on stubborn merchants. Because it borders the city's central markets, the area's three-alarm noise never ceases. Visual diversity is afforded by the proximity of the Acropolis and the quirky interspersion of archaic ruins, such as the **Roman Agora** and **Hadrian's Library,** among windy streets, shops, and restaurants. The old buildings of **Psiri,** north of Ermou, and along the major thoroughfares of **Miaouli, Athinas,** and **Aristofanous** are bounded by **Evripidou** to the north and **Athinas** to the east. These streets now accommodate hot evening destinations and restaurants.

OMONIA. Following Stadiou or Eleftherios Venizelou (Panepistimiou) northwest of Syndagma, you'll find the bustling, commercial melting pot of Pl. Omonia (Ομονια, oh-mo-NEE-ah), or Concord Square. Indian, Arab, Pakistani, Polish, and East Asian tongues are heard as frequently as Greek; between the parallel streets of **Agiou Konstantinou** and **Evripidou,** vendors of shared ethnicities align themselves to sell imports and delicacies from their homelands. Metros run to **Kifisia** (40min.), **Monastiraki** (3min.), and **Piraeus** (20min.), among other destinations. Still the headquarters of the **Greek Communist Party (KKE),** Omonia once served as the hotbed of its activity. Today cheap lodgings, food, and clothing abound. Great efforts have recently been made to clean up the area's image and crime problems. Still beware of pickpockets, mind your own business, and avoid traveling alone at night: Omonia is still one of the less traveler-friendly of Athens's neighborhoods. The **university** and **library** are on Panepistimiou between the two plateias of Omonia and Syndagma. Larisis Station, serving Northern Greece, and Peloponnese Station, serving the south, are both located on **Konstantinoupoleos,** northeast of **Pl. Karaiskaki,** and are accessible from Deligiani (p. 84).

EXARHIA. Pl. Omonia's neighbor to the east, progressive Exarhia (Εξαρχια) was once the spiritual home of Greek anarchists. Over the past 10 years, international models have imported the values of capitalism, and a new population of students has arrived to match. Following Eleftheriou Venizelou (Panepisti-

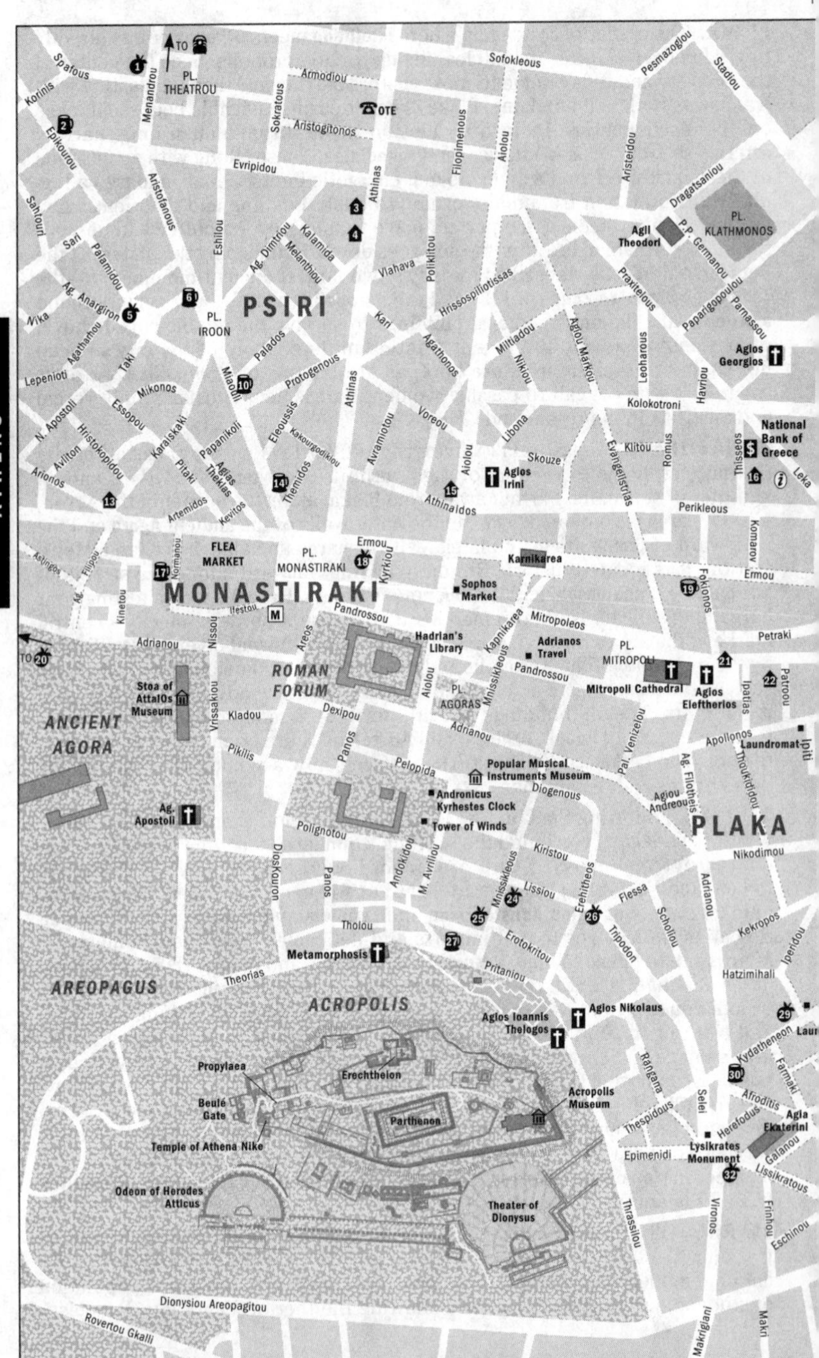
PSIRI
MONASTIRAKI
PLAKA
ANCIENT AGORA
ROMAN FORUM
AREOPAGUS
ACROPOLIS
PL. THEATROU
PL. IROON
PL. MONASTIRAKI
PL. AGORAS
PL. MITROPOLI
PL. KLATHMONOS
OTE
FLEA MARKET
Stoa of AttalOs Museum
Ag. Apostoli
Hadrian's Library
Sophos Market
Karnikarea
Agios Irini
Adrianos Travel
Mitropoli Cathedral
Agios Eleftherios
Agii Theodori
Agios Georgios
National Bank of Greece
Laundromat
Popular Musical Instruments Museum
Andronicus Kyrhestes Clock
Tower of Winds
Metamorphosis
Agios Nikolaus
Agios Ioannis Thelogos
Propylaea
Erechtheion
Beulé Gate
Parthenon
Acropolis Museum
Temple of Athena Nike
Odeon of Herodes Atticus
Theater of Dionysus
Lysikrates Monument
Agia Ekaterini
Sofokleous
Pesmazoglou
Stadiou
Armodiou
Aristogitonos
Evripidou
Sokratous
Menandrou
Spafous
Korinis
Epikourou
Sahtouri
Sari
Palamidou
Aristofanous
Eshilou
Athinas
Filopimenous
Aiolou
Aristeidou
Dragatsaniou
P.P. Germanou
Praxitelous
Paparigopoulou
Parnassou
Ag. Dimitriou
Kalamida
Melanthiou
Vlahava
Polikitou
Hrissospiliotissas
Ag. Anargiron
Nika
Agatharhou
Lepenioti
Taki
Mikonos
Essopou
Palados
Miaouli
Protogenous
Kari
Agathonos
Miltiadou
Nikiou
Agiou Markou
Leoharous
Havriou
Kolokotroni
N. Apostoli
Hristokopidou
Karaiskaki
Papanikoli
Eleoussis
Kakourgodikiou
Avramiotou
Voreou
Libona
Skouze
Klitou
Romus
Thisseos
Evangelistrias
Aviiton
Arionos
Pitaki
Agias Theklas
Themidos
Athinaidos
Perikleous
Leka
Artemidos
Kevitos
Ermou
Komarov
Fokionos
Normanou
Filipou
Astingos
Ag.
Kinetou
Ifestou
Pandrossou
Kyrkiou
Mitropoleos
Kapnikarea
Petraki
Adrianou
Nissou
Areos
Mnissikleous
Patrou
Ipatias
Vrissakiou
Kladou
Dexipou
Apollonos
Ipiti
Pikilis
Panos
Pelopida
Pal. Venizelou
Ag. Filothels
Thoukididou
Diogenous
Agiou Andreou
Polignotou
Kiristou
Nikodimou
Dioskouron
Andokidou
M. Avriliou
Lissiou
Erehitheos
Flessa
Scholiou
Adrianou
Kekropos
Iperidou
Tholou
Erotokritou
Tripodon
Hatzimihali
Pritaniou
Theorias
Kydatheneon
Farmaki
Rangana
Selei
Afroditis
Thespidous
Herefodus
Galanou
Epimenidi
Lissikratous
Thrassilou
Vironos
Frinhou
Eschinou
Dionysiou Areopagitou
Rovertou Gkalli
Makrigiani
Makri
TO
TO

ATHENS

Syndagma, Plaka, and Monastiraki

ACCOMMODATIONS

Adonis Hotel, **23**
Dioskouros House, **31**
Hotel Attalos, **4**
Hotel Cecil, **3**
Hotel Metropolis, **21**
Hotel Tempi, **15**
Hotel Thisseos, **16**
John's Place, **22**
Pella Inn, **13**
Student's & Traveler's Inn, **28**

FOOD

Attalos, **20**
Body Fuel, **12**
Byzantio, **29**
Daphne's, **32**
Eden Vegetarian, **24**
Food Company, **8**
Jackson Hall, **9**
Kentrikon, **11**
Lu Café, **19**
Mandras, **5**
Old Parliament, **7**
Pak Indian, **1**
Savvas, **18**
Sissofos, **25**
T. Stamatopoulos, **26**

NIGHTLIFE

Bee, **14**
Bretto's, **30**
Boite Esperides, **27**
Inoteka, **17**
Revekka, **10**
Soul, **2**
Vibe, **6**

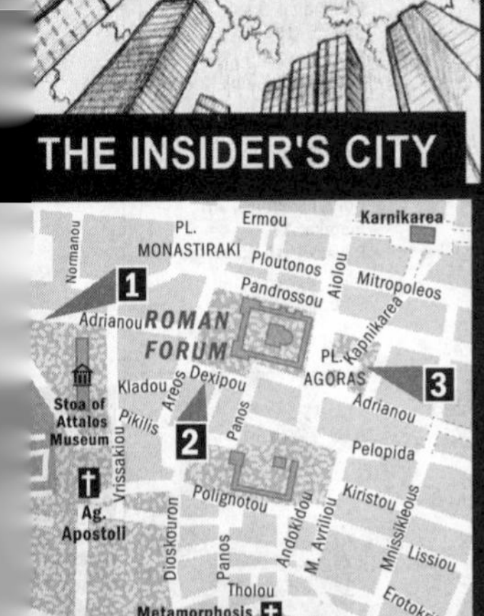

BOHEMIAN RHAPSODY

The marble pathways of Plaka and Monastiraki offer wonderful, bohemian adornments. Unfortunately there is less variety along narrow streets than you might hope. Originality can be found, however, and *Let's Go* will lead you there.

1 **Pericles** (☎210 324 4664) is "a place to create," in its owner's own words. In the factory-like bead room, you can choose from delicately crafted silver leaves (€0.45) and painted ceramic beads (€0.40).

2 **Karambela** (☎210 324 7243) buys from both local and foreign artists. There is a wide collection of dangling silver earrings (€5), shell pendants (€8-15), and coral, malachite, or lapis lazuli beaded necklaces (€40).

3 Find spreads of (naturally) striped and cow-printed shell bracelets within the orange stucco walls of **Agora Ethnic.** Their *palea* (antique) silver cuffs may be fun to try on, but beware the whopping price tag (around €300).

miou) uphill away from Pl. Syndagma will lead you to this district bounded by **Patission** to the west, **Strefi Hill** to the north, and **Mt. Lycavittos** to the east. Thanks to the crazy kids at the **university** on Panepistimiou, Exarhia sports some of Athens's most exciting nightlife, located along main thoroughfares **M. Themistokleous** and **Em. Benaki** and in Pl. Exarhia itself (to which these two lead). Cafes overflow throughout the night, opening a window onto the revelry of students.

KOLONAKI. If you've got money to burn or just want witness how the other half (in Greece) lives, you've found the place. Kolonaki (Κολωνακι), meaning little column, has got the glitz. On this posh foothill of **Mt. Lycavittos,** swanky Greeks drop euros in designer boutiques on **Pat. Ioakeim,** jockey for spots in their BMWs and oversized SUVs, and crowd into the cafes, bars, and restaurants on **Plutarchou, Loukianou,** and **Haritos,** the quaint *pezothromos* (footpath). Kolonaki houses the British Academy, the American School of Classical Studies, and an enclave of expat students. With Plaka just down the hill and a great view of the Acropolis below, Kolonaki shelters Athens's trendiest nightspots and exceptional cuisine.

PANGRATI. Youth and yuppies chat over Fanta or coffee, jabber into cell phones, and play backgammon in Pangrati (Πανγρατι), southeast of Kolonaki. Though close to the city center, Pangrati is remarkably intimate. The tree-lined streets allow for quiet strolls and exploration, and the bevy of cafes provide for a casual evening sipping cocktails or coffee. Several Byzantine churches, the **Olympic Stadium,** and the **National Cemetery** are the area's major monuments. **Pangratiou Park,** a reputed drug hangout (particularly at night), stands as a token of remembrance to the days before the area's gentrification. Take trolley #2, 4, or 11 from Syndagma.

ACCOMMODATIONS

The reception desk at **Youth Hostel #5,** Damareos 75, in **Pangrati** also acts as the **Greek Youth Hostel Association** and lists 10 other affiliated hostels in Greece, found in Thessaloniki, Patras, and Olympia and on Santorini and Crete. (☎210 751 9530; y-hostels@otenet.gr. Open daily M-F 9am-3pm.) The **Hellenic Chamber of Hotels,** Stadiou 24, provides info and reservations for hotels of all classes throughout Greece. Reservations require a cash deposit, length of stay, and number of people; you must contact them a month in advance. (☎210 323 7193 or 323 6962; grhotels@otenet.gr. Open May-Nov. M-F 8:30am-1:30pm.)

ACCOMMODATIONS BY PRICE

UNDER €10 ❶

Athens International Hostel (HI) (98)	OMN
Youth Hostel #5 (98)	PAN

€10-€20 ❷

Hostel Aphrodite (98)	OMN
Hotel Metropolis (95)	SYN
Hotel Orion (98)	EXR
Hotel Thisseos (95)	SYN
Pella Inn (97)	MON
Student's and Traveler's Inn (95)	PLK

€20-€35 ❸

Adonis Hotel (97)	PLK
Dioskouros House (97)	PLK
Hotel Dryades (98)	EXR
Hotel Tempi (97)	MON
John's Place (95)	SYN
The Exarcheion (98)	EXR

€35-€70 ❹

Hotel Attalos (97)	MON
Hotel Cecil (97)	MON
Hotel Omiros (97)	PLK

EXR Exarhia **MON** Monastiraki **OMN** Omonia **PAN** Pangrati **PLK** Plaka **SYN** Syndagma

ATHENS

ACCOMMODATIONS BY AREA

SYNDAGMA

Syndagma is at the heart of Athens. Tourist services and cheap accommodations are plentiful. Though it can be a noisy area, it's a good bet for those looking for dirt-cheap hostel rates and a central location.

Hotel Thisseos, Thisseos 10 (☎210 324 5960). Take Karageorgi Servias, which becomes Perikleous, and Thisseos is down the street about 20m on the right. With pink walls and a retro feel, this hostel is close to Syndagma's sights but far from its noise. Friendly staff speaks English. TV in reception area, full self-service kitchen upstairs, fans, and common baths. Reception 24hr. Towels and sheets free upon request. Dorms in high season €15, in low season €12; singles €30; doubles €44. To sleep on covered roof (€10) in summer, bring a sleeping bag. ❷

John's Place, Patroou 5 (☎210 322 9719), near Mitropoleos. Off the major streets, John's has basic amenities. Dim hallways, high ceilings, and quiet enhance its Old World feel. Singles €25; doubles €30-44; triples €35-53. Bargain for a better price. ❸

Hotel Metropolis, Mitropoleos 46 (☎210 321 7469 or 321 7871; www.hotelmetropolis.gr). Couples and families, as well as kids appreciative of aesthetics, enjoy full amenities and wonderful views of Cathedral Mitropolis and the Acropolis. Elevator, A/C, TV, phones. Free luggage storage. Laundry €6 per 5-6kg load. High season doubles with bath shared with 1 other single €40; doubles with private bath €50. Euro and US$ traveler's checks accepted. Credit cards accepted. ❷

PLAKA

Student's and Traveler's Inn, Kydatheneon 16 (☎210 324 4808 or 324 8802; fax 210 321 0065), has a great location and lively atmosphere, along with A/C, 24hr. restaurant, and around-the-clock cyber cafe (€3 per 30min.) make this inn a popular destination. It courts backpackers with its large courtyard, balconies, and helpful management. Breakfast (6am-noon) €4.50-7. Storage €15 per month, €7 per week. Reception 24hr. Call ahead for reservations; phone in if you are going to be late and your room will be kept without charge. Coed dorms €17-22; singles €40, with private bath €50; doubles €58/€70; triples or quads €75/€120. ❷

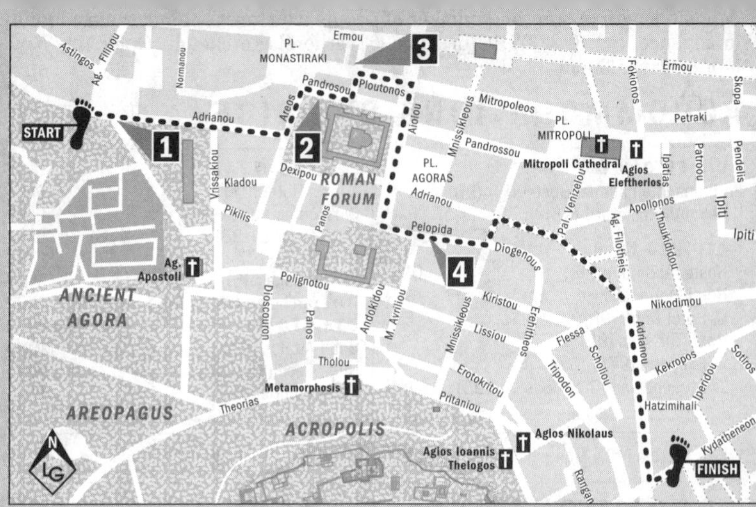

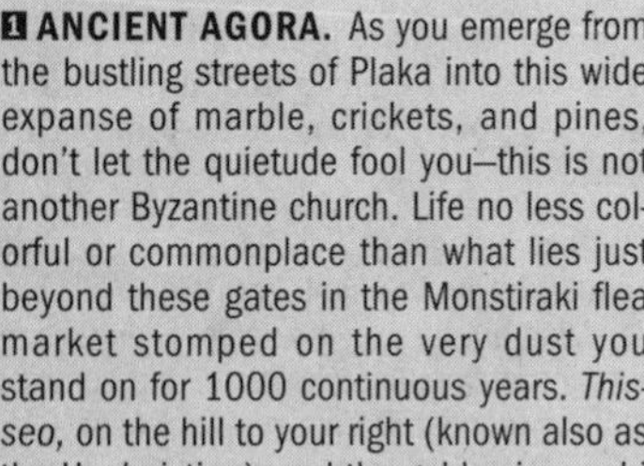

1 ANCIENT AGORA. As you emerge from the bustling streets of Plaka into this wide expanse of marble, crickets, and pines, don't let the quietude fool you–this is not another Byzantine church. Life no less colorful or commonplace than what lies just beyond these gates in the Monstiraki flea market stomped on the very dust you stand on for 1000 continuous years. *Thisseo,* on the hill to your right (known also as the Hephaistion), and the gold coins and jewlery kept in the Stoa of Attalos on your left are still real enough for you to imagine the generations of Greeks and foreigners who came here to haggle over mandarins while Socrates lounged in the shop of his cobbler-friend Simon on the southwestern part of the square. (p. 111)

START: Adrianou, entrance to Agora

FINISH: Kydathinenon 41

DISTANCE: 1.5km

DURATION: 2-3hr.

WHEN TO GO: Late morning

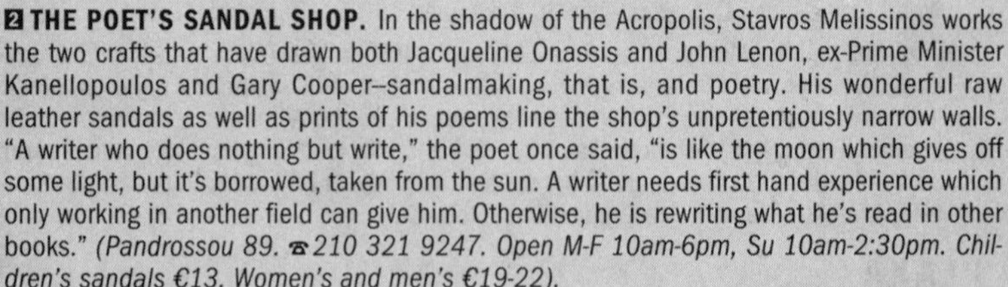

2 THE POET'S SANDAL SHOP. In the shadow of the Acropolis, Stavros Melissinos works the two crafts that have drawn both Jacqueline Onassis and John Lenon, ex-Prime Minister Kanellopoulos and Gary Cooper–sandalmaking, that is, and poetry. His wonderful raw leather sandals as well as prints of his poems line the shop's unpretentiously narrow walls. "A writer who does nothing but write," the poet once said, "is like the moon which gives off some light, but it's borrowed, taken from the sun. A writer needs first hand experience which only working in another field can give him. Otherwise, he is rewriting what he's read in other books." *(Pandrossou 89. ☎210 321 9247. Open M-F 10am-6pm, Su 10am-2:30pm. Children's sandals €13. Women's and men's €19-22).*

3 SAVVAS. Perhaps the most widely renowned among Athenians themselves, this is the best place to order souvlaki and run. Why? Well, first, it's the best souvlaki out there. Secondly, it's a sixth of the price (literally) when you take it away. (p. 102)

4 BRETTO'S. Barrels of wine on the right side of this one-room, high-ceilinged 112-year-old wooden distillery are filled with sweet red wine. In midday, you might prefer a chilled glass of white *topio* ("local") or a small ice-cubed ouzo cocktail, but whatever you do, you must have a taste, a sip, a drink (a whatever) when in Athens. (p. 104)

Adonis Hotel, Kodrou 3 (☎210 324 9737 or 324 9741; fax 210 323 1602). From Filellinon on the way from Syndagma, turn right on Nikodimou and then left on Kodrou, which meets Voulis. A family hotel with private baths, satellite TVs, and phones in each room. Continental breakfast (6:30-9:30am) included and served in the rooftop lounge with Acropolis views. A/C €10 extra per person. Reserve in advance (1 to 2 months for high season). High season singles €41, low season €29; doubles €56/€43; triples €84/€62. Discounts for stays above 2 days. ❸

Dioskouros House, Pitakou 6 (☎210 324 8165), on the southwestern corner of the National Gardens, by the Temple of Olympian Zeus. These simple, wood-floored rooms are sheltered from the city center. Luggage storage (€1) and book exchange. Breakfast included. Singles €40; doubles €60; triples €90; quads €100. Discounts for calling ahead or staying multiple nights. Credit cards accepted. ❸

Hotel Omiros, Apollonos 15 (☎210 323 5486 or 323 3587; omiroshotel@hotmail.com), near Pl. Syndagma, is meticulously clean and conveniently located. Relatively spacious rooms are complete with A/C, TV, private baths, balconies, and telephones. Breakfast included. Call ahead to reserve. Singles €55-65; doubles €85-95; triples €105-117. Bargain for 15% student discount by flashing your ISIC, especially during low season. Credit cards accepted. ❹

MONASTIRAKI

Like Plaka and Syndagma, Monastiraki lies at the center of things. This fun, noisy neighborhood is close to the flea market and the nightlife of Psiri. Stay here to drink regularly, shop cheaply, and unite your soul with the ghosts of antiquity that seem to linger at all hours in the ruins dispersed throughout its streets.

Pella Inn, Karaiskaki 1 (☎210 325 0598; fax 210 325 0598). It's 2 blocks from the Monastiraki subway station or 10min. down Ermou from Pl. Syndagma—literally right on the fault lines of Monastiraki's hip hangouts and Psiri's superlatively cool nightlife. Pella's most distinguishing attribute of all is its unimpeded view of the Acropolis. Nelly, the sweet Bulgarian receptionist suggests you bring a bottle of wine and your pals to the roof and philosophize together on the large terrace before the panorama. Breakfast included in room prices, €3 extra if you stay in dorms. Free luggage storage. Shared bathrooms. Dorms €15; doubles €40-50; triples €60; quads €80. Prices drop in low season, though the hotel remains lively. Credit cards accepted. ❷

Hotel Cecil, Athinas 39 (☎210 321 7079 or 321 8005), on the border of Psiri, just a few blocks down from the Varvakia market and 4 blocks from the Monastiraki Metro, has wood-floored, high-ceilinged rooms. Breakfast included. A/C, TV, private bath, and roof bar with Acropolis view. Free luggage storage. Singles €55; doubles €80; triples €105; quads €129. Ask about low season discounts. AmEx/MC/V. ❹

Hotel Attalos, Athinas 29 (☎210 321 2801; www.attaloshotel.com), next to Hotel Cecil, is extremely pleasant, modernized, air-conditioned, and well located. There are ancient wall-painting replicas about the stairs. A/C, TVs, fridges, baths, and free luggage storage. Breakfast included. Singles €56-60; doubles €70-76. AmEx/MC/V. ❹

Hotel Tempi, Aiolou 29 (☎210 321 3175 or 210 324 2940; www.travelling.gr/tempihotel). Wedged between an assortment of street vendors and garment shops, Tempi rents simple rooms with ceiling fans. Free luggage storage. Check-out 11am. Make your own breakfast using free kitchen facility. Singles €32; doubles €42, with bath €48; triples €60. Prices can be 20% cheaper in low season. ❸

OMONIA

If you're leaving Athens early (or arriving late), you can get some sleep right next to the bus or train stations. The area has been cleaned up recently in terms of crime, but always err on the side of safety and don't travel alone at night.

Hostel Aphrodite, Einardou 12 (☎210 881 0589 or 210 883 9249; www.hostelaphrodite.com). From the Victoria subway station, follow Heiden 2 blocks, then continue along Peioniou for 2 more. Turn right on Michail Voda and left on Einardou. From the train station, take Filadelfias to Michail Voda. Clean, simple rooms with A/C. Full breakfast menu €3-7. Safety deposit box, free luggage storage. Internet access €6 per hr.; laundry €10.50 per 6kg. Reception 24hr. Bus every other day to the Pink Palace in Corfu. Round-trip or one-way (€47) with night stay at Pink Palace included in cost. Dorms €17; doubles €45; triples €60; quads €72. Low season discounts. ❷

Athens International Hostel (HI), Victor Hugo 16 (☎210 523 2049; www.hostelbooking.com). Walk down 30 Septemvriou from Pl. Omonia and take a left on Veranzerou, which becomes Victor Hugo after crossing Marni (minutes from the Metahourgio subway stop). A continental crowd packs this HI-affiliated youth hostel, the only one in Greece—you'll need to be an HI member or buy a membership (€15) to stay here. Hot water 6-10am and 6-10pm. Laundry (€6) and travel office available. Sheets included. Common kitchen available. Reservations required. Email for reservations; priority given to those with previously-purchased HI membership. Dorms €8.16; doubles €16.32. ❶

ATHENS

EXARHIA

Home to much of Athens's student population, Exarhia has some of the city's hippest digs. Near the university bars and the Archaeological Museum, the neighborhood is within walking distance of major public transportation but is quieter and brighter than nearby Pl. Omonia, making it a good choice for budget travelers.

Hotel Orion, Em. Benaki 105 (☎210 382 7362 or 382 0191; fax 210 380 5193). From Pl. Omonia walk up Em. Benaki or take bus #230 from Pl. Syndagma. Filled with hip travelers intent on experiencing Athens away from the tourist machine, Orion rents small rooms with shared baths. Sunbathers relax on the exquisite rooftop with music, TV, and board games. Internet €3 per hr. Laundry €3. Breakfast (€5) is served on the terrace near a kitchen (available 24hr.). Singles €25; doubles €35; triples €40. Bargain for better prices. Major credit cards accepted. ❷

Hotel Dryades, Dryadon 4 (☎210 382 7116 or 210 330 2387). Elegant Dryades offers some of Athens's nicest budget-conscious accommodations, with large rooms and private baths. Full kitchen on the 1st fl. and TV lounge. Breakfast €5. Internet €3 per hr. Singles €35; doubles €50; triples €60. Major credit cards accepted. ❸

The Exarcheion, Themistokleous 55 (☎210 380 0731 or 380 1256; fax 210 380 3296). Although there is a fast elevator, you might enjoy the stairway's modern mural on your way to one of the 50 rooms, which have phones, TVs, views of Exarhia, baths and A/C. Breakfast €4. 24hr. bar. Internet available for guests (€3 per hr.) and a roof garden. Reservations recommended. Singles €35; doubles €45; triples €60. Prices drop 10% in low season. 10% discount for *Let's Go* readers. ❸

KOLONAKI AND PANGRATI

Kolonaki's high prices may scare off budget-wary travelers but its charming neighborhoods and cozy atmosphere make it a pleasant place to spend the night. Though far from the main attractions, Pangrati offers affordable accommodations.

Youth Hostel #5 Pangrati, Damareos 75 (☎210 751 9530; y-hostels@otenet.gr). From Omonia or Pl. Syndagma take trolley #2 or 11 to Filolaou (past Imittou) or walk through the National Garden, down Eratosthenous Efthidiou, then 3 blocks to Frinis, and down Frinis until you come to Damareos; it's on your right. There's no sign for this cheery, family-owned hostel—just the number 75 and a green door. Bulletin boards spread general wisdom; share your own. TV lounge and full kitchen facilities. Hot showers €0.50 for 7min. Sheets €0.75; pillowcases €0.50 each. Laundry token (€3) available at reception; hang items on roof to dry. Quiet hours 2-5pm and 11pm-7am. Dorms €9. When hostel fills up, owner opens roof (€6 per person) to travelers; bring a sleeping bag. ❶

FOOD

FOOD BY PRICE

Restaurant	Area
UNDER €3 ❶	
Antonis Souvlaki (101)	SYN
Carousel Pizza (104)	PAN
Posto Cafe (104)	PAN
CrepeXarhia (103)	EXR
Delikiosk (99)	SYN
Everest (99) and (102)	SYN, OMN
Grigoris (99)	SYN
Healthy Food Vegetarian (102)	OMN
Makrigianni (99)	SYN
Matsoukas (99)	SYN
Mirabelle (99)	SYN
Pita Pan (102)	OMN
Savvas (102) and (102)	MON, EXR
Souvlaki Kavouras (102)	EXR
To Apollonion (99)	SYN
€3-€8 ❷	
Attalos (102)	MON
Body Fuel (100)	SYN
Byzantio (101)	PLK
Dafni Taverna (102)	OMN
Kentrikon (100)	SYN
Mamacas (102)	MON
€3-€8 ❷ CONT'D	
Nikis Cafe (100)	SYN
O Barba Giannis (103)	EXR
Pak Indian (102)	OMN
Roma Pizza (103)	EXR
T. Stamatopoulos (101)	PLK
Yiantes (103)	EXR
€8-€15 ❸	
Chroma (100)	SYN
Eden Vegetarian (101)	PLK
Food Company (103)	KOL
Furin Kazan (100)	SYN
Jackson Hall (103)	KOL
Mandras (102)	MON
Sissofos (101)	PLK
€15-€25 ❹	
Daphne's (101)	PLK
Kallimarmaron (104)	PAN
Old Parliament (100)	SYN
Pluto (103)	KOL
ABOVE €25 ❺	
Orizontes Lycavittou p. 100	KOL

EXR Exarhia **KOL** Kolonaki **MON** Monastiraki **OMN** Omonia **PAN** Pangrati **PLK** Plaka **SYN** Syndagma

FOOD BY AREA

SYNDAGMA

Cheap fast food saturates Syndagma like a grease stain on paper. Chains like Goody's, Wendy's, and McDonald's dispense cheeseburgers and french fries with sodas (€4.50) or local favorite *toast* (τοστ), a grilled sandwich (with feta and lettuce; €1.50). **Delikiosk ❶** and **Grigoris ❶** make cheap sandwiches (ham and cheese croissants €2), while **Everest ❶,** the most worthy by far, grills yummy panini with a generous helping of your choice of centers (no combination of which ever seems to exceed €3). In support of the local economic infrastructure you can also get roughly the same stuff grilled and bagged at family-owned joints on Nikis: **Makrigianni ❶** (#54), **Mirabelle ❶** (#34), or **To Apollonion ❶** (#10). Whatever you end up choosing, you ought to find your way to **Mat-**

soukas ❶, Karageorgios 3, just around the corner from Everest. There, feast on an unbelievably voluminous, inexpensive, and mouthwatering selection of homemade chocolates, gummies, confitures, and traditional cookies (€2-5 per kg).

Body Fuel, Stadiou 3, is a new-age food bar with delights like salmon and fresh vegetable salad (€4.40) or mango, strawberry, and Greek grape fruit salad (€2), which come at lightning speed but are still fresh and gourmet. Sleek steel-halled setting. Green tea served in cool glass bottles €1.50. Open M-F 10am-8:30pm. ❷

Chroma, Lekka 8 (☎210 331 7793). Bright colors abound both in- and outside at this chic restaurant/bar. Dine on fancy penne and smoked salmon (€11.50) while reclining on leather couches listening to lounge music. Stay late for drinks and dancing. Prices range €6-14. Open as a cafe and later as a bar 8am-2am; kitchen open 1pm-midnight. Credit cards accepted. ❸

Kentrikon, Kolokotroni 3 (☎210 323 2482 or 323 5623), near Stadiou and next to the National Historical Museum, serves Greek and selected foreign dishes in a cozy niche with A/C and outdoor seating. The butcher's cut lamb (€9) and the spinach ragout (€5) are expertly prepared along with many vegetarian options. Open M-Sa noon-6pm. ❷

Furin Kazan, Apollonos 2 (☎210 322 9170). Follow Nikis to Apollonos, which is parallel to Mitropoleos and begins 1 block away from the square. Light Japanese fare. The grilled salmon and vegetable platter (€14.80) makes a filling meal. Tuna roll €3.50. Open M-Sa 11am-10:30pm. Credit cards accepted. ❸

Nikis Cafe, Nikis 3 (☎210 323 4971), near Ermou, Nikis serves light fare like fresh baguette sandwiches (€3-4) and quiche into the wee hours of the morning. Margaritas (strawberry or banana €7.10) wash down your meal with style. Tangy chicken teriyaki €7.10. Sweet or savory crepes €5-6. Open Su-Th 8am-midnight, F-Sa 8am-3am. ❷

Old Parliament, Anthimou Gaxi 9 and Karitsi 7, behind the National Historical Museum. Dine and chat on a garden terrace in the shade of the Old Parliament building to the sound of live jazz and Greek music played every night. This gastronomic oasis prepares savory Mediterranean and Italian dishes. For dessert, *panna cotta* with poured espresso (€6.50) or exotic mango mousse with blackberry coulis (€10) delight. Seafood spaghetti €18.50. Cocktails €7. Open 8am-2am; music starts 10pm. ❹

HE BIG SPLURGE

RIZONTES LYCAVITTOU AND CAFE

There's something about seeing a ity from a bird's eye view that makes ou feel like you've conquered it. On ycavittos you can enjoy Athens from among the rooftops—at a comfortable distance from the *fasaria* (hubbub) hundreds of meters below. From here, you can see residences oll out around distant monuments ike little white sugar cubes sparkling n the sun; and the roar of unmuffled motor engines is replaced by the himing of Agios Georgiou church.

Orizontes Lycavittou is an oasis or the aesthetically inclined. Chef Giannis Geldis maintains a dynamic menu, which changes every three months. He reinterprets traditional Greek cuisine, creating delights like gilt-head moussaka (layered grilled eggplant and mashed potatoes opped with a bechemel sauce created from the *joue* of the fish; €90.80). This signature piece, much ike an *haute couture* gown, is one of a kind in both taste and price.

The menu at the **cafe** area, which s much less fussy and generally equires no reservations, is equally delicious and amazingly well priced. ry the risotto of fresh tomato and parmesan cheese (€9.20), penne with minced meat sauce (€8.90), or *sipoura* (porgy, a white fish) with resh vegetables (€14.80), and end t with warm chocolate cake with anilla ice cream (€9.40).

Take the €4 funicular from the op of Ploutarchou in Kolonaki. ☎210 722 7065. Open daily 9am-1:30pm. AmEx/DC/MC/V. ❺

PLAKA

For do-it-yourself meals, **minimarkets** on Nikis sell basic groceries. Most of the tavernas along the main drag of Kydatheneon are roughly equivalent; explore quieter streets like Tripodon and Lysiou for the gems. The restaurants have a traditional feel, many with live Greek music and dancing or stunning views of the Acropolis and Mt. Lycavittos. Check the menus and prices before you sit down—the main tourist area restaurants tend to be expensive.

Daphne's, 4 Lysikratous (☎210 322 7971). The most revered kitchen in Plaka serves rabbit in Mavrodaphne wine sauce (€16.10), a Peloponnesian delicacy, in a lovely, shaded garden. Grilled scallops in orange, Vermouth sauce €17.60. Chocolate mousse gateau €7.30. Open daily 7:30pm-12:30am. AmEx/DC/MC/V. ❹

Antonis Souvlaki, 114 Adrianou. People stand in line here for their pork kebab (€1.50) and *tzatziki*. Mythos beer €1.20. Open daily 10am-10pm. ❶

Sissofos, Mnisikleous 31 (☎210 324 6043; www.sissifos.gr). In a fashion no less aggressive than his competitors, the multi-lingual manager will grab you from the hilly street and set you up on his rooftop patio with dishes like lamb with potatoes (€9) or swordfish souvlaki (€10.90). However, the fuchsia bougainvillea, candlelit views, and large portions make the initial coercion worthwhile. Open M, W-Su 6:30pm-2am. ❸

T. Stamatopoulos, Lissiou 26 (☎210 322 8722 or 694 457 6169). Family-owned since 1882, this restaurant has an outdoor terrace and—the star attraction—Greek dancing to live music (9:30-11pm). Veal in wine sauce €7. Open M, W-Su 7pm-2:30am. ❷

Byzantio, Kydathenaion 18 (☎210 322 7368), perhaps outwardly indistinguishable from neighboring tourist traps, is a real Greek kitchen that knows what's up—even the most local of locals admit to eating here. Greek salad €3.70. Chicken fricassee €6.90. Veal and eggplant stew €6.60. Open daily 8am-1am. AmEx/MC/V. ❷

MONASTIRAKI

Give up fresh breath in exchange for cheap food by eating some *tzatziki*-smothered gyros at the flea market or explore the chic options that stretch the boundaries of regulation Greek cooking at the markets. Stock up on groceries at **Market Sophos,** Mitropoleos 78, near Aiolou. (☎/fax 210 322 6677. Open daily 9am-10pm.)

ON THE MENU

EDEN VEGETARIAN

You can swap greasy, mundane souvlaki for a healthful carrot and walnut salad (€3) at **Eden Vegetarian Restaurant.** This treasure embraces what it calls a "broader ecological philosophy, gradually developing into an alternative form of nutrition." Around it in Plaka, taverna maitre d's aggressively recruit foreigners to consume thickly-cut wedges of moussaka and heavy shanks of pork while, at Eden, international patrons sip fresh apple-pear juice and enjoy slices of delicate whole wheat bread topped with a lovely, mild tapenade. This cozy restaurant seems to be running a mini-totalitarian organic state—the vegetables, beer, wine, cheese, and overhauled taverna staples are exceedingly fresh and natural.

Best of all, a meal doesn't cost you an arm and a leg. A beloved specialty, the "*spanaki* special," is a three-layered gratin of filo, chopped carrots, spinach, and bechemel sauce (€8.80), baked to utter perfection. Since 1982 Eden has been replacing the meat of traditional Greek recipes with soy. The raisin-cinammon apple pie (€3) makes for a nice exclamation point to your meal. When you get your check, you will feel satifisfied but less lethargic than ever after such a complete, hearty meal—certainly at least since you arrived in Greece.

Lyssiou 12, in Plaka, at the top of Mniskleous, just beneath the Acropolis. ☎210 324 8858; www.edenvegetarian.gr. Open M and W-Su noon-midnight. ❸

Savvas, Mitropoleos 86 (☎210 324 5048), tucked away in a corner just off Pl. Monastiraki, across from the entrance of the flea market. This takeout spot is renowned—really renowned. It's a budget eater's dream, with heavenly, cheap gyros (€1.30); just don't sit down because prices will skyrocket. Souvlaki plate €6.50. Open 8am-4am. Credit cards accepted. ❶

Mamacas, Persefonis 41 (☎210 346 4984). Follow Ermou away from Plaka 10min. and bear right to cross Pireos where the avenue ends. Only cool young Greeks come here to the chicest taverna in Athens. *Taramosalata* €3.40. Mykonian sausage €5.80. Open daily 2:30pm-6:30pm and 8:45pm-2am; bar picks up around 11pm. ❷

Mandras, Ag. Anargyron 8 and Taki (☎210 321 3765), in the heart of Psiri. Live, modern Greek music entertains a buzzing young Greek crowd. *Pleurotous* grilled mushrooms, cooked with oil and vinegar (€6.20) make a perfect light meal. Spicy grilled chicken €9.70. Shots €3.30. Open daily 11am-3am, Su closes midnight. ❸

Attalos Restaurant, Adrianou 9 (☎210 321 9520), near the Thisseon area. Frequented by VIPs from the US Embassy, this traditional taverna on the slate patio opposite the Stoa of Attalos (hence the name) serves mussels *saganaki* (€4) and a variety of handmade croquettes—a vegetarian plate of zucchini, eggplant, and tomato croquettes for 2-4 €8. *Bouzouki* photos and pretty antique tapestries adorn the interior walls, while tables outside line the exterior gates of the Agora. Open 9am-1am. ❷

OMONIA

Just as in Syndagma, the immediate area around Pl. Omonia is filled with fast food (**Pita Pan** ❶ and **Everest** ❶ stand a bit above the rest). Busy 30 Septemvriou and 28 Oktovriou (Patission) are alive at all hours. For those with kitchen access, pick up foodstuffs at **Galaxias Discount Market,** 30 Septemvriou 26. To quiet late-night stomach rumblings, stop by the huge daily market on Athinas, between Monastiraki and Omonia, where night-owl restaurants stay open 3pm-7am.

Healthy Food Vegetarian Restaurant, Panepistimiou 57 (☎210 321 0966; fax 210 666 8780). It takes only a few seconds to order a dish of mouth-watering, homemade wholesomeness straight from the kitchen but perhaps a lot longer to decide. Point to freshly made specialties like whole wheat pasta with tomato sauce (€3.55 per kg) or whole wheat zucchini pie (€1.80). The light, moist carrot cake (€2.05) may have no icing but is divine. Carrot-apple juice €1.50. Open M-Sa 8am-10pm, Su 10am-4pm. ❶

Pak Indian Restaurant, Menandrou 13 (☎210 321 9412 or 210 324 2255). From Omonia Metro head down P. Tsaldari (despite street sign identification, known to all as Pireos), turn left on Menandrou, and walk past Indian and Middle Eastern grocery import stores for 1.5 blocks. A nice meal begins with *naan* (€2) and veggie *samosas* (€1.50) with a *tandoori* (€7.50-9) or or curry (€7-8.50) entree. Vegetarian dishes available. Open daily 2pm-midnight (open later in winter). DC/MC/V. ❷

Dafni Taverna, Iolianou 65 (☎210 821 3914). From Pl. Victoria, walk down Aristotelous 2 blocks and turn right on Iolianou. You'll know it's a classic the second you enter the grapevine-shaded courtyard walled by barrels of *retsina*. *Mezedes* €2-3. Moussaka €4.50. Lamb in lemon and olive oil €5. Ask to go to see selections in the kitchen if undecided. Open daily noon-1am. ❷

EXARHIA

Starving twenty-somethings demand cheap food around Exarhia. Many of the options are basic but tasty—think Greek classics and a jug of wine. Pick up a speedy souvlaki (€1-2) for the road at the famous **Savvas** ❶, Spirou Trikouri 3, on Pl. Exarhia. **Souvlaki Kavouras** ❶, Themistokleous 64, will also do the job.

O Barba Giannis, Em. Benaki 94 (☎210 382 4138). From Syndagma, walk up Stadiou and make a right on Em. Benaki; it's on the corner with tall, green doors. Athenian students, CEOs, and artists all agree that "Uncle John's" is the place for cheap food and great service. Fish dishes €5. Moussaka €5.30. Stuffed tomatoes and peppers €4. 0.5L wine €1.60. Open M-Sa noon-1:30am, Su noon-5:30pm. ❷

Yiantes, Valtetsiou 44 (☎210 330 1369), next to the movie theater. Enter this spacious, starkly decorated open-air oasis for organic and ethnic cuisine accompanied by "chill-out" music. *Sougania* (onions stuffed with minted meat, raisins and pine nuts) €6.80. Byzantium chicken €10.50. Vegetarian options €4-8. Fish €5.80-9. Open Tu-Su 1:30pm-1:30am. MC/V. ❷

CrepeXarhia (☎210 384 0773), on the corner of Ikonomou and Themistokleous on Pl. Exarhia, wraps spinach, cheese, and onion (€2.80), or chocolate, strawberry, and hazelnut (€3) into tasty snacks that are always warm and fresh. Make your own combinations from a long list of sweet and savory options. Open daily 11:30am-2am. ❶

Ama Lahei, Kallidromiou 69 (☎210 384 5978), off Themistokleous, behind a gate and down some stairs, at the foot of Strefi Hill. Grilled salmon €10. Country sausage with french fries €5.50. Boiled spinach and zucchini €3.50. Open daily 8pm-2am. ❸

Roma Pizza, Ioustianou 2 and Kallidromiou (☎210 883 6055), nourishes the stressed-out and the hungover of Athens University. Salami, sausage, bacon, gouda, ham, and mushroom pizza €7.80. Vegetarian pizza €7.50. Open daily noon-1am. ❷

KOLONAKI

The surest bargain is the local *laiki* (farmer's **street market**) every Friday morning on Xenokratous. Grab a week's supply of dried fruit, potatoes, and fresh wild strawberries. Otherwise Kolonaki allows you to splurge on a super-swanky meal.

Food Company, Anagnostopoulou 47 (☎210 361 6619), on the corner of Dimokritou, 4 blocks up Lycavitto from Pl. Kolonaki. Dishes you'll never forget, like lentil salad with goat cheese, parsley, and tomato (€4); roast chicken with plums and olives over saffron rice (€6.30); and gnocchi with watercress (€5), are displayed behind glass beneath the counter. Quick and well-priced, Food Company has translated casual, gourmet lunch and dinner into art. Top the visit off with a glass of white wine and a truly divine fudge cake or New York cheesecake (€3). Open daily noon-11:30pm. ❸

Pluto, Plutarchou 38 (☎210 724 4713; www.thepluto.com). Culinary mastermind Constantinos has created a chic restaurant with a warm ambience and an international menu. Greek and international customers line up for seats at the spice-filled glass tables every night. The menu, including grilled eggplant with feta and tomatoes (€9), fillet of sole in saffron and port wine sauce (€15), and strawberry meringue (€9), is always evolving. Open M-Sa 12:30pm-3am. Prominent among the happening venues of Haritos, the bar is open 9am-4am. Daiquiris (€9) are a specialty. Casual and less expensive **Pluto Sushi,** which has takeout, is next door. DC/MC/V. ❹

Jackson Hall, Millioni 4 (☎210 361 6546), is a classic all-wood American bar where Greeks flock for a New York burger (with lettuce, tomato, and onion; €12). After a fluffy chocolate mousse (€6), they gallivant upstairs; the bar there has recently become one of the most popular in Kolonaki. Open daily 9am-2am. MC/V. ❸

PANGRATI

Fresh food is available at the Friday morning *laiki* off Pl. Plastira. Head to Pl. Caravel to relax in cafes and to shop at **Veropoulos,** Formionos 23, a large nearby supermarket. (Open Su-F 8am-9pm, Sa 8am-6pm.)

Kallimarmaron, Eforionos 13 (☎210 701 9727 or 701 7234). From the old Olympic Stadium (with your back to it), take the closest street on the left and walk 1.5 blocks. Some of the best traditional Greek food in the city. Spiced chicken on the spit with raisins is prepared from an ancient recipe (€11.50). For starters, filets of fresh sardines in vine leaves (€5) will wow you. Open daily 8pm-midnight. DC/MC/V. ❹

Carousel Pizza, Eftihidou 32 (☎210 701 6838 or 756 4085). Locals on a break from the job come to this hole in the wall looking for something homemade and real cheap. Margherita pizza €2.90. Cheese bread €0.90. Open daily noon-midnight. ❶

Posto Cafe, Pl. Plastira 2 (☎210 751 0210), in a small storefront tucked into a corner of the square. Try the cheap vegetable pizza (€1.50) or spanakopita (€1.50). ❶

ATHENS

NIGHTLIFE

Athenian nightlife changes with the seasons. In the winter months, the neighborhoods of **Exarhia, Kifisia, Psiri,** and **Syndagma** roar with action. Athens summers, which host some of the best night-clubbing Europe has to offer, usher in the young and sizzling to the beachside clubs of **Glyfada** (p. 118), **Voula, Vari,** and **Vouliagmeni.** Aside from hotspots of the lights-and-dancing persuasion, much of Athens hums with that great Greek hybrid, the cafe/bar, where you can start your day early with a coffee and hang on for a nighttime binge. The new English-language monthly magazine *InsideOut* offers valuable information on all that's happening in Athens.

PLAKA

For a spellbinding 360° view of Athens at night, go up **Pnyx Hill,** opposite the Acropolis, where in ancient times the Assembly of Athenian citizens met to argue and deliberate. The hill now brings locals and tourists together to relish guitar strumming in the city lights. Take care when ascending the smooth, slippery steps. Enjoy a film on a roof garden in the center of Plaka in the cool night breeze at **Cine Paris,** Kedatheneon 22. (☎210 322 2071. 2nd-run English language films with Greek subtitles 8:45 and 11:10pm. Tickets €7.30.)

Boite Esperides, Tholou 6 (☎210 322 5482), at the end of Mniskleous. When you reach the foot of the Acropolis hill, turn right. Eternal legends Hatdzidakis and Dalaras used to come to this local music hall in the 60s "to sing about what was not allowed." Today aspiring *bouzouki* players and honey-voiced girls are invited to the oldest and last-standing *boite* in Athens where they "sing about love and the moon." It's ideal to come F-Sa. Call ahead for performance information. Cover €7.50. Ouzo or wine €7.50. Open T-Su 10pm-4am. Closed Aug.

Bretto's, Kydatheneon 41 (☎210 323 2110), between Farmaki and Afroditis. This wooden room with stools offers a local alcohol-only menu. High walls are shrouded by glass bottles various liquors all made by friendly Dimitris in his family's 112-year-old distilleries. Buy a bottle to take away (5ml-1L) or get immediate satisfaction at the bar. €5 per bottle of sweet red wine; €2 per sizeable glass. Open daily 10am-midnight.

MONASTIRAKI

The Psiri district is the newest place to see and be seen in Athens and Monastiraki's nightlife has revved up to rival Glyfada.

Bee, Miaouli 6 (☎210 321 2624), off Ermou at the corner of Miaoli and Themidos and a few blocks from the heart of Psiri. Pretty, colorfully painted plaster walls and 2 small floors look out in 2 directions to the streets of Psiri. Drinks €3-9. Open Tu-Th noon-3am, F-Su noon-5am. Credit cards accepted.

Vibe, Aristophanous 1 (☎210 324 4794), just beyond Plateia Iroön. The blue orbs hanging above the entrance are just a taste of the weird lighting effects of the bar's interior. Open Tu-Su 9:30pm-5am.

Inoteka, Pl. Avissynias 3 (☎210 324 6446), emerges at night from behind stacks of old wooden chairs and church accessories that aging vendors market. A young set takes yellow tequila shots (€5) under the stars in the hidden plateia. Open daily 9pm-3:30am, with no set closing time Sa-Su.

Soul, Evripidou 65 (☎210 331 0907), in Psiri, plays hip hop, R&B, and dance in a chic garden. *Mojito* €9; simple drinks €7. Open Su-Th 10am-3:30am, F-Sa 10am-5am.

Revekka, Miaouli 22 (☎210 321 1174), on Plateia Iroön and in the center of Psiri. This eclectic cafe/bar blossoms by night, when tables overwhelm the sidewalk and darkness welcomes music and flowing drinks. Beer €2. Open 11am-5am.

EXARHIA

Exarhia exudes funkiness in its many bars, which showcase everything from backgammon to death metal. Check *Athens News* for showtimes of movies played at the outside **Riviera Garden Art Cinema,** Valtetsiou 46 (€7, students €5).

Mo Better, Koleti 32 (☎210 381 2981), off Themistokleous. In fall, winter, or spring, find the tall blue wooden door—it's the entrance to the most popular rock bar in Athens. A staple in the nocturnal schedule of alternative *Panepistimio* (university) students. Whiskey, vodka tonic €6. Open Oct.-June F-Sa 10pm-dawn, Su-Th 10pm-4am.

Rock Underground, Metaxa 21 (☎210 382 2019). For British flavored hard rock, hard core heavy metal, and alternative, try this cafe/bar where young Athenians know all the words. Beer on draft and bottles €2-5; cocktails €5. Open daily 10am-3am.

Wunderbar, Themistokleous 80 (☎210 381 8577), on Pl. Exarhia, plays pop and some techno or electronic. Local DJs often spin. Star-shaped paper lanterns decorate the interior. Vodka *lemoni* €6. Daiquiris €7.50. Su-W 9am-3am, Th-Sa 9am-sunrise.

Wired, Valtetsiou 61. The red parachute on the ceiling and thorn bushes painted on the walls give this rock bar an eerie Alice-in-Wonderland feel. Musical genres each get a turn on the schedule. Drinks €3-5.50. Open Su-Th 11am-1am, F-Sa 11am-3am.

IN RECENT NEWS

COMING TO TERMS WITH THE PAST

On May 29th 2003, PASOK (the Panhellenic Socialist Movement, p 14) vowed to cease bickering and proceed with a plan that, a few decades ago, people in Greece wouldn't have even dreamed of discussing; they are building a mosque in Athens.

Presently, Greece's capital, home to an estimated 100,000 Albanian, Pakistani, Asian, and Middle Eastern Muslims, lacks even one site for Islamic worship—cracked-window tenement rooms have had to suffice as venues of devotion. The Orthodox Church, in a country occupied for four centuries by Ottoman invaders, has claimed that minarets and daily calls to prayer recall too strongly the dark times of ancestral hardship and struggle of ethnic Greeks.

This year's Olympics were the driving force behind the decision to build an Islamic place of worhip in Greece. The Olympic Committee would have been hard pressed to ignore the fact that about half of the athletes planning to live in the Olympic Village are members of some sect of Islam. The mosque will, thus, be built near there, in the area of Paenia, 20km east of Athens's center.

There has been much controversy in this suburban town surrounding the mosque's construction, but the structure is expected to be completed in time for the Games. Interestingly, Saudis are financing the project, perhaps evidence of Greece's apprehension to create (or at least finance) a Muslim venue on its soil.

Korso, Em. Benaki 72 (☎210 384 2077). Artsy and bright, with pipe-lined high ceilings, pale leather couches and chill-out music. The wine bar in the old house next door opens up when the winter months bring colder weather. Engage in a game of pictionary or scrabble over *toast* (€3) and frappés (€3). Open M-Sa 10am-2am.

KOLONAKI

Kolonaki brims with cafes and bars. **Haritos,** to the right of Plutarchou, is the spot for summertime action—if you're prepared to shell out major euros for drinks. **City, Azul, Baila,** and **Mousa** (Μουσα), all at Haritos 43, spill sophisticated patrons sipping beer (€5) and cocktails (€6) into the street late into the night. **Pluto** draws throngs at night and on **Milioni,** where Jackson Hall is located, crowds no less sizeable chat over drinks and little outdoor tables. Summertime performances are staged in Lycavittos Theater as part of the **Athens Festival** (p. 29), which has included acts from the Greek Orchestra to Pavarotti to the Talking Heads. The **Festival Office,** Stadiou 4, sells student tickets. An English-language schedule of events is available in mid-June. (☎210 322 1459 or 322 7944. Tickets range €10-110. Open M-Sa 8am-4pm, Su 9am-2pm and 6-9pm.) In summer, open-air **Dexameni** cinema, in Pl. Dexameni on Lycavittos, shows current movies. (☎210 360 2363 or 210 362 3942. Nightly shows 8:45 and 11pm. €7, students €5, children under 5 free.) **Athinaia,** Haritos 50 (☎210 721 5717), is a second Kolonaki outdoor venue.

Flower, Dorylaou 2 (☎210 643 2111), in Pl. Mavili. Bohemians just want to have fun. No "face control" or high prices (shots €2.50; drinks €5), just a popular dive bar with a varied crowd of cool, European partyers. Open Su-Th 7pm-4am, F-Sa 7pm-6am.

The Daily, Xenokratous 47 (☎210 722 3430). At this small cafe/bar in a shaded enclave on the foot of Lycavittos, chic foreign students converge to imbibe, take in Latin music and reggae, and watch soccer and basketball on TV. Open-air seating in warm months. Pints of Heineken €3, 0.5L €4.95; cocktails €5-6. Open daily 9am-2am.

Briki, Dorylaou 6 (☎210 645 2380), in Pl. Mavili nextdoor to Flower is a lively wooden bar with music that is always hip and fun but not too bass-oriented. Martini €7. Margarita €7.50. Snack on sliced cucumber and green olives splashed with vinegar. Open Su-Th 7pm-4am, F-Sa 7pm-6am.

Cafe 48, Karneadou 48 (☎210 725 2434), 3 blocks downhill Ploutarchou from Haritos, take a left and walk to the end of the block. Expat classicists and student travelers exchange stories and play darts in the back room. Cozy atmosphere makes it a great place for a chill evening with friends. Beer €3. Open M-Sa 9am-3am, Su 5pm-2am.

PANGRATI

The cafes along Imittou let you people-watch in style. A walk between Imittou 128 and 67 resonates with the vitality of relaxing 20-somethings in myriad cafes adorning the street. Most cafes are open daily 9am-2am. Movies show twice nightly at Imittou 107 (€6). **Village Cinemas,** Imittou 10 and Hremonidou, on the second floor of the Millennium Centre, shows the latest blockbusters in state-of-the-art theaters. (☎210 757 2440. Call for listings and times.) The name of **Sideradiko Cafe,** Imittou 128, which means iron, fits the cafe's metal, stone, and mirror interior. Absorb the yuppiness from one of the outside tables. Despite the severe decor, you can enjoy a calm night or Trivial Pursuit or Scrabble. (☎210 701 8700; www. sideradikocafe.gr. Fruit juices €4; beer €5. Open Su-Th 9am-3am, F-Sa 9am-6am.) Next to the movie theater, **Excite,** Imittou 109, neighbors other busy cafes but offers a trendier atmosphere with brightly colored leather couches. (☎210 751 5487. Milkshakes €5; martinis €6.90. Open 9am-4am. MC/V.) **Ellas Espresso,** Pl. Plastira 8, plays pop and Greek music with a shaded terrace and four TVs suspended above the indoor bar. (☎210 756 2565. Frappé €3. Open daily 9am-3am.)

SIGHTS

ACROPOLIS

Reach the entrance on the west side of the Acropolis either from Areopagitou to the south, by following the signs from Plaka, or by exiting the Agora to the south, following the path uphill and turning right. Not wheelchair-accessible. The well-worn marble can be slippery, so wear shoes with good traction. ☎210 321 0219. Open 8am-7pm; in winter 8am-2:30pm. Admission price includes access to all of the sights below the Acropolis (including Hadrian's Arch, the Olympian Temple of Zeus, and the Agora) within a 48hr. period. €12, students €6. Tickets can be purchased at any of the sites.

Looming majestically over the city, the Acropolis complex has served as a city center since the 5th century BC. The brilliant Parthenon at its center towers over the Aegean and the plains of Attica, the greatest achievement of Athens's Classical glory and the era's most enduring architectural contribution. Although each Greek *polis* had an acropolis ("high point of the city"), the buildings atop Athens's central peak simply outshone their imitators and continue to awe even the most jaded traveler. They stand timelessly upright and their energy and extravagance are felt by every onlooker. Visit as early in the day as possible to avoid massive crowds and the broiling, humbling midday sun.

HISTORY

BEGINNINGS. With its view toward both land and sea, the Acropolis began as a strategically located military fortress. In recent years, evidence of a Cyclopean-walled **Mycenaean** city (p. 8) has been found on and around the hill. It was initially controlled by one ruler, who lived in a palace that doubled as a temple to a nature goddess and later to Athena. Around the 12th century BC, wealthy landowners, the city's **aristoi,** ousted the monarch and established themselves as rulers in an aristocracy ("rule of the best"—in practice, the rich). They shifted government away from the Acropolis to the city's northern foothills, in an area that later became the **Agora** (p. 111). The Acropolis became a purely religious center for worshipping Athena, whose wooden shrine celebrated both Athena Polias, goddess of crops and fertility, and Pallas Athena, loving virgin and protectress of the city.

PERICLEAN PROJECT. The Acropolis's world-famous form took shape in 507 BC, when the *aristoi* were overthrown and Athens began its experiment with democracy. In 490 BC the Athenians began constructing a new temple on the Acropolis, this time in marble. Ten years later, Aegean city-states banded together and formed the Delian League to protect themselves against the Persians, and **Pericles** started piling up a slush fund to beautify Athens from the taxes paid by the league. He continued this practice long after the Persian threat evaporated, lavishing money on projects like the temples of the Acropolis, the **Hephaesteion** in the Agora, and the **Temple of Poseidon** at Sounion. His program was mocked as lavish and unscrupulous; Plutarch reports that Pericles was "gilding and bedizening" the city like a "wanton woman adding precious stones to her wardrobe." Nevertheless, after delays caused by the Peloponnesian War (431-404 BC), the Periclean project was completed. Four of the buildings erected thus still stand today on the Acropolis: the **Parthenon,** the **Propylaea,** the **Temple of Athena Nike,** and the **Erechtheion.**

THE HIDDEN DEAL

HELLENIC FESTIVAL AT THE HERODION

The Odeon of Herodes Atticus, known as the Herodion, was built in AD 161 by the ancient Roman philanthropist who inherited the fortune his father found in gold treasure discovered outside of Rome decades before. The 32 amphitheatrically-built rows of stone seats, before an elevated orchestra and ornate multi-arched *skene* wall (means "stage" in Ancient Greece), are more than simply ruins; they still serve their original cultural purpose.

Every summer, from the beginning of June to the end of September, Greece hosts the best the Western, modern world has to offer in terms of performing arts. The Hellenic Festival organizes nearly nightly performances (at 8:30 or 9pm) for a once-in-a-lifetime experience costing €20-110 with prices halved for students and groups. Here the Shakespeare Theatre of Washington performed Euripides's *Oedipus* plays, epic Greek composer Mikis Theodorakis himself presented a series of short songs and epitaphs written in tribute to poet Yannis Ritsos, and the English National Ballet performed Leo Delibe *Copelia*.

This summer of 2004, the festival plans to continue the same prestigious tradition in conjuction with a specific focus on events that "highlight the deeper significance of the [Olympic] Games."

☎210 322 1459; www.hellenicfestival.gr. Odeon box office, in front of the theatre at the foot of the Acropolis: ☎210 323 2771 or 323 5582. Open daily 9am-2pm and 6-9pm.

CAPTURE AND RESTORATION. Almost as soon as the Acropolis was completed, it fell to Sparta; ever since, its function has changed whenever it changed hands. **Byzantine Christians** added the symbolic power of the Parthenon to their faith arsenal; they turned the temple into the Church of Ag. Sophia. In 1205 **Frankish Crusaders** turned back the clock and again made the Acropolis into a fortress/palace/headquarters, this time for the Dukes de la Roche. Eventually, the Parthenon served as a Catholic church, Notre Dame d'Athènes. In the 15th century, **Ottomans** used the Parthenon as a mosque and the Erechtheion as the Ottoman commander's harem. During a 1687 siege, the Venetian attackers fired shells at the Parthenon, and the gunpowder stored on the Acropolis blew off the temple's roof. Squalor ensued as Ottoman guards and their families settled on the Acropolis. It is symbolic of the amazing workmanship that went into the Parthenon that almost all the damage to the building was inflicted in the last 600 years by human hands, not by gravity. In 1833, the newly independent Greeks reclaimed the hill, dismantling remnants of the Turkish occupation and resurrecting the Temple of Nike. The subsequent preservation of the Acropolis has kicked up a swirl of impassioned controversy. The first wave of massive restoration began in 1898 and lasted almost 40 years, transforming the site by demolishing and reconstructing the Temple of Athena Nike. Sadly many of the Parthenon's most important pieces sit in the British Museum in London, having long been chiseled off the building and spirited away by English ambassador Lord Elgin. In the last 20 years, acid rain has forced works formerly displayed outside to take cover in the museum.

RUINS

When you enter the Acropolis, the reconstructed **Temple of Athena Nike** lies before you. Though the Classical ramp that led to the Acropolis no longer exists, today's visitors still make a beautiful climb. The path leads through the Roman **Beulé Gate,** named for the French archaeologist who unearthed it. It continues through the stunning **Propylaea,** the ancient entrance famous for its ambitious multi-level design. Designed by the great engineer and architect Mnesikles between 437 and 432 BC, it was never completed. Mnesikles improved upon the Doric and Ionic styles, pairing the Propylaea's Ionic columns with a Doric exterior.

PARTHENON. Towering over the hillside, the **Temple of Athena Parthenos,** more commonly known as the Parthenon, keeps vigil over Athens and the mod-

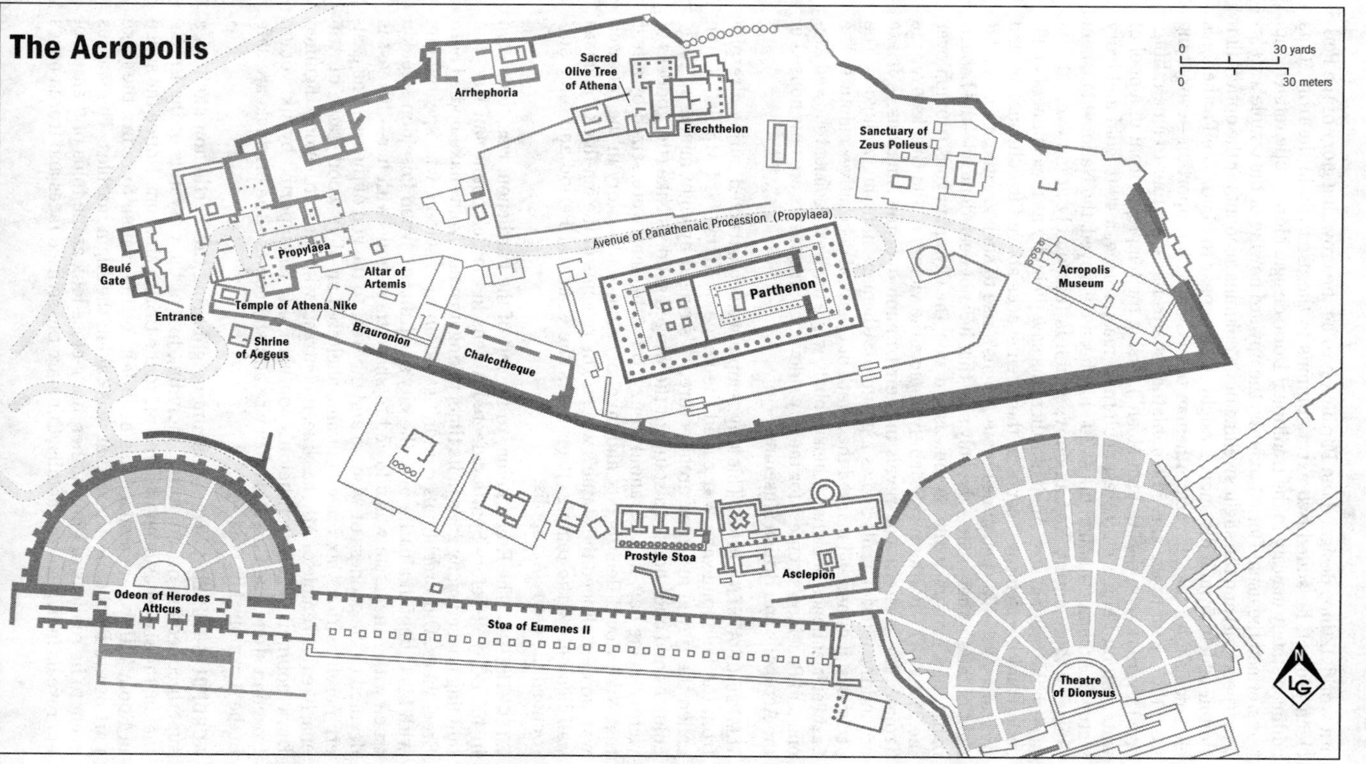
The Acropolis
0
30 yards
0
30 meters
Arrhephoria
Sacred Olive Tree of Athena
Erechtheion
Sanctuary of Zeus Polieus
Avenue of Panathenaic Procession (Propylaea)
Propylaea
Beulé Gate
Altar of Artemis
Temple of Athena Nike
Entrance
Shrine of Aegeus
Brauronion
Chalcotheque
Parthenon
Acropolis Museum
Prostyle Stoa
Asclepion
Odeon of Herodes Atticus
Stoa of Eumenes II
Theatre of Dionysus
N
LG

ern world. Iktinos designed the Parthenon to be the crowning glory of the Periclean project; he added two extra columns to the usual six in the front, thus adding a stately majesty to the traditional Doric design. More subtle refinements transformed the usual Doric boxiness: the upward bowing of the temple's *stylobate* (pedestal) and the slight swelling of its columns account for the optical illusion in which, from a distance, straight lines appear to bend. The Parthenon's elegance shows the Classical Athenian obsession with proportion—everything from the layout to the carved entablature shares the same four-to-nine ratio in size (a variation on the "Golden Mean"). Inside the temple, in front of a pool of water, stood Phidias's greatest sculptural masterpiece, a 40-ft. gold and ivory statue of Athena. Although the statue has been destroyed, the National Museum houses a 2nd-century Roman copy, which is fearsomely grand even at one twelfth the original size. Ancient Athenians saw their city as the capital of civilization and the **metopes** (scenes in the open spaces above the columns) around the sides of the Parthenon celebrate Athens's rise to such greatness. On the far right of the southern side—the only side that has not been defaced—the Lapiths battle the Centaurs, while on the eastern side, the Olympian gods triumph over the Titans. The northern side faintly depicts the victory of the Greeks over the Trojans; the western side revels in their triumph over the Amazons. A frieze around the interior walls shows a group of Athenians mingling with gods. The **pediments** at either end marked the zenith of Classical decorative sculpture. The **East Pediment** once depicted Athena's birth, while the **West Pediment** showed Athena and Poseidon's contest for the city's devotion; fragments are now housed in the Acropolis and British Museums.

TEMPLE OF ATHENA NIKE. This tiny temple was constructed during a respite from the Peloponnesian War called the Peace of Nikias (421-415 BC). Often called the "jewel of Greek architecture," it's ringed by eight miniature Ionic columns and once housed a statue of the winged goddess Nike (the goddess of victory). One day, in a paranoid frenzy, the Athenians were seized by a fear that Nike would flee the city and take any chance of victory in the renewed war, so they clipped the statue's wings. The remains of the 5m-thick **Cyclopean wall** lies below the temple. It predates the Classical Period and once surrounded the entire Acropolis.

ERECHTHEION. The Erechtheion, to the left of the Parthenon, was completed in 406 BC, just before Sparta defeated Athens in the Peloponnesian War. The building housed many gods in its time, taking its name from snake-bodied hero Erechtheus. Old Erechtheus couldn't stand up to Poseidon, who speared him with his trident in a battle over the city's patronage. When Poseidon struck a truce with Athena, he was allowed to share the temple with her—the east is devoted to the goddess of wisdom and the west to the god of the sea. The eastern porch, with its six Ionic columns, sheltered an olive wood statue of Athena; like the Temple of Athena Nike, it contrasts with the Parthenon's dignified Doric columns. The Erechtheion's southern side is supported by six women frozen in stone, the Caryatids. They're actually copies—the originals are safe in the Acropolis Museum.

ACROPOLIS MUSEUM. This museum neighboring the Parthenon shelters a superb collection of sculptures, including five of the Caryatids of the Erechtheion; the sixth has been whisked off to the British Museum. Notice the space in Room VIII, where a space has been left for the British to return the large part of the Parthenon frieze that was taken: the Elgin marbles. The statues seem to be replicas of one another, but a close look at the folds of their drapery reveals individualized details. Compare the stylized faces and frozen poses of the Archaic Period **Moschophoros** (calf-bearer) sculpture to the idealized, more human Classical Period **Kritios Boy** to follow the development of Greek sculpture. *(Open M 11am-7pm, Tu-Su 8am-7pm; low season M 11am-2pm, Tu-Su 8am-2pm. No flash photography; no posing next to the objects. English labels. Avoid going between 10am-1pm, when it is most crowded.)*

ELSEWHERE ON THE ACROPOLIS. The southwestern corner of the Acropolis looks down over the reconstructed **Odeon of Herodes Atticus,** a functional theater dating from the Roman Period (AD 160). Consult *Athens News* for scheduled concerts and plays. You'll also see nearby ruins of the Classical Theatre of Dionysus, the Asclepion, and the Stoa of Eumenes II. *(Entrance on Dionysiou Areopagitou. ☎210 323 2771 or 210 323 5582. Open daily 9am-2pm and 6-9pm. Though the Odeon is closed for general admission, performances are held throughout the summer. Tickets €16-110, but most around €30. Half price for students with ID, children 6-18, members of large groups or families, and tickets in the upper tier and D zone. MC/V. Theater open M-Sa 8am-7pm. €2, students €1.)*

AGORA

Enter the Agora in one of 3 ways: off Pl. Thission, off Adrianou, or as you descend from the Acropolis. ☎210 321 0185. Guide pamphlets provided, but extra reference recommended. Open daily 8am-7:20pm. €4, students and EU seniors €2, EU students and under 18 free.

The Acropolis was the showpiece of the polis; the Agora was the heart and the soul. The Agora served as the city's marketplace, administrative center, and center of daily life from the 6th century BC through AD 500. Many of the debates of Athenian democracy were held in the Agora; Socrates, Aristotle, Demosthenes, Xenophon, and St. Paul all instructed here. After the 6th century AD, the Agora, like the Acropolis, passed through the hands of innumerable conquerors. The ancient Agora emerged again in the 19th century, when a residential area built above it was razed for excavations.

HEPHAESTEION. The Hephaesteion, on a hill in the northwestern corner of the Agora, is the best-preserved Classical temple in Greece. The 415 BC temple still flaunts cool **friezes,** which depict Hercules's labors and Athens native Theseus's adventures. The closer you look, the more impressed you'll be.

ODEON OF AGRIPPA. The Odeon of Agrippa, a concert hall built for Roman Emperor Augustus's son-in-law and right-hand man, now stands in ruins on the left of the Agora as you walk from the museum to the Hephaesteion. When the roof collapsed in AD 150, the Odeon was rebuilt at half its former size. From then on it served as a lecture hall. The actors' dressing room was turned into a porch supported by colossal statues, three of which still guard the site.

STOA OF ATTALOS. The elongated Stoa of Attalos was a multi-purpose building filled with shops and home to informal philosophers' gatherings. Attalos II, King of Pergamon, built the Stoa in the 2nd century BC as a gift to Athens, where he had received his education. Reconstructed between 1953 and 1956, it now houses the **Agora Museum,** which contains relics from the site. The stars of the collection are the excellent black figure paintings by Exekias and a calyx-krater depicting Trojans and Greeks quarreling over the body of Patroclus, Achilles's famous young male lover. *(☎210 321 0185. Open daily 8am-7:20pm.)*

STOA BASILEIOS. Plato reports that Socrates's first trial was held at the recently excavated Stoa Basileios, or **Royal Stoa.** It served as the headquarters for the King Archon, one of the leading political and religious figures in ancient Athens. *(As you cross the subway tracks at the Adrianou exit, it's on the left.)*

OTHER ANCIENT SITES

KERAMIKOS. The Keramikos's rigid geometric design stands out as soon as you enter its grounds. The site includes a large cemetery and a 40m-wide boulevard that ran through the Agora and the Diplyon Gate and ended at the sanctuary of Akademos (where Plato founded his academy in the 4th century BC). **Public tombs** for state leaders, famous authors, and battle victims lined this sacred road, and worshippers began the annual Panathenaean procession along its path. The Sacred Gate arched over the Sacred Way to Eleusis, traversed in annual processions. The **Oberlaender Museum** displays finds from the burial sites; its excellent collection of highly detailed pottery and sculpture is a highlight. *(Northwest of the Agora; archaeological site begins at the acute angle where Ermou and Peiraos intersect. From Syndagma, walk toward Monastiraki on Ermou for 1km. ☎210 346 3552. Open Tu-Su 8:30am-3pm. €2, non-EU students and EU seniors €1, EU students and under 18 free.)*

TEMPLE OF ZEUS AND HADRIAN'S ARCH. At the center of downtown Athens you'll spot traces of the largest temple ever built in Greece. The 15 majestic Corinthian columns of the Temple of Olympian Zeus mark where it once stood. Started in the 6th century BC, it was completed 600 years later by the Roman emperor Hadrian. Ruins of Roman baths are on the right when you first enter the site. Clearly immodest Hadrian attached his name to the centuries-long effort by adding his arch, the boundary between the ancient city of Theseus and Hadrian's new city. Today the arch graces the intersection of four huge thoroughfares: Amalias, Vas. Olgas, Dionysiou Areopagitou, and Syngrou. *(Entrance on Vas. Olgas at Amalias, across from the entrance to the National Garden. ☎210 922 6330. Open Tu-Su 8:30am-3pm. Temple admission €2, students €1, EU students and under 18 free. Arch free.)*

BYZANTINE ATHENS

Hours depend on each church's priest; mornings are best. Modest dress required.

Like their Classical counterparts, Byzantine sanctuaries have become a part of Athens's landscape. Religious Greeks often pause before churches to pay their respects before going about their business. A little time spent in a few churches gives a glimpse of the country's modern culture and faith. Athens had become a political backwater by the time of Byzantine ascendancy. Thus, Byzantine Athens is best represented by religious structures, which are all over the city. Small charming churches pepper tiny streets, squeeze between modern buildings, and hide under concrete porticos. Although many of the churches are not from Byzantine times, they mimic the style quite beautifully. There are, of course, more authentic sites to be found. Shoppers and pedestrians on Ermou will run right into **Kapnikaria Church,** which stands in the middle of the street one block beyond Aiolou. A bas-relief decorates its western wall; it escaped destruction in 1834 only by the clemency of Louis I of Bavaria. Walking down Mitropoleos from Syndagma, you may notice a tiny red church on the corner of Pentelis—it's engulfed in a modern building. You'll also pass **Agios Eleftherios** and the **Mitropoli Cathedral,** flanked these days by scaffolding as a result of damage in the recent earthquake. A frieze with the Attic calendar of feast days adorns the front facade. **Agia Apostoli,** an in-tact Byzantine church, stands at the eastern edge of the Agora in the heart of Athens. White-walled **Metamorphosis,** in Plaka near Pritaniou, was built in the 11th century and restored in 1956. Eleventh-century Russian Orthodox **Agia Triada,** a few blocks from Pl. Syndagma at Filellinon 21, is filled with silver angel icons. Walking down Filellinon, you'll pass the **Sotira Lykodimou,** the largest medieval building in Athens, dating to 1031. It was built as part of a Roman Catholic monastery; now it's the Russian Orthodox Church. The most intriguing juxtaposition of superstitious Byzantine religiosity and commercial development is in the area of **Ambelokipi,** north of Kolonaki next to Areos park. A tiny church named **Panagitsa** (little Virgin) holds its ground literally right in the middle of the driveway to the Alexandros hotel on T. Vassou. Eleventh-century **Aghioi Pantes,** sleeping humbly at the back entrance of the Panathinaiko stadium on A. Tsochas, loses in terms of patronage by frightful measures to cultish Sunday soccer games week after week.

MODERN ATHENS

MT. LYCAVITTOS. Of Athens's seven hills, Lycavittos is the largest. Try ascending at sunset, when you can catch a last glimpse of the densely packed rooftops in the waning daylight and watch the city light up for the night. You can take the **funicular** (2min.; every 15-30min.; round-trip €4, under 5 free; open daily 9am-3am) to the top—the station is a healthy, uphill walk at the peak of Ploutarchou in **Kolonaki.** You can also hike up, a nice 15-20min. walk from any approach. Bring water, watch out for cactuses and slippery rocks, and don't climb alone especially at night. At the top you'll come to the **Chapel of St. George,** where you might spy a couple tying the knot but more likely just the sweet church keeper dozing in his chair. Light a candle (with a small donation) under the ornately painted ceilings. A leisurely stroll around the church provides a 360° view of Athens's seemingly endless expanse. Using the Acropolis as a point of reference, the neighborhoods of Monastiraki, Omonia, and Exarhia are on your right. Continuing clockwise, you will see Areos Park behind a small circular patch of green, which is Strefi, another of the seven hills. The flashy lights and music of the Lycavittos Theater are 180° from the Acropolis. The eastern view looks out onto more parks, Mt. Hymettus, and a glimpse of the Panathenaic Olympic Stadium, the National Garden, and the Temple of Olympian Zeus back toward the Acropolis.

PANATHENAIC STADIUM. Also known as the Kallimarmaro (pretty marble), it is wedged between the National Gardens and Pangrati, carved into a hill. The Byzantines destroyed the Classical stadium, but in 1895 it was restored in Panteli marble. The stadium was the site of the first modern Olympic Games in 1896 and lay under a cloud of disappointment in 1996, when the centennial games were held in Atlanta. Still, in 1997, it held the opening ceremonies of the World Track and Field Championships and the perennial finish line of the **Athens Marathon,** which begins 42km (26.2 mi.) away in Marathon. Seventy thousand people can pack in the stands of this marble preserve for athletes and sunbathing students; military parades and gymnastic displays are held here as well. Marble steles near the front honor Greece's gold and silver medalists and once again, the stadium is undergoing refurbishments in preparation for the largest, most venerated sporting event in the world. In this year's **2004 Olympic Games** (p. 128) it will be the finish line of the men's and women's Marathon events as well as the venue for the **Archery** event. *(On Vas. Konstantinou. From Syndagma, walk up Amalias 15min. to Vas Olgas, and follow it to the left. Or take trolley #2, 4, or 11 from Syndagma. Open daily 8am-8:30pm. Free.)*

AROUND SYNDAGMA. Be sure to catch the **changing of the guard** in front of the **Parliament** building. Every hour on the hour, two *evzones* (guards) wind up like toy soldiers, kick their tasseled heels in unison, and fall backward into symmetrical little guardhouses on either side of the **Tomb of the Unknown Warrior.** Unlike the stoic British beefeaters, *evzones* are known to give a wink and a smile. Their jovial manner matches their attire—pom-pommed clogs, *foustanelas* (short pleated skirts), and tasseled hats. Sundays at 10:45am, there's a special changing of the guard with a band and the full guard troop. Athens's endangered species are kept in the very pretty **National Gardens,** their natural environment. There's a duck pond and a pathetic zoo. Women should avoid strolling here alone.

OUTDOOR MARKETS. Athens's major markets attract bargain hunters, browsers, and award-winning chefs alike—as well as a lot of *yiayias* (grandmothers outfitted in widows' black). The **Flea Market,** adjacent to Pl. Monastiraki, has a festive bazaar atmosphere: picture a massive garage sale where old forks and teapots are sold alongside odd family heirlooms. Try to go on a Sunday. *(Open M, W, Sa-Su 8am-8pm.)* The biggest outdoor food market in Athens, **Varnakios,** is on Athinas between Armodiou and Aristogeitonos. *(Open M-Th 6am-7pm, F-Sa 5am-8pm.)* Not for the faint of heart, its **meat market** which closes earlier (3pm) overwhelms with sights and smells of livers, kidneys, and skinned rabbits. Early risers can jostle with Athenian cooks (restauranteurs and moms alike) for choice meats, fish, fruits, vegetables, breads, and cheeses. Moving farmers' markets or *laikes*, pulsate throughout Athens's central body, stopping every morning to take over a specific *stenodthromos* (narrow street) in a specific neighborhood of the city. Other than following a trail of corn shucks and peanut shells, the best way to track them is to call the Athens office of **Laikes Agores,** Zoodochou Pigis 2-4 (☎210 380 7560).

NATIONAL CEMETERY. The National Cemetery in **Pangrati** holds the graves of politicians, actors, poets, and foreigners who died in Athens—as the gate-keeper puts it, "all the personalities." Family graves differ from rented graves, which must give up their bones to boxes after three years. Soon space limits will only allow all the newly deceased a space in this famous cemetery for merely three years; even VIPs will be moved to the Mausoleum Commons. When entering the main gate, the information bureau with Greek-speaking staff is on your left. The first graves are larger and more elaborate than most, as the rich and famous continue to enjoy their earthly splendor. On the left side of the first courtyard, archaeologist **Heinrich Schliemann,** excavator of Troy and Mycenae, lies in a pseudo-temple. To the left of the statue of an angel is the tomb of **Melina Mercury,** a film icon, who starred in *Never on Sunday* before becoming the Greek Minister of Culture. On the main path there is a chapel where ceremonies are held. *(From Pl. Syndagma walk down Amalias, turn left on Ath. Diakou, and then walk down Anapavseos. ☎210 923 6118 or 923 2550. Open daily. Free. For guided tours call the Cultural Centre, Akadamias 50. ☎210 361 2705 or 210 363 9671; if it is closed call the cemetery office directly. Modest dress required.)*

MUSEUMS

NATIONAL ARCHAEOLOGICAL MUSEUM

Patission 44. A 20min. walk from Pl. Syndagma down Stadiou to Aiolou and right onto Patission. Take trolley #2, 4, 5, 9, 11, 15, or 18 from the uphill side of Syndagma or trolley #3 or 13 from the north side of Vas. Sofias. Or take the subway to Victoria and after exiting, walk straight to the 1st street, 28 Oktovriou. Turn right and walk 5 blocks. ☎210 821 7717. Open Apr.-Oct. Tu-Th 8:30am-3pm, F-Su 8am-7pm; Nov.-Mar. M 10:30am-5pm, Tu-Su 8:30am-3pm. €6, students and EU seniors €3, EU students and classics and art students free; Su free. No flash photography; no posing in front of exhibits.

This jaw-dropping collection deserves a spot on even the most rushed itinerary. Even a few pieces from this, the world's most extensive array of Greek artifacts, would steal the show in any other museum. Check your bags (free) and grab a **free map** of the museum. Hold on to your ticket, since the museum's arrangement redirects you to the entry several times, and you'll have to pay again if you lose it. The museum reopens after nearly two years of renovations in April 2004 and is expected to have a new layout. Look out for prehistoric pieces from Heinrich Schliemann's **Mycenae** excavations (p. 149). At first glance you may think the German archaeologist discovered the Midas touch: it is a world of gold, including the **Mask of Agamemnon** (the death mask of a king who lived at least three centuries earlier than Agamemnon himself). You'll also encounter Greek **sculpture** from the 8th century BC through the AD 5th century. Naked **kouroi** (p. 21), standing young men, allow the viewer to trace every last inch of Greek sculpture's development from early Archaic (marked by rigidity and Egyptian influences) to Classical (emphasizing movement and bodily form) to late Roman (ornate and emotional). Compare the massive 530 BC *kouros* of Sounion to the 520 BC *kouros* named Kroisos; you'll notice how smoothness and fluidity seeped into sculpture over a decade. An inspiration to Renaissance artists in Western Europe, the 460 BC **bronze of Poseidon** poised to throw his trident seems to move. The bronze **Jockey of Atemision,** recovered from the sea and restored this century, is full of life. The luscious neck, lips, and expression of the bust of **Antinous,** a favorite of the emperor Hadrian, will move you, while the suggestive pose of the sleeping *maenad* may arouse something other than your artistic interest. Exquisite wall paintings and other finds come from **Anotiri Thira,** a civilization from the 16th century BC that was buried by volcanic eruption. Resembling both Egyptian and Minoan art, these images of dolphins, reeds, and a boy holding a fish highlight early fresco work. Don't miss the glittering **Stathos Collection,** a family's recent donation.

ATHENS

OTHER MUSEUMS

GOULANDRIS MUSEUM OF CYCLADIC & ANCIENT GREEK ART. This 18-year-old museum, established by the philanthropic Goulandris shipping family, displays a stunning collection that offers a window into the Mediterranean's past. The high-density exhibition space shows off its famous Cycladic figurines: sleek, abstract marble works. Some have painted details that may represent tattoos. Many pieces were either looted from archaeological sites about 100 years ago or found in graves in the Cyclades. The figurines may represent goddesses, concubines, or *psychopompoi* (guides to the Underworld). Bronze jewelry from Skyros, a collection of vases, and Corinthian helmets share the space. Visit the extension of the museum on the corner of Vas. Sofias and Herodotou. *(Neophytou Douka 4. Walk 20min. toward Kolonaki from Syndagma on Vas. Sofias; turn left on Neophytou Douka. It's half a block up. Accessible by trolleys #3 and 13. ☎210 722 8321. Open M, W-F 10am-4pm, Su 10am-3pm. €3.50, students €1.80, archaeologists and archaeology students free with university pass.)*

BENAKI MUSEUM. This museum represents Antoine Benaki's collection, amassed during his European and Asian travels, boasting an impressive assortment of art and archaeological artifacts from around the world. Floors ascend according to chronology and begin with prehistory to the late Roman Period on the ground floor where one finds a mesmerizing and strangely emotional male funeral portrait from Egypt dating back to 325 (Gallery 4). On the first level, check out the Greek costumes and follow the development of Greek culture through the ages; the reconstructed reception rooms, taken from Byzantine Period mansions in northern Greece, are particularly interesting. The third floor, which covers the War of Independence to the formation of the modern Greek state, houses wonderful black and white portraits of poets Palamas, Seferis, Kavafis, Elytis, Sikelianos, and Ritsos as well as multiple key letters penned by Eleftherios Venizelos himself. This museum also happens to have an excellent museum restaurant. *(Vas. Sofias and 1 Koumbari in Kolonaki. ☎210 367 1000. Open M, W, F-Sa 9am-5pm; Th 9am-midnight; Su 9am-3pm. €6, students with ISIC or university ID free.)*

BYZANTINE MUSEUM. Entered from Vas. Sofias through a beautiful mosaic-floored archway, the Byzantine Museum has an excellent collection of Christian art spanning the 4th through 19th centuries. Early Byzantine sculptures, icons from the entire period, and three reconstructed early Christian basilicas squeeze into the space. Room 4 (back left corner of the ground floor) has a ceiling cut in the shape of a cross and a mosaic-studded floor. It centers around an *omphalon* representing an eagle and a snake. Also on the ground floor, you'll find an ornately reconstructed 17th-century Kephalonian church with the 1863 throne of the Patriarch of Constantinople. *(Vas. Sofias 22. ☎210 721 1027 or 210 723 2178. Open Tu-Su 8:30am-3pm. €4; students and seniors €2; EU students, under 18, and classicists free.*

NATIONAL GALLERY. The National Gallery (a.k.a. Alexander Soutzos Museum) exhibits the work of Greek artists, with periodic international displays. The permanent collection from the 18th to 20th centuries includes outstanding works by El Greco, which can be found on the first floor, as well as drawings, photographs, and sculpture gardens. El Greco's large, oil-on-canvas *Concert of the Angels*, on the first wall to your left as you walk in, is a collection highlight. The second floor holds post-war oils and watercolors and a variety of Modern Greek sculpture. Call for information on exhibits. *(Vas. Konstantinou 50, where Vas. Konstantinou meets Vas. Sofias, by the Hilton. ☎210 723 5857 or 723 5937. Open M, W-Sa 9am-3pm, Su 10am-2pm; temporary exhibit also open M, W 6-9pm. €6, students and seniors €3, under 12 free.)*

WAR MUSEUM. Canons and fighter jets mark the museum, which traces Greek armaments from Neolithic times to the present. Best if you're into sub-machine guns, 5th-century BC Persian invasions, or Alexander the Great—or if you harbor a wide streak of Greek patriotism. *(Rizari 2, next to the Byzantine Museum, slightly off Vas. Sofias. ☎210 729 0543. Open Tu-Su 9am-2pm. Free.)*

FOLK ART MUSEUM. Exhibiting *laiki techni* (popular art) from all over Greece, the museum has embroidered textiles, costumes, and household pottery. It is a documentation of modern Greek culture, unfortunately not frequently emphasized in Hellenic studies. The temporary exhibits are its highlights. Paintings of Theophilos Chatzimichael (p. 26) are also found here. *(Kydatheneon 17, in Plaka. ☎210 321 3018. Open Tu-Su 10am-2pm. €2, students €1, EU students and children free.)*

POPULAR MUSICAL INSTRUMENTS MUSEUM. This smart little interactive museum gives you a necessary dose of modern Greek culture, without being at all overwhelming. Cases display antique 18th-, 19th-, and 20th-century instruments that were once functional. You can hear frenetic *kementzes* (bottle-shaped lyres) or *tsambouras* (goatskin bagpipes) music from the islands. *(Diogenous 1-2, in Plaka. Going uphill on Pelopida, it's the green door on your left directly after you pass the Roman Agora on your right. ☎210 325 0198. Open Tu, Th-Su 10am-2pm, W noon-6pm. Free.)*

ILIAS LALAOUNIS JEWELRY MUSEUM. Ilias Lalaounis was a jeweller and goldsmith elected to the Academie des Beaux-Artes. His jewel-studded art is displayed here in his former home. Over 3000 designs from a 50-year period gleam in cases and other displays trace Greek jewelry from ancient to modern times. *(Kallisperi 12, south of the Acropolis. ☎210 922 1044. Open M, Th-Su 9am-4pm, W 9am-9pm. €3, students and seniors €2.30.)*

JEWISH MUSEUM. Occupying a brand-new building, this museum charts 2300 years of Jewish life in Greece. The collection includes textiles, religious artifacts, and a thorough library. A reconstructed synagogue and an exhibit on the Holocaust are on the higher floors. The latter is a poignant reminder of the more than one million Greek Jews who were exterminated under German occupation. The Jewish community that remains today is resultantly tiny: there are only about 4500

START: Where Streit meets Tatoiou

FINISH: Varsos

DISTANCE: About 2.5km

WHEN TO GO: Late morning

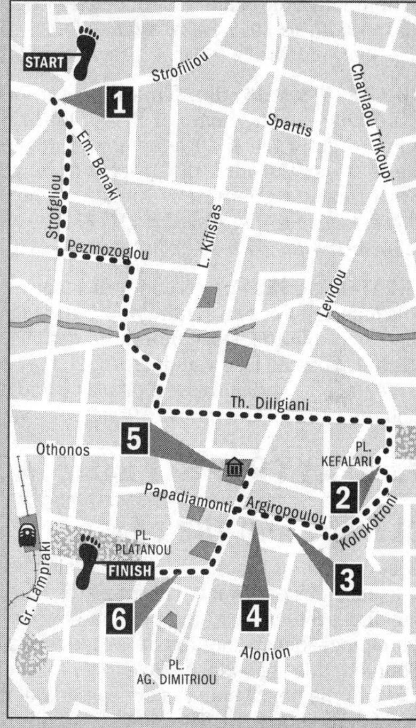

1 VILLAS. A good deal of the enchanting **villas,** which were designed by architect Ernz Ziller at the turn of the century to comfort only the wealthiest of Athenian families, are north of Kifisia's town center. Beginning with a gorgeous 100-year-old mansion at the intersection of Streit and Tatoiou, these villas are located along Strofiliou, Pezmozoglou, and Em. Benaki. They also populate offshooting streets. Specific villa addresses include Strofili 25 and Em. Benaki 8. The opening of the Athens-Kifisia railway in 1885, with a 12-coach engine widely referred to as "the Beast," allowed for easier access (meaning a 40min. trip) to the northern suburb and for aristocrats to flood the temperate hills. Look carefully past fences to see the many lofty turrets.

2 PLATEIA KEFALARI. Here you will see mostly Greek youth indulging in the company of their chic-est friends and in cuisine and refreshments, which guarantee the heaviest bills on the Attican Peninsula. Still, you will pass two majestic edifices, which are not to be missed. The first, the **Church of the Metamorphosis Sotirios,** is on the side of Kefalari's park, in front of a pond. The second is the sprawling, palm-shrouded headquarters of **Latsis Bank,** owned by the famous Greek billionaire family that shares its name. Spiro Latsis currently runs the banking and shipping empire started by his father, John, who resides in Switzerland. The beautiful structure is a bit off the plateia, down the footpath that the church is also on, and across from the confusingly upscale Pizza Hut.

3 GOULANDRIS NATURAL HISTORY MUSEUM. African lions and every kind of bird that exists in Greece stare at you silently on the first floor. Downstairs, you see a full spectrum of the many varieties of marble in Greece. (p. 121)

4 ARISTOKRATIKON. Homemade caramel pistachios (€4 per 125g), strawberry marzipan (€25 per kg), rose turkish delight (€12 per kg), and chocolate pistachio fudge (€28 per kg) line the windows and shelves of this traditional 1928 confisserie. (Argyropoulo 8. ☎210 801 6533). Open M-F 9am-9pm, Sa 9am-4pm.)

5 BOWLING CENTER. A very popular nighttime hangout, local Athenian (often blue-blooded) youth retreat into the air-conditioning in the afternoon for a few cold beers (Amstel €2) while bowling or playing billiards. (p. 121)

6 VARSOS. This is the most famous old gem (created in 1892) of Kifisia. Locals give directions around the town in relation to "Varsos, you know where that is?" Sit outside on bustling but charming Kassavetes with a coffee (€1.80) and any kind of sweet you can imagine. (p. 121) people left from what was once an amazingly rich and worthy tradition in the diaspora. *(Nikis 39, in Plaka. ☎/fax 210 323 1577. Open M-F 9am-2:30pm, Su 10am-2pm. Library open Tu, Th 11am-1pm. €3, students €1.50.)*

CHILDREN'S MUSEUM. This museum offers a colorful, friendly, hands-on experience in the heart of Plaka, faithfully subscribing to the motto, "I hear and I forget; I see and I remember; I do and I understand." Learn about the subway system, the euro, the process of recycling, the combination of primary colors to create secondary ones, or play dress-up in yesterday's bedroom. *(Kydatheneon 14, in Plaka. ☎210 331 2995 or 331 2996. Open Sept.-June M, Th-F 9:30am-1:30pm, W 9:30am-6:30pm, Sa-Su 10am-2pm. Closed July-Aug. Free.)*

THEATER MUSEUM. Mecca for thespians who want to learn about Greek theater, this museum does an admirable job tracing the history of Greek performance with display of photos, stage dioramas, and masks from modern stagings of Classical theater. You can also wander through the reconstructed dressing rooms of famous Greek actors and actresses. *(Akadamias 50, 2 blocks away from the Panepistimiou Metro stop. ☎210 362 9430. Open M-F 9am-2pm; July-Aug. 9am-1pm. Free.)*

DAYTRIPS FROM ATHENS

GLYFADA AND THE COAST ☎210

Join the chic of the Athens summer club scene as they migrate to the big, swanky, seaside clubs of **Glyfada.** The craziness of an Athenian summer starts here, stretching along the coast to the popular—often stunningly pretty but always loud and thumping—beach suburbs of **Vouliagmeni** and **Varkiza.** Located between Faliro and Sounion, this strip is the place to go for a daytime swim and nighttime romp. The clubs in the beach suburbs are spread out along the water, on Poseidonos, each a few kilometers apart. The views from the clubs located along the beach are worth the trip out, even if you're just in Athens for a night or two. **Venue** (☎210 985 2993) in Varkiz; **Island** (☎210 965 3563), on Limanakia Vouliagmeni, in Vouliagmeni; **Balux,** Vas. Georgiou B58 (☎210 894 1620), in Glyfada; and **Privilege** (☎210 985 2995) on Agios Kosmas beach, in Elliniko, are perfect places to enjoy the breezy night air and party to dance music among fashionable Athenians. Also look for **Prime, Envy** and **Plus Soda.** Along Pergamon, look for **Camel Club.** Top 40, funk, and house play until around 2am, when Greek music (often live) takes over. Dance, drink, and eye the beautiful crowd against the backdrop of the ocean, only a few feet away. Hordes of serious-looking bouncers with earpieces guard the doorways to swanky outdoor bars with white furniture. You've got to dress well to get in; no shorts. Cover is usually €10-15. Drinks vary €4-10 but can go as high as €100 for an individual bottle of vodka, complete with mixers, for your table. Take the **A2, A3,** or **B3** bus from Vas. Amalias (along the street to the right of the top corner of Pl. Syndagma, €0.75) to Glyfada, and then catch a cab from there to your club. A **taxi** to Glyfada should cost about €8, but the ride back into the center of Athens in the early morning—due to traffic and nighttime rates—can run €10-15. Beware of greedy taxi drivers; if they pack the cab with more than just your party, don't let them swindle you into a set price per individual. Remember what the total should roughly be and don't pay much more than that. Starting in May 2004, the **tram,** beginning at its Athens Centre stop, will also drop you off in Glyfada by the beach. At any hour, **taxis** can be called (☎210 960 5600 in Glyfada; 210 894 7823 in Varkiza). **Mastro Internet Cafe,** Metaxa 39, on the second floor, charges €3 per 30min. and €0.50 per page of printing. (☎210 894 5426; www.mastronet.gr. Open daily 9:30am-10:30pm.)

During the day, life is spread along **Lazaraki** and **Metaxa,** both U-shaped avenues inland from and parallel to the nighttime strip which runs down the coast. Off Lazaraki, **Hotel Ilion ❸**, Kondili 4, is a slightly aged hotel that offers rooms with private baths. (☎210 894 6011. Singles €35; doubles €45.) **Hotel Avra ❹**, G. Lambraki 5, between Metaxa and the waterfront has A/C, fridges, TVs, free luggage storage, common DVD player, and family discounts. (☎210 894 7185 or 210 898 2264; www.avrahotel.com. Singles from €45; doubles from €70. AmEx/MC/V.) **Garden of Eden ❸**, Zerva 12, is a block from Hotel Ilion away from the center. *Makdous* (baby eggplants, stuffed with walnuts and spices; €3.50) and *kas-kas* (meatballs in spicy tomato sauce; €8) comprise the praised Lebanese fare. (Open daily 8:30pm-midnight. DC/MC/V.) Restaurants fill Konstantinopoleos, including **San Marzano ❷**, Konstantinopoleos 13, serving Italian classics. (☎210 968 1124. Margherita pizza €5.95. Penne arabiate €7.20. Open daily noon-1am. AmEx/MC/V.) Nextdoor is **Sushi Bar ❸**, Konstantinopoleos 15. (☎210 894 2200. Salmon, avocado, cucumber rolls €6.46. Open daily 1pm-12:30am. MC/V.)

ATHENS

CAPE SOUNION PENINSULA Ακρωτηριο Σουνιο ☎22920

Orange-striped KTEL buses travel to Cape Sounion from Athens: 1 leaves from the Mavromateon 14 bus stop near Areos Park and stops at all points on the Apollo Coast (2hr.; every hr., 6:30am-6:30pm; €4.30); the other follows a less scenic inland route that also stops at the port of Lavrio (2¼hr.; every hr., 6am-6pm; €3.90). Get off the bus at the last stop and head up to the right (facing the water), past the cafeteria to a ticket booth. The last coastal route bus leaves Sounion at 9pm, the last inland 9:30pm.

One of the most breathtaking sights in all of Greece is the brilliant evening sun sinking below the **Temple of Poseidon** on Cape Sounion. Bask in front of the giant red orb and the shimmering Aegean in every direction below the 60m rocky promontory. Gracing the highest point on the Cape, the Temple of Posiedon has been a dazzling white landmark for sailors at sea for millennia. Originally constructed around 600 BC, the fortress of Sounion was destroyed by the Persians in 480 BC and rebuilt by Pericles in 440 BC. The 16 remaining Doric columns rise above the coast. Look closely at the graffiti for Lord Byron's name (on the square column as you face away from the cafeteria). Bits of the **Temple of Athena Sounias** litter the lower hill as you ascend to the main temple. (☎22920 39 363. Open daily 10am-sunset except on Christmas, Easter Sunday, and May 1. €4, students and those over 65 €2, EU students and children under 18 free.) After an hour at the temple during the day, many people head down to the **beaches.** To reach the ocean, follow the main road from the inland side of the temple. Swarming with vacationing families, the beaches along the Apollo Coast between Piraeus and Cape Sounion have a carnival atmosphere on summer weekends. Towns often have free public beaches, and some seaside stretches along the bus route remain uncrowded. Drivers will let you off almost anywhere if you ask. If you get stuck, family-run **Hotel Saron ❸** (☎22920 39 144; fax 39 045), 4.5km along the inland road toward Lavrio (ask the bus driver to stop in Assimaki), offers rooms with A/C, private bath, TV and telephone. (Doubles €55. MC/V.) **Camping Bacchus ❶** (☎22920 39 572 or 39 571) is 50m farther toward Lavrio from Saron. Ask to stay closer to the road, near the entrance to avoid the family caravans (€6, €3.30 per small child). Cafe-restaurant **Nao ❶**, to the left as you are walking uphill from the bus stop, offers ham and cheese (€3) and salami sandwiches (€2.65) for a bite. (Open daily 11am-9:30pm.) If you don't want to sit down, pick up snacks and a cold soda at the **roadside stand** 50m before the bus stop.

MARATHON Μαραθωνας ☎22940

The bus from the Mavromateon 29 station in Athens heads to Marathon (1½hr.; every hr., 5:30am-10:30pm; €2.50). Look for the bus's "Marathon" label, sit in front and remind the driver of your destination, and flag the bus down on the way back. Private transportation (local taxi: ☎22940 66 277, 69443 52 943, or 69447 20 215) is the best way to see the sites since they are spread out.

Gasping out two words—*Nike Imin* (Νικη Ημιν), "Victory to us"—**Phidippides** announced the decisive Athenian victory over the Persians in the bloody 490 BC battle of Marathon; he collapsed and died immediately afterward. His 42km sprint to Athens remains legendary and now runners trace his Marathon route twice annually. Today this isn't much more than the site of a small plateia whose satellite businesses cling to the coastline. Most importantly, the town is just south of **Marathonas Olympic Complex,** which will be the venue of two of the 28 sports during the 2004 Olympic Games (p. 128). You can explore nearby sights and beaches by car. At **Ramnous,** 15km northeast, lie the ruins of the **Temple of Nemesis,** goddess of divine retribution, and **Thetis,** goddess of law and justice. **Schinias** to the north and **Timvos Marathonas** to the south are popular **beaches.** To reach the **Archaeological Museum of Marathonas,** it's best to call a taxi, but if you are up for a walk, ask the bus driver to drop you at the "Mouseion and Marathonas" sign, after Marathon Town and the beach. Follow the signs through 2km of farms, bearing right at the fork, to the end of the paved Plateion road at #114. The small museum's five packed rooms focus on **death rituals:** you'll find Neolithic grave pieces (4000-2500 BC), geometric sepulchres (2500 BC), Cycladic funeral offerings, Athenian and Plateian tombs and remains from the battle of Marathon, and a first-century BC baby skeleton surrounded by two beehives. An **Athenian trophy** commemorates the battle with the Persians. Marble heads of Marathon's arts patron Herodes Atticus and his star pupil Polydenkion are on display, as are some Egyptian statues probably from a temple of Isis. Cemeteries from the Neolithic and Classical periods lie 2km from the museum; the oldest site dates from around 2500 BC. Ask for more information at the museum desk. (☎22940 55 155. Open Tu-Su 8:30am-3pm. €3; students €2; EU students, children under 18, student classicists, and archaeologists free.)

Marathon Hotel ❸, Agiou Pantalimonos 25 (☎22940 55 222; fax 22940 55 122), 50m before the plateia on the road coming from Athens, has rooms with private baths. (Breakfast included, served 8am-9:30am. Singles €35; doubles €42; triples €52. From Aug. 13 2004, prices will inflate to €60 per person.) A **supermarket** is half a block inland from the plateia on Dinosthenous. (Open daily 9am-3pm and 5-10pm.) A few buildings to the right of the plateia is beachside taverna **O Vrahos ❸,** Chrisis Aktis 14. (☎22940 55 297. Shrimp spaghetti €55 per kg. *Horta* €5. Open daily noon-1am.) **Avlaia ❷,** Poseidonos 7, on the beach, is a few doors down to the left of the plateia. (☎22940 56 300. Spicy cheese dip €3.50. Beets €3. Fried fish €7.30.)

KIFISIA Κηφισια ☎210

The shaded streets of this cultured suburb feel a good distance more than 12km north of Athens. Perhaps it is the cool breeze that shakes the willowing trees and runs through the Attic pines that has drawn uppercrust Athenians to its pleasing shelter since Roman times. In the last century, Kifisia's modern sidewalks have been tread upon daily by a citizenry composed mostly of the richest and most famous Greece has to boast. Today the neighborhood offers among the country's best—if not *the* best—cuisine and shopping. So close to Marousi's Olympic venues, Kifisia serves as a refuge between athletic events.

TRANSPORTATION AND PRACTICAL INFORMATION

Kifisia is best reached by rail but is also accessible by bus. Take **M1**, the **green line** (Piraeus/Kifisia), all the way to the last, northernmost stop (20min., daily 5am-12:30am, €0.70). You can also take either the **A7** or **B7 buses** (30min., €0.45) from Akademias and Themistokleous in Omonia, which will drop you in front of the National Bank on Kifisias. **Taxis** (☎210 623 3100 or 210 808 4000) are available 24hr.

ATHENS

The **National Bank,** Kifisias 178 (☎210 627 6350), **exchanges currency** and **traveler's checks.** (Take a number and wait in line. Open M-Th 8am-2:30pm, F 8am-2pm.) **Citibank,** Levidou 16, also has 24hr. **ATM. Eleftheroudakis Bookstore** is at Kifisias 268. (Open M-F 9am-9pm, Sa 9am-5pm. AmEx/DC/MC/V.) The **tourist police,** Othonos 94 (☎210 623 4450 or 210 623 4460; open 8am-1:30pm), can be reached 24hr. at ☎171. Dial ☎166 for an **ambulance.** There is a town **OTE,** Papadiamanti 8 (☎210 623 2899; open M-F 7:40am-2pm). The **post office,** Levidou 3a, set in a mini-square off the sidewalk, holds **Poste Restante** packages. (☎210 801 7665. Open M-F 7:30am-2pm.) **Postal code:** 14503.

ACCOMMODATIONS AND FOOD

There is no dearth of upper-echelon hotels with upper-echelon prices in Kifisia. The most reasonable place, **Hotel des Roses ❺,** Militiadou 4, just off of Kyriazi, is centrally located. Comfortable rooms have A/C, TVs, fridges, private baths, and views overlooking the hills. (☎210 801 9952 or 801 8025; fax 210 801 8074. Singles €82; doubles €98.) **AB supermarket,** on the corner of Levidou and Kassaveti, has an extensive selection. (☎210 808 2812. Open M-F 8am-9pm, Sa 8am-6pm. AmEx/DC/MC/V.) **Dos Hermanos ❸,** Kyriazi 24, offers excellent Mexican fare. (☎210 808 7906 or 210 801 7337. Mexican omelette €9.50. Chili *con carne* €13.50. Tostada with black beans €13. Open Tu-Su 7pm-1am; in winter opens for lunch Su 1pm. DC/MC/V.) **Pappa's Restaurant ❷,** Kifisias 222 and Drosini 3, serves spaghetti Neapolitana (€4.80), chicken with mustard sauce (€8.80), and a variety of pizzas (€5-8) in a huge, air-conditioned expanse. (☎210 801 8463. Open daily noon-1am. AmEx/MC/V.) Famous in Kifisia, **Varsos ❶,** Kassaveti 5, is right in the center of the shopping area. This Greek patisserie serves apricot-custard tarts (€2.20), rice pudding (€1.30), brioches (€1), and other tantalizing sweets. (☎210 801 2472. Open M-F 7am-1am, Sa 7am-2am, Su 7am-midnight.) **Far East ❸,** Deligianni 54, offers Cantonese beef fillet (€17.50), chicken with ginger and red peppers (€12.50), and rice chocolate cake (€7.50) in a tranquil garden. (☎210 623 3140; fax 210 801 3636. Open daily 8pm-1am. MC/V.)

SIGHTS AND ENTERTAINMENT

The **Goulandris Museum of Natural History,** Levidou 13, has on its first floor taxidermied birds of Greece and an impressive array of taxidermied mammals. There are also informative overviews of insect, reptile, mollusk, and plant biology—with physical samples of different species for each. On its lower floor, opening out onto a beautiful garden, is a room dedicated to geology with a collection of sample minerals from across the planet as well as a few Jurassic bones and fossils. (☎210 801 5870 or 210 808 6405; fax 210 808 0674. Open M-Th, Sa-Su 9am-2:30pm. Closed Aug. 1-18. €3, students and children 5-18 €1.20, children under 5 free.)

Cine Boubouniera, on the corner of Papadiamanti and Levidou, shows American and English movies in an outdoor garden during the summer. (Ticket office open daily 8:50-11pm. €7.) The **Bowling Center,** Kolokotroni 1, is a popular nighttime destinaton for Athenian youth. (☎210 808 4662. Open daily 10am-2am. Game of bowling or 30min. billiards: Weekdays €3, students €2; weeknights €4; Sa day €4, Sa night €5.30; Su €5.30. Beer €2; cocktails €4-6.) **Plateia Kefalari** comes to life at night when outdoor bars, like **Windows Kefalari,** fill up with chic Athenians. (Open daily 9:30am-1:30am. *Cuba Libre* cocktail with white rum, lime juice, coke, lemon, and sugar €7.50.) **Big Deals,** 50 H. Trikoupi, is a cool restaurant/bar with a 70s flair. (☎210 623 0866. Cocktails €8-9. Open daily 8:30pm-3:30am, later on weekends).

PIRAEUS Πειραιας ☎210

The natural harbor of Piraeus (also transliterated as Pireas or Peiraias) has been Athens's port since 493 BC, when Themistokles concocted a plan to create a naval base for the growing Athenian fleet. A hilly peninsula studded with big apartment buildings, Piraeus has all the dirt and grime of a commercial hub, including a waterfront lined with junk shops, shipping offices, travel agencies, and banks, bordered by grimy neighborhoods. Despite the run-down appearance, Piraeus remains one of the busiest ports in the world and has some of the best restaurants (mainly of the seafood sort) and prettiest outdoor dining in Attica.

TRANSPORTATION

Buses: The **#96** bus shuttles to and from the airport (every 30min., €3). Pick it up across from Philippis Tours on Akti Tzelepi. The **#40** goes between Syndagma and Piraeus (every 15min., 5am-12:45am; €0.45).

Subway: To get to Piraeus, take the **M1** (green) line **Kifisia/Piraeus** from Athens to the last stop **Piraeus** (20min., €0.70). The subway station is the big building adjacent to a busy square on Akti Poseidonos (300m from Akti Tzelepi).

Trains: To get to Northern Greece from Piraeus, take the subway to Omonia, where you transfer trains (on the same ticket) for Larisis Station. Trains bound for the Peloponnese zip from the Peloponnese Station over the ramp beyond Larisis Station.

Ferries: The majority of ferries circling Greece run from Piraeus. Unfortunately the ferry schedule changes on a daily basis; the following listings are only approximate. **Be flexible** with your plans, since ferries are notoriously fickle. Check *Athens News* and the back of the *Kathimerini* English edition or stop by a travel agency for updated schedules before you go. Ferries sail directly to nearly all Greek islands except for the Sporades and Ionians. **Aegina** (1hr., nearly every hr., €5); **Amorgos** (10hr., 6 per week, €17.20); **Anafi** (10hr., 3-4 per week, €22.80); **Astypalea** (12hr., 4 per week, €23.20); **Chios** (9hr., daily, €19.50); **Donousa** (8½hr., 3-4 per week, €16.50); **Folegandros** (11hr., 4 per week, €17); **Hania,** Crete (9½hr., 2 per day, €22.70); **Hydra** (3hr., nearly every hr., €8.10); **Ikaria** (8hr., 1-2 per day, €18.60); **Ios** (7½hr., 2-5 per day, €18); **Iraklia** (8hr., 3-4 per week, €16); **Iraklion,** Crete (8hr., 2-3 per day, €25.50); **Kalymnos** (12½hr., 1-2 per day, €24); **Kastelorizo** (30hr., 1-2 per week, €37.20); **Kimolos** (daily, €15.30); **Kos** (13½hr., 1-2 per day, €25.80); **Koufonisia** (8hr., 3-4 per week, €15.60); **Lemnos** (16hr., 1-2 per week, €24); **Leros** (9hr., daily, €21.90); **Lesvos** (12hr., daily, €24.20); **Milos** (7hr., 1-2 per day, €16.90); **Mykonos** (6hr., 2-5 per day, €17.50); **Naxos** (7hr., 2-5 per day, €17.30); **Paros** (6hr., 2-5 per day, €17.30); **Patmos** (8hr., daily, €21.10); **Poros** (2½hr., nearly every hr., €7.20); **Rethymno,** Crete (11hr., daily, €30.70); **Rhodes** (16hr., 2-5 per day, €30.70); **Samos** (10hr., 5 per week, €22.80); **Santorini** (9hr., 2-5 per day, €20.20); **Schinousa** (8hr. 3-4 per week, €16.50); **Serifos** (4½hr., 1-2 per day, €13.20); **Sifnos** (5¼hr., 1-2 per day, €14.80); **Sikinos** (12hr., 4 per week, €19.90); **Spetses** (4½hr., nearly every hr., €11.20); **Syros** (4hr., 2-5 per day, €15); **Tinos** (5hr., 2-5 per day, €16.10). International ferries (2 per day and around €30 one-way) head to destinations in **Turkey.** Get to: **Kousadassi** via Samos, **Izmir** via Chios, **Marmaris** via Rhodes (see p. 626 for more information).

Flying Dolphins: Run at twice the speed and twice the cost. Every other hour to: **Aegina, Hydra, Poros, Spetses.** 2 per day to: **Mykonos, Naxos, Paros, Syros,** and **Tinos.** Daily to: **Ikaria, Kythnos, Milos, Samos, Santorini, Serifos,** and **Sifnos.**

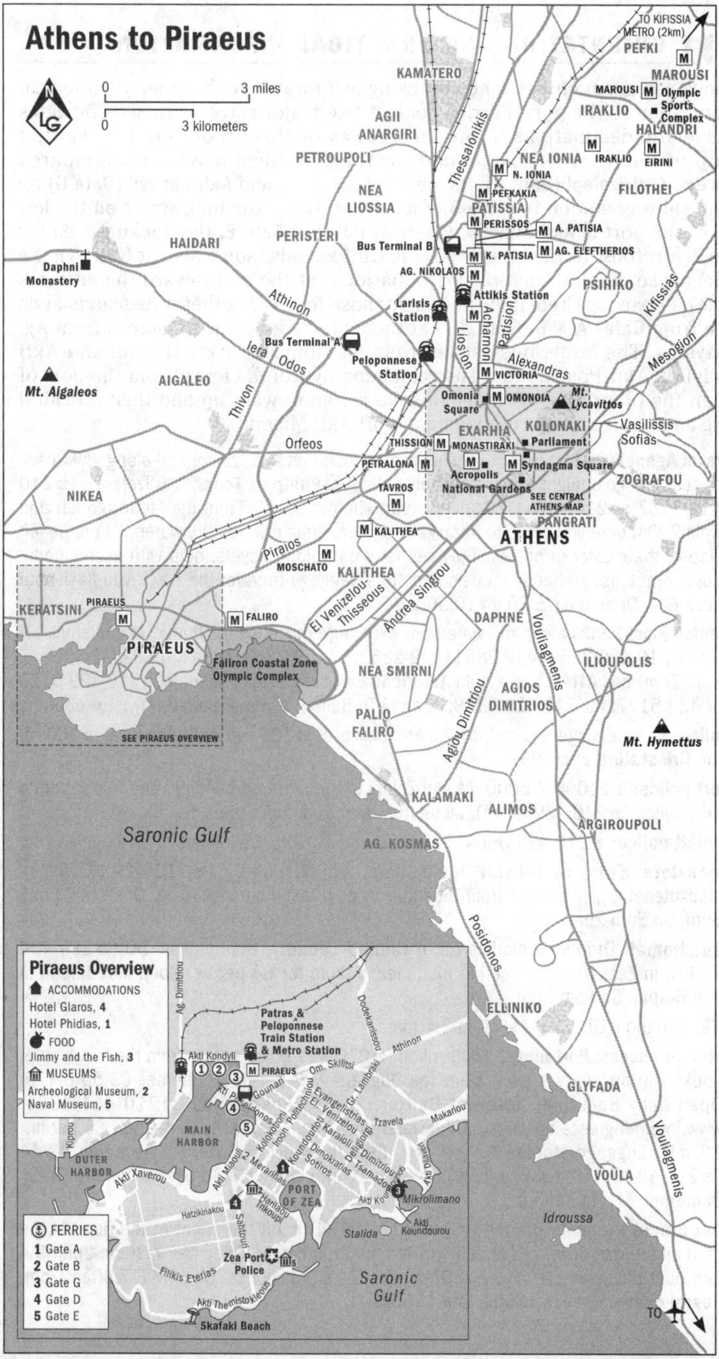

Athens to Piraeus

0 3 miles
0 3 kilometers

TO KIFISSIA METRO (2km)
PEFKI
MAROUSI
MAROUSI
Olympic Sports Complex
KAMATERO
IRAKLIO
HALANDRI
AGII ANARGIRI
IRAKLIO
EIRINI
PETROUPOLI
Thessalonikis
NEA IONIA
N. IONIA
NEA LIOSSIA
PEFKAKIA
FILOTHEI
PATISSIA
PERISSOS
A. PATISIA
HAIDARI
PERISTERI
Bus Terminal B
AG. ELEFTHERIOS
K. PATISIA
Daphni Monastery
AG. NIKOLAOS
PSIHIKO
Attikis Station
Kifissias
Athinon
Larisis Station
Acharnon
Patision
Liosion
Mesogion
Bus Terminal A
Iera Odos
Alexandras
Peloponnese Station
VICTORIA
Mt. Aigaleos
AIGALEO
Omonia Square
OMONOIA
Mt. Lycavittos
Thivon
EXARHIA
KOLONAKI
Vasilissis Sofias
Orfeos
THISSION
MONASTIRAKI
Parliament
PETRALONA
Syndagma Square
Acropolis
National Gardens
ZOGRAFOU
NIKEA
TAVROS
SEE CENTRAL ATHENS MAP
PANGRATI
KALITHEA
ATHENS
Piraios
MOSCHATO
KALITHEA
El Venizelou-Thisseous
Andrea Singrou
KERATSINI
PIRAEUS
FALIRO
DAPHNE
Vouliagmenis
PIRAEUS
Faliron Coastal Zone Olympic Complex
ILIOUPOLIS
NEA SMIRNI
AGIOS DIMITRIOS
PALIO FALIRO
Agiou Dimitriou
SEE PIRAEUS OVERVIEW
Mt. Hymettus
KALAMAKI
ALIMOS
ARGIROUPOLI
Saronic Gulf
AG. KOSMAS
Posidonos
ELLINIKO
GLYFADA
VOULA
Vouliagmenis
Idroussa
TO (airport)

Piraeus Overview

ACCOMMODATIONS
Hotel Glaros, **4**
Hotel Phidias, **1**

FOOD
Jimmy and the Fish, **3**

MUSEUMS
Archeological Museum, **2**
Naval Museum, **5**

FERRIES
1 Gate A
2 Gate B
3 Gate G
4 Gate D
5 Gate E

Ag. Dimitriou
Dodekanissou
Patras & Peloponnese Train Station & Metro Station
Athinon
Akti Kondyli
PIRAEUS
Om. Skilitsi
Gr. Lambraki
Gounari
Akti Poseidonos
Evangelistrias
El. Venizelou
Tzavela
Makariou
Iroon Politechniou
Kolokotroni
Koundourou
Karaoli
Deligiorgi
Dimitriou
MAIN HARBOR
Kiprou
OUTER HARBOR
2 Merarhias
Sotiros
Dimokratias
Tsamadou
Akti Dilaveri
Akti Xaverou
Akti Miaouli
Hanidou
Trikoupi
PORT OF ZEA
Akti Koumoundourou
Mikrolimano
Hatzikiriakou
Santouri
Akti Koundourou
Stalida
Zea Port Police
Filikis Eterias
Saronic Gulf
Akti Themistokleous
Skafaki Beach

ATHENS

ORIENTATION AND PRACTICAL INFORMATION

Piraeus can seem chaotic and confusing at first glance, but there is a logical organization to the port. Ferries dock at five major gates, with specific gates for specific destinations. From the subway or the airport shuttle, the first group of ferries are those bound for the Cyclades, leaving from an area between **Akti Tzelepi (Gate D)**, the heart of the port, and **Akti Kondyli (Gate G)** up to the subway station by **Gate B.** Facing the water, the long street on the left side of the port is **Akti Miaouli,** where you'll find **Gate E,** the docking area for some hydrofoils, ferries to the Saronic Gulf Islands (some also at Gate G), the Dodecanese, and international destinations (at the end toward the customs house). Ferries to Crete dock at **Gate A;** those for the Northeast Aegean Islands leave from **Gates A & B.** Gate A is at the end of Akti Kondyli, across from Ag. Dionysios. The large, busy street running alongside Akti Miaouli and Akti Kondyli is Akti Poseidonos. The remaining hydrofoils leave from the port of **Zea** on the other side of the peninsula, a 10min. walk up and then downhill along any of the streets running inland off Akti Miaouli.

Travel Agencies: Most ticket agencies can be found on Akti Tzelepi and along Akti Poseidonos. Just go straight to the extremely helpful **Philippis Tours,** Akti Tzelepi 3 (☎210 411 7787 or 210 413 3182; filippistours@hotmail.com). From the Metro, go left and walk 200m until you come to Karaskaiki square. Walk towards the water; it's on the left side of the cluster of offices. They sell ferry and plane tickets, help with accommodations, rent cars, exchange money, and store baggage (free for the day if you flash your *Let's Go*). Open daily 5:30am-10:30pm.

Banks: Most **banks** along the waterfront **exchange currency. Citibank,** Akti Miaouli 47-49 (☎210 429 2850, 429 2851, 429 2852, or 429 2853; open M-Th 8am-2:30pm, F 8am-2pm) has **ATMs.** There is an **American Express,** 51 Akti Miaouli (☎210 429 5120 or 429 5127; fax 210 429 5128; open M-Th 8am-2:30pm, F 8am-2pm), next door.

Police: In an emergency, call the Athens police at ☎133, an **ambulance** at ☎166, or the **fire station** at ☎199.

Port police: ☎210 422 6000. At Akti Zelopi in the mirrored building. **Zea** has separate port police (☎210 459 3144), along the water and under the sidewalk.

Tourist police: ☎210 429 0664.

Bookstore: Swing by **Tel-star Booksellers,** Akti Miaouli 57 (☎210 429 3618; telstar@otenet.gr), just down from Citibank, to grab last-minute reading. Open M-F 8am-8pm, Sa 8am-2pm.

Laundromat: Drop your clothes off at **Hionati Laundry,** Bouboulinas 50 (☎210 429 7356), in Zea, where a nice old man cleans them for €4 per kg. Open M-F 8am-2pm and 5-9pm, Sa 8am-3pm.

OTE: Dimitriou 19. Open M-F 7am-2:40pm.

Internet access: Portonet, 2 Loudovikou (☎210 411 058), across from the Metro stop, hooks you up and will even store your luggage (€2 per day). Internet €3.50 per hr. Open daily 8am-8pm. **Internet Center,** 24 Akti Poseidonos (☎210 411 1261; www.internet-greece.com), is on the waterfront drag. Open daily 9am-9pm. €4 per hr., €2 min. Luggage storage €2 per day. **Surf In Internet Cafe,** Polytexneiou 42-44 (☎210 42 27 478; www.surfin.gr), is inland a few blocks. €3.60 per hr. Open Tu, Th-Su 9am-9pm; M, W 9am-5pm.

Post office: The **main branch** (☎210 417 15184) is off the street at the bend in the road all the way down Akti Miaouli toward the expo center. Open M-F 7:30am-2pm. The **Zea** post office (☎210 418 3380) is near Zea's port police. Open M-F 7:30am-2pm. **Postal codes:** Piraeus 18502, Zea 18504.

ACCOMMODATIONS AND FOOD

Inexpensive, quality accommodations are much easier to find in Athens, but **Hotel Glaros ❸**, H. Trikoupi 4, off Akti Miaouli toward the Expo Centre, is an adequate option. (☎210 451 5421; idea@otenet.gr. A/C, TVs, phones, fridges. Singles €36; doubles €50. MC/V.) There's also pleasant and quiet **Hotel Phidias ❹**, Koundouriotou 189, near Zea off Bouboulinas and Akti Miaouli, with spacious rooms, private baths, TVs, and A/C. (☎210 429 6160 or 429 6480; phidiasgr@otenet.gr. Breakfast €7.30. Singles €40; doubles €50; triples €60. MC/V.)

Dockside fast-food joints hawk average food for not too many euros. You can stock up on staples at **supermarkets** around town. There's a little restaurant and cafe area between the buildings near Kolokotroni and Tsamadou. Dine and relax to soft music, a welcome contrast to the jarring madness of the port. At **Jimmy and the Fish ❹**, 46 Akti Koumoundorou, on the water in the Microlimano, the jet-set dine on striped furniture. Try the mussels with tomato sauce and parmesan (€12) or the saffron risotto with porcini mushrooms (€18). Strawberry soup with frozen cream (€7) tops off a light meal. (☎210 412 4417. Open daily 1pm-2am. AmEx/DC/MC/V.) **Varoulko ❺**, Deligiorgi 14, has earned itself a prestigious Michelin Star for its wonderful seafood dishes and excellent service. The dishes are all original and very tasty, but the prices may be the highest in Attica. (☎210 422 1283. Open M-Sa 8pm-1am. Entrees €25 and up. MC/V.) **Belle Epoque ❶** serves an incredible fruit salad (€4) with whipped cream and blackberry sauce and various ice cream dishes with nuts, fruit, and whipped cream. (Open daily 8:30am-1am.)

ATHENS

SIGHTS

The prized possession of the **Piraeus Archaeological Museum,** H. Trikoupi 31, is the second floor's ancient **Piraeus Apollo,** a hulking hollow bronze figure with outstretched arms. A huge grave monument which consists of three statues—the deceased, his father, and his slave—dated to about 330 BC is across the hall as you walk in. Found on the Black Sea coast, it was once painted in full color. Three other bronze statues of Athena and Artemis were found near the port in 1959 and shelved in a storeroom for safekeeping when Sulla besieged Piraeus in 86 BC. The strange spots of color in their eyes are precious stones. (☎210 452 1598. Open Tu-Su 8:30am-3pm. €3, students €2, children 15 and under free.) Farther south at Zea, the ramp to the dock at Akti Themistokleous and Botassi leads to the **Hellenic Maritime Museum,** which traces naval history using detailed ship models. The building itself, if you notice inside the main entrance, includes part of the 5th-century Themistoklean wall, which once protected all three ancient ports on the penninsula—Kantharos, Zea, and Munychia. Of particular note in Room B is a model of an Athenian trireme used in the Persian Wars (490-480 BC). The courtyard holds torpedo tubes, naval weapons, and the top part of a World War II submarine. (☎210 451 6264; fax 210 451 2277. Open Tu-Sa 9am-2pm. €2, children €1.50.)

RAFINA Ραφηνα ☎22940

Rafina seems a smaller, quieter version of Piraeus. It's Attica's secondmost prominent port, though ferry service from Rafina has recently lessened. Compared to its larger counterpart there's less to do, but it's easier on the eyes, ears, and lungs.

TRANSPORTATION AND PRACTICAL INFORMATION. Ferries sail to: **Andros** (2hr., 2 per day, €8.50); **Marmari,** Evia (50min.; 4-6 per day; €7.50, with car €16.50); **Mykonos** (5hr., 2-3 per day, €14.70); **Paros** (€20.40); **Tinos** (4hr., 2-3 per day, €13). **Flying Dolphins** zip daily to: **Mykonos** (1½hr., €29.30); **Paros** (€29.70); **Syros** (€24.70); **Tinos** (€25.90). The **port authority** (☎22940 22 300 or 22940 28 888) supplies info. Along the waterfront, English-speaking **Blue Star Ferries** (☎22940 23 561; fax 22940 23 350); **Rafina Tours** (☎22940 24 660 or 22940 28 518; fax 22940 26 400); and **Hellas Flying Dolphins** (☎22940 22 700; fax 22940 26 100), sell tickets for ferries and catamarans. (All open daily 6am-9pm.) **Buses** from Athens's station at Mavromateon 29 (1hr.; every 30min., 5:40am-10pm; €1.60) or **shuttles** from the airport (every 40min., 6:15am-9:15pm) get you to Rafina at the waterfront ramp.

Both the **Commercial Bank,** two blocks inland from the plateia (☎22940 25 181; open M-Th 8am-2pm, F 8am-1:30pm), and the **Alpha Bank** (☎22940 24 159; open M-Th 8am-2pm, F 8am-1:30pm), one block beyond the far left corner of the plateia, **exchange currency** and have 24hr. **ATMs. Taxis** (☎22940 23 101) line up in front of the plateia. Facing inland at the dock, the **post office** is two streets to the right on El. Venizelou. (☎22940 23 777. Open M-F 7:30am-2pm.) The unmarked building that passes for an **OTE** is inland from the plateia, beside the church. (☎22940 25 182. Open M-F 7:30am-3pm.) There's a **doctor** (☎22940 28 010; available daily 9am-1pm and 6-8pm) on Kyprion Agoniston. Reach the **police** at ☎22940 22 100 and dial ☎166 in a **medical emergency.** There is a **pharmacy** (☎22940 26 526; open M-F 8:30-2pm, also open Tu, Th-F 5:30-9pm) at Kyprion Agoniston 17. **Postal code:** 19009.

ATHENS

ACCOMMODATIONS AND FOOD. Don't stay in Rafina unless you're stuck here: it's boring and expensive. **Hotel Korali ❸,** Pl. Plastira 11, rents standard rooms with private baths and fridges. (☎22940 22 477; owner's home 22940 28 900. Singles €25; doubles €40; triples €50; quads €60.) Down from the plateia overlooking the water to the right (facing the water) the bigger **Avra Hotel ❸** (☎22940 22 780) is expected to be opening at some point in 2004. **O Vrahos ❸,** Vas. Pavlou 1, in front of the plateia, is toward the water on the left. The family catches nearly all fish daily. (☎22940 26 190. Boiled mussels with peppers €10. *Horta* €4. Fisherman's pasta with shrimp, mussels, octopus, and calamari €17. Local wine €7 per L. Open daily noon-midnight.) Head right at the top of the ramp, right again at the end of the blue fence, then follow the coast to find tiny inlets. If you keep walking, you'll get to a long beach with rough sand. Cafes, pizzerias, and tavernas line the plateia and waterfront. Early ferry-catchers can try **Fournos tis Plateias ❶,** a bakery on the right side of the plateia when you're facing the water. (☎22940 26 083. Fresh bread €0.50. Various croissants €1.20 and up. Yogurt €0.90. Open daily 6am-12:30pm.) A **mini-market** (open daily 8am-2pm and 5-10pm) sells fruits, vegetables, and toiletries just off Pl. Plastira, around the corner from the bakery.

MAROUSI Μαρουσι ☎210

Marousi, though a suburb, is paradoxically like Athens's downtown, home to the largest marketing and advertising industries in Greece. It extends outward from its Metro stop. In front and to the right of this stop, (when you are coming from Athens) are the major thoroughfares of Kifisias and Ag. Konstantinos avenues.

Marousi, where Athenians either live or work, is low on accommodations but easily accessible from both the Olympic Sports Complex and Athens accommodations thanks to the **green line.** Marousi is the stop after Eirini on **M1,** the **green line** (Piraeus/Kifisia). In Athens, get on from Omonia. It can also be reached by the **B7 bus** which leaves from the corner of Themistokleous and Akademias in Omonia (25min., €0.45). **Taxis** line up across from the Metro stop in Pl. Ilektrikou Stathmou (on the side of the tracks on which you detrain coming from Athens).

Hotel Marousi ❸, Olympias 8 and Ag. Konstantinos, is 12min. by foot from the plateia. Doubles (€64) have jacuzzi baths, A/C, and TVs. (☎210 689 7697 or 689

8338. DC/MC/V.) **Hotel Nafsika ❹,** Pellis 6, is a 10min. walk from the next Metro stop north of Marousi. (☎210 801 8027; www.nafsika.gr. Breakfast included. Doubles €136.40 for 1-2 days, €124 for 3 or more. MC/V.) Fast-food franchises and a slew of similar cafes speckle both sides of the Metro stop in Marousi. If you walk down Themidos seven blocks until Ag. Konstantinos, **Jaipur Palace ❸,** Themidos 73, serves vegetable *sheek* (juicy minced vegetable rolls with freshly ground spices and herbs; €10.30) and palace *murgh* (chicken breast cooked in cashew gravy; €15), among other specialties. (☎210 805 2762; fax 210 805 2761. Open daily noon-4:30pm and 8:30pm-1am. MC/V.) Much loved by locals, **Ta Pefka ❷,** Haimanta 34, is eight blocks from the other side of the Metro. (☎210 802 2371. Tomato salad €2.10. Veal in milk sauce €7.60. White *retsina* €3.40 per kg. Open M, W-Sa 8pm-12:30am, Su noon-12:30am.) **Dodoni ❶,** Kondili 3, has delicious ice creams. (3 scoops €3.20. Open Su-Th 10am-2am, F-Sa 10am-3am.) Bar/clubs **Envy-Automatic,** Kifisias 7 (☎210 689 8560), and **Cristal,** Kifisias 46 (☎210 618 0603), are open year-round. Take a cab from the plateia (€2.30-3) on the main northern suburban throughfare. **Liberty,** Kifisias 10-12 (☎210 684 0392), is a popular club in the winter. From May to October, it moves to the waterfront.

The **tourist office,** Panathinainon 7, is inset behind another building on the plateia. (☎210 802 1009, 802 5311, or 802 6564. Open M-F 9am-2pm and 5:30-8pm, Sa 9am-2pm.) The **tourist police** (☎171) can be reached 24hr. A **pharmacy,** Ilektrikou Stathmou 1, lies on the plateia on a corner across from the Metro. (☎210 802 0283. Open M, W 8am-2:30pm; Tu, Th-F 8am-2pm and 5:30-8:30pm.) **Fakinos Bookstore,** N. Plastira 8, across from the Alpha Bank **ATM** is a few blocks into town away from the Metro and tourist office. It has foreign press and an **Internet** cafe. (☎210 614 2350. Internet €3.50 per hr., €1 min. Open M, W, Sa 8:30am-3pm; Tu, Th-F 8:30am-2pm and 3:30-9pm. DC/MC/V.) Call ☎166 for an **ambulance. KAT,** Nikis 2 (☎210 801 4411), one of the three largest general hospitals in the greater Athens area, is open 24hr. and located at the next Metro stop toward Kifisia, less than a 5min. cab ride from the square. **Gema Internet,** Aristeidou 5, is on the other side of the Metro stop past the Häagen-Dazs cafe. (Internet €3 per hr. Billiards €6 per hr. Cocktails €3.20. Open daily 10am-1am.) The **post office,** Kondili 5, on the other side of the Metro stop past Dodoni, has **Poste Restante** and sends packages up to 2kg internationally. (☎210 802 0321. Open M-F 7:30am-2pm.) **Postal code:** 15101.

HALANDRI Χαλανδρι ☎210

Halandri is one of many suburban towns close to Athens (around 7km from the city center) that has come into its own in recent years. Within a 30min. walk of the Olympic Stadium in Marousi (p. 132), Halandri is sure to attract crowds of visitors with its thriving nightlife and suprisingly diverse array of restaurants, as well as accommodations, shops, and complete amenities. Halandri is a 5min. (€3-4) cab ride from **Marousi.** From **Athens,** take bus A6 or B6 from Vas. Irakliou in Exarhia near Areos Park and Mavromateon. In Pl. Dourou in Halandri you can catch **#426, 451,** or **423** to get to Penteli. **Links Internet Cafe,** Aristotelous 42, is three blocks into town from Pentelis. (€3.50 per hr., €1.20 min. Open daily 10:30am-11pm.) **Hotel Acropol ❹,** Pentelis 71 (☎210 682 6650; www.acropol.gr), is far up the main avenue. The dated geometric building has singles (€65) and doubles (€90) with A/C, TVs, telephones, and baths. **Kalozimi ❸,** Aristotelous 48, a block from the Internet cafe away from Pentelis, is a quaint Greek taverna. (☎210 683 4784. Zucchini balls €3.70. *Fava* €2.50. Roast chicken €12. Open daily 12:30pm-1:30am. DC/MC/V.) **Santa Pasta ❸,** Penteli 73, is across the street from Hotel Acropol. (☎210 685 4755; www.santapasta.gr. Mozzarella and tomato salad €4.20. Vegetables grilled with provalone cheese €6.20. Spaghetti alla Cabonara €4.70. Open daily noon-1:30am. MC/V.) **Cine Fyla,** farther down Pentelis from Santa Pasta on the right, plays English movies. (☎210 685 8478; www.tourclub.gr. €7.)

VOULIAGMENI Βουλιαγμενη ☎210

Breezy and cool, this area is a great place to spend the afternoon, especially if you happen to be waiting for an evening Olympic event (p. 128). Citibank has 24hr. **ATMs** on Reas, off Poseidonos to the right (coming from Athens) and on Ermou, a little further down Poseidonos on the left. The **fruit store,** Ermou 1, just before the ATM, across from the beach, sells kiwis (€3.40 per kg), nectarines (€3.70 per kg), and others natural goodies. (Open daily 8am-midnight.) **Louizidis ❷,** Ermou 2 (☎210 896 0591), a block left of Poseidonos, on the corner, is a family taverna preparing fresh eggplant salad (€3.50), *horta* (€3), and *pastitsio* (€5.50), among other traditional dishes. (Open daily noon-1am. MC/V.) **Panino ❸,** Orfeos 2 (☎210 967 1046, 967 1047), along the main beach drag a block from Ermou (in the opposite direction from Athens), is an Italian restaurant with a pretty garden. (Spaghetti Neapolitana €6.50. Chicken with spinach and ricotta €12.90. Open daily 7pm-2am. MC/V.) **Dodoni ❶,** Ermou 1, two doors up from the fruit store, has interesting gelato flavors like yogurt with honey (3 scoops €3.20) served in freshly-baked cones. (Open Su-Th 10am-1am, F-Sa 10am-2am.) The main beach of Vouliagmeni, known as the **EOT beach** (€3), is across Poseidonos. Some pleasant beaches down the coast from Vouliagmeni are Agia Marina, Lagonisi, Saronida, Anavissos, Thimari, and Apollonas (in that order as you head south).

2004 SUMMER OLYMPIC GAMES

Nearly three millenia ago (776 BC), the first recorded Olympic Games were held in the olive-shrouded plains of Olympia on the Peloponnese. Two hundred ninety-three *Olympiadas* (the Greeks still call them by this name) later, in AD 393, Roman rulers banned their practice in Greece. A little over a century ago, the tradition was revived in Athens, the then barely developed, ruin-strewn capital of a newly liberated Greece. This summer, from August 13-29, 5.3 million spectators, along with 4 billion viewers across the globe, will watch the Olympic Games return to both the land of their ancient birth and the city of their modern revival.

Since the aforementioned milestones in Olympic history, the Games themselves have become not only the largest but truly *the* paramount sporting event in the world. Since the time of the first Games, the small country located at the crossroads of the world, with one foot in the east and one in the west, has struggled through two millenia of unceasing occupation by a succession of foreign conquerers. After the Romans, among them were the Franks, the Catalans, the Venetians, and perhaps most significantly, the Ottomans of the sprawling eastern empire, whose dominance lasted for more than 400 years. As if the troubled history up to 1821 was not enough, since the Games' 1896 revival, Athens and the rest of Greece has braved one vicious civil war in addition to two consecutive dictatorships.

Today an ancient tradition comes full circle to revive the unique civilization that founded it so many years ago. In Atlanta in 1996 and Sydney in 2000, the pervasive understanding was that long prosperous and modernized nations like the United States and Australia would employ the vast amounts of power and capability at their disposal to put on fabulously extravagant shows for the world out of respect for this valuable tradition—not to mention the profits for Coca Cola and others. In 2004 the issue at hand will be just as much what the Olympic Games will do for the nation of Greece, as what the nation of Greece will do for the Olympic Games.

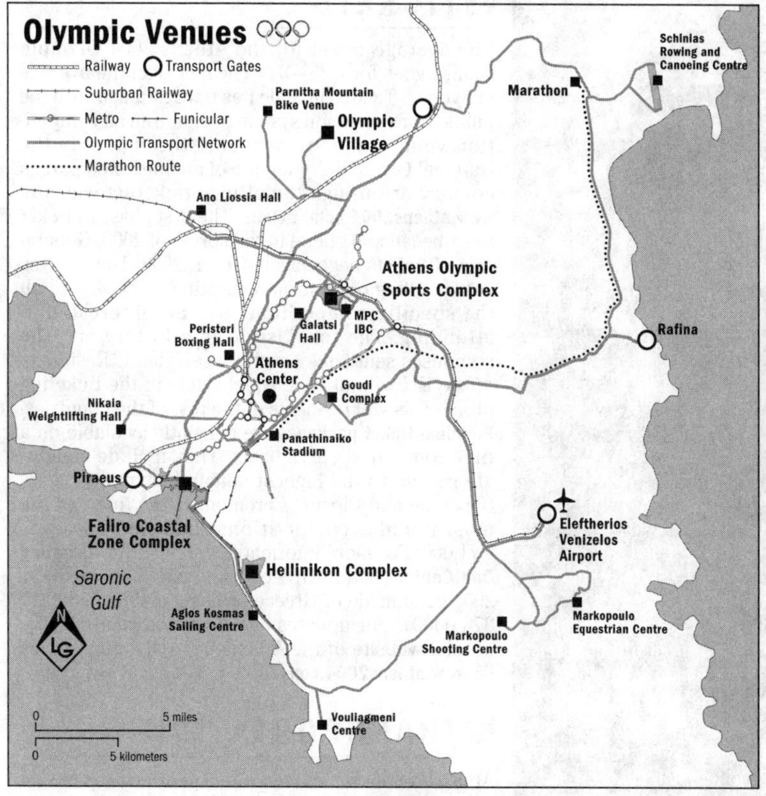

Indeed prospects look bright: after these upcoming Games conclude, the country in which domestic network TV only began in 1981, will be left with an infrastructure to rival the most developed industrial capitals in the world. Among the most impressive of installations will be a revived public transport system, featuring a 24km, two-lined, pollution-free, light-rail tram, a brand new Suburban Rail that will connect the city center's Metro system with the airport, the Peloponnese, numerous international train lines, and, as part of 210km of extended and renovated roads, the Attiki Odos—a six-lane, 70km motorway.

The timing of the 2004 Olympic Games will make them as important as their location will. The 2800-year-old *ethos* upon which the ancient Games were originally founded—and around which the tradition has revolved all along—has rarely in history seemed more ubiquitously apt than it does today. In ancient times, warring city-states would place down their weapons to compete in a nobler medium of human interaction. This year, for the first time in history, the torch relay—which is intended to inspire all countries to unite in the Olympic Truce—will travel to each of the six inhabited continents on the globe. During the Games themselves, "enemies" will for two weeks become "opponents," channeling their energy on the field, court, sea, river, road, or mountain.

ATHENS 2004

THE PLEBS' GAMES

The Olympic Committee might be keener on advertising VIP packages to bring in the big bucks, but there *are* bargains to be found when it comes to the 2004 Olympic Games—and they aren't just family discounts. One of the most exciting and historically significant events on the schedule, the Athens 2004 Marathon, will be entirely, 100% *tzamba* (free). After a 108-year hiatus, the Olympic Marathon will return to Greece to follow the original Marathon route, forged by heroic Phidippides in 490BC.

Wait anywhere alongside the runners' path, from a little after where they begin to a little before the finish line where they end. Unlike some who want to pay to sit and wait (at the Marathon Finish) or pay and to watch the show end in three seconds (at the Marathon Start), you have no committment in terms of vantage points—who knows, some in your position might even decide to run on the sidewalk alongside their favorite stars for a little while, to share in some of their agony and perhaps to also lend to them a little support.

The women's race begins at 6pm on August 22nd; the men's at 6pm on August 29th. See the Olympic Venues map (p. 129) for the exact trail. The road cycling (men's Aug. 14 12:45pm; women's Aug. 15 3pm) and sailing (in 14 sessions on Aug. 14-26 and 28) events can also be viewed free of charge.

TICKETS

The average ticket for the Athens 2004 Olympic Games goes for €35—34% cheaper than the average in Sydney. Tickets include **free transportation** with the public transportation system to and from all competition venues and are available through only the National Olympic Committee of an interested party's country or through the official ticketing website: **www.athens2004.com/tickets.** The first phase of ticket sales began and ended in the spring of 2003. General sale of tickets began again Oct. 1, 2003. The process entails filling out a form requesting admission to all the specific competitions you are interested in attending. The form is put in a lottery and the responses sent back several weeks later. Residents of the EU will all have equal rights in the ticketing process, as will residents of the rest of the countries. **Premium ticket packages** are currently available on a first come, first serve basis. They include sought-after seats to the highest-demand Olympic events (Opening and Closing Ceremonies, the finals of the most popular competitions) and range €3500-€71,000. For more information, contact the **Ticketing Call Center** (within Greece using land line: ☎800 11 2004 02, outside of Greece or using mobile: ☎30 210 373 0000). For updates and more information, the official website of the Athens 2004 Olympic Games is: **www.athens2004.com.**

TRANSPORTATION

Athens's extended and renovated public transport system will be the primary vessel for movement during games time. The **Metro,** along with the new **tram** and new **Suburban Rail** (p. 85), will move approximately one million passengers every day. The largest venue complexes (Athens Olympic Sports Centre, Hellinikon Olympic Sports Centre, Faliro Olympic Coastal Zone) will be directly serviced by one or more of these lines, as will many others near and around the city center. Venues not directly serviced by these lines will be accessible through a combination of the public transport system and specially running **Olympic Transport shuttles** that will leave from Metro, tram, and Suburban Rail terminals, using the 210km of new and upgraded roads scheduled to be ready in the Athens area by Games time. Although public transportation will be free for all ticketed spectators on their way to and from venues the day of their said competition, **parking** will also be available at a distance from the venues, accessed by shuttles and not directly serviced by one of the three main transportation lines.

ORIENTATION

Competitions in **28 sports,** as well as broadcasting services and athlete-accommodations, will be held in **38 Olympic venues** throughout Greece. The great majority of those venues will be concentrated on the Attican Peninsula, which, if you made a full circle around a map of Greece, would be located almost exactly in the center. The capital city of **Athens** (p. 80), is located a little southwest of the center of Attica itself and most of the venues, if not included directly within its greater borders, will be right around it them. The other Olympic cities will be **Thessaloniki** and **Volos** in Central Greece (p. 230), **Patras** in the Pelopponese (p. 160), and **Iraklion**, Crete's large capital on the northern side of the island (p. 585).

ACCOMMODATIONS

Accommodating 5.3 million spectatators (minus the many Athenian resident spectators) has been among the greatest challenges faced by the city and organizing committee. The influx count is going to be over twice that of Athens's normal winter population and, since the city itself was never in the past a specific destination for mass tourism, it lacks the traditional infrastructure for sleeping mass amounts of people. It was over this issue that the 2004 committee derived the term "unique" to describe the Games that they are planning to host. The whole event will be held, on what they call "a human scale."

Though by the time of the Games there will be a total of 31,000 rooms in all new and old **hotels throughout the Athens area** (p. 94), 17,300 of those rooms have already been frozen for use by the press and the Olympic family. Other people are booking at lightning speed but because the number of remaining rooms will not nearly suffice, there are a number of alternative accommodations options for the Olympic Games: A great number of **private residences** in the Athens area will be rented during Games time. There are two joint venture contractor bodies officially responsible for putting owners in contact with tenants for the 16 days of the Olympics: **Alpha Philoxenia 2004** (☎30 210 327 7400; fax 210 327 7444; cpallis@alphaastikaakinita.gr) and **Elliniki Philoxenia** (☎210 327 7403 and 327 7406; gmanzavinatos@eurobank.gr). Docking in the port of Piraeus will be 11 **cruise liners** with a combined total of 6489 cabins in the three- and five-star categories. The ships' draws include cinemas, spas, restaurants, swimming pools, libraries, children's play rooms, Internet cafes, and convenient locations. Among the liners docked will be the German **AIDAvita** (☎49 69 695 801 18; fax: 49 69 695 801 30; Heike-Marie.Ebel@DSM-Olympia.de; ask for Mrs. Heike-Marie Ebel); the **MS OOSTERDAM** and **MS ROTTERDAM** (☎30 210 322 1500; fax 30 210 331 6684; sales@sportius.gr; ask for Mrs. Calli Georgiades); the **Olympic Voyager, Olympic Explorer,** and **Olympic Countess** (☎30 210 429 1000; fax 30 210 459 7482; sales@roc.gr; ask for Mr. Evan Pezas); and the most luxurious of all, the **Queen Mary II** (cruiseships@athens2004.gr). Besides these options, a large number of visitors will stay on nearby islands like **Salamina, Aegina** (p. 320), **Hydra** (p. 331), **Spetses** (p. 335), and **Evia** (p. 355), all of which will be more frequently serviced by high speed ferries than ever before. Nearby towns and cities in the **Peloponnese** (p. 140) will be another option, as they will be serviced by the new Suburban Rail line running directly from El. Venizelos Airport to Patras. Various quiet towns of Attica (p. 120) will also accommodate overflow.

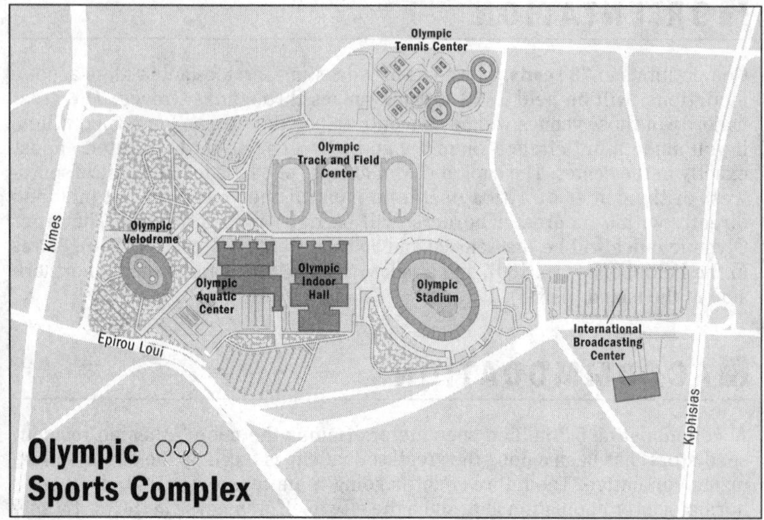

OLYMPIC VILLAGE

The Olympic village, at the foot of striking Mt. Parnitha north of Athens, is a walloping 1240 sq. km complex. It will be used during the Olympic Games to accommodate 16,000 athletes and team officials and again during the Paralympic Games (later in 2004), when it will house 6000. The facility includes a **Residentail Zone** consisting of over 2200 apartments and training facilities among other features. The **International Zone** incorparates the main etrance, **shopping centers,** admistrative buildings, and **Olympic museum.**

ATTICAN VENUES

ATHENS OLYMPIC SPORTS COMPLEX (OCO)

Take Metro green line 1 from Omonia toward Kifisia and get off at Eirini. Using the Suburban Rail (if connecting from blue line 3 or coming from southeast or northwest), get off at Neratziotissa, then board Metro green line 1 toward Piraeus, again getting off at Eirini.

The Athens Olympic Sports Complex, located 9km north of the center of Athens and 11km south of the Olympic Village in Parnitha, where all athletes will reside, is in the residential northern suburb of Marousi (p. 126). Everything in OCO seems to have been constructed on an elephantine scale. The complex will host nine sports including track and field, track cycling, swimming, and diving.

The jewel of the central complex, the **Olympic Stadium (STA)** has the largest capacity of all the sports venues in Attica and will host a modest crowd of 75,000 spectators on August 13 for the opening of the 2004 Olympic Games. It will be revisited by the same volume of people on August 29 for their closing. **Track and field** will take place over 9 consecutive days, August 20-28. It is expected to be fully renovated by April 2004. The vastness of the **Olympic Indoor Hall (OIH)** will add drama to the silent focus of crowd and athletes alike when it hosts 15,000 guests at the **artistic gymnastics** competitions (Aug. 14, 15, 16-19, 22, and 23) and **trampoline gymnastics** (Aug. 20). Near the end of the Games, when 18,000 rowdy fans flood in for **basketball** finals (Aug. 25-28), decibels will multiply and the general effect will exude raw excitement. The OIH should be up and running by October 2003. An expected 16,600 will come to the **Olympic Tennis Centre (TEN)** to watch the **tennis** competitions (Aug. 15-18; finals Aug. 19-22). The center boasts 16 courts; the **main court** seats 8000; the **two semifinals courts,** 4000 and 2000 respectively; the 13 others, 200 each. TEN was completed at the end of summer 2003. The universally popular sports (and disciplines) that will be held here deserve such a grand complex as the **Olympic Aquatic Centre (AQU).** The Aquatic Centre is made up of two outdoor pools, the **main pool** (capacity 11,000) and the **synchronized swimming pool** (capacity 5000), and the **indoor pool,** which seats 6500. The Indoor Pool will host **diving** (Aug. 14, 16, 20-28) and the **water polo** preliminaries (Aug. 15-21). **Swimming** (Aug. 14-21) will come to the main pool, which will afterwards host the water polo finals (Aug. 22-27). **Synchronized swimming** (Aug. 23, 24, and 26; finals Aug. 25 and 27) will be held in the synchronized swimming pool. The Aquatic Centre is expected to be fully renovated by the end of 2003. The sleek and modern **Olympic Velodrome (VEL),** host of **track cycling** (Aug. 20-25), has been totally overhauled for the 2004 Games. The eyes of 5000 anxious onlookers will follow the quick elliptical movement pulsing around the venue. It will be finished around January 2004.

FALIRO COASTAL ZONE OLYMPIC COMPLEX (FCO)

Take tram line 1 from Zappeio; switch to tram line 2 at the junction on Poseidonos and continue in the opposite direction to the last stop (Neo Faliro). You can alternatively take Metro green line 1 toward Piraeus and get off at Faliro.

The Faliro Coastal Zone Olympic Complex is a blessing for the southern Attican coastline. It has polished what was for so long just a diamond in the rough. The beautiful stretch between Piraeus (to the west) and the beach suburbs of Gyfada, Vouliagmeni, and Varkiza (to the east) have been covered with piles of old boats and unfinished construction, and utterly neglected since anyone can remember. Now beautiful gardens, walkways, and a state of the art marina embellish the new or refurbished sites, invaluable for future use. Faliro will host four of the 28 sports. The closest venue to the bustling docks of Piraeus, the **Peace and Friendship Stadium (SEF)** is a graceful oblong edifice with gently sloping sides. It will be, like the Olympic Stadium, a one-sport stop. The newly renovated stadium, which has been around since the 80s, is scheduled to host the main event for a crowd of 14,000 teeming **volleyball** fans (Aug. 14-23; finals Aug. 24-29). Renovations should be finished in December 2003. In the brand-new **Sports Pavillion (FSP),** 8000 spectators are scheduled to come see the **handball** preliminaries (Aug. 14-24) and **Taekwondo** (Aug. 26-29). Construction will be done by early 2004. Right in front of the sea, the impressively sleek, new **Olympic Beach Volleyball Stadium (BVF),** will host 10,000 **beach volleyball** fans (Aug. 14-21; finals Aug. 22-25). The training will take place out in front in a similar, sandy court. The completion date is in early 2004.

HELLINIKON OLYMPIC COMPLEX (HCO)

Take tram line 1 from Zappeio to the last stop, Helliniko.

The Hellinikon should be the worldwide symbol of recycling or involved in a campaign for its merits. It is the site of the old airport (the only airport Greece ever had before Eleftherios Venizelos was built in 2001). Parts of many of the buildings, like the **Indoor Arena** and **Fencing Hall,** are reconstructed using the skeleton of old aviation buildings; in July 2003 there was still a lingering "International Flights" sign hanging from an entrance. The Hellinikon will host seven sports.

Built by Greeks generally unfamiliar with the sport but ready and willing to learn, the **Olympic Baseball Centre's** two fields will accommodate 7000 and 12,000 **baseball** fans (Aug. 15-18, 20-22, and 24; finals Aug. 25) from across the globe. It's expected to be completed in January 2004. The venue for **softball** (Aug. 14-20 and 22; finals Aug. 23), the **Olympic Softball Stadium** has also been built from the ground up. There is a **main field,** where competitions will take place, and two satelllite warm-up fields. The fields will be ready in January 2004. The **Olympic Hockey Centre,** where **field hockey** games will be held (Aug. 14-23; finals Aug. 24-27), has a capacity of 8000. The neighboring warm-up field has a capacity of 2000. They should be done in January 2004. The impressive, high-ceilinged structures of the **Indoor Arena and Fencing Hall** may not have been built from scratch, but their frames were modified from what were once the Olympic Airways hangars of the former airport. The **Indoor Arena** (capacity 15,000) will host **basketball** preliminaries (Aug. 14-24) and then **handball finals** (Aug. 26-29). The two-roomed **Fencing Hall** (5000 and 3500 capacity) will host the age-old sport of **fencing** (Aug. 14-22). The facility will be completed in January 2004. The sprawling **Olympic Canoe Kayak Slalom Centre,** with winding, elevated canoe paths positioned on an incline toward its vast pool, will only be used for four consecutive days during the Olympics for **canoe/kayak slalom racing** (Aug. 17 and 19; finals Aug. 18 and 20). It will have seats for 5000 people, but the surface area of the enormous structure will end up larger than almost anything else in the Hellinikon. It will be completed in February 2004.

ATHENS

ATHENS CITY CENTRE CYCLYING ROAD RACE COURSE (ARR)

In the center of Athens; take Metro green line 1 from Omonia toward Kifisia and get off at Thissio or take blue line 3 from Syndagma and switch to green at Monastiraki.

On a course around Athens's center, **road-race cycling** will take place August 14-15. Crowds will look on in awe as the most capable road-race cyclers in the world zip around the Acropolis and other major landmarks of the ancient city. The precise route will be determined in July 2004.

MARATHON START (MRS)

Take Metro green line 1 from Omonia to Neratziotissa and switch to the Olympic shuttle. Martathon is 26 mi/42km (the distance of a marathon) from Athens's center.

Perhaps some of the most historically stirring hours of the Olympics will be those of the **marathon,** since the course itself will follow the precise path believed to have been run by the first runner of the marathon, the ancient hero Phidippides, who in 490 BC fell to his death after booking it from Marathon to Athens to declare Attica's miraculous defeat over the Persians. The marathon will start in a small renovated stadium and end in the enormous ancient Panathenaic stadium of central Athens. The women's race will take place August 22; the men's, August 29.

PANATHENAIC/KALLIMARMARO STADIUM (PAN)

In Athens's center, the Panathenaic is a 7-10min. walk from Syndagma, on the other side of the National Gardens. Stoll down Irodou Atikou to get there.

The product of ancient aristocrat Herodius Atticus's boasting that he would build a stadium entirely out of marble for the Panathenaic Games, the Kallimarmaro in Athens's center hosted the 1896 revival of the Games after it was refurbished by wealthy Athenian George Averof. Though it may be only one of 38 venues slated to host 2004 Olympic contests, this breathtaking, elliptical edifice cannot be overshadowed in gracefulness or historical significance. **Archery** events (Aug. 15-17; finals Aug. 19-21) will attract an estimated 5500 spectators. The women's marathon finish will be attended by 45,000 spectators on the evening of August 22; the men's, August 29. Renovations should be completed November 2003.

SCHINIAS OLYMPIC ROWING AND CANOEING CENTRE (SCH)

Take Metro green line 1 from Omonia to Neraztiotissa and switch to the Olympic shuttle. Continue past the Marathon start to Schinias.

Southen Greece doesn't have many rivers and has taken it upon itself to provide an exception. In northeastern Attica, set about 250m back from the long coastal beach, the 2222m-long, 3.5m-deep lake shares the Olympic venue's name. It has been miraculously and masterfully created out of dry land to accommodate two Olympic sports. **Rowing** (Aug. 15-20; finals Aug. 21-22) and **canoe/kayak flatwater racing** (Aug. 23-26; finals Aug. 27-28) will come to this venue. There is a smaller, slightly more shallow lake that will be used for practice and training purposes.

NIKAIA OLYMPIC WEIGHTLIFTING HALL (NIH)

Take Metro green line 1 toward Piraeus; get off at Petralona and take Olympic shuttle.

Wedged at the foot of dramatically jutting rocks in Nikaia, this is the westernmost Olympic venue of the Attican peninsula. The circular **indoor gym,** its foremost attraction, which is cutting-edge but still intimate enough to promise a fabulous experience, will host 5000 spectators for **weightlifting** (Aug. 14-16, 18-21, and 23-25), one of the most popular Olympic sports in Greece. One of the first to be started and first to be finished, this project was completed in the summer of 2003.

ANO LIOSSA OLYMPIC HALL (LIH)

Take Metro green line 1 from Omonia toward Kifisia. After switching to the Suburban Rail at Neratziotissa, get off at the stop before Ano Liossa; then switch to Olympic Shuttle.

This major new sporting center promises to encourage the regional developent of three age-old spectator sports which, as of now, are not so familiar in Greece. **Judo** (Aug. 14-20) will draw 8000 fans, while **freestyle wrestling** (Aug. 22 and 27; finals 23 and 28-29) and **Greco-Roman wrestling** (Aug. 24-25; finals 26) will draw 9300 each. The venue is expected to be finished by the end of December 2003.

PERISTERI OLYMPIC BOXING HALL (PBH)

Take Metro red line 3 from Syndagma or Omonia and get off at either Sepolia or Agios Antonios to catch the Olympic shuttle.

Boxing (Aug. 14-21; quarterfinals Aug. 22-25; semifinals Aug. 27; finals Aug. 28-29) will draw intense fans to this indoor venue (capacity 8000) in western Attica.

GALATSI OLYMPIC HALL (GAL)

While Metro line 1 is currently the easiest way to get to the northwestern suburban town and venue, there are plans to extend line 3 from Athens's center to Galatsi.

A sprawling indoor complex of 32,000 sq. m with a modern design and asymetrically sloping roof, the Galatsi Olympic hall will host 6000 spectators for the nail-biting **table tennis** matches (Aug. 14-19; finals Aug. 20-23). Fans will gather to watch the graceful **rhythmic gymnastics** competitions (Aug. 26-27; finals Aug. 28-29). The complex is due at the end of summer 2003.

MARKOPOULO OLYMPIC EQUESTRIAN CENTRE (EQU)

Take Metro green line 1 to Neratziotissa or blue line 3 to Doukissis Plakendias; switch to Suburban Rail headed toward El. Venizelou; disembark at stop where rail and Attiki Odos make a 90° turn for the airport and board Olympic Shuttle.

Over 21,000 sq. m of the rolling inland plains of eastern Attica beside the rural town of Markopoulo have been marked and manicured in a fashion that would make Ascot blush. **Eventing equestrian competitions** (Aug. 15-17; finals Aug. 18), **dressage** (Aug. 20 and 23; finals Aug. 21 and 24), and **jumping** (Aug. 22; finals Aug. 24 and 27) will draw whopping crowds of 40,000, 8000, and 20,000 respectively. The facility is expected to be finished in January 2004.

MARKOPOULO OLYMPIC SHOOTING CENTRE (SHO)

Take Metro green line 1 to Neratziotissa or blue line 3 to Doukissis Plakendias; switch to Suburban Rail headed towards El. Venizelou; disembark at stop where rail and Attiki Odos make a 90° turn for the airport and board Olympic Shuttle.

This complex in the inland country side on the outskirts of the sleepy village of Markopoulo, composed of 305 acres and four main buildings will host a total of 8000 spectators for the **shooting** events schedules to take place from August 14-22. The center is due for completion in December 2003.

AGIOS KOSMAS OLYMPIC SAILING CENTRE (AGK)

Take tram line 1 from Zappeio in the center of Athens, switch to tram line 2 headed towards Glyfada Sq., and get off at Agios Kosmas stop.

August in Greece is *meltemi* season, a time of wind storms and strong marine tumult, generally feared by fishermen and ferry captains. Agios Kosmas Sailing Centre, however, jutting out off of the southern Attican coast into the sea, is exposed enough to capture the season's propitious gusts but protected enough to avoid the waves that normally accompany them. **Sailing** (Aug. 14-20 and 23-24; finals Aug. 21-22, 25-26, and 28) will be held at this breezy venue with panoramic views of the Aegean blue. This venue is expected to be finished by January 2004.

GOUDI OLYMPIC COMPLEX (GOC)

Take Metro blue line 3 from Syndagma; get off at Katehaki and catch Olympic shuttle.

Built in the middle of an evergreen thicket of northeastern Athens, Goudi consists of a gymnasium and a **modern pentathlon** center. Designing the complex, says the Athens 2004 Committee, was a structural challenge, to say the least, considering the complexity of the pentathlon. Its completion date is March 2004. In the **Olympic Hall,** the **badminton** competitions (Aug. 14-18; finals Aug. 19-21) will be held before 5000 spectators. The **shooting** and **fencing** disciplines of the modern pentathlon (Aug. 26-27) will take place here before a crowd of 4500. The remaining three disciplines of the modern pentathlon, **swimming, riding,** and **running** (Aug. 26-27), will be held at the **Olympic Modern Pentathlon Centre.** Two thousand fans will get to witness the swimming leg, while 5000 will watch the riding and running portions.

VOULIAGMENI OLYMPIC CENTRE (VOU)

Take tram line 1 from Zappeio; switch to line 2 and ride toward Gylfada Sq. (the last stop) from where you can catch the Olympic Shuttle.

The **triathlon** (Aug. 25-26) will be held in the beautiful beachside region of Vouliagmeni, farther down the southern coast from most of Athens's crowded summer 2004 chaos. Three thousand fans will behold some of the most capable all-around athletes in the world striving to swim, cycle, and run faster than they ever have before. **Road race/time trial cycling** (Aug. 18) will use a venue nextdoor called the **Vouliagmeni-Agia Marina Route.**

PARNITHA OLYMPIC MOUNTAIN BIKE VENUE (MTB)

Take either Metro green line 1 from Omonia toward Kifisia or Metro blue line 3 toward Doukissis Plakentias; get off at Neratziotissa (from the green line) or Doukissis Plakentias (from the blue line). Switch to Suburban Rail going toward Patras; get off before Ano Liossa and take Olympic shuttle.

This venue, the closest to the Olympic Village, hosts the **mountain bike cycling** event (Aug. 27-28). A temporary overlay will supply the necessary surface on the winding trail around Parnitha. The atmosphere around the trail alone showcases inland Attica's rugged beauty. Construction completion is expected by December 2003.

KARAISKAKI STADIUM (ATH)

Take Metro green line 1 from Omonia toward Piraeus and get off at the Faliro stop (in Nea Faliro, just before the Piraeus terminal). You can also take tram line 1 from Zappeio and switch to line 2 toward the terminal in Neo Faliro.

Used over 100 years ago at the Olympic revival games as the velodrome, Karaiskaki was renovated in the 1960s and has been transformed once again into an impressively modern **soccer** stadium (capacity 35,000) for the Athens 2004 Olympic Games. It is the second largest stadium in Athens proper, after the Kallimarmaro. Some of the most important soccer games will take place here (Aug. 14-15; quarterfinals 17-18, 21, and 23; semifinals Aug. 24; finals Aug. 28-29). The completion date for construction is August 2003.

OTHER VENUES

Though Athens is the sole host of the 2004 Olympic Games in Greece, the city is sharing its responsibilities with other Greek metropoli. Patras, Volos, Thessaloniki, and Iraklion will host mostly soccer competitions and surely many fans.

PATRAS'S PAMPELOPONNISIAKO STADIUM

The Suburban Rail runs all the way from Athens to Patras. Trains and buses (p. 81) also run to Patras. When in Patras take bus #7 (20min., €1) from the Europa Centre.

Known around the city as the "Jewel of Patras," the new Olympic complex will play host **swimming** and **soccer** (Aug. 11-12, 14, 17-18, and 20; quarterfinals Aug. 21 and 23; semifinals Aug. 26) events and also serve as the **athletic training halls.** Added demands from the city, the Greek Althletic Association, and the Athens 2004 Committee have pushed the projected date of completion to February 2004 .

VOLOS'S PANTHESSILIKO STADIUM

To get to Volos from Athens, see p. 81. The stadium is 5km out of Volos's city center, north of the suburb of Nea Ionio.

The stadium (capacity 20,000) will host limited **soccer** (Aug. 11-12, 14-15, 17, and 20) competitions. Another smaller stadium is set next to the Panthessiliko.

THESSALONIKI'S KAFTANSOGLIO STADIUM

To get to Thessaloniki from Athens, see p. 81.

This techinoligcally enhanced stadium (capacity 28,000) will host a smattering of preleminary and semifinal **soccer** matches (Aug. 11-12, 14-15, 17-18, and 20; quarterfinals Aug. 21, 23, and 26).

IRAKLION'S PANKRITIO STADIUM

Iraklion is most often reached by plane or ferry from Athens (see Intercity Transportation, p. 81). The stadium is located 2km outside Iraklion; follow Kalokerinou through the center of town; the stadium is on your right.

This venue, seating up to 27,000,will play host to a variety of **soccer** matches (Aug. 11-12, 14-15, 17-18, and 20; quarterfinals Aug. 21 and 23).

ILLUMINATING THE MODERN FACE OF GREECE

The ATHENS 2004 Olympic Games will clearly draw from the extraordinary history and culture of Greece for its themes, iconography, and focus on the human scale. The Greek people will be proud to show the world the country in which the first recorded Games took place in 776 BC and the city that hosted their 1896 modern revival. At another level, the Games are important to Greece not so much for what they show about our past and our traditions, but for what they show about our present and our future. The Games are an opportunity to introduce the world to a growing, vibrant, cosmopolitan country. At the same time, they not only reflect the emergence of modern Greece, they are one of the important forces behind this emergence.

As nations around the world—especially our European neighbors—increasingly recognize, Greece is strategically located and internationally engaged. Our position at the crossroads of the Balkans, the Middle East, and Western Europe place us in the center of regional diplomacy and politics. We are members of the European Monetary Union and NATO. Our economy, driven in part by Olympic preparations, has been growing more rapidly than the EU average for several years. We will show the modern face of Greece to the world in 2004. It is important to understand, the Olympic Games are a source of growth themselves and the force behind tremendous changes in our infrastructure and urban life. Recent visitors to Greece had the chance to follow the successful tenure of our Prime Minister as President of the European Union, as well as the chance to notice our new airport; perhaps the most modern and secure international airport in Europe. And while the average visitor might not track GDP figures, he or she will undoubtedly benefit from the track laid over the last several years for the Metro and Suburban Rail systems that will link Athens's neighborhoods and its suburbs together.

In a city whose growth has often been unplanned, Olympic preparations have changed the way Athens does business. For the first time, we are building our city with the future uppermost in our minds. Our new Metro system combines modern efficiency and our ancient heritage. It moves hundred of thousands of Athenians daily, rapidly and efficiently, while turning stations into museums displaying the rare artifacts that were unearthed during their construction. In combination with the new 32km suburban train and new tram, we will move a million riders a day by the time the Olympic Games open on August 13th. This is a major transformation in the infrastructure of the region and one of several reasons air quality in Athens has improved dramatically in recent years. In addition to mass transportation, Athenians will find their commutes improved by 210km of new and upgraded roads, including major arteries that will keep through-traffic out of downtown, reducing congestion in the most crowded areas.

New Olympic facilities are being built not only to serve athletes and spectators during the Games, but also neighbors and neighborhoods after the Games. These sites are expected to bring economic development to hard-pressed areas and serve communities as local sports centers as well. Present in several ways is a new environmental sensibility, which will become a model for future non-Olympic development. Olympic venues will create new open spaces and green areas for Athenians. Hundreds of thousands of trees and large bushes are being planted. Our Olympic rowing center, situated on a former airport, preserves and restores acres of wetlands. The marathon route, which traces the route first followed by a herald announcing Athens's victory over Persia, will be lined with ancient olive trees, rescued from another, non-Olympic construction site. The Olympic Village incorporates bioclimatic design principles, using sunlight and airflow to minimize the need for artificial heating and cooling. After the Games, the Village will become housing for middle-income Greeks, much of it accessible for the disabled.

The ancient Olympic Games were emblematic of the nation that gave the world democracy, and the ideas and philosophies on which Western civilization was built. The 2004 Olympic Games will give us a chance to show what we have accomplished in recent years, give us the opportunity to embrace our potential in future years and give the world a chance to rediscover the roots of Olympism in their natal country.

Mrs. Gianna Angelopoulos-Daskalaki is the president of the ATHENS 2004 Organizing Committee. She was appointed to her current position in 2000.

PELOPONNESE

Πελοποννησος

Stretching its fingers into the Mediterranean, the Peloponnese transports its visitors to another time and place through its rich history and folklore. The remnants of ancient civilizations and their achievements mark the present-day peninsula, and its timeless natural beauty remains unchanged. Here rest the majority of Greece's most significant archaeological sites, including Olympia, Mycenae, Messini, Corinth, Mystras, and Epidavros. Breathtaking landscapes, from the barren crags of the Mani to the forested peaks and flower-blanketed pastures of Arcadia, grace Pelops's former home. The serenely beautiful and sparsely populated Peloponnese displays the fruits borne of 5000 years of continuous habitation.

HIGHLIGHTS OF THE PELOPONNESE

EXPERIENCE an ancient city in Monemvasia, where cobbled streets and castle-like buildings line streets traversed only by donkeys and pedestrians (p. 204).

BE INVITED into the Byzantine ghost town of Mystras, once the capital of the Greek part of the empire, now a living architectural museum (p. 198).

TAKE A BREAK from antiquity in the exquisite Arcadian mountain villages of mountainside Dimitsana (p. 181) and medieval Stemnitsa (p. 183).

BE A CONTENDER at ancient Olympia, where pan-Mediterranean Greek city-states squared off every four years in the original Olympic Games (p. 175).

DROP A COIN on the center stage of the acoustically marvelous theater of Epidavros, and a friend can hear it in the last row (p. 159).

CORINTHIA AND ARGOLIS

Κορινθια AND Αργολιδα

Legend holds that Argos, a monster endowed with 100 unblinking eyes, once stalked the northern Peloponnese subduing unruly satyrs and burly bulls. While these mythical creatures have left no tangible evidence behind, the region does provide impressive archaeological sites from the ancient past near secluded villages and bustling cities. Make Nafplion (p. 154) your base for exploration, since this sweet city allows access to Mycenae, Corinth, and other destination points.

NEW CORINTH Κορινθος ☎27410

New Corinth rests on the Gulf of Corinth, west of the canal separating the Peloponnese from the Greek mainland. Efforts to make the city more than a transportation hub have largely failed. Consequently the streets are supersaturated with fast food , designer shops, and 24hr. ATMs. The trend has even affected the local taxi drivers, who now conduct business in either purple Mercedes Benzes or

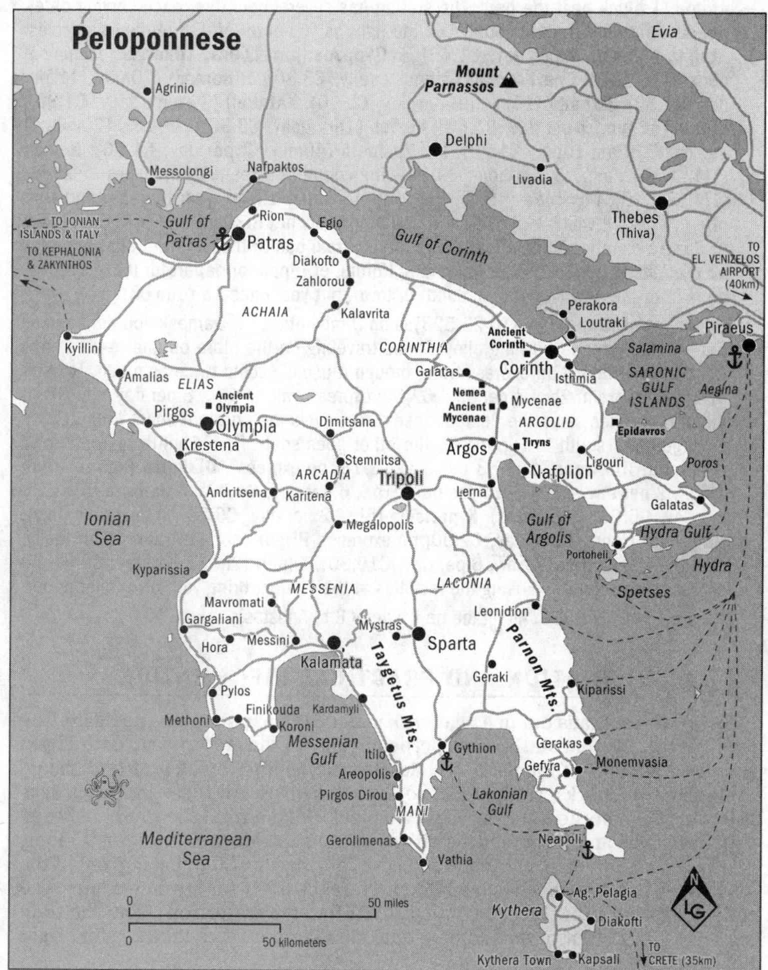

red Alpha Romeos. Despite an attractive harbor and a few cafe-lined pedestrian streets, New Corinth remains unworthy of special consideration. Bypass the headache by staying at out-of-town campgrounds or in nearby Loutraki (p. 146).

TRANSPORTATION

Buses: Terminal A: Beyond the train station on Dimokratias. To: **Athens** (1½hr.; 29 per day, 5:30am-9:30pm; €6). **Terminal B:** Walking inland on Eth. Anistasis, turn right on Koliatsou, halfway through the park; the terminal is outside a bakery. To: **Ancient Corinth** (20min.; 8 per day, 8:10am-9:10pm; €0.90). **Terminal C:** The **Argolis Station** (☎27410 24 403 for Nafplion or Mycenae, 27410 25 645 for Isthmia, Nemea, Loutraki) is also outside a bakery, at the intersection of Eth. Antistasis and

Aratou, 1 block past the park. The station has several counters, each serving different destinations. The 1st counter on the right as you enter off Eth. Antistasis serves: **Athikia** (30min., 7 per day, €1.40); **Eofiko, Almipiri, Loura, Xilkeriza** (15min.; 9 per day, €1.30); **Epathovouni** (30min., daily, €3.30); **Hiliomodi** (20min., 11 per day, €1.30); **Isthmia** (15min., 6 per day, €0.90); **Katakali** (30min., daily, €1.80); **Klenia** (40min., 7 per day, €1.60); **Korfos** (1hr., daily, €3.30); **Loutraki** (20min.; 2 per hr., 7:30am-10pm; €1.20); **Lg. Vasiaeio** (40min., 2 per day, €1.90); **Nemea** (1hr.; 7 per day, 7:30am-5pm; €3.20). The counter on the left has buses to: **Argos** (1hr., €3.20); **Mycenae** (45min., €2.60) via Fihtia, 1.5km from the site; and **Nafplion** (1½hr.; 4 which leave at 7am, and then every hr., 8:30am-9:30pm; €4). To get to **Sparta** or other points south, take the Loutraki bus to the Corinth Canal and pick up the Athens bus to Sparta, Kalamata, Koroni, or Tripoli; or depart for these destinations from the new bus station south of town, but you'll need a taxi (€3).

Trains: The **station** (☎27410 22 523) is on Dimokratias, off Damaskinou right across from an abandoned bowling alley. Those traveling on the more popular routes have the option of taking an express train, though it usually costs twice as much. To: **Athens** (normal train: 2hr., 7 per day, €2.60; express train: 1½hr., 6 per day, €5.70). 2 major train lines serve the Peloponnese: one travels the northern coast from Corinth to Pirgos and south to Kyparissia; the other goes south from Corinth to Tripoli and Kalamata. To: **Argos** (1 hr., 3 per day, €1.18, no express); **Diakofto** (normal train: 1½hr., 2 per day, €2.10; express train: 1hr., 6 per day, €4.70); **Kalamata** (4½hr., 3 per day, €5.60, no express); **Kyparissia** (5hr., 2 per day, €6.80 express train only); **Nafplion** (1½hr., 2 per day, €2.90, no express); **Pirgos** (normal train: 4½hr., daily, €5.60; express train: 3½hr., 6 per day, €10.30); **Tripoli** (2hr., 3 per day, €2.90, no express). If you plan on using the facilities at the station, bring your own toilet paper.

Taxis: ☎27410 73 000. Along the park side of Eth. Antistasis.

ORIENTATION AND PRACTICAL INFORMATION

New Corinth spreads out in a neat grid, making it fairly simple to navigate. The main street, **Eth. Antistasis,** runs perpendicular to the waterfront. Both **Ermou** (on the other side of the park) and **Kokolotroni** (another block up from Ermou, away from the park), run parallel to Eth. Antistasis. All three intersect **Damaskinou,** which borders the harbor. Two blocks inland from the shore, between Eth. Antistasis and Ermou, is the city's central **park.** Most of the town's shops, restaurants, and hotels are found on these four streets. Standing in front of the park, the **Court of Justice** makes a good reference point for any newcomer. The train station is a few blocks southeast. To find the waterfront from the train station, turn left out of the building onto Dimokratias, then take the first right onto Damaskinou

Tourist Police: Ermou 51 (☎27410 23 282 or 100). Doubles as the tourist office, providing maps, brochures, and assistance. Some English spoken. Open daily 8am-2pm.

Banks: National Bank, Eth. Antistasis 7, 1 block up from the waterfront, offers **currency exchange** and a 24hr. **ATM.** An unusual number of banks with these services are also within a few blocks of Eth. Antistatis. Normal hours in New Corinth are M-F 8am-2pm.

Public Toilets: Across from the park on Eth. Antistasis. Open 8am-11pm. €0.50.

Police: Ermou 51 (☎100 or 27410 81 100), across the park from the courthouse. Open 24hr.

Pharmacies: On Eth. Anastasis, Koliatsou, and Ermou. Open M-F 8am-2pm and 5-8pm.

Hospital: ☎27410 25 711. On Athinaion; cross the train tracks and turn left. It's a long walk, so take a cab or call the hospital for an **ambulance** (☎100) in an emergency. Open 24hr. Closer **medical sevices** by the intersection of Notara and Ag. Orous.

OTE: Kolokotroni 32 (☎27410 24 499). Walk down Eth. Antistasis away from the waterfront, turn right onto Adimontou, and then make a right onto the next street; it's on the left. Open M-F 7:30am-1:30pm.

Internet Access: Stretto, Pilarinou 70 (☎27410 25 570), right off the first block of Eth. Antistasis. Sip coffee (€2) and check your email (€3 per hr., €1.50 min.). Open M-Sa 9am-11pm. Or try **Dia Diktio** (☎27410 73 707; bar@cafe.korinthia.net.gr), by the corner of Damaskinou and Eth. Antistasis. Coffee (€2) and Internet (€3.50 per hr., €3 after the first 10min.) available. Open daily 8am-11:30pm.

Post Office: ☎27410 80 050. On Adimantou, facing the park, between Eth. Antistasis and Ermou. Open M-F 7:30am-2pm. **Postal code:** 20100.

ACCOMMODATIONS

Most travelers find themselves merely passing through New Corinth for the ancient sites or to catch connecting trains; as a result, the selection of accommodations in the city is very limited. New Corinth's few hotels, which lie mostly along Eth. Antistasis and Damaskinou, tend to be pricey. Campgrounds can be quite a distance from the city, making it difficult for those who need to catch an early bus. **Hotel Korinthos ❸,** Damaskinou 26, two blocks on the right after the intersection of Damaskinou and Eth. Antistasis, boasts that it's the first to sell out for local soccer matches, though the roof garden and nightclub keep it popular year round. A/C, TV, private bathrooms, and breakfast are included with each of the 34 rooms. (☎27410 26 701; www.korinthoshotel.net. Reservations strongly recommended. Singles €45; doubles €70; triples €80; quads €90. MC/V.) Renovations completed in 2003 have given birth to New Corinth's most technologically up-to-date hotel, **Hotel Apollon ❸,** Damaskinou 2, one block before the train station. Each room comes with TV, A/C, and Internet access. (☎27410 25 920; hotelapol@otenet.gr. Reservations recommended. Singles €40; doubles €60; triples €70. Cash preferred.) **Hotel Akti ❷,** Eth. Antistasis 3, offers the best choice for the financially conscious traveler hoping to stay downtown. All rooms come with sink and towels for the shared shower. Some have balconies with great views of the water, but some are less well maintained. (☎27410 23 337. Singles €15-20; doubles €30-35. Cash only.) Tourist-friendly campgrounds of Blue **Dolphin ❶,** on Lecheon beach, cater to the true minimalist, as well as to those with BMWs by their tents. Kitchen and laundry facilities are available, as well as an on-site restaurant. (☎27410 25 766; www.camping-blue-dolphin.gr. Lockout midnight. Check-out 2pm. Parking for cars and electricity extra. Prices lower in low season. €12 per person, €6 tent rental. Cash preferred.)

FOOD

After 9pm, downtown perks up a bit, as residents flock to the waterfront to dine outdoors in the balmy evening air. As in the daytime, hustle seems to be a virtue; waiters deftly dodge the traffic on Damaskinou to shuttle between restaurants and outdoor seating areas on the waterfront plateia across the street. As fast, generic, and cheap foods abound, visitors often find themselves deciding where, not what, to eat. The snails in devil sauce (€5.50) or rigatoni with four cheeses (€7.50) at **Pros Korinthions ❷** (Προς Κορινθιους), Ap. Panlon 19, suggests the best food in New Corinth isn't even Greek but Italian. Walk toward the waterfront on Eth. Antistasis, turn right on Pilarinou, and then turn left on Ap. Panlon; it's on the left. (☎27410 81 250. Appetizers €2-15. Entrees €6-20. Desserts €4. Wine €12-30. Open daily 5pm-1am. MC/V.) One of the few tavernas open for breakfast (omelette €3.60), **Akhinos ❸,** Damaskinou 41, across the street from the waterfront plateia, serves classic staples. In warm weather, enjoy jazz renditions of early 90s pop songs as you sit outside in a tactlessly festive dining area. (☎27410 28 889. Prawns *saganaki* €12. Rabbit *stifado* €7. Beer €2. Open daily 10am-2am. Cash only.)

NIGHTLIFE

After sunset the incessant din of moped-mounted, cell-phone-crazed teenagers goes west of the city to **Kalamia beach;** follow them for a soon-to-be-forgotten evening of Corinthian entertainment: food and people-watching. To reach Kalamia without a moped, walk four blocks past the park along Eth. Anistasis, turn right, and proceed for 10 blocks. As the neighborhood is disconcertingly dark and empty at night, women may prefer taking a taxi from the park (€1.50); tell the driver "Kalamia" or "*thalassa*" (the sea). Kalamia's strip has something for everyone. Mixed crowds of older couples, teens, and families with small children share a single walkway overlooking the sparkling lights of Loutraki. Late-night favorites include the ironically ultra-trendy club **Unique** (beer €3; mixed drinks €6). A slightly older crowd frequents **Pilarinou,** off the first block of Eth. Antistasis.

PELOPONNESE

DAYTRIPS FROM CORINTH

ANCIENT CORINTH Αρχαια Κορινθος ☎27410

7km southwest of New Corinth. Buses leave from outside the bakery on Koliatsou (20min.; every 2hr., 10am-9:10pm, return buses leave at half past the hr.; €0.90). ☎27410 31 207. Open daily 8am-7pm; low season 8am-5pm. Guidebooks €4-7. Museum and site €6, students €3, EU students free.

Strategically located on the isthmus between the Corinthian and Saronic Gulfs, Ancient Corinth was once a powerful commercial center and one of the most influential cities in ancient Greece. Its opulent wealth attracted *hetairai* (courtesans) as well as merchants, earning it a reputation as a sinfully delightful city. At its height in the 5th century BC, Corinth joined forces with her southern neighbor, Sparta, against the naval muscle of Athens—a power struggle that led to the Peloponnesian Wars (p. 9). While the war won dominance for Sparta, the long struggle weakened Corinth significantly. After the Romans sacked and virtually razed the city in 146 BC, it remained deserted until Julius Caesar rebuilt it in 44 BC. Unfortunately not even his efforts could prevent the city from crumbling at the hands of violent earthquakes time and time again.

FORTRESS AND ACROCORINTH. It's located 3km uphill from the museum. Hiking to the fortress at the top of the Acrocorinth is both a strenuous and dangerous 2hr. climb up a road regularly traveled by fast moving cars. Taxis (☎27410 31 464; €6) are an easy alternative and will even wait an hour and drive you back down (€10). Those truly dedicated should head past the first three gates and towards the summit. Here, the Temple to Aphrodite, once served by "sacred courtesans" who initiated diligent disciples into the "mysteries of love," remains largely intact. Though the courtesans may be taking their days off, you can still enjoy the amazing bird's-eye view of Corinthia. Time permitting, venture around the rest of the relatively empty fortress which contains acres of towers, mosques, gates, and walls. Don't forget sturdy shoes, sunscreen, and a bottle of water.

ANCIENT SITE. The remains of the ancient Roman city stand at the base of the **Acrocorinth,** a fortress atop a large mountain. Past the exit of the museum, the archaeological site is down the stairs to your left. Most conspicuous and breathtaking, the seven columns from the **Temple of Apollo** have defiantly endured the trials of time since the 6th century BC. As you walk toward the remains of the temple, climbing over the engraved friezes and pediments that scatter the courtyard, a small edifice with hollowed entryways is on the left. Here, located behind the museum, is the **Fountain of Glauke,** named after Jason the Argonaut's second wife, who was consumed by the flames of an enchanted robe given to her by Jason's bitter ex-wife Medea. Ahead of you, from the Temple of Apollo, facing the mountainous Acrocorinth, lie the remains of the **forum,** the center of Roman civil life. Walk down the middle of the row of central shops and you'll see the **Julian Basilica,** which served as the forum's entry.

To the left, near the exit at the edge of the site farthest from the museum, a broad stone stairway descends into the **Peirene Fountain,** which once stood over 20 feet tall. Although smoothed by the water that still flows today, the columns and fresco-covered tunnels inside the fountain have survived the centuries unharmed. According to legend Peirene was the daughter of the river god Asopus; when one of her sons (by Poseidon, no less) was accidentally killed, she shed "endless tears" and was turned into the spring. Just past the fountain is the **Perivolos of Apollo,** an open-air court surrounded by still more columns. On the uphill edge of the site, on the side farthest from the museum, somewhat ragged sheds cover the mosaic floors of a Roman villa. Unfortunately, like the Roman Odeum and ancient Theater in front of the museum, entry is not permitted; you'll have to settle for a view through the rusted chain link fence.

ARCHAEOLOGICAL MUSEUM. Tracing Corinth's history through Greek, Roman, and Byzantine rule, the Archaeological Museum proudly showcases its restored collection of impressive statues, well-preserved mosaics, and tiny clay figurines. The expansive genres of ancient works in the permanent exhibit range from a marble statue of a sphinx to a Corinthian soldier's helmet. The Roman frescoes and mosaics date from the same period as Pompeii, and changes in pottery technique trace Greece's evolution from Neolithic to Byzantine times. The museum's collections of sarcophagi—including one with a skeleton under glass—and headless statues in the open-air courtyard are morbidly appealing. While the exhibits are noteworthy, it's worthwhile to purchase a guidebook (€4-7) because there is little explanation given. *(Open Tu-F 8am-7pm, Sa-Su 8:30am-3pm.)*

NEMEA Νεμυα ☎27460

5km from modern Nemea; coming by bus from Corinth (1hr., 7 per day, €2.80), ask to be let off at the ancient site (☎27460 22 739). Site and museum open Tu-Su 8am-2:30pm; call to confirm. €3, students and seniors €2, EU students and under 18 free. Same for stadium.

Ancient Nemea is a refreshing alternative for those feeling claustrophobic at more commercialized ancient sites in Corinthia. An airy museum proudly displays the history of both the site and its excavation with a well-sized collection of coins, tools, and statuettes. Excellent explanatory notes and videos in English help convey the historical significance of an area that once held the **Temple of Nemean Zeus.** Outside the museum, three massive columns still stand starkly against the mountainous backdrop. Visitors are also greeted by an encased skeleton from an early Christian tomb. Self-guided tours of the stadium, 200m up the road to the left, allow visitors to occupy the cery track that once hosted Panhellenic contests.

ISTHMIA Ισθμια ☎27460

At Terminal C, catch the bus from New Corinth to Isthmia (10min., 6 per day, €0.90). Ask to be let off at the green museum (☎27460 37 244), or get off at the Isthmia stop, go straight 1km, turn right for 300m, and then turn left on the uphill road; the museum is on the right. Open Tu-Su 8:30am-3pm. €3, students and seniors €2, EU students free. Guidebooks €6.

Held every other year during the Festival of Poseidon, the Isthmian games attracted the best Panhellenic athletes in a series of contests that rivaled those of Olympia and Delphi. According to legend the games grew out of funeral rites put on by Sisyphus for the child Melikertes, in whose honor the champions donned pine and laurel crowns. Today little of the site remains, save the foundation of the **Temple of Poseidon.** The adjacent museum holds a humble collection. Of particular interest are the glass **opus sectile,** 87 mosiac panels which miraculously survived the earthquake at Kenchreai in 375.

LOUTRAKI Λουτρακι ☎27440

Since ancient times travelers have visited the pebbled beach of Loutraki, just over the isthmus from Corinth, to soak in the natural springs with reputed medicinal powers. The waters are also bottled and sold all over Greece. Although hotels dominate the streets and waterfront, and tourists crowd the beach, the vacation atmosphere and beautiful surroundings allow for a pleasant overnight stay.

TRANSPORTATION. To get to Loutraki from Isthmia, cross the canal bridge and find the bus stop next to a railroad station sign. Stay on the bus until the last stop, a triangular road island where **El. Venizelou,** the main street, meets **Periandrou** and **Iasonos.** Running parallel to the water, El. Venizelou curves away from Corinth at the northern end of the strip and becomes **Giorgiou Lekka.** The change from Venizelou to G. Lekka marks the central square of Loutraki, but the beach and most of the tourist activity are along the boardwalk and on Venizelou. **Buses** also leave the station on El. Venizelou for **Athens** (1¼hr.; M-Sa 8 per day, 6:05am-9pm, service reduced Su; €6) and **Corinth** (20min.; 2 per hr., 6am-10:30pm, service reduced Sa-Su; €1.20). **Boat excursions** are available at the dock past the park. Cruises sail to Lake Vouliagmeni and down the Corinth Canal. Times and prices vary; contact the tourist office or call ☎27440 64 919 for more information. For a **taxi** (☎27440 61 000 or 27440 65 000), stop by the stand next to the tourist info center on El. Venizelou. **Moto-Rent** (near the bus station) has **moped rentals.** (☎27440 67 277. €18 per day.)

PRACTICAL INFORMATION. Loutraki has no lack of tourist information. There are two **tourist information kiosks:** with the water on your right, one is located on El. Venizelou, one block south of the bus station; the other is after the curve at the central square on G. Lekka, at the end of the town park. (Both open daily 8am-2pm and 7-9pm.) The **Municipal Enterprise for Tourism** office, in the central square, is a wonderful resource for any and all adventures in Loutraki: water parks, scuba diving, hang-gliding, tours, and cruises. (☎27440 26 001 or 26 325; loutraki@kor.forthnet.gr. Open M-F 7:30am-3pm.) To get to the **National Bank,** follow El. Venizelou, with the water on your left, to the central square. (☎27440 22 220; fax 27440 64 945. 24hr. **ATM** available. Open M-Th 8am-2:30pm, F 8am-2pm.) Periandrou, the first side street on the right across from the bus island, is home to **Laundry Self-Service,** on the first block on your left, which provides wash and dry for €10. (☎27440 67 367. Open M, W, Sa 8:30am-2pm; Tu, Th-F 8:30-2pm and 5:30-9pm.) The **police,** El. Venizelou 7 (☎27440 63 000; open 24hr.), are in the same building as the **tourist police,** 3km from downtown Loutraki, on El. Venizelou as it heads south toward Corinth. The **health center** is roughly 5km from the center of town; walk five blocks up from El. Venizelou, follow the signs by turning right then continuing straight. (☎27440 26 666. Open 24hr.) One of several **pharmacies** is at El. Venizelou 24. (☎27440 64 528. Open daily 8:30am-2pm and 5:30-9:30pm.) **Las Vegas Internet Cafe** is just past the information kiosk on El. Venizelou. (☎27410 24 872. €4 per hr.; 15min. minimum. Open daily 9am-2am.) The **OTE** is at El. Venizelou 10, on the left if you walk from the bus station with the water on your left. (☎27440 61 999. Open M-F 7am-2pm.) From the bus station, walk up El. Venizelou, with the water to your right, one block past the gas station to find the **post office** on your right. (Open M-F 7:30am-2pm.) **Postal code:** 20300.

ACCOMMODATIONS. Loutraki draws a near-constant stream of moneyed vacationers, so there are many hotel options. Those on a budget can try the hotels in the center of town, where El. Venizelou becomes G. Lekka, while those looking to splurge should head to the waterfront, particularly the quieter stretch past the park. For **domatia,** call ☎27440 22 456 or consult the tourist office in the central square. Most hotels on El. Venizelou offer A/C and private baths in room. To reach **Le Petit France ❸,** M. Botsari 3, take El. Venizelou from the bus station in the direction you face when exiting the station; M. Botsari is your third right. The friendly owners of this quaint, blue-shuttered hotel extend their hospitality in every way. Visitors may take breakfast in a lovely garden; rooms come with balconies, ceiling fans, and baths. (☎27440 22 401; www.geocities.com/lepetitfrance. Breakfast €3.50. A/C €5 extra. Call ahead for reservations in summer. Singles €25; doubles €30-35. Larger, family-style rooms available.) Nearly on the beach, **Hotel Marko ❸,** on L. Katsoni, has lovely rooms with bathrooms, TVs, A/C, and balconies. Enjoy complimentary breakfast in the cafe downstairs and return later for a drink at the bar. (☎27440 63 542; markohl@otenet.gr. Singles €40; doubles €50; suite for up to 5 €70.) For a quieter stay, head to **Hotel Galaxy ❹,** just after the waterfalls on G. Lekka, overlooking a small, secluded beach. Newly renovated rooms have TVs, A/C, mini-fridges, balconies, and private baths, and friendly owner Tatiana speaks good English. (☎27440 28 282. Breakfast €5. Singles €48; doubles €55.) **Hotel Possidonion ❷** overlooks the central square. Friendly owner Alexandros speaks English and his clean rooms have phone, A/C, TV, private bath, and balcony. (☎27440 22 273; htlposid@otenet.gr. Breakfast €3. Singles €20-25; doubles €30-36.) **Camping ❶** (☎27410 91 230 or 91 229) is available 16km away at stunning Lake Vouliagmeni. To get there, take G. Lekka out of town and follow the signs. You can also camp at Isthmia beach on the Corinth Canal (☎27410 37 447 or 37 720; www.isthmiacamping.gr). Consider taking a taxi; otherwise take the bus and walk the rest of the way to the campsite.

FOOD AND NIGHTLIFE. There are a number of good cafes and fish tavernas on the beachfront—stroll along the promenade and enjoy the

THE BIG SPLURGE

THE WATERS OF LOUTRA

The ancient city of Thermai, toda known as Loutraki, has beer acclaimed throughout history for its healing waters. Thermai was home to temples of Apollo and Hera and it wa first made famous in Xenophon's *Hellenica.* It is reputed that while Greece was under Roman control, Genera Sulla came to Loutraki to be cured by the therapeutic waters of the city's Roman Baths. During the Byzantin Period, a number of churches were built around Loutraki's springs and spas, and today, a thriving "healtl tourism" industry has developed ir Loutraki.

There are two types of water ir Loutraki—medicinal and mineral Both are renowned throughou Greece. The mineral water ir Loutraki is bottled in seven bottling plants around the city and is sold throughout the country and the res of Europe. Residents of Loutrak enjoy this same fresh and pleasan tasting water straight out of the tap The medicinal waters are said t allieviate arthritis, skin conditions kidney disorders, gynecologica problems, and various other cond tions. Both drinking and bathing ir the medicinal water is advised as treatment for these ailments, and visitors to the Loutraki Spa put the water to use in a number of ways.

Hydrotherapy Thermal Spa, G Lekkas 26, past the central square along Venizelou, offers 4-, 5-, 6- and 10-day programs. ☎27440 22 215; www.city-of-loutraki.gr/spa €15-20 per day. Open daily 7an 1pm; in winter M-F 8am-noon.

process of choosing one that suits you. Hotels on El. Venizelou and the streets between it and the water also have some good options. There is certainly no shortage of places to eat, though prices tend to be high. **Supermarkets** are on El. Venizelou; the one across the street from the post office is a good bet. (Open M-F 8am-9pm, Sa 9am-2pm.) On the beach behind the OTE, **Caravella Beer House ❷** serves pasta, salads, meat dishes, seafood, ice cream, coffee, and—clearly—beer. Stop in for a snack while you're soaking up the sun or make this your last stop and throw down a few cold ones as you admire the beautiful bay of Corinth. (☎27440 65 204. Entrees €5-10.) Locals flock to **Strougka ❸,** at the Corinth end of the waterfront, where meat dishes like beef tenderloin (€10) and souvlaki (€6) are scrumptious. (☎27440 65 747. Entrees €5-10. Open daily until 1:30am.) **Grill House 71 ❶,** El. Venizelou 71, a few blocks past the post office on the left, is a slight distance from the center of town but certainly worth the trip. Locals claim it has the best souvlaki (€1.10) around. (☎27440 61 776. Takeout and delivery available. Open 5pm-4am. Closes earlier in winter.) Tiny **Il Guosto Pizza ❷,** three blocks past the bus station on El. Venizelou with the water on your right, has an impressive variety of pizzas (€5.50-7) and Italian dishes. (☎27440 69 200. Open daily 24hr.)

Nightlife in Loutraki means eating and dancing. Waterfront restaurants swell in summer, staying full well past midnight. Along the boardwalk, **Cameo, Sax, Paul's, Cafe Coral, Jamaica,** and **El Niño** pump music for steady crowds. After midnight, taxis transport the party-hungry to discos on the city's edges. **Hype** (formerly Baby-O), near the Pepsi/Loutraki Water bottling plant on the road to Corinth, pulses past dawn. (Cover €10, includes 1 drink. Open F-Sa.) **CoCoon,** at the Corinth end of the boardwalk, is a space-aged venue serving food by day and alcohol by night. (Beer €4; mixed drinks €5.50-6. Open daily 10am-3am.) Feeling lucky? Follow the road to Corinth past Hype and look right. Loutraki is also home to Europe's largest **casino** (☎27440 65 501), according to the tourist office.

WATER. If you seek solace in Loutraki's healing waters, indulge at **Therma: Hydrotherapy Thermal Spa** (see **The Waters of Loutraki,** p. 147). At the well maintained **waterfalls,** a 12min. walk from the central square on G. Lekka, admire the fountains at the cliff's base. (Open daily 10am-3am.) The water park **Water Fun** is between Loutraki and Corinth on Lake Vouliagmeni. (☎27410 81 400; www.water-fun.gr.) Loutraki's many **beaches** shouldn't confine you to the boardwalk area.

MYCENAE Μυκηνες ☎27510

Excavations of ancient Mycenae have continued for 130 years, since Heinrich Schliemann first turned a spade here (p. 150). When ancient Athenian sites become oversaturated with pin-swapping tourists during the Olympics, Mycenae, with its famed Lion's Gate and Tomb of Agamemnon, will most likely be inundated with the overflow. Most travelers make Mycenae a daytrip from Athens or Nafplion, but the tourist-friendly modern village can be a pleasant place for a night.

TRANSPORTATION AND PRACTICAL INFORMATION

The only direct **buses** to **Mycenae** are from **Nafplion** (45min.; 5 per day, 7:30am-7pm; €1.80) via **Argos** (30min., €0.90). The site is on the Corinth-Argos road; follow the signs to Mycenae from Fihtia. Four buses make the return trip to **Argos** and **Nafplion,** stopping in the town of **Mycenae** (in front of Hotel Belle Helene) and at the site (a 25min. walk from the town). **Trains** (5 per day) run from **Athens** to Fihtia via Corinth. Mycenae has **no bank,** but a mobile **post office** booth at the site offers **currency exchange.** (Open mid-Mar.-Oct. M-Sa 9:30am-4pm.) **Postal code:** 21200.

ACCOMMODATIONS AND FOOD

Mycenae is well equipped to accommodate travelers with various preferences and (perhaps more importantly) budgets. Hotels, **domatia,** and campgrounds can all be found in the village and on the road to the ancient site. Without an ATM in town, most establishments and shops accept credit cards and traveler's checks. A new **youth hostel ❶** (☎27510 76 224) currently under construction, above Iphiggeria Restaurant, 50m downhill from Belle Helene, is scheduled to be completed by 2004. On the main road to the site, **Hotel Belle Helene ❸** is just uphill from the strip of restaurants. Opened in 1862, the oldest hotel in the village once hosted Heinrich Schliemann and his archaeological posse. With the exception of room #3 (where Schliemann stayed and which still has an iron bed and period furniture), all rooms come with shared baths, fans, private sinks, and comfortable beds. (☎27510 76 225; fax 27510 76 179. Breakfast included. Singles €20-30; doubles €40-50; triples €50-55. AmEx/MC/V.) Next door, **Dassis Rent Rooms ❸,** despite being less historic, has balconies, baths, A/C, and even some bathtubs which keep this place constantly brimming with travelers and even contemporary archaeologists. (☎27510 76 123 or 76 385; fax 27510 76 124. Reservations strongly recommended. Singles €40; doubles €50; triples €60. MC/V.) **Rooms to Let ❷,** above Restaurant Aristidis Dikeos on the main road, may not have much going on in the way of decor but they are admirably clean with A/C and big private baths. (☎27510 76 852. Singles €25; doubles €25-30. Cash only.) Across from Dassis Rent Rooms in the middle of town and shaded by pine trees, **Camping Mykines ❶** offers laundry facilities (€3), free hot showers, and a nicely-priced, completely renovated taverna. The owners also sell wine (€3) from their own vineyards, 5km from the camp. (☎27510 76 121. Breakfast €1-4. €4.50-5.50 per person, €3-3.50 per child; €3-3.50 per car; €3.50-4.50 per small tent, €4-5 per large tent. Electricity €4-4.50. 10% off in low season or if you inquire about a reduction. Cash only.)

A few good restaurants hide among the overpriced multitude of tour bus troughs bearing the name of unfortunate members of the Atreus clan, ancient Mycenae's infamous ruling family. Local favorite **Spiros Restaurant and Taverna ❶,** 50m downhill from Belle Helene, serves wonderful Greek dishes. (☎27510 76 115. Omelettes €2-3. Grilled meats €4.50 and up. Stuffed tomatoes €4.50. Pizza €6.50. Cash only.)

DAYTRIP FROM MYCENAE: ANCIENT MYCENAE

Walk 25min. uphill from the town, or take the bus to where it stops at the end of the asphalt road; the ruins are on the right. Open Apr.-Sept. daily 8am-7pm; Oct.-Mar. 8am-5pm. €6, students €3, EU students free. You must hold onto your ticket after entering the main site to access Agamemnon's Tomb. Bring a flashlight for the tombs and cistern.

The excavated remains of ancient Mycenae rest on a rocky knoll between Mt. Ag. Elias to the north and Mt. Zara to the south. The gargantuan **Cyclopean walls,** 13m high and 10m thick, surround the site; they inherited their name from ancients who believed that the city's founders, Perseus and his descendants, could only have lifted such stones with the help of a superhuman Cyclops. Outside the central fortified city, several *tholoi* (domed tombs)—most notably the so-called **Treasury of Atreus**—unsubtly hint at the magnificence that lies over the horizon. Today the bulk of the ruins left standing date from 1280 BC, when the city was the center of a vast Mycenaean Empire. Many of the unearthed relics number among the most celebrated archaeological discoveries in modern history, and are consequently housed in the National

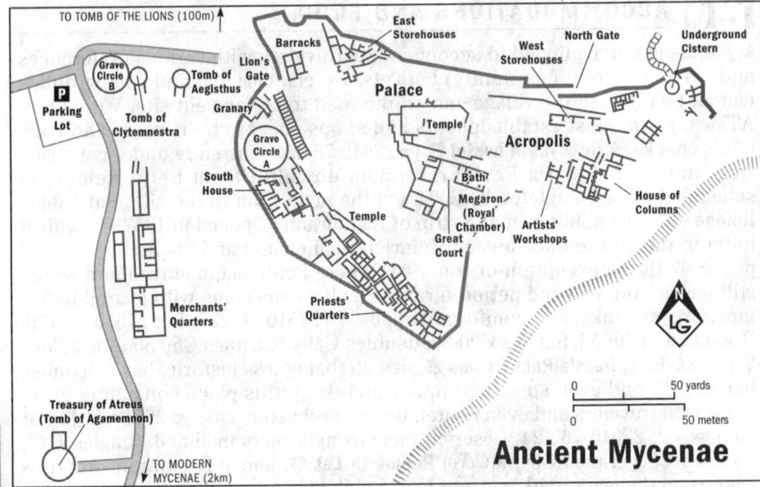

Archaeological Museum in Athens (p. 114). A guidebook can add to the experience: S.E. Iakovidis's *Guide to Mycenae and Epidavros* (€7.50) includes a map. Another by George E. Mylonas, director of the excavation, takes a more scholarly approach and focuses on Mycenae (€5.50). For info on other nearby ruins, try *The Peloponnese*, by E. Karpodini-Dimitriadi (€10).

HISTORY. Mycenae's origins, interactions with other Near Eastern civilizations, and subsequent decline have long puzzled historians. Thought to have been settled as early as 2700 BC by a tribe from the Cyclades, Mycenae, along with other nearby cities, remained under the control of the Minoan capital Knossos for centuries. It wasn't until the cataclysmic collapse of Minoan civilization in the mid-15th century BC that Mycenae surged to the head of the Greek world (p. 8). Mycenaean culture flourished for centuries until the 12th century BC, when the belligerent Dorians attacked from the north. Burning and looting anything in their path, the Dorians successfully conquered Greece, and Mycenae lost its grasp on the culture it had helped to create. Mycenae contined to be inhabited through the Roman Period but by Byzantine times had been swallowed by the earth and forgotten.

In 1874, the German businessman, classicist, and amateur archaeologist **Heinrich Schliemann** burst onto the Mycenaean scene. Fresh from his lucrative dig at Troy and eager to further establish the historical validity of Homeric epics, he began a quest to uncover Agamemnon's city. To his delight, he found massive walls which surrounded elaborate tombs laden with dazzling artifacts. It was impossible to overlook the possible connection between these finds and Homer's description of a "well-built citadel... rich in gold." Schliemann began his dig just inside the citadel walls at the spot where several ancient authors described royal graves. Discovering 15 skeletons "literally covered with gold and jewels," Schliemann decked his new 17-year-old Greek bride with the baubles and had her pose for photographs. Believing he had unearthed the skeletons of Agamemnon and his disciples, he sent a telegram to the Greek king that read, "Have gazed on face of Agamemnon." Moments after he removed its mask, the "face" underneath disintegrated. Modern archaeologists, who still today cringe at the thought of such reckless excavation, now date the tombs to four centuries before the Trojan War.

RUINS. Uphill from the entrance booth, you'll spot the imposing **Lion's Gate,** the portal into the ancient city, with two lions carved in relief above the lintel (estimated to weigh some 20 tons). They symbolized the house of Atreus, and their heads—now missing—once bore eyes of precious gems. The sculpture is one of the earliest known examples of statuary incorporated into a structure's support system. Schliemann found most of his artifacts in **Grave Circle A,** a large hollow area to the right, just outside the city walls, which contains six 16th-century BC **shaft graves** that have yielded 14kg worth of gold. Don't listen to dilettantes who claim that the graves were the resting place of Agamemnon; the graves date back to the 17th-16th centuries BC, while the reign of the legendary king occurred in the 13th or 12th century. The barracks are up the stairs to the left after the gate. The gate and the walls of the upper citadel date from the 13th century BC.

The ruins on the hillside are the remnants of various homes, businesses, and shrines. The **palace** and the **royal apartments** are at the highest part of the citadel on the right. The open spaces here include guard rooms, private areas, and public rooms; look for the **megaron,** or royal chamber, with its round hearth framed by the bases of four pillars. To the left of the citadel sit the remaining stones of a Hellenistic **Temple of Athena.** At the far end of the city, between the palace and the **postern gate,** is the **underground cistern,** a vital component of the ancient city which guaranteed water during sieges. Silently offering solitude and complete darkness, visitors can still enter at their own risk. A flashlight is essential to explore its depths. Be careful: the steps are worn and slippery, dropping off suddenly.

Follow the asphalt 150m back toward the town of Mycenae to the **Tomb of Agamemnon** (a.k.a. the Treasury of Atreus), the largest and most impressive *tholos,* named by Schliemann for the king he desperately wanted to discover here. On your way, stop at two often-overlooked *tholoi*, the **Tomb of Aegisthus** and the even more interesting **Tomb of Clytemnestra,** both outside the Lion's Gate on the site of the town. Take the paths on your left and make sure to hang on to your flashlight. Once you get to the main event, head down a 40m passage cut into the hillside that leads to Agamemnon's resting place, looking up at the 120-ton lintel stones above you. The dim interior of the *tholos* conveys a ghostly majesty befitting the grave of such a famous and tragic figure. But, to the dismay of archaeologists and tourists alike, the tomb was found empty, having lost its valuables to robbers.

ARGOS Αργος ☎27510

According to Homer, Argos was the kingdom of the hero Diomedes and claimed allegiance to Mycenae's powerful king, Agamemnon. Later Dorians invaded and captured the city in the 12th century BC, using it as their base for control of the Argolid Peninsula. Argos remained the most powerful state in the Peloponnese through the 7th century BC, defeating even Kleomenes and the Spartans, who, in the famous 494 BC battle, were unable to penetrate the city walls. Later Argos stood with Corinth and dominant Sparta as the pillars of the Peloponnesian League. As with other Greek cities, over time Argos laid new foundations over the old. The modern city is built almost entirely on top of previous layers of habitation, and, despite a healthy ribbon of archaeological red tape, it has managed to grow into a crowded, lively city. Argos may not be the most picturesque city that the Peloponnese has to offer, but the excellent museum and the ruins of the ancient theater, agora, and Roman baths are worth seeing if you're in the area.

TRANSPORTATION

The **Argolida** station (☎27510 67 324), on Kapodistriou, which runs parallel to and one block beyond the side of the plateia with Hotel Morfeas, sends buses to: **Athens** (2½hr.; 15 per day, 5:30am-8:30pm; €8.10) via **Corinth** (€3.20); **Mycenae** (30min., 5 per day, €1); **Nafplion** (20min.; every 30min., 6:30am-9pm; €0.80); **Nemea** (1hr.; 6:30am, 1pm; €2); **Tripoli** (1hr., 4 per day, €3.70). Service is reduced on weekends.

The **train station** (☎27510 67 212) is 1km from the plateia. Walk down Nikitara past the OTE and follow the signs to Nafplion from the five-point intersection. Follow signs for the police station until you reach the intersection with 25 Martiou; the station is directly ahead. Trains go to: **Athens** (3hr.; 5 per day, 2:37am-7:36pm; €3.50) via **Fihtia** (€0.60), **Nemea** (20min., €0.70), and **Corinth** (1hr., €1.80); **Kalamata** (4hr.; 3 per day, 1:29am-5:13pm; €4.40) via **Tripoli** (1hr., €2).

ORIENTATION AND PRACTICAL INFORMATION

Argos has few landmarks and can be tough to navigate, so pick up a **map** (available at the Archaeological Museum). Most amenities, hotels, and restaurants are in or around the plateia, marked by the large **Church of St. Peter.** If you ride the bus into town, go right out of the station and turn left at the first significant intersection onto **Danaou.** The plateia will be on your left and a small park on your right.

Bank: National Bank (☎27510 29 911), on Nikitara, off the plateia behind the small park to the left as you face Hotel Morfeas, has **currency exchange** and a 24hr. **ATM.** Open M-Th 8am-2pm, F 8am-1:30pm.

Police: ☎27510 67 222. On the corner of Inaxou and Papaoikonomou; head out from Vas. Sofias or follow the signs from the train station. Some English spoken. Open 24hr.

Hospital: ☎27510 24 455. 1km north of the plateia on Korinthou. Open 24hr.

OTE: Nikitara 8 (☎27510 67 599). Facing the park from the main plateia, take the street along the left side of the park past the National Bank ATM. Open M-F 7am-2pm.

Internet: Center for Youth Information (☎27510 25 314), 50m to the left of the bus station as you face the plateia, in the building at the end of the grassy playground, provides free Internet access. Open daily 10am-10pm.

Post Office: ☎27510 67 366. 3 blocks down from the bus station. Follow the signs from the plateia. Offers **currency exchange.** Open M-F 7:30am-2pm. **Postal code:** 21200.

ACCOMMODATIONS AND FOOD

It's a good idea to make Argos and Mycenae a daytrip from Nafplion since the sights can be seen in a day and Argos has few accommodations. If you stay overnight, try the **Hotel Apollon ❷,** Papaflessa 13. Walk past the National Bank ATM and follow the road closest to Micky's Fast Food. Budget-conscious visitors can get a solid night's rest in spacious rooms with ceiling fans, TVs, telephones, and sinks. Private baths and A/C are available at an extra charge. (☎27510 68 065; fax 27510 61 182. Singles €17.60-22; doubles €24-31; triples €29.76-37.20. Cash only.) The brand-new **Hotel Morfeas ❸,** Danaou 2, has the classiest rooms in town at unexpectedly reasonable prices. All guests are treated to roomy private baths, A/C, TVs, and balconies with views of St. Peter's. (☎27510 68 317; fax 27510 66 249. Singles €25-35; doubles €35-45. MC/V.) The **Hotel Palladion ❸,** Vas. Sofias 5, just off the plateia, offers centrally located rooms with A/C, TVs, telephones, private baths, and balconies. During hot afternoons, guests can siesta on the red velvet couches that occupy the hallways. (☎27510 67 807. Singles €22-35; doubles €40-96; triples €50-65. MC/V.)

Argos has the Peloponnese's largest **open-air market** (see **Argos Agora,** p. 153) in the empty parking lot across from the museum. (Open W, Sa 8:30am-2pm.) Fast-food junkies will be thrilled by the greasy gyro joints that clog the arteries of the plateia and the surrounding area. Those who prefer a more formal meal, may be disappointed by the sit-down options. There are many supermarkets scattered throughout the center of town including **Atlantik Supermarket,** 50m to the right of the bus station as you face the plateia. (Open M-F 8am-9pm, Sa 8am-6pm.) Next to the Hotel Mycenae, **Cafe Retro Pizzeria** ❷ serves piping-hot pizzas (€5-11) and pastas (€2.50-5) that make up for slow service and discordant decor. (Salads €2.50-7. Grilled entrees €5-11. Cash only.) If you do find yourself tempted by the fast-food options, try local favorite **La Prima** ❶, in the park by Dia Discount Supermarket. This joint serves Italian fare, but a few Greek options are on the menu. (☎27510 68 188. Salads €2.35-3.52. Crepes €2.93-3.23. Pasta €2.34-4.40. Chicken souvlaki €4.40. Takeout and delivery available. Cash only.)

SIGHTS

ARCHAEOLOGICAL MUSEUM. Argos's superb archaeological museum has a large Mycenaean collection, Roman sculptures, and much weaponry, as well as a garden courtyard with more sculptures and the notable **Roman mosaics.** In the most striking of the mosaics, 12 figures personify the months of the year in their dress, expressions, and accoutrements—and if that strikes your fancy, make sure to check out the mosaic that portrays the four seasons in a similar manner. On the ground floor of the museum, a detailed shard of a *krater* from the 7th century BC depicts Odysseus putting out the eye of Polyphemus. In the same room, the well-preserved helmet and breastplate from the Geometric Period also deserve perusal. Make sure not to skip over the **Lerna Exhibition,** which features pottery, roof tiles, and a hearth from the early Helladic Period. *(Off the plateia on Vas. Olgas. ☎27510 68 819. Open Tu-Su 8:30am-3pm. €2, students and seniors €1, EU students and children free.)*

ANCIENT ARGOS. Archaeologists hope to uncover a large part of the ancient city of Argos, but at this point, most of it remains buried beneath the modern version. Major excavations have taken place on the city's western fringe at the site of the ancient agora. With a seating capacity of 20,000, the 5th-century BC **theater** was the largest of its

THE HIDDEN DEAL

ARGOS AGORA

If your trip to Argos's ancient theater and Archaeological Museum has left you wishing you were born in the Bronze Age instead of the information age, don't panic. Twice a week, in the vast space adjacent to the museum, you can still partake in one ancient Greek tradition that has managed to survive through Dorian invasions and devastating earthquakes: the open-air market.

In need of fresh fruit? Designer fanny-packs? Jewelry, sarongs, or used clothing? Whatever it is you're looking for, one of the hundreds of merchants who sets up shop in the Peloponnese's largest agora is sure to have it. Early in the morning, truckloads of goods are unloaded onto massive tables. By noon, no claustrophobe would stand a chance against the crowds that fill every possible space beween the vendors.

But unlike similar open-air markets in Athens, there is very little interaction between buyers and sellers. Once the goods are set out, customers become entrenched in what quickly becomes a shopping free-for-all. Consequently, buyers need not be concerned about the strength of their bargaining skills, but rather their wilingness to fight other customers for what they want. Even the ordinarily stern elderly women get into it; don't be surprised if one elbows you or snatches the last pair of sandals straight from your hands.

Open W and Sa 8:30am-2pm. In the empty parking lot across from the museum.

time in the Greek world, although it's not as well preserved as its famous counterpart in Epidavros. Across from the theater are the remains of the extensive **Roman bath complex,** whose two remaining red brick walls convey the structure's magnitude. Many of the original floor mosaics are intricate, colorful, and intact. The **Roman Odeum,** 30m to the left of the baths (with your back to the entrance), survives mostly as an outline, as the rows dissolve into the hillside. Across the street are the scattered remains of the agora, built in the 5th century BC and destroyed by Alaric's Visigoths in AD 395. *(From the museum, turn left, and walk towards the large space that holds the open-air market. Turn left onto Phidonos, and walk 5min. until the road ends. Make a right on Theatrou and walk to the end. Open daily 8am-3pm. Free.)*

THE CASTLE OF LARISA. In medieval times, Franks, Venetians, and Ottomans in turn captured and ruled Argos. As a result, the fortress is an architectural hodgepodge, combining these disparate medieval elements with Classical and Byzantine foundations. The ruins are mainly of interest to scholars—though all visitors can appreciate the castle's view over the city. The Cyclopean walls are nearly 4000 years old. *(Walk along Vas. Konstantinou for roughly 1hr. or climb the foot path from the ruins of the ancient theater. The road to the castle is mostly unshaded, and sweltering heat in the summer months can make it very unpleasant. A taxi (€5) provides relief. Open all day. Free.)*

OTHER SIGHTS. The **Argive Heraion,** 10km northeast of Argos, dedicated to Hera, goddess of the Argives, was built in the 5th century BC. It prospered well into the 2nd century AD, hosting the celebrations that followed the official ending of the Heraia Games (archery contests held at Argos in the second year after each Olympiad) and other annual festivals. Nearby **Prosimni,** 5km past the Heraion, is home to prehistoric graves. Fifteen kilometers from Argos, and a few kilometers east of Agias Trias, are the remains of the city of **Dendra,** where tombs yielded the preserved suit of bronze armor now in the Nafplion Archaeological Museum (p. 158).

NAFPLION Ναυπλιο ☎27520

Beautiful old Nafplion shines with Venetian architecture, fortresses, a pebble beach, and hillside stairways. Though it's the perfect base for exploring the ancient sites of the Argolid, Nafplion may entice you to spend a few days away from the ruins. A delightful central park links the two sides over shady, flower-lined paths and a large children's playground. Before the Venetians built Nafplion—named for Poseidon's son Nafplius—on a swamp in the 15th century, the city consisted entirely of the two hilltop fortresses. Nafplion has vastly expanded, swallowing neighboring villages and acquiring chain stores. Though the New Town has little to offer, the charming Old Town is a maze of bougainvillea-trellised alleys packed with tavernas and craft shops—certainly worth a day of wandering.

TRANSPORTATION

The bus terminal is on **Syngrou,** near the acropolis. To reach **Bouboulinas,** the waterfront promenade, go left when exiting the station and follow Syngrou to the harbor—the **Old Town** is on your left. The **bus station** (☎27520 28 555) is on Syngrou off Pl. Kapodistrias, with service to: **Argos** (20min.; 2 per hr., 5am-10:30pm; €1); **Athens** (3hr.; every hr., 5am-8pm; €9) via **Corinth** (2hr., €4); **Epidavros** (45min.; 4 per day, 10:15am-7:30pm; €2); **Mycenae** (45min., 3 per day, €2); **Tripoli** (1½hr., 4 per day, €3.50); **Tolo** (20min.; every hr., 7am-9:30pm; €.85). **Taxis** (☎27520 24 120 or 24 720) congregate on Syngrou near the bus station. Past the post office, away from the Old Town, **Motortraffic Rent-A-Moto,** Sidiras 15 (☎27520 22 702), rents mopeds. (€13.50-40 per day. Includes helmet and insurance. Open daily 8:30am-10:30pm.)

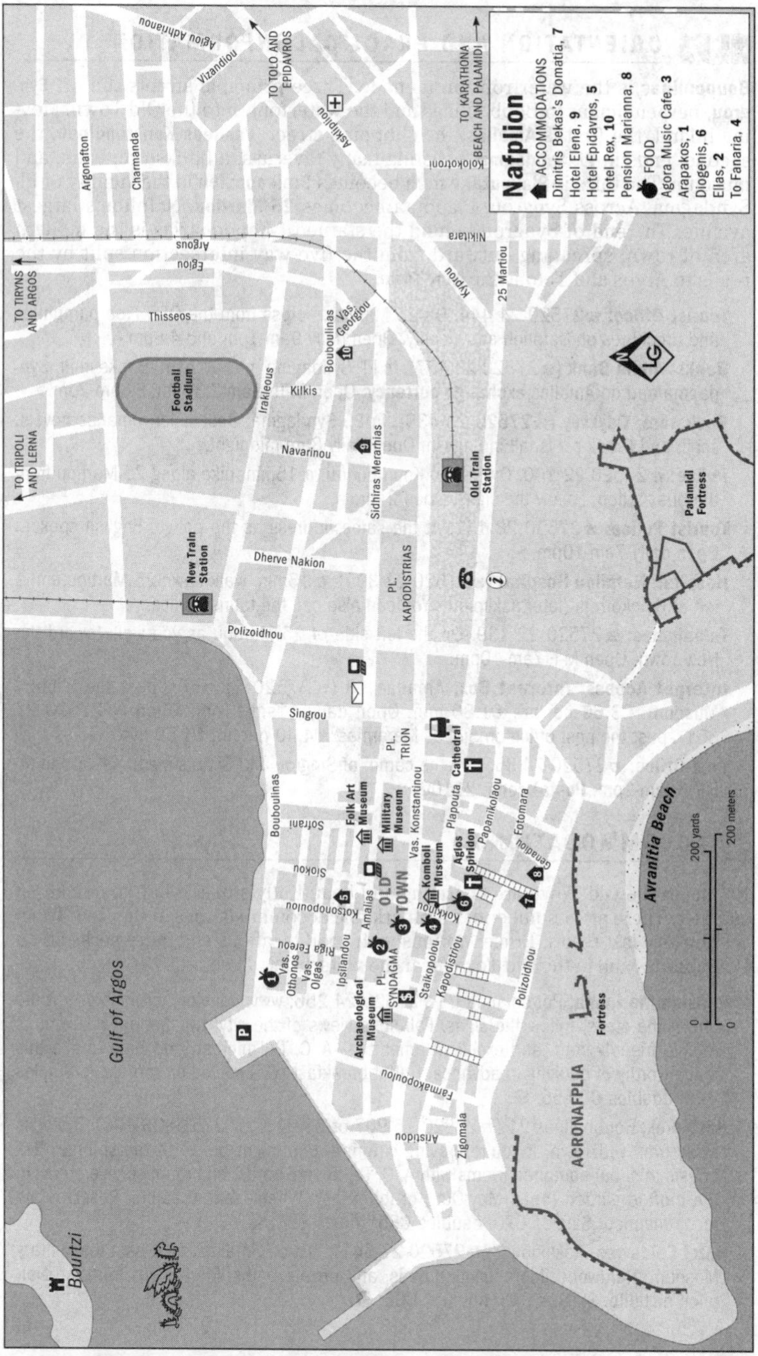

Nafplion

ACCOMMODATIONS
Dimitris Bekas's Domatia, 7
Hotel Elena, 9
Hotel Epidavros, 5
Hotel Rex, 10
Pension Marianna, 8

FOOD
Agora Music Cafe, 3
Arapakos, 1
Diogenis, 6
Ellas, 2
To Fanaria, 4

TO TOLO AND EPIDAVROS
TO KARATHONA BEACH AND PALAMIDI
TO TIRYNS AND ARGOS
TO TRIPOLI AND LERNA
Agiou Adhrianou
Vizandiou
Argonafton
Charmanda
Asklipiou
Kolokotroni
Argous
Egiou
Nikitara
Kyprou
25 Martiou
Thisseos
Vas. Georgiou
Bouboulinas
Football Stadium
Irakleous
Kilkis
Navarinou
Sidhiras Merarhias
Old Train Station
Palamidi Fortress
New Train Station
Dherve Nakion
PL. KAPODISTRIAS
Polizoidhou
Singrou
PL. TRION
Cathedral
Bouboulinas
Sofrani
Folk Art Museum
Military Museum
Vas. Konstantinou
Plapouta
Papanikolaou
Fotomara
Avranitia Beach
Siokou
OLD TOWN
Komboli Museum
Agios Spiridon
Genation
Kotsonopoulou
Amalias
Kokkinou
Riga Fereou
Vas. Othonos
Vas. Olgas
Ipsilandou
PL. SYNDAGMA
Staikopoulou
Kapodistriou
Polizoidhou
Archaeological Museum
Fortress
Gulf of Argos
Farmakopoulou
ACRONAFPLIA
Aristidou
Zigomala
Bourtzi

0 — 200 yards
0 — 200 meters

PELOPONNESE

ORIENTATION AND PRACTICAL INFORMATION

Bouboulinas is the waterfront promenade. Three principal streets run off **Syngrou,** perpendicular to Bouboulinas and the waterfont, into the Old Town. Moving inland, the first is **Amalias,** the shopping street. **Vasileos Konstandinou,** the second, ends in **Pl. Syndagma,** boasting many tavernas, a bookstore, bank, and museum. The third is **Plapouta,** which becomes **Staikopoulou** in the vicinity of Pl. Syndagma. Across Syngrou, Plapouta becomes **25 Martiou,** Nafplion's largest avenue. The end of Syngrou behind the statue of Kapodistrias is the modern area of town; spreading outward from the five-way intersection split by the roads to Argos and Tolo is the **New Town.**

Tourist Office: ☎27520 24 444. On 25 Martiou, across from the OTE. Free pamphlets and brochures on Nafplion and vicinity. Open daily 9am-1pm and 4-8pm.

Banks: Alpha Bank (☎27520 23 497), in Pl. Syndagma, has an **ATM.** Banks in Pl. Syndagma and on Amalias **exchange currency.** Open M-Th 8am-2:30pm, F 8am-2pm.

Bookstore: Odyssey (☎27520 23 430), in Pl. Syndagma. Best-seller romance novels, sci-fi, and Greek plays, all in English. Open daily 8am-midnight.

Police: ☎27520 22 100. On Pavlou Kountourioti, a 15min. hike along 25 Martiou from the bus station. Follow the signs. Open 24hr.

Tourist Police: ☎27520 28 131. At the same address as the police. English spoken. Open daily 7am-10pm.

Hospital: Nafplion Hospital (☎27520 27 309), a 15min. walk down 25 Martiou and a left at Kolokotroni (later Asklipiou). You can also call the tourist police.

Telephones: ☎27520 22 139. On the left side of 25 Martiou as you walk toward the New Town. Open M-F 7am-10pm.

Internet Access: Internet Box, Amalias 18 (☎27520 25 556), past the Military Museum. €3.60 per hr., €1.80 min. Open daily 11am-11pm. **Filion** (☎27520 27 651), past the post office on Sidiras Merarhias. €4.40 per hr., €1.50 min.

Post Office: ☎27520 24 855. On the corner of Singrou and Sidiras Merarhias. Open M-F 7:30am-2pm. **Postal code:** 21100.

PELOPONNESE

ACCOMMODATIONS

Rooms in the Old Town are charming and beautifully situated but go quickly in summer. There are a number of unremarkable accommodations in the New Town serving as a last resort. Pricier options with good locations and more perks lie on Bouboulinas and in the Old Town near the waterfront.

Pension Marianna, Potamianou 9 (☎27520 24 256; www.pensionmarianna.gr), at the top of the steps; follow the signs. Fabulous views of the city, traditional yet luxurious rooms, friendly staff, and excellent amenities–A/C, TV, minibar, and bath–make this place worthy of booking in advance. Buffet breakfast (€5) served on roof deck. Singles €45; doubles €50-55. ❸

Hotel Rex, Bouboulinas 21 (☎27520 26 907 or 26 917; fax 27520 28 106), 3 blocks away from Old Town. If you're craving catering, this might be worth the splurge. Rex boasts mini-bar-equipped rooms with A/C, TV, private baths, and room service. Relax in the rooftop garden (open May-Oct.) or lobby bar. Wheelchair-accesible. Reservations recommended. Singles €70; doubles €85; triples €97. ❹

Hotel Epidavros, Kokkinou 2 (☎27520 27 541), just off Amalias, right past the Military Museum. Hardwood floors, inviting beds, and private baths. Mere steps from the Nafplion nightlife. Singles €45; doubles €66. ❸

Hotel Elena, 31 Sidiras Merarchias (☎/fax 27520 23 888; www.nafplio-gr.com\elenahotel.htm). Standard rooms with A/C, TV, phone, balcony, and bath. Singles €37; doubles €48. ❸

Dimitris Bekas's Domatia (☎27520 24 594). Turn up the stairs onto Kokkinou, following the sign for rooms off Staikopoulou; climb to the top, turn left, then go up another 50 steps. Its best feature is its view from the roof deck. Small, somewhat shabby rooms have shared baths and fridges, some with balconies. Prices vary with room size. Space is limited; reservations recommended. Singles €16; doubles €20-22. ❷

FOOD AND NIGHTLIFE

The beautiful alleys of the Old Town have an endless number of romantic tavernas lit by soft flood lights and strewn with plants, balconies, and people. The waterfront is lined with fish restaurants that charge as much as €60 per entree. The best dining options are on Staikopoulou, the street inland from Pl. Syndagma, behind the National Bank. **Marinopoulos,** an excellent modern supermarket, is behind the Filion Internet cafe. The trellised alleyway of **To Fanaria ❷,** a street above the plateia on Staikopoulou, provides an intimate atmosphere in which to enjoy tantalizing entrees. (Soups €2.50-3. Spaghetti bolognese €4.50. Fish dishes €6-8.) **Ellas ❷,** in Pl. Syndagma is refreshingly inexpensive, with a cheerful staff and seats facing the plateia action. (☎27520 27 278. Veal with potatoes €6. Pasta dishes €4.) Old Town's first fast-food enterprise, **Diogenis ❶,** Staikopoulou 28, focuses on the souvlaki and gyros food groups. A mixed grill plate (€5.50) would satiate the truly ravenous. (☎27520 29 519. Pork or chicken souvlaki €1.50. French fries €2.) The waterfront **Arapakos ❸,** Bouboulinas 81, toward the parking lot, serves only local fish, prepared in the traditional Greek style. Enjoy typical taverna fare (appetizers €2-3.50), or treat yourself to a fish specialty. (☎27520 27 675. Fish €26-60.) **Agora Music Cafe ❶,** Vas. Konstandinou 17, is perfect for an evening cocktail or ice cream, with friendly staff and both indoor and outdoor seating. International and Greek pop play inside. (☎27520 26 016; www.cafgeagora.gr. Beer €2.50; drinks €4-5. Ice cream €4-5.) Although trendy cafes strung along the waterfront and Pl. Syndagma bustle far into the night, the search for spicier nightlife may land you in a taxi (€7) for the 15min. ride to **Tolo,** a packed beach resort where locals find themselves far outnumbered. You can also take a **minicruise** of the harbor and get a close-up view of the *bourtzi*. Small *caïques* leave from the end of the dock.

PELOPONNESE

SIGHTS AND BEACHES

The Old Town's architectural diversity is a historical sight in itself. Pl. Syndagma alone boasts a Venetian mansion, a Turkish mosque, and a Byzantine church, while the alleyways are home to Ottoman fountains, cannons, monuments, and statues. After passing from the Venetians to the Ottomans and back again, in 1821 Nafplion served as headquarters for the Greek revolutionary government and later as Greece's first capital (1821-1834). President John Kapodistrias was assassinated here in Ag. Spyridon Church; the bullet hole is still visible in the church wall. The city's three fortresses stand as testaments to Nafplion's politically checkered past.

PALAMIDI FORTRESS. The grueling 999 steps (though travelers attest that there are fewer—around 860) that once provided the only access to the 18th-century fort have since been supplemented by a 3km road (taxis €3). If you opt to brave the steps, they begin on Plizoidhou across the park from the bus station; bring water and try to go in the morning when the steps are shaded. There are spectacular views of the town, gulf, and much of the Argolid at the top of the fortress. Years ago there were eight working cisterns at the site; today you can tour the cool interiors of the two remaining underground reservoirs. During the last ten days in June, there are nightly concerts. *(☎27520 28 036. Open daily 8:30am-6:45pm; low season 8:30am-5:45pm. €4, students and seniors €2, EU students and children free.)*

ACRONAFPLIA. The fortress walls of the Acronafplia were fortified by three successive generations of conquerors—Byzantines, Franks, and Venetians. To reach the fort take the tunnel that runs into the hill from Zigomala to the Xenia Hotel elevator or follow the signs from the bus station. The views of the Palimidi Fortress, the Gulf, and the Old Town are fantastic. Ludwig I, King of Bavaria, had the huge Bavarian Lion carved out of a monstrous rock to guard the graves of the men who died in an epidemic in 1833-34. Today the lion guards only a small park.

MUSEUMS. The fascinating **Komboloi Museum,** Staikopoulou 25, in the heart of the Old Town, allows visitors to explore all facets of the famous Greek *komboloi* (worry beads). *(☎/fax 27520 21 618. Open M-Sa 9:30am-9:30pm, Su 10:30am-9:30pm. €1.50, students free.)* Nafplion's **Folklore Museum** is housed in a lovely yellow building in the heart of the Old Town on Sofrani. The award-winning collection includes an exhibit devoted to fashion. *(☎27520 28 379. Open M, W-Su 9am-3pm. €4, students and children €2.)* The **Archaeological Museum,** in the former Venetian armory in Pl. Syndagma, has a small but esteemed collection of pottery and idols from Mycenaean sites, plus a Mycenaean suit of bronze armor. *(☎27520 27 502. Open Tu-Su 8:30am-3pm. €2, students and seniors €1, EU students and children free.)* The **Military Museum,** toward the New Town from Syndagma on Amalias, displays artifacts from the burning of Smyrna, the population exchanges of the 1920s, and the World Wars. *(☎27520 25 591. Open Tu-Su 9:30am-2pm. Free.)*

PELOPONNESE

BEACHES. Arvanitia, Nafplion's tiny pebbly beach, is along the road that curves around the left-hand side of Palamidi. On hot days the shore is packed, and pop music blares over the noise of the sun-drenched crowd. Lounge chairs (€2.50) and beach umbrellas (€2) are available for rent. For a cleaner, more serene alternative, take the footpath that runs along the water from the Arvanitia parking lot. The scenic 45min. walk will reveal three quiet, rocky **coves.** If you're desperate for a long, sandy beach, try the mostly undeveloped **Karathona** beach, a 3km hike along the coast from Avranita (taxi €5), or head to **Tolo,** where you can rent watersports equipment (€8-15). Buses head there from Nafplion hourly (€0.85).

DAYTRIPS FROM NAFPLION

TIRYNS Τιρυνθα

Take the Argos bus from Nafplion (10min.; 2 per hr., 5am-10:30pm; €1). ☎27520 22 657. Guidebooks (€5) outline the history of the city. Open daily 8am-7pm; low season 8am-3pm. €3, students €2, EU students free.

About 4km northwest of Nafplion on the road to Argos lie the Mycenaean ruins of Tiryns, or **Tiryntha,** birthplace of Hercules. Heinrich Schliemann's excavation of the site began in 1875 and has been continued by the German Archaeological Institute ever since. The site is now one of the finest in the region. Perched atop a 25m high hill that provides a 360° view of the Argolid, Tiryns was nearly impregnable during ancient times, until its stunning capture and destruction by the Argives in 468 BC. Parts of the stronghold date as far back as 2600 BC, but most of what remains (including the walls) was built 1000 years later in the Mycenaean Era. At 8m tall the massive walls surrounding the site reveal the immensity of the original fortifications; on the eastern and southern slopes of the ancient acropolis, they reach a width of 20m. Vaulted galleries are concealed within these structures. While gems like the palace's frescoes have been taken to the National Archaeological Museum in Athens (p. 114), a huge limestone block remains to form a bathroom floor. Follow the signs to the left from the site to a preserved *tholos* tomb from the Mycenaean era in a hillside.

EPIDAVROS Επιδαυρος

Buses travel to and from Nafplion (45min.; 10:15am, noon, 2:30pm; €2). A snack bar and cafe serve the site but visitors may want to bring lunch. Museum ☎27530 22 009. Open daily 8am-7pm. Ticket office open daily 7:30am-7pm, F-Sa until 9pm during festival season. For a detailed explanation of the ruins, visitors may want to purchase a guidebook (€4.50-10). Ticket includes museum entrance and small map of the ruins; €6, students and seniors €3, EU students and children free.

Like Olympia and Delphi, Epidavros was once both a town and a sanctuary—first to an ancient deity Maleatas, then to Apollo, who assumed the former patron's name and aspects of his identity. Eventually the energies of the sanctuary were directed toward the demigod Asclepius, the son of Apollo who caught Zeus's wrath (and even worse, his fatal thunderbolt) when the good doctor got a little overzealous and began to raise people from the dead. Under the patronage of Asclepius, Epidavros became famous across the ancient world as a center of medicine. The prestige of the ancient health center reached its peak in the early 4th century BC, when, after an onslaught of plagues hit cities all over Greece, the sick would travel across the Mediterranean for medical and mystical cures. Recent finds indicate that both surgeries and direct divine intervention took place here—diagnoses were made by the god (or by one of his sacred creatures, the dog and the snake) in dream visitations. Over the centuries, the complex became increasingly lavish with the former patients' assistance, growing to include temples dedicated to Themis, Aphrodite, and Artemis. Operating until 426, the sanctuary complex was closed along with all other non-Christian sanctuaries by Emperor Theodosius II.

The theater, built in the early 2nd century BC, is without a doubt the most splendid structure at the site. Initially constructed to accommodate 6000 people, its capacity was expanded to 12,300 in the next century. Despite severe earthquakes in 522 and 551, the theater is still almost perfectly intact. Fortunately for today's visitors, Greece's most famous ancient theater has come alive again after centuries of silence: during July and August it hosts the **Epidavros Theater Festival.** the National Theater of Greece and visiting companies perform Classical Greek plays translated into modern Greek. Performances begin at 9pm, and tickets can be purchased at the site. (€17-40, students and children €8.50; children under 6 prohibited.) You can also buy tickets in advance at the Athens Festival Box Office (☎210 322 1459) or Nafplion's bus station. On performance nights, KTEL buses make a round-trip trek from Nafplion (7:30pm, €4).

THEATER. Built into a hillside in the 3rd century BC, the 55 tiers of the **Theater of Epidavros** face half-forested, half-flaxen mountains so awe-striking they almost distract from the tragedies played out on the stage. Though it is often said that the theater was designed by Polykleitos the Younger, architect of an even larger companion theater at Argos, it is not old enough to have been his work. The theater's acoustics are legendary, as yelling, singing, coin-dropping, whispering, and even match-lighting tourists from all nations enthusiastically demonstrate from the stage area—every sound can be heard, even in the last row. The secret to the theater's acoustic perfection is its symmetrical architecture; the entire amphitheater, , was built in proportion to the **Fibonacci sequence.**

MUSEUM. The **Archaeological Museum** lies between the theater and the ruins. While most of the museum's exquisite pieces have been hidden from visitors because of restoration efforts, three open rooms still display a worthwhile collection. The room closest to the entrance holds a very interesting array of ancient medical instruments, as well as a series of engraved stone tablets, some of which describe the miraculous cures of Asclepius in lengthy detail. The second room is filled with elaborately decorated architectural reconstructions and a parade of statuary. Make sure to check out the marble statue of bearded Asclepius, complete with thigh-high *caduceus.* The room farthest from the entrance is filled with intricate **entablatures** from the Temple of Asclepius and the *tholos.* Most impressive, however, is the perfectly preserved, authentic Corinthian capital, regarded as the architect's prototype for all of the capitals of the Temple of Asclepius.

SANCTUARY OF ASCLEPIUS AND THOLOS. The extensive ruins of the sanctuary, currently undergoing restoration, can be confusing to decipher. Walking from the museum, you'll first pass the **Xenon,** an ancient hotel that now resembles little more than a a maze of foundations. The **gymnasium** containing the remains of a **Roman odeon** is the first structure of the more concentrated complex of ruins. To the left is a **stadium,** of which only a few tiers of seats and the athletes' starting blocks survive. Two of the most important structures of the ancient sanctuary, the **Temple of Asclepius** and the famous **tholos,** are in front and to the left as you approach the ruins from the museum area. The *tholos*, thought to have been built by Polykleitos the Younger in the mid-4th century BC, is considered to be an architectural masterpiece, richly decorated with carvings. Beside the *tholos* are the remains of the **abaton,** where ailing patients would wait for Asclepius to reveal the proper treatment. Farther from the *tholos*, along the path on the eastern edge of the site, lie the ruins of 2nd-century **Roman baths.** Restoration efforts have limited visitors' access to some of the ruins, including the *tholos* and the odeon.

PELOPONNESE

ELIAS AND ACHAIA Ελειας AND Αχαια

In rural Elias and Achaia, tomatoes and beachgoers alike redden beneath the blazing sun. Cornfields, golden beaches, and occasional ruins stud the road between their capitals, Pirgos and Patras. First settled by Achaians from the Argolid, the region was later ruled by Romans. Afterward Franks, Ottomans, and Venetians all violently disputed this land, leaving a visible wake.

PATRAS Πατρας ☎2610

Greece's third-largest city, one of the official sites of the **2004 Olympic Games,** spreads from its harbor in a mixture of urban and classical, Greek and international styles. Location, location, location—on the northwestern tip of the Peloponnese—makes Patras a busy transportation hub. Island-bound tourists often see Patras as a stopover, never looking beyond the tourist agencies and cafes. Yet a closer look proves that Patras is transforming itself from a means to an end. Its noisy exuberance makes for a lively social atmosphere; cafe-lined plateias and pedestrian-only streets overflow nightly. From mid-January to Ash Wednesday, Patras breaks out with pre-Lenten Carnival madness—music, food, and an all-night festival. The port becomes one vast dance floor and for once the people stand a chance against speeding vehicles.

TRANSPORTATION

If you're coming from Athens by car, choose between the **New National Road,** which runs inland along the Gulf of Corinth, and the slower, scenic **Old National Road,** which hugs the coast. From the north take a ferry from **Antirio** across to **Rion** on the

Peloponnese (30min.; every 15min., 7am-11pm; €1 per person, €5.50 per car), then hop on bus #6 from Rion to the stop at **Kanakari** and **Aratou** (30min., €1) four blocks uphill from the main station.

Ferries: From Patras boats reach **Kephalonia, Ithaka,** and **Corfu** in Greece, and **Brindisi, Trieste, Bari, Ancona,** and **Venice** in Italy. Most ferries to Italy leave at night. Daily ferries to **Vathy** on Ithaka (3½hr., €11.70) via **Sami** on Kephalonia (3hr., €11.50) and **Corfu** (6-8hr., €21-25). Deck passage to **Brindisi** is €27-30 including port tax. Several ferry lines make the trip, so check the travel offices along Iroön Polytechniou and Othonas Amalias; discounts are available for those under 25. **Railpasses** won't work for domestic ferries, and they may or may not work for international ferries; some companies accept the railpass while others do not; make sure you check with more than one line. The folks at **Manolopoulos,** Oth. Amalias 35 (☎2610 223 62), sell tickets for destinations both domestic and abroad. Open M-F 9am-8pm, Sa 10am-3pm, Su 5-8pm. For info on ferry departures, call the **Port Authority** (☎2610 341 002) or contact the Info Center or tourist police (see below).

Buses: KTEL (☎2610 623 886, 887, or 888), on Oth. Amalias between Aratou and Zaïmi. Buses go to: **Athens** (3hr.; 33 per day, 2:30am-9:30pm; €12.90); **Egio** (14 per day, 8am-10:15pm; €2.50); **Ioannina** (4hr.; 4 per day, 8:15am-5:30pm; €15.30); **Kalamata** (4hr.; 8am, 2:30pm; €14.70); **Kalavrita** (2hr.; 3:15, 4pm;

€5.40); **Pirgos** (2hr.; 5 per day, 5:30am-5pm; €6.40); **Thessaloniki** (8hr.; 8:30am, 3, 9pm; €29.70); **Tripoli** (4hr.; 7:15am, 2pm; €11); **Volos** (5½hr., 2:30pm except Sa, €17.90). The **blue buses** around town are city buses. Buy tickets at the many white kiosks; there's one in Pl. Giorgiou. Tell the person at the kiosk your desired bus number and your destination, and make sure to get a ticket for the return trip. Otherwise just pay the driver when he has a moment. Ask at the Info Center (see below) for more information.

Trains: Oth. Amalias 47 (☎2610 639 108 or 2610 639 109 for info, 2610 639 110 for tickets abroad). To: **Athens** (8 per day, 2:39am-7:23pm; €10); **Egio** (8 per day, 6am-7:20pm; €3.80); **Kalamata** (5½hr., 6:18am, €5); **Pirgos,** where you can catch a bus to Olympia (1½hr.; 8 per day, 2:41am-9:45pm; €5.50). The trains to Athens are packed, so reserve seats even if you have a railpass. **Ticket booth** open daily 6am-2am. MC/V.

Car Rental: Many along Ag. Andreou. **Hertz Rent-A-Car,** 2 Kavolou (☎2610 220 0990), across from Europa Center. Rates as low as €55 per day. Open M-Sa 8:30am-2pm and 4-8:30pm. AmEx/MC/V.

Taxis: ☎2610 346 700 or 2610 425 201. Line up in plateias and by the bus station. Respond to calls 24hr.

PELOPONNESE

ORIENTATION AND PRACTICAL INFORMATION

Patras is divided into an upper and a lower city, both of which are arranged in a grid; most hotels, restaurants, and shops are in the heart of the lower city. **Iroön Polytechniou** runs parallel to the water. As you walk south with the water on your right, the road curves just before the train station and becomes **Othonos Amalias.** Just beyond the train station, it runs past the palm trees, cafes, and kiosks of **Pl. Trion Simahon.** Car-free **Ag. Nikolaou,** full of hotels and cafes, runs inland from the plateia and intersects the major east-west streets of the city. From the corner of Ag. Nikolaou and **Mezonos,** walk three blocks from the water and turn right to find **Pl. Giorgiou** and its sculpted fountains near the waterfront. The heart of New Patras lies between Pl. Giorgiou and **Pl. Olgas,** three blocks to the north. Access the upper city by walking away from the water on Ag. Nikolaou.

Tourist Office: The **Info Center** (☎2610 461 740 or 2610 461 741; infopatras@hol.gr), on Oth. Amalias between 28 Oktovriou and Astingos, provides information about Patras and the area. Transportation info, **free maps,** brochures, and general information are readily available. Open daily 8am-10pm. The **Greek National Tourist Agency** (☎2610 430 915) is on the waterfront at the customs entrance. Staff hands out bus and ferry schedules, lodgings advice, and **maps.** Open M-F 8am-3pm and 5:30-8pm.

Banks: National Bank (☎2610 278 042), in Pl. Trion Simahon on the waterfront, has a 24hr. **ATM,** as do other banks on the plateia and all over the lower city. Open M-Th 8am-2pm, F 8am-1:30pm.

Luggage Storage: Europa Center (see **Food,** p. 143) will store your bags for free. You can also store them at the port (€1.20) from 8am-10pm.

International Bookstore: Lexis Bookshop, Patreos 90 (☎2610 274 831). Useful selection for travelers: language dictionaries and various books about Greek history and culture. Open M-Sa 8:30am-2pm and 5:30-8pm. MC.

Laundromat: Zaïmi 49 (☎2610 620 119), past Korinthou. Self-service wash and dry €7. Open M-F 9am-3pm and 5-8:30pm, Sa 9am-3pm.

Tourist Police: ☎2610 695 191. In the customs complex. Offers the same services as the tourist office. Open daily 8am-2:30pm.

Police: ☎100. On the corner of Ermou and Kanakari, 6 blocks up from waterfont.

Hospital: Red Cross First Aid (☎2610 227 386), on the corner of 28 Oktovriou and Ag. Dionysiou. Open daily 7am-midnight. **St. Angelou Hospital** (☎2610 227 000) is located on Orevatikou past the church and on the left. For an **ambulance,** dial ☎100.

OTE: At the corner of D. Gounari and Kanakari. Open M, W, Sa 8am-3pm; Tu, Th-F 8am-3pm and 5:30-8pm.

Internet Access: There's no lack of Internet cafes in Patras. In Pl. Giorgiou, facing the upper city, **Pl@teia** (Πλ@τεια; ☎2610 277 828) will be on the right. €3 per hr., 15min. minimum. Open daily 9am-midnight. Heading toward the upper city on Gerokostopoulou from Pl. Giorgiou, **Plazanet** (☎2610 222 190) is on your right. Have a drink in the roomy cafe while checking your email. €3.50 per hr., €1.50 min. Open daily 8am-midnight. Just up the street is the quiet **Joy@Net** (☎2610 242 640). €2.50 per hr., €1.50 min. Open daily 10:30am-2am.

Post Office: ☎2610 223 864 or 2610 224 703. On Mezonos at the corner of Zaïmi. Open M-F 7:30am-8pm, Sa 7:30am-2pm. **Postal code:** 26001.

ACCOMMODATIONS

Most hotels in Patras are on Ag. Andreou, to the left of Pl. Trion Simahon, facing inland, or on Ag. Nikolaou. Of those nearest to the water, many are often budget in appearance but not in price. There are, however, some diamonds in the rough.

Pension Nicos, Patreos 3 (☎2610 623 757), 2 blocks off the waterfront. The best bet in Patras, cheery and conveniently located. Sent down from the backpacking gods, this place features wood-paneled rooms with fans and large, modern shared baths with tubs. Bar and roof terrace with perfect sunset harbor views. Singles €20; doubles €35; triples €50. Cash only. ❷

Hotel El Greco, Ag. Andreou 145 (☎2610 272 931; fax 2610 272 932). Walking along Andreou with the water on your right, it's 4 blocks past Pl. Trion Simahon. Clean but small rooms have baths, TVs, fridges, and A/C for less than you'll pay for similar rooms in town. Check-out noon. Singles €38; doubles €50; triples €60. Cash only. ❸

Youth Hostel, Iroön Polytechniou 68 (☎2610 427 278). From the port walk away from town with the water on your left for about 1.5km. The slightly remote hostel occupies a creaky turn-of-the-century mansion that sat empty for 40 years after being used by occupying Germans in WWII. Minimalism is the key word here, but the location near the water and the relative quiet make for a pleasant atmosphere. Free hot showers 24hr. Leave valuables at reception desk. Check-out 10:30am. Dorms €9. Cash only. ❶

Primaloria Art Hotel, Othonos Amalias 33 (☎2610 649 900; www.arthotel.gr). With the water on your left, it's 50m past the train station on the right. Featuring 14 spacious, well-furnished rooms that will make you never want to leave, this hotel could be the most elegant in all of Patras. Individually themed suites like "Old Glory," "Just Married," and the premier "Black Room" come with beautiful beds and bathrooms, A/C, TV, telephones, and gorgeous views. Singles €118; doubles €147. MC/V. ❺

Hotel Olympic, Ag. Nikolaou 46 (☎2610 224 103), 2.5 blocks from the waterfront, on the right. Though perhaps a little rough around the edges, this place may be the best compromise between location and price. At the epicenter of the lower city's pedestrian flow, the Olympic offers decent rooms with A/C, private bathrooms, and TV. Singles €48-77; doubles €66-172; triples €79-146. V. ❹

Rion Camping (☎2610 991 585 or 2610 991 450), 9km east in Rion, a beach-and-club suburb of Patras. Catch bus #6 at the corner of Aratou and Kamakari, get off at the port in Rion, and follow signs. Check-out noon. €22 for 2 people with RV and electricity, €18 for 2 people with tent and car, €15 for 2 people with tent. €5 per tent. Electricity €4. Cash only. ❶

PELOPONNESE

FOOD

Patras has an abundance of fast-food joints and cafes, while more typical restaurants and tavernas are a bit harder to come by. Free-flowing food, frappés, and alcohol entice flocks to the outdoor tables along the waterfront and in the plateias. **Supermarkets** can be found throughout town (most open M-Sa 8am-3pm).

Europa Center (☎2610 437 006), on Oth. Amalias between the information center and bus station. This friendly cafeteria-style eatery is run by Greek-Americans ready to assist weary backpackers fresh from the ferries. In addition to tasty, low-priced dishes with large portions, they provide services such as free luggage storage, maps, book exchange, Internet access, and valuable local tips and resources. Appetizers €2.50. Salads €2.50-4. Entrees €3-7, including many vegetarian options. MC/V. ❶

Mythos (☎2610 329 984), on the corner of Riga Ferou and Trion Navarhon. This whimsical eatery sells itself as a cafe, but they do have a food menu with a fairly large selection of Greek salads (€4.70-5) and pastas (€5-8.50). The draw is the amazing outdoor and indoor decor: bright pots of flowers and shrubs are adorned with pinwheels, lanterns, and lights, while various plates and serving dishes hang from the walls. Open daily 7pm-late. Cash only. ❷

To Palaion, Ag. Nikolaou 13 (☎2610 266 435), between Mezenos and Mihalakopoulou. One of the few cafes on Ag. Nikolaou where local customers are willing to (temporarily) put down their coffee cups and pick up their forks. Entrees €7-14.80. Coffees €1.50-3. Desserts €2.80-5. Open 8:30am-1:30am. Cash only. ❸

Signore (☎2610 222 212), on Ag. Andreou near Ag. Nikolaou. Bustling with younger crowds after sunset, this quasi-Italian sit-down or takeout place serves everything from calzones (€2-3) and pizza (€1.75 per slice) to sweet and savory crepes (€2.50-3.50). Pasta €4.80-7.40. Wine €7.50-25. Delivery available. Open 24hr. Cash only. ❶

Majestic, Ag. Nikolaou 2 (☎2610 272 243). An older clientel frequents this small restaurant that caters to a variety of caffeinated and alcoholic tastes. The extensive wine list features Achaia Clauss wines (see below). Entrees €3.50-8.50. Open 8pm-late. ❸

SIGHTS

ACHAIA CLAUSS WINERY. A narrow road meanders uphill through grapevines and shaded countryside to the castle-like, internationally renowned Achaia Clauss winery, 8km southeast of Patras. Founded in 1861 by German-born Baron von Clauss, its weathered stone buildings have aged well along with its wine. Try a complimentary sample of their famous Mavrodaphne, a superb dessert wine named for the black eyes of Clauss's ill-fated fiancée Daphne. Not only is the wine amazing by international standards—numerous awards, diplomas, and letters from grateful ambassadors adorn the walls—but the staff is friendly and incredibly knowledgeable about the winery. Be sure to take a tour of the old wine cellars to see and learn how Mavrodaphne is made and stored. *(☎2610 368 100. Take bus #7 (30min., €1) from the intersection of Kolokotroni and Kanakari; it stops at the main gate to the winery. Free English tours every hr. from noon-5pm between Mar. and Oct., 10am-3pm between Nov. and Feb. Open Mar.-Oct. 11am-8pm; Nov.-Feb. 9am-5pm. Free.)*

THE CASTLE OF PATRAS. Built atop ruins of an ancient acropolis and continuously in use from the 6th century to World War II, Patras's castle remains relatively intact, considering its turbulent history. Controlled at various times by the Byzantines, Franks, Turks, Venetians, and even the Pope, the castle serves as a tribute both to the importance of the city below as well as to the various influences that have helped shape it. While the Slavs and Saracens have left, the castle maintains its aggressive spirit by hosting the occasional death-metal concert in the courtyard. *(Walk to the upper city from Ag. Nikolaou. If the nearest entrance through the playground is closed, walk around to the main entrance at the opposite side of the castle, along Athinas. ☎2610 623 390. Open M-Sa 8am-7pm. Free.)*

ANCIENT ODEION. Southwest of the castle in the upper city, this ancient Roman theater, which held an audience of 2500, was built before AD 160 and used until the 3rd century. Ancient travel writer Pausanias described it as the second most impressive in Greece—after Athens's Theater of Herodes Atticus. Excavated in 1889, the theater was later restored after World War II. As a result visitors can now make out the ancient cavea, orchestra, and *proskenion*, the wall at the end of the stage. *(☎2610 220 829. Open Tu-Su 8am-2pm. Free.)* The theater hosts the **Patras International Festival,** where Greek and international music groups play nightly. *(Every summer June-Aug.; check at Info Center for performance times and prices.)*

AGIOS ANDREAS. The largest Orthodox cathedral in Greece, it is dedicated to St. Andrew, a Patras native martyred here on an X-shaped crucifix (he felt unworthy of dying on a cross like Jesus's). A decade ago the Catholic Church presented the Bishop of Patras with the grand relic, St. Andrew's holy head. The crown of the head is visible through its reliquary, an ornate silver replica of the cathedral itself. The cathedral's frescoes, gold mosaics, and delicately latticed windows enhance its beauty. To the right of the cathedral is the equally beautiful **Church of St. Andrew,** with shining silver icons and chandeliers, as well as a small well allegedly built by the saint himself. Find the well through a doorway to the right of the church. Legend holds that anyone who drinks from it will return to Patras again. *(Walk along the waterfront or Ag. Andreou with the water to your right until you reach the cathedral, roughly 1.5km from the port; it will be on your left. Open daily 7am-dusk. Modest dress required.)*

PAMPELOPONNISIAKO STADIUM. Known around the city as the "Jewel of Patras," the new Olympic complex will host swimming and soccer events and serve as athletic training halls. Construction, expected to cost upwards of €30 million, ought to be completed in February 2004. *(Take bus #7 (20min., €1.) from outside Europa Center.)*

NO WORK, ALL PLAY

PARTY ON THE PORT

The city of Patras plays a great front a well-populated port city that blends rural efficiency with tight-clothed urban flare. But for seven and a half straigh weeks, even the most stoically en *vogue* will be crawling on hands and knees in a city-wide scavenger hunt o be blindsided by fudge in one o Europe's largest chocolate fights. In the pre-Lenten madness of Patras's annual *karnival,* anything goes.

The 19th-century merchant Moreti is credited with the establishment of the festival after he hosted an intimate, VIP only Carnival ball in 1829 in the city o Patras. Since then, the guest list has been extended to anyone who can fi into the streets from mid-January to Ash Wednesday. In 1966 organizers introduced the very first treasure hunt game still one of the most popular events on the calendar, which unites all of Patras in a quest to unlock clues spread throughout the city.

The festival now offers adults the *Bourboulia*, a night filled with myster and seduction. Men, having paid the "symbolic entrance fee," come to the historical Apollo Municipal Theater and await their imminent mistresses, who wear black costumes and masks known as "dominos." The children have thei time in the sun as well, putting on theater of their own and participating in myriad parades, activities, and games On the Sunday before Ash Wednesday the festivities culminate in the 7hr. Carnival Parade and, 72hr. later on the fina night, Patras experiences an all-nigh harbor-side party including the burning of King Carnival's effigy. The event draws some 300,000 revelers.

ARCHAEOLOGICAL MUSEUM

This small museum's most striking pieces are Roman. Make sure to see the two cases containing amazingly intact gold jewelry, including a pair of earrings shaped like birds. *(Mezonos 42, next to Pl. Olgas at the corner of Mezonos and Aratou. ☎2610 620 413. Open Tu-Su 8am-3pm. Free. Guidebooks €3.)*

ENTERTAINMENT AND NIGHTLIFE

For an even more relaxed night out, head along the waterfront with the water on your right. Walk about 10min. past Agios Andreas Cathedral and you'll come to the two-story entertainment complex **Veso Mare** (☎2610 362 000 or 2610 625 115 for movie times). Featuring a 16-lane bowling alley (€3 per game), eight movie theaters, and live music, the complex pleases Greek families and teens alike.

At night, cafes and pubs swell with patrons of all tastes: hardcore beer-swillers rub elbows with spiked-frappé sippers. Cigarette smoke disperses through the air as everyone jabbers into cell phones. The three main plateias, Ag. Nikolaou, Radinou (a pedestrian-only alley one block south of Pl. Olgas), and the upper part of Gerokostopoulou (extending uphill from Pl. Giorgiou) are especially dense with cafe umbrellas. Yet at the base of the steps to the upper city on Gerokostopoulou, **Naja** (ni-YAH) provides patrons with an unparalleled ambiance. Flickering candles and echoed voices mellow the mood of the only bar in Patras that resembles a cave. Let the bartender make you a cocktail (€6) from ingredients you request. (☎2610 624 140. Beer and mixed drinks €3-6. Open daily 10pm-3:30am. Cash only.) Adorned with photos of Elvis and James Dean, **Blue Monday,** along Radinou, is a veritable shrine to 1950s America, playing a mix of soul and American and British rock. Though it may be placed on an abnormally obscure side street, locals, tourists, and cockroaches alike have been glad they took the time to search it out. (☎2610 277 716. Beer €2-3; mixed drinks €4.50-6. Open 9am-3am. Cash only.)

PELOPONNESE

Though Patras itself has much to offer in the way of bars and cafes, some of the wildest party-goers head out of town. **Rion,** a beach satellite 9km to the northeast, accommodates Patras's club junkies. To get to there, take bus #6 from Kanakari and Aratou (30min., €0.85) all the way to the port, past the beach. Get off the bus just after the port, before it turns left to head back to Patras; the strip is ahead as you walk with the water on your right. Buses to Rion only run until 11pm, so count on taking a cab home (€3-6). If none are immediately available, head over to the port near the beginning of the strip. Along the strip beer will run €2-3, while cocktails are generally €4.50-5. Though a popular location, clubs rarely last long.

DIAKOFTO Διακοφτο ☎26910

Though famous among travelers for its 19th-century rack-railway trains, the small town of Diakofto remains largely isolated from the droves of tourists that have infested the more famous sights. In the residential area, the roads are lined with houses planted between citrus trees and shaded by bougainvillea. Even the beaches, speckled with stray dogs and abandoned boats, remain mostly empty. Those with a penchant for liveliness would be better suited to nearby Kalavrita.

TRANSPORTATION AND PRACTICAL INFORMATION. The **train station** (☎26910 43 206) intersects Diakofto's main road about 10min. from the beach. As the town's social center, it is flanked by mini-markets, bakeries, and casual coffee cafes. Undergoing renovation and closed until March 2004, tiny rack-railway trains to **Kalavrita** (1hr., 4 per day, €3.80) make for an exhilarating ride; halfway rides to **Zahlorou** (30min., €1.90) are also available. Trains to **Athens** (3hr.; 8 per day, 7:53am-3:22am; €8.50, express €9.70) via **Corinth** (1hr.; €2.10, express €4.70) leave from the opposite side of the tracks and **Patras** (40min.; 8 per day, 9:43am-1:17am; €4.40, express €4). The station also offers **luggage storage.** (€3.20 per item, €1.60 if traveling by train. Open daily 7am-9:30pm.) Walk down the main road (perpendicular to the railroads) toward the sea to pass through a picturesque residential area and end up at the harbor and public beach. If you walk inland on the winding main road toward the mountains, you will see a **pharmacy** (☎26910 42 885; open M-Sa 8am-1pm and 5-9pm) and the **National Bank,** which offers **currency exchange** (open M-Th 8:45am-12:45pm, F 8:45am-12:15pm) and a 24hr. **ATM.** The nearest **hospital** is 20min. away in Egio. It is accessible only by bus or by **taxi** (☎26910 72 424). The **post office** (☎26910 41 343; open M-F 7:30am-2pm) is on the left side of the road as you walk inland from the train station. **Postal code:** 25003.

ACCOMMODATIONS. Considering the number of visitors to Diakofto every year, the complete lack of **domatia** and severe shortage of hotels is almost laughable. **Hotel Lemonies ❷,** halfway between the train station and the beach on the main road, offers adequate rooms with private bathrooms, comfortable beds, A/C, balconies, and occasionally functioning TVs. The hotel's proximity to a playground may bring back fond memories of handball and four-square, or they may disturb an otherwise good night's rest. (☎26910 41 820; fax 20691 43 710. Singles €24-30; doubles €36-40. Cash only.) For a bit more money, you can stay at the well-advertised **Chris Paul Hotel ❸,** located one block inland from the train station, left off the main road. Twenty-four clean, carpeted rooms offer A/C, TVs, balconies, and private bathrooms; the hotel is proud to also have the benefits of handicapped access, a private pool, and a dining room. Here you'll find the only formal sit-down breakfast (€4.50) in town. (☎26910 41 715 or 26910 41 855; www.chris-paul-hotel.gr. Singles €35.50; doubles €65; triples €80.50. MC/V.) Though formal campgrounds along the beach have shut down, travelers have been known to take their RVs to the shoreline and camp out for the night.

FOOD AND ENTERTAINMENT. Though cafes and bars cluster around the train station, actual restaurants are just as uncommon as hotels. The best bet for a cheap but filling meal is the unnamed **taverna ❶** with the red and white sign, just past the National Bank on the right. Make a meal out of a big tomato salad (€1.75) and a hot gyro (€1.20) or souvlaki (€1). Or, for something less traditional, try the *pastitsio* (€4.40), a dish that combines spaghetti and meatballs into a delicious layered cake. Next door, **Psistaria Pizzeria ❶** (Ψηστaρια Πιτσαρια; ☎26910 42 474) is *the* place for cheap food and an authentic Greek atmosphere. Don't be surprised when you see the owner sipping beer as he prepares your meatballs (€5.50) or *tzatziki* (€1.70) on the grill; just sit back and enjoy the soothing singing of the elderly Greek gentlemen as the recordings play a little too softly in the background. After dinner young people leave behind their espresso-sipping parents and head towards the beach. At the end of the main road on the right, **Fuego** offers patrons a pleasant evening of drinks (beer and ouzo €2; mixed drinks €4), music, and large straw umbrellas under the stars. During the summer season, crepes (€3) and ice cream (€4) are also served. (Open daily 4pm-midnight.) A slightly older crowd tends to frequent **Relax Place,** opposite the train station on the inland side. Music, two TV screens, and a fully stocked bar (ouzo €1.50; beer €1.50-1.80; wine €2) keep locals here until closing time. (Open daily 4pm-midnight.)

GREAT CAVE MONASTERY Μονη Μεγαλου Σπηλαιου

Located 26km inland from Diakofto, this famous monastery is accessible primarily by a combination of 19th-century rack-railway and hiking. Getting there is half the fun; the 30min. railway ride winds into smoke-blackened tunnels, through spectacular canyons and gorges created by the Vouraikos River, and over old bridges, offering rollercoaster-esque excitement (€1.90). For the monastery, get off at **Zahlorou,** the midway point on the line. The small mountain village conjures up stock images of mining or timber towns in old Western movies. A few well-shaded, rustic buildings cluster around the tracks where they pass over the river. From Zahlorou you can either hike up to the monastery or drive (taxis are rare). If you decide to hike, be prepared for a challenging walk with loose ground underfoot; this is not recommended for elderly people or small children. The path that leads to the monastery is marked in English. Don't forget a water bottle, long-sleeved shirt, and sturdy shoes. After about 1¼hr. of walking, you should reach a paved road; turn left and follow the road to the sign for Megalou Spilaiou on your right. Stairs in front of the monastery lead to the main entrance, a large green door that stands below a set of Biblical paintings. As you walk in, head towards the staircase that lies just to right of the small gift shop. Four cannons point the way to the museum (€2), where a black-robed monk will lead you to the various exhibits. Captions in both English and Greek help differentiate between all the centuries-old manuscripts, communion cups, and clerical vestments. Especially noteworthy is the group of handmade crosses on the left wall. As you exit the museum, one of the cliff's caves is accessible on the left. Follow the sounds of running water down the stairs, where you'll be able to peer into the darkness in search of its miraculous icon, a painting of the Virgin Mary supposedly by St. Luke.

KALAVRITA Καλαβρυτα ☎26920

Resting in a valley at the end of the rack-railway line, the close-knit mountain village of Kalavrita caters mostly to winter skiers. The mountain vistas and quiet streets certainly make the warmer months a pleasant time to visit.

TRANSPORTATION AND PRACTICAL INFORMATION. By March 2004 Kalavrita should be accessible by a completely renovated, tiny, fun-to-ride rack-railway line from **Diakofto** (1hr.; 8am-3:45pm, 9:15am-5pm return; €3.80). Until then a taxi may be the best alternative. Ask your driver to take you either directly to Kalavrita (€28) or take you from Diakofto to the Great Cave Monastery, wait for you for an hour there, then on to Kalavrita (€35). The two roads perpendicular to the train station that lead to the plateia are **Konstantinou** (which becomes **Ag. Alexiou**) to the left and **Syngrou** to the right (initially a pedestrian road, later becomes **25 Martiou**). Contained within the two streets is the **central square,** 100m away from the train station. A **bus station** (☎26920 22 224) has service to: **Athens** (3hr.; 3 per day, 9am-4:45pm; €11.40); **Patras** (2hr.; 5 per day, 6:15am-4:45pm; €5.40); **Tripoli** (2hr., 9:30am, €5.70). To get there, take your first right off Syngrou onto Kapota, walking away from the train station. Walk several blocks until the road merges; the bus station will be on your left. **Taxis** (☎26920 22 127) line up along the side of the plateia closest to the train station. The **National Bank,** 25 Martiou 4, 100m in front of the church, offers **currency exchange** and a 24hr. **ATM.** (☎26920 22 212. Open M-Th 8am-2pm, F 8am-1:30pm.) Walking from the train station, the **police,** Fotina 7, are to the right off of Ag. Alexiou, three blocks beyond the OTE. (☎26920 23 333 or 26920 22 213. Open 24hr.) **Pharmacies** are sprinkled throughout the town; find one a block up Syngrou from the train station. (☎26920 22 131. Open M-F 8am-2pm.) Another pharmacy is across the street from the hospital. (☎26920 23 047. Open M-F 8am-2pm.) To reach the **hospital** (☎26920 22 724), walk to the right of the train station for three blocks; it's on the right. The **OTE** is at Ag. Alexiou 10 (☎26920 22 599), one block past the central square. **Internet access** is located at the ultra-modern **CyberNet,** Ag. Alexiou 17. (☎26920 23 555; kalavryta@cy-net.gr. €2.20 per hr., €0.80 min. Open daily 9am-midnight.) The **post office,** on 25 Martiou, is to the right of the town hall. (☎26920 22 225. Open M-F 8am-2pm.) **Postal code:** 25001.

ACCOMMODATIONS. Hotels in Kalavrita are pleasant but expensive, especially during ski season. Luckily, affordable, well-appointed **domatia** abound; numerous signs near the train station will lead you to them. **Domatia Hrysa ❸** is behind the train station, 50m down the road running perpendicular to the tracks. Comfortable ground-floor singles with TVs and baths open onto a garden. Guests staying during the summer may be lucky enough to land one of the more luxurious rooms on the third floor for the price of a normal single. (☎26920 22 443. Singles €25-35; doubles €50-60. Cash only.) Make a right after the first block of Syngrou and **Hotel Filoxenia ❹,** Eth. Antistaseos 10, is one block down on the left. Filoxenia certainly lives up to its name, which means hospitality. Twenty-eight rooms delicately combine modern comforts with old-fasioned European beauty. A/C, private bathrooms, TV, telephone, and an electronic key card system come with every wood-paneled single and triple. (☎26920 22 443; www.hotelfiloxenia.gr. Breakfast included. Reservations recommended. Singles €49-76; triples €81-117. MC/V.) **Anesis Hotel ❸,** just off Ag. Alexiou facing the plateia, is a lovely stone hotel, which holds 15 well-furnished rooms with phones, TVs, baths, and temperature controls during the winter. After a long day of skiing, guests can come home to a fireplace with additional charge. (☎26920 23 070; www.anesishotel.gr. Breakfast included. In summer: singles €30; doubles €40. In winter: all rooms €70. V.) Turn right after the hospital, continue two blocks, and **Lehoupitis ❷** will be on the right. This is the place for anyone thinking about spending more than just a few nights in Kalavrita. Apartment-style doubles feature TV, small fridge, desk, and a coffeemaker. Quads come with the same amenities in addition to a cozy loft. (☎26920 22 440. In summer: doubles €30; quads €50. In winter: doubles €50; quads €65. Cash only.)

FOOD AND NIGHTLIFE. A collection of indistinguishable tavernas line Ag. Alexiou and Syngrou (or 25 Martiou). They tend to have inconsistent hours and be closed on some days of the week. **Taverna Aistralos ❷,** part of the Anesis Hotel, just off Ag. Alexiou facing the plateia, serves traditional Greek dishes including a meatball with stuffed cheese (€5) and lamb with vegetables (€5.60). Right next door is **Tzaki Taverna ❷,** opposite the church, with good prices for Greek classics. (*Tzatziki* €1.80. Moussaka €5. Stuffed tomatoes €4.20.) Much to the joy of the town's teenage crowd, night clubs in Kalavrita have begun to flourish on Thursday, Friday, and Saturday nights. The **Tehni Music Club,** one block to the right of the post office, can be heard throughout the square. For a slight change of scenery, head to **Portokali,** the tiki-hut club just to the right of the train station. Those in the mood for live music would prefer **Skinko,** two blocks to the right of the station, 300m past the church. Cafes on the pedestrian block of 25 Martiou serve unti late.

SIGHTS AND THE OUTDOORS. Of the few sights in Kalavrita, the one held most dear to the townspeople is the **Martyrs' Monument,** a tribute to the Kalavritan men who were killed on December 13, 1943. In retaliation for the murder of one of their troopers, the occupying Nazis gathered all of the town's men and boys over age 15 on a hill outside of town under the pretext of a stern reprimand for the murder. Instead, at 2:34pm, lurking troopers opened fire on the men and their sons. Immediately afterward, just as the Ottomans had done 115 years before, the Nazis set fire to the town and the church. Today one of the clocks of the town's reconstructed church is set permanently to 2:34, and an extensive memorial stands at the site itself. Massive gravestones detail the names and ages of the victims, commemorating them eternally beneath an overarching Greek flag. In an accompanying room, hundreds upon hundreds of hanging oil lamps symbolize the anticipated resurrection of the murdered men. If they wish, visitors may light a candle in memory of the victims. To reach the memorial, follow Ag. Alexiou from the train station. Signs in English point the way.

To make an afternoon of the beautiful countryside, continue walking past the memorial on the road that winds up the mountain beyond. After about an hour and a half you will see signs pointing to the **Kalavrita Castle,** which appears to be an old chapel built high up on the hillside. Wear good shoes and take plenty of water. There are also several summer **hikes** around Mt. Helmos; ask around for information or a guide. In the winter months, travel to nearby **Mt. Helmos** for fantastic **skiing.** One of the town's many ski stores and offices, the **Ski Centre,** on 25 Martiou, provides information and rentals. (☎26920 22 175. Open Dec.-Apr. daily 8:30am-3:30pm.) Worth the trip if you have private transportation is the **Cave of the Lakes,** 16km away. English signs point the way from the road behind the memorial.

KYLLINI Κυλληνη ☎26230

For a port town that handles almost all the tourist traffic to Zakynthos, Kyllini is surprisingly undeveloped; the town has almost no bus service, few accommodations, and—outside of an overabundance of cafes and bars crowded with bored and/or drunk travelers—very little to occupy the passing traveler. If you find yourself stuck here, make the best of it by spending the afternoon at the sandy beach adjacent to the port. If you're considering bypassing Kyllini entirely, keep in mind that some buses from Zakynthos Town take ferries and continue on to more noteworthy destinations on the Patras-Athens route (p. 160).

To leave Kyllini, take the **bus** from the kiosk near the port gate to **Pirgos** (1½hr.; 9:30am, 1, 4:30pm; €3.50). Once in Pirgos, catch a bus to **Olympia** (30min., 14 per day, €1.40) or a train to **Athens, Ioannina, Patras,** or **Thessaloniki.** For all other bus connections you will have to spend €10 on a **taxi** (☎26230 71 764) to **Lehena,** the nearest town on the main Patras-Pirgos highway. Taxis line up by the same kiosk where the buses depart. **Ferries** sail from Kyllini to: **Argostoli,** Kephalonia (2hr., 11:30am, €10.10); **Poros,** Kephalonia (1½hr.; 7am, 7:30, 10:30pm; €6.50); **Zakynthos** (1hr.; 5 per day, M-Sa 8am-9:45pm; Su 10:30am-9:45pm; €5.10). Buy tickets from one of the two kiosks on the dock; the kiosk on the right sells tickets to Zakynthos and the one on the left tickets to Kephalonia. The **port police** are on the dock. (☎26230 92 211. Open 24hr.) To find the **police** station (☎26230 92 202), walk past the centrally located Sea Garden Restaurant (straight ahead as you exit the dock) and turn left; it's a block and a half down on the right side. A 24hr. **ATM** is on the dock directly in front of Killini Port Restaurant. The town's **pharmacy** is 6m to the right of the police station (facing inland). The **post office** is one block past the police station on a side street. (Open M-F 7:30am-2pm.) **Postal code:** 27068.

If you plan on spending the night, **Sea Garden Domatia ❸,** above the Sea Garden Restaurant two blocks inland from the port, offers nothing spectacular but is your best bet for a relatively inexpensive night's rest. Rooms located above a somewhat noisy street have ceiling fans, TVs, balconies, and some private baths. (☎26230 92 165. Singles €20-30; doubles €36-55. Cash only.) **Hotel Ionion ❸,** one block inland from the port and to the right, rents fairly spacious but unattractive rooms with A/C, TVs, and private baths. (☎26230 92 318; fax 26230 92318. Singles €36-48; doubles €48-60; triples with mini-fridges €66. Cash only.) **Stivas ❸,** down the street from the port gate, one block past Sea Garden domatia on the right, serves well-portioned dishes cooked in a tiny, family-run kitchen. Eat under a vine-laden trellis on the side patio while caged birds sing above you. Dishes change daily, so ask before you look at a menu. (☎26230 92 045. Salad €2-4. Entrees €4-16. 0.5L wine €2. Cash only.)

PIRGOS Πιργος ☎26210

Not unlike Kyllini, Pirgos is often seen as the rusted last link in the golden chain to Olympia. In fact, most traveler's experiences of Elias's capital are confined by a tour bus window. Beneath streets oversaturated with fast-food joints and designer-clothed mannequins lies a town proudly clinging to traditional Greek culture. So if traveling for history and tradition, consider immersing yourself in Pirgosian culture for the night; Olympia, after all, is only one link in the chain away.

TRANSPORTATION. Pirgos has earned its reputation as an important Peloponnesian transport hub. A relatively reliable bus and train system will most likely get you where you need to go and as close to on time as possible (by Grecian standards, that is). The **train station,** Ypsilantou (Υψηλαντου) 12 (☎26210 22 576), 450m downhill from the intersection of Mitrop Antoniou and Manolopoulou, has trains to: **Kiparissia** (1hr.; 6 per day, 4:21am-8:46pm; €1.80); **Olympia** (45min.; 5 per day, 6:50am-2:09pm; €0.70); **Patras** (1½-2hr.; 7 per day; express €5.40, normal €2.80). For bus service, **KTEL** has two stations, one serving those traveling locally and the other serving those traveling greater distances. Those looking for tickets to destinations within 1hr. of Pirgos should go to the **bus station** at Manolopoulou 15 (☎26210 23 703), two blocks to the right of the intersection of Mitrop Antoniou and Manolopoulou (facing uphill), which has service to: **Amaliada** (25min.; M-F 5 per day, 7am-6pm; Sa-Su 7:30am-6pm; €1.30); **Kyllini** (1½hr.; 10:30am, 2:35pm; €3.50); **Olympia** (35min.; M-F 14 per day, 5:15am-9:30pm; Sa-Su 9 per day, 5:15am-9:30pm; €1.40). Travelers who are taking longer trips should consult the other **bus station,** Manolopoulou 18 (☎26210 22 592), 20m farther down the same street, which sells tickets to: **Athens** (normal trains: 5hr.; 8 per day, 5:30am-12:30am; €18.60; express trains: 4¼hr.; 9:30am, 2:30, 5:15pm; €18.60); **Patras** (2hr.; 10 per day, 5:30am-8pm; €6.40); **Thessaloniki** (9hr., daily, €34.20). Service to Athens and Patras is reduced on Saturday and Sunday. **Taxis** (☎26210 25 000), which offer reasonable rates, line up in the center of town by the OTE.

ORIENTATION AND PRACTICAL INFORMATION. Pirgos's layout forms a loosely structured grid that slopes uphill. Both bus stations drop off on centrally located **Manolopoulou.** As you walk to the left of the bus station (start out facing it), you'll find yourself face-to-face with a rather large bronze statue of a stern-faced man gripping a weapon; this marks the center of town. The statue, in addition to its debatable aesethic value, more practically marks the division of two important streets. **Themistokleous** runs perpendicular to Manolopoulou on the far side of the statue. At this point Manolopoulou becomes **Meg. Alexandriou.** The street on the near side of the statue is the main street which, if followed downhill, leads directly to the train station. Known locally as "Patron," the street signs identify it first as **Eth. Adistaseos,** which then becomes **Mitrop Antoniou,** and eventually **Ermou** (the main shopping sector of town). The beautiful plateia, known as **Pl. Kiprou,** is accessible from the intersection of Mitrop Antoniou and Manolopoulou. Facing uphill, make a right onto the steps of Miaouli and then make a left onto 28 Oktovriou.

The **National Bank of Greece** (☎26210 22 911), in Pl. Kiprou on the side closest to 28 Oktovriou, has a 24hr. **ATM** and **exchanges currency.** (Open M-Th 8am-2pm, F 8am-1:30pm.) Other banks surround the plateia and other 24hr. ATMs can be found along Mitrop Antoniou. The **police station** (☎26240 22 100) is three blocks uphill from the train station on Karkarvitsa, next to Hotel Olympus. (Open daily 7:30am-10pm, for emergency 24hr.) The local police also serve as the **tourist police.** In the event of an **emergency,** dial ☎100. **Pharmacies** (most open M-F 8am-2:30pm) are found around the intersection of Mitrop Antoniou and Manolopoulou. The **hospital** (☎26210 22 222) is 1km past the bus stations on Manolopoulou; signs point the way. The OTE (☎26210 31 299) is by the intersection of Themistokleous and Manolopoulou, directly behind the bronze statue. (Open M-F 7am-2:40pm.) The appropriately named **Internet Cafe** (☎26210 24 025), in Pl. Kiprou on Letrinon, has two computers. (€3 per hr., €0.80 min. Open daily 8:30am-midnight.) The **post office** is on

Kanari street; walk three blocks past the intersection of Manopoulou and Antoniou, make a left onto Girmanou, and turn right after two blocks. (☎26210 33 117. Open M-F 7:30am-2pm.) **Postal code:** 27100.

ACCOMMODATIONS AND FOOD. Backpackers who love the smell of pre-owned hostel sheets and high-rollers who thrive off complementary bath robes will be disappointed by the accommodations choices in Pirgos. Options are limited to a group of C-level hotels, which cluster between the bus and train stations. Rates and amenities tend to be consistent so don't be surprised if you end up making a choice based on arbitrary details like color scheme or headboard shape. Bargain for the best price. **Hotel Ilida ❸,** Eth. Adistaseos 50, to the right of the train station and one block uphill at the intersection with Deligianni is the classiest of the C-level hotels. These rooms provide the most pleasant stay in Pirgos with A/C, TVs, telephones, big private baths, and plush, shell-shaped headboards. (☎26210 28 046; fax 26210 33 834. Singles €30-40; doubles €50-60. MC/V.) **Hotel Pantheon ❸,** Themistokleous 7, two blocks uphill from the train station, caters to those who need a little color in their accommodations. Lime-green doors lead to fully carpeted rooms with A/C, fridges, hair dryers, spacious yellow beds, and blue-tiled private bathrooms. (☎26210 29 746; fax 26210 36 791. Singles €35-45; doubles €50-60. MC/V.) One block uphill from the train station, **Hotel Marily ❸,** at the intersection of Themistokleous and Deligianni, has 30 fairly plain but spotless rooms with A/C, TVs, telephones, hair dryers, freezers, and private baths. (☎26210 28 133; fax 26210 27 066. Singles €30-54; doubles €40-76. MC/V.)

PELOPONNESE

For a town that prides itself on hard work and authenticity, it seems strange that most of the eateries serve little but fast food. Still travelers sick of greasy gyro wrappers have no reason to despair; with a little wandering, you can find wonderful restaurants that perfectly fit the demeanor of the town. **To Spitiko ❷,** halfway between the train station and Hotel Olympus on Eth. Adistaseos, serves marvelous Greek food in a family-run, local taverna. The owner promotes the calamari (€6), but with staples like meatballs in red sauce (€4.50), you can't go wrong. (☎26210 29 948. Salads €2-4. Entrees €3-7. Open daily 11am-midnight. Cash only.) **Restaurant Milano ❷,** on Themistokleous, 70m downhill from the OTE, is a perfect choice for vegetarians and Italian cuisine-enthusiasts. (☎26210 23 291. Appetizers €2-3.50. Salads €2-3.50. Pizza €4-6. Pasta €3-4.30. Open 6pm-12:30am. Cash only.) **O Vasilis** (Ο Βασιλης) **❷,** in Pl. Kiprou across from the Internet cafe, gets even Pirgos's most chic to roll up their sleeves and dig into fast food. (☎26210 31 104. Entrees €5 and under. Open daily 10am-12:30am. Cash only.)

OLYMPIA Ολυμπια ☎26240

Though set among quiet meadows of cypress and olive trees, modern Olympia is anything but relaxed. With the 2004 Summer Olympic Games on their way, the small town is in a frenzy to make a name for itself.

TRANSPORTATION

Facing the tourist office, the **train** station is three blocks to the right. Signs point the way down the hill. To: **Pirgos** (45min.; 5 per day, 7:30am-3:14pm; €0.70). **Buses** leave Olympia from in front of Town Hall, two blocks from the tourist office and go to **Pirgos** (35min.; M-F 15 per day; Sa 12 per day; Su 9 per day, 6:30am-10pm; €1.40) and **Tripoli** (4hr.; M-F 8:45am, 12:30, 5:30pm; Sa-Su 8:45am, 5:30pm; €8).

PRACTICAL INFORMATION

Olympia consists primarily of a 1km main street called **Kondili;** buses stop in front of the tourist office on this street. Facing the tourist office, walk to the left to reach the ruins and Archaeological Museum; signs point the way. On the side road that intersects Kondili at a fork near the youth hostel sits the train station, convenience store, and pricey tavernas.

Tourist Office: ☎26240 23 100; fax 26240 23 125. On Kondili, toward the ruins. Helpful staff, photocopier, **currency exchange,** and **free maps.** Open M-F 9am-4pm.

Bank: National Bank (☎26240 22 501), on Kondili next to the tourist office, has an **ATM** and **currency exchange.** Open M-Th 8am-2pm, F 8am-1:30pm.

Police: Em. Kountsa 1 (☎26240 22 100), 1 block up from Kondili, directly behind the tourist office. Open daily 9am-9pm, emergency 24hr. Also serve as **tourist police.**

Health Center: ☎26240 22 222. Olympia uses **Pirgos's hospital** (☎26210 22 222) but has its own brand-new health center. Walk from the ruins down Kondili and turn left before the church on your left. Continue straight as the road winds to the right and then take a right. Open M-F 8:30am-2pm.

OTE: ☎26240 22 163. On Kondili by the post office. Open M-F 7:30am-2pm.

Internet Access: Olympia's **Internet Cafe** (☎26240 22 578 or 26240 23 841) is a hip and spacious cafe/bar, blaring American and British tunes late into the night. Turn off Kondili with the youth hostel on your right and walk uphill two blocks; Pension Achilles is on the same street. €3 per hr., €1.50 min. Open daily 9:30am-2am.

Post Office: ☎26240 22 578. On a nameless uphill side street just past the tourist office. **Poste Restante** available. Open M-F 7:30am-2pm. **Postal code:** 27065.

ACCOMMODATIONS

Though Olympia's many hotels offer similar amenities like private baths and balconies, there is much price diversity. You can pay anywhere from €15-40 for a single and €20-70 for a double.

Youth Hostel, Kondili 18 (☎26240 22 580). A great place to get to know international backpackers, this hostel offers clean rooms and a friendly owner. In a good location, this hostel definitely has the cheapest rooms in town. Breakfast (€2.50) served 8-10am. Free hot showers. Sheets €1. Check-out 10:30am. Lock-out 10:30am-12:30pm. Dorms €8; doubles €20. Cash only. ❶

THE LOCAL STORY

THE GAMES RETURN

Apostolos Apostolopoulos, a 16-year member of the Olympia Town Council, currently serves as Special Cooperative to Mayor Skoularikis. Let's Go *spoke with him on June 17, 2003.*

LG: How are the people of Olympia reacting to the upcoming Gmes?

A: Positive to all this, positive to the Olympics taking place in Athens in 2004, and they have great expectations, hoping it will be very successful, not only in the stadiums, but especially in terms of the cultural aspects.

LG: What do you mean by that?

A: The Olympic Games, when they started in 776 BC in Olympia, they were giving to all the people the opportunity for transferring the beautiful humanistic ideas of the Greek spirit of that time. So the games were the instrument for these ideas.... These are the same ideas of world peace: friendship between all nations and races, no matter if they were speaking different languages, had a different color, or believed in a different dogma. The third part of this spirit, the gentle rivalry between participating athletes, which if we take into a larger meaning, means that we should all try to be better than the ones next to us, but in a nice, gentle way.

LG: What else do you have planned to promote Greek culture?

A: Before, during, and after the Games, there will be music, theater, Ancient Greek tragedies and comedies taking place in all of Greece.

New Olympia (☎26240 22 506; fax 26240 22 112), on the road that diagonally leads to the train station. Located away from the hubbub of the main road, this hotel is perfect for travelers who need extra amenities at cheap prices. You'll find spacious rooms with A/C, TVs, telephones, and large private baths. Be prepared; some bargaining skills may be in order. Breakfast buffet included. Singles €25-52; doubles €45-70; triples €90. ❹

Pension Poseidon (☎26240 22 567), on the same street as the Internet Cafe. Turn off Kondili with the Youth Hostel on your right or follow the signs. Teal hallways introduce guests to astonishingly clean rooms, some with decently-sized private baths. Singles €25-35; doubles €35-40. Cash only. ❸

Zounis Rooms, 13 Avgerinou and Spiliopoulou (☎26240 22 644), 2 blocks to the right and then a left when facing the tourist office; it's up the hill opposite the large hotel. Inquire about vacancies at the Anesi Cafe-Taverna. Immaculate rooms come with the bare essentials. Shared fridge available. Singles €25; doubles €35. Cash only. ❸

Olympia Palace, Kondili 2 (☎26240 23 101; www.olympia-palace.gr). As close to Ancient Olympia as you can get, the 5-star Palace surely has won nods of approval from the gods of luxury. Complex features shops, a cafe, a restaurant, and a gorgeous marble lobby. Rooms are no less elegant or modern, with A/C, satellite TVs, room service, private baths with large bathtubs, Internet connection, and huge balconies. Breakfast included. Singles €60-70; doubles €75-85. Breakfast included. MC/V. ❺

Camping Diana (☎26240 22 314), uphill from the Sports Museum, has hot water, helpful info, swimming pool, mini-market, and restaurant serving ouzo, snacks, and breakfast (€5). €5.50 per adult, children €3.50; €3.50 per small tent, €5 per large tent; €3.50 per car. Electricity €3.50. 10% student discounts. Cash only. ❶

PELOPONNESE

FOOD

Along Kondili, **mini-markets, bakeries,** and **fast-food** joints compete for your attention (and money). Most Kondili eateries are overpriced, but a short walk toward the train station or up the hill can lead to enticing, relatively inexpensive tavernas. The constant influx of crowds keeps most restaurants open 8am-1am. To find **Ambrosia** ❷, face the train station, head to the left, and follow the road as it bends. Don't let the loads of wide-eyed tourists deter you from enjoying exceptional food overlooking a cypress-lined meadow. (☎26240 23 414. Veal with pasta €7. Stuffed vine leaves €5.50. AmEx/MC/V.) **Taverna Olympia** ❷ is on the diagonal road to the train station next to the hotel New Olympia. Vegetarians and carnivores alike can enjoy meals somewhat removed from the cafe crowds. (Salads €2.50-3. Greek entrees €7. Pastas €2.50-8. Grilled dishes €4.80-5.30. Cash only.) **Pension Poseidon** ❷, two blocks uphill from the Youth Hostel, draws patrons with its *retsina* (€4 per L), made from the grapes that hang on the lattices overhead. (☎26240 22 567. Entrees €3.20-7.20. Omelettes €2.80. Cash only.)

SIGHTS

MUSEUM OF THE OLYMPIC GAMES

☎26240 22 544. Open M-Sa 8am-3:30pm, Su 9am-4:30pm. €2, children and EU students free. Guidebook €6. Two blocks uphill from Kondili, on Angerinou.

Also known as the Sports Museum, it houses a collection that should not be missed by any sports enthusiast. Pins, stamps, photographs, and posters from each Olympiad are among the many media which illustrate the history of the Modern Games. Don't miss an actual silver medal from the 1996 games in Atlanta, donated to the museum by the women's high-jump medalist.

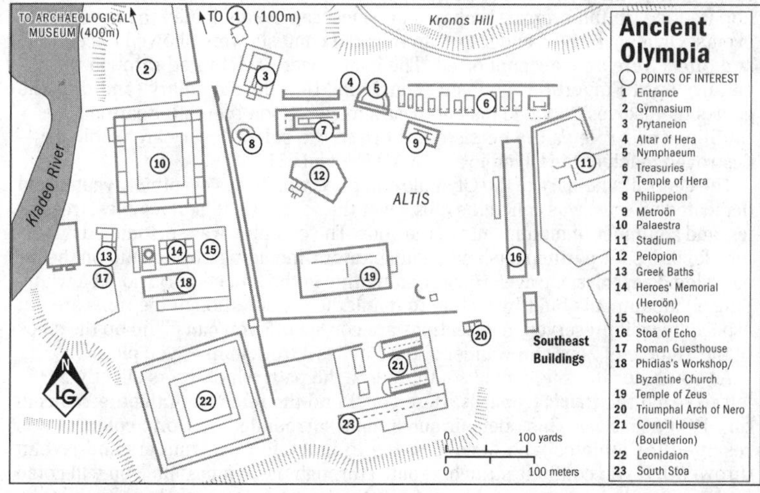

ANCIENT OLYMPIA

Site: ☎*26240 22 517. Open in summer daily 8am-7pm. Museum:* ☎*26240 22 742. Through the parking lot opposite the ancient site. Open M noon-3pm, Tu-Su 8am-7pm. Flash cameras prohibited. Museum and site €9 (individually €6), seniors and non-EU students €5, EU students and children under 18 free. The ruins are practically unmarked. Several guides are available at the site–try* Olympia: Complete Guide *(€7) by Spiros Photinos or the* Guide to the Museum and Sanctuary *by A. and N. Yalouris (€7.50). Maps €2-4.*

For two weeks in the summer of 2004, the world's attention will be focused on Greece. Amidst pin-trading travelers and ubiquitous corporate sponsorships, men and women will battle each other and the clock in the world's most historically significant athletic forum. But before there were photo-finishes, drug-tests, and aerodymanic unisuits, there were the games of Olympia. A green tract between the rivers Kladeo and Alphios, the city was one of the most important cultural centers of the ancient world for a millennium. Participants from Sicily, Asia Minor, North Africa, Macedonia, and Greece once convened here to worship, compete, and mature among the most cultured poets, musicians, and masterpieces of art and architecture. Every four years, warring city-states would call truces and travel to Olympia for the most splendid Panhellenic assembly of the ancient world. Yet remember that, despite their intensity, the games were never just about athletic ability; rather, they were deliberate instruments of peace and diplomacy.

Olympia was settled in the 3rd millennium BC, when it was dedicated to **Gaia,** the Earth Mother, who had an oracle at the site. The first athletic games commenced in Zeus's honor, only to be forgotten again until 884 BC. Ancient history credits divine intervention for the first Olympic revival, which took place on the Oracle of Delphi's orders to Iphtos, King of Elias; prophecy held that the games would save Greece from civil war and plague. The first recorded Olympiad was in 776 BC, with **Koroibos of Elias** emerging victorious. Every four years thereafter, another champion added his name to the illustrious list, which became the first accurate chronology of Greek history. Initially the most athletic men, naked as the day they were born, competed only in a simple 192m (the stadium's length) foot-race. As time wore on and the Games' popularity broadened, longer races, wrestling, boxing, the pentathlon (long jump, discus, javelin, running, wrestling), the hoplite race (in full bronze regalia), and equestrian events joined the schedule of events. Olympia thrived under Roman rule; the contests were allowed to continue and often were actively supported. The games were celebrated through the 4th century until Emperor Theodosius concluded that the sanctuary (and thus the games themselves) violated his anti-heathen laws. Soon thereafter earthquakes—fulfilling their role as the persistent thorn in the side of every archaeologist—destroyed much of the Olympic site in AD 522 and 551.

The central sanctuary of the Olympic complex, which was eventually walled and dedicated to Zeus, was called the **Altis.** Over the centuries, it held temples, treasuries, and a number of monuments to the gods. The complex was surrounded by various facilities for participants and administrators, including the stadium on the far east side. **Pausanias,** a traveler/historian writing in the 2nd century, noted a whopping 69 monuments built by victors to thank the gods. Although the ruins are not especially well preserved, few sections are corded off; you can climb up the steps of the Temple of Zeus and wander about Phidias's workshop as you please.

As you enter the site, facing south, follow the path which veers slightly to the left to reach the **training grounds.** Here you'll find the remains of the the 2nd-century BC **gymnasium.** This open-air quadrangle surrounded by Doric columns was reserved for athletes who needed space to practice (e.g., runners and javelin throwers). If you continue straight (south) through the gymnasium, you will come to the re-erected columns of the square **Palaestra,** or wrestling school, built in the 3rd century BC. More than an athletic facility, the Palaestra ensured that competitors wouldn't become one-dimensional, uncivilized brutes. The young trained their minds and bodies, wrestling one moment and studying metaphysics the next.

As you continue south and slightly west (out the far right corner of the Palaestra), the next group of structures includes a reddish, suprisingly intact, walled-in building. At this point you've reached the **workshop of Phidias,** the marvelous sculptor who came to Olympia after his banishment from Athens under a cloud of scandal which concerned the statue of Athena he had created for the Parthenon. Commissioned to sculpt for the Temple of Zeus, he produced an ivory and gold statue of the god so magnificent that it was later called one of the **Seven Wonders of the Ancient World.** It stood 12.4m tall and portrayed the god with an expression revealing benevolence and glory, seated on his throne. In rhythm with the Olympic Games, Zeus cupped a statue of Nike, the goddess of victory, in his right palm. After viewing this magnum opus, poet Philip of Salonika wrote, "Either God came down from Heaven to show you his image, Phidias, or you went to see God." When the Games were abolished in the 4th century, the statue was moved to Constantinople; it burned in a fire there in 475. Adding insult to injury, the Byzantines built a **church** on top of the sculptor's workshop in the 5th century, constructing new walls but leaving the foundation intact. As a result, the identity of the site was debated for years. However, the traditional sources have been affirmed by recent excavations, which have uncovered moulds, sculpting tools, and, most amazing of all, shards of a plain wine jug that, when they were cleaned and mended, bore the inscription "I am Phidias's." These finds are currently in the museum (p. 178). The entrances to the workshop are to the south (away from the Palaestra) and east (toward the Temple of Zeus). Just beyond the workshop to the south and slightly east (straight and left) is the huge **Leonidaion,** built in 330 BC by a wealthy man from Naxos named Leonidas. Though the building was officially dedicated to Zeus sometime after 350 BC, it served a primarily secular role, often hosting officials and other VIPs.

At the **Bouleterion,** east of the Leonidaion, to the right as you face the entrance, lie the remains of the South Processional Gate to the Altis. The procession of athletes and trainers entered the sacred area on their way to the Bouleterion (to the right of the Gate), where the ancient Olympic council met. Each athlete was required to make a sacrifice to Zeus and take the sacred oath, swearing his eligibility and intent to abide by the rules of the Games.

To the north of the Bouleterion (toward the entrance) are the ruins of the once-gigantic **Temple of Zeus,** the centerpiece of the Altis after its completion in 456 BC. Home to Phidias's awe-inspiring statue of Zeus, the 27m-long sanctuary was the largest temple completed on the Greek mainland before the Parthenon. The temple's elegant facade, impressive Doric columns, and accurately modeled pedimental sculpture exemplified the Classical design that evolved before the Persians invaded Greece. Today only a half-column stands, while the rest of these tremendous pillars, toppled in segments, lie as they fell after a 6th-century earthquake.

Continuing east past the temple (to the right as you face the entrance), you will reach the remains of the **Stoa of Echo,** which was used for competitions between trumpeters and heralds, whose musical prowess was no doubt enhanced by the seven-fold echo the Stoa is said to have had. At the northern edge of the Stoa (toward the hill), stone blocks that once supported statues of victorious athletes lead to the **Krypte,** the official entrance to the **stadium** (farther to the right and east) used by athletes and judges. This domed passageway (of which only one arch survives) and the stadium as it stands today are products of the Hellenistic Period, built over the remains of the earlier, similarly positioned stadium. Having survived the effects of powerful earthquakes, the stadium appears much as it did 2300 years ago. The judges' stand and the start and finish lines are still in place, and the stadium's grassy banks can still seat nearly 40,000 spectators. You may feel inspired to take a lap or two to bond with Olympians of millennia past. As you leave the passageway to the stadium, the remains of treasuries erected by distant states to house votive offerings are in a row on the northern hillside to your right. Continuing west, or left as you face the hill, you'll see the space that once held the **treasuries,** small-scale temples donated by individual cities. Beyond the treasuries are the remains of the **Nymphaeum** and the **Metroön,** an elegant Doric temple dedicated to Zeus's mother, Rhea. Archaeologists date the temple to the 4th century BC. Along the terrace of the treasuries stand the remains of the bases of 16 bronze statues of Zeus, built with money from fines collected from cheating athletes.

Westward (to the left facing the hill) past the Metroön and the Nymphaeum are the dignified remains of the **Temple of Hera.** Erected around 600 BC, the temple is the oldest building at Olympia, the

ATHENS 2004

ULTRA-MODERN OLYMPIA

While Athens claims ownership of the 2004 Olympics, efforts made by the small town of Olympia will keep the world from overlooking the Games' first home. The Greek Ministry of Culture is pumping €45 million to complete a series of renovations that will spruce up both the town of Olympia and its prestigious archaeological site and museum.

In regards to Modern Olympia, one of the most important renovations is taking place at the Hotel Spap, a presence in town since the beginning of the 20th century. It will be transformed into a modern convention center with a capacity of 300, serving the archaeological department based in Olympia. The entire southern side of the hotel will serve as spacious offices for archaeologists. The lobby of the edifice (which is one of the closest in town to the actual site) will eventually serve as Olympia's new Town Hall.

The town has reserved €7.5 million for the improvement and beautification of modern Olympia itself. Though urgent care was once only available at Pirgos Hospital, the city will proudly renovate its health center, which will be kept open 24hr. per day. Even the park around the train station, which is nearly 100 years old, will be glamorized. Finally, to ensure safe and peaceful enjoyment of the town's new look, pedestrian walkways are to be installed throughout the town.

oldest Doric temple in Greece, and the best-preserved structure at the site. Originally built for both Zeus and Hera, it was devoted solely to the goddess when Zeus moved to grander quarters in 457 BC. The cella of the temple is where the magnificent **Hermes of Praxiteles** was unearthed during excavations; you can see the statue in the site's museum. This temple figured prominently in the **Heraia,** a women's foot-race held every four years. Today, every fourth year in the last week of May or the first week of June, the Olympic **flame** is lit at the Altar of Hera, at the northeastern corner of the temple. From here, it is borne to Athens by runners who each travel 1km, then pass it from hand to hand to the site of the Modern Games. It can involve thousands of runners or draw upon more modern methods of transportation like boats, planes, and even laser beam (as in the unique case of the 1976 Montreal Games). The **Prytaneion** is northwest (toward the entrance) of the Temple of Hera and contains a hearth, the Altar of Hestia. The spirit of the Games reached its culmination here with feasts held on behalf of the victors and official guests, that expressed an appreciation for the virtues of discipline and honor that the athletes embodied.

Many find the gleaming new **Archaeological Museum** a greater attraction than the actual ancient site. A team of French archaeologists began unearthing the site from 1400 years of silt in 1829; the systematic excavations that continue today commenced in 1875. Most of what has been extracted in these 129 years resides in the museum. Since military victors from across the Greek world sent spoils and pieces of their own equipment to Olympia as offerings to the gods, the new museum doubles as a museum of Greek military history, with entire rooms filled with helmets, cuirasses, greaves, swords, spear points, and other military paraphernalia. The most spectacular military offering is a common **Corinthian helmet** (490 BC), partially destroyed by oxidation. While richer, better preserved headgear can be found elsewhere in the museum, the helmet's attraction is the faint inscription on the chin guard, which reads "Miltiades dedicated this to Zeus." The victor of one of the most famous battles in all antiquity, **Miltiades** led the outnumbered Greeks to victory over the Persians at Marathon in 479 BC; he may have worn the helmet in the battle. Beside it is another headpiece, whose inscription reveals it to be from the Persian side of the same battle. The museum's array of sculpture includes some of the greatest extant pieces in the world. Gape at the graceful perfection of the **Hermes of Praxiteles** (340-330 BC) and the **Rape of Ganymede** (470 BC) and observe the **Nike of Paionios** (421 BC). The pedimental sculptures and metopes depicting the Hercules's 12 labors from the Temple of Zeus are in the main room. Even the overlooked objects astound—every case holds objects that would be highlights of a lesser collection.

ARCADIA Αρκαδια

Beyond the noisy bustle of Tripoli, mountainous Arcadia is heavily forested and lightly speckled with red-roofed villages and lonely monasteries. Ushered into mythology and literature with its serene landscape, the pastoral archetype was home to Pan, Dionysus, and the nymphs, satyrs, and lucky mortals who cavorted with them. While few foreign tourists venture as fas as Arcadia's outer reaches, those who do enjoy the company of mountain goats clinging to precipitous slopes.

TRIPOLI Τριπολη ☎2710

At first Tripoli may seem like just another gritty, modern city. Although crowded and fast-paced, Tripoli has pushed to beautify its urban landscapes. Cafes and tavernas brim with energy at the park's edge. You can settle back with a leisurely game of backgammon or by watching children wreak havoc in the park.

TRANSPORTATION

Buses: Tripoli has 2 bus stations; 1 is in Pl. Kolokotronis; the other is farther southeast, outside the center of town. The **KTEL Arcadias Station** (☎2710 222 560), in Pl. Kolokotronis, runs buses to: **Andritsena** (2hr.; 11:45am, 7:30pm; €5.40); **Athens** (3hr.; 14 per day, 5am-9:30pm; €11); **Dimitsana** (1hr.; M-F 1:30 and 6:30pm, M and F 8:30am, Sa-Su 1:30pm; €4.60); **Megalopolis** (45min.; 9per day, 4:30am-10:15pm; €2.40); **Nafplion** (1hr..; 5 per day, 7am-4:20pm; €3.70) via **Argos; Pirgos** (3½hr.; M-F 8:30am and 6:30pm, Sa-Su 11am; €8.40). **Blue buses** leave from Arcadias Station for **Mantinea** and **Tegea** (1hr., every 15min., €1). The **KTEL Messinia and Laconia** depot (☎2710 242 086) is across from the train station. From Arcadias Station turn right onto Lagorati, which runs 1 block behind the eastern side of Pl. Koloktroni; follow it past the curve near Atlantik Supermarket until it ends at the train station–the depot is on the left. Buses go to: **Kalamata** (1½hr.; 10 per day, 8am-11pm; €5.50); **Patras** (3hr.; 6am, 2:45pm; €11); **Pylos** (3hr.; 10:30am, 5:30pm; €8.80); **Sparta** (1hr.; 8 per day, 9:15am-10pm; €3.70).

Trains: ☎2710 241 213. Facing the Messinia and Laconia bus depot. Trains to: **Argos** (1½hr.; 10am, 7pm, 1am, €1.90); **Athens** (4hr.; 9:30am, 6:25pm, 1am; €6); **Corinth** (2½hr.; 9:30am, 6:25pm, 1am; €2.90); **Kalamata** (2½hr.; 10:20am, 6pm; €5).

PELOPONNESE

ORIENTATION AND PRACTICAL INFORMATION

Think of Tripoli as a cross. At the central joint is **Pl. Ag. Vasiliou,** marked by the Church of Ag. Vasiliou. Four other plateias form the ends of the cross, at the ends of the four roads that branch out from Ag. Vasiliou. Most buses arrive at Arcadia station in **Pl. Kolokotronis,** to the east of the center. From the station, **Giorgiou,** to the left as you face the National Bank, takes you to Pl. Ag. Vasiliou from behind the church. Facing the church in Pl. Ag. Vasiliou, turn left and head north on **Eth. Antistasis** to reach **Pl. Petrinou,** recognizable by the large, Neoclassical Maliaropouli Theater. Along with Pl. Kolokotronis, Pl. Petrinou sees most of the city's activity. Continue on Eth. Antistasis, the main shopping boulevard, past pedestrian-only **Deligianni,** which runs perpendicular to Eth. Antistasis. Travel farther up Eth. Antistasis and the city **park** will be on your right. At the center of the park is **Pl. Areus,** with a 5m-tall statue of Kolokotronis, War of Independence hero.

Bank: National Banks, in Pl. Kolokotronis (☎2710 371 110), another on Eth. Antistasis (☎2710 234 878), 1 block from Pl. Agios Vasiliou. Both **exchange currency** and have a 24hr. **ATM.** Both open M-Th 8am-2pm, F 8am-1:30pm.

Police: ☎2710 224 847. On Eth. Antistasis in Pl. Petrinou. Open 24hr.

Hospital: ☎2710 238 542. On Panargadon. Walk due west (straight ahead with your back to the church) from Pl. Ag. Vasiliou; the road becomes E. Stavrou, which intersects with Panargadon after 500m. At the intersection, turn left. After 300m, look right, and you'll see the hospital. In an **emergency,** dial ☎166 or 100.

OTE: 28 Oktovriou 29 (☎2710 226 399). From Pl. Agios Vasiliou, take Eth. Antistasis and bear left on 28 Oktovriou. Open M-Sa 7am-5pm.

Internet Access: Concept Cafe (☎2710 235 600), on Dareioutou off Eth. Antistasis, before Deligianni. €3 per hr., €1.20 min. Open 9am-1:30am. **Forth Net** (☎2710 226 407) is on Deligianni, inside Cinema Classic Billiards Club. €3 per hr. Open until 1am.

Post Office: ☎2710 222 565. 1 block behind the Galaxy Hotel. Open M-F 7:30am-8pm. **Postal code:** 22100.

ACCOMMODATIONS AND FOOD

Tripoli has many mid-range hotels better suited to business conventions than budget travelers. Unless you're carrying a briefcase, you may want to consider setting up shop in a smaller village like Dimitsana, where rooms are less expensive and better equipped. In Tripoli's Pl. Kolokotronis, **Arcadia Hotel ❸** offers charmingly old-fashioned rooms with leather-backed chairs and classy furnishings. While each room comes with private bath, A/C, and TV, each features a unique wallpaper pattern and color scheme. (☎2710 225 551. Singles €30-50; doubles €45-72; triples €80-85. V.) **Hotel Alex ❸,** Vas. Georgios 26, is between Pl. Kolokotronis and Pl. Ag. Vasiliou. Ongoing renovations have provided an elegant lobby that leads to spotless white-walled rooms with A/C, TVs, phones, baths, and balconies. (☎2710 223 465; alexhotel@icn.gr. Singles €30-40; doubles €50-60; triples €65. Suites available. Cash only.) **Artemis Hotel ❸,** on Dimitrakopulou by Pl. Areus, has a location made for the adventurous. Dimly lit, run-of-the-mill rooms have A/C, TVs, phones, and baths. (☎2710 25 221; fax 2710 22 629. Singles €35; doubles €50. Cash only.)

The restaurants in Tripoli will not wow you in general, but there are a few good options bordering the park. Sandwich shops on Eth. Antistasis and Giorgiou pile baguettes with meat and cheese (around €2). **Atlantik Supermarket,** on Lagorati, is well-stocked. (Open M-F 8am-9pm, Sa 8am-6pm.) **Klimataria ❸,** on Eth. Antistasis, four blocks past the park as you walk from Pl. Petriou, has garden seating with fountains and grape vines that accent the traditional delicacies. (☎2710 222 058. Goat in egg-lemon sauce €8.20. Beef with tomatoes and onions €5.50. AmEx/MC/V.) **El Forno ❷,** at the edge of the park as you approach from Pl. Vasiliou, is a good choice for those tired of tiropita and *tzatziki*. The chef at this Italian and Mexican eatery serves up a slew of vegetarian-friendly pizzas (€5.25-10.15) and pastas (€3-5.50), while the more carnivorous types can feast on chimichangas (€3) and other Mexican fare. (☎2710 221 138. Cash only.)

PELOPONNESE

SIGHTS AND ENTERTAINMENT

The **Archaeological Museum** is on Evangelistrias, in a pink building surrounded by rose bushes and sculpture. Walking from Pl. Kolokotronis to Pl. Ag. Vasiliou, take the first left and then turn left again. The museum has a large prehistoric collection, with rooms of pottery and weaponry from the Neolithic to Mycenaean Periods. Among the more significant pieces is a Hellenistic relief showing a figure with a scroll in hand; it's one of the few surviving artistic depictions of the predecessor to modern books. The clay figurine of a dancer, complete with conical hat, also stands out from the collection. (☎2710 242 148. Open Tu-Su 8:30am-2:45pm. €2, students and seniors €1, children free. Photography strictly prohibited.) Walk to the left of the Galaxy Hotel in Pl. Ag. Vasiliou to find the **War Museum** on the left side of the street. Of particular interest is an old photograph of Peristera Kraka, the female "Captain of West Macedonia." (Open Tu-Sa 9am-2pm, Su 9:30am-2pm. Free.) The large **Church of Ag. Vasiliou** is in the plateia of the same name.

In summer, posters advertise dance groups, choirs, and plays performed in the city's main plateias and nearby villages. Traveling companies and local performers stage Greek shows in the attractive, recently renovated **Maliaropoulio Theater,** on Eth. Antistasis between Pl. Vasiliou and Pl. Petrinou. The **Lera Panigyris** is a 10-day **theater festival** beginning in the middle of August. At night you can rub shoulders with Tripoli's high school students at the downtown hot spot, pedestrian-only Deligianni. Especially popular is the **Cinema Classic Billiards Club,** to the right of Deligianni from Pl. Petrinou. With a big TV, A/C, and cheap drinks, this place fills up with males showing off their pool skills or complete lack thereof. (Beer €1.50-

2.50; cocktails €3-4. Pool €5 per hr.) Numerous cafes crowd the narrow area around Deligianni and Eth. Antistasis. **Faces,** like many others, caters to an older clientel who watch the younger people walk by on their way to window-shopping. **The American Music Bar,** found below a "Mobile" sign near the Billiards Club, is a smaller pub with wall-space devoted to all types of pop icons. If you party around the cafes, expect to pay €3 for beer; €5 for mixed drinks.

DIMITSANA Δημητσανα ☎27940

About 60km west of Tripoli lies the quintessential Arcadian village of Dimitsana, clinging to a steep, pine-covered mountainside. Built on the ruins of ancient Teuthis, Dimitsana has been a center of Greek learning and revolutionary activity since the 16th century. Greek city dwellers have been resettling Dimitsana, bringing the money and energy to keep the town's historic buildings in good repair.

TRANSPORTATION AND PRACTICAL INFORMATION. Transportation can be tricky in the mountains and locals are roughly indifferent to the passage of time. When planning connections, keep in mind that the two taxi drivers in some towns might siesta all afternoon. Unfortunately the bus system is also unreliable. There exists no Dimitsana bus station, only a bus kiosk with a posted schedule. Talk to the locals about the buses to find out approximate times, but don't be shocked if your bus comes an hour late or not at all. **Buses** are supposed to run to **Olympia** (1hr., at least 1 per day, €4.30) and **Tripoli** (2 per day, around 7:30am and 7:30pm; €4.60). There are morning (7am) and afternoon (2:30pm) buses that connect Dimitsana to the nearby **Stemnitsa** (€1). When you leave the bus kiosk, make sure to tell the driver where you want to go. If your final destination is **Olympia, Pirgos,** or **Tripoli,** you'll probably be dropped off at the nearby village of **Karkalou.** Occasionally other buses will be waiting for passengers making those connections; otherwise, flag down the first bus you see heading in the direction you want to go. The bus deposits those arriving on **Labardopoulou** (the main street), near the **taxi** stand (☎27950 614 001), 30m downhill from the town center.

Walking uphill into the town center, you'll pass a string of cafes, stores, and the worn-down **police station** (☎27950 31 205; open 24hr.) to the left, followed by a small grocery store just before a turn in the road. Opposite this road is an alley leading to rooms and an ecclesiastial museum. As you continue around the corner, a **National Bank** (☎27950 31 503; open M-Th 8am-2pm, F 8am-1:30pm) with a 24hr. **ATM** will be on your left. The **health center** (☎27950 31 401 or 31 402; open 24hr.) is a 10min. walk along the road toward Karaklou and a **pharmacy** is on your right as you walk uphill from the bus stop. The closest **hospital** is in Tripoli. The **post office** is next to the bank. (☎27950 31 234. Open M-F 7:30am-2pm.) **Postal code:** 22100.

ACCOMMODATIONS AND FOOD. For its small size, Dimitsana has an impressive number of rooming options. Though **domatia** tend to be just as expensive as some rooms in Tripoli, there's no doubt that you get what you pay for; most establishments are beautifully furnished and include breathtaking views of the nearby mountains. If you decide to visit the village, come during the summer; the high and low seasons are reversed, making rooms cheaper when its warm. Penny-pinching travelers will probably be most satisfied with the **Rooms to Let ❸** above the grocery store next to the police station. Beautiful hardwood floors support spacious rooms with TVs, kitchenettes, and private baths. (☎27950 31 084 or 31 562. Singles €25-30; doubles €30-40; apartment-style space €70. Cash only.) If you're looking for something slightly more isloated, check out the rooms at the home of **Vasilis Tsiapa ❸.** As you walk up the main road from the bus stop, take the last right before the road bends and follow the signs past the icon museum. Each elegant

THE BIG SPLURGE

TAMING THE WILD LOUISOS

Though hard to believe, a few minutes below the quiet towns of Dimitsana and Stemnitsa, where elderly men sit in front of cafes for what seems to be an unhealthly amount of time, a wild afternoon of adventure awaits.

Thirty kilometers outside Dimitsana lies the area of Vlahorafti, where the Louisos river is wide enough to allow for small river-rafting boats. All you need to bring is a towel, a bathing suit, and extra pair of shoes for the boat. **Trekking Hellas,** which has been leading tours in the area for 15 years, will take care of the rest (like professional guides, all equipment, and a picnic lunch.)

After a 30min. crash course on the fundamentals of rafting, you and the rest of your group will be ready to take on the river. An hour and a half of rafting (sometimes of the white-water variety) culminates with the river trek, in which members of the group get out of the rafts and physically walk through the remaining part of the river to a small waterfall.

The full experience lasts 4-5 hr. Rafting is most popular during the winter and fall months. However, because the river is so close to the springs, it never runs dry, allowing adventure-lovers to head out all year long.

River-rafting €52 per person; group discounts available. Expeditions leave at 9am and 1pm. For more information, contact the Dimitsana Trekking Hellas (☎27950 31 750) or check out www.trekking.gr.

room comes equipped with big beds, TVs, kichenettes, and private baths. All guests have access to a fragrant garden, cozy common room, and balcony overlooking the mountains. (☎27950 31 583. Breakfast included. Singles €30-38; doubles €35-50.) Guests at **Pyrtos Zeniou ❺** relax in the tallest brick-and-stone building in all of Greece. Originally constructed in 1850, the five floors are now occupied by extraordinary rooms with beautiful beds, wooden-balconies, fridges, stereos, large private baths, and a pair of complimentary slippers. If that's not enough, the third floor still hosts the original wine cellar, and students and professors from the University of Fine Arts have recently restored the original murals in the hallways. To get there, follow the road across from the police station and turn right after 25m. The hotel is just after the bend on the right. (☎27950 31 750. Rooms €150-200. MC/V.) At the home of **Georgios Velissaropoulos ❸,** the small gardens and magnificent views are perfect for budget-conscious honeymooners. Immaculate rooms come with TVs, fridges, cabinets, private baths, balconies, and kitchenettes. To find the house, simply follow the road across from the police station and turn right after 25m; signs point the way. (☎27950 31 617. Singles and doubles €30. Cash only.)

The dining options in Dimitsana prove both limited and generic, so if you're looking for something more ethnic, you'll probably have to cook it yourself. At **Barougadiko ❸** (Μπαρουγαδικο) down the main street by the bus stop, traditional Greek dishes are skillfully prepared in a castle-like building with low arched doorways and small stone rooms. (☎27950 31 629. Lamb with potatoes €6.50. Salads €2.50-5.50. Entrees €4-8. Open daily noon-11pm. Cash only.) **Drumonas ❸,** 200m past the post office on the road leading to Stemnitsa, offers a rotating menu of classic Greek staples. Vegetarians can enjoy stuffed tomatoes (€4.20), while meat-eating types can indulge in lamb chops (€21 per kg), the house specialty. (☎27950 31 116. Salads €4.50. Entrees €4-23. Open daily noon-midnight. Cash only.)

SIGHTS. Two small museums commemorate the town's ecclesiastic, scholarly, and revolutionary heritages. The **Historical Museum** was formerly the library to a ministry school established in 1764. Its collection of over 5000 books was decimated when the books were used as gunpowder during the War of Independence. A donation by Nikolaos Makris revamped the library/museum, which now holds over 35,000 books. It displays some books from the original library, including a handful of Greek-Latin **incunabula,** 16th-century books from Venice and Basil that are some of the first printed books in history. To find the museum and library, walk up the alley next to the police station and look for the courtyard with the statue near a large church; the entrance to the museum is on the wall closest to the mountains. (☎27950 31 219. Open Tu-Sa 9am-2pm. Free.) Walking up from the bus station, the **Icon Museum,** in an old mansion, is just off the main road on the final right before the bend. (☎27950 31 465. Open M-Tu, Th, Sa-Su 10am-1:30pm and 5-7pm. Free.) Dimitsana gets pretty busy in the winter, when tourists flock to the nearby ski slopes of Menalo Mountain. The Lousios River attracts both adventurers and seekers of serene entertainment. To reach it, ask a local for directions or follow the paths off the road to Stemnitsa. Strolling the banks and swimming are popular in the summer. Rafting (sometimes of the white water variety), horseback riding, and river tours are available and popular in fall and winter months. For more information, contact **Hellas Trekking** (☎27950 31 750 or 210 331 0323).

STEMNITSA Στεμνιτσα ☎27950

From Dimitsana, walk an easy, scenic 11km (about 2hr.) along the winding road, catch the morning bus, or pay for a taxi to Stemnitsa (€4). With its unspoiled mountain scenery and abundant flowers, greenery, and hidden courtyards, it is easy to see why this town has been called one of the most beautiful in Greece.

At the town's **Folk Art Museum,** 300m on the road leading away from Dimitsana, a series of recreated rooms display antiquated techniques for the rural tasks of cobblers and candlemakers. (☎27950 81 252. Open M-F 11am-1pm, Sa-Su 11am-2pm. Free. Guidebook €6.) Between Dimitsana and Stemnitsa there are several monasteries, some built right into the mountain face. Some of the roads and paths leading to them are unsuitable for cars and are best attempted on foot. A loop from Dimitsana to a monastery and then to Stemnitsa could be up to 30km. The monastery of **Ag. Ioannis Prodromos,** 10km from Stemnitsa and 16km from Dimitsana, is still inhabited by a small group of monks. You can see icons painted on the bare stone walls and gravity-defying monastic cells that seem to hang off the mountain. Follow the road as it goes from asphalt to dirt and finally becomes a footpath. (☎27950 81 385. Open dawn-dusk. Men only. Modest dress required. Free.)

There are **buses** that come through Stemnitsa, but as with Dimitsana, they are not necessarily regular or on time. According to the locals, there are 7:30am buses to **Tripoli** and 2:30pm buses to **Dimitsana** on weekdays and some weekends. The people in the **town hall** (☎27950 81 280; open M-F 8am-3pm) in the plateia are extremely friendly and helpful, and they speak English. **Postal code:** 22024.

IN RECENT NEWS

PROVINCIAL PAGEANTRY

These days everything in Greece is getting a facelift in preparation for the 2004 Games. Hotels are remodeling, restaurants renovating, and contractors redoubling their efforts to ensure that, come August, Greece wears its Sunday best.

Away from the Athenian spotlight, the fervor has infected the countryside at Diakofto and Kalavrita, between which runs the delightful rack-railway trains. With the primary goal of providing tourists easy and entertaining access to popular sights like Mega Spiliou, construction of the railway began in 1896. By 1903, 22km of track less than 1m wide had been laid; the rack-railway route was soon famed among travelers. Following a path created by the erosive flow of the Vouraikos river, the trains climbed through magnificent gorges, rumbled over waterfalls, and sharply descended into narrow valleys. The trains (locomotives until 1959) were cartoonishly small–passenger cars were 5m long and 3m tall.

Visitors arriving in Diakofto in the summer of 2003 found only a multicolored sign explaining that the beloved rack-railway had been shut down for renovations. New, wider tracks are being implemented for trains with air conditioning, heating, and bigger windows. Plans also include the destruction of and subsequent reconstruction of the bridges over which the trains pass. Though officials claim the trians will be ready in time for the Summer Olympics, many are skeptical the project will be completed in time.

The only hotel in town, the splendid **Hotel Triokolonion ❸**, on the left side of the main road as you head away from Dimitsana, has a terrace, which is a relaxing place to unwind after a day of hiking. Rooms have hardwood floors, private baths, and amazing views. (☎27950 81 297; fax 27950 81 483. Buffet breakfast included. Call ahead to reserve. Singles €25-30; doubles €40; triples €53.) **Domatia** in Stemnitsa do exist, though they tend to be expensive and require some effort to locate. You're best bet may be in the **rooms ❸** above Drakopoulou, the general store halfway between the plateia and the Folk Art Museum on the main road. Despite simple furnishings and shared baths, rooms are spacious enough to provide a pleasant stay. (☎27950 81 218. Singles €30-35; doubles €40-50. Cash only.) Another decent option is **Sophia's Rooms to Rent ❸**, where small but comfortable rooms come with fridges, private baths, and homemade honey and marmalade. (☎27950 81 368 or 81 375. Inquire at the religious art store closest to the Folk Art Museum on the main road. Singles and doubles €40. Cash only.) Unless you can satisfy your hunger with honey, you may initially be disappointed by the food options in Stemnitsa; however, the unimaginatively named **Restaurant Stemnitsa ❷**, in the plateia, serves exceptional Greek meals in very filling portions. (Grilled chicken €3.50. Lamb with potatoes €4.70. Entrees €3-5. Retsina €1.20. Cash only.) Otherwise consider tiny **Taverna Klinitsa ❷**, just outside the plateia on the way to Dimitsana, for an inexpensive meal. The special fried bread is particularly tasty. (Entrees €3-5.)

MESSINIA Μεσσηνια

Messinia is an oasis on the arid Peloponnese. Renowned olives, figs, and grapes spring from the rich soil on the rocky coastline, which remains largely tourist-free. Most Messinians live at the head of the gulf around sprawling Kalamata, though visitors may prefer to stay in the sleepy coastal towns of Pylos, Methoni, Koroni, Kardamyli, or Finikounda, with clean beaches and quiet streets.

KALAMATA Καλαματα ☎27210

Kalamata, the second-largest Peloponnesian city, played a key role in igniting the War of Independence, when on March 23, 1821, two days before a Greek revolt was to begin, a group of impatient Kalamatans massacred local Ottomans as they slept. A yearly reenactment of the grisly Greek victory is followed by parades and dancing. Fast-growing Kalamata has all the characteristics of any other large city, some of which may detract from its appeal. Still it exudes a pleasant, summery feel with open-air markets, cafes, and a clean, if crowded, 4km-long beach.

TRANSPORTATION

Trains: ☎27210 95 056. Where Sideromikou Stathmou dead ends at Frantzi. As you walk away from the Old Town and toward the waterfront in Pl. Giorgiou, turn right on Frantzi at the far end of the plateia and walk a few blocks. To: **Argos** (4hr., €4.40); **Athens** (6½hr.; 7:11am, 4:03, 11:01pm; €7) via **Tripoli** (2½hr., €2.80); **Corinth** (5¼hr., €5.60); **Kyparissia** (2hr.; 5:19, 11:30am; €1.90); **Patras** (5½hr., 3:19pm, €5); **Pirgos** (3¼hr., 7:45pm, €2.80).

KTEL buses: Leave from the station on Artemidos (☎27210 22 851; open 7am-10pm), inland from Pl. Giorgiou and across the river from Aristomenous. To get to the waterfront from the bus station, take a taxi (€3) or walk down Artemidos and eventually cross to parallel Aristomenous, which leads to Pl. Giorgiou. Buses go to: **Athens** (4hr.; 12per day, 4:45am-10:45pm; €15.10) via **Megalopolis** (1hr., €3.70); **Finikounda**

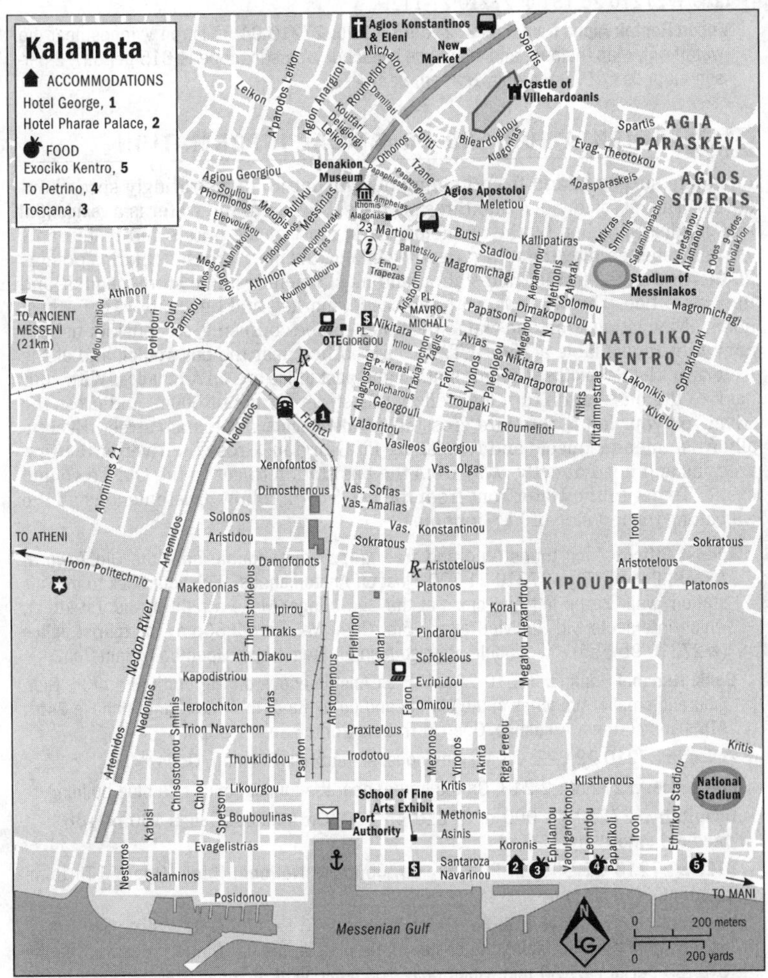

(2½hr.;5am, 3:15pm; €4.90); **Koroni** (1½hr.; 8 per day, 5am-7pm; €3.20); **Mavromati** and **Ancient Messini** (1hr.; 5:40am, 2pm; €2); **Methoni** (1¾hr.; 6 per day, 5am-7:45pm; €3.90); **Patras** (4hr.; 8:30am, 2:30pm; €14.70) via **Pirgos** (2hr., €8.30); **Pylos** (1½hr.; 8 per day, 5am-7:45pm; €3.20); **Sparta** (2hr.; 9:15am, 2:30pm; €2.80) via **Artemisia** (30min.; 5 per day, 5am-4pm; €1.60); **Tripoli** (2hr., €5.50). To get to **Areopolis** (15min., €0.80), go to **Itilo** (2hr.; 4 per day, 5:15am-5pm; €4.70) and change buses. Bus stops in **Kardamyli** (€2.30) and **Stoupa** (€2.80) before Itilo.

Intercity buses: Unfortunately for the traveler without a vehicle, the local city bus system (€0.80 per ride) is definitely limited. City buses depart from near Pl. 25 Martiou in the Old Town; look for the large street off Aristomenous. **Bus #1** goes down Pl. Aristomenous to the water and then runs along the water. Buy your ticket on the bus.

Taxis: ☎27210 28 181 or 27210 21 112.

Moped Rental: Alpha Rental (☎27210 93 423 or 27210 94 571), on Vyronos near the waterfront. Map, helmet, and insurance included. 1-person mopeds €15 per day, 2-person mopeds €20. Open daily 8:30am-8pm.

ORIENTATION AND PRACTICAL INFORMATION

Kalamata surges inland from its long beachfront in a frustratingly spread-out design. The city is divided into three sections. Closest to the water is a **residential section,** distinguished by the municipal park; most of the hotels and restaurants are here, clustered by the water. Heading inland, the next largest gathering point is **Pl. Giorgiou,** home to the train station and most amenities, like stores, banks, and the post office. The **Old Town,** with the castle, market, and bus station, is farthest inland. Navigating from one end to the other can be confusing, so consider using a map; they're available at the DETAK tourist office near the **bus station** and at the waterfront **tourist police.** The bus station and **post office** are on **Artemidos.** With your back to the bus station turn left, follow this street for about 500m, and cross the "river" on your left at the third crossing to **Aristomenous,** the main street. Eventually Aristomenous meets and runs along Pl. Giorgiou. Cross the river at the first crossing and head directly away from the bus station to get to the Old Town and castle. To get to the waterfront from the Old Town, follow Aristomenous all the way along the left side of Pl. Giorgiou.

Tourist Office: Much tourist info and **free maps** are available near the Old Town at **DETAK,** Poliviou 6 (☎27210 21 700), just off Aristomenous. With your back to the bus station, walk to the left and cross at the 2nd bridge. Make a right at the 1st street, which intersects with Poliviou after 75m. Open M-F 7am-2:30pm. The **tourist police** (☎27210 95 555), on Miaouli, are also helpful. **Free maps.** Open daily 8am-2pm.

Bank: National Bank (☎27210 28 047), on Aristomenous off the north end of Pl. Giorgiou and smaller branches in the plateia and on Akrita at the waterfront. All have **24hr. ATMs** and **currency exchange.** Open M-Th 8am-2pm, F 8am-1:30pm.

Police: ☎27210 22 622. On Aristomenous, south of Pl. Giorgiou. Open 24hr.

Port police: ☎27210 22 218. On the harbor near the tourist police in a blue building.

Hospital: ☎27210 46 000 or 27210 45 500. On Athinou. Call ☎100 or 166 in a **medical emergeny.**

OTE: ☎27210 92 999. In Pl. Giorgiou, opposite National Bank. Open M-Th 8am-1:30pm, F 8am-1pm.

Internet Access: Diktyo Internet Cafe, Nedontos 75 (☎27210 97 282), just off Aristomenous and, when facing the center of the plateia, it's to 50m to the left of the the OTE. €3 per hr., €1.50 min. Open daily 10am-midnight. If you're staying closer to the waterfront, try **Matrix,** on Faron, about 5 blocks up from the waterfront. €3 per hr., €1.50 min. Open daily 9:30am-1:30am.

Post Office: Iatropolou 4 (☎27210 22 810). Follow this street from the south end of Pl. Giorgiou. Offers **currency exchange** and **Poste Restante.** There's another branch on the waterfront next to the tourist police. Open M-F 7:30am-2pm. **Postal code:** 24100.

ACCOMMODATIONS AND FOOD

Hotels in Kalamata tend to cluster around Pl. Giorgiou and the waterfront. Budget accommodations are few and far between. **Hotel Nevada ❷,** Santa Rosa 9, is off Faron, one block up from the water. Heading inland on Faron, take the first left or take bus #1 from town and get off as soon as it turns left along the water. The best prices in town provide wildly decorated rooms with shared baths and kitchen. (☎27210 82 429. Singles €10.50-13.50; doubles €15-19; triples €18.50-23.50. Cash only.) **Hotel George ❸** is visible on Frantzi as you walk from the waterfront end of Pl. Giorgiou. The mirrors may be cracked and the TVs dysfunctional, but this hotel has well-sized rooms, conveniently near the train station. (☎27210 27 225. A/C €30 extra. Singles €25-32; doubles €30-35. Cash only.) **Hotel Pharae Palace ❹,** on the waterfront at the intersection of Navarinou with R. Feraiou, has beautiful rooms equipped with all the comforts: TVs, big beds, large private baths, A/C, and balconies overlooking the water. (☎27210 94 420; fax 27210 93 969. Buffet breakfast included. Singles €62-74; doubles €100-120. AmEx/MC/V.)

The immense **New Market** is a must-see; with your back to the bus station, walk across the first bridge on your right. The market holds a huge collection of meat, cheese, and fruit shops. You can sample the famous Kalamata Olives and figs at the daily farmer's market. If you prefer something more formal, sit down for a meal along the waterfront. One fantastic option is **To Petrino ❸.** Incredible bread and interesting dishes make this outdoor eatery stand out from the crowd. (Ostrich €14. Bison €27. Stuffed tomatoes €3.50. Kalamata Olives €3. Greek entrees €3.50-8. Cash only.) It may not have an expansive menu or a flashy facade, but there's reason why **Exociko Kentro ❶** (☎27210 20 985), 150m past To Petrino with the sea on your right, is packed with locals night after night. This waterfront restaurant shines when it comes to a hearty meal with a savory lamb and potatoes (€5), and veggie-lovers can still enjoy stuffed tomatoes (€4) and pasta dishes (€3-4.50). At **Toscana ❸,** on the waterfront by Hotel Pharae Palace, vegetarians can indulge in an array of well-portioned pastas (€4.50-7.50) and calzones (€8); meat-eaters can select an entree (€6-10) and combine it with a sauce (€1.50-2) of their choice. (☎27210 95 500. Cash only.)

SIGHTS

Having survived quite the turbulent history, the **Castle of the Villehardouins** crowns a hill above the Old City. From Pl. 25 Martiou, walk up Ipapandis past the church on the right and take the first left. Built by the Franks in 1208, it was destroyed by Ottomans in 1685 and rebuilt by Venetians a decade later. The restoration process, begun following the 1986 earthquake, continues today, meaning you may have limited access to the site on certain days. The castle also encircles an open-air theater, which hosts **Cultural Summer of Kalamata** in July and August, with jazz,

THE BIG SPLURGE

SEWING SISTERS

With fantastic food, pulsating nightclubs, and wowing ancient sites, the city of Kalamata can easily persuade a traveler to extend his vacation's duration. But quietly tucked away from the loud olive vendors and absent-minded window shoppers is one of the most extraordinary places in the Peloponnese. Believe it or not, it's actually a nunnery.

Founded in 1796 by a monk from Kalamata, the Convent of Ag. Konstantinos and Ag. Elena was first built under the pretense of an orphanage. The convent was able to generate funds by partaking in silk-weaving, a intricate skill for which the people of Kalamata had been renowned. Around 1826, sisters of the convent became known as some of the most skillful weavers in the region, especially after a group of nuns returned from Constantinople (where they were serving time as part of a nine-year punishment) with improved knowledge of the trade.

The sisters of the convent continue the tradition that began over 200 years ago. And, fortunately for travelers, the fruits of the nuns' labors are available for purchase by the entrance of the nunnery. Beautifully handwoven silks and linens that could easily run upwards of hundreds of euros are priced at a fraction of the retail value.

From Pl. 23 Martiou, walk uphill on Ipapandis and make a right when you reach the large church; the convent is on a side street labeled Mystras. Signs point the way. Silks €9-29. Linens €5-95. Hours vary.

rock, and Greek drama. (Open daily 10am-1:30pm. Free.) Near the castle in the Old Town is one of Kalamata's most hidden gems, the **Convent of Ag. Konstantinos and Ag. Elena.** Founded in 1796, the convent houses nuns who spend their days hand-weaving silks. Closer to the new town by Pl. 23 Martiou is the 14th-century **Church of the Ag. Apostoloi** (Holy Apostles). The church first gained recognition when a doe-eyed icon of the Virgin Mary was found at the site. The name of the city reflects this miraculous icon's appearance—kala mata means "good eyes." (Most churches open 7am-noon and 5-7pm. Modest dress required.)

After a five years of restoration, the Old City's **Benakeion Museum** proudly exhibits its small collection, with captions in both English and Greek, highlighted by an exceptionally preserved mosaic floor from a ruined Roman villa nearby. (☎27210 26 209. Open Tu-Su 8:30am-3pm. €2, seniors €1, EU students free.) Kalamata's **School of Fine Arts,** Faron 221, just off the waterfront, exhibits works by contemporary Greek artists. (Open M-F 10am-1pm and 7-10pm, Sa 7-10pm. Free.) Kalamata also supports two professional **theaters** and **cinemas;** ask DETAK or the tourist police for info on events in the **Pantazopoulion Cultural Center** on Aristomenon. (☎27210 94 819, or call the municipality at 27210 28 000.) For information on the July **Kalamata International Dance Festival,** contact the Kalamata International Dance Center (☎27210 83 086; dikeho@conxion.gr).

NIGHTLIFE

When the sun sets over Kalamata, the youth don their skin-tight garb and flock to the strip, 1km east of the port. While the small cluster of clubs may lack the intensity of those found on the islands, hard dance beats and a continuous flow of alcohol manage to keep the locals happily entertained. Along the strip, expect a €5 cover usually going toward your first drink. Beer generally costs €3; mixed drinks €5. You'll find the city's most hardcore hip-thrusters at **Heaven** and **XL,** two of the first (and largest) clubs as you approach the strip from the port. If you prefer a change of scenery, head 50m down the road to **De Luxe,** where art deco couches and multicolored spotlights surround the circular bar.

DAYTRIP FROM KALAMATA: ANCIENT MESSINI

Take the bus to Mavromati (1hr.; leaves M-Sa 5:40am and 2pm, returns 2:30pm; €2). Taxis €16-18. If you rent a moped, you'll need 50ccs to handle the steep hills. ☎27240 51 046. Site open 8am-8pm. Free. Museum open Tu-Su 8am-2:30pm. €2, seniors €1, EU students free.

Continuous excavations on **Mt. Ithomi** over the last two decades have uncovered what is quickly becoming one of the most impressive archaeological sites in Greece. Archaeologists believe they are uncovering a city which dates back 2300 years. When the battle of Leuctra in 371 BC ended Spartan domination of the Peloponnese, Theban general and statesman **Epaminodas** built Messini, naming the town for the region's first queen. While the remains of a theater, stadium, gymnasium, public baths, and nine different temples have been uncovered, it is the city's **defensive walls** that receive attention. The 3m-thick walls circle 9km and represent the massive heft of 4th- and 3rd-century BC military architecture. The partitions were constructed so well that the city lay unharmed for 700 years. Originally huge gates reinforced with towers and battlements interrupted the circuit, taking their names from the roads that they barricaded. Of the four surviving, the Arcadian gate is the best preserved. Purchasing a guidebook (€13) is a good idea at this unmarked site. A **museum** houses marble statues and other ancient objects. Also outside Mavromati, the 17th-century **Monastery of the Vourkan** was a staging point for rebels in the War of Independence. Its library holds priceless manuscripts.

KARDAMYLI Καρδαμυλη ☎27210

It would be a crime to miss this sleepy, one-road town (the first major bus stop south of Kalamata near Taygetus) when visiting the southern Peloponnese. The flower-scented streets of this seaside village possess a few stone houses and restaurants, but its gorgeous white-pebble beach and views of the surrounding mountains captivate an increasing number of foreign visitors.

TRANSPORTATION AND PRACTICAL INFORMATION. Four buses run from Kalamata every day, dropping off near the *periptero* off the main plateia. There is no posted schedule, but the locals will tell you when the buses stop in town. If you're headed to **Athens,** take a bus to **Kalamata** (1hr.; 5 per day, 7:15am-8pm; €2.30). Buses also run to **Itilo** (30min.; 4 per day, 6am-6pm; €2.40), where you can transfer to the **Areopolis** bus (20min., €0.90). A bus headed to Aeropolis sometimes will wait for connecting passengers; inquire with the driver. Weekend service is reduced. Through the main plateia, on the road to Itilo, are the **post office** (open M-F 7:30am-2pm), a **bank** (open M, Th 9:30am-1pm) with 24hr. **ATM,** and a **pharmacy** (☎27210 73 512; open daily 8am-2pm and 5-9pm), across from the post office. The **book shop,** two doors down from the post office, offers a large selection of best-sellers in English. To get to the **police station** (☎27210 73 209; open 24hr.), walk 5min. along the road to Kalamata and over the bridge; the station will be on a street to the left—look for signs. Walking toward Itilo, turn right on the side street across from the post office to **Cafe Internet Kourearos,** next to Olympia Domatia. (☎27210 73 148. €3 per 30min., €5 per hr. Open 5pm-1am.) **Postal code:** 24022.

ACCOMMODATIONS AND FOOD. Travelers to tiny Kardamyli will be glad to discover that there's suprisingly no shortage of reasonably priced rooms for rent. **Olympia Domatia ❷,** on the side street across from the post office, offers immaculate rooms with personal fans and a shared kitchen. Olympia herself is the gem of the town; not many domatia owners hand weary travelers cold glasses of water, ice cream, and maps upon their arrival. She also prepares coffee for tenants every afternoon. (☎27210 73 623. Singles €17-23; doubles €25-38. Cash only.) Across the way from Olympia Domatia, the amiable **Stratis Bravakos ❸** lets spacious rooms that have fridges, private baths, wood-paneled furnishings, and balconies that overlook the more forested parts of town. (☎27210 73 326. Singles €22-35; doubles €24-40. Cash only.) Travelers who plan extended stays in the area may want to consider a room at **Hotel Anniska ❹,** at the end of the street to the right of the bank. You can stay at either of its two buildings; both offer studios and apartments. The studios in the old hotel have ceiling fans and beach access, while those in the new hotel come with A/C and pool access. Both have lovely dining areas and book exchanges. All rooms are decorated in shades of blue, and come equipped with balconies, small kitchens, TVs, phones, and private baths. (Old hotel: ☎27210 73 601; fax 27210 73 000. New hotel: ☎27210 73 600; fax 27210 73 000. Studios €50-75; apartments €85-110. MC/V.) If you're looking for something a little more rugged, walk toward Kalamata, turn left at the signs for **Camping Melitsana ❶,** and walk 1.5km down the main beach. Campers have access to a nearby cafe, bar, communal showers, shared kitchen, and laundry facilities. (☎27210 73 461. Depending on season, €4-4.25 per person, €2.40-2.70 per child; €3.50-3.70 per small tent, €3.70-3.90 per large tent; €2-2.30 per car. Cash only.)

Tavernas in Kardamyli tend to cater to the small tourist population; nearly all the menus are multilingual and generally include the most traditional of Greek dishes. Travelers should keep in mind that two well-sized **supermarkets** can be found past the plateia on the road to Kalamata. If you are going to go out for a meal, the family-run **Taverna Kiki ❶,** downhill from the main plateia, offers some wonderful dishes in front of the water. Rotating through entrees like stuffed tomatoes (€4) and lamb with olive oil and oregano (€7), the menu changes daily. (☎27210 73 148. Entrees €4-8. Cash only.) **Kourmaristria ❸**, two blocks past the post office on the road leading to Kalamata and on the left, adds a twist to classic Greek staples. Traditional moussaka is not on the menu, but you'll find minced pork stuffed with cheese and tomatoes (€6). The locals recommend the *tzatziki* (€2), made with local greens. (☎27210 73 250. Cash only.) **Anemokiklion ❷** (☎27210 73 943), on the road across from the post office, has a crowded outdoor eating area where both locals and tourists enjoy filling Greek entrees. The grilled chicken (€6.50) is exceptional. (Appetizers €2-5. Entrees €0.70-7.50. Cash only.)

SIGHTS AND BEACHES. Beaches are Kardamyli's main attraction, but there are a few other things to see. A short stroll up the road to Kalamata will bring you to the small but interesting ruins of the **Old Town** (across from the supermarkets), highlighted by the Church of Ag. Spyridon and the Mourtzinos Tower. Nearby the frescoed **Monastery of Dekoulo** and the 17th-century Ottoman fortress are poised on a hill. One kilometer along the waterfront toward Kalamata, you'll spot the magnificent **Ritsa beach.** On an enormous natural bay encircled by barren mountains, the white-pebble shore is ideal for an early-evening stroll. The roads that wind through the mountains from Kalamata to Areopolis offer stunning vistas of the small villages and aquamarine harbors of Messinia and the Mani, including tiny **Limani**, the old harbor of Areopolis and home to the **Castle of Potrombei.**

PELOPONNESE

DAYTRIP FROM KARDAMYLI: TAYGETUS MOUNTAINS. **Hiking** the terrain surrounding the village competes with enticing beaches as Kardamyli's main draw. Southeast of Kalamata, the limestone mountain range of the Taygetus divides Messinia and Laconia, running from Megalopolis down through the Taenarian promontory. Sacred to Apollo and Artemis, the mountains were named after **Taygete,** daughter of Atlas, mother of Lacedaemon, and lover of Zeus. Since those mythological origins, ancient and modern poets alike have glorified the range for its sheer size. Lampito declares in Aristophanes's *Lysistrata*, "I would climb as high as the peak of Taygetus, if thus I could find peace," while Nikiforos Vrettakos describes the mountain as "the masculine child of [the Peloponnese]." With such a prestigious reputation, it is not hard to see why many travelers make the mountain a necessary stop on their trips through southern Greece; adventure-seekers find themselves drawn to the challenging paths that lead to the mountain's peak at Profitis Ilia (elev. 2704m), and history buffs can't help but treasure the lower regions for their assortment of Byzantine churches, Venetian towers, Frankish forts, and **Mycenean tombs.** But human hikers aside, 26 species of plants, 58 species of birds, and 35 species of amphibious reptiles (including the rare *testudo marninata* turtle) call the mountain home. If you are interested in going on a day-hike, the entrance from Kardamyli offers many paths with different levels of difficulty. One popular 1½hr. trail begins at Kardamyli, goes through Old Kardamyli, up to Agia Sophia (elev. 300m) and back to town via Petrovouni (elev. 180m). The trail is initially marked with yellow and black rectangles. Toward Petrovouni, follow the signs with red circles inside the white and red squares. More experienced hikers may be interested in the 4hr. path that leads from Agia Sophia to Kato Chora (elev. 450m) and past the Vyros Gorge to Moni Satiros (elev. 150m). Be forewarned: you'll have to walk through a river bed to return to Kardamyli. Regardless of what path you choose, carry lots of water, wear good shoes, and be familiar with your route. **Brochures** and **maps** with suggested routes are available in tourist shops and bookstores, as well as in many of Kardamyli's accommodations.

PYLOS Πυλος ☎27230

With its delightful beaches, Ottoman fortress, museum, splendid views of Navarino, and the Peloponnese's largest natural bay, Pylos is mystifyingly untouristed. It was also the site of an important battle in the War of Independence.

TRANSPORTATION AND PRACTICAL INFORMATION. Most of the town's businesses line the plateia and the roads leading uphill to Methoni and Hora. The tiny **beaches,** one sand and one pebble, lie to the right of the waterfront as you face inland, as does the 16th-century Ottoman **Neocastro** on a forested hill. **Buses** (☎27230 22 230) go to: **Athens** (6½hr.; 9am, 7:30pm; €18.30); **Finikounda** (1hr., 4 per day, €1.10); **Kalamata** (1½hr.; 9 per day, 6:30am-9:20pm; €3.20); **Methoni** (15min.; 6 per day, 6am-9pm; €0.90). No buses travel directly to **Koroni,** but you can go through Finikounda and take a bus to **Horokorio,** the stop nearest Koroni. Buses leave Pylos for **Kyparissia** (1½hr.; 5 per day, 6:40am-7:30pm; €4), stopping at **Nestor's Palace** (30min., €1.10) and **Hora** (45min., €1.20). Service is drastically reduced on weekends. Tickets are sold and schedules posted at the tiny KTEL office in a corner of the plateia; buses leave from the back of the plateia. **Rent-A-Bike,** 100m off the back left corner of the plateia on the road running by the police station, has a moped monopoly. (☎27230 22 707. €15-25 per day. Open daily 9am-1pm and 5:30-8:30pm.) **Taxis** (☎27230 22 555) line the left side of the plateia and park by the port police as well. A **National Bank** with a 24hr. **ATM** is in the plateia. The **police** are in a building on the left side of the waterfront. (☎27230 22 316. Open 24hr.) The **tourist police** (☎27230 23 733; open daily, hours vary) are in the same building. Continue around the curve of the waterfront road with the water on the right to reach the **port police.** (☎27230 22 225. Open M-Th 8am-2pm, F 8am-1:30pm.) To get to the **hospital,** take the road right from the plateia. (☎27230 22 315. Open 24hr.) For the **OTE,** pass the post office, take your first left, and then your second right. (Open M-F 7:30am-3pm.) The **post office** is on the road toward Hora and Kiparissia, uphill from the bus station; it offers **currency exchange.** (☎27230 22 247. Open M-F 7:30am-2pm.) **Postal code:** 24001.

ACCOMMODATIONS AND FOOD. You'll spot Rooms to Let signs as the bus descends into town from Kalamata. Expect to pay €15-20 for singles, €20-35 for doubles, and €25-37 for triples. A cheap option is the **pension ❷,** just before the OTE as you walk up the hill, which has high-ceilinged rooms with TVs, private baths, and A/C. (☎27230 22 748. Singles €20; doubles €25; triples €30. Cash only.) **Hotel Nilefs ❸,** Rene Pyot 4, has big rooms with colorful bathrooms, A/C, TVs, and some balconies. It's on the road uphill from the waterfront on the right side of the plateia, facing inland. (☎27230 22 518. Singles €25-30; doubles €35-42; triples €40-50. Cash only.) **Navarino Beach Camping ❶,** 6km north at Yialova beach, has a mini-market, restaurant, communal kitchen, shared showers, public toilets, and laundry facilities. (☎27230 22 761. €2.80 per person, €2.50 per child; €4 per large tent; €2.30 per car. Electricity €2.60. Cash only.) The less frugal traveler will find luxury at **Karalis Beach Hotel ❹,** a 5min. walk from town with the water on your right. (☎27230 22 980. Buffet breakfast included. Reservations recommended. Prices change by season. Singles €35-80; doubles €70-150. V.)

Many waterfront restaurants prepare taverna staples served alongside sunset views over the waterfront. The road leading uphill from the left of the plateia is also packed with excellent options. The best of four eating establishments with the same name, the **Navarino ❷,** around the corner from the port police on the waterfront, has good, cheap meals away from the bustling cafes of the plateia. (☎27230 22 564. Salads €1.35-2.50. Entrees €3.80-8.60. Open daily 10am-4pm and 7pm-midnight. Cash only.) **Four Seasons ❷** (Τεσσερα

Εποχες, TEH-seh-rah eh-po-CHES), the last taverna on the water to the right of town (facing inland), serves cheap, nicely prepared, traditional dishes. (☎27230 22 739. Salad €1.50-3. Moussaka €4. Spaghetti €3-4. Fish €4.50-40. Open daily 11am-midnight. Cash only.) Behind the bus station, **La Piazza ❷** creates wonderful pastas and pizza. Try the "Vesuvio" pizza (€5.30-6.30), made with hot peppers and hot salami. (☎27230 23 780. Salads €2-4.30. Entrees €3-4.80. Open daily 6pm-midnight. Cash only.) Classy **1930 Restaurant ❸,** on the road from Kalamata, is accented by wood paneling and antique fishing gear. (☎27230 22 032. Salads €4.50-8.50. Grilled octopus €7.35. Entrees €6-13. Greek dishes €4.50-9. Open daily 1-3pm and 6pm-midnight. V.)

SIGHTS AND BEACHES. Fortresses guard both sides of Navarino Bay. **Neocastro,** to the south, is easily accessible from the town; walk up the road to Methoni and turn right at the sign reading "Φρουριο" (Frourio). Built by the Turks in the 16th century, the fortress was won by the Greeks during the 1821 War of Independence. The well-preserved walls enclose a citadel and quickly-decaying church, which was originally a mosque. Take a look at the pictures of the Peloponnese as it was 100 years ago. The restored hexagonal courtyard, up the hill to your right after entering the castle, contains a series of photographs detailing its restoration. The **Museum of the Rene Puaux Collection,** to the left as you enter the site, contains artistic works celebrating the Greek triumph in the war. (☎27230 22 010. Open Tu-Su 8:30am-3pm. €3, seniors and students €2, EU students and children free. Guidebook €13.) At the **Archaeological Museum,** a Mycenaean boar's tusk helmet catches the eye. (☎27230 22 448. Open Tu-Su 8:30am-5pm. €2, seniors and students €1, EU students and children free.)

PELOPONNESE

Just offshore is the island of **Sfakteria,** famed as the site of a rare Spartan defeat during the Peloponnesian War (p. 9). To see the island up close, you can take a **boat tour** from the port. They stop at monuments to the allied sailors of the Battle of Navarino and show a sunken Ottoman ship. Inquire at the small booth on the waterfront around the corner from the port police. (1½hr., €30 for 4 people. July-Aug. only.) Small **beaches** surround the town. Although the sand is devoured by the ocean when the tide is in, families take to the waters on most summer afternoons. The sandy and much wider **Yialova beach** is 6km north of town; sunken ships poke out from its shallow waters. Buses to Athens and Kyparissia pass by. Because of the infrequency of public transportation (especially on weekends), you may want to use private transportation. The **Navarino fortress** lies at the end of the beach.

DAYTRIP FROM PYLOS: NESTOR'S PALACE. Pylos was second only to Mycenae during Mycenaean times in wealth and artistic development. The centerpiece of the archaeological site is the **palace** where, according to Homer, Nestor met Telemachus, Odysseus's son. The palace is thought to have been built in the 13th century BC by Nestor's father Neleus, the founder of the Neleid Dynasty. It was destroyed by fire around 1200 BC. Under excavation since the early 20th century, the thigh-high remains of the site comprise three buildings. The main building, thought to be the king's residence, originally had a second floor with official and residential quarters and storerooms. Archaeologists believe an older, smaller palace stood to the southeast. To the northeast lie the ruins of a complex of isolated workshops and storerooms. Archaeologists have turned up pottery, jewelry, various bronze and ivory objects, and a cache of over 600 **Linear B tablets** explaining some of the palace's administrative operations. Most finds are displayed at the National Archaeological Museum in Athens, though some pottery and surviving fragments of wall paintings are at the **museum** in Hora, 5km away. You can supplement your tour with the University of Cincinnati's Guide to Nestor's Palace (€5). **Buses** from Pylos run through

Kyparissia (1½hr., 5 per day, €4) and stop at **Nestor's Palace** (30min., €1); service is reduced on weekends. The last bus returns at 5:30pm. (☎27230 31 437 or 31 358. Open daily 8:30am-3pm. €2, seniors and non-EU students €1, EU students and children free.) A **Mycenaean tholos tomb** is across from the lower parking lot. Fortunately for achaeologists, hasty thieves left much of the tomb untouched during a gold-hoarding escapade. Today visitors can still look down into the grave pits of the tomb. Signs point the way from the palace.

METHONI Μεθωνη ☎23530

With a relaxed atmosphere, Methoni is a restorative reprieve from the bustle of Kalamata and Tripoli. Treasured for millennia, Methoni was used as bait by Agamemnon to lure the sulking Achilles back to war in *The Iliad.* A spectacular castle, where Miguel de Cervantes penned romances while imprisoned under Ottoman guard, shoots its stone walkways onto the Turkish *bourtzi* in the bay.

The town's two main streets form a Y where the Pylos-Finikounda buses stop. Facing the fork, the lower road is on the left and leads to the beach and castle. There's no bus station nor posted schedule; you should ask at hotels or the *periptero* just before the fork about bus schedules. **Buses** go to **Finikounda** (30min., at least 3 per day, €0.90) and **Pylos** (15min., at least 5 per day, €0.90); service is reduced on weekends. There are two daily buses to **Athens** (6hr., €19) via **Pylos** and daily buses to **Kalamata** (2hr., €3.90). The town's main **beach** is a few blocks to the left end of the lower street, beside a beachfront plateia. The campgrounds and several beach bars are on the beachse road. The **police** are near the bus station on the upper street, just past the bank. (☎23530 31 203. Open 24hr.) The **National Bank** with a 24hr. **ATM** is 40m down the right fork. (☎23530 31 295. Open M-Th 8am-2pm, F 8am-1:30pm.) The **OTE** is in a cream-colored building with blue shutters; go down the lower fork and turn left toward the beachside plateia. (☎23530 31 121. Open M-F 7:30am-3pm.) The **post office** is two blocks down the lower street on the left side. (☎23530 31 266. Open M-F 7:30am-2pm.) **Postal code:** 24006.

Since Methoni receives a fair amount of August tourism, rooms can get pricey. Several Rooms to Let signs hang along both forks of the road. Although the rooms usually lack luxurious amenities, their prices are a bit cheaper than many of the hotels in the area. Near the end of the lower road, eight blocks from the bus stop, make a left at the small plateia with a waterless fountain to find **Hotel Giota ❷** in the beachfront plateia. Oversized single beds dominate rooms with A/C, fridges, balconies, and private baths. (☎27230 31 290; fax 27230 31 212. Singles €20-30; doubles €30-45. Cash only.) Giota's owners also run nearby **Hotel Alex ❸,** which has more spacious rooms but smaller beds. (☎27230 31 219; fax 23530 31 291. Cash only.) Six blocks past the post office and away from the noise of the plateia, **Achilles Hotel ❹,** the gleaming white building on the lower road past the cafe, provides 11 of the most elegant rooms in Methoni with full amenities. Some have views of the ocean and the fortress. (☎27230 31 819; fax 23530 28 739. Singles €30-44; doubles €44-60. Ask about discounts for longer stays. Cash only.) **Seaside Camping Methoni ❶** is a 5min. walk down the beach to the right of the plateia with the sea on your right. (☎27230 31 228. €3.50-3.70 per person, €2-2.50 per child; €2.50-2.70 per small tent, €2.80-3 per large tent; €2-2.50 per car. Electricity €2.60. Cash only.)

Several excellent tavernas and restaurants pepper Methoni. In the waterfront plateia, the multilingual proprietor of **Meltemi ❸** serves excellent traditional entrees. Stuffed tomato and pepper (€4) or a hot plate of vegetables (€4) keep vegetarians content. (☎27230 31 187. Olives €1.50. Salad €2-3.50. Chicken souvlaki €5.50. Meatballs €4.50. Squid €5. Open daily 7pm-midnight. Cash only.) Quaint **Nontas ❷** accents its tourist-free atmosphere with high quality and low prices. Walking from the bus stop, turn left one block down the lower road and continue 30m. (☎27230 31 791. *Tzatziki* €1.80. Gyros €1.30. Souvlaki €0.90. Cash only.) **Nikos ❷**, on the road closest and parallel to the castle near the waterfront plateia, serves staples that cater to vegetarians and meat-eaters alike. The vine leaves with lemon sauce (€4) come highly recommended. (☎27230 31 282. Sandwiches and entrees €4-7. Open daily noon-midnight. Cash only.)

No visitor to the southwest Peloponnese should miss Methoni's **Venetian fortress,** a 13th-century mini-city. To get to the castle, follow the upper or lower street to its end. Walk to the right along the path outside the castle for a great view of the open sea and fortified back wall. Venture behind the fortified gate of the fortress to wander paths above overgrown fields strewn with bright wildflowers and crumbling walls. Frankish foundations, Venetian battlements, and Turkish steam baths testify to the castle's turbluent history. (Open M-Sa 8:30am-7pm, Su 9am-7pm. Photography prohibited. Free.) The town's main **beach** is a few blocks to the left of the end of the lower street, beside a little beachfront plateia.

FINIKOUNDA Φοινικουντα ☎27230

The tiny **beach** hamlet of Finikounda lies just 20km south of Methoni and is quickly becoming the ultimate tourist attraction of the area. Fortunately, its secluded location still prevents overcrowding. Although the town has no bank, police station, or post office, it does offer several large hotels, domatia, campsites, and a vast array of bars, cafes, and tavernas, scattered along the beachfront road. You'll find some of the best **beaches** on the Peloponnesian coast within easy walking distance of Finikounda. Grab a towel and some sunscreen, and find one to your liking. Ask around town for directions to the top beaches of the moment. **Buses** head to **Kalamata** (2½hr., €4.90) three or four times per day via **Pylos** (45min., €1.10) and via **Harakopio** (1hr., €1.25). Service is reduced on the weekend. The bus drops off and picks up at the plateia one block up from the waterfront, outside the Hotel Finikounda. A booth by the water offers **currency exchange. Postal code:** 24006. Should you opt to stay in Finikounda, try to find a **domatia** or head to **Hotel Finissia ❸**, at the far right of the waterfront as you face inland. Nicely furnished rooms with shiny clean floors include A/C, TVs, phones, and private baths. (☎27230 71 457. Singles €25-40; doubles €35-50. Cash only.) The closest to town of three campsites, **Camping Anemomilos ❶**, on the beach just north of town, lies among flowering shrubs and has easy beach access. The camping site has good facilities, which include laundry, mail drop, restaurant, bar, showers, and **Internet** access (€3 per hr.). To reach the campsite, walk out of town via the road past Hotel Finikounda, then walk 5-10min. toward Methoni, turning left at its signs. (☎27230 71 360. Depending on the season, €4.50-5 per person, €2.50 per child; €3.50 per small tent, €4 per large tent; €2.50 per car. Electricity €2.50.) Restaurants are by no means hard to find, but, if you're after a view, walk to the left end of the waterfront (facing inland) to the enormous taverna **Elena ❷**. This popular establishment serves seafood. (☎27230 71 235. Entrees €3.60-24. Salads €2.60-7. Vegetarian items €3.60-4.60.)

LACONIA Λακωνια

Laconia, the territory of the ancient Spartans, has long prided itself on its minimalist image. The Spartans were ferocious to their enemies, simple in lifestyle, and terse in speech. Such a regional disposition seems to have worn off on the landscape, with the stark, imposing Taygetus Mountains beyond row after row of ancient olive trees. Although it boasts touristed Mystras, as a whole Laconia offers a break from the more touristed urban hustle of other Peloponnesian towns.

SPARTA Σπαρτη ☎27310

Citizens of today's quiet Sparta make olive oil, not war. Built directly on top of the ancient warrior city, modern Sparta offers meager ruins to occupy tourists. Still, it's by far the best base for exploring the ruins of Byzantine Mystras, 6km away. Warrior Sparta dominated the Peloponnese with its legendary sense of discipline and invincible armies. Spartans traced their austere daily regimens back to 8th-century BC law-giver Lykurgus, who demanded plain dress, simple food, and strict training for all citizens from a young age. Men and women were educated differently, but with equal severity. The Spartans produced almost no literature, art, or architecture, as they preferred to expend their creative energy in the art of war. Finally capturing upstart Athens in 404 BC to end the 28-year Peloponnesian War (p. 9), Sparta won its greatest victory and effectively ruled Greece. Though its historical place as the military giant of Greece was assured, Sparta's hold on Classical power declined following challenges from the Thebans and the Macedonians in the 4th century BC. Earthquakes and slave revolts didn't help matters, and further losses in 222 and 195 BC to the Macedonians and the Romans, respectively, sapped the city's strength. Sparta slipped slowly into obscurity, where it remained, until the modern city was founded in 1843.

TRANSPORTATION

To get to the **bus station** (☎27310 26 441), walk downhill on Lykourgou away from the plateia or toward the Archaeological Museum, continuing past a small forested area on your right; the station will be on your right, 10 blocks from the center of town. Buses go to: **Areopolis** (1½hr.; 9am, 5:45pm; €4.60); **Athens** (3½hr.; 8 per day, 5:45am-5pm; €13.40) via **Corinth** (2½hr., €8.30) and **Tripoli** (1hr., €3.70); **Gerolimenas** (2hr.; 10:15am, 5:45pm; €6.90); **Gythion** (1hr.; 5 per day, 9am-9:15pm; €3.90); **Kalamata** (1hr.; 9am, 2:30pm; €2.20); **Monemvasia** (2hr.; 11:30am, 1:30, 8:10pm; €6.80); **Neapoli** (3½hr.; 4 per day, 7am-8:30pm; €9.50); **Pirgos Dirou** (1½hr., 9am, €5.10). Buses to **Mystras** (20min.; 11 per day, 6:50am-8:20pm; €0.90) also stop at the corner of Lykourgou and Leonidou on the left, two blocks past the plateia away from the main station.

ORIENTATION AND PRACTICAL INFORMATION

Sparta is built in a grid. The main streets, **Paleologou** (named for the family of Byzantine emperors) and **Lykourgou** (named for Lykurgus), hold the necessary amenities and intersect in the center of town. From this intersection, the town plateia is one block west, away from the bus station, on Lykourgou. To reach the center of town from the bus station, walk about 10 blocks west slightly uphill on Lykourgou. The **bus station** is often crowded and not particularly tourist-friendly. There are often confusing and unmentioned transfers on the bus routes, but if you pay attention to the drivers and ask questions, you'll end up where you want to be. Make your life easier and find a Greek traveler heading to your destination; follow him or her to ensure that you end up on the right bus.

Tourist Office: ☎27310 24 852 or 27310 26 771. In the plateia, on the 3rd floor of the town hall. English spoken. Bus schedules, hotels, **maps,** and information are available when requested. Open M-F 8am-2pm.

Banks: National Bank (☎27310 26 200), on Paleologou, 3 blocks north (toward Ancient Sparta) from Lykourgou and the town center, has a 24hr. **ATM** and **currency exchange,** not to mention long lines. Open M-Th 8am-2:30pm, F 8am-2pm.

Police: ☎27310 26 229. On Ep. Vresthenis, on a side street off Lykourgou, 1 block past the bus station heading toward the plateia. Open 24hr. English-speaking **tourist police** (☎27310 20 492) in the same building. Open daily 8am-9pm. In an **emergency,** dial ☎27310 29 106.

Hospital: ☎27310 28 671 or 28 675. On Nosokomeio, 1km to the north of Sparta. **Buses** run to the hospital (7 per day, €0.90). Open 24hr.

Pharmacies: There's one on Lykourgou across from Aerodromi (☎27310 22 609). Or try the one next to the National Bank (☎27310 25 041). Many are on Lykourgou and Paleologou. Most open M-F 8am-2pm and 6-9pm.

OTE: Kleomvritou 3 (☎27310 23 799), accessible from Lykourgou, across from the museum. Open M-F 7:30am-12:30pm.

Internet: Aerodromi (☎27310 29 268), on Lykourgou between the bus station and the Archaeological Museum. Check email and play darts, pool, or ping-pong. €5 per hr., €1 min. Open daily 10am-1pm. **Hellas Internet Cafe,** Paleologou 34 (☎27310 21 500), south of Lykourgou, away from Ancient Sparta; it's on the 2nd fl. of the video rental store. €3.50 per hr., €1 min. Open M-Sa 8am-11pm, Su 11am-11pm.

Post Office: ☎27310 26 565. On Archidamou off Lykourgou. Open M-F 7:30am-2pm. **Poste Restante** available. **Postal code:** 23100.

PELOPONNESE

ACCOMMODATIONS

A bargain is hard to find among the numerous mid-range hotels on Paleologou, but TVs and private baths are widespread. **Hotel Cecil ❸,** Paleologou 125, five blocks north of Lykourgou toward Ancient Sparta, on the corner of Paleologou and Thermopilion, has a pale yellow facade. Pleasant rooms all come with TVs, A/C, phones, private baths with curtainless showers, and plenty of light. (☎27310 24 980; fax 27310 81 318. Reservations recommended. Singles €28-33; doubles €33-37.50. Cash only.) **Hotel Apollon ❸,** Thermopilion 84, across Paleologou from Hotel Cecil, has a flashy, mirrored lobby. The colorful rooms have TVs, faded private baths, phones, and A/C. (☎27310 22 491; fax 27310 23 936. Breakfast €5. Singles €27-33; doubles €38-45. V.) At the intersection of Paleologou and Lykourgou, in the heart of the city, **Hotel Maniatis ❹** offers modern, carpeted rooms with wood-paneled furniture. Rooms feature TVs, A/C, phones, and sizeable private baths with bathtub. Large and comfortable couches dot the marble lobby and restaurant lounge. (☎27310 22 665; fax 27310 29 994. Breakfast buffet €7.30. Singles €40-59; doubles €50-74. MC/V.)To find **Camping Castle View ❶,** near Mystras, take the Mystras bus and get off at the signs. The site boasts a pool, modern showers, toilets, mini-market, restaurant, cafe, bar, and market. (☎27310 83 303; spiros@panafonet.gr. €5 per person, €2.50 per child 4-10, under 4 free; €2.90 per car; €3.30 per small tent, €4 per large tent. Electricity €2.90. Cash only.)

FOOD AND NIGHTLIFE

Sparta's restaurants provide standard menus at pretty reasonable prices. **Supermarkets** and **bakeries** fill the side streets of Paleologou, while cheap fast-food joints hedge the main plateia. **Menelaion Restaurant ❷,** in the Menelaion Hotel on Paleologou, two blocks north of Lykourgou toward Ancient Sparta, is one eatery not to be overlooked. Elegant poolside seating comes a distant second to excellent meals at low prices and in very generous portions. (☎27360 22 161. Beefsteak €4.50. Quiche Lorraine €4. Pasta €3-6.50. Fish €4-9. MC/V.) **Parthenon ❶,** on Vrasithou, two blocks east of the intersection with Paleologou and one block south of the National Bank, boldly claims to serve "the best food in Greece." While their self-image may be a little bloated, the unrivaled gyros (€1.30) and souvlaki (€1-1.30) at least make them a contender for the best food in Sparta. (☎23767 20 444. Cash only.) **Diethnes ❷,** on Paleologou, a few blocks north of the main intersection, serves tasty Greek food in a vibrant garden with orange trees and the occasional turtle. The stronger-stomached may be interested in making meals of sheep's head or intestine, though less adventurous dishes, like stuffed tomatoes and peppers (€3.70) are still available. (☎27310 28 636. Salads €2.20-4. Entrees €4.50-6. Cash only.) A large selection and unusual specials spice up **Elyssé Restaurant ❷,** on Paleologou just past Diethnes. Meat-lovers can indulge in the veal *kikinisto* (€6.50) or pepper steak (€8.90). Vegetarian options are limited, though one of the pasta dishes (€3.50-5.80) should satisfy dietary restrictions. (Cash only.)

At night, the side of the plateia near the town hall fills with young people who while away the hours at outdoor cafes. **The Imago,** on the far side of the plateia as you approach from the museum, offers its mostly artsy 30-year-old clientele a choice between prime people-watching plateia seating and a more relaxed outdoor garden ambience. (Beer €2.50-4.50; cocktails €5-6. Open in high season daily 8am-3am; in low season 8am-1am.) At **Caprice,** another popular club on the far side of the plateia, 25m from the Imago, white leather-backed chairs support Sparta's most chic as they stiffly sip on drinks of choice. (Beer €2.30-4.50; cocktails €5. Open daily 11pm-3am.) Outside the plateia, stop in for a drink at the always-packed **Ministry Music Hall,** on Paleologou one block north of the intersection with Lykourgou. Brimming with more energy than its plateia counterparts, this bar offers patrons a large drink selection, booth seating upstairs, and walls decorated with unicycles and mandolins. (Coffee €1.50-3.50; juices €2.30-5; beer €2.50-4.50; mixed drinks €2.30-6. Open daily noon-3am.)

SIGHTS

What little remains of **Ancient Sparta** lies in an olive grove 1km north of the town plateia down Paleologou. At the northern end of Paleologou stands an enormous statue of **Leonidas,** the famous warrior king who fell at the Battle of Thermopylae (p. 229) in 480 BC. The Spartans built a large, vacant tomb for their leader, but his body was never found. The tomb is in a public park, to the left of the road heading up to the ruins. Along with a few fragments of the acropolis, the otherwise unimpressive site is highlighted by the outline and lower rows of an **ancient theater.** To reach this theater, which was one of the larger ones in the ancient world, walk down the path to the left as you reach the site of the acropolis.

Sparta's **Archaeological Museum,** on Lykourgou across from the OTE, lies in a beautiful, well-kept park with a fountain and assorted ancient statuary. Headless statues usher visitors into the entrance of the museum, whose varied collection definitely deserves at least an hour; it includes haunting votive masks used in ritual dances at the sanctuary of Artemis Orthia, a large marble statue of a warrior thought to be Leonidas, and various representations of the Dioskouri—the brothers Castor and Pollux—locally revered as symbols of brotherly love and honor. One room is devoted to prehistoric pottery, weaponry, and jewelry. Especially impressive are the incredibly well preserved mosaics from the Roman Period. Adequate English captions accompany all the artifacts. (☎27310 28 575. Open Tu-Sa 8:30am-3pm, Su 9:30am-2:30pm. €2, students and seniors €1, EU students and children free.) The **National Art Gallery,** Paleologou 123, near Hotel Cecil, has a small collection of 19th-century French and Dutch paintings, including one by Gustave Courbet. Upstairs is an exhibit by modern Greek artists. (☎27310 81 557. Open Tu-Sa 9am-3pm, Su 10am-2pm. Free.)

For history buffs, finding the various ruins surrounding Sparta is worth the challenge. Ask the tourist office or tourist police for a map before heading out. Three remaining platforms of the **Shrine to Menelaus and Helen** are 5km away. The remains of a **Shrine to Apollo** are south on the road to Gythion in the town of Amiklai. From the northeastern corner of town, near Hotel Apollon, a 10min. walk east along Odos Ton 118 leads to the **Sanctuary of Artemis Orthia,** where Spartan youths proved their courage by enduring floggings.

DAYTRIP FROM SPARTA: MYSTRAS

Buses leaving Sparta's main station (see above; 20min.; 11 per day, 6:50am-8:20pm; €0.90) drop off at the restaurant near the main entrance and then at the kastro entrance. Ask your driver if the bus goes to the kastro. If you get off at the lower stop, you're in for a 45min. uphill walk to the castle. Buses pick up at the restaurant beneath the lower entrance, though some buses also pick up at the castle gate. It gets hot–go early, bring water, and wear good hiking shoes. Consider Guidebook Mystras, *by Manolis Chatzidakis (€6.50), to supplement your exploration. Modest dress required. ☎27310 83 377. Open daily 8am-7pm; low season 8:30am-3pm. €5, EU students and children free.*

Once the religious center of all Byzantium and the locus of Constantinople's rule over the Peloponnese, Mystras now rests as a site saturated with remains of Byzantine churches, chapels, and monasteries. Like other cities of cultural and political significance, Mystras suffered from a turbulent history. Founded by French crusader **Guillaume de Villehardouin** in 1249 with the building of a central castle, the city first experienced a change of ownership in 1262, won over by the Greeks, giving them an important military base and cultural center. Under Greek rule, the city flourished; in the following centuries it grew from a village to a city, draining Sparta of its inhabitants as they sought protection in the city's fortress. By the early 15th century, Mystras was an intellectual and cultural center with a thriving silk industry. But even economic booms couldn't keep the lower classes at bay. Unhappy under the thumb of repressive feudal lords and clergy, restless country folk eventually surged into town, set up schools, and created an early bourgeoisie. However, the glory days ended when Turks invaded in 1460. Over the next few centuries, the city crumbled to ruin. When King Otto founded modern Sparta in 1834, Mystras's fate was sealed with a table-turning exodus to its revived neighbor.

An intricate network of paths traces through three tiers of ruins, descending from royalty to nobility to commoners. Although less preserved than many of the religious edifices that encircle it—they're almost completely intact, if a bit faded at the frescoes—the dramatic **castle** delivers a breathtaking view of the site and the surrounding countryside. Most people choose to take the bus to the upper entrance, climb to the castle, and then work their way down through the rest of the site. Particularly beautiful is the **Metropolis of Ag. Demetrios** on the lower tier, with its detailed frescoes, flowery courtyard, and small museum of architectural fragments, clothing, and jewelry. Also on the lower tier are the two churches of the fortified monastery of **Vrontochion.** The first, **Aphentiko,** glows with magnificent two-story frescoes; **Ag. Theodoros** is its neighbor. Slightly higher up in the center of the site is the **Pantanassa,** a convent with an elaborately ornamented facade, frescoes, and a miracle-working icon of Mary. Finally, quietly tucked away in the far corner of the lower tier, every centimeter of the awe-inspiring **Church of Peribleptos** is bathed in exquisitely detailed and colorful religious paintings.

At some point during your visit to Mystras, make sure to stop at the elegant though small **museum.** The air-conditioned room holds everything from 14th-century manuscripts to marble sculptures to a reconstruction of a Byzantine woman's shoe. However, travelers who visit around the Olympics may find the artifacts have been moved to the **Palace,** where renovations have been underway for a number of years in an effort to create a space large enough to display all the artifacts.

MANI Μανη

The name of Mani comes from *manis* (wrath or fury). Sparsely settled and encircling the unforgiving Taygetus Mountains (p. 190), the region vulnerably juts out into the surrounding sea. In Roman times, Mani founded the league of Free Laconians and broke free of Spartan domination. Ever since Maniots have ferociously resisted foreign rule, boasting even today that not one Ottoman set foot on their soil. While historically fierce and lastingly proud of that history, Maniots today are warm hosts to those who visit their villages and unique gray stone tower houses.

GYTHION Γυθειο ☎27330

Gythion has a much livelier feel than the desolate landscapes to its south. Bright fishing boats bustle in and out of the port, where dockside restaurants hang strings of octopi out to dry. A short causeway connects Gythion to the tiny island of Marathonisi, where Paris and Helen consummated their ill-fated love. Gythion is the only town in the Mani region that rents motorbikes.

TRANSPORTATION. The **bus station** (☎27330 22 228), on the northern end of the waterfront, opposite a park, sends buses to: **Areopolis** (1hr.; 10:15am, 1, 6:45pm; €1.80) via the **campgrounds** (€0.80); **Athens** (4hr.; 6 per day, 7:30am-7pm; €16.30) via **Sparta** (1hr., €2.90) and **Tripoli** (2hr., €6.50); **Corinth** (3hr., €11.60); **Gerolimenas** (2hr.; 1pm, 6:45pm; €4); **Pirgos Dirou** (1¼hr., 10:15am, €2.50). To get to **Kalamata** (2hr.; 5am, 1pm), you must switch buses at **Itilo** (1hr., €2.90). **Ferries** go to **Diakofti,** Kythera (2½hr., 5 per week, €8.70) and **Kasteli,** Crete (7hr., 2 per week, €19.20). **Taxis** (☎27330 23 423, 27330 23 492, or 27330 22 755) are available 24hr. **Moto Makis Rent-A-Moped** (☎27330 25 111), on the waterfront between the plateia and the causeway, has €16 per day rentals including tax, insurance, map, helmet, and 50km. (Each additional km €0.25. Open daily 8:30am-1:30pm and 4:30-8:30pm.)

ORIENTATION AND PRACTICAL INFORMATION. As you head south from the bus station along the main harbor road with the water on your left, most of the hotels are on your right. The small **Pl. Mavromichali,** consisting mostly of cafe seating, appears as the road curves and continues to the dock. The bus stop is on the far right of the waterfront as you face inland. A number of other stores and offices crowd around the inland plateia by the bus station.

To find the **EOT,** facing the bus station, go around the left corner, and straight along a small plateia to the right. Archaiou Theatrou will head to the right; continue straight for 200m. (☎27330 24 484. Open M-F 8am-2:30pm.) **Rozakis,** a travel agency on the waterfront near the police station, is the most convenient place in town to buy ferry tickets. (☎27330 22 650. Open daily 8am-2pm and 5-9pm.) The **National Bank,** just beyond the bus stop toward the water, has **currency exchange** and a 24hr. **ATM.** (☎27330 22 313. Open M-Th 8am-2pm, F 8am-1:30pm.) The **police** (☎27330 22 100), on the waterfront, halfway between the bus station and Pl. Mavromichali, are open 24hr. The **port police** (☎27330 22 262) sit before the causeway, past the plateia. One **pharmacy** lies across from the bus station. (☎27330 22 009. Open M-F 8am-2pm and 5-9pm.) You'll find other pharmacies scattered throughout the town. While the nearest hospital is in Sparta, a **health clinic** (☎27330 22 001, 22 002, or 22 003) is on the water just past Saga toward the causeway. For an **ambulance,** dial ☎ 166. As you face the bus station, take a sharp right around the left-hand side of the station onto Herakles, to find the **OTE,** at the corner of Herakles and Kapsali. (☎ 27330 22 799. Open M-F 7:45am-1:30pm.) **Mystery Cafe,** on Kapsali at the corner, one block behind the National Bank from the bus station has **Internet** access. (☎ 27330 25 177. €4.50 per hr., €1 min. Open daily 10am-12:30am.) As you face the bus station, go around the left hand corner and follow the plateia to the Archaiou Theatrou. Follow it to the right for two blocks to find the **post office** on Ermou. (☎ 27330 22 285. Open M-F 7:30am-2:30pm.) **Postal code:** 23200.

ACCOMMODATIONS AND FOOD. While seaside accommodations are prohibitively expensive, you'll find cheap, but charming options farther inland. Gythion's campgrounds are a pleasant, more interesting alternative to city lodgings—all are about 4km south of town toward Areopolis and can be reached by city bus (10:15am, 1, 6:45pm; €0.90). Taxis (€3) are inexpensive. If you stay in Gythion, get some wheels for beach access. At **Xenia Karlaftis Rooms ❷,** on the water 20m north of the causeway toward town, the charming Voulas family has been letting spacious rooms for over 20 years. They offer a kitchen with free coffee, fridges on every floor, laundry, and clean rooms with private baths. (☎ 27330 22 719. Singles €15; doubles €22; triples and quads €30; apartments €30-60. Cash only.) **Hotel Aktaion ❹,** the first hotel on the waterfront away from the bus station, offers elegant, recently renovated rooms with TVs, hairdryers, A/C, phones, baths, and balconies. (☎ 27330 23 500; fax 27330 22 294. Reservations recommended. Singles €45-65; doubles €60-80. AmEx/MC/V.) **Meltemi Camping ❶,** 4km south on the road toward Areopolis, has hot showers, cooking area, washing machines (€4), market, restaurant, and pool. (☎ 27330 22 833. €5 per person, €3.20 per child; €4 per small tent, €4.40 per large tent; €3 per car. Electricity €3.50. Cash only.) **Gythion Bay Campgrounds ❶,** 5km south on the road toward Areopolis, has laundry (€3), mini-market, restaurant, and showers. (☎ 27330 22 522. €5.28 per adult, €2.93 per child; €3.23 per tent; €3.23 per car. Electricity €3. Cash only.)

Virtually identical waterfront tavernas serve up fresh seafood and lovely views at moderate prices. A **fruit store** and **bakery** are across the street from Masouleri Kokkalis and a **supermarket** is behind the bus station. The charming outdoor **Taverna To Nisaki ❷,** on Marathonisi, a provides a romantic setting for anyone looking to escape the noise and crowds of the waterfront tavernas. (☎ 27330 23 830. *Tzatziki* €2.50. Grilled entrees €3-5.50. Fish €6-50. Cash only.) Upscale **Saga ❹,** on the water between the causeway and the plateia, prides itself on serving only the freshest fare. (☎ 27330 23 220. Salads €3 and up. Shrimp *saganaki* €17. Fish €35-60 per kg. Entrees €6-8.40. MC/V.) **La Gondola ❸,** on the waterfront 50m to the left of the police station (facing the water), specializes in pizzas (€6.40-9.50) and pastas (€5-15); the seafood spaghetti (€15) comes highly recommended by staff. (☎ 27330 24 477. Cash only.) **Masouleri Kokkalis ❶,** behind the plateia, does greasy fast food well. (Gyros €1.20. Pork souvlaki €0.80. Salads €1.50-3. Cash only.)

SIGHTS AND BEACHES. The compact, masterfully built, 240° ancient theater of Gythion has endured the centuries remarkably well. Even its class distinctions remain—note the differences between the seats for dignitaries in front and the simpler seats farther back. Arrive early in the evening to join the soldiers getting their nightly pep talk; any other time of day it will most likely be deserted. Crumbling Roman walls are scattered up the hill. (Heading away from the bus station, walk past the post office on Archaiou Theatrou until it deadends at the theater entrance. Open daily 8am-8pm.) One of the last of its kind in the Peloponnese, the authentic **Paliatzoures Antique Shop** has furnished a number of museums in its day, as owner Costas will gladly tell you. The majority of the collection consists of 18th-

and 19th-century household items, artwork, pistols, clocks, furniture, coins, and other assorted trinkets with a few medieval and even ancient items interspersed. (#25 on the waterfront, near the police. ☎27330 22 944. Open daily 11am-2pm and 6-9pm.) When traveling from Gythion to Areopolis, look for the Frankish **Castle of Pasava** on the right. The road is dangerous; check to see if it has been improved by asking domatia owners or by calling the local consulate at ☎27330 22 210. (Roughly 10km down the road; taxi €5.50; tours available.) Farther along, the **Castle of Kelefa** looks out to sea. (Catch the bus to Areopolis and ask the driver to take you as close to the castle as possible; a taxi will cost around €6. Open all day.)

There is a disappointing **public beach** just north of the bus station; better beaches lie outside town. Four kilometers south, near the campgrounds, is the wide beach of **Mavrovouni.** Winds and deep waters make the beach a popular surfing spot, though those who leave their boards at home can still crash at any one of the nearby bars, where beer runs €2-3.50; mixed drinks are €3-4.50. (From Areopolis, take one of the 4 daily buses, a €4 taxi ride, or a 50min. walk.) Three kilometers north is rocky **Selinitsa,** known for its incredibly clear water. (Signs point the way. Walk or take a €3 taxi.) **Vathy,** 15km away on the road to Areopolis is a quiet cove, great for topless sunbathing. (To the left as you face inland, after the river.)

PELOPONNESE

AREOPOLIS Αρεοπολη ☎27330

Areopolis neighbors both the sea and the mountains, yet the incredible buildings of the town dominate the scenery: stone tower houses and cobbled streets just wide enough for donkey carts are framed by the dramatic peaks of the Taygetus. Tourists flocking to nearby coastal towns often pass right through Areopolis, leaving plenty of romantic accommodations available in the traditional tower houses that once defended the insular, suspicious clans of the Mani. Close by you'll find the breathtaking caves at Pirgos Dirou alongside the beautiful beach at Limenas (which doubles as Areopolis's port), quiet and sternly beautiful Itilo, and lively Gythion, the harbor town on the opposite side of the peninsula.

TRANSPORTATION AND PRACTICAL INFORMATION. All services can be found in the plateia or off **Kapetan Matapan,** the main road running into the Old Town from the plateia. The **bus station** (☎27330 51 229), just a table with a single employee, is next to the Romeo Pub and Europa Grill, on the eastern edge of the plateia, opposite Hotel Kouris. The road running perpendicular from the bus station is Kapetan Matapan. Follow it along the plateia, past the statue, and into the Old Town. Buses from Areopolis go to: **Athens** (6hr.; 4 per day, 8am-6pm; €18) via **Gythion** (45min., €1.80) and **Sparta** (2hr., €6.50); **Itilo** (20min.; 6:30, 9am, 1:45pm; €0.90). From Itilo, you can catch a bus to **Kalamata.** A bus running into the Mani takes you to **Vatheia** (1hr.; noon, 1:45, 7:30pm; €2) via **Gerolimenas** (40min., €1.60) and the **Vlihada Lake Caves** (leaves 11am, returns 12:45pm; €0.90), with limited service on Sunday and holidays. To find the **National Bank** (☎27330 51 293; open M-F 9am-noon) with a 24hr. **ATM,** walk down Kapetan Matapan, turn right at the first small church, and continue up the street or walk on the road away from Pirgos Dirou making a left on the street closest to the gas station. The **police** are 500m out of town toward Pirgos Dirou. (☎27330 51 209. Open 24hr.) As you walk facing the sea, a **pharmacy** is two doors down from the post office. (☎27330 29 510. Open 8am-2pm and 5-9pm.) A 24hr. **health center** (☎27330 51 242 or 51 259) is 50m down a street that starts in the main plateia and runs away from the ocean. Opposite is the **OTE.** (☎27330 51 299. Open 8am-1pm.) The **post office** (☎27330 51 230; open M-F 7:30am-2pm) is on the street with National Bank, across from Hotel Mani. The post office **exchanges currency** and **traveler's checks** for a hefty fee and offers **Poste Restante. Postal code:** 23062.

ACCOMMODATIONS. Though you won't find much variety in the way of price, the styles of rooms in Areopolis range from century-old tower houses to modern hotels. Follow Kapetan Matapan and turn left at the end to get to **Tsimova's Rooms ❸**, behind the church in the Old Town. Kolokotronis supposedly slept in one of these narrow rooms. Unfortunately, the war hero wasn't timely enough to enjoy the newly installed A/C. War memorabilia, religious pictures, and various knick-knacks give each room in this 300-year-old house distinctive character. (☎27330 51 301. Shared and private baths. Continental breakfast €3. Singles €25-32; doubles €35-60. Cash only.) Tsimova's neighbor and rival, **Pierros Bozagregos Pension ❸**, across from Tsimova, has large, airy rooms with private baths in a classic stonework building. (☎27330 51 354. Breakfast included. Singles €20-40; doubles €35-50. Cash only.) Facing the bank, turn left and walk 50m down the road; make a left on the side street and **Passales ❸**, a two-story stone building, is on the left. Follow the signs to Elena's Rooms. Quiet rooms come equipped with A/C, TVs, and baths. (☎27330 51 474. Singles €20-30; doubles €30-60. Cash only.) **Hotel Mani ❸** is 50m from the bus station on Kapetan. Turn right at the first small church and walk another 200m; it's across from the post office near the National Bank. Spacious, generic rooms come with baths, balconies, TVs, and wood furnishings. (☎27330 51 190; fax 27330 51 269. Singles €30-40; doubles €35-50. Cash only.)

PELOPONNESE

FOOD. Tourist-traps dominate Areopolis's dining options. The plateia and Old Town, however, offer some pleasant alternatives. In the plateia, **Nicola's Place ❷** serves wonderful Greek dishes in plentiful portions. Since his mother makes all the food, the owner is hesitant to declare any dish more special than the others, but you can't go wrong with the stuffed tomatoes (€5) or chicken with lemon (€5.50). The tasty grilled and seasoned bread is included in the €0.55 cover. (☎27330 51 366. Cash only.) Across from the church in the Old Town, **Lithostroto ❸** serves more upscale meals (with a €1.20 cover charge) at more upscale prices. Though vegetarians will overlook the menu's grilled options like rabbit (€7.50) or young goat with potatoes (€7.50), dishes like stuffed vine leaves (€6.50) provide enjoyable alternatives. (☎27330 54 240. Salads €2.50-4.50. Grilled entrees €4-26. Main dishes €5-35. Cash only.) A simple sign reading "Taverna" hangs in front of **Oinomageireio ❷**, the yellow building on the left of Kapetan Matapan as you walk from the plateia towards the Old Town. The intimate garden seating is its main draw. (☎27330 51 205. Mixed vegetables €5.50. Meatballs €6. Grilled entrees €6-13. Cash only.) You can also head to one of the **supermarkets** in the area. There's one just off the plateia on the road away from Pirgos Dirou and another on the road from the plateia to the Old Town.

DAYTRIP FROM AREOPOLIS. Part of a subterranean river, the unusual **Vlihada Cave (Spilia Dirou or Pirgos Dirou)** is cool, quiet, and strung with tiny crystalline stalactites. Vermillion stalagmites slice the 30m-deep water's surface. Discovered at the end of the 19th century, it was opened to the public in 1971 and has yet to be fully explored. Experts speculate that the cave is 70km long and may extend all the way to Sparta. The 1300m boat ride through the cave lasts about 30min.; the tiny boats guided only by a small oar rock their way through the narrow, incredibly low channels of the cave, forcing passengers to duck and lean at times to avoid low-hanging stalactites. Luckily, life-vests double as body-armor, proving useful when the stalactites graze unsuspecting tourists' shoulders. Floating lights illuminate the tour, but unlit recesses branch off on each side. Don't miss **Poseidon's Foot,** a striking hanging formation resembling a giant foot. (☎27230 52 222. Open year-around 8am-3pm. Tickets, including tour, are checked at the entrance and again at the exit. €12; students, seniors, and children €7. Video cameras prohibited.)

GEFYRA Γεφυρα ☎27320

Byzantine enthusiasts on the way to their paradise, Monemvasia, may be puzzled when the bus drops them off in the unabashedly modern—albeit pleasant—coastal town of Gefyra ("bridge"). Just beyond the breaking waves off Gefyra's shore lies an impressive island, dominated by spectacular vertical cliffs. "The Rock," as it is known, looks uninhabited from the mainland; only after crossing the causeway and walking along the main road for 15min. does Monemvasia appear. Before you cross, however, it's wise to take care of your needs in cheaper Gefyra.

TRANSPORTATION AND PRACTICAL INFORMATION. During late July and August, an **orange bus** runs between the causeway and the Monemvasia gate all day long (every 15min., 8am-midnight; €0.30). In Gefyra, the main throughfares form a fork, the tail of which leads to the causeway connecting Monemvasia to the mainland. The main branch of this fork, **23 Iouliou,** runs inland from the causeway, later becoming **Spartis.** With the causeway before you, the harbor is to the right, and a pebbled beach to the left. On 23 Iouliou is the **bus station,** located in the helpful **Malvasia Travel Agency,** where superwomen Eva and Mary provide a multitude of services, including **moped rental** (€6 per day), **currency exchange** (with the standard 3% commission), and **tickets** for **Flying Dolphins** and **ferries.** (☎27320 61 752; fax 27320 61 432. Open M-Sa 7:15am-3:15pm and 6-9pm, Su 1-2:15pm). All **buses** connect or stop in **Molai.** Daily buses at 4:10, 7:15am, and 2:15pm leave for: **Athens** (6hr., €20) via **Molai** (20min., €1.80); **Corinth** (5hr., €15); **Sparta** (2½hr., €6.80); **Tripoli** (4hr., €10.40). On Monday and Friday there is an additional bus at 8:30am. Twice weekly **Flying Dolphins** go to **Piraeus** (€32) via **Spetses** (€20). **Taxis** (☎27320 61 274) line up across from the police. Across from the bus station, the **National Bank** has a 24hr. **ATM.** (☎27320 61 201. Open M-F 9am-1:30pm; open 1-2 days per week in the low season.) The **police** are on 23 Iouliou, 50m to the left of Malvasia Travel, facing the bank. (☎27320 61 210. Open 24hr.) **Internet** access is available at the **Baywatch Cafe,** 50m down the beachfront road with the water on your right. (€4 per hr., €2 min. Open daily 10am-1am.) The **post office** is next door to the National Bank. (☎27320 61 231. Open M-F 7:30am-2pm.) **Postal code:** 23070.

ACCOMMODATIONS AND FOOD. As Gefyra's hotels tend to be expensive—expect to pay at least €30 for singles and €40 for doubles, the waterfront **domatia** are your best bet (doubles €15-30). A room (doubles €50 and up) in one of nearby Monemvasia's traditional hotels will cost even more. **Hotel Akrogiali ❷,** directly across from Malvasia Travel on 23 Iouliou, is a perfect place for penny-pinching travelers who can overlook less than immaculate sheets and focus instead on small personal fans, TVs, private baths, and shared fridge. (☎27320 61 260. Singles €20-23; doubles €28-35. Cash only.) The rooms of **Hotel Aktaion ❸,** just before the causeway, have an unimaginative decor but offer balconies with harbor views, private baths, and TVs. (Singles €30-41; doubles €40-46; triples €40-45. Cash only.) Rooms in Old Monemvasia are generally reserved for the most spendthrift of travelers. But if you feel like splurging, check out **Hotel Byzantino ❺,** in the Old Town's plateia. Thirty gorgeous rooms all come with A/C and private baths. To help you get into the medieval feel, only some rooms have phones, and none have TVs. (☎27320 61 254; byzantino@yahoo.gr. Reservations recommended. Singles €40-120; doubles €115-180; triples €126-148. MC/V.) Beachfront rooms are available at **Hotel Pranataris ❹,** a short walk down the beachfront road away from the causeway, 75m past Baywatch Cafe with the water on your right. Spacious, well-lit rooms have private baths, mini-fridges, TVs, A/C, and balconies—half with seaside views. (☎27320 61 833; hotelpr@hol.gr. Breakfast €4.40. Reservations recommended during high season. Singles €25-60; doubles €30-75. MC/V.) **Camping Paradise ❶,** 4km along the water on the mainland, offers free 24hr. hot water, a restaurant, communal toilets, a cafe, and a mini-market. (☎27320 61 123. €5.50 per person, €3 per child; €3 per car; €3 per small tent, €4 per large tent. Electricity €0.50-3. Discounts for extended visits. Cash only.)

Pipinellis Taverna ❷, 2km from Monemvasia on the road to Camping Paradise, has featured homegrown produce for the past 25 years. It may be out of the way, but unrivaled meals like rabbit *stifado* show why it continues to be a favorite with locals. (☎27320 61 004. Salads €2-4.50. Entrees €5-8. Cash only.) If you're looking to stay in town, the many harbor-front tavernas of Gefyra are the best option for dining in the immediate area. **To Limanaki ❶,** offering waterside seating on the mainland between the causeway and the harbor, serves exceptional Greek food, including some of the best *pastitsio* (€5), moussaka (€5), and stuffed tomatoes (€4) around. (☎27320 61 619. Cash only.) Otherwise, **To Votoalo ❷,** 150m from Baywatch Cafe with the water on your left, offers beachfront seating away from the noisier areas of the waterfront. Before a trip to the Old Town, sit and enjoy large portions of Greek classics and fresh seafood. (☎27320 61 486. Appetizers €3.50-8. Vegetarian-friendly pasta €3. Fish €5-9.50. Grilled dishes €4.50-5.50. Cash only.) If you choose to dine in Old Monemvasia, try **Restaurant Matoila ❸.** The first taverna you come to in the town, Matoila offers a wonderful ocean view from the outdoor garden. Favorites like *dolmas* (€6) and more decadent veal and seafood entrees (€8-15) adorn the menu. (Open daily until midnight. V.) For lighter meals, try one of the town's **bakeries ❶,** or follow the road forking off 23 Iouliou to find the well-stocked **Lekakis Supermarket.** (Open daily 8am-9pm.)

PELOPONNESE

DAYTRIP FROM GEFYRA: MONEMVASIA. This ancient town deserves the constant attention it receives; an undeniable other-worldliness shrouds the city, adding an aura of medieval mystery to every tunnel and turn. Entering through the single gateway (hence the town's name, which means "one way") into old **Monemvasia,** you feel as though you've passed into a city frozen in time. No cars or bikes are allowed through the gate, so packhorses bearing groceries and cases of beer are led back and forth to restaurants. Upon entering the gate, a winding cobbled street passes the town's tourist shops and continues to the central plateia. Scramble down the nearby alleys toward the ocean to take a stroll along the fortified sea wall. Back in the plateia, the church of **Christos Elkomenos** (Christ in Chains) is on the left as you face the ocean. On the right, the small but well-labeled (and nicely air-conditioned) **Archaeological Museum** has a single room full of items attesting to Monemvasia's 13th-century prominence and strong commercial ties to the Western world. (☎27320 61 403. Open M 8am-3pm, Tu-Su 8am-7pm. Free.) To get to the often-photographed 12th-century **Agia Sofia,** balanced on the edge of the rock cliffs that also hold the remains of the city's **castle,** head through the tunnel across from Matoila and work your way through the maze of narrow streets—with hidden stairways, child-sized doorways, flowered courtyards, and the occasional cactus—to the edge of town farthest from the sea at the base of the mountain. There, a slippery path climbs the cliffside to the tip of the rock; you'll find the church on the far side of the rock. Although invading Turks defaced the faded frescoes, the beauty of the structure is still awesome. The top of the rock, about a 30min. climb from the Old Town, offers unparalleled views of the town and sea below. There are no signs that point the way to Agia Sofia, so you may want to purchase a map (€2) from a local store or the Archaeological Museum. The hike may be unsuitable for elderly travelers and young children.

NEAPOLI Νεαπολις ☎27340

A necessary stop on the path between Kythera and the southeastern Peloponnese, Neapoli is a small coastal town with lots of waterfront restaurants, a few luxury hotels, and an increasing number of tourists. The pebble and dark sand beaches are an uncrowded and refreshing break from the towel-to-towel sunbathers of more popular vacation spots. Grilled octopus is available everywhere. Though there's not much other than Neapoli's waterfront to keep visitors occupied, you may be convinced by the sea, the sun, and the friendly locals to spend a day and catch a later boat or bus out of town.

TRANSPORTATION AND PRACTICAL INFORMATION. The **bus station** (☎27340 23 222) is on an unmarked street off the right side of the waterfront as you face inland, two blocks from the pier. **Buses** leave at 8:15am, 1:30, and 5pm for: **Athens** (6hr., €22.90) via **Ag. Nikolaos** (20min., €0.90); **Molai** (1hr., €4.50); **Sparta** (2½hr., €9.50). **Ferries** go to **Kythera** (1hr.; July 6-July 20 8am, 2, 5pm; July 21-Aug. 31 4 per day; €5.20). To the left of the pier as you face inland, a blue and white hut on the water's edge provides **information** and posts ferry schedules. Schedules and tickets can also be obtained at the **ticket agency** on the strip between Hotel Aivali and Hotel Limira Mare. A sign along the road points the way. (☎27340 23 980. Open M-F 8:30am-2pm and 6-8pm, Sa-Su 8:30-11am. Extended hours during high season.) The **National Bank** and a 24hr. **ATM** are on the waterfront across from the pier. (Open M-Th 8am-2pm, F 8am-1:30pm.) The **port police** (☎27340 22 228) are one block from the National Bank. The **post office** is one block inland on Dimokratias on the left of the waterfront as you face inland, past the bridge. (Open M-F 7:30am-2pm.) **Postal code:** 23053.

PELOPONNESE

ACCOMMODATIONS AND FOOD. If you decide to stay in Neapoli overnight, scour the streets for **domatia,** or stay at **Hotel Arsenakos ❸,** a 5min. walk from town with the water on your left and run by a friendly ex-New Yorker and his wife. A cheery lobby with a large aquarium leads to spacious, clean, brightly painted rooms with A/C, TVs, phones, private baths, balconies, and fridges. And unlike other hotels in the area, it's only 15m from the beach. (☎27340 22 991 or 22 691; arsenakos@yahoo.com. Singles €20-30; doubles €25-45. Prices vary by season, highest in Aug. V.) Since rooms at Hotel Arsenakos tend to book quickly during the high season, consider **Aivali ❸,** at the corner of the street that leads to the post office. Confined but comfortable rooms all come with A/C, TVs, phones, balconies, small fridges, and low beds. (☎27430 22 561. Singles €25-37; doubles €30-42. Cash only.) Fans of domatia may be disappointed by their options in Neapoli. Most rooms for rent set up for families or independent travelers with extended itineraries and come loaded with amenities but high price tags. Still you may want to try the rooms owned by **Stavros Katoulis ❸** (Σταυρος Κατουλης), on Ag. Triados, the street one block to the right of the pier as you face inland. Centrally located rooms have A/C, TVs, fridges, balconies, and clean private baths. (☎27340 22 458. €25-50 per person. Cash only.) **Hotel Limira Mare ❹,** 300m from the port with the water on your left, caters to travelers who vacation in luxury. Over 100 rooms include balconies (half with sea-views), A/C, TVs, telephones, marble desks, and fridges. (☎27340 22 236; www.limiramare.gr. Singles €48-63; doubles €55-70; triples €66-84; quads €80-105. MC/V.)

The local cuisine is one of the first things travelers to Neapoli encounter as they stumble off the ferry; most restaurant owners grill octopi in front of their eateries all day long and the smell permeates the town. So if the thought of tentacles doesn't rub you the right way, check out **Gorgona ❷,** directly in front of Hotel Arsenakos. The owner, who doubles as the chef and sometimes the waiter, cooks up wonderful Greek dishes in portions that could feed two. Menu rotates daily, but ask if the meatballs in tomato sauce (€4.40) is being served. (☎27340 22 720. Appetizers €1.80-2.20. Salads €1.30-1.90. Pastas €3-5.50. Vegetarian dishes €3.50. Fish €4-36. Other entrees €4-14.60. Cash only.) Two blocks past Ailavi with the water on your left, **Moreas ❷** doles out delectable dishes of meat and fish primarily to locals. Tables are pulled as close to the beach as they can get, so you can watch the waves crash as the waitress lists dishes from the rotating menu. (☎27340 23 845. Salads €2-4. Fish €30-40 per kg. Main dishes €5-9. Cash only.)

KYTHERA Κυθηρα

According to ancient myth, the island of Kythera rose from the waters where Zeus cast his father Chronos's severed head into the sea after castrating him. Springing from Chronos's foamy misfortune, Aphrodite washed up onto Kythera's shores and made it her homeland. In antiquity, the island supported a large temple to the goddess, where she was worshipped as Aphrodite Urania, goddess of chaste love. Though one might not associate the island's barren, mountainous landscape with Aphrodite's famous and worship-worthy fertility, its flowering shrubs, sandy beaches, and secluded villages hold a potent beauty. Like the Ionians to the west, Kythera passed through the hands of the Venetians and the French before ending up as a British possession. But unlike its western counterparts, it remains distinct with its extremely rugged scenery—desert-like in places—and its untouristed feel. Improved ferry schedules have made it a more convenient destination for budget travelers. The two main island ports are northern Agia Pelagia and the newer, less accessible eastern port of Diakofti. Bus service is nonexistent, making some sort of vehicle virtually essential to taking full advantage of all the island has to offer.

AGIA PELAGIA Αγια Πελαγια ☎27360

If you plan a short stay on the island—especially if you're catching a ferry—Agia Pelagia is a good place to set up camp to avoid paying for an overpriced cab. The town is smaller and less picturesque than southerly Hora or Kapsali, but accommodations and moped rentals are cheaper and its long, convenient stretch of beaches offer up both sand and pebbles.

TRANSPORTATION AND PRACTICAL INFORMATION. The island's main road runs between Agia Pelagia and **Kapsali** in the south, with small villages connected by subsidiary roads. This road also passes through **Potamos** (the island's largest town), **Livadi,** and **Hora (Kythera). Ferries** leave from Agia Pelagia for **Neapoli** (1hr., daily, €5.20) and from **Diakofti** to **Gythion** (2½hr., 5 per week, €8.70) and **Kasteli,** Crete (7hr., 2 per week, €18.70). **Flying Dolphins** leave Diakofti for **Piraeus** (5hr., 2 per week, €18.60). Ferry tickets are also available at the two tiny shacks at the end of the pier when ferries are docking. In Agia Pelagia, a cottage to the left of the dock as you face inland is a **tourist office,** where friendly staffers provide information about accommodations and sights. (☎27360 33 815. Open July-mid-Aug. daily 9am-1pm and 5-8:30pm.) The nearest **bank, hospital, pharmacy,** and **post office** are all in Potamos. **Easy Rider,** a 10min. walk with the water on your left, rents mopeds. The shop has no signs, so call ahead. (☎27360 33 486. Motorbike license required. €15-20 per day for 100cc. 21+.) During high season, you can also rent vehicles from **Panyotis Rent-A-Car,** 200m to the right of the port as you face inland. (☎27360 31 600. Scooters €15 per day; cars €25 and up.) The **port police** (☎27360 33 280) are 50m to the right of the port, facing inland. **Postal code:** 80100.

ACCOMMODATIONS AND FOOD. The tourist office has a list of the few **domatia** owners in town and can put you in contact with them. Blue-and-white **Hotel Kythereia ❸,** directly opposite the dock, has rooms with colorful private baths, A/C, shared fridge, and lovely views (of either mountains or sea) for prices that compete with any other hotel on the island. Even better, this hotel is run by an extremely hospitable Greek-Australian family. (☎27360 33 321; fax 27360 33 825. Breakfast €3. Singles €18-30; doubles €30-60. MC/V.) Out of town, along the waterfront toward Potamos in the building with the dolphins on it, **Maneas Domatia ❸** lets rooms with private baths, shared kitchens, and phones. (☎27360 33 503. Singles €20-25; doubles €25-35. V.) The other hotels in town are more luxurious and, consequently, more expensive. An expensive C-class hotel is the **Pelagia Aphrodite Hotel ❸,** a 10min. walk from town with the water on your left. Marble steps lead to immaculate, spacious rooms with A/C, TVs, fridges, mini-bars, and telephones. Most rooms have balconies with unbeatable seaside views. (☎27360 33 926; fax 27360 34 242. Reservations and deposit required during high season. Singles €39-73; doubles €47-88; triples €56-105. MC/V.) The **Vernados Hotel ❹,** just 50m inland on the road opposite the tourist office cottage, has a score of amenities, among them A/C, TV, free laundry, 24hr. room service, and a buffet breakfast. The owner is proud that all rooms have sea-view balconies. (☎27360 34 205 or 34 206. Singles €47-70; doubles €65-80; triples €78-96. MC/V.)

Taverna Faros ❸, the first taverna to the right of the pier (facing inland), has waterfront seating away from the crowds. Travelers with different eating habits can quietly enjoy meals like tomatoes or the delicious fish entrees (€38-44 per kg). Farther north (to the right as you face inland) on the waterfront, **Restaurant Kaleris ❷** serves mostly local cuisine to natives and vistors alike. Enjoy dishes like fried squash with cheese and fresh mint (€4) as children play in the surrounding area. (Appetizers €2-4.50. Salads €2.50-6. Fish €4.50-9. Entrees €4.50-6. Cash only.) Agia Pelagia has a **supermarket** opposite the beach, beside the fruit market.

BEACHES. In addition to its convenience as a port town, Agia Pelagia is the only town on Kythera that boasts six beaches all within convenient walking distance of the town center. Starting from the town's main beach, continue south, toward Potamos, with the water on your left, to five more beaches. The road is initially paved as you pass the second, dark sand beach, and turns to dirt after the Aphrodite Pelagia Hotel. Each beach offers its own unique combination of coves, sand, and pebbles; a local favorite is small, secluded **Lorenzo beach,** just past the hill with the monastery. The most distant beach is only a 45min. walk away.

AROUND KYTHERA

The island has a lion's share of sights, enough to keep any visitor occupied. The peaceful beach town of **Kapsili,** east of Hora, has clear waters and a long shore. At Paleohora, in the east, are the ruins of the former fortified capital of the island, **Agios Dimitrios,** built during Byzantine rule. The town was destroyed by pirates led by the notorious Barbarossa in 1537. Even more compelling are the island's natural wonders, including the **Cave of Agia Sofia** (open Tu-Su 10am-5pm; €3), near the village of Milopotamos (home to the splendid Milopotamos waterfall) on the western side of the island. The most impressive of the island's several caves, Agia Sofia also has beautiful **frescoes** painted on the cave walls and is an easy walk or taxi ride away from Milopotamos. Kythera's **beaches** are gorgeous, with the ocean's blue contrasting with the brown landscape. The best beaches are a bit difficult to reach, accessible only by dirt roads that can be perilous for mopeds—a car is safer. On the eastern coast, a staircase leads down to spectacular **Kaladi beach,** with sparkling coves and striking rock formations. **Halkos,** near Kalamos on the southern coast, is another isolated beach; its quiet beauty makes it worth the trip.

POTAMOS Ποταμος ☎27360

Potamos is on a hill 9km south of Agia Pelagia on the main road, with narrow streets ornamented by flowers and fresh fruit markets. Though accommodations are scarce, it's still worth a visit after a trip to the Cave of Agia Sophia or one of the many footprint-free beaches. As you stroll through the town streets, notice the traditional architecture and take advantage of the services in the small central plateia. There's an **Olympic Airways** office down the left road of the plateia as you face the bank, although the airport is a taxi ride away on the eastern half of Kythera. (☎27360 33 362. Open M 12:30-2pm, W-Th noon-2pm, F 9am-1pm.) Olympic runs **flights** to and from **Athens** (daily, €43). **Taxis** park in the plateia. (☎27360 33 720. To Diakofti €12-15.) The **National Bank** with 24hr. **ATM** is in the plateia. The bank offers **currency exchange.** (Open M-Th 8am-2pm, F 8am-1:30pm.) The **police station** is off of the plateia; turn right on the street that runs across from the ATM. (☎27360 33 222. Open daily 8am-10pm.) There is a **pharmacy** next to the Olympic Airways office, on the road that runs to the left of the plateia. (☎27360 33 364. Open M-F 8:30am-2pm and 6-9pm.) The **hospital** is on the road to Hora. (☎27360 33 325. English spoken.) **Selana Cafe,** in the plateia, has a single computer for **Internet** access. (€7 per hr. Open 8:30am-11pm.) The **post office** with **Poste Restante** is uphill from the plateia. (Open M-F 7:30am-2pm.) **Postal code:** 80200.

If you're looking to spend a night in town, be forwarned that your options are very limited. Fortunately the town's small hotel comes reasonably-priced and rather well-equipped. Uphill from the plateia, **Pension Parfira ❸** offers spacious rooms with A/C, TVs, fridges, kitchenettes, telephones, private baths, and a shared patio. (☎27360 33 329. Singles €20-30; doubles €35-50. Cash only.) **Panapetos ❷,** in the plateia, provides a quiet ambiance. The shrimp *saganaki* (€7) and tortellini with cream sauce (€4.50) are good selections, though the servings may not be huge. (☎27360 34 290. Salads €3.50-5. Entrees €4-8. Cash only.) Travelers who don't feel like dining out (or spending a fair amount of money) can always make their way over to the **supermarket** (open daily 8am-11pm), located in the plateia.

HORA Χωρα ☎27360

The whitewashed plaster houses of the island's southern capital gleam in the bright sun. During high season, tight-knit Hora (also called Kythera) is overwhelmed with visitors who come from the ports of Diakofti and Kapsali. **Taxis** (☎27360 31 720) are a good way to get to both Diakofti (€18) and Agia Pelagia (€18). Travelers under time contraints should be aware that many taxi drivers on the island will siesta all afternoon, so it's best to plan your ride ahead of time. There is a **National Bank** with 24hr. **ATM** in the plateia. (Open M-Th 8am-2pm, F 8am-1:30pm.) **Public toilets** are below the plateia; follow the steps by the National Bank. Facing the water, Hora's main street begins in the plateia's lower left-hand corner and runs downhill; along it you'll find the **police** (☎27360 31 206; open 24hr.), 150m down toward the water, on the left side of the street once you make a right at the fork in the road. **Kithira Travel** has **Flying Dolphin** schedules, **currency exchange,** and tickets for **Olympic Airways.** (☎27360 31 390; fax 27360 31 490. Open daily 9am-2pm and 7-10pm.) The nearest **hospital** is in Potamos. **Internet** access is available at **Typographics,** on the main road leading to the police station. (☎27360 39 016. €4 per hr. Open daily 9am-2:30pm.) The **post office** with **Poste Restante** is in the plateia. (Open M-F 7:30am-2pm.) **Postal code:** 81200.

The few accommodations catering to visitors tend to offer similar views and amenities. If you do decide to go hotel hunting, most are clustered around and along the main road leading to the police. At **Castello Apartments ❷,** to the left of the main road as you approach the fork from the plateia, airy rooms all come with ceiling fans and clean private baths. Guests can also stay in rooms with kitchenettes and/or verandas. (☎27360 31 069; fax 27360 31 869. Singles €25-30; doubles €25-38. MC/V.) Though a little more removed from the center of town, the unnamed **rooms ❷** above the restaurant Mirtuon (Μυρτωον; see below) provide ordinary doubles with A/C, TVs, phones, kitchenettes, and balconies with beautiful views. Walk up the stairs to the right of the post office and turn right at the road; the rooms are 20m on the right. (☎27360 31 404 or 31 705. Singles and doubles €30. Cash only.) **Camping Avlemonas ❶,** near the town of Frilingianika, is a solid choice for the most budget-conscious travelers. There is no charge to stay overnight at the grounds, which also have free hot showes, a shop, easy beach access, and public toilets (€4). From Hora, drive north along the main road towards Frilingianika. Signs will point the way to Avlemonas. (☎27360 33 742.)

While the brightly-colored awnings that shade the plateia's small cafes may be intriguing, the best bet for food is found on the road just outside of town. Head up the stairs to the right of the post office and turn right on the road to find **Mirtuon ❷** Μυρτωον. This family-run eatery doles out piping-hot portions of Greek staples, like homemade tiropita (€2.50) to start. Work your way to grilled rabbit (€6) or *pastitsio* (€5), which make this place a local favorite. (☎27360 31 705. Appetizers €1.50-2.50. Salads €1.50-3.50. Vegetarian dishes €3-3.50. Cash only.)

A Day In the Fields

Picking olives in December is a national tradition and an annual rite. All over Greece, men and women can be found spreading large tarmacs and nets below olive trees, thwacking at the branches with sticks, climbing into olive groves, shaking trees, and raking leaves with short plastic "combs." More sophisticated olive pickers buy machines that sort the olives from the leaves.

When a friend suggested I join him to shed his 40 trees of their olives, I took him up on the offer. We left Athens in the early morning, drove along the national highway, and arrived at his plot near Corinth, next to the sea. The water was calm and in the grayish light looked thick as mercury.

We were joined by two of his cousins from nearby Ellinohori, two men from northern Epirus, and a Greek-Russian. The most important member of the troop turned out to be his Aunt Tasia, a woman who'd been picking olives since she was 10 years old. A brawny, attractive woman in her late forties, she wore sweatpants and a sweatshirt. She surveyed the eight stremmata (two acres) with a knowing eye, walked up to a few trees, plucked an olive, and bit into it. "Two thousand kilos worth of olives on these trees," she said. "I estimate 180 kilos of olive oil. A little ripe, but you'll be able to smell the olive oil in your salad, and that's what counts."

I beat a branch laden with black and yellow olives with a long six-foot wooden rod. The olives rattled onto the ground like heavy rain. When the ripest ones had been dislodged, we had to get to the ones that were harder to remove. Using ladders we climbed into the trees and combed the branches with small plastic rakes, sending a second school of olives to the ground. From inside the tree itself, I could uncover new bunches of olives, and these too soon joined their brethren on the ground.

When I stood back to admire a whole section of a tree that I'd combed of all its fruits, satisfied that no twig had remained untouched, eagle-eyed Tasia shouted at me, "No, no! You've le enough olives on there to feed an army! Ther can't you see? Are you blind? Look, up there!"

By midday my jeans were graced with two kne spots of olive oil, and my sweatshirt was full shavings from the saw and a heaviness of oil. M shoes were slippery from stepping on raw olive. We stopped at two o'clock for a lunch of kokk neli wine, feta cheese, pastitsio prepared b Tasia, and large chunks of bread. Slightly drun we were back at it by 3pm, less jubilant, mor serious, and determined to finish before the su went down. There were only two hours of ligh remaining, and the clouds were starting to hudd above our heads.

Suddenly it started to rain, a light drizzle. Tasi quickly cleaned the remaining piles of olives; w covered the bags with branches and soon walke around in mud. There were only three trees le My friend would return in a week, when th weather cleared up.

A small lorry came, and we piled the bags into i We went to the olive press and left the bags olives inside a small warehouse. This was a ne olive press, which Tasia said didn't carry with the smell and age of the old ones. "The o presses," she explained, "made even sour olive taste good." Within a few hours the olives ha been pressed and poured into large tins. M friend poured some oil into a plate. It was sti clouded, of a light green color. We dipped our fi gers into it. Extra virgin olive oil.

Driving back to Athens, I recalled the day. At on point, I stood on the ladder, my body thrust u through the top of the tree like some sort Christmas decoration. To my left, the wind rip pled along the sea's surface, leaving its famili treads. To my right, the impressive Corinthia landscape jutted into the sky, raw and ragge dotted with patches of dark green cypress tree Cottony clouds drifted above with serene nobi ity. And on the earth, Tasia, the cousins, and th emigrant workers: four Greeks, two Albanian and one Russian, cutting, pruning, gathering, co lecting, and laughing.

Nicholas Papandreou is a writer living in Greece. He is the author of two novels, A Crowded Heart *(Picador) and* Klepto nemon: The Thief of Memories. *He is currently an advisor to the Ministry of the Aegean, where a major effort is underwa to preserve the architectural integrity of the area. His articles and columns appear in weekly and monthly newspaper and magazines throughout Greece.*

CENTRAL GREECE

Under 19th-century Ottoman rule, Thessaly and Sterea Ellada acquired a Byzantine aura; seek it along forgotten mountain-goat paths that lead to the treasures of this era. Along the way, you'll encounter glorious mountain-top vistas that look out over silvery olive groves, fruit-laden trees, and patchwork farmland.

STEREA ELLADA

Small mountainside villages, monumental ruins, the country's finest honey, and superb ski slopes characterize Sterea Ellada (the "Greek Continent"), the only section of the mainland to join the new Greek state after the War of Independence (p. 13). For thousands of years, pilgrims from all over the Mediterranean and Asia Minor headed to the Delphic Oracle, where ponderous questions met cryptic replies. The 10th-century monastery of Osios Loukas, a modern religious center near Delphi, displays Byzantine architectural mastery. Be kind to strangers you meet on the road below the monastery: at the crossroads, an unknowing Oedipus met and murdered his father on the way to Thebes, where he married his mother.

HIGHLIGHTS OF CENTRAL GREECE

ASCEND to cloud-swept Meteora monasteries as the Byzantine saints did (p. 244).

MARVEL at the frescoes and gold mosaics at the Monastery of Osios Loukas (p. 215), an oasis of Byzantine decorative art.

ABANDON PSYCHIC HOTLINES for the real deal–Apollo's oracle at Delphi (p. 217).

FORGET YOUR TROUBLES at the springs of Krya: *Lethe* and *Mnemosyne* (p. 219).

HIT THE SLOPES on Mt. Parnassos, Greece's premier ski mountain (p. 213).

THEBES (THIVA) Θηβα ☎22620

Buried beneath the low-rise apartment buildings and lazy tavernas of modern Thebes lies its claim to fame: an illustrious—and notorious—past. History has literally surfaced in scattered spots throughout the city, as attempts at construction have often revealed the buried edifices of Ancient Thebes. Thebian buildings grace the avenues of Cadmus (the city's legendary first king), Oedipus (exiled king and namesake of the Complex), and Epaminonda (the general who ended Spartan dominance). Rising to prominence in the heyday of the Greek city-state (600-400 BC), Thebes capitalized on its fertile plains and strategic location between Northern Greece and the Peloponnese. Alexander the Great's army cut this prosperity short around 335 BC by maliciously setting fire to the city, reducing it to rubble, sparing only temples and Pindar's ancestral home. Thebes, it seems, is still attempting to recover from that blow; it barely warrants a brief daytrip.

TRANSPORTATION. From Terminal B, Platform 4 at Liossion 260 in Athens, take the **bus** to Thebes (1½hr.; every hr., 6am-8pm; €5.25). Buy tickets inside the station from the desk labeled ΘΗΒΑ (Thebes). The main **bus station** (☎22620 27 512) is in the valley below Thebes on Estias. From Thebes, buses depart from the station for **Athens.** To travel to **Halkida,** take the Athens bus to the Skimatari stop (30min., €1.70); across the street from the stop, catch the Athens-Halkida bus (10min., every 30min., €1.20). The direct bus between Thebes and Halkida runs twice a day (7:20, 10am; €2.80). Regular buses run to **Livadia** (45min.; every hr., 6:30am-9:30pm; €3.10) from a stop about 2km out of town; walk all the way down Pindarou past the Archaeological Museum and go down the steps. Take the left fork then the right onto Laiou (Λαιου). Take a left onto St. Athanasiou and follow the blue signs to Livadia (Λειβαδια) to the small bus shelter just before the Shell gas station on your right. Buy your ticket on board. For **taxis,** call ☎22620 27 077.

ORIENTATION AND PRACTICAL INFORMATION. When traveling by bus, if you ask nicely upon arrival, the driver might let you off in the center of town. Otherwise, to get to town from the station, cross the parking lot with your back to the station and turn right, following the first road uphill. Follow **Eteokleous** up the hill to a plateia where first **Pindarou** and then **Epaminonda** veer off to the right. Turn right onto Epaminonda to find hotels, tavernas, and other comforts. Thebes is built on a high hill. Two parallel main streets, Epaminonda and Pindarou, run from the top of the hill into the valley below. Epaminonda hosts a variety of cafes and shops; Pindarou is lined with **banks** and **pharmacies.** The **National Bank,** Pindarou 94, has a 24hr. **ATM.** (☎22620 23 331 or 22620 25 144. Open M-Th 8am-2pm, F 8am-1:30pm.) The **hospital,** Pindarou 105 (☎22620 24 444), is between the church and Archaeological Museum—look for Greek and Red Cross flags. An **OTE,** 14 Vourdouba, is off Epaminonda (open M-F 7:45am-1pm). For **Internet** access, go to **Internet Cafe,** Pindarou 44. (€2 per hr. Open 10:30am-midnight.) The **post office,** Drakou 17, lies on a side street between Pindarou and Epaminonda, at the end closest to the bus station. (☎22620 27 810. Open M-F 7:30am-2pm.) **Postal code:** 32200.

CENTRAL GREECE

ACCOMMODATIONS AND FOOD. If you decide to spend the night in Thebes, there are only two options in town. The English-speaking staff at **Hotel Niobi ❸,** Epaminonda 63, offer rooms with TVs and beautifully-tiled private baths. (☎22620 29 888. Breakfast €3. Singles €35; doubles €40; triples €45.) The rooms at **Hotel Meletiou ❸,** across the street, feature the same amenities (TVs and private baths) but are lower quality and ridiculously priced. (☎22620 27 333. Singles €45; doubles €65; triples €80.) By evening, people of all ages fill the pedestrian-only sections of Epaminonda as tavernas move tables into the street. A multitude of tavernas tumble across Epaminonda and its side streets to Pindarou offer similar fare at similar prices (€3-6). **Dionysos ❷,** on Epimanonda just before the main plateia, has been serving traditional kitchen fare longer than the others, first opening its doors in 1922. Bakeries, fruit stands, and gyro and souvlaki restaurants scattered among the tavernas provide cheaper eats (€1-3).

SIGHTS. Thebes's antiquities are its main attraction. The **Archaeological Museum** at the end of Pindarou has an extensive collection of Mycenaean artifacts. The museum also displays Boeotian statuary from the 5th and 4th centuries BC and pottery galore. Especially notable are the Geometric-style vases *(larnakes)*, dating from 900 to 700 BC. (☎22620 27 913. Open M 12:30-7pm, Tu-Su 8am-7pm. €2, seniors €1, children and EU students free.) Peer into the open **excavation pits**—the source of the museum's collection—sprinkled between buildings throughout the central city. Segments of a Mycenaean palace and acropolis (c. 1400 BC) are partially visible. The largest of these, the **House of Cadmus,** shows its ancient palace walls; it is along the way to the museum on Pindarou, just between the church and the hospital. Also nearby are uninspiring ancient **Mycenaean Chamber Tombs.** Take Vourdouba downhill from Pindarou, passing the remains of **Proetides Gate,** turn left on Avlidos and right on Katsina before the high school.

PARNASSOS AND ARAHOVA Παρνασσος AND Αραχωβα ☎22670

Winter is peak season on Mt. Parnassos (elev. 2455m), as Apollo and the muses share their abode with ski buffs and bunnies flocking to the best slopes in Greece. By night the frostbitten masses thaw out in the village of Arahova, the country's largest ski resort, thanks to its prime location (24km away from Parnassos). In the summer months, the crowds desert both mountain and village, all the more reason to discover their low season appeal. Outdoor enthusiasts will adore Parnassos regardless of season and summer trekkers can hike the broad slopes undisturbed. Peaceful Arahova offers local delights like delicious unresinated red wine, Boeotian honey, and that peculiar grape-seed brandy called *tsipouro* (p. 19) along with an overwhelming view of the valley below. A three-day festival in April commemorates Arahova's role as the site of a pivotal victory over the Turks during the War of Independence. In honor of St. George, the renowned dragon-slayer and the town's patron saint, the festival consists of athletic competitions, dances, and general merrymaking; during the festivities, residents don their best costumes.

TRANSPORTATION AND PRACTICAL INFORMATION. From Terminal B in **Athens** (p. 84), take the Delphi bus to **Arahova** (2hr., 6 per day, €10.30). The bus stops at the end of town closest to Delphi, next to the kiosk in front of the main plateia. There is no bus station—ask at the information office for bus schedules. From the bus stop, buses make the run from Arahova to: **Athens** (2hr.; 6 per day, M-Sa 5:45am-6:15pm, Su 7:45am-9:15pm; €10.50); **Delphi** (20min.; 6 per day, 9:45am-10pm; €0.90); **Livadia** (30min.; M-F 3 per day, 7am-8pm; Sa-Su 7am, 8pm; €2.70). Getting from Arahova to Parnassos is slightly easier during ski season when a **bus** runs from the plateia (leaves 7:30am, returns 3pm). During the summer months, go by **car;** those without cars can hire a **taxi** (☎22670 31 566; round-trip €32-40).

Arahova centers on a single road, **Delphon,** which points downhill toward Delphi and has all the essentials. Three main plateias lie in town; directions assume you are heading into town from Delphi. An **information office** with English-speaking staff is just to the right off the main plateia. (☎22670 29 170; detpa@internet.gr. Open 8am-10pm.) For the **police,** call ☎22670 31 333. Among several **pharmacies,** one lies just past the second plateia, down an alley to the right. A little past the post office, on the left, lies the **National Bank** (☎22670 31 496; open M-Th 8am-2pm, F 8am-1:30pm) with a 24hr. **ATM. Alpha Bank,** in the second plateia of cafes on the right, **exchanges money** and also has an **ATM.** (☎22670 32 561. Open M-Th 8am-2pm, F 8am-1:30pm.) Turning right on the cross-street in the main plateia, you'll find the **post office** (open M-F 7:30am-2pm), uphill and on the right. **Postal code:** 32004.

ACCOMMODATIONS AND FOOD. Several hotels, pensions, and **domatia** cluster near the first plateia and more sit along Delphon and at the other end of town. The low-end prices listed refer to summer prices; high-end prices refer to ski season rates. **Pension Petrino ❷** (Πετρινο), down the first small alley on the right after the main plateia, offers gorgeous rooms with TVs, private baths, and sometimes balconies. (☎22670 31 384; fax 22670 32 663. 40% discount M-F in ski season; 10% off for stays longer than 3 days in summer. Breakfast included. Singles €20-65; doubles €40-80.) Spend a hard day's night at **Pension Nostos ❸,** located down the road to the right off the main plateia. Its cozy, well-appointed rooms (fridge, TV, private bath, balcony) once hosted the Beatles. (☎22670 31 385; nostos@otenet.gr. Breakfast included. Singles €25-75; doubles €35-75; triples €50-90.) Down the road past the town center, **Hotel Parnassos ❷** has comfortable rooms with shared hall bathrooms. Some rooms have balconies with uninterrupted views of the surrounding mountains. (☎22670 31 307. Doubles €25.)

The **bakeries** along the road to Delphi sell fresh bread and savory pastries (€0.50-2). Nondescript tavernas can be found along the main road; many close for the summer. The moderate prices, like everything else, increase in winter. **Pizzaria Kellaria ❶,** on the right past the second plateia, serves many pizzas and calzones (€5-7.50) from its brick oven, as well as savory and sweet crepes (€3.50-4.50). **Taverna Karathanassi ❷** (Καραθανασση), up from the second plateia on the right, serves the usual fare including grilled meats (€3-6.50) and features rooftop dining.

SKIING, HIKING, AND THE OUTDOORS. Winter activities at Parnassos are accessible at either of its two main **ski centers, Kelaria** (☎22340 22 689 or 22 624) and **Parnassos Ski Center** (☎22340 22 693). There are tavernas, equipment rental shops, and childcare services at each one. The ski season runs from December 15 to May 1. (Sa-Su €25 per day, M-F €15 per day; full week €80. Ask about discounts for students and children and family passes.) There are 14 lifts servicing the 20 slopes, which have a combined length of 14,000m. Though more goats than tourists frequent Parnassos in the summer months, it's a peaceful spot for hiking and rock climbing, with literally breathtaking views—the air becomes noticeably thinner higher up. Ski centers on the mountain provide free parking and an easy starting destination for most trips; Kellaria is the best starting point for a climb to the summit. Consult the **Greek Alpine Club** in Athens (☎210 321 2429) or the **Skiing and Mountain Climbing Association of Amfissa** (☎22650 28 577 or 22650 29 201) about routes and refuges for climbers. In most cases, the hike will take no more than 3hr. Summer hikers should note that trails are poorly marked and usually deserted (goats aside). Bring water and beware the thin air and rocky paths.

OSIOS LOUKAS Οσιος Λουκας ☎22670

Osios Loukas delights the eye with its mountain vistas and stunning Byzantine architecture. The exquisite **monastery,** built in the 10th and 11th centuries and still in use today, overlooks the fruit orchards and vineyards of Boeotia and Phokis from the green slopes of Mt. Elikon, more than 500m above sea level. (☎22670 22 797. Open May 3-Sept. 15 daily 8am-2pm and 4-7pm; Sept. 16-May 2 8am-5pm. Modest dress required; no bare shoulders. €3, seniors €2, under 18 and students with ID free.) Gold-laden mosaics, vibrant frescoes, and intricate brick- and stonework adorn Osios Loukas, the most famous and perhaps the most striking monastery in Greece. Ironically Christian saint Osios Loukas was born in AD 896 in Delphi (p. 216), a former religious center of the Olympian gods and polytheistic worship. Inclined to an ascetic life from early on, he became a monk at the age of 14. In AD 946, Osios Loukas settled at the lush and enchanting site of the monastery that now bears his name, building a cell, a small church, and a garden. Rumors that his relic worked miracles brought believers to his church, which led to an expansion of the grounds and the beginning of a monastery. With aid from fellow hermits and money from admirers, Osios Loukas began construction of two churches. The first, the **Church of the Panagia** (Church of the Virgin Mary), was finished soon after the saint's death in 953. The larger **Katholikon of Osios Loukas,** built in 1011, became the site of his reliquary. Osios Loukas was famed as a miracle worker during his lifetime; since his death, thousands have found cures at his tomb. Unfortunately, the monastery still bears the damage from 13th-century Frankish occupation and, more recently, from German bombing during World War II.

Today the monastery consists of the two churches, a crypt, a bell-tower, and monks' cells. Also on the grounds are a museum and several tourist shops. The **Archaeology Museum,** on the right after the arched stone gate, sells tickets for entrance into the monastery. The museum holds a few relics from the monastery's architectural past (chunks of molding and such) and merits only a glance. The **Katholikon,** on the right after the museum, is the most impressive piece of the monastery. Built on the classic "Greek cross" basilica plan, the church is resplendent with frescoes and mosaics. The mosaics, crafted from minute pieces of stone, enamel, and gold, depict scenes of Christian lore: the birth, baptism, and crucifixion of Jesus and **Christ Pantokrator** (Jesus in heaven, reigning in glory) on the dome.

A small passageway in the Katholikon's northwestern corner links it to the smaller **Church of Panagia.** In this passageway is the monastery's most prized relic: the desiccated body of the saint himself, lying in a transparent glass coffin. Orthodox pilgrims come here to pray at Osios Loukas's velvet-slippered feet. Some have been even bolder: Loukas's left hand, which protrudes from his habit to hold a rosary, has lost a few fingers to relic-seekers. The Church of Panagia down the passage features extremely fine exterior brickwork and an inlaid mosaic floor. Between the museum and the churches and accessible by an entrance in the southern exterior of the Katholikon is the **crypt;** its stunning frescoes should not be missed. Protected from the elements, the frescoes retain their original brilliance, giving onlookers an idea of what the churches looked like originally. Past the crypt entrance is a small courtyard; take a peek inside the two doors on the left for a glimpse at the luxurious digs enjoyed by medieval monks. After that, be sure to climb the tower at the far end of the courtyard for a stunning view.

So few **buses** from Arahova force you to take a **car** or **taxi** (☎22670 31 566; €20).

DELPHI Δελφοι ☎22650

As any local will proudly attest, this town of 2500 marks the *omphalos* (belly button) of the earth. According to the ancient myth, Zeus simultaneously released two eagles, one toward the east and one toward the west. They collided, impaling each other with their beaks, directly over Delphi—a sacred stone marks the spot. Nearby stood the most important oracle of the ancient Mediterranean. The oracle was initially devoted to Gaia (Mother Earth), but she was overthrown by the Olympian gods around 800 BC, when Apollo defeated the Python, Gaia's snaky, underworldly son and ruler of the site. The Apollonian oracle drew pilgrims from far and wide who sought guidance from the Pythia, priestess of the oracle. The temples and treasury of the ancient oracle have mostly crumbled to rubble, but Delphi remains a place of pilgrimage—for tourists. Jewelry stores, expensive restaurants, "Greek Art" trinket shops, and hotels now decorate the town. Beyond tourism, the town's mountainside perch and beautiful ruins make Ancient Delphi a must-see.

TRANSPORTATION. From **Terminal B** in Athens (p. 84), take a **bus** to **Delphi** (3hr., 6 per day, €10.20). Buy your ticket at the booth labeled "Δελφοι" (Delphi). From Delphi, buses go to: **Amphissa** (30min.; 3 per day, 6:30am-8:15pm; €1.50); **Itea** (30min.; 3 per day, 7am-10:15pm; €1.30; **Lamia** (2hr., 3 per day, €6.10); **Nafpaktos** (2½hr., 3 per day, €7) via **Galaxidi** (1hr., €2.50); **Patras** (3hr., daily, €8.70); **Thessaloniki** (5hr.; M-Th, Sa 10:15am; F and Su 3:15pm; €24) via **Volos, Larisa,** and **Katerini. Taxis** (☎22650 82 000) wait at the eastern end of Pavlou.

ORIENTATION AND PRACTICAL INFORMATION. Delphi's main street, **Friderikis-Pavlou,** runs east-west through town. **Apollonas** runs uphill from and parallel to Friderikis-Pavlou. The **bus station** (☎22650 82 317; open daily 8am-10:30pm) is at the western end of town, on Pavlou. The oracle and museum are on Pavlou at the opposite end of town, toward Athens. The **tourist office,** Pavlou 12 or Apollonas 11, is housed in the town hall. From Friderikis, the office is up a flight of stairs, in a stucco courtyard to your left as you walk toward Athens, marked by an "Information" sign. Quadrilingual **Efi Tsiropoulou** can assist you with buses and accommodations. (☎22650 82 900. Open M-F 8am-2:30pm.) If the office is closed, the bus station can provide directions and bus information. (Open 7:30am-10:30pm.) The **National Bank,** Pavlou 16, has a 24hr. **ATM.** (☎22650 82 622. Open M-Th 8am-2pm, F 8am-1:30pm.) The **police** (☎22650 82 222) are directly behind the church at the peak of Apollonas. **Public toilets** are at the eastern end of Pavlou behind the taxi stand. The **OTE** is in the town hall. (Open M-Th 7:30am-1pm, F 7:30am-12:30pm.) **Cafe Delfikon,** on the right side of Pavlou past Hotel Sibylla (facing Athens), has **Internet** access. (€4.50 per hr., €2 min. Open daily 9am-midnight.) The **post office** is at Pavlou 25. (☎22650 82 376. Open M-F 7:30am-2pm.) **Postal code:** 33054.

ACCOMMODATIONS. Delphi is full of expensive hotels. Almost all can be found on Apollonas or Pavlou. Prices rise during ski season. **Hotel Sibylla ❷,** Pavlou 9, provides TVs, fans, wonderful views, some balconies, private baths, and the best prices in town. (☎22650 82 335. Singles €15; doubles €22; triples €27. Discount for *Let's Go* readers.) **Hotel Artemis ❸,** on the left side of Pavlou, about 250m from the bus station, just completed evident renovations—rooms have refreshingly bright decor, balconies, A/C, and private baths. (☎22650 82 294 or 82 494.

Breakfast included. Singles €35; doubles €50.) **Hotel Pan ❷**, across the street from Artemis, is under the same management and offers the same amenities with a little less polish but lower prices and better views. (☎22650 82 294 or 82 494. Singles €28; doubles €45.) Find camping on the road west from Delphi. The bus can drop you at **Delphi Camping ❶**, 4km out of town. (☎22650 82 745. €5 per person, €3 per tent, €2.50 per car.) **Chrissa Camping ❶**, 10km out of town, is also accessible by bus. (☎22650 82 050. €5 per person; prices vary by season.) Both have pools.

FOOD AND ENTERTAINMENT. Several **mini-marts** and a **bakery** along Pavlou and Apollonas provide for self-caterers. Four **pizza** places beckon from the western end of Pavlou. The town's tavernas are indistinguishable, providing the same Delphic view and slightly pricey entrees.

Delphi's only two nightclubs are within stumbling distance of most hotels on Pavlou. Both open at 10pm and stay open until the customers leave (substantially later in the more crowded winter season). **Katoi Cub,** across the street and about 75m up from the bus station attracts young tour groups with its large dance floor and view of the gulf. (Cover €6, includes 1 drink. Beer €3; cocktails €5.) Rub elbows with tourists and the local youth at **Down Town Club,** Pavlou 33. (Cover €3, deducted from the price of your 1st drink. Beer €3; cocktails €5.) The **European Cultural Center of Delphi** (☎22650 82 731) puts on a **Festival of Greek Drama** with performances in the ancient stadium in July and August. They also present temporary international art exhibitions. Contact their office in Athens (☎210 331 2781; epked@culture.gr) for more information. (For more on Greek drama, see p. 28.) Follow the Amphissa/Itea road down the hill out of town to the blue signs, turn right and head up the hill. (Open daily 9am-2pm.) Delphi is home to several other summer **festivals,** so ask around and keep an eye out for posters.

THE ORACLE OF DELPHI

A sacred site from 1500 BC or earlier, the Oracle of Delphi became the most important source of sacred wisdom in the ancient world from around the 7th century BC until the advent of Orthodox Christianity after the 4th century AD. Pilgrims ventured to the Delphic oracle from all over Greece and the Near East (where Alexander the Great had brought Greek culture). After all, the Delphic oracle foretold Cadmus's founding of Thebes and prophesied the horrific fate of Oedipus—to kill his father and marry his

THE LOCAL LEGEND

KNOW THYSELF (OR ELSE

Prophesizing at Delphi followed a strictly regimented procedure. Prophesies were made one time per mont[h] except during 3 winter months, whe[n] it was believed that the spirit of Apoll[o] was absent at Delphi. Arriving pilgrim[s] would cleanse themselves in th[e] Kastalian Spring, pay a tax, and the[n] sacrifice an animal at the Altar o[f] Apollo. Pythia (priestess) uttere[d] prophesies in response to pilgrim[s'] questions. The priests of Apollo woul[d] then interpret the Pythia's words.

The Delphic Oracle was known for giv[-]ing obscure answers to questions. Man[y] a suppliant went home more confuse[d] than he had come, having failed to dra[w] meaning from the answer or havin[g] drawn the *wrong* meaning.

Croesus of Sardis came to the ora[-]cle in the 6th century BC with co[n]cerns about the Persian threat. Th[e] oracle told him, "A great empire wil[l] be destroyed." The king returned t[o] Sardis confident that he woul[d] emerge victorious over the Persian[s,] whose empire was as large as hi[s] own. The oracle had meant his ow[n] great empire would crash—he watche[d] his home fall to Persian invaders. Athenian leader Themistocles fare[d] better when he asked the oracle ho[w] to prepare for another war with eve[r] pesky Persia. He was told to "buil[d] wooden walls." Instead of enclosin[g] Athens's in wooden walls, Themisto[-]cles set to work building a fleet o[f] ships. Only after Athens' decisive vi[c]tory in the First Persian War at th[e] naval battle of Salamis did the Athe[-]nians realize their leader's wisdom.

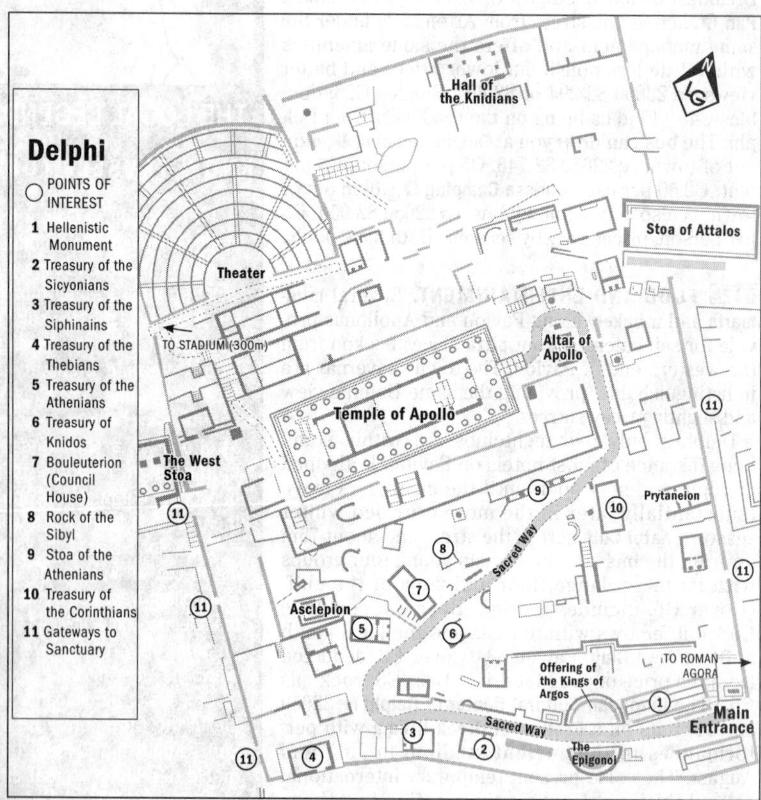

mother. The oracle's authority extended beyond religious matters and personal fortune-telling; Delphic approval sanctioned many political decisions, including the reforms that led to democracy in Athens. The oracle's pronouncements altered nations and set off (or extinguished) military conflicts. Hoping to make powerful friends, city-states from all over the Greek world erected treasuries and donated immense sums in respect to the oracle.

From Delphi, head out of town on the road toward Athens; follow the highway to a paved path on the left, leading to the ruins and museum. At the time of publication, most rooms of the museum were closed for renovations, scheduled to be completed in 2004. Until the rest of the museum opens, admission is free to all. (☎22650 82 312. Open daily 7:30am-6:45pm. Site €6, students and seniors €3, EU students free.)

ARCHAEOLOGICAL SITE. The inscription "Know thyself" (Γνοθι σεαυτον) has long since crumbled from the portal of the ancient temple, but it still governs the meditative atmosphere of peaceful, windswept Delphi. Cut into the steep mountainside, the ancient oracle reigns over the brush-dotted valley below and overlooks eagles that fly below the lofty temple. Now, as then, the **Temple of Apollo** is the centerpiece of the oracle site. A largely wooden incarnation of the temple was burned in 548 BC. It was again shattered, this time by an earthquake, in 373 BC, and it still lies in ruin today. Ancient proclamations etched along the stone base are still visible. To reach the Temple of Apollo, visitors follow the **Sacred Way,** which winds up the site in the footsteps of ancient pilgrims. To the left, the treasuries of the supplicant cities line the Sacred Way, including the reconstructed **Treasury of the Athenians,** excavated in the early 20th century. Past the Temple of Apollo, the **theater,** with its geometric perfection and amazing acoustics, is no less impressive. For a taste of ancient Delphi as a Roman site, make your way up the slick steps to the **stadium** at the very top of the hill. Take a break from the thin air to sit among Roman ghosts in the stadium's seats; then before you go, take a few laps around the stadium and imagine the turning posts and cheering crowds.

ARCHAEOLOGY MUSEUM. The museum contains many artifacts mined from the site: the frieze and two *kouroi* (p. 22) from the Siphian Treasury, the haunting bronze **Charioteer of Delphi,** the altar from the temple of Athena Pronaia, enormous 7th-century bronze shields, and many trinkets offered to the oracle. Nearly all of the collection was unearthed in 1939 by the **Ecole Française d'Athens.** Most labels are written in French and English, but a **guidebook** (€3.50-12) is still helpful.

OTHER SITES. Before calling upon the oracle, pilgrims cleansed themselves both physically and spiritually in the **Kastalian Spring,** 300m past the main ruins along the road to Athens. The remains were covered by rocks until the beginning of this century, when a clever archaeologist cleared them out of the lush ravine. You can still see the niches carved into the rock for votive offerings. Drinking from the spring is said to confer the gift of eloquence. Just past the spring, on the opposite side of the road, are the remains of an ancient **gymnasium.** About 200m farther down the road (also accessible from the gymnasium), the **Temple of Athena Pronaia** served as a lounge for pilgrims before they entered the sanctuary. The three remaining Doric columns of the **Tholos,** a round building used for an unknown purpose, are the sole evidence of its architectural mastery.

GALAXIDI Γαλαξιδι ☎22650

The town shares its name with a drink made of *gala* (milk) and *xithi* (vinegar), which may allude to the bittersweet existence of a seaman's wife—Galaxidi was once a prominent naval base. In its modern incarnation, seafaring has evolved into pleasure boating, as locals lead tours for vacationing Swedes and Germans. Quiet during most of the year, Galaxidi delights visitors with its peaceful waterfront, pebble beaches, and gorgeous views of the surrounding mountains.

On Kon. Satha, off Nik. Mama, the **Church of Agios Nikolaos** houses many fine mosaics. The 13th-century **Monastery of the Metamorphosis,** with sublime wood carvings and a great view of town, is 6km from Galaxidi on the uphill road outside of town. Though the unshaded trip takes an hour by foot, on a cool day the views make it an enjoyable hike; follow K. Papapetrou out of town past the school, beneath the highway, and follow the signs through the terraced orange orchards. Rocky shoreline stretches out past the docks on the forest side of the harbor; small, pebbly **beaches** are scattered throughout. Walk Nik. Mama to the waterfront, then follow the harbor toward the forest to your left until you find a resting place that suits you. Several tiny islands are within easy swimming distance.

Galaxidi shakes off its sleepiness with the Bacchanalian frenzy that is **Carnival,** just before Lent. Ouzo bottles are emptied as fantastically costumed people come from miles around for once-a-year carousing. Revelers gyrate around a fire in traditional dances and throw brightly colored pigments at each other.

Galaxidi's main street, **Nik. Mama,** leads from the town plateia and **bus station** down to the harbor. **Buses** run to **Nafpaktos** (1hr.; 3 per day, 11:30am-5pm; €5) and **Itea** (1hr.; M-F 5 per day, 7:30am-8pm, Sa-Su 4 per day; €1.60), where you can transfer to **Delphi.** Buy tickets at **Kourdisto Portokali Cafe,** around the corner from the bus stop on the right. The **National Bank** with 24hr. **ATM** is several blocks farther down Nik. Mama, past Hotel Poseidon on the left. (Open M-Th 8:30am-2pm, F 8:30am-1:30pm.) **Public toilets** are across the harbor from Nik. Mama before the forest on the right. The **police** (☎22650 41 222) are in the main plateia across from the bus station. A **pharmacy** is one block to the right of the bus station up Nik. Mama. (☎22650 41 122. Open M-Sa 8:30am-1pm and 6-9pm.) Galaxidi's **post office** is next to the bank on Nik. Mama. (Open daily 7:30am-2pm.) **Postal code:** 33052.

From the bus stop, turn right and head down Nik. Mama to find **Hotel Poseidon ❸,** a home-turned-hotel blessed with a friendly manager, Costas, who just may break open a bottle of ouzo on the evening of your arrival. Rooms have A/C, TVs, and sometimes private baths. (☎22650 41 426. Breakfast included. Singles €25-40; doubles €35-50; triples €50-60. Cash only.) Several **domatia** can be found on side streets off Nik. Mama and above the restaurants along the waterfront. **To Perasma ❶,** across from the National Bank, sells typical mainstays at typical prices. (Gyros €1.50. Souvlaki €1.) For a splurge, head to one of the tavernas along the harbor for a great view and tasty seafood. **O Tasos ❸** leads the pack, with a constant crowd vying for their fresh fish (€12-44 per kg) and grilled dishes (€5-6).

NAFPAKTOS Ναυπακτος ☎26340

Nafpaktos has something for the whole family, from *paidi* (child) to *pappou* (grandfather), but shows no signs of becoming the generic, family resort town. Vacationing urbanites and Greek children sunbathe side by side on the city's long, pebbly beaches, which stretch out on both sides of the picturesque Old Port. The tree-lined waterfront avenues are packed with cafes, tavernas, and playground equipment, and are mercifully closed to traffic—you might even see a 14-year-old riding a bicycle instead of a fancy moped.

CENTRAL GREECE

TRANSPORTATION AND PRACTICAL INFORMATION. Buses from points east stop at the base of the main town plateia on **Athinon,** which becomes **Tzavela** and ultimately converges with **Mesologgiou** by the Old Port. One block toward the water from Athinon is Mesologgiou, which runs one way in the opposite direction to Athinon (away from the Old Port). There are two **bus stations** in town, both near the church one street below the main plateia on Athinon. The **first station** is located across the street and just around the corner to the left (standing with your back to the front door of the church). It serves **Delphi** (2hr., 4 per day, €7.20) and **Larisa** (5hr., 8:45am, €19.30). The **second station,** across from the back of the church, serves all other destinations. Buses to: **Athens** (3½hr.; 1 per hr., 4:45am-11:15pm; €13); **Lamia** (3hr.; 10:30am, 3pm; €9.50); **Thessaloniki** (8 hr.; 10:30am, 3pm; €25.30). Take a bus to **Antirrio** (15min.; 2 per hr., 6am-4pm; €1) to catch the ferry that serves the Peloponnese. **Taxis** (☎26340 27 792 or 27 678) and phones are next to the main plateia. In an emergency, contact the **police** (☎26340 27 258). The **National Bank** and **Alpha Bank,** both on Athinon just off the main plateia, **exchange currency** and have 24hr. **ATMs.** (Both open M-Th 8am-2pm, F 8am-1:30pm.) There are **pharmacies** around the plateia and down Athinon, all with varying hours; if one is closed, there should be a sign indicating which others are open. **Hobby Cafe,** on Psani beach, past the Old Port, has **Internet** access. (€5 per hr., €2 min.) The **post office** is several blocks down Athinon from the banks, on the right side of the street. (☎26340 27 232. Open M-F 7:30am-2pm.) **Postal code:** 30300.

ACCOMMODATIONS AND FOOD. **Pension Aphrodite ❷,** on Apokaykou, is two blocks down from the bus stop at the far right end of Gribovo beach (when facing the water). Follow the signs for Hotel Xenia. Just across the street, Aphrodite has private baths, TVs, A/C, and phones. (☎26340 27 370. Singles €20; doubles €30; triples €35. Note there is confusingly also an Aphrodite Hotel in town. Cash only.) Beachfront digs at **Lepanto Beach Hotel ❸**, a short walk down Gribovo past Aphrodite, have A/C, phones, TVs, balconies, and bathtubs. (☎26340 23 931. Breakfast €5. Singles €40-50; doubles €50-60; triples €60-70. AmEx/MC/V.) **Hotel Diethnes ❷** (Διεθηνες), on Mesologgiou, has hardwood floors, balconies, and blindingly white private baths. Look for the purple shutters just past the Old Port plateia. (☎26340 27 342. A/C €2 extra. Singles €25; doubles €30; triples €35.)

Bakeries, souvlaki stands, and fast-food restaurants clutter the central plateia area and Old Port. Head to the waterfront along Gribovo beach (just a few blocks down from the main plateia) for tavernas; veer left for the best prices. The first of the bunch, **O Stavros ❷**, offers a variety of succulent dishes and a great view. (☎26340 27 473. Entrees €3-8. Open daily 11am-1am.) If you find yourself near Psani beach, **Krisiakti ❷**, a couple hundred meters from the Old Port, offers similar fare. (☎26340 29 446. Entrees €3-7. Open daily 10am-midnight.)

SIGHTS AND ENTERTAINMENT. The **Venetian Castle,** one of the most important examples of fortress architecture in Greece, dominates the picturesque town. Besides having the best vista around, the citadel also encloses the tiny **Church of the Prophet Elias,** the remains of a **Byzantine bath** and **church,** and a large **cistern** to help the fortress weather sieges. Its walls, which reach down to the port, formed five zones of fortification, and are now woven into the construction of modern houses on the hill. Footpaths wind around the walls, past fountains, and through century-old gates; one begins off Athinon just past the post office. Look for the cobblestone steps and the sign that says "ΚΑΣΤΡΟ/Castle" on the right. A leisurely walk up to the fortress will take about 30min. When you hit the road just below the main fortifications, follow it uphill 1km to reach the **castle.** Alternatively, drive to the castle by following Athinon-Tzavella past the Old Port where it becomes Mesologgiou; veer right on Thermou and follow the signs.

The **Old Port,** enclosed by low walls and watchtowers, is the site of the town's hottest cafes, and forms a romantic backdrop for any outing. Plaques on the walls commemorate the October 7, 1571 **Battle of Lepanto** and its hero, **Miguel de Cervantes Saavedra.** Both the castle and the Old Port are lit up spectacularly at night. Most leisure time around Nafpaktos is spent on the town's beaches; many locals take an afternoon break to relax on the beach. Nafpaktos's

IN RECENT NEWS

HEY, HEY, WE'RE THE MONKS

Using "the same tools as the Devil," a band of musical monks have successfully worked their way onto the Greek pop scene over the past several years. In addition to spreading their religious message and saving the souls of young people from the temptations of the modern world, the monks have secured chart-topping success—their first two CDs boasted platinum sales in Greece. Their third, *By Your Side,* was launched in 2002.

The 12 unlikely pop stars hail from the monastery of Saint Augustine and Seraphim Sarof in the village of Trikorfo, not far from Nafpaktos. Their catchy tunes have had young Greeks tapping their feet to songs addressing a myriad of issues: loneliness, depression, drug abuse, politics, and globalization to name just a few. However, their deviation from traditional monastic practices has caused a stir among the Orthodox community. A number of bishops have condemned the monks' unique approach to preaching as scandalous.

Yet the monks, who actually perform in their appropriate black Orthodox priest attire, unperturbed by such sharp reprimands, have taken their act on the road, heading to the US to hold concerts in the metropoli of New York, Chicago, and Boston. Trying to conquer the international market, they perform not only in Greek but also in English as their popularity and following grows. All proceeds from the concerts will go toward legal fees for death row inmates of Greek descent in the US.

beaches form a large crescent with the Old Port at its center. Facing the water at the Old Port, **Gribovo beach** is to the left and **Psani beach,** the better choice, to the right. Families dominate Psani beach; small amenities, like playgrounds and a few **public showers,** add to the experience. Cafes and *ouzeria* along Psani beach and in the Old Port are filled with customers 8:30-11:30pm, when those who don't hit the hay hit the clubs.

Club Cinema, featuring a large dance floor and pulsing DJ mixes, is conveniently located one block off Gribovo beach on Apokaykou. (☎26340 26 026. Open F-Sa 11pm-late.) Down Apokaykou (walking away from the Old Port) by Pension Aphrodite is ultra-hip **Macuba,** whose fluorescent lights illuminate the beachfront. (☎26340 26 400. Cover €3. Beer €4; drinks €6. Open daily midnight-late.) Many other clubs open only in the summer—watch out for posters around town. On the roof of Club Cinema is the outdoor movie theater **Ciné-REX,** which features American movies and an incredible vista. (Movies usually 9:30 and 11:30pm. €6.) Nafpaktos's week-long **Carnival** is a fun time for all (though some townsfolk migrate to **Patras's** larger scale festivities), with music, dancing, and free wine and souvlaki.

EVRITANIA Ευριτανια

Often called the "Switzerland of Greece," this mountainous land was once a refuge for Greeks escaping Ottoman rule. Since then it has evolved into a wildlife sanctuary where hikers and adventurers can explore clean air, green forests of fir and walnut, and trails that wander past tiny mountain villages to the highest peaks of the Louchi Mountains. Old churches and shrines dot the mountains and overlook steep gorges where water enthusiasts hop in their rafts, canoes, and kayaks and try to tame the rushing Karpenisiotis, Krikelopotamos, and Tavropos Rivers. The best way to explore Evritania is by foot. Take a stroll up and down the sunny streets of a hillside town or hike to the peak of the closest mountain for a breathtaking change of perspective. A car, however, is the most sensible (and frequently the only) option for reaching the more remote villages—rent one elsewhere before you come; no car rental exists; buses are sporadic and rare in the afternoons.

In winter, backpackers can contact the **Hellenic Alpine Club (EOS),** which runs several mountain refuge huts throughout Evritania. (Karpenisi Office ☎22370 23 051, Lamia 22310 26 786.) The adventurous can outfit themselves at **Trekking Hellas,** past the Karpenisi plateia down Karpenisioti on the right (☎22370 25 940), which offers kayak, rafting, and ski packages. A map of the region is on sale at the *periptero* in the plateia in Karpenisi and is well worth the €6 for hiking routes, a topographical key, and an invaluable guide to the area's history.

KARPENISI Καρπενησι ☎22370

Karpenisi (pop. 10,000), at the tip of a long stretch of hairpinned roadway, is Evritania's relaxed capital and the perfect base for outdoor explorations in the surrounding countryside and villages. Founded when five agrarian settlements in the foothills of Mt. Timfristos merged early in the era of Ottoman rule, Karpenisi suffered for years as an economic backwater, weakened by emigration and unemployment. In the broad main plateia, a floor mosaic spells out the names of the region's old towns. However, in recent years a thriving tourism industry has breathed new life into the city, bringing increased prosperity as Greek and foreign outdoor enthusiasts discover the region's extraordinary beauty. South of Karpenisi, the streets give way to rolling pastures and the Karpenisiotis River gorge.

TRANSPORTATION. **Buses** run to: **Agrinio** (3½hr.; Sa-Th 9am, F 3:15pm; €7.20); **Athens** (5hr.; 9am, noon, 3:30pm; €16.50); **Koryshades** (10min., M-Sa 7:20am, €2.80); **Lamia** (1¾hr.; 4 per day, 6:30am-3:30pm; €4.40); **Megalo Horio** and **Mikro Horio** (20min.; 7am, 1pm; €0.80); **Proussos** (M and F 5:30am and 1pm; €2). Ask at the station about bus service to smaller villages. In winter, buses to the **Velouchi Ski Center** (12km) can be arranged for larger groups. **Taxis** (☎22370 22 666 or 22 100) line up at the stand just downhill from the bus station.

ORIENTATION AND PRACTICAL INFORMATION. Karpenisi sits at the foot of Mt. Velouchi, about 70km west of Lamia in central Sterea Ellada. Everything of importance is within a 5min. walk from the **bus station.** From the station, **Tsamboula** leads downhill to the spacious plateia, where it changes its name to **Zinopoulou.** Past the plateia, the road splits in a "V," with **Karpenisioti** heading down to the right and Zinopoulou continuing on the left. Most of the town's shops are on these two streets. The other main road, **Eth. Antistaseos,** forks off to the right from Zinopoulou at the top end of the plateia. As Eth. Antistaseos passes the plateia, **Grigoriou Tsitsara** branches off to the left, between the church and the OTE, running roughly parallel to Zinopoulou and Karpenisioti. The largest **church** and the **town hall** are on the northern end of the plateia, near a **monument** to Greek soldiers who died in 20th-century wars. Above the bus station, the town climbs up the hillside in a tangle of steep, winding streets and narrow stairways.

Directly across the street from the taxi stand, the **tourist office** is behind an inconspicuous door beneath a green sign. The friendly English-speaking staff offers regional maps and brochures and can help you with hiking, rafting, camping, canyoning, and parachuting excursions. (☎/fax 22370 21 016. Open M-Sa 10am-2pm and 5-8pm, Su 10am-2pm.) A map of Karpenisi and the surrounding villages, including extensive hiking trails, can be purchased at the *periptero* across the street (€6). There are a number of 24hr. **ATMs,** including one at the **National Bank** in the plateia. (Open M-Th 8am-2:30pm, F 8am-2pm.) The 24hr. **police station** (☎22370 89 160 or 22370 22 966) and the **OTE** (open M-F 7:30am-1:30pm) are on Eth. Antistaseos. The **hospital** (☎22370 80 680) is a 10min. walk past the police station; signs point the way. Free **Internet** access is available at the **library** (M-F 4-9pm). To get there, take the first left after the police station and head straight through two intersections. After the second intersection, the library is up the hill about 200m on the left. You can also get connected after 1pm at **Anzonopoulos,** a computer shop on the first street left off of Karpenisioti. (€3 per hr.) The **post office** (open M-F 7:30am-2pm) is off of Karpenisioti, in an alley on the left, before the Dia Discount Supermarket. **Postal code:** 36100.

ACCOMMODATIONS. Though there is no shortage of hotels in Karpenisi, prices aren't budget-friendly, particularly on weekends and during the winter high season. The cheapest option is one of the local **domatia.** The tourist office lists rooms and prices. **Hotel Galini ❷,** Riga Feriou 3, is set back on a quiet side street; to reach it, walk down G. Tsitsara from Eth. Antistaseos and take the second right. True to its name ("serenity"), it offers quiet, comfortable rooms with balconies, fridges, TVs, phones, and private baths. (☎22370 22 914; fax 22370 25 623. Singles €20; doubles €30; triples €40.) Conveniently located to the left of the plateia, **Hotel Apollonion ❸** features modern rooms with TVs, balconies, phones, and gleaming private baths. (☎22370 25 001; www.hit360.com/apollonion/gr. Breakfast €5. Singles €35; doubles €40; triples €50. Prices higher in winter.) Friendly former Bostonian **Konstandinos Kousigos ❸** offers rooms at his house straight up the steps behind the taxi stand, under the white sign advertising domatia. (☎22370

CENTRAL GREECE

21 400. Singles €30; doubles €40.) **Hotel Elvetia ❸,** Zinopoulou 17, has pleasant rooms with TVs, large private baths, phones, and balconies. (☎22370 80 111; fax 22370 80 112. Breakfast included. Singles €30; doubles €40; triples €50.)

FOOD. **Klimatria ❷,** Kosmai Etolou 25, 100m downhill from the top of Eth. Antistaseos, though decorated with antique local handicrafts, has a 1953 Rock-Ola American jukebox that vaults it into the 20th century. The gregarious owner, whose family has owned the restaurant for over a century, will happily translate the Greek menu for you. Excellent seasonal dishes (€4.50-7), including rabbit and rooster, are made from local ingredients. Look for a large yellow awning. (☎22370 22 230. Open 10pm-late.) A short walk beyond Hotel Galini away from the plateia, **Taverna Panorama ❷** serves meat dishes *tisoras* (charcoal grilled) under a thick canopy of leafy vines. (Entrees €3-6.) Directly off the plateia, **Kitsios ❶,** Zinopoulou 13 (☎22370 25 504), soothes the sweet tooth with fresh Greek pastries (€0.40 and up). To scrounge up your own meal, visit the **Panemporiki Supermarket,** down Karpenisioti on the right (open M-F 8am-9pm, Sa 8am-6pm), or **Dia Discount Supermarket,** farther down on the left.

NIGHTLIFE AND ENTERTAINMENT. The afternoon and evening blend seamlessly in Karpenisi as the small cafes, where young Karpenisians chat over iced coffee, slowly evolve into crowded bars with hopping music. Three doors down from the plateia, mild-mannered **Peros** sheds its cafe image around midnight, serving beer with marvelous speed and efficiency. (☎22370 22 382. Beer €3; frappé €2. Open daily 9am-2am.) Later head down the street to **Byzantio,** the late-night bar of choice for most young Karpenisians; pulsing beats give way to more melodic Greek songs as the night wears on. (€3 cover includes 1 drink. Open daily 10pm-3am.) Just past the police station (be on your best behavior) on Eth. Antiostaseos, a number of bars draw revelers out into the night. The most popular is the recently opened **Cinema Cafe.** Its breezy summer bar has great mountain views nearer the plateia. (Beer €2; cocktails €5. Open 9am-late.) **De Facto** has an all-Greek jukebox and outdoor seating. (☎22370 24 455. Cocktails €3-3.50. Open 9am-3am.) About 1.5km south of town on the road to Koryshades, two clubs fill up on weekends with dancers who migrate down from the slopes of the city. At Karpenisi's most popular club, **Nemesis,** tourists and Karpenisians alike groove to house, trance, and Greek pop. (Cover €5, includes 1 drink. Drinks €3-6. Open F-Sa midnight-6am.) Down the road from Nemesis, a replica stagecoach indicates the Old American West-themed **Saloon,** a log cabin where stereos blare American music and would-be cowpokes slug Jack Daniel's and munch on BBQ-flavored potato chips. (☎22370 24 606. Beer €2-5; cocktails €5-6. Open daily 10am-6am.) For live traditional Greek music, head to **Musikes Epafes,** Kosma Aitovou 17, a door down from the Klimataria Restaurant, above the billiard parlor. (☎22370 25 555. Open F-Sa.) Throughout the summer, saints' days are celebrated with morning religious services and revelry at night. In mid-July, the town hosts a 15-day **Yiortes Dassous** ("Celebrations of the Forest") replete with exhibitions, food, and music.

DAYTRIP FROM KARPENISI. Getting to **Proussos** is an adventure in itself; enjoy the roadside scenery and admire your driver's uncanny ability to maintain control of his vehicle as it swerves alongside steep ravines past intermittent, flimsy guardrails, and shrines to drivers killed on the road. The **Monastery of the Virgin of Proussiotissa** is well worth the trip. Clinging spectacularly to the cliffside, the monastery's innermost sanctuary is blasted out of the stone itself and contains a miracle-working icon of the Madonna, said to have been painted by St. Luke the Evangelist. Visitors must dress modestly. They can expect to be offered a piece of *loukoumi* (Turkish jellied candy covered in powdered sugar) by the hospitable monks. In the evenings, monks' chants mingle with the sound of rushing water from the Karpenisiotis River echoing through the ravine. Proussos's **clock tower** belts out the hour from its precarious hilltop perch. The Castle of Karaiskakis is a small stone fortress, now more of a crumbling tower than a castle, near the monastery. The dark **Black Cave,** allegedly an ancient oracle and a hideout for Greek women and children during the War of Independence, is along a trail that begins on the far side of the village near a bridge. Bring a flashlight to explore. Proussos has no hotels, but like most of Evritanian villages, has many homes that offer **domatia** for fairly inexpensive prices; most are on the road through the main village. On the road above the monastery complex, **Proussiotissa ❷** (☎22370 80 768) has a fabulous location with balcony tables overlooking the monastery, clock tower, and gorge below. The friendly, English-speaking owner cooks up local specialties like roast goat with tomato sauce (€5).

Proussos is 15km beyond Megalo Horio. Buses (M and F 5:30am, 1pm; €2.30) run from Karpenisi. You can also catch the bus as it heads by Megalo or Mikro Horio: walk back down to the main road or to the tiny hamlet of Gavros. Ask to be let off at the monastery, on the left side of the road before you enter the village. The afternoon return bus to Karpenisi leaves Proussos at about 3pm.

NEAR KARPENISI

Outside Karpenisi, small villages and traditional settlements lure visitors to gorgeous rural views and hikes; old-fashioned stone houses rest on the shores of lakes while herds of goats snooze on hillsides. Hotels can be expensive in the area; **domatia** offer much better deals. The map of Evritania (€6), available at the *periptero* in Karpenisi's plateia, is crucial for navigating the area.

Closed in by ominous peaks on three sides, **Koryshades** (5km southwest of Karpenisi) is a traditional Evritanian village. To get there, take the early bus from Karpenisi or hire a taxi for the short ride. Stone houses outfitted with elaborate wooden balconies, red slate roofs, and terraced gardens dot the hillsides. The National Council convened in 1944 in the schoolhouse in Koryshades; the site has been turned into a small **museum.** The only hotel and restaurant in the village, named simply **Koryshades ❹** (☎22370 25 102; fax 22370 23 456), offers spectacular but expensive rooms (€40-70) and can provide information on nearby hikes and outdoor activities. West of Karpenisi lies the village of **Klafsion** (8km away), the name of which—derived from the Greek verb "to cry"—is a tribute to the hardships endured by the townspeople when they survived a 279 BC disaster caused by Galates. The church dates from the 5th century and features an ancient mosaic floor. Most of the homes in Klafsion are inhabited by vacationing Greeks for two to three months a year. Beyond lie **East** and **West Frangista** (40km from Karpenisi), home of a fresco-covered church well worth a visit. A hometown Greek feast awaits at the village tavernas where local trout, traditional sausages, *katiki* cheese, and scrumptious country bread satisfy hungry patrons. The **Monastery of Tatarnas,** west of Frangista and 70km from Karpenisi, served as a refuge for rebels against the Turks. The extensive Byzantine art collection includes an icon of "The Lord of Glory," painted in 1350. Backpackers can take the **Trans-European Footpath E4** all the way to **Mount Oxia** in the southwestern extreme of Evritania.

MIKRO HORIO

Fifteen kilometers down the road from Karpenisi and accessible by bus (15min., €0.80) are the "Little Villages," Neo (new) and Paleo (old) Mikro Horio. Paleo Mikro Horio was largely destroyed by a landslide; only a 19th-century church and the village square, consisting of five old water fountains, survived. The cool, shaded plateia overlooks terraced farmland rising from the gorge below. After the disaster, the population relocated down the hill to Neo Mikro Horio (pop. 250) on the slopes of Mt. Helidona. But they couldn't shake their bad luck—bombs scarred the new village and occupying Nazis executed the town's 13 leading dignitaries in 1944. The route to the top of the mountain (3hr.) starts near the bus stop; a view of the river valleys and Kremaston Lake is the reward for the uphill trek. Lodgings range from simple, cheap **domatia** to expensive ski lodge-style hotels. **Taverna Nyonia ❹** has white-walled, tiled rooms, with bathrooms and a small communal kitchen. (☎22370 41 393. Doubles €35.) A small, narrow pathway leads through beautiful farm gardens to an outdoor **taverna ❷** patio where a small menu of mostly grilled meats and salads is offered. (Entrees €5-6.) **Horiatiko ❸,** just as you enter the village from the main road, offers good deals on rooms during low season. Colorful flowers pave the way to beautifully furnished, spacious rooms with large balconies facing the mountains. Guest houses, ideal for families and small groups, are also available for rent. (Singles €30 and up.)

MEGALO HORIO

Megalo Horio (pop. 200) is not so much a village as a handful of stone houses tossed haphazardly down an Evritanean hillside. It is an M. C. Escher utopia precariously tilted to 45 degrees. Houses lean on the mountain and each other for support. Roads turn into staircases and back to roads again. As you stroll from the top of the village down, tin-roofed weather-torn huts gradually develop into sparkling mountain vacation homes. Perched midway up the hillside, the *kafeneion* tables on the plateia overlook the breathtaking gorge of the Karpenisiotis River. An enormous gnarled plane tree shades the plateia and a semi-circle of lime trees tint the summer air with the delicate scent of their blossoms. A few meters above the plateia, the main road in Megalo Horio splits in two. From the left branch begins the trail for the 3hr. climb up Mount Kaliakouda, marked clearly to the top with red blazes. The right branch curves quickly downhill and meanders past gorgeous homes where flowers fill every unused space. Take the same road to the **Folk Art Museum.** (☎22370 41 502. Open F-Su 10am-2pm. Free.)

Reach Megalo Horio by the **bus** (7am, 1pm; €0.80) that runs from **Karpenisi** and through Mikro Horio. Like the rest of Evritania, Megalo Horio has a number of rooms to let scattered around the village. Cheap rooms can be hard to find during high season, however, so look around before settling somewhere. The rooms at **Petrino ❸** have TVs and fireplaces. (☎22370 41 187. Doubles €38.) The **taverna ❷** downstairs has a wide selection of meat dishes as well as a few vegetarian options. Enjoy the clean mountain air, the shade of a twisted old tree, and the view of a river gorge at **Antigoni ❷** (☎22370 41 395) in the plateia. Its staff serves sandwiches, omelettes, and Greek coffee all day.

CENTRAL GREECE

LAMIA Λαμια ☎22310

Drab Lamia serves as a jumping off point for travelers bound for Northern or Central Greece. The city was important during the War of Independence and became the border gateway for the newly independent Greece in 1884. If you find yourself in Lamia for any length of time, its snappy Archaeological Museum, swinging nightlife, and the gardens of Agios Loukas may make your visit more palatable.

TRANSPORTATION. With six intercity bus stations and one local station, Lamia makes for a strangely inconvenient transportation hub. A new, centralized **bus station** is scheduled to open south of the city in early 2004. Directions to the bustling heart of the city depend on where your bus or train pulls in. The local **train station** is on **Kostantinopoulos;** head east (left as you face the tracks) and turn left on **Satovriandou,** which runs northwest to **Pl. Parkou,** one of the city's four central plateias—the southeastern corner of the quadrangle they form. From the bus station serving Karpenisi on **Botsari,** head east (right facing away from the station) half a block to Satovriandou and turn left. If arriving from Athens or Thessaloniki, Satovriandou is just to your left as you face away from the station; turn right to the city center. Buses from Delphi pull in on the west side of **Thermopylon** while those from Larisa, Patras, Trikala, or Halkida stop just off Thermopylon on the eastern side. Walk uphill on Thermopylon, crossing the railroad tracks, until it dead-ends into **Kapodistriou,** where a left brings you to Pl. Parkou. Buses from Volos, Agia Marina, and Raches pull in on **Rozaki Angeli,** to the east of the city center. Facing away from the station, cross the miniscule triangular park and turn right on Kapodistriou. The large bus station at **Papakiriazi 27** (☎22310 51 345 or 51 346), south of the town center and left off Satovriandou, sends buses to **Athens** (3hr.; every hr., 5am-9pm; €13.50) and **Thessaloniki** (4hr.; M-Th, Sa 9am, 3:15pm; F, Su 9am, 3:15, 7pm; €19.10). Take the Athens bus and ask to be let off at **Agios Kostantinos** (45min., €3.30) for the nearest ferries to the **Sporades.** The **Botsari 3** station (☎22310 28 955), just off Satovriandou, sends buses to **Karpenisi** (1½hr.; 5 per day, 7am-9pm; €4.80) and the **Evritania** region. The local station, **Konstantinopoulos 2** (☎22310 51 348), at the southern end of Satovriandou, serves **Thermopylae** (15min.; 5 per day, 8:30am-4:35pm; €1.40) and other small destinations. The station at **Thermopylon 58** (☎22310 35 494), along Kapodistriou from Pl. Parkou and right on Thermopylon, serves **Delphi** (2hr.; 3 per day, 10:40am-7pm; €6.10). The **Thessaly station** (☎22310 22 802), farther down Thermopylon and to the left when it intersects with Nikopoleos has buses to: **Halkida** (2½hr.; 12:45, 7:45pm; €10.10); **Larisa** (2hr.; 3 per day, 11am-6pm; €9); **Patras** (4hr.; noon, 7pm; €12); **Trikala** (2hr.; 8 per day, 9:45am-7:45pm; €6.40). The sixth station, **Rosaki Angeli 69** (☎22310 22 627), down Kapodistriou, runs buses to: the beaches of **Agia Marina** (20min.; every hr., 8am-9pm; €1.10); **Raches** (5min.; 7 per day, 9am-10pm; €2.40); **Volos** (2hr.; Su-F 9am, 3pm; Sa 9am; €8.50). **Local buses** marked "Stavros" (Σταυρος) make stops at **Lionokladi,** departing from the corner of Drosopolou and Hatzopolou at Pl. Parkou. The **town train station,** Konstantinopoulos 1 (☎22310 22 990), across from the local buses, has trains to **Athens** (6am, 5:25pm). Trains from **Lionokladi Station** (☎22310 06 161) go to: **Athens** (3½hr.; 7 per day, 10:15am-7:20pm; €7.10) and **Thessaloniki** (3¾hr.; 8 per day, 9:28am-3am; €9.40). Take the local bus (10min.; 13 per day, 9:10am-7:10pm; €1.40) from the OTE, Averof 28, the third right down E. Venizelou from the southwestern corner of Pl. Parkou.

ORIENTATION AND PRACTICAL INFORMATION. Just inland off the Maliakos Gulf and 160km north of Athens, Lamia climbs gently to a northwesterly ridge, crowned by the **kastro** in the north. The city sprawls outward from the roughly rectangular arrangement of its four central plateias. Southeastern **Pl. Parkou** is broad, crowded, and lined with banks. Maps of Lamia are posted at its northern edge. From Pl. Parkou's northeastern corner, past the National Bank, **Kolokotroni** leads north to leafy and mellow **Pl. Laou,** filled with *kafeneia* and currently torn up by construction. West from Pl. Parkou up **Karagiannopolou** is sleepy, spacious **Pl. Diakou.** Head up Riga Feriaou in the northwestern corner of Pl. Parkou to reach pulsing **Pl. Eleftherias,** home to Lamia's trendiest nightlife. Pl. Eleftherias connects with Pl. Diakou via **Diakou** on its southern side and with Pl. Laou via **Kounoupi** on the east. On the northern side of Pl. Eleftherias, Lamia's largest **church** and the **regional prefecture** (town hall) face each other on the corner of **Ipsilandon.** A network of small streets including **Rozaki Angeli** and **Karaiskaki** interlace the squares and burst with small cafes, shops, and bakeries.

A **tourist kiosk** lies on the western side of Pl. Parkou. Pl. Parkou teems with banks, including a **National Bank** on the corner of Kapodistriou with a 24hr. **ATM.** (Open M-Th 8am-2pm, F 8am-1:30pm.) The **police** are on Patroklou, one street below Pl. Parkou off Satovriandou. (☎22310 22 331. Limited English spoken. Open 24hr.) The 24hr. **hospital** (☎22310 56 100 or 56 200) is north of the city. On the western side of Pl. Eleftherias sits the **OTE.** (Open M, W, Sa 7:30am-2pm; Tu and Th-F 7:30am-2pm and 5:30pm-9pm.) **Bet.Net,** across the street from Hotel Athena on Rozaki Angeli has **Internet** access (€3 per hr; open 8am-2am), as does **Internet Cafe,** Ipsilandon 6 (☎22310 46 315), just north of Pl. Eleftherias. (€4.40 per hr. Frappé €2.50. Open 9am-3am.) The **post office,** on Pl. Diakou, offers **Poste Restante.** (☎22310 23 237; fax 22310 33 727. Open M-F 7:30am-8pm.) **Postal code:** 35100.

ACCOMMODATIONS AND FOOD. Few travelers see more than the bus station on their way through Lamia, so hotels are scarce and expensive. **Thermopylae Hotel ❷,** Rozaki Angeli 36, two blocks east of Pl. Laou, has 15 small but clean and comfortable rooms with TVs, phones, A/C, and baths. (☎22310 26 393 or 22310 21 366. Singles €25; doubles €35; triples €40.) **Hotel Athena ❷,** Rozaki Angeli 41, has cozy rooms featuring wooden floors, private baths, TVs, A/C, and balconies. (☎22310 20 700 or 22310 27 700. Singles €25; doubles €35; triples €40.) **Hotel Neon Astron ❷,** on Pl. Laou, offers unspectacular accommodations at decent prices. (☎22310 22 246. Doubles €32; triples €35.) Lamia is a diner's paradise: virtually every street and side alley is crammed with pizza joints, gyro stands, *ouzeria*, tavernas, pastry shops, and coffee bars. For fresh fruits and veggies, head to the markets along Rozaki Angeli and Othonos, both off Pl. Laou. **Ouzo Melathron ❷,** off Pl. Laou on Aristoteli (the stairs on the northern side), delivers grilled specialties in a romantic courtyard separated from the bustle of the plateias. The *pilino* (pork with cheese, mushrooms, and tomato sauce; €4.70) is worth a try. (☎22310 31 502. Entrees €4-7. Open daily 1-5pm and 9pm-1am.) **Aman Aman ❷,** on Androutsou (the alley to the right on Kounoupi coming from Pl. Laou), serves tasty *mezedes* for €3.50-6.50. (Open 9pm-12:30am.)

SIGHTS. The imposing remains of the **kastro** loom eerily over the city in nighttime illumination. Built in the Classical Period, it has undergone many renovations under the Romans, Franks, Catalans, and Ottomans. Before Greece's 1884 annexation of Thessaly and Domokos, Lamia's kastro served as the core of the country's border defenses. The barracks building, built by King Otto in 1880, was used until World War II. It now serves as a spacious and well-organized **Archaeological Museum,** displaying finds from the Neolithic to Roman Periods found in tombs outside Lamia. Aside from the numerous ceramic figurines and amphoras, highlights include the earliest preserved vase depicting a naval battle and a fearsome collection of rusty weaponry. (Head east out of Pl. Parkou on Kapodistriou and make the 2nd left onto Amalias. Walk up the hill and cross Eklision when Amalias dead-ends to walk up a stone stairpath. Turn right and follow the road at the top of the stairs, with the kastro on your left. ☎22310 29 992. Castle open Tu-Su 8:30am-2:30pm during the summer. Museum open Tu-Su 8:30am-3pm. €2, students and under 18 free.) The way to the **Gardens of Agios Loukas** (on Agios Loukas hill) begins at the top of Pl. Diakou behind a gloriously posed **Statue of Athanasios Diakos,** his sword broken in battle. A War of Independence hero, he was burned to death in Lamia by the Turks in 1821. Continue up the steps beyond to reach the gardens.

NIGHTLIFE AND ENTERTAINMENT. Young people congregate nightly in Pl. Eleftherias. For those looking to dance, there are plenty of clubs; for a more sedentary night, find a table at one of the bars in northeastern Pl. Eleftherias. **Venezia,** on Dikou between Pl. Diakou and Pl. Eleftherias, is *the* place to see and be seen for Lamia's cosmopolitan youth. (☎22310 46 525. Beer €3.50; cocktails €5. Open 9am-late.) **Aroma Musicafe,** next door to Venezia, vies fiercely for the title of Best in Show. (☎22310 36 808. Beer €5; cocktails €7). The **Municipal Theatre** (☎22310 33 325), on Ipsilandon, past the Internet Cafe, offers plays, music, and movies.

DAYTRIP FROM LAMIA. More a highway roadstop than a destination in itself, **Thermopylae** (Θερμοπυλες), 18km south of Lamia, is richer in history than anything else. As the gateway to southern Greece, Thermopylae's strategic location has made it a prime target for invading armies for thousands of years. **Leonidas** and his army of 300 Spartans fought to their heroic deaths here in 480 BC, holding back Xerxes's vast Persian army (estimated by the hyperbolic historian Herodotus to be five million strong) long enough for the united city-states to consolidate their power for victories at Salamis and Plataea. More recently Ottomans and Nazis fiercely attacked the straits. Today the sulfurous **hot springs** (☎22310 30 065; open daily 6:30am-1:30pm), originating in the mountains above, attract visitors suffering from rheumatism, arthritis, gynecological complaints, and respiratory illnesses, among others, as well as those just looking to relax. There is a small swimming pool (€3) and numerous private bathtubs (€3.50) filled with the 42-44°C waters. Legend holds that Thermopylae's waters once helped Hercules regain his strength.

From the hot springs parking lot (with your back to the baths) take a right down the dirt path. Continue through a highway underpass, heading right once you emerge. When you reach the building with the orange roof, turn right on the paved road that crosses a stream. The road leads to a highway rest stop with a **plaque** commemorating the battles in Greece and Crete during World War II, the **Monument to the Thespians,** and the **Statue of Leonidas.** The defiant inscription on the statue reads "Molon Labe" ("come and get it"). Across the highway is the **archaeological site,** where you can scramble around a network of trails, see the ruins of a Classical-era wall, and catch the views from craggy outlook points. Just beyond the Leonidas monument, a dirt road runs between an olive grove and the highway to Thermopylae village, consisting of a deserted square with a bone-dry fountain and some crumbling benches. Flag down one of the frequent buses to **Lamia** (€1.20) here at the rusty **bus stop.** (Take the bus from Lamia's local station (15min.; 6 per day, 8:30am-4:30pm; €1.20). Ask to be let off at the baths (μπανιο, BAN-yo) not the village of Thermopylae. To return, walk 1.5km to the village and catch the bus there.)

AGIOS KONSTANTINOS Αγιος Κωνσταντινος ☎22350

Agios Kostantinos is situated at the meeting point of the mountainous mainland and the Aegean. As the closest port to Athens with ferries to the Sporades, it serves as a gateway for those taking to the sea. It doesn't warrant a long stay, but its small town charms make waiting for ferry or bus easy to bear.

When arriving by ferry, the **bus station** (☎22350 32 223) is 150m to the left (facing inland) along the waterfront, just before Galaxias Supermarket. **Buses** go to: **Athens** (2½hr.; 15 per day, 5:45am-10pm; €10.30); **Lamia** (45min.; every hr., 7:30am-7:30pm and 8:45-11:45pm; €3.20); **Thessaloniki** (4hr.; 7am, 2pm; €22). The pier, immediately seaward of the plateia, serves both **ferries** and **Flying Dolphins** (☎22350 31 874). Buy your tickets at the right side of the plateia (facing inland). Two high-speed ferries with prices and schedules varying with the season leave daily for **Skiathos** (2hr., €20.80) and **Skopelos** (3hr., €27.90). Ferries also go to **Alonnisos** (5½hr., 2 per week, €13.60). Flying Dolphins go daily to: **Alonnisos** (2¾hr., €27.60); **Skiathos** (1½hr., €20.80); **Skopelos** (2½hr., €27.90). Check departure times posted outside of the ticket offices or call ahead. (☎22350 32 444 or 32 445; fax 22350 32 234.) **Taxis** (☎22350 31 850) line up behind the church. The **port police** (☎22350 31 920), along the harbor, can help with ferry schedules. Facing seaward from the plateia, a right-hand turn toward the bus station takes you past the **National Bank** (open M-Th 8am-2pm, F 8am-1:30pm) with its 24hr. **ATM.** A left turn from the plateia takes you past the **OTE** (open M-F 8am-3:10pm) and a sign for the **post office,** 20m inland on a street just parallel to the park. (Open M-F 7:30am-2pm.) **Postal code:** 35006.

Accommodations in Agios Kostantinos are somewhat limited. The first on the strip of hotels along the water to the right of the plateia (facing inland), **Hotel Olga** ❷ is both classy and reasonably priced. Rooms have A/C, phones, TVs, and views from private balconies. (☎22350 31 766; fax 22350 32 266. Singles €23-26; doubles €33-40; triples €40-48.) In the center of town, **Hotel Poulia** ❷, on a street off of the right side of the plateia, features small rooms with varying levels of amenities, from stark singles to the works: TVs, A/C, and private baths. (☎22350 31 663. Singles €20-25; doubles €29-35; triples €38.) You can devour delectable souvlaki (€1-1.50), play backgammon, and do some quality people-watching just past the main plateia. The bakery **Aggelozumoton Asteriou** ❶, sells bread and pastries.

THESSALY Θεσσαλια

Thessaly provides travelers with a rare mix of the mundane and the ethereal. The region is the earthly anchor to the transcendent Meteora monasteries; at the same time, it harbors some of Greece's drabber cities. Medea supposedly dropped her witch's potions in Thessaly after returning here with Jason from Colchis (modern Georgia), and the legend won the region a reputation for sorcery and magical plants in ancient times. Thessaly's plains were once home to farmers who tended sheep and goats in summer before returning home to fish from the waters of the Pinios River. In these out-of-the-way places to the north of Karpenisi and in the green Pelion Peninsula, you'll find little English and much genuine hospitality, folk songs, and reverence for all things *hiropitios* (hand-made; "poetry of the hands").

VOLOS Βολος ☎24210

Volos looms large in some of ancient Greece's best-loved myths. Jason and the Argonauts set sail from Volos on their quest for the Golden Fleece, a legend the city won't let its visitors forget: two important streets and half a dozen hotels are named after the voyaging Argonauts. A century ago, Volos was a quiet hamlet on the Pagasitic Gulf. But after the 1922 population exchange (p. 13), Orthodox refugees from Turkey invigorated the port town with their love for carousing: Volos quickly became famous for the *ouzerias* that popped up along the water. Today Volos is a fast-growing industrial center and transportation hub, but on the short waterfront walk eastward from the bus station toward the beach, the cranes and oil tankers quickly become a memory. Two of the four main roads running parallel through the city are pedestrian avenues. Come nightfall, strolling couples fill the harborside, fruit vendors hawk their sweet produce, and dozens of cafes and seafood restaurants push tables up to the water.

TRANSPORTATION

Ferries: To: **Alonnisos** (5hr., daily, €15.76); **Skiathos** (2¼hr., 2-3 per day, €14); **Skopelos** (3½hr., 1-2 per day, €14). Ferries for the more distant islands of **Tinos, Paros, Santorini,** and **Crete (Iraklion)** are less frequent. Several waterfront agencies sell tickets.

Flying Dolphins: 3 per day to: **Alonnisos** (2¾hr.; 9:30am, 1:15, 7:30pm; €26.30) via **Glossa** (1½hr., €21.20); **Skiathos** (1¼hr., €19); **Skopelos** (2¼hr., €24.60). Tickets available at any of the ticket agencies near the ferry pier such as **Falcon Tours** (☎24210 21 626 or 24210 25 688; www.dolphins.gr).

Trains: ☎24210 24 056 or 24210 28 555. 1 block west of the tourist office. From town, turn right at the first street past the tourist office. Walk 2-3min. down the road parallel to the track. Intercity to **Larisa** (45min., 6:15am, €5.90). Regular train to **Larisa** (1hr.; 12 per day, 7am-11:21pm; €2.10). For **Athens** and **Thessaloniki,** passengers must travel to Larisa and change trains.

Buses: ☎24210 33 254 or 24210 25 527. In the Old Town, all the way at the end of Lambraki. To: **Athens** (4½hr.; 11 per day, 5:45am-10pm; €18.70); **Larisa** (1hr.; 12 per day, 6am-9pm; €3.80); **Makrynitsa** (45min.; M-F 9 per day, 6:15am-8:45pm; €0.95) via **Portaria; Milies** (1hr.; 6 per day, 5:45am-6pm; €1.80); **Thessaloniki** (3hr.; 8 per day, 5:45am-8:30pm; €12.50); **Trikala** (2½hr.; 4 per day, 6:30am-7pm; €9.30); **Tsagarada** (1½hr.; 3 per day, 5:15am-3:30pm; €3.50); and other destinations. Inquire at the bus station or tourist office. Most villages have daily service and can be reached in less than 3hr. Service reduced Sa-Su and in winter.

Taxis: ☎24210 27 777.

Car Rental: Avis, Argonafton 41 (☎24210 20 849; fax 24210 22 849), rents mopeds (€30 per day) and cars (€55 per day and up). **European Car Rental,** Iasonos 83 (☎24210 36 238; fax 24210 24 192) also rents cars (€50 per day and up).

ORIENTATION AND PRACTICAL INFORMATION

Volos's **bus station** lies west of town on **Lambraki,** an easy 15min. walk from the city and the waterfront. This main road, which leads from the bus station to town, runs past the train station and **Riga Fariou Park.** Lambraki splits at a fountain to become **Dimitriados** on the left and **Iasonos** on the right; both run parallel to **Argonafton** on the waterfront. Dimitriados and Iasonos are covered with fast-food joints and ice cream shops for the local youth while the waterfront Argonafton is filled with overpriced tourist tavernas and trendy local bars. Escaping the waterfront you pass the long seaside park, and in about 10min. reach the large **Church of Agios Konstantinos,** easily visible from the docks jutting out into the harbor. Here, Argonafton and Dimitriados join to become **Nik. Plastira.** This quieter street leads past the locals' ouzeria to the hospital and the Archaeological Museum before ending at the pleasant **beach** in the residential section of town. **Ermou,** the next street inland after Dimitriados and running parallel to it, is a pedestrian street lined with shops selling women's clothes, shoes, and the occasional icon. Ermou leads to an open plateia containing the **Church of Agios Nikolaos.**

Tourist Office: Koumoundourou 31, (☎24210 20 273). Walk east along Ermou with the sea on your right and take a left onto Koumoundourou; it's on the left. Information about Volos as well as the Pelion Peninsula. **Maps** available. Open M-F 8am-2:30pm.

Banks: Major banks are found on Iasonos including the **National Bank** (☎24210 23 382); **Agricultural Bank** (☎24210 23 411 or 24210 54 030); and **Bank of Greece** (☎24210 23 442.) Most offer **currency exchange** (M-Th 8am-2pm, F 8am-1:30pm) and **ATMs.** There's also a **Citibank** on the corner of Argonafton and El. Venizelou with a 24hr. **ATM.**

Police: ☎24210 39 061. Open 24hr.

Tourist Police: 28 Oktovriou 179 (☎24210 39 065). Helpful staff speaks English. Open daily 8am-10pm.

Hospital: ☎24210 27 531. Next to the museum on the eastern waterfront. A gorgeous new facility built specifically in time for the Olympics. Open 24hr.

OTE: On the corner of El. Venizelou and Sokratous, across from the fruit market. Open 7:30am-3pm.

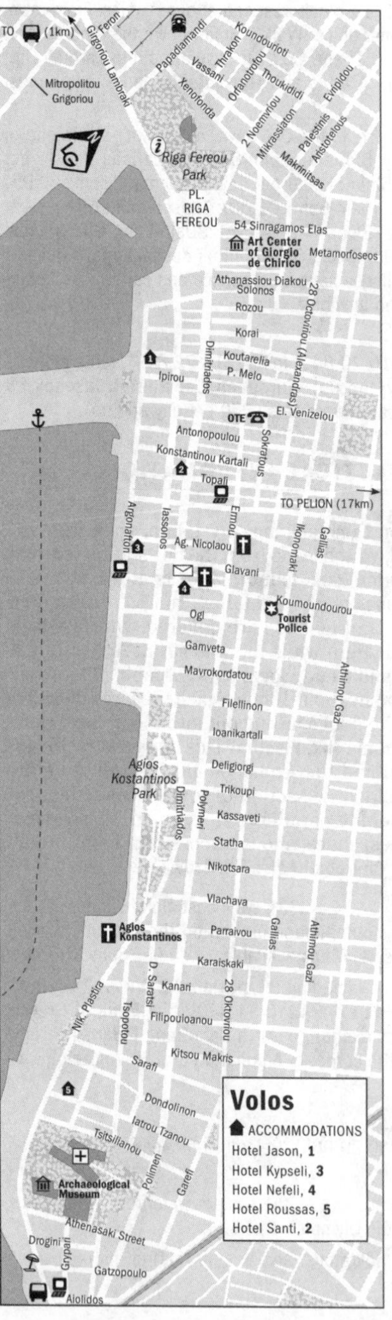

Internet Access: Magic Cafe, Dimitrides 124 (☎24210 25 291), in a game arcade, has 25 terminals and a printer. €3.50 per hr.; black and white printing €0.29 per page, color €0.88. Open 1pm-3am. **Diavlos Youth Center,** Topali 14 (☎24210 25 363), off Dimitriados, has superior Internet prices. €1.50 per hr. Open 10am-3pm and 5-10pm. **M@gic Cafe,** Aiolidos 2 (☎24210 27 310), at the end of Nik. Plastira and directly across from the bus station, has 3 computer terminals. Internet €3 per hr. Frappé €2.50. Open 9am-1pm.

Post Office: ☎24210 31 815. At the intersection of Dimitria and Ag. Nikolau. **Poste Restante** available. Open M-F 7:30am-8pm. **Postal code:** 38001.

ACCOMMODATIONS

Volos's hotels vary little in size, location, appeal, and amenities and are almost all relatively expensive. Most of the cheaper options are clustered along the waterfront or on the small streets that lead away from the harbor. As usual, negotiating is a potent price slasher.

Hotel Roussas, Iatrou Tzanou 1 (☎24210 21 732; fax 24210 22 987), on the corner of Plastira and Iatrou Tzanou, midway between Ag. Konstantinos church and the beach; look for the purple balconies. In a peaceful section of town, the recently renovated Roussas features rooms with refreshing sea breezes, baths, phones, A/C, TVs, and balconies. The owner speaks fluent English. A computer in the lobby has Internet access. Singles €25; doubles €32; triples €38. ❷

Hotel Nefeli, Koumoundourou 10 (☎24210 30 211 or 30 313; ababis@kentavros.gr). Particularly nice rooms with smooth wood flooring, yellow walls, and wood furniture. TVs, A/C, phones, balconies, and spotless baths with tubs. Singles €33; doubles €47; triples €55. ❸

Hotel Jason, P. Melo 1 (☎24210 26 075; fax 24210 26 975), easy to find on the waterfront, across from the ferry dock. A good deal considering its convenient location. Most of the gleaming, white rooms have balconies overlooking the waterfront. All have phones, baths, fans, and TVs. Singles €25; doubles €40; triples €50. ❸

Hotel Kypseli, Ag. Nikolaou 1 (☎24210 24 420 or 24210 26 020). The prominent sign for this harborside hotel is visible from the waterfront. Spacious rooms with views, balconies, A/C, baths, phones, and TVs. Singles €30; doubles €40; triples €50. ❸

Hotel Santi, Topali 13 (☎24210 33 341; fax 24210 33 343), off Argonafton. Basic, dim rooms with interesting color scheme—green linoleum floors and pink walls. All rooms have private baths, TVs, phones, A/C, and small balconies. Singles €27; doubles €41; triples €50. ❸

FOOD

A **supermarket,** on Iasonos, one block up from the ferry dock, and a **farmers' market,** along Lambraki toward the bus station, provide provisions for a seaside picnic. For those with a little change remaining, a euro binge of ouzo and *tsipouradika* at one of Volos's signature waterfront ouzerias is sure to be memorable. Each has a delightful selection of *mezedes*—seafood plates with *garides* (prawns) and *ohktopodthi* (octopus). **Halabalias** ❷ is hidden on a side street off the plateia of Ag. Nikolaos church. Walk to the church and ask any local to point you there. A quiet neighborhood taverna, Halabalias has no menu. Walk inside to view the three or four deliciously filling homestyle meals prepared for the day. (Entrees €4-6.) **Klasico** ❸, on Argonafton by the ferry docks, is a typical ouzeria. (☎24210 32 891. Entrees €4.50-14.) **Rotonda** ❷, Plastira 15, past the Church of Ag. Konstantinos on the eastern edge of town, specializes in fresh fish served whole, Rotonda offers delicious grilled calamari and swordfish souvlaki. Walk into the kitchen to pick your critter, which they'll grill up fresh. (☎24210 34 973. Entrees €5.50-9.) Find Italian fare at **Casa Pizzeria** ❷, on the waterfront between Ag. Nikolaou and Koumoundourou and next to Goody's. (☎24210 24 500 or 24 211. Entrees €3.50-€7.)

SIGHTS

The **Archaeological Museum,** Athonassaki 1, a 20min. walk along the water from the ferry docks, occupies a lovely Neoclassical mansion. Check out the painted grave *steles* from ancient Demetrias in Room 4 and the rather morbid reconstructed tombs in Room 6. The panoply of miniature Neolithic objects in Room 3 includes figurines, seals, spindle wheels, bits of jewelry, carbonized seeds, and small tools of bone and stone. (☎24210 25 285. Open Tu-Su 8:30am-3pm. €2, students and seniors €1, EU students free.) Inquire here to pick up English pamphlets with information on the nearby archaeological sites at **Dimini** and **Sesklo.** Sesklo is the oldest known settlement in Thessaly and has the oldest acropolis in Greece; the sites represent two of the oldest sites in the region: Dimini dates from 4000 BC and Sesklo from 6500 BC. The **Art Center of Giorgio de Chirico,** Metamorphoseos 3, around the corner from Hotel Ialkos, showcases Greek landscape paintings. (☎24210 31 701. Open M-F 10am-1pm and 6-9pm, Sa 10am-1pm, Su 6-9pm. Free.) The **Kitsos Makris Museum,** Afendoli 50 (a.k.a. Kitsos Makris 50), includes works by folk painters **Theophilos** (p. 26) and **Christopoulos.** (☎24210 37 119. Open M-F 8:30am-2pm, Su 10am-2pm. Free.)

Volos, like other Greek metropolises, will play a part in the **2004 Olympic Games.** The **Panthessiliko Stadium,** which can accommodate up to 20,000 screaming fans, will host limited soccer competitions. Another smaller stadium accompanies it. Both venues are located 5km out of town, just outside the suburb of Nea Ionio. At the time of the Games, when the city is expected to swell with tourists, large cruise liners anchored in Volos harbor will supply extra accommodations.

NIGHTLIFE

The waterfront between the docks and Ag. Konstantinos turns into a hive of activity at night with revelers spilling out of cafes onto the streets. In the quiet morning or afternoon, you'll wonder how the thousands of tables that stretch for 0.5km down the waterfront are ever as packed as they are at night. Each of the myriad cafes has its own character; you can window shop while taking a traditional Greek *volta* (evening stroll) down the water's edge. Young Greeks congregate at **Cafe Memory** and **Cafe Magic,** sitting side by side on Argonafton, chatting over the loud music and pings of arcade games. A few doors down, **Lirikon** is a little more mellow; the focus here is soccer on the two big-screen TVs. By the museum and the beach, bars toward the east dominate with pounding beats and tight black pants. **Ammos** and **Yiousouri,** side by side on the beachfront across from Rotonda, play Pop and house music. (Beers €3-4; cocktails €4. Open nightly.) After imbibing your fill, head to one of the local clubs including **Blaze** (☎24210 88 332) or **Plastique,** by the train station. For a truly wild time with a slightly heftier price tag, grab a cab (€4) to **Alykes.** This beach suburb hosts the locals' favorite dives: **Astra** (☎24210 62 182), meaning "the stars," and **Domata** (☎24210 88 079), more humorously meaning "tomatoes." For traditional Greek *bouzouki* dancing and *rebetika* tunes head to equally massive **Fengaria** (☎24210 88 733), also in Alykes.

MOUNT PELION PENINSULA Ορος Πηλιο

Way back before propriety, the Pelion Peninsula was home to a group of rather rowdy centaurs. These mythical half-men, half-horses, well known for their insatiable sex drives, had their way with whatever hot, young nymphette they could find. Chiron, a healer and tutor to Achilles, settled in Pelion despite its citizenry; its abundant supply of over 1700 medicinal herbs lured him here. The cool, moist peninsula is conducive to this variety of flora, and tourists tired of the scorching sun appreciate this climate. Over the years, the mountains of Pelion have protected the area from invasion. While the rest of Greece groaned under Ottoman rule, the peninsula was a virtually autonomous center of Greek nationalism.

MAKRYNITSA Μακρυνιτσα ☎24280

In Makrynitsa, one of Pelion's most popular villages, a wide flagstoned path bends around well preserved *archondika* (mansions) to one stunning lookout point after another. Thanks to its designation by the European Community as a protected traditional settlement, the town's roads are closed to cars. While this may bring peace and quiet within town, the outskirts are a mess of traffic and tour bus gridlock. On the plateia, five immense age-old trees form a dome of green overhead, keeping the square in perpetual shade. Nicknamed "the balcony of Pelion," the town overlooks the Pagasitic Gulf like a box seat in a giant opera house. At nightfall, the valley fills with deep indigo, broken only by the shimmer of city lights from Volos far below.

TRANSPORTATION AND PRACTICAL INFORMATION. Makrynitsa is accessible by daily buses from **Volos** (45min.; 9 per day, 6:15am-8pm), which twist their way up the mountainside and through the neighboring village of **Portaria.** From the bus turn-around, take a short walk up the hill to the town parking lot, where a low road (17 Martiou) and a high road lead to the plateia. The low road passes various shops purveying both tourist kitsch and local medicinal and kitchen herbs. The high road begins with a steep flight of stone steps and runs past the village **clock tower** and the **Kimisi Theotokou church.** In Portaria you can catch buses to other Pelion destinations, including the beaches at **Agios Yiannis** and **Milopotamos.** A **tourist information booth,** on the side of the road leading to the village just after the bus stop, offers helpful maps and advice on touring the area. (☎24280 90 150. Open Sa-Su.) A **mailbox** and **payphones** are readily available in the plateia. 24hr. **ATMs,** a **post office,** and a **police station** (☎24280 99 105) can also be found in Portaria, a 20min. walk from the parking lot along the mountain road.

ACCOMMODATIONS AND FOOD. Because of its protected status, staying in Makrynitsa at high season will cost a fortune (average single €65). Luckily for summer travelers, this is perhaps the only Greek region where longer days herald the low season. For further savings, nearby Portaria offers several exceptionally cheap **domatia** (average single €20; double €30). Portaria is also filled with upscale winter tourist hotels, which offer somewhat cheaper prices and the same posh rooms to summer travelers. In Makrynitsa, **Hotel Achilles ❸,** on the right just before you reach the plateia via the low road, has wood-panelled walls and red-tiled floors covered with colorful mats. Gorgeous rooms have TVs, phones, baths, and priceless views; some have balconies. (☎24280 99 177; fax 24280 99 986. Singles €30; doubles €40; triples €50.) Next door is **Hotel Centavros ❸,** which offers similarly well decorated rooms with TVs, phones, and bathrooms. (☎2428 99 075; fax 2428 90 085. Singles €33; doubles €39). In Portaria, two adjacent accommodations on the northern side of the plateia, **Hotel Pelia ❸** (☎24280 99 290; fax 24280 99 840; singles €40; doubles €50) and **Hotel Filoxenia ❸** (☎24280 99 160; singles €35; doubles €45), offer rooms perched on top of the immense patio below. Both hotels have TVs, baths, and breakfast.

A number of small restaurants offer outdoor dining and spectacular views from elevated verandas. Most affordable is the local ouzeria **A-B ❷,** past the plateia on the small trail that skirts the church. From their porch perch at the end of town, patrons have a superb view of Makrynitsa as well as Volos and the gulf far below. (☎24280 99 083. Entrees €4-6.) Slightly more touristed is **Galini ❷,** which overlooks the northern end of the plateia and is next to the large fountain. Sentimental Greek tunes saturate the atmosphere as patrons feast on *spetsofai* (spicy sausage) and rabbit stew. (☎24280 99 256. Open 9am-midnight.) Across the way, **Pantheon ❷** monopolizes the spectacular view of the Pagasitic Gulf. Tables for two against the railing provide a romantic setting to sip a frappé and while away an afternoon. For dinner, the *moschari* and *kotopoulo kokkonisto* (braised veal and chicken, respectively) are equally delicious. (☎24280 99 143. Entrees €4-7.)

SIGHTS. Makrynitsa's **Museum of Folk Art and the History of Pelion** lies down a path that begins to the left of the church in the plateia. Follow the signs about 75m down the windy path. Housed in a converted 1844 mansion, the museum highlights old *tsipouro* stills and paintings by **Christopoulos,** all of which depict ships, gorgons, and sundry sea-related subjects. (☎24280 99 505. Open Tu-Su 10am-2pm and 6-10pm. €2.) In the plateia, the building across from the church contains a somewhat dim wall mural painted by folk artist Theophilos himself (p. 26). Remarkable **churches** include the diminutive **Church of Agios Yiannis the Baptist** in the main plateia and the peaceful, functional church of **Kimisi Theotokou,** which once housed the *Krifto Skolio,* a secret school that taught the forbidden Greek language during the Ottoman Era. The town's churches remain open at the whim of their caretakers; early to mid-morning and evenings are your most likely opportunities for a visit. From the main parking lot, the narrow road leads steeply uphill to the **Monastery of Agios Gerasimos** (20min. by foot). The view alone is worth the trip. (Open 7am-noon and 4-6pm.) The town's old houses are a sight unto themselves; stained glass lanterns, false painted windows, and symbols to protect against evil spirits festoon the outer walls. If you've ever wondered what it must be like to live inside a tree trunk, Makrynitsa is well equipped to give you some idea. Just by the door or the main church in the plateia stands a tall, leafy tree with a hollowed out trunk and a handy opening that lets you slip in and out.

AGIOS IOANNIS Αγιος Ιωαννης ☎24210

If Makrynitsa seduced you with its voluptuous views, the neighboring towns on the opposite side of Pelion will have you panting at first sight. In contrast to the brown scrub covering the western slope of Pelion, the east is a wonderland of forests, ferns, and fog. In the mornings the area assumes the character of a dewy wet coast, but when the fog burns off in the afternoon it becomes a hiker's and quiet beach-goer's paradise. Basically a tourist resort town created by the Volos-based tour operator Les Hirondelles, Ag. Ioannis has little to offer travelers not staying with them. Having the cheapest prices in the area, however, makes it an excellent base for exploring the coves and *kalderimi* (laid stone trails) of Mouresi.

TRANSPORTATION AND PRACTICAL INFORMATION. Buses (☎24210 33 254) leave daily for **Volos** (1½hr.; 2 per day, 7:30am-4:30pm; €3.50) from in front of the kiosk in the center of the strip. The town lies completely along a beachfront main street. Beginning at the docks just beyond the road leading up to the main highway 6km above, the beach road runs past the Les Hirondelles office, hotels, bars, and restaurants to the town parking lot beside the river. Here a branch continues across the river ford—only pedestrians can use the bridge—to end 100m further at the beach of **Papa Nero.** A right turn at the parking lot leads 100m up to a left turn onto the windy seaside lane for **Damouhari.** Continuing instead to the right leads one back to the highway. The **tourist police** located in the parking lot dispense maps and pamphlets. (☎24260 31 218; www.dimosmouresiou.gr. Open M-F 10am-4:30pm.) More detailed information, taxis (€15 to Tsangaradha), boats (€55 per day), motorbikes (€20 per day), and hotel accommodations are available from the **Les Hirondelles** office. (☎24260 31 181; www.les-hirondelles.gr. Open daily 9am-10pm.) The **police** can be reached at ☎24260 49 222, and for **first aid,** call ☎24260 31 950. For more serious problems, a **hospital** (☎24260 22 2222) is 30km away in Zagora. **Internet** access is available but expensive (€10 per hr.) at Hotel Kentrikon, in the alley between the pizzeria and Kyma Taverna. A **post office** and **ATM** are available 1hr. away in Tsangaradha (p. 237).

ACCOMMODATIONS AND FOOD. Many of the hotels in Ag. Ioannnis proper are controlled by Les Hirondelles and are rather expensive for travelers not associated with their package tours. The best area deal, hidden on a gravel path 300m past the river on the coastal road to Damouhari, is well priced **Hostel Katerini ❷,** complete with views, kitchens, and private baths. (☎24260 31 624. Singles €25; doubles €40.) Another budget option is **Eleni ❸,** just across the river on the road to Papa Nero beach. Its large clean rooms have baths, TVs, and often kitchenettes. (☎24210 62 157 or 24260 31 664. Singles €30; doubles €40.) **Hotel Martha ❸,** located toward the parking lot end of the strip, has clean rooms, which could not be any closer to the ocean, with private baths. (☎24260 31 406. Doubles €30-40; triples €45.) Also notable is **Hotel Kochyli ❸,** in the direction of the docks. It has TVs and telephones in addition to bathrooms. (☎24260 31 229; fax 24260 31 092. Singles €30-45; doubles €40-55.) There is also a campground **Papa Nero ❶,** near its namesake beach beyond Eleni. The campground offers clean baths and ocean-front sites. (☎24260 31 319. €4.50 per person, €4 per tent, €3 per car. Electricity €2.50.) The strip is dominated by tavernas, cafes, and bars. Of note are the two inexpensive **sweet shops** ❶ (ζαχαροπλαστειες, zah-cha-ro-plah-STEE-es) and reasonably priced pizzeria **Plazza** ❷. (☎24260 32 110. Pizzas €4 and up.). For a truly good meal at the same price as an Ag. Ioannis pizza, follow the trail to Damouhari (below).

DAMOUHARI Δαμουχαρη AND TSANGARADHA Τσαγαραδα

In contrast to the packaged tourism of Ag. Ioannis, both Damouhari and Tsangaradha are quiet, traditional villages. Damouhari consists of a handful of houses and a gorgeous cove. Next to the cove is a telephone and a convenience store for snacks. In the secluded cove you will find **Palia Damouhari** ❷. (☎24260 49 175. Feta €2.40. Octopus €7.50. Chicken €4.40. *Halva* €1.50. Open 8am-midnight.)

Stunning Tsagaradha offers views of both immaculate gardens cascading downhill into the violent bluffs and the peaceful Sporades sitting in the far distance. Though reachable from Ag. Ioannis by climbing far up to the highway and then descending back down again, it is most quickly and most spectacularly approached by walking the coastal lane to its end in Damouhari, then climbing the bluffs on a *kalderimi*. Tsangaradha has succumbed to some tourism of the expensive variety, but its sprawled layout preserves the village's charm. Spread across a wide area on the slope just below the highway, Tsangaradha consists of four hamlets: Ag. Kyriaki, Ag. Paraskevi, Ag. Stefanou, and Ag. Taxiarhon. The stone-covered **bus stop** is opposite the ATM, across the highway. Buses go to **Volos** (1½hr.; 7:45am, 4:45pm; €3.50). Visitors arriving by way of the Damouhari-Tsangaradha *kalderimi* will enter at Ag. Paraskevi, emerging onto the road by the charming **Villa Ton Rodon** ❹, which offers rooms with private baths, TV, and complementary breakfast. Shuttered doors opening onto porches, perched above charming rose bushes and a panoramic view of the brilliant sea justifies heftier price tags. (☎24260 49 201; fax 24260 49 667. Singles €40; doubles €59.) Turning left at the road, the hamlet's plateia is about 50m down and to the right. Here you will find the eponymous church and a massive 1000-year-old plane tree. From the plateia, a well marked path leads 1hr. down to the blue-green waters and pearl white stones of photogenic **Milopotamos beach.** Up the road 20m in the other direction you'll pass the **post office** (☎24260 49 218; open M-F 7:30am-11:30am and 2pm-5pm) and **tourist office** (☎24260 48 993; open daily 9am-3pm), which has friendly English-speaking staff, before reaching the highway. The **ATM** is on your left when coming up to the highway.

CENTRAL GREECE

WESTERN THESSALY

LARISA Λαρισα ☎2410

As any Greek will tell you, Larisa is no tourism hotspot. Pockets of English spill from cafes and bars, associated with one of the city's claims to fame: a NATO headquarters. Larisa boasts excellent local *halva*, ouzo, and the highest summer temperatures in Greece. If you get stranded here, Larisa isn't completely uninviting. Tree-lined plateias, stork-stalked church domes, trendy boutiques, and a number of chic cafes and bars will keep you busy for a couple of days.

TRANSPORTATION

Buses: ☎2410 537 777. 150m north of Pl. Laou at Olympou and Georgiadou has buses to: **Athens** (4¼hr.; 6 per day, 7am-midnight; €21); **Ioannina** (4hr.; 2 per day, 9:30am and 3pm; €12.60); **Kastoria** (4hr.; 3 per day, 7am-1pm; €13.60); **Thessaloniki** (2hr.; M-F 14 per day, 6am-9pm; fewer Sa-Su; €10.30); **Volos** (1hr.; M-F 12 per day, 6am-9:30pm; €3.80). 2 counters at either end of the terminal sell tickets for different destinations. **Branch station** (☎2410 610 214), on Iroön Polytechniou, has buses running to **Karditsa** (4hr.; 11 per day, 6am-8:15pm; €4.20) and **Trikala** (1hr.; 18 per day, 6am-8:30pm; €4.05). To locate the station, head south on Olympou to Plateia Laou, where Panagouli begins; continue south on Panagouli, turn right at the 5-way intersection, and walk about 600m to the deceptively camouflaged gas station/bus stop on your left.

Trains: ☎2410 236 250 or 2410 590 263. At the end of Paleologou, head south on Panagouli and bear left (while avoiding a sharp left) onto Paleologou at the 5-way intersection; the station is on the southern side of the small park. Intercity express trains run to: **Athens** (4hr.; 7 per day, 7:04am-3:38am; €10-30); **Thessaloniki** (2hr.; 5 per day, 7:50am-midnight; €7.40-20); **Volos** (45min., 12:12pm, €5.90). Also **regular service** to: **Athens** (5hr.; 5 per day, 10:15am-2am; €10); **Thessaloniki** (2½hr.; 8 per day, 4am-12:45pm; €4.70); **Volos** (1hr.; 13 per day, 4:50am-11:12pm; €2.10).

ORIENTATION AND PRACTICAL INFORMATION

Surrounded by miles of fertile corn and wheat fields, Larisa is directly southeast of the **Pinios River,** smack in the middle of eastern Thessaly. The bus station in the north and the train station in the south mark the boundaries of the city's main commercial district, which follows a grid layout. From the bus station, **Olympou** heads south to **Pl. Laou,** one of Larisa's three main plateias. **A. Panagouli** begins here and heads to the bottom of the city where it crosses **Iroön Polytechniou** at a five-way intersection. A. Panagouli marks the eastern border of **Pl. Ethnarhou Makariou** (a.k.a. Pl. Tahydromiou, "Post Office Square"), which is the town's center. The northern edge of this plateia is formed by **Papakyriazi,** which can be taken west three blocks to **Papanastasiou.** From here, Papanastasiou runs north to **Pl. Mikhali Sapka,** and south past the post office and tourist office. If this sounds bewildering, the city will be even more so. Maps are essential. Detailed maps are posted around the train station and Pl. Tahydromiou. Pocket maps are available at magazine stores, many *periptera,* and some hotels.

CENTRAL GREECE

Tourist Office: ☎2410 670 437 or 2410 618 189. On Ipirou near the intersection with Botsari. Doles out city **maps,** pamphlets on Larisa, and advice in broken English. Open M-F 7am-2:30pm.

Police: ☎2410 683 171. On Papanastasiou, 7 blocks south of Papakryiazi.

Hospital: ☎2410 230 031. On Georgiadou, east of the main bus station. Open 24hr.

OTE: ☎2410 995 376 or 2410 622 999. On Filellinion. Take Papanastasiou north and turn right on Kyprou. The OTE is down the 1st block on the left. Open M, W, F 8am-1:30pm and 5:30-8:30pm; Tu and Th 8am-1:30pm.

Internet Access: Yahoo.gr, just off Pl. Eth. Markariou where Papakiriazi meets Rousvelt, has over 20 speedy terminals and a full bar. Internet €2 per hr. 9am-3pm; Internet €2.50 per hr. 3pm-3am. The chic cafe **Traffic,** Patroklou 14 (☎2410 250 210), nearby at Patroklou and Rousvelt, has fast computers. Internet €2 per hr. Drinks €5. Multiple **arcade parlors,** along pedestrian Rousvelt south off Pl. Tahydromiou, offer other Internet options.

Post Office: ☎2410 532 312. On the corner of Papanastasiou and Diakou, a block north of the tourist office. Open M-F 7:30am-8pm. **Poste Restante** and **currency exchange. Postal code:** 41001.

ACCOMMODATIONS

Mid-range to upper-level hotels can be found among the side streets that connect the three main plateias. The cheapest options are near the train station and not too far from the smaller bus station, but they're a 1.5km hike south from the main bus station. **Hotel Diethnes ❷,** on Paleologou on the left after exiting the train station, is a brand-new hotel with immaculate rooms, pretty interior decoration, and sparkling bathrooms. (☎2410 234 210. Singles €20, with bath and A/C €26; doubles €30; triples €45.) **Hotel Pantheon ❷,** on Paleologou near the train station, sits above a small taverna. Its inexpensive, serviceable rooms have TVs and phones—ask for one with a balcony. (☎2410 234 810. Singles €20, with bath and A/C €27; doubles €35.) **Hotel Doma ❸,** Skarlatou Soutsou 1, offers spacious, carpeted rooms with basic baths, A/C, TVs, phones, and small balconies in a central location. (☎2410 535 025. Singles €25; doubles €38; triples €50.)

FOOD

Most of Larisa's cafes, bars, and tavernas are centered around **Pl. Tahydromiou** and its surrounding pedestrian streets, where eateries blend into a ceaseless series of chairs, tables, and blaring TVs. Dissatisfied frappé and hot Nescafé drinkers who yearn for fresh ground beans will find them at various *kafekopteia* (coffee sellers), including one just north of Pl. Laou on the corner of Olympou and another particularly excellent one on Skarlatou Soutsou. Overpoweringly rich aromas pervade these old-fashioned stores, which also sell imported foodstuffs, candies, nuts, dried fruit, and herbs. If you prefer to pick up groceries among neat, straight aisles, head to the southern end of Panagouli, where you'll find a large **supermarket.** For the famed local *halva*, duck into one of the plentiful *zacharoplasteias.*

Because of Larisa's relatively inactive tourism industry, restaurants are rare. Tempting scents might entice you to the *psistarias* (grills) on Panos, north of Kyprou and one block east of the OTE, where lamb and whole chickens slowly turn on spits in the window of each establishment. On the southern side of Plateia Tahydromiou, **To Sidrivani ❷** offers old favorites like *pastitsio* and *moschari* at reasonable prices. Vegetarians will enjoy rice-stuffed tomatoes and green peppers as well as palate-pleasing string beans. (☎2410 535 933. Entrees €4.50-8.) For a special treat try the **Frourio ❸,** located in the Byzantine fortress on the summit of Larisa's highest hill. The ancient stone wallings, flowing trees, and stork-topped cathedral make a great setting for fine dining. (☎2410 937 173. Entrees €7-10.)

SIGHTS

Larisa's archaeological sites cluster on the city's northern hill. The **Greek theater** is at the corner of Venizelou and Papanastiasiou. In a bramble field above the theater are one or two column sections from the ancient **acropolis.** Beyond the acropolis is the **Byzantine fortress.** Down the opposite side of the hill is the Peneios River. Crossing the river on Ag. Haralabous and turning right, you'll find shady **Alkazar Park.** The park is without a doubt the most serene spot in the city—even the graffiti here is a bit more decorative. At the intersection of Venizelou and 31 Augustou is a small mosque with a single minaret, now the **Archaeological Museum.** (☎2410 288 515. Open Tu-Su 8:30am-3pm. Free.) The modern art museum, **Pinakothiki,** Roosvelt 59, has one of the best 20th-century art collections in Greece. (☎2410 621 205. Open W-Su 10am-2:30pm and 6-8pm. €1.) The **Museum of Folk Art,** Mandilara 74, features rotating temporary exhibits with captions in both Greek and English. (☎2410 287 516 or 287 493. Open Su-F 9am-2pm. Free.)

NIGHTLIFE

For after-dinner entertainment, the lively bars of Larisa will not disappoint. Find hip settings at **Cafe del Mar** (☎2410 252 464), **Ermes** (☎2410 611 205), on the corner of Roosvelt and Mandilara, and **De-Tox** (☎2410 257 838), at Asklepiou one block down, where music blares until 3am. Larisa also shows off its dynamic discos, which generally have a €6 cover (goes toward your first drink). **Venga** (☎2410 288 845), a €3 taxi ride from downtown, is an enormous open-air nightclub boasting a row of towering fountains, 10 bars, and a mini-club within the club: **Planet Babe.** The crowd usually starts to arrive around 1am, but the ultimate exhibitionism doesn't start until at least 4am. A €5-6 taxi ride in the other direction brings you to Larisa's most popular club, **Kika** (☎2410 661 112 or 661 312), on the outskirts of town. Three thousand people gyrate nightly to American and Greek favorites under the enormous Thessalian night sky.

TRIKALA Τρικαλα ☎24310

Greeks may snicker when they hear you've visited Trikala—many consider it a provincial knock-off of Larisa. Trikala, however, is actually more pleasant than either Larisa or Volos. The Letheos River, named for the ancient Underworld's river of forgetfulness, carves Trikala in half; acacias, chestnuts, plane trees, and pedestrian-friendly footbridges give the town some charm. The remains of a mosque designed by Ottoman-Era master architect Sinan, views from the frourio (fortress), the labyrinthine old quarter, and the slight remains of an Asclepion (ancient hospital sanctuary)—Trikala was the birthplace of Asclepius god of healing—can keep you from twiddling your thumbs at the bus station. At night young locals strut down the pedestrian arcades and dance in packed clubs outside town.

TRANSPORTATION. The **bus station** (☎24310 73 130) is on the river's southern bank about 150m downstream of Pl. Riga Feriou, at the corner of Othonos and Garivaldi streets. After crossing the bridge, make a left onto Othonos and continue one block down the river. It's on your right at the corner and has buses going to: **Athens** (4½hr.; 6 per day, 7am-8:30pm; €19.10); **Ioannina** (3½hr.; 2 per day, 8:30am-3pm; €9.70); **Kalambaka** (30min.; 22 per day, 5:15am-9pm; €1.50); **Larisa** (1¼hr.; 21 per day, 5:45am-8:30pm; €4.20); **Pyli** (30min.; 13 per day, 5:45am-9pm; €1.30); **Thessaloniki** (3¼hr.; 6 per day, 7:30am-8pm; €12.70); **Volos** (2½hr.; 4 per day, 7am-7pm; €9.30). The **train station** (☎24310 27 214) is at the far southern end of Asklepiou, about 700m south of Pl. Riga Feriou. Continue straight along Asklepiou and 10 blocks from the river the yellow building will come into view. The recently renovated station has a modern ticket counter and electronic departure boards. Trains go to: **Athens** (regular: 5½hr., 9:55am, €10; express: 4½hr.; 7:25am, 2:55, 5:40pm; €16.50); **Kalambaka** (20min.; 4 per day, 8:10am-8:20pm; €1.05); **Larisa** (3 per day, 9:55am-9pm; €3.20). **Taxis** (☎24310 22 022) convene in Pl. Iroön Polytechniou.

ORIENTATION AND PRACTICAL INFORMATION. Trikala lies 58km west of Larisa. The Letheos River divides the town roughly northwest to southeast and the two main plateias lie directly across the river from each other: **Pl. Riga Feriou** in the south and the rectangular **Pl. Iroön Polytechniou** in the north. The latter is home to a charming statue of a boy perpetually relieving himself into a small pond. The bus station is on **Othonos,** on the southern bank of the river, downstream from Pl. Riga Feriou. **Asklipiou,** Trikala's main road, runs south from Pl. Riga Feriou, where it begins as a broad pedestrian arcade designed for strutting and coy ogling. It turns into a car-laden street after Kapodistriou, on its way to the train station south of town. **Vyronos** and **Garivaldi** cut diagonally across Asklipiou in succession. On the north bank, **Sarafi** leads west out of Pl. Iroön Polytechniou to **Varousi,** the old Turkish quarter, and the fortress in the northwest.

A **National Bank** with an **ATM** is located right on the northern side of Pl. I. Polytechniou. (Open M-Th 8am-2pm, F 8am-1:30pm.) There's also a 24hr. ATM on Asklepiou just south of Pl. Riga Feriou. The **police station** (☎24310 27 303) is four blocks down Asklepiou at its intersection with Kapodistriou. The 24hr. **hospital** (☎24310 22 222) is on the main road to Kardista. For **Internet** access, turn left on Vyronos, one block down Asklepiou from Pl. Riga Feriou. **Neos Kosmos** has nine terminals, a printer, and a full bar. (☎24310 72 591. €3 per hr. Open 8am-3am.) There is an **OTE,** 25 Martiou (☎24310 95 328 or 95 315). Martiou runs parallel to Sarafi, 2 blocks away from the river; turn left after Pl. I. Polytechniou. The main **post office,** Sarafi 15, provides **currency exchange** and **Poste Restante.** (☎24310 27 415. Open M-F 7:30am-2pm.) Walk across the bridge from Pl. Riga Feriou and turn left on Sarafi, which is directly in front of you. **Postal code:** 42100.

ACCOMMODATIONS AND FOOD. The most affordable digs in town are at the **Hotel Palladion ❷,** Vyronos 4, along the riverbank and one street west of Pl. Riga Feriou. All types of travelers amble across the marble floors of these spacious, comfortable, colorful rooms with phones, sinks, and TVs that receive more than 20 channels. (☎24310 28 091 or 24310 37 260. Shared baths. Singles €21; doubles €30; triples €36.) Other hotels are readily available but often expensive. **Hotel Dinas ❸,** two blocks down Asklepiou, is right above the hippest cafes in town (the sign reads Hotel Ntina). The brightly painted rooms have bathrooms, TVs, and A/C and are moderately priced for Trikala hotels. (☎24310 74 777; fax 24310 29 490. Singles €37; doubles €50; triples €60.) Easily spotable **Hotel Achilleion ❹,** just south of the main bridge on Pl. Riga Feriou, offers cozy, carpeted rooms with large beds and wooden furniture. Rooms have TVs, phones, A/C, and simple baths. (☎24310 28 192; fax 24310 74 858. Breakfast included. Singles €45; doubles €70; triples €90. MC/V.)

Katzinetrou, one block west of Pl. Iroön Polytechniou off Martinou, is a lively spot for an evening meal. Tavernas line the streets, their colorful outdoor tables wrapping around street corners. Join crowds of chatty locals at **Taverna Thea Artemis ❷,** Ypsilandou 4, three blocks north of Martinou. Located in a quiet cafe-lined alley, this taverna offers a large selection of Greek wines to complement its traditional menu. (☎24310 77 533. Entrees €4.70-7.70.) A few blocks farther south, **To Dipylo ❷** serves up an assortment of souvlaki and schnitzels, as well as the Drunkard's Delicacy (€4.40), a spicy pork dish. (☎24310 72 722. Entrees €4.10-8.80.) A **supermarket** on Vyronos, next door to Palladion Hotel, sells mini-icons of the Panagia (Virgin), in addition to average foodstuffs. (Open M-F 8am-9pm, Sa 8am-6pm.)

SIGHTS AND NIGHTLIFE. Looming above Varousi are the grand stone walls and bell tower of **Fort Trikkis,** first constructed in the 4th century BC and dedicated to Artemis. The fountain-decked park and cafe in the lower half of the fort is an ideal setting for a frappé with a view (€2.50). The upper half contains the bell tower and a small garden; from mid-June to mid-September, an open-air theater shows movies (10pm nightly; €5, students €3) in English with Greek subtitles. Pl. Riga Feriou and Asklipiou are packed with loud cafes blasting dance music and serving drinks until daybreak. In the afternoons and early evenings, the chairs are lined up like cinema seats facing the pedestrian street—prime positioning for people-watching. For a cool drink any time of the day, take a taxi to nearby Pyli for **Neromylos,** a 17th-century water mill converted to a cafe and meticulously landscaped by its owner. (☎24340 22 085. Frappé €2.50. Beer €3. Open 10am-2am.)

KALAMBAKA Καλαμπακα ☎23420

Its name in Turkish means roughly "rocks in the air." The lone main road channels countless package-tour buses past the town, to the rocks' summit, but staying in this inexpensive and welcoming town is a must to fully embrace the area.

TRANSPORTATION. The main **bus station,** downhill from Pl. Dimarhiou on Rodou, past the taxi stand, has buses to: **Athens** (5hr.; 8 per day, 7am-8:30pm; €19.10) via **Lamia** (2½hr., €6.50); **Ioannina** (3½hr.; 8:50am, 3:50pm; €8.30) via **Metsovo** (1½hr., €4.30); **Patras** (6hr., 9:45am and 3pm, €19.40); **Thessaloniki** (6 per day, 7:30am-8pm; €12.70); **Trikala** (30min.; 25 per day, 6:15am-10:30pm; €1.50); **Volos** (3hr.; 4 per day, 7am-7pm; €10.80). Buses bound for **Kastraki** (5min.; 24 per day, 6:40am-9:40pm; €0.70) and **Meteora** (20min.; 9am, 1:20pm; €0.90) pick up in front of Pl. Dimarhiou at the foot of the large fountain. The 9am bus to Meteora allows time to hike around the monasteries. Most walk back to Kalambaka (6km downhill), visiting monasteries along the way; you can take a bus back from Grand Meteoron at 1:30pm. The distinctive yellow **train station** (☎24320 22 451), on the corner of Pindou and Kondyli, is clearly visible 50m to your left, one block down from the bus station, with trains to: **Athens** (4hr.; 5 per day, 6:30am-5:40pm; €19.10) and **Thessaloniki** (5hr.; 11:09am, 5:40pm; €8.50) via **Larisa** (1½hr.; 5:40, 8:48pm; €3.80). **Taxis** (☎23420 22 310 or 22 822) congregate at a small kiosk across from the central plateia. (To Meteora €4-5. Available 6:30am-midnight.)

ORIENTATION AND PRACTICAL INFORMATION. Kalambaka is in the northwestern corner of Thessaly, 25km north of Trikala near the border with Epirus. Centrally located **Pl. Dimarhiou** is uphill from the bus station. Standing there with your back to the fountain and the Meteora cliffs, **Vlahava** is behind you, **Rodhou** in front, and **Ioanninon** downhill to the right. **Patriarchou Dimitriou** goes uphill to your right, while **Trikalon** leads left to the sunny **Pl. Riga Fariou,** home to various banks and restaurants. A horde of cafes and bars can be found open at all hours on the pedestrian street **Dimoula,** two blocks down Trikalon from Pl. Riga Fariou.

With the cliffs on your left, Kondyli branches off to your right at the end of Pl. Riga Feriou. Through a well marked gate half a block down on the right, the **tourist office,** Kondyli and Hatzipetrou 38, supplies **maps,** hotel listings, and monastery opening hours. (☎24320 75 306; fax 24320 25 343. Open M-F 8am-3:30pm.) The **kiosk** by the taxi stand also provides maps of the town and of Meteora. Both the **National Bank** in Pl. Riga Fariou and the **Agricultural Bank** near the central plateia have 24hr. **ATMs.** On the road to Ioannina, a 10min. walk from the center of town, the **police** (☎24230 76 100) are open 24hr. and also house the **tourist police.** A 24hr. **health center** (☎24230 22 222) lies 1km from town, on the road to Ioannina. The **OTE** is on Ioanninon. (☎24230 22 121. Open M-F 7:30am-2pm.) A block down Dimoula off Trikalon, **Koktel** has **Internet access** in the back of the well-lit cafe. (☎24230 22 370. €0.05 per min. Open 8am-3pm.) **Ouranio Toxo,** Trikalon 100 (☎24320 24 688), on the right at Trikalon's entrance to Pl. Riga Feriou, has three terminals (€3 per hr.) beside its bar. The **post office,** between the two plateias on Trikalon, has **Poste Restante.** (☎24230 22 467. Open M-F 7:30am-2pm.) **Postal code:** 42200.

ACCOMMODATIONS. Do not accept **domatia** offers from dock hawks, locally infamous for luring travelers with promises of good prices only to hit them with exorbitant surcharges. Pouncing on disembarking tourists is an ominous—and illegal—beginning. Kalambaka has many cheap and well run options anyway. The best accommodations for views, comfort, and hospitality are in the quiet, high-rise free, Old Town up near the foot trail to Meteora. Many less personal, moderately priced hotels are at the end of Trikalon. A number of campsites line the roads around Kalambaka and Kastraki; many also rent rooms at cheap prices.

In the quiet Old Town at the base of the footpath to the rocks and monasteries, **Koka Roka ❷,** offers large rooms with views. Aussie-accented Arthur serves souvlaki nightly to guests from around the world. It's an 8min. walk from the central plateia; follow Vlahava until it ends, then follow signs. (☎24230 24 554;

CENTRAL GREECE

kokaroka@yahoo.com. Laundry €3 per hr. Internet access €3 per hr. Singles €15; doubles €27, with bath €32; triples €42.) In the Old Town just before Koka Roka, follow signs from the end of Vlahava to find **Alsos House ❷,** Kanari 5. Recently remodeled spacious rooms with breathtaking views of Meteora's pinnacles and Ag. Triada Monastery have baths, A/C, and balconies. Amiable English-speaking proprietor Yiannis Karakantas can arrange guides for climbers and hikers. (☎24230 24 097 or 6972 544 825; www.kalampaka.com/alsos-house. Internet, printing, laundry machine, and communal kitchen available. Singles €20-25; doubles €30; triples €40; apartment with kitchen €50.) **Hotel Meteora ❷,** at the end of short Ploutarhiou, one block up Patriachou Dimitriou from Pl. Dimarhiou, is ensconced beneath its namesake cliffs. Tight, but charming rooms have bath, TV, A/C, and balcony—half open onto a wall rather than onto the cliffs. (☎24320 22 367; fax 24320 75 550. Internet access and breakfast included. Prices for *Let's Go* readers: singles €15; doubles €20; triples €30; family suite €50.) **Hotel Kaikis ❷,** Trikalon 146, past Pl. Riga Feriou, set amongst a cluster of similar, mid-level hotels. Brand-new rooms have baths, telephones, TVs, and balconies. (☎24320 75 280; fax 24320 75 282. Internet available. Breakfast €6. Singles €25; doubles €30; triples €40.)

Vrachos Camping ❶, 1km out of town toward Kastraki and the monasteries, is the largest, most popular, and best kept of the area's campsites boasting a pool, restaurant, great views, and a separate quiet area. (☎24320 22 293. €6 per person. €5 per car.) **Kalambaka Camping ❶,** 1km down the road toward Trikala, on the opposite side of town from Vrachos Camping, offers decent facilities. (☎24320 22 309. €3.70 per adult, €2.60 per tent, €2.25 per car. Electricity €2.60.)

FOOD AND NIGHTLIFE. To save some cash or to slap together a picnic for the monasteries, there's a **supermarket** just off of Trikalon on Dimoula and various **fruit stands** on Vlahava. Fridays Vlahava and its main intersector Kondyli turn into a full-scale **marketplace** for fresh produce and sundry household goods. **Restaurant Panellinio ❷,** perched on a cobblestone platform next to the fountain, is the life of Pl. Dimarhiou. Mrs. Soula cooks up a mean moussaka and many grilled meat and vegetable dishes. (☎24230 24 735. Entrees €4.50-6.) Join in on the lively conversation at **Koka Roka Taverna ❷,** inside its namesake hotel, while enjoying some home cooking. Spectacular views of the cliffs whet appetites with reminders of the calorie-crunching hike to come. (☎24230 24 554. Entrees €3.20-5.10.) The patrons of **Arhondariki ❷,** at the left end of Pl. Riga Feriou when facing the cliffs, enjoy views of the Meteora. (☎24320 22 449. Signature lamb €5.30. Entrees €4-7.)

Nightlife centers on **Trikalon,** south of Pl. Riga Feriou, where fast-food joints and neon signs line the streets. Ouzeria **Plaka,** just past Pl. Riga Feriou, has live nightly *bouzouki* music. A hipper atmosphere surrounds fountain-lined **Dimoula,** home to entertaining, indistinguishable bars, offering beer (€4) and cocktails (€5.50).

SIGHTS. In the land of monasteries, it comes as no surprise that Kalambaka's foremost attraction is the Byzantine **Church of the Assumption of the Virgin.** Follow signs in the central plateia; after several blocks you'll spy the graceful bell tower of the antique basilica. Built in the 5th century atop a Classical temple whose pagan mosaics still survive entombed beneath the floor, the main structure was remodeled in 1573. Most of the soot-darkened interior frescoes were painted by the Cretan monks at this time, though some pictures from the church's 12th-century renovations remain. Next to a severed temple column in the churchyard beneath Meteora's looming monasteries, the southern wall's hell fresco draws attention. (Open 8am-1pm and 4-6pm. €1.50. Modest dress required.) For monastery visitors wondering how all those gorgeous yet rigidly standardized icons were produced, the **Workshop of Dimitris Zervopoulos,** across from Camping Kalambaka 1km down the road to Trikala, offers free tours. While sipping free ouzo or lemonade, you will see monks painting the world's next generation of icons from holy originals. (☎24320 75 466; fax 24320 24 003. Open daily 9am-7pm.) In late July, the town honors its patron saint with a celebration complete with music, dance, and food. Nearby Kastraki holds a three-day **wine festival** with free samples in late August.

METEORA Μετεορα

Meteora (meh-TEH-o-rah; "rocks of the sky") formations are the remains of a large delta in the primordial Thessalonian Sea. A careful glance at the rock will reveal its conglomerate structure of fused sand and stone run-off. A few epochs (modern Greek for season) after the sea dried up, rivers carved most of the easily eroded sandstone away, leaving the present towers. In the 14th century, some monks decided these peaks would make the most awesome tree houses ever, so they built the 24 gravity-defying, frescoed Byzantine monasteries that cling to them. Six of these monasteries are still inhabited by religious orders and are open to the public. The largest monasteries, Grand Meteoron and Varlaam, have the most spectacular displays and attract hordes of tourists. The other monasteries are quieter and more intimate; if you're lucky, you might even meet one of the reclusive monks. Meteora requires a full day's visit and it's well worth the time and the walk.

TRANSPORTATION AND PRACTICAL INFORMATION

Buses leave for Meteora from the **Kalambaka** fountain. (M-F 9am, 1:20pm; Sa-Su 8:20am, 1:20pm; €0.90. Buy tickets on the bus.) Each monastery closes one day per week, and opening hours vary slightly. (All open Apr.-Sept. Sa-Su and W 10am-12:30pm and 3:30-5pm. €2 per monastery, children under 12 free.) Modest dress is required and bare shoulders deny you entrance. Wraps and shawls are available at some monasteries for the forgetful. Men with long hair may be asked to wrap it in a bun (as the monks do). Photography and filming are forbidden inside most of the monasteries; pack a picnic for the siesta-time midday closing.

CENTRAL GREECE

WALKING THE MONASTERIES

The origins of the settlements perched atop the Meteora rocks are unknown: one likely story holds that the first recluse was a monk named **Barnabas,** who founded the *skite* of the Holy Ghost in the mid-10th century. By the 11th century, hermits and ascetics followed his example, moving to the wind-beaten pinnacles and crevices of the Meteora, worshipping in a church dedicated to the **Theotokos** (Mother of God), which can still be seen below the Agios Nikolaos monastery. As religious persecution at the hands of Turkish and Frankish marauders increased in the 12th century, devout Orthodox Christians scurried to the summits of these impregnable columns of rock.

In 1344 the region's first monastic community was founded when the monk **Athanasios,** his spiritual father **Gregorios,** and 14 fellow mountain-climbing monks began to build Grand Meteoron. Athanasios was a highly educated monk whose journeys brought him from his native Patras to Constantinople, Crete, and finally Mt. Athos, from which he fled to avoid Turkish invasions. He preferred to occupy his time weaving baskets in a nearby cave, referring to women as "the sling" (that vaults the stones of sin into men's hearts) or as "the affliction" (addicting men to the sinful pleasures of the flesh). When the Ottomans ruled most of Greece, Meteora served as an outpost of Christianity along with Mount Athos (p. 303), growing in the 16th century into a robust, rich community of 24 monasteries, each embellished by the age's finest artists. In the late 1700s when donations fell off and the popularity of monastic life waned, the Greeks sold off many treasured manuscripts and books to foreign visitors for a fraction of their actual worth. A small brotherhood still exists at **Grand Meteoron, Varlaam, Agia Triada,** and **Agios Nikolaos,** while **Agios Stephanos** and **Roussanou** are now convents.

The first ascetics scaled the sheer cliffs of Meteora by wedging timbers into the rock crevices to construct small platforms; traces of these platforms can still be seen along the Meteora walls. After the monasteries were completed, visitors usually arrived by means of extremely long rope ladders. Once these were pulled up, the summit became virtually inaccessible. Visitors who were either too weak or too timid to climb the ladders were hoisted up in free-swinging rope nets. Motorized winches have since replaced rope-spool cranes, and today only provisions, not pilgrims, are yanked up by rope, though monks can be seen riding miniature cable cars over the chasms. In 1922 steps were carved into the rocks and bridges built between the pillars, so even the vertigo-prone could feel secure.

It's easiest to begin your tour of Meteora in the morning at Grand Meteoron, the uppermost monastery and bus stop, and then work your way down through its neighbors, Nikolaos, Roussanou, and Varlaam, while catching the dazzling views from the highway. When the monasteries close for siesta, you have two options: you can catch the afternoon bus back to Kalambaka or flag down one of the many taxis always happy for another passenger. You can also grab a bite from your bagged lunch and start the hike to Ag. Triada and Stephanos. A sign on the highway between Varlaam and Roussanou marked "Ag. Triada" points into the bush to a short trail to Triada (20min.). This scenic but overgrown trail allows plenty of opportunity for creativity. Others may choose the clearly marked road (45min.).

GRAND METEORON. The **Monastery of the Transfiguration,** known as Grand Meteoron (Μεγαλου Μετεορου, MEH-gha-loo meh-teh-OH-roo), is the oldest, largest, most important, and most touristed monastery in the area. Built in the late 14th century on the most imposing of the inhabited stone columns, **Platys Lithos,** the Grand Meteoron complex, looms 613m above Thessaly's plain. It reached its peak in the 16th century, when it was visited by the reigning patriarch and accorded the same privileges as the autonomous Mt. Athos. Around this time the **Church of the Transfiguration** was built, to be capped by an exalted dome with a *Pantokrator* (a central image of Christ). The sounds of chanting monks—diappointingly emanating from a stereo in the folk museum—fill the monastery. The monks keep mostly to their private quarters on the monastery's eastern side. *(Open W-M 9am-5pm. €2.)*

VARLAAM. Some 800m downhill from Grand Meteoron stands Varlaam, the second-largest Meteora monastery. Varlaam was founded in the 14th century by a contemporary of Athanasios who, in a show of monkish humility, named the monastery after himself. The 16th-century frescoes of the *katholikon* depict hermits, martyrs, an apocalyptic sea serpent swallowing doomed sinners, as well as St. Sisoes looking pitifully upon Alexander the Great's skeleton (symbolic of the vanity of worldly achievements). The monastery's **library** contains 290 manuscripts, including a miniature Bible from 960 that belonged to Emperor Constantine Porfitogenitou. Varlaam also has every science teacher's dream—an extensive **net and pulley system,** now used for supplies, which shows how earlier visitors were hoisted. Recently the monastery has gotten a face-lift—new walkways, handrails, and a clock tower have been added. *(Open M-W and F-Su 9am-2pm and 3:20-7pm. €2.)*

ROUSSANOU. Bear right at the fork in the road to reach Roussanou. Visible from most of the valley, it is one of the most spectacularly situated monasteries in the area. With its steep sides, three of which overlook the sheer drop to the valley below, Roussanou feels less like a creation of man than a natural continuation of the boulders. Despite continuous renovation, the interior, which includes paintings of the criminal in paradise and a portrait of Constantine the Grea, can't match the heavenly exterior, accessible without a ticket. Still the *katholikon*, illuminated by stained glass, is beautiful. Roussanou celebrated its greatest moment when it housed Greek refugees fleeing the Turks in 1757 and 1897. Today the monastery is home to an order of nuns. *(Open daily 9am-6pm. €2.)*

AGIOS NIKOLAOS. Farther down the road lies the 16th-century monastery of Agios Nikolaos Anapafsas, only 2.5km from Kastraki. Situated on a very narrow boulder, Agios Nikolaos grew vertically rather than horizontally; it is now the second tallest of the monasteries, next to Grand Meteoron. Visitors are admitted only in small groups; wait at the top of the steps for the door to open. Allow 30min. for the walk past Roussanou to the next monastery, Agia Triada. *(Open M-Th and Sa-Su 9am-3pm; closed in winter. €2.)*

AGIA TRIADA. A shortcut from Roussanou bypasses a large section of road on the way to Agia Triada. Standing on the metal bridge into Roussanou, face away from the monastery, get out your walking stick, and take the (mostly) paved path uphill on the right. When the path hits the road, bear right and keep bearing right to find Agia Triada ("Trinity"); movie buffs will recognize it from the James Bond flick *For Your Eyes Only*. Looming above Kalambaka, the peak of Agia Triada gives a soul-searing view of the red-roofed town and the distant Pindos Mountains. Ambitious monk Dometius built the monastery in 1438, but most of the **wall paintings** weren't added for another 200 years. Most of the monastery's prized manuscripts and heirlooms were lost in WWII. Triada is now one of the least-touristed and most intimate monasteries. For hikers hoping to interact with monks, Triada is the best bet. Many visitors report having had illuminating discussions with superior Father John. To get to **Kalambaka** from Agia Triada, take the unmarked 2km footpath leading from the bottom of the monastery's staircase. At the base of the cliff and with your back to the monastery, walk a few meters to your left, and then descend on the small left-hand fork in the path. The overgrown trail soon evolves into a cement-paved stone path. *(Open M-W and F-Su 9am-12:30pm and 3-5pm. €2.)*

AGIOS STEPHANOS. At the end of the road, past Agia Triada, is Agios Stephanos, according to an 18th-century report, originally a convent; it became a monastery in the early 15th century. Today it is once again home to a large, active community of nuns. Of its two churches, only the more modern **Agios Haralambos,** built in 1798, is open to the public. The **museum** displays well-preserved icons, manuscripts, liturgical vestments, and crosses. Its wooden iconostasis is intricately carved into figures of birds, animals, and people. The peaceful garden out back offers spectacular views of the entire valley. *(Open in summer Tu-Su 9am-2pm and 3:20-5pm; in winter Tu-Su 9:30am-1pm and 3-5pm. €2.)*

Christianity has been a part of Greece and the life of the Greek people for nearly 2000 years. About 49 AD, St. Paul and his companions arrived at Philippi and then traveled to Thessaloniki, Athens, and Corinth. In each ity, they aided the establishment of Christian ommunities. Five of Paul's letters were sent to hese communities and passed on to others, and t. John the Evangelist composed the Book of evelations on Patmos about 95. By this time, ther missionaries were active throughout the egion, leading to the rapid expansion of these hristian communities. At that time, the Greek eninsula and islands were within the Roman-yzantine Empire and the Church in Greece was art of Eastern Christianity, centered in Constan-inople. But discrepancies in understandings of he relationship of the Pope of Rome to other ishops eventually led to a schism between the hristian East and West, emphasizing the two hurches' differences in theological ethos. Since hat time, the Roman Catholic Church and the rthodox Church have developed on their own ith little positive contact until recent decades.

reek Orthodox believers today are devoted to he apostolic origins of their Church; they con-inue to pray at locations where Christ's first fol-owers taught, worshipped, and were sometimes artyred. They take pride in the fact that the ew Testament was written in Greek and that he earliest theologians taught in this language. s part of the family of Orthodox Churches hroughout the world, the Greek Church's teach-ngs are centered upon Jesus and his Gospel. rthodoxy affirms a loving God who entered nto this life in the person of Jesus for the sake of he world's salvation. Jesus revealed the one od as Father, Son, and Holy Spirit. In prayers, he Church proclaims that the Triune God is the *hilanthropos*, lover of the human person. rthodoxy also teaches that Jesus revealed that od treasures human persons (meant to be *heophoros*, bearer of God) and calls them to ve in communion with Him and others in the idst of this creation—and in the life to come. ooted in God's revelation in Christ, these affir-ations are expressed in the scripture and tradi-on of the Church. They are celebrated through orship, especially in the Holy Eucharist or ivine Liturgy, and expressed in the Sacraments and prayer services that accompany the life of the believer. The saints are honored as persons who embodied these convictions.

Orthodox Christianity is embedded in the fabric of Greek life. Greeks recognize that the Church and the Christian faith helped preserve their identity during the difficult centuries of Ottoman rule.On their way to school, work, or market, many Greeks enter their local church to offer a prayer and light a candle—and not surprisingly, since in Greece, every road leads to a church. In fact, the country's greatest Christian monuments are churches, some of which date from as early as the 5th century. In spite of their potential value to art historians or archaeologists, however, Greeks refuse to turn these ancient churches—often constructed over even older edifices where the earliest Greek Christians gathered—into museums, and most are still in use today. In addition to the remnants of early churches at Delphi, Agia Sophia and St. Demetrios in Thessaloniki are poignant examples of the ancients' giving older structures a facelift in order to turn them into powerful representations of their religious belief. Many structures, including the Parthenon in Athens and the Roman Rotunda in Thessaloniki, were also used as Christian churches for centuries despite their modern association with the Hellenic pantheon. And today, Greek religious architecture is still drawing on the past to create a vibrant present. Many churches built recently reflect earlier Byzantine designs, which center on a large dome built over the intersection of the two branches of the cross, in which shape the church is constructed. In many cities, exquisite churches from the Byzantine period barely survived Ottoman rule and have only been restored in the past century. In both Byzantine and more modern churches, icons, depicting Christ, Mary, or other saints, are of particular importance. Greeks also prominently display these icons in homes, shops, roadside shrines, taxis, and buses, but they are best appreciated in a religious setting. The churches of Osios Lucas, Daphni, Mistra, Mount Athos, and Meteora contain particularly outstanding examples of Greek iconography. Taken all together, the design of the church and the icons it contains nurture, instruct, and inspire worshippers in their relationship with God and with each other. So it is not for nothing that it is said that Greece is truly a pilgrim's delight.

Thomas FitzGerald, Th.D., is an Orthodox priest and Professor of Church History and Historical Theology at Holy Cross Greek Orthodox School of Theology in Brookline, MA. Among his published works are The Orthodox Church *and* Happy in The Lord: The Beatitudes for Everyday. The Ecumenical Movement *is due for 2004 publication.*

NORTHERN GREECE

Northern Greece rarely finds its way into package tours, but not because of a lack of appeal. Robust and pretension-free, the region draws adventurous travelers looking to flee the packed plateias and bikini-filled beaches of the islands. From the peaks of Mt. Olympus to the depths of the Vikos Gorge, the diverse landscape holds countless opportunities to commune with nature, while age-old monasteries offer access to the gods of your choice. In ancient times, snide Athenians regarded the residents of Macedonia and Thrace as primitive barbarians. Yet today Thessaloniki's trendsetting residents outshine even Athens's hip.

HIGHLIGHTS OF NORTHERN GREECE

SIDESTEP scorpions while trekking through Vikos Gorge (p. 267), the world's steepest canyon.

GENUFLECT in reverence to Agios Dimitrios, Thessaloniki's oldest church, before being floored by the ancient mosaics inside (p. p. 280).

GET LOST in the clouds atop Mt. Olympus; the gods await your ascent (p. 289).

ABIDE by 10th-century monastic doctrine at Mt. Athos's monasteries (p. 303).

FLIRT WITH FATE amid the rustling leaves of Dodoni's oracular oak (p. 262).

EPIRUS Ηπειρος

If you came in search of idyllic isolation, consider roaming Greece's northwestern coast. The postcard-worthy towns and beaches of Parga see their share of visitors, but the mountains and timeless Zagorohoria villages near the Vikos Gorge remain undisturbed. Epirus links itself to a living past—the old Latin dialect of Vlach is still spoken in the mountain towns, and the almost perfectly preserved mosques of the once dreaded Ali Pasha still grace the city of Ioannina.

The region's mountains draw international hikers for some of Greece's best outdoor rambles. Those who enjoy exhilaratingly fresh natural air and quality hiking will delight in the beauty of the Pindos Mountains Region. Rushing rivers and waterfalls, towering mountains, steep ravines, fertile forests, and blossoming wildflowers constitute the breathtaking scenery that provides a refreshing change from the typical Greek tourist attractions. The European E6 path and national O1 and O3 routes run through the area near Ioannina (p. 257), a good base city from which to explore the mountains. The O3 brings hikers through the Vikos Gorge and past an array of mountaintops and villages known to offer some of the best hiking in Greece. The tourist office in Ioannina has an informative, Greek-only contour map that marks all the trails. Rock climbers can scale the faces of Eamila, Tsouka Rossa, and Pirgos Astraka, and avid spelunkers can attempt the Provatihas Cave, the second-deepest cave in the world at 407m. Most of these expeditions are best undertaken with an experienced guide or after consulting an outdoors agency in Ioannina, as maps of the region tend to be unreliable.

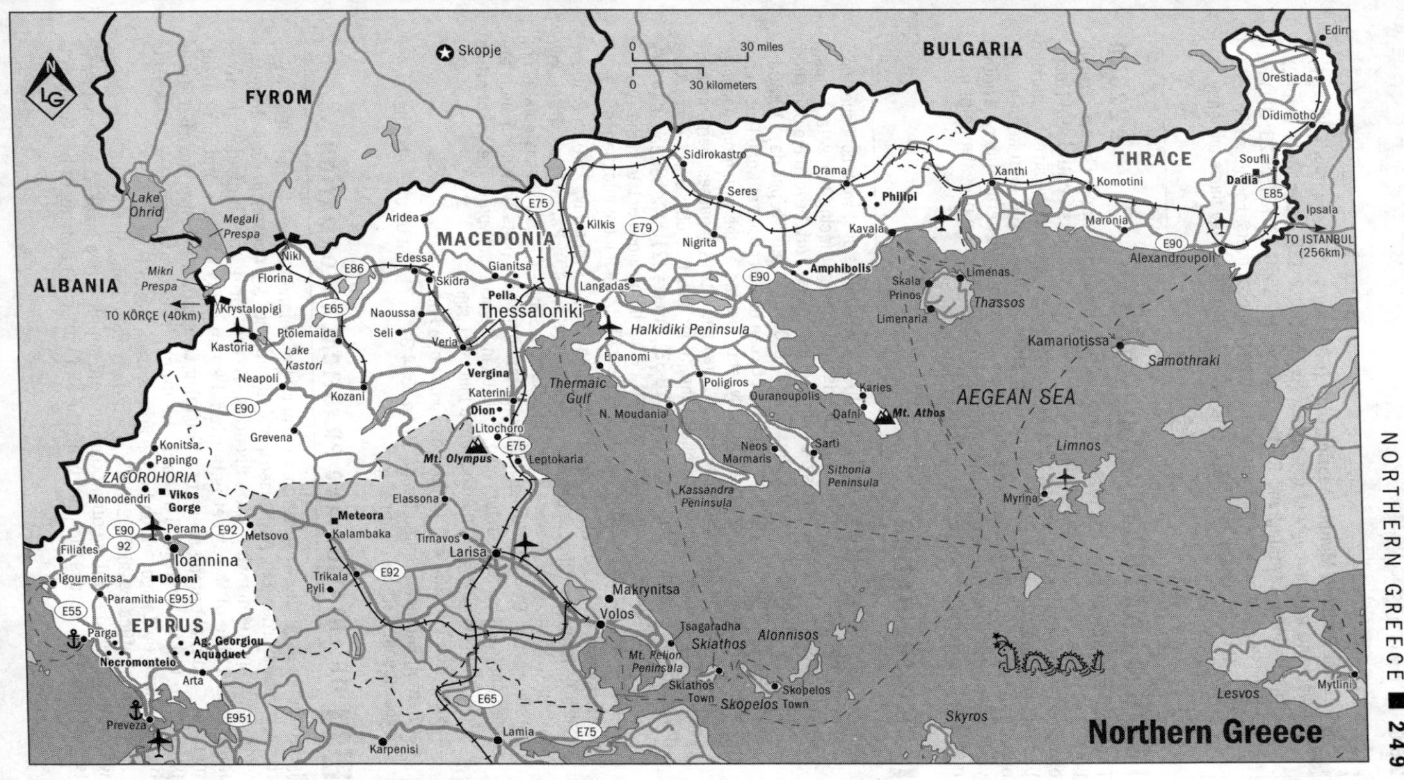

NORTHERN GREECE

The Hellenic Mountaineering Club (EOS) supplies information and leads weekend trips throughout the region. (☎26510 22 138. Open M-Sa 7-9pm.) The **Paddler Kayaking and Rafting School** (☎26550 23 777 or 23 101) in Konitsa gives lessons and oversees outings to local rivers. For alpine flowers, April through June is the best hiking season; colored foliage flares brilliantly in the dry autumns.

IGOUMENITSA Ηγουμενιτσα ☎22650

For many, Igoumenitsa is the first glimpse of the Greek mainland. Greece's third-largest port and consummate transportation hub, the city links Central and Northern Greece, the Ionian Islands, and Italy. Tourist agencies line the streets, harried backpackers scurry about in search of their ships, loitering old men keep an eye on all the comings and goings, and everyone seems in a desperate hurry. Though you may prefer to avoid staying the night in Igoumenitsa, the prevalence of early morning ferries makes this easier said than done.

TRANSPORTATION

Ferries: Igoumenitsa's endless **port** currently has 3 subdivisions; work continues on a 4th. **Old Port,** on the waterfront's north edge (to the right facing the water), mostly sends boats to Italy. **Corfu Port** is the middle of the 3. **New Port,** beyond the Corfu Port, sends boats to both Italy and Corfu. Tickets to **Corfu** (1½hr.; 5 per day, 10:30am-10pm; €5.10, students €3.60, children €2.60) can be purchased at Corfu Port, in one of several white kiosks. For tickets to **Italy,** shop around at the waterfront agencies. Some have student rates and some accept Eurail and Inter-Rail passes; bargain before you buy. Destinations include: **Ancona** (15hr., 3 per day, €50-60); **Bari** (9½hr., 3 per day, €35-45); **Brindisi** (8hr., 2 per day, €28-33); **Trieste** (21hr., 2 per day, €44-57). Prices do not include port duties. Most boats depart before noon or late in the evening. Contact **Nitsas Travel** (☎26650 29 140; anitsas@hol.gr) for more information.

Buses: Kiprou 17 (☎26650 22 309). To: **Athens** (8hr.; 6 per day, 7:30am-8:30pm; €21.80); **Ioannina** (2hr.; 9 per day, 6:30am-8pm; €6.40); **Parga** (1hr.; 4 per day, 5:45am-5:15pm; €4); **Preveza** (2hr.; 11:45am, 3:30pm; €7.40); **Thessaloniki** (7hr.; 10:30am, 7pm; €27.70). To reach the **bus station** from the ports, walk north along the waterfront to 23 Februariou, turn right, then left in 2 blocks on Kyprou. The **ticket office** is behind a cafe on the left marked with a blue KTEL sign.

Taxis: ☎26650 23 200 or 23 500. Line up by Corfu Port.

Car Rental: Europcar, Spirou Livada 19 (☎2684 32 777), just off the waterfront at the police station. €30 per day and up.

ORIENTATION AND PRACTICAL INFORMATION

Igoumenitsa is on the westernmost corner of mainland Greece, about 20km from the Albanian border. **Eth. Antistaseos,** which becomes **Ag. Apostolon,** runs along the waterfront and teems with travel agencies. To the north, after it divides, the tree-lined inland side of the street is bordered by an array of cafes and bars. Igoumenitsa's main shopping area is on **Grigariou Lamprari,** the first pedestrian street parallel to the waterfront. To reach the uninspiring central plateia, walk four blocks inland on **Zalogo,** which begins across from Corfu Port.

The **tourist office** (☎26650 22 227; open daily 8am-2pm), in the Old Port, helps with transportation and accommodations and supplies **free maps.** A **National Bank** (☎26650 22 415), across the road from the Old Port, is in a string of banks including a **Merchants Bank** and an **Agricultural Bank.** All have **ATMs** and **exchange currency.** (Open M-Th 8am-2:30pm, F 8am-2pm.) The **police,** Ag. Apostolon 5 (☎26650 22 100), across from Corfu Port, are available 24hr. The **port police** are in a Corfu Port booth, near customs and passport control. The 24hr. **medical center** (☎26650 24 420) offers basic health care. They can help you reach the **hospital** (☎26640 22 203), 15min. away. The **OTE** (☎26650 22 499; open 7am-2:30pm) is at pedestrian Grigariou's end. The New Port also has an OTE (☎26650 27 757; open 7am-10pm). **Netronio,** on the northern end of the waterfront in the cafe strip, has **Internet** access. (€3 per hr. Frappé €1.75; beer €2. Open 8am-2pm.) The **post office,** Tzavelenas 2, 1km north along the waterfront on the corner of a playground, accepts **Poste Restante.** (☎26640 46 100. Open 7:30am-2pm.) **Postal code:** 46100.

ACCOMMODATIONS

Hotel Acropolis ❷, on the waterfront in Old Port, has rooms with sinks, beds, and windows. The feel created by the owner's family is contagious. (☎26650 28 346. Singles €20; doubles €30; triples €35.) Looking out over the Old Port, **Jolly Hotel ❸** makes for a comfortable alternative with its spacious, carpeted rooms and marble-tiled hallways. All rooms have bath, A/C, TV, and phone. (☎26650 23 971; jolligm@otenet.gr. Singles €35; doubles €45; triples €60.) Look for **Hotel Egnatia's ❸,** in the central plateia's far right corner. Rooms have baths, TVs, phones, and A/C. (☎26650 23 455. Singles €30; doubles €40; triples €45.)

FOOD AND NIGHTLIFE

Mykonos ❷ (☎26650 27 567), at the beginning of the waterfront strip, north of the ports, has a vine-covered patio full of loquacious Greeks. The menu includes pizza, pasta, Greek mainstays, and a few fish specialties. The feta-stuffed souvlaki (€4.40) is a stimulating, inexpensive change of pace. **Alekos ❷,** next to Mykonos, specializes in fish caught in the harbor waters. (☎26650 23 708. Entrees €4.20-5.60.) **Strada Marina ❸,** facing the police station between the Old Port and Corfu Port, has a multilingual menu of Greek favorites. (Entrees €6-12.) The best and most popular among locals of the city's restaurants are on the northern edge of the waterfront, past the ports. Dozens of **bakeries** and **markets** line the pedestrian street just inland from the harbor.

Igoumenitsa's bland nightlife centers on a strip of bars along the waterfront. **Privilege** and **Traffic** (☎26650 23 505), a few doors down from Taverna Aleko, pump American and Greek tunes all night on the weekends over their cafe tables. (Cover €3, includes 1 drink. Beer €2; cocktails €4. Open until 5am.) A short distance from the city, **Clik** and **Ostria** attract a trendy local crowd. (Cover €3, includes 1 drink. Beer €2; cocktails €4.) Buses (€0.80) run hourly from the center. There's also a **cinema** (shows 9:30 and 11:15pm, €5), next to Taverna Aleko.

PARGA Παργα ☎26840

Birthplace of Süleyman the Magnificent's famed second in command, Vezir Ibrahim Pasha, Parga, like much of Greece, has a rich history with an ignoble end. Founded in 1204 by refugees from the crusader sack of Constantinople, the town's heyday began in 1401 when the Venicians fortified its high peninsula, establishing their Epiriote foothold here. The lion of Venice can still be seen over the gate to the well preserved kastro. Parga remained Venetian despite Ottoman attacks, during one of which young Ibrahim Pasha was enslaved, until Napoleon's sack of Venice transferred the city to France. The Gallic remains can be found on the island in the harbor. From France the town bobbled to the British, the Russians, Ali Pasha, the

Ottomans, and finally the Greeks. Its current occupants are T-shirt vendors and sun-toasted fuchsia-nosed Scandinavian children wielding inflatable alligators. Attached to the mainland by an arc of mountains and hosting luxurious beaches, Parga looks and feels like a Greek island town. A bustling waterfront, an effervescent nightlife, and overpriced beachside convenience stores complete the picture.

TRANSPORTATION. **Buses** run from Parga to: **Athens** (8½hr.; 3 per day, 7am-5pm; €28); **Igoumenitsa** (1¼hr.; 4 per day, 7am-6:30pm; €4); **Preveza** (1½hr.; 5 per day, 7am-9:15pm; €4.80); **Thessaloniki** (8½hr., 7am, €32.20). The **bus station** (☎26840 31 218) is a small booth next to the Chinese *(Kineziko)* restaurant at the top of Sp. Livada. **Ferries** run to **Corfu Town** (2hr., Th 8:30am, €35).

ORIENTATION AND PRACTICAL INFORMATION. Parga is organized around its waterfront. The main waterfront road, which brims with tavernas, bars, and tourist agencies, has three different names: from west to east, they are **Lambraki, Anexartissias,** and **Ag. Athanassiou.** At **Krioneri beach,** which runs alongside Athanassiou, the road forks: its uphill branch is **R. Feraiou.** Running inland from the waterfront is **Al. Baga,** which leads uphill to most of Parga's municipal buildings. Al. Baga meets **Sp. Livada** at the town's main intersection. Sp. Livada runs up to the highway and bus stop. Running parallel to the waterfront, **V.E. Vasila,** packed with tourist ships, leads up to the **Venetian castle** at the far southwestern corner of town. From here, a stone path leads down the other side to **Valtos beach.**

Tourist agencies pack the streets around the waterfront. Ready to help you find rooms, arrange daytrips, or rent a boat or car, they're generally open Monday through Saturday 9am-2pm and 5:30-10pm. Try **ITS,** beyond the ferry dock next door to a pharmacy. (☎26840 31 833. Open 9am-1:30pm and 6:50-10pm.) With the **OTE** (☎26840 31 699; open M-F 8am-1pm and 3-8pm) on your left and the shore behind you, the **police station,** with a helpful tourist bureau (☎26840 31 222; open 24hr.), and **post office** (☎26840 31 295; open M-F 7:30am-2pm) are straight ahead. To the left, across from the church, is the **National Bank** (open M-Th 8am-2pm, F 8am-1:30pm) with a 24hr. **ATM;** 100m down the road is the 24hr. **health center** (☎26840 31 233). Going right will bring you to a junction with the main road and the bus stop. For **emergencies,** you can also call the **port police** (☎26840 31 227). **Internet** access is available at **Cafe Terra** (€1.50 per 20min.; open 8am-3am), on the waterfront, halfway between the dock and the beach; at **Flamingo** on Riga Feriou (☎26840 32 207; €1.50 per 20min.); and at the cheap **Net Zone** (☎26840 32 895; €2 per hr.; open 1pm-2am). **Postal code:** 48060.

ACCOMMODATIONS AND CAMPING. Parga's hotels can be expensive; prices spike in July and August by about 30%. Look near the highway, around the southern end of the town and at the top of the hill for **domatia.** Just below the entrance to the fortress, above a small bakery in a bright yellow building, **Kostas and Martha Christou ❷** rent clean, simple rooms with private baths and balconies, just a 5min. walk to the pebbly shores of Valtos beach. (☎26840 31 942. Singles €15; doubles €25; triples €35.) The **Andreou Rooms ❷** (☎26840 31 306), just below, have balcony views, kitchens, and baths. **Hotel Galini ❷,** behind an orchard off Sp. Livada at the top of town has a friendly proprietor, even through hand gestures. Mr. Drakos offers quieter rooms with balconies baths, and phones. (☎26840 31 581; fax 26840 32 221. Breakfast €5. Singles €25; doubles €35; triples €50.) About 50m beyond Krinoeri beach's end, **Pavlos Vergas ❸** has tidy rooms with bath, kitchen, TV, and balcony. Enjoy a drink on the beautiful marble patio. (☎26840 31 617. Doubles €45; triples €55.) Camping on nearby beaches is a good option to stay on budget. English-speaking **Camping Valtos ❶** is cleanest and close to both town and Valtos beach; the grounds close at midnight. (☎26840 31 287; www.campingvaltos.gr.

Laundry available. €4 per person, €3.50 per tent, €2.40 per car. Electricity €2.60.) Closest to a beach, though far from Parga, is **Camping Lichnos ❶**, whose terraced, vine-trellised sites are appealing, if not over polished. A small market is on site and laundry is available; the entrance closes at 9pm. (☎26840 31 171; holidays@enjoy-lichnos.com. Laundry available. €5 per person, €3.60 per tent, €2.20 per car. Electricity €2.) **Parga Beach Camping ❶**, outside of town, also has nice sites. (☎26840 31 161. €4.30 per person, €4 per tent, €3 per car. Electricity €3.20.)

FOOD. The price discrepancies between boardwalk corn-on-the-cob stands 50m apart, should alert you to the erratic pooling of euros in this land of loose tourist cash. Although there are some reasonable menu items along the waterfront, those who would trade a view for value should head back to town alleys or the highway. Perched on the hilltop just below the entrance to the fortress, **Kastro Entasis ❸**, with its soft music and sea-blue tablecloths, serves up superb food and sweeping views. (Salads €3-8. Entrees €6.50-12.50.) For budget options try the deck-top taverna **Altana ❷** (☎26840 31 361), on Pl. Ag. Dimitrios, or the delicious but noisy **Dokos Taverna ❷** (☎26840 31 574), 150m toward Preveza along the highway outside of town. The excellent *yiovetsi* and service make the journey worthwhile. A few doors beyond the ferry dock as you head toward Krioneri beach, **To Souli ❷** cooks up lamb and feta *kleftiko* (€5), salads, and fresh fish (€23 per kg). By Krioneri beach, **Restaurant Ionio ❷** (☎26840 31 402) has a prime location and honest prices. If you're looking to splurge, swanky **Rudis ❹** (☎26840 31 693) serves creative Greek and Italian cuisine at the end of the dock.

NIGHTLIFE AND ENTERTAINMENT. Scuttling waiters and rambunctious children run through crowds of jovially inebriated Northern Europeans at Parga's many waterfront bars and cafes. During the day **Tango Club** on Valtos beach is most popular. Students crowd the bar, while children reign in the club's pool (☎26840 31 252). **Caravel,** near the ferry dock, is also popular, with an upstairs balcony. Tourists fill the seats all day sipping either a morning orange juice, afternoon iced coffee, or evening cocktail. (☎26840 31 359. Drinks €3.50-4.50.) The more removed **Blue Bar** (☎26840 32 067), on the road leading to the castle, is a hipper choice, with stunning views of the sea and Art Deco blue-light and mirror decorations to go with the 93 cocktails mixed up by the bartenders. Try the "Happy Company" (€18), served in a massive ceramic jug; it packs a punch powerful enough to floor you and three of your friends. Though the tourists here are of the family ilk, there are a couple of discos that don't really fill up until around 2am. Clubs stay open until 4am on weekdays and at least 6am on weekends; the cover is usually €3, which includes one drink. The biggest scenes are at **Camares** (☎26840 32 000), behind Caravel, and **Arena,** down behind the beach. Camares teems with freshly tanned Northern Europeans, showing off their drunken dance moves. Arena caters to the young, hip set behind its mirrored facade. **Factory,** whose neon signs point up side streets from near the ferry dock, is slightly less packed but funky with furniture transformed from the original factory machinery. After July 10, **Rendezvous,** a local *bouzouki* club, opens its pounding doors.

SIGHTS AND BEACHES. High on Parga's rocky headland, the massive **kastro** was built by the Normans but was controlled by the Venetians from 1401 to 1797. In its glory days, the castle held 500 homes and 5000 Pargiotes. A surprising number of walls still stand; the cannons, however, which lined their tops, have long since fallen and are now strewn about the cobblestone enclosure. Although under reconstruction, the castle remains a perfect spot for a shady picnic, stroll, or dramatic reenactment of a Venetian-Ottoman battle. It's 5min. from the water; follow the steps from the harbor up the hill. (Open 7am-10pm.)

Krioneri beach, Parga's little waterfront, may be popular, but travelers should heed the sweet smell coming from the rocks behind the shoreside dumpsters and head to one of the more pristine beaches for a swim. Paddleboats (€8 per hr.) are available for water-wary swimmers who still want to make the 100m journey to the island. From the island's small beach, a hike past the **spring** and small **Church of the Panagia** takes you to remains of the Napoleanic fortifications. One building has the telltale inscription "De la Patrie 1808." On the other side of the island is a quiet pine-covered pinnacle with views of the distant islands Paxos and Antipaxos. **Piso Krioneri,** a 5min. walk around the rocks at the end of Krioneri beach, is a bit more secluded. For long sands and hip sunbathing head to **Valtos beach,** on the other side of the castle: a voluptuous crescent of sole-tickling pebbles turns to sand near the middle. You can enjoy anything from a beach ball to a paragliding trip or hit the packed **pool club.** Boats from **The Parga Mariners** travel to the smaller beaches, including the cafe-lined **Lichnos beach** (2km), accessible by car or boat (€4 round-trip), and quiet **Pogo beach** (€3), accessible only by boat, with a single cafe.

Tour companies along the waterfront and on the ferry dock book a variety of pre-packaged **excursions.** Most popular are 2hr. trips to uninhabited Antipaxos, with a lunch stop on its occupied Ionian neighbor Paxos, and cheery voyages up swampy **River Acheron**—better known as the River Styx, mythical gateway to the Underworld and to **Necromanteion** (the Oracle of the Dead; €9). From atop the rocky site you can gaze at miles of low surrounding farms and imagine how dismal the site must have been before this flat breadbasket, once a malarial swamp, was drained. It's a 1hr. voyage past coastal cliffs, caves (brief swimming stop), and coves and up the turtle and snake inhabited Acheron to the ancient swamp, now a corn field. A 30min. walk past fields and the occasional reed brings you to Necromanteion. The site is excellently preserved with clay offerings, jugs larger than a man, a labyrinth meant to exclude sound from the windowless inner sanctum, and a subterranean arched vault for communing with the dead. It was here that Odysseus supposedly conversed with the Shades, who spoke to him only after drinking offerings of blood. (☎26840 41 206. Open 8am-3pm. €2, students with ID free.) Food is available in the nearby town **Mesopotamo.** The site can also be reached in about 20min. by taking the bus for Preveza. To return, wait at the bus-stop on the highway, just outside Mesopotamo, for the Preveza-Parga bus. From the end of Valtos beach a trail leads past a **neromylos** (watermill) up to **Ali Pasha's castle** on the top of the cliff with wonderful views.

PREVEZA Πρεβεζα ☎26510

Sixty kilometers south of Igoumenitsa and 75km southwest of Ioannina, at the tip of a peninsula capping the Amvrakikos Gulf is the merchant port of Preveza, home to the Greek naval school. The sheltered gulf and its strategic peninsula have enjoyed naval significance since ancient times. It is at the bottom of the strait, sprinkled around the new tunnel to Aktio, that most of Antony and Cleopatra's ships lie: sunken by Octavian in the battle that made him emperor. The huge archaeological remains of Octavian's victory city, Nikopolis, are Preveza's main attraction. The remainder of the few tourists that visit this tiny city are en route to the long sandy beaches and secluded coves that dot the Adriatic coast from here to Parga; few visitors stay here for more than a day or two.

TRANSPORTATION

Buses, leaving from Byzaniou and Irinis (☎26820 22 213), go to: **Arta** (1hr.; 10 per day, 7:15am-5:45pm; €3.50); **Athens** (6hr.; 7 per day, 9am-8pm; €7); **Igoumenitsa** (2½hr.; 4 per day, 11:15am-2:30pm; €7.40); **Ioannina** (2hr.; 20 per day, 6am-7:30pm; €6.90); **Parga** (1¾hr.; 8 per day, 7am-8pm; €4.80); **Thessaloniki** (7½hr., 9:10am,

€27.90). **Flights** run from **Aktio Airport** (☎26820 22 355), 3km away. To: **Athens** (50min.; M, W, Th, Sa; €61.60); **Corfu** (30min.; Tu, Th, Su; €34.60); **Kephalonia** (20min.; Th, Su; €29.60); **Thessaloniki** (40min.; Tu, Su; €84.60); **Zakynthos** (30min.; Th, Su; €34.60). An **airport bus** (€1.50) runs from the **Olympic Airways** office, Irinis 37 (☎26820 28 343), to Aktio Airport 1hr. before departure. (Open M-F 8am-2:30pm.) **Taxis** (☎26820 22 887, 26820 28 470, or 26820 23 750) wait by the bus station and at a stand at the waterfront's northern end, by Klemanso. The **car rental** agencies **Europcar** and **Avis** are just past the post office at Spilaiou and Vokli.

ORIENTATION AND PRACTICAL INFORMATION

Preveza lies parallel to its harbor waterfront on the Amvrakikos Gulf. The main road in from Arta and Ioannina is **Irinis.** Both the KTEL office, and just past it, the Olympic Airways office, with its airport bus, are off this highway. Beginning with **Vizaniou** at the KTEL, streets branch left off Irinis to the waterfront two blocks away. On their way there these streets cross the two roads parallel to Irinis, **21 Oktovriou** and **Ethn. Anastasis.** Shops, banks, and bakeries cover Ethn. Anastasis, a pedestrian road. The town's center, **To Roloi,** named after the clock tower, is on Anastasis. Nearby side streets, **Dardanellion** and **Parthenagogio** in particular, host the locals' tavernas. **Venizelou,** the waterfront road, starts at the **ferris wheel** in the south port and runs north past the tourist office, taxi stand, and nightclub Portokali. Below the ferris wheel, the waterfront road is called **Spiliadou;** after passing the post office it quickly becomes more friendly to pedestrians. The tunnel (cars €3, motorbikes €0.70) is on the other side of town.

The **tourist office** (☎26820 21 078; open M-F 8am-2:30pm), off the waterfront on Balkou, provides **maps** and pamphlets. **National Bank,** on Ethn. Anastasis at Parthenagogio, and **Merchants Bank,** just down Pathenagoiohas have **ATMs.** (Both open M-Th 8am-2:30pm, F 8am-2pm.) The **police** (☎26820 22 223) are on Dodonis off Irinis past the KTEL on the way out of town. The **hospital** (☎26820 46 200) is at the far southern end of the waterfront; pass the ferris wheel and follow Spiliadou for 600m. The **OTE** is on Karyotaki just off Irinis (open M, Th 8:30am-1:45pm; Tu-W, F 8:30am-1:30pm and 6-9pm). Find **Internet** access at **Ascot Internet Cafe,** Balkou 6 (☎16820 27 746), opposite the tourist office by the waterfront. Access is cheap (€2.50 per hr.), as are the frappés (€1.80). **Net Cafe,** on Spiliadou in front of the kastro, also offers Internet (€2.50 per hr.) as well as scanners and printers. (☎26820 27 230. Open 9am-1am.) The **post office,** on Spiliadou three blocks past the ferris wheel, has **Poste Restante.** (Open M-F 7:30am-2pm.) **Postal code:** 48100.

ACCOMMODATIONS

Like in other mainland Greek cities, Preveza's hotels are not especially cheap. The best value is **Hotel Avra ❸,** Venizelou 19, which offers harbor views, along with private baths, TVs, telephones, and A/C. (☎26820 21 230; www.epirus.com/hotelavra. Singles €30; doubles €40; triples €50). **Hotel Minos ❸,** 21 Oktovriou 11, has simple but comfortable rooms with telephones, TVs, A/C, and baths. (☎26820 28 424; fax 26820 24 644. Singles €25; doubles €30; triples €40.) **Hotel Dioni ❸** has TVs, A/C, telephones, fridges, baths, and balconies. (☎26820 27 381; fax 26820 27 384. Singles €35; doubles €40; triples €55. AmEx/V.)

FOOD AND NIGHTLIFE

The traditional Greek restaurants in Preveza often have delicious prices to go with tasteful locations. If you want to hang with tourists, you'll see a few at the *psistarias* on Parthenagogio; you won't find anything but Greek spoken on the other side of Ethn.

Anastasis. For those stocking up for a long day's tramp around Nikopolis, there is a large **Atlantik Supermarket** across from the OTE at Karyotaki and Irinis. **Taverna Psatha ❷,** Dardanelion 4 (☎26820 23 051), under a kitten-haunted awning formed by flowering vines teems with the chattering of Greek families. Step into the kitchen to inspect the night's mouth-watering dishes. **Seitan Pazap ❷,** Kontou 18, a local fish taverna in a quiet venue, has excellent harborside prices. (☎26820 60 863. Squid €4. Octopus €6.50. Cuttlefish €5.50.) **Kaixis ❷,** Parthenagogio 7, is another *psarotaverna* (fish taverna) with excellent prices. (☎26820 24 866. Menus available in English and German.)

Preveza's ultimate party spot is **Club Nikopolis,** a huge cafe, bar, and beach complex 10km along the road to Parga. Another popular club is **Portokali** (☎69440 41 591), meaning "orange"—as in the fruit—whose orange jellyfish lamps line Venizelou at the far northern end of the harbor. (Both open F-Sa until late.) Along Venizelou are many typical Greek cafes, where trendy youngsters sip beer until 3am.

DAYTRIPS FROM PREVEZA

NIKOPOLIS

The Arta, Ioannina, Parga, and Igoumenitsa buses (€1) will drop you at the site 7km outside the city. To return, wait for an Arta or Ioannina bus at the Smyrntoula highway stop. Alternatively, take a taxi (€5). ☎*26820 41 336. Site open 8am-7pm; museum 8am-5pm. €3, seniors €2, students and under 18 free.*

In 31 BC former allies **Octavian Caesar** and **Mark Antony** met in the waters off Preveza for the naval battle of **Actium,** which would secure Octavian's power. Antony brought with him one of the strongest fleets in the Mediterranean—that of Egypt—along with Egypt's queen, his lover, **Cleopatra.** Many of Antony's Roman friends ended up abandoning him, throwing the battle to Octavian. In celebration of his *nike* (victory), Octavian built **Nikopolis** at the point where he had camped on the eve of the battle. Surrounding cities where emptied as inhabitants were resettled in this new capital of Epirus. The well-preserved **odeon,** parts of the walls, the **baths,** and the **nymphaion** (fountain pools at the end of the aqueduct) survive from this period. All these structures are within 10min. of the site museum. You'll also find the **stadium, gymnasium,** and **Actium Victory Monument,** perched above the city with a sweeping view of the fateful waters. These latter structures were built outside the ancient city and are a 25min. walk away in modern Smyrntoula. In addition, St. Paul wrote his famous **Letter to Titus** here in the first century.

The barbarian raids and the fall of the western empire in the 5th century led to a contraction of the city, which the **Emperor Zeno** surrounded with a new Byzantine fortification. This is the impressive tower-studded **wall** that still stands. Look closely for pieces of friezes and reused Roman blocks in the wall, which reveal the fate of many of the city's lost monuments. The remains of three basilicas, whose mosaics are now covered with sand, date from this time. The site is extensive; keep in mind that this was once a sprawling city and requires a good deal of walking, sometimes through high grass and thistles. Long pants are recommended. The flocks of sheep, reed-filled basilicas, ocean views, and olive grove-shrouded ruins make for a delightful day's romp. The **museum,** housing some tombstones, friezes, and a sculpture of Octavian's victorious admiral, **Agrippa,** deserves a visit too.

AG. GEORGIOS AQUEDUCT

Buses (1hr.; 20 per day, 7am-8:30pm; €3.50) from Preveza to Ioannina run in pairs; the later lags 30min. behind. Ask to be let off at Ag. Georgios, then hustle back to flag down the later bus. The stop at Ag. Georgios is only for the Ioannina bound. Those traveling to Preveza must walk 10min. toward Ioannina for the next bus stop. Walk 3min. down the Ag. Georgios road to the bridge; the ruins are on the right.

Those traveling to Ioannina from Preveza should not miss the impressive remains of Nikopolis's **aqueduct** in Ag. Georgios. The ruins' location alone, high in the mountains 40km north of Preveza, is impressive, but the well-preserved section crossing the Louros rapids has a beauty of its own. One sees why it took over 50 years to lay the aqueduct from the springs to the **nymphaeum fountain** of Nikopolis.

IOANNINA Ιωαννινα ☎26510

On the shores of Lake Pamvotis, 96km east of Igoumenitsa, lies Epirus's capital, largest city, and transportation hub. Ioannina itself might not detain you for long, but the surrounding mountains and calm lake below deliver scenic views and an uplifting breeziness to the city. The city's post-World War II architecture is redeemed by the narrow cobblestone streets and the magnificent fortress of the Old City. No visitor to Ioannina from Byron to the present has been able to escape the foreboding, half-legendary Ali Pasha, "Lion of Ioannina." The Albanian-born Pasha from Trikala seized Ioannina in 1788 and built himself a palace. Intending to make the city the capital of his Greek-Albanian empire, Ali ruled with an iron fist, alternately fighting with and serving the Ottoman Sultan, who was theoretically his ruler. Ali has certainly left his imprint on the city: his immense fortress and torso are here, and he was shot in a monastery on a nearby island in 1822.

TRANSPORTATION

Flights: Daily service to: **Athens** (50min.; 10:35am, 5:25pm; €79) and **Thessaloniki** (40min.; M 1:35pm, Tu 3:35pm, F and Su noon; €60). To reach the airport, take bus #2 or 7 from the stop in front of the clock in the central plateia. Find **Olympic Airways** (☎26510 26 218; reservations 26510 23 120), where G. Averoff splits into Napoleonda Zerva and Leoforos Dodoni, above the city center. Open M-F 9am-2:30pm.

Buses: There are 3 terminals in town.

Main terminal, Zosimadon 4 (☎26510 27 442). To: **Athens** (6½hr.; 10 per day, 7:15am-midnight; €26.10); **Igoumenitsa** (2hr.; 9 per day, 5am-7:30pm; €6.40); **Konitsa** (1¼hr.; 7 per day, 5am-7:30pm; €4); **Metsovo** (1½hr.; 3 per day, 5am-2pm; €3.80); **Monodendri** (M, W, F 5:30am and 1:15pm); **Papingo** (M, W, F 5am and 1pm); **Parga** (2½hr., 8:30am, €8); **Trikala** (8am, 2pm; €9.70); **Thessaloniki** (7hr.; 6 per day, 7:30am-10:30pm; €21.50) via **Larisa** (4hr., €12.50); **Volos** (3pm).

Minor station, Vizaniou 21 (☎26510 25 014). To: **Agrinio** (3hr.; 6 per day, 5:30am-7:15pm; €10.30); **Arta** (1½hr.; 10 per day, 5:45am-8pm; €4.60); **Dodoni** (30min.; M, W, F 6:30am and 3:30pm; €2); **Patras** (4hr.; 4 per day, 9am-5:30pm; €15.30); **Preveza** (2hr.; 10 per day, 6am-8pm; €6.90).

KTEL Kastorias, G. Papandreou 58 (☎26510 30 006 or 26510 25 868) serves **Kastoria** (3hr.; 10:30am, 4pm; €12.90).

Taxis: ☎26510 46 777, 46 778, or 46 779. Convene in the city center and at the bus station.

ORIENTATION AND PRACTICAL INFORMATION

Ioannina is at the center of Epirus, at the edge of steely Lake Pamvotis, and circled by the peaks of Pindos. Not far into the lake is a small, hilly island simply called Nisi or Nissaki ("the island" or "the islet"). The city center is a major intersection near the **clock tower** *(To Roloi)* in Litharitses park. **G. Averof,** lined with jewelry stores and souvlaki stands, is a broad avenue that runs from the main gate of the Old City to the city center. To reach the city center from the main **bus station,** walk uphill about 20m from the station to an intersection, where you'll see an **Agricultural Bank.** Facing the bank, walk uphill along the street on the left, which begins as **Dagli** but becomes **M. Botsari** after a block—the enormous Hotel Egnatia sign makes a useful landmark. You'll pass the **post office** (the **OTE** is behind it, but not visible from Botsari) and emerge next to the **Alpha Bank** on Averof, facing the park. On your right, past the long building labeled "Prefecture of Ioannina" (Νομαρχιον Ιωαννινων, νο–μαρ–ΧΗΕΕ–ον ΨΑΗ–νεε–νον), the road splits. The right side (not the sharp right) is **Napoleonda Zerva,** to the left is **Leoforos Dodoni.** At the set of street lights before the Prefecture building, a road leads downhill to the smaller of the two intercity bus stations. To reach the **Frourio** (fortress) and the **waterfront,** follow the signs from the city center to Averof's opposite end, and veer left at the Frourio walls. You will now be on **Karamanli,** which passes the main gate of the Frourio to the dock and waterfront.

Tourist Office: EOT office (☎26510 46 662; eotioan@otenet.gr), about 500m down Leoforos Dodoni on the left immediately after the playground. Has **maps** and Ioannina Prefecture propaganda, with a list of **domatia** in the province. Worth the 10min. walk from the city center. Open M-F 7:30am-2:30pm. Hours extended July-Sept. M-F 5-8:30pm, Sa 9am-1pm.

Banks: There are a number of banks with 24hr. **ATMs,** including **National Bank,** on Averof, just after the Archaeological Museum as you walk toward the waterfront. Open M-Th 8am-2pm, F 8am-1:30pm.

Police: ☎26510 65 93. Walk along Botsari to the post office; the police are around the corner on 28 Oktovriou. Open 8am-10pm. Available 24hr. for **emergencies.**

Tourist Police: ☎26510 65 922; www.uoi.gr/tourist_police. In the same building as the police. **Free maps** and other info available. Open 8am-10pm.

Hospital: 2 hospitals, each about 5km from the center of town. **Hatzikosta** (☎26510 80 111) handles emergencies on even dates; the **University Hospital** (☎26510 99 111) does so on odd dates.

OTE: ☎26510 22 350 or 26510 42 777. On 28 Oktovriou, next to the post office. Open M-F 7:30am-2pm.

Internet Access: Online i-cafe (☎26510 72 512), on Pirsinella, the last street on your right as you walk south along Averof away from the waterfront, is stylish with 75 speedy terminals. Open 24hr. €2.20 per hr. noon-midnight, €2 per hr. midnight-noon. Frappé €2. Down Pirsinella, **The Web** (☎26510 26 813) is a cheaper alternative. €1.50-2.50 per hr. Frappé €0.75. Open 24hr.

Post Office: ☎26510 25 498. At the intersection of 28 Oktovriou and Botsari. Open M-F 7:30am-8pm. **Postal code:** 45110.

ACCOMMODATIONS

There is little value to be found in Ioannina. Hotels are either comfortable and expensive or uncomfortable and cheap. This is a good place to consider **camping.** Try **Limnopoula ❶**, 10 Kanari (☎26510 25 265; fax 26510 38 060) with laundry, cooking, swimming, and shade. Otherwise head to one of the pricey but livable hotels on Averof. You can try one of Ioannina's cheap—for good reason—options if you're not concerned with surroundings and amenities. **Hotel Tourist ❸**, Kolleti 18, just behind Hotel Metropolis, on the right a few blocks up Averof from the kastro section, has well-decorated rooms with A/C, baths, telephones, and TVs, set back slightly from Averof's incessant motorbike racket. (☎26510 25 070; fax 26510 20 002. Singles €30; doubles €40; triples €50.) **Hotel Bretania ❸**, Central Plateia 11a, is on Averof across from the clock in the city center. Central location and the sugar-coating from Bretania sweet shop downstairs make sour prices more paletable. Clean rooms have baths, A/C, and TVs, and street noise. (☎26510 29 396, fax 26510 33 589. Singles €35; doubles €45; triples €55. MC.) **Hotel Metropolis ❷**, Kristali 2, is on the corner to your left as you walk down Averof toward the water-

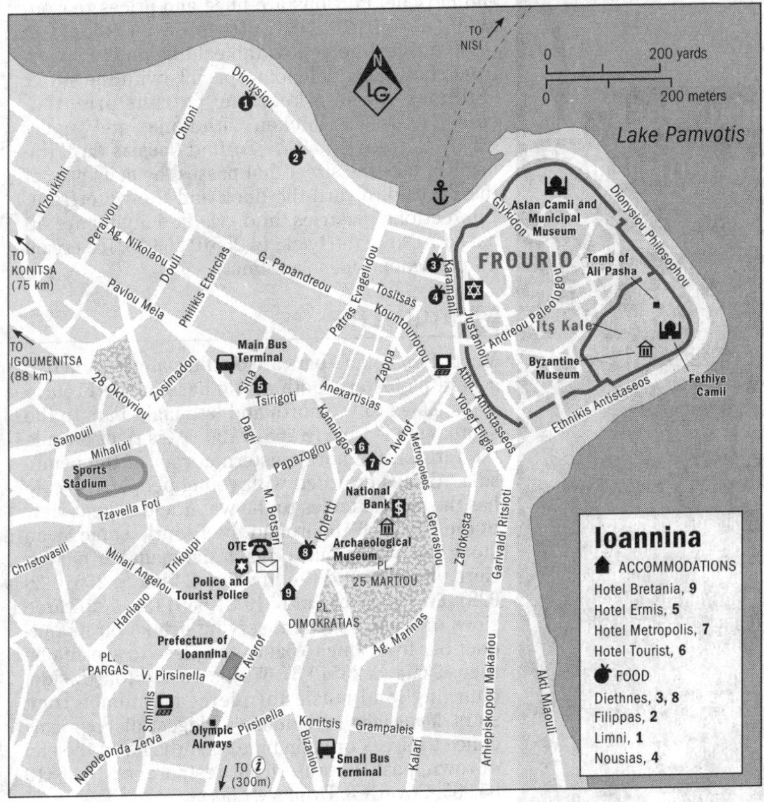

front. Look for the red and yellow sign. Colorful rooms are noisy but conveniently located. (☎26510 26 207. Singles €15; doubles €20; triples €35.) **Hotel Ermis ❷**, Sina 2, at Tsirigoti across from the main bus station, has bare, uncomfortable rooms with no private baths and much street noise. Still it's cheap and convenient. (☎26510 75 992. Singles €18; doubles €25; triples €33.)

FOOD

Souvlaki, gyro, and hamburger joints coat Averof as thickly as cholesterol on arteries. More substantial dining can be found on Papagou by the waterfront. Follow Averof to the Frourio, skirt the walls to the lake. Walking away from the Frourio, cafes will soon give way to scenic tavernas. After a meal head to one of Ioannina's sweet shops, where you can sample the regional speciality: baklava. Ioannina also has excellent Turkish ice cream, called *kaimaki*. Its unique flavor, deriving from gum resin, should not be missed. **Diethnes ❶** (☎26510 74 366) is a sweet shop carrying the town's sticky specialty. It also has excellent *kaimaki* (€1 per scoop). One is located in the park on Averof after the clock tower. Another is found on Karamanli by the waterfront. **Limni ❷** means "lake," and, like other restaurants in this area, it has a charming lakeside patio with views of the mountains

THE LOCAL LEGEND

BUT A WHIMPER

Though Greek historians can't agree on whether Ali Pasha of Ioannina was a hero or villain, local legends agree that his semi-independent Albanian *bey* had a mean streak. Finding a local girl, Kura Frosuni, to his taste, Ali sought to add her to his harem, and when she refused, he drowned each of her 17 servants, so she could fully savor the fate she soon shared. Ali was also known to cruelly torture his enemies, and Byron was particularly impressed by his sadism. But his years of strangling dissidents to build a totalitarian empire were numbered.

After siding with the British against the very Sultan who appointed him, and then double crossing them too, Ali's friends grew thin, and in 1822 the Sultan sent an army to crush his rebellious, power-hungry pasha. Ali holed up on Nisi island and gave orders to Selim, his most trusted servant, to stand guard over the castle's immense casks of gunpowder with a lighted torch. If Selim heard gunshots from the island, he was to blow himself, the castle, and the city with all its inhabitants clear into Lake Pamvotis. If anyone arrived bearing Ali's rosary, all was well and he could put out the torch. The sultan's envoys, however, managed to convince Ali's Greek wife, Vasilikis, to betray Ali's instructions, telling her it was her duty as a Greek to save the town from destruction. Vasilikis stole Ali's rosary as he slept, and presented it to the Turks, who immediately used it to convince Selim to put out his torch. The gun battle which ensued the next day saw the end of Ali Pasha–not with a bang.

and mosque. Portions are huge and prices reasonable. (☎26510 78 988. Entrees €5-7.) **Filippas ❷** (look out for the yellow tablecloths on the waterfront) has many delicious specials with the suffix "Filippas" to help keep the patrons oriented. (☎26510 31 170. Chicken with honey and yogurt €6.50. Entrees €4.50-7.) To find **Nousias ❶,** Karamanli 1, take the street that passes the main gate of the Frourio toward the dock and the waterfront. Confections, pastries, and crispy delights are all baked fresh in the back. (☎26510 25 075. Ice cream €1 per scoop. Open 9am-1am.)

NIGHTLIFE

Most of Ioannina's bars are on the waterfront in two separate clusters, both at the base of the Frourio walls: cafes to the north and late-night bars to the south. **Kura Frosuni** (☎26510 73 984) is right outside the fort, on the northwestern corner of the peninsula. Always crowded with young people, the cafe has the closest tables to the water and a great view of the island. Walk around the Frourio some 300m along the waterfront to reach the main bar center. Here you will find the low-key **N-Club** (☎26510 28 028). **Ev. Ioanninos** (☎26510 21 669) takes up three sides of a small square, serving drinks on its outdoor bar from 9pm to 5am—the place to see and be seen. **Skala** (☎26510 37 676) is on the fourth side, churning loud music for pierced wannabe rock stars. **Monopolio** is Ioannina's biggest disco; locals dance to Greek or Latin tunes nightly. It's at the end of town, past the waterfront restaurants. (☎26510 35 985. Cover €3. Drinks €1.50.)

SIGHTS

FROURIO. The town's fortress, the **Frourio** (a.k.a. the **kastro** or **Old City**) presides regally over the shore, a slender minaret at each end. Its massive, overgrown stone walls enclose a placid neighborhood of narrow streets and old Turkish-style homes. Like any self-respecting fortress, the Frourio's main entrance on Karamanli has several sharp turns, making invasion tricky. Just outside this entrance is the shrine to **St. George the Neomartyr,** Ioannina's patron saint, whose Turkish overlords tortured and hanged him in 1838 for marrying a Christian. Most of the castle was built in the 14th century by **Thomas Preljubovic,** the Serbian ruler of Ioannina who was also known as **Albanitoktonos** ("Albanian-killer"). In order to secure the city's bloodless surrender in 1430, the Turks assured the

Greeks that they could remain in their houses within the walls. However, after a failed 1611 Greek insurrection led by **Skilosofos,** the fanatical Bishop of Trikala, the Turks cracked down. One Sunday, when all the Greeks were in church, the sneaky Turks seized their houses. Skilosofos, the rebellious bishop, was captured and skinned alive. When Ali Pasha came to power in 1795, he forced his Greek subjects to rebuild the Byzantine walls on a grander scale to fortify the capital of his dreamed-of empire.

ITŞ KALE. To reach the Itş Kale from the main entrance, walk forward, veering left, following the signs. The small ruined buildings on both sides as you enter the walls were guard posts, and the cafe on the left was originally a kitchen. Over to the immediate right along the wall are the remnants of Ali Pasha's **hamam** (baths). Around what is now the Silverworks Gallery, the *serai* once housed Ali, his harem, and his ornately decorated audience chambers. Ali Pasha held most of his notorious tortures and executions at the plane tree near the *serai*, running the gory gamut from skinning to impaling and suspending on hooks hung from the tree's branches. War of Independence hero **Katsandonis** is said to have sung patriotic hymns while being brutally hammered to death here, a scene re-enacted frequently in Greek folk shadow puppet theater. The ruins on the right of the complex are partially preserved, and are well worth a scramble. *(Open 8am-10pm.)* The **Byzantine Museum** in the Itş Kale has a small collection of intricately carved wooden sanctuary doors, stone carvings, calligraphic manuscripts, and post-Byzantine icons. English-language wall plaques chronicle the history of Epirus and Ioannina. *(☎26510 27 761 or 26510 39 580. Open M 12:30-7pm, Tu-Su 8am-7pm. €3, students €2.)* The **Fethiye Camii** (Victory Mosque) next to the museum is the third mosque in its location, a space once occupied by a 13th-century church. The current mosque was rebuilt in 1795 by Ali Pasha himself. In front of the mosque, weeds and rubble obscure the **Tomb of Ali Pasha,** a sarcophagus that contains his headless body; from the neck up, he's buried in Istanbul. The tomb was originally decorated with a gilded cage that was looted by Nazis in 1943, but it was recently replaced by a green iron approximation. Ioannina is the silversmith capital of Greece, and at the **Silverworks Gallery,** you'll find snuffboxes, tea services, and belt buckles to prove it. An etching beside the desk depicts the Frourio's former glory. *(☎26510 25 989. Show your Byzantine Museum ticket for admission to the gallery.)*

MUNICIPAL MUSEUM. The smaller of the Frourio's walled inner areas is a little farther to the left of Itş Kale—follow signs through the crooked streets to the museum housed in the lovely **Aslan Pasha Camii.** On the left as you enter is the long, rectangular former *medrasa* (school for Quranic study). The tombstones engraved in Arabic are the remains of an **Ottoman cemetery,** and the small building behind the mosque is Aslan Pasha's mausoleum. In 1618 following Bishop Skilosofos's rebellion, the Turks destroyed the former church of St. John Prodromus and replaced it with this elegant mosque. The Municipal Museum focuses on Ioannina's diverse ethnic past and is divided into Jewish, Greek, and Muslim exhibits. Highlights include a sword that belonged to War of Independence hero Karaiskaki and a golden dress worn by Ali Pasha's wife, Lady Vasilikis. *(☎26510 26 356. Open June-Sept. 8am-8:30pm; Oct.-May 8am-3pm. €2, students €1.)*

ARCHAEOLOGICAL MUSEUM. Aside from local finds, Paleolithic to Roman, the museum's highlights are the **lead tablets** used by puzzled ancients to inscribe their questions to the oracle to Zeus in nearby **Dodoni** (p. 262). Check out the **copper statues** from the oracle, which would speak the words of Zeus through batons they held in their hands. *(On a small road off Averof near the city center, across from the yellow town hall building. Currently under renovations. ☎26510 33 357 or 26510 25 490. Open Tu-Su 8:30am-3pm. €2, students free.)*

NISI (THE ISLAND). Wandering chickens, cheap silver shops, a tiny whitewashed village, and five deteriorating monasteries cover Ioannina's peaceful island, a 10min. ferry ride from the harbor. Ali Pasha met his death on Nisi after falling out of the sultan's favor in a big way. Discovered and trapped in the second story of the island's **St. Pantaleimon monastery,** he was killed by shots fired up through the floorboards (now, complete with bullet holes, in the museum). The victors hung Ali's severed head for public viewing for several days before transporting it on horseback to the sultan back in Constantinople. The monastery now houses the **Ali Pasha Museum,** which displays Ali Pasha's enormous *nargileh*, from which he happily puffs in almost every portrait and a large painting of the sultan ceremoniously receiving the head of his fearsome ex-governor. *(Open daily 8am-10pm. €0.75.)*

Signs point the way to St. Pantaleimon and the other four monasteries. A short walk from the museum, the **frescoes** of St. Nicholas Philanthropinos, painted by Katelanou in 1542, depict saints, the life of Jesus, and seven ancient sages (including Plato, Aristotle, and Plutarch, just inside the door on the left) who were said to have proclaimed the coming of Jesus. If the monastery is locked, ask politely at the house next door for a tour. At the nearby *krifto scholio* ("secret school"), the forbidden Greek language was kept alive during the Ottoman reign. The monastery of **St. John Prodromos** has a crypt leading to a secret exit and path to the lake. *(☎26510 25 885. Take one of the little 10 min. ferries from Ioannina's waterfront. They run every hr., 6:30-11:30am, and every 30min., 11:30am-11pm; in winter every hr., 7am-9pm; €1.)*

DAYTRIPS FROM IOANNINA

DODONI Δωδωνη

Buses to Dodoni run from Ioannina's smaller station (30min.; M, W, F 6:30am and 3:30pm; €1.70). Ask to be let off at the theater. The return bus passes by at about 4:45pm; however, this doesn't leave you with much time to view the site. Alternatively, you can hire a taxi (at least €15 one-way) and take the bus back. ☎26510 82 287. Open 8am-7pm. €2, students and seniors €1, EU students free.

Ancient Dodoni, the site of mainland Greece's oldest oracle, lies at the base of a mountain 22km southeast of Ioannina. The name Dodoni originates from Linear B (p. 8) and may mean "great mother of civilization;" Dodoni was probably the deity worshipped there by pre-Hellenic Pelagians before being supplanted by Zeus. Excavations suggest the oracle was used from the Bronze Age (2600-1100 BC) through Christianity's arrival in the late 4th century. Worship of Zeus at Dodoni was well established by Homer's time; Odysseus himself came to the oracle at "wintry Dodona" for advice on ridding his house of Penelope's suitors. At its height, Dodoni was one of the ancient world's greatest oracles and home of the **Naia festival,** a series of athletic and dramatic contests held every four years in Zeus's honor.

The large **amphitheater** near the entrance to the site was built in the 3rd century AD. The original design seated 18,000 before the Romans replaced the lowest rows with a retaining wall and improved the still visible drainage system to accommodate their blood sports. The theater is currently undergoing restoration and much of it is off limits. Locals report, however, that the famed acoustics are so good that derogatory whispers made on stage have been heard by headmasters high in the gallery. Beyond the amphitheater are the ruins of the oracle itself, where Zeus would answer queries through an oak tree, recently replanted. Legend says a dove from Egypt settled at the oracle. Because the Ancient Greek words for dove and old woman are the same, historians believe an Egyptian priestess may have started the oracle. A clan of priests called the **Hellopes, Helloi,** or **Selloi** succeeded her, interpreting the wind's effect on the oak leaves and the sound of wooden batons, held by a bronze statue of a boy striking a row of copper cauldrons. Using their sonic data, the priests made prophecies; trying to absorb the god's messages through the soil, they walked barefoot. Wild priestesses prone to divine frenzy eventually replaced the male Selloi. Little remains today of the original building that housed the tree and its horde of pilgrims. A 5th-century BC temple and the 350 BC **bouleterion** and **prytaneion,** now almost totally vanished, once surrounded the oracle. Following the Aetolian sack in 219 BC, a larger Ionic temple to Zeus was built in 167 BC and the great amphitheater in the early 3rd century AD.

PERAMA CAVES

Take local bus #8 from the park behind the city center (15min.; every 20min., 8am-7pm; €1.20 round-trip). At Perama, follow the signs (reading ΣΠΗΛΑΙΟ) for the cave. ☎26510 81 251 or 26510 81 440. Tours every 25min. Open in summer daily 8am-8pm; in winter 8am-5pm. €5, students €2.50.

A 163-step stairway leads through the spectrally lit, glimmering yellow Perama Caves, among the largest in the Balkans. Excavations have turned up bears' teeth and bones in the almost two million-year-old stalagmites and stalactites, as well as **paintings** devoted to the ancient worship of Hades and Persephone. The path leads from narrow passageways to immense **caverns** hanging with eerie rock formations. The 45min. Greek-only guided tour mainly introduces selected stalagmites that have been named after other objects they uncannily resemble: "Tower of Pisa," "Egyptian Sphinx," and so on. Always a comfortable 17°C/62°F inside, the cave makes for a great excursion during the scorching Greek afternoons.

METSOVO Μετσοβο ☎26560

On the western slope of the 1690m Katara Pass lies the quaint alpine town of Metsovo. The town itself is a piece of art, maintained in pristine condition through the fortune left by Metzovite expatriate, who turned to Swiss banking, Baron Tositsas. Though frequented during the day by tour buses taking a rest during their transmontane journey, the self-proclaimed Vlach capital has much to offer the more dedicated traveler. Amateur linguists can discover what a Vlach is and try to decipher their unique old Latin tongue. Craft seekers can enjoy the exquisite local costumes and rugs, and hikers will find the town a cozy base for treks into the Northern Pindos. Visitors in mid- and late July will receive a full dose of Metsovite culture as festivals and traditional weddings kick off.

TRANSPORTATION AND PRACTICAL INFORMATION. Metsovo is about 100km inland in eastern Epirus, halfway between Kalambaka and Ioannina. On a stone wall in the main plateia a large, nearly illegible English-language **town map** lists hotels, sights, monasteries, restaurants, and discos. From the main plateia, **buses** depart for **Ioannina** (1½hr.; 4 per day, 6:15am-4:30pm; €3.50) and to **Trikala** via **Kalambaka** (1½hr.; 1:15am, 3:15pm; €4). Buses to **Thessaloniki** (5 per day, 8:45am-8:15pm) stop at the main highway above town. For **schedule info,** ask at the *periptero* by the central square bus stop. Some six or seven unlabeled streets are off the large plateia, but locals neither know nor use names for them. Standing with your back to the big town map, the street on the left side of the souvenir shop leads slightly downhill to the municipal **police** (☎26560 41 233 or 41 222; open 24hr.) and the **OTE** (☎26560 42 199; open 8am-2pm). There is a 24hr. **hospital** (☎26560 41 111) at the top of the town by the highway. Following the path around to your right from the police will bring you to Hotel Apollon where **Internet** access is available for a pricey €5 per hr. The main road is on your left, choked with souvenir stands and tavernas; it leads uphill to the path toward the Tositsas Museum

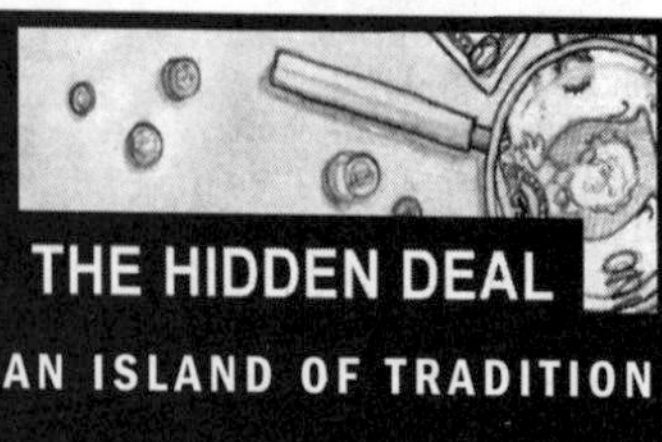

THE HIDDEN DEAL

AN ISLAND OF TRADITION

Metsovo is famous for the colorful mountain costumes and rugs produced by Vlach locals. Originally shepherds of enormous herds migrating across the Balkan mountain pastures, Vlachs were skilled in creating textiles from wool before their settlement by the government in the 1800's. The skill has since been passed from generation to generation, and George Boubas is one of its current masters continuing on this important and distinctive tradition.

Though George laments not having any apprentices who want to learn the old techniques—his children have all sought more "modern" employments—for the present his mastery is enough. Sought by French designers and supplier to Micheal Dukakis, George is a giant in the traditional Greek clothing industry. Visitors can enjoy his beautiful Vlach wears display, and those looking for a worthwhile souvenir from Greece should conisider his smaller textiles. George uses the traditional natural dyes—onion for yellow and various flowers for the bright red and blues—which do not photo-bleach or age as their artificial brethen hawked on the street will. Indeed George has textiles on display that are over 100 years old and still exploding with color.

Come enjoy this Vlach tradition before, like the sheep herds, it is swallowed by modernity.

The workshop of George Boubas is open daily 9am-8pm. ☎26560 42 580 or 25560 41 411.

and the **post office,** which has **Poste Restante.** (☎26560 41 245. Open M-F 7:30am-2pm.) The **town hall,** on the second floor of the large pale yellow building where the main road meets the plateia, can provide you with a few glossy brochures of the area. (☎26560 41 207. Open 7am-2pm; walk around to the building's back entrance.) On your right, a road runs downhill to Agios Nikolaos monastery and to **Tsigas's Super Game Club,** which has **Internet** access (€2.50 per hr.); another road wraps around the plateia past the **National Bank** and **Agricultural Bank** (both with 24hr. **ATM**), the art museum, and Hotel Filoxenia. **Postal code:** 44200.

ACCOMMODATIONS. Room prices peak during the two high seasons: from mid-July through September and December through March. During these times, Metsovo is best visited between the arrival of the morning bus and the departure of the evening bus. In the low season, its accommodations provide tranquility, village charm, and excellent value. By far the most welcoming option is **Hotel Filoxenia ❷**, whose Greek name (hospitality) says it all. British-educated propreitor Ioannis is perhaps your best source in Metsovo for hiking assistance. He offers tips, humor, maps, guides, lore, and gear storage even for hikers not staying at the hotel. His rooms offer TVs, extraordinary mountainside balconies, and baths. (☎26560 41 021. Breakfast €4. Singles €25; doubles €30; triples 50.) **Domatia** are found by veering left before the OTE, past the super market. **John Xaralabapoulos's Rooms ❷** are large and comfortable. All have TVs and phones; some have fridges and stoves. An oval, handpainted sign labeled "Domatia-Rooms" marks the entrance, just past the basketball court. (☎26560 42 086. Singles €20; doubles €30; triples €40. Prices rise in high season.) **Hotel Olympic ❸,** located just behind John Xaralabapoulos's Rooms, has carpeted rooms, which have bath, TV, and phone. (☎26560 41 337; fax 26560 41 837. Singles €30; doubles €36; triples €42. MC/V.)

FOOD AND ENTERTAINMENT. Many of the restaurants in Metsovo are very similar and cater to large groups of tourists. If you'd like to eat in the plateia, try tourist favorite **Kryfi Folia ❷** (☎26560 41 628) for its grilled meats, like *kokoretsi* (€6) and *kontosoufli* (€5.50). Also on the plateia are **Kria Vrisi ❷,** which specializes in *hilopittes fournou* (a pasta), and **Galaxias ❷** (☎26560 41 202), on the patio atop the grassy hill overlooking the plateia. Galaxias has a large selection of dishes, all cooked within an ivy-covered mansion. A local favorite, serving trout from Lake Metsovo as well as the town's speciality, vegetable pies, is **To Koutouki Tou Nikola** ❷ (☎26560 41 732). The taverna is found, as its name implies, in Nikola's basement on the street towards the post office. For something a little different, and much cheaper, try local fast-food favorite **Mangare** ❶ (☎26560 41 101), located just up the left branch of the road which forks at the post office. Home-grown origins and €0.75 souvlaki make this lively joint more than bearable. Try the *jizbernger* (τζιζμπεργκερ; €2) for a real surprise. Metsovo has little nightlife, but if you need a drink (€2-3.50) or three after dinner, head to the cafes by Mangare. There's little difference between bars, which calm by midnight, when the thrifty Metsovites turn in to prepare for another day of work.

SIGHTS. Thanks to the generosity of Baron Tositsas, a Metsovo-born Swiss baron who donated his fortune to the town, and Evangelos Averof-Tositsas, Metsovo has far more sights than you'd expect from a 3500-person town. Off the main plateia, the spacious **E. Averof Gallery** exhibits 19th- and 20th-century Greek art labeled in English and Greek, including the private collection of Averof-Tositsas. (☎26560 41 210. Open M, W-Su 9am-1:30pm and 5-7:30pm. €3, students €2.) Next door in the conference center (Diaselo), there's an exhibition of letters, postcards, and newspaper clippings from the Balkan War, as well as a small but interesting collection of seashells. (Open Tu-F, Su 11am-2pm, Sa 10am-1pm. Free.) Just off the central plateia, sandwiched by the National and Agricultural Banks is the **Workshop of George Boubas** (☎26560 42 580). Those looking for their own souvenir will be much safer making purchases here, where George can guarantee that non-fading natural dyes (*physica*) were used. The **Tositsas Museum,** in a mansion to the left of the main road, honors the generosity of the town benefactors. (Open M-W, F-Su 9:30am-1:30pm and 4-6pm. Visitors are admitted only in small groups; wait at the museum's door for the guide, who appears every 30min. €3.) A 30min. walk from the plateia brings you to **Agios Nikolaos Monastery;** signs point the way. Built in the 14th century and subsequently abandoned, the crumbling chapel was a refuge for itinerant shepherds for years. The smoke from their fires completely covered frescoes painted in 1702 by noted saint biographer Efsiat Chios, perfectly preserving their colors until they were rediscovered in 1950 by Averof-Tositsas. A Greek woman now lives in and cares for the monastery.

For information about outdoor activities in Metsovo and **Valiakalda National Park** (Vlach: "warm valley"), contact the town hall (☎26560 41 207) or the

THE LOCAL LEGEND

SPEAK SOFTLY AND CARRY BIG CROOK

Legend has it that a disgracec Ottoman vezir once fled to the secluded valley of Metsovo. Here h was adopted by a kindly Vlach shep herd, all the while hiding his true identity. When the political climat in Istanbul cooled and it was safe fo the vezir to return, he revealed himself and asked the astounded shepherd what type of personal rewarc he desired. The clever Vlach repliec that he wanted nothing *himsel* rather he wished for his whole towr to be granted special privleges.

Thus, Metsovo came to have a garr son of only three Turks, to be placec under direct ecclesiastical control o the patriarchate in Constantinople, anc to be included in the tax district of the island Euboia. Because Euboia is across the Pindos Mountains some 180km southwest of Metsovo in the Aegean, the tax collector's journey alone, not to mention risk of brigandage, prevented him from ever visiting this peaceful hamlet. Thus Metsovc became a bastion of independance during the *Turkokratia* (period of Turkisl domination), attracting many Greeks fleeing the Sultan's army—though no all were fleeing for savory reasons.

The clever Metsovetzes continue to maintain their tradition of privileges to this day. One of Greece's six delegates to the EU has consistenly been Metzovian; the province's executive in Ioannina is traditionally fron Metzovo; and several of Greece's foreign ministers have hailed from this tiny town with a big crook.

owners of Hotel Filoxenia (☎26560 41 725). Around the end of July each year, the village hosts a *yiorti* (celebration). In old times it was the Vlach courting day, so today all of the women and most men dress in traditional bright costumes for the festivities. Also on a day between July 20 and July 26 the town leads its yearly hike up to the refuge for general carousing in celebration of the Greek gods. Town elders have decided that this is the only way to legitimately use the fortune donated by an eccentric local believer in the Olympian pantheon. Accommodations for this period must be reserved in advance.

ZAGOROHORIA Ζαγοροχωρια

The Zagorohoria are a collection of 46 hamlets between Ioannina and the Albanian border in the North Pindos Range. Historically a peaceful refuge from Ottoman domination, the Zagorohoria received special privileges in return for surrendering their mountain sanctuary to Murad II in 1431. The hamlets have had less luck in recent times; Italy's abortive 1940 invasion centered on the North Pindos and much of the Zagorohoria was burnt by the more successful Germans. The Greek Civil War of the late 1940s devastated villages that survived the World War. The region has only seen positive growth since, so expect to find natural beauty, a thriving tourism industry, and wizened reminders of a traditional past. Although the villages themselves are well worth a day or two, most tourists come to this rugged region for hiking around rough-riding rivers, stark peaks, and the renowned Vikos Gorge. Outdoorsmen of every skill level will find more than enough to satisfy them in Zagoria and the surrounding Vikos-Aoös National Park.

MONODENDRI Μονοδενδρι ☎26530

Many an enchanted traveler has tripped dreamily through Monodendri's cobbled maze, illuminated only by twinkling stars and the summertime multitudes of synchronized fireflies. Despite a few hikers, skiers, and city-escapees in summer and winter, this village of 150 remains perfectly peaceful. Its natural and architectural beauty, location at the top of Vikos Gorge, proximity to Ioannina, and inexpensive yet beautiful hotels, make it a base for hikers unmatched in Greece.

The single paved road in Monodendri runs through the upper end of the village; the bus stop, all of the hotels, and most of the restaurants cluster there. **Buses** infrequently go to **Ioannina** (1hr.; M, W, F 7am, 5pm; €3). For those who miss the bus there are **taxis** (€25). Hikers can also avoid being marooned in expensive Ioannina by catching one of five daily buses to **Konitsa** (p. 257). Monodendri's plateia is accessible via a footpath descending to the right as you leave the bus stop; follow the path downhill and turn left when the road forks. The plateia hosts a cafe, a **phone, post box,** and signposts for all the trailheads. The narrow cobblestone paths of Monodendri can be a disorienting maze of gray rock, but most paths meander in one way or another toward the plateia. There is **no bank;** the closest are in Kalpaki and Konitsa. Some hotels may cash traveler's checks or **exchange money.** For **medical care,** the nearest hospital is in Ioannina. The town kiosk has good trail **maps.**

A major local outfitter is **Alpine Zone,** Josef Eligia 16 (☎26550 24 822; www.alpinesone.gr), located just off Averof in Ioannina. For more information, contact Mario at **Pension Monodendri** (☎26530 71 300) or Nikos at **Koulis Restaurant** (☎26530 41 138), in Monodendri and Papingo respectively. Rafting and kayaking trips can be arranged in spring through **Konitsa's Paddler School** (☎26550 24 536 or 24 500). The best times for hiking are late May, early June, and September.

NORTHERN GREECE

Monodendri's plentiful accommodations are generally high in quality and low in price, making it one of the most affordable villages in the Zagorohoria. On the left as you walk up from the bus station, **Arhondiko Zarkada Hotel ❷** offers a pool as well as large comfortable rooms with modern baths, TVs, phones, and gorgeous stone balconies providing scenic views. (☎26530 71 305; www.epirus.com/zarkadas. Breakfast €5. Singles €20; doubles €35; triples €45. AmEx/MC/V.) A bit farther up the road, **Pension Monodendri ❷** has cheerful rooms with colorful rugs. The owner's English-speaking son Mario is full of info on trekking in the area and does pick-up (€30) from Vikos village or Megali Papingo after your dayhike. His parents, Dimitris and Katerina Daskalopoulou, can provide a bagged lunch (€3) for the trail. (☎26530 71 300; fax 26530 71 410. Breakfast €5. Singles €25; doubles €35; triples €45.) Close to the bus station is **Ladia ❷,** a castle-like structure at the entrance to the village offering modern rooms with private baths, TVs, rugs, and the occasional fireplace. (☎26530 71 483; www.epirus.com/ladias. Singles €25; doubles €33; triples €35. MC/V.)

A few tavernas are interspersed among these pensions on the main road. The friendliest is **Katerina's ❷,** on the porch of Pension Monodendri, where Pension Monodendri's Mrs. Daskalopoulou prepares an ever-changing menu, including an array of delicious and savory pies. (Entrees €3-5.50.) Usually the most crowded, **Restaurant Vikos Gorge ❶,** just above Pension Monodendri, has a spectacular view from its wide porch. An array of local wines complements the stuffed tomatoes (€3.50) and *kotopita* (€4). **Taverna Oxya ❷,** below the hotel, serves up a limited selection of salads and meat dishes. (Open daily 8am-midnight.)

As gateway to the steepest canyon in the world, Monodendri's sites are mostly gorge-oriented. There are breathtaking, unparalleled views of the entire **Vikos Gorge** (p. 267) from the must-see natural overlook, about a 1½hr. walk on the main road uphill from the village. A large section of the road can be bypassed by following a red-blazed trail that begins behind Pension Monodendri. The road eventually ends and gives way to a small footpath, leading to a vantage point for gazing down on the gorge's three main chasms. The sunset glow is spectacular. Also a must is the hike beyond the abandoned **Monastery of Agia Paraskevi,** about 600m from the plateia. Though the monastery also has some impressive views, it is the edgeless meter-wide path beyond, cut straight into the sheer rock wall, that will make you feel the gorge's power. The treacherous path leads to a small cave in which monks could hide from marauders. Signs from the plateia point the way to **Megali Spilia,** another nearby cave where Zagorians used to stock food and water and hide from Albanian marauders.

VIKOS GORGE Χαραδρα Βικου

According to the *Guinness Book of World Records*, the Vikos Gorge, whose walls are 900m deep but only 1100m apart, is the steepest canyon on earth, stretching from the village of Kipi in the south to Megalo Papingo at its northernmost tip, winding its way through the center of the Zagorohoria. In spring, the river that has taken millions of years to form the eponymous gorge rushes along the 15km stretch of canyon floor. By summertime this mighty force is reduced to a feeble trickle crawling through the massive white boulders in a bone-dry riverbed. Rusted iron deposits in the gorge's sedimentary rock leave an orange-pink tint on the walls. Even more colorful are the spring wildflowers, summer butterflies, autumn foliage, and views of the bright-green spring running below Vikos village. When night falls, listen for the shrill chirping of crickets and watch fireflies dance among the trees. The long hike through the gorge is stunning: the nearly vertical canyon sides, softened by hundreds of stubborn trees, tower hundreds of meters overhead.

THE LOCAL STORY

VLACHS: THE ROMANTIC GREEKS

Hikers in the mountains of Greece, Albania, and FYROM may be surprised to hear the villagers speaking a language not at all resembling Greek—indeed, a Romance language—to one another. There are two theories on the origins of this tongue, known as Vlach. The first, drawing on its similarity to Romanian and the tendency of the once nomadic Vlach shepherds to migrate long distances with their herds, postulates that the two are common ancestors of medieval "Wallachian," noted by 12th century crusaders and Byzantine chroniclers.

According to this theory, the Vlachs descended from Roman military colonists of cities like Phillipi. These urban Romans took to the rustic mountains in the 7th-11th centuries when the Byzantines temporarily abandoned the Balkans to Slav invaders, retreating to more populous Asia Minor.

The second theory, favored by political Vlachs, holds that the Vlachs are descendants of Greeks who learned Latin as guards on the high passes of Rome's Balkan roads. Either story is equally romantic, as are the charming Vlachs themselves.

Ioannis Papapostolou is a Vlach from Metsovo, who was educated in the United Kingdom, with a penchant for the history of his people. Let's Go spoke with him on June 25, 2003.

LG: What kinds of examples demonstrate the Vlach language's antiquity?

A: The word for chair, for instance, does not exist. The word for bench exists, "bangu," which is pretty similar

The well-marked Vikos **trail** is part of the **Greek National O3 route,** which runs from the Aoös River near Konitsa all the way to Kipi. Before you go, be sure to get a **map.** The *periptero* on the main road through Monodendri and EOS in Papingo sell detailed maps (€7) of all the trails in Zagorohoria. If you get confused, just look for the red diamonds on white square backgrounds with "O3" stenciled on them, which consistently mark the path. Most enter the gorge from **Monodendri,** the highest of the villages, but it can also be accessed from **Kipi,** the **Papingo** villages, and from **Vikos** village. It takes 4½hr. to walk between Vikos village and Monodendri and 6hr. between the Papingos and Monodendri.

To reach the gorge from Monodendri, take the marked path from the plateia. After about 40min. along the steep descending trail, you'll reach a fork in the path (700m). Go left to enter the canyon's dry riverbed of smooth rocks and head toward the far-off villages of Papingo and Vikos. To the right, about 1½hr. (4km) away, lies the village of Kipi with its trademark stone bridges. Take the left fork as it climbs above the left bank of the riverbed. The path continues for some time, fairly level and pleasant, through a mossy, shady woodland along the riverbank.

After about 2hr., there will be a sign for a **water tap** where you can fill your bottle—this is the halfway point. Continuing straight on the trail after the water tap, you'll pass some open groves mowed clean by grazing horses. About 4-5hr. from Monodendri (9km) you reach the confusing crossroads for Vikos village. Coming from Monodendri the trail suddenly becomes a meticulously cobbled stone path, which, after about 2m, makes a 90° turn up toward Vikos (800m; about 45min.). If you're Papingo-bound you'll want to maintain a straight course hugging the riverbanks into the grassy pasture. This area is a popular freelance camping site among backpackers looking to avoid the steep, northern gorge room rates. Keep your eyes on the stream's opposite bank, because, about halfway through the grassy clearing, a frenzy of red arrows on the boulders marks the ford and continuation of O3 to Papingo. There are some powerful springs here as well. Another long hour out of the gorge brings you to the well marked Megalo Papingo-Mikro Papingo split. From here its about 30min. to either village for a total of 13km.

Hikers entering from Papingo villages should again follow signs from the plateias. The trailhead in **Vikos Village** is just outside town across from Dinoulis Rooms. The only other accommodations in this tiny 30-person hamlet are at **Sotiris Karpouzis ❸.** (☎26530 41 176. Rooms €35.) Both have tavernas; there is a third place in the plateia, whose obliging owner provides lifts (€30) to Monodendri on off-hours.

THE PAPINGOS Τα Παπινγκα

☎26530

The two Papingo villages, Megalo (Μεγαλο; big) and Mikro (Μικρο; small), are the most developed towns of the Zagorohoria. Their position at the end of the Vikos Gorge ensures their popularity with backpackers and independent travelers. In recent years, Megalo Papingo, has also become a favorite spot for wealthy vacationing Greek families seeking a retreat from Thessaloniki and Ioannina. These villages boast 22 separate lodging choices, while most of the 44 other Zagori towns don't have 22 full-time residents. Luckily the influx of visitors hasn't diminished the villages' peaceful, rural seclusion and peculiar, stony beauty.

TRANSPORTATION AND PRACTICAL INFORMATION. The large, austere stone church and its attendant **bell tower** stand at the entrance to Megalo Papingo, at the end of the road to the outside world and next to the **bus stop.** From here, one cobblestone main street snakes around the town, containing most of the pensions and restaurants. The road to Mikro Papingo is clearly marked to the right of the church; the **trailhead** for Vikos Gorge is 20m down this road at the end of a well marked dirt lane on the right. Note another 50m down the road there is an old, yellow, metal sign for the Vikos trail that will lead you astray if you follow it. Buses go to **Ioannina** three days a week (1½hr.; M, W, F 5:15am and 2:30pm; €3.80). A more dependable alternative is to hike the 2hr. trail to **Klidonia** (see below). Klidonia is on the better served Konitsa-Ioannina bus route (1hr.; 7 per day, 7am-8:30pm; €4). Megalo Papingo has a **phone,** by the church, and a **mailbox,** by Lakis Cafe. Mikro Papingo also has a **phone** at the town entrance by what was once the public school; a **mailbox** is farther into town by the trail signpost. There is an alternative entrance for Vikos Gorge here as well as the trailhead for **Drakolimni, Mt. Astrakas,** and the **SEO refuge.** For information on all outdoor activities, ask for Nikos, the EOS representative, at **Koulis Cafe** (☎26530 41 138). To find him, walk uphill, to the left when facing the Megalo Papingo church from the main road, and quickly take another left at the wrought-iron fence.

to Italian. The word stove also does not exist, although it's a cold place here, so it should exist. There is only the word for fireplace. Consider how old the language is. Modern words like chair do not exist.

LG: What examples show the language's origins?

A: The word we use for Metsovo is "Aminchu." This word must derive from a small river in northern Italy. Probably the Romans who came to guard the road here came from that area.... Also we have a word "Imperitiuarai," which means emperor's place. There is a story here that when Antoninus [Mark Antony] used to go and see his girlfriend, Cleopatra, in Egypt, he used to send his wife up here. This should be true, because if you go in the mountains there is still a large Roman building.

LG: How did the Vlach people make their livings and survive?

A: The area here does not produce anything, so in order to survive we had to go around. Most went to Egypt or parts of Russia. They worked there; they made a lot of money, but they forgot to get married, that's the important thing. When they approached dying they decided to leave their fortunes for Greece or for Metsovo.

LG: What Vlach contributions can be seen in other parts of Greece?

A: People from Metsovo have built the [first] Olympic stadium in Athens. Also they built the Polytechnique of Athens, which is called Metsovo Polytechnique. Also they have built a lot of churches around Greece. One of them, I think, has built around 150 churches in Greece and many schools.

ACCOMMODATIONS AND FOOD. The lodgings in the chic Papingo can be quite expensive. If Koulis is full and **domatia** prices are at high season levels, backpackers may want to huff it up to the EOS Refuge by Mt. Astrakas. Though technically illegal, many hikers have also been known to freelance camp at the Vikos town crossroads in the gorge (see above), or in a small clearing on the left, halfway down the road from Megalo to Mikro Papingo. The beautifully furnished rooms at **Pension Koulis ❷**, with fireplaces, wooden floors, TVs, and baths, are a great deal, even if the overpriced attached cafe is not. Facing the village from where the surfaced road ends, continue along the main road and take the first left after the church. The pension is on the corner of the next crossroads to the left. (☎26530 41 115; fax 26530 41 484. Breakfast €5. Singles €20; doubles €30; triples €40-45.) The homey domatia of **Georgios Reppas ❸** offer quilted beds, TVs, shared baths, and tranquility. Look for his house immediately opposite the church. (☎26530 41 711. Breakfast €5. Singles €30; doubles €40.) At **Vasiliki Nikolaus ❸,** a kind, energetic lady lets simple, spacious rooms in her stone-roofed farmhouse with its communal bathroom, fridge, and washing machine; the rooster might wake you at dawn. Standing where the smooth main road meets cobblestone, facing the church, take the first right heading uphill. Fifty meters farther, go left up a small lane. The first left off this lane takes you on a small path that leads directly to the farmhouse door. (Singles and doubles €35.) Another impeccably decorated bed-and-breakfast kind of establishment, **Kalliope ❸,** just behind Hotel Papingo, is visible behind the central *estiatorio* by the church. (☎26530 41 081. Breakfast €4. Singles €35; doubles €40; triples €55; quads €60.) Behind its grape vine entryway, the 120-year-old **Astraka ❸,** on the other end of the main road, offers comfortable rooms with baths, fireplaces, and TVs, plus a cozy living room. (☎26530 41 693. Singles €35; doubles €45; triples €50; quads €60.)

Just outside town beside the path to Vikos Gorge on the road to Mikro Papingo is the **restaurant ❷** (☎26530 42 108) of Christoforos Tsoumanis. Christoforos prides himself on lamb from his father's flock, vegetables from his gardens, and his own feta. The prices (vegetarian *briam* €4.20; trout €5) are as appealing as the food is fresh. Downhill to the right of the main road, **Estiatorio ❷** has the best views of the gorge's craggy outcrops. Choose from a selection of Zagorian pies and pork or veal dishes. (☎26530 42 108. Entrees €5-7.) **Restaurant Papingo ❸,** to the right of the belltower in the Papingo Pension, is a popular choice among visitors to the village and serves a selection of meat dishes and salads. (Entrees €7.50-12.)

SIGHTS. Mikro Papingo hosts the Zagorohoria regional **World Wildlife Federation (WWF).** The office, located on the right at the entrance to town in the old public school, has a small number of nice exhibits on local wildlife, history, and culture. (☎26530 41 071; papingowwf@forthnet.gr. Open Su-Tu, Th 10:30am-6pm, F-Sa 11am-3pm and 4-7pm.)

THE HIKES. The most spectacular Zagoria hikes begin in Mikro Papingo. Besides Vikos Gorge, village visitors can climb **Mt. Astraka** (2436m), which has the second deepest straight plunge cave in the world, or trek to the pristine **Drakolimni** ("Dragon Lake"). This cloud-reflecting alpine pool (2000m) is filled with newts who hang motionless on the wind-whipped grasses. Both hikes can be paired with a stay in the **EOS refuge** (1900m), perched on a ridge nearby.

For trekkers stranded in Ioannina or Papingo because of the limited buses, a fun solution is to hike in from the Klidonia bus stop on the Ioannina-Konitsa line (1hr.; 7 per day, 7am-8:30pm; €4). From the bus stop follow the Konitsa-bound bus along the highway to the town's main road on the right across from a gas station. Ask at the petrol station, or any of the homes along the town's road, to be pointed to the

Klidonia-Papingo Trail (Κλιδονια–Παπιγκο; 5km). From the trailhead, at a church visible above town, a well marked path, highlighted by red blazes, leads up the mountain side. If you slip off the track just follow the electric line, which follows it, albeit without switchbacks. At the top (1hr., 2km; elev. 900m), are stunning views of the Aoös River flood plain and a small abandoned church. This is the town of **Ano Klidonia** (Upper Klidonia) withered from lack of a highway. There is a small English speaking cafe just beyond, otherwise it is a ghost town. Follow the dirt track to the large antenna, where the red blazed trail begins again. From here you have a sweeping view of **Mt. Astrakas** on the left and **Vikos Gorge** on the right. Perched in the distance on the ridges flanking this gaping crack are clustered houses. The right hamlet is Vikos; the left is your destination (Papingo). It is 1hr. (skirting two ridges) to the dirt lane, marking the final kilometer of the route.

To get to the **refuge** (Drakolimni and Mt. Astrakas), follow signs from Mikro Papingo reading "To the Refuge" (Μπρος Κατεφυγειο); the trail climbs past three **springs:** a chapel-topped faucet (Ag. Pandeleimon; 10min.), another faucet (Antalki; 30min.), and a frog-filled trough (2hr.). The path is well marked with O3 triangles and red blazes throughout. Occasionally the trail spiderwebs, through the work of industrious goats. Usually all are valid; keep a look-out for blazes. After the last spring, the trail is exposed and the ridge-resting refuge is visible. Another hour of views and knee-crunching brings you to the 60-bed **EOS refuge ❶**, 3km from Mikro Papingo. (☎26530 26 553 or 26530 41 335. €10 per person, members of any mountain club €8.) From here a 1½hr. trail scales **Mt. Astrakas** (1km) while a path (1hr.) descends into the blossom-dotted valley and then climbs the rattling meadow of the opposite ridge to Drakolimni (1.8km). In the summer the meadow's grasses are home to **sheep** and their shepherds, who are friendly and happy to gesture directions to the few visitors who make it up here. Give the flocks a wide berth as the sheep dogs are very protective. From the refuge, multi-day **treks** deep into the Pindos are possible and hikers can usually plan to end their day in the luxury of some valley village.

MACEDONIA Μακεδονια

Some of the most captivating Greek landscapes and sights belong to Macedonia, including the sublime Olympian hiking trails, millions of sparkling mosaic *tessarae* from Thessaloniki's Byzantine churches, Kavala's Ottoman *imaret*, the Royal Tombs from Vergina, the austere monasteries of Mt. Athos, the remote mountain lakes of Prespa, and the surf and sand of Halkidiki's three peninsulas. Greece's largest province tops the mainland like an ancient gold-wrought crown. You'll encounter the region's symbol, a 16-pointed star, on everything: the sidewalk at the OTE, bumper stickers saying "Macedonia is Greece," and even Philip II's gold casket in Vergina. Though rarely touristed, it's far from a backwater: hip, lively Thessaloniki, Greece's second-largest city, keeps the whole region on its toes.

THESSALONIKI Θεσσαλονικη ☎2310

Thessaloniki (also called Salonica or Saloniki; Σαλονικη) a jumble of Byzantine, Turkish, Balkan, and Greek cultural and historical debris, fans out from its hilltop fortress toward the Thermaic Gulf. From its peak, the fortress oversees the Old Town's placid streets stretching down to the city's long, congested avenues. Among glitzy concrete facades, fashion-conscious young Salonicans rub shoulders with old, black-clad widows and long-bearded monks. Golden mosaics, frescoes, and floating domes still gleam in the city's Byzantine churches.

Macedonia's capital and Greece's second largest city, Thessaloniki was founded in 316 BC when Cassander (the ruler of Macedon) needed a new city to name after his wife. He selected a spot on the Thermaic Gulf shore and transplanted the citizens of 26 pre-existing towns to his new Thessaloniki. Despite frequent and bloody raids by Goths, Avars, Slavs, Bulgars, and Latin Crusaders, Thessaloniki rose to become the Byzantine Empire's second-most important city, after Constantinople. The Turks ended these glory days, conquering the city by siege in 1421 and ruling until 1912. Although the cosmopolitan city began the 20th century with a Greek minority, the Turkish population exchange (p. 13) and the death of 96.5% of the city's 50,000 Sephardic Jews during the Holocaust, have left Thessaloniki as homogenous as the rest of Greece. To complete the transformation, the Great Fire of 1917 destroyed most of the city. French rebuilding plans were mostly ignored with the sudden influx of over a million Greek refugees from Turkey five years later. In the 1960s disaster struck again when the American supported junta allowed the city's stately houses to be sold for apartment complexes, in return for inhabitants receiving two flats. The result: today's concrete forest.

INTERCITY TRANSPORTATION

BY PLANE

The **airport** (☎2310 408 400), 16km east of town, can be reached by **bus #78** (€0.45) from the train station or Pl. Aristotelous, and also by **taxi** (€10). There's an **EOT** branch (☎2310 985 215) at the airport. Flights go to: **Athens** (55min., 9 per day, €90); **Chios** (3hr.; Su, Tu-W, F; €60); **Corfu** (50min.; M, Sa; €64); **Cyprus** (2½hr.; Tu, Th, Sa-Su; €134); **Hania** (2hr.; W, Sa; €114); **Ioannina** (50min.; M, W, F, Su; €59); **Iraklion** (2hr., 2 per day, €109); **Lesvos** (2hr., daily, €63); **Limnos** (50min.; M, W-Th, Sa; €64); **Rhodes** (3hr., daily, €116); **Samos** (1hr.; Tu, Th-Sa; €70). To purchase tickets, head to the **Olympic Airways,** Koundouriotou 3. (☎2310 368 311; fax 2310 229 725. Open M-F 8am-3:45pm. Reservations ☎2310 368 666; open M-Sa 8am-4:30pm.)

BY TRAIN

To reach the **main terminal** (☎2310 517 517), on Monastiriou in the western part of the city, take any bus down Egnatia (€0.44). **International trains** go to: **Istanbul, Turkey** (12hr., 7am, €40); **Skopje, FYROM** (4hr.; 8am, 5pm; €13); **Sofia, Bulgaria** (8hr., 11:28pm, €18). Tickets are sold at the **International Trains booth,** at the train station. (☎2310 599 033. Open daily 7am-2pm and 3:30-9pm.) Both regular *(aplo)* **domestic trains** and IC (intercity) trains, a high speed alternative, serve most destinations. Trains to: **Alexandroupoli** (regular: 7hr.; 3 per day, 7am-10:25pm; €9.70; IC: 5hr.; 3 per day, 7am-2:30pm; €16.20); **Athens** (regular: 8hr.; 5 per day, 8:24am-midnight; €20; IC: 6hr.; 6 per day, 6:40am-2am; €40); **Drama** (regular: 3½hr., €5.60; IC: 2½hr., €8); **Komotini** (regular: 4hr., €8.20; IC: 5hr., €12.50); **Larisa** (2½hr.; 9 per day, 7:30am-2am; €4.70); **Volos** (4hr., 7:20pm, €6.70); **Xanthi** (regular: 5hr., €7; IC: 4hr., €10). The **Travel Office** (☎2310 598 112) provides updated schedules.

BY BUS

KTEL buses connect Thessaloniki with most major Greek cities; with the exception of the bus to Halkidiki, all leave from one central, dome-shaped **bus station** west of the city center. **Bus #1** is a shuttle service between the train station and bus station throughout the day (every 15min., €0.45). **Bus #78** connects the train station to the airport passing through the waterfront corridor en route (every 30min., €0.45). **International buses** (☎2310 599 100) leave from the **main train station** (☎2310 517 517), on Monastiriou in the city's western part; take any bus down Egnatia to get there (€0.45). Buses go to: **Istanbul, Turkey** (12hr., 7am, €44); **Koritsa, Albania** (6hr., 10am and 1am if demand permits, €20); **Sofia, Bulgaria** (6hr.; 4-6 per day,

7am-10pm; €19.10). **Domestic buses** leave from a dome 3km west of town. Take local bus #1 from the train station. Inside the dome sit offices for each of the KTEL district booths. If you don't know in which district your destination lies, just pick a promising booth and ask.

In addition, domestic buses leave from the **Halkidiki Station** (☎2310 924 444), located past the end of Egnatia; walk down Kanari for 2 blocks and turn right onto Karakassi. Buses go to: **Armenistis** (2½hr.; 4 per day, 8:45am-6:30pm; €9.40); **Ierissos** (2½hr.; 7 per day, 6:15am-6:30pm; €7.40) and **Ouranoupolis** (7 per day, 6:15am-6:30pm; €7.70); **Kalithea** (1½hr.; 27 per day, 5:40am-10pm; €6.10); **Nea Marmaras** (2½hr.; 8 per day, 6am-7pm; €8.90); **Sarti** (3hr.; 6 per day, 7:30am-7pm; €12.50).

DESTINATION	TIME	FREQUENCY	PRICE	TELEPHONE
Athens	6hr.	11 per day, 7:30am-11:45pm	€28	☎2310 595 495
Alexandroupoli	5hr.	7 per day, 7:30am-11:30pm	€20.50	☎2310 595 439
Corinth	7½hr.	11:30pm	€32	☎2310 595 405
Drama	2¼hr.	Every hr., 7am-9pm	€9	☎2310 595 420
Edessa	2hr.	6 per day, 6am-8pm	€5.10	☎2310 595 435
Florina	3hr.	7 per day, 7:30am-9pm	€10.60	☎2310 595 418
Grevena	3hr.	4 per day, 8:30am-6pm	€10.70	☎2310 595 485
Igoumenitsa	7hr.	8pm	€27.70	☎2310 595 416
Ioannina	7hr.	5 per day, 7:30am-9:30pm	€21.50	☎2310 595 442
Karditsa	3¼hr.	5 per day, 8am-8pm	€13.00	☎2310 595 440
Kastoria	3½hr.	7 per day, 7:30am-8pm	€13.20	☎2310 595 440
Katerini	2½hr.	Every 30min., 6:30am-10:30pm	€4.60	☎2310 595 428
Kavala	2½hr.	Every hr., 6am-8pm and 10pm	€10.20	☎2310 595 422
Komotini	4hr.	7 per day, 8:30am-1am	€15.80	☎2310 595 419
Kozani	2¼hr.	Every hr., 6am-8:30pm	€8.20	☎2310 595 484
Lamia	4hr.	9am, 3:15pm	€19.70	☎2310 595 416
Larisa	2hr.	Every hr., 7am-9:45pm	€10.50	☎2310 595 430
Metsovo	5hr.	5 per day, 7:30am-9:30pm	€17.70	☎2310 595 442
Parga	9hr.	10am	€32.20	☎2310 595 406
Patras	7hr.	3 per day, 8:15am-8:30pm	€29.70	☎2310 595 425
Ancient Pella	40min.	Every 45min., 6:30am-10pm	€2.30	☎2310 595 435
Pirgos	14hr.	M-Th, Sa-Su 10:30am, F 3:30pm	€34.20	☎2310 595 424
Preveza	6hr.	10am	€27.90	☎2310 595 406
Serres	1½hr.	Every 30min., 6am-10pm	€5.25	☎2310 523 210
Trikala	3hr.	6 per day, 8am-9pm	€12.70	☎2310 595 406
Veria	55min.	Every hr., 5:45am-6:55pm	€4.60	☎2310 595 432

BY BOAT

Buy ferry tickets at **Karacharisis Travel and Shipping Agency,** Koundouriotou 8 (☎2310 524 544; fax 2310 532 289), across from the Olympic Airways office. (Open M-F 8:30am-8:30pm, Sa 8:30am-2:30pm.) **Ferries** during high season (mid-June-early Sept.) go to: **Chios** (20hr., Su 1am, €30.70) via **Lesvos** (14hr., €30.70); **Iraklion** (24hr.; Tu 3pm, Th 7:30pm, Sa midnight; €41); **Kos** (20hr., Sa, €38.21); **Limnos** (8hr., M, €19.80); **Mykonos** (15hr.; Tu, Th, Sa; €31); **Naxos** (16hr., Th, €29); **Paros** (17½hr.; Tu, Sa; €31); **Rhodes** (24hr., Sa, €45.71); **Samos** (16hr.; Tu, Th; €31.40); **Santorini** (19½hr.; Tu, Th, Sa; €33); **Skiathos** (4hr.; Tu, Th; €16); **Skopelos** (6½hr., Th, €16.10); **Syros** (10hr., Th, €28); **Tinos** (12hr.; Tu, Sa; €30). Buy **Flying Dolphin** tickets at Karacharisis. Hydrofoils go to: **Chios** (9hr., W 9:30am, €61.40) via **Lesvos** (6½hr., €61.40) and **Limnos** (4hr., €39.60).

LOCAL TRANSPORTATION

Thessaloniki and its suburbs are connected by an extensive public transportation network. **Local buses** cost €0.45 and run throughout the city. An **office** across from the train station provides limited schedules, and **maps** posted at many of the bus stops show the city routes. Buy tickets at *periptera* (kiosks) or at depot ticket booths. The **depot** most frequently visited by travelers is at the train station. Among the many buses here are bus **#1,** which runs to the KTEL dome, **#8,** which goes to the White Tower stop, and **#73, the airport express,** which also stops at the White Tower. Another small depot is at Pl. Eleftherias by the harbor. Here one can catch **#5, 6,** and **33,** which navigate the waterfront on Tsimiski and Mitropoleos, and **#24,** which goes uptown to the Old City. Bus **#73** also runs the waterfront on its way from the train station to the post-tower suburb of **Kalamaria** and finally the **airport,** but be aware that because it's express, **#73** skips many stops. Buses **#10, 11,** and **31** run up and down Egnatia. **Taxis** (☎2310 551 525) run up and down Egnatia, Tsimiski, and Mitropoleos, but have specific queues at Ag. Sophia, Mitropoleos, and the White Tower.

ORIENTATION

Thessaloniki stretches out along the waterfront of the Thermaic Gulf's northern shore from the iconic **White Tower,** *Levkos Pyrgos*, in the east to the equally prominent **harbor** in the west. Its rough grid layout—established by the French city planner Hebrard after the Great Fire of 1917—and the orienting presence of the sea make it nearly impossible to get lost. The most important arteries run, like the city, parallel to the water. Farthest from shore is **Egnatia** the city's busiest thoroughfare, a bidirectional six-lane highway. Next comes **Ermou,** named after the god of merchants (Hermes) and home to many stores, then **Tsimiski, Mitropoleos,** and **Nikis.** Tsimiski's traffic and buses run from tower to harbor, while Mitropoleos hosts buses running the other direction. At the White Tower end, Tsimiski terminates in **Pl. Hanth** (XANΘ), Greek for YMCA. The plateia is a common reference point, bus stop, and base for museum exploration. The final route, Nikis, borders the harbor on one side and the city's main cafe strip on the other. Intersecting all these streets and leading from the water into town are, in order from harbor to tower, **I. Dragoumi, El. Venizelou, Aristotelous, Ag. Sophias,** and **Eth. Aminis.** Aristotelous, a wide boulevard where breezes sweep unobstructed from the ocean to the acropolis, is the city's center. Had Hebrard had his way after the 1917 fire, the whole city would look like this. Inland from

Egnatia is **Ag. Dimitriou** and the **Old City.** The roads north of Ag. Dimitriou grow increasingly tiny and steep towards the Old City's ancient fortress walls, panoramic views, and cheap tavernas. Between Tsimiski and the Arch of Galerius, **Pl. Navarinou,** with the ruins of Galerius's palace, is a meeting ground for youth. The mature converse in the taverns of **Ladadika,** just behind the northern side (tower-side) of the port. Formerly the home of olive oil merchants, the back alleys have become a pocket of upscale cafes, bars, and tavernas.

PRACTICAL INFORMATION

TOURIST AND FINANCIAL SERVICES

Tourist Offices: EOT (☎2310 222 935), inside the port at the Passenger Terminal, has **free maps,** hotel listings, transportation schedules and prices, and festival information. Open M-Sa 7:30am-3pm. Another EOT office (☎2310 985 215) is at the **airport. UTS,** Mitropoleos 28 (☎2310 286 256; fax 2310 283 156), is near Pl. Aristotelous; ring the bell by the door labeled "28" and go to the 7th fl. English-speaking Liza is a great help. Open M-F 9am-5pm.

Permits for Mt. Athos: Visit the **Holy Executive of the Holy Mt. Athos Pilgrims' Bureau,** Kou. Karamanli 14, 1st fl. (☎2310 861 611; fax 2310 861 811), opposite a Harley Davidson motorcycle shop. Karamanli is the eastern extension of Egnatia; take **bus #12** from Mitropoleos at Pl. Aristotelous and ask to be let off at Papafio. Letter of recommendation not needed but make sure you bring your passport. Only men are allowed to visit Mt. Athos (p. 303). English spoken. Open M-F 9am-1:30pm, Sa 10am-noon.

Consulates: Canada: Tsimiski 12 (☎2310 256 350). Open M-F 9am-noon. **Cyprus:** L. Nikis 37 (☎2310 260 611). Open M-F 9am-noon. **Turkey:** Ag. Dimitriou 151 (☎2310 248 452). Open M-F 9am-3pm. **UK:** Aristotelous 21 (☎2310 278 006). Open M-F 8am-1pm. **US:** Tsimiski 43 (☎2310 242 900). Open M, W, F 9am-noon.

Banks: Banks with currency exchange and 24hr. **ATMs** line Tsimiski, including **National Bank,** Tsimiski 11 (☎2310 230 783). Open M-Th 8am-2pm, F 8am-1:30pm. No bank, not even Greece's National Bank, will accept the volatile currencies of neighboring states Bulgaria or Albania. Overland travelers coming from these countries must head up Venizelou to its intersection with Ermou, where **exchange booths** will convert any currency at terrible rates.

Work Opportunities: Cafe Extrablatt (see **Alternatives to Tourism,** p. 76) will consider foreign applicants for part-time waitstaff and kitchen help. Good level of Greek needed. Contact the manager upon arrival. Pay negotiable.

LOCAL SERVICES

International Bookstores: Molchos Books, Tsimiski 10 (☎2310 275 271), across from the National Bank, has an excellent selection of English, Classical, religious, and art history books, plus international daily newspapers. Open M, W, Sa 8:30am-3pm; Tu, Th, F 8:30am-2pm and 5:30-9pm. **Malliaris,** Aristotelous 10 (☎2310 276 926), has a large selection of English travel and leisure reading as well as stationary supplies. Open M-Tu, Th-Su 8:30am-3:30pm, W 8:30am-9pm. **Newsstand,** Ag. Sophias 37 (☎2310 287 072), offers a wide selection of international newspapers and magazines.

Travel Books: For English travel guides, including *Let's Go* titles, head to **Traveller Books,** Proxenou Kopomila 41 (☎2310 275 215), 1 block inland from Nikis east of Aristotelous. Open M-Sa 9:30am-3:30pm, also open W 5:30pm-9pm.

Backpacking Supplies: SurfoMania, Proxenou Kopomila 48 (☎2310 231 351), across from Traveller Books, carries backpacking, mountain biking, and boating equipment. Open M-Sa 9:30am-3:30pm, Tu, Th additional evening hours.

Laundromat: Bianca, L. Antoniadou 3 (☎2310 209 602), behind the church to the right, facing the Arch of Galerius. Wash and dry €6. Open daily 8am-3pm.

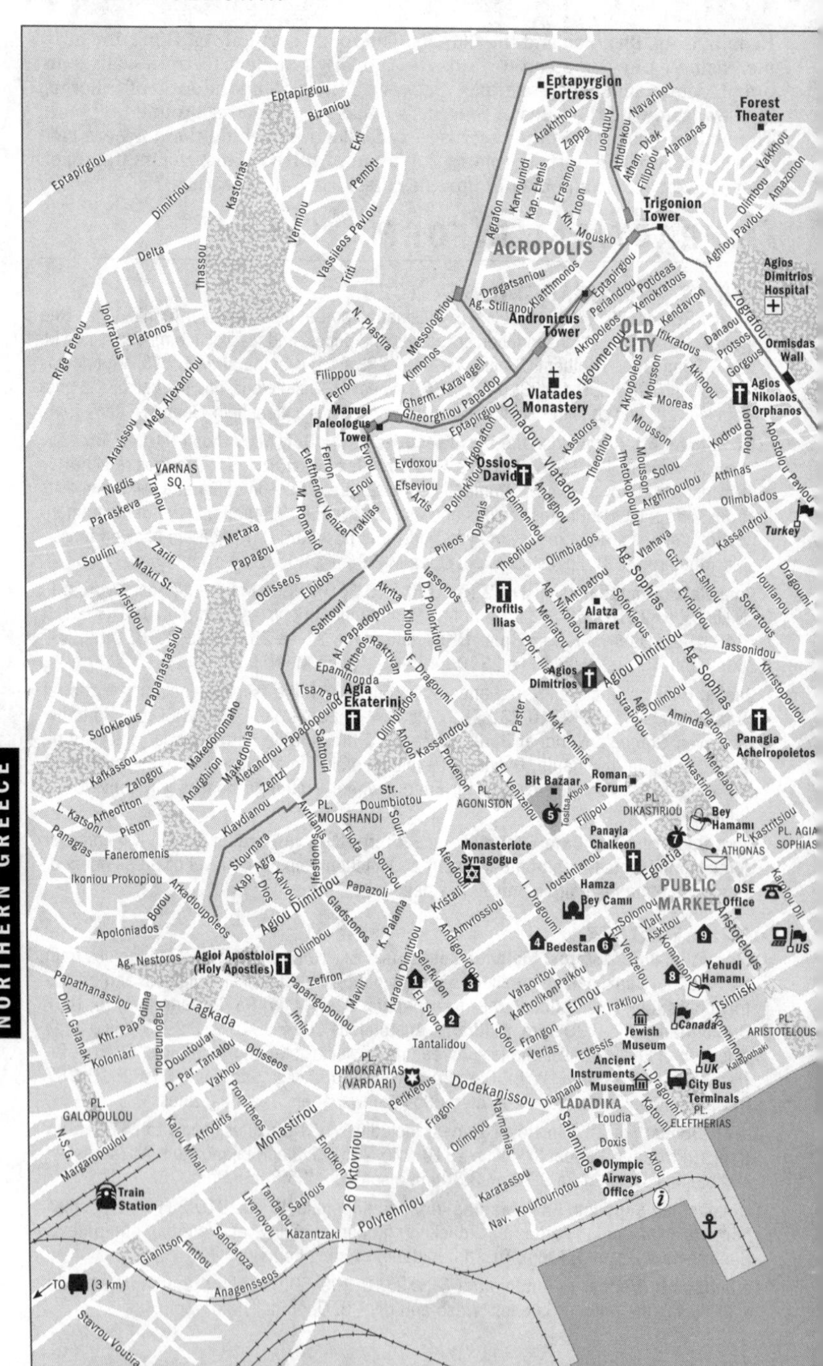
Eptapyrgion Fortress
Forest Theater
Trigonion Tower
ACROPOLIS
Agios Dimitrios Hospital
Andronicus Tower
OLD CITY
Ormisdas Wall
Vlatades Monastery
Agios Nikolaos Orphanos
Manuel Paleologus Tower
Ossios David
Turkey
VARNAS SQ.
Profitis Ilias
Alatza Imaret
Agios Dimitrios
Agia Ekaterini
Panagia Acheiropoietos
Bit Bazaar
Roman Forum
PL. AGONISTON
PL. MOUSHANDI
PL. DIKASTIRIOU
Bey Hamamı
PL. AGIA SOPHIAS
Panayia Chalkeon
ATHONAS
Monasteriote Synagogue
PUBLIC MARKET
OSE Office
Hamza Bey Camıı
US
Bedestan
Agioi Apostoloi (Holy Apostles)
Yehudi Hamamı
Canada
Jewish Museum
PL. ARISTOTELOUS
UK
PL. DIMOKRATIAS (VARDARI)
Ancient Instruments Museum
City Bus Terminals
LADADIKA
PL. ELEFTHERIAS
PL. GALOPOULOU
Olympic Airways Office
Train Station
TO (3 km)
Eptapirgiou
Bizaniou
Ekti
Pembti
Kastorias
Dimitriou
Delta
Thassou
Vermiou
Vassileos Pavlou
Triti
Arakhthou
Zappa
Antheon
Navarinou
Athdiakou
Athan. Diak
Filippou
Alamanas
Karvounidi
Kap. Elenis
Erasmou
Kh. Iroon
Mousko
Agrafon
Vakkhou
Amazonon
Olimbou
Agiou Pavlou
Zografou
Dragatsaniou
Klafthmonos
Ag. Stilianou
Eptapirgiou
Periandrou
Potideas
Xenokratous
Kendavron
Akropoleos
Igoumenou
Ifikratous
Danaou
Protsos
Gorgous
Ipokratous
Platonos
Rige Fereou
N. Plastira
Messologhiou
Kimonos
Filippou
Ferron
Gherm. Karavagelli
Gheorghiou Papadop
Meg. Alexandrou
Aravissou
Dimadou
Argonafton
Vlatadon
Kastoros
Theofilou
Mousson
Moreas
Akinou
Iordotou
Kodrou
Apostolou Pavlou
Nigdis
Tranou
Paraskeva
Evrou
Eleftheriou Venizelou
Ferron
Enou
M. Romanid
Iraklias
Evdoxou
Efseviou
Artis
Poliorkitou
Andighou
Epimenidou
Thetokopoulou
Solou
Arghiroulou
Athinas
Olimbiados
Kassandrou
Soulini
Zarifi
Metaxa
Papagou
Makri St.
Danais
Pileos
Odisseos
Epidos
Akrita
Iassonos
D. Poliorkitou
Aristidou
Sahtouri
Al. Papadopoul
Pitheos
Raktivan
Kilous
F. Dragoumi
Antipatrou
Ag. Nikolaou
Meniatou
Ag. Sophias
Vlahava
Gizi
Sofokleous
Eshilou
Evripidou
Ioulianou
Dragoumi
Sokratous
Iassonidou
Khristopoulou
Papanastassiou
Sofokleous
Epaminonda
Tsamad
Olimbiados
Prof. Ilia
Agiou Dimitriou
Stratiotou
Agn. Olimbou
Aminda
Platonos
Menelaou
Dikastirion
Kafkassou
Makedonomaho
Anarghiron
Makedonias
Alexandrou Papadopoulou
Zalogou
Zentzi
Andon
Kassandrou
Proxenou
Paster
Mak. Aminis
El. Venizelou
Tositsa-Kbola
Filipou
Kastritsiou
Karolou Dil
Arheotiton
L. Katsoni
Piston
Panagias
Faneromenis
Klavdianou
Avrilianis
Str. Doumbiotou
Souri
Filota
Stournara
Kap. Agra
Dios
Kalvou
Ifestionos
Soutsou
Papazoli
Afendoulis
Ioustinianou
I. Dragoumi
Egnatia
Solomou
Vlalr
Askitou
Komninon
Aristotelous
Ikoniou Prokopiou
Borou
Arkadioupoleos
Apoloniados
Gladstonos
K. Palama
Kristalli
Amvrossiou
Andigonidon
Ag. Nestoros
Olimbou
Zefiron
Paparigopoulou
Irinis
Mavili
Karaoli Dimitriou
Selefkidon
El. Svoro
Valaoritou
Katholikon
Paikou
Ermou
V. Irakliou
El. Venizelou
Tsimiski
Komninon
Papathanassiou
Dim. Galanaki
Khr. Papadima
Dragoumanou
Lagkada
Koloniari
Dountoular
D. Par. Tantalou
Vakhou
Odisseos
Tantalidou
L. Sofou
Frangon
Verias
Edessis
I. Dragoumi
Kalapothaki
Promitheos
Afroditis
Kalou Mihail
Monastiriou
Perikleous
Dodekanissou
Diamandi
Navmanias
Salaminos
Katouni
Loudia
Doxis
Fragon
Olimpiou
N.S.G.
Margaropoulou
Enotikon
26 Oktovriou
Tandalou
Sapfous
Livanovou
Karatassou
Nav. Kourtouriotou
Polytehniou
Kazantzaki
Sandaroza
Fintiou
Glanitson
Anagensseos
Stavrou Voutira

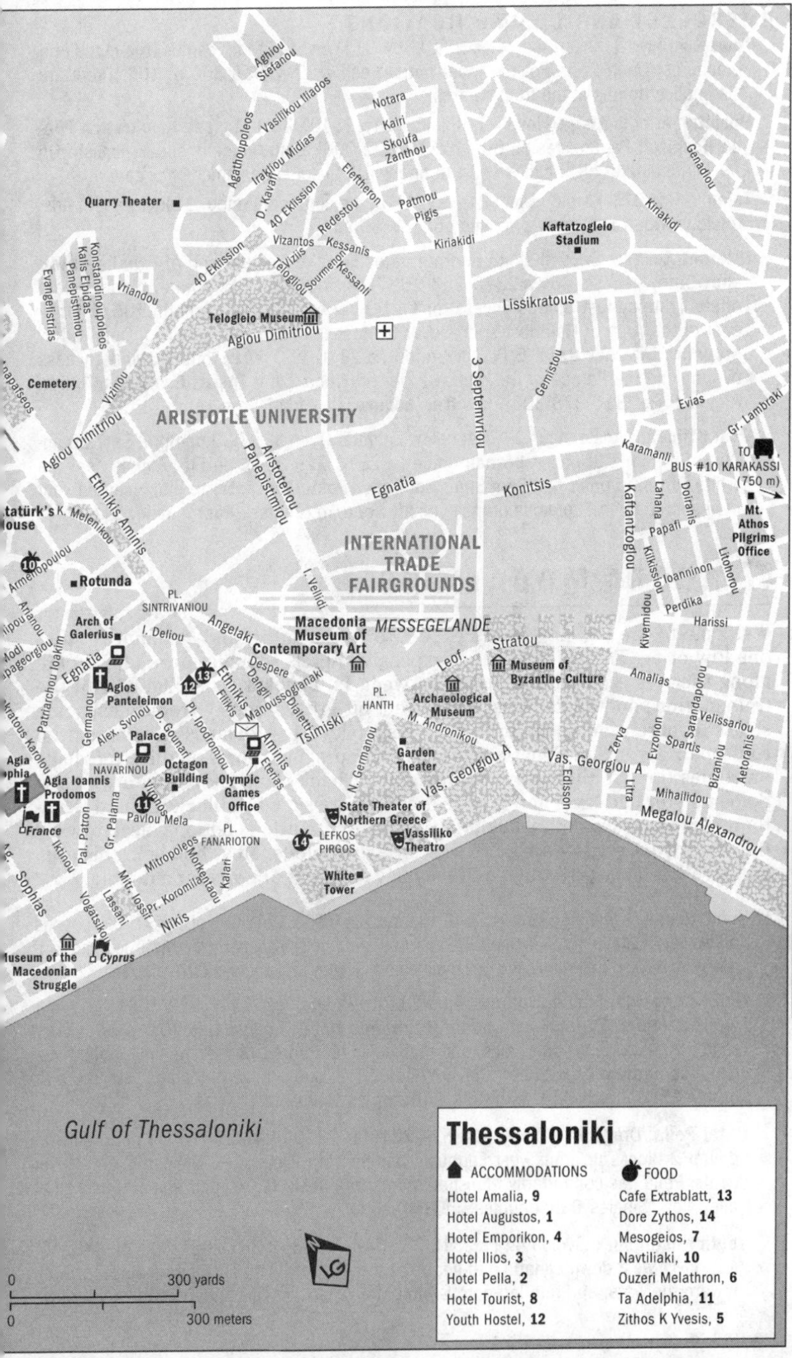

Aghiou Stefanou
Vasilikou Iliados
Agathoupoleos
Iraklilou Midias
Notara
Kairi
Skoufa
Zanthou
Eleftheron
Patmou
Pigis
Genadiou
Kiriakidi
Quarry Theater
D. Kavafi
40 Eklission
Redestou
Vizantos
Kessanis
Kaftatzogleio Stadium
40 Eklission
Viziis
Sourmenon
Teloglou
Kessanli
Konstandinoupoleos
Kalis Elpidas
Panepistimiou
Evangelistrias
Vriandou
Teloglelo Museum
Agiou Dimitriou
Lissikratous
3 Septemvriou
Gemistou
Cemetery
Vizinou
ARISTOTLE UNIVERSITY
Evias
Gr. Lambraki
Agiou Dimitriou
Aristoteliou
Panepistimiou
Karamanli
TO
BUS #10 KARAKASSI
(750 m)
Ethnikis Aminis
Egnatia
Konitsis
Kaftantzoglou
Lahana
Doiranis
Mt. Athos Pilgrims Office
Atatürk's House
K. Melenikou
Papafi
INTERNATIONAL TRADE FAIRGROUNDS
Kiikissiou
Litohorou
Armenopoulou
Ioanninon
Rotunda
I. Vellidi
PL. SINTRIVANIOU
Kivemidou
Perdika
Harissi
Arianou
Arch of Galerius
Angelaki
I. Deliou
Macedonia Museum of Contemporary Art
MESSEGELANDE
Stratou
Modi
Papageorgiou
Egnatia
Despere
Dangli
Leof.
Museum of Byzantine Culture
Amalias
Patriarchou Ioakim
Agios Panteleimon
Ethnikis
Filikis
Manoussoglanaki
Dialetti
PL. HANTH
Archaeological Museum
Sarandaporou
Velissariou
Germanou
Alex. Svolou
D. Gounari
Pl. Ipodromiou
M. Andronikou
Evzonon
Spartis
Zerva
Aetorahis
Palace
Tsimiski
Aminis
N. Germanou
Garden Theater
Vas. Georgiou A
Bizaniou
Agia Sophia
PL. NAVARINOU
Octagon Building
Olympic Games Office
Eterias
Vas. Georgiou A
Edisson
Litra
Agia Ioannis Prodomos
Gr. Palama
Vlahou
Mihailidou
Pavlou Mela
State Theater of Northern Greece
Megalou Alexandrou
France
Pal. Patron
Iktinou
PL. FANARIOTON
LEFKOS PIRGOS
Vassiliko Theatro
Mitropoleos
Morkentaou
Kalari
Ag. Sophias
White Tower
Mitr. Iossif
Pr. Koromila
Lassani
Vogatsikou
Nikis
Museum of the Macedonian Struggle
Cyprus
Gulf of Thessaloniki
0
300 yards
0
300 meters
Thessaloniki
ACCOMMODATIONS
Hotel Amalia, 9
Hotel Augustos, 1
Hotel Emporikon, 4
Hotel Ilios, 3
Hotel Pella, 2
Hotel Tourist, 8
Youth Hostel, 12
FOOD
Cafe Extrablatt, 13
Dore Zythos, 14
Mesogeios, 7
Navtiliaki, 10
Ouzeri Melathron, 6
Ta Adelphia, 11
Zithos K Yvesis, 5

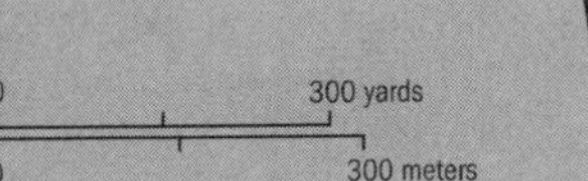

EMERGENCY AND COMMUNICATIONS

Tourist Police: Dodekanissou 4 (☎2310 554 871) on the 5th fl., carries **free maps** and brochures. Open 24hr. For the **local police,** call ☎2310 553 800 or 100. There are also police booths at the train station.

Hospital: At both **Ahepa Hospital,** Kiriakidi 1 (☎2310 993 111), and **Ippokration Public Hospital,** Papanastasiou 50 (☎2310 892 000), some doctors speak English. On weekends and at night call ☎1434 to find which hospital has emergency care.

Telephones: OTE, Karolou Diehl 27 (☎134), at the corner of Ermou, 1 block east of Aristotelous. Open M-F 7am-3pm, also open W 7-9pm.

Internet Access: Several small Internet cafes line the western end of Egnatia. **Interspot Cafe,** Tsimiski 43 (☎2310 253 2697), inside the mall with an American flag, offers lightning-fast 3Mbps access for €1.50 per hr. **E-Global,** Egnatia 105, 1 block east of the Arch of Galerius, sports over 50 fast terminals. €2-3 per hr. Open 24hr. **Meganet Internet Cafe,** 5 Pl. Navarinou (☎2310 250 331), offers 2Mbps access overlooking the Palace of Galerius. €2 per hr. Open 24hr. The **British Council,** Eth. Aminis 9 (☎2310 378 300), has **free access.** Open M-F 9am-1pm.

Post Office: At Aristotelous 27, just below Egnatia. Open M-F 7:30am-8pm, Sa 7:30am-2pm, Su 9am-1:30pm. A **branch** office (☎2310 229 324), on Eth. Aminis near the White Tower, is open M-F 7am-8pm. Both offer **Poste Restante;** to make certain your mail gets to the Aristotelous branch specify *Kentriko* (Center). **Postal code:** 54101.

ACCOMMODATIONS

Welcome to the big city—don't expect to find comfort and cleanliness all at one low price. Thessaloniki's less expensive hotels (doubles around €25) are along the western end of **Egnatia,** between **Pl. Dimokratias** (500m east of the train station) and **Aristotelous.** Most are a bit gritty, ranging from ramshackle sleaze to merely cheerless, but all are easy to locate, with signs stretching from rooftop to pavement. Egnatia is loud at all hours, but rooms on the street have balconies (i.e. air circulation), while quieter back rooms have just a window. Some quieter mid-level hotels (€40 doubles) are set a few blocks behind Egnatia on **Dragoumi** around **Pl. Diikitiriou.** For more luxurious options, head toward the waterfront area two blocks west of Aristotelous. Most hotels in this area come with a hefty price tag—you may pay upwards of €150 for a double.

NORTHERN GREECE

Hotel Atlantis, Egnatia 14 (☎2310 540 131; fax 2310 536 154). One of many cheap options on western Egnatia, Atlantis offers standard budget furnishings, complete with bed and window. The hallway bathrooms are well maintained. Singles and doubles €20, with bath €30. ❷

Hotel Augustos, Elenis Svoronou 4 (☎2310 522 955; fax 2310 522 500). From the western end of Egnatia, turn north at the Argo Hotel; Augustos is 20m ahead. Cozy rooms with wooden floors, rugs, and high ceilings. Rooms vary; some have balconies. Doubles and triples with bath have A/C and TVs; some have balconies. Singles with bath €25; doubles €30, with bath €40; triples with bath €50. ❷

Hotel Pella, Dragoumi 63 (☎2310 524 221; fax 2310 524 223), to the north on Dragoumi 2 blocks up from west Egnatia's budget strip. One of Pl. Diikitiriou's mid-level deals, Pella has comfortably furnished rooms with desk, TV, telephone, bath, and quiet alley view. Singles €35; doubles €50. MC/V. ❸

Youth Hostel, Alex. Svolou 44 (☎2310 225 946; fax 2310 262 208). Take bus #8, 10, 11, or 31 west down Egnatia and get off at the Arch of Galerius (Kamara stop), or walk toward the water and turn left onto Svolou after 2 blocks. This cheap option finds backpackers talking long into the hot nights on its balconies, but you get what you pay for. On Let's Go's last visit, the showers ran cold, and Let's Go strongly prefers other accommodations in Thessaloniki to this one. €9 per person, July 15-Sept. 15 €10 per person. 10% discount with ISIC. ❶

Hotel Tourist, Mitropoleos 21 (☎2310 270 501; fax 2310 226 865), just west of Aristotelous has an excellent location and rooms with TV, phone, A/C, and bath. Singles €50; doubles €70; triples €90. ❹

Hotel Emporikon, Singrou 14 (☎2310 525 560 or 2310 514 431), has clean rooms with bright balconies overlooking leafy, tranquil Singrou. There are newly-tiled shared bathrooms and hallway fridges. It is a little quieter than most other hotels on Egnatia. Singles €20; doubles €40; triples €43. ❷

Hotel Ilios, Egnatia 27 (☎2310 512 620), on the western Egnatia budget strip, offers modern rooms with big windows, A/C, TVs, phones, fridges, and gleaming white baths. Rooms away from the street are quieter. Singles €35; doubles €49; triples €58. ❸

Hotel Amalia, Ermou 33 (☎2310 268 321; thess@hotelamalia.gr). From Egnatia, turn right at Aristotelous and right again at Ermou. Amalia's bright rooms have TVs, A/C, bathrooms, and large balconies. A bar on the 1st fl. serves drinks (€3-4.50). Breakfast €5. Singles €55; doubles €69; triples €81.60. MC/V. ❹

FOOD

Thessaloniki proper has eight main dining districts. Just behind the port is the upscale **Ladadika.** Farther inland at the corner of **Dragoumi** and **El. Venizelou** are a bevy of youthful restaurants. Between **Egnatia** and **Aristotelous** a network of alleyways support some fine vine-canopied *ouzeria* where roaming musicians squeeze their way through the tightly packed tables to strum a tune for your dinner (and for theirs). A bustling **public market,** with everything from fresh meat to Italian leather sandals, operates every day in the alleys between Egnatia and Aristotelous. Continuing eastward **Pl. Athonos** is a student favorite, while **Pl. Navarino** acts as a porch for the tables of a number of well-priced *ouzeria,* which overlook the ruins of Galerius's Palace. Either behind the **Rotunda** or before the **White Tower,** find some ostentatiously positioned, but nevertheless tasty, avant-garde *ouzeria.* Lastly, the **Old City** brims with tavernas and restaurants near the **fortress** which have sweeping views of the gulf. Thessaloniki restaurants have a delightful custom of providing their patrons watermelon or sweets gratis after a meal. The local syrup-drenched cake known as *revani,* a gift of the many refugees from Asia Minor, is especially good. Late city work hours mean eateries don't fill until 3:30pm and again around 11pm.

Dore Zythos, Tsiroyianni 7 (☎2310 279 010), is behind the grassy triangular plot across from the White Tower. Sea breezes and superb views of the White Tower combine with the avant-garde menu to make this hot-spot a local favorite. Try the *Its Pilaf* (€7) for an Anatolian treat. Entrees €6-€8. ❷

Ouzeri Melathron, Karypi 21-34 (☎2310 275 016). From Egnatia, walk past the Ottoman Bedesten on El. Venizelou and make a right into the passageway between storefronts. Witty, 4 ft.-long subtitled menus feature the "transsexual special" ("tastes like lamb, but is a chicken dish") and snails ("for friends of the hermaphrodite"). Also serves lamb, octopus, and a variety of cheese dishes. Entrees €3.50-12. ❷

Navtiliaki, Pl. Ag. Georgiou 8, just beside the Rotunda. An *ouzeri* with excellent seafood. Has some fine meaty and vegetarian options. The cool, tree-covered setting is quite relaxing. Octopus €7. Entrees €5-9. ❷

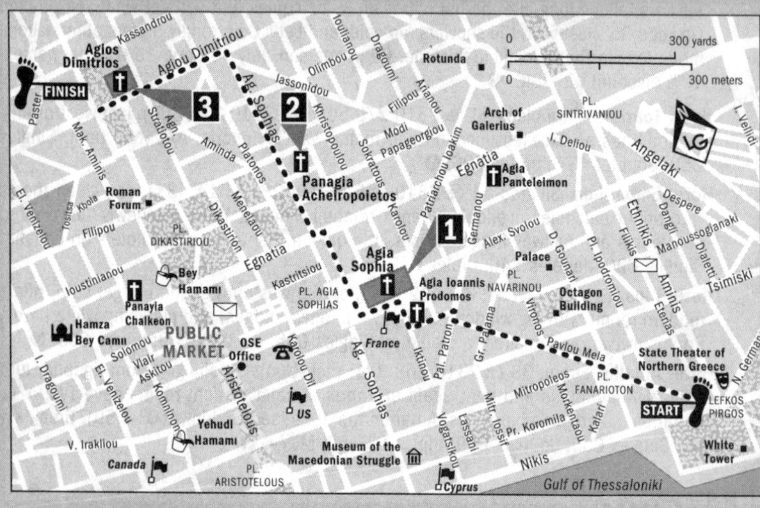

During the Byzantine Empire, Salonica was graced with enough churches to keep devout old women crossing themselves at an aerobic rate all day. Over the centuries, earthquakes, fires, and Muslim appropriations have severely damaged most of Salonica's 90 original churches, but many—such as Agios Dimitrios and Panagia Acheiropoietos—have been beautifully restored and deserve a visit. Most churches open early (6-7am), close sometime between noon and 2pm, and re-open for a few hours in the evening (usually around 5-8pm). Modest dress is required; donations are appreciated.

START: The White Tower

FINISH: Agios Dimitrios

DISTANCE: 1.5km

WHEN TO GO: Morning

1 AGIA SOPHIA. Walk northwest from the White Tower up Pavlou Mela to Agia Sophia Square. Sunk into the ground at the eastern end of Ermou, the magnificent, domed 7th-century **Agia Sophia** offers a brilliant introduction to the splendor of Byzantine churches. Gold *tesserae* gleam on the dome's 9th-century circular **mosaic of the Ascension,** where the awe-struck Apostles, angels, and Virgin witness a truncated Christ ascending in a blue globe. (Open daily 7am-1pm and 5-7pm.)

2 PANAGIA ACHEIROPOIETOS. Follow Ag. Sophias north past Egnatia until you arrive at the three-aisle, 5th-century **Panagia Acheiropoietos** to your right, once the city's official mosque. On the underside of the church's arches you will see late Roman mosaics heavily influenced by pagan naturalistic themes. They portray heavenly delights—glittering fruits, birds, vases of water, and fish. (Open daily 8am-1pm and 6-9pm.)

3 AGIOS DIMITRIOS. Continue north along Ag. Sophias; turn left three streets later onto Agiou Dimitriou and the massive **Agios Dimitrios** will appear on your right. The city's oldest and most famous church is named for its patron saint, a Christian Roman officer speared to death by order of Galerius in the bath complex. Although fires (in 620 and 1917) decimated the church, the surviving fragments of the mosaics that once covered the inner sides of the colonnades are precious because they comprise the few figural mosaics in the empire that survived 8th-century iconoclasm. The **crypt** contains the shell of the original tiny church, the Roman road now below ground level, and the fountain where Dimitrios was killed. (Open daily 6am-10pm. Crypt hours reduced Su-M. Holy Liturgy every F 9:30-11pm.)

Mesogeios, Balanou 38 (☎2310 288 460), east of Aristotelous, 1 block south of Egnatia, is the largest *ouzeri* in the area. A popular spot among locals, Mesogeios serves large portions of meat and seafood under a canopy of vines. Mediterranean-style entrees €4-6. Seafood €7-9. ❸

Ta Adelphia, Pl. Navarion 7 (☎2310 266 432). Excellent prices (even the seafood tops out at €6), 1930s pictures, and seating in a quiet plateia overlooking Galerius's Palace make Adelphia a student favorite. Entrees €5-6. ❷

Cafe Extrablatt, Alex Svolou 46 (☎2310 256 900), next to the youth hostel. This cheerful, family-run restaurant offers a rare blend of German and Greek cuisine. Crepes, pasta, and sausage and mushroom dishes make up the eclectic menu. Wash your meal down with one of over 50 beer options. Entrees €6-12. ❸

Zithos K Yvesis (☎2310 268 746), hidden away near the intersection of El. Venizelou and Filipou. Head up Tositsa and look for an alleyway entrance between 2 tall buildings. Laughter and loud conversation continue well into the night in the triangular "Bit Bazar" area where this taverna is located. Delicious meat and vegetarian dishes are served by friendly, English-speaking waiters. Entrees €2.50-6. ❷

SIGHTS

ARCH AND PALACE OF GALERIUS. At the intersection of D. Gounari and Egnatia stands the striking Arch of Galerius, known to locals simply as *Kamara* (arch). A colonnaded processional led north from the arch and nearby palace to the cylindrical rotunda. Caesar Galerius built his arch to commemorate a victory over the Persian Shah Narses in 297, covering it with relief sculptures detailing his triumphs and close rapport with father-in-law, and Augustus, Diocletian. Christians, who suffered greatly under Galerius's persecutions, rubbed out his face in every panel. Much of the lower panels have faded, but one can still make out the Persians with their distinctive headgear, along with some elephants, in the upper panels. A tiny piece of the once 150,000 sq. m royal complex is open for viewing in Pl. Navarino, another two blocks seaward. One can admire some weathered geometrical **mosaic floors** and the partially preserved **octagonal hall.** *(Open daily 8am-7pm.)*

THE ROTUNDA. From the arch, turn up D. Gounari to see the most dramatic reminder of Thessaloniki's Roman heritage. The enormous cylindrical rotunda, now **Ag. Georgiou,** was originally built as a temple to the patron gods of the tetrarchy, Diocletian's administrative system wherein governance was divided between two Augusti and two lower ranking Caesars. In the 5th century, the rotunda became a church filled with **mosaics** of saints martyred at the hands of Galerius and Diocletian, and from 1590 to 1912 it sojourned as a mosque. The walls once displayed some of the city's most lavish and gleaming mosaics. An estimated 36 million *tesserae* were assembled to represent gilded facades, birds, and saints. Only those highest in the dome have survived and renovation work from the 1978 earthquake obscures most of these; bring binoculars. *(Open Tu-Su 8am-7pm.)*

ROMAN AGORA. At the top of Aristotelous, the 2nd-century odeon and covered market survive. On the south side of the Agora's lower square was once the Hellenistic colonnade that held eight **caryatids** of mythological women. Known in Ladino, the language of the Sephardic Jews, as *las Incantadas* ("the enchanted women"), they were thought to have been magically petrified. When the portico was demolished in 1865, the statues were sent to the Louvre. *(Open 8:30am-8pm.)*

WHITE TOWER. The city's most recognizable site, the White Tower presides over the eastern part of Thessaloniki's seafront like an oversized chess piece, often acting as an easy rendezvous point. Originally part of a 15th-century seawall, the tower later became the Ottoman Death Row where **Janissaries,** an elite corps of Ottoman soldiers recruited from the Christian populace, carried out notoriously gruesome executions. Blood was so often seen seeping from the tower's stone walls that locals began calling it the Bloody Tower. In 1890 a prisoner white-washed the whole building and inaugurated the current name. *(At the far eastern end of Nikis. ☎2310 267 832. Open M 12:30-7pm, Tu-Su 8am-7pm. Free.)*

OLD WALLS. Starting from the White Tower, walk inland along Filikis Eterias. Occasional strips of rubble mark the route of the old walls. After Egnatia head right one block and continue up on Ethn. Aminis. At Ag. Dimitriou the walls rise back up to their ancient 10m glory and a footpath begins. Here, just across from the hospital, a massive 8m-long 5th-century **Greek inscription** built into the high rampart's brick arrogantly proclaims, "Ormisdas fortified the city with these indestructible walls." As the walls climb, the path improves toward the 15th-century **Trigonion Tower,** built as a guard post at the intersection of the city and acropolis walls. Enter the Old City, or acropolis, here through holes in the indestructible walls. Following the wall along Eptapyrigiou, you'll see multiple pretty brick crosses and a large late Byzantine inscription, built into sporadic towers.

HEPTAPYRGION. Meaning the seven towers, this Byzantine and Ottoman fortress was a high security prison until 1989. It's more morbid monument to the Greek penal system than historical landmark. *(☎2310 204 134. Open Tu-Su 8am-7pm. Free.)*

OTTOMAN SIGHTS. The Ottomans ruled Thessaloniki for almost 500 years, leaving an indelible imprint on the city's landscape. **Bey Hamami,** a 15th-century bathhouse, once featured a labyrinthine interior, with a cool antechamber leading to a "tepid" room and the immense domed sauna beyond. *(On Egnatia, east of Aristotelous. Open daily 8am-9pm. Free.)* Built by a *bey's* daughter in 1467-68 as a *mesçid* (a hall of worship minus the minarets), **Hazma Bey Camii** gained a minaret and official mosque status in the late 16th century; today it is the largest mosque in Greece. *(On Egnatia, just past Venizelou.)* A late 15th-century covered marketplace and craftsmen's workshop, the Ottoman **Bedesten** was said to emit delicious perfumes of musk and amber. Inscriptions carved into the domes in French, Greek, Southern Slav, and Turkish evoke the variegated ethnicities of Thessaloniki in its cosmopolitan heyday. The market has lost a lot of its bustle, but the interior still houses merchants selling fabrics and sewing supplies. *(On Venizelou, 1 block south of Egnatia.)*

MUSEUMS

ARCHAEOLOGICAL MUSEUM. The treasures from Vergina's royal Macedonian tombs, once the highlight of Thessaloniki's collection, were returned to Vergina (p. 285) in 1998, but the museum still shelters many jewels, including a permanent exhibit on Macedonian gold with some foil myrtle wreathes, whose splendidly frail leaves vibrate with your footsteps. Sculptures of a famously erotic Aphrodite and parts of an enormous statue of Athena share space with a grand mosaic depicting Dionysus with Ariadne, Apollo stalking Daphne, and Ganymede in Zeus's eagle talons. There are also finds from 121 graves at Sindos, including gold death masks and jewelry, soldiers' swords and helmets, and figurines. The museum is a good place to visit before exploring the local Roman Forum and the nearby sites of Vergina and Pella. *(At the western end of Tsimiski, across from the International Helexpo Fairgrounds. ☎2310 830 538. Open M 12:30-7pm, Tu-Su 8am-7pm; hours reduced in winter. €4, students and seniors €2, EU students and under 18 free.)*

MUSEUM OF BYZANTINE CULTURE. Throughout Greece a Byzantine museum is synonymous with a deeply religious exhibition of holy icons, usually dating from the empire's dying days and sometimes even later. In keeping with its exhaulted postion as second city of the Byzantine Empire, Thessaloniki uses its huge museum to tell a much more cosmopolitan and secular tale. Through the displays of everyday life, economics, engineering, and imperial dynasties, visitors may discover for the first time that the Byzantine Empire was neither the theocracy nor monocultural Greek state that domestic museums often portray it to be. As visitors will learn, one of Thessaloniki's churches (Ag. Chalkeon) was actually rebuilt by a noble of Byzantine Lombardy and the city's walls were repaired by the Emperor Leo, a Syrian. *(Stratou 2. Behind the Archaeological Museum, across Septemvriou 3. ☎2310 868 570 or 868 571. Open M 12:30-7pm, Tu-Su 8am-7pm; hours reduced in winter. Wheelchair-accessible. €4, students and seniors €2, EU students and under 18 free.)*

MUSEUM OF THE MACEDONIAN STRUGGLE. Once the Greek consulate to Turkish Thessaloniki (1892-1912), this large house now contains memorabilia to the wars that made the city Greek. Through pictures, artifacts, and dioramas in the basement, the museum tells the tale of Macedonia's brutal guerrilla wars. From Greek and Bulgarian Christians killing Turks to killing one another, the **Balkan Wars,** which ripped the multi-ethnic north apart, are portrayed through an understandably tinted glass. The exhibits include personal artifacts of the famous rebel leader **Pavlou Melas** (including the bullet that killed him) as well as captured war booty like Turkish and Bulgarian arms and treasure. The museum is happy to provide English pamphlets with facts about the collection and a historical overview of the Macedonian War. *(Koromila 23, 1 block from the water, halfway between the White Tower and Pl. Aristotelous. ☎2310 229 778. Open Tu-F 9am-2pm, Sa 10am-2pm. Free.)*

JEWISH MUSEUM OF THESSALONIKI. "Thessaloniki: The Metropolis of Sephardism," proclaims a sign over the museum's entrance. In the 15th century waves of Jewish refugees, fleeing Reconquista Spain, were invited by the Ottoman sultan to settle in his lands. The museum's first two rooms use pictures, gravestones, and folk artifacts to tell the subsequent 500-year history of Thessaloniki's community, the largest in Europe. A third exhibit tells the story of the Jews' migration to Palestine—founding ports like Tel Aviv—in the 1920s and 30s in response to Thessaloniki's 1917 fire and pressure from Greek nationalism. The last room remembers the terrible holocaust story, when 96.5% of the city's remaining 49,000 members were murdered in the camps of Auschwitz and Bergen-Belsen. Only some 1000 remain in the city today. *(Agiou Mina 13. ☎2310 250 406; www.jct.gr. Open Tu, F, Su 11am-2pm; W-Th 11am-2pm and 5-8pm. Free.)*

ATATÜRK'S HOUSE. If you've just come from Turkey and miss the ubiquitous statues, streets, and museums dedicated to the creator of the modern Turkish state, here's a chance to get your fix. The three-story concertina wire enclosed house, which was the birthplace and childhood home of Atatürk, now displays various relics from his life. Pictures of the great leader adorn all the walls and many items of clothing (including his bathrobe) are also on view. Display signs are in Turkish and Greek only. *(Apostolou Pavlou 17. Open daily 10am-5pm. Free. Ring the bell then present your passport next door at the Turkish Consulate, Ag. Dimitriou 151.)*

TELOGLION FOUNDATION OF ART. The large museum of Teloglion is part of the Aristotle University complex. Here some excellent rotating exhibits focus on topics from archaeology to modern art. *(Agiou Dimitriou 159A. ☎2310 991 610; www.auth.gr/teloglion. Open Su 11am-2pm, Tu-F 10am-1pm, also open W 5-8pm.)*

MUSEUM OF ANCIENT, BYZANTINE, AND POST-BYZANTINE MUSICAL INSTRUMENTS. Three floors of this upscale museum display replications of ancient musical instruments, tracing their evolution from 2800 BC to the early 20th century. The concert hall hosts a series of Byzantine music performances throughout the year—details can be found in local newspapers and at the front desk. *(Katouni 12-14, at the western end of Tsimiski near the Ladadika district. ☎2310 555 263. Open M 9am-3pm, Tu-Su 9am-3pm and 5-10pm. €4.40, students and children €2.)*

WAR MUSEUM. Located inside a new building in the War Department of Thessaloniki, the museum features military paraphernalia used by Greeks from the War of Independence through the Civil War. Also on display are some Ottoman military artifacts and various captured weapons (Turkish, Bulgarian, and German) from Greece's many enemies. *(G. Labraki 4. ☎2310 893 731. Open Tu-F 9am-2pm. Free.)*

ENTERTAINMENT

Summer visitors looking for live *rembetika* music should spend a weekend night at **Iyoklima,** on tiny Axiou south of Nikis near the port, or **Palios Stathmos** (Old Station), Voutira 2 (☎2310 521 892). **Alpha Odeon** in the mall with the US Embassy, Tsimiski 43, is an indoor **movie theater** (☎2310 290 100) with many American films (€7). When skies are clear, head outside to waterfront **Natali Cinema,** Vas. Olgas 3 (☎2310 829 457), 5min. past the White Tower, or **Ellinis** (☎2310 292 304), at Pl. Hanth, across from the Archaeological Museum. (Films 9 and 11pm. €6.) You can't miss the posters plastered all over town for the theater, music, and dance performances at venues like the **Dhasos "Forest" Theater,** uptown in the forest near the acropolis (☎2310 218 092), **Kipos "Garden" Theater** (☎2310 256 775), by Pl. Hanth, **Damari "Quarry" Theater** in an old quarry in the **Saranda Ekklesias** district, **Moni Lazariston** (the old catholic monastery), and **Kratiko and Vassiliko Theaters** near the White Tower (☎2310 223 785 for both). The **International Fairgrounds,** across from the Archaeological and Byzantine Museums, holds festivals throughout the year, including the **International Trade Fair and Song Festival** (Sept.), the **Dimitria Festival** celebrating the city's patron saint (Oct.), the internationally revered **Thessaloniki Film Festival** (Nov.; www.filmfestival.gr), and the new **Documentary Festival** (Mar.). A **Wine Festival** is celebrated in the park of **Nea Elvetia** district in September.

NIGHTLIFE

There are three main hubs for late-night fun in Thessaloniki: the bars and cafes of the **Ladadika** district, once the city's red-light strip; the bustling **waterfront;** and the big open-air discos around the **airport** (€8-9 from the center). Most of the clubs (cover €9, includes 1 drink) around the airport feature live modern or traditional Greek music. Call ahead and dress well. Although the clubs boom until dawn, summer nightlife in the city doesn't amount to much by Salonican standards—most head to the mega-beach clubs of **Kalithea** on Kassandra (p. 300).

Shark, Themistokli Sofouli and Argonavton 2 (☎2310 416 855), in Kalamaria around the gulf 4km from the city center. Waterfront views of the city skyline and a throbbing clientele. Mostly young professionals who haven't yet forgotten how to party.

Night Club Arabian (☎2310 471 135), along the highway toward the airport 13km from the city. Arabian supplies the standard Greek fare in a pseudo-Islamic venue with colonnades to shelter its flashy revelers from their powerfully sophisticated selves. Cover €9.

Rodon (☎2310 476 720), 11km east of the city along the main highway. The most sophisticated club in Thessaloniki has an equally sophisticated cover (€10, includes 1 drink). Rub elbows with Thessaloniki's hipsters in the club's amphitheatric bowl, or join the crowd on stage with the live Greek pop band. Open until 4:30am.

Stala, L. Nikis 3 (☎2310 228 237), right at the western end of the waterfront, by the port, has breezy tables outside, deafening rock music in the cavernous interior. It's a great place to sip a drink and people-watch before heading to the clubs of Ladadika, 2 blocks away. Cocktails €5.50-6.50.

Mylos, Andreou Georgiou 56 (☎2310 516 945), in the far west of the city; take bus #31 or a taxi. Once an old mill, now an entertainment center with art exhibits, a restaurant, and bars. Try the Turkish dessert *ek mek,* served nowhere else in the city.

DAYTRIPS FROM THESSALONIKI

ANCIENT VERGINA Βεργινα

Buses (☎26100 70 785) run from Thessaloniki (55min.; every hr., 5:45am-6:55pm; €4.60) to Veria. From Veria take the bus to Vergina (20min.; 8 per day, 6:50am-8pm; €1). You'll be dropped off in the Vergina plateia; follow the signs to the archaeological sites. Buses run out of Vergina for Veria (20min.; 10 per day, 7:20am-8:20pm; €0.95) but are less reliable. Open M noon-7pm, Tu-Su 8am-7pm; winter Tu-Su 8am-7pm. An €8 ticket will grant admission to all of Vergina's sights. Students €4, EU students free.

Unearthing the ancient Vergina ruins was an archaeological watershed—among the enlightening finds were Greek inscriptions that proved the ancient Macedonians were a Greek tribe. The findings in the tombs display such superb artistry that scholars believe they could have belonged only to the royal Macedonian family of Philip II, father of Alexander the Great; it's likely too since the tombs date 350-325 BC, years during Philip's rule.

MUSEUM. At once uncannily morbid and dazzlingly beautiful, Vergina's museum will no doubt be the highlight of your visit. Visitors enter the **Great Tumulus,** itself a massive burial mound, the largest in Greece (over 12m tall and 110m in diameter). The Tumulus was built before the mid-3rd century BC and housed the graves of Vergina's average citizens in addition to the massive royal tombs. The atmospherically lit museum displays artifacts found in the Great Tumulus including Attic vases, clay and ivory figurines, gold jewelry, and the carved funerary *steles* of the commoners' graves. Four of the majestic **royal tombs** lie in their original locations. The designs of all four are similar: each has an anterior Ionic or Doric colonnade decorated with mythological scenes. The large room behind the colonnade contains the remains of the deceased and various items to accompany him or her into the afterlife. Tombs I and IV belong to unknown royal family members. Tomb IV, looted in antiquity, stored unusually beautiful and well-preserved **frescoes,** possibly the work of master artist **Nikomachus.** The most intact depicts an anguished Persephone being abducted by a grim Hades, while Demeter watches with cold sorrow. The **Tomb of the Prince** probably belongs to Alexander IV, son of Alexander the Great; he was murdered along with his mother Roxana at age 13 by his not-so-close relative, Cassander at Amphipolis. The silver hydra containing his bones and his spectacular leaf-mimicking gold myrtle wreath are on display, along with other artifacts. The grand **Tomb of Philip II** is accompanied by a magnificent gold chest and exquisite myrtle wreath, and by fragments of his chryselephantine couch. The wood has rotted, but the ivory faces, arms, and legs of the couch's diorama, depicting Philip II hunting with a young Alexander, still remain. A huge glass case displays the charred remains of the bountiful offerings thrown on Philip's funeral pyre; they include animal offerings, figurines, and all his treasured possessions. Philip's tomb also contained the remains of a woman, probably **Cleopatra,** one of his seven consorts. Her gold couch remains, as do shreds of the gold-embroidered purple cloth that wrapped her bones.

RUINS. To get to the **Palace of Palatitsa,** turn right as you exit the museum and follow the road as it veers to the left. A short-cut through the bus parking lot followed by an uphill walk will get you to the ruins in about 20min. What remains of the 3rd-century BC palace is now little more than a collection of toppled columns and ancient rubble; as of summer 2003, the mosaic on the southern side of the palace floor was undergoing conservation work and could not be viewed. *(Open M noon-7pm, Tu-Su 8am-7pm.)* On the walk up to Palatitsa, you'll encounter the **Macedonian Tomb** believed to be that of Philip II's mother **Queen Evridiki.** Walk down the steps to its opened doors to see a stately marble throne. Next to it is a second tomb, with a fresco of Persephone and Hades in the underworld. Farther up the road, a sign off to the left past a prickly meadow indicates the site of the **ancient Theater.** It was here, overlooking the plains of his kingdom below, that Philip II was assassinated while celebrating the marriage of his daughter, Cleopatra.

ANCIENT PELLA Πελλα

It's along the main Edessa-Thessaloniki highway, 38km west of Thessaloniki. Buses go to Pella (40min.; every 45 min., 6:30am-10pm; €2.30). Make sure you are let off at "Ancient Pella," not "New Pella." You will see the site off to the right. Buses to Thessaloniki (2-3 per hr.) pass the site; the bus stops across from the cafe by the archaeological site. ☎23820 31 160. Open Apr.-Oct. M noon-7pm, Tu-Su 8am-7pm; Nov.-Mar. Tu-Su 8:30am-3pm. Site and museum €6; students €3; seniors, EU students, and under 18 free.

As the remains of 26 Neolithic settlements indicate, the area around Pella was heavily inhabited in prehistoric times. Around 400 BC, King Archelaus opted to move his capital here from Aigai (Vergina); the new location fostered eastern trade and cultivated a rapport with southern Greece. Later the birthplace of Philip II, the capital prospered under his reign. The construction of a splendid new palace attracted great minds and talents from the entire Hellenic world to the court; Alexander was born here. By the mid-4th century BC, however, the recession of the sea had made Pella a now inconvenient port—its glory days came to an end in 168 BC when the city was ransacked by Roman general Aemilius Paulus.

Pella only takes an hour to see, but the **museum** alone makes the trip worthwhile. Its treasures include gold-leaf jewelry, terracotta figurines, glazed and unglazed Macedonian pottery, and unusual molded pottery depicting some rather racy episodes. The collection's important objects are the exquisite **mosaics** of Dionysus riding a leopard, a lion hunt, and a gryphon devouring a deer, highlighted by grisly splashes of blood. The mosaics are composed of small sea pebbles outlined with thin lead strips; the missing eyes were likely semi-precious stones. They're the earliest-known mosaics to mimic a three-dimensional look. Directly across the highway from the museum is Pella's vast **archaeological site,** still under excavation by young go-getters from the University of Thessaloniki. At the heart of the site are the remains of the **agora,** the commercial center of the city in ancient times, with the three wells from which much of the ancient discarded pottery in the museum was collected. To the left, the **House of Dionysus** and the **House of the Abduction of Helen** both have expansive, well-preserved mosaic floors. The beautifully-executed scenes in the mosaics seem to breathe, with subtle muscle gradations and shadows in the stag-hunting scene, and the swirling skirts and rearing horses in Helen's abduction. The **House of Plaster** has no mosaics, but it does have a splendid rectangular Ionic colonnade. North of the houses and the agora are the **acropolis** and **palace** (off-limits to visitors). The palace, built in 10 stages, is a makeshift blend of architectural styles. Expanded by Philip, it fell with the rest of Pella at the hands of Aemilius Paulus.

NORTHERN GREECE

LITOCHORO Λιτοχωρο ☎23520

For most tourists, Litochoro is just the gateway to Mount Olympus. But it actually offers a whole lot more—a charming small-town atmosphere, partying in nearby Plaka, and proximity to the breathtaking archaeological site at Dion. The upper town's twisting cobblestone paths lead down the mountainside to the central plateia known as *kentro* (center), where friendly locals relax in the shadows of Olympus. It's also possible to make the ascent from the western side of Olympus, beginning in Kokkinopilos village, but this treeless route can't compare to the lush canyon trails that originate in Litochoro.

TRANSPORTATION AND PRACTICAL INFORMATION. **Trains** from Litochoro's station run to: **Athens** (6hr.; 4 per day, 9:10am-11:30pm; €11.70); **Larisa** (1½hr.; 6 per day, 8:11am-8:29pm; €2.90); **Thessaloniki** (1hr.; 4 per day, 7:49am-7:12pm; €3). Call the Katerini station (☎23510 23 709) or the Litochoro tourist office for more information. A **taxi** from the train station should cost around €6. **Buses** (☎23520 81 271) from Litochoro's KTEL station, under the blue awning opposite the tourist office, travel to: **Athens** (5½hr.; 3 per day, 9:30am-midnight; €25); **Larisa** (2hr.; 8 per day, 6:30am-7:45pm; €5) via **Katerini** (€1.60); **Plaka** (10min.; every hr., 10:15am-7:15pm; €1); **Thessaloniki** (1½hr; 18 per day, 6:15am-9:45pm; €6) via **Katerini. Trains** (☎23520 22 522) stop at **Litochoro** on the **Thessaloniki-Volos** and **Thessaloniki-Athens** lines. Buses run from the bus station to the train station every hour (6:15am-9:50pm, €1). Ask for the Health Center stop.

Litochoro lies 90km southwest of Thessaloniki, with Olympus to the west and the Aegean Sea to the east. **Ag. Nikolaou** runs east-west leading up to a fountain at the central plateia. Down Ag. Nikolaou near the police station, you'll find the town's **tourist office** by the park, providing **free maps** of the town and a €3 map of the mountain. (☎23520 83 100. Open July-Nov. 8:30am-2:30pm and 5-9pm.) There's a **National Bank** (☎23520 81 025; open M-F 8am-3pm) with a 24hr. **ATM** in the main plateia. The **police station** is just below the plateia, on the left as you walk downhill. (☎23520 81 100 or 81 111. Open 24hr.) The **health center** (☎23520 22 222) is about 5km outside of town by the beach and has 24hr. **emergency** facilities. **Internet** access is available at many of the trendy cafe-bars toward the lower end of town. One such establishment is **Cafe Artio,** across from Hotel Park. (☎23520 84 038. €3 per hr.) From the plateia, cobblestone 28 Oktovriou leads left, up to the **post office.** (Open M-F 7:30am-2pm.) The **OTE** sits across from the tourist booth farther down the main street. (Open 7:20am-3pm.) **Postal code:** 60200.

ACCOMMODATIONS AND FOOD. Accommodations prices in Litochoro are pretty constant and any price discrepancies can be eliminated by the usual negotiating. That said, a hotel with an affordable starting price is **Hotel Park ❷,** Ag. Nikolaou 23, down Ag. Nikolaou from the plateia and past the long park; the comfortable rooms have optional A/C (€5 extra), baths, TVs, fridges, and large balconies. (☎23520 81 252. Singles €20; doubles €30; triples €40.) **Hotel Mirto ❸,** on the left at the end of the first block coming from the plateia has large, quiet rooms with private baths, TVs, and A/C. (☎23520 81 398; www.galaxynet.gr. Breakfast €4. Singles €28; doubles €30; triples €40.) **Papa Nikolau ❸,** behind the plateia on a road that veers off to the left, has tidy, well-maintained rooms looking out over Litochoro's red roofs. Each room is equipped with a kitchenette, TV, fridge, and fan. Flower gardens line the entrance to this friendly family-run domatia. (☎23520 81 236; xenpap@otenet.gr. Doubles €35; triples €45.) The **Hotel Aphrodite ❸,** next to the plateia and behind the bank, offers rooms with mountain views, private baths, phones, TVs, fridges, and A/C. Though the owners are rather indifferent, the large, comfortable family lounge downstairs, the outdoor terrace, and a second-floor dining area make it a reasonable base. (☎23520 81 415; fax 23520 83 646. Breakfast €5. Singles €25; doubles €30; triples €40.) Opposite the entrance to Hotel Aphrodite, **Hotel Enipeas ❸** provides clean rooms with phones, A/C, balconies, and private baths. Ask for a room with a view of the mountains. There's a lovely balcony upstairs that looks down over the plateia, and a communal kitchen is available in the basement. (☎23520 84 328; fax 23520 81 328. Singles €30; doubles €35; triples €40; quads €45.) The beach, 5km from town, is full of campgrounds, of which **Olympus Zeus ❷** (☎23520 22 115) and **Olympus Beach ❷** (☎23520 22 112 or 23520 83 477; www.olympos-beach.gr) are the largest and best located. Due to their waterfront position, expect to pay at least €11 for a site. Avoid freelance camping on the northern side of the road between the town and the highway—army training grounds.

For a final feast before you head for the hills, try **Gastrodromio En Olympo ❷,** just off the plateia near the church. Enjoy the backgammon and laughter of the old men below, the plateia's bustle, and the sheep grazing in the idyllic pastures beneath immutable Olympus. (☎23520 21 300. Entrees €4-10.) Local favorite **Fistaria Dias ❷,** under a yellow awning on the left as you walk toward the plateia, serves grilled chicken (€5), fish, octopus, and other meat dishes. (☎23520 83 335. Entrees €3.50-6.50.) **Ta Mezedakia ❷,** on the street that forks right at the police station, has porch seating and cooks up a range of tasty Greek classics over a charcoal grill. (☎23520 84 574. Entrees €3.50-7.) Those wisely seeking water and trail snacks for the arduous hike up Olympus should steer away from the expensive one room "supermarkets" just above the plateia. Instead head to the locals' market **Arvanitides,** at the end of the short windy Odos Ermi, which branches off Ag. Nikolaou opposite the *Demotic* (Public) School just below the tourist office.

NIGHTLIFE. If you want to party before—or instead of—hiking, the evening begins in the **bars** around the bottom of Ag. Nikolaou and moves over to Plaka by midnight. In Litochoro, **Bolero** and **Maskes** are popular for their selective American tunes. **Status,** which blasts house music, and **Garage,** playing heavy metal, see a younger and hipper crowd. In Plaka, elegant **Caprice,** and techno-blasting **Cavo Dimo**—both popular waterfront clubs—cede to the town hotspot **White Shark,** where the sleekest and trendiest Litochorians get down until 8 or 9am. Partying in Plaka can get expensive: a taxi costs around €6, covers are around €8, beer also around €8, and cocktails up to €10. Fueling up on *retsina* and ouzo at one of the tiki torch-lit *psistarias* (seafood grills) can be a cheap experience enhancer.

ANCIENT DION Διον ☎23510

A goat herder quietly tending his flock under the gaze of Olympus's windswept snowfields provides much material for meditation. So, too, a heron stalking a frog in a clear pool. But when the frog darts behind a reed shrouded Doric column and the flock passes over the walls of a 4th-century basilica, there is really something to think about. Dion was the Macedonians' sacred city devoted to the worship of Zeus; Dion is derived from a form of Zeus's name. It was here at the temple to Zeus that Alexander the Great made sacrifices to seal the oaths of his assembled armies on the eve of the immortal campaign. Later the city was Romanized, gaining baths (whose subterranean "hypocaust" steam system is well preserved), villas with mosaics (the Dionysus mosaic is particularly spectacular), and a cosmopolitan taste for fashionable foreign gods (the Temple of Isis set now among the reeds). Destroyed by a combination of earthquakes and the first German tourists—the Visigoths—in the 4th century, subsequent mudslides preserved a pre-Theodosian city in which official Christian basilicas could still live in harmony with temples of the empire's old religions. (A taxi from Litochoro should be about €5. ☎23510 53 206. Site open daily 8am-7pm. €4, students and seniors €2.) If the bubbling brooks, mountain vistas, and stately trees aren't enough to make you fall in love with life in classical Dion, visit the outstanding **museum,** just a 5min. walk into town. On display are several of the sites' lively mosaics, along with a 2nd-century water organ, and perfectly mud-preserved sculptures. (Open M 12:30pm-7pm, Tu-Su 8am-7pm. €4, students and seniors €2.) For those visiting Dion for the day, some reasonable **tavernas** are located just opposite the museum.

MOUNT OLYMPUS Ολυμπος Ορος ☎23520

Erupting out of the Thermaic Gulf, the formidable slopes of Mt. Olympus (nearly 3000m) mesmerized the ancients so much that they believed it to be the divine dwelling place of their immortal pantheon. The sharp peaks saw no successful mortal ascent until 1913, when Christos Kakalos, a Litochorian hunter, guided two Swiss adventurers up to Mytikas's zenith. Since then, Olympus has been harnessed by a network of well maintained hiking trails that make the summit accessible to just about anyone with sturdy legs, a head for heights, and a taste for adventure; the climb is a strenuous but fantastic must-do. As you ascend, you'll pass leafy green woodlands and shadowy pine forests before emerging above the treeline to truly spectacular views. Mt. Olympus has eight peaks: Antonius (2817m), Kalogeros (2701m), Mytikas (The Needle; 2919m), Profitis Ilias (2803m), Skala (2866m), Skolio (2911m), Stefani (The Throne of Zeus; 2909m), and Toumba (2785m). The entire region became Greece's first national park in 1938, and the mountain is said to contain all the climates of Europe, from the Mediterranean climate of Litochoro to snowy tundra at the summit.

LOGISTICS OF THE CLIMB

You'll find the most reliable resources for all aspects of hiking—updates on weather and trail conditions, advice on itineraries and routes, and reservations for any of the **Greek Alpine Club** (EOS) refuges—from EOS refuge **Zolotas,** known as "Spilios Agapitos"(see **Accommodations,** below). The staff has years of experience and is happy to distribute information over the phone in fluent English. You will find the **EOS office** in the parking lot below Litochoro off Ithakisiou. The parking lot is just below **Gastrodromio** (p. 288) and the plateia. Here you'll get helpful information and some friendly banter from fellow hikers. (☎23520 82 444. Open M-F 9:30am-12:30pm and 6-8 pm, Sa-Su 9am-noon.) The SEO office (Association of Greek Mountain Climbers; ☎23520 83 262), behind Hotel Mirto, acts more as a clubhouse than as an official resource, but if you happen to catch someone there, they can answer questions. You can buy a colorful bilingual fold-out map with contour lines and all the major trails at most local shops for €3. Produced with data from Greek Army Geographical Service, the best map is made by Anavasi and comes with a handy plastic sleeve.

Each winter, well over 2m of snow buries Mt. Olympus, and even in late July snowfields linger in the ravines. Unless you're handy with an ice-pick and crampons, you'll want to make your ascent between May and October, when Persephone supposedly returns to Olympus from the Underworld, and her mother, Demeter, warms the earth. Mytikas, the tallest peak, is not accessible without special equipment until June. **Weather** conditions can change extremely rapidly near the summits; even in the peak of summer, be prepared for chilly, damp clouds, rain, and unrelenting sun above treeline. If you make the ascent between June and September, you'll need to carry typical hiking **equipment:** sturdy shoes, sunglasses, sunscreen, head covering, some snacks, at least 2L of water, a warm wool or synthetic fleece sweater or jacket, and, ideally, an extra shirt and waterproof windbreaker. Some hikers swear by trekking poles for maintaining balance and climbing steep terrain. Take a small day-pack and leave your luggage in Litochoro, as you'll come to resent every extra pound on your shoulders.

ACCOMMODATIONS AND FOOD

For those who can climb 8km straight up 2000m, braving a continuous 6hr. steep ascent, and then wish to finish off their knee caps with a 4hr. race down, Mytikas can be conquered in one day. For those who can't, want to savor the summit trails, or are concerned with the possible altitude sickness of leaping from the Aegean to 3000m and back in one day, an overnight stay in one of the mountain's social **refuges** is a good idea. The refuges provide beds, blankets (no bedsheets or towels), meals, and water, but you'll still want a full suit of warm clothes, a flashlight, and possibly earplugs. There are three refuges near the summits. The EOS runs **Zolotas refuge** ❶ (elev. 2100m), called "Spilos Agapitos" or "Refuge A," after its owner, about 800m below Skala and Mytikas peaks. It has 110 beds, making it the largest and cushiest, with a telephone and very cold showers. The Zolotas family has nearly 50 years of experience and takes great pride in the refuge's cleanliness. The **kitchen** ❶ offers salads (€2.20) and meat dishes (€5) and serves meals until 9pm. (☎23520 81 800; zolotam@hol.gr. Open mid-May-Oct. 6am-10pm. Lights-out 10pm. €10 per bed, €8 for members of any mountain club. Tent nearby while using refuge's facilities €4.20.) The other EOS refuge is on the other side of the mountain: **Kakalos** ❶ (elev. 2650m), called "Refuge C," has 22 beds, no phone, and charges the same prices as Agapitos. Make reservations through Agapitos. (Open mid-June-Sept. 15. Meals served 6am-9pm. Doors open 24hr.) Fifteen minutes from Kakalos, beneath Stefani and Profitis Ilias, **G. Apostolidis** ❶ (better known as **SEO Refuge;** elev. 2760m) sleeps 90 and can accommodate extras and late-comers in its glass-walled porch or living room. The friendly proprietor will cook up a delicious meal for €5. (Open June-Sept. Meals served 9am-9:30pm. Doors open 24hr. €10 per bed, €8 with any mountain club membership.) Make reservations through the **Thessaloniki SEO,** which runs the refuge. (☎2310 244 710. Open M-F 8am-10pm; leave a message for a reservation.) Although Kakalos is smaller than the other refuges, it boasts the best views of dawn rising above the clouds. All of the refuges, particularly Zolotas, tend to fill up on weekends between June and October. Call at least a few weeks in advance for **reservations.** Otherwise, call one to two days ahead and try your luck. At refuge kitchens, soups and salads tend to run about €2.50-3.50; pasta and meat dishes €3-5; breakfast €3. Bring a **flashlight** to navigate your way to the bathroom after the generator is shut down in the evenings. The refuges' managers are also prepared to handle emergency rescues if needed.

THE HIKE TO THE HEAVENS

There are three ways to take on Olympus; all originate in **Litochoro** (elev. 340m). Two involve heading straight to the trailheads. The first and most popular trailhead begins at **Prionia** (elev. 1100m), 18km from the village. This trails ascends 4km through a sheltered, forested ravine to Spilios Agapitos. The second trailhead is at **Diastavrosi** (also called **Gortsia;** elev. 1300m), 14km away, which leads 11km up to Kakalos and the SEO refuges. There are no buses to Prionia or Diastavrosi so you must walk, drive, or take a taxi (Prionia €20; Diastavrosi €8) along the asphalt road that winds upward starting next to the police station in Litochoro, just below the plateia. The third route is more challenging and involves hiking to Prionia via a trail along the **Enipeas Gorge;** you begin in Litochoro and eventually arrive at the Prionia trailhead. After spending the night at the Agapitos refuge, you'll ascend to the summit the next day and head around to the SEO and Kakalos refuges. Hikers can stay another night there and walk down the next day to Diastavrosi (3-4hr., depending on how you fare going downhill), or pass the refuges and arrive at Diastavrosi in late afternoon. All of the trails to the refuges are easy to follow, and most are marked with red blazes.

ASCENDING FROM PRIONIA. The most popular route begins at Prionia, where you'll find drinking **water, toilets,** and a small **restaurant.** From here, a 4km walk uphill takes you to the Spilios Agapitos refuge ("Zolotas;" elev. 2100m). The trail is well marked, and is part of the **European E4 path** from Spain to Greece. There's one

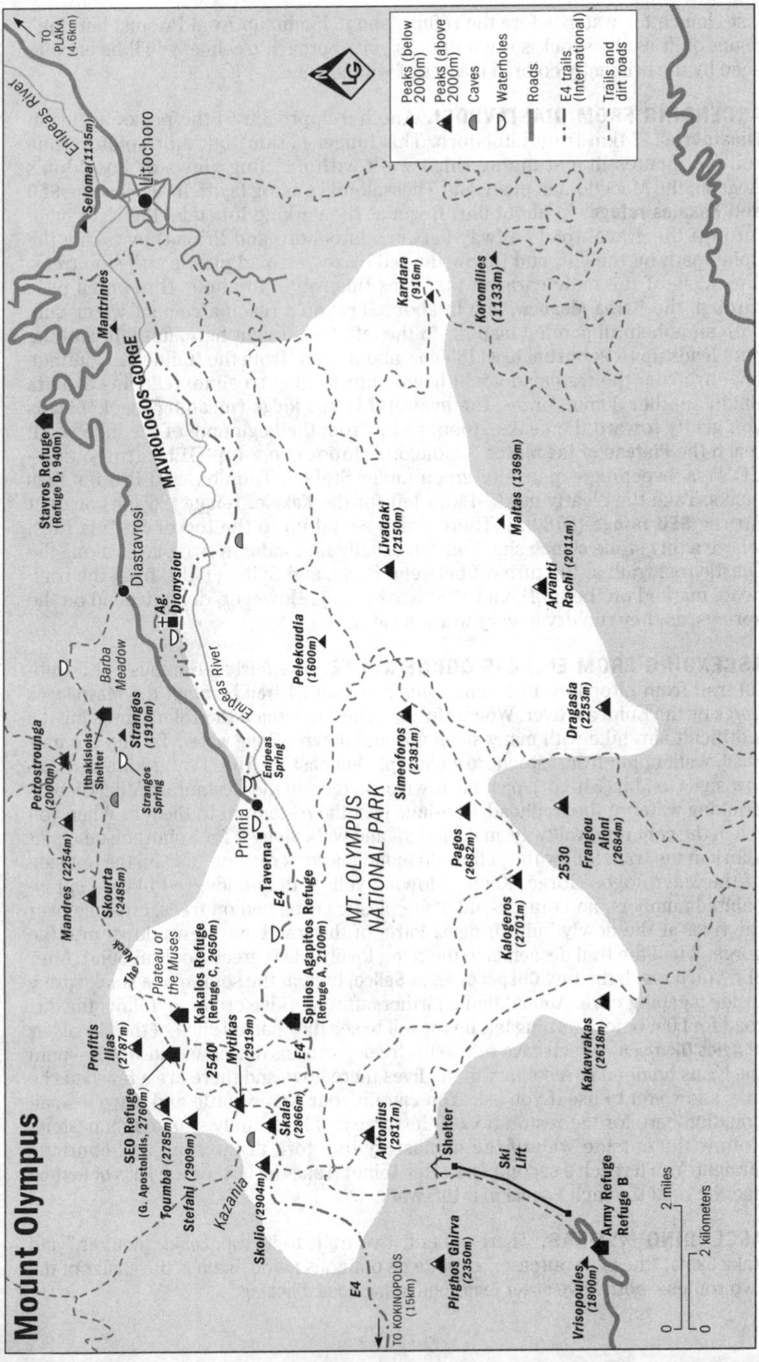

Mount Olympus

Peaks (below 2000m)
Peaks (above 2000m)
Caves
Waterholes
Roads
E4 trails (International)
Trails and dirt roads

last chance for water before the refuge, about 45min. up from Prionia, but don't count on it as the spout is often dry. As you approach treeline, you'll be encouraged by the brilliantly colored masses of wildflowers.

ASCENDING FROM DIASTAVROSI. Another approach to the peaks begins at Diastavrosi, 14km from Litochoro. This longer (11km) but more picturesque route climaxes in a stunning ridge walk with dazzling views of Poseidon's Aegean, the Macedonian plain, and Thessaloniki's smog layer. It reaches the **SEO** and **Kakalos refuges** in about 6hr. Begin at the parking lot (take the right hand turn off the gravel road halfway between Litochoro and Priona) by taking the uphill path on the left, and follow the red blazes, striped plastic strips on trees, and signs of the mule caravan that uses this route. In about 1hr., you'll pass through the **Barba Meadow,** and in about 2hr. you'll reach a cement water tank with an unhelpful painted map off to the left. Go straight here, not left, and the path leads up to **Petrostrounga** (1800m), about 2½hr. from the trailhead. Continue on; 4hr. from the trailhead you'll begin approaching treeline, reaching **Skourta Hill** in another 30min. or so. The beautiful **Lemos Ridge** (meaning "neck") leads you gently toward the peaks. About 5½hr. from the beginning of the hike you'll reach the **Plateau of the Muses** (Οροπεδιο Μουσον; ορ–οη–ΠΕΗ–δτηι–ο μοο–ΣΟΝ), a sweeping expanse of green under Stefani, Toumba, and Profitis Ilias peaks. Take the clearly marked fork left for the **Kakalos refuge** (2650m) or right for the **SEO refuge** (2760m). There's also a trail up to the top of Profitis Ilias, where a tiny stone **church** sits. You can usually find **water** in two places along the Diastavrosi trail: at the turn-off between Barba and Spilla (1½hr. from the trailhead, marked on the trail), and at Stragos spring. However, don't depend on the springs, as they run dry in very warm weather.

ASCENDING FROM ENIPEAS GORGE ROUTE. The fairly strenuous but beautiful trail from Litochoro to Prionia runs along an **E4 trail** through the **Mavrologos Gorge** by the Enipeas River. Wonderful stretches punctuate the 18km climb, but it's a difficult 5hr. hike with many steep ups and downs. **Bring water.** To find the **trailhead,** walk uphill from Litochoro's main plateia past the Hotel Aphrodite, and follow signs to Mili (Μυλοι), past the town cemetery, to the Restaurant Mili. There is drinking water at the trailhead. Continue past the restaurant to the left. When you reach the concrete walkway, make a right and walk along it for a short distance. At a fork in the trail, follow the yellow diamond markers reading "E4" up the left side of the Mavrologos Gorge. Keep following yellow diamonds, red blazes, spray-painted numbers, and orange-and-white plastic strips tied on trees, crossing over the river at the newly built bridges. Parts of the trail have views down into the gorge. When the trail descends to the river, lovely, clear green pools abound. After 3hr. you'll reach the tiny **Chapel of Agios Spileo,** built at the source of a small spring inside a gaping cave. About 20min. farther, after a bridge crossing, follow the dirt road for 60m before turning left up the hill to see the charred shell of the **Monastery of Agios Dionysiou,** which gave refuge to Greek partisans during World War II—until the Nazis bombed it. A solitary monk lives there now, and there are a few beds he may allow you to use if you ask. You can fill your water bottle and leave a small donation here for the restoration of the large and beautifully situated monastery. Follow the outside wall of the monastery to a fork in the road and continue straight. You'll reach a second fork after 15min. Take the left for the **Falls of Perivoli** and the right to reach **Prionia** in a 1hr. walk.

ASCENDING MYTIKAS. There are only two trails to its top: **Louki,** "couloir," and **Kaka Skala,** "the evil staircase." Despite its ominous name Skala is the easier of the two routes—both have **sheer drops** and some **hand climbing.**

Slightly longer, and a large detour for hikers ascending from Kakalos or the SEO refuge, Kaka Skala climbs the ridge behind Zolotas on a broad but steep path to the Skala peak (2861m). From Zolotas, walk uphill. After about 45min. (1.2km), you'll find a **map** at a fork in the road. The left takes you along the E4 trail to Skala and Skolio peaks; the right is the **Zonaria** trail, which leads to the Louki trail fork and the SEO and Kakalos refuge paths. If you're going via **Skala,** 50m beyond the signpost you'll find an unmarked fork. Make a right and continue ascending for about an hour (1km) along exposed terrain until you reach Skala peak. From here hikers may turn up to the Skolio peak (2904m) for a sweeping view of Mytikas and Profitis Ilias, or grab handholds on the mostly vertical "path" plummeting down to the sharp saddle point between Skala and Mytikas and then back up "The Needle." Those distracted by rocks loosed from climbers above should glance to their left. The 500m drop into **Kazania,** "The Cauldron," named for clouds of mist that steam up from it, will brush away all extraneous concerns. The total climb usually takes about 3hr.

The Louki trail should be used only for ascent, and then only by serious climbers, Alpine-bred Europeans, and students who have not yet decided whether their lives are worth living. Those who use the trail for descending will have the decision made for them. Louki branches off Zonaras about halfway (45min. or 0.7km) between its endpoint on the Skala trail and SEO path respectively. After strolling the pleasant, precipitous Zonaras trail, hikers must turn straight up Louki's red blazed couloir. During a pause in the shower of rocks coming from climbers above, those with particularly good handholds should peruse the plaques commemorating their intrepid predecessors, whose final handholds were not as secure as you hope your next one will be. After 300m you may arrive at the top. A little closer to the SEO side of the Zonaras path a slightly more dangerous trail goes up to **Stefani** peak marked by a bent, rusted signpost. Past this is the SEO path, a 20min. walk to the SEO refuge and Plateau of the Muses. The bowl-shaped slopes are known as the **Throne of Zeus.** The god of gods rested his enormous cranium on the Stefani (crown) peak above. Approaching the peaks from the Plateau of the Muses, it's about 1½hr. up to Mytikas via Louki, or 4hr. by the Skala route.

ASCENDING SKOLIO. If you decide to resist tempting the gods by ascending Mytikas, you can take the 20min. hike from Skala to Skolio, the second highest peak (2911m; 6m shorter than Mytikas). The best view of Olympus's sheer western face looks out from here. It takes about 2½hr. to reach the Skolio summit from the Agapitos refuge. From Skolio, a 1hr. walk south along the ridge takes you to Agios Antonis summit and a path descending to Zolotas.

EDESSA Εδεσσα ☎23810

An equidistant 50km from Kastoria and Thessaloniki, the town of Edessa spreads along the edge of a great cliff with sweeping views of Classical ruins and the plains, which stretch to Thessaloniki, some 70m below. Its many rivulets race along side streets and under bridges to leap off the cliffs, forming the country's only notable waterfalls. Its beautiful 19th-century cliffside water mills, along with waterfall overlooks, make it an ideal layover for travelers of Macedonia. Indeed, for many Greek tourists it is the destination.

TRANSPORTATION

Edessa's main **bus station,** Pavlou Mela 13 (☎23810 23 511), is at the intersection near the center of town. **Buses** to: **Athens** (7hr.; 3 per day, 8am-8pm; €31.40) via **Litochoro** (3hr., €6.80) and **Larisa** (4½hr., €11.70); **Thessaloniki** (2hr.; 13 per day, 7am-8pm; €5.70); **Veria** (1¼hr.; 6 per day, 8am-4pm; €3.20). From a stop outside a fast-food joint next to the fruit market on Filippou, one block past the main bus station toward the city center, buses go to: **Florina** (2hr.; 6 per day, 6am-8:15pm; €5.70); **Kastoria** (2hr.; 3 per day, 11:20am-5:20pm; €7.40); **Kozani** (2hr.; 6 per day, 10am-8:45pm; €7.04). Look for schedules on the sign above the storefront or inquire inside. From the **train station** (☎23810 23 510), at the end of 18 Oktovriou, trains run to: **Athens** (7hr., €28.30) via **Plati** (€14.70); **Florina** (1½hr., €2.80); **Kozani** (2hr., €2.60); **Thessaloniki** (2hr., €2.80) via **Veria** (€1.30) and **Naoussa** (€1.20). **Taxis** (☎23810 23 392 or 23810 22 904) congregate on Dimokratias, near the National Bank in Pl. Megalou Alexandrou.

ORIENTATION AND PRACTICAL INFORMATION

With your back to the bus station, facing the kiosk across the street, **Pavlou Mela** is in front of you. On the left it leads two blocks to the cliffside; on the right, three blocks to **Dimokratias** at the town center. Here in front of the Pella and Alfa Hotels is the drop-off for buses stopping on the way from Kastoria or Florina to Thessaloniki. Standing in Pavlou Mela, Dimokratias leads on your left to the ubiquitous **Egnatia,** which leads to the hospital and Thessaloniki. On your right Dimokratias charges past cafe-covered **Pl. Megalou Alexandrou** to an intersection near the stadium, marked by a large, leafy park full of bars and cafes. The right fork is **25 Martiou,** the left **18 Oktovriou,** and the sharp right **Filellinon.** Filellinon leads to the old district of **Varosi,** 25 Martiou leads to a series of right-branching side streets for the waterfalls, and 18 Oktovriou marches nine blocks to the train station. Street maps are posted at many of the city's major intersections.

The **Tourist Information Office,** to the right of the waterfalls, provides **maps** and brochures with information in English about sights, hotels, and transportation for Edessa, the prefecture of Pella, and much of northern Greece. (☎23810 20 300. Open daily 10am-8pm.) The **National Bank,** Arch. Panteleimonos 2 (☎23810 23 322), and the nearby **Bank of Pieraeus** (☎23810 21 889) have **ATMs.** To find the 24hr. **police station** (☎23810 23 333), follow Dimokratias toward the waterfalls and turn left on Iroön Polytechniou; the station is at the intersection with Arhelaou. The large **hospital** (☎23810 27 441) is just outside town on Egnatia. The **OTE** is a blue and white building facing the Byzantine clock tower on Ag. Dimitriou. (Open 7am-2:40pm.) **Internet** access is available at **Net Cafe,** Filellinon 17, on the street that flanks the stadium. (☎23810 29 629. €2.30 per hr. Open 8:30am-1am.) Edessa's **post office** (open 7:30am-2pm), Pavlou Mela 10, one block up from the bus station, offers **Poste Restante** and **exchanges currency. Postal code:** 58200.

ACCOMMODATIONS AND FOOD

There are a few good deals among Edessa's handful of hotels. The luxurious option, **Hotel Xenia ❹,** Filippou 35, offers well-furnished rooms with A/C, baths, TVs, fridges, and spectacular cliffside views. The hotel also has Internet access and a pool; the latter is open to the public for €2-3 per person. (☎23810 29 706 or 29 707; www.xenia-edessas.gr. Singles €60; doubles €85; triples €100; quads €120.) **Hotel Alfa ❸,** Egnatia 28, is conveniently located for those traveling by bus, a block uphill along Pavlou Mela from the station and directly in front of the Kastoria-Thessaloniki bus stop. Bare but colorful rooms have baths, TVs, A/C, and phones. Internet access and **free maps** are available at reception. (☎23810 22 221 or 22 231. Singles €30; doubles €45; triples €60. MC/V.) **Hotel Pella ❷,** Egnatia 26, next to Hotel Alfa, is a cheaper alternative. Basic rooms have small balconies, TVs, phones, and baths. (☎23810 23 541. Singles €20; doubles €30; triples €40.) **Hotel Elena ❸,** D. Rizou 4, is centrally located near Varosi just off

Pl. Timendon. Standard rooms have telephones, TVs, baths, and balconies. A/C is included in the price if you are shrewd about it. (☎23810 23 218; fax 23810 23 951. Breakfast €5. Singles €30; doubles €40; triples €50.)

Edessa suffers no shortage of **fast food**—cheese pies, rotisserie chickens, and gyro stands crop up on every street. Inexpensive restaurants are easy to find near the waterfall park. The largest and most popular restaurant in town is the **Public Waterfall Center Restaurant ❷,** at the top of the falls. It serves local and traditional specialties like *stamnato* (€5.68), a concoction of pork, potatoes, vine leaves, and cheese. The *tsoblex* (€5.68), a potato and eggplant pie filled with juicy chunks of veal, is also delicious. (☎23810 26 810. Entrees €5.50-9.)

ENTERTAINMENT

The most popular of Edessa's cafes is the picturesque **Cafe High Rock,** M. Alexandrou 2, in the southwestern corner of town on—surprise, surprise—a high rock perched over the cliff. (☎23810 26 793. Coffee €2; beer €2. Open 9am-2am.) You'll find the complete night—dinner, drinks, and dancing—at **Kanavourgeio,** at the bottom of the glass elevators inside the huge old mill. The name, that of the old mill, derives from *kanabis*. Yes, this was a hemp factory. The tableside machinery inside once twisted fibers from that bountiful plant into thick ship's rope; samples now fence off the dance floor. The DJ blasts American music straight into space every Friday, Saturday, and Sunday night. Cliff-edge dancers are exempt from the city's standard 3am curfew, so the partying often lasts until 9am. (☎23810 20 070 or 20 102. Entrees €3.50-8. €5 cover, includes 1 drink.) Another club popular with locals, **Vanilla,** is a short taxi ride outside of town. In the town center, the heart of nightlife is a tree covered park off Dimokratias just before a Goody's fast-food restaurant, where eight similar cafe-bars draw masses of people into tight clusters on the sidewalks. In the summer starting at 9pm, the town shows nightly open-air **movies** (€3) just below the aquarium.

SIGHTS

WATERFALLS AND ENVIRONS. Edessa's best sights revolve around the *katarrakton* (waterfall), where the town's rivers spill over into the plains below. Walk down Dimokratias past the stadium, where it becomes 25 Martiou, and watch for the large waterfall signs—they'll tell you when to turn right. The descending concrete terraces let you survey the falls and the agricultural plain below while catching a little spray on your face. Look for the marble column ruins of the ancient city near a convent to the right of the valley. The cliffside was once home to a collection of water mills and textile factories. A European grant redesigned and renovated the entire area as Edessa's open-air **Water Museum,** featuring pre-industrial mills and tanneries, modern textile factories, the wool mill, and the **cannabis factory,** which produced rope. Water still runs through the chutes alongside each mill, and plans are in the works to return them to working condition. The tourist office has a great free brochure showing the mill locations. The sesame oil mill has been converted into a rapidly growing **aquarium,** displaying indigenous amphibians, reptiles, and freshwater fish all hand caught by town embryologist Tasos. For an interesting story, ask how he catches the vipers. *(Open M, W-Su 10am-2pm and 5-9pm. €1.50.)* To reach the Kanavourgeio, you can follow the steps down along the waterfalls, but a more unconventional mode of transport are Edessa's two **great glass elevators.** Descending about 13 stories along the cliffs, they provide sweeping views and relief to ascending tourists

VAROSI DISTRICT. The old church-dotted town, which retained a Christian population even during Ottoman occupation, rests along the cliff's edge, beginning to the right of the waterfall park and continuing on behind the walls of the stadium. Examples of traditional architecture abound: upper stories miraculously protrude out on creaky old wooden beams over stone bases. The quarter's location near the "safe escape" of the lowlands made it a popular spot for World War II resistance fighters—much of the area was burned by the Nazis in 1944. The new **Museum of Traditional and Folk Life** occupies one of the old buildings on the side of the drop, a block down from the intersection of Arch. Panteleimonos and Megalou Alexandriou (ignore the yellow "museum" sign and go left, away from Cafe High Rock). Ring the bell if the door is locked. *(☎23810 28 787. Open Tu-Su 10am-6pm. €1.47.)*

OTHER SITES. Below the town, about 3km to the southwest, you'll find the ruins of the ancient city of **Loggos.** Though little remains of the 4th-century BC city, a few columns along the main avenue still stand, including one from a temple devoted to **Mas,** the goddess of fertility. Try going in the evening, when the dying light makes the columns glow with celestial beauty. An archaeologist is usually on duty until 7pm and can give information. The fastest way to the ruins begins at the landing between the two elevators. Walk to the right on the sandy path over the little mound to find a windy path. Follow it downhill (don't go through the gates on the left) and go straight; you'll reach the city in 15min. The **Byzantine Clock Tower** occupies a block in the upstream direction from Dimokratias at Pl. Megalou Alexandrou. The very dilapidated, neglected remains of a 19th-century **Ottoman mosque** sink down on a side street: walk along Dimokratias a few blocks away from the city center, turn right after the Alpha Credit Bank, and veer left when the mosque's dome and de-crowned minaret come into view. To see Edessa's rivers united, follow any of the tributaries upstream until you hit the **Byzantine Bridge.** The uninspiring footbridge arches over the main stream that eventually splits off to form the town's countless rivulets and narrow channels.

KASTORIA Καστορια ☎24670

Named after the once prolific beaver *(kastoras)* that perished at the hands of a thriving fur industry, Kastoria remains famous for fur. Though hides are now imported and Jewish tradesmen gone, the city still claims to hold 90% of the world market. Travelers on tighter budgets can visit the town's multitude of Byzantine chapels or marvel at the bizarre mountain lake set into the dry, scrub hills.

TRANSPORTATION. **Aristotelis International Airport** (☎24670 42 515 or 24670 21 701), 13km from the city has flights to **Athens** (1hr.; M, W, Th, Sa; €76). The **Olympic Airways** office is just past the public park at the corner with Dioikitiriou when walking on Megalou Alexandrou away from Ath. Diakou. (☎24670 22 275. Open M-F 8am-3:30pm.) **Buses,** Ath. Diakou 14 (☎24670 83 455), go to: **Amyntaio** (1¼hr., 2pm, €4.40); **Athens** (9hr.; 3 per day, 7:30am-7:30pm; €34.40); **Ioannina** (3hr.; 9am, 3:30pm; €12.90); **Kozani** (2¼hr.; 4 per day, 7:30am-7:30pm; €6.20); **Thessaloniki** (3hr.; 7 per day, 6am-6:30pm; €13.20) some via **Amyntaio.** Connect to **Florina** in **Amyntaio. Taxis** (☎24670 82 100) line up by the public park on Ath. Diakou at the intersection with M. Alexandrou.

ORIENTATION AND PRACTICAL INFORMATION. Kastoria occupies a bulbous peninsula in Lake Kastoria. The bus station is in the peninsula's northern groin on **Ath. Diakou,** one block from the waterfront **Kyknon.** One block farther inland, and parallel to these two, is **Grammou.** All three run into **M. Alexandrou,** which passes the city's main action—a concert park (between Ath. Diakou and Kyknon), cafes, and restaurants—before changing names to **Orestiados.** The southern waterfront's much quieter hotel and residential strip is served by **Nikis,** which runs from the ferry dock at the base to a boat house at the bulb. The peninsula is mountainous and becomes more difficult to cross towards the tip. A few punishing stair paths make the climb, but few roads attack the grade past the base. Here, **11 Noemvriou** connects Grammou to the southern shore and the city's large military reserve, and **3 Septemvriou** connects Ath. Diakou to bank covered **Pl. Davaki** at the base's center. From there **Ioustinianou** completes the peninsular crossing, while **Mitropoleos** and **Ag. Athanasiou** lead up the peninsula spine on the north and south respectively.

The **Tourist Office,** a kiosk in the public park between Ath. Diakou and M. Alexandrou, has an excellent English tourist booklet, **free maps,** and an album of Kastoria chapels. (☎24670 26 777. Open 7:30am-3pm.) Also try the **Nomarchio** (prefectorial building; ☎24670 55 297), on M. Alexandrou just after the park. There's an **Agricultural Bank** (☎24670 22 712), in Pl. Davaki at the intersection of Mitropoleos and 3 Septemvriou, and an **Alpha Bank** (☎24670 27 312), at 11 Noemvriou 9. Both have **ATMs.** (Open M-Th 8am-2:30pm, F 8am-2pm.) To find the **police,** Grammou 25 (☎24670 22 100), just behind the KTEL, walk one block inland on Averof and turn right; the police are on your left. The 24hr. **hospital** (☎24670 55 60) is on Nosokomeiou, uptown near its intersection with Papathoma. The **OTE,** Grammou 209, is outside town. (☎24670 87 099. Open 7:30am-8pm.) Find **Internet** access at **Cafe Ilion,** along the M. Alexandrou waterfront just past the post office. (☎24670 21 444. €3 per hr. Frappé €2.) The local teenage hangout, **Aeras,** Ag. Athanios 48, also has Internet. (☎24670 23 232. €3 per hr.) The **post office,** M. Alexandrou 47, two blocks along the peninsula beyond the public park, accepts **Poste Restante.** (☎24670 80 779. Open daily 7:30am-2pm.) **Postal code:** 32100.

ACCOMMODATIONS. Kastoria has no budget deals, but its hotels are surprisingly cheap considering its size and wealth. Most are located either along the road from Kozani or on the Nikis waterfront. Some are also found on Ag. Athanasiou. **Hotel Europa ❸,** Ag. Athanasiou 12, has a friendly staff and lake views. The huge rooms have desks, TVs, telephones, and balconies. (☎24670 23 826; fax 24670 25 154. Singles €25; doubles €35; triples €45; quads €65. AmEx/MC/V.) The luxurious rooms at **Hotel Kastoria ❹,** Nikis 122, lie at the end of Nikis's waterfront strip by the boathouse. Comfortable rooms with quiet lake views, TVs, telephones, A/C, and baths. (☎24670 29 453; www.hotelkastoria.com. Breakfast €5. Singles €30; doubles €50. AmEx/MC/V.) Rooms at **Hotel Keletron ❸,** 11 Noemvriou 52, two blocks in from the south shore, have phones, TVs, baths, and balconies with lake views. (☎24670 22 525; fax 24670 23 264. Singles €30; doubles €35; triples €45.)

FOOD AND ENTERTAINMENT. Kastoria's cafe/restaurant strip extends from the public park on M. Alexandrou to the end of the lakeside walk. Restaurants cluster around the peninsula's end while cafes fill the section near the park. **Miltos ❷,** M. Alexandrou 125, at the end of the strip, serves tasty Greek homestyle dishes on tables inches from the lake. (☎24670 21 101. Entrees €4-7.) **Nostalgia ❷,** on Nikis past the dock heading out to the peninsula, offers grilled souvlaki, steak, veal, and lamb. The quiet setting on the southern waterfront is the real draw. (☎24670 22 630. Entrees €5-7.) **Cibo ❶,** M. Alexandrou 17 (☎24670 28 888), is a little shop across from the public park selling tasty sandwiches (€1-2).

Nights in Kastoria are often cold, so when summer arrives in Kastoria, action moves outdoors at M. Alexandrou's **waterfront cafes** or at **concerts** in the public park. Don't expect any indoor action when Kastorians are savoring their rare balmy nights, but if the air chills, head for heat to popular club **Apollon Live,** Mitropoleos 12, just behind the M. Alexandrou waterfront strip. (☎24670 25 235. Open Th 11:30pm-late, F-Sa midnight-late, Su 10pm-late.) During the first week in

August, the **Nestorio River Party,** brings thousands of campers to the banks of the Aliakmonas River for live music concerts and outdoor revelry. Activities include kayaking, climbing, and archery along with daily trekking excursions to the concerts's majestic backdrop: **Mt. Grammos,** a rugged peak straddling the Albanian border that saw the brutal last stand of Greece's communists in 1949. (☎24670 31 204; www.cultureguide.gr. Camping €10 per day or €25 for all four days).

SIGHTS. The **Byzantine Museum** has an extensive display of icons, many from after the 1453 fall of the Byzantine Empire, along with some equally modern manuscripts. Its main function is providing keys for tourists to visit the city's ancient chapels. (☎24670 26 7781. Open Tu-Su 8:30am-3pm. Free.) The **city walls,** built by Emperor Justinian, have a noble history of failure—the city fell to Bulgars, Normans, crusaders, Serbs, and Ottomans. The remains of these fortifications now lie along the right of Ioustinianou as one walks to the Nikis waterfront. Two **tour boats** (☎24670 26 777) leave daily (noon and 7pm) from the southern docks on Nikis for a trip around the lake and a view of the peninsula's skyline. From March 7-10, 2004, Kastoria will host the **International Fur Fair** (☎24670 22 353; www.furfair.gr).

FLORINA Φλωρινα ☎23850

Transportation hub for Greece's northern borders—FYROM is 18km away, Albania 36km—and gateway to the Prespas, Florina sees more tourists than its attractions would suggest. The good transportation out of this oversized village of block apartments leaves little reason for travelers to stay more than one night.

Travel to Albania requires a **visa** (€15) which can be purchased at the border, where they speak English and **exchange currency;** remember to exchange currency upon return to Greece. No tellers will accept Albanian Leke in Greece. From Florina, you can take the bus (see below) or a taxi (€32) to **Krystallopigi.** From here, an informal bus (1hr., €1.50) takes travelers to **Korçe, Albania,** which has service to Tirana; you'll have to wait until it fills while fighting off taxi offers (€25). For more on travel within Albania, see *Let's Go: Eastern Europe 2004.*

TRANSPORTATION. Florina's main **bus station** (☎23850 22 430), Makedonomachon 2, across from the stadium, sends buses to: **Amyntaio** (30min.; 4 per day, 5:30am-8pm; €2.50) en route to **Kastoria; Athens** (8½hr.; 8:30am, 8:30pm; €34.30); **Kozani** (2hr.; 6 per day, 7am-6pm; €5.80); **Krystallopigi** and **Albanian border** (1hr.; 7am, 2:30pm; €3.30); **Niki** and **FYROM border** (1hr.; 10am, 1:30pm; €3); **Prespa** (1hr.; M, W, F 7am and 2:30pm; Sa-Su 2:30pm; €4.30); **Thessaloniki** (3hr.; 6 per day, 6:45am-6pm; €10.60). One block up Makedonomachon, two blocks right on Nikis, and right one block on Arti Ioannis brings you to the **train station** (☎2310 517 517) with service to **Thessaloniki** (3½hr.; 4 per day, 5:30am-4:25pm; €4.90). The **taxis** (☎23850 22 700 or 23850 23 800) go to the Albanian border (€35) and to Prespa (€30). They prowl the Dragoumi-Saradaporou-Makedonomachon intersection.

ORIENTATION AND PRACTICAL INFORMATION. Facing the stadium across **Makedonomachon** from the bus station, **Saradaporou** is the first street to your right, descending two blocks to **Pavlou Mela,** while **Nikis,** leading to a rotary at **Pl. Megalo Alexandrou,** is one block to your left. **Pavlou Mela,** a pedestrian street, is the best place to find shops, fast food, banks, and cafes. Turning right on Pavlou Mela off Saradaporou takes you in two blocks to the cafe-covered town center, **Pl. Modi.** From the plateia, **Stephanou** leads back up the hill to **Dragoumi,** which ends back at

Makedonomachon by the taxi stand. Back at the rotary, **Arti Ioannis** leads downhill to the train station, museum, and town drainage-ditch-cum-river. The **OTE** is on the right one block down Tyrnovou off Pavlou Mela. (Open M-Sa 7:30am-2:30pm.) Across the street, **Cafe Amsterdam,** Tyrnovou 8, has **Internet** access (☎23850 23 283; €3 per hr.) as does **Info,** Vas. Georgiou 7. (☎23850 22 274. €3 per hr. Open 10am-3pm.) There is a **Merchant's Bank** (☎23850 46 946), Dragoumi 17, with an **ATM.** The **post office,** Kallergi 22, which accepts **Poste Restante,** is just off Stephanou. (☎23850 22 236. Open daily 8am-2pm.) **Postal code:** 53100.

ACCOMMODATIONS. Florina has neither cheap accommodations nor attractions that warrant a night's stay. If transit schedules necessitate a bed, **Hotel Antigoni ❸,** Arrianou 1, at the intersection of Dragoumi and Makedonomachon, has tidy rooms. (☎23850 23 180; fax 23580 45 620. Baths, A/C, and telephones. Singles €30; doubles €42; triples €55. V.) **Hotel Ellinis ❸,** 31 Pavlou Mela, offers spacious rooms along the city's central pedestrian avenue. (☎23850 22 671; hellinis@line.gr. Balconies, telephones, TVs, and baths. Singles €25; doubles €35; triples €45. MC.)

SIGHTS. There is just enough in Florina to keep the stranded occupied for a day. The town's rough gem is the **Archaeological Museum.** (☎23850 28 206. Open Tu-Su 8:30am-3pm. €2, EU students free.) The lower floor focuses on some fine sculptures from Roman Florina, while the upper contains Hellenistic finds from both Florina and nearby Petres. A back room has some beautiful mosaic fragments and icons from the Prespa churches. Labels for that exhibit are in Greek only. Florina's **archaeological site** is 1km up the hill outside town. Follow Arti Ioannis past the museum towards the town river. Make a left onto Panosopoulou; the road becomes Ag. Georgiou. The site is currently under excavation.

PRESPA Πρεσπα ☎23850

In the cold waters of Lake Megalo Prespa some 50km north of Florina and Kastoria, meet the borders of FYROM, Albania, and Greece. Shallow, reed-shrouded Mikri Prespa lies just south, across a narrow, marshy isthmus. The shores of these two lakes contain the towns of Prespa, some of the most remote villages in all of Greece. Surviving on fishing and bean fields, these once Slavic towns still seem a world apart from the rest of Greece. The region is studded with beautiful ancient chapels, reminders of the days when exiled Byzantine bureaucrats whiled away their lives on the frigid shores of the Prespa Lakes.

TRANSPORTATION AND PRACTICAL INFORMATION. Buses run to **Florina** from **Ag. Germanos** five days a week (1hr.; M, W, F 7:30am and 4 pm, Sa-Su 4pm; €4.30). The Wednesday bus passes through all the Prespa villages; on other days call the station in Florina (☎23850 22 430) to verify the stops, which vary with demand and school busing schedules. **Taxis** (€30) will go to Kastoria or Florina.

After slipping through the Greek **border checkpoint** in Trigono, visitors to Prespa pass over a mountain and find Mikri Prespa laid out below them. At the end of Mikri Prespa, the road forks. Regional centers **Laimos** and **Ag. Germanos** are to the right and **Psarades** and **Ag. Achillios** on the left. Laimos houses the **OTE, post office,** and **mayor's office,** which distributes some information. The official **Prespa Information Center** is just up the road in Ag. Germanos. Ag. Germanos also hosts the cheapest accommodations options, though, like Laimos, this village is a bit distant from either lake. There are **no banks** or **ATMs** in the Prespes, though the grocer of Psarades is willing to **exchange currency.** Taking the fork to Psarades one crosses a marshy isthmus between Megalo Prespa on the right and Mikri on the left. At the end of the isthmus is the small channel of **Koula** and a

beach (on the Megalo side) of the same name. Turning left takes you to the causeway for Ag. Achillios, an 11-house village on the island of Mikri Prespa. Continuing straight over the mountain the road, and Greece, end in Psarades.

ACCOMMODATIONS AND FOOD. Though inland Ag. Germanos offers the cheapest lodging, the best value is found in Psarades, where local **domatia** combine budget rates with serene lake views and an end-of-the-world sense of isolation. **Tasos's Domatia ❷,** on the right at the end of the lakefront road (ask at the taverna next door for Tasos), offers four quiet, homey rooms with views of the inlet and private baths. Listen to a frog chorus at night and wake up to waterfowl. (☎697 826 4775. Singles €25; doubles and triples €30.) **Arhondiko ❷,** set back to the right of the lake lane (ask at the lakeside taverna, Akrolimnia), has rooms with balconies and baths. (☎23850 46 260. Singles €30; doubles €35; triples €45.)

Psarades has a handful of shoreline tavernas that serve tasty fresh fish from the lakes. **Syntrofia ❷** (☎23850 46 107), at the very end of the village's waterfront, offers the most remote setting imaginable. Views of dwarf cattle, reeds, and Macedonian waters go excellently with Lazaros's fresh fried trout.

SIGHTS. Each village is separated by about 10km, so traveling requires a car or bike; the extra planning is well rewarded. The shallow Mikri Prespa, with a maximum depth of only 8m, lies almost entirely in Greece and hosts the 15-person village of **Ag. Achillios** on its islet. Separated from shore by an 800m causeway, Ag. Achillios contains the famous ruins of a 10th-century **basilica** of the same name. This cathedral was built by the powerful Bulgarian Tsar Samuel to house the remains of St. Achillios, Bishop of Larisa. Difficult as it is to believe now, the Prespes were briefly at the center of the Balkan world, when Samuel used the region as his capital. The lake party ended when Byzantine Emperor Basil II "Bulgarian-killer" crushed his defiant northern neighbor. Other sights of note are the 10th century **Church of St. Germanos** in landlocked **Ag. Germanos,** and a unique breed of dwarf-cows, which wander the cobblestones and pebble shores of **Psarades.** In Psarades contracted **boat trips** in the Greek waters of Megalo Prespa are also available. The excursions are run by many a taverna and hotel owner. They include a tour of the lakeside Byzantine rock paintings, ascetic caves, and monasteries. (☎697 826 4775. About €30 per hr. for 4-5 people.) The isthmus between the lakes has a number of observation areas for **bird watching.** The Prespes have over 260 species of avian inhabitants.

HALKIDIKI Χαλκιδικη

The three fingers of Halkidiki peninsula—from east to west: Agion Oros (Mt. Athos), Sithonia, and Kassandra—point south into the Aegean, sporting spectacular scenery and some of Greece's finer beaches. Central Europeans and Thessaloniki urbanites sprawl their oily bodies onto the two fingers of Sithonia and Kassandra to sunbathe in the shadow of Agion Oros, "The Holy Mountain," which continues its thousand-year tradition of Orthodox asceticism. Female mammals are still forbidden to enter the theocratic republic where devout monks fill twenty ancient monasteries and numerous hermitages. Male visits to Mt. Athos are strictly regulated. Reservations for serious pilgrims should be made up to six months in advance, both for permits and for accommodations (p. 275). Visitors to Kassandra and Sithonia have no hoops to jump through, other than the Halkidiki public transportation system. Frequent buses run between the Karakassi 68 station in Thessaloniki (☎231 924 444) and the three peninsulas, but bus service does not run from finger to finger; you'll have to return to Thessaloniki. Kassandra is the most heavily developed; some of the largest night clubs in Greece are located in Kalithea, a favorite night-trip for Thessaloniki's youth. Sithonia is still heavily forested and less developed. Private transportation allows for splendid cruises along Halkidiki's quiet, beautiful roads to your own private beach just around the corner.

SITHONIA PENINSULA Σιθωνια

Tranquility persists on the isolated beaches of the southern and southwestern coasts of Sithonia, though like Kassandra, the peninsula has begun to sell its soul to tourism, plunging into the plastic world of souvenirs and tour buses. Nevertheless much of the land remains untouched, yet accessible to budget travel. Excellent campsites dot the coves off the single road which loops around the coast.

NEOS MARMARAS Νεος Μαρμαρας ☎23750

Many Sithonian towns begin with the moniker Neos, "new," followed by a region in modern Turkey. These villages were founded in 1923 on land appropriated from Mt. Athos's estates to provide housing for Greek refugees displaced by the nationalism of a nascent Turkey. Neos Marmaras was the refuge for one such fishing community until a more subtle "ism"—tourism—once again claimed the community. Though the local charm is gone, Neos Marmaras's beaches and sunsets remain gorgeous, making the area a favorite destination.

TRANSPORTATION AND PRACTICAL INFORMATION. The town of Neos Marmaras is a single strip with restaurants and hotels on one side and water on the other. The **first bus stop** is at Dionysios restaurant. Facing the sea, the town stretches to the left. Immediately left is the **taxi stand** followed by the docks, the police station, banks, and finally the **first plateia.** The road angles right to follow the shoreline, heading uphill. Appropriately, a seaside **church** follows on the high promontory; the road descends, and you pass the **Internet** cafe. Arriving at the **second plateia,** which has a *periptero*, a **map** with accommodations, the post office, and the **second bus stop,** the road bends inland. The waterfront becomes a stone path, which winds past domatia before meeting the road at the **beach,** where the **third bus stop** stands. **Buses** (☎23710 22 309) run to: **Thessaloniki** (2½hr.; 7 per day, 6am-7:30pm; €8.90) and nearby small towns, including **Nea Moudania** (6 per day, 6am-7:30pm; €5.30) and **Sarti** (6 per day, 9:15am-9pm; €3.70). Schedules are posted outside Dionysios. **Taxis** (☎23750 71 500) gather by the beach and at the stop by Dionysios. **Ferry** service to the Sporades runs from Nea Moudania.

The English-speaking staff at **Marmaris Tours,** next to Dionysios, recommends rooms and books excursions. (☎23750 72 010; www.marmaras.co.yu. Open daily 9am-2pm and 6-11pm.) The **National Bank,** with 24hr. **ATM,** is on the main street just before the first plateia after Dionysios and offers **currency exchange.** (☎23750 72 123. Open M-Th 8am-2:30pm, F 8am-2pm.) The **police station** is three doors up from the National Bank. (☎23750 71 111. Open 7am-5pm.) **Internet** access is available at **Stadium,** opposite the small church. From Maramaris Tours, turn right and walk about 300m; it's on the left. (☎23750 71 234. €3 per hr. Frappé €2.50; beer €3. Open 8am-2am.) For **laundry,** see the attendant in the second plateia's *periptero*. She works with the cleaners **Ariston** (☎23750 71 059), who charge a steep €10 per load. The town **post office,** in the second plateia, tucked away to the left of La Plazza, accepts **Poste Restante.** (☎23750 71 334. Open M-F 7:30am-2pm.) **Postal code:** 63081.

ACCOMMODATIONS. Even with an astounding 104 proprietors in town, vacancies are scarce on midsummer weekends. A sign with a map by the beach lists every **domatia;** most singles run around €30; anything below €25 will take a little haggling. **Domatia Pella ❷** has exceptionally clean rooms with balconies, baths, fridges, TVs, and shared kitchens (sink and electric hot plate). Walk from the first plateia between the two banks; the rooms are 20m uphill on the left. (☎23750 71 226. Singles and doubles €25; triples €35.) **Grigoris Rooms ❸**, in the second plateia above Alkano Grill, offers bright, colorful, rooms with A/C, TVs, fridges, balcony views, and sparkling clean bathrooms. (☎23750 71 944. Singles €30; doubles €40; triples €45.) For something cheaper and closer to Sithonia's natural beauty, try one of the numerous campsites. Among the better equipped and forested beachfront sites outside of town are **Areti ❶** (☎23750 71 430), **Castello ❶** (☎23750 71 094), and **Marmaras ❶** (☎23750 71 901).

FOOD AND NIGHTLIFE. Escape the afternoon heat for lunch under the namesake trees of **Tavern Pevka ❷** ("pines" in English), which overlooks the water and the stone footpath between the town and beach. There are no cars here to disturb an intimate meal of aphrodisiac octopus (€6.50). For a tempting selection of delicious Greek classics, head to waterfront taverna **Dionysios ❷.** (☎23750 71 202. Entrees €6-8.) On the left as you approach the second plateia from Dionysios, tree-lined **Taverna Gonia ❷** offers picturesque views of the harbor along with cool shade and tasty meat and fish dishes. (Entrees €6-12.50. Open daily 6pm-late.) Popular pagoda imposter **Zoe's Little China ❸,** in the second plateia, serves a variety of Chinese dishes. (☎23750 72 064. Entrees €8-14.) Nightlife in Neos Marmaras centers on the strip of bars between the two plateias and a pair of discos on the beach. The most happening bar in town is the centrally located, wave-side **Ploton,** where the floating pier's undulating tables mix with strong drinks and loud music to achieve a wonderful, often desperately sought disorientation. (☎23750 71 704; www.sithonianet.gr/ploto. Drinks €5-8. Open until 4am.) Next door at **Molos,** things are more laid back: Greeks and foreigners rub elbows, drink, and watch the surf. (☎23650 71 331. Drinks €4.50-8.) The big disco, **Vareladiko** (☎23650 72 900), about 2km away, plays Greek music.

SARTI Σαρτι ☎23750

NORTHERN GREECE

The main town on Sithonia's eastern coast, Sarti is nothing but a cluster of cafes, restaurants, and accommodations. It provides amenities to campers on its beaches, which have startling views of Mt. Athos, 25km across the gulf.

Buses run to **Thessaloniki** (3hr.; 7 per day, 5am-7pm; €12.50) by way of nearby towns. Four of the Thessaloniki buses run to **Neos Marmaras** (7:15, 11:30am, 5:45, 7pm; €3.70), while the others circumvent the peninsula in the opposite direction. Ask at the **periptero** by the bus stop two blocks in from the water for timetables. Standing at the bus stop, a 10m stroll past the *periptero* takes you to a sea-destined side street on the right. Here is **Taousanis Tours** (☎23750 94 141), a travel office offering **currency exchange** and the usual set excursions. One block down is the **Internet** cafe **Sartios.** (☎23750 20 160. €3 per hr. Frappé €2.) Another block brings you to the waterfront road with a **taxi** stand (☎23750 94 293) and many tavernas and cafes with tables under awnings over the sand. There is no post office, but a **post box** is by the **pay phone** at the bus stop *periptero*. A 24hr. **first aid** office (☎23750 94 511) is one block seaward along the side street in the opposite direction of the *periptero*, walking from the bus stop sign. Following the bus stop street past the *periptero* some five blocks, you'll find the main **plateia** littered with fast-food joints.

Sarti is full of **domatia,** but the most relaxing and best located accommodations—not to mention cheapest—are campgrounds. Of particular note for its proximity to the town is **Axladha Camping ❶,** which has clean bathrooms and a gorgeous location in a secluded, wooded cove. The site is easily accessible on foot by a beautiful trail which leaves the end of Sarti's beach facing Mt. Athos to climb a scenic goat-inhabited bluff. From here the campground's cove, beach, and harbor are visible below. The descent to the site, along with the ascent to the bluff, take about 10min. (☎697 877 3721. €3.50 per person; €3.20 tent; €2.30 car, €4.20 caravan.) Notable is **Kivotos ❷** (☎23750 94 143), halfway down the Mt. Athos end of the beach. Well priced seafood dishes and gratis dessert make it a good pick.

RURAL SITHONIA ☎23750

Explore more of Sithonia by taking the **bus** around the peninsula. The bus passes by the most deserted, unblemished turf on the peninsula. From Neos Marmaras you cross the extensive forests and olive orchards of shipping magnate Carras. The resort's white behemoths—wonderful accommodations for those already missing the city—crash into the skyline of Neos Marmaras. On the eastern side those looking to camp should try the famous **Camping Armenistis ❶,** accessible from Thessaloniki by bus (2½hr.; 11:15am, 2:45, 6:15pm; €9.40). A king among campgrounds, it has every amenity imaginable at an isolated site in the golden sands and coves of the forested eastern shore. This nomad village has numerous music festivals every summer. Check out the website for upcoming events. (☎23750 91 497, in winter 23770 71 183; www.armenistis.com.gr. AmEx/MC/V.)

MOUNT ATHOS PENINSULA

OURANOUPOLIS Ουρανουπολις ☎23770

The last settlement in secular Athos, Ouranoupolis functions dually as a gateway to monastic Athos and as a hedonistic beach resort popular among Germans. Halfway down the peninsula 125km southeast of Thessaloniki, it lies just beyond a trans-peninsular depression dug by Xerxes as a canal for his invasion fleet. There isn't much to see in Ouranoupolis beyond the beaches. Tickets for the **cruise around Athos** can be purchased from the offices near the tower. (☎23770 71 370. 9am, 7pm; €15.) Also interesting are the **offshore isles.** Explore the nearby coves in a rented boat or take the ferry to inhabited **Amouliani.**

The town of Ouranoupolis centers on the distinctive, medieval **Fosfori Tower** by the sea. The **bus stop** (☎23770 22 278) and posted schedule are just in front of the tower in the parking lot. Buses go to **Thessaloniki** (2½hr.; 7 per day, 5:30am-6:15pm; €8.50) and **Athens** (7hr., 2:15pm, €29.50). The sea makes a 90° angle at the tower. Facing town with your back to the tower, the main taverna strip as well as the Athos **ferry office** (☎23770 71 149) are along the left waterfront paralleling the road out of town. On a righthand side street two blocks down this road out of town is an **Agricultural Bank** with 24hr. **ATM.** (Open M, W 9am-2:30pm, F 9am-2pm). Three blocks down is **MaMoynia Internet Cafe,** which offers steep €4 per hr. access. Several blocks further is the **Pilgrim's Office,** which issues permits for Athos. (☎23770 71 422. Open 8am-2:30pm.)

Those staying overnight in Ouranopolis have several reasonably affordable choices. Dozens of houses offer **domatia,** and on your arrival you will probably be greeted at the bus by offers. **Camping Ouranoupoli ❶** lies on a beach 1.5km outside of town along the highway. (☎23770 71 165; www.camping-ouranoupoli.gr.) **Hotel Athos ❷,** above a supermarket one street back from the waterfront, offers elegant rooms with baths. (☎23770 71 368. Singles €20; doubles €25; triples €35.) Most places will also store luggage while you're on Athos. Those looking for a last supper before their entrance into Mt. Athos—or a triumphal reward after the monks' spartan cuisine—should head to the row of tavernas on the waterfront.

IN RECENT NEWS

ORTHODOXY OR DEATH

Athos monks have much to gripe ıbout. In 2000 prime minister Costas imitis removed the religion line from ireek identity cards to harmonize with the EU's secularism. The monks, and many ireeks, were furious at this "betrayal," vhich they believe erases from the cards precisely what makes them Greek. Monks ılso worry about accepting EU cultural unds to renovate the medieval monasteres, a trend evidenced by rampant construction, cranes, cement mixers, and guest workers across the Holy Mountain. Besides bringing electricity and private bathrooms, some fear they might have to open up to more daily visitors.

For Athos's Esfigmenou monastery, he final straw came with Patriarch Vartholomew's rapprochement with he "illicit community headed by the Pope." The churches have been in schism since 1054 when the bishops f Rome and Constantinople mutually excommunicated one another. So vhen Vartholomew's championed ecunenism led his representative to kneel with the pope, the Esfigmenou monks stopped mentioning Vartholomew in their prayers. The patriarch ordered the state to evict the 113 schismatics, and the deadline was set or January 28, 2003. On February 10 a monk, whom Esfigmeniotes claim was fleeing Greek police, drove his ractor off a cliff. In March 2003 the nighest court in Greece, the Council of State ordered police to lift the seige. Police have relaxed their presence and pilgrims can even visit(☎23770 23 796). At press time, the Council of State was expected to rule on the egality of the eviction.

MOUNT ATHOS Αγιον Ορος ☎23770

The monasteries on Mt. Athos (the "Holy Mountain"), the easternmost peninsula of Halkidiki, have been the paradigm of Orthodox asceticism for more than a millennium. The community has existed since 883, when Basil I issued an imperial charter to Athos preventing local military officials from interfering with the monks. Today the Holy Community of Mount Athos is an autonomous state comprised of 20 Orthodox monasteries and countless hamlets *(skites)*, with some 1800 monks who live there and at least as many full-time workers. By limiting development to the construction of a few unsurfaced roadways, the monks have preserved the peninsula's luxuriant foliage. Only the jagged marble peak of Mt. Athos itself, soaring 2033m above the waves, is exposed, and wildlife like eagles and jackals roams the peninsula. Against the background of this lush sanctuary, the monks sequester themselves from the outside world, shunning material pleasures to pursue a spiritual life. Emperor Constantine's *avaton* (edict) of 1060 forbids women and female domestic animals from setting foot on the peninsula

ORIENTATION AND PRACTICAL INFORMATION. With **permit** in hand, arrive at the western port of **Ouranoupolis** or the less frequently used eastern port of **Ierrissos** the night before your entry date to Athos. **Buses** leave Thessaloniki's Halkidiki station, Karakassi 68 (☎2310 924 444), for **Ouranoupolis** (2½hr.; 7 per day, 6:15am-6:30pm; €8.50) and **Ierrissos** (2½hr.; 7 per day, 6:15am-6:30pm; €7.40). For Ouranoupolis, there is also a daily bus direct from **Athens.** (☎210 515 4800. 7hr., 11pm, €29.50.) You can also catch the 6:15am bus from Thessaloniki the day of your visit, but this is a hectic approach. From Ouranoupolis two **boats** per day go to **Daphni** (1½hr; daily 9:45am and M-F 6:30am, Sa 7am, Su 10am; €4) and stop at each of the monasteries on the way there. The early morning boat, Agia Anna (8am, €2.40), continues from Daphni at 8am to the *skitic* community of **Kafsokalivia** at the peninsula's tip, stopping twice at each monastery and *skite* en route both going and returning. Arriving back at Daphni by 11:10am, the Ag. Anna connects with the 11:30am arrival of the second boat from Ouranoupolis for a second trip down the peninsula at 12:45pm. Upon completing this trip, Ag. Anna stops at Daphni at 3:30pm then returns to Ouranoupolis at 5:15pm. The second daily ship to Ouranoupolis from Daphni leaves at noon. To reach the peninsula's eastern monasteries, take the **bus** from Daphni to Karies (30min.; 10:30am from Karies, noon from Daphni; €2), or sail with **Captain**

Spiro, who travels to **Vatopedi** from **Ierrissos** (☎23770 22 576 or 6974 060 743; M, W, F-Su 8:30am; €8). You can also hike (p. 308) or take pricey monk-driven **taxis** (☎23770 23 266) between monasteries.

OBTAINING A PERMIT. Men who wish to see Mt. Athos must secure a permit in advance; call the **Mt. Athos Pilgrims' Bureau** (☎/fax 2310 861 611), in Thessaloniki, six months in advance. If you can be flexible with your dates, you may call later and find a day that hasn't been fully booked yet; only 14 non-Orthodox visitors are admitted to Mt. Athos per day. Then mail (don't fax) a copy of your passport to the office at Kon. Karamanli 14, Thessaloniki, 54638; call two weeks ahead of your visit to confirm the reservation and visit the office with your passport to pick up the permit. (Open M-F 9am-2pm, Sa 10am-noon; call ahead.) If leaving from Ouranoupolis, **bring your permit and passport** to the Athos office (☎23770 71 422; open 8am-2:30pm), uphill from the bus stop by the gas station, by 9am on the day your visit begins. You will receive your entrance pass called the *Diamonitirion,* complete with the blue seal of the monastic community, which you must present before boarding the ferry to Mt. Athos. For the early morning ferry, and for the boat from Ierrissos, officials will be at the dock. Arrive early as lines are long, especially when the 9am bus gets in. The regular permit is valid for a **four-day stay.** Passes cost €35 for foreigners and €18 for students with ISIC under age 27. You must strictly observe the date of arrival on your permit–if you arrive a day late, you will be turned away. You will not be admitted without your **passport.** To extend your stay, you must ask at the peninsula's capital, Karies. Unless you have an extremely compelling reason (i.e., to become a monk), your request will almost certainly be denied. Unofficial extensions are easier to come by, especially in low season, monks often allow considerate, interested visitors to stay longer.

Because Athos's hikes can be long and arduous, grab a green **Mount Athos Tourist Map** (€8) or buy a **guidebook** with a map (€4-10) in Ouranoupolis or Karies. Leave your pack in Ouranoupolis. **Karies,** the capital of Mt. Athos, has an **OTE** next to the Athonite Holy Council Building, a **post office** (open M-F 7:30am-2pm), and a **hotel** ❷ (€12 per person). Two Karies **restaurants** ❷ serve spartan meals (€4.40), resembling those of the monasteries. Daphni also has a restaurant, convenience store, and **post office** (open M-F 7:30am-2pm). **Postal codes:** Daphni 63087, Karies 63086.

THE HOLY MOUNTAIN. Derived from the name of a Thracian giant buried by Poseidon beneath the mountain, "Athos" predates both Christianity and Hellenism. The Christian tradition began here when the **Virgin Mary,** on a trip from Ephesus to visit Lazarus on Cyprus, is said to have been thrown off course and led by divine sign to the Athonite coast. The peninsula, known as **Akte,** had been a notorious center of paganism; the moment Mary's foot graced its soil, the false idols disintegrated in realization of their own worthlessness. Even before Mary's time, many had tried to tame the rowdy peninsula, from Alexander the Great to Xerxes.

Although legend claims that the first monastic settlements were founded by Constantine the Great and his mother, Helen, record of monkish habitation does not come until the 7th century. The first monastery, **Megistis Lavras,** was built in 963 by **St. Athanasios** with Arab spoils from the reconquest of Crete. Over the centuries that followed, Athos periodically flourished—at one point it contained 40 settlements and 40,000 monks—but its low points ached with natural disasters, pirate invasions, and internal squabbling. The edict banning women from the area was enacted in 1060, perhaps out of respect for the Virgin Mary, but likely because of scandalous frolicking between the monks and Vlach shepherdesses who had settled on the mountain. Unlike most of Greece, Mt. Athos retained autonomy during the Turkish occupation by surrendering promptly to the Ottomans and accepting their rule. During the centuries preceding the Greek liberation of 1821, Mt. Athos was supported and populated by Serbs, Bulgarians, Romanians, and Russians, who still have affiliations with particular monasteries. At the height of imperial Russia's expansionist policies, some 3000 Russian monks inhabited **Agios Panteleiomon,** supplied weekly by cargo ships arriving straight from Odessa.

After World War I, the Treaty of Lausanne made Mt. Athos an official part of Greece while still allowing it to retain much autonomy. A body of monks, elected from each of the 20 monasteries, was set up to legislate and govern the peninsula. Dwindling vocations through the 1950s threatened the stability of Mount Athos, and it soon became a prime target for greedy real estate developers. In recent years, however, Athos has been rejuvenated by hundreds of young men, many from Australia and Cyprus, inspired to take vows of Orthodox monasticism.

LIFE ON MOUNT ATHOS. Today all the monasteries are cenobitic, with communal money and duties. Athos retains an unsurpassed wealth of Paleologian and late Byzantine art, manuscripts, treasure, and architecture. Each monastery houses *lipsana*, remains of dead saints that only Orthodox Christian men are allowed to see. Especially impressive are the **Hand of Mary Magdalene,** who bathed Jesus, which remains (skin intact) in **Simonos Petra,** and the **belt of the Theotokos** in **Vatopediou,** the only extant relic of the Virgin Mary. Several monasteries possess fragments of the **True Cross.** The **Gifts of the Magi,** presented to Jesus at his birth, are housed in **Agios Pavlou;** five of the 28 pieces are displayed for nightly veneration.

BEING A PILGRIM. Mt. Athos will likely induce complete culture shock. The monks operate on a schedule twice removed from the outside world: they use the **Julian calendar** (not Gregorian), which lags by 13 days, and set their watches to **Byzantine time,** marking the sunset as midnight. At most monasteries, the morning liturgy begins at 3am (normal time) and stretches until 8am. Although only the most devout pilgrims attend the service's beginning, the ringing of bells and tapping of wooden planks, called *semanitron*, keep visitors turning in bed until they too get up and go to church. Breakfast is served directly after service in fresco-covered *trapezaries* to the sound of a **chanter,** who reads the story of a different saint's life at every meal. Only the chanter talks during meals, and everyone stops eating the moment the chanter stops. Non-Orthodox pilgrims often sit at a separate table from both the monks and Orthodox visitors; at some monasteries they must eat after everyone else. Breakfast and dinner both generally consist of homegrown vegetables, bread, water, and fruit, with fish and other delicacies on feast days.

Always reach the monastery where you plan to stay by 4pm and make sure you are inside the monastery walls before the gates close at sunset. When you arrive, look for the *arhodariki* (guest house); a monk will welcome you with a glass of ice-cold water, some *tsipouro*, and a Turkish Delight as he explains the monastery's rules. The evening *esperino* church service usually starts at 5pm and lasts until 6:30pm or so, with dinner served immediately afterward. Both food and lodgings are free at every monastery, although it is a good idea to make a reservation.

While there, be as courteous and cooperative as possible: always address monks by their title, *Patera*, and instead of hello and goodbye, use the more formal HAIR-eh-teh with monks and pilgrims. Orthodox visitors may also say ev-lo-YEE-teh (bless us, father) when encountering monks. Avoid talking loudly, especially during siesta and after nightfall. Also, sitting cross-legged or standing with hands behind your back is considered disrespectful and arrogant respectively, and might earn you a few sharp frowns. Be aware of each monastery's chapel restrictions for non-Orthodox visitors.

MONASTERIES. On the northwestern tip of the peninsula, **Megistis Lavras** (☎23770 23 745) is the oldest, largest, and richest of the monasteries. Its monks are known to be stern and conservative. Though it is one of the most visited monasteries, you may find it somewhat impersonal. It's also the most isolated: to get here, you will need to get a ride (€60 per car) from Karies. All other monasteries require telephone reservations. Beautifully situated near a meadow overlooking the northern coast, **Iviron** (☎23770 23 643) was founded by Georgian monks in 980 and was the second monastery on Mt. Athos. Today it is completely Greek and one of the most popular monasteries. Moated and turreted like a medieval castle, **Vatopediou** (☎23770 23 219; reservations 9am-1pm) lies on the northern coast in a secluded bay and is now populated largely by Greek-Cypriot monks. Vatopediou is the most visited monastery on Athos; call at least two weeks ahead for a reservation. **Pantokratoros** (☎23770 23 880) and nearby **Stavronikita** (☎23770 23 255; reservations 10am-noon) lie on the northern coast, close to Karies and accessible by bus. Home to a small community of friendly monks, Pantokratoros is one of the few monasteries that imposes no special restrictions on its non-Orthodox visitors. Stavronikita is the smallest and "youngest" monastery, completed in 1536; it's also one of the friendliest and most peaceful. Greek for "God-loving," **Philotheou** (☎23770 23 256; reservations noon-3pm) is one of Mount Athos's most stunningly located monasteries, sitting on a plateau over the northern coast. The abbey is surrounded by orchards, gardens, and lush chestnut forests. Philotheou is also one of the stricter monasteries: non-Orthodox guests must eat after the faithful and may not enter the church at all. Perched on the edge of a sheer cliff on the southern coast, **Simonos Petra** (☎23770 23 254; reservations 1-3pm) is spectacular but only has room for ten guests. Travelers can relax in the roomy guest quarters, which extend out on a balcony overlooking the cliff to the sea. Under constant renovation, the monastery is frequently booked; you'll need to call at least two weeks in advance to get a bed. In a secluded bay just east of Simonos Petra, **Grigoriou** (☎23770 23 668; reservations 11am-1pm) is one of the more liberal monasteries. Guests are treated to their own private quarters just outside the monastery walls, with breeze-blown balconies. Following Grigoriou, and accessible from the next monastery Agios Pavlou (St. Paul's) by a 30min. shore path, imposing **Dionisiou** (☎23770 23 687) perches on a rocky bluff over the Aegean. The monks are welcoming, English is prevalent, and guest quarters are luxurious. Most rooms are singles, and showers (rare on Athos) with hot water (still rarer) are available. With thickly forested hills to the north and the sparkling ocean to the south, **Karakallou** (☎23770 23 225) is exceptionally picturesque. Karakallou's rules for non-Orthodox visitors are particularly strict.

SLAVIC MONASTERIES. In addition to these predominantly Greek monasteries, the Slavs, not to be outdone, inhabit several abbeys. At one time, there were nearly equal numbers of Greek and Slavic monks on the mountain. However, political turmoil (notably the 1917 Russian Revolution) cut off the supply of funds and novices at the source. Today just three Slavic monasteries remain: onion-domed Russian **St. Panteleimon,** Bulgarian **Zagrafou** (☎23770 23 247), and Serbian **Hilandariou.**

SKITES AND HERMITAGES. Many of Athos's monks choose to live as ascetic hermits, eschewing the material comforts of the monasteries in favor of caves and huts on the harsh slopes of the peak. Dozens of huts, cells, and tiny churches dot the southernmost end of the island, between Megistis Lavras and Ag. Pavlou, all occupied by monks who have given their lives to the reclusive study of sacred texts and the contemplation of God. Many hermits will allow you to stay with them, but you must bring your own food and sleeping bag and be careful not to disturb their constant meditations. The barren southeastern slope of Athos, called **Karoulia** after the pulleys the monks use to bring food to their caves, is home to some of the most extreme ascetics.

HIKING. Hikes through Mt. Athos's winding mountain paths, high above emerald coves and speckled by fluorescent butterflies, rival any in Greece. The trail from **Megistis Lavras to Skiti Agia Anna** is one of the wildest and most scenic among the Holy Mountain's family of trekking superlatives. The lack of auto accessibility and the breathtaking bluffs plunging into the blue Aegean beside rocky peninsulas make this region a favorite among the most reclusive hermits. The path takes a good 6hr. but can be shortened to four by stopping at Kafsokalivia and taking the afternoon ferry to Agia Anna. Other popular hikes include the ascent of **Athos's peak,** a hot, dry 5hr. trek from *skiti* **Agia Anna** (☎23770 23 320). A 4hr. climb will take you to the **Church of the Panagia,** with beds for an overnight stay, just 1hr. from the summit. Take along a copy of the green **Mount Athos Road Editions Map** (€7.50) or another Athos guide. **Paths** can be narrow and poorly marked; furthermore, the ones on the map might have been swallowed by brush. Stop frequently en route to verify directions with the monks. Bring lots of water and bear in mind the lay of the peninsula: western shore hikers will enjoy Athos's shadow until 11am, while the eastern shore is perfect for late afternoon rambles—but be back by sunset. The light monastic fare is insufficient for a long day's hike, so make sure to bring some nourishment from the outside world. Alternatively, you can join most Greek pilgrims and hop into a monk-driven minibus for a bumpy ride back to Karies. From there, ask around for another bus traveling in your direction.

EASTERN MACEDONIA

KAVALA Καβαλα ☎2510

Be forewarned: "Kavala" stems from the Greek verb meaning "to ride" (as in cavalry), a word connoting the same sexual innuendo as its English equivalent—that's why people may get excited when you say you're vacationing "in Kavala." The modern town stretches from the oil rig dotted Thassos strait to the slopes of Mt. Simvolo, 160km east of Thessaloniki. Modern Kavala rests upon the ruins of the ancient Thassian gold mining colony Neapolis (later Byzantine Christopolis), where the apostle Paul first set foot in Europe. In the 18th century, Mehmet Ali, a future pasha of Egypt and founder of the dynasty that lasted until Nasser, was born here. Most visitors make Kavala a departure point for the nearby islands.

TRANSPORTATION

Flights: Most ferries leave from the eastern end of the port in front of the string of restaurants. Thassos boats all leave from the western dock. The **airport** (☎25910 53 272) is 32km away, accessible by buses to **Chrissoupolis,** which run every 30min. (every hr. on Su) followed by a short taxi. You can take a taxi (€15) direct from the city center. **Olympic Airways,** Ethn. Anastassis 8 (☎2510 223 627), a little west of the Thassos ferry dock on the corner with Mitropoleos, has daily flights to **Athens** (1hr., 14 per week, €89). Open M-F 8am-4pm.

Buses: ☎2510 223 593. At the corner of Eterias and Kavalas, 1 block north from Vas. Pavlou and the waterfront and 1 block south of the post office. To: **Athens** (9½hr.; 3 per day, 9:15am-7:15pm; €39.50); **Drama** (1hr.; every 30min., 6am-9pm; €2.40); **Ioannina** (8hr.; 3 per day, 7am-6pm; €34); **Philippi** (30min.; every 30min., 6am-9pm; €1.20); **Thessaloniki** (2¼hr.; 20 per day, 5:30am-8:30pm; €10.20); **Xanthi** (1hr.; 20 per day, 4:45am-8:40pm; €3.70). To get to **Alexandroupoli** (2hr.; 7 per day, 9:30am-2am; €10.60), go to **Seven-Eleven,** a fast-food restaurant located directly opposite the main entrance of the bus station. There you'll find schedules, tickets, and the bus itself.

Ferries: Nikos Milades (☎2510 220 067 or 2510 223 421), in a back corner of the main harbor, has ferry info for islands other than Thassos. Look behind the small park to the left of the row of tavernas. Open daily 9am-1:30pm and 6-8pm. Ferries to: **Chios** (24hr., Sa 1:30am, €26); **Lesvos** (12hr.; W, Sa, Su ; €24); **Limnos** (5hr., 3 per week, €14); **Piraeus** (35hr., Su, €35.50). **Arsinoi Travel,** K. Dimitriou 16 (☎2510 835 671), a few doors down from Milates, sells tickets to **Limnos** (4½hr.; Tu, Th; €14) and **Samothraki** (4hr., 4-5 per week, €15.50); schedules change monthly. Open daily 8am-noon and 5-8pm. Buy tickets to **Thassos** (1hr.; 10 per day, 8am-10pm; €3, students and children €1.50, cars €14.40) at the white ticket kiosk on the Thassos ferry dock, located on the busy corner 1 block south and 1 block east of the bus station.

Flying Dolphins: Hydrofoils leave from near the Thassos ferry dock for **Thassos** (40min.; 4 per day, 7:10am-2pm; €8).

Taxis: ☎2510 232 001. Just behind the port in Pl. Eleftherias. Available 24hr.

ORIENTATION AND PRACTICAL INFORMATION

The city's main attraction, the **Panagia District,** is southeast of the port on its own peninsula, hemmed in by ancient walls under the turrets of the Byzantine fortress. The entrance is on **Poulidou** at the end of **El. Venizelou.** Venizelou runs parallel to the waterfront two blocks inland. The next parallel street seaward is hotel-lined **Erithrou Stavrou,** followed by **Ethn. Andistassis,** which skirts the waves from the Thassos ferry dock to beyond the Archaeological Museum and municipal park. A detailed **map** of Kavala can be found next to the small port police kiosk, at the Thassos ferry dock. For paper copies head to the **municipal information office.**

Tourist Office: Municipal Information Office (☎2510 231 011), the large windowed kiosk off Venizelou just behind the port at Pl. Eleftherias, is an English-language oasis of accurate information. City maps (€3) and walking guides to Thassos's ruins (€9) are available. Ferry schedules, bus schedules, and accommodations information are free. Purchase tickets to local performances at the ticket office window outside. **Internet** access is also available (€2 per hr.). Open M-Sa 8am-9pm.

Police Station: Omonias 119 (☎2510 622 273 or 622 274), 4 blocks north of the port. Follow Averof to the OTE then bear left. **Tourist police** (☎2510 622 246), on ground floor. Open 8am-3pm. **Port police** (☎2510 223 716), at both ports. Open 24hr.

Bank: Pl. Eleftherias on Venizelou by the tourist office, directly behind the port, is surrounded by banks with **ATMs.** Most open M-Th 8am-2:30pm, F 8am-2pm.

Hospital: Stavrou 113 (☎2510 830 260), 4 blocks past the Panagia district.

OTE: ☎2510 561 160. On eastern side of Pl. 28 Oktovriou, near El. Venizelou. Open M, W 7:30am-3pm; Tu, Th-F 7:30am-2:30pm and 6-8:30pm; Sa 8:30am-2:30pm.

Internet Access: Funtazia, Venizelou 43 (☎2510 83 6660), has fast DSL connections (€1.70 per hr.). **Cyber Club,** El Venizelou 56, has over 50 high-speed terminals. €1.50 per hr. Frappé €1.50; beer €1.80. Open 24hr.

Post Office: Main branch (☎2510 833 330), at Kavalas and Stavrou, 1 block north of the bus station, **exchanges currency.** Open M-F 7:30am-8pm. **Postal code:** 65110.

ACCOMMODATIONS AND CAMPING

Domatia are scarce, hotels aren't cheap, and many of Kavala's rooms overlook the port (the shipping industry doesn't shut down when you do). In Panagia at Th. Poulidou 38, the cliffside sea of domes that was once the imaret, a type of Ottoman hostel for pilgrims and Sufi holy men, will soon be an operating hotel. There is a

GNTO campground ❶, Batis beach, with a supermarket 4km outside of Kavala. (☎2510 227 151. €1 to swim in the pool. €3 per person; €7 per large tent, €4 per small tent.) Blue **bus #8** goes to Batis from Kavala every 30min.

George Alvanos Rented Rooms, Anthemiou 35 (☎2510 221 781, 2510 228 412, or 6994 221 781). Enter the Panagia District on Poulidou, bear left uphill on Mehmet Ali, and make a sharp left on Anathemiou. A centuries-old house in the heart of the scenic Panagia District has beautifully furnished rooms far from the noise and fumes of the port. Many of the spacious, homey rooms look out over the sea; all allow free use of a laundry machine and full kitchen. Singles €18; doubles €25. ❷

Hotel Acropolis, El. Venizelou 29 (☎2510 223 543; fax 2510 830 752). From the bus station, walk 2 blocks away from the water and turn right on El. Venizelou. It's 1 block ahead on your right. Friendly management and bare but clean rooms with high ceilings, sinks, and TVs. Singles €26; doubles €33, with bath €44. ❸

Oceanis Hotel, Erythrou Stavrou 32 (☎2510 221 981; fax 2510 225 270), at the intersection with Dagli. Colorful, spacious rooms are fully equipped with TVs, A/C, phones, large balconies, and sparkling bathrooms. The bar and swimming pool on the 8th fl. provide great views. Singles €40; doubles €60; triples €70. ❸

Hotel Panorama (☎2510 224 205), across from Hotel Acropolis, has basic rooms with small balconies, TVs, and colorful drapes. Singles €26; doubles €34; triples €40. ❸

FOOD AND NIGHTLIFE

Tavernas line the water and Poulidou in Panagia. **Oraya Mytilini ❷** (Οραια Μυτιληνη; ☎2510 224 749), by the port under the Old Town, among a row of similar tavernas. Friendly, English-speaking staff is happy to give you a guided tour of the kitchen. Tastefully decorated with hanging cloves of garlic and a clothesline of gutted fish, the restaurant serves up delicious seafood entrees (€4-8). **Mikros Mylos Bakery ❶**, on the corner of El. Venizelou and Dangli, a block south of the Municipal Museum, is a first-rate bakery. (☎2510 228 132. Marzipan and fruit tart €1.50.) After hours, Kavala remains relatively calm, though a few lively cafe-bars line the waterfront. Winter clubbers inhabit the restored tobacco warehouses on Paleologou, but the real summer action moves to Kavala's suburban beaches. Take a taxi to nearby **Palio** (€5) or the beach at **Aspri Amos.**

SIGHTS

Follow signs from the Panagia's entrance to reach the **kastro.** Originally built in the 5th century BC, the castle and its surrounding walls were later augmented by the Byzantines and the Ottomans. The well-preserved, turreted walls survey the wide panorama of the city and the island of Thassos to the south. The small **amphitheater** hosts occasional musical and cultural performances. In the **Eleftheria Festival** in late June, students celebrate Kavala's liberation from the Ottomans by performing dances at the castle. (Open daily 8am-9pm. €1.) The **Archaeological Museum,** one of the region's largest museums, nicely complements any trip to Amphibolis or the sites of Thassos, of which it houses many antiquities. Much of the pre-WWII artifacts were plundered by the Bulgarians, but the museum has recovered. Don't miss the gold jewelry and wreaths from Amphibolis's Macedonian tomb and the elaborate Hellenistic funeral scene painting. (On the waterfront, 3 blocks from the port in the opposite direction from the Old Town. ☎2051 222 335 or 2051 224 717. Open Tu-Su 8am-3pm. €2, students €1.) The ground floor of Kavala's small **Municipal Folk Museum** houses works by famed Thassian sculptor Polygnotos Vagis (p. 513). The marble, stone, and wooden pieces blend archaic Greek styles with modern influences like Chagall and Matisse, seen in the roughly chiseled faces of *The Moons.* (Filippou 4. Take Venizelou west from the Old Town and turn away from the water onto Mitropelous. ☎2510 222 706. Open M-F 8am-2pm, Sa 9am-1pm. Free.)

Once home to the Thassian colony of Neapolis, the **Old Town** is now the **Panagia** district. This spiderweb of steep narrow streets and old Ottoman-style stone houses with projecting second stories folds atop the promontory beside the port. Start your walk on Poulidou, which branches off Koundouriotou just after its intersection with Venizelou. Don't miss the Muslim **imaret,** Th. Poulidou 38, currently closed but soon to be a hotel. An imaret is a type of hospice often funded by wealthy Muslims to fulfill the Islamic principle of charity; this one was financed by local boy and self-made pasha of Egypt, Mehmet Ali. Well situated, **Ali's House** also survives at the very tip of the promontory next to his equestrian statue at the end of Polidou (inside closed for renovations). From here there are splendid views of the sea. In front you see green Thassos, an oil rig to your left, and beyond that the uninhabited islet of Thassopoula. Zigzag back along the opposite side of the promontory following first M. Ali, then Navarinou, then Issidorou to enter the kastro. Continue on Issidorou to Katsoni, which passes under the splendid 14th-century **aqueduct** built under Sultan Süleyman the Magnificent, to rejoin Koundouriotou, thus completing the circuit. Kavala's 18th-century fortunes came from its surrounding tobacco fields. There are a number of **tobacco-related sights,** including the Folk Museum, which was the house of tobacco trader Zachos Zachou, and the stately tobacco warehouse, soon to be the new art museum, one block in from Venizelou at Pl. Kapnergati. Follow Averof, which runs inland from the port, up four blocks. In the square there is a monument to the tobacco workers.

Kavala's waterfront is home to three **beaches.** Although it's not an arduous walk from town, the best bet is an intercity bus—get off on impulse or consult the tourist office. The sandy beach of **Perigali,** northwest of the city beyond the Panagia district, is a favorite. The closest beach is near the city of **Kalamitsa,** 1.5km east of the city center. The city's main resort beaches, complete with hot summer nightlife and long sands, are **Palio,** 10km south, **Nea Iraklitsa,** another 5km, and **Nea Peramos,** the largest, some 20km south.

DAYTRIP FROM KAVALA: PHILIPPI

Take the bus from Kavala (every 30min., 6am-9pm; €1.20). Make sure to tell the driver you want the archaeological site. ☎2510 516 470. Open daily 8am-7pm, the pavilioned mosaics 8am-3pm. €3, students and seniors €2, EU students free.

Roughly 15km north of Kavala, the once-proud city of **Philippi** lies in splendid ruins. Philip of Macedon founded Philippi to protect Thassian goldminers from Thracian attacks and named it all by himself. A 42 BC Roman Civil War battle made it famous: here, Octavian (later Augustus) and Antony defeated Cassius and Brutus, the assassins of Julius Caesar. In AD 50 missionaries St. Paul and St. Silas arrived from Anatolia to preach Christianity, soon baptizing a woman named **Lydia,** the first European Christian. The **Cell of Paul** is the apostle's own budget accommodation. Check out the Roman **latrines** behind the tall bascilica ruins, where most of the 42 marble seats are intact—and all the lids have been left up.

THRACE Θρακη

Thrace is halved by the Evros River—Greece holds the west, Turkey the east. Geographically it is a continuation of the Bulgarian Rhodopi Range, which terminates suddenly some 20km from the Aegean wherein lie the main cities (Xanthi, Komotini, Sapes). Tobacco and tomato fields spread out to the south; the mountains and their Slavic villages flow heedlessly through the Bulgarian border to the north. Historically Indo-European (non-Hellenic) Thracians, "barbarous" and not fully subdued until their late Roman conquest in AD 46, inhabited the mountainous province. Ruled by the Ottomans until 1913, the west fell to Bulgaria after the Balkan Wars and then passed under Allied control during World War I. In 1920 all of Thrace, then only 11km from Istanbul at its border, joined Greece. The area was then split again by the 1923 Treaty of Lausanne, which granted the eastern part back to Turkey. The scarring 1922 population exchange (p. 13) relocated Greeks in Turkish territory to Greece, and vice-versa; many of the region's Greeks arrived at this time. Interestingly Thracian Muslims, mostly Slavic Pomaks, were exempted from the exchange, giving the region a multi-cultural flavor. Within the last decade Orthodox Georgians and Armenians from the former USSR joined the stew.

XANTHI Ξανθη ☎25410

Xanthi, Thrace's most charismatic city, may be the most pleasant place to experience Thracian multiculturalism. Strolling the sidewalks you'll see both the Turkish and Slavic Pomak Muslims, Christians, and Roma. Getting lost among the cobbled streets of Xanthi's Old Town threads you through neighborhoods of Ottoman houses and elegant old mansions, the bounty of a tobacco industry that still buoys much of the town's economy. A student population from the University of Thrace gives the modern city a smart, sophisticated feel year-round.

TRANSPORTATION. Trains go to: **Athens** (regular: 14hr., 5:22pm, €22.30; express: 9½hr.; 9:53am, 10:18pm; €38); **Istanbul, Turkey** (11hr., 10:30am, €26); **Komotini** (45min.; 6 per day, 3:11am-7:22pm; €1.50); **Thessaloniki** (regular: 4hr.; 3 per day, 11:27am-2:47am; €8.20; express: 4hr.; 9:53am, 8:08pm; €10). Tickets are sold at both the train station and the **OSE Office** in the Agora Nousi shopping area on Tsaldari, just east of the central plateia. (☎25410 22 277 or 25410 27 840. Open M-F 10am-2:30pm and 6-9pm.) Xanthi's **train station** (☎25410 22 581) is about 2km southeast of the central plateia. To get there, head down Karaoli, go right at the rotary of Pl. Baltati, and then left onto Kapnergaton (a.k.a. Kondili). You will see signs 100m past the stadium and the tennis courts. You can also take a taxi (€2) from the central plateia. From the **bus station,** Dimokritou 6 (☎25410 22 684), buses go to: **Athens** (11hr.; 9:30am, 7pm; €43); **Avdira** and **Myrodato beaches** (30min.; 6 per day, 11am-6:30pm; €3.50); **Drama** (2hr.; 6 per day, 8am-6:45pm; €6); **Kavala** (1hr.; every hr., 6am-11pm; €3.70); **Komotini** (45min.; 14 per day, 6:30am-8:30pm; €3.45); **Lagos** (30min.; 7 per day, 8:40am-5pm; €3.50); **Mangana beach** (30min.; 4 per day, 12:20pm-7pm; €3); **Thessaloniki** (3½hr.; 8 per day, 6am-7pm; €13). **Taxis** (☎25410 25 900 or 25410 22 702) wait in Pl. Dimokratias and Pl. Baltatzi.

NORTHERN GREECE

ORIENTATION AND PRACTICAL INFORMATION. Xanthi is Thrace's westernmost city, about 50km northeast of Kavala. Its central plateia, **Pl. Dimokratias,** is recognizable by the clock tower in the center. From the bus station, standing at the door in front of the seating area, **Dimokritou** is on your left. Facing the street with your back to the station, head left past **Pl. Baltatzi,** a small traffic circle, as Dimokritou becomes **Karaoli** and leads into the central plateia. The main street, **28 Oktovriou,** runs south to **Pl. Eleftherias,** parallel to Karaoli. **Vas. Konstantinou** runs north to the Old Town, across from the clock tower. Xanthi has no tourist office, but the **town hall** (☎25410 24 444), on the upper end of Vas. Konstantinou, provides city **maps.** The **National Bank,** which has a 24hr. **ATM,** is north of the main plateia. Take the first right off Konstantinou as you head toward the Old Town. (Open M-Th 8am-2pm, F 8am-1pm.) Two blocks southeast of Pl. Baltatzi is the 24hr. **hospital** (☎25410 47 100 and 47 200). The 24hr. **police,** Neston 2 (☎25410 84 116), are north of Karaoli near the bus station. The **OTE** is left of the central plateia as you face the

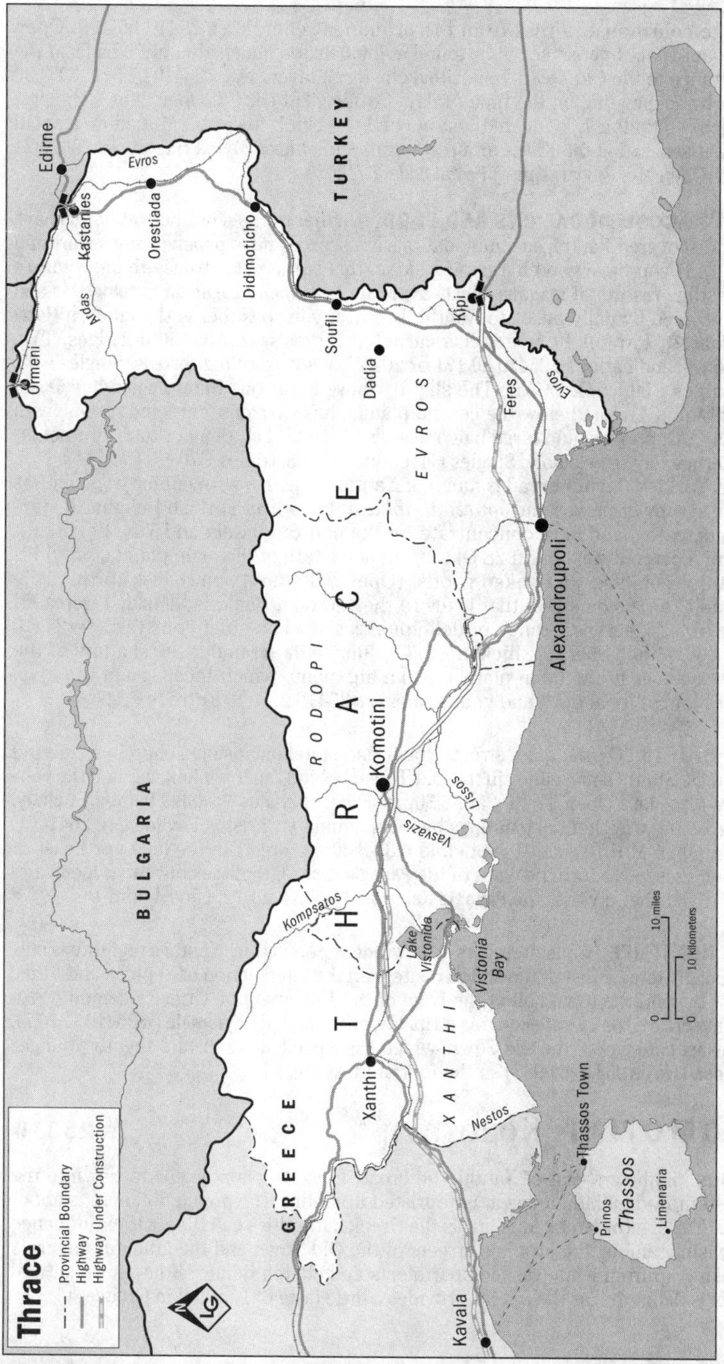

Thrace
Provincial Boundary
Highway
Highway Under Construction
BULGARIA
GREECE
TURKEY
THRACE
RODOPI
EVROS
XANTHI
Edirne
Kastanies
Orestiada
Didimoticho
Evros
Ardas
Ormeni
Soufli
Dadia
Kipi
Feres
Alexandroupoli
Komotini
Lissos
Vasvazis
Kompsatos
Lake Vistonida
Vistonia Bay
Xanthi
Nestos
Thassos Town
Thassos
Prinos
Limenaria
Kavala
0 10 miles
0 10 kilometers

large courthouse across from the prominent church. (☎25410 56 199. Open 7:30am-1pm.) **Internet** access is found at **InfoCafe,** on Maletsidou of Pl. Lada, at the entrance to the Old Town, opposite a cluster of tavernas. (☎25410 67 871. €1-2.20 per hr., depending on the time of day. Coffee €2; beer €3. Open 24hr.) The **post office,** Miltiadou 7, is located just beyond the clock tower on Miltiadou, a small street separating the Klimataria restaurant and Mikros Mylos Bakery. (☎25410 21 166. Open M-F 7:30am-2pm.) **Postal code:** 67100.

ACCOMMODATIONS AND FOOD. Neither tourists nor budget hotels have yet discovered Xanthi; accommodations are scarce and expensive (singles around €40). If you have good bargaining skills, this is the place to use them. Xanthi's coastline resorts of **Magana beach, Myrodato beach,** and **Lagos** have **campsites** and are served by daily buses to Xanthi. In town, your best bet is the modern **Hotel Orfeas ❸,** Karaoli 40, which has carpeted rooms with A/C, mini-fridges, TVs, phones, and baths. (☎25410 20 121 or 20 122; www.ixanthi.gr/orfeas. Singles €32; doubles €50; triples €58.) The slightly more luxurious **Hotel Democritus ❹,** 28 Oktovriou 41, just below the central plateia, has spacious, carpeted rooms, with TVs, A/C, phones, and large balconies. (☎25410 25 111; democritus@internet.gr. Internet access available. Singles €41; doubles €58; triples €70.)

A Turkish flavor pervades much of Xanthi's cuisine, with culinary specialties like syrupy *kariokes* and *soutzouk-lokum*, known as Turkish Delight. Restaurants, cafes, and bars concentrate on the central plateia and Vas. Konstantinou. A **covered market,** off 28 Oktovriou just south of the main plateia, provides fruit, vegetables, and baked goods. (Open daily until 3pm.) Just north of the plateia, on a side street that leads to the National Bank, is **Midos Taverna ❷,** Stavrou 18, serves a range of delicious classics in a quiet courtyard. (☎25410 77 060. Midos Special Chicken €5.30.) **Klimataria ❷,** under the shadow of the clock tower in the main plateia, has a big menu, which locals seem to enjoy, with lots of local pork and goat dishes. (☎25410 22 408. Entrees €3.50-7.)

SIGHTS. On the quiet streets you'll find stately mansions, churches, and old homes. Xanthi's museums, in the Old Town, behind the town hall, include the **Folklore Museum.** (Open Tu-Su 8am-2:30pm. Free.) **Christos Pavlides Painting Gallery,** across the way, houses paintings by local luminary Christos Pavlides. (☎25410 76 363. Open M-F 10:30am-1:30pm and 6:30-8:30pm. Free.) In the hills northeast of town, frescoes adorn the walls of the **Panagia Archangeliotissa** convent. (Open 7am-7pm.) Farther down is the **Panagia Kalamou.** (Open 8am-1pm and 4-8pm.)

NIGHTLIFE. Considering its large student population, Xanthi's nightlife is surprisingly tame. Most of the action centers on the intersection of Sophias and Idras, just beyond the town hall at the edge of the University of Thrace's campus. Students crowd the 12 cafes on this strip. Favorites include **Kyverneio** (☎25410 77 577), the last cafe before the Old Town, which has a packed porch, and slightly younger **Rodon Live** (☎25410 64 988), at the foot of Idras.

KOMOTINI Κομοτηνη ☎25310

Forty kilometers east of Xanthi, the broad Thracian plain begins to rise into the eastern Rodopi Mountains at untouristed Komotini. The population here is about 15% Turkish (or Greek Muslim, as the Greek authorities call them); their influence is visible among the crooked streets of the Old Town and the graceful minarets poking up from whitewashed apartments and church domes. Komotini's cultural mix is delightful, as the bazaar provides a little taste of Istanbul in Greece.

TRANSPORTATION. The town has an **OSE office,** Zoidou 50. (☎25310 26 804. Open M-F 8am-3pm.) Komotini's **train station** (☎25310 22 650) is at the far southwestern corner of the city, a 20min. walk from the city center. Standing on Orpheos, facing the main plateia, go right and keep walking as the street becomes Makedonias then Ipsilandou. At the railroad tracks, turn right on Kyprillou; it's seven more blocks to the station. **Trains** go to: **Athens** (regular: 12hr., 4:42pm, €22.30; express: 8½hr.; 9:20am, 9:45pm; €47.70); **Istanbul, Turkey** (10hr., 11:15am, €24.10); **Komotini** (45min.; 6 per day, 9:20am-2:10am; €1.50); **Thessaloniki** (regular: 3½hr.; 3 per day, 10:50am-2:10am; €8.20; express: 2½hr.; 9:20am, 7:35pm; €14.70). The **bus station,** G. Mameli 1 (☎25310 22 912 or 25310 26 111), is on the corner of Tsounta. **Buses** go to: **Alexandroupoli** (1hr.; 13 per day, 6am-8pm; €4.20); **Athens** (11hr.; 8:30am, 6:30pm; €45.40); **Kavala** (1½hr.; 8 per day, 5:30am-9:30pm; €6.50); **Thessaloniki** (4hr.; 7 per day, 5:30am-6:30pm; €15.80); **Xanthi** (45min.; 14 per day, 6:30am-8:30pm; €3.70). **Taxis** (☎25310 37 777 or 25310 32 223) are available 24hr. by the OTE, below Pl. Eirinis, or in front of Hotel Olympus on Orpheos.

ORIENTATION AND PRACTICAL INFORMATION. To get to the city center from the **bus station,** turn right from the bus station door and then left at the first intersection; follow this road all the way to the central plateia, **Pl. Eirinis. Orfeos** runs east-west directly above it and **Zoidi** runs east-west a few blocks below it. Across Orfeos from the plateia is the maze of pedestrian streets *(pezodromos)*, markets, and mosques that is the Turkish part of town. The open-air **bazaar** centers on **Ermou,** which runs from an elegant ashlar **mosque** in the west to another mosque, made to resemble a church, in the east. Following Orfeos east (to your right when facing away from Pl. Eirinis) takes you to **Pl. Vizinou,** with a large white obelisk and wooded city park. Here at the intersection of **Sismanoglou** and **Souzou** is the **town hall** *(Dimarhio)*. **Maps** and regional tourist pamphlets are available here as well as at the downstairs information office in the **Nomarhio** (district offices) on Dimokratias at the other side of the park (☎25310 22 858. Open 8am-8pm). Three blocks farther down Dimokratias by the prominent church is the **police station** (☎25310 83 205), which provides **free maps.** The **National Bank,** Thisauis 1, north of Pl. Eirinis at the east end of Orfeos, has a 24hr. **ATM.** (☎25310 54 901. Open M-Th 8am-2:30pm, F 8am-2pm.) There is a **Bank of Greece,** Ag. Georgiou 1, at the eastern end (closest to Pl. Vizinou) of Pl. Eirinis (☎25310 34045. Open M-Th 7:45am-3:15pm, F 7:45am-2:45pm). Underneath the bank is another **information office** and next door is a **supermarket. Laundry** is done in 2hr. at the corner of Zoidou and Ambelon. (€7.30 per load. Open 8am-2:30pm and 6-9:30pm.) The local **hospital** (☎25310 22 222 or 25310 24 601) is on Sismanoglou in the southeastern part of town; follow Georgiou east out of Pl. Eirinis. The **OTE** is on Parasiou, a side street of Pl. Eirinis opposite Orfeos and next to Hotel Orpheus. (☎25310 37 799. Open M-Th 7:30am-1:30pm, F 7:30am-1pm.) One block farther down is the **post office.** (☎25310 22 344. Open M-F 7:30am-2pm.) Find **Internet** access at **Easy Surf,** A. Souzou 8. (☎25310 70 111. €1-2.50 per hr., depending on time of day. Open 10am-3am.) **Postal code:** 69100.

ACCOMMODATIONS. Unlike nearby Xanthi, Komotini has some budget accommodations. Campers can save even more at the **EOT's campsite ❶** (☎25350 31 217), in the beach resort Fanariou. **Olympos Hotel ❸,** Orfeos 37, to your right when facing Pl. Eirinis from Orfeos, offers bright rooms with TVs, phones, fridges and A/C. (☎25310 37 690; holympos@otenet.gr. Shared bathrooms. Singles €26, with bath €35; doubles €33/€45; triples with bath €57. MC/V.) **Hotel Hellas ❷,** Dimokritou 31, is a building bereft of balconies on a large intersection just north of the Archaeological Museum. With Pl. Eirinis on your left follow Orfeos as it becomes Makedonias; pass its first intersection with Dimokritou, which bends back and re-intersects Makedonias three blocks farther along at the hotel. Find bare rooms with shared baths off hallways adorned with the artwork of the manager's wife. (☎25310 22 055. Singles €20; doubles €28; triples €32.) **Hotel Orpheus ❸,** Parassion 1, on Pl. Eirinis across from the OTE, has cheerful rooms with TVs, fridges, A/C, baths, and balconies. (☎25310 37 180; fax 25310 28 271. Breakfast €4. Singles €33; doubles €47; triples €53. AmEx/MC/V.)

FOOD. Dining centers on **Pl. Eirinis.** Excellent local fare abounds among the winding streets of the bazaar. Sweet shops display colorful cubes and long sausages of Turkish Delights; back alleys host Muslim eateries. One favorite, **Taverna Petrino ❸,** Serron 25, prevents any traffic traversing its vine-covered alley and side streets, filled with crimson tablecloths and lively conversation. Look for the crimson spilling out onto Ermou, the bazaar's main road. (☎25310 73 650. Open in summer only. Entrees €4.50-7.) **Restaurant Ydroxos ❷,** Papaflessa 2 (☎25310 33 786), on a side street connecting Orfeos to Pl. Eirinis, has tasty dishes and standard souvlaki and salads. Directly opposite Hotel Orpheus, the balcony tables at **Oinopion ❸** let you survey the plateia from a high point. The tasty menu includes meat dishes and salads. (☎25310 36 082. Entrees €7-13.50.)

SIGHTS. To reach Komotini's interesting **Archaeological Museum,** follow Zoidi westward and bear right onto the cement footpath at the park. Arranged in meticulous chronological order with helpful explanations in English, the museum's defensive exhibits focus on establishing the Hellenic heritage of Thrace. There are also a few early Thracian wall-paintings and some artifacts from what must have been a barren end-of-the-world Roman fortress at Nestos, whose often raided walls protected the Via Egnatia and port of Neapolis. Don't miss the golden bust of Emperor Septimius Severus and the carefully molded phallic altar. (☎25310 22 411. Open daily 8am-3pm. Free.) A 30min. taxi ride from Komotini brings you to the beaches of **Maronia** and **Fanari.** Maronia has a few archaeological sites.

ALEXANDROUPOLI Αλεξανδρουπολη ☎25510

Travelers often rush through Alexandroupoli on their way to Turkey, the Northeast Aegean Islands, and the hinterlands of northern Thrace. In the haste to get somewhere else, don't overlook the charms of Thrace's most bustling city. Rows of fashionable stores, cobblestone streets, and a lovely wooded waterfront make Alexandroupoli a pleasant pit-stop or comfortable enough place to get stranded.

TRANSPORTATION. Dimokritos Airport (☎25510 45 198), 6km east of town, flies to: **Athens** (1hr., 3 per day, €101); **Sitia,** Crete (2hr., 3 per week, €79); **Thessaloniki** (1hr., 3 per week, €65). Buy tickets at **Olympic Airways,** Ellis 6 and Koletti (☎25510 26 207); follow M. Alexandrou two blocks past the post office and take Ellis one block inland. The **train station** is about 400m east of the lighthouse along Alexandrou, in front of Pl. Eleftherias. (☎25510 26 395. Open daily 6am-10:30pm.) Three trains per day (9:45am, 3:38pm, 1am) go to **Thessaloniki** (6½hr., €9.70) via **Komotini** (1hr., €1.50) and **Xanthi** (1½hr., €2.70). One (3:38pm) continues to **Athens** (14hr., €23.80). Three Intercity (express) trains travel the same routes (8:22am, 6:37, 8:46pm) about 30% faster for twice the cost. Two continue to **Athens** (8:22am, 8:46pm). Trains run daily to **Istanbul, Turkey** (8hr., 12:15pm, €25). The **bus station** (☎25510 26 479) is at the corner of El. Venizelou and 14 Maiou, 500m from the docks, with service to: **Athens** (11hr., 6:15pm, €46.40); **Didimotiho** (1½hr.; 18 per day, 4:15am-8:45pm; €5.70) via **Soufli** (1hr., €4) and **Feres** (30min., €1.80); **Kipi** (45min.; 5 per day, 6:50am-7:30pm; €2.60); **Komotini**

(1hr.; 14 per day, 6:10am-8pm; €4.20); **Thessaloniki** (regular: 5hr.; 8 per day, 8am-10pm; express: 11am, 6:30pm; €20.50) via **Kavala** (2hr., €10.60) and **Xanthi** (1½hr., €7.40). There are two main **ferry** lines. **Saos,** on Kyprou, with ferries to **Samothraki** (2½hr.; 2-3 per day; €7.90, students €5.25), lies a few doors up from the waterfront. (☎25510 26 721 or 25510 23 512. Open M-Sa 8am-9:30pm, Su 8am-5:30pm.) **Kikon Tours,** Venizelou 68 (☎25510 25 455; open M-F 9am-2:30pm and 6:30-9:30pm, Sa 8:30am-2:30pm), sends a weekly ferry to: **Chios** (18hr., M noon, €24.40); **Kos** (14hr., M noon, €24.40); **Lesvos** (10hr., M noon, €18.60); **Rhodes** (24hr., M noon, €39) via **Limnos** (4hr., M noon, €13.30); **Samos** (20hr., M noon, €30). Saos also sends **Flying Dolphins** to **Samothraki** (1hr., 2-3 per day, €15.80). **Taxis** (☎25510 22 000 or 25510 27 700) are available 24hr.

ORIENTATION AND PRACTICAL INFORMATION. Everything the traveler needs or wants is within 10min. of the waterfront center, marked by a lighthouse. Standing at the lighthouse facing inland, the waterfront road, **Megalou Alexandrou,** stretches left to the row of cafes and right toward the **train station.** Halfway between the lighthouse and the train station, **Kyprou** leads inland to small, leafy **Pl. Kyprou.** The three main streets running parallel to Alexandrou (**L. Dimokratias, El. Venizelou,** and **Paleologou**) lie about three blocks inland, linked by a row of narrow cobblestone streets. The **tourist police,** Karaisaki 6, supply **maps** and tourist information. (☎25510 37 411. Open M-F 8am-2pm.) L. Dimokratias is one long string of banks with 24hr. **ATMs,** including an **Alpha Bank** (☎25510 25 742). The 24hr. **police** (☎25510 37 424) share a building with the tourist police, two blocks inland from the water, just before the lighthouse. There is a 24hr. **hospital,** Dimitras 19 (☎25510 74 000). **Planet Games,** Xarilaou Trikouri 2, supplies **Internet** access. Head west along Dimokratias until the road splits; take the left fork onto Trikouri. (☎25510 29 751. €3 per hr.) The **post office,** M. Alexandrou 42, is on the water 20m west of the lighthouse. (☎25510 23 122. Open M-F 7:30am-2pm.) **Postal code:** 68100.

ACCOMMODATIONS AND FOOD. Alexandroupoli offers lodgings in all price ranges. Inexpensive choices cluster near the bus and train stations. Call ahead, especially for weekend stays. **Hotel Lido ❷,** Paleologou 15, behind the bus station, has functional rooms. (☎25510 28 808. Singles €27, with bath €35; doubles €35/€43.) **Hotel Vergina ❷,** Karaoli 74, directly across the street from the train station, has 10 clean, well-furnished rooms, with showers, TVs, and phones. (☎25510 23 025. Singles €25; doubles €35; triples €60.) **Hotel Alex ❸,** Dimokratias 292, one block south of the bus station next to the town hall, has comfortable rooms with baths, balconies, TVs, phones, and ceiling fans. (☎25510 26 302; fax 25510 27 417. Singles €33; doubles €43; triples €48.) **Camping Alexandroupolis ❶,** 1km west of the town center on the water, is open all night. (☎25510 28 735. €4.40 per person, €3.20 per tent, €1.80 car. Electricity €2.60.)

Plenty of cheap fast food can be found on the waterfront and on Dimokratias, while a number of good seafood restaurants have tables along the shore. **Taverna Mylos ❸,** across from the post office (look for the windmill), has delicious fresh seafood, served to tables overlooking the Aegean. Plunge into the impressive ouzo and *tsipouro* selection. (☎25510 35 519. Entrees €3.50-12. Open until midnight.) **Neraida ❷,** Kyprou 5, diagonally across from I. Klimataria on Pl. Kyprou, is popular with locals. (☎25510 22 867. Octopus pasta €3.82. Entrees €3-7.50.) Patrons flock to **Methistaris ❸,** 5min. east of the lighthouse on the waterfront, for the impressive fish selection. (☎25510 82 645. Entrees €5-15.) The modest nightlife in Alexandroupoli centers almost exclusively around the waterfront, where the street closes to traffic and locals stroll past cafes.

SIGHTS. Alexandroupoli's **Ecclesiastic Art Museum** is housed within the Cathedral of Ag. Nikolaos, two blocks inland from the National Bank. An 18th-century icon of Jesus, with his legs forming a heart, is the highlight of a collection of icons and church frescoes. If you can, get an English-speaking priest to give you a tour. (☎25510 37 205. Open M-Sa 8am-1pm. Donation €1.)

DAYTRIPS FROM ALEXANDROUPOLI. The lush green expanse of the **Dadia Forest Reserve** lies 40km northeast of Alexandroupoli, covering 7300 hectares of thickly-wooded hills near the Turkish border. "Protected" in 1980, the forest serves as home and breeding ground for hundreds of endangered raptors. Of the 38 European species of these huge hunters, 36 are found only in Dadia. A well-maintained network of clearly marked hiking trails runs throughout the sanctuary. Blazes light the way along rugged ridges that break up the golden, untouristed Thracian plain. From the Ecotourist Center, a main trail leads up a hill to a bird hide, complete with free binoculars, where you can cringe as raptors, vultures, and other early birds catch worms in the valley. Follow the orange blazes uphill from the center for about an hour along the clearly-marked hike. The center also runs a frequent bus to the bird hide (10min., every 20min., €1.50). From the hide, trails extend in all directions, with most leading back to the center. To head straight back down to the center, take the trail marked with yellow blazes. (Take the bus from Alexandroupoli to Didimotiho; it stops in Soufli (1hr.; 18 per day, 4:15am-8:45pm; €3.85). From Soufli, catch the bus to Dadia. Get maps of the reserve at the Ecotourist Center, across from the bus stop. They rent mountain bikes. (☎25540 32 463. €3 per hr. Open June-Aug. daily 8:30am-8:30pm; Sept.-May 9am-7pm.)

Long before "diversity" became a sought-after attribute for companies, colleges, and network news shows, the city of Ioannina (p. 257) was a multicultural mix of nationalities and religions, and each made its mark within the confines of the kastro. The Turks who ruled Ioannina from 1430 to 1913 left behind two mosques-cum museums, and Greek Orthodox Christians still attend the chapel of the Agioi Anargyri. But there's another fascinating house of worship within the Kastro—the still-functioning Kahal Kadosh Yashan synagogue.

The current building, which dates back to the early 1800s, is a historic artifact of the vibrant Jewish community that was a substantial part of Ioannina's population before World War II. But it is also a spiritual center for the tiny group of Greek Jews who still live in Ioannina, and for the descendants of Ioanniote Jews in the diaspora.

A self-described "minority within a minority," the Jews of Ioannina are Romaniote Jews, a community that has existed in Greece since the first century AD. Legend holds that they were sent to Rome in slave ships after the destruction of the Second Temple in 70 AD, but a fateful storm forced them to land in Greece. Regardless of how they traveled, Romaniotes arrived in Greece over 2300 years ago, and many settled in the thriving commercial center of Ioannina. They communicated in Greek and hybrid Judeo-Greek, and preserved their unique culture and language even after tens of thousands of Judeo-Español-speaking Sephardic Jews, who were expelled from Spain and Sicily, arrived in Greece in the late 15th century.

By 1904 the Romaniotes in Ioannina had established two synagogues and a Jewish school, the Alliance Israelite Universelle. That year there were about 4000 Jews in Ioannina, but economic depression, the Greek war for independence in the region, and surges of anti-Semitic activity prompted many to emigrate to Palestine or to America. The number of Romaniotes had dwindled to 1950 by September 1943, when the city came under the control of the German forces.

Ioannina's Jews knew that 48,674 Jews from Thessaloniki had been deported between March and August 1943, but the occupying Germans assured Sabethai Cabilli, a prominent Romaniote businessman, that his community would not be harmed. Cabilli urged total cooperation with the Germans, only to realize his fatal error on the morning of March 25, 1944, when the Jews were rounded up for deportation, and he cried, "I have sinned." Upon arrival at Auschwitz, the elderly Cabilli was among the first group sent to the gas chambers.

Elsewhere in Greece, some Jews did manage to escape the Holocaust. The Greek Orthodox Archbishop Damaskinos and Evangelos Evert, the Chief of Police, issued false identity cards to Athenian Jews, saving two-thirds of the community. The 275 Jews on Zakynthos were unharmed after the Germans requested a list of Jews and the mayor and local bishop gave him only two names: their own.

But most Greek Jews were not so lucky: about 87% died in the Holocaust, with the number of Jews in Greece dwindling from 78,000 to about 10,000 after the war. Only 163 returned to Ioannina, many to homes inhabited by squatters. The returnees built an apartment building on the site of the dilapidated second synagogue. These apartments are now home to much of the surviving community, about 50 inhabitants.

Due to emigration and intermarriage, the number of Romaniotes in Ioannina continues to dwindle. But although it is a small community struggling to survive, it is also a far-reaching one. The Ioanniote Jews are working to refurbish and protect the Ioannina's Jewish cemetery and to turn the women's gallery of the Kahal Kadosh Yashan into a museum. Assisting them are the members of the only Romaniote synagogue and museum in the Western Hemisphere, the Kehila Kedosha Janina in New York (280 Broome St.; ☎212-431-1619; www.kehila-kedosha-janina.org). As Rose Eskononts, the president of the Sisterhood of the Kehila Kedosha Janina says, "We all think of Ioannina as our home."

To visit the cemetery or synagogue, contact the Jewish Community of Ioannina office (18B Josef Eliya St.; ☎26510 25 195). For more information, read *The Jews of Ioannina*, by Rae Dalven, or visit the Jewish Museum of Greeces.

Eleni N. Gage, a former Researcher-Writer and Editor of Let's Go: Greece and Turkey 1995, *is the author of* North of Ithaka, *a travel memoir about Northern Greece to be published by the Free Press in Spring 2004.*

SARONIC GULF ISLANDS

Τα Νησια του Σαρωνικου

When five million Athenians flee the city each summer in search of beaches and *pareia* (literally meaning a "posse of friends" but Greek for something like "food, folks, and fun"), they don't flee far. Many head to the Saronic Gulf Islands. This means two things: first, you've chosen a destination approved by discriminating Greeks; second, you're not the only one. Despite their geographic proximity, each of the gulf islands retains a distinct character: relaxed Spetses attracts Greek hipsters on summer weekends, artsy Hydra boasts pollutant-free streets, Poros holds hands with the mainland to the west, and Aegina retains shades of suburbia while catering to swarms of beach-hungry vacationers.

HIGHLIGHTS OF THE SARONIC GULF ISLANDS

BEHOLD the 360° view of Aegina's coastline from the 5th-century BC Temple of Aphaia (p. 324).

PUCKER UP after looking out over the thousands of lemon trees in Lemonodassos (p. 330), near Poros.

DON'T LOOK BOTH WAYS while crossing the street on vehicle-free Hydra (p. 331), but watch out for donkeys and bicycles as you wander through the art fairs.

REFRESH yourself with a slice of watermelon and a dip in the sea on Spetses's stunningly colorful Xylocheriza beach (p. 335).

AEGINA Αιγινα

Bright, white-washed Aegina is an easy daytrip for city-weary Athenians and summer weekends find the island saddled by the bustle of Greece's capital. Agia Marina, on the far side of the island from Aegina Town, boasts great beaches and wild nightlife. A pleasant drive through olive-terraced mountains leads to the massive Church of Agios Nektarios. The clean beaches of Marathonas, a quiet hamlet outside of Aegina Town, are ideal for a late-afternoon swim. The well-preserved remains of the Temple of Aphaia, a fascinating reminder of the island's ancient glory, stand high on the western coast.

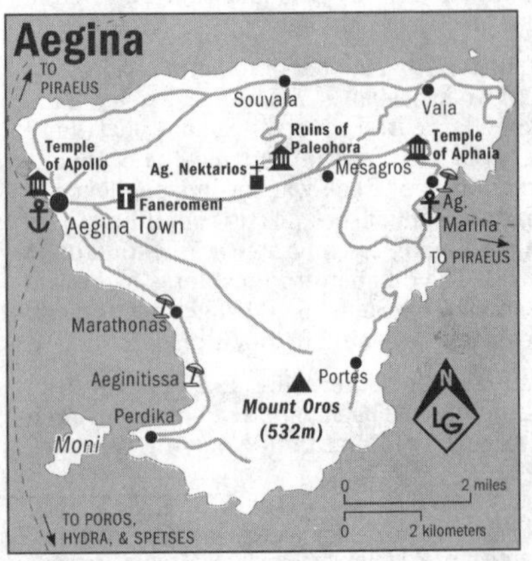

In ancient times, relations between Athens and Aegina were not so chummy, which might explain the zoo-like resort town that contemporary islanders have fashioned for their visitors from the north.

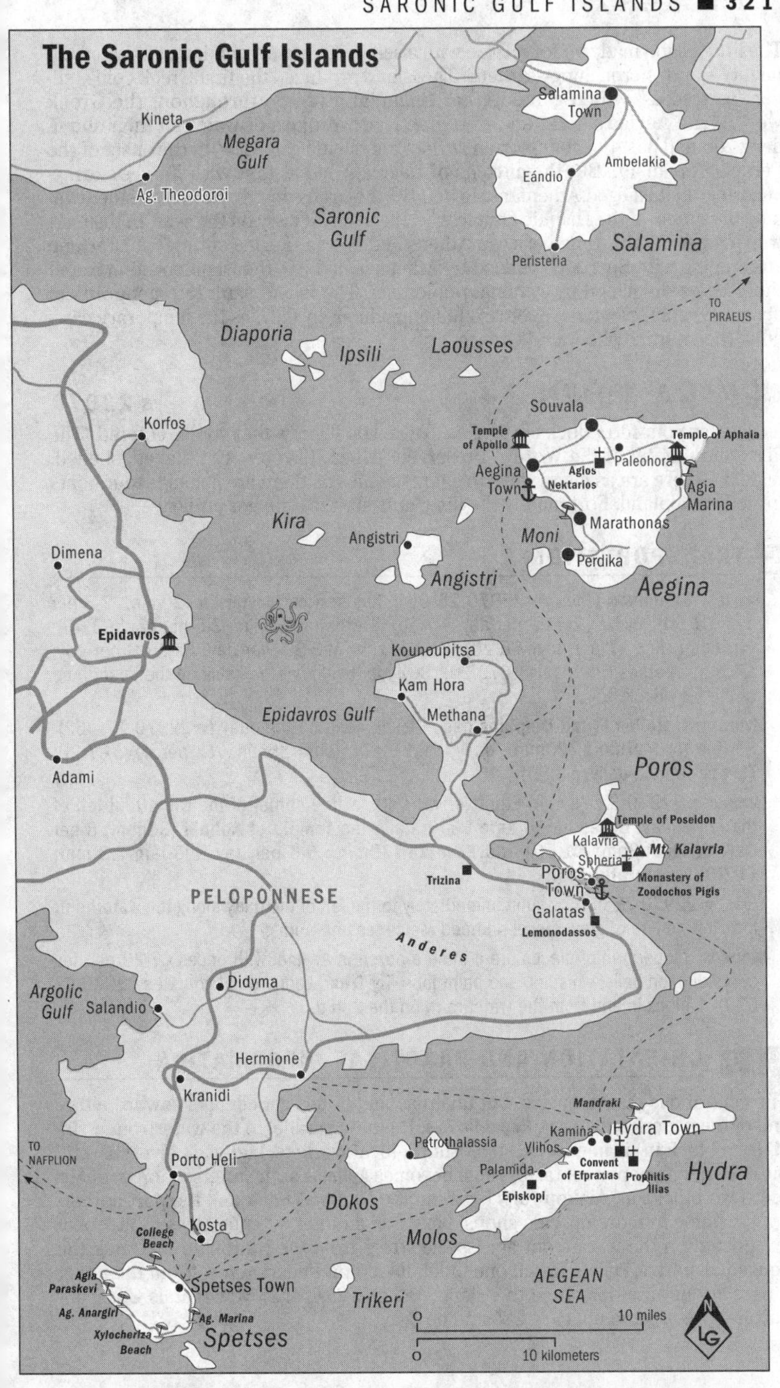

SARONIC GULF

The little island made up for its size with a self-determining spunk that irritated the mighty—and encroaching—Athens. The island produced the first Greek coins (silver "tortoises," which gained great financial leverage throughout the Greek world), and Aegina's sprinters, who practiced with jugs of water on their shoulders, zoomed past the competition at the Panhellenic games. With the onset of the Persian War in 491 BC, the citizens of Aegina sided at first with Xerxes's army, angering the besieged Athenians. In 480 BC they returned to the Greek side, winning the praise of the Delphic Oracle with the swiftest navy on the seas. In the next warring period, this time between Athens and Sparta, Aegina suffered misfortune after siding with Sparta. Trounced by Athens in 459 BC, the islanders soon found themselves displaced by Athenian colonists. The island sank into geopolitical obscurity, only to emerge over two millennia later, in 1827, as the temporary capital of then partially liberated Greece.

AEGINA TOWN ☎22970

As soon as your ferry docks in Aegina Town, you'll know that you've entered "The Pistachio Capital of the World." Preserved, jellied, flavored, red, flaked, shelled, regular—there are as many ways to eat pistachios as there are package tour boats from the mainland. Fortunately the tasty nuts are the stronger influence.

TRANSPORTATION

Ferries: Saronikos Lines (☎22970 25 951) has service to: **Agistri** (20min., 2-3 per day, €1.50); **Hydra** (2hr., 2 per day, €7.50); **Methana** (45min., 3-5 per day, €3.40); **Piraeus** (1hr., 11 per day, €5.20); **Poros** (1hr.; M-F 3-5 per day, Sa-Su 6 per day; €4.50); **Spetses** (3hr., daily, €10.20). Buy your tickets at the kiosk on the inland end of the ferry dock.

Hydrofoils: Hellas Flying Dolphins has a ticket stand on the quay (☎22970 27 462). Service to: **Methana** (20min., daily, €6.70); **Piraeus** (35min., 12 per day, €7.20; **Poros** (40min., daily, €8.80).

Buses: ☎22970 22 787. In Ethnegarcias Park, at the corner of the waterfront left of the ferry quay. Buses run to **Agia Marina** and the **Temple of Aphaia** (30min.; 8 per day, 6:30am-8pm; €1.50) and **Perdika** (20min.; 5-6 per day, 6:30am-7:30pm; €0.90) via **Marathonas.**

Taxis: ☎22970 22 635. Station immediately to the left of the quay along the waterfront; look for the line of grey, diesel-pumped Mercedes and Audis.

Mopeds: Moped rental places are a dime a dozen in Aegina, with prices €7-20 per day depending on bells, whistles, and paint jobs. Try **Trust,** Leonardou Lada 1 (☎22970 27 010), 1 block inland from the waterfront, on the 2nd fl.

ORIENTATION AND PRACTICAL INFORMATION

The central quay is expensive, but tavernas and hotels get cheaper toward either end of the waterfront street, **Republic Ave.** Running parallel to the waterfront, **P. Irioti** (one block in) is lined with small shops, local markets, laid-back tavernas, and the occasional moped rental. **Sp. Rodi** becomes **Aphaias** at the intersection with **Aiakou.** Two blocks in, Aiakou runs between the National Bank and the port authority. It's home to more upscale shops, bars, and an Internet cafe. **Maps** of the town are posted on the waterfront across the street from the National Bank. Ask the congenial staff at **Pipinis Travel,** one block inland on Kanari across from the ticket kiosks, for information about the island. (☎22970 25 664. Bicycle rentals €4.50 per day; mopeds €8 and up; cars €35 and up.)

Bank: National Bank (☎22970 26 930), to the right of the waterfront quay, past the port police. **Currency exchange** and 24hr. **ATM.** Open M-Th 8am-2pm, F 8am-1:30pm.

Police: ☎22970 22 100.

Tourist Police: Leonardou Lada 11 (☎22970 27 777). Open daily 8am-8pm. Tourist and regular police are in the same courtyard.

Port Authority: ☎22970 22 328. On the waterfront. Ferry schedules. Open 24hr.

Pharmacy: There are 3 along Aiakou. Open at 7:30am and 1 stays open until midnight on a rotating basis.

Medical Center: ☎22970 22 222. 2km along the waterfront to the left of the ferries. Call the tourist police and they will arrange transport or refer you to doctors in town.

OTE: Paleas Choras 6 (☎22970 22 399; dial 161 for assistance), up Aiakou to the right. Open M-Th 7:30am-1:30pm, F 7:30am-1pm.

Internet access: Nesant Internet Cafe, Aphaias 13 (☎22970 24 053). €6 per hr. Open daily 9am-11pm. Your other option is **Prestige Internet Cafe,** at Sp. Rodi and Aiakou. €6 per hr. Open 10am-3am.

Post Office: Kanari 6 (☎22970 22 398), in Pl. Ethnegersias, behind the bus station. Express Mail Hellenic Post and **Poste Restante** available. Open M-F 7:30am-2pm. **Postal code:** 18010.

ACCOMMODATIONS

Rooms here are cheaper than those on any of the other Saronic Gulf islands. In the high season, doubles go for around €25-40. **Domatia** owners often meet the ferries, but always bargain and discuss location before committing.

Hotel Avra (☎22970 22 303; fax 22970 23 917), at the far left end of the waterfront. Typical rooms have A/C, TVs, phones, and baths. Singles €45; doubles €60. ❸

Hotel Artemis (☎22970 25 195; fax 22970 28 779), set back to the left of the post office, away from the waterfront. Rooms with A/C, private bath; some with balconies. Settle your bill the night before if you're catching a pre-10am boat. Continental breakfast €4.50. Singles €30; doubles €45. Discount for stays over 10 days. ❸

Hotel Plaza, Kazatzaki 4 (☎22970 28 404; plazainaegina@yahoo.co.uk), at the far left end of the waterfront. Rooms are modestly furnished and cheap. They vary in price according to amenities (A/C, TV, balcony). Singles €25-45; doubles €28-50. ❷

Hotel Pavlou, Aeginitou 21 (☎22970 22 795), behind the church on the far right of the quay. Come for the stylish 70s decor and comfortable rooms with balconies overlooking the town church. Some rooms with private bath. Payment required in advance. Owners also run the **Athina,** quietly tucked back 200m into the town on Telemonos, which features charmingly decorated rooms with private baths and fridges. Singles €35; doubles €40-47; triples €50. Discounts for stays of multiple days. ❸

FOOD AND NIGHTLIFE

No-frills tavernas line P. Irioti, which runs parallel to the waterfront one block inland along the right side of the harbor. For make-your-own meals, try the **supermarkets** on P. Irioti. In an alley to the left, after a short walk up Aikaou, **To Patitiri** ❷, serves marvelous, fresh Greek meals in a bougainvillea-filled courtyard. (☎22970 51 520. Entrees €4.50-8.50. Open 6pm-midnight.) If you can't eat another souvlaki, walk upstairs to the **Panagakis Cafe Bar/Crêperie** ❷, on the waterfront. Fillings range from ice cream and strawberries to cold cuts and mayo. (Crepes €4.70-9. Cocktails €6.80.) Just down from the Nesant Internet cafe, **Leo Confections** ❶, Aphaias 48, serves ice cream (€1 per scoop) and other mouthwatering desserts. (Open daily 8am-11pm.) **Zachastiki Bakery ❶,** at the intersection of Aphaias and Telemonos, will lure you in with the scent of fresh bread (€0.50), large croissants (€0.75), and a multitude of cookies (€5.50 per kg).

For a low-key evening, watch American movies outdoors at **Anesis,** to the right off Aiakou, 100m from the waterfront, or **Olympia,** to the far right of the waterfront, just before the athletic complex. Both have shows (€7) nightly at 9 and 11pm. Get your groove on at Aegina's dance club, **Ellinikon,** a 10min. walk along the water to the right. (www.ellinikon.net. Beer €4-5; cocktails €6-7. Cover €6, includes 1 drink. Open daily 10:30pm-late.) The bar **Inn on the Beach,** just before Ellinikon, gets going on summer weekends. (☎22970 26 440. Cover €3, includes 1 beer.)

SIGHTS

Aegina Town's archaeological fame teeters on the last half-column of the **Temple of Apollo.** The 8m-tall Doric column dates to 460 BC and stands on Kolonna Hill, ancient Aegina's acropolis. Archaeology enthusiasts will delight in seeing the ongoing excavation of the site, now known to have been an important settlement since the Early Bronze Age (3000 BC). Today Byzantine-Era cisterns and the foundations of prehistoric houses keep mute vigil with the monolithic column. The site's **archaeological museum** features a magnificent early Classical sphinx (460 BC), artifacts from the Temple of Aphaia, a statue of Hercules from the Temple of Apollo, and some Neolithic pottery. (☎22970 22 248. Museum and site open Tu-Su 8:30am-3pm. €3.) The underground church of **Faneromeni,** a 15min. walk inland just south of the town, houses a rare icon of the Virgin Mary. Locals say that the night before construction was to begin on a site above Faneromeni, the architect had a vision in which he was instructed to dig instead of build. Doing just that, he discovered the church and unearthed the icon.

DAYTRIPS FROM AEGINA TOWN

MARATHONAS

7km south of Aegina Town.

Tranquil beaches reverberate with the murmur of the Aegean in unassuming **Marathonas.** Approaching the town on the main road, veer right onto the unpaved road after the first stand of umbrellas to reach the peaceful beachfront, which is lined with small tavernas and pebble beaches. **Cafe Ostria ❶** serves specialty *melizano* (eggplant) salads and calamari; juicy slices of watermelon (€1.50) accompany the perfect Aegean sunsets nicely. (☎22970 26 738. Entrees €4-6.) Family-owned **O Tassos ❶,** accessible from the main road just before the church, is renowned for its homemade pastries, pita creations, and fresh vegetables from the family farm. (☎22970 24 040. Entrees €3-6.)

TEMPLE OF APHAIA

A small museum opens for 15min. periods at 9, 11am, noon, and 1pm. The Agia Marina bus from Aegina Town stops in front. Open M-F 8:15am-7pm.

The fifth-century BC remains of the Temple of Aphaia rest 2km uphill from Agia Marina. Legend holds that Aphaia, daughter of Zeus and Karme, fled to Aegina from the amorous overtures of King Minos. There she became invisible. Her temple, built on the foundation of a 6th-century BC temple, boasts a spectacular set of standing double-tiered columns. At night, peacocks roam the hills by the temple.

AGIOS NEKTARIOS

A 15min. bus ride from Aegina Town; ask to be let off at Agios Nektarios. Modest dress required; no bare shoulders.

The bronze and white church of Agios Nektarios is one of the largest places of worship in the Balkans. It's part of a complex that includes a monastery and the Orthodox saint's personal residence. There are several English language publications (€5-25) available in the **bookshop** that will let you read up on the details of Nektarios's life. The turn-off just after Agios Nektarios leads up to **Paleohora** (about 1km), the "town of 300 churches," where locals once took refuge from pirate invasions. It's worth making the short climb to explore the 15 churches that remain and take in the spectacular view from the top of the hill.

AGIA MARINA

A 30min. bus ride from Aegina Town through the island's lovely interior.

If you find yourself inexplicably yearning to see hordes of sunburned tourists, overpriced beach toys, and tacky towels, then swing by Agia Marina. This summer resort town offers some quality nightlife along with pleasant, sandy, albeit often crowded, beaches. The town is built around a main avenue, called **Aphaias,** parallel to the sea. It's lined with bars, tourist shops, and moped rentals. A multitude of hotels surround the port. Most are open only in the summer. **Internet** access is available from 7pm-midnight at **The Bell Inn Bar** on Aphaias. (☎22970 32 049. €6 per hr.) **Hotel Myrmidon ❷,** off Aphaias, sports a courtyard with a swimming pool and a lovely footbridge. The rooms have A/C, private baths, and fridges, and *Let's Go* readers enjoy a 20% discount. (☎22970 32 691; fax 22970 32 558. Singles €20; doubles €35; triples €45.) Buy **bus tickets** at the kiosk in the plateia where the bus lets off. Pricey water's-edge restaurants crammed with tourists mingle with gyro and fast-food shops along Aphaias. **Restaurant Paradise ❷,** along the beach, affords a great view of the water underneath a cool canopy of trees. Try the spaghetti bolognese (€4.50). A **supermarket** on Aphaias offers an alternative to eating out. You can rent paddle boats at the beach (€8 per hr.), but consider saving your money to buy drinks at **Crystal,** located 200m out of town, keeping the water on your left. This "snack bar" opened in August 2002 and features a gorgeous swimming pool, pool tables, and two outdoor patios. (☎22970 32 170. Open 10am-5am. Cocktails €3-6.) Trendy **Zorba's Castle** is a popular disco close to the waterfront; take a right on Praxitelous two blocks past the bus stop, then follow the signs. (Opens daily 11pm.) Summer dance club **Manos** lies across the street from Crystal.

POROS Πορος

Poros is actually two islands separated by a shallow channel: Sphaeria hugs the Peloponnesian mainland and is covered by the sprawl of tourist-heavy Poros Town, while Kalavria preserves stretches of woods and dark-watered beaches. The name Poros ("passage") refers to the channel separating it from the Peloponnese. In the 6th century BC, the Kalavrian League met in Poros to ward off hostile naval powers and ordered the construction of the Temple of Poseidon. The great orator Demosthenes, who improved his diction by speaking with marbles in his mouth, committed suicide beside its columns. Poros was sparsely populated until Greek refugees arrived from the newly created Turkey in the 1920s.

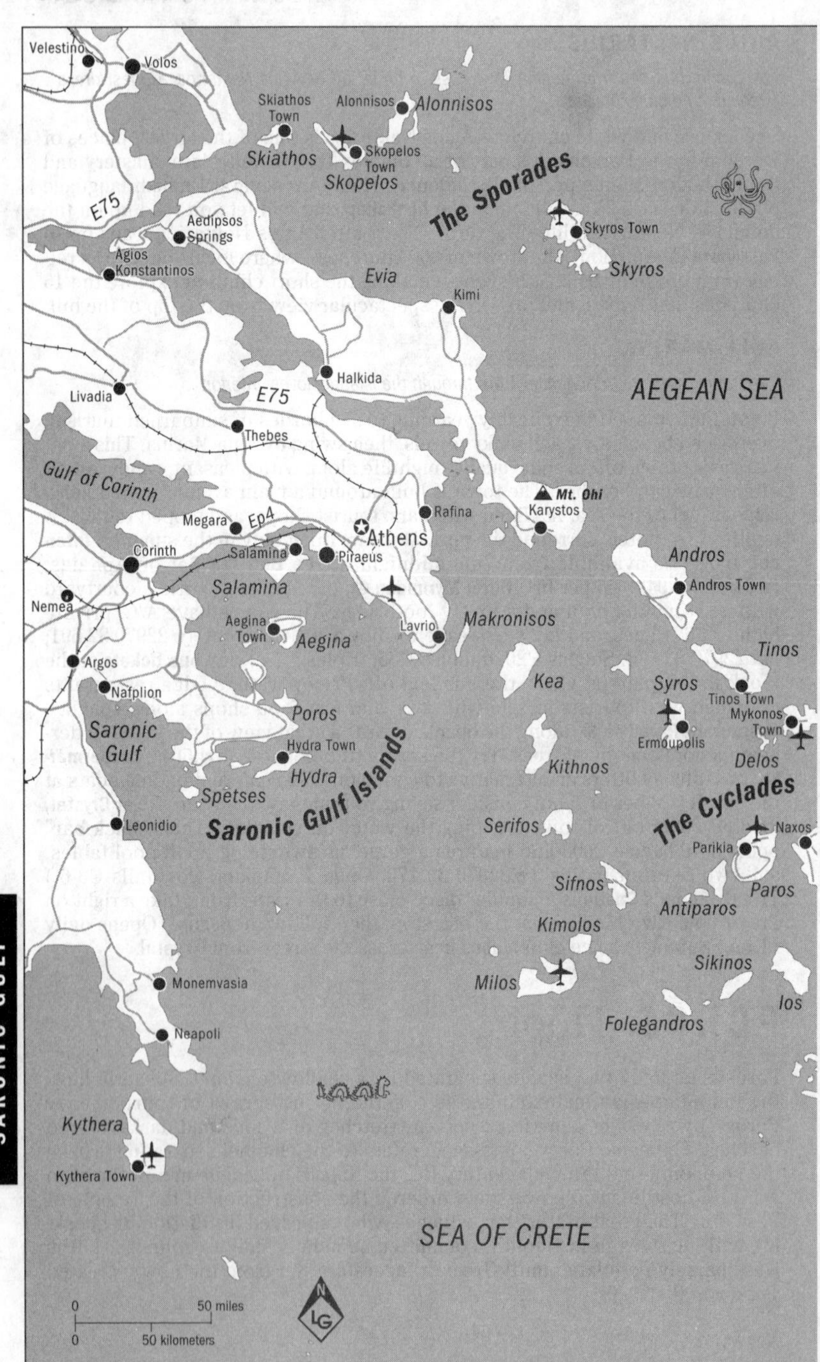

SARONIC GULF

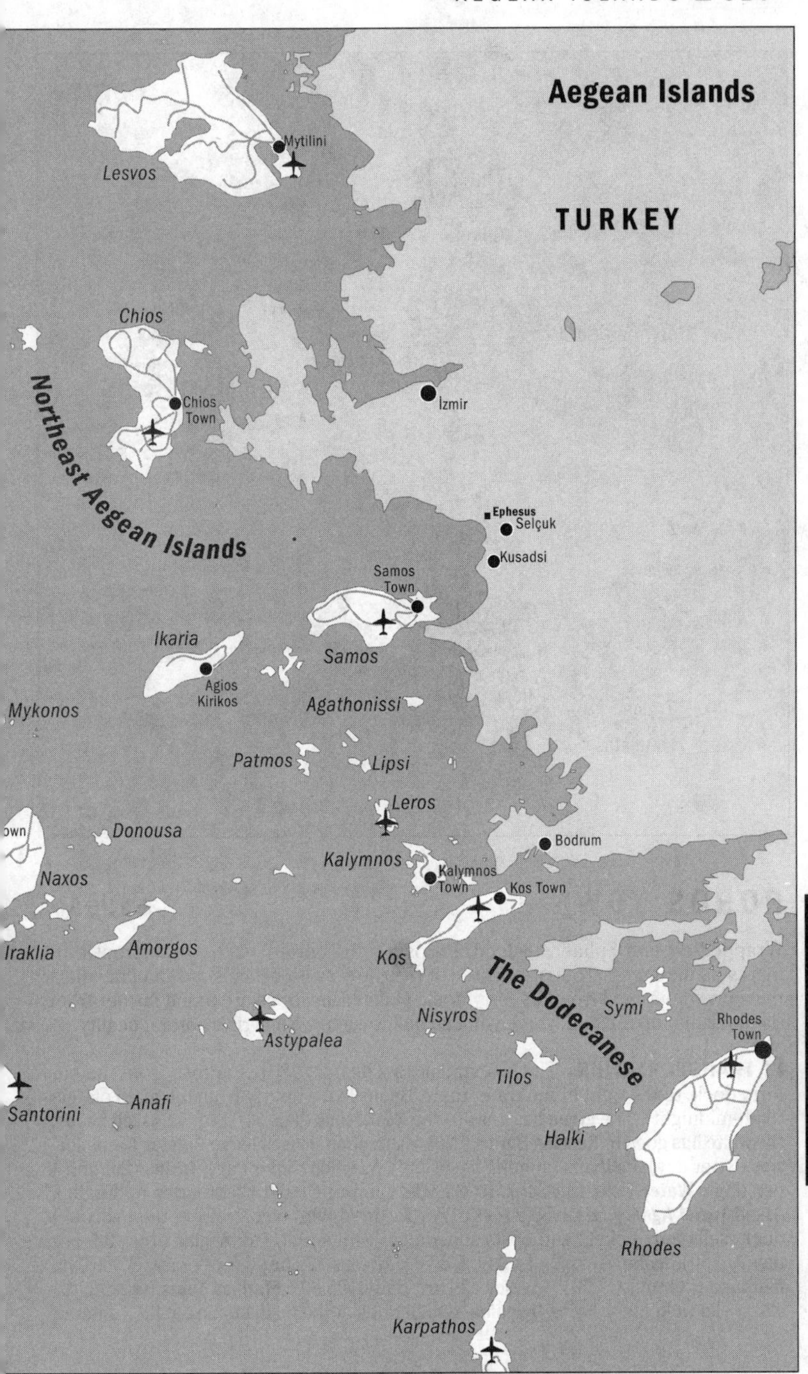
Aegean Islands
TURKEY
Mytilini
Lesvos
Chios
Chios Town
Northeast Aegean Islands
İzmir
Ephesus
Selçuk
Kusadsi
Samos Town
Samos
Ikaria
Agios Kirikos
Mykonos
Agathonissi
Patmos
Lipsi
Leros
Donousa
Kalymnos
Kalymnos Town
Bodrum
Kos Town
Naxos
Iraklia
Amorgos
Kos
The Dodecanese
Symi
Nisyros
Rhodes Town
Astypalea
Tilos
Santorini
Anafi
Halki
Rhodes
Karpathos

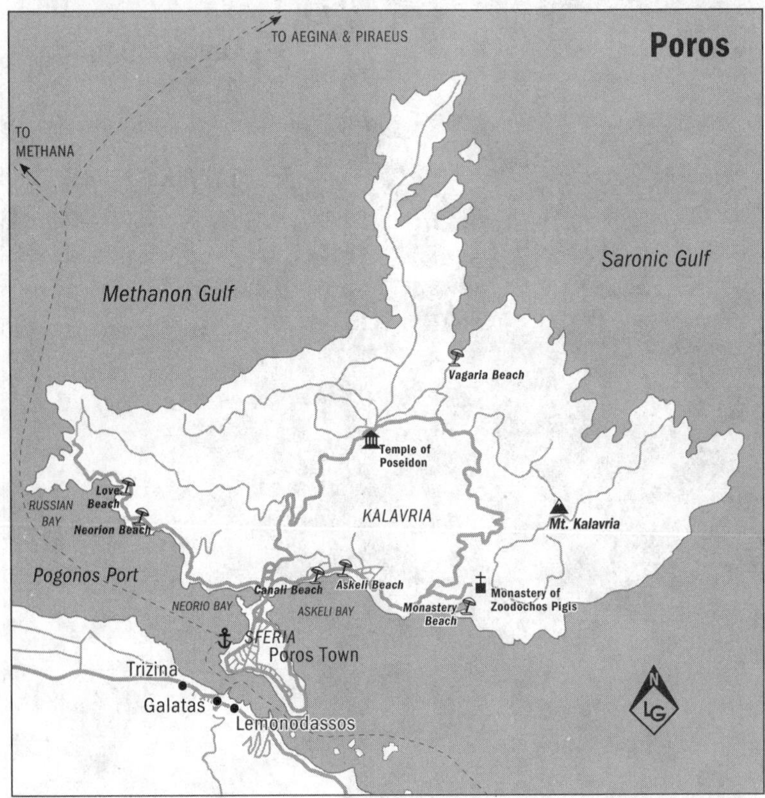

POROS TOWN ☎22980

Wrapped around Sphaeria island, Poros Town centers on the waterfront that marks its perimeter. Tourist-oriented, it overflows with beach shops and tavernas that sprawl outward from the ferry dock. Quieter locations are found farther from the dock and up the hill, where you can acknowledge Kalavria's natural beauty.

TRANSPORTATION. The **bus station** (☎22980 22 480) is across from the car ferry dock, to the right of the water taxis. Buses leave hourly from the main plateia (8am-midnight). The **green bus** goes to the **Zoodochos Pigis** (€0.90) via **Askeli beach;** the **white bus** goes to **Russian Bay** (€0.70) via **Neorion.** Buses leave **Galatas** for: **Epidavros** (3 per day); **Methana** (45min., 5 per day); **Nafplion** (3 per day); **Trizina** (20min., 4 per day). **Water Taxis** run 24hr. to **Galatas** (2min.; €0.50, €0.80 after midnight). **Askeli Travel Agency** (☎22980 24 900, 24 767, or 24 566), across from the hydrofoil dock, sells **ferry** tickets and posts schedules, with service to: **Aegina** (1hr., 3-5 per day, €4.50); **Hydra** (1hr., 2 per day, €3.70); **Piraeus** (2½hr., 3-5 per day, €7.50) via **Methana** (30min., €2.50); **Spetses** (2½hr., daily, €5.80). **Marinos Tours** (☎22980 24 423) sells tickets for **Flying Dolphins,** which dock at the main landing in the center of town and go to: **Hermione** (1hr., 3-5 per day, €9.10); **Hydra** (30min., 6-7 per day, €6); **Piraeus** (1¼hr., 8 per day, €13.80); **Portoheli** (1½hr., 1-2 per day, €11.50); **Spetses** (1hr., 2-3 per day, €10.80). Left of the main ferry docks, about 300m down the waterfront, **car ferries** go to **Poros-Galatas** (every 30min., 7am-11pm; €3.70 per car). The 24hr. **port authority** (☎22980 22 274) is one street in from the harbor by Seven Brothers. Go up the stairs and down a long hallway. **Kosta's Bike Rental,** rents mopeds (€7-12 per day) and bikes (€2.50), to the left of the waterfront past Diana Cinema. (☎22980 23 565. Open daily 9am-9pm.) **Taxis** (☎22980 23 003) wait on the waterfront to the right of the ferry landing, facing inland.

ORIENTATION AND PRACTICAL INFORMATION. Ferries and hydrofoils dock in the center of the waterfront, which traces around the edge of the small island; the main plateia is to the right facing inland. **Galatas,** across the strait, has cheaper food and lodgings. The **Alpha Bank,** in the plateia to the right before the port police, has a 24hr. **ATM.** (Open M-Th 8am-2:30pm, F 8am-2pm.) **Suzi's Launderette Service,** left of the dock in an alley just past International Press does wash and dry for €10. (Ironing extra. Drop-off only. 2hr. service. Open July-Aug. M-Sa 9am-2pm and 5-9pm; Sept.-June M-Sa 9am-2pm.) From the post office in the main plateia turn right and head up the stairs to the left of Igloo Ice Cream. Turn right at the church and continue downhill past Platanos Taverna to reach the **police** (☎22980 22 256). The **tourist police** (☎22980 22 462) are in the same building. There is a **pharmacy** across from the ferry dock. (☎22980 25 523. Open daily 8:30am-2pm and 5-10pm.) The **OTE,** on the waterfront left of the main landing, sells telecards and telegrams. (☎22980 22 199 or 22 399. Open M-F 7:30am-3pm.) **Webworld Internet Cafe,** above Coconuts Bar, is in the plateia to the right of the ferry dock. (€6 per hr., €1.50 min. Open daily 10:30am-3pm and 6:30-11pm.) **International Press,** left of ferry dock, also has access. (€6 per hr., €1.50 min. Open 8:30am-11pm.) **Galatas clinic** (☎22980 22 222) is open 24hr. Emergencies including minor surgery can be handled at the **Naval School;** contact the tourist police. The **post office,** in the first plateia to the right along the water. Specify Poros Trinzinias for **Poste Restante.** (☎22980 22 275; fax 22980 23 451. Open M-F 7:30am-2pm.) **Postal code:** 18020.

ACCOMMODATIONS AND FOOD. The best deals in Poros Town are the **domatia** advertised in almost every window; expect to pay €20-30. There's no pressing reason to stay in Poros Town, as **Galatas,** 2min. across the strait by boat (every 10-15min., 24hr.; €0.50), has similar, less expensive hotel rooms. **Hotel Seven Brothers ❸,** to the right of the ferry dock and inland past the Alpha Bank, provides one of the better deals for a portside hotel. Rooms come equipped with private baths, TVs, and A/C. (☎22980 23 412; fax 22980 23 413. Singles €40; doubles €50. Discounts for longer stays.) Across from the water taxi landing in Galatas, **Saronis Hotel ❸** has simple rooms with A/C, TVs, and private baths. (☎22980 22 356; fax 22980 25 642. Doubles €30.) To find **Manos Pension ❷** in Galatas, walk left when you debark the small boat from Poros Town and go just past the playing field. Friendly Manos and Beatrix can rent you motorbikes and tell you all about the region, and cozy rooms will make you feel at home. (☎/fax 22980 22 000 or 697 708 0791. Singles €20-22; doubles €24-26; triples €30-32.)

Similar restaurants line the harbor and "charming" waiters try to coax tourists to sit down; make your choice based on the view. Several grocery stores and produce markets cluster along the waterfront to the right of the dock. Cafes are open all day; more hard-core places open at 10:30pm. **Bobby's Taverna ❷** (Ο Μπαμπης), in Galatas to the right of the water taxis (facing inland), across from the ATM, is the place for fresh seafood. (☎22980 23 629. Seafood dishes €5 and up. Grilled dishes €4-7.) **Igloo Ice Cream ❶** is around the corner to the right of the post office. (☎22980 25 515. Ice cream €1.40 per scoop. Crepes €2.20 and up.) **Colona ❶,** just down the waterfront to the right of the dock, meets all your fast-food needs. (☎22980 22 366. Gyro €1.35). **Taverna Poros ❷,** across from the water taxi dock, is one of the more relaxed waterfront spots. (☎22980 25 267. Entrees €6 and up.)

SIGHTS AND ENTERTAINMENT. The **Archaeological Museum,** in the middle of the waterfront, has some interesting inscriptions and photographs of the ruins at Trizina in the Peloponnese; very little of the collection is actually from Poros. (☎22980 23 276. Open Tu-Su 8:30am-3pm. Free.) For a pretty view of the harbor, climb the **clock tower.** The stairs are next to the library, one block inland. The 18th-century **Monastery of Zoodochos Pigis** (Virgin of the Life-Giving Spring) is sequestered in an overgrown glade 6km from Poros Town. Monks have been drinking blessed curative waters here since 200 BC. The monastery once served as a meeting place for Greek naval leaders Miaoulis, Jobazis, and Apostolis, who strategized the uprising of 1821. Before hopping on the bus back, stop for delicious ice cream (€1.30 per scoop) at **Samali's ❶,** opposite the monastic complex. If you're curious, ask nicely about the tiny church next door. Between the cafe and the small church is a fountain from the **life-giving spring,** so fill up your water bottle and be invigorated. To get to the monastery, take the 20min. green bus (€0.90) from the stop next to the main port; it runs hourly 7am-11pm. (Open sunrise to sunset but closed 2-4:30pm in summer. Modest dress required.) If you bear left instead of right at the fork in the road before the monastery, you can find the 6th-century BC **Temple of Poseidon** (take a moped–it's a few kilometers). The ruins may be best appreciated by Greek history buffs, but the view will inspire all.

Not much of a party town, Poros has several options for a night out. Check billings by the bus station for **Diana open-air cinema,** to the left of Lela Tours, where you can see American movies (9 and 11pm; €6, children €4). Fashionable locals and tourists alike head to the waterfront for late-night fun; **Malibu** dominates the scene. (☎22980 25 267. Drinks €5-7.) Clubs are farther from town; two popular places to satisfy your dance music cravings are **Sirocco,** a short cab ride to the southern point of Sphaeria on the waterfront road, and **Illusions,** in the Askeli area.

BEACHES AND THE OUTDOORS. The white bus line runs hourly along the shore to **Russian Bay,** where Russian ships once docked to aid the Greek rebellion. Along the way are **Neorion,** featuring a sand beach, tavernas, and a watersports center, and the secluded blue-green waters and rocky sands of local favorite, **Love beach.** The tiny island near the beach was an undercover school during the Turkish occupation, when Greeks were denied education. Ironically, it's now a sunning rock for playing hookey. On the way to the monastery, the green bus passes crowded **Askeli beach,** which has tavernas, shops, and watersports.

If you look across a thin strait to the Peloponnesian mainland from Poros, you'll spy **Galatas** (Γαλατας), a working village with a grittier feel than tourist-frequented Poros. Surrounded by beautiful farmland and cut with flat, well-paved roads, Galatas is great for bike riding (rent them at Manos Moto) and there are a few gems waiting to be uncovered. If you follow the road heading left (facing inland from the ferry dock) about 3km out of town, you'll reach the enormous lemon grove of **Lemonodassos** ("lemon forest"). Follow the signs to **Kardassi Taverna** (☎22980 23 100), taking the first turn-off if you are in a car or moped, and the second if on foot, to get a glass of the freshest **lemonade** (€1.50) and a view of 38,000 lemon trees. If you follow the road heading left (facing inland from the ferry dock) about 15km out of town you'll reach **Artemis,** where the ruins of a temple to the goddess are visible underwater. Fifteen kilometers from Galatas lies **Trizina,** mythical home to the hero **Theseus.** Take a bus (20min., 3 per day) or a taxi (about €7—tell the driver where you're going and he'll take you a bit closer than where the bus lets off) from Galatas and follow the signs up the hill out of town. Meager ruins have been unearthed near the town, but of far more interest is the lovely **Devil's Bridge,** so named for the cloven hoof footprint found in one of the rocks at the gorge's base. The shady, verdant area is a pleasant change of scenery from the scrubby growth of the islands. The rushing water and cool mountain pools take the edge off the heat. Head uphill from the bus stop in the center of town and go right, following the paved road past olive trees and fragrant citrus groves. At the fork in the road, follow the dirt path heading left and uphill (right and downhill will take you to the ruins), passing the ancient **Tower of Diateichisma.** At the next fork, go right. Stay on the worn path (though you'll have trouble believing you weren't the first person to discover this magical place) and climb down to the bottom. Ropes guide the way at the steepest points. Sturdy footwear is advisable.

HYDRA Υδρα

Even bicycles are illegal on Hydra (EE-dthrah)—the steep, scaling streets only accommodate pedestrians, donkeys, and three garbage trucks—making the island both smog- and screech-free. Despite its aqua-inspired name, Hydra's land has always been too arid for prosperous agriculture, so the islanders turned to managing foreign exports. The impressive Venetian-built mansions of the merchants of Hydra's past dot the hills behind the harbor. During Ottoman rule, the Hydriots made a deal in return for the island's freedom, providing the Turkish navy with the service of 30 young men every year. Hydriot youth thus learned the art of naval battle, a perk when, in 1821, Admiral Miaoulis and the Hydriot elite dedicated their fleet to the fledgling Greek revolution. Pride in this military courage persists today; the main thoroughfare is named for Miaoulis. George Koundouriotis was one of the many Hydriot leaders in the Greek War of Independence; his grandson, Pavlos Koundouriotis, became the President of Greece in the 1920s.

HYDRA TOWN ☎22980

The sometimes baffling, cobbled streets of Hydra Town twist up the island's parched hills as they rise from the rich blues of the sea. Donkeys and wheelbarrow-pushing fruit vendors share the quiet alleys while the port below bustles with art students and smiling tourists during the summer months. As gorgeous as the summers are, the pink-blossomed spring and salt-winded fall give the town a low season like no other. Outside Hydra Town, the island's main settlement, hidden beaches are yours for the price of a sea taxi.

TRANSPORTATION

Ferries: Saronikos Ferries (☎22980 54 007). Ticket office upstairs in the building with the gray door across from the ferry dock. Open daily 9:30am-6:30pm. 2 ferries per day to: **Aegina** (2¼hr., €7.20); **Methana** (1½hr., €5); **Piraeus** (3¼hr., €7.80) via **Poros** (1hr., €3.40); **Spetses** (1hr., daily, €3.90).

Flying Dolphins: ☎22980 53 813. Ticket office located on the same floor in the same building as Saronikos Ferries. Open daily 6:30am-6:30pm and 8:30-10:30pm. To: **Hermione** (30min., 3 per day, €6.60); **Piraeus** (1½hr., up to 12 per day, €16.70); **Poros** (30min., 5 per day, €7.30); **Portoheli** (45min., 4-5 per day, €10.20); **Spetses** (30min., 8 per day, €8.50).

Water Taxis: ☎22980 53 690. Brightly colored motorboats parked by the mule stand in the southeastern corner of the harbor. Priced per boat (not per person), reflecting length of journey. Service to: **Agios Georgios** (€36); **Agios Nikolaos** (€45); **daytrip** around the island with beach stops (€98); **Hydra beach** (€45); **Kamina** (€6.80); **Mandraki beach** (€9.80); **Metohi** (€21); **Palamidas** (€14); **Vlihos** (€9.80).

ORIENTATION AND PRACTICAL INFORMATION

The buildings of Hydra Town form an amphitheater around its famously picturesque harbor with its opening facing north. Yachts and fishing boats bob in the center, accompanied by water taxis in the southeastern corner. Ferries and Flying Dolphins dock on the eastern edge of the harbor. Jewelry and tourist boutiques share harbor front space with pricey restaurants, bars, and cafes. **Tombazi,** in the southeastern corner of the harbor, runs inland past the Internet cafe and several restaurants. **Miaouli** runs inland from the center of the harbor and **Votsi,** in the southwestern corner beyond the clock tower, runs inland past the OTE, police, and medical center; you'll rarely hear locals call these alleys by name.

Bank: National Bank (☎22980 53 233), on the waterfront. 24hr. **ATM.** Open M-Th 8am-2pm, F 8am-1:30pm.

Laundromat: Yachting Center, in the southwestern corner of the harbor, has laundry service upstairs. Wash, dry, and fold up to 4kg for €12. Showers also available (€4). Open daily 8am-noon and 5-9pm.

Tourist Police: ☎22980 52 205. Follow the street to the right of the clock tower inland and turn left at the fork. Look for the coat of arms, opposite the OTE. Open 24hr.

Port Police: ☎22980 52 279. Upstairs in the big gray building flying the Greek nautical flag, in the northwestern corner of the harbor. Open 24hr.

Pharmacy: Inland on Tombazi, just before the Amarillis Hotel. Open daily 9am-1:30pm and 5-8:30pm.

Hospital: ☎22980 53 150. Inland on the street to the right of the clock tower, set back on the right, just past the tourist police. Look for a brown door with grates set in a stone wall. Open M-F 9am-1pm and by appointment. In an **emergency,** call the 24hr. nurse (☎22980 53 150) or the tourist police.

Telephones: OTE (☎22980 52 199 or 52 399), facing the tourist police. Open M-F 8am-2pm. **Card phones** are just past the OTE entrance on the left.

Internet Access: Flamingo Cafe (☎22980 53 485), 20m up Tombazi. €4.40 per 30min., €8 per hr. Open daily noon-3pm and 6-9:30pm. Also offered at the **Yachting Center** (see above). €3 per 15min., €7 per hr. Open daily 8am-noon and 5-9pm.

Post Office: ☎22980 52 262. 1 block inland in the alley just before Vicky's Shop. Open M-F 7:30am-2pm. **Postal code:** 18040.

ACCOMMODATIONS

Hydra has the most expensive accommodations in the Saronic Gulf and among the most expensive in Greece. Singles are practically nonexistent and doubles generally cost at least €40 during high season. Rooms in one of Hydra's famous old mansions are particularly expensive. Without reservations, weekend accommodations are almost impossible to get due to the influx of vacationing Greeks; try to call ahead or arrive on a Thursday for the weekend. You may also be met at the ferry dock by Hydriots offering **domatia** (probably your cheapest option), but don't expect luxurious accommodations.

Hotel Amarillis (☎22980 53 611 or 22980 52 249; fax 22980 53 446). Walk inland on Tombazi; hang right at the fork. Rooms at this welcoming, family-run hotel have fridges, TV, and A/C. Singles €44; doubles €53; triples €60. MC/V. ❸

Pension Antonios (☎/fax 22980 53 227), on Spilios Charamis across from Christina's, a 5min. walk inland on Tombazi. Bright, clean rooms off a quiet courtyard feature baths, fridges, and A/C. Singles €30-35; doubles €50. ❸

Hydra Hotel (☎22980 52 102 or 22980 53 085; www.hydrahotel.com) looms high over the waterfront on the west side, down the street from the Koundouriotis mansion. Walk 1 block inland on Votsi, take the hard right up the stairs and around the corner, and turn right again on L. Koundouriotis (another long staircase). Wood-accented rooms have balconies with unsurpassed views and private baths. Doubles €63; triples €78; quads €92. Discounts for longer stays. ❸

Hotel Mira Mare (☎22980 52 300), at Mandraki beach. All rooms have large patios and beach access. Complimentary water taxis shuttle guests from the ferry and into town. Rooms have TV, A/C, bath, and fridge. Restaurant/bar on site. Doubles €85. ❹

FOOD

Most waterfront establishments have average food, many tourists, and prices that reflect the rent. Hidden treasures compensate for location with superb food and significantly lower prices.

Barba Dima's (☎22980 52 967), a few minutes walk up Tombazi and bearing right at Hotel Amarillis. Shouts of "Amalia! Amalia!" ring out as you approach this tiny taverna. While the locals are very demanding of the busy owner, the traditional Greek cuisine she serves meets even the highest expectations. Entrees €3.50-6. Open daily 10:30am-1am. ❷

Christina's Taverna (☎22980 53 615), on Spilios Charamis to the right of Douskos. Another local favorite, here you'll find terrific home cooking. Don't bother with the menu—just order whatever Christina has in the kitchen. Most entrees €4-10. Open daily 11am-11:30pm. ❷

Douskos (Taverna Xeri Elia; ☎22980 52 886), in a trellised courtyard 5min. inland on Tombazi. With a wide range of Greek dishes and live traditional music every night, this well-known taverna attracts large crowds. Entrees €4-9. ❷

Artopoieion (☎22980 52 886), in the 1st alleyway to the left off Tombazi and next to Vassilis Tours, delivers savory baked goods (€1.60 at most) and has a small market. Open daily 7am-10pm. ❶

Anemoni (☎22980 53 136). Bear left uphill from the OTE. Greek pastries (€1.50) in generous portions. Stop in after dinner for fresh ice cream (€2 for 2 hefty scoops) and almond confections. Open daily 8am-11pm. ❶

SIGHTS

The **Tombazis mansion,** on the west side of the harbor, now houses the famous **Fine Arts School;** look for paint-smeared artists on the balcony. The works of

THE BIG SPLURGE

BRATSERA

A converted sponge factory, Brat sera may seem like an unlikely place to find luxurious accommodations Indeed, a walk into the dim lobby with its low ceiling and rough stone walls feels more industrial than homey. Bu let your eyes adjust to the light and you'll understand why Bratsera sets the standard on an island with such discerning taste. The lobby's antique furniture and tapestries balance modern features. A quick stroll through the courtyard should be enough to win you over—a serene garden of carefully tended bougainvillea, oleander, and jacaranda provide shaded sanctuar from the bustling streets of Hydra. A welcoming swimming pool lies jus beyond, teasing the occasional passerby with its aqua blue waters.

The rooms themselves pamper visitors with full amenities—TVs, A/C, ful baths, telephones—and the luxury o pleasing decor. Wood rafters give a comforting sense of space; nautica antiques add a Hydriot touch. While the external architecture enchants mosquito nets in bedrooms are a nice touch to the interior decoration. The hotel's restaurant serves breakfast lunch, and dinner. Take a seat unde the wisteria-covered trellises of the courtyard and enjoy the surroundings.

Summer ☎22980 53 971, winte 210 721 8102; summer fax 2298 53 626, winter 210 722 1619; brat sera@yahoo.com. High season regu lar double €116, low season €100 high season double with balcony €180, low season €165. Open end o Feb.-Oct.

Hydriot painter Periklis Byzantios, who taught at the school, and those of his son, Constantinos, are now on display in the basement of **Lazaros Koundoriotis Historical Mansion,** the yellow building high on the west side of town. Take the first hard right off Votsi and turn right again on L. Koundouriotis; head left at the top of the long stairway. On the first and second floors, the museum exhibits an extensive array of traditional Hydriot costumes and has a brilliant view of the town. (Open Tu-Su 10am-5pm. €4, students and children 11-18 €2, children 10 and under free.)

Those in search of peace need only check beneath the large clock tower that dominates the port. The calm, white courtyard of the **Church of the Assumption of the Virgin Mary** contrasts with the busy harbor streets that lie just through the alleyway. The small church is certainly worth a trip, if only for a peek at its gilded ceiling and a few wonderful moments of quiet contemplation. Before becoming a monastery, the structure was a convent from 1648 to 1770, housing 18 nuns. It is now dedicated to the *kemesis*, the Ascension of Mary. The courtyard surrounds the tomb of Koundouriotis, his statue, and another of Miaoulis. Hidden away upstairs are the treasures of the **Byzantine Museum.** Especially noteworthy are the brightly colored, beautifully preserved scenes from the life of Christ produced in the 18th and 19th centuries. (Open Tu-Su 10am-5pm. €1.50. Modest dress required.) The **Historical Archives Museum,** to the left of the ferry building, houses old Hydriot costumes, census records, naval treasures, relics of the revolution, and a library. The heart of Admiral Andreas Miaoulis is stunningly preserved in a silver and gold urn. (☎22980 52 355. Open daily 9am-4:30pm. €3, students €1.50.) A visit to Hydra wouldn't be complete without a peek at the art that the island inspires, and it is nearly impossible to walk a few blocks in Hydra without coming upon at least one gallery. **Lagioudera,** on the northwestern corner of the harbor, and **Melina Merkouri,** on the northeastern corner, are rented out by local artists for brief shows.

An arduous 1½hr. hike will take you to the **Monastery of Prophitis Ilias** and the **Convent of Efpraxia,** located on the lower peak overlooking the harbor. Hike up A. Maiouli from the waterfront; signs point the way as you go higher up. Monks may show you around the monastery, the prettier of the two structures. A donkey ride up the rocks costs about €30 and seems to wear out the donkey—inquire at the harbor. (Both open daily 9am-5pm. Modest dress required.)

If you're in Hydra town during the **Miaoulia** (the fourth weekend in June), celebrate the feats of Admiral Andreas Miaoulis via an explosive mock battle held in the harbor. The celebration of Greek Orthodox **Easter** (April 11 in 2004) is reputedly one of the best in the land. Throngs of visitors crowd Kamini beach on Good Friday, where men of the church, in full attire, carry the Epitaph into the sea.

NIGHTLIFE

Hydra is more an island for lovers than for swingers. Known internationally as a romantic honeymoon destination, it doesn't offer much kicking nightlife. Still, **Disco Heaven,** perched high on a cliff on the west side of town, may be the answer to your partying prayers. Take the white-trimmed stairs just before the Sunset Restaurant. There's an indoor dance floor as well as an outdoor bar overlooking the sea. (☎22980 52 716. Cover €3. Cocktails €7. Open in summer only, daily 11pm-late.) As the large contingent of artists might suggest, the Hydriot scene is about strolling the moonlit harbor, getting invited onto yachts for drinks, and wandering through the waterfront bars. The Hydriot pub crawl begins around 12:30am in the lounge seats of the **Pirate Bar,** tucked into the southwestern corner of the harbor. (☎22980 52 711. Beer €4; cocktails €6-8. Open daily 10am-late.) It then meanders to the west side of the harbor through the crowds to trendy **Nautilus** (☎22980 53 563; cocktails €7.50; open daily 10pm-late) and **Saronicos** (☎22980 52 589; cocktails €7.50; open daily 9pm-6am), and ends with an early morning swim in the deep waters off the landing past Sunset Restaurant. On a quieter night in town, enjoy the intimate setting of **Amalour,** a short walk up Tombazi (cocktails €5-7).

BEACHES

Landings and stairs, cut into the rocks around the point across the harbor from the ferry dock, provide access to the finest swimming on Hydra, with waters that are cool, crystal, and instantly deep. The first landing on the right is open to the public, but head to the next few to grab a drink at one of the cafes that serve them; daiquiris at **Hydronetta** are a delicious treat (€5). A 15min. walk west along the coast takes you past the high-walled, cobbled artists' colony of Kamini. Just beyond it is a tiny, pebbly beach where the drop to the sea is less severe and water reasonably shallow. Walking another 20min. brings you to slightly more populous **Vlihos beach,** guarded by a regiment of Hawaiian-style beach umbrellas. East of town (30min. hike or 10min. water taxi ride) lies manicured **Mandraki beach,** a genuine but coarse sand beach. This isn't the secluded beach of your dreams, but there are plenty of fun water toys to keep you busy. (Paddle boats €8, canoes €5, windsurfing €16, sailboat €6-16; all prices per hr.) If you have time and money, hire a water taxi to the far side of the island; there's room for you to find a quiet beach of your own—just be sure to agree on a pick-up time before getting out.

SPETSES Σπετσες

A green cloak of pine trees and a rounded landscape distinguish Spetses from its rockier neighbors. Years ago, visitors were welcomed to the island by an air of mystery: the vegetation combined with an abundance of honey to produce a sweet, magical odor—hence the name "Spetses," derived from the Venetian term *spezzie* (aromatic or spiced). Perhaps the fact that there was something in the air can explain past Spetsiots' passionate devotion to their homeland. They played a crucial role in the War of Independence, fighting courageously and offering their fleet to the cause. Today Spetses is a haven for Athenian tourists. In summer the streets are crowded with motorbikes and swimsuit-clad Greeks and Brits.

SPETSES TOWN ☎22980

The vast majority of Spetsiots live in Spetses Town, as close to the water as possible. Cafes and bars line the 4km of water, interspersed with little pebble beaches every 50m, turning the town into a round-the-clock beach club that attracts many young Greeks on the weekends. Jet-setters dock in Spetses's Old Harbor. Although topless sunbathing is technically illegal, Spetsiots know how to bend the rules.

TRANSPORTATION. **Bus** schedules and prices are posted at stops. From Ag. Mamas beach 500m down the waterfront from the dock, buses go to **Ag. Anargiri beach** (20min., 4 per day, €2), from the plateia by the Hotel Poseidono to **Anargyrios College** and **Lioneri beach** (15 per day, every hr. at half past; €1). **Ferries** depart once daily to: **Aegina** (3hr., €8.70); **Methana** (2½hr., €7.40); **Piraeus** (4hr., €11.70) via **Hydra** (1hr., €4.20); **Poros** (2hr., €5.80). **Alasia Travel,** on the waterfront, sells tickets and posts schedules. (☎22980 74 098. Open daily 8am-9pm.) **Flying Dolphins** (☎22980 73 141) are inland from the dock, with service to: **Hydra** (30min., 8-10 per day, €8.50); **Piraeus** (2hr., 6-8 per day, €22.20); **Poros** (1hr., 1-4 per day, €11.60). **Water Taxis** (☎22980 72 072) are docked across from the Flying Dolphin ticket office, just inland of the ferry dock and go to: **Agia Marina** (€18); **Anarghiri beach** or **Paraskevi beach**

N RECENT NEWS

ASH THAT BUTT

As almost half the Greek population mokes on a daily basis (45% of those ver 15 years old), perpetual cigarette moke seems part of the Greek experince. But change is in the nicotine-saturated air. In the summer of 2002, the Health Ministry began a vigorous camaign to ban smoking in public places.

According to the regulations mposed by the Health Ministry, restauants and tavernas must designate ion-smoking areas for patrons, though oars and nightclubs are exempt. Smoking is no longer tolerated in pubic transportation systems, schools, universities, airports and other transort stations, hospitals, pharmacies, and government buildings. Furthermore, the government has begun an ambitious anti-smoking awareness campaign in schools and a joint effort vith the Greek Orthodox church. The goal of all these measures is to discourage tobacco use and significantly cut smoking rates, especially among Greek teenagers.

In May 2003, officials passed furher regulations banning smoking in all oublic areas within the private sector such as conference rooms, lecture ıalls, and business reception areas, to oe implemented starting October 2003. At the conclusion of negotiations between employers and workers' unions, smokers will be confined o selective specially designated areas n the workplace by March 2004.

The question on the minds of officials remains: will the smoke clear in ime for the Games or will the athletes ıave an added obstacle?

(€38); **Costa** (€12); **Costoula** (€15); **daytrip** around the island (€50); **Emilianos** (€25); **Hinitsa** (€22); **Old Harbor** (€11); **Porto Heli** (€30); **Zogeria** (€25). **Taxis** wait in front of the travel agencies to the left of the ferry dock. Several rental agencies cluster just past the Ag. Anarghiri bus stop; veer right at the kiosk. Expect to pay €15-20 per day. **Rent-a-Bike** (☎22980 74 143) on the street parallel to the waterfront, behind the Hotel Soleil, rents **mountain bikes** (€4 per day).

ORIENTATION AND PRACTICAL INFORMATION. The waterfront road runs from the left (facing inland) of the ferry dock around the base of the town to the **Old Harbor,** past **Ag. Mama's** beach. To the right of the ferry dock are several restaurants and cafes on the way up the hill to **Plateia Bouboulina.** The first street inland parallel to the water hosts shops, pharmacies, and tavernas. The Old Harbor, home to waterfront bars and tavernas, is a 20min. walk or €7 carriage ride; carriages wait near the ferry dock.

Several **travel agencies** lie around the corner on the left side of the boat landing. The friendly Kentros brothers at **Mimoza Travel** (☎22980 73 426) can help you find accommodations, book Saronic Dolphin Ferries, and are a great source of information about the island. **Alasia Travel** sells ferry tickets. (☎22980 74 130, 74 903, or 74 098; fax 22980 74 053; alasia@otenet.gr. Open daily 8am-2:30pm and 4-9pm.) The **National Bank** next to the OTE, on the waterfront to the right of the ferry docks, has a 24hr. **ATM.** (☎22980 72 286. Open M-Th 8am-2pm, F 8am-1:30pm.) Follow signs to the Spetses Museum; 150m before the museum are the 24hr. **police** (☎22980 73 100) and the **tourist police** (☎22980 73 744). The **port police** are in the rear of the OTE building; walk up the street between the National Bank and the OTE and follow the signs. (☎22980 72 245. Open 24hr.) For the **first aid station,** dial ☎22980 72 472. (Open 24hr. for **emergencies.** Call the police to reach a doctor.) The plateia has a **pharmacy** off the street running parallel to the waterfront. (☎22980 72 256. Open M-Sa 8:30am-1:30pm and 5-9pm, Su 10am-1:30pm and 5:30-9:30pm.) The **OTE** is around to the right of the ferry dock, next to the National Bank. (☎22980 72 199. Open M-Th 7:30am-1:30pm, F 7:30am-1pm.) **Delfinia Net-Cafe** is to the left of the ferry docks, next to O Roussos, just before the beach. (☎22980 75 051; delfinianet@usa.net. €4.80 per hr., €2.40 min. Open daily 9am-2am.) There is also Internet access at **Politis,** around to the right of the ferry dock. (☎22980 74 519 or 74 652. €4.40 per hr., €2.20 min.) The **post office** is to the left of the dock on the road parallel to the waterfront. (☎22980 72 228. Open M-F 7:30am-2pm.) **Postal code:** 18050.

ACCOMMODATIONS AND FOOD. Accommodations are expensive, with prices slightly higher and rooms scarcer on weekends. A few **domatia** are advertised around town. Be sure to bargain. While unimpressive, **Pension Brazos ❷**, just inland of the ferry docks, is convenient. Rooms have baths, fridges, fans, TV, and balconies. (☎22980 75 152. Singles €30; doubles €45.) **Villa Mimoza ❸**, past the Bouboulina Museum, is in a peaceful location, away from the hustle and bustle of town, boasting expansive gardens and an outdoor patio with bar. (☎22980 75 170. Free transportation from ferry dock. TV, A/C, kitchenette, bath, and big balconies. Doubles €60-70.) **Hotel Klimis ❹** is on the waterfront to the left of the ferry docks. (☎22980 73 725 or 73 334. Baths, TVs, balconies, and A/C. Breakfast €4.20-6.80. Singles €40-50; doubles €50-55; triples €70-80.)

Tavernas abound in this tiny town, but they tend to be rather pricey. You can economize by buying groceries at one of the island's many supermarkets. **O Roussos ❸**, on the waterfront just before the beach, calls octopus (around €6) its specialty. (☎22980 72 212. Fresh seafood and traditional Greek entrees €4-11. Open daily 11am-midnight.) **Quarter Pizza ❷**, in the plateia off the road running parallel to the water, offers pizzas (€6-10) cooked on a wood-fire stove. (☎22980 72 027. Pasta €4-7. Beer €2. Takeout and delivery available. Open daily 11am-midnight.) **Politis ❷**, on the waterfront just to the right of the ferry docks, serves decadent baklava (€1.50), delicious waffle breakfasts with bottomless cups of coffee (€4.70-6), and a wide variety of cocktails. Also connect to the Internet (€4.40 per hr., €2.20 min.) upstairs. (☎22980 74 519 or 74 652. Open daily 8am-late.)

SIGHTS AND ENTERTAINMENT. The **House of Laskarina Bouboulina**, next to the park behind the National Bank and the OTE, was home to a ship's captain who played a major role during the War of Independence. Mme. Bouboulina, a woman of unchecked patriotism and courage, is to date the only female admiral in Greek history. Despite her valor, she did not enjoy a hero's death—she was shot by her daughter-in-law's father during a dispute. (☎22980 72 416. Open for guided tour only; English tours run every 1½hr., 10:30am-6pm. €4, children €1.) The **Spetses Museum** is housed in the center of town in the crumbling, 19th-century mansion once owned by Spetses's first governor. The collection includes a casket of the remains of Laskarina Bouboulina (see above), folk art, and religious artifacts. (Follow the signs near the OTE and the National Bank. ☎22980 72 994. Open Tu-Su 8:30am-2:45pm. €3.) The **Monastery of Agios Nikolaos** stands above the old harbor, across from a square of traditional Spetsiot mosaics. A plaque to the left of the entrance commemorates Napoleon's nephew, Paul Marie Bonaparte, who was pickled in a barrel of rum after he died in the War of Independence. The barrel was stored in a monastic cell at Agios Nikolaos from 1827 to 1832. (Modest dress required.)

Spetses hosts many animated festivals, the best of which is certainly the **Armada**, a mid-September celebration reenacting Spetses's fleet's victory over the Turkish Armada early in the War of Independence. Islanders construct a flimsy Ottoman-style ship, which quickly sinks in the harbor after dramatic fireworks are set off from it. Greeks, particularly Athenians, flood Spetses for this rowdy, memorable event; book accommodations early to join in on the fun. At **Socrates**, soccer fans gather to catch their favorite teams on the big-screen TV during Happy Hour (9:30pm-midnight; all cocktails €3). A younger crowd heads to **Mama's**, at Ag. Mama's beach for expensive, chic drinks (€3-7). **Rendezvous**, next door to Mama's, is also popular. The second inlet of the Old Harbor, around the bend from the inlet closest to Dapia, is host to many of the prime bars and clubs on the island. **Remezzo** features live traditional music on the weekends after 11pm; **Thrubie**, a relaxed ouzo bar, serves up selections of organic food. If a night on the dance floor is what you desire, head for the bumping rhythms of **Brachera**; those craving company should try **Figaro**, across the inlet, which boasts a 2000-person capacity.

BEACHES. Spetses's warm waters are invitingly shallow and a major reason why people come to the island. Hop on a moped and see them all on the 24km jaunt around the island; cool off with a refreshing dip in the ocean and a frappé from the tavernas found at every beach. Big sandy **Ag. Anargiri,** on the opposite side of the island from Spetses Town, is the most popular beach, boasting two tavernas and a host of watersports. (Windsurfing €12 per hr.; waterskiing €15 per person; canoes €10 per hr.) In the rear of the beach's sole restaurant **Manolis** are showers, changing rooms, and impeccable bathrooms. **Ag. Paraskevi,** about 1km to the right when facing the sea, has the same blanket of pine trees and a sand and pebble surface without the accompanying hubbub. Midway along the bus route between Anargiri and Spetses Town is utterly peaceful **Xylocheriza.** Pure white, smooth stones contrast with the still, brightly colored waters of the bay. Refresh yourself after a swim with a hunk of watermelon big enough for two at the snack bar. Although it is most easily accessible by moped, the bus passes by the dusty road to the beach (10-15min. walk); check with the driver about return times before you hop off. **College beach,** in front of Anargyrios College, is home to a popular bar and tanned tourists. **Agia Marina** beach is about a 30min. walk from the far left end of the waterfront in Spetses Town, taking a right at the kiosk.

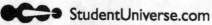

THE SPORADES AND EVIA

Circling into the azure depths of the Aegean, Evia and the Sporades form a family of enchanting sea maidens. Evia, the matriarch, nudges the coast of Central Greece, stretching from Karystos in the south, through bustling Halkida, to the warm waters of the northern coast. Her children, the Sporades, arc across the sea to the north. Sophisticated Skopelos, the eldest, quietly welcomes the moonlight to her shores with echoing jazz melodies. Wild and independent Skiathos pays homage to the sun, flaunting her beach-ringed shores for travelers from around the world. Little Alonnisos harbors pristine wilderness crossed by hiking trails and is home to *Monachus monachus* (MOM), an endangered species of seal, and its wildlife preservation organization. Austere Skyros watches from afar as a keeper of the old ways. They have beckoned visitors for millennia: 5th-century BC Athenians, 2nd-century BC Romans, 13th-century Venetians, and 20th-century tourists have all basked on their sun-lit shores and trod their shaded forests.

HIGHLIGHTS OF THE SPORADES AND EVIA

PEEL OFF your Fruit of the Looms on Skiathos's Little Banana beach (p. 340).

LISTEN UP where punk meets folk on Skopelos, home of Giorgios Xintaris, one of Greece's last great *rembetika* performers (p. 346).

PONDER poetry by Rupert Brooke among pirate spoils in Skyros Town (p. 352).

SIP FROM a divine aphrodisiac with your eyes—the view from Mt. Ohi on Evia, where Zeus and Hera fell in love (p. 359).

SPORADES Σποραδες

SKIATHOS Σκιαθος

Having grown up almost overnight from an innocent island daughter to a madcap dancing queen, Skiathos is the tourism (and party) hub of the Sporades. Its long waterfront, lined with travel agencies and rental shops, gives little hint of the island's raw beauty. The traveler who escapes the tourist temptations of Skiathos Town finds majestic pine forests, ethereal beaches, and dignified monasteries.

SKIATHOS TOWN ☎24270

Arriving in Skiathos Town can be overwhelming; Skiathans crowd the ferry landing hawking domatia and cafes and tavernas line every street with tacky beach shops and expensive boutiques. Yet beyond the crowds Skiathos reveals a charm and exhilaration. From bars packed with talkative travelers to the picturesque backdrop of the port with lively discos, Skiathos offers something for everyone.

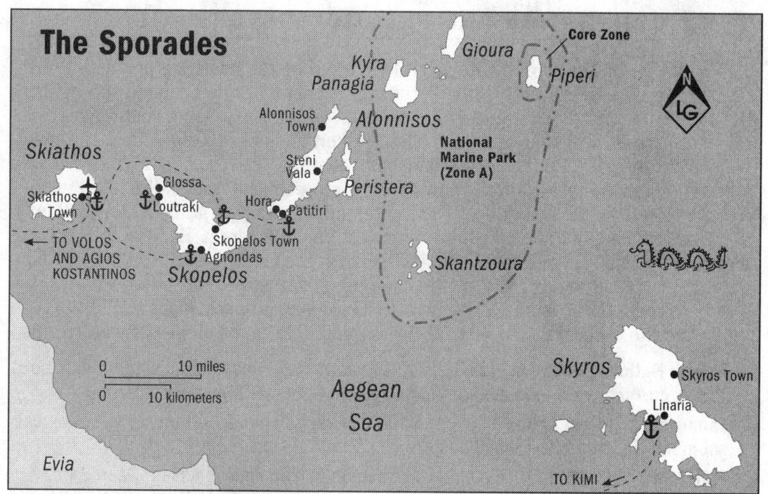

TRANSPORTATION

Ferries: Hellas Lines (☎24270 22 209), on the corner of Papadiamantis across from the ferry landing. Prices slightly higher July-Aug. Ferries run to: **Agios Konstantinos** (3½hr., 1-3 per day, €10.10); **Alonnisos** (2hr., 1-2 per day, €7.80); **Glossa** (30min., 1-2 per day, €5.60); **Skopelos** (1½hr., 1-3 per day, €5.40); **Volos** (2½hr., 2-3 per day, €11.60). Some ferries are jet ferries, which have similar prices and durations to Flying Dolphins. To get to Skiathos from **Athens,** take the daily bus from the station at Liossion 260 to **Ag. Konstantinos** (2½hr., 16 per day, €10.20), then take the ferry.

Flying Dolphins: Minoan Lines (☎24270 22 018), at the same office as Hellas. Trips to: **Agios Konstantinos** (1¼hr., 1-2 per day, €20.80); **Alonnisos** (1hr., 3-6 per day, €12); **Glossa** (15min., 5 per day, €5.60); **Skopelos** (35min., 9 per day, €9.10); **Volos** (1¼hr., 4 per day, €19.30).

Flights: Olympic Airways (☎24270 22 229 or 22 220), at the airport. Call 24hr. prior to take-off to confirm flight. Open M-F 8am-4pm. Taxis (€3) get you from the harbor to the airport. 1 flight per day to **Athens** (50min.).

Local buses: Facing inland, the **bus stop** is at the far right end of the wharf past the park. The bus to **Koukounaries beach** (every 15min., 7:15am-1am; €1.10) makes stops at southern beaches. Heading outbound, sit on the driver's side for the best view. A schedule and list of stops is at the bus stop in Skiathos Town and at Koukounaries.

Taxis: ☎24270 21 460. Line up along the waterfront. Prices posted on a small wooden kiosk on the waterfront. Open 24hr.

Moped Rental: Euronet (☎24270 24 410), **Avis** (☎24270 21 458), and **Heliotropio** (☎24270 22 430) all along the waterfront include insurance in the rental price (€15-20 per day).

Charter Boats: Boats run from the Old Port. Circuits around the island, including Lalaria and Castro beaches, cost €10-12 per person and leave before 10am, returning in the afternoon. Boats to the small island of Tsougria, which is a popular location for swimming and snorkeling, cost €8 per person and leave between 10am and noon, returning in the afternoon. Ask at the information kiosk next to the ferry dock.

ORIENTATION AND PRACTICAL INFORMATION

The midpoint of Skiathos's waterfront is marked by the **Bourtzi,** a peninsula fortified by the Venetians in the 13th century. The **main waterfront** runs to the right of the Bourtzi, facing inland, and is the location of the ferry dock, rental agencies, tavernas, cafes, and tourist shops. The **Old Port** runs perpendicular to the main waterfront from the Bourtzi. **Papadiamantis,** Skiathos Town's main drag, overflows with cafe-bars, souvenir shops, and clothing stores; it intersects the main waterfront across from the ferry dock. Farther inland, **Pandra** (left at the National Bank) and **Evangelistra** (by the post office) intersect Papadiamantis. Parallel to Papadiamantis, **Polytechniou** contains a string of bars. On the far right of the waterfront facing inland, a road winds from the bus stop up to the airport and then follows the southern coast of the island all the way to **Koukounaries beach. Maps** (€1.50) of Skiathos and the other Sporades islands are available in shops along the waterfront.

Banks: National Bank (☎24270 22 400), midway up Papadiamantis on the left side, offers **currency exchange** and an **ATM.** Open M-Th 8am-2:30pm, F 8am-2pm.

Laundromat: Miele Laundry, about 200m up Papadiamantis on a side street across from the National Bank. Wash and dry €9. Soap €1. Open 8am-11pm.

Police: ☎24270 21 111. Upstairs past where Papadiamantis forks left. Open 24hr.

Tourist Police: ☎24270 23 172. A small white building on the right side of Papadiamantis next to the school, just past where the road forks around an electronic info kiosk. Open daily 8am-10pm.

Pharmacies: Several pharmacies line Papadiamantis and its side streets.

Hospital: ☎24270 22 040. On the Acropolis hill behind Skiathos Town. Open 24hr.

OTE: ☎24270 22 399. On Papadiamantis, past the post office on the right. Open M-Th 7:30am-1:30pm, F 7:30am-1pm.

Internet Access: Internet Zone Cafe (☎24270 22 767), on Evangelistra, to the right off Papadiamantis. €3 per hr. Open daily 10:30am-2pm and 6pm-1am.

Federal Express: ☎24270 22 006; fax 24270 23 204. On Simeonis, 1 block to the left of Papadiamantis before the National Bank. Open M-F 9am-2pm and 6-8pm, Sa 9am-1pm.

Post Office: ☎24270 22 011. At the intersection of Papadiamantis and Evangelistra. Open M-F 7:30am-2pm. **Postal code:** 37002.

ACCOMMODATIONS AND CAMPING

Most tourists make reservations in advance for July and August and tour groups book most of the summer hotel rooms a year in advance. Dock hawks flock to meet the ferry and promote their **domatia,** which are generally the best deal in town. Be sure to bargain. Typical doubles run €20-30 in spring and fall; €30-50 in summer. Try the **Rooms to Let office** in the port's wooden kiosk, which can give you a list of rooms currently available. (☎24270 22 990. Open daily 9am-8pm.) In August, forget about finding a room, much less a cheap one—if you arrive without accommodations lined up, forego sleep and just party the night away.

Australia Hotel (☎24270 22 488), on Evangelistra off Papadiamantis and in an alley to the left, is convenient. Rooms have A/C, TVs, private baths, fridges, balconies, and some kitchenettes, and are a steal before Aug. Singles €20; doubles €25-30; triples €36; quads €44. Prices double late July-Aug. ❷

Pension Nikolas (May-Sept. ☎24270 23 062; Oct.-Apr. 23940 32 756), off Polytechniou to the left past Kirki bar. Centrally located, it offers private baths and fridges. Some rooms have A/C. Doubles €35-65; triples €43-73. ❷

Pension Lazou (☎24270 22 324), on the hill overlooking the Old Port. Walk along the Old Port with the water to your left and climb the stairs to the right at the end. Quiet Lazou has rooms with great views and private baths. Doubles €35-50. ❸

Hotel Pothos (☎24270 22 324), next to Pension Nikolas off Polytechniou. Brightly decorated, with marble floors, handcrafted furnishings, and full amenities. Singles €50; doubles €60; triples €75. No singles in Aug., and prices increase by €30 per room. ❹

Camping Koukounaries (☎24270 49 250), on the bus route to Koukounaries, just before stop #23. Has a restaurant, mini-market, and campground a short walk from the beach. €6.50 per person; €3-3.50 per tent, €5.50 per tent rental; €3 per car. ❶

FOOD

Skiathian eating establishments accommodate a wide range of tastes and wallet sizes. While traditional Greek tavernas abound, Italian, English, Chinese, and Mexican restaurants can also be found in town. Not surprisingly, more exotic food tends to be pricey; back-alley souvlaki stands and tiny tavernas off the main strip feed locals and broke backpackers. Cheap Greek food stands pack Papadiamantis.

Primavera (☎24270 24 086), tucked behind a church among labyrinthine streets. Turn left on Pandra before the National Bank and then left again when it intersects the end of Polytechniou. Delicious Italian food (pizza €7-9.50; pasta €5.50-8) in a romantic, Old World setting. Open daily 6:30pm-12:30am. ❷

Hellinikon (☎24270 23 225), next to Primavera. Traditional Greek fare in large portions with live music nightly. Accommodating owner. Open daily 11am-3pm and 6pm-late. ❷

Desperado (☎24270 24 024), on the waterfront, above Remezzo. Dishes up Mexican grub before a view of the Aegean. Pricey entrees (€9.50-11) are a nice change of pace. Margaritas €7; Coronas €4. Kitchen open 7:30-midnight; open later for drinks only. ❸

Crepes Krepali (☎24270 23 840), way up Papadiamantis on the right, before the school. Serves sweet and savory crepes at decent prices (€3-4.50). Open 24hr. ❷

To Bourtzi (☎24270 21 834), coincidentally the only cafe on the *bourtzi*, offers an unparalleled view of the sea and surrounding islands from a spot quietly removed from the glitz of Papadiamantis. Drinks and snacks only. Frappé €3. ❷

SIGHTS

Author Alexandros Papadiamantis's tiny 140-year-old house, set back off Papadiamantis about 1.5 blocks inland, now serves as the **Papadiamantis Museum,** housing his few possessions. The museum honors the 19th-century realist who was one of Greece's best-loved prose writers. Info and short stories are available in English. (Open Tu-Su 9:30am-1pm and 5-8pm. €1.) **Panagia Eikonistra** or **Kounistra** ("The Blessed Icon Painter") is the most important monastery on the island. The **Festival of the Presentation of the Virgin** on November 21 celebrates the monastery's miracle-working icon and the island's patron saint, the Blessed Virgin. Get off the bus at stop #18 and follow the road signs to the monastery. The **Convent of Evangelistra,** 4km north of Skiathos Town on the slopes of Karaflitzanaka, is the site where the first **Greek national flag** (a white cross on a blue background) was raised in 1807. Ten kilometers from Skiathos Town on the northern coast of the island, accessible by private vehicle or by boat, stand the ruins of a medieval walled **castle** built in the 16th century as a refuge from marauding pirates. With independence in the 19th century, the castle's occupants moved to Skiathos Town. Presently only two of the kastro's original 30 churches remain standing, notably the **Church of Christ,** which houses rare icons and frescoes and a magnificent iconostasis.

BEACHES

A single paved main road runs along the southern coast of Skiathos, between Skiathos Town and the island's most famous beach, Koukounaries. The bus makes many stops along the road, mostly at other beaches. A list of stops is available at the bus station in Skiathos and at Koukounaries. **Koukounaries beach and Biotrope** (stop #26) has been voted one of the most beautiful beaches in the Mediterranean. Plush sand arcs between blue waters and the verdant pines of the Biotrope, a protected forest area. It is the most popular on the island—expect crowds in July and August. Koukounaries offers a full slate of water sports (water skiing €20; parasailing €35) and is well-equipped with showers, bathrooms, and bars. **Banana** and **Little Banana beaches** (stop #26) are at the end of the road up the hill across from the Koukounaries bus stop. Signs lead the way. To get to curvy Little Banana from Banana, walk around the rocks on the right as you face the sea. Both are technically **nude beaches,** though it's a guideline more than a rule.

The bus also stops at other beaches, including **Megali Ammos** (stop #5), **Nostos** (stop #12), **Vromolimnos** (stop #13), and **Kolios** (stop #14). All of the beaches on the southern part of the island tend to be very crowded because of their proximity to the bus route. From the later stops, a 30min. walk through a pine forest brings you to the northern beaches, where winds are stronger and beach umbrellas less prominent. **Mandraki,** one of the better ones, is up a sandy road from stop #23. If you prefer to steer clear of the bus route altogether, a 45min. walk north of town past the airport will get you to **Xanemo beach,** frequented by locals. Private beach-hunters will enjoy exploring the coastline that stretches toward town.

NIGHTLIFE AND ENTERTAINMENT

Indulge yourself at the bars in **Pl. Papadiamantis,** on **Polytechniou,** or on **Evangelistra.** Island novelists traditionally write from real life, and if you're lucky, you may be immortalized as a minor character by a latter-day Papadiamantis. Expect to pay €2-5 for beer, €5-6 for cocktails, and €3-5 cover on very popular Saturday nights. **Admiral Benbow Inn,** on Polytechniou, is a cozy place to begin (or end) the night, with plenty of comfy couches, an older crowd, and a €2-per-pint Happy Hour (9pm-midnight) most weekends. (☎24270 22 980. Beer €1.50-3.50; cocktails €4-5.) **Kentavros** is off Papadiamantis to the right beyond the Papadiamantis Museum. From British to Brazilian pop, this bar plays it all. (☎24270 22 980. Beer €2.50-4; cocktails €5-6.50.) **Rock and Roll Bar,** in the Old Port, is a relaxing place for a drink. Pillows serve as chairs on the hill outside. (☎24270 22 944. Beer €3.50-5; cocktails €6.60-8. Half-price drinks daily 7-9pm.) **Spartacus,** on Polytechniou, attracts a young Scandinavian and British crowd. Stop by on "14 Beers Around the World Night" and try winning a free t-shirt. (☎24270 21 891. Beer €2.50-3; cocktails €5.)

From October to May, it's a ghost town; by July it hops. Party until dawn at one (or many) of the discos that line the waterfront on the right edge of the harbor, facing inland. Clubs get going around 10pm and play everything from techno to Top 40. While there is no cover, beer costs about €5, so get your drinks beforehand. **Kahlua** is one of the better venues, with both interior and exterior bars and wooden dance floors. Space-aged **Remezzo,** below Desperado, is also popular. For more sedate entertainment, the open-air **Cinema Attikon,** just past the Papadiamantis Museum on the right, screens recent Hollywood hits in English with Greek subtitles. Schedules are available out front and on signs along the waterfront. (☎24270 22 352. Tickets €6. Twice per night, 9 and 11:30pm.) Concerts play at the **bourtzi,** the small peninsula jutting out next to the Flying Dolphin dock, during July and August. Ask at the information kiosk in the harbor for program schedules.

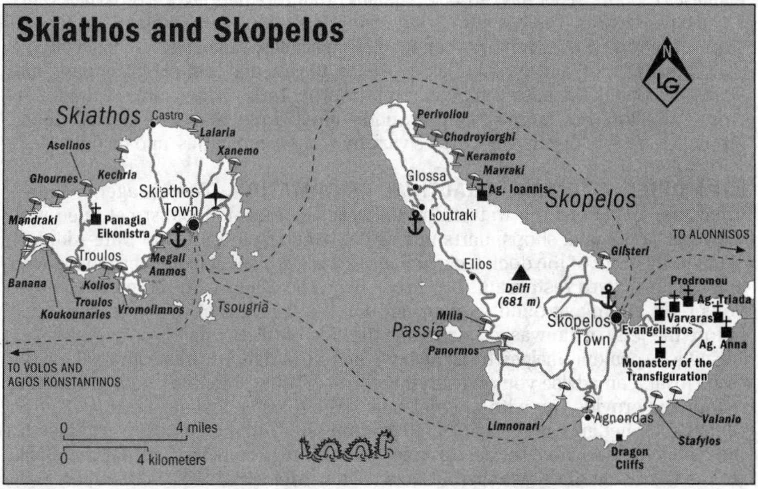

Skiathos and Skopelos

SKOPELOS Σκοπελος

Skopelos sits between the whirlwind of Skiathos and the largely untouched wilderness of Alonnisos, incorporating the best elements of both. Hikes and moped rides through shady forests of tall pine lead to numerous monasteries, bright beaches, and white cliffs that drop into a dazzling blue sea. By night, the town's waterfront strip closes to traffic, and crowds swarm the streets to scour boutiques. A number of low-key bars and a few quality clubs keep the kids on their feet until the wee hours of the morning.

SKOPELOS TOWN ☎24240

Skopelos Town winds up the steep hills above the harbor. Close to the waterfront, the plethora of moped rental shops, cafes, and tavernas contrasts with the narrow streets farther up the hill, which twist among whitewashed buildings, beautiful churches, and precariously perched cafes. These alleys, still in the night, are a joy to wander. If the silence spooks you, the waterfront bars and clubs are never far.

TRANSPORTATION. In good weather, ferries and Flying Dolphins dock at the concrete landing on the left side of the harbor, facing inland. When it's windy, they dock at **Agnondas,** 8km south of town. If you find that you have landed in Agnondas, wait for the bus at the end of the dock, which will take you to Skopelos Town (€1). In Skopelos Town, **taxis** wait near the ferry dock; the **bus station** is just down the street to the left. **Hellas Lines** (☎24240 22 767 or 24240 23 060; fax 24240 23 608), directly across from the ferry dock, runs ferries to: **Agios Konstantinos** (4hr., daily, €13.80); **Alonnisos** (30min., 1-2 per day, €4.10); **Skiathos** (1hr., 3-4 per day, €5.50); **Thessaloniki** (1 per week, €40.20); **Volos** (4hr., 2-3 per day, €11.50). Some of the ferries are jet ferries, which have the same trip durations and prices as Flying Dolphins. Prices are slightly higher in July and Aug. **Minoan Lines** (☎24240 22 767 or 24240 23 060; fax 24240 23 608) sells **Flying Dolphin** tickets, which are also sold directly across from the ferry dock, to: **Agios Konstantinos** (2hr., 3 per day, €27.70);

Alonnisos (30min., 6 per day, €7.50); **Skiathos** (45min., 9 per day, €9.80); **Volos** (2hr., 4 per day, €23.30). The **bus** stop is left of the ferry dock facing inland, on the left side of the road. Buses run between **Stafilos, Agnondas, Panormos,** and **Milia** (12 per day, 7am-10:30pm) and another between **Elios, Glossa,** and **Loutraki** (8 per day, 7am-10:30pm). Check the posted schedules at the stop. **Taxis** are available at the waterfront 7am-2am. For **rentals,** shop around—most travel agencies arrange them. Mopeds run €10-15; cars €40. Prices vary by season, amenities, and distance.

ORIENTATION AND PRACTICAL INFORMATION. Tourist agencies, tavernas, and cafes line the waterfront. **Galatsaniou,** a fashionable street lined with souvenir and snack shops, darts upward between Cafe Cafe and Cafe Aktaion, 100m to the right of the dock facing inland. **Platanos,** a small plateia brimming with souvlaki and gyro restaurants, is across from the dock, with the monument on your right and playground on your left. On the far right of the waterfront, just before the jetty, whitewashed stairs line the side of the town.

English-speaking **Thalpos Travel Agency,** 5m to the right of Galatsaniou along the waterfront, can advise you on everything from Flying Dolphin tickets to catching octopi and provide you with a useful **map** of the town and island. (☎24240 22 947; thalpos@otenet.gr. Open May-Oct. 10am-2pm and 6-10pm; Oct.-May available by fax or telephone.) Most tourist agencies can **exchange currency.** The **National Bank,** on the right side of the waterfront, has a 24hr. **ATM.** (☎24240 22 691. Open M-Sa 8am-2pm.) The **police** (☎24240 22 295) are behind the National Bank. Follow the left-hand road inland from Pl. Platanos past Ag. Ioannis to the dead end, then go right at the signs to find a **medical center.** (☎24240 22 222. Open M-F 9am-2pm for free walk-ins; open M-F 24hr. for **emergencies.**) The **OTE** is 100m up from the water on Galatsaniou. (☎24240 22 139 or 22 121. Open M-F 7:30am-3:10pm.) **The Internet Cafe** is on the road that runs through the back of Platanos. Coming from the waterfront, take a left at the end of the plateia; the cafe is 150m down the road on the left. (€4 per hr. Printing €0.30 per page. Faxing to Europe €2.50 per page; US €3.50 per page. Beer €2. Open daily 9am-3pm and 5pm-1am.) Look for the yellow postbox, 50m beyond the Internet Cafe on the same road, for the **post office.** (☎24240 22 203. Open M-F 7:30am-1:30pm.) **Postal code:** 37003.

ACCOMMODATIONS AND FOOD. In general, Skopelos's hotels cater to all-inclusive-resort tourists. The **Rooms and Apartments Association of Skopelos** (☎24240 24 567; open daily 10am-2pm and 6-10pm), in the stone building next to the town hall, around the waterfront to the right (facing inland), can provide a list of **domatia.** Prices vary but run around €15-30 for singles and €20-40 for doubles. Dock hawks may also offer reasonable rooms. **Pension Sotos ❷,** on the corner of Galatsaniou on the waterfront, has a fantastic location at a diamond-in-the-rough price. A renovated Skopelian house, the pension provides A/C and baths, a common kitchen, a quiet courtyard, a roof terrace, and book exchange. (☎24240 22 549; fax 24240 23 668. Singles €22; doubles €32; triples €55.) Also known as "Souvlaki Square," Pl. Platanos abounds with quick bites. For slower-paced dining, **Taverna O Molos ❷,** around the waterfront to the right facing inland, serves delicious Greek food with a harbor view. (☎24240 22 551. Entrees €4-8. Lamb *kleftika* €7.)

SIGHTS AND ENTERTAINMENT. Skopelos Town has an abundance of **churches.** Thalpos Travel (p. 346) can provide a map that pinpoints many of them. A good place to start your tour is around the harbor to the far right, where beautiful whitewashed **Panagia ston Pirgho** perches on the rocks. Follow the stairs below the church and up along the sea-edge of the city. Along the way pass tiny, simple **Evangelismos and Athanasios,** just below the kastro, the town's oldest church, built in the 11th century. Just off to the left is **Genesis tou Christou,** a larger cruciform church with a round cupola and clock tower. Continuing up the side of the city, walk over the **kastro,** originally built by King Philip of Macedon in the 4th century BC. Today it is the site of a traditional taverna featuring live Greek music. On the uphill side of the kastro, wind your way into town and head for the top of the hill, where **Spiridon** rewards tired hikers. Slightly farther into the city lies **Papameletiou,** a cruciform basilica built in 1662 with a red-tile roof and small clock tower. Closer to the waterfront, **Ag. Nikolaos,** just up Galatsaniou on the left, exhibits brightly colored icons and a marble statue of the Virgin. In **Mikhail-Sinnadon,** a stone cruciform basilica features a remarkable iconostasis. Skopelos draws international students and recognition for its **Photographic Center of Skopelos** (☎24240 24 121); call for more info. The **Folklore Museum,** 100m left past the OTE, has a dull collection of island artifacts, but the meticulously researched first-floor exhibit on popular religion is worth a look. (☎24240 23 494. Open daily 10am-2pm and 7-11pm. €2.)

A 10min. walk up the stairs on the far right of the waterfront leads to the taverna **Anatoli,** the haunt of one of the world's last great *rembetika* singers, Giorgos Xintaris. Stop by for a drink after dinner (usually a little before midnight), and you may be lucky enough to catch him with a group of friends singing the old songs. The sounds and setting are phenomenal. (Beer €2.50; cocktails €5.50-6.50. Open daily 8pm-late.) For new jazz and blues, **Platanos Jazz Club,** on the far right of the harbor facing inland, near the jetty, lets you relax with a drink by candlelight under a gargantuan tree. (☎24240 23 661. Beer €3; cocktails €6.50. Open 8am-3am.) **The Blue Bar,** two blocks up Galatsaniou in an alley on the right (just past the church of Ag. Nikolaos), plays folk, rock, and blues music that accompanies the €3 beers just fine. Skopelos's **dance clubs** cluster midway up a street off of Pl. Platanos. Chat with American painting students at **Metro.** (☎24240 24 446. €3 cover includes 1 drink. Open May-Oct. daily; Oct.-May weekends only.) **Kounos** is Skopelos's oldest club—it's a whopping 10 years old and counting. Top 40 and foreign hits shake the speakers. (☎24240 24 300. Cover €3 includes 1 drink.)

BEACHES. Traveling Skopelos's asphalt road by bus or car to Loutraki or Glossa gives you your pick of the lovely southern beaches. Archaeologists discovered the tomb of the ancient Cretan general **Stafylos** on a nearby hillside, along with a 15th-century BC gold-plated sword that's now in the Volos museum. Stafylos beach is crowded with families. Nearby **Valanio,** over the hill to the left as you face the sea, is less jam-packed. Named for the trickling spring that was a gushing fountain in Roman times, today Valanio is advertised as the only nude beach on Skopelos. Past the small town of **Agnondas,** a paved road leads about 1km to the sparkling blue beach of **Limnonari;** ask the bus driver to let you off at the top of the road or take a water taxi. Farther along the asphalt road is the wide, deep bay of **Panormos.** A 5min. walk leads to the **Adrina beaches,** named for the female pirate who terrorized the islands, leaping to her death in this cove after being cornered by angry islanders. Silvery **Milia,** the island's largest beach, has water sports and rough surf on windy days. It's accessible by bus. Closer to Loutraki, dirt paths lead to the northern beaches of **Spilia, Mavraki, Keramoto,** and **Chondroyiorghi.**

HIKES FROM SKOPELOS TOWN. Due to Skopelos's predominantly dirt roads, the island is best explored by moped or on foot. The island's 35km asphalt road runs from the Skopelos bus station through **Stafylos** (4km), **Agnondas** (8km), **Panormos** (18km), **Elios** (24km), **Loutraki** (30km), and **Glossa** (32km). Thalpos Travel and souvenir shops carry *Skopelos Trails* (€10.25), a great guide to island hikes. According to local lore, a fierce dragon went on a fiery bender, eating almost everyone on Skopelos until Ag. Rigine killed it and became the island's protector. The **Dragon Cliffs** *(Drakondoschisma)*, where the creature was hurled to its death, are now a quiet picnicking spot with a sea view and an altar portraying the dragon's grisly demise. To find it, take the asphalt road from Skopelos Town through Stafylos and turn left down a small dirt road which disappears into the woods about 2km before Agnondas beach.

Two paved roads leave the town from the bus depot on the right end of the waterfront. To reach the monasteries, follow the road out of the harbor to the left (facing inland)—signs mark the way to the monasteries ascending **Mt. Palouki. Evangelismos** was built in the 18th century as part of the Monastery of Xiropotamos of Athos, but its enormous altar screen—the genuine article from Constantinople—is 400 years older. Take the left-hand fork up the hot, winding mountain road for 45min.; start early in the morning before the heat and bugs intensify and in time to reach the monasteries before their 1-5pm daily closing. Up the right fork, another 45min. walk leads you to the **Monastery of the Transfiguration** *(Metamorphosis)*. Its chapel, set in a flowered courtyard, dates from the 16th century. Another hour up the hill along the road takes you to two monasteries perched on precipitous ridges overlooking the sea. The first, the **Monastery of Ag. Varvaras,** was built as a fortress in 1648. Nearby **Prothromou** contains icons dating back to the 14th and 15th centuries and wall paintings. Once a functioning monastery, Prothromou is now a cloister dedicated to St. John the Baptist; its astounding setting surveys the entire coast. The dirt path that begins behind the building leads to the smaller monasteries of **Agia Triada** and **Agia Taxianches.** Farther up the road, a trail leads to the beautiful monastery of **Agia Anna.** At the end of the road on the opposite side of the island from Skopelos Town, the quiet hilltop town of Glossa looks down on Skopelos's second port. For a 4hr. round-trip hike from **Glossa,** walk the dirt track across the island to the **Monastery of Agios Ioannis,** clinging spectacularly to a boulder above the ocean. Take the main road east from Glossa and turn left on the first dirt road to Steki Taverna; it's smooth sailing after that. At the road's end, a path drops to the sea, and stone steps, cut in the escarpment, lead up to the monastery. The road is navigable by motorbike, up to the stairs. A paved road also leads to the church from the road above Glossa, but watch out for loose gravel.

ALONNISOS Αλοννησος

Of the 20-odd islands within Greece's new National Marine Park, only Alonnisos is inhabited, and its fledgling tourism industry remains friendly to those who come to explore its natural treasures. In the past, visitors to the island might have been regarded suspiciously. Until about a century ago, Alonnisos was a refuge for people hiding from the government—pirates, maligned activists, Communists, and the like. Of course, time spent on Alonnisos is more a blessing than a punishment. Hikers take to the highland trails in the north, where aromatic herbs spice the air and the coastal cliffs, awash in green pine and white sand, form an unspoiled boundary with the sea. In the south, there are beaches aplenty to satisfy sun-worshippers. Gioura, a small island to the northeast of Alonnisos, is believed to have been the home of Polyphemus, the Cyclops whose eye was gouged out by Odysseus's sizzling lance. Though many islands claim this distinction, Gioura hosts a rocky landscape that best fits Homer's description of Polyphemus's cavern and herds of the now-endangered brown goats with black crosses on their backs.

PATITIRI Πατητηρι ☎24240

All boats dock at Patitiri, the only town on the island. Sharp-angled and hastily built, it's not a postcard harbor, but it serves as an easily accessible base to explore the rest of Alonnisos and the surrounding Marine Park. Work has recently been done to expand the dock and provide better seating for the waterfront cafes.

TRANSPORTATION AND PRACTICAL INFORMATION. From the docks, two main parallel streets run inland: **Pelasgon** on the left and **Ikion Dolophon** on the right. **Ferries** run to: **Agios Konstantinos** (5½hr., 2 per week, €13.70); **Skiathos** (2hr., 2 per day, €6); **Skopelos** (30min., 1-2 per day, €4.10); **Volos** (5¼hr., daily, €12.80). **Flying Dolphins** go to: **Agios Konstantinos** (2¾hr., 1-2 per day, €27.70); **Glossa** (35min., 3-5 per day, €8.80); **Skiathos** (1¼hr., 4-7 per day, €9.50); **Skopelos** (25min., 4-7 per day, €8.10); **Volos** (2½hr., 2-3 per day, €25.40). Prices go up in July and August. The island's **bus** runs from its waterfront stop to **Hora** (every hr., 9am-3:20pm and 5pm-midnight; €0.90) and to **Steni Vala** (9:20am, 2:35, 6:20pm; €1). Schedules are posted at the Patitiri, Hora, and Steni Vala stops. **Taxis,** lined up along the waterfront, run until 2am; they respond to calls any time (taxi phone numbers are posted on phone booths). **Motorbikes,** the fastest way to explore Alonnisos, are available for rent at the numerous shops on Pelasgon and Ikion Dolophon. Expect to pay about €15 for a 24hr. rental.

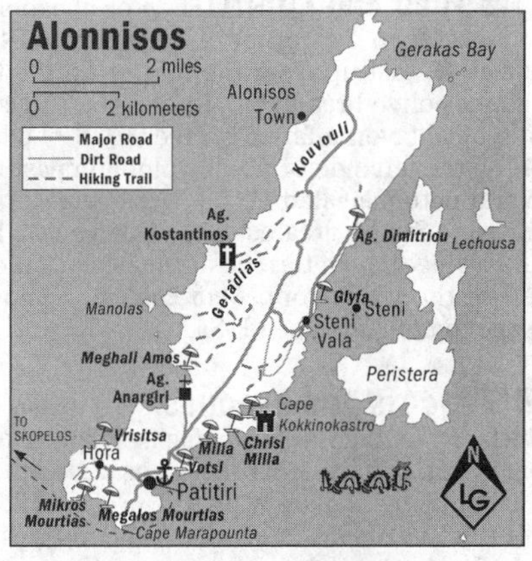

Alonnisos Travel, centered on the waterfront, **exchanges currency,** helps with accommodations, books excursions, and sells ferry tickets. (☎24240 65 188; fax 24240 65 511.) Up Ikion Dolophon, the 24hr. **port police** are on the corner. (☎24240 65 595.) The **National Bank,** with 24hr. **ATM,** lies on the left. (☎24240 65 777. Open M-Th 8am-2pm, F 8am-1:30pm.) The **police** (☎24240 65 205) are on the hill, near the **hospital.** (☎24240 65 208. Open daily 9am-1pm; 24hr. for emergencies.) Find **Internet** access at **Il Mondo** on Ikion Dolophon, on the right just before the post office. (☎24240 65 834. Internet €4 per hr.; €1 min. Printing €0.50 per page. Fax €2.50 per page. Open daily 9:30am-11pm.) The **post office** is a 5min. walk up Ikion Dolophon. (☎24240 65 560. Open M-F 7:30am-2pm.) **Postal code:** 37005.

ACCOMMODATIONS. The **Rooms to Let Office,** next to Ikos Travel can aid travelers looking for a place to stay. (☎24240 66 188. Open daily 9:30am-2pm and 6:30-10pm.) To reach **Panorama ❸,** down the first alley on the left up Ikion Dolophon, walk up the stairs to the top of the hill and turn in at the courtyard on the right. It rents bright rooms and studios with private baths, common fridges, some kitchens, and large, bougainvillea-covered common balconies with a port view. (☎24240 65 240. Singles €25; doubles €40; 2-bedroom suite with kitchen €40-60.) Inquire at Boutique Mary, on the right side of Pelasgon, about simple rooms with private baths at the **Dimakis Pension ❷,** next door. (☎24240 65 294. Singles €15-32; doubles €20-32.) Magdalini and Ilias Besinis rent **Rooms and Studios ❸** with baths, kitchens, and fridges, about 200m up Pelasgon on the left, across from I'M Motorbikes. A gorgeous stone staircase and hand-painted decor add to the atmosphere. (☎/fax 24240 65 451. Book exchange. A/C €5. Singles €20-35; doubles €25-40.) **Camping Rocks ❶** is a 25min. walk; begin in the first alley on the right of Pelasgon and continue uphill. The sites, 50m from some swimming rocks, have showers. (☎24240 65 410. €7 per person, €2 per tent.)

FOOD AND NIGHTLIFE. For cheap souvlaki and gyros (€1.50), stop by **To Steki ❶**, on the corner of Pelasgon. (☎24240 65 816. Open 9pm-late.) **Artolikoudies ❷**, just up from the harbor on the right of Pelasgon, serves delicious summer olive bread (€1.50) and traditional pastries (€0.90-1.40), in addition to typical taverna fare. (Entrees €6-8.) Locals adore the little ouzeri **To Kamaki ❶**, on the left side of Ikion Dolophon past the National Bank. (☎24240 65 245. Warm octopus salad €8.50. *Ouzo meh mezedes* €3. Open daily 11am-2am.) Listen to Sting's greatest hits while you sip a cocktail (€6) under a gnarled tree and a vine-draped terrace at the island's oldest cafe-bar, **Pub Dennis,** on the far left of the waterfront. **Club Enigma,** a short walk up Pelasgon, is the (only) place to boogie. (Open F-Sa.)

SIGHTS AND BEACHES. The **History and Folklore Museum** of Alonnisos, to the far left of the waterfront facing inland and up the stairs, features a wide variety of cultural artifacts from Alonnisos. Exhibits include weaponry used in major conflicts from the Balkan Wars to World War II, historical maps of the Sporades and Greece, and, downstairs, an excellent series of **trade exhibits** on everything from winemaking to pack-saddle construction. (Open daily 11am-5pm. €3.)

Many **beaches** are accessible from the island's main road, which runs along the spine of the island from Patitiri to the port of Gherakas in the far north. A 1½hr. walk on this road from Patitiri takes you to **Votsi,** the island's other major settlement. Local boys dive off the 15-20m cliffs near Votsi beach, just outside the village. Beyond Votsi, the road passes separate turn-offs for the pine-girded beaches of **Milia** and the shallower, sandier **Chrisi Milia.** Locals will tell you that **Ag. Dimitriou,** at the end of the coastal road, is the island's most beautiful beach. The beaches are also accessible by **water taxi** (€6); inquire at the port. Farther up the coast from Chrisi Milia is the beach and archaeological site of **Kokkinocastro,** where swimmers occasionally find ancient coins. The tiny fishing village of **Steni Vala,** 12km north of Patitiri, with a population fluctuating between 25 and 60, is the only other bus stop (20min., 3 per day, €1)—be sure to stop by one of the fantastic **fish tavernas. Glyfa beach** is along the shore, north of the village.

HIKES AND THE OUTDOORS. Only the southern end of the island is inhabited, leaving stretches of mountain wilderness to the north. Though a moped remains the quickest way to explore—Patitiri to Gerakas takes about 45min.—it's worth **hiking.** Trails are marked at regular intervals and include both paved roads and steep, rocky trails. **Blue maps,** scattered throughout the island, mark trailheads and show trail routes, marked by **numerical yellow signs,** but the purchase of a trail map (€3-5) or *Alonnisos on Foot* (€9), a walking and swimming guide, available in Patitiri, is recommended. Numbers below refer to those of marked trails.

The **Meghalo Nero-Ag. Anarghiri-Meghali Amos-Raches- Votsi trail** (#5, 6km, 2½hr.) takes you along the southeastern side of Alonnisos, to the secluded **monastery** of Ag. Anarghiri and **beach** of Meghali Amos. The trailhead is just up the main road from Votsi. Head out Ikion Dolophon from Patitiri to get to the main road, then follow the signs to Votsi and Steni Vala. From Meghali Amos, two trails (#7, 1½hr. and #8, 1½hr.) lead north to **Meghalo Chorafi,** east of the main road, the hub for hikes to **Ag. Laka beach** (#14, 45min.) and the church of **Ag. Kostantinos** (#6, 2hr.). From Ag. Kostantinos, hikes lead north to the church of **Ag. Georgios** (#12, 1hr.) and **Meleghakia** (#13, 1½hr.) in the more rugged part of the island. Hikes #12 and 13 both bring you back to the main road. From **Steni Vala,** hike #10 (1hr.) takes you south past **Ag. Petros beach** to **Isomata** and on to the main road. From Isomata, hike #9 winds its way down to **Leftos beach** (45min.). Far north, past Ag. Georgios, a dirt road leads to the trailhead for trail #11, leading down to **Ag. Dimitrios beach** (1hr.).

DAYTRIPS FROM PATITIRI. Set high on a hill to ward off pirates, **Hora** (Χωρα) now welcomes visitors looking for the island village charm that Patitiri lacks. Its quiet, crooked alleys which open suddenly on to incredible views of the island and wind their way into the dusty hills, have an interesting explanation. When settlers first came to the island, they performed a goat sacrifice, beheading the animal and then cutting it into pieces. They placed the pieces of meat at potential building locations. Over subsequent days, if the meat had kept, they reasoned the spot a prime building location, sheltered from the sun, pests, and other elements, disregarding ease in getting around. From here, you can spy out your own private beach (see below). Tiny 12th-century **Christ Church** is run by Father Gregorias, the village priest and local legend. Newly renovated **Hiliadroma ❸**, up behind the church, has beautiful wood-accented rooms with stone floors, tiled private baths, A/C, TVs, fridges, and fantastic balcony views. (☎24240 65 814. Doubles €45; studios with kitchen €75.) Hora is host to a variety of quaint cafes and tavernas, some perched on beautiful overlooks. From the bus stop, veer left up the hill past the old church, continuing up the stairs to reach a charming paved street with several cafes; the best views are at the end of the street. **Taverna Aloni ❷**, up the right-hand fork from the bus station at the base of an old windmill (sans blades), serves Greek food with views of the island. (Starters €2-3. Entrees from €5.) For a similar view, try the Italian fare at **Nappo ❷**, past the church. (☎24240 65 579. Pastas €7. Pizza €8. Open 7pm-midnight.)

Four hiking trails lead down from Hora to beaches and overlooks in the southern part of Alonnisos. The trail to **Mikros Mourtias** (#1, 1.5km, 45min.) begins at the bus stop. Walk through town, past the church, and up the stairs to a street lined with cafes. Turn left before the street ends and walk down the narrow side street to the trailhead. A dirt road also leads down to the beach from the village. Mikros Mourtias is a small beach replete with perfectly-shaped skipping stones. The tiny inlet is perfect for a quiet swim. **Kalovoulos** (#2, 1.5km, 45min.) is an enchanting overlook, a wonderful place to take in the sunset on the rocky coast east of Hora. Continue on the main road past the bus stop and the trail is on the left. A miniature beach on a secluded cove, **Vrisitsa** (#3, 1km, 30min.) is accessible by trail on the left of the main road, heading away from Hora. Farther down the road on the right, **Patitiri** (#4, 1.5km, 35min.) connects the Old and New Towns. Buses

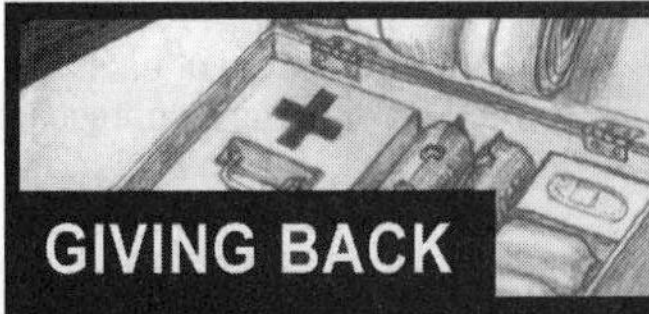

GIVING BACK

HI MOM

Established in 1992, the National Marine Park of Alonnisos-Northern Sporades was created in large part to protect the Mediterranean monk seal, Europe's most endangered marine mammal. The monk seals number only about 500 total in the Mediterranean; a growing colony of approximately 50 monk seals is now carefully monitored by MOM, an Alonnisos-based sea patrol unit named for the seal's Latin monicker, *Monachus monachus*. MOM also runs a Seal Treatment and Rehabilitation Center on Alonnisos, and conducts a number of education and public awareness programs throughout the coastal regions of Greece.

Each year, a team of volunteers conducts summer information programs, informing and instructing locals, tourists, and fishermen about ongoing conservation and protection efforts. Volunteers must have at least a basic knowledge of spoken Greek. Contact MOM for more information on becoming a volunteer.

Visit MOM's headquarters, at the ferry dock in Alonnisos, to make a "Save the Seals" poster and pick up some literature on their programs. You can also tour the Marine Park in a specially-licensed boat. Most trips, advertised and sold along the Patitiri harborfront, are all-inclusive single-day trips for €40.

If you happen upon a seal, MOM asks that you record its color, length, and other charteristics. Call them immediately with any information.

☎21052 22 888; fax 21052 22 450. www.mom.gr; info@mom.gr.

run from Patitiri (10min.; every hr., 9am-3:20pm and 5pm-midnight; €0.90); schedules are posted at each bus stop. A round-trip taxi will run €10.

Surrounding Alonnisos are the 25 ecologically protected islets of Greece's National Marine Park. The largest and most important are Peristera, Skantzoura, Piperi, Kyra Panagia, Jura, and Psatnoura. They're strictly regulated and visited only by organized tours in summer. Psatnoura, Kyra Panagia, and Skantzoura are owned by nearby Mt. Athos (p. 303) and are used in part for grazing goats. Visiting Jura and Piperi is forbidden in an effort to protect their rare species, including the Mediterranean monk seal (see **Hi Mom,** p. 351). Unless you're a MOM official, forget about seeing the monk seals. Enthusiasts are free to draw a "Save the Seals" poster for the gallery in MOM's Alonnisos ferry dock headquarters. They provide crayons, paper, and info in English about ecology and conservation efforts.

The park islands are accessible by specially licensed boat. Most trips, advertised and sold along the Patitiri harborfront, are all-inclusive single-day trips (€40). MOM's headquarters are on the corner of Ikion Dolophon. (☎21052 22 888; www.mom.gr. Open May-Oct. daily 10am-2pm and 6-10:30pm.)

SKYROS Σκυρος

Skyros is dominated by two forces—modern tourism and local tradition—that are as diametrically opposed as the terrain found on each side of the island. But while the barren landscape of the south and the green hills of the north will always remain separate, the two influences on Skyrian life are beginning to coexist more happily. The preservation of the island's folkways has been recognized as an important priority, as well as a major draw for those travelers weary of the typical tourist-infested vacation island. The trend promises to continue, as there is no longer a link to Skyros from the other Sporades. Those who visit the island are most likely in the market for more than just a whirlwind beach and bar tour.

SKYROS TOWN ☎2220

Like a gleaming pocket of snow, Skyros Town (Horio—"the village"—to locals) stands out in bright white contrast to the greens, yellows, and browns of the hills that surround it. Beyond the requisite tavernas, cafes, and bars lie the features that give the island its distinctive character. Among its maze of whitewashed houses, old men sew sandals by porchlight late into the evening, women embroider patterns learned from pirates, and Carnival is truly an wild affair.

TRANSPORTATION. The **military airport** (☎22220 91 607), 20km from Skyros Town on the island's northern tip, flies to: **Athens** (35min., 2 per week, €33) and **Thessaloniki** (2 per week, €57). Take a cab (€11) to get there; **taxis** (☎22220 91 666) wait by the central plateia or the bus stop (unavailable late or during siesta). The best way to get to Skyros is to take the **bus** from **Athens** to **Kimi,** Evia (3½hr., 2 per day, €9.95), then the **ferry** from Kimi (M-Sa noon and 6pm, Su 11am and 5pm; €7.50). Buses to Kimi stop in the town, 5km from the port; less frequent buses go directly to and from the dock. If you land in Kimi proper, either take a **taxi** from the bus station or walk down the long winding road. No ferries or hydrofoils run to the other Sporades making Skyros a difficult destination to reach on an island hopping tour. The ferry to Skyros arrives in **Linaria,** the tiny western port; a **local bus** to Skyros Town picks up when ferries arrive (20min., 3 per day, €0.90) and leaves Skyros Town about 1hr. prior to ferry departures; another bus runs from Skyros Town to **Molos** (10min., daily, €0.90). Skyros Travel posts schedules (see below). Buses stop in Skyros Town at the base of **Agoras,** the town's backbone road, which heads straight uphill from the stop. Veering left and downhill from the stop, the road winds around the base of the hill, passing Magazia on its way to Molos.

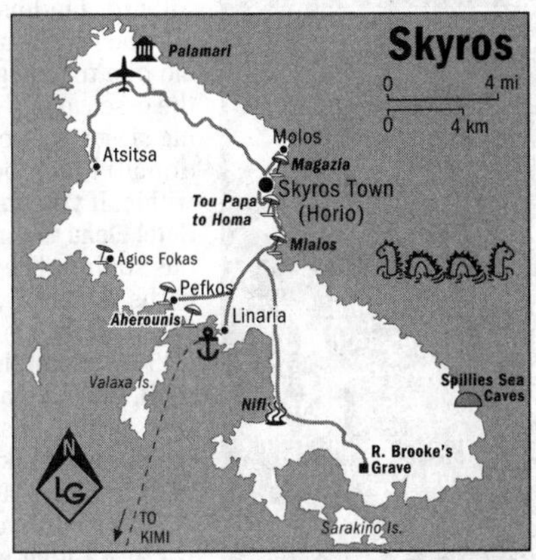

ORIENTATION AND PRACTICAL INFORMATION. Shops, pharmacies, bars, and restaurants ascend the hill in Skyros Town along **Agoras.** Maze-like residential streets scatter out in every direction along the hillsides. Buildings are numbered counterintuitively, and few streets are named; when venturing off Agoras, pick out landmarks on your way. At the far end of town, looking out across Molos and the sea, is **Pl. Rupert Brooke,** dedicated to British poet Brooke and to "immortal poetry" (αθανατη την ποιησι, ah-THAH-nah-tee TEEN PEE-ee-see). To reach Pl. Brooke, walk up Agoras through town until it forks left at Kalypso Bar. Head left along the wall and walk up until you reach a sign pointing to "ΜΟΨΣΕΙΟ/MUSEUM." Veer right and follow the narrow street to the plateia. At the top of the hill, before descending to the plateia, a sign points the way up marble-edged steps to the **Monastery of Ag. Georgios** and the **castle.** Both are closed, but make the climb anyway for a great view of both the entire village and the sea. At Pl. Rupert Brooke, the stairs to the right pass the **Archaeological Museum** on a 15min. descent to the beach; stairs straight ahead lead to the **Faltaits Museum.**

Skyros Travel, past the central plateia on Agoras walking away from the bus station, sells **Olympic Airways** tickets, organizes bus and boat excursions, and helps find lodgings. Their port office in Linaria is open when ferries arrive. (☎22220 91 123 or 91 600; fax 22220 92 123. Open daily 9am-5pm and 6:30-10:30pm.) The **National Bank,** just past the central plateia, has a 24hr. **ATM.** (Open M-Th 8am-2:30pm.) The **hospital** (☎22220 92 222) is just out of town behind Hotel Nefeli. Ask at the **police** station, beyond Nefeli across from the gas station, for **doctors** in town. (☎22220 91 274. Open 24hr., but small staff may be away on another call.) There are **pharmacies** on the right near the central plateia (☎22220 91 617; open 8:30am-1pm and 6:30-10pm) and on the right past Skyros Travel. (☎22220 91 111. Open daily 9am-2pm and 6pm-1am.) **Internet** access is available at **Meroi Cafe** on Agoras. (☎22220 91 016. €4.50 per hr., €1.50 min. Printing €0.50 per page. Open daily 9am-1pm and 7pm-2am.) To get to the **OTE,** turn right just past Skyros Travel, walk to the end of the road, and take another right; it's on the right. (☎22220 91 399. Open M-F 7:30am-1pm.) The **post office** is on the far side of the central plateia from Agoras. (☎22220 91 208. Open M-F 7:30am-2pm.) **Postal code:** 34007.

ACCOMMODATIONS AND FOOD. Coming to Skyros and staying in a hotel is like coming to Greece to paddle in a pool—you've got to stay in a Skyrian house. You'll be met at the bus stop by old women offering **domatia.** The thick-walled houses are treasure troves, brimming with Delft ceramics, Italian linens, icons, embroidery, metalwork, and fine china bought from long-dead pirates who looted throughout the Mediterranean. Expect to pay €15-35 for a room, depending on size and season. If you decide to stay in a Skyrian house, always bargain over the price and look care-

THE BIG SPLURGE

EXPERIENCE SKYROS

Traditional Skyrian homes were remarkably miniature, around 40 sq. m. They consisted of one large room, divided by a wooden screen into three sections: a sitting room for entertaining guests, a kitchen/living area, and one small loft which served as the bedroom for the entire family. To save space in these cramped quarters, the furniture was tiny—a traditional Skyrian table and chairs looks as though it was made to serve the needs of a five-year-old's tea party, not a full-sized family. What these homes lacked in space, however, they made up for in character. The small furniture was finely carved, and beautiful ceramics and tapestries covered the walls.

Domatia offer a wonderful opportunity to experience these Skyrian traditions first-hand. But if you don't want to haggle with the old women at the bus stop or if you desire more upscale accommodations, you can rent a Skyrian-style home of your very own. Hotel Nefeli, just outside Skyros Town, rents apartments decorated in the traditional style, with a touch of luxury.

Far exceeding the usual 40 sq. m, the three-level apartments feature a kitchen and bath on the first floor, a room with two single beds on the second, and a room with a double bed on the third. The hotel also boasts a lovely swimming pool and a poolside snackbar, as well as a friendly English-speaking staff.

☎22220 91 964; fax 22220 92 061; amica@otenet.gr. Apartments €97-120.

fully for landmarks and house numbers; the streets may be confusing, and it's easy to lose your way. The aid of a travel agency will cost you an arm, a leg, and the essence of the whole experience. If you arrive during siesta, the town will be dead, and your calls for a domatia may be answered only with snores from within. If you don't feel like searching for a room, try **Hotel Elena ❷**, on the first right off of Agoras past the bus station. The newly renovated rooms have private baths, A/C, TVs, fridges, and balconies. (☎22220 91 738 or 91 070. Singles €15-20; doubles €35-45; triples €45-55.) **Hotel Nefeli ❹**, just before town on the main road, boasts classy, well-equipped rooms with TVs, A/C, private baths, phones, and some balconies, which overlook the swimming pool and snackbar. (☎22220 91 964 or 22220 92 060; amica@otenet.gr. Singles €54-75; doubles €66-82; triples €75-90.)

After a long afternoon swim, you can't go wrong with Skyrian food. Look for the light green chairs outside the incredible **O Pappou Kai Ego (Grandpa and Me) ❷**, immediately after the sharp bend in Agoras, on the right. Known in town as "Pappou's", this popular spot concocts a brilliant Chicken *O Pappous* floating in a light cream sauce over rice (€6.80), a nanny goat au lemon (€6.80), and many other Skyrian specialties. (☎22220 93 200. Entrees €4-8. Open daily 7pm-late. Get there early to avoid a long wait.) **To Metopo ❷**, on the left just heading into town from the bus stop, serves a number of seafood dishes like the octopus BBQ (€9) as well as meat dishes. (☎22220 93 515; www.inskyros.gr/tometopo.htm. Entrees €5-10.) Just before Pappou's, **Obelistirio ❶** serves up a slow-cooked, just-shy-of-healthy, incredibly delicious €1.35 gyro. (☎22220 92 205. Open daily 7pm-2am.)

SIGHTS AND ENTERTAINMENT. The **Faltaits Museum,** just past Pl. Rupert Brooke, is the wonderful private collection of a Skyrian ethnologist. Tours (available in English) take you through the frozen-in-time ancestral home of the Faltaits family. The extensive holdings include beautiful embroidery, carved furniture, pottery, costumes, copperware, rare books, and relics from the island's annual carnival—it's an excellent introduction to the island's traditional culture. The wise, friendly staff speak perfect English, affectionately calling the museum "a place where the nine muses meet." Conferences and cultural activities are held here throughout the year, including a **theater and dance festival** in late July and August; ask the staff for dates and times. (☎22220 91 232; faltaits@otenet.gr. Open daily 10am-2pm and 6-9pm. Admission and basic guided tour €2, guided historical tour €5.) Down the stairs to the right of Pl.

Rupert Brooke is the **Archaeological Museum.** (☎22220 91 327. Open Tu-Su 8:30am-3pm. €2.) Both museums have rooms decorated in the manner of traditional Skyrian homes, but if you decide to venture out on to the labyrinthine streets of the village, don't be afraid to knock on a door or two and ask to see the real thing. Skyrians are often proud to show you their homes, decorated with distinctive scarves, plates, and furnishings of the island. Closer to the beaten path, on Agoras after going left at Kalypso, is the "upper village," a stronghold of island tradition. In several shops in the area, jewels, sandals, and other Skyrian items are crafted and sold. The museum shop, **Argo,** can also be found here. (Open daily 9:30am-1:30pm and 6:30-10:30pm.) The shop's proprietor, Niko Sikkes, gives occasional talks on Skyros and leads walking tours of the island. Contact him to find out times (☎22220 92 707 or 92 158).

For an action-packed night, join the younger crowds at the two bars across from the central plateia, **Iroon** and **Kata Lathos.** (Beer €2.50-4.50; cocktails €4.50-5.50.) For those wanting calm, **Kalypso Bar,** at the top of Agoras past Pappou's, is a mellow place to sip a nightcap after a tasty Skyrian meal. (Cocktails €5-6.)

BEACHES. The pleasant beach below town stretches along the coast through the villages of **Magazia** and **Molos,** and continues around the point. To get there, head down the stairs after the Archaeological Museum. Crowded and crawling with children in July and August, it's undeniably convenient. The local nude beach, ironically named **Tou Papa to Homa** (The Sands of the Priest), remains clean and uncrowded, just south of the local beach. To get there, follow the seaside road south past Club Skyropoula and some low-ceilinged concrete structures (10-12min.); a narrow, spiky plant-lined, slippery dirt path leads downhill along a wire fence. Be especially careful on the last 4m of the trail. From here, you'll have a beautiful view of the **Southern Mountain,** famous in local literature and poetry for its hourly color changes in the sloping island light. Once home to nymphs, the deserted **natural spring** at **Nifi,** south of Linaria, allows you to frolic solo. Locals recommend the beach at **Pefkos,** which is accessible by taxi. Barren beaches and British national hero **Rupert Brooke's grave,** on the southern portion of the island, are accessible only by dusty paths or by boat. If you ask, buses from Linaria to Skyros Town may stop at the beaches of **Aherounis,** on the west coast, and **Mialos** on the east. Boats can explore the one-time pirate grottoes at **Spillies,** on the southeastern coast, and **Sarakino Island** (formerly Despot's Island), and one of the largest pirate centers in the Aegean. During Ottoman rule, it was an important hiding-place for ships. Keep an eye out for the rare wild **Skyrian ponies.**

EVIA Ευβοια

The second-largest island in Greece, Evia is paradise to any sort of pleasure-seeker, with warm waters, forested highlands, archaeological treasures, charming villages, and therapeutic baths. Its capital, Halkida, reaches out to the mainland via a new suspension bridge. Ferries from ports near Athens connect the mainland at other locations along the western coast of the island: Aedipsos, Marmari, and Karystos. Because of this proximity to Athens, floods of Greek vacationers arrive during the summer months, but Evia absorbs the masses with ease and manages to retain its immense appeal.

HALKIDA Χαλκιδα ☎22210

Sprawling, modern Halkida (also known as Chalkis)—the ninth most populated city in Greece—is the capital of Evia as well as its major transportation hub, connecting the island to the mainland. Its sparkling waterfront promenade and archaeological artifacts, nearby beaches, and fresh seafood make Halkida a prime starting point for exploration of the island.

TRANSPORTATION. Halkida's hangar-like **bus terminal** is just off **Papanastasiou,** which intersects with El. Venizelou. Heading out the front of the station, take a left, a right, and another left to get to El. Venizelou. **Buses** travel to: **Aedipsos Springs** (2½hr.; 3 per day, 10:15am-5:15pm; €6); **Athens** (2 per hr., €4.70); **Karystos** (3½hr.; 3 per day, 6am-5:30pm; €7.80); **Kimi** (1½hr., 9 per day, €5.70); **Limni** (2hr.; 4 per day, 8:30am-5:15pm; €5.30). **Trains** go to **Athens** (17 per day, €3.70). From the train station, cross the Old Bridge and take a left along the waterfront; Venizelou intersects it five blocks down. **Taxis** (☎22210 25 220) are available 24hr.

ORIENTATION AND PRACTICAL INFORMATION. Halkida's main thoroughfare is tree-lined **El. Venizelou,** which runs inland perpendicular to **Voudouri** (the waterfront) for about 12 blocks before bending left into **Eikosi Oktovriou.** The **Erippon Bridge,** or **Old Bridge,** connects Halkida to the mainland at the end of the waterfront to the left off El. Venizelou and points due west with Halkida at your back. Halkida also joins the mainland via the new **suspension bridge** on the city's southern edge now the connection for most ground transportation.

The **port authority,** across the Old Bridge in the white building with blue shutters, offers information about the city. (☎22210 28 888. Open daily 8am-3pm.) The **National Bank** is on El. Venizelou two blocks from the water, with a 24hr. **ATM** and **currency exchange.** (Open M-Th 8am-2pm, F 8am-1:30pm.) The English-speaking **tourist police** (☎22210 77 777) are only available in the mornings and are fairly inconvenient; their office is a 25min. walk up Venizelou and on to Oktovriou, in the same building as the regular 24hr. **police** (☎22210 83 333). To get to the **hospital** (☎22210 21 901), head up Venizelou away from the water and turn left on to Arethoussas (just after Papanastasiou). Follow the street as it curves and turn left on Chatzopoulou; it's two blocks down on the right. **Pl. Agios Nikolaos** borders the waterfront and is host to the **public library** and the **Church of Agios Nikolaos.** (Dress modestly to enter the church.) The **OTE** (☎22210 22 599) is at the intersection of El. Venizelou and Papanastasiou. For fast **Internet** access, go to **Orionas Net Cafe,** a 15min. walk up Avanton, the street parallel to Karamourtzouni on the other side of Pl. Agios Nikolas. (☎22210 29 123. €3.60 per hr. Open M-Th, Su 9:30am-1pm and 4:30pm-midnight, F-Sa 9:30am-1pm and 4:30pm-1am.) The **post office** is on Karamourtzouni between El. Venizelou and Pl. Agios Nikolas, the second left from the waterfront. (Open M-F 7:30am-8pm.) **Postal code:** 34100.

ACCOMMODATIONS. Most hotels here are of the €75-per-night variety catering to business travelers or Athenian families. That said, there a couple inexpensive options. **Hotel Kentrikon ❸,** Ageli Gobiou 5, in a peach-colored building, has immaculate rooms with TVs, phones, sinks, and shared fridges; some have A/C and private bath. The Greek-Canadian proprietor, George Grontis, will be happy to help you make sense of the city. (☎22210 22 375 or 22210 27 260; www.geocities.com/hotel_kentrikon. Continental breakfast included. Reception 24hr. Singles €25-37; doubles €32-46.) **Hotel Hara ❸,** a short walk up Karoni (the street that runs uphill behind the port authority) has bright white rooms with TVs, private baths, and balconies that are a bargain for larger groups. (☎22210 76 305; fax 22210 76 309. Breakfast included. Singles €40; doubles €60; triples €72.) **John's Hotel ❹,** next to Kentrikon on the road closest to the waterfront has comfortable, clean, carpeted rooms with baths, A/C, phones, and balconies. (☎22210 24 996; www.johns-hotel.gr. Breakfast €5. Singles €45; doubles €60.)

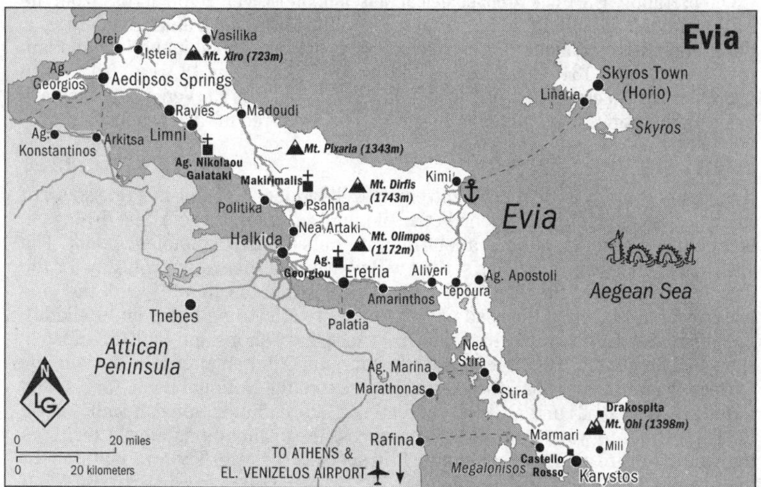

FOOD AND NIGHTLIFE. Like hotels, restaurants in Halkida are budget-busting, though the fresh seafood available along the waterfront may justify the cost. Several bakeries hide on streets around Ag. Nikolaos; fast-food joints are bunched at the base of El. Venizelou and near the Old Bridge on the waterfront. Deliciously named pizzas like the Inferno and the Erotica (tomato, cheese, salami, pepper; €8) emerge from the igloo-shaped oven at **La Fiamma ❷,** an Italian eatery on the waterfront. (☎22210 75 006. Entrees €4-9. Open daily 7pm-2am.) **Tsaf ❷,** around the corner from the OTE serves seafood dishes at more reasonable prices than waterfront establishments. (☎22210 80 070. Entrees €4.50-10.50. Open daily 1pm-midnight.) For a traditional meal go to **Folia ❷** (Φωλια), across from the park on the Evia side of the Old Bridge. (Entrees €5-8.)

Halkida's thriving nightlife is not to be missed; follow the party-hungry hordes to one of the bars on the waterfront—**Yacht Cafe** and **Jam** are both packed around 1am. (Beer €3-5; cocktails €6. Open 8:30am-late.) Later on, hop a cab to the suspension bridge and take your act on to the dance floor of **Gaz** or **Mist** (cover €10).

SIGHTS. Breezy and palm-lined **Venidou,** Halkida's kilometer-long waterfront promenade, makes for a splendid evening stroll. The fresh seafood available at many restaurants along its length, though pricey, may be worth the splurge. Or save a few euros by sipping a frappé and do some quality people watching. If you're looking for some exercise, take a hike up to the **Fortress of Carababa,** on the other side of the Old Bridge, for a great view of the city, the ocean, and the surrounding hills. From Halkida, cross the Old Bridge and head right. Once you reach the park, take the stairs on the left, which lead all the way up the hill to the fotrtress. Built by Turks in 1688 to protect Halkida from Greek and Venetian invaders, the fortress is extremely well-preserved. You can picnic, climb on the walls, and check out the lookout posts where tTurks once guarded the city. Stop by the **castle,** at the west end of the fortress, where the friendly staff will give you historical information about the site. Occasionally the castle hosts exhibitions of art or historical artifacts. On the way down, grab a cold drink or a bowl of ice cream at **Xenia Cafe ❷,** built into the hillside just below the fortress. (Ice cream €4-5. Beer

€3.50-5; frappé €3.) The **Archaeological Museum,** on El. Venizelou across from the National Bank, is full of findings from the Neolithic, Classical, and Roman Eras. It has a impressive collection of marble statuary, pottery, and shimmering gold laurels. (☎22210 76 131. Open Tu-Su 8:30am-3pm. €2, under 18 free.) The white **Church of Ag. Nikolaos,** just off of Venidou to the right of El. Venizelou, displays beautiful paintings and vaulted arches. (Modest dress required. Open 9am-1pm.)

LIMNI Λιμνι ☎22210

If there are tourists here, they're extremely well-hidden. A 45min. bus ride south of Aedipsos takes you to the wooded cove of Limni (meaning "lake"). The fishing village remains friendly, curious about the rare outsider that stumbles upon it. The splendid scenery and gorgeous setting will wow you, especially if you stay for the dazzling sunset and the star-filled night. Limni is laid out in a "T" with the long waterfront intersecting the road upward and outward (to Aedipsos and Halkida). Facing inland, turn right on the waterfront for pastry shops and Pl. Eth. Antistassis, the main plateia. Turn left for most restaurants. After an afternoon dip, stop by **To Neon ❶** (☎22210 31 262), the pastry shop next to the National Bank, for a scoop of ice cream (€0.50) and a Greek confection. Before dinner, you can walk out on the fishing pier to watch the sunset bend across the distant mountains. After 10pm the waterfront restaurants serving nightly specials pick up. Try **Avra ❷,** just past the plateia, for a traditional Greek meal. (☎22210 31 479. Entrees €4-10. MC/V.) If you stay for the stars, **Hotel Limni ❷,** to the far right, facing inland, past the small boat dock, is the only hotel in town. It has unadorned rooms with baths. (☎22210 31 316 or 31 748. Singles €16; doubles €30; triples €35. Rates lower in the low season.) For **domatia,** call ☎22270 31 640. Limni is on the Halkida-Aedipsos Springs bus line (3 per day, €5.40). Buses stop at the main intersection in town; ask before you get off when the next one comes.

ERETRIA Ερετρια ☎22210

Now a popular destination for French tourists and beach-bound Athenians, Eretria's former status as one of ancient Evia's most important cities has waned. Its past, however, is magnificently preserved in the archaeological excavations which provide the best reason for a stop here. The **Archaeological Museum,** at the inland end of Archaiou Theatrou in a courtyard brimming with marble statues, friezes, and pillars, displays some quality pieces, including three large *pithoi* (clay jugs used for holding agricultural produce) south of the House of the Mosaics—the remaining six are in the museum at Athens. The mysterious six-fingered **Centaur of Lefkandi's** body and head were inexplicably found in separate tombs. Exhibits are in Greek and French but you can buy an English guidebook (€6). Museum admission lets you into the **House of the Mosaics,** a 10min. walk from the museum; just trade your passport for the keys at the front desk of the museum. Coming out of the museum, head left to the main road, and bear right for three blocks, turning left at the marked road. The 4th-century BC mosaics are incredibly well-preserved and are among the oldest in existence. (☎22210 62 206. Open Tu-Su 8:30am-3pm. €2, students and under 18 free. Brochure €3.) On the other side of the main road from the museum is a large excavated portion of **Ancient Eretria;** highlights include the ancient **theater** and city's residential section.

Should you choose to spend the night in Eretria, inexpensive options are few and far between. Try **Pension Diamado ❸,** on Archaiou Theatrou, past the traffic circle. Wood-panelled rooms and feature TVs, private baths, and A/C at additional charge. (☎22210 62 214. Singles €28; doubles €38; triples €45.) A number of cheap fast-food establishments center on the traffic circle. For more upscale dining, head to the tavernas along the waterfront.

Eretria is accessible by bus from Halkida. **Buses** (1-2 per hr., 5am-8pm; €1.40) headed to **Karystos, Kimi,** and **Amarinthos** all stop in Eretria. Buses stop three blocks inland from and parallel to the waterfront. Facing the street from the bus station, turn left and walk to Archaiou Theatrou. The waterfront is to the right,the museum and House of the Mosaics to the left. At the water, Archaiou Theatrou intersects in a traffic circle with Amar. Artemidos runs along an edge of the L-shaped harbor; Archaiou Theatrou continues along the other.

KARYSTOS Καρυστος ☎22240

A sanctuary between mountains and sea, Karystos blooms in summer, delighting nature-lovers and party fiends alike. Both crowds owe thanks to Otto, the first King of Greece, who ordered German architect Bierbach to lay out the modern city's streets in a grid. It is easy to find your way from one attraction to the next within town, though your eyes may be distracted by the sparkling panorama. The long bus ride from Halkida passes some unexciting strip towns, but the view of Marmari's bay more than compensates; wind-generators stand guard over the sea while sunlight flashes from wave to wave.

TRANSPORTATION AND PRACTICAL INFORMATION. The central plateia along the waterfront is connected by **I. Kotsika** running straight uphill to the **city hall;** the long waterfront, **Kriezotou,** is lined with tavernas and melts into beaches in both directions along the shore. Facing the water, **Kremala beach** is to the right. **Psili beach** curves around the bay on the left, past the **bourtzi,** the stone building on the waterfront. The city hall sits above a plateia circled by **El. Amerikis,** which heads out of town to the west.

The **bus** stops on I. Kotsika, the street running along the right side of the city hall. Buses from Karystos travel to: **Athens** (4hr., daily, €8.10); **Halkida** (3hr., 2 per day, €7.60); **Marmari** (30min., 4 per day, €1.10); **Stira** (45min., 2 per day, €2). No buses run from Karystos on Sundays. Take the bus to Marmari for the ferry to Rafina, a hub for travel to the Cyclades. At **South Evia Tours,** on the left side of the central plateia (through Kozmos), Nikos, his sister Popi, and their friends can help you with everything from **car rental** (€30-40 per day) to local excursions. (☎22240 26 200 or 22240 29 010; www.eviatravel.gr. Open daily 9am-midnight.) **Taxis** (☎22240 22 200) line up in the plateia.

The **National Bank,** just uphill from the bus stop at the intersection of I. Kotsika and Karystou, has a 24hr. **ATM.** (Open M-Th 8am-2:30pm, F 8am-2pm.) To find the **police** (☎22240 22 262), turn into the small alley just past the bank and climb the stairs. A **pharmacy** (☎22240 23 505) is at the head of the central plateia. The **OTE** is on Amerikis, to the right off I. Kotsika one block above the plateia. (☎22240 22 399. Open M-Th 7:30am-2pm, F 7:30am-1:30pm.) **Internet** access is available for €3.50 per hr. at **Cafe Kalypso,** on the left side of Kriezotou, 150m past the *bourtzi*. (☎22240 25 960. Open daily 10am-10pm.) The **post office** is on Th. Kotsika, one street over from I. Kotsika, to the left facing inland, just above El. Amerikis. (Open M-F 7:30am-2pm.) **Postal code:** 34001.

ACCOMMODATIONS AND FOOD. Hotel Als ❸, on the corner of Th. Kotsika and the waterfront, offers plain rooms with TVs, A/C, private baths, and balconies. (☎22240 22 202; fax 22240 25 002. Singles €24-35; doubles €38-50.) To the right of the waterfront, facing the water, **Hotel Galaxy ❸,** run by a hospitable English-speaking couple, has rooms with TVs, A/C, and baths. (☎22240 22 600; fax 22240 22 463. Breakfast included. Singles €30; doubles €42.) Fresh seafood abounds in the many waterfront restaurants; all have similar entrees at comparable prices. **Marino's ❷,** on the waterfront to the right as you face the water, serves typical kitchen fare and seafood. (☎22240 24 126. Entrees €5-10.) Revive your inner teen at **Tastyland** ❶ (☎22240 25 000), on the waterfront. Patrons, donning their disco gear, stop in to grab a burger (€1.40) to go.

NIGHTLIFE AND ENTERTAINMENT. Lazy during the day, Karystos hosts an active nightlife on weekends. Start your night at either pseudo-tropical **Oasis** or mellow **Ostria Bar,** on Kremala beach at the right edge of the waterfront, with a drink and a moonlit bay view. (Beer €2.50-4; cocktails €5.) Around 3am the party staggers uphill to **Barbados** disco, about 1.5km out of town to the west on Amerikis. You can catch a cab at the central plateia, though the walk might be more gratifying. (☎22240 24 119. Beer €3; cocktails €4 and up. Open 11:30pm-late.) For a quieter evening, **Ciné Aura,** one block in from the waterfront on Sachtouri, shows American movies (9 and 11pm; €6).

SIGHTS. Peek into one of the holes at the back of the **Fort of Bourtzi,** the impossible-to-miss structure on the left side of the waterfront. In the 11th century, the peep-hole was used to pour boiling oil on attackers. Today the fort is regularly invaded by theater-goers crowding in to watch student productions in August; inquire at South Evia Tours (see above) about schedules. The **Archaeological Museum,** on Kriezotou just past the *bourtzi*, houses a small collection of marble statues and inscripted tablets, as well as artifacts from the *drakospita* of Stira and Mt. Ohi. (☎22240 25 661. Open Tu-Su 8:30am-3pm. €1.50, free Su.)

DAYTRIPS FROM KARYSTOS. The widely varied terrain of the Karystos region features many spectacular daytrips. Some are most easily accessed by private vehicle. The 3hr. hike up **Mt. Ohi** affords inspiring views of southern Evia and the surrounding sea. A set of mysterious and massive **columns** appears on the side of the trail 45min. into the hike. The haunting ruins of the **Dragon House** *(drakospitsa)* rest on the summit. Believed to date back to Megalithic times, it may have served as a temple dedicated to Zeus and Hera; local legend holds that it was inhabited by a dragon who terrorized the region. To get to the trailhead, take a cab to the village of **Mili** (€4), or make the 3km hike yourself by following Aiolou, one block east of the plateia, out of town. A 1hr. hike from the summit, there is an **alpine hut** ❶ (elev. 1300m), where you can spend the night (€6) and catch the glorious sunrise from the peak of Ohi the next morning. Make arrangements beforehand at South Evia Tours.

Running from the heights of Mt. Ohi to the sea below, the **Dimosari Gorge** is a natural wonder that those with an extra day should not miss. Clear, cold water cascades down its length in pools shaded by verdant forest. The gorge is accessible by car or taxi (about €60) at **Kallianou** (41km north of Karystos), or by foot—hike over the summit of Mt. Ohi and follow the gorge down the northern slope of the mountain (the trip from the Dragon House to the sea is a 6-7hr. downhill hike). Bring food and water for the hike, though you can stop for a bite at **Klimataria Taverna** ❷ (☎22240 71 300), at the base of the gorge at the end of your journey. The owners also rent **rooms** ❷ above the taverna (€13). On the slopes above Karystos is the majestic **Castello Rosso** (Kokkino Kastro or Red Castle) named for the blood spilled there in the many battles for its control. From Mili, it's a 20min. hike up the hill on the left and across the stone bridge. Other interesting sites in the region include the **Roman aqueduct** past the Red Castle and the **stone church** and **cave** at **Agia Triada,** accessible by hike from **Nikasi,** where the bus (€1.30) can drop you off. **Hiking maps** (€3) are available at South Evia Tours.

CYCLADES Κυκλαδες

When people speak longingly of the Greek islands, they are probably talking about the Cyclades. Whatever your sense of the Aegean might be—peaceful cobblestone streets and whitewashed houses, breathtaking sunsets, vigorous hikes, bacchanalia—you will find it here. The archipelago derives its name from its spiral shape: the *kyklos* (cyclical) pattern around sacred Delos. Although quiet villages and untouched spots still hide in their corners, the Cyclades are known as a tourist's mecca. Santorini is the most chic and expensive, with spectacular views along its black-sand beaches. Mykonos ranks a close second in sophistication (and price), though it also uncorks some of the wildest nightlife on earth. Beer-goggled Ios can be summed up in two words: frat party. Paros, Naxos, and Amorgos also get their share of visitors, but they're less frantic, more pristine, and attract more families and hikers. Few non-Greek vacationers sprawl in the sand on the rest of the isles. The pint-sized Little Cyclades are isolated oases blissfully uncorrupted by tourism.

HIGHLIGHTS OF THE CYCLADES

SPLISH, SPLASH, take a bath in hot sulfur springs while the sun sets over lava-made cliffs and smoke-colored sand on Santorini's western coast (p. 414).

DO AS DIONYSUS DID on the streets of Mykonos (p. 371), the Aegean's premier party destination.

LEND AN EAR to the clatter of electromagnetic art in Andros Town (p. 365).

LOSE YOUR MIND Lose your pants. Party naked on Ios (p. 407).

TRAIPSE through pearly sands and stunning rock formations–products of centuries of volcanic eruptions–on Milos (p. 424).

ANDROS Ανδρος

The magnificent 1hr. drive from the ferry landing at Gavrio to Andros Town winds above Andros's famous, beloved beaches. This island is *the* weekend destination for Greece's wealthy ship captains, whose families' originate here and who restrict ferry access to the island in their zeal to keep their hideaway unspoiled. Stone walls outline green and purple fields, and the island's 300 sandy beaches glow in solitude beneath the sun, each more breathtaking than the last. Andros has the distinction of being the only island in the Cyclades with a source of natural spring water. The flowing streams in the island's interior are bottled and exported for use throughout Greece. Though Athenians crowd in on the weekends, Andros remains an escape for those who delight in untrammeled ground and quiet nights.

BATSI Μπατσι ☎22820

Humming along a stretch of golden sand, Batsi is the tourist capital of Andros, with varied food and accommodations options and the liveliest nightlife. Visitors stroll the waterfront by night, pausing for a drink at a *kafeneion* or maybe to dance the night away in bars and clubs swelling with Athenian visitors.

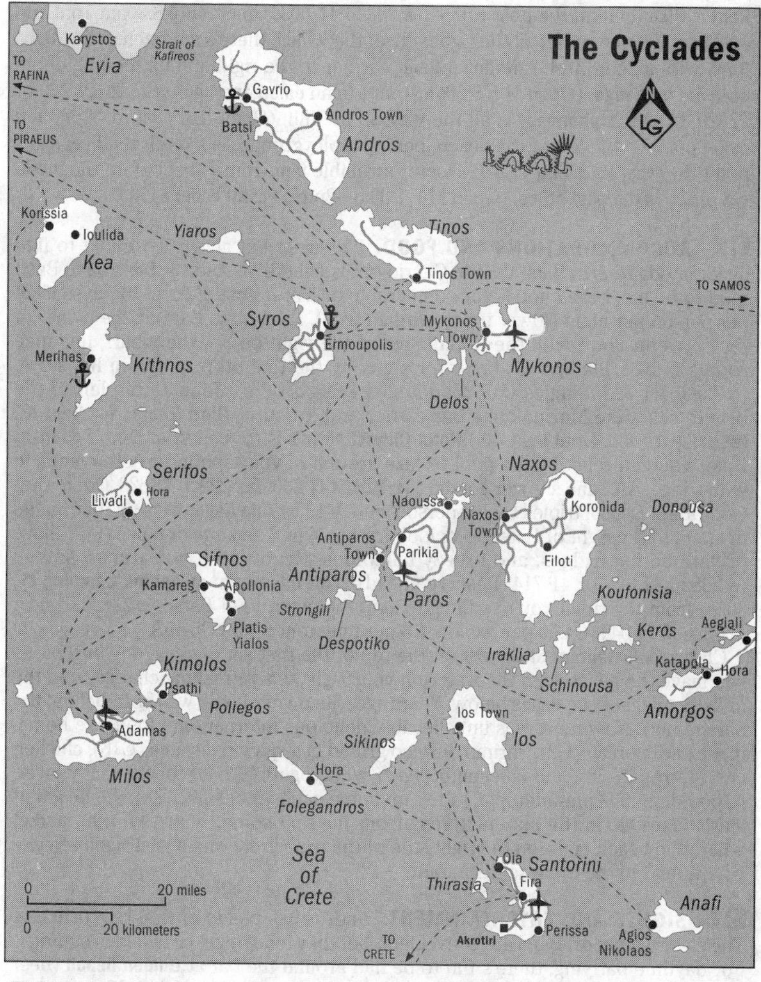

TRANSPORTATION AND PRACTICAL INFORMATION. The main **bus stop** and the **taxi stand** are at the beach's end in a small plateia. A single **bus** motors four to six times per day between **Andros Town** (€2.50), the port of **Gavrio** (€1), and Batsi. From Gavrio, **ferries** sail to: **Mykonos** (2½hr.; 3 per day, 9:45am-7pm; €9); **Rafina,** (2hr.; 3-4 per day, 9:45am-7pm; €8.90); **Tinos** (2hr.; 3 per day, 9:45am-7pm; €6.50). Check schedules and prices in Batsi at **Greek Sun Travel,** on the right of the wharf, above an ice cream parlor. Here you can rent cars and learn about walking tours. (☎22820 41 198 or 41 771; www.travelling.gr/greeksun. Open 9am-1:30pm and 6-9pm.) Alternatively, stop by **Andros Travel,** past the left end (when facing inland) of the beach. (☎22820 41 252 or 41 751; androstr@otenet.gr. Open 8:30am-2pm and 6-10pm.) In Gavrio, **Hellas Ferries** is a good choice. Beach-bound **taxi boats**

dock at the end of the wharf (round-trip €13). For a **moped** (€16 and up), try **Dino's Rent a Bike,** behind the post office. (☎22820 41 003. Open daily 8:30am-1pm and 5:30-9pm.) In the square at the right side of the wharf, there's a branch of the **Alpha Bank** with a 24hr. **ATM.** A **National Bank,** farther to the right and up the hill, offers **currency exchange.** (Open M-F 8:30am-1pm.) In an **emergency,** call ☎22820 22 222 or 22820 23 333. A **pharmacy** is all the way up the hill. (Open daily 9am-1:30pm and 6:30-9pm.) To the left of the beach, behind a playground, is a **medical office;** signs point the way. (☎22820 41 326. Doctor available 9am-1pm.) Just before the medical office is the **post office.** (Open M-F 7:30am-2pm.) **Postal code:** 84503.

ACCOMMODATIONS AND FOOD. It's easier but generally pricier to find accommodations in Batsi than in Gavrio or elsewhere on Andros. **Domatia** in Batsi tend to be nicer than hotels for comparable or lesser cost. Expect to pay €15-25 per person per night (lower if you bargain well). Panayiotis Barous, the owner of the souvenir shop with the Kodak sign at the right end of the wharf, lets nice rooms at his **Villa Lyra ❷.** Look for signs by the taxi stop or ask in his store. (☎22820 41 322. Singles €19-25; doubles €22-30.) For rooms to the left of the beach, see Mike Marinakis, a bar owner and artist, at **Glari Rooms for Rent ❸.** (☎22820 41 350. Doubles €40.) **Hotel Chryssi Akti ❹** is to the left of Dino's Rent-A-Bike. You can relax by the pool or laze around in your spotless room complete with fridge, A/C, and shower goodies. (☎22820 41 236; fax 22820 41 628. Open Apr.-Oct. Doubles €60; triples €72; 5-person suite €100.) **Villa Aegeo ❸** is up four flights of stairs to the right of Batsi Gold; look for the sign. The large doubles (€50) have private baths, fridges, and breezy balconies. Negotiate if you want a single. (☎22820 41 327 or 41 714. Reserve ahead.) You can camp at **Andros Camping ❶,** 300m from Gavrio, if you're willing to skip the nightlife of Batsi. (☎22820 71 444; fax 22820 71 044. €4.50 per person; €3 per tent, tent rental €5-15.)

Classy **Restaurant Sirocco ❸,** at the top of the first set of steps on your left as you leave the beach with the water on your right, is a refreshing change from the indistinguishable tavernas below. Years ago, the owner Louie was born behind the bar (really). Now he serves unbelievably delicious international food like homemade garlic bread (€2), Shrimp Sirocco grilled in a spicy red sauce (€15), chicken cacciatore (€7.50), and chicken *biryani* with yogurt (€7.50) for the curry lover. (Open daily 6:30pm-midnight.) Pick up some sandwiches (€2) for the beach at **Villy's Place ❶,** in the plateia across from the taxi stand. There's a **fruit market** where the beach ends, on the right side of the waterfront and a **mini-market** by the wharf, next to the Chinese restaurant.

SIGHTS AND ENTERTAINMENT. Andros has plenty of first-rate beaches. The clear waters off Batsi are convenient, but they tend to get crowded in summer. For daytime partying, there's fun to be had around the bar at **Golden beach** (beer €2.50-4), accessible by water taxi (round-trip €13), taxi (round-trip €8, arrange a pick-up time before getting out), or foot (45min.). Here visitors play beach volleyball, recline under straw umbrellas, and swim in calm, shallow water. If you're looking for something more low-key, walk back along the road 400m toward Batsi and descend to **Kipri.** Following the road toward Gavrio, you'll find **Agios Petros,** another secluded stretch of sand. Take a taxi to the ruins of the ancient capital of **Paleopolis,** where you can explore the remains of a theater and a stadium, or to the **Bay of Korthion** and Andros's finest swimming. Remnants of the **Castle of the Old Woman** are north of **Korthion,** 33km from Batsi, and are accessible by car or moped.

Begin a night out at **Select** (☎22820 42 039), a funky bar all the way up the hill to the right of the wharf (past the pharmacy). Happy Hour, every night 6-10pm, offers fun, psychedelic cocktails (€3) replete with plenty of toys and shiny decorations.

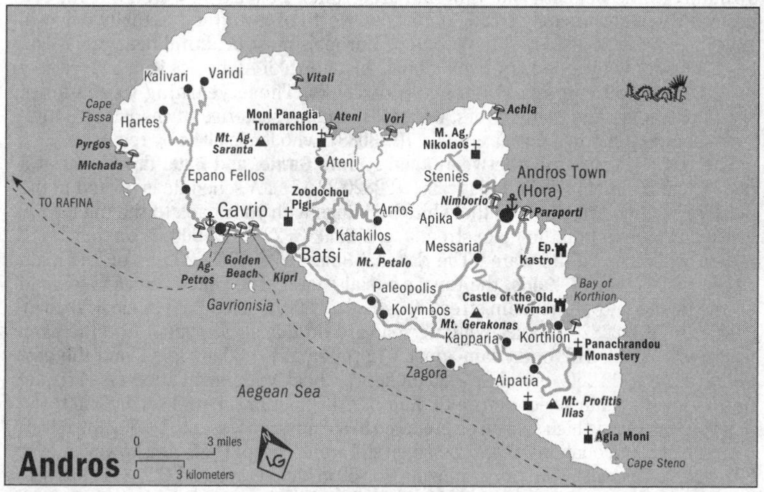

Sip a Heineken (€4) or do one of Andros's local shots on the patio at **Capriccio Music Bar** (☎22820 41 770), above the fruit market across from the taxi stand. The party moves to the indoor dance floor around midnight. Follow the Greeks to **Nameless** (☎22820 41 698) after midnight to experience how they really party; look for the artificial flames in the back right corner of the wharf's plateia.

ANDROS TOWN ☎22820

Andros Town (commonly known as Hora) is built on an Aegean peninsula capped by a medieval castle. The quiet, cobbled streets lead past hotels, shops, and homes ending at the water, where blue waves pound the black rocks. Sit and watch the world go by from a table at one of the many cafe-bars in Pl. Kairis

The **Archaeological Museum,** a large white building with a brown tile patio across from the Heaven Rock Cafe, has an excellent display on the geometric village of Zagora and other artifacts marking Andros's ancient history, including a marvelous marble **statue of Hermes.** The museum patio offers a lovely view of Andros Town. (☎22820 23 664. Open Tu-Su 8:30am-3pm. €3, students and seniors €2, EU students free.) Turn down the lane to the left upon exiting, and travel down four small sets of stairs (following the blue arrows on the left wall) to find the **Museum of Modern Art.** The building displays a number of works by 20th-century Greek sculptor Michael Tombros and by other Greek artists. The weird noises from downstairs are not a mechanical failure—they're the clatter of the wonderful kinetic, **electromagnetic art** by Takis. Two sets of steps farther down on the right is the large space set aside for the traveling exhibitions that visit the museum every summer. (☎22820 22 444. Open Oct.-May M, Sa-Su 10am-2pm.; June-Sept. M, W-Sa 10am-2pm and 6-8pm. €6, students €3, seniors and children under 12 free.) At the end of the main road is the **Maritime Museum of Andros.** (Open daily 8am-11pm. Free.) Continue on the main road for a view of the **Venetian turret.**

Gazing at peninsular Hora from the sea, **Paraporti beach** is to the left; **Nimborio beach** is to the right. To reach Paraporti, head down any of the alleys on the right after Pl. Kairis. Nimborio is most easily accessed via the stairs across the street from Alpha Bank. Down the rocky face at the end of the peninsula is an excellent swimming hole beneath old Venetian arch ruins. Be sure to watch out for sea urchins and a surprisingly strong undertow. North of town (and virtually inaccessible) lies **Achla,** considered to be one of Europe's most beautiful beaches. It can be reached only by moped or fishing boat. Just north of Alcha lies **Vori,** a close second, where you can swim among shipwrecks. Those yearning to see more secluded spots—the many rivers, **waterfalls,** and monasteries of the island's interior—should pin down **Cosmas** (☎697 707 3088), who leads **hikes** by request.

The **bus** (€1) that runs between **Andros Town, Gavrio,** and **Batsi** drops you at a depot near a plateia where **taxis** wait (☎22820 22 171). A schedule is posted in the outdoor waiting area. Facing the white buildings with your back to the hills, walk down any lane to find the main street. **Alpha Bank** (☎22820 23 900) is on this street as you walk toward the water. The **National Bank** (☎22820 22 232) is on the main street, just before **Pl. Kairis,** the town's social center. The **police station** is located on the inland end of the main street. (☎22820 22 300. Open 24hr.) In **medical emergencies,** dial ☎22820 22 222. Walking seaward on this street, you'll find the **pharmacy** (☎22820 22 210; open 8am-3pm), **OTE** (open M-F 7:30am-3pm), and the **post office** (☎22820 22 260; open M-F 7:30am-2pm). Check your email at **e-waves Internet Cafe** along the main street before Pl. Kairis (€4.50 per hr.). **Postal code:** 84500.

If you visit during high season be prepared to spend, spend, spend. During the rest of the year, accommodations in Andros Town still aren't cheap. There are, however, over 50 registered **domatia,** with prices ranging €35-50 in high season and €25-35 in low season. Keep an eye out for signs along Nimborio beach. **Hotel Egli ❸** is up the lane from Alpha Bank. Rooms have TVs, sinks, and phones; each floor has a sofa lounge. Reception is next door at the hotel bar. (☎22820 22 303 or 22 159; fax 22820 22 159. Private bath and breakfast extra. Singles €30-33; doubles €44-52.) **Karaoulanis Rooms ❸,** on the left corner of Nimborio beach (as you face inland), are top of the line with kitchens, microwaves, bathrooms, A/C, and TVs. (☎22820 24 412; riva@otenet.gr. Moped rental €14. Doubles €30 and up; doubles with fridges, A/C, and kitchenettes €60 and up. Rooms for 2-5 people available.) If you wish to experience high society, check into **Paradise Hotel ❺** (☎22820 22 187; fax 22820 22 340), on the main road 500m before Hora. Lie by the pool and order a drink, or just take a siesta on your canopy bed in the tastefully decorated rooms. (Doubles €90-120; triples €115-150.) *Mezedes*, milkshakes, and pizza are among the tasty options served by friendly locals in Pl. Kairis. Family-owned cafes, restaurants, and markets line the main street and Nimborio beach.

TINOS Τηνος

Tinos spreads below from the summit of hulking Mt. Exobourgo. In one direction, Hora's buildings, ferries, and mystic beaches cluster together. Away from the port, wildflowers, medieval dovecotes, and villages untouched by time contrast with the green mountains. The island's allure is perhaps most apparent to the thousands of pilgrims who have flocked to the Panagia Evangelistria Church in Tinos Town every year since the 1812 War of Independence. Its miracle-working Icon of the Annunciation—the *Megalohari* (Great Joy) or *Panagia Evangelistra*—was found by a nun in an underground church. Each year on the Feasts of the Annunciation (March 25) and Assumption (August 15), close to 30,000 pilgrims crawl on their knees up a red carpet from the port to the church; they then follow the icon in a 10km procession to the Kechrovouni convent.

TINOS TOWN ☎22830

A stroll past the barrage of waterfront tourist shops reveals Tinos Town's dual role as tourist and religious mecca: peddlers sell both standard tourist wares and the jugs pilgrims use to carry Panagia's sacred waters home. The town is also politi-

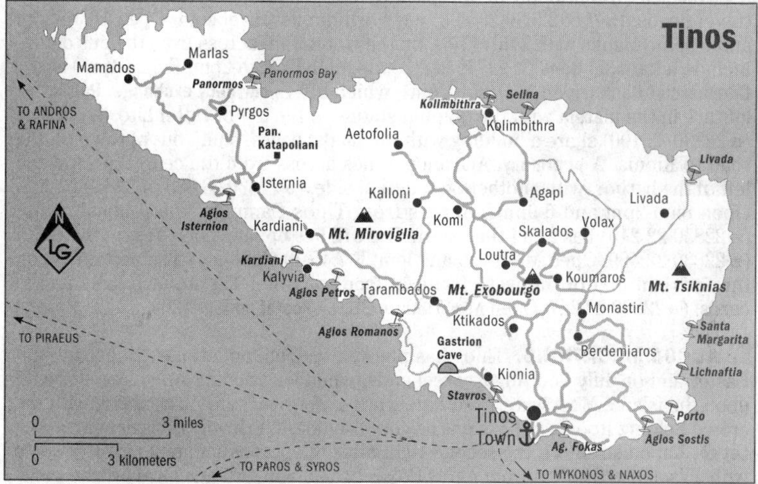

cally significant. On August 15, 1940, an Italian submarine torpedoed the Greek cruiser Elli as it docked in the harbor for the observance of the Feast of the Assumption of the Virgin Mary. Mussolini declared war two months later. The ancient Greeks believed Tinos to be the home of the wind god Aeolus; today, the cool sea breezes that buffet the island speak to his legacy.

TRANSPORTATION. **Ferry** schedules vary, so check with the port police (☎22830 22 348) in the central port or **Blue Star Travel** (☎22830 24 241). Ferries run to: **Andros** (2hr., 3-4 per day, €6.50); **Mykonos** (30min., 4-5 per day, €3.70); **Naxos** (4hr., daily, €7.85); **Paros** (1hr., daily, €9.60); **Piraeus** (5½hr., 3-4 per day, €20.40); **Rafina** (4hr., 3-4 per day, €12.90); **Syros** (20min.; 3-4 per day, 10:15am-3:15pm; €4.30). There are three ferry ports in Tinos (see below), so ask which is yours when purchasing tickets. Across the street from the National Bank, **buses** go three to five times daily during the summer to: **Kalloni** (€2); **Kionia** (€0.90); **Panormos** (€2.50); **Porto** (€1); **Pyrgos** (€2.50); **Skalados** (€1.50); **Steni** (€1.30). A **schedule** is posted in the KTEL ticket agency across from the central port, next to Blue Star Travel. (☎22830 22 440. Open 8am-5pm.) Bus service in winter is limited. **Taxis** sit next to Commercial Bank. (☎22830 22 470. Available 6am-1:30am.) If you want your own wheels, go to a waterfront rental place. Try **Vidalis,** Zanaki Alavanou 16 (☎22830 23 400; vidalis@thn.forthnet.gr), on the road running inland from the right of the waterfront, across from Commercial Bank. (Mopeds €10-23; cars €27 and up. English-speaking staff. **Free maps.** Open 8:30am-9pm.)

ORIENTATION AND PRACTICAL INFORMATION. Most ferries land at the central port across from the bus depot; catamarans and hydrofoils dock at the port to the left, as you face inland. The outside port is located near a playground farther to the left. Activity centers on two main streets: sprawling **Megalochares** and parallel pedestrian street **Evangelistras** (known as "Bazaar") to the right. Both streets lead uphill to **Panagia Evangelistria Church.** Many domatia are off Evangelistras and **Alavanou,** on the right of the waterfront. Hotels, tavernas, ticket agencies, and banks face the main dock. A labeled map of Tinos is to the left of the central port.

Windmills Travel, opposite the park by the outside port, will handle all your travel needs. (☎/fax 22830 23 398; www.windmills-travel.com. Open 10am-2pm and 6-8pm.) Banks with 24hr. **ATMs,** on the waterfront across from the bus depot, include a **National Bank** (☎22830 22 328; open M-Th 8am-2pm, F 8am-1pm) and a **Commercial Bank** (open M-F 8am-2pm), which offers **currency exchange. Public toilets** are in the plateia with the dolphin statue, to the left of Hotel Lito. The **police** (☎22830 22 100) share a building with the **tourist police,** 5min. out of town on the road to Kionia. A **pharmacy,** Alavanou 7, lies across from the central port at the left of the harbor, with another on the right side. (☎22830 23 888 or 22830 22 438. Open 8am-2pm and 6-9pm.) Across from Tinos Camping, the **medical center** (☎22830 22 210) has a full-time staff. The **OTE** lies up Megalochares on the right. (☎22830 22 499. Open M-Th 7:45am-3pm, F 7:45am-12:30pm.) The **post office,** on the far right end of the waterfront, in front of Hotel Tinion, also sells phone cards. (☎22830 22 247. Open M-F 7:30am-2pm.) **Postal code:** 84200.

ACCOMMODATIONS. Tinos has plenty of accommodations, except around Easter and on July and August weekends, when vacationing Athenians descend upon the island. Most waterfront hotels are expensive, so try bargaining with the crowd holding Rooms to Let signs as you disembark. Friendly **Nikoleta Rooms to Let ❷,** Kapodistriou 11, the second right after the post office, rents lovely rooms with TVs and A/C, 100m from Agios Fokas beach. Some rooms have private baths and kitchenettes. (☎22830 24 719; nikoleta@thn.forthnet.gr. Common kitchen, laundry, and BBQ facilities available. Call ahead to be picked up at the port. Singles €20-25; doubles €30; triples and quads €35.) **Dimitris-Maria Thodosis Rooms ❸,** Evangelistrias 33, midway up the road to the left, on the second floor, is a traditional home with a central kitchen, and common bathrooms. Families or groups of five to eight should ask about their more upscale apartments on G. Plati. (☎22830 24 809 or 694 686 8495. Open Mar. 25-Oct. 31. Doubles €30; apartments for 2 €60, €12 for each additional person.) Up the stairs to the left of Windmills Travel, turn left at the top of the stairs to find **Faros ❸,** Foskolou 2, on the right. Rooms have views, baths, and TVs; some have A/C. (☎22830 22 712. Singles €25; doubles €35-45; triples €60.) If you're in the mood for high-class service, call ahead to reserve one of the spacious rooms at **Hotel Tinion ❹.** Follow the main port road to the right (with your back to the water); it's on the left. (☎22830 22 261; kchatzi@ath.forthnet.gr. Doubles €55-80. MC/V.) After a 10min. walk from the waterfront to the right, signs point the way to **Tinos Camping ❶,** which has kitchen, laundry, showers, restaurant, and a bar. (☎22830 22 344; fax 22830 24 551. July-Aug. €6 per person; May-June and Sept.-Oct. €4.50 per person, €3-4 per tent, tent rental €6-6.50. Bungalows for 2-5 with baths, TVs, and kitchenettes €40-47.)

FOOD AND NIGHTLIFE. Small **Cafe Italia ❷,** Akti Nazou 10, behind the children's park near Windmills Travel, is a hidden jewel, serving a range of pastas (€6-8) made to the exacting standards of its Italian chef Dora. (☎22830 25 756. Open 9am-12:30am.) **Mesklies ❷,** on the left side of the waterfront below a green awning, is both a fine pastry shop (€3.50-4) and a pizza restaurant (€8-14). Wrap up your meal with *tyropitakia*, the cheesecake-like local specialty. (☎22830 22 151. Open 7am-3am.) There's a **supermarket** two doors to the left of the post office.

Late-night partyers buzz around the square to the left of the hydrofoil port. Most bars are open all day and late into the evening; clubs are open 9pm-3am. Pop music encourages bar-top dancing under the starlight at **Koursaros Music Bar** (also known as **Corsaire**), near the water, 10m seaward from Mesklies restaurant. (☎22830 23 963. Drinks €3-6.50. Open 8am-3am.) At **Plori Cafe Yacht Club** (☎22830 24 824), a 10min. walk to the left along the beach road toward Stavros beach, sit back and relax on your choice of indoor or outdoor lounge chairs. Those who are just raring up when the bars shut down head for the thatched roof of **Paradise,** an "after-club" 5min. past Plori. (Open 3am-9am.) **The Kaktos Club,** inside a windmill on the hills above the Panagia Evangelistria Church, opens its incredible hilltop view to lovers of American music; it also hosts special live music nights.

SIGHTS. In 1822 the Tiniote nun Sister Pelagia had a vision of the Virgin Mary telling her about an icon buried in an uncultivated field (once a church destroyed by 10th-century pirates). A year later, amid great rejoicing, the prophesied icon was unearthed, and **Panagia Evangelistria** was built to house it. The church continues to draw daily visits from believers who consider it evidence of the Virgin's power and presence. The relic is said to have healing powers and is credited with ridding Tinos of cholera, saving a sinking ship, and giving a blind man sight. Gifts of gold, diamonds, and jewels, and countless *tamata*—plaques praising Mary's healing powers—cover the chapel, the "Lourdes of the Aegean." The **icon** is housed in the upper part of the church. Head up the red-carpeted flight of steps on the right side, facing the church. Pilgrims process in the front door, and the icon is ahead on the left. It is customary for pilgrims to cross themselves three times (touching forehead, chest, right shoulder, then left shoulder), and then kiss the icon, before filing past. The **Well of Sanctification** is a natural spring that appeared when the icon was unearthed. Today it flows from one of many faucets in the church between two sets of marble entrance stairs to the chapel; visitors scoop up a bottle of it to drink or to carry as a talisman. To the right is the mausoleum of the Greek warship Elli, sunk by an Italian torpedo in 1940. (Church open daily 7am-8pm. Free. Modest dress required. Museum open M-F 8am-3pm, Sa-Su 9am-2pm. Free.) Tinos's small **Archaeological Museum,** halfway up Megalochares on the left and uphill from the OTE, exhibits sculptures from the coastal sanctuary of Poseidon and Amphitrite at Kionia, an ancient sundial, a 5th-century BC relief from a cemetery at Xombourgo, and wonderful 7th-century BC relief pottery showing Athena bursting from Zeus's head. (Open Tu-Su 8:30am-3pm. €2, students €1, EU students free.) Tinos is strewn with medieval-era **dovecotes,** large birdhouses that number over 1000. The island's symbol, they are built of intricate white lattices and are full of nesting birds. Take the KTEL **bus** from Tinos Town (3-5 per day, €0.90) or drive left along the waterfront road to explore the ruins of the 4th-century BC **Temple of Poseidon and Amphitrite** and enjoy the fine-sand beach.

Take a bus 29km northwest of Tinos Town to the artsy, picturesque town of **Pyrgos** (1hr., 3-5 times per day, €2.50), home to a School for Fine Arts and inhabited by Tinos's renowned marble sculptors.

IN RECENT NEWS

GREECE'S CLEAN-UP

With the influx of attention it received for both assuming the 2003 European Union presidency and hosting the 2004 Olympic Games, Greece has come under harsh criticism for its environmental record. In fact, in 2003, when charges were filed for the unsanitary practices of the overflowing Para Galini Landfill in Iraklion, Greece became the first nation in the EU to be fined for failing to comply with environmental legislation.

Since then, the EU has charged Greece with a barrage of other environmental encroachments, from the hazardous state of the Kouroupitas Landfill in Hania to the failure at protecting the Loggerhead *(Coretta coretta)* turtle on the Ionian islands. Chastisement has not only come from the EU. Greenpeace, which traditionally rates the environmental friendliness of approaching Olympics, gave Greece a zero out of ten, lamenting that the country was doing little to organize green Games. In the past year, however, Greece has made a concerted effort to respond to environmental issues. The 2003 Rio conference with the EU set out a list of long-term goals that paved the way for forest protection in wilderness areas, had amendments for cleaner seas, and eliminated subsidies damaging to the environment. In the meantime, Greece had made advances toward noninvasive farming, clean technology, and sustainable consumption. The changes, however, are not limited to abstract legislation; look around cities for new brightly-colored recycling bins throughout the streets.

Several museums and exhibitions are dedicated to past residents, such as Giannouli Chalepas, whose *Sleeping Daughter* graces Athens's central graveyard. For classy souvenirs, head to **The Blue Trunk** (☎22830 31 870), where marble and terracotta statues are for sale; it's on Sardela, near a cluster of tavernas and cafes frequented by locals.

HIKING MOUNT EXOBOURGO. If you have a car or moped, the villages that ring Mt. Exobourgo (Εξοβουργο Ορος; 14km north of Tinos Town) and the site of the Venetian Fortress **Xombourgo** are great places to explore. After withstanding 11 assaults, the 13th-century capital fell to the Ottomans in 1715, becoming their last territorial gain. For a panoramic view of the entire island, drive up to the foot of the fortress itself. If you're feeling energetic, climb the mountain from the eastern foothill (near Xinara or Loutra) on a trail lined with wildflowers and brilliant orange moss. At the gated entrance to Xombourgo, head left into the plateia to the little gate where the rocky trail to the top starts. The road detours to a church at a fork. Go straight to get to the fort. Strong winds buffet Exobourgo, causing the fort to close occasionally ; stay low to avoid getting blown off the mountain.

The delightful hike from Tinos Town to Mt. Exobourgo takes 3-4hr. Alternatively, the trip from Tinos Town to Loutra and back takes 3-4hr., taking you over much of the island's interior. Other direct routes up Mt. Exobourgo don't cut through all the villages; wooden signposts mark these trails. Whatever your route, bring water, provisions, comfortable shoes, and a buddy. Stick to the trail and be prepared for extremely high winds at all times. There are signs for hikes around Tinos. Ask a travel agent about various difficulties and lengths.

To make the ascent to the village of **Kitikados,** begin by heading left behind the Panagia Evangelistria Church to unmarked **Agios Nikolaos** (ask if you can't find it). Follow this road straight up and to the left, where the asphalt gives way to a broad cobblestone path that takes you past two white chapels within 45min. Along the ascent, look behind you to see the ferries coming into port. Past the second white chapel is a small stone bridge with an arch; either go over the bridge for a 15min. visit to the unremarkable Kitikados or continue on the main trail up to the island's main asphalt road and turn left. Continue across the road until you see a small trail marked with a wooden sign bearing a hiker and the word "Ksinara." Follow this path up to the right of the windmill. Once you pass the windmill, there is another trail marker on your right. Written in Greek, it indicates a direct ascent up to Mt. Exobourgo, looming in the distance, topped by a cross revealing the **fortress** Xombourgo. **Ksinara** is straight ahead and **Tripotamos** is behind you. You can ascend Exobourgo from here or continue 1½hr. through the quiet town of Ksinara.

To get to the village of **Loutra To Xombourgo** (2hr.), follow the road through to the church plateia and then head left to the narrow dirt and stone trail. This pathway begins your descent to the village; turn right when you hit the asphalt road. Continue on the asphalt past Loutra to Skalados; turn right to find a nice hillside taverna. From the taverna, head up and right on a street with steps to another asphalt road. Walk to the right about 15min. until you see the blue sign pointing toward **Volax.** It's worth stopping here to meander through the narrow, low-arched streets and to peek into one of the many basket-weaving workshops in town. Retrace your steps to the blue Volax sign and turn left onto the road. At **Koumaros,** look for the **Association Lounge,** offering hospitality and dirt-cheap drinks and snacks. Once through Koumaros, the road turns into a stone stair trail that will take you up the northeast side of Mt. Exobourgo. At the foot of **Sacred Heart,** an impressive Catholic monastery, go diagonally through the plateia to the little gate on the left. Ascend 20min. to the Xombourgo fortress for a view of the island.

MYKONOS Μυκονος

Mykonos has long been the object of envy and desire. In ancient times, merchants here competed with each other to serve pilgrims en route to the holy island of Delos. In the Byzantine and Ottoman times, pirates patrolled the seas hankering for riches. In the 1970s, Mykonos's gay scene and wild nightlife secured the island's place among the premier resorts of the Mediterranean. The island is now the playground of sophisticates, called *kosmopolitikoi*. Though Mykonos's gay scene has lost its former preeminence, it's anything but dead and nightlife still commands the attention of hard-core hedonists the world over.

MYKONOS TOWN ☎22890

Mykonos Town owes its labyrinthine streets, now closed to motor traffic in the afternoon and evening, to Mediterranean pirates. The city's maze of streets was planned expressly to disconcert and disorient marauders—it has a similar effect on tourists. Despite the influx of visitors, the town has resisted large hotel complexes and is anything but a generic tourist town. The drag queens and high fashion models seem to complement, not corrupt, the traditional fishing boats, basket-laden donkeys, and king-like pelicans of the harbor.

TRANSPORTATION

Flights: Olympic Airways (☎22890 22 490 or 22 495; airport 22890 22 327). Flights to: **Athens** (40min., 6-7 per day, €90); **Rhodes** (1hr., 2 per week, €109); **Santorini** (30min., 4 per week, €78); **Thessaloniki** (3 per week, €120). A taxi (€8) from Mykonos Town is the only way to the airport.

Ferries: To: **Andros** (3hr., 2 per day, €9.20); **Naxos** (3hr., 1-2 per day, €7.10); **Piraeus** (6hr., 2-3 per day, €24); **Rafina** (5hr., 1-2 per day, €15); **Samos** (2 per week, €18.80); **Santorini** (6hr., 3 per week, €13.40); **Syros** (2½hr., 1-3 per day, €5.90); **Tinos** (45min., 3 per day, €4).

Flying Dolphins: To: **Ios** (daily, €25.10); **Naxos** (daily, €14.40); **Paros** (daily, €13.10); **Piraeus** (3-5 per day, €36.20); **Santorini** (daily, €24.80); **Syros** (2-5 per day, €11.50); **Tinos** (4-5 per day, €7.60).

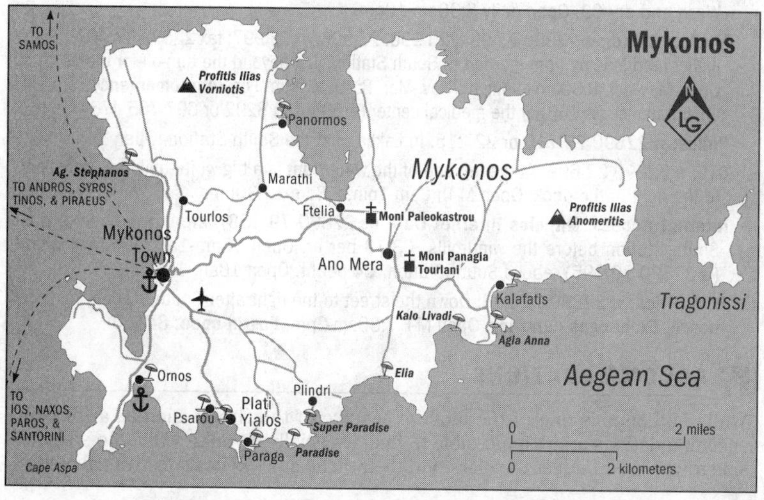

Buses: KTEL (☎22890 23 360) has 2 stations in town. Unless noted otherwise, buses are €0.90 during the day and €1.20 after midnight. **North Station,** uphill from the ferry dock, serves: **Ag. Stefanos beach** (every 30min.); **Ano Mera** and **Kalafatis** (10 per day); **Elia beach** (30min., 8 per day, €1); **Psarou beach** (15min.; every 30min., 8:15am-2am). **South Station,** uphill from the windmills at the opposite edge of town, serves: **Ag. Ioannis** (every hr.); **Paradise beach** (every 30min.); **Plati Yialos beach** (every 30min.); **Ornos beach** (every 30min.). Schedules are posted at the stations.

Taxis: ☎22890 22 400 or 22890 23 700. Available at "Taxi Square," along the water.

Rentals: Agencies ring both bus stops. Be sure to bargain. **Mopeds** €9-25 per day. **Jeeps** €35-50 per day.

PRACTICAL INFORMATION

Facing inland, incoming boats dock at a pier on the far left of the waterfront. One road leads to the right along the water, past the beach to the center of town. Another parallel road, north of the first, heads uphill to the **North Station** bus depot, and wraps around the back of Mykonos Town to **South Station.** A turn-off on the road to South Station leads to the **airport.** The action centers around the **waterfront,** but much of the real shopping, fine dining, and partying occurs among the narrow, winding back streets, including **Matogianni, Kalogera, Mitropoleas,** and **E. Dinameon.** On the right side of the waterfront is a pier that docks excursion boats usually headed to Delos. Past the pier is a series of churches, a lovely part of town called **Little Venice,** home to the islands' classiest bars and cafes, and a windmill-lined hill. The town's essentials—post office, police, markets, and so forth—mostly lie in the **inland** vicinity of Lakka and South Station, reached by following Mitropoleas.

Tourist Police: ☎22890 22 482. In an office at the ferry landing. Very helpful English-speaking staff. Open daily 8am-11pm.

Banks: National Bank (☎22890 22 932), around the corner from South Station, **exchanges currency** and has an **ATM.** Open M-Th 8am-2pm, F 8am-1:30pm.

International Bookstore: International Press (☎22890 23 316), in a small plateia opposite Pierro's; follow signs from the waterfront. It sells eclectic books, magazines, and newspapers in English. Open daily noon-midnight.

Laundromat: ☎22890 27 600. On Psarou, toward the windmills from the bus terminal. Wash and dry €9. Open daily 8:30am-10pm.

Medical Center: ☎22890 23 994, 23 995, 23 996, or 23 997; fax 22890 27 407. On the higher road leading from the port to South Station, just beyond the turn-off for the hospital. Open May-Oct. 8:30am-midnight; Nov.-Mar. 8:30am-9pm. For 24hr. **emergency** care, call an ambulance (☎166) or the medical center (☎694 433 8292 or 697 765 4737).

Police: ☎22890 22 716 or 22 215. In Lakka past the South Station. Open 24hr.

OTE: ☎22890 22 699. At the left end of the waterfront in a big white building, uphill and to the right of the dock. Open M-Th 8am-1pm, F 8am-12:30pm.

Internet Access: @ngelos Internet Cafe (☎22890 79 138), around the corner from South Station before the windmills. €3.79 per hr. Open 10am-1am. **Internet World** (☎22890 79 195), above South Station. €4 per hr. Open 10am-1am.

Post Office: ☎22890 22 238. Down the street to the right after South Station, near the police. **Exchanges currency.** Open M-F 7:30am-2pm. **Postal code:** 84600.

ACCOMMODATIONS

While Mykonos is one of the most expensive of the Greek islands, affordable accommodations aren't impossible to find, especially if you're willing to stay outside town. Most budget travelers find their niche at Mykonos's festive campsites,

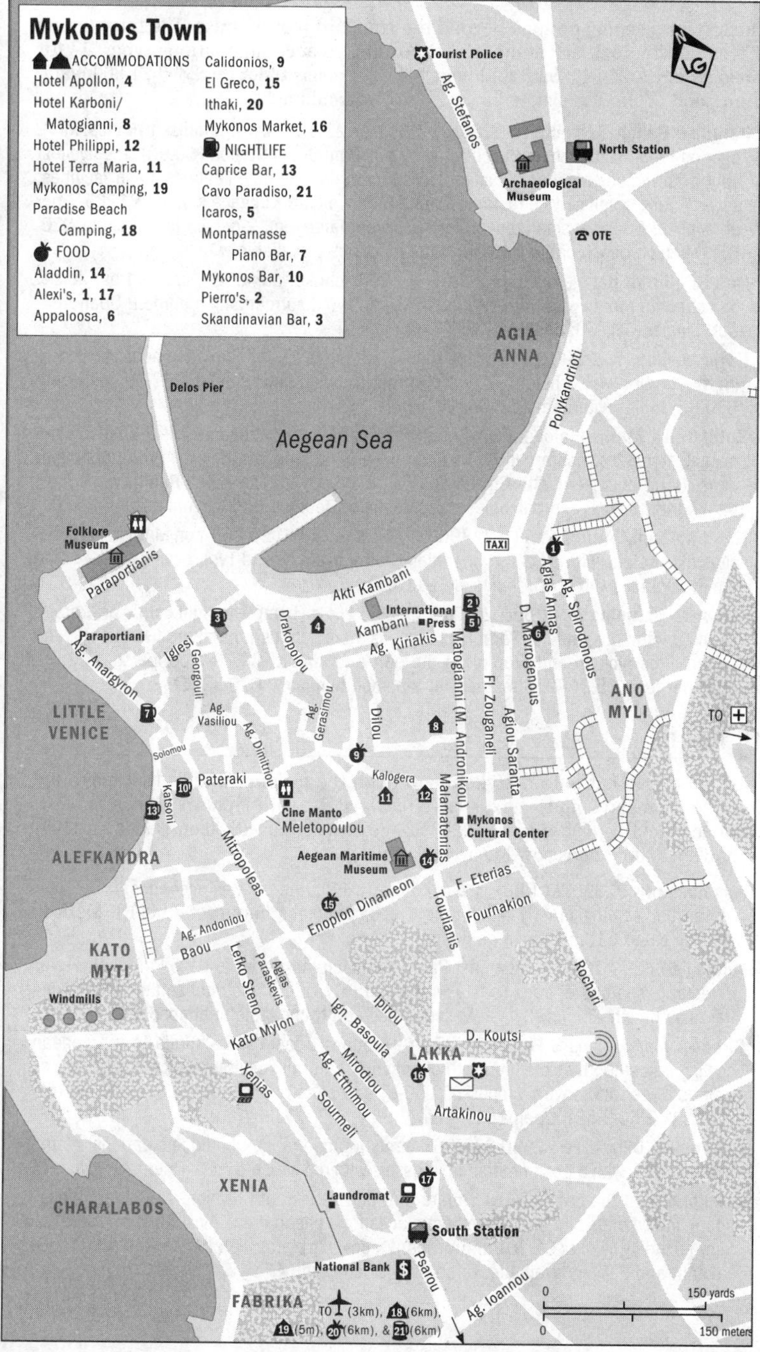

Mykonos Town
ACCOMMODATIONS
Hotel Apollon, 4
Hotel Karboni/ Matogianni, 8
Hotel Philippi, 12
Hotel Terra Maria, 11
Mykonos Camping, 19
Paradise Beach Camping, 18
FOOD
Aladdin, 14
Alexi's, 1, 17
Appaloosa, 6
Calidonios, 9
El Greco, 15
Ithaki, 20
Mykonos Market, 16
NIGHTLIFE
Caprice Bar, 13
Cavo Paradiso, 21
Icaros, 5
Montparnasse Piano Bar, 7
Mykonos Bar, 10
Pierro's, 2
Skandinavian Bar, 3
Tourist Police
Ag. Stefanos
North Station
Archaeological Museum
OTE
AGIA ANNA
Polykandrioti
Delos Pier
Aegean Sea
Folklore Museum
Paraportianis
TAXI
Akti Kambani
International Press
Kambani
Paraportiani
Ag. Anargyron
Iglesi
Georgouli
Drakopolou
Ag. Kiriakis
Matogianni (M. Andronikou)
Agias Annas
Ag. Spirodonous
D. Mavrogenous
Fl. Zouganeli
Agiou Saranta
ANO MYLI
TO
LITTLE VENICE
Ag. Vasiliou
Ag. Dimitriou
Ag. Gerasimou
Dilou
Solomou
Pateraki
Kalogera
Malamatenias
Katsoni
Cine Manto
Meletopoulou
Mykonos Cultural Center
ALEFKANDRA
Mitropoleas
Aegean Maritime Museum
F. Eterias
Fournakion
Enoplon Dinameon
Tourlianis
Ag. Andoniou
Baou
KATO MYLI
Lefko Steno
Agias Paraskevis
Rochari
Windmills
Ipirou
Ign. Basoula
Kato Mylon
D. Koutsi
LAKKA
Mirodiou
Ag. Efthimou
Xenias
Sourmeli
Artakinou
XENIA
Laundromat
CHARALABOS
South Station
National Bank
Psarou
Ag. Ioannou
FABRIKA
TO (3km), 18 (6km), 19 (5m), 20 (6km), & 21 (6km)
0
150 yards
0
150 meters

which offer sleeping options beyond the standard plot of grass. The information offices on the dock are numbered according to accommodations type: "1" for **hotels** (☎22890 24 540; 9am-midnight), "2" for **rooms to let** (☎22890 24 860; 9am-11pm), and "3" for **camping** (☎22890 23 567; 9am-midnight).

Paradise Beach Camping (☎22890 22 852 or 22 129; www.paradisemykonos.com), right on Paradise beach and accessible by bus from South Station (€0.90). The liveliest spot in town sees most of the island's visitors during the day. Features clean facilities, several bars, a self-service restaurant, and a dance club. Luggage storage €1. €5-7 per person; €2.50-3 per small tent, €2.50-3.50 per large tent; 2-person beach cabin €20-45; 4-person beach cabin €40-90; hotel rooms also available. ❶

Hotel Philippi, Kalogera 25 (☎22890 22 294; chriko@otenet.gr), across from Zorzis, has cheerful rooms with baths, fridges, TVs, and A/C surrounding a garden. Open Apr.-Oct. Singles €35-60; doubles €45-75. ❹

Hotel Apollon (☎22890 22 223), on the waterfront, is an antique-laden house overlooking the harbor with a helpful, cheerful owner. Singles and doubles €42-50, with bath €50-65; triples with bath €56-65. ❸

Hotel Terra Maria, Kalogera 33 (☎22890 24 212, low season 22890 22 957; tertaxma@otenet.gr), has a central location on a quiet side street next to the public gardens. Don't confuse it with Chez Maria or the nearby Marios Hotel. Rooms have A/C, baths, fridges, TVs, and balconies. Breakfast €6. Doubles €46-82; triples €55-99. ❹

Hotel Karboni/Matogianni (☎22890 22 217; fax 22890 23 264), on Matogianni, consists of 2 hotels, with different amenities (both have A/C and TVs), owned by the same family. Doubles €40-100; triples €63-110. ❹

Mykonos Camping (☎22890 25 915 or 25 916; mycamp@hotmail.com), on Paraga beach, on the bus route to Paradise beach, is more subdued than Paradise but still animated. Free pick-up and drop-off at the port and airport. €4.70-7 per person; €2.60-3.50 per tent, €5.30-7.50 tent rental; 2-person bungalow €20-30. ❶

FOOD

Most choose to eat out on Mykonos, though the produce stands that surround South Station can supply inexpensive meals along with **Mykonos Market,** a short distance from the post office. (☎22890 24 897. Open 8am-12:30am.) Cheap creperies and souvlaki joints crowd nearly all streets.

Appaloosa (☎22890 27 086), 1 block from Taxi Square on Mavrogeneous, is a classy restaurant serving mostly Mexican entrees. Delicious burritos €8.50-13. Mexican chicken salad €10.50. Open daily 8pm-1:30am. ❸

Ithaki (☎22890 26 850), just past Paradise beach, next door to Cavo Paradiso, serves delectable seafood entrees (pasta with shrimp €18) in a beautiful setting overlooking Paradise beach. The lovely marble sculptures add to the tasteful atmosphere. ❹

Sirocco, Metropoleos 8 (☎22890 27 669), brings a taste of California to the Aegean serving fruit smoothies blended with either sorbet, frozen yogurt, or ice cream (€5-6), as well as sweet and savory crepes (€3.50-8) and sandwiches made with real New York bagels (€2.50-3.50). Open 10am-1am.

Calidonios, Dilou 1 (☎22890 27 606), offers a broad range of unique creations, made-from-scratch, with a posh ambiance. Mussels with red sauce €7.50. Open 1pm-1am. ❷

Alexi's, one at the back of Taxi Square and one near South Station. The oldest greasy spoon in Mykonos and one of the best places for a cheap meal. Alexi's has all the favorites, including gyros (€1.70) and a hearty souvlaki platter (€5.50). Breakfast €5.50. Takeout and delivery available. Open daily 10am-7am. ❶

El Greco (☎22890 22 024), on E. Dinameon. Take your pick from over 70 wines before digging into a meal of Greek favorites and Mediterranean hybrids while enjoying the very professional service. Octopus salad €9. Grilled swordfish €13. Open 1pm-1am. ❸

Aladdin (☎22890 24 783), on E. Dinameon near Malamatenias, offers unusual varieties of baklava (€1.50), including tiramisu and apple, other interesting pastry creations, and many coffees. Open daily 10am-1pm. ❶

SIGHTS

The prime daytime activities on Mykonos are tanning and shopping. Losing yourself in the colorful alleyways of Mykonos Town at dawn or dusk is one of the cheapest and most exhilarating experiences the island has to offer. A stroll to the **kastro** area—behind the Delos ferry pier, at the far left of the port when facing the water—will take you to the **Paraportiani,** a cluster of white churches you might recognize from postcards. From there, walk through **Little Venice,** where the turquoise waters of the eager Aegean lap at the legs of cafe tables and chairs. The line of stalwart **windmills,** farther south along the waterfront, also offers prime sunset seating.

Although cultural enrichment may not be Mykonos's primary draw, several museums on the island are worth a look. The **Archaeological Museum** is on the paved road between the ferry dock and the center of town. (☎22890 22 325. Open Tu-Su 8:30am-3pm. €2, students and seniors €1, EU students free.) The **Aegean Maritime Museum,** around the corner from the inland end of Matogianni, thrills with a beautifully manicured garden housing immense nautical instruments. (☎22890 22 700. Open Apr.-Oct. 10:30am-1pm and 6:30-9pm. €2, students €1.) **Lena's House,** part of the town's **Folklore Museum,** is an 18th-century home exactly as its owner left it. (☎22890 22 591. Open Apr.-Oct. M-Sa 5:30-8:30pm, Su 6:30-8:30pm. Free.) The **Cultural Center of Mykonos** hosts a rotating exhibition of shows, featuring up-and-coming Greek artists. (Hours generally 11am-2pm and 7pm-2am.)

NIGHTLIFE

Come nightfall, the young and beautiful mix with mere mortals at chic cafes, illustrious nightclubs, and a handful of pubs. After 11pm, the bars get packed. The most popular watering holes are around Little Venice and Taxi Square. If you tire of dancing, head to **Cine Manto,** in Pl. Lymni off Meletopoulou, which shows English-language films. (☎22890 27 109. 2 shows per day. €6.)

Skandinavian Bar, near Niko's Taverna and the waterfront. There's something for everyone in this 2-building party complex, which includes a disco, 2 bars, and a cafe-esque seating area. Though large enough to accommodate massive crowds, it's intimate enough to contain the energy of the night. Beer and shots €3-3.50; cocktails €7 and up. Open Su-F 8:30pm-3am, Sa until 4am.

Caprice Bar, on the water in Little Venice, is a popular post-beach hangout with breathtaking sunsets, funky music, and lively company. Gathering its party steam earlier than most other establishments on the island, it's a good place to kick off your night. Cocktails €7. Open Su-Th 6:30pm-3:30am, F-Sa until 4:30am.

Mykonos Bar, in Little Venice, next to the inland side of Caprice, plays mostly Greek tunes. Cover €3 and up. Beer €3.50; cocktails €5 and up. Open daily 10pm-4am.

Cavo Paradiso, on Paradise beach. Considered one of the world's top dance clubs, Paradiso hosts internationally renowned DJs. Despite a very steep cover (€20 and up), free bus service is provided to and from Mykonos Town every hr. Open daily 3am-11am.

Pierro's, on Matogianni, is the oldest gay bar in Mykonos and still *the* place to go for a good time. Spontaneous theme nights (e.g., glitter night, drag shows) keep the crowd on their toes. Beer €5; cocktails €6-7.

Icaros, next door and upstairs from Pierro's, shares customers, atmosphere, and a nightly drag show with its downstairs neighbor. Beer €5. Open daily 11:30pm-4am.

Montparnasse Piano Bar, Ag. Anargyron 24. Savor the good life with a cocktail by the bay, while being serenaded by cabaret tunes from a live piano. The clientele is mostly gay. Beer €5; cocktails €7. Open daily 7pm-3am.

BEACHES

Mykonos has a beach to please everyone. Although all the beaches on Mykonos are **nude,** the degree of nudity depends on where you go. To avoid the unspectacular Mykonos Town beach, get on a bus and head out of the city (see **Transportation,** above). **Paradise, Paraga, Plati Yialos,** and **Super Paradise** are the most popular and offer water sports. Except for Super Paradise, all are accessible by bus from South Station (€0.90). Hourly *caïques* (water taxis) also shuttle beach bums between them for about €1.50. Small **Ag. Stefanos beach,** an easy bus ride from the North Station, is close to the busy roadway leading to the airport. Litter often covers its sands. The clear, shallow water of little **Ornos beach** is a short hop away from South Station, as is crowded **Psarou beach.** Super Paradise beach has the craziest reputation among Mykonos's beaches. On the far reaches of **Elia's** quiet shores (accessible by bus from North Station), contemplative naked people while away the daylight hours. Majestic and remote **Kalo Livadi beach** is about a 5km walk back along the road to Mykonos from Elia. The bus to Elia stops at the turn-off, so ask the driver to let you off at Kalo Livadi to shorten your trek.

DAYTRIP FROM MYKONOS: DELOS

Excursion boats leave from the dock (35min.; 3 boats per day in each direction, leave 9:30-11:30am, return 12:20-3pm; round-trip €10). An additional boat per day makes the trip from Mykonos's southern beaches. Most trips let you explore for only 3hr., but each boat line has several return trips in the afternoon, allowing you some flexibility. Guided tours are offered by each company (€26, including admission to the ruins). A more affordable option is to buy a guidebook (€5-15; available in town or at the entrance to the site), which includes info, color pictures, and a map of the site. Freelance guides offer their services on the island (€10 per person). Tinos, Naxos, Paros, and other islands offer joint trips to Mykonos and Delos but allow less time to explore. Open Tu-Su 8:30am-3pm. €5, students and EU seniors €3, EU students free.

An excursion to Delos—the sacred navel around which the Cyclades whirl—is a must-see, even for those who take little interest in mythology or history. Delos claims the most important **Temple of Apollo,** built to commemorate the birthplace of the god and his twin sister, Artemis. A site of religious pilgrimage in the ancient world, today Delos is something of a giant, island-wide museum.

HISTORY. After impregnating **Leto** with Artemis and Apollo, womanizing **Zeus** kicked her out, afraid of his wife **Hera's** wrath. Desperately seeking a place to give birth, Leto wandered the Aegean, rebuffed by island after island. At last Leto came upon a rocky, floating island shrouded in mist. She swore by the river Styx that it would come to no harm. The reassured island stopped drifting, but Hera soon conned the goddess of childbirth, **Eilythia,** into prolonging Leto's labor for nine days. When the infants finally arrived, born by the Sacred Lake, the mist disappeared and the island basked in radiance. Its name thus changed from Adelos ("invisible") to Delos ("visible"). Grateful Leto made the island the seat of her son's worship; with Apollo's sanctuary attracting pilgrims and money, Delos was transformed into a major religious and commercial center.

With a central position among the Aegean islands, Delos's role as a maritime and political powerhouse is hardly surprising. The 5km-long island is paired with larger **Rheneia,** whose inhabitants are also called Delians. Although first settled in the 3rd millennium BC, it was during the Mycenaean Period (1580-1200 BC) that Delos began to flourish. Mycenaean rule ended around 1100 BC, and a century later the Ionians dedicated the island to worshipping Leto. By the 7th century BC, Delos had become the political and mercantile center of the Aegean League of Islands, starting off three centuries of struggle for power between the Delians and the Athenians. The Delians put up a good fight but slowly bled power to the mainlanders. During these years, the Athenians ordered at least two "purifications" of the island, in honor of Apollo. The second, in 426 BC, decreed that no one should give birth or die on its sacred grounds, meaning that all graves had to be exhumed; the bodies within moved to a "purification pit" on nearby Rheneia. After the **Persian Wars,** Delos served as the treasury and the seat of the **Delian League,** an alliance of independent city-states becoming the de facto Athenian empire. After Sparta defeated Athens in the **Peloponnesian War** (p. 9), Delos enjoyed independence and wealth. Sweet prosperity soured during the Roman occupation in the 2nd century BC, when prestigious Delos was reduced to the slave-trading center of Greece. By the end of the 2nd century AD, after successive sackings, the island was left virtually deserted. Today its only residents are legions of leaping lizards and members of the French School of Archaeology, excavating here since 1873.

SIGHTS. Occupying almost an entire square mile, the **archaeological site** includes, in the center of the ancient city, the Temple of Apollo and the agora, in the outlying parts of the city, Mt. Kythnos and the theater quarter. While it takes several days to explore the ruins completely, you can see the highlights in around 3hr. Most ferry passengers follow a similar route when they disembark, so reverse the route for some privacy. Bring a hat, good shoes, sunblock, and a water bottle. The cafeteria beside the museum is exorbitantly priced, so it's wiser to bring snacks.

The path beyond the admission booth points you toward the **Agora of the Competaliasts,** where Roman guilds built their shop-shrines. Continue on in the same direction and turn left onto the wide Sacred Road. Decorating your walk are two parallel **stoas,** the more impressive of which (on the left) was built by Phillip of Macedon in 210 BC and dedicated to Apollo. Bear right and follow this road around to the **Sanctuary of Apollo,** a collection of temples built in the god's honor that date from Mycenaean times to the 4th century BC. The sanctuary begins when you reach the **Propylaees.** The biggest and most important of the temples is on the right. The famous **Temple of Apollo,** or Temple of the Delians, was completed at the end of the 4th century BC. Its immense, partially hollow hexagonal pedestal once supported an 8m marble statue of the sun god. Following the direction of the Sacred Road north, 50m past its end, leads to the **Terrace of the Lions.** In the 7th century BC, at least nine marble lions looked onto the sacred lake from the terrace. Only four remain standing on Delos, and the body of a fifth, pirated by the Venetians, guards the entrance to the arsenal in Venice.

Proceed up the small crest left of the terrace to the **House of the Hill.** Because the building was planted deep into the earth, this archetypal Roman house is still intact. Downhill lies the **House of the Lake,** with a well-preserved mosaic decorating its atrium, and the desecrated **Sacred Lake,** drained in 1925 to protect against malaria. The round form of the former lake today appears as a leafy oasis with a lone palm tree at its center. On the lake's south side is the expansive **Roman agora.**

From the **Archaeological Museum** you can hike up the path to the summit of **Mt. Kythnos** (elev. 112m). Its peak offers such a good view of the island's entirety that Zeus chose it to spy on the birth of Apollo and Artemis. Although the climb is not too difficult, wear sturdy, comfortable shoes—the trail can be steep and some of the rocks dislodge easily. Ascending the mountain coming from the direction of the Temple of Apollo, you will pass temples dedicated to Egyptian gods. The elegant bust in the **Temple of Isis** depicts the sun. The immense building blocks of the nearby **Grotto of Herakles** reverberate Mycenaean architecture while some experts suggest they're knock-offs. Coming down the mountain, bear left away from the museum to reach the **House of the Dolphins** and **House of the Masks,** which contain intricate mosaics of dolphins and *Dionysus Riding a Panther.* Continue on to the **ancient theater,** which has a sophisticated cistern (as cisterns go) called **Dexamene,** with nine arched compartments. As you weave down the rough path back toward the entrance, you'll see the **House of the Trident,** graced by a mosaic of a dolphin twisted around a trident, the **House of Dionysus,** containing another Dionysus and panther mosaic, and the **House of Cleopatra.** The famous statue of Cleopatra and Dioscourides is sheltered in the site's Archaeological Museum.

SYROS Συρος

Syros is the capital of the Cycladic islands and, despite its small size, is also home to almost half of the Cyclades's permanent residents. Syros first rose to commercial power as a Phoenician seaport; the 13th-century Venetians turned it into the trading capital of the Cyclades until steam-powered ships and the rise of Piraeus as the national port finally ended Syros's glory days. In the last 20 years, the island has regained its economic footing, largely due to the shipbuilding industry. Escape the madness of the port town Ermoupolis by following legions of Greek families to one of the island's many crowded seaside villages or by heading to the medieval settlement of Ano Syros, high above Ermoupolis on one of Syros's two peaks.

ERMOUPOLIS Ερμουπολις ☎22810

Bustling Ermoupolis, the Cyclades's largest city and capital, is the city of the winged messenger Hermes, god of commerce and travel. Elegant Neoclassical buildings of Greek, Italian, and Bavarian design in Pl. Miaouli and Dellagrazia give the island an international appearance and offer a peek at the city's opulent past. They also explain its former nicknames—the "Manchester of Greece" and "Little Milan." Though the city's roles in government and shipping make tourism a secondary concern, its vitality makes Syros an exciting, lively island. Athenian vacationers jam Ermoupolis's hotels from mid-July to September; you'll probably want to head for the island's countryside.

TRANSPORTATION

Flights: 5 flights per week go to **Athens** (€64). You must take a bus or a taxi to the **airport,** southeast of Ermoupolis (☎22810 81 900).

Ferries: To: **Crete** (10hr., 1 per week, €28); **Ios** (4hr., 4 per week, €12); **Mykonos** (2hr., 4-6 per day, €7.30); **Naxos** (2½hr., daily, €9.50); **Paros** (1hr., 2 per week, €7.50); **Piraeus** (4½hr., 5-7 per day, €21); **Santorini** (5hr., 4per week, €17.30); **Tinos** (45min., 4-6 per day, €4.70). Most boats depart from the right side of the harbor. **Flying Dolphins** depart daily for **Piraeus** (2hr., €32) and **Rafina** (2hr., €26) and several times per week for **Mykonos** (1hr., €11.40); **Naxos** (1½hr., €15.50); **Paros** (30min., €12); **Tinos** (30min., €7.30). Schedules vary by season; check with a travel agency.

Buses: ☎22810 22 575. Green **KTEL** buses leave from the depot near the ferry dock. 1 beach loop runs every 30min., passing through **Azolimnos** (45min., €1), **Galissas** (15min., €1), **Finikas** (25min., €1.20), **Komito** (30min., €1.20), and **Megas Yialos** (35min., €1.20). The 2nd loop leaves 5 times per day for the interior towns of **Episkopio** (€0.90), **Parakopi** (€1), **Posidonia** (€1.30), and **Manna** (€1). 3-5 shuttle buses per day go to: **Ano Syros** (€0.90); **Dili** (€0.70); **Vrontado** (€0.70).

Taxis: ☎22810 86 222. Line up 24hr. by the Hermes statue to the right of the port.

Rentals: Rental agencies line the waterfront. Try **Enjoy Your Holidays Rent a Car,** Akti Paeidou 6 (☎22810 87 070 or 22810 81 336; fax 22810 82 739), by the central port. Scooters €10-15; cars €30. Open daily 8am-11pm.

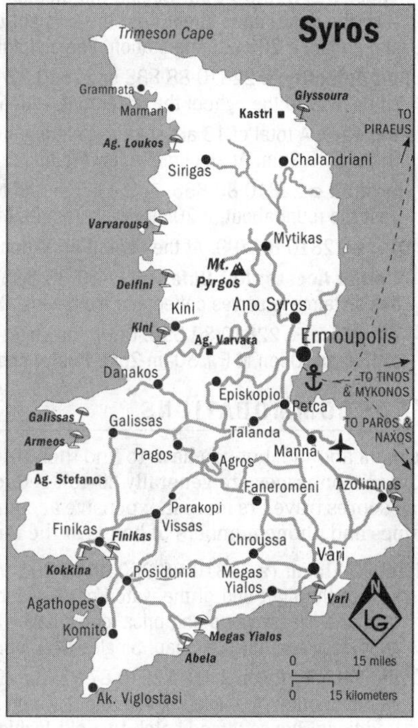

ORIENTATION AND PRACTICAL INFORMATION

Facing inland when you get off the ferry, head right and walk down the waterfront for 3min. to **El. Venizelou,** the town's main street, beginning at the winged **statue of Hermes.** Venizelou runs inland to **Pl. Miaouli,** a large marble plaza marked by the Neoclassical town hall. Social life centers on this plaza, and along the right side of the harborfront. Hotels and domatia can be found all along the waterfront and the surrounding streets. A labeled map of Ermoupolis and a listing of domatia are posted on two large signs at the bus depot.

Tourist Information: ☎22810 87 360. Look for the "i" as you head right off the ferry. The booth, behind the Hermes statue, offers free info on accommodations, good **maps** (€1), and books on the island. Open daily 10am-2pm and 6-10pm.

Tourist Agencies: Team Work, 30 Eth. Antistasis (☎22810 83 400), at the left end of the waterfront. Open daily 9am-10pm. **Vassilikos Tours** (☎22810 84 444; vassiliko@syr.forthnet.gr), on the port across from the bus depot. Open daily 9am-11pm. Both provide ferry, hydrofoil, and flight schedules, prices, and tickets.

Banks: National Bank (☎22810 85 350), at the end of the 1st main street on the right off El. Venizelou (going away from the waterfront), **exchanges currency** and has a 24hr. **ATM.** Open M-Th 8am-2:30pm, F 8am-2pm.

Public Toilets: On the right side of the first alley off the street with the National Bank and the post office on it. Look for the "WC" sign.

Police: ☎22810 96 105. Behind the theater off the upper right corner of Pl. Miaouli. Take the right inland street from the far right corner of Pl. Miaouli, go right at the fork and continue 200m to the station. Very helpful. Open 24hr.

Port Authority: ☎22810 88 888 or 22810 82 690. The office is at the end of the dock all the way to the right of the waterfront, with a Greek flag in front. Open 24hr.

Pharmacy: A total of 18 are scattered throughout the city. Most open M-F 8am-2pm; Tu, Th-Su 5:30-9pm. At any time, a few are open.

Hospital: ☎22810 86 666. At the left end of the waterfront (facing inland) at Pl. Iroön past the roundabout, a 20min. walk from Pl. Miaouli. Open 24hr.

OTE: ☎22810 82 799. At the right of Pl. Miaouli. Open M-Sa 7am-2:40pm.

Internet Access: Net Cafe (☎22810 85 330), in Pl. Miaouli, to the left of the town hall's staircase serves coffee and ice cream. €6 per hr., €2 min. Open daily 9am-3am.

Post Office: ☎22810 82 596. Down the street from the National Bank. Offers **currency exchange.** Open M-F 7:30am-2pm. **Postal code:** 84100.

ACCOMMODATIONS

Domatia abound, but you have to find them—look around for "Rooms to Let" signs. Low season prices are generally 20-40% reduced. Venturing out of the capital city also scores travelers more inexpensive accommodations. There's a large map with names and phone numbers of hotels at the ferry dock.

Hotel Aktaion (☎22810 88 200 or 88 201; romana@otenet.gr). Look for the rooftop sign at the right end of the waterfront. Location is only the 1st of Aktaion's attractive qualities–classy wood and brick rooms have TVs, A/C, telephones, and complimentary goodies like candy and soap. Singles €40; doubles €55. ❹

Villa Votsalo, Parou 21 (☎22810 87 334 or 693 830 0557; fax 22810 86 760). Walk inland on Hiou (to the left of Venizelou); Parou is the first left off Hiou. Housed in a cozy, traditional house-turned-hotel, this old fashioned pension offers rooms named after Cycladic islands and equipped with TVs, phones, A/C, and private baths; the comfy rooftop veranda boasts a full harbor view. Breakfast included. Doubles €35-50. ❸

Hotel Almi (☎22810 82 812), on the left side of the alleyway across from the bus depot and port. Look for the dark wooden doors. Luxuriant pink perfumed rooms cash in on the Neoclassical feel of the city, albeit with more modern conveniences; TVs, balconies, baths, and fridges complement the pastoral prints of the walls. Doubles €20-45. ❸

Ariadni Rooms to Let, Nikolaou Filini 9 (☎22810 81 307 or 22810 80 245), near the ferry dock. Turn left at the kiosk before the Hermes statue and head up the stairs (look for signs). Inordinately proud of the class-A rating, this hotel sports rooms with kitchenettes, private baths, TVs, telephones, and A/C. Doubles €30-56; triples €36-68. ❸

FOOD

For groceries, head to the **mini-market** halfway up from Hiou's plateia. (☎22810 81 008. Open 8am-9pm.) **Hiou** hosts fruit and seafood stalls and aromatic bakeries.

To Archontariki, Em. Roidi 8 (☎22810 81 744). On the 2nd street over from corner of Pl. Miaouli. Lose yourself in this local legend's atmosphere amidst the crowds of sophisticated diners and white-clad waiters. Mussels bakes with feta and tomato €9. Eggplant stuffed with 7cheeses €6. Open daily 11am-late. AmEx/MC/V. ❸

Restaurant Bakhos, (☎22810 84 597). Walking along Hiou, turn left on Peloponnisou; the restaurant is at the end under a leafy awning. The elegant 1843 building was a functioning pottery factory until 1922. Today it spins out a modest menu of seafood (€5-7), pasta (€3-5.50), and Greek specialties. Open daily 11am-1am. ❷

Kechayia Sweet Shop (☎22810 88 076), on the waterfront corner of El. Venizelou. Fabulous renditions of traditional local specialties such as *chalvathopita* (sweet concoction of almond paste, nuts, and chocolate; €1.40) and *loukoumi* (sweet fried dough; €1.50). Open daily 8am-noon. ❶

Mavros (☎22810 82 244), in the center of the ocean end of Pl. Miaouli. An ideal location, big-screen TV, and a broad menu make for a relaxed meal. Sandwiches €2.50-3.50. Crepes €3-5. Pizza €5-7. Open daily 8am-1am. ❷

SIGHTS

At the **Church of the Assumption** *(Kimisis Theotokou)*, on Ag. Proiou at the end of the alley opposite the bus station, contemplate a 1562 painting by a 20-year-old Domenikos Theotokopoulos before he was known as **El Greco.** (Open daily 7:30am-1:30pm and 4-10:30pm.) Ascend the steps (20min.) at the far left of Pl. Miaouli or take the bus (€0.90) from the waterfront to **Ano Syros,** a medieval Venetian settlement which Syros's Catholics still call home. Continue past the summit church through labyrinthine streets of chalky, crowded houses to the lofty Church of Ag. George, and look over a panorama of Ermoupolis and the coast below. The town hall's **Archaeological Museum** has a small collection of Cycladic and early Roman art. (☎22810 88 487. Open Tu-Su 8:30am-3pm. Free. No cameras.)

NIGHTLIFE

At night, the waterfront and Pl. Miaouli buzz with cafes, restaurants, dance clubs, and bars. Most of the popular waterfront locales open as cafes in morning, morph into bars by night, and feature DJs and dancing after midnight. **Liquid** lures young Syrians to a sleek atmosphere replete with copious portside seating, a waterfall behind the bar, and a DJ till dawn. (☎22810 82 284. Beer €3-4; cocktails €6. Open daily 8am-4am.) **Kimbara** is packed with wall-to-wall bodies. (☎22810 80 878. Cover €5 after midnight, includes 1 drink. Beer €3; cocktails €6. Open daily 8am-3:30am.) Cavernous **Arxaion** creates a clubbing atmosphere with modern Greek music, disco balls, and a dim-lit dance floor. (☎22810 84 774. Beer €3; cocktails €6. Open daily 9am-4am.) If you want some high rollin', try your luck at **Kazino Eyeou** (Aegean Casino), the only sin center around. Men must wear pants. All must leave passports and €15 at the door. (☎22810 84 400. Gambling starts at 2pm.)

BEACHES

The closest beach is sedate **Agios Nikolaos.** To get there, walk up El. Venizelou through Pl. Miaouli to the right of the Archaeological Museum. Head right and pass through Pl. Vardakas up to the right of the church of Agios Nikolau. Continue on the street until you see an archway and a stone stairway leading down to the beach. Family vacationers (sometimes with inflatable alligators) frolic on the main beach at **Galissas.** Fight for your eight inches of sand or climb past the chapel of Agia Pakou on the left side (facing the water) to discover a nudist paradise: tiny, beautiful **Armeos beach.** From Ermoupolis **buses** travel to Galissas (13-18 per day, €1), alternating between a direct 15min. route and a 45min. route that stops in other villages first. Taking the scenic route to Galissas allows you to see the rest of Syros's southern beaches. **Finikas** and **Komito** are ideal for watersports like windsurfing. **Megas Yialos** offers many small coves that allow for a semblance of solitude; **Azolimnos** features a large metal waterslide. The beach resort of **Vari** is popular with families and package tour groups because of its shallow waters and relaxed atmosphere. North of Galissas is the quiet fishing village of **Kini,** ideal for the quintessential romantic sunset. If you happen to be in this hamlet on June 29, the **Church of Ag. Peter** invites you and every other living thing within earshot to an all-night festival where *bouzouki* accompanies plentiful *kakavia* (fish soup).

NAXOS Ναξος

The gleaming marble Portara, the lone remaining arch of the grandest Greek temple to Apollo, serves as the portal into diverse and splendid Naxos. The island is the largest of the Cyclades; olive groves, wineries, small villages, and chalky white ruins fill its interior, while sandy beaches line its shores. Though the ancients believed it to be the island home of Dionysus, Naxos has had a colorful history independent of mythology. Prosperous since ancient times, the island has wielded greater power than its small size would suggest. When the Venetians conquered the region in 1207, they made Naxos the capital of their empire. To properly experience Naxos, it's essential to escape the clutter of Naxos Town and get to the interior. Mopeds are invaluable for combining trips to the beaches south of town and the inland sights and villages. Just be wary of the serpentine roads that aren't always well-paved. The villages of the Tragea highland valley (a vastly green olive grove) are Naxos's best features. Hikers should stop by the tourist office to pick up any number of the 33 walking tour maps (€0.50 each), a detailed map of the island (€4.50), or a copy of *Walking Tours on Naxos*, by Christian Ucke (€15).

NAXOS TOWN ☎22850

Naxos's capital reaches out to you before you've stepped off the ferry—as you drift into the harbor, the Portara juts out into the sea on a peninsula, and the Chapel of Myrditiotissa floats on an island. Once inside Naxos Town, the twisting historic quarter and the hard-nosed modern area step forward. Tightly-packed on the hill leading up to the Venetian castle, Old Naxos snoozes behind the waterfront shops. Low stone archways and trellises of flowers drape the homes that crowd the labyrinthine streets descending from the castle. Hip bars and clubs near Agios Giorgios beach call you to cut loose after a day exploring the island.

TRANSPORTATION

Flights: An **Olympic Airways** desk is in **Naxos Tours** (☎22850 22 095 or 22850 24 000), at the left end of the waterfront. 1 flight per day to **Athens** (€70).

Buses: ☎22850 22 291; fax 22850 22 999. Check the **schedules** at the bus station across the street from the ferry dock and to the left; also available at the tourist office. Buses to **Apollonas** (2hr.; 5 per day, 9:30am-3pm; €4) and **Filoti** (30min.; 6 per day, 9:30am-7pm; €1.60) are often packed. Buses also run to: **Apiranthos** (1hr.; 5 per day, 9:30am-7pm; €2.10); **Engares** (daily, €1.20); **Halki** (30min.; 6 per day, 9:30am-7pm; €1.20); **Koronos** (3 per day, €2.70); **Melanes** (3 per day, 9am-3pm; €1); **Plaka beach** (15min.; every 30min., 8am-1am; €1.20) via **Ag. Prokopios beach** and **Ag. Anna beach; Pyrgaki beach** (1hr.; 5 per day, 7:30am-5pm; €2) via **Tripodes** (€1).

Ferries: All **ferries** to Naxos dock in Naxos Town. There are 2 docks at the left end of town: the larger for large ferries; the other for smaller ferries and daily cruises. To: **Amorgos** (4½hr., daily, €9.30); **Crete** (7hr., 1 per week, €20); **Donousa** (4hr., daily, €6.30) via **Iraklia** (1hr., €5.50); **Koufonisia** (3hr., €6.50); **Ios** (1hr., daily, €8.20); **Kos** (7hr., 1 per week, €16); **Mykonos** (3hr., daily, €9); **Paros** (1hr., 4 per day, €5.50); **Piraeus** (6hr., 4 per day, €20); **Rhodes** (13hr., 1 per week, €20); **Santorini** (3hr., 3 per day, €13); **Schinousa** (2hr., €5.50); **Syros** (2½hr., daily, €9.30); **Thessaloniki** (14hr., €30); **Tinos** (4hr., daily, €9.50).

Hydrofoils: Flying Dolphins and new **Flying Cats** to: **Astypalea, Crete, Ios, Mykonos, Paros, Piraeus**, and **Santorini.**

Taxis: ☎22850 22 444. On the waterfront, next to the bus depot.

Rentals: Fun Cars (☎22850 26 084) is inland and to the right from the roundabout. In Pl. Protodikiou, try **Rental Center** (☎22850 23 396). Friendly staff, good rental rates, and lots of info on Naxos. Also has **Internet** access (€4 per hr.). Open 8:30am-11pm.

ORIENTATION AND PRACTICAL INFORMATION

Avoid the dock hawks and quasi-tourist office and make your way to the waterfront Tourist Information Centre (look for the "i") to find a suitable rooming situation. The waterfront to the right of the harbor, along **Protopapadakis,** is lined with cafes, tavernas, and clubs. After 500m the road forks inland; 70m and to the right is the roundabout of **Pl. Protodiokiou,** the central square—authentic establishments are located anywhere but here in Naxos Town. The **Old Town** lies to the left as you walk toward Protodikiou, accessible via any of the alleyways running inland.

Tourist Information Centre: ☎22850 24 358, 22850 25 201, 22850 22 993, 22850 24 525 or 22850 26 123; chateau-zevgoli@nax.forthnet.gr. 300m from the dock, by the bus depot. Accommodations assistance, bus and ferry schedules, car rental, **cur-**

rency exchange, international telephone, **luggage storage** (€1.50 for the whole day until plane/ferry departure), safety deposit (€1.50), and **laundry** service (€7.50). English-speakers **Despina** and **Stavros** are marvelous. Open daily 8am-11pm.

Tourist Agency: Zas Travel (☎22850 23 330, 22850 23 331, or 22850 24 330; zas-travel@nax.forthnet.gr), 2 doors down from the tourist center along the waterfront. **Car rental** (€26.60 per day) and ferry and plane tickets. Open daily 8:30am-11pm.

Bank: National Bank (☎22850 23 053) is one of many banks on the waterfront offering **currency exchange** and an **ATM.** Open M-Th 8am-2pm, F 8am-1:30pm. Citibank has 2 ATMs, one in front of Zas Travel and one farther down on the waterfront.

International Bookstore: Vrakas (☎22850 23 039), in the back of a jewelry shop mid-way down the waterfront. Look for signs reading "gold-silver, used books." Charming owner buys at half original price, sells for €2-10. Open 9:30am-11:30pm. **Zoom** (☎22850 23 675), to the right of the National Bank, offers international magazines and photocopying (€0.30 per large page). Open daily 7:30am-12:30am.

Public Toilets and Showers: Behind Grotta Tours on the street parallel to the waterfront. Turn left by the dock after Zas Travel and turn left again. Toilets €0.40; showers €3. Open daily 6am-midnight.

Police: ☎22850 22 100. On the main road heading toward Ag. Giorgios beach from Pl. Protodikiou, 1km out of town. Open 24hr.

Port Police: ☎22850 22 300. On Protopapadakis, across from the small port dock.

Health Center: ☎22850 23 333. Turn inland at the fork in the road past the OTE, at the right end of the waterfront. Follow that road for about 500m; the center will be on your left. Helicopter to Athens available for **emergencies.** Open 24hr.

OTE: Left of the fork in the road to the right of the waterfront, inland from Cream night-club. Open M-F 7:30am-3pm.

Internet Access: At almost every corner. Near the ferry, **Zas Travel** has access for €4 per hr. **Vaporia Play Room** (☎22850 22 003), 1 block toward Ag. Giorgios beach from Pl. Protodikou. Satellite TV, video games, pool. €3 per hr. Open daily 2pm-3:30am.

Post Office: Walk down the waterfront with the water on your right, and continue just beyond the main street that turns left. Pass a long playground on the right and the post office will be on your left, up 1 floor. Open M-F 7:30am-2pm. **Postal code:** 84300.

ACCOMMODATIONS AND CAMPING

Most hotels on Naxos fill to capacity in late summer. Accommodations of all types can be arranged through the tourist office. Prices vary according to season. If you're looking for a unique experience and are a planning a slightly longer stay, ask the tourist agency about renting century-old houses in the Old Town, but be prepared to spend quite a bit of money. Naxos has three roughly equivalent beach **camping** options and their representatives wait eagerly at the dock. All of the sites are complete with mini-markets, restaurants, Internet access, moped rentals, and laundry facilities. Prices are set to be equivalent. Inquire at the camping booth on the dock (camping €5, tent €2). **Plaka Camping ❶** (☎22850 42 700), 12min. by van, next to Plaka beach, has a trellis overhead for shade. **Naxos Camping ❶,** 1500m to the right along Ag. Giorgios beach, has a swimming pool. (☎22850 23 500; fax 22850 23 501.) **Maragas Camping ❶,** on Ag. Anna, a 15min. drive from Naxos Town, also has studios and apartments. (☎22850 42 552 or 42 599. Doubles €16-29.)

Pension Irene (☎22850 23 169), with 2 facilities, both located 100m from Ag. Giorgios. Well-equipped rooms with A/C, TVs, and showers are not far from the center of Naxos Town. 1 site has a swimming pool. Free port shuttle. Dorms €10; singles €15; doubles €20-30; triples €25-35; apartments for 5 €40-50. AmEx/MC/V. ❷

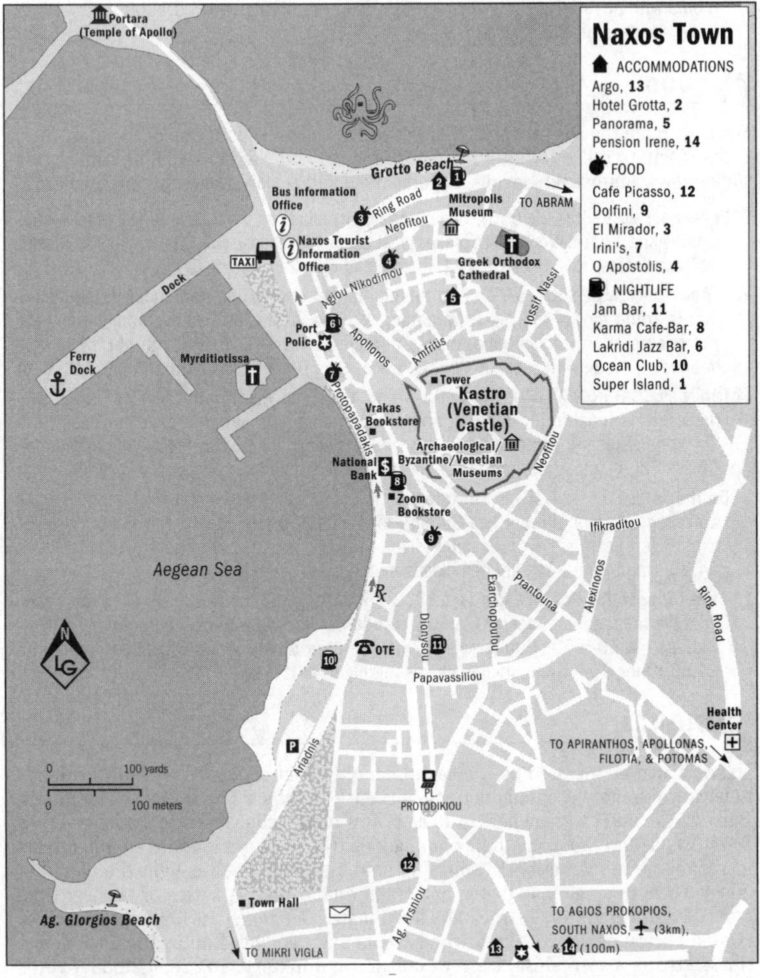

Panorama (☎22850 22 330), in Old Town, make a left on the street labeled "Old Market" and make a left again, following signs inland to "Panorama" and "Chateau Zevgoli." Enjoy the calm of the town in your breezy room with fan and fridge. Doubles high season €40 and up, low season €25. Cash only. ❸

Hotel Grotta (☎22850 22 215 or 22 101; www.hotelgrotta.gr), in Grotta, 500m northwest of Hora. Call for free shuttle or follow upper Ringroad along the water until you see the sign on your left and head up the dirt path. For a little luxury, check into this hotel situated on a bluff overlooking the Aegean. Indoor pool with jets. Rooms have fridges, A/C, balconies, hair dryers, satellite TV, safe-deposit box, telephone, and laundry service (€8). Buffet breakfast €5. Doubles €40-60. MC/V. ❹

Argo (☎22850 25 330 or 22850 23 059; info@argo-hotel.com), 150m from Ag. Giorgios and 400m from the square; call for a port shuttle. Multilingual owners offer rooms with private baths, phones, and A/C. Buffet breakfast €5. Doubles €24-50; 2-room apartments €30-80. ❸

FOOD

Wade through the sea of waterfront tables and grab a seat at one of the many new cafes if what you're looking for is a crepe. In Old Naxos, you'll stumble upon tucked-away moussaka havens. **Supermarkets** and **grocery stands** are everywhere.

El Mirador (☎22850 22 655), one of the first buildings on the beach as you enter the ringroad. Anna, born in Mexico City, makes great beans with cheese (€2.50), chicken enchiladas (€7), and tacos (€7). Open daily 11am-2pm and 6pm-2am. MC/V. ❷

O Apostolis (☎22850 26 777), on the old market street. This traditional Greek restaurant is at the foot of the Old Town among whitewashed walls and overhanging flowers. The cook prepares exceptional dishes at incredible prices. To start, try the distinctive *dolmades,* made with zucchini flour and rice (€5). Open 6:30pm-2am. AmEx/MC/V. ❷

Irini's (☎22850 26 780), the 2nd taverna along the waterfront after Zas Travel, prepares divine local food. Beetroot salad with homemade garlic and walnut sauce €3. Chickpea salad with fresh onions, red peppers, and dill €3.50. Fresh grilled calamari €6.50. Fried eggplant in tomato sauce €4.50. Open daily 11am-2am. MC/V. ❷

Dolfini (☎22850 24 320), up the steps from Ergo Bank, 1 winding block inland from the waterfront. A slice of India (via Britain), the self-proclaimed Mystic Fire Priest of Naxos challenges patrons to down spicy dishes. Curry and Thai entrees €7-10. Cocktails €4.50. Open 9am-2am; kitchen closes midnight. ❷

Cafe Picasso Mexican Bistro (☎22850 25 408), 1 block toward Ag. Giorgios beach from the main square, serves Mexican standards. Nachos with chili *con carne* €5. Quesadillas €4.50-5.50. Guacamole €2.50. Sangria by the glass €2; frozen margarita €4.50. Open 7pm-2am; kitchen closes midnight. MC/V. ❷

SIGHTS

Naxos Town is crowned by the **kastro,** an old Venetian castle. Of the 12 original houses within its walls, only one remains entirely intact. The Domus Della Rocca-Barozzi, vacated by its owners in 1999, is now a **Venetian museum** that showcases furniture, decorations, and household goods from past generations of inhabitants of the castle. A "Venetian Evening" is held monthly; candles light the castle as guests revel in singing, dancing, and traditional drinks. A series of "Sunset Concerts" feature traditional Greek shadow theater *(karaghiozis)* and traditional or contemporary music with renowned artists and dancing. Run by local islanders, the kastro is a refreshing dose of culture and history. (☎22850 22 387; venetian@aias.gr. Open daily 10am-3pm and 7-10pm. Multilingual 30min. tours throughout the day. €5, students and seniors €3.) The **Byzantine Museum,** just around the corner, features artifacts from the 8th to the 10th centuries found on Naxos and surrounding Cycladic islands. (Open M-Sa 8am-2pm. Free.) Also inside the kastro sits the **Archaeological Museum,** located in the former Collège Français where Nikos Kazantzakis (p. 28) studied. (Open Tu-Su 8:30am-2pm. €3, students €2.) The impressive **Catholic Church** is just around the corner. (Open 10am. Free. Modest dress required.) The **Mitropolis Museum,** on the left side of town next to the Orthodox Church, is an architectural achievement. Elevated walkways lead you through the reconstructed buildings of a 13th-century BC settlement. (☎22850 24 151. Open Tu-Su 8:30am-3pm. Free.)

Stop by **Vallindras** and **Promponas** distilleries to sample **Citron,** a liqueur unique to the island. From the waterfront, you can see the white chapel of **Myrditiotissa,** floating in the harbor on a man-made islet, and the marble **Portara** archway, on its own peninsula. Climb up to it and view the unfinished beginnings of an ambitious temple dedicated to Apollo, begun on the orders of the tyrant Lydamis in the 6th century BC. With no admission and no guards, and open 24hr., the temple is an ideal place to catch romantic sunsets or star gaze deep into the night.

NIGHTLIFE

After-hours Naxos serenades evening wanderers with music from cafes and clubs. Take advantage of half-price Happy Hours, then relax all night, or get ready to join the masses at the waterfront clubs; mobilize around 11pm. Alternatively, spend a low-key evening under the stars at **Cine Astra** (☎22850 25 381), on the road to Agia Anna from Pl. Protodikiou; it's a 15min. walk from the waterfront. (Movies in English shown 9 and 11pm. Open daily May-Oct. €6.)

Super Island Bar and Club (☎694 693 7462), on the water along the paved road next to the bus depot. All the Greeks on Naxos come here to be seen and to dance to adrenaline-pumping Euro beats. Drinks €4.50. Open 11pm-3:30am, later on weekends.

Jam Bar (☎694 201 9426), first left after Klik Cafe, behind the OTE. Sit back and experience the wide variety of music while sipping an exotic concoction such as the Naxos Butterfly (€4). Shots €2-2.50. Open 7pm-3:30am, later on weekends.

Karma Cafe-Bar (☎22850 24 885), right in the center of the waterfront. Start your evening here grooving to the wide variety of music in this uniquely constructed building with marble walls and a view of the port. Daily Happy Hour until midnight offers 2-for-1 beers. Open 9pm-3:30am, later on weekends.

Ocean Club (☎22850 30 285), facing the water at the right end of the harbor. Ocean churns enough to make its namesake proud. Do your best Ricky Martin atop the gogo box. Frozen strawberry daiquiri €4. Open 9pm-3:30am, all night on weekends.

Lakridi Jazz Bar, in Old Naxos, on the old market street; take the first right when you walk in. Chill with a frozen cocktail (€4) to the sounds of Billie Holliday in the hot Naxian night. Open 8pm-3:30am.

BEACHES

North of Naxos Town, you can snorkel among caves in search of rocks and sea urchins, but head south for Naxos's busiest beach life, with hotels, rooms to let, bars, tavernas, discos, and creperies. The most remote, uncrowded beaches with the clearest waters are the farthest from town. Scantily-clad bathers frolic among visiting windsurfers who come from all over. Near town, **Agios Giorgios, Agios Prokopios, Agia Anna,** and long and sandy **Plaka** border crystal-blue water. Beware: you may have to vie for your share of sand. On Plaka, stunning nude sunbathers stud the shore. Naxos is overflowing with opportunities for athletes and outdoor enthusiasts. You can sign up for windsurfing lessons, rent a mountain bike, or go for a sail in a catamaran at **Naxos Surf** (☎22850 29 170; info@naxos-surf.com), **Flisvos Sport Club** (☎22850 24 308; flisvos@otenet.gr), on Ag. Giorgios, or **Plaka Watersports** (☎22850 41 264; kpigos@otenet.gr), at Plaka and Ag. Anna. A **bus** (€1.20) goes from the port to the beaches every 30min. Desert meets sea at the more secluded beaches of **Mikri Vigla, Abram, Aliko, Moutsouna,** and **Pyrgaki,** where scrub pines, prickly pear, and century plants grow on the dunes. All are accessible by bus from Naxos Town. There is a small **nude beach** on the southern protuberance of **Kastraki beach.** If you're tired of the water, you can explore the island on horseback through the **Stamatis Riding Center** (☎22850 41 879).

DAYTRIPS FROM NAXOS TOWN

APOLLONAS AND NORTHERN NAXOS

From Naxos Town, catch the bus to Apollonas for an exhilarating ride on a beautiful coastal road (2hr.; 5 per day, 9:30am-3pm; €4). This bus service can be easily made round-trip (in either direction) of the central Naxian villages and the island's northern coast; the bus travels on an interior route. The coast is lined with secluded, sandy beaches; by moped, pick a spot and hike down along the goat trails.

On the road to Apollonas you'll pass the secluded beach at **Amiti** on your left, down the road from Galini; farther on is the monastery of **Faneromenis** (the Virgin Revealer). One of the more famous **kouroi** of Naxos is just a short walk from the harbor. This *kouros* (p. 22) is nearly 11m-tall. From the Apollonas bus stop, walk back along the main road uphill to the fork in the road. Take a sharp right and walk up until you see the stairs at the sign reading "Προς Κουρο" (toward the Kouros).

CENTRAL NAXOS AND THE TRAGEA

Buses run the 17km from Naxos Town to Halki (30min.; 6 per day, 9:30am-7pm; €1.20). Look for the turn-off to Ano Sangri, an isolated town of winding flagstone streets 1km west of the road. You can get off the bus at the turn-off and hike 1½hr. the entire way.

If you're up for the 30min. amble south of Ano Sangri, you can see the 6th-century BC **Temple of Demeter** being reconstructed with original fragments and new Naxian marble. If you have a motorbike or car, an alternate route takes you from Naxos Town through Melanes to **Flerio,** where another magnificent, 6.4m-tall Naxian **kouros** dated to the 7th century BC sleeps in a garden. This one was probably abandoned in its marble quarry because it broke before completion. Its owner runs a small *kafeneion* in the garden. From Flerio, backtrack and follow a road through three charming villages in a river valley—**Kato Potamia, Mesi Potamia,** and upstream **Ano Potamia**—before reaching Halki. (Maps available at the tourist office in Naxos Town. €4.50 for a large map, €0.50 each for maps of individual hikes.)

Halki, a placid village surrounded by Venetian towers, marks the beginning of the magnificent **Tragea,** an enormous, peaceful Arcadian olive grove. Restoration work in the **Panagia Protothonis,** across from the bus stop, has uncovered frescoes from the 11th through 13th centuries. The priest can let you in if it is closed. A 30min. walk northwest of Halki takes you to the village of Moni, where you can admire the **Panagia Drosiani,** one of the best preserved early Christian monuments in southern Europe, which houses frescoes dating back to the 7th century. A 20min. walk southwest of Halki, you will reach **Filoti,** a village at the far end of the Tragea valley. Footpaths off the main road will lead you into the dense **olive grove.** It is easy to get delightfully lost wandering among the scattered churches and tranquil scenery of the Tragea. If you do, take note of the sun and head west to return to the main road. Naxos's largest celebration, the **Feast of the Assumption of Panagia** (the Virgin Mary) is held in Filoti from August 14 to 16.

The slopes of **Mt. Zeus,** near Filoti, offer superb views extending to Poros and the sea beyond. Serious hikers may want to check out the **Cave of Zeus,** the spot where an eagle gave the king of the gods the power to hurl thunderbolts. This 150m-deep cave is a good 1½hr. trek uphill from Filoti. Determined mythologists, or those simply looking for a good hike with excellent views, should bring a flashlight to fully appreciate the cave. Head up the road to Apiranthos for 20-30min. until a sign points to the right for Mt. Zeus. Follow this road to its end, passing through a gate, just before a clearing with a potable **spring water fountain.** From there, keep going, staying on the left (uphill) whenever possible. Look for red arrows on stones. After 45min. you'll reach the cave's mouth, marked with a simple sign that reads "cave." The grotto itself is large, cool, slimy, and fun to explore.

APIRANTHOS

Buses run from Naxos Town (1hr.; 5 per day, 9:30am-7pm; €2.10) and Filoti (15min.).

With its narrow marble paths, the small town of Apiranthos is the most beautiful in Naxos. Lord Byron was so impressed he once said he wished to die here. Apiranthos houses an **Archaeological Museum** in a white building on the right side of the main street. Also in Apiranthos are a modest **folk art museum,** a **natural history museum** (near the bus stop), and a **geological museum** (beside the large church). All four are "officially" open 10am-1:30pm, but it all depends on tourist traffic; many owners moonlight as goat herders. (Single ticket to all 4 €1.)

Many Apiranthos homes are 300-400 years old and lie in the shadow of the two Venetian castles that preside over the town. The Zevgolis family lives in the castle by the square. If you are interested in looking around, call Despina Zevgolis one or more days ahead (☎697 661 8384) or find her in the port town's tourist information center. The mountain views from the edges of the town are stunning and locals are cordial to the few tourists who come this way. More information is available at the unofficial **info center,** inside the pricey Yasou Snack Bar, on the right past the geological museum. The road from Apiranthos through **Koronos** and **Koronida,** a 1hr. drive, snakes through interior mountain ranges. Near Koronos, once famous as the mining center of the island, you'll find the newly restored loading station and cable for the mines where you can catch a glimpse into the beginnings of the industrial history of the island. Interestingly, the industrial history of the island has also affected its current cultural makeup. Among other migrants, the mines drew a large number of Cretans for employment during the Turkish occupation. Many descendants of the old "Naxian" families who live in Apiranthos have green eyes; when a Naxian has green eyes, a trait among a few select regional groups in Greece, you can be pretty certain they are of Cretan heritage.

Stou Leftheris ❷, 100m up the marble road from the bus stop after you pass the main church, is one of the most beautiful places in all of the Cyclades to have lunch. The taverna also has some of the most savory local food. Try the *bifteki tou lefteri* (large spiced meatball; €8.50) or zucchini balls (€5), both specialties. (☎22850 61 333. Open daily 9am-midnight. MC/V.)

LITTLE CYCLADES

These tiny Cycladic isles provide the perfect opportunity to escape their larger, increasingly crowded counterparts. Jumping off the beaten island-hopping track allows you perfect isolation in tiny towns where goats outnumber human inhabitants, locals gather around the single town cafe every night, and a rural Greek culture still prevails. Peaceful walks, refreshing solitude, and a breathtaking nighttime sky await the adventurous traveler.

KOUFONISIA Κουφονησια ☎22850

The smallest of the inhabited Little Cyclades (and the most popular), Koufonisia surrounds itself with a sparkling selection of beaches on the southeastern side of the island, called Ano Koufonisia. The name, meaning "hollow," refers to the caves perforating the island's surface; the small town of Hora is found here. Tales of serene beaches and Cycladic relics lure visitors off of Ano Koufonisia to neighboring Kato Koufonisia and rocky Keros. There are few alternatives to the beaten path, but the simplicity of the setting lends itself to complete relaxation.

TRANSPORTATION AND PRACTICAL INFORMATION. The **ferry ticket office,** up the second road parallel to the beach and a few buildings past the blue-domed church, posts a ferry schedule on its door. (☎22850 71 438. Open daily 9am-

2:30pm and 6-10:30pm.) Ferries to: **Aegiali** (2hr., 5 per week, €5.50); **Iraklia** (1hr., daily, €4); **Katapola** (3hr., 5 per week, €5.50) via **Donousa** (1½hr., €4.50); **Naxos** (2½hr., daily, €6) via **Schinousa** (30min., €3.50); **Paros** (3hr., 4 per week, €12.50); **Piraeus** (6hr., 4 per week, €20.50). Head straight off the ferry dock toward winding Hora. The heart of Hora can be reached by turning left at the second road, just past the card phone. Be sure to bring enough money, as there is **no bank** and **no ATM** on the island. Koufonisia's commercial center consists of two main streets. One runs inland from just beyond the port to the left of the mini-market; the other springs from its left side, about 100m inland and parallel to the beach. The **medical center** (☎22850 71 370; open M, W, F 9am-2pm and 6-8pm; Tu, Th 9am-2pm; 24hr. emergency service) is on the right side on the road leading inland from the port, next to the the 24hr. **police** (☎22850 71 375). A few **mini-markets** are on the main road. **Internet** access is available at **Kohili** and **Kalamia Music Cafe** (see below). The **OTE** (☎22850 22 392; open 8am-2pm and 5-10pm) is on the main road inland, across from Pension Melissa. **Currency exchange** is available at the **post office;** heading inland, take a left before the mini-market on the first road parallel to the beach. (☎22850 74 214. Open 8:30am-noon and 6:30-11pm.) **Postal code:** 84300.

ACCOMMODATIONS AND CAMPING. The small pensions around town fill up fast; call ahead. Many homes with rooms to let are along the main road; prices for doubles run €40-55 in high season, €20-30 in low season. **Pension Melissa ❸** is attached to the taverna, 70m along the street leading inland from the telephone. **Maria Prasinou ❷** boasts beautiful beach views (☎22850 71 454. Doubles €20-45; triples €25-50. V.) **Akgrogiali ❷,** along the beach road, provides rooms with sea views, fridges, private baths, and balconies. (☎22850 71 685. Doubles €20-45; triples €30-52.) **Keros Hotel ❸,** just before the post office, provides a view of the harbor from large rooms with private balcony, bath, phone, fridge, and A/C. (☎22850 71 601; fax 22850 71 961. Doubles €55-67; triples €65-79.) **Harakorou Camping ❶** is a bare site with a beautiful location, affiliated with the taverna of the same name on Finikas beach. (☎22850 71 683. €3 per person, €4 per tent, cars free.)

FOOD AND NIGHTLIFE. The town is filled with traditional, tasty seafood and standard Greek fare (entrees €5-8.50). **Remezzo ❷,** 100m past Pension Melissa heading inland, serves up fish specialties to zealous locals year-round. (☎22850 71 468. Lobster with spaghetti for 2 €19. Fish with garlic and vinegar €7.50. Eggplant *dolmades* €5.50. Open daily 6pm-late.) **Kohili ❶** is the perfect spot for a croissant sandwich (€1.80-3.50), relaxed coffee (€1.50-3), and great views of the harbor. (☎22850 74 279. Internet access €3 per hr. Open daily 8am-2am.) **Kalamia Music Cafe ❶,** 150m along the inland road, by the public phones, provides drinks (frappé €2.50), sweets (€2-4.50), and an eclectic blend of world music to a crowd of chic customers. (☎22850 71 741. Open daily 8am-3am. Cocktails €6-7. Internet access €8 per hr.) For late-night dancing, set sail for **Emplo,** a word signifying the beginning of a sea voyage. Walk up the hill path to the left of the port and listen for Greek music to find the purple-draped, DJ-sporting disco. (Beer €3; cocktails €5. Open daily 10pm-late.)

BEACHES. Koufonisia's beaches spool out in a continuous ribbon along the southern coast. **Ammos beach** is closest to Hora, just to the right of the ferry dock (facing inland); here you can spot nearby fishing boats and watch spirited kids' soccer games. Continuing 10min. down the road behind the sand leads you to family-packed **Finikas,** with a convenient taverna beside it. Just on the other side of the ridge from Finikas waits much quieter **Fanos.** The farther you walk, the fewer people (and clothes) you'll see. A 30min. walk from Hora brings you to **Pori beach,** the best on the island, with water and sand that is magnificent even by Greek island standards. If the sand begins to broil, head for the shaded rocks behind the beach to cave-lined coves that provide perfect snorkeling spots. Regular boats (4 per day, round-trip €3) also make trips to Pori from the dock at Hora. For those who hate sharing the sand, there is always the daily ferry (4 per day, round-trip €3) to **Kato Koufonisia,** where total peace awaits.

DONOUSA Δονουσα ☎22850

A trip to Donousa will give you a dose of local culture in the rural Cyclades. Lacking banks, public transportation, or a reliable tourist office, Donousa beckons those eager to abandon modernity and swarms. Isolated, golden-sanded beaches abound beyond the town's scattering of tavernas and pensions. The small **town beach** provides children shallow splashing room amidst fishing boats. **Kedros beach,** a nicer piece of shore, stretches out just over the ridge. Follow the road perpendicular to the town beach to the right of the white sign to get to the tent-lined sand. A 1hr. walk down this road lies even more pristine **Livadi beach.** Taxi boats also leave daily at 10am from the port for Livadi (round-trip €4).

The **tourist office** is across from the ferry dock; it sells ferry tickets and **exchanges currency.** If closed during your visit, you can buy your ticket on the boat. (☎22850 51 648; fax 22850 51 649. Open 8am-2pm and 5-10pm.) **Ferries** travel four times per week at 8am to: **Amorgos** (2hr., €5); **Koufonisia** (1hr., €4.50); **Naxos** (2hr., €6); **Schinousa** (1½hr., €5). Travel to other islands is more sporadic. **To Kima ❶,** the island's main hangout, sells phone cards, tasty dishes (entrees €3.50-5.50), and some groceries; it's right beside the dock. (☎22850 51 566. Open daily 7am-2am.) Up the hill to the right of To Kima is the island's **public phone.** You can reach the **doctor** 24hr. (☎22850 51 506). The few **domatia** in town lie to the left and across the bay from the main port; doubles go for €20-45. Newly constructed **Firoa Studios ❷** offers the most luxurious accommodations in town, with flower-lined patios, full kitchenettes, immaculate bathrooms, and spacious interiors. (☎22850 51 658; www.donoussa.net/firoa-studios. Doubles €20-35.) **Christos Sigalas ❷,** at the massive blue "Rooms to Let" sign, offers bare, large rooms with fridges and private baths. (☎22850 51 570; fax 22850 51 607. Doubles €20-40.) The rooms of **Venetsanou Eleftherie ❷,** in the first complex at the right of the beach, boast the best views in town, as well as basic kitchenettes and small bathrooms. (☎22850 51 609. Doubles €25-45; triples €30-50.) Catch a ride with the owners when you come into port. **Camping** is permitted only on **Kedros beach,** over the hill to the right of the domatia. Join the daily raid on the delicious goods dished out by the **bakery ❶,** above the tourist office. (☎22850 51 567. Bread €1 and under. Pastries €1.20-1.80. Open daily 7:30am-2:30pm and 5-10:30pm.) Bear right from the dock to find the small **mini-market.** (☎22850 51 582. Open daily 8am-10pm.) There are several tavernas all visible from the dock, all serving similar Greek food (entrees €3.50-6.50). **Meltemi ❷,** just to the right of the tourist office when facing inland, serves simple dishes in view of spectacular sunsets. (☎22850 52 241. Entrees €4-6. Open May-Oct. daily 9am-1am. MC/V.) **Ekatzohoros,** just to the left of the dock facing inland, is the only nightlife option in town, serving cocktails in a beach bar with cushy couches and tropical umbrellas. (☎22850 51 783. Beer €2.50-4; cocktails €5-6. Open June-Sept. daily 9am-4am.)

IRAKLIA Ιρακλια ☎22850

Visitors to Iraklia tend to return: this underpopulated hideaway is a relaxed respite from the summer swarms. Whether exploring its caves, basking on its beaches, or sipping coffee under a starlit cafe, you'll enjoy the breathtaking scenery.

TRANSPORTATION AND PRACTICAL INFORMATION. Ferries run to: **Amorgos** (2½hr., daily, €7); **Donousa** (1½hr., daily, €6); **Koufonisia** (45min., daily, €4); **Naxos** (1½hr., daily, €5); **Paros** (3-4 times per week, €10.50); **Piraeus** (6hr., 3-4 times per week, €19.50); **Schinousa** (15min., daily, €3.50); **Syros** (3 hr., 1 per week, €14). Schedules are posted around the harbor or consult a travel agent. **Iraklia Rent a Scooter** in Panagia rents **mopeds.** (☎22850 71 564. €12-16 per day.) From the **port,** head right past the town beach to get to **Ag. Giorgios.** This main road splits at **Perigali** (☎22850 74 234; open daily 8am-11pm), the local mini-market where you can score a **map** (€0.90). A small ravine runs through the center of town; two roads run alongside it and merge at the top. The **medical center** is just above Perigali on the right branch. (☎22850 71 388 or 697 667 7833. 24hr. emergency service. Open M-F 8am-2:30pm.) Fifty meters farther along the right-hand road is all-purpose **Melissa,** a general store, ferry ticketer, telephone operator, domatia (see below), and post office. (☎22850 71 539. Open daily 6am-11pm.) One of the island's two card phones is just outside; the second is in Panagia. **Postal code:** 84300.

ACCOMMODATIONS AND FOOD. In July and August, call ahead to reserve accommodations—in most cases, your hosts will pick you up at the port. **Anna's Place ❷,** up the hill on the first left from the left fork of the main road, looks out over the port from its spacious balconies. The rooms are basic but comfortable and pristine with fridges and showers; the studios are palatial. (☎22850 71 145. Doubles €25-40; 3-person studios €40-65.) **Alexandra ❷,** at the top of Agios Giorgios just beyond Anna's, has four small, breezy rooms with baths and fridges, a shared kitchen, and a spacious common veranda. (☎22850 71 482. Doubles €15-40; triples €20-45.) **Maria's ❷,** across the road, offers cramped, homey rooms with full kitchenette, private bath, and shared balcony. (☎22850 71 485. Doubles €20-40.) **Melissa ❷** offers rooms with shared bath. (☎22850 71 539. Doubles €15-25.) Right on the road after Anna's and then left on the second gravel road, **Prasinos Nikolas ❷** boasts luxurious modern rooms with built-in beds, fridges, stone floors, TVs, private baths, and balconies. (☎22850 71991. Doubles €20-40.)

Ten minutes down the road to Livadi, you'll find a delicious variety of grilled fish and Greek specialties (€5-7) with free camping overlooking the water at **Giorgios Gavalas's Place ❷.** Dance late into the night with his sons or ask Giorgios if you can participate in the next all-male Miss Iraklia contest. Rave about your exploits to the folks back home at their **Internet** station (€5 per hr.) or on the **international phone.** (☎22850 29 034 or 22850 71 226. Open May-Sept. 24hr. Traveler's checks accepted.) **Maistrali ❷,** up the hill just before Alexandra, sells postcards, foreign papers, and books, has an **international telephone, exchanges currency,** and offers **Internet** access (€3 per hr.); an attached **restaurant ❷** serves standard Greek cuisine. (☎22850 71 807 or 71 648; maistralinick@hotmail.com. Entrees €3-8. Open daily 8am-late. AmEx/MC/V.) Across the road **O Pevkos ❷** (☎22850 71 568), the island's oldest restaurant, sells fresh fish caught by its owner. Raw fish (€10-20 per kg) can also be bought there to be prepared at home. (Prepared fish €20-40 per kg. Open daily 10am-10pm). For a more raucous hangout try **Bar Aki Music-Dance,** the island's only club, down the dirt road from Maistrali. (☎22850 71 487. Beer €3; cocktails €6. Open daily from 10pm.)

SIGHTS AND BEACHES. The shallow, clear waters of **Livadi beach** epitomize Iraklian serenity. Wade out and look at the ruins of the **Venetian Castle** overhead. The water taxi "Anemos" (M, W, F-Sa departing 11am, returning 4pm; round-trip €6) will take you to **Karvounlakos** or **Alimia beaches;** buy tickets at Perigali. To get a feeling for the Greece of 40 years ago, continue along the main road past Livadi to the town of **Panagia** (45min. from Agios Giorgios), where you'll find a small taverna, a church, some cows, and not much else. The taverna **To Steki ❷** (☎22850 71 579; open daily 8am-2am) also serves as a general store, bakery, and the only "gas station" on the island—fill up from a canister.

THE OUTDOORS. The stalactite- and stalagmite-scattered **Agios Ioannis Cave,** with tiny waterways, dramatic depths, and seemingly endless series of chambers will fascinate the adventurous. There is a rough but helpful map of the path on the back of the Iraklia map available in Perigali. Bring a flashlight, many candles, matches, and a walking stick if possible—and get ready to get filthy. The steep, 1½hr. **hike** begins in Panagia, where a red arrow and the word "cave" are scrawled on a barn just after the blue-domed town church—if you don't see it, ask in To Steki. After 20min. along the stone wall-lined dirt path, you'll reach a wooden fence and another painted arrow pointing you through it. Follow the stone wall on your right until it meets another stone wall. The beaten path of the ascent becomes difficult to follow; just stay near this wall. After your climb, another wooden door stands at the intersection of two fences. Go through this door and follow the stone piles until you reach a more clearly defined pathway that marks the beginning of a 30min. descent along the back side of **Mt. Pappas** toward the tiny, bright white cave entrance; painted signs will start directing you within 5min. of the entrance. Crawling through the small entrance (marked by a hanging bell) brings you into the caves. You'll need the flashlight right away; leaving lighted candles along the way will mark your path. To the left as you enter is an icon of St. John, who is celebrated in an August **festival** at the cave. There are said to be 15 rooms inside the cave; the final chamber is so deep that there is no oxygen inside. Be careful: the rocks are slippery and daylight vanishes quickly.

SCHINOUSA Σχινουσα ☎22850

A multitude of isolated yet accessible beaches line the coast of untouched Schinousa, all but guaranteeing a peaceful communion with nature. The island is best enjoyed on foot; explore its dusty, donkey-patrolled interior and get to know the affable population—250 at last count.

TRANSPORTATION AND PRACTICAL INFORMATION. All boats dock at the tiny port of **Mersini,** with **Hora** a 10-15min. walk uphill. Call ahead for accommodations and you'll be picked up from the ferry or grab a ride with a pension owner at the dock. **Flying Dolphins** or **ferries** go to: **Amorgos** (3 hr., daily, €6.50) via **Koufonisia** (30min., €3.50); **Donousa** (1½hr., 5 per week, €6); **Iraklia** (15min., 5 per week, €3.50); **Naxos** (1½hr., 5 per week, €5); **Piraeus** (7hr., 2 per week, €21.60). Check the posted schedules for daily routes. Nearly everything you'll need in Hora is found on the main road, a 5min. walk from end to end. At the dock end of the main road you'll see a sign pointing to Tsigouri beach. Following this road to town travel guru **Giorgios Grispos,** who offers one-stop tourist shopping with a **travel agency,** domatia (see below), and taverna. (☎22850 71 930; grispos@nax.forthnet.gr. Open daily 9am-2pm and 6-9pm.) Buy **ferry tickets** here or at the port and **exchange currency** at poor rates. Note that there is **no bank** in town. **Maps** and **phone cards** are available at the mini-markets lining the main road. The **doctor** (☎22850 71 385) is on the same road as Agnantema bakery in a clearly marked white building; 24hr. emergency care is available. Two public **card phones** are down at the port and in the plateia of Hora. The **post office** (☎22850 714 032) is in a private home on the main road; look for the hand-painted sign. **Postal code:** 84300.

ACCOMMODATIONS AND FOOD. Nearly every restaurant or general store in town offers several rooms to rent in addition to moussaka and Fanta. **Girogios Grispos's domatia** ❸ have A/C, TVs, fridges, and a pleasant beachside location (see above; doubles €32-65). Centrally located **Anesis** ❷ has large, clean rooms with fridges, private baths, and panoramic balcony views. (☎22850 71 180. Doubles €28-40. Be sure to bargain.) **Agnantema** ❸, in a new building, has a prime location right above the bakery and restaurant. The rooms, with bath, fridge, kitchenette, phone, and TV, overlook a rocky terrace with tables and a gazebo. (☎22850 71 987; fax 22850 74 077. Reserve in advance during high season. Doubles €25-40; 4-person studios €45-60. Cafe open 8am-11:30pm.) **Iliovasilema Hotel ❷**, run by the same family as Anna Rooms, offers small, simple rooms with fridges and private baths. (☎22850 71 948. Doubles €15-35; triples €25-40). **Anna Rooms ❸**, down the road to the left just before the bakery, has a similar but slightly more modern atmosphere with phones, private balconies, and a cafe/terrace overlooking the ocean. (☎22850 71 161. Doubles €32-48; triples €36-55.)

There are mini-markets about town. Off the main road, heading left, you'll find a street marked by signs for **Agnantema bakery ❶.** (☎22850 71 987. Open daily 8am-11pm). Traditional music, tasty food, and talkative locals abound at **Loza Pizzeria ❷**, on the main plateia. (☎22850 71 864. Pizzas €6-7. Pastas €5.50-6.50. Open daily 8am-2am.) Gaze at the sea from the balcony as you wait for your moussaka (€5) or octopus (€8) at **Panorama ❷**, a few meters past the beach turn-off on the main road. (☎22850 71 160; fax 22850 71 957. Open June-Sept. daily 8am-midnight. V.)

NIGHTLIFE AND BEACHES. **Ostria Cafe**, an outdoor beach bar and restaurant perched on the edge of Tsigouro beach, provides a pleasant setting for the only nightlife to be found on the island. (☎22850 71 174. Beer €2.50-3; cocktails €5. Open June-Sept. daily 10am-late). Schinousa's rocky, pothole-littered dirt roads are virtually car-free, and make exploring the island on foot easy. Grab a bottle of water, glance at a map, and walk until a particularly alluring cove catches your eye. **Tsigouri beach**, 450m down the first road on the right heading into town from the port, provides an easily accessible and more developed option. **Livadi**, a long thin stretch of sand cradled by a small bay, lies at the end of the right fork of the road heading through Hora. The pristine cove of **Psili Ammos** sprawls on the other side of the island, about 2km (30min.) past the bakery.

PAROS Παρος

Paros's enduring legacy is its opaque, pure marble. Many of the great statues and buildings of the ancient world have shone because of Parian rock: the Venus de Milo, the Nike of Samothrace, and parts of Napoleon's mausoleum in Paris all derived their materials from this locale. A late bloomer in the tourism business, Paros had 20 donkeys for each car as recently as 15 years ago. Yet not even the headstrong residents of Paros could resist the call of foreign dollar; today the local population inflates to 10 times its low-season size in the heart of the summer, when the golden beaches and lonely mountains swell with travelers.

PARIKIA Παροικια ☎22840

Behind Parikia's commercial facade, flower-filled streets wind through archways, past whitewashed houses, and by one of the most treasured basilicas of the Orthodox faith. Wander through the agora to find trendy clothing, snappy jewelry, local art, homemade goods, and many coffeehouses. While the small, pebbly beaches are overpowered by souvenir shops and touristy tavernas, this transportation hub is a convenient base for reaching the more pristine outlying island locations.

TRANSPORTATION

Flights: Olympic Airways (☎22840 21 900), in the plateia by National Bank. Open M-F 9am-2:30pm. To **Athens** (around 2 per day, €55). Taxi to airport €7.

Ferries: To: **Amorgos** (3hr., 1-2 per day, €10.60); **Crete** (8hr., 5 per week, €21.40); **Ikaria** (4hr., 5 per week, €13.20); **Ios** (2½hr., 7-9 per day, €8.30); **Kos** (1 per week, €16.60); **Naxos** (1hr., 5-10 per day, €5.30); **Piraeus** (5-6hr., 5-8 per day, €19.20); **Rhodes** (16hr., daily, €26.10); **Samos** (6hr., 6 per week, €16.20); **Santorini** (3½hr., 7-9 per day, €11.80); **Sikinos** (3hr., daily, €6.20); **Syros** (1hr., 3-6 per day, €6.20).

Flying Dolphins: To: **Crete** (3½hr., June-Sept. 6 per week, €42.40); **Ios** (2½hr., 2-3 per day, €17.40); **Mykonos** (50min., 2-4 per day, €12.90); **Naxos** (1hr., 4-7 per day, €10.20); **Piraeus** (3hr., 3 per day, €37.40); **Rafina** (3hr., 8 per week, €31.40); **Santorini** (1¾hr., 3-4 per day, €23.10); **Syros** (45min., 6 per week, €12.40); **Tinos** (1½hr., 4-5 per day, €17).

Buses: ☎22840 21 395 or 21 133. Schedule posted a few blocks to the left of the windmill (facing inland). To: **Aliki** and the **airport** (30min., 8 per day, €1.10) via the **Valley of the Butterflies** (€0.90); **Chrisi Akti** (50min., 2 per day, €1.80); **Drios** (1hr., 12 per day, €1.80); **Kamares** (20min., 2 per day, €0.90); **Lefkes** (25min., 8 per day, €1); **Marpissa** (35min., 15 per day, €1.30); **Naoussa** (15min., 33 per day, €1); **Piso Livadi** (40min., 15 per day, €1.60); **Pounda** (15min., 15 per day, €1.50).

Taxis: ☎22840 21 500. Facing inland, walk to the right of the windmill and take the 1st left inland; the taxis line up at the corner of the plateia. Available 24hr.

ORIENTATION AND PRACTICAL INFORMATION

Cheap hotels, tourist offices, and the town beach lie to the left of the ferry dock. The plateia is straight ahead, past the windmill. To the right, a whitewashed labyrinth brims with shops, restaurants, and cafes. To the far right and around the bend, the island's party district awaits.

Travel Agency: Polos Tours (☎22840 22 092; www.polostours.gr), next to the OTE, has transportation schedules and car rental (€24-41 per day). Open daily 9am-midnight.

Banks: National Bank (☎22840 21 298). From the windmill, head inland to the plateia and to the right. It's in the fortress-like building at the far corner, past the playground. 24hr. **ATM** and **currency exchange** machine. Open M-Th 8am-2:30pm, F 8am-2pm.

Luggage Storage: Agencies around the port charge €2-3 per piece per day.

Laundromat: Top (☎22840 23 424). Pass the bus station and turn right after the ancient cemetery. Wash and dry €10. Open daily 9am-midnight.

Public Toilets: Beside the small blue and white church to the left of the windmill and others to the right of the windmill beside the signs for the Frankish Castle. Free.

Police: ☎22840 23 333. Across the plateia behind the OTE, on the 2nd fl. Open 24hr.

Tourist Police ☎22840 21 673. Share the police's building. Open daily 7am-2:30pm.

Port Police ☎22840 21 240. Off the waterfront, past the bus station. Open 24hr.

Medical Clinic: ☎22840 22 500. Across from the small blue and white church to the left of the windmill. Open M-F 8:30am-2:30pm. **Emergency** care available 24hr.

OTE: ☎22840 21 399. 1 block to the right of the windmill (facing inland). Open M-F 7am-2:40pm.

Internet Access: Internet cafes are all over Parikia. **Cybercookies** (☎/fax 22840 21 610), on Agora, charges €4.80 per hr. Free 20min. with a food order, 40min. with 2 orders. Open daily 8am-1am. **Memphis Cafe** is to the left of the windmills on the waterfront, past the bus station. €3.75 per hr. Open daily 9:30am-11pm.

Post Office: ☎22840 21 236. On the left side of the waterfront facing inland, 2 blocks past the bus stop. Open M-F 7:30am-2pm. **Postal code:** 84400.

ACCOMMODATIONS AND CAMPING

There are many hotels and **domatia** along the waterfront and in the Old Town; a slew of new, inexpensive pensions have opened behind the town beach to the left of the plateia. Dock hawks are known to offer good deals in Naoussa, Piso Livadi, and Antiparos, among other places; remember to insist on seeing rooms before you pay. The **Room Association** (☎22840 22 772) can help you hunt.

Rena Rooms (☎22840 22 220; www.cycladesnet.gr). Turn left from the dock and take a right after the cemetery or call ahead for a port shuttle. Owners George and Rena provide detailed information on the island, a welcoming atmosphere, and bright, clean rooms with fridges, ceiling fans, baths, and balconies. Free luggage deposit. A/C €5 extra. Doubles €18-39; triples €27-45. 20% discount for *Let's Go* readers. ❸

Pelagos Studios (☎22840 22 725; fax 22840 22 708). Find Vassilis, the voluble owner, in the port, or call ahead and get picked up. Furnished rooms with kitchens, baths, TVs, A/C, and radios in a peaceful location just out of town. Barbecues on the patio contribute to a familial atmosphere and Parikia's nightlife lies only 300m down the road. Breakfast €3. Doubles €30-50; triples €40-60. ❹

Parian Village (☎22840 23 187; inter@otenet.gr), about 1km north of the port; public buses run past the site on the way to Krios beach. Small rooms a bit out of town offer spectacular bay views and easy beach access. A/C, phones, fridges, and Parian marble decoration come standard; media-hungry patrons can request a TV. A gleaming pool and a cafe serving simple dishes and breakfast (€1.50-4) are downstairs. Singles €45-65; doubles €53-73; triples €62-88. MC/V. ❹

Parasporos Camping (☎22840 22 268 or 22840 21 100), 1.5km south of the port, away from the bustle of town, beside Delphini beach. Shuttle service available. Showers, laundry, and kitchen. €6 per person; €3 per tent, €4 tent rental. ❶

Koula Camping (☎22840 22 081; www.campingkoula.gr), 400m north of the dock, across the street from the town beach. A market, kitchen, and easy access to the town from a beachside location keeps the backpackers flowing. €6 per person, €3 tent rental; small, simple cabins €6 per person. MC/V. ❶

FOOD

Happy Green Cow (☎22840 24 691), 1 block inland off the plateia in the narrow walkway behind the National Bank, provides vegetarian food in a psychedelic setting designed by the artist-owners. The "Cow's Orgasms" (pastries with cheese and peppers; €10) may not induce the desired effect on bovines but are sure to produce ecstasies for diners. Open Apr.-Nov. daily 7pm-midnight. ❸

Nick's Hamburgers (☎22840 21 434). Walk right from the port; it's tucked away in Ventouri's square along the water. "Pure 100% Beef" declares a sign, welcoming foreigners hankering for a taste of home to the land of beefy goodness. Paros's 1st hamburger joint, established in 1977, Nick's serves mouth-defying large dishes including vegetarian options for few euros. Cheeseburger €1.80. Hot dog €1.50. Fish and chips €4.20. Nikfeast (2 burgers, chips, and salad) €3.80. Open Apr.-Oct. daily 11am-2am. ❶

Porphyra (☎22840 23 410), next to the ancient cemetery on the right side of the waterfront. Serving seafood exclusively, it entices diners with exotic offerings fresh from the water including the namesake *porphyra* (the inhabitant of a conch shell; €4) and sea urchin (€4) harvested by the owner. Open Mar.-Oct. 7pm-1am. AmEx/MC/V. ❷

Ephesus (☎22840 21 491), behind the hospital. Combining Anatolian and Greek cooking, Ephesus dishes out a delectable variety of dips (hummus €2.50; spinach €3.50), wonderfully messy stuffed pitas oozing toppings (€5.50-6.50), and a variety of kebabs (€6.50-7.50). Open daily 10am-midnight. ❷

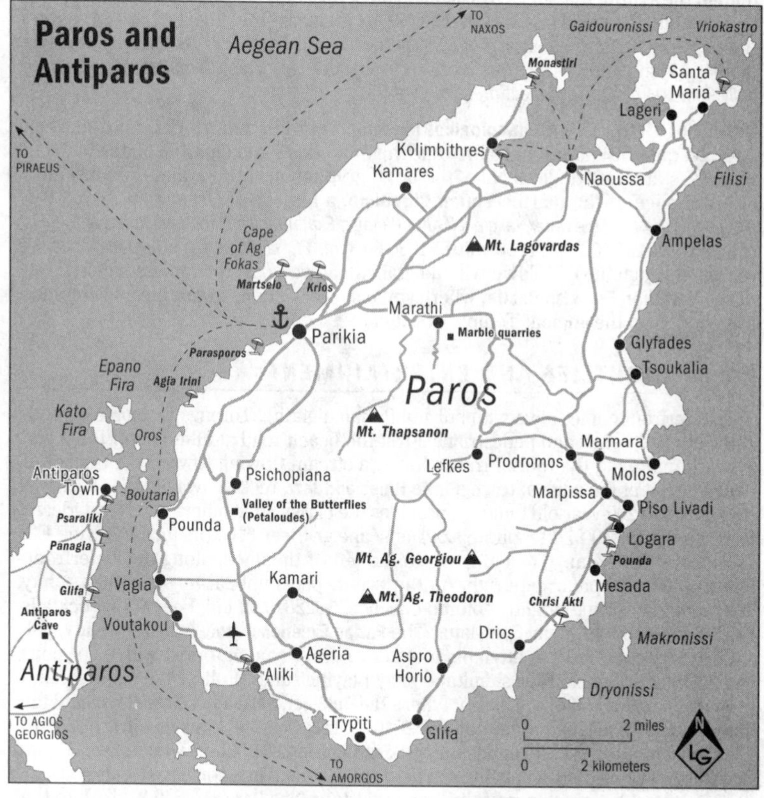

Apollon Garden Restaurant (☎22840 21 875). Follow Agora away from the main plateias and keep an eye out for the signs. Overflowing with operatic music and lush plantlife, Apollon caters to a sophisticated crowd of tourists with a rotating menu of fresh fare. Chicken with mango €12.50. Salmon fillet €12.50. Open May-Oct. daily 6pm-1am. AmEx/MC/V. ❸

SIGHTS

PANAGIA EKATONTAPILIANI. The **Church of Our Lady of 100 Gates** looms over Parikia's plateia in the shape of an imperfect Greek cross. Tradition holds that only 99 of the church's 100 doors can be counted—when the 100th appears, Constantinople will once again belong to the Greeks. The Ekatontapiliani was supposedly conceived in the 4th century when **St. Helen,** the mother of Constantine, stopped here on her way to the Holy Land. While praying, Helen saw the True Cross and vowed to build a church befitting the site of her vision. She died before she could fulfill her promise, but in the 6th century the Emperor Justinian commissioned young Ignatius, student of Isidorus of Miletus, to build her church. According to legend, the church's beauty drove Isidorus to a fit of jealousy, and both men died in the scuffle that ensued. The main structure of the complex is the mammoth **Church of the Assumption.** The **Church of Agios Nikolaos** (the oldest of the three) and the **baptistry** flank this centerpiece to the north and south, respectively. A **museum** displays 17th-century religious icons. *(Church open daily 7am-10pm; free. Museum open daily 9am-10pm; €1.50. Modest dress required.)*

OTHER SIGHTS. The **Archaeological Museum** contains more prized pieces than your average antiquities museum. Ogle the infamous Parian marble on the 5th-century BC statue of wingless Nike, the large gryphon sculpture, and the museum's beloved slice of the marble **Parian Chronicle,** a history of Greece up to 264 BC. *(Heading away from the water, take a left after Panagia Ekatontapiliani; the museum is at the end of the road. ☎22840 21 231. Open Tu-Su 8:30am-3pm. €2, students €1, EU students free.)* A ramble through the Old Town will inevitably lead you past the lone remaining wall of the Venetian **Frankish Castle,** where you can see sections of marble and columns removed from the ancient Temple of Athena.

NIGHTLIFE AND ENTERTAINMENT

The waterfront comes alive with pulsing Parian nightlife. Throngs assemble on both sidewalk and beach and pedestrians stroll the beach road at all hours of the night. Toward midnight, the tourist traffic forms a stream flowing toward the thicket of clubs that sit at the edge of town. **Pirate Blues and Jazz,** tucked away in the Old Town on Agora in a 200-year-old building, provides the classy atmosphere of a New Orleans jazz club. (☎22840 21 114; piratejazz@netscape.gr. Beer €3; cocktails €7; wine €3. Open daily 7pm-3am.) The cafes are to the left of the dock, along the waterfront. **Saloon D'Or,** a popular cafe right on the water, plays upbeat music amidst funky checkered floors and brightly colored couches. (☎22840 22 176. Beer €2-3; cocktails €5-7. Open Apr.-Oct. daily 6pm-4am.) The **Parian Experience** consists of a sweaty, pulsating party complex that attempts to cater to every type of tourist with a spacious central courtyard and four simultaneously playing tunes. Follow the spotlight and crowds to the far end of the harbor where **The Dubliner, Salsa Club, Scandi Bar,** and the **Paros Rock Cafe** all share one roof. (☎22840 21 113. Cover €3 includes 1 drink. Beer €2-3; cocktails €5-6.) The subtly-named **Sex Club** (☎22840 25 115; open F-Su 11pm-late) next door proffers a dancing-oriented environment in a converted warehouse.

If a night of boozing doesn't thrill you, outdoor **Cine Rex** (☎22840 21 676), to the left of the dock along the waterfront and **Cine Paros** (☎22840 21 423), two blocks past the post office, show American movies in their original versions. (Showings 9 and 11pm. €6. Check signs in the plateia.)

BEACHES

Almost every beach on the island can be reached in under an hour's drive. In the immediate area of Parikia, though, there are some outstanding and easily accessible beaches. **Parasporos** lies 2km to the south and attracts only the occasional guest from a nearby resort (take the bus to Pounda; every hr., €0.90). **Krios beach** lies across the harbor from Parikia. The sand is less pebbly and more welcoming than the beaches in town. It is accessible by bus (3 per day, €1.80) and taxi boat (every 30min., 9:30am-7pm; round-trip €2).

DAYTRIPS FROM PARIKIA

Just 10km south of town is the shady, spring-fed **Valley of the Butterflies,** or Petaloudes, where the rare (and tongue-twisting) *Panaxiaquadripunctaria* moths return to the place of their birth to breed, lured back by their strong sense of smell;

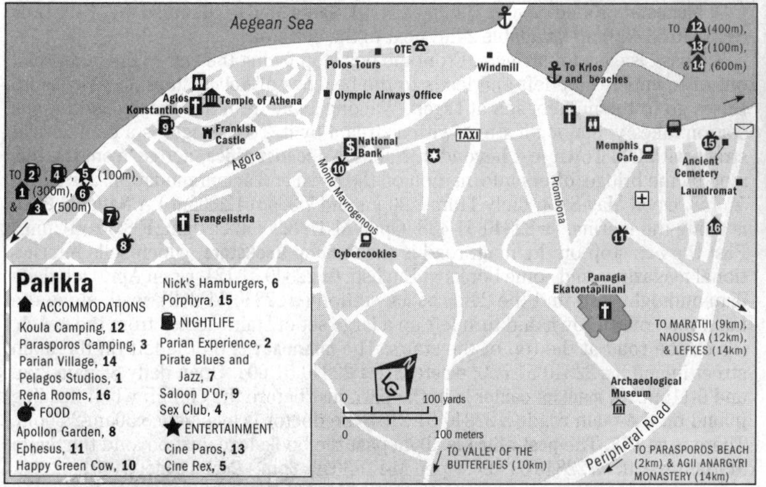

Petaloudes is one of the rare surviving sanctuaries for the moths. June provides only a speckling of the brightly striped, black and yellow moths, while the height of mating season (late July-late Aug.) sometimes draws millions in a miraculous display. The moths do not eat for their entire mating season so they can ill afford to expend energy entertaining photo-hungry guests. Be considerate: don't clap or talk loudly; don't shake the bushes. Take the bus from Parikia to Aliki (10min., 8 per day, €0.90) and ask to be dropped off at Petaloudes. Follow the signs up the steep road for 2km. (☎22840 91 211. Open June-Sept. daily 9am-8pm. €1.50.)

Five kilometers from Parikia in the center of the island, **Marathi** is home to Paros's idle marble quarries. Still considered to be among the finest in the world, Parian marble is translucent up to 3mm-thick, with one-third the opacity of most other marble. A visit to the quarries is a serious undertaking: bring a flashlight, strong shoes, and don't go alone. Nearby **Lefkes,** 5km from Marathi, was the largest village on the island through the 19th century, as Parians moved inland to escape plundering coastal pirates. Today it's a quiet village of 400 inhabitants with classic Cycladic architecture—the most attractive and unspoiled town in Paros's interior. Buses run to Marathi on the way to several destinations, every other hour. From the bus stop, signs will direct you to the quarries.

NAOUSSA Ναουσσα ☎22840

Naoussa is Paros's second port, a natural harbor cradled by long, sandy beaches in the shape of crab claws. Persian, Greek, Roman, Venetian, Ottoman, and Russian fleets have anchored here over the years, but the upscale environment of the tiny town will make it difficult for a budget traveler to last too long amidst the posh nightclubs, pricey pensions, and scenic waterfront.

TRANSPORTATION AND PRACTICAL INFORMATION. **Buses** run continuously between **Parikia** and Naoussa (15min., every 30min., €1). Buses run to: **Ampelas** (4 per day, €0.90); **Drios** (15 per day, €1.60); **Santa Maria** (4 per day, €0.90). Check the schedule at the bus stop booth. **Taxi boats** leave for nearby beaches. The blue booth across from the waterfront cafes sells round-trip tickets to: **Kolimbithres** (12min.; every 30min., 10am-6pm; €3); **Lageri** (20min., every hr., €4); **Monastiri** (15min., every 30min., €3.50); **Santa Maria** (40min., daily, €7). **Taxis** (☎22840 53 490) are available 24hr. next to the bus stop.

Naoussa is easy to navigate. From the bus stop facing the water, the main road out of town is to the left and leads to the beaches of **Kolimbithres** and **Monastiri.** Buses go to the nude beach at **Lageri.** Walking away from the water past the bus station takes you along a street with a stream by it. To the right is a commercial street with Old Town just beyond it. Naoussa's **tourist office,** across from the bus stop by the bridge, offers information on the town and accommodations. (☎22840 52 158. Open May-Sept. daily 11am-3:30pm and 7:30pm-12:30am.) A **National Bank** is along the marina. (☎22840 51 438. Open M-Th 8:30am-2:30pm, F 8:30am-2pm.) Past the bus stop on the main road is the **General Bookstore,** which sells international magazines and some books in English. (☎22840 51 121. Open Apr.-Oct. daily 9am-midnight.) To find the 24hr. **police** station (☎22840 51 202), walk along the main road out of town and turn left up a large set of stairs across from the beach; it's on the road at the top of the stairs. The **pharmacy** is on the left on the main street inland. (☎22840 51 550; **emergencies** 22840 51 004. Open daily 8:30am-2pm and 5-11pm.) A **medical center** is in the park just before the church when heading inland on the main road (☎22840 51 216); the doctor is available 8:30am-2:30pm. There is **no OTE.** The **post office** is 400m past the bookstore, just beyond the Santa Maria turn-off. (☎22840 51 495. Open M-F 7:30am-2pm.) **Postal code:** 84401.

ACCOMMODATIONS. For a small town, Naoussa has many places to sleep, but the prices skyrocket in the summer when package-tour groups book most hotels months in advance. Rooms to let cost roughly €30-45 for doubles, €35-50 for triples. Ask at the tourist office for help finding accommodations. **Villa Galini ❷** is inland past the bus stop and 700m to the right; signs mark the way. It boasts a gregarious owner, a peaceful setting, and airy rooms with private baths, phones, and fridges. Call several days in advance to arrange free shuttle pickup at the port at Parikia. (☎22840 53 335; fax 22840 53 336. Open Apr.-Sept. Doubles €25-50. MC/V.) To the right of the waterfront with your back to the water lie a number of upscale pensions with spectacular views of the harbor. To reach **Pension Hara ❹,** walk along the main road out of town 300m past the port and climb the stairs that lead to the police station. Impeccably clean rooms with balconies, TVs, A/C, and fridges, located only 150m away from the beach. (☎22840 51 011; fax 22840 51 500. Doubles €40-60. AmEx/MC/V.) Around the corner to the right and up the hill 20m is **Sakis Rooms ❸,** which provides weary travelers with luxurious lodgings in a welcoming atmosphere. Amenities include private baths, TVs, A/C, fridges, and balconies overlooking the sea. (☎22840 52 171; www.paros-online.com. Doubles €35-60; 5-person apartments €50-130. MC/V.) The upscale **Atlantis Hotel ❹** sits just around the corner from the bus station on the road out of town. Bare but well-equipped rooms with A/C, phones, baths, and fridges are complemented by a pool and jacuzzi in the garden area. (☎22840 51 340; fax 22840 52 087. Breakfast included. Doubles €50-70; triples €65-85. AmEx/MC/V.) **Camping Naoussa ❶** is on the road to Kolimbithres. Call for the free port shuttle. (☎22840 51 595. €5 per person; €4 per tent, €6 per tent rental.) **Camping Surfing Beach ❶,** 3km toward Santa Maria, offers watersports, a mini-market, pool, self-service taverna, free safety deposit boxes, and a location right on the beach. (☎22840 51 491; fax 22840 51 937. €5-7per person; €3.50 per tent, €5.50 tent rental; €3 per car. AmEx/MC/V.)

FOOD AND ENTERTAINMENT. Naoussan kitchens cook up famously delicious seafood; their local specialty is the fish plate *gouna*. **Diamantis ❷,** behind the church on the commerce road about 300m from the bus station, is an excellent choice for meat-heavy Greek fare. Feast on the specialty called Lamb Diamantis

(€7), which is stuffed with feta, tomatoes, peppers, and onions. (☎22840 52 129. Open daily 6pm-1am. MC/V.) **Pervolaria ❸** offers a more sophisticated setting for a plentiful variety of pizzas and pastas, served in a peacefully secluded garden, about 200m inland on the road along the stream. (☎22840 51 721. Pesto calamari €8. Tagliatelle with salmon €12. Open daily 7pm-late. AmEx/MC/V.) Across from the water, you'll find **Moufagio ❷**, a simple taverna with a limited, seafood menu. (☎22840 51 405. Crab €5. *Taramasalata* €2.50. Open Apr.-Nov. daily 10am-1am.) For a late-night dose of sweet little *loukamades* (€2.50), turn left off the commercial street at the Naoussa pastry shop and continue past the white church to tiny **To Paradosiako ❶.** (☎22840 51 240. Open 6pm-4am).

Posh **clubs** with painfully high covers and cavernous dance floors dominate Naoussa's nightlife. Up the road with the stream 100m from the bus stop, a number of dance clubs grind away late into the night. **Varelathiko** is a huge wooden disco that draws crowds to its outdoor deck with modern Greek music. Reminiscent of an old-fashioned barn, the place is decorated with wine barrels and lanterns hanging from the ceiling. (☎22840 53 251. Cocktails €8-10. Cover €8-10 includes 1 drink. Open Apr.-Sept. midnight-late.) Two doors down, **Privilege** lures chic customers with gauze-draped couches in a palm-lined courtyard and a spacious dance floor playing American music (☎22840 53 450. Cocktails €8-10. Cover €8-10, includes 1 drink. Open daily midnight-late.) Neighboring **Nosto** (☎22840 53 450) draws dance-hungry patrons to a sea-faring-themed interior replete with windmills, wine bottles, and mock rivers. The **Aqua Paros water park** (☎22840 53 271), at Kolimbithres, is a pricey option for water-slide aficionados. On the first Sunday in July, eat, drink, and be merry as you cruise Naoussa's harbor and watch traditional dancing at the **Wine and Fish Festival;** call the tourist office for details.

EASTERN COAST OF PAROS

The quiet town of **Piso Livadi,** 11km from Lefkes, provides an escape from the bustle of the larger touristed ports. If Parikia's nightlife is not your scene, Piso Livadi is close to Paros's nicest beaches (from **Logara** to **Chrisi Akti**), which will warm your heart and roast your skin. **Perantinos Travel & Tourism,** across from the bus stop, provides information on accommodations and ferries. (☎/fax 22840 41 135. Open daily 9am-5pm and 6-9pm.) Doubles generally run €35-50, depending on season and quality. Up the street from the bus stop 100m toward Parikia are two simple hotels. **Hotel Piso Livadi ❸** offers rooms with fridges, private baths, balconies, A/C, phones, and sea views (☎22840 41 387. Doubles €40-50; triples €45-55. MC/V.) At the family-run **Londos Hotel ❸,** rooms come with fridges, private baths, balconies. (☎22840 41 218. Doubles €45-55; triples €50-60.)

ANTIPAROS Αντιπαρος

Literally "opposite Paros," Antiparos is so close to its neighbor that, according to local lore, travelers once signaled the ferryman on Paros by opening the door of a chapel on Antiparos. The small island is mostly undeveloped, with a modest population to match Antiparos's size. Most travelers encounter Antiparos as a daytrip to see the caves, but it's easy to find a place to stay on the tiny island, which makes even peaceful Paros look frenetic.

ANTIPAROS TOWN ☎22840

Virtually all of the island's 900 inhabitants live in town, where the ferry docks and most accommodations are found.

TRANSPORTATION AND PRACTICAL INFORMATION. You'll arrive in Antiparos Town by ferry; a few waterfront restaurants and several hotels and pensions are at the harbor. Tourist shops, tavernas, and bakeries line the street leading from the dock to the tree-shaded central plateia, where a cluster of bars and cafes have opened. Go through the stone archway to the right of the plateia to reach the **Castle of Antiparos,** a village built in the 15th century and once the haunt of such infamous inhabitants as famed pirate Babarossa. Take a direct **ferry** from **Parikia** (30min., 8 per day, €2) or a **bus** to **Pounda** (15min., 15 per day, €0.90), followed by a boat to Antiparos (10min., 30 per day, €0.60). The only **bus** service on the island goes to the **stalactite caves** (20min., 1 per hr., €1).

Waterfront **Oliaros Tours** assists with accommodations and has boat and bus schedules, **Internet** access (€6 per hr.), and **currency exchange.** (☎22840 61 231, low season 22840 61 189; oliaros@par.forthnet.gr. Open daily 9am-10:30pm.) It may be better to get cash in Parikia; the **National Bank** is open only from April to October. (☎22840 61 294. Open M-F 9am-1pm.) The **laundromat** is behind the windmill, to the left of the port facing inland. (Wash, dry, and soap €8. Open 8am-9:30pm.) Reach the **police** 24hr. at ☎22840 61 202. To find the **doctor** (☎22840 61 219; open M-F 9am-2pm), walk 200m inland on the main street and take a left before the post office. The **post office** is on the left side of the street leading from the water to the plateia. (☎22840 61 223. Open M-F 7:30am-1pm.) **Postal code** 84007.

ACCOMMODATIONS. The **Mantalena Hotel ❸,** to the right of the dock when facing inland, has recently renovated rooms with private baths, fridges, A/C, TVs, and balconies. A family-owned establishment for 37 years, the hotel welcomes guests with island savvy and tasty almond cookies called *kourabiedthes*. (☎22840 61 206. Doubles €35-60; triples €42-72. AmEx/MC/V.) At **Hotel Antiparos ❷,** the small, basic rooms are stuffed with amenities, including A/C, kitchens, balconies, and phones. (☎22840 61 358; www.otenet.gr/antiparoshotel. Breakfast €4. Doubles €20-35; triples €24-45.) To the right of the harbor facing inland, around the bend on the road to Camping Antiparos, **Theologos Rooms to Let ❷** offers rooms with gleaming bathrooms and balconies off a shady central courtyard. (☎/fax 22840 61 045. Breakfast €2.50-4.50. Doubles €20-40; triples €35-55. AmEx/MC/V.) On the road out of town towards Camping Antiparos, Kaloudia offers rustic rooms with bath, balcony, ceiling fan, and fully-equipped kitchenettes. (☎22840 61 032 or 61 708. Doubles €20-35. AmEx/MC/V.) **Camping Antiparos ❶** is 800m northwest of town, on the well-marked way to Ag. Yiannis Theologos beach. The undeveloped beachside has its own mini-market and restaurant. (☎22840 61 221. Open May-Sept. €5 per person, €5 per tent rental, €4 per car.)

FOOD AND ENTERTAINMENT. Inland on the main street and right after the bookstore, **Taverna Klimataria ❷** trades in the sea view for an idyllic garden setting, roofed with pink azaleas. A family-run establishment dishes out deliciously fresh dishes; the meat and many of the other ingredients come from the proprietor's farm. (☎22840 61 298. Most entrees under €6. Open June-Sept. 5pm-1am.) To the right of the dock on the waterfront, **O Statheros ❷** serves up fresh, hefty-portioned plates of seafood under a canopy of hanging octopi. (☎22840 61 172. Cuttlefish €5. Swordfish €6. Open daily noon-midnight.) **Amargyros ❷** provides a similarly seafood-oriented menu in a more formal environment (☎22840 61 204. Fried octopus €5. Seafood pasta €5. Open Apr.-Oct. daily 7am-midnight. MC/V.) For a post-meal/pre-pub stop, **The Shipwreck ❶,** just past the post office heading inland, plays jazz and mellow music in a schooner-themed interior. (☎22840 61 012. Frappé €2.50. Crepes €2-4. Cocktails €4-5. Open Apr.-Oct. daily 9am-3am.)

Bars, clubs, and late-night eateries cluster around the main plateia inland. **The Stones,** a spacious bar with a dance floor and patio for people watching, and **The Doors,** a more intimate bar playing live Greek music on Wednesdays, both open nightly at 9pm, and serve beer for €2-4 and cocktails for €4-5. The posh wooden patio of **Cafe Yam,** in the alley next to the bookstore, is a trendy spot to sip cocktails. (☎22840 61 055. Beer €2-3.50; cocktails €6. Open Apr.-Oct. daily 9pm-3am.)

SIGHTS AND BEACHES. The dank, wet stalactite **caves** at the southern end of the island are Antiparos's main attraction. (Open daily 10am-3:30pm. €3.) Names of ancient visitors are written on the walls with their years of entry. Unfortunately, some of the stalactites were broken off by Russian naval officers in the 18th century and "borrowed" on behalf of a St. Petersburg museum, while still more were destroyed by Italians during World War II. Despite all this defilement, the caves, which plunge 100m into the earth, are dramatic; the stalactites stretch to over 25 feet in length, and the cavernous interior feels like a surreal, otherworldly landscape. Excursion **buses** (20min., round-trip €3.50) run from Antiparos Town's port every hour from morning through early afternoon. **Psaraliki beach,** a 5min. walk just to the south of town, is a pleasant place to bathe, as is **Glifa,** a 15min. ride to the east on the bus (1 per hr., €1) heading toward the caves .

AMORGOS Αμοργος

Much of Amorgos resembles its most enduring sight, the Hozoviotissas Monastery, which burrows into the cliffs near Hora. The steep cliffs and clear waters were captured 20 years ago in the film *The Big Blue (Le Grand Bleu);* they remain just as startlingly big and blue now. King Minos of Crete was said to rule a kingdom on Amorgos in ancient times, a legend affirmed by the 1985 discovery of artifacts atop Mt. Moudoulia. Despite the recent tourism boom, Amorgos's small size and tight-knit local community have preserved the pervasive peace. Infrequent ferry connections generally stop at Amorgos's two ports in succession—Aegiali in the northeast and the larger Katapola in the southwest.

KATAPOLA Καταπολα ☎22850

Whitewashed houses, narrow streets, and the overhanging Venetian castle make up Katapola, Amorgos's central port. Free from the bustle of many other Cycladic port towns—even as Amorgos grows more touristed—the town retains a serene, communal atmosphere. The small streets extend only a little ways beyond the water; a few minutes' walk will get you to deserted beaches and Minoan ruins.

TRANSPORTATION AND PRACTICAL INFORMATION. Ferries from both ports of Amorgos go to: **Astypalea** (3hr., 3 per week, €9.26); **Donousa** (1½hr., 5 per week, €5); **Koufonisia** (7 per week, €5.50); **Naxos** (3-6hr., daily, €9); **Paros** (4hr., daily, €10.20); **Piraeus** (10hr., daily, €22); **Schinousa** (5 per week, €6.80); **Syros** (4½hr., 4 per week, €11.20). **Speedboats** go to **Mykonos** (2 per week, €22); **Syros** (2 hr., 2 per week, €22.50); **Tinos** (1½hr., 2 per week, €23). The bus station lies to the left of the dock facing inland. Frequent **buses** connect villages in summer, running from Katapola to: **Aegiali** (45min., 6 per day, €1.60); **Agia Anna** (25min., 6 per day, €1); **Hora** (15min., 1 per hr., €1); **Hozoviotissas Monastery** (20min., €1); and to several beaches (around €1).

The town surrounds the ferry dock in a horseshoe shape, with restaurants, bars, and accommodations on either side. The large port rests at the center; most tourist services are between the ferry dock and the road to Hora. Across from the ferry dock is **Synodinos Tours,** which **exchanges currency, rents cars** (€35), and sells ferry and hydrofoil **tickets.** (☎22850 71 201 or 71 747; fax 22850 71 278. Open daily Sept.-May 8am-2pm and 6-10pm; June-Aug. 8am-10pm.) **Agricultural Bank,** across from the ferries, has a 24hr. **ATM.** (☎22850 71 872. Open M-Th 8am-2:30pm, F 8am-2pm.) The **laundromat** is inland at the left of the waterfront; take the first left after Pension Amorgos. (☎22850 71 723. Wash and dry €10. Open M-Sa 8:30am-4:30pm and 6:30-10pm.) Free **public toilets** are at the start of the town beach across from Auto Moto Thomas. The **police** (☎22850 71 210) are in Hora while the **port police** (☎22850 71 259; open 24hr.) are on the right on a side street heading inland from the main plateia. The nearest **pharmacy** is in Hora. The **medical center** is at the far left end of the waterfront, in the white building behind the two statues. (☎22850 73 222. Open M-F 9am-2:30pm.) For **medical emergencies,** dial ☎22850 71 805. There is **no OTE** in Katapola. **Internet** access can be found at Minoa Cafe in the central plateia. (☎22850 71 480. €5 per hr. Open daily 9am-2pm and 6pm-midnight.) The small **post office** is located at the back left of the main plateia facing inland. (☎022850 71 884. Open M-F 10am-1pm and 6-9pm.) **Postal code:** 84008.

ACCOMMODATIONS AND FOOD. Katapola is a small town with few hotels and many **domatia. Pension Amorgos ❸,** at the left of the plateia above the cafes, offers small rooms directly on the water and has a rooftop veranda with a view. (☎22850 71 013 or 71 121; fax 22850 71 814. Doubles €35-55.) To reach **Big Blue Pension ❷** from the ferry dock, walk toward town, turn right after the plateia and follow signs. The pension, one of many establishments cashing in on the popularity of the French film *The Big Blue*, is big, with blue windows and doors. Flower-studded walkways and spectacular veranda views complement private baths, fridges, TVs, and a free port shuttle (☎/fax 22850 71 094. Doubles €30-40; triples €35-45.) **Titika Rooms ❷** sits under grape and flower trellises at the far left end of the beach. Free port shuttle and pleasant, if cluttered, rooms with private bath, fridge, and balcony are completed by mosquito netting, hair dryers, and large mirrors. (☎/fax 22850 71 660. Breakfast €2.50. Doubles €30-40; triples €35-50.)

Katapola's nightlife consists of laid-back cafes that cater to sun-worshippers during the day and light drinkers at night. **Aigaion Cafe ❶,** in the center of the main plateia, serves fruit juices (€3), crepes (€3-5), omelettes (€2-4.50), and cocktails (€5.50-6) to lounging locals at waterfront seats; Inside there's groovy decor and a host of board games. (☎22850 71 549. Open Apr.-Oct. daily 8am-2am; Nov.-Mar. 9am-midnight.) **Mourayio ❷,** across from the dock, dishes out authentic meals like boiled octopus (€5.50), fried cod (€5), and moussaka (€4.40) in a simple outdoor seating area. Pop inside to get a sneak preview of your meal or point to whatever looks particularly tempting in the coolers of fresh fish.

SIGHTS AND BEACHES. In front of Katapola's main church, a sign points to a 40min. hike to the ancient town of **Minoa,** inhabited between the 10th and 4th centuries BC. Look for the base of the temple among the otherwise unimpressive ruins and the bust of a statue rising from within—the barely distinguishable acropolis once stood on the plateau above the temple. Thorough signs explain the history of the site and the former location of the city's main buildings. Various **nude beaches** provide sand and sun outside of town, opposite the dock. Smooth-stoned, bare-skinned and rocky **Plakes** and the sandier **Agios Panteleimonas** are quiet, yet easily accessible by foot or boat—taxi boats leave from the left of the dock facing inland (5 per day, round-trip €2).

DAYTRIP FROM KATAPOLA. A trip to Amorgos is incomplete without a visit to otherworldly **Hozoviotissas Monastery**—one of the most exhilarating spectacles in all of Greece and an inspiration to Le Corbusier among others. Built into the sheer face of the cliff, the 11th-century Byzantine edifice looks like a whitewashed epiphyte. Legend has it that attempts to build the monastery on the shore were thwarted; when the workers discovered their tools inexplicably hanging from the cliff, they figured it was an omen and started construction there. If you complete the hike (up 350 stairs), the monks may treat you to cold water, sweet, ginger-flavored liquor, and *loukoumi* (a kind of Greek sweet). Inside visitors must lean to the left when climbing the narrow staircase to avoid the brittle cliff face, which protrudes into the building's cave-like interior. To see more of the building, come in November when the entire island celebrates the **Feast of Panagia Hozoviotissa** at the monastery. If you miss the bus back, take the stone stairway (10m uphill from the fork in the road leading away from the monastery). A 15min. climb up the stairs will lead you back to Hora. The road from the monastery also takes you to the crystal waters of **Agia Anna** and its two beaches; from the bus stop, one is at the end of the path through the clearing, the other at the bottom of the central steps. Catch a **bus** (20min., 6 per day, €1) from Katapola to the monastery. (☎22850 71 274. Open daily 8am-1pm and 5-7pm. Modest dress required. Free.)

HORA Χωρα ☎22850

Katapola means "below the town"—the eponymous town is Hora. Also known as Amorgos Town, the island's tiny, relatively untouristed capital lies 6km from the harbor along the island's only significant paved road. A typically frustrating example of Byzantine village planning, Hora's winding streets were constructed to deter and confuse raiding pirates; they now allow visitors to meander along the cafe-lined walk to **Pl. Loza,** at the far end of town. Sights include a 14th-century Venetian **fortress,** a row of retired windmills perched on the mountain ledge above town, Byzantine churches, and the first secondary school in Greece, built in 1821 (on your left as you head up to the OTE). Check out the remnants of Amorgos's Minoan civilization at the **Archaeological Museum,** downhill from the large church at Pl. Loza. (Open Tu-Su 9am-1pm and 5-7pm. Free.)

Hora is home to Amorgos's main **post office** (☎22850 71 250; open M-F 7:30am-2pm), tucked in a corner up from Pl. Loza , and its main **OTE** (☎22850 71 339 or 71 099; open M-F 8am-2pm), on the right at the top of town. The **police** are in the main plateia with the big church, next to Cafe Loza. (☎22850 71 210. Open daily 8am-3pm.) The **medical center** is on the main road into Hora from Katapola. (☎22850 71 207. Open M-F 9am-2:30pm; 24hr. emergency care.) The **pharmacy** is across from the bus stop. (☎22850 71 166. Open M-F 9:30am-2pm and 6:30-9pm.)

If you decide to spend the night, you can strike a deal with the **domatia** owners that meet your boat, or look for "Rooms to Let" signs in town. **Maria Economidou ❸** has rooms furnished with modern class; all come with balconies, kitchenettes, and impeccable bathrooms. (☎22850 71 111; kstp@otenet.gr. Doubles €38-45; large 2-person apartments €45-55.) **Pension Kastanis ❸,** located next door, offers slightly less luxurious lodgings, with bathroom, common balcony, and fridge. (☎22850 71 277. Rooms €35-45.) Both establishments offer free port shuttles if you call ahead.

Liotrivi ❷, below the bus station, prepares delicious twists on Greek standards—*kalogiros* (eggplant with veal, cheese, and tomato) and *exohiko* (lamb and vegetables in pastry shell) are the house specialities. (☎22850 71 700. Entrees €5-7. Open May-Oct. daily noon-midnight). **Zygos ❶** (☎22850 71 350; open daily 8am-3:30am), on the cafe-lined alley leading from Liotrivi toward Pl. Loza, serves peerless apple pie (€2.50), coffees (€2-3), and cocktails (€5) in a mellow, cave-like interior. **Bayoko,** by the bus station, caters to coffee-sipping locals with a relaxed cafe downstairs. Upstairs, one of Hora's only clubs provides a small dance floor, nightly DJs, and Greek dance hits from 9pm till dawn. (Beer €2-4; cocktails €5; ouzo €1.50. Open daily 8am-late.)

Rugged mountains and a placid coast run alongside the road from Hora to Aegiali. The clearly-marked, sun-exposed 4hr. **hike** begins behind Hora and stretches up the mountains to Potamos. Forty minutes into the hike, you'll find the crumbling Byzantine church of **Christososmas** (The Body of Christ), hewn out of a small cave that was once a hermit dwelling. The trail ascends past a series of monasteries before descending to views of miniature **Nikouria** island, which experienced swimmers can reach from the beach by the main road. Lonely and deserted **Ag. Mammas** church is the last significant marker before Potamos appears.

AEGIALI Αιγιαλη ☎22850

Aegiali, the island's other port, is as close as Amorgos comes to feeling touristy. As a result, the locals seem a little wearier of travelers than on other parts of the island. With a town beach and many accommodations, leisurely Aegiali serves best as a base for exploring the beaches clustered along the island's northern edge.

TRANSPORTATION AND PRACTICAL INFORMATION. For **ferry** and **Flying Dolphin** schedules, see the listings for Katapola (p. 403). **Buses** run **Aegiali-Hora-Katapola** (3 per day, €1.60); **Meria-Hora-Katapola** (2 per day, €1); **Ormos-Lagada** (6 per day, €1); **Tholaria** (4 per day, €1). **Taxis** (☎22850 73 003 or 73 570) can be reached 24hr. Aegiali is built up the slope of the mountain foothills. Most tourist facilities are along the waterfront. Facing inland, clubs are to the left along the beach, cafes are to the right. **Nautilus Travel** (☎22850 73 032; fax 22850 73 231; open daily 10am-9pm) handles all ferries, accommodations, and other travel services. Across the street, **Aegialis Tours** (☎22850 73 394; fax 22850 73 395) offers **Internet** access (€5.60 per hr.), **stores luggage** (€1.50 per piece per day), and handles accommodations, **car rental** (€45), and bus or boat excursions. (Open Apr.-Oct. daily 9am-1pm and 6-10pm.) Both agencies are just inland from the waterfront. Note that there is **no bank** in Aegiali. The **police** (☎22850 73 320) are located in Langada; the 24hr. **port police** (☎22850 71 259) lie on the road inland to the bakery. A **first aid station** is 100m beyond the pharmacy near the road to Potamos. (☎22850 73 322. Open M-F 9am-2:30pm. Available 24hr.) A **pharmacy** is up the road by the Island Market, on the right. (☎22850 73 173. Open M-F 9:30am-2:30pm and 6-9pm.) **Phones** are next door. The **post office** is across from the pharmacy, in the mini-market. (☎22850 73 001. Open daily 9am-10pm.) **Postal code:** 73032.

ACCOMMODATIONS AND CAMPING. **Lakki Village ❸,** at the left side of the beach across from the campgrounds, has rooms and apartments with private baths, balconies, and phones; some include A/C and television. The flower-filled hotel, owned by the Gavala family, exudes a friendly, resort-like atmosphere. (☎22850 73 253; lakki@aigialis.com. Breakfast included. Laundry service €10. Free port shuttle available. Doubles €40-90; triples €60-120. AmEx/MC/V.) **Camping Aegiali ❶** is just outside town, near the road to Tholaria. Though it's a 10min. walk from the port and beach, they provide free port pick-up and drop-off. The site boasts laundry and cooking facilities, free safety deposit boxes, impeccable showers, restaurant, and bar. (☎22850 73 500; fax 22850 73 388. €4.50 per person, €2.50 per tent rental, €2.50 per car.) You can also look for "Rooms for Rent" signs going up the paths in the middle of town. **Pension Christina ❸** (look for the large sign up the road from the pharmacy) has gleaming rooms with private baths, microwaves, stoves, fridges, sinks, and balconies with the best views in town. (☎22850 73 236; fax 22850 73 109. Doubles €25-50.) **Poseidon Pension ❸,** just beyond Christina's on the road inland, provides neat, trim rooms with kitchenettes, floor fans, private baths, and spacious outdoor seating. (☎22850 73 007. Doubles €40-60; triples €45-68.) **Captain Nikos ❷,** to the right just before the medical center, provides clean but plain rooms with kitchenettes and private baths. (☎22850 73 026. Doubles €15-40).

FOOD AND NIGHTLIFE. Lakki Village Restaurant ❶ offers delicious home-grown vegetables and souvlaki (€5) grilled in the open air. (☎22850 73 253. Moussaka €4.40. Grilled octopus €6.80. Open daily 7am-1am. AmEx/MC/V.) **To Steki ❷**, at the edge of the beach, serves traditional food on a limited menu in a simple, outdoor setting on the water. (☎22850 73 003. Fava €3. Fish €4-6. Pasta dishes €3-4. Open daily 4pm-2am. MC/V.) Follow the signs (and your nose) uphill from the waterfront to the aromatic **bakery ❶**. (☎22850 73 225. Pastries €1.20-1.50. Breads €1 and under. Open daily 6:30am-10pm.) Relax by the port at **To Limani ❷**, serving up traditional dishes with fresh ingredients to outdoor diners (☎22850 73 269. Fava €3. Pastas €4. Seafood €5-7. Open daily 7am-2am. MC/V.) Later cut loose under the stars at **Delear** (☎22850 73 205), a club down the beach from To Steki.

IOS Ιος

Ios has little room for any functional daylight spaces. Daytime activity generally spreads to its coasts, as beachgoers soak up the sun's energy in preparation for the long night ahead in Ios Town, the only city. The island has settled down a bit in the past few years, making a sincere and successful effort to bring families and an older set to enjoy its more peaceful side. Of its 36 beaches, only three have been fully developed for tourism, so there's plenty of unexplored territory.

IOS TOWN ☎22860

If you're not drunk when you arrive, you will be when you leave. On Ios, beers go down and clothes come off faster than you can say "Opa!" You'll see everything your mother warned you about—wine swilled from the bottle at 3pm, all-day beachside drinking games, men and women dancing madly in the streets, people swimming less than 30min. after they've eaten, and so much more. Those in search of quieter pleasures stay in Yialos (the port), while the party animals cavort in Hora. Still, visitors to this mecca should prepare for loud music, hangovers, and the lustful stares of the inebriated.

TRANSPORTATION

Ferries: To: **Anafi** (3hr., 2 per week, €7.30); **Folegandros** (1hr., 4 per week, €5.13); **Naxos** (1¾hr., at least 3 per day, €8.12); **Paros** (3hr., at least 3 per day, €8.92); **Piraeus** (8hr., at least 3 per day, €19.92); **Santorini** (1¼hr., 3 per day, €6.12); **Sifnos** (3 per week, €10.42); **Sikinos** (30min., 2 per week, €3.82); **Syros** (4hr., 5 per week, €16.52).

Flying Dolphins: To: **Iraklion,** Crete (2½hr., 3 per week, €32.52); **Milos** (3½hr., 3-4 per week, €13.02); **Mykonos** (2hr., daily, €22.82); **Naxos** (45min., daily, € 15.92); **Paros** (1½hr., daily, €17.42); **Santorini** (45min., daily, €11.92).

Rentals: Jacob's Moto Rent (☎/fax 22860 91 047), by the bus stop at the port. Bikes €12; small cars €38. **Ios Rent-A-Car** (☎22860 92 300), located in Acteon Travel in the port, offers similar rates. MC/V. Other agencies are scattered about.

ORIENTATION AND PRACTICAL INFORMATION

The action goes down around three locations, each 20min. apart along the island's paved road. The **port (Yialos)** is at one end; the **village (Hora)** sits above on a hill; frenzied **Mylopotas beach** is 3km farther. During the day, the winding streets behind the church are filled with charming wares and postcard pushers; as the sun sets, they become the focus of nocturnal activity. Buses shuttle between port, village, and beach (every 10-20min., 7:20am-midnight; €0.90). After midnight, while the road from Hora to Mylopotas is generally walked, one of the three island **taxis** (☎693 268 0896, 697 776 0570, or 697 703 1708) can take you to and from Yialos.

Tourist Information: Acteon Travel (☎22860 91 343; fax 22860 91 088), adjacent to the bus stop, but booths are set up all over the island. Open daily 8am-midnight. Sells **ferry tickets,** offers info on accommodations, **exchanges currency,** and rents vehicles.

Banks: In Hora, **National Bank** (☎22860 91 565), next to the main church, has an **ATM** and handles all your MasterCard needs. Open M-Th 8am-2pm, F 8am-1:30pm. **Acteon Travel** in the village around the corner from the main church has a 24hr. Citibank ATM. The **Commercial Bank** (☎22860 91 474), by the main plateia next to the Lemon Club, has 24hr. ATM, too. There is also a 24hr. Commercial Bank ATM at the port, to your left as you disembark from the ferry, and at Mylopotas beach, in the Acteon Travel office.

Laundromat: Sweet Irish Dream Laundry (☎22860 91 141), next to the club with the same name. Wash and dry full load €8; half load €6. Drop-off laundry services also available at **Far Out Beach Club** (€3 per kg).

Police: ☎22860 91 222. On the road to Kolitsani beach, past the OTE. Open 24hr.

Port Authority: ☎22860 91 264. At the harbor's far end by Camping Ios. Open 24hr.

Pharmacy: ☎22860 91 562. In Hora, next to Acteon Travel. Open daily 9am-2:30pm and 5-11:30pm.

Medical Center: ☎22860 91 227. In new public facilities at the port, 100m from the dock. Specializes in drunken mishaps. Open daily 9am-2pm and 6-7pm. In Hora, reach a **doctor** (Yiannis) 24hr. at ☎22860 91 562 or 693 242 0200. His office is on the main road next to Fun Pub; you can ring the bell at any hour.

Internet Access: Located all over the port and village. At the port, **Acteon Travel** charges €5 per hr., €1.50 min. Open daily 8am-midnight. In the village, **Francesco's** (€1.50 per 15min., €6 per hr.) and **Hotel Sunrise** (€0.10 per min.) have access. On Mylopotas beach, **Far Out Beach Club** offers access for €0.10 per min.

Gym: Ios Gym, by the basketball courts. €5.50 per day; €26 per week.

Post Office: In the village on the main road toward Mylopotas, take your 1st right after Sweet Irish Dream. Receives **Poste Restante** and sends packages abroad. Open M-F 7:30am-2pm. **Postal code:** 84001.

ACCOMMODATIONS AND CAMPING

Affordable accommodations can be found in the frenetic village or in the quiet port. Each area has its own personality, so weigh your interests before making your bed (and sleeping in it). A tent, bungalow, or room on Mylopotas beach lets you roll hazily from blanket to beach, foregoing coffee for a tequila sunrise.

Francesco's (☎22860 91 706; www.francescos.net), in the village. With your back to the bank, take the steps up from the left corner of the plateia, then take the 1st left. Francesco oversees a family of hotels. Rooms (some with private baths) sit atop a convivial terrace bar that supplies the perfect pre-party social atmosphere and a beautiful view. Additional fee for A/C in low season. Dorms €8-14; rooms for 2-4 €10-25. ❶

Far Out Camping (☎22860 92 301 or 92 302; www.faroutclub.com), at the center of Mylopotas beach. A luxurious campsite with rock-bottom prices, a restaurant, bar, minimarket, volleyball court, swimming pool, bungee jumping, new movies (shown every evening), showers, laundry, Internet access, live music, and nightly Happy Hours (5pm-7pm; 2-for-1 cocktails €5). Just about every visitor to the island under 25 congregates here during the day. Open Apr.-Oct. €4-7.50 per tent, tent rental €1.50; cabins €5 and up; bungalows €7-18; hotel rooms €10-35 per person. MC/V. ❶

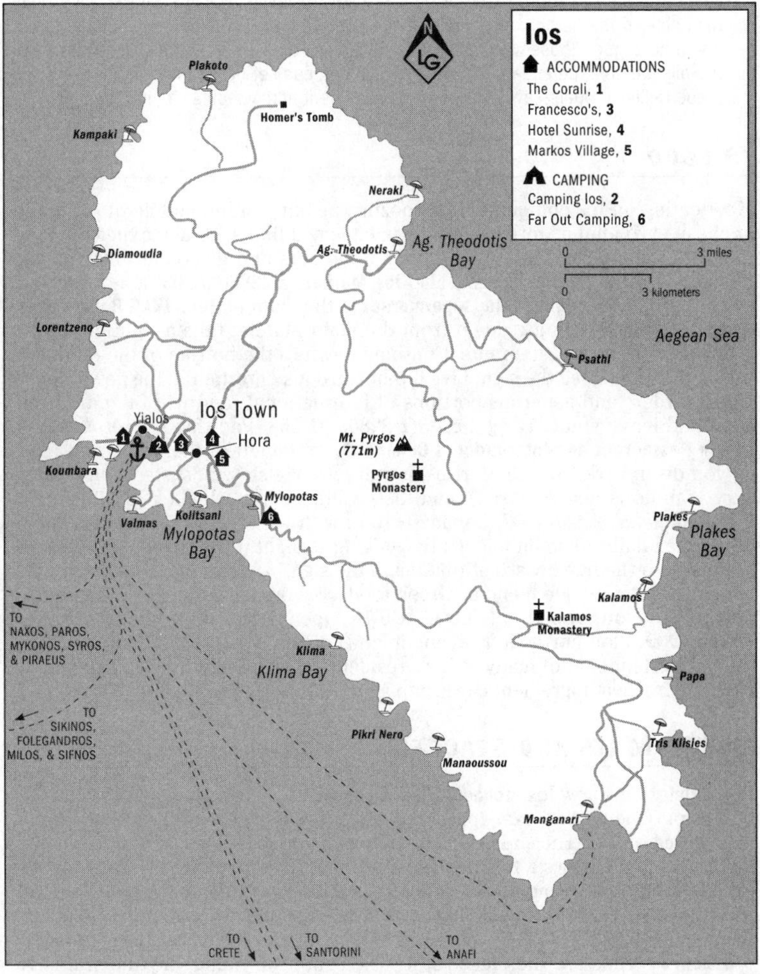

Markos Village (☎22860 91 059 or 22860 92 260; marcovlg@otenet.gr), a block up from the main road of the village. From the bus stop coming from Yialos, go uphill and to the left. Markos knows how to entertain. Chill by the hopping poolside bar and sip frozen daiquiris while admiring the view. Dorms €9-14; doubles €20-45. MC/V. ❶

Hotel Sunrise (☎22860 91 074 or 91 527; www.thegreektravel.com/ios/sunrise), just beyond Markos Village further up the hill. Fine amenities including swimming pool and restaurant-bar (open 9am-midnight). Breakfast served all day. Doubles with A/C €40-84; triples and quads also available. DC/MC/V. ❸

The Corali (☎22860 91 272; coraliht@otenet.gr), on the peaceful port beach where umbrellas and beach volleyball spill onto the sand. At this family-oriented hotel, you can find cool both in the flowered garden and A/C-equipped rooms. Doubles €58; triples €65; quads €80 in high season. MC/V. ❹

Camping Ios (☎22860 92 035 or 92 036; www.camping.ios.com), all the way to the right side of the harbor when you're getting off the boat in Yialos, has pretty grounds and a huge pool. Those who want similar amenities to those at Far Out Camping minus the high volume, potentially wearying excitement, can set up tent here in the shade of grape trellises. Open May-Sept. €7 per person, tent and sleeping bag included. ❶

FOOD

Most eating on Ios coincides with boozing, peaking in the middle of the night at cheap gyro joints. More discerning palates will find several inexpensive restaurants interspersed among the ubiquitous bars and discos in town, at the port, and on the beach. There's also **Ios Market** (☎22860 91 035), across from the bus stop in Hora, and the **supermarket** in the main plateia. **Ali Baba's** ❷ is next to Ios gym; coming down from the main plateia, take a right after you reach the fast-food restaurants. Continue down to the bottom of the road and take a left; you'll see the sign. Live hip-hop groups entertain in the newly renovated garden, and generous portions of international food will fill you to the brim and leave you craving more. (☎22860 91 558. Pad thai €8.50.) **Waves Indian Restaurant and International Cuisine** ❷, to the left of the waterfront road as you disembark from the ferries, is run by a Welsh windsurfer couple who serve fabulous hearty curries and tasty Chinese stir-fries. (☎22860 92 145. Chicken *tikka masala* €7. Banana fritters with ice cream €5. Takeout available. Open daily 10am-midnight.) By walking straight through the main church plateia onto the narrow street that bears the sign, you can find **Lord Byron's** ❸, which serves a unique blend of Greek foods. Savory specialities will undoubtedly satisfy your appetite. (Entrees €9-15. Open daily 7pm-midnight. MC/V.) **Polydoros** ❷, 2km north (left, facing inland) of the port on Koubara beach, is the beloved hideout of many of Ios's residents, who delight in dishes prepared with the freshest ingredients. (Shrimp *saganaki* with feta €6.50.)

SIGHTS AND BEACHES

Pay a visit to the new Ios **Archaeological Museum,** in the town hall across from the bus stop. (Open Tu-Su 8am-2pm. Free.) According to legend, Homer died and was buried on Ios. The supposed site of **Homer's tomb** has been worn to rubble, but the site still draws a few dedicated tourists. To repent the previous night's excess at the solitary monastery, walk toward the windmills to the path near the top of the hill. There's an **Open Theatre Festival Program** every summer, held above the windmills on the island—inquire at a travel agency for more information.

Beaches on Ios are the place to be. The center of young, daytime life is at **Mylopotas beach,** a 20min. walk downhill from Hora. Like the town at night, it has music blasting everywhere, and all parties are welcome at the debaucherous Far Out Sports Club (part of the campsite). The farther you go, the fewer clothes you will see (or wear). Alternatively, for those who just want quiet and beauty, buses (25min., 2 per day, €5) go to the more secluded **Manganari,** the nicest stretch of sand. **Dimitris Taverna** ❶ is in the middle of the main cove with the Australian and Greek flags. (☎22860 91 483. Fava purée €3. Stuffed tomatoes €4. Cantaloupe €1.90. Open daily 9am-midnight.) **Yialos** (the port beach), **Mylopotas,** and **Manganari** all offer watersports, from tubing (€12-22) to wakeboarding to windsurfing (€14-40). Continuing uphill from the OTE, look for the path leading to the secluded beach and crystal pool of water at the little bay of **Kolitsani** (a 15min. walk from Hora). Secluded, nudist **Psathi** on the eastern coast, is accessible by moped.

NIGHTLIFE

Most of Ios's extraordinary number of bars are densely packed into the old village making it easy to hit all the hotspots in no time. People tend to walk around to decide where to go considering the central focus of the party can't really be determined until the night is underway. Larger and louder discos line the main road, lined with revelers. Bacchantes warm up at beachside bars, like **Francesco's** and **Markos,** swilling liquor from the bottle in the main plateia at sunset, hitting the village before 1am, then migrating to the discos and private liaisons before sunrise.

Dubliner (☎22860 92 070), near the basketball courts on the main road, across the street from the bus stop coming from the port. This Aussie-Kiwi bar which serves big drinks at pub prices (beer €2.50) is a good place to start the night. If you plan to make it a longer night (or a much shorter one), get wasted for your money's worth by entering the nightly drinking-challenge-cum-kamikaze-mission. Open daily 2pm-3am.

Scorpion Disco (☎693 229 3834), on the main road in town, en route to the beach after Q Club. This crazy techno emporium, the island's largest club, is strategically located for those heading to Mylopotas after they get sloshed. Cover after 1am. Open Su-Th midnight-3:30am or later; F-Sa midnight-7am.

Blue Note, walking from the main plateia away from the church, past the fast-food joints. Get trollied at this Scandinavian bar straight ahead at the end of the road on your left which features tequila shots, bar dancing, the latest hits, and a little Swedish Pop. Open weekdays 9:30pm-3:30am, weekends 9:30pm-late.

The Slammer Bar, in the left inland corner of the main plateia in the village. Have the bartender whack your helmeted head before you get hammered in a different way, downing the tequila slammer (tequila, Tia Maria, and Sprite €3). Open weekdays 10pm-3:30am, weekends 10pm-late.

Disco 69 (☎22860 91 064; www.disco69club.com), on the main bar street toward the church from the plateia on the right hand side. Blares mainstream dance music, inviting all comers to get smashed and bar dance. Cover €5 after 2am. Open 10pm-3:30am.

Red Bull (☎22860 91 019), in the main plateia in the village. Kick-start the night to the tune of 90s rock before heading out to tackle the rest of the scene. Get plastered on the Red Bull and vodka energy special (€4.50). Shots €2.40. Open 10pm-3:30am.

Sweet Irish Dream, in a large building near the "donkey steps." Come here after you get pissed (or after 2am) to dance on tables–most save it as the night's last stop. No cover before 1am. Beer €2.50. Open daily 3pm-3am.

Q Club, on the right side of the road to Mylopotas, after "Munchies." Showcase your breakdancing skills to the hip hop and house spun by visiting international DJs. Then get soused. Open weekdays midnight-3:30am or later, F-Sa midnight-7am.

FOLEGANDROS Φολεγανδρος

Named after the son of King Minos, who, according to legend, made the first footprints on the island's shores, Folegandros was secluded from outside influences for many centuries due to its high, rocky cliffs and inaccessible port. The dry, steep hills are terraced with low, snaking stone walls worn by centuries of fierce wind—the only tumultuous presence on the island.

HORA Χωρα ☎22860

The main town and the capital of Folegandros, cliffside Hora is friendly and beautiful, the perfect place to stay during your time on the island.

TRANSPORTATION AND PRACTICAL INFORMATION. After disembarking from the ferry, you can board the **bus** that runs from the port **Kararostassi** to the Hora. Buses head to the port (45min.) before each ferry and then return with new arrivals (19 per day, 7:30am-12:15am; €0.90). Irregular **ferries** run to: **Ios** (1½hr., 6 per week, €4.90); **Kimolos** (1½hr., 2 per week, €4.90); **Milos** (2½hr., 2 per week, €6.40); **Naxos** (3hr., 5 per week, €8.30); **Paros** (4hr., 2 per week, €7.10); **Piraeus** (10-12hr., daily, €18.40); **Santorini** (1½hr., 6 per week, €6.20); **Serifos** (5hr., 2 per week, €9.10); **Sifnos** (4hr., 2 per week, €7.10); **Sikinos** (1hr., 4 per week, €3.80). Several times per week, **hydrofoils** zip to **Milos, Santorini,** and **Sifnos** for doubled prices and halved durations. Once a week, they also head to **Amorgos** (€22.30). **Taxis** are available at ☎22860 41048 or 694 469 3957. **Moped rental** is cheaper at the port than in town. Try **Jimmy's** (☎22860 41 448). The **post office** will be on your left as you enter town (open M-F 8:30am-2pm). From the post office, follow the heliport sign toward town to **Sottovento Travel Center** for **maps** (€2.10), ferry and bus schedules, **currency exchange,** and general information. (☎22860 41 444; fax 22860 41 430. Open 10am-1pm and 5-9pm.) If you continue straight down the main road past the post office, turn left after Pl. Pounta, and to your left 50m down will be **Maraki Travel,** which offers similar services as well as **Internet** access for €6 per hr., with a €1.50 min. (☎22860 41 273; fax 22860 41 149. Open daily 9:30am-noon.) The only **ATM** is in Pl. Kontarini, the main square in town; make a right after Folegandros Snack Bar and it's tucked into the far left corner of the plateia. Past Maraki Travel, head straight past the next two tree-filled plateias, cut across to the right, then head left. A sharp right before the **market** leads to the **police** (☎22860 41 249). The 24hr. **medical center** (☎22860 41 222) is directly across from you on Pl. Pounta as you are entering town from the main road. The **pharmacy** is on the road to the port, after the post office and before Hotel Polikandia. **Postal code:** 84011.

ACCOMMODATIONS. Folegandros's increasing popularity has created a minor shortage of space, so be sure to reserve ahead of time in high season. Most housing is pricey, but welcome relief can be found at **Pavlo's Rooms ❷.** About 200m before town on the road coming from port, this charming converted stable has simple rooms in a valley filled with cactuses, crickets, and reeds. (☎/fax 22860 41 232. Laundry €6. Breakfast and free port shuttle available. Doubles €15-54. You can sleep on the roof for €6.) **Hotel Polikandia ❸,** just past the pharmacy on the way into town, offers rooms with breezy balconies surrounding a very pretty flagstone garden. (☎22860 41 322; fax 22860 41 323. Buffet breakfast €6. Singles €17-50; doubles €25-65; triples €35-73.) **Rooms to Let Embati & Evgenia ❸,** next to and across the street from Hotel Polikandia, Embati and Evgenia offer simple rooms with private baths and fridges. (☎22860 41 006; fax 22860 41 469. Doubles €20-53; studio for 4 €40-90.) To find **Livadi Camping ❶,** set back from the sparkling aqua port beach, on the road from the port to Hora, take a left at the sign or call for a port shuttle. (☎22860 41 204 or 41 478. €5 per person, €2.50 per tent.)

FOOD AND NIGHTLIFE. Fresh fruit and bread **markets** line the road from Kararostassi through Hora. **Kritikos ❷,** to the left after Pl. Pounta then straight through two more plateias, serves the freshest meat on the island. The grilled lamb (€6) or *kontosouvli* (pieces of pork and lamb roasted on the spit; €6) should be savored. (☎22860 41 219. Open daily noon-12:30am.) In a beautiful stone garden, find **Pounta ❷,** on your left just as you enter Pl. Pounta, the first square from the port road—don't miss the view from its far right corner. (☎22860 41 063. Crepe with tomato, cheese, and *tzatziki* €3.50. Eggplant risotto with feta, tomatoes, and peppers €6. Open daily 8am-4pm and 6pm-12:30am.) **To Sik ❶**, right across the plateia from Kritikos, puts a twist on traditional Greek dishes; try the stuffed aubergine (€4.40) or vegetarian *pastitsio* (€4.50) among other vegetarian specialties. (☎22860 41 515. Almond-raisin lamb casserole €8.50. Saffron chicken with chickpeas €6.50. Open daily 6pm-12:30am.) At **Folegandros Snack Bar ❶**, across from Maraki Travel, owner Michailidia makes what could be the best cappuccino outside of Italy. He also provides a wide array of fresh meals, snacks, and intangibles starting quite early and ending quite late, including a grilled vegetable platter (€8), 40 varieties of tea, games, books, maps, and info about the island. (☎22860 41 226. Open Apr.-Oct. daily 7am-2am.) Pause to appreciate the prime location of **Piatsa ❶**, in the center of Pl. Kontarini, as you wait for a delicious traditional Greek meal. The *matzata* (pasta with rabbit or chicken; €7.50) is an island speciality. (☎22860 41 274. Open daily 9am-1am. MC/V.)

In summer, when the island's permanent population of 650 triples with the influx of mostly Greek tourists, Hora starts to party. Summer weddings fill the town's plateias with roasting goats and local music. **El Greco**, on the path right next to Sottovento, is a bohemian cafe-bar adorned with artistic lighting and paintings. (☎22860 41 456. Cocktails €6. Open Apr.-Oct. daily 10am-3pm and 6pm-4am.) **Carajo**, which is left down the narrow fork that begins from the far left corner of the plateia near Kritiko, has a lively atmosphere accented by a mix of funk and Latin music. (☎22860 41 463. Cocktails €6. Open daily 10pm-4am.) **Kellari Wine Bar**, in Pl. Pounta next to the medical center, boasts an amazing selection of Greek wines in a small stone-walled room reminiscent of a castle wine cellar. Ask the hostess for the perfect selection. (☎22860 41 119. €3-6 per glass. Open daily 7:30am-3am or later.) **Avissos**, beyond El Greco on the same road, away from town to the left, is the only dance club in town. A mixture of Top 40 and Greek tracks keeps things moving at the outdoor bar. (☎22860 41 100. Beer €4; cocktails €6. Open daily 10pm-4am or later.)

SIGHTS. The **Church of Panagia**, above the town on Paleokastro Hill, is an excellent place to watch the sunset or photograph whitewashed domes against mountains and sea. When you get to Pl. Pounta, take two sharp rights and hike up the zigzagging path past a tranquil three-level cemetery. The torso of a marble statue, dated to Roman times, a prodigal artifact suggesting that perhaps Folegandros was more than simply a place of exile during that period, rests in the masonry of the bell tower. (Open daily 6-8pm in summer, in winter for religious festivals only.) Walking into town from Pl. Pounta, take your first right up the stairs through the narrow archway labeled "Kastro," into the triangular fortification of houses built during the period of Venetian rule in the years following the Fourth Crusade of 1204. On your left after the church of **Agia Anargyron**, walk through a tiny wooden-roofed corridor that townspeople used to hide in from Romans, Franks, Venetians, and Turks. During the times of hardship and fear on Folegandros, when conquerors frequently plundered and pirates ascended the hills to raid, 150 to 200 large families dwelled in this small clifftop enclosure, each in their own *monospito*, or one-roomed house. Continuing straight through the rows of these *monospitia*, you will come to the church of **Our Lady Pantanassa** at the end of the road. From the balcony outside its door, you can catch one of the best views on the island. To the left is the edge of Hora and the terraced hills leading to Ano Meria, while to the right is a panoramic vista towards Milos, Kimolos, and Sifnos, all three of which you can see on a clear day. A demanding hike beyond the church across Paleokastro Hill leads to **Chryssospilia** (Golden Cave), once a refuge for islanders during pirate invasions. Local lore insists that there is a secret tunnel connecting this uncharted cave to Panagia. Go by boat if you're not up for a climb.

HIKES. The hike from Hora to **Agali** and **Agios Nikolaos** takes about 1hr. to Agali and another 30min. to **Ag. Nikolaos beach.** Start from Hora, following the elevated road toward Ano Meria. After 20-30min. of asphalt, take one of two dirt paths leading left off the road and down to the glassy aquamarine beaches and beige, earthen-terraced countryside. Across from one of several small white churches, you'll see the trail snaking down toward Agali. You'll traverse rocky terraces and pass olive trees down the main dirt track (hang left) that heads straight to Agali. There you'll find a few tavernas, **domatia,** and several tents. A rocky trail past the first tavernas on the right leads to Ag. Nikolaos beach. Between the two beaches are intimate, stony coves and beaches made for cool, quiet dips. Alternatively, the bus from Agali leaves you at a stop 10-15min. to sea and sand by foot.

ANO MERIA Ανο Μερια ☎22860

Ano Meria has many footpaths leading to secluded **beaches,** including **Livadaki,** the island's best. The steep, winding trails—the only access to these beaches—take at least 1hr. each; there is no taverna at the end. The Sottovento tourist office heads day-long boat tours around the island that stop at several beaches; inquire upon arrival. For a superb glance into Ottoman life, check out the **Folklore Museum** in Ano Meria. On an island whose history is empty of epoch-defining events, the olive presses, looms, and fishing nets detail the perpetual struggle against infertile soil and stormy harbors. Take the bus to Ano Meria and ask the driver to let you off there. (Guidebook €6. Open June-Aug. daily 5-8pm.) Those planning an extended stay in Folegandros or who want to acquaint themselves with island culture should look into **The Cycladic School,** which leads six- to 12-day courses that focus on drawing and painting, as well as theater, music, sailing, diving, history, and philosophy. A day at the school includes a lecture, practice time, and excursions around the island. (☎22860 41 137; fax 22860 41 472. For more information, contact Anne and Fotis Papadopoulous, GR-84011, Folegandros, Greece.)

SANTORINI Σαντορινη

Whitewashed towns balanced on plunging cliffs, burning black-sand beaches, and deeply scarred hills make Santorini's landscape nearly as dramatic as the volcanic cataclysm that created it. This eruptive past—and startling beauty—has led some to believe that Santorini is the lost continent of Atlantis. According to Greek mythology, the island arose from a clod of earth given by the sea god Triton to the Argonauts. The island, called Thira in Greek, was an outpost of Minoan society by 2000 BC. Around the turn of the 17th century BC, an earthquake destroyed the wealthy maritime settlement of Akrotiri. All hope of recovery vanished when a massive volcanic eruption spread lava and pumice across the island around 1625 BC. The destruction of Santorini heralded the fall of Minoan prominence; the volcanic eruption possibly also led to a tidal wave that wreaked havoc on Crete. Natural disaster continues to threaten the safety of Santorini's residents: as recently as 1956, an earthquake caused serious damage to much of the island. Yet the volcanoes have enriched the soil, making Santorini a green oasis among the mostly barren Cyclades and creating the basin that now forms its harbors and western rim. Santorini is an easily accessible mob scene. It's one of the most beautiful islands in the world; tourists pour in from all over in gawking parades of weddings, honeymoons, and curious beach-combers. The prices on the island tend to be steep, mostly due to the cost of importing water and, of course, its popularity.

FIRA Φηρα ☎22860

The island's activity centers in the capital, Fira. Atop a hill and far from the black sand beaches, the congested assemblage of glitzy shops, whizzing mopeds, and hyperactive tourists can be overwhelming to newcomers. Tourist traffic has made it almost too easy to find a hamburger or wiener schnitzel, and jostling groups of hotels fearlessly peer over steep cliffs and defy the actively seismic island to send them tumbling into the sea. All the kitsch and overcrowding, however, still can't negate the pleasure of wandering the tiny cobbled streets and arriving at the caldera (basin) on the western edge of town in time to watch the sunset.

TRANSPORTATION

Boats dock at one of three ports: Athinios, Fira, or Oia. Athinios is the most trafficked and has frequent buses to Fira and Perissa beach (30min., at least 20 per day, €1.50). Be aware that even if your ferry ticket says "Fira," you may be landing in the town of **Athinios.** The **port** of Fira is down a 587-step footpath from the town; you can take a **cable car** (every 20min., 6:40am-10pm; €3, children €1.50, luggage €1.50) or hire a **mule** (€3). Both methods of transportation are fun and scenic. Santorini's **buses** run frequently and can take you anywhere you want to go, but be warned that their convenience leads to overcrowding. Arrive at the station 10min. early to make your bus. The estimated journey lengths below are based on ideal circumstances; busy buses often move much slower.

Flights: Olympic Airways (☎22860 22 493) flies to: **Athens** (daily, €81.60); **Mykonos** (4 per week, €64.60); **Rhodes** (5 per week, €89.60); **Thessaloniki** (2 per week, €111.60). From the bus depot, turn left on the main street and left again at the next road. Walk to the end of the road and head right by the hospital. Open M-Sa 8:30am-8pm, Su 8:30am-3pm. **Aegean** also has flights to **Athens, Mykonos,** and **Thessaloniki.**

Ferries: To: **Anafi** (2hr., 2 per week, €6.60); **Folegandros** (1½hr., 3 per week, €6.60); **Ios** (1½hr., 3-5 per day, €6.30); **Iraklion** (4hr., daily, €13.60); **Mykonos** (7hr., 2 per week, €12.60); **Naxos** (4hr., 4-8 per day, €10.80); **Paros** (4½hr., 3-5 per day, €11.50); **Piraeus** (9hr., 4-8 per day, €21.60); **Sikinos** (4½hr., 2 per week, €6.50); **Syros** (8hr., 3 per week, €15.60); **Thessaloniki** (15hr., 5 per week, €34.50). **Flying Dolphins** run similar routes in half the time but at twice the price.

Buses: To: **Akrotiri** (30min., 16 per day, €1.30); **Athinios** (25min., 20 per day, €1.30); **Kamari** (20min., 30 per day, €0.90); **Monolithos** via the **airport** (30min., 5 per day, €0.90); **Oia** (30min., 30 per day, €0.90); **Perissa** (30min., 20 per day, €1.50).

Taxis: ☎22860 22 555 in Pl. Theotokopoulou beside the bus station. Available 24hr.

Moped Rental: Marcos Rental (☎22860 23 877), 50m north of the plateia. €15 per day, discounts for extended rentals. Helmets included. Open daily 8:30am-7pm.

ORIENTATION AND PRACTICAL INFORMATION

From the bus station, walk uphill (north) to **Pl. Theotokopoulou,** which is full of travel agencies, banks, and cafes. At the fork in the road, the street on the right with the large National Bank building is **25 Martiou,** the main paved road. It leads from the plateia north toward Oia and hosts accommodations, including the youth hostel. Head onto the left branch of the fork and turn onto any westbound street to find back streets with many of the best bars, stores, and discos. Farther west is the caldera, bordered by **Ypapantis,** where expensive restaurants and art galleries are overshadowed by the spectacular view.

Banks: National Bank (☎22860 22 662), on the road branching off 25 Martiou south of the plateia. **Currency exchange.** 24hr. **ATM.** Open M-Th 8am-2:30pm, F 8am-2pm.

American Express: In the office of **X-Ray Kilo Travel and Shipping Agency** (☎22860 25 025). Turn at the National Bank to reach the caldera; the office is another 100m up the street. Open May-Oct. daily 8:30am-2:30pm; Nov.-Apr. M-F 9am-2pm.

International Bookstore: International Press (☎22860 25 301), in the plateia, has many magazines and a selection of popular reading books. Open daily 7am-midnight.

Library: The Greek Cultural Conference Center and Library (☎22860 24 960), off 25 Martiou, on the side street before the post office. The island's only library, with info about island events. Open M-F 9am-2pm and 6-9pm, Sa 10am-2pm.

Public Toilets: On 25 Martiou, beside the bus depot. Free.

Medical Center: ☎22860 22 237. Go downhill (south) from the bus station, take the first left, and look for an unmarked building at the end of the street on the left. Open for routine problems M-F 8:30am-2:30pm. **Emergency** care 24hr.

OTE: ☎22860 22 135. Off the plateia on 25 Martiou. Open M-F 7:30am-3:10pm.

Laundromat: 100m from the main Plateia toward the youth hostel. Wash and dry €6. Open daily 9am-8:30pm.

Internet Access: PC World (☎22860 25 551), in the main plateia next to the international bookstore, boosts their appeal with extra perks like free coffee with an hour's worth of Internet time. €3.50 per hr. Open M-Sa 10am-11pm. **Diverso** (☎22860 24 405), on the other side of the international bookstore from PC World, hooks you up for the same price in more chic surroundings. €3.50 per hr. Open daily 7:30am-11pm.

Post Office: ☎22860 22 238. 50m downhill (south) from the bus stop. Open daily M-F 7:30am-2pm. **Postal code:** 84700.

ACCOMMODATIONS

In summer, the pensions and hotels fill up quickly and prices skyrocket out of budget range. The cheapest options are the quality youth hostels in Fira, Perissa beach, and Oia. Call ahead. You can find cheaper places in Karterados, 2km south of Fira, or in the small inland towns along the main bus routes—try Messaria, Pyrgos, or Emborio. Hostels and many pensions will pick you up at the port.

Thira Youth Hostel (☎22860 22 387 or 22860 23 864), on the left roughly 300m north of the plateia, set back 25m from the road to Oia. Lonely travelers join the throng in the courtyard of this old monastery neighboring Fira's caldera. Cleanliness is not the priority, but the dorm rooms and pension-quality private rooms with baths are friendly. Quiet after 11pm. No smoking in dorms. Open Apr.-Oct. Dorms €8-12; doubles €20-40. ❶

Pension Petros (☎22860 22 573; fax 22860 22 615). From the bus station, go 1 block up 25 Martiou and make a right. Make a left at the bottom of the hill; take your 1st right. Owner Petros shares stories and bottles of wine with travelers. Rooms have baths, TVs, and fridges; some have A/C. Free port shuttle. Doubles €45-60; triples €55-70. ❸

Hotel Leta (☎22860 22 540; fax 22860 23 903). Just 100m from the plateia: walking up the main road, follow signs to the right after the laundromat. This colorful building hidden in the alleyways of Fira provides a quiet escape from the caldera's crowds. Upstairs rooms with A/C, TVs, baths, and fridges: doubles €25-60; triples €40-70. Downstairs rooms with bath €15 per person. ❹

Panorama Hotel (☎22860 22 271; fax 22860 22 481), on Ypapantis, over the caldera. The view? Out of this world. The prices? *Out of this world.* The rooms are fully stocked—A/C, TVs, balconies, fridges—as is the hotel itself—sauna, fitness center, jacuzzi. Breakfast included. Singles €78; doubles €120-140; triples €160-180. MC/V. ❺

Costa Marina Villas (☎22860 28 923; www.pelican.gr), 2 doors down from Pension Petros. Costa Marina has spacious rooms, classy wrought-iron beds, A/C, fridges, private bathtubs, and the occasional kitchen. Breakfast included. Singles €60-80; doubles €80-100; triples €100-130. MC/V. ❹

Santorini Camping (☎22860 22 944 or 22860 25 062; fax 22860 25 065). Follow the blue signs leading east of the plateia. This shady campsite is the most festive spot in town, with a pool, poolside bar, cafe, and mini-market on the premises. 24hr. hot showers. Washing machine €4 (soap included). Internet access €2 for 30min., €3 for 31-60min. Quiet hours midnight-8am. Open Apr.-Oct. €7 per person; €3 per tent, €6 per tent rental; €3 per car, €1.70 per motorbike. MC/V. ❶

FOOD

Inexpensive restaurants are hard to find in Fira, but the few that exist are crammed between shops on the tiny streets sandwiched between the plateia and the caldera. The caldera is lined with fine dining options that impose a hefty fee for their priceless views. Generic but convenient snack shops dot the plateia.

Mama's Cyclades Cafe (☎22860 23 032). Head north on the road to Oia; it's on the right side. Advertised as the best American breakfast in Greece, it lives up to the claim. Mama is chatty, endearingly loud, and wants to feed all her "babies" generously. Pancakes with 2 eggs, bacon, hash browns, and OJ €5.50. Open daily 8am-midnight. Free glass of wine for *Let's Go* readers. ❷

Calderimi (☎22860 23 050), on the caldera, behind Hotel Atlantis. Don't be fooled by the classy decor and tasteful food; you're paying for the magnificent view. If your pizza looks almost as small as the boats down on the bay, take solace in the spectacular sunset. Pizzas €10.50-15. Pastas €11-18. Open daily 6:30pm-midnight. MC/V. ❸

Poldo (☎22860 24 004), up the street from the National Bank. Salivating devotees swarm this modest stand to savor vegetarian picks like falafel (€3.50), tabbouleh (€2.70), and hummus (€2.70). Poldo also provides oustanding gyros (small €1.50, large €3.80) for those feeling more carniverous. Open daily 11am-3am. ❶

Nikolas (☎22860 24 550), on Ethivrou Stavrou, across from Kira Thira Jazz Club; look for the line out the door. The menu, updated daily on the board inside, doesn't come in English. Entrees €5-8. Open daily 6-11pm. ❷

Corner Creperie (☎22860 25 512). Walking into town from the bus stop, turn right after the main plateia; the restaurant will be on your left. Thick, hearty crepes (€4-6) and light fare (omelettes €4-5.50; waffles €4-5) are served up in a pleasant, palm-lined restaurant. Open Apr.-Oct. daily 8am-2am. ❷

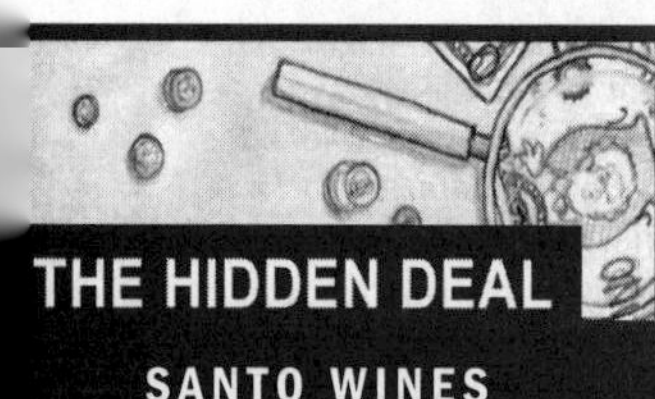

THE HIDDEN DEAL

SANTO WINES

Known for their wine, locals might consider it a near felony to leave Santorini, however reluctantly, without visiting a vineyard or at least sampling their wonderful creations.

Santo Wines, bastion of class, allows regal connoisseurs to hone their taste and gives amateurs a chance to sample without abandoning their budget.

Even better, the location provides some of best panoramas on the island, ensuring nightly sunsets that put even infamous Oia to shame. Santo's organic grapes are grown without pesticides. The winery is communally owned; 70% of the island's grapes come here and profits are distributed among the farmers.

Founded in 1947, the winery has won innumerable gold medals at global competitions. Dabble in this luxury by tasting the famous Santorini *Vinsanto*, *Nykteri*, or any one of Santo's 15 other varieties (€0.70 per tasting). Enamored patrons can upgrade to a full glass (€1.80), or order 12 tastings plus petite plates of bread, cheese, and Greek olives (€10). Even bottles (€4.50-€12.50) lie in budget range.

Take the bus toward Perissa to the crossroads with Pyrgos (€.90); the bus will drop you just outside the winery. ☎22860 22 596; fax 22860 23 137; www.santowines.gr. Open daily 10am-9pm. Antoniou Winery (☎22860 23 557), 100m down the road from Santo Wines toward Perissa, offers a lighter take on the Santorini Vinsanto. €2 per glass; €10-20 per bottle. Open Apr.-Oct. daily 9am-9pm. AmEx/MC/V.

Restaurant Poseidon (☎22860 25 480), in a garden down the stairs next to the plateia taxi stand. Enormous traditional Santorini dishes, like *tomatoklefdes* (tomatoes breaded with fried dough; €3.85) and *potmapavia* (beef with lemon sauce; €7.05) separate Poseidon from typical tourist traps. Open daily 10am-1am. MC/V. ❷

SIGHTS

The **Petros M. Nomikos Conference Center,** north of the cable car station, houses an exhibition center that currently displays life-size reproductions of the magnificent **wall paintings** of Ancient Thira; the originals are some of the most prized pieces at the National Archaeological Museum in Athens (p. 114). Coupled with the ruined city itself, the brightly colored and intricately detailed murals hint at the quotidian existence of Santorini's ancient Minoan culture, as well as an unhealthy infatuation with blue monkeys. (☎22860 23 016. Open May-Oct. daily 10am-9pm. €3, seniors and students €1.50, children under 18 free; audio tour €3.) Just steps away from the cable cars you'll find Fira's **Archaeological Museum,** which holds a plethora of geometric vases, large-scale statues, and well-preserved figurines pillaged from Ancient Thira. (☎22860 22 217. Open Tu-Su 8:30am-3pm. €3, students and EU seniors €2, EU students free.) The same ticket will get you into the newly-renovated, sleek **Museum of Prehistoric Thira,** across from the bus station. The large collection attempts to unravel the mystery of Santorini's pre-volcanic eruption civilization through preserved frescoes, fossils, marble vessels, reconstructions of the ancient city, and plentitudes of explanatory signs. (☎22860 23 217. Open Tu-Su 8:30am-3pm.) The **Megaro Gyzi Museum,** just northwest of Thira Youth Hostel, attempts to chart Santorini's more recent history. (☎22680 23 077. Open May-Oct. M-Sa 10:30am-1pm and 5-8pm, Su 10:30am-4:30pm. €2, students €1).

BEACHES AND OUTDOOR ACTIVITIES

Fira is a convenient base for exploring the beaches of neighboring towns. The closest, though least spectacular, of these beaches is **Vourvoulos,** about 1hr. walk north of town (follow the signs). It is one of the more secluded (though pebbly) of Santorini's famed black-sand beaches. Remember that the island's black sand

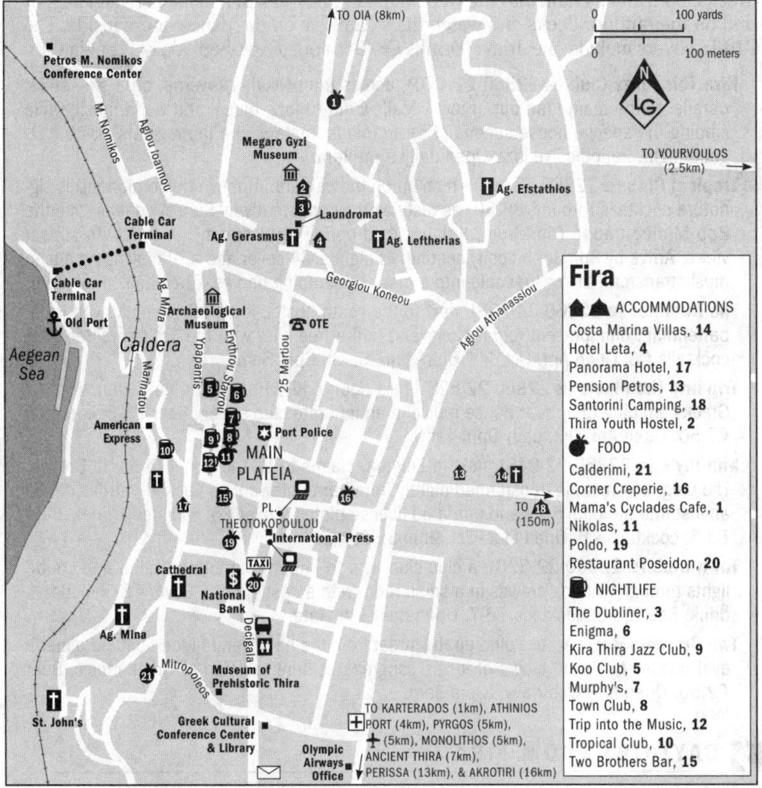

is hot, so bring **sandals.** The little islands along Santorini's caldera rim cater to curious visitors tired of viewing the volcanic strata from afar. The most popular boat excursion goes to the **active volcano,** with a 30min. hike up the black rocks to see the crater. Most boats make a stop afterward in nearby waters that are warmed by hot sulphur springs. Be prepared to swim through cold water to get there. A longer excursion goes to the inhabited island of **Thirasia;** on the standard daytrip, you'll only have 2hr. to wander through the tiny towns and fish taverna-lined streets of the island. Built along Thirasia's upper ridge, the villages of **Manolas** and **Potamos** have overwhelming views of Santorini's western coast. Tour groups dock at **Korfos** or **Reeva.** From Korfos, you'll have to pant up 300 steps or you can hail a donkey (€3) to get to the villages; Reeva provides a paved road. Agencies all over Santorini can arrange **boat tours** (volcano and springs €12, with Thirasia €17).

NIGHTLIFE

Fira is host to one of the hippest late-night scenes in Greece. The clubs on the northern end gear up around 2am. Beer costs €3-4; cocktails €5-8. Covers vary with the season starting at €5 and soaring up toward €15 in high season. **Koo Club** (☎22860 22 025) and **Enigma** (☎22860 22 466) face each other. Cavernous, posh, and crowded with hip

Greeks, both clubs crank into the wee hours. Carve yourself a niche between bars or chill on the outdoor decks and watch the steam rise on the dance floors inside. The €10-15 covers include one drink. (Drinks €8. Both open Apr.-Sept. daily 11pm-late.)

Kira Thira Jazz Club (☎22860 22 770), across from Nikolas Taverna, on a side street parallel to the main road out of town. Mellow out to jazz, blues, and world music while sipping the special house sangria (€5). In this intimate venue the regulars kiss the DJ good night. Periodic live jazz. Open daily 9pm-3am.

Tropical Club (☎22860 23 089), high up on the caldera. A native Californian mixes signature cocktails (around €6.50) as tasty as they are creative. "Sunset coffees" like the Bob Marley frappé (dark rum, Kahlua, iced coffee, and cream) go well with sunset views. Arrive by 8pm for balcony seating. At night a €4 cover and a DJ playing American music transform the casual cafe into a mass of bumping bodies. Open daily noon-4am.

The Dubliner (☎22860 24 888), next to the youth hostel, kicks off the night with jovial bartending, omnipresent four-leaf clovers, and a free shot with the 1st drink. Beer €4; cocktails €6. Open Apr.-Oct. M-F 6pm-3am, Sa-Su 6pm-5am.

Trip into the Music (☎22860 22 628), next door to Kira Thira Jazz Club, features young Greeks grinding to upbeat dance music in an intimate club space. Beer €3-5; cocktails €7.50. Open Apr.-Oct. daily 9pm-4am.

Murphy's (☎22860 22 248), next to Enigma, claims to be the first Irish bar in Greece. The long, thin room is transformed nightly from bar to blowout as packed patrons dance amidst international flags and outdated license plates. Cover €5, includes 1 drink. Beer €3-5; cocktails €6. Open Mar.-Oct. 2pm-3:30am.

Town Club (☎22860 22 820), a chic club next to Murphy's, pumps techno and strobe lights through writhing crowds in a small room with a castle motif. Cover €8, includes 1 drink. Beer €3-5; cocktails €6-7. Open daily 9pm-late.

Two Brothers Bar, next to Poldo up the street from the banks and hidden behind a medieval prison. A relaxed crowd of locals congregates here to listen to Greek music. Beer €2.50. Open May-Oct. daily 10pm-3am.

DAYTRIPS FROM FIRA

AKROTIRI. The volcanic eruption that rocked Santorini in the 17th century BC blanketed Akrotiri with lava that, despite destroying the island, preserved the maritime city of Akrotiri more completely than almost any other Minoan site. In 1967 the paved streets of Akrotiri were uncovered by Professor Spyridon Marinatos who was later killed by a fall at the site in 1974. Only an estimated 5% of the massive city has been excavated, but the sprawling remains attest to the sophistication of Minoan society in multi-storied houses, extensive sanitary, sewage, drainage systems, and evidence of writing and numeric codes. Each house had at least one room decorated with wall paintings, some of which are the most advanced in Greece; the originals are at the National Archaeological Museum in Athens (p. 114). Since no skeletons were found in the city, the theory goes that everyone escaped before the 1625 BC eruption devastated the area. Signs guide you through the excavation. *(Take the bus (16 per day, €1.30) from Fira. ☎22860 81 366. Open Tu-Su 8:30am-3pm. €5, students €3.)*

For sustenance and a fabulous sea view, head down the road perpendicular to the archaeological site to reach **Dolphins Fish Restaurant ❸,** where diners enjoy the daily fresh catch (€10) on sun-drenched piers that extend onto the water. (☎22860 81 151. Open daily 11am-midnight. AmEx/MC/V.) Away from the ancient site and past the Dolphin Fish Restaurant lies the magnificent **Red beach,** a 20min. walk from the Akrotiri bus stop. Though Santorini is famed for its black beaches, this ruddy beach is prized for its remote location, smooth sand, and brick-red cliffs.

PYRGOS AND ANCIENT THIRA. Once a Venetian fortress, the lofty town of Pyrgos is girded by medieval walls. Twenty five blue- and green-domed churches highlighting the horizon are the legacy of Ottoman occupation, which lasted through 1828. One of these colorful sanctuaries (near the top of town) houses the **Museum of Icons and Liturgical Objects.** *(☎22860 31 812. Open Tu-Su 8:30am-4pm. Free.)* To find the museum in the maze of alleyways leading up the hill, follow the signs for adjacent Kafe Kasteli. The deteriorated walls of the old fortress still ring the town; continuing upwards past the church leads to the fortifications and their panoramic views of Fira and Oia. Continuing through the town on the main road, a 40min. hike takes you to the **Profitis Ilias Monastery.** Built in 1711, it graciously shares its site with a radar station installed by the Greek military, who thought that the station would be safe from attack alongside this ancient monastery. Visitors are no longer allowed inside the monastery, though the lofty location provides an island panorama. On July 20, the monastery hosts the **Festival of Profitis Ilias,** a primarily religious ceremony involving eating, drinking, and dancing.

From Profitis Ilias, the ruins of **Ancient Thira** are approximately a 1½hr. hike away. *(Open Tu-Su 8:30am-2:30pm. Free.)* This trek, along the mountain that separates Kamari and Perissa, leads to fantastic views of all the island. Be warned that the path consists of slippery gravel on a windy mountainside, so shoes with good traction are a must. The ancient theater, church, and forum of the island's former capital are still visible, replete with carved dolphins and ruined columns. *(Take the bus (15min., 30 per day, €0.90) from Fira to Perissa. Ask the driver to let you off at Pyrgos. Ancient Thira can be reached as a hike from Pyrgos. Or take a bus from Fira to Kamari (20min., 2-3 per hr., €0.90). Climb the mountain beside the water to reach the ruins.)*

MONOLITHOS. More popular with locals than with tourists, small **Monolithos beach** is comparatively umbrella-free and easily accessible due to its proximity to the airport (5 buses per day, €0.90). The black sand is much finer than at many of Santorini's other beaches, though this means the winds can whip up dark-hued sandstorms at times. The fish taverna **Skaramagas** ❷ dishes out seafood caught by the owners. Locals lounge over calamari (€6), *horiatiki* (€3), and the taverna's famed *kakavia* (€9), a fish soup. *(☎22860 31 750. Open Apr.-Oct. daily 8am-11pm.)*

PERISSA Περισσα ☎22860

Perissa becomes a ghost town in the winter, when the storming hordes of youthful tourists dissipate; during the summer, chic clubs, open-air bars, and endless rounds of drinks turn tiny Perissa into a playground for the young. Lacking the crammed, careening pace of Oia and Fira, Perissa also lacks the stunning views and picturesque cafe-lined caldera. Nonetheless, the umbrella-filled black-sand beaches beckon sun-bathers and students looking for a relaxed and comparatively inexpensive retreat from the more major tourist destinations.

TRANSPORTATION. To get there take the bus from **Fira** (30min., 20 per day, €1.50). If black sand seems passé, take the ferry to **Red beach** at Akrotiri. (☎22860 82 093. Leaves 11am; returns 4pm. €6 one-way.)

ACCOMMODATIONS. Domatia offer privacy; proprietors hang around the dock at Athinios, but you shouldn't agree to anything before seeing a room. Doubles run €20-35. **Stelio's Place** ❸ is a 7min. walk from the plateia. From the road leading out of town, turn left after passing Cafe Del Mare on your right; it's 50m down on your left. Stelio's has 21 rooms with private baths, fridges, A/C, a crystalline pool, an adjacent bar (beer €1.50), easy beach access, and free shuttles to the airport or seaport. (☎22860 81 860; splace@otenet.gr. Breakfast €3-4.50. Reservations recommended. Doubles €30-55; triples €45-70.) If the 1min. walk to the beach from Stelio's doesn't suit you, **Ostria ❷** is located on the waterfront. Walking away from the main square, turn left about 250m down the road after a small gravel clearing; then turn right on the beach road. Spacious studios with A/C, TVs, and kitchens are imbued with a sea-themed decor and a sailing boat print. (☎22860 82 607. Doubles €35-40; triples €40-50.) **Youth Hostel Perissa-Anna ❶** is 50m before the first bus stop heading into town. From the final stop at the main plateia by the beach, walk inland along the main street for 500m. This popular spot provides decent women's and co-ed dorms and private rooms, with discounts on services around Perissa, use of a nearby pool, and a social atmosphere. The hostel is also affiliated with a travel agency and organizes discount excursions (€15-25), car rental (€25), and plane tickets. (☎22860 82 182; annayh@ote.net. 20% discount at the restaurant across the street. Luggage storage €3. Linens €1. Internet access €5 per hr. 36-bed dorm €6; 10-14 bed dorm €7; rooms for 3-4 €8-10 per person.) **Perissa Camping ❶** is adjacent to the beach in one of the few forested spots on the island. Enjoy their beach bar, mini-market, kitchen facilities, clean restrooms, discounted scuba diving excursions, and taverna. (☎22860 81 343; camp@otenet.gr. Internet access €5 per hr. €6 per person, €3 per tent rental, €2 per car.)

FOOD AND NIGHTLIFE. Where the main road meets the plateia, **Santo Food ❶** offers hungry sunbathers inexpensive gyros (€1.50), breakfast (€3-5), and pleasantly plump sandwiches (€3) in a wood lined interior. (☎22860 82 893. Open Apr.-Oct. 24hr.) Across the street, calzones, 15 varieties of pizza, and pasta await at **Bella Aurora ❷.** The infamous super-calzone (€6.50) is crammed with 10 toppings; finishing it might be an intimidating prospect. (☎22860 81 176. Calzones €4.50-6.50. Pizzas €4.50-6. Pastas €3-5.50. Open May-Oct. daily 8:30am-11:30pm. AmEx/MC/V.) Head back across the street to the **Full Moon Bar,** where the loquacious Canadian owner taps Guinness (€4), hosts nightly DJs and frequent themed parties, and boasts a Happy "Hour" that actually lasts seven. (☎22860 81 177. Beer €3; mixed drinks €3-6. Open Apr.-Oct. daily 4pm-4am.)

KAMARI Καμαρι ☎22860

Although renowned for its black sand, Kamari beach is actually covered in black pebbles and the slippery seaweed-covered rock bottom makes wading especially difficult. The notoriety of the town has translated into inflated prices and an overdeveloped waterfront; the narrow beach area, pressed against the ocean by pricey hotels, shops, cafes, and nightclubs, is covered in umbrellas (€7). Still, the surrounding mountains, sun-drenched strollers, and stretches of beach attract storms of devotees who gawk at the scenery and absorb the relaxed resort atmosphere.

TRANSPORTATION. Buses come from **Fira** (20min., 2-3 per hr., €0.90) and deposit passengers about a block from the south side of the waterfront. A bumpy shuttle boat scoots between Kamari and **Perissa** (every 30min., 9am-5pm; €3). The boat leaves from in front of the Hook Bar at the right end of the waterfront.

ACCOMMODATIONS. Doubles throughout town range €30-70. **Hotel Preka Maria ❸** (☎22860 31 266) rents rooms with fridges and baths (€30-45) and spacious, well-furnished 3-person apartments (€40-60), replete with A/C, TV, and balcony views. It's on the northern end of town; heading away from the mountain on the beach road, take a left before the barbecue restaurant. The hotel is 70m farther along. Past Preka Maria on the left lies **Pension Spiridoula ❸**; look for the gargantuan sign. The rooms, though simple, have baths, balconies, and fridges. (☎22860 31 767. Doubles €25-45.) **Hotel Roussos ❺** provides a luxurious stay on the water, with a pool and a classy outdoor bar. The well-equipped, small rooms have A/C, TVs, fridges, and fantastic views fronting the ocean. (☎22860 31 590; rousbeach@otenet.gr. Doubles €110; triples €119. MC/V.)

FOOD AND ENTERTAINMENT. The waterfront is lined with indistinguishable tavernas. **Eanos ❷** differentiates itself with a menu that fuses traditional cuisine with non-standard options including 21 kinds of pizza. (☎22860 31 161. Greek dishes €4-7. Pizza €5-8. Open Apr.-Oct. daily noon-1am. MC/V.) For an inexpensive snack, head to **Ariston ❶**, a bakery and market selling fresh bread (under €1), at the northern end of the waterfront. (☎22860 312 603. Open daily 7am-11pm. MC/V.) Nearby, **Mango ❶** caters to chic young tourists sipping cocktails and nibbling on light fare. (Pizza, pasta, and crepes €3-5. Open Apr.-Oct. daily 9am-2am. MC/V.)

Near Mango is the futuristic indoor club **Dom.** (☎22860 33 420. Cocktails €6. Open Su-Th 11pm-3:30am, F-Sa 11pm-dawn.) For quieter entertainment, see a flick at the **Open-Air Cinema Kamari** (☎22860 31 974; tickets €7 for evening shows), 500m out of town on the road to Fira. The **Canava Roussos** winery, 1km from Kamari Camping, is the oldest winery in Santorini. The house favorite *mavrathiko* (€1 per tasting; €9.50 per bottle) is a dessert wine made with purple grapes instead of the traditional white. The bus between Fira and Kamari can drop you there. (☎22860 31 275. Open daily 10am-8pm.)

OIA Οια ☎22860

Dazzling sunsets have made the posh cliffside town of Oia (EE-ah) famous; the little stucco buildings on the cliffs make it breathtaking. In the aftermath of the 1956 earthquake that leveled the town (and much of the northwestern tip of the island), inhabitants carved new dwellings among the crumbled debris of the old, making for a romantic jumble of whitewashed houses cleft into the brittle cliffside. The budget traveler, however, will not survive long in this spectacular setting. Window-shopping pedestrians rule the narrow cobblestone streets at the town's many upscale boutiques, while glitzy art galleries and craft shops dominate. If browsing isn't your bag, hightail it to the cliffs and secure a prime sunset view.

TRANSPORTATION AND PRACTICAL INFORMATION. Buses run from **Fira** (25min., 30 per day, €0.90), and ferries dock at Oia before continuing to Fira or Athinios. **Karvounis Tours** (☎22860 71 280; mkarvounis@ote.net.gr; open Apr.-Oct. daily 10:30am-2:30pm and 6:30-10:30pm), on the main street beside the largest church in town, answers questions about Oia and Santorini, in addition to selling ferry and airline tickets. To find the agency from the bus stop, walk uphill away from Fira and turn left at the first alley; it's to the right at the end.

ACCOMMODATIONS. The Karvounis family of Karvounis Tours' **Youth Hostel Oia ❷** has impeccable rooms with baths featuring large mirrors for the narcissistic (or insecure), a courtyard, and a bar open for breakfast and evening drinks. This luxurious hostel makes painfully expensive Oia bearable. Get more bang for your buck during Happy Hour (7:30-8:30pm), with cheap drinks and a sunset free from the caldera crowds up on the roof patio. (☎22860 71 465; fax 22860 71 281. Single-sex and co-ed dorms. Laundry €7.80 per load. Free safety deposit boxes. Breakfast included. Open May-Oct. Dorms €12-14.) Short-term **domatia** are rare in Oia; most proprietors expect a 5-day stay. **Lauda ❸**, perched on the cliffs 100m from the main church in the direction of Fira, offers traditional stucco cave houses with built-in beds, private baths, fridges, A/C, and a rooftop jacuzzi. (☎22860 71 204 or 71 157; fax 22860 71 274. Doubles €50-70; apartments with kitchen €60-90.)

FOOD. Dining here will cost you a bit more than in Fira, but some restaurants serve exceptional food. **Petros ❷,** Oia's oldest restaurant, at the southern end of the town's main road (turn left at the main church and walk down about 300m), overlooks the sparkling sea. Seafood fried up in front of customers is complemented by old Greek culinary touches and a modest seating area. Wine production (€3-12 for 0.5L) continues as a family tradition by Petros Jr. (☎22860 71 263. Entrees €6-13. Open Apr.-Oct. daily 6pm-midnight. AmEx/MC/V.) Petros's family extends up the street to **Thalami Taverna ❷,** where they serve more standard dishes in a more sophisticated atmosphere. (☎22860 71 009. Chicken with blue cheese and mushrooms €10. Santorini salad €8. Open May-Sept. daily noon-1am. AmEx/MC/V.) **Restaurant Lotza ❸,** about 100m to the north of the main church, serves well-seasoned dishes like curried chicken (€9), *yioourtlou* (minced meat, pita bread, and yogurt; €9), and spaghetti with seafood (€13) in an upscale atmosphere on the caldera. (☎22860 71 357. Open Apr.-Oct. daily 9am-midnight.) Flowering terraces, obsequious waitstaff, and omnipresent antiques make **1800 ❹** the town's classiest bistro. Situated in a 19th-century mansion, 50m north of the main church, with much original furniture, this self-titled "slow-food" restaurant serves up a rotating menu of creative dishes. (☎22860 71 485. Entrees €15-30. Open daily 7:30pm-12:30am. Reservations recommended. AmEx/MC/V.) In restitution for the splurge, prepare your other meals at the small **grocery/bakery** near the plateia where the buses stop. Follow the signs to fresh loaves and croissants. (☎28860 71 121. Bakery items €0.60-1.20. Open daily 7am-3pm and 5-8:30pm.)

BEACHES. A 20min. trip down the 252 stone stairs at the northern end of the main road (to the right of the church) leads to rocky **Ammoudi beach,** where a few boats are moored in a startlingly deep swimming lagoon. There is no sand and no obvious beach, but the path to the left leads to pleasant swimming holes of stunning blue water and volcanic rocks. Weary bathers unwilling to walk up the cliffside for dinner can nab fresh fish at one of the three **tavernas** at the bottom of the stairs or simply hire a **donkey** (€3 per person) to get them up the steep slope.

MILOS Μηλος

The Venus de Milo may indeed have been uprooted from her hometown of Trypiti on Milos to make camp in the Louvre, but fortunately the French can never steal the most breathtaking of treasures Milos has to offer. Mineral deposits and volcanoes have collaborated to create a wealth of the most sublime and dramatic beaches in the Cyclades. At the feet of lofty, cliff-like dunes, the pale, cerulean waters of Papafragas, Tsigrado, and Kleftiko beaches are to be rivalled by none. The winding streets of Trypiti, the ancient theater, and the catacombs deserve an evening of aimless wandering.

ADAMAS Αδαμας ☎22870

This port town stuffs most of Milos's accommodations, food, and nightlife into only several blocks, causing congestion that dwindles into the vibrance and fun of the outer regions of town. Milos's sights and graphic, untouched beauty is better found elsewhere, but the centralized bus system makes Adamas a solid base for exploring the rest of the island; renting a car or moped is a good idea. Follow the waterfront to the right from the ferry landing to reach the center of Adamas.

TRANSPORTATION

Flights: Olympic Airways (☎22870 22 380, airport office 22870 22 381), on 25 Martiou. Planes go once daily to **Athens** (€35-55). Open M-F 8am-3pm.

Ferries: From Milos, ferries follow a complex but posted schedule to: **Folegandros** (2hr., 4 per week, €6.10); **Ios** (1hr., 7 per week; €12.40); **Kithnos** (2½hr., 2-3 per day, €9.10); **Piraeus** (7hr., 3 per day, €18.20); **Santorini** (4hr., 8 per week, €13.40); **Serifos** (2hr., 3 per day, €6); **Sifnos** (1½hr., 3 per day, €5.40). The small Karamitsos ferry and a local fishing boat also go to **Kimolos** (30min., 7 per day, €1.73-3) from Pollonia.

Flying Dolphins: Twice as fast and roughly twice as expensive as ferries. 6 per week to: **Piraeus, Serifos,** and **Sifnos.** 3 per week to **Amorgos.** 2 per week to **Iraklion,** Crete.

Buses: ☎22870 51 062. Stop by the Agricultural Bank on the waterfront for almost hourly buses to **Plaka (Horio), Pollonia, Trypiti,** and other destinations (€.90-1.30 one-way). They also travel regularly to **Paleohori, Hivadolimni** (both the beach and nearby campsite), and **Provatas.** Check schedules posted in the bus station and travel offices.

Taxis: ☎22870 22 219. Line up along the waterfront when they're free. They are also available by phone 24hr.

Moped and Car Rental: Milos Rent a Car (☎22870 21 994; fax 22870 24 002), across from the port. Bikes €10-30 per day; cars €35-60 per day. 21+. Must have held license for 3 years to rent mopeds and cars.

ORIENTATION AND PRACTICAL INFORMATION

Tourist Office: ☎22870 22 445. Across from the dock. Ask for brochures, **maps,** ferry, bus timetables, and a complete list of the island's rooms and hotels. Open daily 10am-4pm and 6-11:30pm. Pick up a free *Welcome to Milos* guide.

Tourist Agencies: Sophia's Tourist Office (☎22870 24 052). With your back to the boat, to the right of the official agency, has friendly and knowledgeable staff. **Milos Travel** (☎22870 22 286; fax 22870 22 396) and **RIVA Travel** (☎22870 24 024; fax 22870 28 005; rivatr@otenet.gr) are also comparably useful; both located farther down the waterfront. All 3 agencies sell ferry tickets and help with bus schedules.

Banks: National Bank (☎22870 22 077), near the post office along the waterfront, has 24hr. **ATM.** There's an **Agricultural Bank** (☎22870 22 330) in the central plateia by the harbor. Both open M-Th 8am-2pm, F 8am-1:30pm.

Laundromat: ☎22870 22 228. Take your 1st left after the waterfront up a narrow street; after taking a sharp right at the "Corali" sign, take the next left and it's straight up at the end of the street on your left. €8.80 per 5kg.

Police: ☎22870 21 204. By the bus stop in Plaka. Open 24hr.

Port Authority: ☎22870 22 100. Open 24hr.

Pharmacy: ☎22870 21 218. Located past the Agricultural bank, on your 1st right after the supermarket. Open daily 9am-2pm.

Medical Center: ☎22870 22 700, 22 701, or 22 702. In Plaka. Open 24hr.

Internet Access: Internet Info (☎22870 28 011). Walk uphill on the street across from the Agricultural Bank (same left as you take for laundromat). Take sharp right at "Corali" sign and continue straight until the end of that road. It's on your left. €6 per hr. Open daily noon-3pm and 6pm-midnight.

Post Office: ☎22870 22 288. Take the waterfront road past the bus station and turn right after the Agricultural Bank; it's 100m down this road. Offers **Poste Restante** and express mail services. Open M-F 9am-2pm. **Postal code:** 84801.

ACCOMMODATIONS

High season prices may wound your wallet, but fear not—persistence will reveal affordable private rooms in **domatia** hiding in Adamas's side streets. Book far in advance to stay here.

Camping Milos (☎22870 31 410; fax 22870 31 412), located at Hivadolimni beach, 7km from port; buses pick up at the dock before 6:30pm. Set on a cliff in the more rural, western half of the island, it has dramatic sea views. New and sharp, with kitchen, laundry, car and bike rental, mini-market, and restaurant. €5-8 per person, including tent rental. Bungalows for 2 with fridges and baths €35-66. ❶

Semiramis Hotel (☎22870 23 722; www.hotelsemiramis.gr). Follow the main road past the bus station and bear left after the supermarket; it's straight ahead. Free minibus runs from ferry. Nikos and Petros tend excellent rooms with a shaded garden outside. Phones, fridges, TVs, and private baths. Additional €6 for A/C. Breakfast €3.50. If you seek a step up in modernity and luxury (same amenities but with free A/C and newer rooms for about €15 more), ask about its sister hotel, nearby **Dionysus,** 50m farther along the main road. Doubles €25-47; triples 20% more. Cheaper rooms downstairs with common bath €25-33. Traveler's checks accepted. MC/V. ❸

Kanaris Rooms to Let (☎22870 22 184 or 69467 52 275), 200m from the town center–look for the "Anezina" minibus when you disembark the ferry. If walking, take left just before Internet cafe and it's down the street on your right. Private baths, fridges, balconies, and ceiling fans. Doubles €20-42. ❷

Anezina (or Iliopetra), set back from the waterfront about 50m. If you want slightly fancier rooms with A/C and fridges, stay at one of these sister hotels. Doubles €30-80, depending on room and season; singles 20% less. MC/V. ❸

Hotel Corali (☎22870 22 216; fax 22870 22 144), when walking downhill from Kanaris Rooms around the corner to your right. Private baths, ceiling fans, TV, fridge, and phones. Port shuttle available at no extra charge. Doubles €35-65 in high season; cheaper rooms available downstairs for €30. MC/V. ❹

FOOD

Large waterfront restaurants where you can watch the moon sparkling on the harbor's surface draw tourists every night. Several cafes also pepper the waterfront. The multitude of bakeries, creperies, and sandwich shops in the main square allow for quick, cheap meals. **Pitsounakia ❶,** opposite the Agricultural Bank, serves snappy and tasty souvlaki (€2.95). About 250m along the waterfront road you'll find **Navayio ❸,** a popular taverna with delicious, affordable fish dishes. (☎22870 23 392. Swordfish fillet €10.30. Open 9am-10:30pm.)

NIGHTLIFE AND ENTERTAINMENT

Though there isn't much of a bar or disco scene in Adamas, there are a few places to dance to Greek tracks. Sip a drink at **Aragosta Cafe,** located both above and beside Milos Travel. The late-night dancing is at the upstairs cafe. (Piña colada €7. Cafe open 8am-3am; club open 8pm-3 or 4am. MC/V.) Next door, you'll find **Vipera Lebetina,** where DJs spin mainstream foreign and then Greek music into the wee hours of the morning. If you're looking for some impressive man-made scenery, head to **La Costa.** With your back to the port, make your way left past the tourist agency and around the curve of the beach cove adjacent to Adamas; you can't miss the massive reconstructed ship that hovers above the bar. (☎22870 24 008. Open 9pm-3am.) **Faros** booms with Greek tunes and has dancing on a wooden deck overlooking the harbor. (With your back to the water, it's 1km right of Adamas along the beach. Drinks €5-7. ☎22870 31 403. Open M-Sa 9pm-3am or whenever people choose to retire.) A cinema, **Cine Milos** (☎22870 23 625), can be found by taking a left before "KozzmoKar" as you walk along the beach toward the strip of restaurants; it's about 150m down on your right.

BEACHES

Because of centuries of volcanic eruptions, Milos has impressive **beaches** (they're *all* pretty incredible) covered with exceptional rock formations and unique sand. Twenty-four distinctive beaches line the island's northern and southern coasts. In the north, the pools of **Papafragas** are embraced by a stone arch and arms of white, powdery rock reaching into the sea, creating the impression of that you're next to snow-covered mountains. Take the bus to **Pollonia** and ask the driver to let you off at the beach (1.5km before Papafragas on the coast). Seven buses per day journey to crowded **Hivadolimni** beach (15min.). On the southern side of the island, lively **Provatas** and **Paleohori** beaches sport bars, music, and comfy beach chairs. You can take the bus to Adamas (25min., about 8 per day). The real gem sits between them at **Tsigrados,** where natural stores of perlite make for deep, soft sand that glimmers magnificently in the afternoon sun. It can only be reached by braving the steep and towering dune that borders it; get there by moped, or make the 1½hr. trek from Provatas. Ask at the travel agencies about boat excursions that stop at several beaches on a tour (most run 9am-6pm, about €18) around the island. If you want to get a little exercise, explore the island by kayak. Contact **Sea Kayak Milos** (☎22870 21 365 or 22870 23 597; www.seakayakgreece.com) to find out details on the various excursions ranging €30-50.

DAYTRIPS FROM ADAMAS

PLAKA AND TRYPITI Πλακα AND Τρυπητη

Buses from Adamas run to Plaka and Trypiti (15min., every 30min., €0.90.)

From the bus stop, head along the cobblestone path down the steps and bear right to find the large, yellow **Archaeological Museum,** which houses artifacts unearthed at Fylakopi—including the mesmerizing *Lady of Fylakopi*. (☎22870 21 620. Open Tu-Su 8:30am-3pm. €3, students and seniors €2, EU students free.) For a truly spectacular view, climb upward for 15min. from the bus station to the **Panagia Thalassitra Monastery** at the top of the old castle. The town of **Plaka** rests on this and neighboring knolls all of which are located 6km from Adamas. Opposite the police station, follow the signs downhill through twisting streets to the terrace of the **Church of Panagia Korfiatissa,** which opens onto a view of lush countryside and blue sea only an arm's length away. Next door is the **Folk Museum.** (☎22870 21 292. Open Tu-Sa 10am-2pm and 6-9pm, Su 10am-2pm. €2, students and children €1.)

A 3min. walk from the Archaeological Museum (follow signs that begin across the street from it to the left) leads to the tiny town of **Trypiti.** From there a paved road winds down past several sights. A sign marks the spot where the **Venus de Milo** was buried around 320 BC; it was moved to the Louvre in Paris in the 19th century after being discovered by a farmer tilling his fields. Farther off the path a well-preserved **theater** with free entry dates back to the Roman occupation and provides a riveting ocean view; ask at the tourist office about performances there. At the end of the road and down a set of stairs are signs for the **catacombs,** hewn into the cliff face, the oldest site of Christian worship in Greece. These open-air ruins are small and lack on-site plaques, but peering into the unlit corridors of the cool catacombs sparks the imagination. Of the five chambers, only one is open to the public. (☎22870 21 625. €2, students €1; Su free. Open Tu-Su 8am-7pm.) You can also still see part of a Dorian stone wall built between 1100 and 800 BC. Archaeology buffs will want to scramble among the ruins of **Fylakopi,** 3km from the fishing village of **Pollonia** toward Adamas, where British excavations unearthed 3500-year-old **frescoes** now displayed in the National Museum in Athens.

KIMOLOS Κιμωλος

Transportation from Pollonia to Kimolos is provided about 7-8 times a day by both a small car ferry (€1.70), and 2 alternating fishing boats, "O Nikos" (☎22870 51 061; €3) and "Tria Athelfia" (☎69726 04 977; €3). They offer tasteful, relaxed tours making a ring around the island and stopping at the most worthwhile restaurant (To Kima) and most remarkable beaches. Boats leave directly from Adamas; inquire at tourist office.

A quiet island with tilled, naked hills, Kimolos is loveliest at sunset when the colors are most vivid over both the sea and Kimolos's shining white rock. Valued for centuries, the Venetians called the island Argentiera after the silver sands on the southeast part of the island. Disembark at the small port of **Psathi** where, directly on the beach, you'll find taverna **To Kima,** a family establishment that has a mouth-watering local menu. (☎22870 51 001. Zucchini pie €3.50. Fava bean purée €2.40. Chicken in fresh tomato sauce €5. Open M-Sa noon-midnight.) From here, you might head left for **Aliki beach** where pleasant and quiet **Sardis Domatia** ❷ lie a bit set back from the sands. (☎22870 51 458 or 69772 38 244. Fridge, A/C, private bath. Taverna attached. Doubles €25-50.) Otherwise, continue up to Hora, where you can wander through alleyways and peer into the empty houses. From the Kastro, a 1hr. hike will take you through mountains to the beautiful beaches of the eastern shore. Travel around the island is difficult, but the island's single **taxi** (☎22870 51 552 or 69454 64 093) is always available and you are allowed to bring rented cars or motorbikes over from Milos four to five times per day. A watertaxi is also available to drop you off and pick you up at hard-to-reach beaches. Contact **Delphini Sea Taxi** (☎22870 51 437 or 69722 72 111). For more information on the island, pick up a free *Kimolos Tourist Guide* in Psathi at To Kima.

SIFNOS Σιφνος

Sifniots are a festive bunch, dropping everything 13 times a year to celebrate religious festivals with food, drinking, dancing, and merriment that lasts for days. Even when they return to work, Sifnos has much with which to relax them—animated nightlife, distinctive cuisine, and majestic beaches, where people are as likely to be snorkeling or leaping from cliffs as they are to be basking in the warmth of the sun.

KAMARES Καμαρες ☎22840

Kamares is an unaffectedly charming harbor filled with sailboats and yachts and surrounded by formidable brown cliffs, which stand in fierce contrast to the emerald sea that laps gently at their bases. The town beach known as Ammouthia sweeps the harbor rim and a few tavernas line its shallow perimeter. Days here seem to drift away. Here you can find a room, swim, dine, and peruse shops full of ornate local pottery; look for signs reading *keramiko* (ceramic) throughout the village.

TRANSPORTATION. From Sifnos, **ferries** head to: **Ios** (2 per week, €9.60); **Kimolos** (1hr., daily, €5.10); **Kithnos** (1½hr., daily, €6.80); **Milos** (1½hr., 3 per day, €5.10); **Piraeus** (5½hr., 3 per day, €15.40); **Santorini** (5hr., 9-12 per week, €10.70); **Serifos** (45min., 3 per day, €4.70); **Sikinos** (4½hr., 2 per week, €8.10). As always, you have the option of cutting your travel time in half by shelling out twice the cash—**Flying Dolphins** speed daily to: **Kithnos** (45min.); **Milos** (45min.); **Pireaus** (3hr.); **Santorini** (2½hr.); **Serifos** (20min.). Four **buses** travel daily from the main stop in Kamares, in front of the tourist office near the ferry landing, to: **Apollonia** (10min.; every hr., 7:30am-midnight; €0.80), **Artemonas, Faros, Herronisos, Kastro, Platis Yialos,** and **Vathy;** consult schedule in the tourist office for exact frequency and prices. A number of **taxis** (☎22840 33 719, 22840 31 626, or 22840 31 347) are available 24hr. on the island. You can also call the drivers' cell phones directly (☎69446 96 409, 69446 42 680, and 69444 44 904; entire list available in the tourist office). **Niki Rent a Car,** 200m down the main road from the dock, has some of the best rates. (☎22840 33 993 or 69456 56 147. Bikes €10-20; cars €38-60. Prices vary with season, increasing steadily from mid-June to Aug. MC/V.)

ORIENTATION AND PRACTICAL INFORMATION. Just opposite the ferry dock, extremely helpful and friendly anglophones in the **Information Office** help visitors find rooms, decipher boat and bus schedules, **store luggage** (free), and **exchange currency.** (☎22840 31 977; fax 22840 33 916. Maps €1.30. Open daily 9am-midnight.) The **port authority** is next door. (☎22840 33 617. Open 24hr.) Along the waterfront as you walk from the dock to town, the English-speaking staff at **Aegean Thesaurus Travel Agency** are equally willing and able to provide the services offered at the tourist office; they also sell tickets for ferries and Flying Dolphins. (☎22840 33 151; thesaurus@travelling.gr. Open daily 9:30am-10pm.) **Public toilets** are behind the kiosk next to the information office—bring your own toilet paper. An international press **"The Bookshop,"** a few stores down on the main strip, provides a carefully selected array of wares from island maps with hiking trails (€1.30) to English fiction. (☎22840 33 521. Open daily 9am-midnight, July-Aug. 8am-1am.) In an **emergency,** call the **police** (☎22840 31 210) in Apollonia. A **doctor** can be reached 24hr. at the **medical clinic.** (☎22840 31 315. Open M-F 10am-1pm, Tu, Th 5-7pm). Call the **pharmacy** at ☎22840 33 541. **Postal code:** 84003.

ACCOMMODATIONS AND CAMPING. During high season, you're unlikely to find a budget hotel room; inquire at **Room to Let** signs or ask at one of the many waterfront tavernas. Ten meters uphill from Niki's Car Rental on the main road, turn right; the second building of its kind on your left, **Hotel Kiki ❹** offers spotless rooms with baths, TVs, A/C, fridges, and balconies overlooking Kamares and the harbor. (☎22840 32 329; fax 22840 31 453. Doubles €45-59; triples €49-62.) **Meltemi Rooms ❸,** behind Hotel Kiki, has clean rooms with A/C and private baths. (☎22840 31 653 or 22840 33 066. Doubles €25-50.) **Maki's Camping ❶,** across the main road from Niki's Car Rental and down the dirt path 200m on your left, lies 50m behind the beach. It has a taverna, mini-market, Internet (€6 per hr.), laundry facilities, common baths, and showers. (☎22840 32 366; www.makiscamping.gr. €6 per person, €6.50 including tent.) Another, more secluded campsite is calm, clean **Platis Yialos Camping ❶,** 30min. by bus from Kamares, then a 10min. walk down a rocky country road away from the beach; follow the signs. (☎22840 71 286. €4 per person, €2.40 tent rental.)

FOOD. The local Sifniot specialty *revithada*, a chickpea soup, can be found most everywhere that serves Greek cuisine (€2.50-5.50). There are also several **groceries** and **bakeries.** Most of the tavernas serve food of roughly the same quality and price, but some have seaside seating. **Ristorante Italiano de Claudio ❷,** up the main street toward Apollonia, makes incredible pizza (€6.50-10) and *rigatoni delicati* (€8.50), a pasta with chicken, asparagus, and cream sauce. (Open 6pm-1am. MC/V) Across the street, **O Kapetan Andreas ❷** specializes in seafood. Try the *astakomakaronada*, a lobster pasta dish (€65 per kg). Lights adorn the tree-filled terrace, creating a romantic ambience. (☎22840 32 356. Open daily noon-midnight.)

NIGHTLIFE. A choice sunset-watching spot is **Cafe Folie,** about 150m along the beach. Colorful, funky decor, Caribbean flavor, and fruity cocktails (€6-7.50) enhance the delight of being so close to the water. The **Old Captain Bar,** midway along the waterfront strip, serves milkshakes (€4.50) and a variety of rum punches (€7). Tap your toes in the sand to the beat of calypso and string music. (☎22840 31 990. Open daily 11am-3am.)

APOLLONIA Απολλωνια ☎22840

The streets of Apollonia, the island's capital and heart, meander haphazardly about the hilltop. Pick a landmark by the main road where all of Sifnos's roads converge to get your bearings. A few steps from the main road, you can wander narrow lanes, where you'll find a maze of shops, bars, charming houses, and all the locals and Athenians who have adopted Sifnos as their island home.

ORIENTATION AND PRACTICAL INFORMATION. All the necessities and luxuries a traveler needs can be found in the main plateia, where the **bus** from Kamares makes its first stop. Buses to **Kamares** (10min., €0.80) wait in front of the post office, while those to villages and beaches such as **Kastro** (€0.80) and **Platis Yialos** (€1.50) stop around the corner on the mountain road next to the Hotel Anthousa. Buses run to these three destinations at least once every hour. For exact times consult schedules posted by the plateia stop, outside the travel agency. **Aegean Thesaurus,** near the post office, is your source for **currency exchange,** accommodations assistance, bus and ferry schedules, and €2 island information packs. (☎22840 33 151. Open daily 10am-10pm.) The **National Bank** is down the main road from the bus stop, directly after Hotel Anthousa on the right. It has a 24hr. **ATM.** (☎22840 31 317. Open M-Th 8am-2pm, F 8am-1:30pm.) Heading up the hill toward Hotel Anthousa on the road to Artemonas, you will find the **police station** in a white building on your right. (☎22840 31 210. Open daily 9am-1pm.) The **medical center** (☎22840 31 315) should be on your left. There's an **OTE** 50m down the road back to Kamares on the right. (☎22840 31 699 or 22840 33 499. Open daily 7:30am-2:30pm.) The **Billiard Cafe,** on the road out of Apollonia to the right, offers **Internet access.** (€5.50 per hr. Open daily 11am-midnight.) The **post office** is in the main plateia and offers all services. (☎22840 31 329. Open M-F 7:30am-2pm.) **Postal code:** 84003.

ACCOMMODATIONS. Summer vacancies are rare in Apollonia. Plans for the months of July and August in particular are best made as far in advance as possible. **Nikoleta Rooms ❹,** across from the Eko gas station, offers quiet, clean rooms with balconies overlooking the city and the sea. Added perks include TVs, A/C, kitchenettes, phones, and private baths. (☎22840 71 348. Doubles €35-53.) Located in the heart of the village, **Sifnos Hotel ❹** has spacious, inviting rooms with little carpets and colored bedspreads. It's close but not too close to the town's nightlife. (☎22840 31 624. TV, A/C, fridge, and private bath. Doubles €39-69, depending on the season. MC/V) **Hotel Sofia ❸** is just off the plateia; head up the wide paved road from the main plateia until you see it on your left, above the supermarket with the same name. (☎22840 31 238. TV, A/C, fridge, and private bath. Doubles €36-45.) **Hotel Anthousa ❸,** on the mountain road to Artemonas and above the pastry shop around the corner from the main plateia, offers A/C, TVs, fridges, private baths, and phones in very clean rooms. (☎22840 31 431; fax 22840 32 220. Self-service laundry €12. Singles €30-40; doubles €40-50. MC/V)

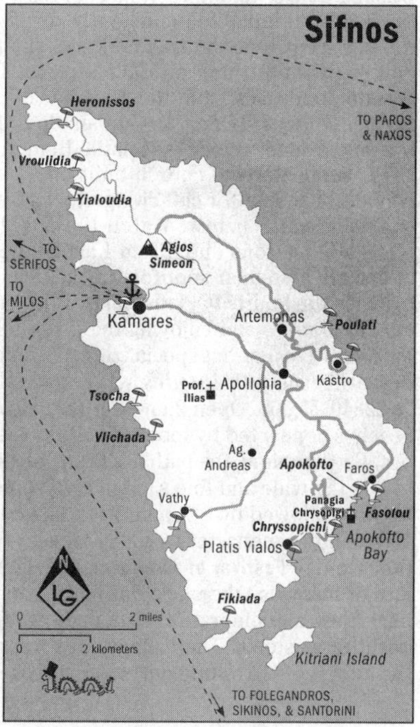

FOOD AND NIGHTLIFE. For the most part, restaurants are excellent—and not as expensive as their beautiful exteriors suggest. The better tavernas are along the path across from the police. Beginning at the top of what is called Apollonia's *stenodthromos* (narrow road, ultimately leading down to the plateia), **Apostolos ❷** ladles it up along with years of wisdom about the island. Both the fricassee of goat and rice in a ceramic pot (€6.50) and the *arnaki mastelo* (lamb with red wine and dill; €8.50) define true classics. (Open 4pm-1:30am. MC/V) **Vegera ❶,** on the road to Artemonas, just before the National Bank, brews strong coffee and makes crepes (€3.50-5) on a veranda, pleasant for viewing one of the island's spellbinding sunsets. The caramel cake is sinfully delicious. (☎22840 33 385. Open daily 9am-3am.) Across the street from Apostolos, the restaurant at the **Sifnos Hotel ❷** serves the island specialty, *revithada* (€4.50), on Sundays. *Imam baldi* (eggplant baked with onions and tomato; €4.50) is another favorite. (☎22840 31 624. Open 8am-1am. MC/V)

Stroll along the street behind Hotel Anthousa to tap into the Sifniot nightlife. **Bodzti,** a popular cafe-bar, on the *stenodthromos* down from Apostolos and Sifnos, closer to the plateia, is likely to catch your eye and ear: candles light up both levels and the outside terraces the trip-hop beats your eardrum. (Drinks €5-7. Open nightly 4pm-3am.) For a few good beers or more sophisticated prosciutto with melon (€10.50), stop by **Okiyialos** (next to Apostolos, open daily 7pm-2am), which serves more than 40 kinds of ale and lager. Live Greek music plays every night until sunrise at the local hangout **Aloni.** Take the road about 75m toward Artemonas to get there. The **Camel Club** (open 9pm-4am or later), up the road toward Platis Yialos past the Eko gas station, blares international tunes.

DAYTRIPS. Travel in Sifnos is easy with the assistance of maps available at kiosks, bookstores, travel agencies, and tourist offices (€1.30). Pack a picnic to nibble on as you explore Apollonia's neighboring hillside villages. The quiet but expansive village of **Artemonas,** 1.5km from Apollonia (about a 10min. walk) boasts a magnificent view and several fine mansions built by Greek aristocrat refugees from Alexandria. The enchanting village of **Kastro,** 2km east of Apollonia, can be reached by bus (10min., €0.80) or on foot (take a shortcut via the stone path about 300m along the paved road). This cluster of whitewashed houses and narrow streets rests on a mountain facing the ocean. Kastro has been inhabited constantly for five millennia and the architecture has not changed since the 14th century. The tiny **Archaeological Museum** lies at the center of the former capital's streets. There you will find clay figurines of female goddesses from the Mycenaean period and the head of a remarkable archaic *kouros*. (Open Tu-Su 8am-3pm. Free.) There are no hotels in Kastro, but ask around to locate **domatia**. Behind Kastro and below the tiny Epta Martires **(Seven Martyrs)** church built on a naked, elevated rock, you can find the island's best spot for **cliff diving.** Rocks form natural platforms for jumping into the deep water below. Watch the weather; foolish courage and rough seas make a dangerous duo. From Kastro, the footpath leads to the sparkling cove at **Poulati,** a popular spot for snorkeling.

Buses run hourly to **Platis Yialos,** 12km from Apollonia, where you'll find locals sipping frappés and enjoying the beautiful views. For a delicious meal, head to **Kalimera,** a restaurant specializing in French and Greek cuisine as well as sugary desserts. The *gahliatelles* with smoked salmon (€9) are particularly good. (☎22840 71 365. Open 9am-midnight.) To the south, **Faros** has several popular beaches connected by footpaths. Busy **Fasolou** and **Apokofto** beaches have tavernas. Farther along the path is the striking **Panagia Chrysopigi Monastery** (and next to it is the wide and fine-sanded Chrysopigi beach), accessible by the Platis Yialos bus followed by a 10min. walk down toward the sea. A bridge connects the 17th-century monastery's rocky islet to the mainland. Forty days after Easter, the two-day **Festival of Analipsos** is celebrated at Chrysopigi. Other renowned Sifniot festivals take place during the summer (one in July and four in September); they all celebrate the namedays of their respective saints and maintain beautiful customs. The Panagyri festival at Chrysopigi is the largest. Inquire at the tourist office to find out when you can join in the fun.

SERIFOS Σεριφος

Stony Serifos gets its name from mythology. After Perseus hunted down the Medusa and turned her shocking ugliness against her with a mirror, he took her head back to King Polydictes of Serifos. When he found the monarch putting the moves on his mother, Danae, irate Perseus flashed Medusa's head at Polydictes, turning his royal court (and the island) to stone. Serifos, the most ruggedly romantic of the Cyclades, is one of the smallest islands in the archipelago but has a topographical scale fit for the Rockies or Alps. Sitting above crumbling Kastro, you can take in from a distance the breathtaking panorama of Serifos: the fertile arc of the port to the mining-ravaged hills and untouched beaches. Poor roads confine the great majority of Athenian vacationers to the port, leaving the rest of the island blissfully undiscovered.

LIVADI Λιβαδι ☎22810

Livadi, Serifos's port, keeps visitors rested and full for daytime trips to other island destinations. This town has reached a good level of tourism—it boasts all the amenities a traveler might desire but lacks the hordes than drive them insane. Hora, the island's other main town, hangs above the port; you can hike there (30min.) or catch one of the frequent buses (€0.90).

TRANSPORTATION AND PRACTICAL INFORMATION

A walk along the waterfront takes you past the most important services offered on the island. An island map that lists useful phone numbers can be purchased at kiosks (€1.50). Regular **ferries** from Piraeus and other western Cyclades arrive in Serifos. From Serifos, ferries travel to: **Folegandros** (5½hr., 1 per week, €9.10); **Ios** (6hr., M, €10.80); **Kimolos** (2½hr., 6 per week, €6.80); **Kithnos** (1¼hr., F, €6.30); **Milos** (2¼hr., 1-3 per day, €6); **Piraeus** (4½hr., 1-3 per day, €13.80); **Santorini** (7hr., 2 per week, €14.30); **Sifnos** (45min., 1-3 per day, €5.10); **Sikinos** (6½hr., 2 per week, €10.20). **Catamarans**—paying twice as much gets you moving twice as fast—go once per day to **Milos, Kimolos, Piraeus,** and **Sifnos. Buses** travel from Livadi to **Hora** (14 per day, 8am-10:30pm; €0.90); a return bus follows the same schedule with a 15min. delay. Another bus (Tu, Th, Sa-Su) travels to the beach towns of **Megalo Livadi** and **Koutalas.** Buses also go to the **monastery** daily, waiting 30min. before rumbling back to Livadi. For exact departure times, consult the schedule posted at the bus stop (on your left, directly across from the second newsstand you pass on the way from the ferry landing to town). **Krinas Travel,** your first left as you walk away from the dock, rents **cars** (€30-50 per day) and **mopeds** (€12-20) at the most competitive prices on the island. (☎22810 51 500; fax 22810 51 073. Open daily 9am-11pm.) For **taxis,** call either ☎22810 51 245, 22810 51 435, or the drivers' cell phones directly (☎69324 31 114, 69738 01 051, 69444 73 044, and 69449 08 637).

Apiliotis Travel, on the waterfront, inset on the left just before the butcher shop/fruit market, sells hydrofoil and ferry tickets and has English schedules. (☎22810 51 155. Open daily 9am-2pm and 6-8:30pm.) The **Alpha Bank,** on the waterfront up the second flight of stairs on your left, has a 24hr. **ATM.** (☎22810 51 780 or 51 739. Open M-Th 8am-2pm, F 8am-1:30pm.) The **port police** (☎22810 51 470) are up the narrower first flight of steps. For 24hr. **police,** dial ☎22810 51 300. To get to the **pharmacy,** take a left after the first supermarket from the dock, walk past the bakery, take a right, and proceed about 30m. (☎22810 51 205. Open M-F 9am-2pm, Sa 10am-2pm.) Drop off your dirty clothes at **Oreo Mou Plintirio Laundromat** (☎69749 07 586; open 10am-2pm and 6-10pm), located right above Krinas Travel. **Internet** access can be found at **Vitamine C.** (☎22810 79 352; vitamine@hol.gr. €3 per hr. Open 8am-1:30am.) **Postal code:** 84005.

ACCOMMODATIONS AND FOOD

Though small in size, Livadi is big on rooming options. **Hotel Areti ❹,** up the hill (take the 1st left from the dock then continue about 60m to the end of a one-way road) has a harbor view, a backyard terrace, private balconies, A/C, and fridges. (☎22810 51 479 or 51 107; fax 22810 51 547. Breakfast €5. Open Apr.-Oct. Singles €30-50; doubles €46-64; elegant studio quads €50-90.) **Hotel Serifos Beach ❸** is away from the main strip, a block back from the beach and under a large blue sign on the main waterfront road. Rooms are quiet and comfortable. (☎22810 51 209 or 51 468. Free port shuttle available. Breakfast €7.50. Singles €33-41; doubles €40-50.) For a splurge, head to **Asteri Hotel ❺,** located on the beach. Rooms are spacious and have sea views along with A/C, TV, and fridge. (☎22810 51 789; www.asteri.gr. Doubles €75-100; triples €90-120.) To walk to **Alexandros-Vassilias ❹,** located on Livadakia beach, take an immediate left when you get off the boat. Bear left and follow the road up the hill for about 500m. You will eventually come to a fork in the path. Take the left and you will get to this clean, pretty establishment hidden among beautiful flowers. Its four-person studios with divided rooms (€70-90) are perfect for families. (☎22810 51 903. Doubles €30-50; triples €47-72.) The **Coralli Campgrounds ❶**, popular with backpackers, lie 20m from Livadakia beach and 700m left of the port. Call for the free minibus or take the right at the aforementioned fork and continue toward the Coralli flags. Bungalows have TVs, A/C, fridges, and private baths. Grounds have a mini-market, laundry facilities, swimming pool, common kitchen, and small restaurant. (☎22810 51 500; www.coralli.gr. €5.50 per adult, €2 for children 10 and under; €5.50 per tent. Singles €24-25; doubles €39-60; triples €47-70; quads €57-84.)

For the ripest fruit on the island, go to **Frutopoleio O Petros ❶** (also a butcher's shop inside), next door to Apiliotis Travel. It has to-die-for apricots (€7 per kg) and local oranges (€1 per kg). Restaurants and cafes spring from hotels and line the waterfront. For an inexpensive, stick-to-your-ribs meal, head to **Stamadis ❶**, the locals' choice, at the right end of the waterfront on the beach. The stuffed vine leaves (€3.50) and rabbit casserole with onions (€5.30) are delightful. Meatless stuffed peppers (€3.20) and boiled zucchini with lemon (€2) provide good vegetarian alternatives. (☎22810 51 309 or 51 729. Open daily 8am-1am). Visit **Vitamine C ❷**, near the Hotel Serifos Beach (see above), for a breakfast sandwich (€5.30). The restaurant at **Hotel Anna ❷** serves a Greek and Italian menu. Penne with eggplant, mushrooms, and tomatoes (€5) does the trick. (☎22810 51 666 or 51 484; fax 22810 51 277. Meat dishes €11. Open daily 6:30am-2am.)

NIGHTLIFE AND BEACHES

Karnayia, just on the waterfront, a few doors past Hotel Anna and before Vitamine C (look for the red chair), blasts classic tunes from the 70s and 80s. (Cocktails €6.50. Open daily 9am-3am.) **Hook** is a rooftop dance club, next door to Vitamine C, playing a mix of American Top 40 and Greek hits. Look for its red sign and large globular patio lights. (Drinks €3-7. Open daily 11pm-late.) During Happy Hour (5-8pm) before the dancing starts at Hook, the **Yacht Club,** 50m down the waterfront, past Serifos Beach Hotel, hosts pre-party chilling on a porch overlooking the water. Shots, cocktails, or beers readily flow from the nautical bar inside. (☎22810 51 888. Drinks €3.50-7; shots €1. Open 5pm-3am.)

Serifos has many secluded sandy **beaches** awaiting your lone footprints. Follow the signs to the right of the waterfront for the 2km walk to **Psili Amos.** In a calm bay at the base of a mountain, this quiet beach has a single taverna. To reach unnamed beaches, follow the paved and dirt roads of northern Serifos. For those without a vehicle or swift-footed mule, a bus travels once daily to **Mega Livadi** and **Koutalas.**

DAYTRIPS FROM LIVADI

HORA Χωρα

The 40min. walk from Livadi begins at a stone staircase next to the Marinos market and then continues straight up. Attempt it in the more pleasant morning or early evening. Alternatively the hourly bus from Livadi stops in Hora.

Hora with its whitewashed houses tumbling down the hill like a handful of white dice is postcard perfect. Those less keen on hiking can catch the hourly bus and get deposited by Serifos's only **post office** (☎22810 51 239; open M-F 7:30am-noon) and **OTE** (☎22810 51 399) across the street, while the second leaves you in front of a well-stocked **supermarket** and a few **tavernas.** From here you can climb up the first series of steps on your right to the small **chapel** that crowns the town. The crumbling remains of **Kastro** invite you to poke around; follow the signs painted along the numerous steps up. Getting lost in Hora's maze of stony, twisted streets can be even better than actually knowing your way around. You'll discover quiet tavernas and markets along the alleyways. The **Archaeological Museum,** open only during high season, houses artifacts from Hora's Roman years (open M-F 6-9pm, Sa-Su 10am-noon). If you cannot be torn away from this town, **Apanemia Domatia** ❷ (doubles €24-30) are straight across the intersection from the second bus stop, 200m along the mountain path. Other domatia are available in town for similar prices.

NORTHERN SERIFOS

Serifos's interior isn't easily accessible without a car or moped, a map, and excellent driving skills. Taxis will, however, leave and pick you up at a set destination; buses run once or twice a day to the Monastery of the Taxiarchs and to nearby Galani.

Traditional villages, scattered churches, monasteries, and traces of ruins mark the northern part of the island. The **Monastery of the Taxiarchs** (☎22810 51 027), 10km beyond Hora toward Galani, was built in 1400 where a Cypriot icon mysteriously appeared and where it returns whenever removed. The monastery also houses an Egyptian lantern and several Russian relics. Upon entering the church, look up at the frescoes by the doorway. There is also a 17th-century stone plate in the middle of the floor depicting the Byzantine Double Eagle. Between 1600 and the 1940s, 12 to 40 Orthodox monks lived together in this castle-like edifice. Today if you arrive by bus, you may meet the lone monk who has lived here on his own for 30 years. Call ahead to arrange a visit. By foot, the trip takes 2hr.; the monastery and town around the port have no facilities so bring provisions if you choose to hike.

KITHNOS Κυθνος

At dusk local teenagers promenade the horseshoe-shaped perimeter of Kithnos's quaint harbor. The inlet is so well protected by surrounding rocks, that besides the "meltemi" season in August and the few time a day when the ferries arrive, Greeks generally describe it as being *san lathi* (as calm as oil). It's safe to say that the local attitude follows suit—Kithnos's locals are famously laid-back and welcoming, embodying simple small town life. Nothing else makes Kithnos stick out among its neighbors except for Kolona beach, thought by some to be one of the most beautiful in the Cyclades.

MERIHAS Μεριχας ☎22810

The main port of the island, Merihas harbors most of the island's tourists in addition to its ferry landing. Making it your base of operations will help you explore the rest of Kithnos.

TRANSPORTATION AND PRACTICAL INFORMATION

The port town offers an abundance of rooms to let, a few tavernas and businesses, and several waterfront markets. **Ferries** sail to: **Folegandros** (6hr., 2 per week, €12.70); **Kea** (1½hr., 3 per week, €5.40); **Kimolos** (3hr., 5 per week, €8.10); **Milos** (4hr., 2 per day, €8.50); **Piraeus** (3hr., 1-2 per day, €10.90); **Santorini** (8hr., 2 per week, €17.40); **Serifos** (1¼hr., 1-2 per day, €6.30); **Sifnos** (2½hr., daily, €6.80); **Sikinos** (7hr., 2 per week, €13.40); **Syros** (2½hr., 2 per week, €6.70). **Catamarans** dash to: **Mykonos** (1½hr., 6 per week, €19.70); **Rafina** (3½hr., 6 per week, €17.40); **Santorini** (2 per week); **Syros** (1hr., 6 per week, €13.50); **Tinos** (2hr., 6 per week, €21.50) for roughly double the ferry price. Two **buses** stop at the waterfront and go to **Driopis** (30min., on an infrequent schedule); **Hora** (15min.; every 1½hrs., 7:15am-9:15pm); **Loutra** (30min.; every 1½hr., 7:30am-9:30pm). All trips run €1-2; return buses follow a schedule 15min. behind this one. For a **taxi,** call ☎22810 31 272 or 31 407. Especially useful at night, some cellular numbers of individual drivers are ☎6944 743 791, 6944 271 609, and 6944 276 656.

The **tourist office** (☎22810 32 250; open mid-June-Aug. 9:30am-1:30pm and 5:15-9pm) is by the dock. Heading into town from where the boat arrives, take a left and go up the first flight of stairs. On the left is the helpful **Antonis Travel Agency,** with information on rooms and ferries. Cars (€27-65) and mopeds (€10-17) are available to rent. (☎22810 32 104; fax 22810 32 291. Open 9am-2pm and 5-10pm.) Call the **tourist police** at ☎22810 31 201; the **port police** (☎22810 32 290) can help with ferry info. Farther along the waterfront, veering right as if you were going to walk along the beach, a store labeled "Cava" will be on your left; inside a representative of the **National Bank** will not only **exchange currency** and traveler's checks but will also withdraw money from a pint-sized **ATM** machine for a €3 fee. The **pharmacy** is two doors to the left when you are facing Antonis Travel Agency. (Open 8am-2pm and 6-8:30pm.) A **doctor** is available at ☎22810 31 202 or via cell at ☎69775 69 231. **Internet** is available (€3 per hr.) at **Yachting Club Restaurant** (☎22810 31 436) in Loutra. There is **no OTE or post office** in Merihas; the post office is in Hora. **Postal code:** 84006.

ACCOMMODATIONS AND FOOD. The accommodations in the area surround the small beach in town. As you disembark the ferry, look up at the first white building at the top of the town to find **Paradise Rooms ❸.** Its panoramic view of the waterfront compensates for the many stairs that lead there. It also boasts newly renovated rooms equipped with kitchens, A/C, and private bathrooms. (☎22810 32 206. Doubles €35-45.) Continuing along the port about 200m (with the sea on your right), turn left just before the arched mini-bridge to locate a series of **domatia** including **Panayota Rooms To Let ❸.** Spacious, clean rooms are equipped with two or three beds, kitchen, baths, and fridges. Panayota also has four rooms available two buildings to the right of Kythnos Hotel when facing away from the water. (☎22810 32 268. Rooms €25-35.) **Kythnos Hotel ❹** is left of Antonis Travel Agency when facing inland. Rooms with verandas, A/C, TVs, and fridges are simple but comfortable. Its highlight is the chic cafe downstairs. (☎22810 32 247; kythnoshotel@in.gr. Breakfast €5. Doubles €30-45; triples €45-60.) **Bouriti ❸** rooms with kitchenettes and baths are great for families. They can be found by walking along the beach, turning left after Remezzo, and walking past the supermarket; owners may be behind the supermarket counter. (Triples €30-40; quads €50-60.)

Ikos Araps Pizzeria ❶ is on the left corner of the harbor, diagonally across from Cava (with the ATM), and has white plastic chairs beneath a white awning. Local school kids grab ham, cheese, and bacon omelettes (€3.60) before the bus comes, and teenagers with late-night munchies order bowls of macaroni with tomato, meat, and cheese (€5) at the steel counter inside. (☎22810 32 190. Open daily 8am-2:30pm and 7pm-2am.) **Sailors Restaurant ❸,** on the central waterfront, waves flags out in front. Take your pick from its selection of locally caught fresh fish—they're still flopping. Lobster spaghetti (€60 per kg), mixed fish (€15), onion pies (€5), and Kithnos goat cheese croquettes (€4) are specialties. (☎22810 32 056. Open daily 9am-midnight. MC/V.) Two doors down the friendly staff at **Yialos Restaurant ❸** serves traditional home-cooked food (€3.50-10) raved about by locals.

NIGHTLIFE. After dinner bring the crew for ice cream (€5) and/or cocktails (€8) to laid-back **Byzantio Club.** (☎22810 32 259. Open daily 9am-late.) Later you can groove to international tunes literally all night long at **Remezzo,** right next to Yialo on the waterfront. Trek uphill at the right of the harbor to find **Agnanti**—you can't miss colored lights that illuminate the entrance. Ask the DJ to play your favorite song (all the Greeks do), so you can hear the best of both worlds. **Akrotiri**

is the only place in town with a huge outdoor dance floor. Spectators convene on either of the two bars on the multi-tiered balcony. (☎22810 32 755. Beer €3; cocktails €8. Open daily 6-11pm for coffee and ice cream, 11pm-late as a club.)

BEACHES. The road that leads toward the beaches of Hora and Loutra also passes a turn-off for the small town of **Kolona.** After the turn-off, head left before a white building and follow this path until you reach a long beach. Because it is protected from ocean currents, the right side is warm and the left cool (when facing the ocean). **Taverna Loukas** ❷ (open during beach hours, loosely 10am-8pm) sits above the beach, waiting to relieve your hunger and thirst with grilled meat dishes and local wine. A road that heads in the other direction from Merihas takes you past little **Driopis** with its **Folk Museum** and **Byzantine Museum.** (Follow the signs from the church in the main plateia. Both open 10am-2pm and 7-9pm.)

KEA Κεα (Τζια)

The predominant crowd on this verdant island—such lushness is uncharacteristic among the Cyclades—consists of Greeks who return regularly. They come to bask in the well-kept secret that is Kea. Athenian weekenders and other visitors who know to escape the main port discover the island's preserved beauty. Lofty oak-covered mountains harbor Ioulida, the island capital seemingly frozen in time. *Ammouthitses* (little sandy coves) speckle the island's perimeter.

KORISSIA Κορισσια ☎22880

Falling short in terms of aesthetics and vitality, the main port seriously trumps the rest of the island in terms of immediate utility. Take advantage of its car rentals, bus schedules, taxi contacts, and information on accommodations.

From Kea, **ferries** depart for: **Lavrio** (1¼hr.; M-F 3 per day, Sa-Su 5 per day; €6) and **Kithnos** (1½hr., 1 per week, €6). **Catamarans,** costing roughly twice as much, zip passengers to **Kithnos** once daily. The new **Flying Cat** ticket office is directly across from the ferry landing. Tickets for normal ferries can be purchased at the **ticket office,** a few doors to the left and next to Yiannis Rent a Car. Two **buses** (€1-2) travel to: **Ioulida** (12min., 5 per day); **Katomeria** (3 per day); **Otzias beach** (3 per day); **Pisses beach** (3 per day); **Vourkari** (7min., 5 per day). Schedules for times and stops are posted at the main stop directly in front of the landing dock in Korissia. **Taxis** line up here; reach them individually. (☎69730 12 813, 69373 82 702, 69773 31 431. €5 to Ioulida; €4 to Vourkari.) Although prices are steep, travelers looking to explore multiple beaches should consider renting a car. **Yiannis Rent a Car** is on your right before the ticket office as you are walking away from the dock. (☎22880 21 898 or 69326 23 150. €40-50 per day. AmEx/MC/V.)

In the Flying Dolphin ticket office across from the landing, you will find Stephanos Lepouros, who is capable of answering any logistical question you have about the island—he has written multiple guidebooks and is also the owner of **Stegathi Bookshop** (☎22880 21 435; lepoura@pel.forthnet.gr). Mr. Lepouros does **currency exchange.** The **tourist police** (☎22880 21 100) are located on the right, two blocks away from the dock. The **port police** (☎22880 21 344) are across from the beach's center. A **National Bank ATM** is a short distance down the waterfront from the ticket office; **Alpha Bank** is one block down on the left and **Piraeus Bank** 200m left of Karthea Hotel. **Our Tzia Laundromat** has dry cleaning. To get there, continue from Piraeus Bank along the bay, make a right at the far side of the river, and turn left after 100m. (☎22880 21 154. Open M-Sa 8am-1pm.) **Internet** access is available at **Art Cafe** (☎22880 21 181; elio@sound.gr) on the waterfront next to the National

Bank ATM (€2.50 for first 30min., rates decrease for longer time increments). The **medical clinic** is in in Ioulida and can be reached at ☎22880 22 200. The **pharmacy** is also located in Ioulida. (☎22880 22 277 or 69455 47 567. Open M 9am-2pm; Tu, Th-F 9am-2pm and 6-9pm; Sa 10am-1pm; Su 10am-2pm.) **Postal code:** 84002.

Korissia boasts most of Kea's accommodations which, coupled with its amenities found nowhere else on the island, makes it a good base. The first hotel on the bay's corner is **Hotel Karthea** ❸ (☎22880 21 204), in an angular, modern building with clean but unexciting singles (€40) and doubles (€50) with private bath, A/C, and TV. Half of the rooms have bay views. Past Piraeus Bank, turn right on the near side of the "river" (a stream of water trickling toward the ocean), walk 120m, and look on your right to find **Domatia Athina** ❷ (☎22880 21 175 or 21 467). It has doubles with kitchenettes and private baths (€30). Farther down, **Hotel Korissia** ❸ is partially hidden from the main road by reeds. It has colorful rooms with TV, A/C, private baths, and verandas. (☎22880 21 484. Doubles €50-55; triples €60-65. AmEx/MC/V.) Past the school yard is slightly older **Hotel Tzia** (☎22880 21 305) with doubles with private baths and terraces that open onto the beach (€45-52). **Camping Kea,** 50m from Pisses beach, is about 30min. by bus from Korissia. It has a mini-market, laundry facilities, and common baths. Pine trees shade a nearby taverna. (☎22880 31 302, 31 303, 31 304, or 69443 87 834. €4.40 per person, €4.40 per tent.)

Kafeneion To Akrogiali ❶**,** left of the ferry landing, serves sandwiches (€4.50) and sweets like local specialty *ekmek pagoto* (€2.40), made of sweet cream and ice cream. (☎22880 21 493. Open 8am-1am.) **Akri** ❷ (☎22880 21 196 or 69775 74 957), after the supermarkets at the start of the beachside road, serves delicious homemade food like *strapatsiata* (tomato, egg, and cheese casserole; €3.50).

IOULIDA Ιουλιδα (Χωρα) ☎22880

Steep, windy-pathed Ioulida (also known as Hora), perched on a rocky and arid orifice, overlooks lush ravines of oak trees and stores Kea's history and heart.

The **Lion of Kea** is a sculpture, surrounded by white-washed stones, thought to have been carved by Kean men in the 6th century BC to ward off evil nymphs who were harming and killing their wives. It lies 1.5km northeast of Ioulida (about a 10min. walk). Follow the main road leading northeast out of town past Agios Spyridon church and bear left when the road veers right; continue down that path until you reach a metal gate; down the stairs you'll find the rock sculpture you've come to see. Shaded by pine trees, **Pisses beach** (30min. from Korissia by bus) has emerald-tinted waters. Family-run taverna **Christophoros** ❶ (☎22880 31 308) specializes in *souzoukakia* (spiced meat balls; €5). Crickets hum from the trees and shrubs around **Otzias beach,** 3km from Vourkari and about 15min. by bus from Korissia, famously clean due to changing tides.

The port town of **Vourkari,** about 7min. by bus from Korissia, is a hotspot for young, wealthy Athenians with massive sailboats. Let the chic main strip provide the backdrop for your night; lounge on the terraces of cafe and bar **Vinilio** (☎22880 21 080), on your right as you enter town, or at **Brachera** (☎22880 21 940) where you can enjoy a cool *karpousi* watermelon cocktail (€7). Both are open roughly 9pm-3am. Brand-new **Koundouros Beach Bar,** on the beach about 40min. outside of Korissia, blares a mix of the Greek and foreign music of the moment, serving up Nescafé with Kahlua (€3) and Mai Tais (€8) until (or even after) sunrise.

From the bus stop go through the stone arch and bear right. A **National Bank ATM** is 200m up on the left, by the supermarket. Climbing the stairs to the right of the bus stop and then following the signs, you'll find the **pharmacy.** (☎22880 22 277 or 69455 47 567. Open M, W 9am-2pm; Tu, Th-F 9am-2pm and 6-9pm; Sa 10am-1pm; Su 10am-2pm.) The **post office** sits between the bus drop-off and the ATM, about 150m up the hill. (☎22880 22 325. Open M-F 9am-1pm.) **Postal code:** 84002.

Ioulida has no true hotels and few **domatia.** Up the hill, past the post office on the right, **Filoxenia** ❷ (☎22880 22 057) is a godsend. Four charming, traditional rooms have very clean bathrooms. (Double €30; triple €40-45; quads €50-60.) The narrow streets of Ioulida hide many culinary gems including **En Lefki** ❶, a hip cafe serving grilled sandwiches (€2.50), interesting *karithopites* (warm walnut pie with ice cream; €4.20), and *milopites* (similar to *karithopites* but with apple; €4.20) on a wide terrace overlooking both mountains and sea. Find live music here on some nights and spirited owners daily. (☎22880 22 155. Open daily 8am-1:30am.) **Kalofagadon** ❶ next door has a similar view and also serves delicious food. (Whole eggplant, topped with minced meat and bechemel sauce €5.95. Pumpkin in lemon sauce €5.60. Stewed okra €4.70. Open daily 11am-1am.)

IONIAN ISLANDS

Νησια Του Ιονιου

Just to the west of mainland Greece, the Ionian Islands exude an air of mystery etched into their rugged mountains, patchwork farmland, shimmering olive groves, and pristine beaches, all surrounded by an endless expanse of turquoise sea. Rapacious invaders have conquered and re-conquered these islands: Venetians, British, French, and Russians have all left cultural and architectural fingerprints. Today the islands are a favorite among Western Europeans and ferry-hopping backpackers heading to Italy. Multicultural for millennia, each of the Ionian Islands maintains a unique identity while sharing an unparalleled beauty.

HIGHLIGHTS OF THE IONIAN ISLANDS

PARK YOUR YACHT and stroll past the rainbow array of Neoclassical buildings of Fiskardo on Kephalonia (p. 468).

SUBMIT TO THE MATING RITUALS of party animals at Corfu's Pink Palace (p. 451).

WASH ASHORE on the beaches of Ithaka, Odysseus's kingdom (p. 458).

CORFU Κερκυρα

Homer first sang Corfu's praise, writing of its "honeyed fig," "unctuous olive," and "boisterous waves;" since then, Goethe, Wilde, the Durrell brothers, Sisley, and Lear have all thrown in their own two cents about Corfu's perfection. Handed down from the Franks to the Venetians to the British to today's tourist hordes, Corfu (Κερκυρα, KEHR-kee-rah) has captivated them all. As in most of Greece's beautiful places, those who stray from the beaten path encounter uncrowded, unspoiled beaches. Try the less frenetic resorts at Pelekas, Kalami, or Agios Stefanos, or make Corfu Town your daytripping base. Regardless of where you set up camp, even the most skeptical visitor will begin to understand the Homeric fuss.

CORFU TOWN ☎26610

Corfu Town flutters with activity both day and night. Techno-blasting Peugots yield to horse-drawn carriages on winding roads that balance an antiquated Venetian feel with a modernizing Greek culture. When in Corfu Town, give yourself half a day to get lost. Focus on the peripheral: laundry lines stretching from ornate iron balconies, yellow roses, Venetian buildings, and green-shuttered alleyways all exhibit the area's most genuine flavors.

TRANSPORTATION

Flights: Olympic Airways, Iak. Polila 11 (☎26610 38 694; reservations ☎26610 38 695). From the post office, walk 1 block on Rizopaston Voulefton toward the Old City and turn right. Open M-F 7:30am-7:30pm. Flights to: **Athens** (1hr., 4-5 per day, €80-

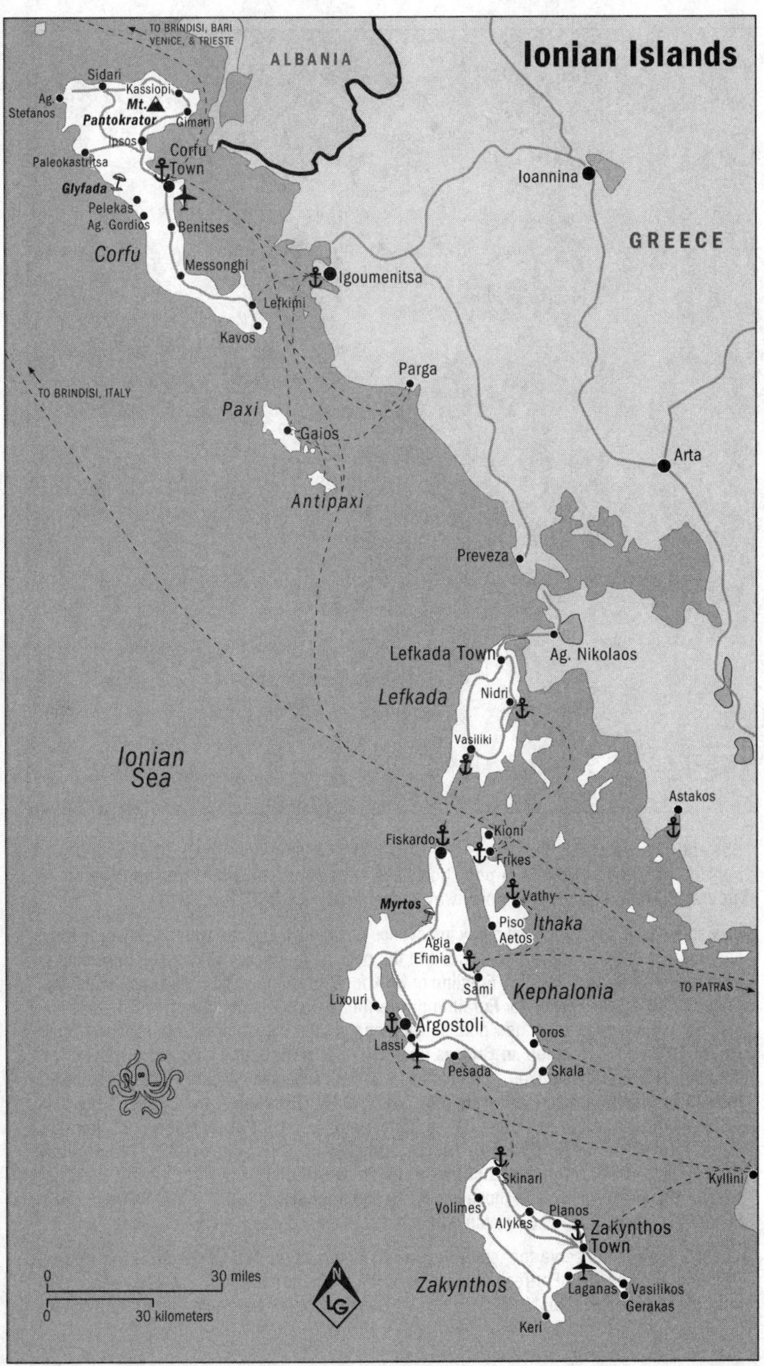
Ionian Islands
TO BRINDISI, BARI VENICE, & TRIESTE
ALBANIA
GREECE
Sidari
Kassiopi
Ag. Stefanos
Mt. Pantokrator
Gimari
Ipsos
Corfu Town
Paleokastritsa
Glyfada
Pelekas
Ag. Gordios
Benitses
Corfu
Messonghi
Igoumenitsa
Lefkimi
Kavos
Ioannina
TO BRINDISI, ITALY
Parga
Paxi
Gaios
Antipaxi
Arta
Preveza
Lefkada Town
Ag. Nikolaos
Lefkada
Nidri
Vasiliki
Ionian Sea
Astakos
Fiskardo
Kioni
Frikes
Vathy
Myrtos
Piso Aetos
Ithaka
Agia Efimia
Sami
Kephalonia
TO PATRAS
Lixouri
Argostoli
Poros
Lassi
Pesada
Skala
Skinari
Kyllini
Volimes
Planos
Alykes
Zakynthos Town
Zakynthos
Laganas
Vasilikos
Gerakas
Keri
0
30 miles
0
30 kilometers

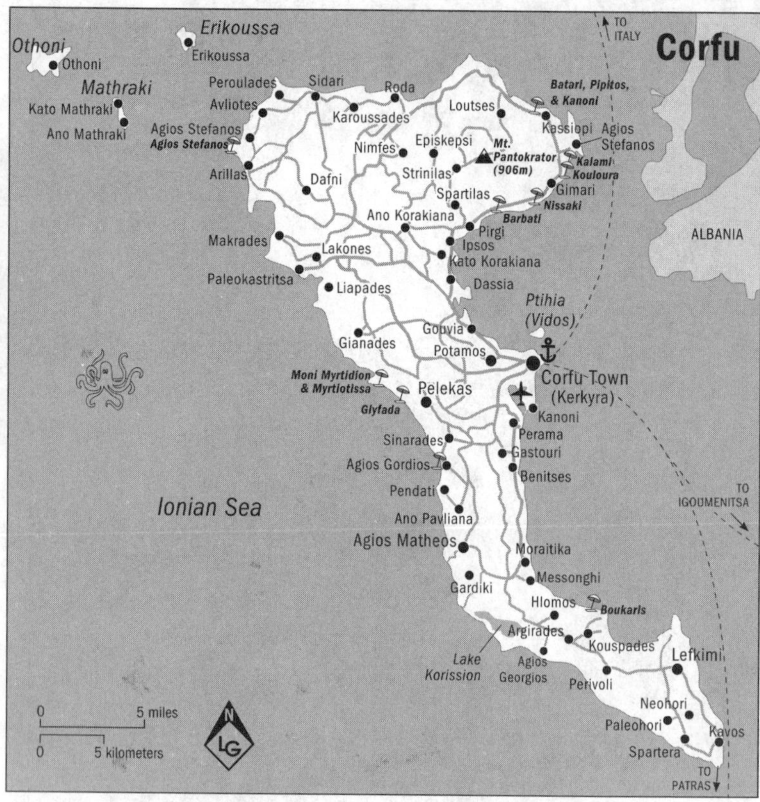

95) and **Thessaloniki** (1hr.; Tu, F, Su; €80-100). In summer, almost 50 charter flights per day fly through Corfu's airport; book 2-3 days ahead. A 5min. taxi ride (agree on around €8 beforehand) is the only way to the **airport** (☎26610 33 811).

Ferries: Get your tickets at least a day in advance during high season; when traveling to **Italy,** find out if the port tax (€5-6) is included in the price of your ticket. Prices vary according to season, ferry line, and class. Try **Fragline** or **HML** for **Brindisi** and **Strindzis Lines** for **Venice.** Check at **Blue Star Ferries** for **Eurail** and **InterRail** passes. Shipping company agents line Xen. Stratigou, opposite the new port, so shop here for the lowest fares. **International Tours** (☎26610 39 007) and **Ionian Cruises** (☎26610 31 649), both located across the street from the Old Port on Venizelou, can help you with your scheduling woes. Ferries to: **Ancona, Italy** (20hr., daily, €58); **Bari, Italy** (9hr., daily, €46); **Brindisi, Italy** (6-7hr., 3 per day, €30); **Igoumenitsa** (1½hr.; 8 per day, 6:30am-9pm; €5.10); **Patras** (6-7hr., 1-2 per day, €25); **Paxi** (5 per week, €12.90); **Trieste, Italy** (24hr., 4 per week, €52); **Venice, Italy** (24hr., daily, €57). High-speed **catamarans** go to **Brindisi, Italy** (4hr.; 9am; check for prices, up to 30% discount for those under 26) and **Kephalonia** (3hr., W and Sa 9am, €38). Schedules vary and some routes run only in high season, so check before planning your trip.

Buses: 2 main lines serve the island: **green KTEL buses** (☎26610 39 862), between I. Theotoki and the New Fortress (accessible from I. Theotoki or Xen. Stratigou) and **blue municipal buses** (☎26610 37 595), at Pl. San Rocco. For a detailed green bus schedule with return times and prices, ask at the white info kiosk at the station (open 6am-8pm); equally detailed blue bus schedules are available at the ticket kiosk window in Pl. San Rocco (open 6:30am-10pm).

Green buses: Agios Gordios (45min.; M-Sa 5 per day, 8:15am-8pm; Su 3 per day, 9:30am-3:30pm; €1.50); **Agios Stefanos** (1½hr.; M-Sa 6 per day, 5:30am-7:30pm; Su 9:30am; €2.60); **Barbati** (45min.; 9am, 6:30pm; €1.50); **Glyfada** (45min.; M-Sa 6 per day, 6:45am-8pm; Su 4 per day, 9am-4pm; €1.50); **Ipsos** and **Pirgi** (30min.; M-F 10 per day, 7am-8pm; Sa 7 per day, 9am-6:30pm; Su 9:30am; €1); **Kassiopi** (1hr.; M-Sa 6 per day, 5:45am-4pm; Su 9:30; €2.40); **Kavos** (1½hr.; M-F 11 per day, 5am-7:30pm; Sa 8 per day, 5am-7:30pm; Su 4 per day, 9am-7:30pm; €3); **Messonghi** (45min.; M-Sa 5 per day, 9am-3:30pm; Su 4 per day, 9am-7:30pm; €1.50); **Paleokastritsa** (45min.; M-Sa 7 per day, 8:30am-6pm; Su 5 per day, 9am-4pm; €1.60); **Sidari** (1hr.; M-Sa 8 per day, 5:30am-7:30pm; Su 9:30am; €2.20). Buy tickets on board. **KTEL** also runs buses to **Athens** (9hr.; 8:45am, 1:45, 7:15pm; €29.50) and **Thessaloniki** (9hr., 6:45am, €28.50); prices include ferry. Buy tickets at green bus station.

Blue buses: #10 to **Achilleon** (30min.; M-Sa 6 per day, 7am-8pm; Su 4 per day, 9am-8pm; €0.85); **#6** to **Benitses** (25min.; 13 per day, 6:45am-10pm; €0.85); **#8** to **Ioannis** and **Aqualand** (30min.; 13 per day, 6:15am-10pm; €0.85); **#2** to **Kanoni** (M-F 2 per hr.; Sa 1 per hr., 2:30-9:30pm; Su 1 per hr., 9:30am-9:30pm; €0.60); **#11** to **Pelekas** (30min.; M-F 7 per day, 7am-8:30pm; Sa 2:15, 5, 8pm; Su 10am, noon, 5, 8pm; €0.85). Buy tickets at the kiosk.

Taxis: ☎26610 33 811. At the new and old ports, the Spianada, Pl. San Rocco, and G. Theotoki. Taxis respond to calls 24hr.

Car Rental: A small car starts at €55-60 per day, but price varies by season. Ask if price includes 20% tax, 3rd-party insurance, and mileage over 200km. Both **Europcar** (☎26610 46 931; www.europecar.com.gr; AmEx/MC/V) and **InterCorfu Rent a Car** (☎26610 93 607), on the water at the new port, offer reasonable rates.

Moped Rental: Travelers should note that many roads, especially those remote from Corfu Town, are not well-paved and present serious risk to moped drivers. With this in mind, you can rent from a place on Xen. Strategiou, near customs. You shouldn't have to pay more than €25 per day. Make sure the brakes work and get a helmet. Rental fee should include 3rd-party liability and property damage insurance.

ORIENTATION AND PRACTICAL INFORMATION

Befuddling alleys and ubiquitous waters may add to the charm of Corfu Town, but they can also cause stress for anyone with a plane or ferry to catch. Most visiting Corfu Town arrive in the **New Port,** which sits adjacent to the **Old Port** on the northern coast of the town. The **New Fortress** is the conspicuous edifice by the ports that can provide a good reference point at any time. From the customs house at the New Port, it's about 1km to the center of Corfu Town, known as both **Pl. San Rocco** and **Pl. G. Theotoki.** To get there cross the intersection at the light, turn left, and walk uphill on **Avriamou,** which eventually turns into I. Theotoki. The long driveway for the **KTEL (green) bus terminal** will be on your left as you pass, and the station for the **blue bus terminal** is on the left as you enter the center of town. If you make a left onto **G. Theotoki** (which becomes Ev. Voulgareos), you'll find yourself in the town's social center, a long park known as the **Spianada.** Two streets encircle the Spianada: **Eleftherias** (which runs into **Kapodistriou**) is the street more inland; **Polytechniou** goes around the outside. As you face the Spinada and the **Old Fortress** behind it, a left on Kapodistriou will bring you toward the **Old Town,** the tourist-friendly heart of the historic city. To enter the maze that is the Old Town, just make another left at any straight street above **N. Theotoki.**

Tourist Office: EOT (☎26610 37 520), at the corner of Rizopaston Voulefton and Iak. Polila. The building is marked and a sign directs you up the 1st flight of stairs. **Free maps** and information. Open M-F 8am-1:30pm.

IONIAN ISLANDS

Banks: Banks with 24hr. **ATMs** line the larger streets and the waterfront by the ports. **Ionian Bank** is in Pl. San Rocco in front of Ag. Spyridon in the Old Town; **National Bank** on the corner of Alexandras and Rizopaston Voulefton across from the post office.

Work Opportunities: The Pink Palace (see **Agios Gordios,** p. 451), hires hotel staff, nightclub staff, and DJs. Mail a letter of introduction, a resume, and a photo in advance of arrival. Minimum 2 month commitment required.

Luggage Storage: In the customs building at the new port (€2 per bag per day). Confirm what time you will be returning for your bags. Open 7am-11pm.

International Bookstore: Xenoglosso, Markora 45 (☎26610 23 923). From the police station, make a left onto Markora; the bookstore is on the right. This wonderful collection includes classic novels, books on Greece, and language materials. Open M, W, Sa 8am-2pm; Tu, Th-F 8:30am-2pm and 5-8:30pm.

Laundromat: Snowman (☎26610 46 193), by the entrance to the Old Gate. Wash and dry €11 per 5kg. Open daily 7am-2:30pm and 5:30-9:30pm. **New Port Laundry** (☎26610 23 923), on Eth. Antistaseos near number 12A, has dry cleaning; wash and dry €10 per load. Open M-F 8:30am-2:30pm and 6-9pm, Sa 8:30am-2pm.

Police: ☎26610 39 509. Heading toward the New Port, turn right off I. Theotoki along Pl. San Rocco onto the short street that intersects Markora. Open 24hr. In an **emergency,** dial ☎100. The **tourist police** are located on the 4th floor of the police building. **Maps** available. Open daily 7am-2pm.

Port Police: Contact either the port police (☎26610 30 481), in the customs house at the new port, or the **port authority** (☎26610 32 655 or 26610 40 002). They also provide ferry schedules.

Hospital: Corfu General Hospital (☎26610 88 200 or 26610 45 811), on I. Andreadi. The tourist office or tourist police can help find an English-speaking doctor. For an **ambulance,** call ☎166.

OTE: Mantzarou 3 (☎26610 30 099), off G. Theotoki. Open M-F 7:30am-2pm. Card **phones** on the Spianada, at the post office, and in white mobile buildings at the Old and New Ports.

Internet Access: Netoikos Cafe, Kaloheretou 14 (☎26610 47 479), behind Ag. Spiridon church. €4 per hr. Open daily 9am-midnight. **Cafe Online** (☎26610 46 266), after the McDonald's as you walk along Kapodistriou with the Old Fortress on your left. €6 per hr. Open M-Sa 9:30am-midnight, Su 5:30pm-1am.

Post Office: ☎26610 25 544. On the corner of Alexandras and Voulefton. **Poste Restante** and **currency exchange** available. Open M-F 7:30am-8pm. **Postal code:** 49100.

ACCOMMODATIONS

There's no getting around the fact that Corfu Town is expensive. But even though pricier places tend to lie among conveniently located Dimokratias and Kapodistriou, relatively cheaper accommodations are still available. Monetarily mindful travelers may have better luck with the **Association of Owners of Private Rooms and Apartments in Corfu,** Iak. Polila 24, which has a complete list of rooms in Corfu as well as the phone numbers of the landlords who lease them. (☎26610 26 133. Open M-F 8:30am-2pm and 5:30-8pm.) During high season, give them a ring several weeks prior to your trip to ensure availability. Otherwise, towns and campgrounds just outside the city can often provide a worthwhile alternative.

Hotel Hermes, G. Markora 14 (☎26610 39 268; fax 26610 31 747), around the bend from the police station and by the noisy public market. Has a central location, decent rates, and a verdant entrance to make up for the hotel's minimalist rooms. Singles €28, with bath €33; doubles €33/€44; triples €50. MC/V. ❸

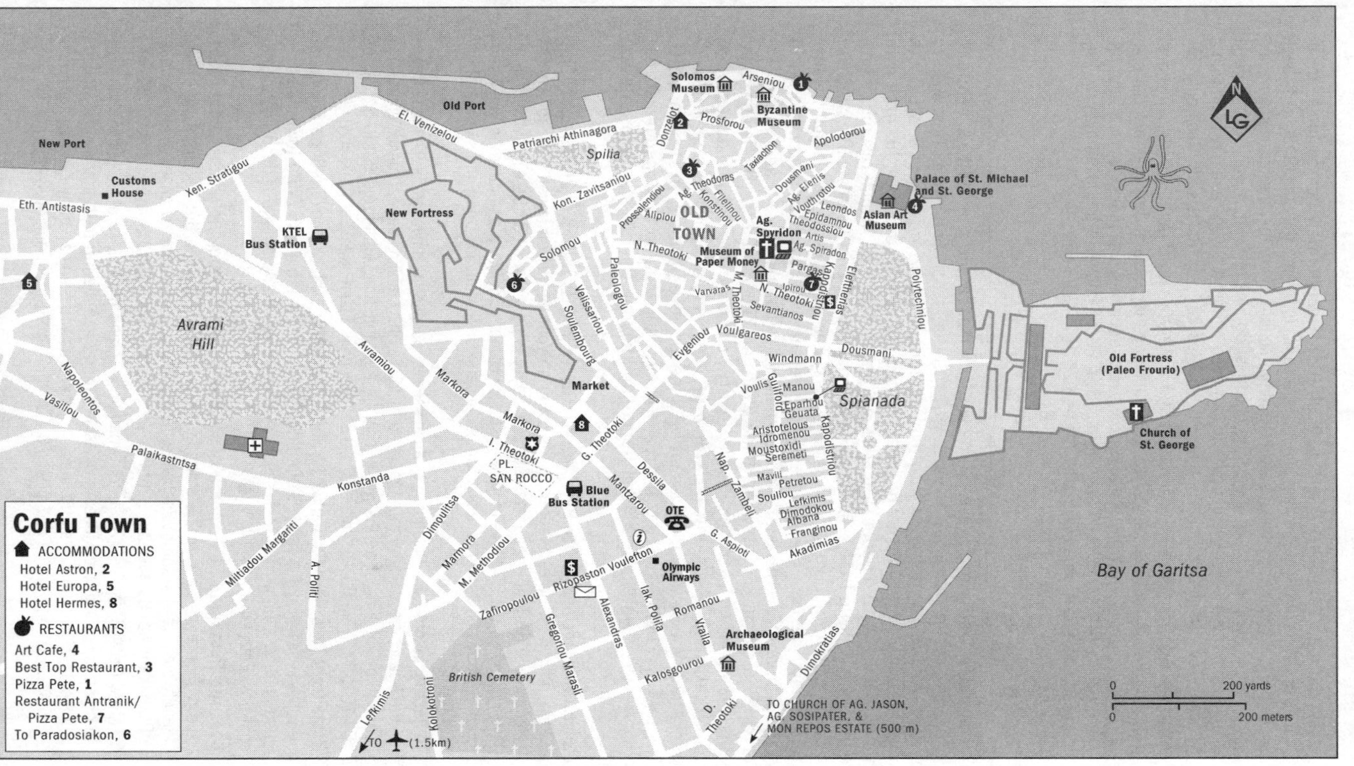
Corfu Town
ACCOMMODATIONS
Hotel Astron, 2
Hotel Europa, 5
Hotel Hermes, 8
RESTAURANTS
Art Cafe, 4
Best Top Restaurant, 3
Pizza Pete, 1
Restaurant Antranik/
Pizza Pete, 7
To Paradosiakon, 6
New Port
Old Port
Customs
House
KTEL
Bus Station
New Fortress
Avrami
Hill
Spilia
OLD
TOWN
Solomos
Museum
Byzantine
Museum
Palace of St. Michael
and St. George
Asian Art
Museum
Ag.
Spyridon
Museum of
Paper Money
Market
Spianada
PL.
SAN ROCCO
Blue
Bus Station
OTE
Olympic
Airways
Archaeological
Museum
British Cemetery
Old Fortress
(Paleo Frourio)
Church of
St. George
Bay of Garitsa
TO CHURCH OF AG. JASON,
AG. SOSIPATER, &
MON REPOS ESTATE (500 m)
TO (1.5km)
0
200 yards
200 meters

Hotel Europa, Giantsilio 10 (☎26610 39 304). From the New Port customs house, cross the main street at the light and make a sharp right onto the street that leads back from the waterfront; Giantsilio is a tiny road on the left, where the road turns sharply left to become Napoleonta. As one of the cheapest options in town, it won't put you in a convenient nor a well-lit location. It will, however, offer you a white and airy room with a decent view. Singles €25, with bath €30; doubles €30-35; triples €36. Cash only. ❷

Hotel Astron, Donzelot 15 (☎26610 39 505 or 39 986; Hotel_Astron@hol.gr), just past the Spilla with the water on your left. The building may have an imperial feel, but spacious rooms hold modern price tags along with amenities, including TVs, fans, and private baths. A/C €6 extra. Breakfast included. Prices inflate to the listed high by Aug. Singles €45-90; doubles €55-100; triples €75-100. Cash only. ❺

FOOD

The premier restaurant areas are near the **Spianada** and the **Old Port.** While in Corfu, if you're carnivorous, experiment with the many meat specialties: *sofrito* (veal stewed in a wine sauce with pepper and garlic), *stifado* (beef stewed with onions), and *pastitsada* (lamb or beef with noodles and tomatoes, flavored with cinnamon, onion, and pepper). Traditional pork *nuombolo*, which resembles prosciutto, can be found at Corfu's famous butcher shops. Corfiot treats like *chadilia* (a dense cake of almonds, pistachios, rose water, and special citrus marmalade) are served at bakeries throughout town. The kumquat plant, introduced to Corfu by the British, fills bottles of "koum kouat" (κουμ κουτ) liqueur and jars of preserves. You can also taste homemade wines and beers all over the island: light white *kakotrygis*, richer white *moscato*, dry *petrokorintho* red, and dark *skopelitiko*. Bottles of light yellow *tsitsibira* (ginger beer) are another imperial holdover. A daily open-air public **market** sells inexpensive produce on Dessila, off G. Theotoki and below the new fortress. (Open daily 6am-2pm.) **Supermarkets** are located on I. Theotoki, in Pl. San Rocco, and beyond the bus station on Alexandras. (Open M-F 8am-9pm, Sa 8am-6pm.)

Restaurant Antranik/Pizza Pete, Arseniou 21 (☎26610 38 858 or 26610 23 301), a 2min. walk past Hotel Astron with the water on your left. If you haven't already stuffed yourself with its renowned pizza (€6 for a small) or *pastitsada* (€7.30), make sure to try 1 (or more) of the 20 types of homemade ice cream (€5-7). As an added bonus, waterfront seating allows you to relish Corfiot sunsets. Open daily in spring and summer 9am-midnight. Cash only. ❷

To Paradosiakon, Odos Solomou 20, on the street opposite the stairs leading to the entrance of the New Fortress. Highly recommended by locals, this small restaurant makes great traditional food for a meal on the run or a relaxed get-together. Appetizers €2.50-6. Entrees €4.10-8.50. Wine €6-13. Coffee €1.50-3. Open daily 11am-midnight. Cash only. ❷

Restaurant Rex, Kapodistriou 66 (☎26610 39 649), 1 block back from the Spianada. The freshest fish make this restaurant one of the most famous in Corfu Town, but they also make it a bit pricey. Their savory *sofrito* (€12.50) and *stifado* (€11.50) are good options. Entrees €7.40-14. V. ❸

Best Top Restaurant, Filellinon 33 (☎26610 24 010). From the plateia at the Spilla end of Donzelot, walk up the stairs to the left; Best Top is in the 2nd little plateia. A friendly staff serves Corfiot specialties and other dishes at cheap prices to the sounds of Greek music. Salads €2-6. Entrees €2.50-12. Open daily 9:30am-midnight. MC. ❷

Art Cafe (☎26610 37 775), in the small park behind the Palace of St. Michael and St. George; as you exit the Museum of Asian Art, keep to the left path that curves around. Join young Corfiot families and chess amateurs as you enjoy an early evening sandwich (€2.10-3.80) and coffee (€1.50-4.10). Open daily 11am-midnight. Cash only. ❶

SIGHTS AND MUSEUMS

After invading Vandals and Goths destroyed ancient Corfu (Paleopolis) in the 5th and 6th centuries AD, Corfiots built a more defensible city between the twin peaks of the Old Fortress. Wary of Ottoman raids, the Venetians strengthened this fortress, constructed the New Fortress, and built thick walls around the growing city. A series of underground tunnels, now closed, connected the Old and New Fortresses and all parts of Corfu Town. They later provided refuge for Corfiots after the first World War II air raids in 1940.

MON REPOS ESTATE. In a grandiose effort to please his Corfiot wife, Sir Frederic Adam mandated the construction of one of the most elegant and expansive estates in Corfu. With the British High Commissioner of the Ionian Islands long since gone, the estate now hosts the intriguing **Museum of Paleopolis,** which forms an eclectic collection of replica period rooms from the palace as well as archaeological finds from excavations around Corfu. Visitors may be especially interested in the ancient version of a cosmetics kit as well as 510 silver Corinthian and Corcylaen coins. Full explanations in English and Greek are provided for each display. *(To reach the palace, head up the path to the right just inside the main gate. Estate open 8am-7pm. Free. Museum open Tu-Su 8:30am-3pm. Free.)* After touring the museum you can venture out into the grounds of the estate to see some of the sites of excavation. From the palace, with the water on your left, follow the forested path overlooking the sea to reach the tiny pebble **Kardaki beach.** Legend has it that anyone who drinks from its spring will remain on the island forever. To the right of the palace as you face the museum entrance, a path leads to two Doric temples, the decrepit **Temple of Hera** and the more impressive **Kardaki Temple,** which is thought to have been dedicated to either Poseidon, Apollo, or Asclepius. *(Take the #2 bus towards Mouse Island; just tell the driver that you want to be dropped off at "Mon Repos." 10min., €0.60.)*

ARCHAEOLOGICAL MUSEUM. Relics from Corfu's Paleolithic and Classical pasts appear in this large collection. Ancient coins, laurel leaves of bronze, and detailed statuettes are sure to catch any visitor's attention, but the hands-down highlight is the fantastic **Gorgon Pediment** from the Doric Temple of Artemis in ancient Corfu. The pediment depicts the ghoulish Medusa with her children: the winged horse Pegasus and the Chrysoar. According to mythology the creatures were born at the moment when Perseus cut off their mother's head, though in the pediment she appears full of life. *(Vraila 1, down the steps leading to the Spianada, past Hotel Corfu Palace on the right. ☎26610 30 680. Open Tu-Su 8:30am-3pm. €3, students and seniors €2, children and EU students free. Combined tickets for the Old Fortress, Byzantine Museum, Archaeological Museum, and Museum of Asian Art can be purchased for €8 at any of the sights.)*

OLD FORTRESS (PALEO FROURIO). Of all the sights in the vicinity of the Spianada, the Old Fortress is surely the most conspicuous. Finished in the late 14th century by the Venetians, the Paleo Frourio was isolated by the surrounding waters and a still-present moat. In short, it was considered invincible—that is, until the British blew it up in 1864. Today after a short period of renovation, much of the fortress remains intact. Most visitors find themselves drawn to the red **bell tower** near the summit, as well as the **Church of St. George.** Consider buying a guidebook from the museum (€4-6), for explanations in English are sparse. *(Just east of the Spianiada. ☎26610 48 311. Open daily 8am-7pm. €4, students and seniors €2, EU students free.)*

NEW FORTRESS. The result of the Venetians' second attempt to protect their city, the 350-year-old walls of the New Fortress were once considered the paradigm of military architecture. Currently the massive edifice hosts two small art galleries, as well as a playground, a small cafe, and an occasional stray dog. This younger fort, located above the ferry docks, offers panoramic views of Corfu Town ideal for sun-drenched picnics. The fort has one small **gallery** of etchings, maps, and watercolors with nautical motifs and another with contemporary exhibits. Concerts and theatrical events are staged here during the summer. *(Look for signs as you walk along Velissariou from the Old Port. ☎26610 45 000. Open daily 9am-10pm. €2.)*

BYZANTINE MUSEUM. Unbeknownst to most tourists, this rather impressive collection of religious artifacts is housed in the small 15th-century aisle-less **Church of the Most Holy Virgin Antivouniotissa.** Eighteenth-century priestly vestments, gold communion cups, and iron-covered gospel books highlight the permanent exhibit in the room adjacent to the church. The museum's collection of **Cretan School** icons is also worth seeing, if only to observe the painted "wallpaper" and wood carvings on the room's ceiling. The many styles and influences reflected in the collection is attributed to the influx of Cretan artists who stopped in Corfu on their way to Venice after the 1646 fall of Rethymno. *(Look for signs on Arsenion as it curls downhill from the palace. ☎26610 38 313. Open Tu-Su 8am-3pm. €2, students and seniors €1.)*

PALACE OF SAINT MICHAEL AND SAINT GEORGE. Built by the British Lord High Commissioner Sir Thomas Maitland, this neoclassical palace presiding over the Spianada was originally intended to be both a home and an office space. Once the headquarters of Corfu, it holds an impressive "throne room" and the **Museum of Asian Art,** which displays over 11,000 Oriental artifacts from five formerly private collections. Samurai weapons and a set of six-fold screens prove to be of particular interest in this well-organized collection. *(☎26610 30 443. Open Tu-Su 8:30am-3pm. €2, students and seniors €1, EU students free.)* The **Municipal Modern Art Gallery (Dimotiko Pinakothiki),** behind the Palace and through the garden, has a small-collection of Corfiot paintings and rotating special exhibits. *(☎26610 48 690. Open daily 10am-6pm, but hours may vary with special exhibits. €1.50, students €1.)*

CHURCH OF AG. SPYRIDON. Housing the embalmed body of the island's patron saint, St. Spyridon, this church prides itself on being an important pilgrimage point for Orthodox Christians. The biblical scenes on the beautiful baroque ceiling certainly draw secular tourists in addition to pilgrims. Inside, a silver casket holds the remains of the 3rd-century saint whose spirit is thought to wander the streets and perform good deeds for the island's people. Rumor has it that if the priest opens the gold cover of Spyridon's casket during your visit, you can still catch a glimpse of his blackened face. *(Take Ag. Spyridon off the Spianada; it's on the left, as is the rose-colored onion dome. Open daily 6am-9pm. Be respectful and dress modestly.)*

OTHER MUSEUMS. Located in the house in which he spent the last 20 years of his life, the **Solomos Museum** pays tribute to the country's beloved national poet, Dionysios Solomos. The first to use Demotic Greek in poetry, Solomos's *Hymn to Freedom* eventually became the lyrics of Greece's national anthem. Beyond myriad photographs and photocopies, the museum holds actual pieces of the tree that was said to have inspired the poet. *(Look for the sign in an alleyway on Arseniou just west of the Byzantine Museum, toward the New Port. ☎26610 30 674. Open M-F 9:30am-2pm. €1.)* Fanatical capitalists will enjoy the **Museum of Paper Currency,** in the Ionian Bank Building down N. Theotoki from the Spianada. In addition to examples of all Greek currency ever in circulation, the museum is the proud owner of the first bank note ever printed in Greece. *(☎26610 41 552. Open M-F 10am-2pm. Free.)*

FESTIVALS. Corfu's animated **Easter** celebrations are reflected in the ornate Palm Sunday procession of the embalmed body of St. Spyridon, Corfu's conspicuous saint. On Holy Saturday (the day before Easter), Corfiots throw pots full of water out of their windows at 11am. **Carnival** season, which begins 40 days before Easter, is largely secular in Corfu; celebrating generally means dining, drinking, and dancing. The most entertaining Carnival traditions include "the Gossip," on the final Thursday of Carnival. In something like a street theater performance, women call out the latest gossip from windows across alleys in the center of the Old Town. On the last Sunday, the festival culminates with the burning of King Carnival, when the effigy "King" is tried and sentenced to death by fire for his hand in all the year's misfortunes. Corfu seems to always be celebrating something. In August, Corfiots are at it again, celebrating the worthy **Barcarola** festival.

NIGHTLIFE AND ENTERTAINMENT

Located 2km west of the New Port, the so-called **Disco Strip** is the undisputed epicenter of nightlife in Corfu Town. Crowds of locals and tourists intermingle at the plethora of bars and cafes, each of which offers its own take on the ideal evening out. If you strut out of your hotel with dancing boots tied tight, **Hippodrome,** situated at the end of the strip, may be your best bet for an international soiree. Though popular **Sodoma** blasts Greek music under dizzying flashes of strobes, **Bouzoukia** wins out as Corfu's bona-fide hot spot. The club for Greeks who know how to party, Bouzoukia often has no cover, but you won't find a drink for under €6. If you're going to try and snag a table for the night, be ready to shell out up to €130. Above the creperie, the **Opera Music Cafe** provides a perfect alternative to a rigorous night of pelvic gyrations. Hanging marionettes, quality music, and unbeatable cocktails cater to your senses' highest demands. The best way to get to the strip, located on Eth. Antistaseos, is by taxi (€3-5, more if the taxi is coming after midnight). Once there, beer generally costs €2.50-4.50; cocktails €4-7.40.

If you're looking to stay in town, make your way to **Liston,** an arcade (adjacent to the Spianada) of elegant little cafes which remain lively until around 1am. By far the most popular among them is **Magnet,** at the top of Kapodistriou, where the buzz of multilingual conversations spills out onto the shady plateia. The **cinemas** on G. Theotoki are a few blocks from Pl. San Rocco, on the corner of Akadimias and G. Aspoti. Walk one block uphill from the OTE and the theater will be on the right. Movies in English play regularly. Look for placards on G. Theotoki (tickets €6). The **municipal theater** (☎26610 33 598), between Dessila and Mantzarou one block from G. Theotoki, has occasional drama, dance, and music performances, publicized on bulletin boards all over town.

DAYTRIP FROM CORFU TOWN: ACHILLION PALACE

In Gastouri. From Corfu Town, take bus #10 from a spot 200m west of Pl. San Rocco, on Methodiou (30min.; M-Sa 6 per day, 7am-8pm; Su 4 per day, 9am-8pm; €0.85). ☎26610 56 210. Open daily 9am-7pm. €6, groups €3, children free.

From the home of an estranged empress to the filming location of the 1981 James Bond flick *For Your Eyes Only*, the Achillion Palace has continually intrigued visitors with its exquisite architecture, ornate designs, and flourishing gardens. Achillion Palace is heavily touristed, but its crowds are entirely justified. The property first belonged to Empress Elizabeth of Austria, a woman whose turbulent familial affairs forced her out to this secluded Corfiot estate. Having developed a penchant for classical literature, she christened her palace after the nearly-invincible Greek hero Achilles. After her assassination in 1898, the palace had short lives as the home to German Kaiser Wilhelm II, a hospital, and even the first Grecian casino. Today the palace itself has become a museum; its most impressive works are two outdoor statues of Achilles, portrayed in both "dying" and "triumphant" form. The latter statue stands an enormous 8m tall.

WESTERN CORFU

A beach lover's paradise, western Corfu showcases wide expanses of golden sand and hidden crystal coves, majestic cliffs, and rock formations serving as a backdrop to the glimmering turquoise sea. While it sees its share of tour buses, it doesn't suffer from the same degree of overdevelopment that mars the east and south. Instead, its towering, untouched natural beauty makes exploring its towns and more remote beaches a continual delight.

PELEKAS Πελεκας ☎26610

Removed from the mass tourism of the resorts, the village of Pelekas sits at the top of a hill, with great views and famously beautiful sunsets. Pelekas has some of the best of what Corfu has to offer—beaches, natural beauty, great food, and fun bars—with the added benefit of being off the typical tourist path. Take **bus #11** from Pl. San Rocco in Corfu Town (30min.; 7 per day, 7am-8:30pm; €0.75). The long, sandy **beach** is a pleasant 30min. walk from town down a very steep road. (Plan on an hour return hike. A free shuttle bus to and from town picks up at the left side of the beach facing inland and runs 6 times per day from 11:45am-8:30pm; signs are posted all over town.) Rooms to let are plentiful and well priced in Pelekas, but call ahead in high season to secure a spot. **Pension Tellis and Brigitte ❷**, down the hill from the bus stop, has the friendliest hosts in town and lovely rooms in a little, yellow house covered with bougainvillea. Balconies offer superb views of the surrounding countryside. (☎26610 94 326. Laundry around €5. Doubles €25. Some rooms with private bath.) Near the **Church of Ag. Nikolaos,** around the corner and above the bus stop, **Takis Kontis's ❷** rooms are comfortable and airy; half have fantastic balcony views and all have shared baths. (☎26610 94 742. Singles €15; doubles €20.) On the road to the beach, next to the fork for Glyfada, **Pension Paradise ❷** offers a good deal. Rooms have bathroom and kitchen and the management is very nice. (☎26610 94 530 or 26610 36 217. Singles €30; doubles €30.) Just outside of town on the road to Glyfada, the **Taverna Pink Panther ❷** restaurant and bar serves up terrific Greek and Italian food. (Pizzas start at €5.50. Greek entrees €5-6.) If you get there at the appropriate time, the pink balcony offers great sunset views; revelry begins around midnight. Next to the church, the well-situated **Pelekas Cafe ❶** purees superb milkshakes (€3) from a view over the island. **Zanzibar,** across the street, has Caffrey's and Guinness on tap. (Open 5pm-late.)

GLYFADA Γλυφαδα

Glyfada attracts more tourists than tiny Pelekas, 5km down the coast, but its seemingly endless shore accommodates the throngs admirably. Scrubby cliffs bracket both of Glyfada's shallow **beaches,** where crashing waves make swimming a bit more unpredictable. An eclectic crowd of internationals basks on the sun-speckled sand. Young sun-worshipers scope each other's tans and amuse themselves parasailing (singles €30; doubles €45), water-skiing (€18 per 10min.), or jet skiing (15min.; singles €30; doubles €45). Motorboats, kayaks, inner tubes, and paddle boats are also available. Green KTEL **buses** leave from Corfu Town at the intersection above the Grand Louis Hotel (30min.; 10 per day, 6:45am-8pm; €1.25), and a free bus connects **Pelekas** to Glyfada (10min.; 6 per day, 11am-8:30pm; the bus leaves from the parking lot, and schedules are posted in both towns). Budget accommodations are scarce, but it's easy to make the trip from Pelekas or Corfu Town. The nearest camping site is at **Vatos Camping ❶**, Linou Koyevino 30 (☎30661 36 064; www.vatoscamping.com), in Vatos Village. North of Glyfada, accessible via dirt path off the main Pelekas road, lie the isolated **beaches** of **Moni Myrtidion** and

Myrtiotissa, extolled by Lawrence Durrell as the most beautiful in the world. A section of Myrtiotissa serves as an unofficial nude beach—unless local monks complain to the police, who reluctantly bring offending nudists to court.

PALEOKASTRITSA Παλαιοκαστριτσα

Paleokastritsa **beach** rests among six small coves and sea caves that cast shadows over the blue. Although the beach is a bit narrow and can get crowded, a swim in the calm, dark-blue water encircled by cliffs more than makes up for it. Green KTEL **buses** arrive from Corfu Town (45min.; 17 per day, 8:30am-6pm; €1.50). You can hire a motorboat (30min. one-way; €8 per person) or rent a pedal boat (€8.80 per hr.) or kayak (singles €3; doubles €6 per hr.) to reach the caves where, according to legend, Phaeacian princess Nausicaä found the shipwrecked Odysseus washed ashore. Jutting out on a hill over the sea, bright white **Panagia Theotokos Monastery** boasts a museum with a collection of Byzantine icons, engraved bibles, and a so-called **sea monster's skeleton.** Sunlight reflects off the whitewashed walls and highlights the colors in the lovely little garden next to the courtyard; step over the railing for startlingly beautiful views. Come as early as possible—by midmorning it's a mess of tour buses—and take a little bread with you to feed the monastery's very tame peacocks (up the little road past the vegetable garden). The paved road up the hill leads to the monastery. The 12th-century fort of **Angelokastro** sits above Paleokastritsa. A natural balcony with a magnificent view, the appropriately named **Bella Vista,** is a 1½hr. walk from Paleokastritsa. Take the road from the bus stop to the Odysseus Hotel, turn left on the path through the olive groves, and continue on the trail through a village to the fort.

AGIOS GORDIOS Αγιος Γορδιος ☎26610

Ten kilometers south of Pelekas, Agios Gordios is highlighted by impressive rock formations and a lovely, wide **beach.** The main road runs perpendicular to the sand, with a short stretch of restaurants, mini-markets, and souvenir shops lining both sides. But in truth, most visitors to Agios Gordios could not tell you where those shops are; most visitors never make it beyond the premises of the town's debaucherous **Pink Palace Hotel ❸,** a favorite with American and Canadian backpackers in search of instant (and constant) gratification. Regardless of when you arrive, an energetic (and occasionally hungover) staff member greets you with open arms and a mandatory, eye-opening shot of pink ouzo. From then on, it's up to you how to sin away the day. The Palace's impressive list of amenities makes it a self-contained party resort: there's a laundry service (€7.50); book exchange; Internet access (€2 per 30min.); a jacuzzi; basketball, volleyball, and tennis courts; a nightclub; massages (€11); car rental (€18-30); clothing-optional cliff-diving (€15); boat daytrips (also known as the "booze cruise"); and various watersports. If possible, plan your stay around the Saturday night dance-and-drink-fest, when some pseudo-Greek traditions heighten the fun: pink toga-wrapped partyers have been known to down countless shots of ouzo as the hotel's owner, Dr. George, breaks plates on willing guests' heads in a spirit of revelry that would make Dionysus proud. In short, nights at the Palace are not for the faint of heart, nor the weak of liver. (☎26610 53 103 or 53 104; www.thepinkpalace.com. To get to the palace from Corfu Town, take the green bus to Agios Gordios (45min.; M-Sa 5 per day, 8:15am-8pm; Su 3 per day, 9:30am-3:30pm; €1.50). Buses go both ways between Athens and the Pink Palace, bypassing Patras (€38 one-way to Athens; €47 one-way from Athens). When you return from Athens, the Pink Palace guarantees the availability of a room for you. Breakfast, dinner, and pick up/drop off at the Corfu Town ferry included. Check-out 9am. Dorms €19; rooms with A/C, telephones, private balconies, bonfire-proof furniture, and baths €25.)

EASTERN CORFU

The eastern coast of Corfu is the most developed and least aesthetically pleasing part of the island. The first 20km north of Corfu Town are thoroughly Anglicized by throngs of rowdy expats, and the beaches are thin strips along a busy, clamorous coastal road. Despite its low points, eastern Corfu is convenient and relatively inexpensive. Everything—beach, restaurants, hotels, nightlife—is consolidated into one strip, so you won't need to rent a moped. It's cheaper than beautiful Corfu Town, but close enough to enable frequent trips. **Gouvia** and **Dassia,** the first two resorts north of town, thrive off package tours despite beaches stretched thin by the crowds. A bit farther north, the visitors to the small but notorious town of **Ipsos** have unlimited access to a myriad souvenir stands, fast-food joints, and C-class hotels that line the flat stretch of road from across the mountain. Guests guzzle the day away at countless tacky bars and discos like the depressingly named bar "Alcoholics Anonymous," only to collapse a few hours later onto the yellow sand like beached whales. The scene is identical during the night, as clubs offer gimmicks like free shots and foam parties to anyone willing to drop a few euros. **Pirgi,** a quieter extension of Ipsos, offers much of the same €2-per-pint atmosphere. Hotels do tend to fill up quickly with package tour groups, so reserve ahead if you plan on staying. Your best bet may be to settle down at a nearby campground like **Karda Beach Camping ❶,** located in between Dassia and Ipsos on the main road. The campground's relative proximity to the bus station makes Corfu town, and therefore the rest of Corfu, easily accessible. (☎26610 93 595. €4.40 per person with his/her own tent. Electricity €3.25. Apartment-style bungalows €35.) **KTEL green buses** serve **Ipsos** and **Pirgi** (30min.; M-F 10 per day, 7am-8pm; Sa 7 per day, 9am-6:30pm; Su 9:30am; €1). **Blue buses** head to **Dassia** via **Gouvia** (every 30min., 7-9am and 7-10:30pm; every 20min., 9am-7pm; €0.75). Buy tickets on the bus.

NORTHERN CORFU

Past Pirgi the road begins to wind below steep cliffs. Mt. Pantokrator, a bare rock jutting out of the forested hills, towers 1000m above on your left, while dramatic vistas of dark, wooded Albania appear across the straits. Emperors Tiberius and Nero of Rome once vacationed here, though tourism has erased most traces of the ancient world on the northern coast. The farther you get from overbuilt beach towns like Kassiopi and Sidari, the better off you'll be.

AGIOS STEFANOS Αγιος Στεφανος

The most remote northern beach town is Agios Stefanos (not to be confused with the northeastern village of the same name). A mere 15min. drive from bustling Sidari, Agios Stefanos is mercifully underdeveloped; the wide, sandy beach is set in a long curving gulf of high sandstone cliffs. The long waves roll in toward the few determined souls who have escaped Sidari and Kassiopi. The trip there is a treat in itself: the coastal road curves inland west of Sidari, past ferny hillsides of figs, olives, and cypresses, and through a picturesque mountain village. **Buses** run from **Corfu Town** (1½hr.; 6 per day, 5:30am-7:30pm; €2.60) and **Kassiopi** via **Sidari** (4 per day, 9:30am-4pm). The few who make it to town will find expensive hotels but also plenty of **domatia,** some at reasonable prices (€25-35); check the signs in front of tavernas along the main road to track them down. Be warned: there is **no bank or ATM** in town, so bring enough cash for your stay.

The sheer slopes of northeastern Corfu cradle several fine **beaches** including **Barbati,** 10km north of Ipsos, nearby **Nissaki,** and the twin beaches **Kalami** and **Kouloura.** A **green KTEL bus** from Corfu Town runs to **Kassiopi** (1hr.; 7 per day, 5:45am-4pm; €2.20) and stops at most beaches along the northeastern coast;

ask to be let off at less popular destinations. Kouloura and Kalami beaches are a brief walk from the main road north of Gimari village. Head down from the bus stop on the main road. Soon you'll see a yellow sign on the right marking the shortcut path to Kalami. If you're heading for Kouloura, continue down the road until you reach a fork with signs for Kouloura and Kalami. Head right down this road; blue "To the Beach" signs on the left mark the path down to Kouloura. Signs on the right side of the road point you toward Kalami.

Kalami, with its wide flat-stoned beach, was home to author Lawrence Durrell and his family in the 1930s. His small white house is still "set like a dice on a rock" in the southern end of town; now it houses the pleasant **Taverna White House ❷**, which serves typical Greek fare under wisteria vines with a sea view (entrees €5.50-11.50; appetizers €1.90-5.40). Super-secluded Kouloura, a 10min. walk along the road from Kalami, is a small, partially-shaded beach composed of mixed sand, eucalyptus leaves, and stones, with nary an umbrella or paddle boat in sight. **Taverna Kouloura ❷** has a nice view of the marina and lots of veggie options. (Entrees €4-8. Fish dishes €11-28.) It can be expensive to stay in the area overnight, and there are no accommodations in Kouloura.

To hike to the high plateau of **Mt. Pantokrator** for breathtaking views of all Corfu, start at Spartillas, a village 7km north and inland from Pirgi, along the bus route. From there, follow the same path used each summer by villagers on their way to the annual festival at Pantokrator Monastery. For the nature-weary or wild, a club called **Monaco** holds foam parties twice a night; one at around 2am, the other at 3am. (☎26936 35 7535. No cover. Drinks €2-5. Open June-Sept.)

LEFKADA Λευκαδα

Thucydides reports that Lefkada was part of the mainland until 427 BC, when the inhabitants dug a canal and made their home an island. A bridge now connects Lefkada to the mainland, just 50m away; it only recently replaced an archaic chain-operated ferry built by Emperor Augustus. The modern bridge has brought the tourism industry to Lefkada—souvenir shops and overpriced restaurants abound, especially in Nidri, compromised primarily of tourist traps and liquor stores. Still, miles of white-sand beaches and natural beauty remain; with a little effort, you can skirt the patches of tacky tourism and find the island's unspoiled secrets.

LEFKADA TOWN ☎26450

Lefkada Town, facing the mainland, is a frenetic little city packed into a space that feels far too small to hold it. The waterfront and pedestrian streets near the main plateia are the centers of the town's social scene, offering locals and travelers plenty of shopping, eating, and interaction with the most conspicuous of tourists. Still, meandering into the tiny alleys off the main street will quickly convince you that Lefkada Town retains a quiet allure beneath its bustling surface.

TRANSPORTATION. From the **bus station** (☎26450 22 364), a yellow waterfront building with a gray and yellow-striped awning 5min. to the left of the beginning of Dörpfield as you face inland, **buses** cross the canal to **Athens** (5½hr.; 8 per day, 6am-7pm; €22.50). **Local buses** run to: **Agios Nikitas** (20min.; 6:40am, 12:15, 2:15pm; €0.90); **Nidri** (30min; 15 per day, 5:30am-7:30pm; €1.10); **Poros** (45min.; 6:05am, 1:25pm; €1.70); **Vasiliki** (1hr., 4 per day, €2.30). Pick up a bus schedule at the station for additional routes and return times; service is reduced on Sundays.

Ferries leaving from **Nidri** and **Vasiliki** link Lefkada with **Ithaka** and **Kephalonia** to the south. **Taxis** (☎26450 21 001) are available but expensive. They line up by the entrance of Dörpfield and by the bus station.

ORIENTATION AND PRACTICAL INFORMATION. Based on his analysis of island topographies, archaeologist William Dörpfield claimed that Homer's Ithaka was actually Lefkada; Lefkada Town thanked him by naming one of its main roads **Dörpfield** (later **Strategou Mela**) a pedestrian-friendly street by the park that runs down the middle of the peninsula that defines the city's downtown. Dörpfield and all the little winding branches off it are for pedestrians and bikes only for the first few blocks until they reach the central **plateia** packed with cafes and the occasional traveling music act. A beltway, which becomes the waterfront road to the right of the beginning of Dörpfield as you face inland, envelops the entire downtown area. This road is identified on maps as **8th Merarhias,** but on street signs it also becomes D. Golemi, I. Polytechneiou, and Ag. Sikelianou for some stretches.

There is no tourist office, but the **tourist police** can be found on 8th Merarhias. Facing the bus station, walk left and follow the road as it leads away from the water; the police building will be on your left. (☎26450 29 379. General info and island contacts for accommodations. Open 8am-10pm.) The 24hr. **police station** (☎26450 22 346) is in the same building. For info about ferries, tours, or sights, try the travel agencies around the bus station. There is a **National Bank** (open M-Th 8am-2pm, F 8am-1:30pm) with a 24hr. **ATM** and several **pharmacies** on Str. Mela. For the **OTE,** turn right off Str. Mela onto Skiardesi, just before the National Bank; turn left when it dead-ends at I. Marinou. (Open M-F 7:30am-1pm for purchases, 7:30am-11:30pm for information.) **Internet C@fe Lefkada,** past the police station on 8th Merarhias on the left, offers **Internet** access. (☎26450 21 507. €2.40 per hr. Open M-Sa 8am-2am, Su 10am-midnight.) The **post office** is on Str. Mela past the National Bank. (☎26450 24 225. Open M-F 7:30am-2pm.) **Postal code:** 31100.

ACCOMMODATIONS. There are few **domatia** in town, so if you're pinching pennies, consider staying elsewhere. Hotels cluster on the waterfront near Dörpfield and on the first few blocks inland. Lefkada Town is expensive—most rooms start at €40. Advance booking and longer stays could ease the cost. Travel agencies suggest you check in **Lia,** a domatia-packed village 4km outside of town; frequent buses to and from Nidri and Vasiliki pass through Lia. For those unwilling to compromise class for cost, one relatively affordable option is **Pirotani Pension ❸,** on Dörpfield, two blocks from the waterfront. Beautiful rooms have tile floors, full baths, TVs, A/C, fridges, balconies, and tasteful wood furniture. (☎26450 22 270 or 26450 25 844; fax 26450 24 084. Singles and doubles €35-50. Cash only.) In a higher price range is **Hotel Nirikos ❹,** at the end of Dörpfield and on the waterfront. A shiny lobby and dining room give way to spacious but simple rooms with TVs, phones, and baths. (☎26450 24 132; fax 26450 23 756. Breakfast included. Singles €30-50; doubles €45-70. AmEx/MC/V.) Another hotel on the pricier side is **Hotel Lefkas ❹,** at the entrance to Dörpfield, opposite the Park of Poets. Ninety-three spacious rooms come equipped with A/C, telephones, TVs, and pleasant sea views. (☎26450 23 916; fax 26450 24 579. Singles €35-45; doubles €45-65. V.)

FOOD AND NIGHTLIFE. Dining in Lefkada Town is pricey and tourist-oriented; you'll have to work a little harder to find authenticity. One of the oldest local favorites is the family-owned **Taverna Regantos ❶,** 75m down Dimarmou Verrioti, the first right as you approach the plateia from the waterfront. Peek into the pots as your palate-pleasers are prepared in this wood-paneled eatery. (☎26450 22 855. Beef in red sauce €5. Stuffed peppers €3. *Retsina* €2 per 0.5L. Open 6pm-2am. Cash only.) Travelers looking for variety hunt down **Alkiona ❸,** 100m to the left of the bus station (facing inland). Fresh fish (€5-13) and calamari (€9.50) are the most popular dishes, while pasta (€3.5-5) and vegetable pies (€4) cater to vegetarian palates. (☎26450 22 458. Open daily noon-4pm and 7pm-1am. AmEx/V.)

As the sun begins to set, the party gets started at the small cafe/clubs located to the right of Dörpfield (as you face inland). At **Cafe Excess** and **Coconut Groove,** small rooms swell with sweaty locals dancing to the sounds of hard music. Nightlife elitists find themselves returning to **Capital,** the two-storied club that makes any club in town look like a middle school mixer. Featuring good music, a swimming pool, and a bridge that connects to a cafe, Capital reigns supreme. To get there, walk with the water on your right past the large white museum building and then follow that road past two schools; its on the left. Women should avoid walking alone; taxis cost roughly €4. (Cover €7. Beer €3; mixed drinks €6-7. Open daily mid-July-mid-Aug. and on weekends in low season.)

SIGHTS AND BEACHES. The **Archaeological Museum** is located 1km down the waterfront road; make a left as you exit Dörpfield and follow the road with the water on your right for 1km; it's the big white building on the right. This wonderful museum houses a collection of artifacts from ancient Lefkas, a prominent island city from the 7th century BC. Panels thoroughly explain the objects in English and give interesting information on Lefkas's history and culture. The sarcophagus with the original skeleton and burial goods still inside and the terracotta figurines of dancing nymphs from the 6th century BC are focal points of the collection. (☎26450 21 635. Open Tu-Su 8:30am-3pm. Free.) The **folklore museum** gives a taste of Lefkada's Italian legacy. From the waterfront make a right onto Dimarmou Verrioti (the first right as you approach the plateia) and then make a left at the next road and follow the signs. It may be temporarily closed for renovations, so call ahead. (☎26450 22 473. Open M-F 11am-1pm and 6-10pm. €2.) In the second half of August, Lefkada hosts the annual **Folklore Festival,** with music and dance performed in the outdoor theater just off the plateia. While Lefkada Town has no sandy beaches, the northwestern coast has miles of white pebbles and clear water. To get there, rent a **moped** (€10 per day) at **Eurocar** (☎26450 23 581), on Panagou, to the right of Hotel Nirikos. You can also catch a bus to the best stretch of beaches, starting at **Agios Nikitas** (6 per day, €0.90) and continuing to the sweeping views from the serene **Faneromenis Monastery.** (☎26450 21 105. Open 7am-2pm and 4-10pm. Free. Modest dress required.)

NIDRI Νιδρι

The last stop on the delightful Fiskardo-Frikes-Nidri ferry, Nidri is unfortunately an anti-climactic end of the line. The waterfront, crowded with pleasure boats, has a handsome view of the dappled coves of offshore islands; meanwhile, the town itself is a crowded strip of tourist shops and cafes. From Nidri, **ferries** (☎26450 31 520) sail to **Fiskardo,** Kephalonia (2-3hr., €5) and **Frikes,** Ithaka (2hr., €4.20). From Vasiliki, a ferry leaves once daily for **Fiskardo** (1hr., €5). Check travel offices for current schedules. Beware that ferry schedules change from month to month. **Excursion boats** (€20) leave Nidri each morning at 9:45am and return at 6pm, cruising to **Ithaka, Kephalonia, Madouri, Meganisi,** and **Skorpios.** (Call ☎26450 92 658 or check at a travel agency for more information.) For other boat excursions, ask at waterfront travel offices, or read the boats' hard-to-miss signs. The **buses** stop at a small KTEL bus sign on the main street; **taxis** make the trip for €10-15.

The crowds and glitz that make Nidri unpleasant during the daytime transform it into a party zone at night when strobe-lit clubs on the main street throw open their doors. Those in the mood for a healthy dose of dancing have some good options. Coming from Vasiliki, at the very beginning of the street just after the post office and on the left, you'll hit **Club Tropicana.** This expansive disco is only for die-hard partyers; it's the place everyone goes when the more timid clubs shut down at 3am. Its doors don't even open until midnight, but, if you last long enough, you can catch the morning bus back to town. (Cover €3, includes 1 drink. Beer €3; mixed drinks €5-6.) At the other end of the strip, 100m past the flashy Bel Air Hotel, **Sail Inn** dabs on some makeup and converts itself from a harmless hot dog and hamburger cafe during the day to the host of some of the town's wildest nights. Focusing on atmosphere, it's complete with straw umbrellas and an outdoor dance floor that opens onto the beach. (Cover €4, includes 1 drink. Beer €2-3; mixed drinks €5-6.) **Status Bar,** perhaps the most mainstream on the strip, is 50m beyond and across the road from Byblos. Its international clientele enjoy a lone pool table and the small garden bar outside.

VASILIKI Βασιλικη ☎26450

Vasiliki's unique position between mountains creates distinct wind patterns that make it one of the world's premiere windsurfing towns. Despite the visitors, the town keeps a neighborly, close-knit atmosphere. Smaller than Lefkada Town and less touristy than Nidri, Vasiliki is the best Lefkada has to offer. The long beach provides a great view of multicolored windsurfing sails, while boats run to nearby beautiful pebbled coves. With an attractive waterfront with excellent restaurants, Vasiliki is full of all the quiet pleasures of a small beach town.

ORIENTATION AND PRACTICAL INFORMATION. Almost everything in Vasiliki lies either along the waterfront or on the main road running inland between Penguin Restaurant and the bakery. To reach the road from the ferry docks, walk 5min. with the water on your left; it will be before the road curves to the left. Coincidentally, the main road's bakery doubles as the town's **bus stop.** Four buses per day (7:15am-8:45pm) run to and from **Lefkada Town** (1hr., €2.30) and **Nidri** (30min., €1.40). For **ferry** information, inquire at Samba Tours (see below). Renting a **moped** or a **car** is a good idea if you plan to avoid overly touristed beach towns. **Christo Alex's Rental,** at the intersection of the road inland with the road to Lefkada, is the cheapest. (☎26450 31 580; fax 26450 31 780. Mopeds €6 per day; motorcycles €10 per day; cars start at €20. MC/V.) If you walk for about 2min. up the road inland, on the left you'll find the incredibly helpful **Samba Tours.** They offer a vast array of services including **ferry** and **bus information,** boat excursions, faxes, car hire, plane tickets, photocopying, safety deposit, **currency exchange,** book swap, accommodations, and **Internet** access. (☎26450 31 555 or 31 520; sambatours@otenet.gr. Internet €2 per 15min. Open daily 8am-11pm.) The **National Bank** has installed a 24hr. **ATM** on the far left of the waterfront as you face inland. The 24hr. **police station** (☎26450 31 218) is inland along the main road. For medical **emergencies,** contact the **health center** (☎26450 31 065); on the main road, go straight through the intersection with the road to Lefkada Town and Nidri. To reach the **post office,** walk uphill along the main road; it's just after the crossroads. (Open M-F 7:30am-2pm.) **Postal code:** 31082.

ACCOMMODATIONS. Rooms for rent are plentiful along the waterfront, the main road, and the side streets branching off them. With a little work you should be able to find **domatia** for €15 per person or less in the low season; it's possible to get a room for as low as €20-25 in high season. The owners of the ostensibly worn-down fruit market (now more of a mini-market), to the right side of the waterfront when facing inland, opposite the ferry dock, let spacious **rooms** ❸ with private baths, balconies, and fabulous views of the water. (☎26450 31 221. Singles €20-25; doubles €30-40. Cash only.) **Hotel Lefkatas** ❸, on the left 100m inland from the waterfront on the main road, has simple, clean, and comfortable rooms featuring private baths, A/C, telephones, and some ocean-view balconies. (☎26450 31 801; lefkatas@otenet.gr. During high season call ahead for reservations. Singles €20-30; doubles €35-45. MC/V.) A 1km walk along the road inland or along the beach leads to a bit of luxury at **Porto Fico ❹.** Gorgeous rooms come with tiled floors, dark wood furniture, A/C, TVs, balconies, and private baths. Easy beach access and a swimming pool may make this place worth the money and the effort of getting there. (☎26450 31 402; portofico@lantisworld.com. Breakfast included. Call ahead for reservations. Doubles €45-50 from Sept.-June, €55-60 from June 15-July 15, €90 from July 15-Aug. MC/V.) **Vasiliki Beach Camping ❶,** popular among the windsurfing crowd, provides guests with a clean, affordable campsite. Amenities like bar, mini-market, laundry, showers, and a great waterfront location will make travelers glad they traded in air conditioning for a tent. Walk about 500m along the road inland, past the intersection with the road to Lefkada Town; the campsite is on the left. (☎26450 31 308; fax 26450 31 458. €5 per person; €4.50 per small tent, €5 per large tent; €3 per car. Cash only.)

IONIAN ISLANDS

FOOD AND NIGHTLIFE. Nearly all the restaurants in Vasiliki are on a short stretch of the waterfront and generally serve similar dishes at similar prices. Yet if you can sift through the ordinary, you can manage to find a quality, well-prepared, and still inexpensive meal. **Miramare ❷,** toward the far right side of the waterfront facing inland, is essentially on its own pier—both literally and figuratively. (Pizzas €7.50-8.10. MC/V.) At the corner where the waterfront meets the road running inland, Aussie and Greek tag-team Gary and Mary cater to a multitude of tastes at their **Penguin Restaurant ❷.** Vegetarians can find joy in many dishes here while their meat-eating friends indulge in traditional Greek favorites. (Entrees €2-7. Pasta €4-9.50. Vegetable dishes €3. Cash only.) Check out how the Greeks take on Chinese food at **Jasmine Garden ❷,** with your back to the boats, at the far right corner of waterfront. Szechuan beef (€7) and satay shrimp (€10.50) may be the house specialties, but indulging in one of the various vegetable dishes (€4-5) satisfies vegetarian tastes. (Entrees €4-15. MC/V.)

After dark, try **Zeus's Bar,** on the waterfront between Penguin and Dolphin restaurants, which serves up a slew of shots and cocktails to soothe the salt- and sun-weary. The place comes alive with a more mature crowd of revelers during Happy Hour (7-9pm), when cocktails go for €4. **Remezzo Beach Bar,** on the beach all the way to the left of the waterfront (facing inland), offers the most popular nightlife in Vasiliki for the younger crowd. Featuring solid DJs as well as indoor and outdoor bars, carousers show their elders they know what island partying means. Doors don't open until midnight and on weekends the dancing doesn't end until the sun comes up again. (Cover €3, includes 1 drink. Beer €3; cocktails €4.)

SIGHTS. **Boat tours** to several of the island's beaches leave from Vasiliki. During high season, Samba Tours offers weekly trips to Lefkada's best beach, breathtaking **Porto Katsiki** (Port of the White Goat), at the base of towering white cliffs. (40-50min. Round-trip leaves 11am and returns 5pm. €8.) Porto Katsiki is also accessible by car or moped: drive to the end of the main road and turn left and keep an eye out for signs. The drive takes about 1hr. and then you have to walk the rest of the way. A **lighthouse** built on the site of the **Temple of Lefkas Apollo** sits at the southernmost tip of the island. Worshippers were under the impression they could exorcise evil with an annual sacrifice at the temple—the victim, usually a criminal or a person thought to be possessed, was launched from the cliffs into the sea. It is said that it was from these 70m cliffs that the ancient poet **Sappho,** rejected by her lady lover Phaon, leapt to her death. The best views of Sappho's Leap are experienced from the various boat excursions.

ITHAKA Ιθακη

Perhaps the most beautiful of the Ionian Islands, Ithaka retains a close-knit feel and is genuinely Greek amid heavily-touristed neighbors. Discovering Ithaka means delighting in the island's pebbled beaches, rocky hillsides, and terraced olive groves. Villages, where the ambling pace of life creates a far more relaxing and quiet atmosphere than that found on nearby Kephalonia or Lefkada, surround the many natural harbors on the island. Ithaka was the kingdom that Odysseus left behind to fight in the Trojan War (and to wander for 10 years on his way home). His wife Penelope faithfully waited 20 years for his return here, while crowds of suitors pressed for her hand—and Odysseus's kingdom.

VATHY Βαθυ ☎26740

Ithaka's lovely capital wraps around a circular bay, where garish fishing and pleasure boats bob in the water and precipitous green hillsides nudge against the water. At dusk witness an explosion of color as the dying sun deepens the tint of the red-shingled roofs and pastel-painted houses.

TRANSPORTATION AND PRACTICAL INFORMATION. Facing inland, Vathy's **ferry docks** are on the far right of the waterfront, about a 4min. walk to the right of the town plateia. Depending on where you're coming from or heading to, you may need a taxi (☎26740 33 030) from Piso Aetos (10min., €12-15) or Frikes (30min., €20-25). Be sure to call ahead for a taxi, as there are not many on the island. **Ferries** depart from Frikes, on the northern tip of Ithaka, to **Vasiliki** on Lefkada (2½hr., 10:10am, €4.20). Departures from Piso Aetos go to **Sami** on Kephalonia (45min., 4pm, €2.50) or from Vathy to **Sami** (6:45am, €4.50). Ferries also go to mainland **Patras** in the Peloponnese (4½hr.; 7am, 4:30pm; €11.50). Schedules vary seasonally; check with the staff at **Delas Tours** (☎26740 32 104; fax 26740 33 031; open daily 9am-2pm and 3:30-9:30pm), in the main plateia. Or consult **Polyctor Tours,** along the far side of the plateia as you approach from the port police. (☎26740 33 120; fax 26740 33 130. Open daily 9:30am-1:30pm and 3:30-9pm.) **Rent a Scooter,** on a side street off the waterfront directly across from the port police, has standard rates of €10 per day, plus gas. (☎26740 32 840. Open daily 8:30am-9pm.) For car rental, try **AGS Rent a Car,** on the waterfront 2.5 blocks to the right of the plateia, near Andriana Domatia. (☎26740 32 702; fax 26740 33 551. €45 per day for a small car, including insurance. Open daily 8:30am-9pm.) **Taxis** (☎26740 33 030) tend to be pricey; they line up by the water, in front of the plateia.

To reach the **police station** (☎26740 32 205) headed from the plateia, turn right on the first street after Drakouli (Δρακουλη), the mansion turned cafe, and walk inland. (Open 24hr.) There is a **pharmacy** 20m to the right of the post office. (☎26740 33 105. Open daily 8am-2pm and 5-10pm.) To get to the **hospital** (☎26740 32 222), walk along the waterfront with the water on your left for about 1km until you see a sign. For **laundry** service, **Polifimos** is behind the National Bank, in the far right corner of the plateia. (☎26740 32 032. Wash and dry €4 per kg. Open M-Sa 8am-1pm and 6-9pm.) The **National Bank** is in the upper left corner of the plateia with Polyctor Tours on your left; it has a 24hr. **ATM.** (Open M-Th 8am-2pm, F 8am-1:30pm.) **Alpha Bank,** a few doors left of Net, offers the same services. (Open M-Th 8am-2pm, F 8am-1:30pm.) The **OTE** is on the waterfront, just before Hotel Mentor when coming from the plateia with the water on your left. (☎26740 32 299. Open M-F 8am-noon.) **Internet** access is available at **Net,** on the left side of the plateia, facing inland. (€4 per hr. Open 8am-11pm.) A lone computer offers Internet access at **Nirito Cafe,** in the plateia. (€4 per hr. Open daily 7am-2am.) The **post office** is in the plateia. (☎26740 32 386. Open M-F 7:30am-2pm.) **Postal code:** 28300.

ACCOMMODATIONS AND FOOD. As you get off the boat, cheap, private **domatia** are definitely the way to go over tempting hotel rooms. If the well advertised domatia are fully booked (which occurs frequently during high season), wander the streets inland from the waterfront, ask friendly locals for advice, or contact Delas Tours to see what they have available (though their offerings tend toward pricier options). Be sure to discuss price and distance before leaving the town center. Her rooms may be slightly out of the way, and the oddly-decorated rooms' lack of A/C may initially be a turn off, but every traveler would benefit from the graces of Ithaka's gem, elderly **Ms. Martha ❷,** who offers old domatia with private baths, kitchenettes, fans, and balcony access. To find her, walk uphill two blocks from the plateia straight past Nikos's Taverna, turn right at the T intersection, walk one more block, and turn left; the rooms are on your left. (☎26740 32 252. Singles €20-26; doubles €26-50. Cash only.) Another good bet is **Andriana Domatia ❸,** across from the ferry dock on the far right side (when facing inland) of the waterfront. Immaculate rooms include baths, TVs, and A/C; some have pleasant waterfront views. (☎26740 32 387. Singles €25-35; doubles €40-50. Negotiate for discounts in the low season. Cash only.) Facing inland, **Hotel Mentor ❹** is on the far left of the waterfront. Despite being the most expensive hotel in Vathy, it has nothing too extravagant to offer its guests. The ritzy lobby leads to basic but spacious rooms with linoleum floors. Some come with stunning harbor views and bathtubs; all have baths, balconies, A/C, and TVs. If the hotel is a bit out of your price range, ask about renting one of its apartments (€35), a great deal for big rooms with TV, private bathrooms, and kitchens. They are closer to the plateia than the hotel itself. (☎26740 32 433; fax 26740 32 293. Breakfast included. Singles €52-62; doubles €68-82. Cash only.)

Local favorite **Taverna To Trexantiri ❶,** one block behind the post office off the plateia, serves big portions of mostly beef-based dishes. Check out whether they're serving *clarini* (€5) or other house specialties. (☎26740 33 066. Salads €2.50-3. Entrees under €6. Cash only.) If you're overwhelmed by stictly Greek cuisine, **Lo Sputino ❷** (☎26740 32 021), on the waterfront next to the port authority, offers a variety of appetizing pizzas, pastas, and other Italian dishes. (Entrees and pizzas €7.50. MC/V.) At **Kantouni ❷** (☎26740 32 910), on the right side of the waterfront facing inland, the carnivorous can delight in the selection of beef, rabbit, goat, lamb, and snail dishes. But fear not, vegetarians; plates of mixed vegetables (€4) are available as well. (Entrees €4-8. MC/V.) **O Nikos ❷,** just down the street along the left side of the National Bank, is a good choice for grilled octopus (€9), fish soup (€7.34), and other fresh fish. (☎26740 33 039. Entrees €5-9. Cash only.)

SIGHTS. By far the best entertainment in Vathy is found outdoors on the several lovely **beaches,** on the water, or relaxing while sipping a frappé in open-air cafes. But museum enthusiasts aren't entirely out of luck. The **Folklore and Nautical Museum,** two blocks inland from the waterfront near the plateia, houses a rather large collection of nautical equipment and memorabilia as well as artifacts from Ithaka's colonial period. Art buffs will appreciate early 19th-century illustrated renditions of Homer's literary characters on the second floor. (☎26740 33 398. Open Tu-Sa 9am-1pm. €1.) To the left of the Folklore and Nautical Museum sits the **Vathy Archaeological Museum.** Displaying finds from ongoing excavations at the **Sanctuary of Apollo at Aetos,** a site that may have been Odysseus's palace, the tiny collection consists mostly of ceramics. Animal-shaped ritual vases from the 7th or 6th century BC are museum highlights. (Open Tu-Su 8:30am-3pm. Free.)

BEACHES AND THE OUTDOORS. Ithaka's beaches are slightly out of the way, but their beauty is well worth the effort of reaching them. Because most tourists are disinclined to make the long trips shuttling from shores to seaports, you

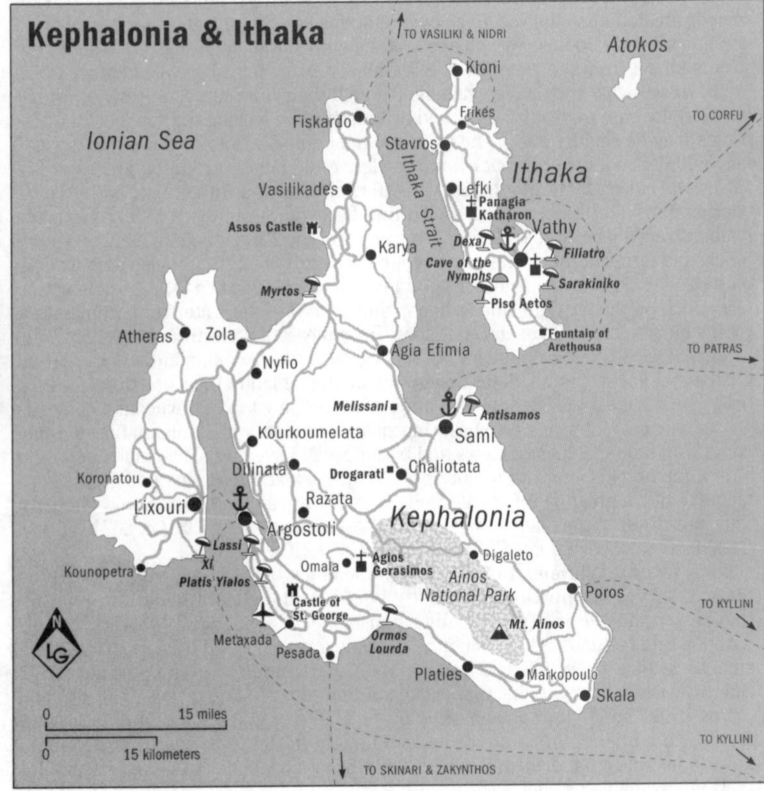

may find yourself pleasantly alone. The closest beach to the plateia is family-oriented **Dexa,** with a long, pebbled shore and shady trees to recline under. To get there from Vathy, follow the main road out of town (with the water on your right) up and over the hill with the gas station on it; the walk will take about 20min. Still within walking distance are the jaw-dropping, secluded beaches of **Filiatro** and **Sarakiniko;** walk with the water to your left and after Hotel Mentor turn right and keep heading toward the mountain to the left of town as you face inland; take the steep uphill road. Eventually the road to Filiatro will turn left off the main road—it's about a 40min. walk. Near the village of **Agios Ioannis,** on the island's western side, are several stunning pebble beaches with views of Kephalonia. A taxi from the plateia should cost €8-12. To spend a languid afternoon on the shores of first-rate **Gidaki,** you'll need to take a boat (€2-3), which makes the trip twice a day during high season.

Fans of Homer, exercise fiends, and those who simply love a great view can make the challenging 4km **hike** (about 1hr.) up to the **Cave of the Nymphs,** where Odysseus supposedly hid the treasure the Phaeacians gave him. Archaeologists have been excavating the cave in recent years and consequently it is sometimes closed to visitors. If it is closed, you can still walk around the site and view the two separate entrances (one for the gods and one for mere mortals) and perhaps chat with a few archaeologists. To get there, walk around the harbor with the water on your right on the road out of town leading to Piso Aetos and Stavros; then follow the signs along the road that winds up the mountain. The entrance is up a flight of steps to the right, just before the paved roads ends. The hike provides impressive views of Vathy. Make sure to bring a flashlight for the cave. A strenuous, 2hr. **hike** southeast leads to the Homeric **Arethousa Fountain,** along a steep mountain path through orchards and spider webs. Unfortunately the fountain runs dry in the summer. To find the trail from the plateia, follow Ermeou, your first right after Drakouli, for about 5km. A small blue sign on the left side of the road marks the start of the rocky but clearly marked path to the fountain.

The island's sole **bus,** which doubles as a school bus, runs north from Vathy to **Frikes** (45min., €1.20) and **Kioni** (1hr., €1.80). The line ends at exceptionally beautiful **Kioni,** a small village whose crystal blue harbors and white pebble beaches make it a favorite of the locals. In high season, the bus generally runs twice a day: once at 5:30am, returning immediately, and later in the morning at 7:30am, returning after a few hours (so you have time to wander the towns). You'll want to bring a bagged lunch. Around 3km south of Kioni, little **Stavros** sits high in the mountains. The **Archaeological Museum** houses a collection of excavated items from Pilicata Hill, another contender for the site of Odysseus's palace. Keep an eye out for signs; it's 700m past the town's church. (Open Tu-Su 8am-2pm. A small donation is expected.) Wander down the steep road to the small beach and harbor or sit in a pine-shaded taverna eating *rovani,* a sticky and sweet island specialty made with rice and honey. You can also visit the **Monastery of Panagia Katharon,** on Ithaka's highest mountain, Mt. Neritos; take a taxi or moped to Anoghi and follow the signs. Make sure to close the door when you get there. Goats from the surrounding area like to amble onto the premises, bringing great distress to the monks, who are also distressed by women with bare legs exposed in their sanctuary.

PERAHORA

For an amazing view and a literal taste of modern Grecian culture, make your way up to the **Perahora,** the small village that rests on the frighteningly steep mountainside 4km above Vathy. The residents are renowned for their devotion to the vine; they produce Ithaka's best wine and play host to the **wine festival,** held annually on the final Sunday of July. If you make it up to Perahora and have time to kill, visit the ruins of **Paleohora,** the capital of the island until it was abandoned in the early 16th century. To find it, follow the signs in Perahora to the community center until you reach the beginning of a footpath that leads through olive groves. You'll first encounter the ruins of the town church; though the roof is gone and the walls nearly crumbled, you can make out where frescoes once clung to the inner walls. The road leading to Perahora is on the far right of the waterfront as you face inland (opposite the road to Stavros)—follow the signs. The road is extremely steep as you near the village and there is little shade so sturdy shoes and a store of water are advisable. This hike is not recommended for elderly people or children.

KEPHALONIA Κεφαλονια

Massive mountains, subterranean lakes and rivers, caves, dense forests, and more than 250km of sand and pebble coastline make Kephalonia a nature-lover's paradise. Its profound beauty has been fought over by the Byzantine, Frankish, Ottoman, Venetian, Napoleonic, and British Empires. Today Kephalonia's beauty draws in a diverse crowd—from the upscale yachting set to budget-conscious backpackers. Many a traveler has learned that the island may be large, but its natural splendor runs deep. Because of the island's astonishingly (perhaps infuriatingly) inconvenient bus schedules, Kephalonia is a perfect place for a longer stay.

ARGOSTOLI Αργοστολι ☎26710

The capital and by far the largest town on both Kephalonia and Ithaka, Argostoli is a lively city packed with yellow and orange buildings that dot the hills. Other places on the island may be more picturesque, but the crowds flock to Argostoli for its balance between urban convenience and island allure. There's no shortage of hotels, restaurants, or shops and if you're looking for true Kephalonian nightlife, the main plateia is the only place to go.

TRANSPORTATION

Flights: Olympic Airways, R. Vergoti 7 (☎26710 28 808 or 28 881), has 2 flights per day to Athens (€75) during high season. Open M-F 8am-3:30pm.

Ferries: Kephalonia has multiple ports for different destinations. Buses connect Argostoli to other ports, including **Sami** (p. 466), where ferries leave for **Corfu, Ithaka,** and **Patras,** in addition to **Italy** in July-Aug. Prices and times are seasonal; inquire at a travel agency. From Argostoli boats go to: **Kyllini** on the Peloponnese (1-2 per day, €10.10) and **Lixouri** in western Kephalonia (1 per hr., until 10:30pm; €1.10). From Poros, on the southeastern coast, ferries leave for **Kyllini** (2 per day, €6.50). Ferries head to the tiny port of **Skinari** on the northern end of Zakynthos from Pesada, a similarly small and inconvenient port on the southern coast of Kephalonia. Buses do not go from Pesada to Argostoli, so you'll have to take a taxi (€12-15). You should seriously consider arranging private transportation in Zakynthos as buses do not go regularly get you to Skinari.

Buses: ☎26710 22 281. On the southern end of the waterfront, in a light pink building all the way to the left as you face inland. Brochures with schedules, prices, and return times available. Open 7am-8pm. Buses head to: **Agios Gerasimos/ Omala** (10am, 12:30, 2pm; €1); **Fiskardo** (2hr.; 10am, 2pm; €4); **Lassi/Platis Yialos** (9 per day, 10am-6:30pm; €1); **Poros** (10:30am, 2pm; €3.50); **Sami** (7, 11am, 1pm; €3); **Skala** (10am, 2pm; €3). For **Travliata,** take either the Skala or Poros buses (€1). Buses meet the ferry and continue on to **Athens** (4 per day, €25.50). Buses to Argostoli meet the ferry arriving in **Sami** (3-4 per day, €2). Local service is reduced Sa; none Su.

Taxis: ☎26710 28 505 or 26710 22 700. Plenty of taxis, which are very useful on this particular island, line up in the plateia. Available 24hr.

Rentals: Sunbird, Antoni Tristi 139 (☎26710 23 723), near the Port Authority, rents cars (€40) and mopeds (€13.50). Gas (€5-30) not included. Open daily 8:30am-3pm and 5-8:30pm. **Thrifty,** G. Vergoti 7 (☎26710 27 461). Head inland up Vyronos for 3 blocks. Cars €32-92 per day, including 1st 100km; €0.20-0.46 per km thereafter, depending on the type of car. Open daily 8am-2pm and 5-9pm.

ORIENTATION AND PRACTICAL INFORMATION

The town's cafe-packed and hotel-lined main plateia is two blocks inland from the water on **21 Maiou,** near the Port Authority and GNTO/EOT. South of the plateia, **Lithostrotou** is a pedestrian shopping area with high-rent stores like Diesel and Benetton and dozens of leather, postcard, and jewelry shops.

Tourist Office: ☎26710 22 248 or 26710 24 466. Beside the port authority near the ferry docks. Provides **free maps,** helpful information about sights and beaches, and some assistance with accommodations and restaurants. Open fall, spring, and summer, M-Sa 8am-2:30pm.

Banks: National Bank, offering **currency exchange** and 24hr. **ATM.** Open M-F 8am-2pm. Other banks and ATMs line the waterfront.

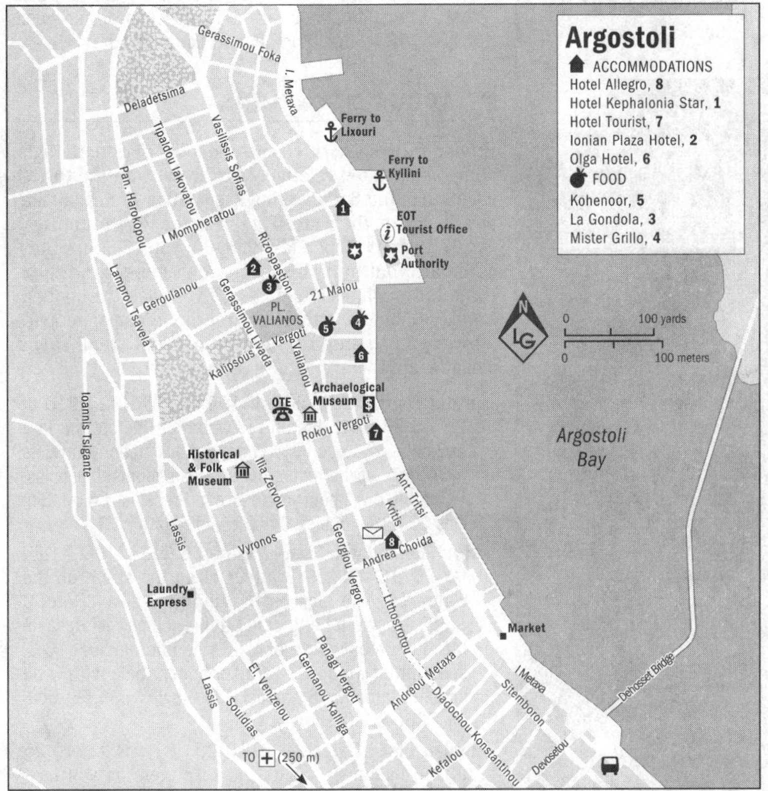

Work Opportunity: Milos Beach Bar and Cafe (☎26710 83 188 from May-Oct.; in winter 26710 83 231), in Skala, Kephalonia. Hires waitstaff, bartenders, and chefs for tourist season; summer hiring in Feb., Mar., Apr. Call and ask for Joya Grouzi.

International Bookstore: Petratos Bookstore (☎26710 22 546), on Lithostrotou across from a small church, 2 blocks up from the water. English-language and foreign newspapers, magazines, and best-sellers. Open M-Sa 8am-9:30pm.

Laundromat: Laundry Express, Lassis 46b. Walk inland on Vyronos for 9 blocks, turning left onto Lassis. The place is 2 blocks farther on your right. Self-service. Bring soap. Wash and dry €5.40 per load. Open daily 9am-10pm.

Police: ☎26710 22 200. On I. Metaxa across from the tourist office. Open 24hr.

Tourist Police: ☎26710 22 815. In the police station. Open daily 7am-10pm.

OTE: ☎26710 91 339. On Rokou Vergoti and Georgiou Vergoti, near the Archaeological Museum. Open M-Sa 7am-2:40pm.

Internet Access: Check your email to the sounds of blasting pop music at **Cafeland** (☎26710 24 064), on Andrea Choida, 1 block uphill from Hotel Allegro. €5 per hr., €2.50 min. Open daily 9am-11pm.

ON THE MENU

WINE FROM STONE

According to legend, Kephalos was the first settler on the island that now bears his name. Born and raised in the Attican hills of Athens, the young man knew such a drastic change in scenery would be a difficult transition and so upon arrival Kephalos immediately scaled the hills and planted a vine to remind him of his former home. Today while gorgeous coastlines have captured the imaginations of many a traveler, still those hills are what Kephalonians hold most dear, for, on what seems to be just barren crags jutting up 1000m above the sea, some of the best wine that Greece has to offer is born.

Kephalonian white wine *(Robola)* comes from the vines, which flourish on steep limestone slopes. The vineyards are quite a sight; scattered throughout the rocky mountaintops, green vines and blonde grapes grow literally out of the stone. The wine, with a "medium body" and "long aftertaste," is enjoyed complementing white meat or seafood.

Six wineries in Kephalonia create the award-winning *Robola*, now exported internationally. Two of the most highly regarded of the wineries are the Kephalonian Robola Producers Co-Operative and Metaxas Estate, within driving distance of Argostoli.

The Kephalonian Robola Producers Co-Operative (☎26710 86 301), by St. Gerasimos monastery, is open daily Oct.-May 8am-3pm and June-Sept. 7am-9pm. Metaxas Estate (☎26710 81 292), in the southwest, is open daily May-Oct. 10am-6pm and in winter by appointment.

Post Office: ☎26710 23 173. 2 blocks up from the water on Lithostrotou, at the intersection of Kerkyras. Open M-F 7:30am-2pm. **Postal code:** 28100.

ACCOMMODATIONS

Private rooms are often the cheapest option, though many are located relatively far away from the town. Check out the **Self-Catering Association of Kephalonia and Ithaka,** on the waterfront near the Port Authority. (☎26710 29 109. Open M-F 9am-3pm and 6-8pm.) Bargain hard, but in high season don't expect to find a room for much less than €25. If you plan to stay in a hotel, call ahead. Otherwise renting a car or moped allows you to stay in the omnipresent small town **domatia** and to have access to the beach.

Hotel Tourist, Antoni Tristi 109 (☎26710 22 510 or 26710 23 034). It's on the waterfront before the Port Authority as you approach from the bus station. Travelers may cringe at the name, but spacious rooms, balconies, TV, and A/C will help you forgive it. Breakfast €4.50. Singles €30-36; doubles €46-52. AmEx/MC/V. ❸

Hotel Kephalonia Star, I Metaxa 60 (☎26710 23 180; fax 26710 23 180), farther down the street on the waterfront; the sign on the door just says "Hotel C Star." 42 colorful and comfortable rooms feel upscale but have reasonable prices. Amenities include A/C, soundproof windows, TV, telephones, balconies, and small bathrooms. Breakfast €5. Singles €35-55; doubles €60-80. Cash only. ❹

Ionian Plaza Hotel (☎26710 25 581; fax 26710 25 585), on the right side of the plateia as you face inland. The unbeatable views and central location of this hotel satiate even the fussiest guests. All modern rooms come with A/C, TV, telephones, spacious bathrooms, and wood furnishings. Buffet breakfast included. Reservations recommended for high season. Singles €41-53.50; doubles €60-78. AmEx/MC/V. ❹

Olga Hotel, I Metaxa 82 (☎27610 24 981; fax 27610 24 985), on the waterfront between Hotel Tourist and Mister Grillo. One of the more expensive of those facing the water, this hotel features 42 small, somewhat elegant rooms with A/C, TV, telephones, balconies, and private baths. Reservations recommended for high season. Singles €45-52; doubles €55-60. V. ❸

Hotel Allegro, Andrea Choïda 2 (☎26710 28 684), up from the waterfront on Andrea Choïda (also spelled Hoïda and Xoïda), halfway between the bus station and Port Authority. Eccentric hall decorations lead to anticlimactic, simple, and decent rooms with telephones, fans, and shared fridge; some rooms with balconies and privates baths. Singles €25-50; doubles €30-60. Cash only. ❸

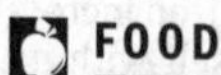 FOOD

Food may be cheaper on the waterfront, but selection and quality are better in the plateia. Those visiting on Saturdays can enjoy the well organized **farmer's market,** which takes over the waterfront near the bus station in the morning; less ephemeral are the fruit shops, bakeries, and supermarkets that line the water between the bus station and port. **Mister Grillo ❷,** near the Port Authority, has a constant local crowd that loves to sing along to live Greek music. The great food in very large portions caters to a multitude of tastes, including that of vegetarians. Traditional grilled octopus (€8.50) and moussaka (€5) satisfy carnivorous tastes. (Entrees €6-14. Cash only.) If you feel like spending extra to eat in one of the plateia restaurants, **La Gondola ❸,** with ample but often packed seating on 21 Maiou and in the plateia, is a worthy option. It serves Greek dishes, but people come for the divine Italian food like *risotto d'oro* with pumpkin and shrimp (€6.90). Rest assured that the steeper prices will also get you comfortable chairs, red roses on the table, and excellent service. (Pizza €5.90-9. Pasta €4.20-9.10. Greek entrees €5.90-8.80. Wine €8.50-25. Open noon-1am. MC/V.) For a more ethnic meal, **Kohenoor ❷,** at the intersection of Metaxa and Lavraga, by the plateia, doles out delicious, relatively well-priced Indian food. Lamb *vindaloo* (€8) and chicken *jalfrezi* (€8) are a couple of house specialties. (Appetizers €3.40-4.20. Curry dishes €6.50-8. Open 6:30pm-midnight. MC/V.)

SIGHTS

Argostoli's requisite and worthwhile **Archaeological Museum** is housed in a beautiful building a few blocks south of the plateia, near the Municipal Theater on R. Vergoti. Pottery and jewelry from excavated sites around the island, and Melissani lake, are displayed with explanations in both Greek and English. Though artifacts from the collection date back to the Paleolithic period, the most interesting items come from Roman times. Make sure to stop by the preserved mosaic from the temple of Poseidon from the 2nd century. (☎26710 28 300. Open Tu-Su 8:30am-3pm. €3, seniors and students €2, children and EU students free.) The **Historical and Folk Museum,** two blocks from the Archaeological Museum, on the road to the left of the theater, contains an exhaustive display of 19th-century objects. Of particular interest are the photographs of Argostoli during the 20th century, including shots of damage from the devastating 1953 earthquake. (☎26710 28 835. Open M-Sa 9am-2pm. €3, students €1.50, children free.)

DAYTRIPS FROM ARGOSTOLI

Renting a moped or car allows you to roam between sights and beaches, unrestrained by inconvenient bus schedules. You can also get to **Myrtos beach** (p. 469) on the western coast, considered one of Europe's best beaches.

CASTLE OF ST. GEORGE. The Venetian castle is 9km southeast of Argostoli, overlooking the village of Travliata. From its battlements, you can admire the panorama that once inspired Lord Byron. *(By moped, head toward Skala and bear left when the road splits or take either the Poros or Skala buses (10min., €1). Open M-Sa 8am-8pm. Free.)*

LIXOURI. In the center of the western peninsula, Lixouri offers a quiet alternative to the often heavily touristed plateias and beaches of Argostoli. The convenient boat schedule allows you to access miles of uncommercialized coastline at your leisure. If you wish to spend the day, you can rent **mopeds** at several places in Lixouri and explore the charming towns and villages in the area. You can also take one of the local **buses** including the one that runs twice a day to **Xi** (€1), an incredible red sand beach surrounded by cliffs. Alternatively the town itself with its small cafes and family bakeries is a wonderful place to settle down and unwind. For a change of scenery, a small beach lies at the far left of the waterfront as you face inland; it's about a 5min. walk along a lovely tree-lined promenade. *(Get there from Argostoli by boat (30min., every hr., €1.10). Buy tickets on board.)*

SOUTHERN COAST BEACHES. A few beaches and noteworthy towns dot the area south of Argostoli. Closer to the capital city than white-sanded **Ormous Lourda, Makris Yialos** and **Platis Yialos** share breathtaking shorelines below an enormous, steep cliff. You can sit above the sands and listen to the crashing waves or join the ever-present tanning population on the royal blue lounge chairs below. *(Take the Lassi bus; it's a 30min. ride and costs €1.)*

EAST OF ARGOSTOLI. The **Monastery of Ag. Gerasimos** was built around the underground cove where St. Gerasimos spent his last days on earth. Today a small ladder toward the back of the church allows guests to access that cove. When a large enough crowd forms at the monastery, the monks will open the silver casket which holds his preserved body. On the night of August 15, nearby **Omala** hosts a festival and a vigil in the saint's church. On the saint's namedays (Oct. 20 and Aug. 16), the whole town goes wild. *(Ask at the tourist office for info on the festival. Buses run from Argostoli to Omala/Agios Gerasimos at 10am, 12:30, 2pm; €1.)* **Skala** is yet another Kephalonian village with an exquisite beach; this one's pebble and sand. Sun-soaked history buffs will be glad to see that the remains of a 2nd-century Roman villa are also in town; almost all of its structure is gone but the mosaic floors are remarkably well preserved. In fact you can still make out one scene of an unfortunate man being devoured by various beasts. *(Look for the signs as you walk down the road from the bus stop toward the water. Open M 8:30am-3pm, Tu-Su 8:30am-10pm. Free.)* Eat at the **Sun Rise Restaurant ❸**, all the way to the left of the beach, facing inland. It's on the expensive side, but the seafood, such as the seafood platter for two (€17.90) is reasonably priced and fresh. (Fish entrees start at €4.90. Pizza €5.90-6.30. Pasta €4.80-5.80. Greek entrees €5.90-10.80. Children's menu available. V.) Also keep in mind that on August 15, the village of **Markopoulo,** on Kephalonia's southeastern side, celebrates the Assumption of the Virgin Mary with a festival involving an all-night church liturgy. According to local belief, hundreds of small snakes with black crosses on their heads slither over the icons during the service.

SAMI Σαμη ☎26740

As you stroll through Sami, stunning views in all directions make it difficult to decide which is more lovely: the tempestuous blue waves crashing on the long, white-sand beach or the lush, green hills cradling the town. Unfortunately reminders are everywhere that Sami served as the set for the movie *Captain Corelli's Mandolin,* based on the similarly named (and much better) novel. Despite this brief brush with Hollywood and constant tourism in the high season, Sami remains fairly quiet and peaceful. It's close to the natural wonders of Melissani Lake, Drogarati cave, and Antisamos beach, whose beauty makes it a good place to spend the afternoon and night before catching a ferry from its small but busy port.

TRANSPORTATION. Buses leave the station on the left end of the waterfront for **Argostoli** (7:15, 8am, 3:15, 5:30pm; €2.50) and **Fiskardo** (10:15am, 2pm; €3). Buy tickets on board. From Sami, **ferries** sail to: **Vathy,** Ithaka (1hr., 4 per day, €2.50) and **Patras** (2½hr.; 8:30am, 5pm; €11.50). In summer, international ferries go to **Brindisi, Italy** (daily beginning in early July, €35). **Taxis** (☎26740 22 308) line up on the waterfront beside the plateia but are very expensive.

ORIENTATION AND PRACTICAL INFORMATION. The waterfront street, lined with restaurants and cafes, intersects the main plateia. White sandy beaches lie both to the left and right of the town center. Ferries land on either side of the town plateia. From the bus station, facing the water, turn left to reach the plateia. You may be able to see the top of the blue and white Hotel Kyma, which sits on the (unmarked) main road of Sami; this road runs parallel to the water one block inland. The plateia lies between the road and the waterfront. If you follow it with the water on your right, this main road leads to Argostoli. **Sami Star Travel,** next to the bus station on the waterfront, sells ferry tickets; a receptive staff also offers general information. (☎26740 23 007. Open daily 9am-10pm.) The 24hr. **police station** (☎26740 22 100) is located on the main road that leads to Argostoli; it can be found three blocks from the plateia on the right. There is no official tourist office, but the police may be able to answer your questions. There are several **banks: Emporiki Trapeza** on the waterfront, to the right of the plateia as you face inland, has an **ATM.** (Open M-Th 8am-2:30pm, F 8am-2pm.) **Pharmacies** are on the main road to Argostoli. The **OTE** is one block past Emporiki Trapeza. (Open M-F 7:30am-10pm.) For **Internet** access, try **Melissani Restaurant and Snack Bar,** next to Karavomilos Beach Camping. (☎26740 22 395. €6 per hr. Open daily 11am-2pm and 5:30-11pm.) Follow directions to Karvomilos beach (p. 467) The **post office** is on the road to Argostoli, two blocks off the right corner of the plateia across the street from the supermarket. (Open M-F 7:30am-2pm.) **Postal code:** 28080.

ACCOMMODATIONS AND FOOD. Because Sami is a convenient base for travel within Kephalonia, there's a high demand for rooms, which are relatively expensive. The nearby village of **Karavomilos,** on the way to Melissani lake, offers more **domatia.** If you insist on staying in town, try the **Hotel Kyma ❸,** in the middle of the plateia, for fairly sizable rooms with private sinks, fans, and anti-mosquito plug-ins. (☎26740 22 064. Singles €18-28; doubles €26-55; triples €31-66. Cash only.) **Hotel Melissania ❸,** two blocks inland from the port authority, on the far left of the waterfront, has funky hallway decor that leads to 15 small, somewhat dim rooms crammed with amenities: private baths, TVs, telephones, radios, balconies, fans, and fridges. (☎26740 22 464. Singles €25-37; doubles €30-58; triples €45-70. Cash only.) **Karavomilos Beach Camping ❶,** a 15min. walk from town with the water on your right, is set in a huge field. Guests enjoy cleanliness, hot showers, electricity, laundry facilities, Internet access,

IN RECENT NEWS

SAMI GOES HOLLYWOOD

Before the streets were filled with souvenir stands and the beaches with tanning tourists, Kephalonia underwent some tremendously turbulent times. Foreign troops occupied the island during both world wars, while the post-World War II Civil War had threatened to tear all of Greece apart at the seams. Finally the destructive legacy left by a massive 1953 earthquake haunts the minds of every Kephalonian.

Later Louis de Bernieres published a Western novel about Kephalonia set during World War II. The critically acclaimed *Captain Corelli's Mandolin* became progressively more popular despite upsetting many Greeks. So when producers of the major motion picture bearing a similar title, *Corelli's Mandolin,* came knocking on Kephalonia's door with the intention of converting de Bernieres's book into a shot-on-location film, many Greek eyebrows were furrowed. Though Greek officials had dodged allowing the big-time producers to film scenes on their shores, a desperate, deep-walleted Hollywood, dreaming of filming in Greece, gave the Kephalonian town of Sami little choice but to comply.

By the end of the shoot, they had actually grown attached to their guests. The film had brought a moderate economic boost to the town since local manual laborers were employed and islanders were even hired as extras. Ultimately when *Corelli's Mandolin's* filming was wrapped up, a mediocre (at best) blockbuster was completed but an island community strangely contented.

and a mini-market. (☎26740 22 480. Depending on the season €4.50-6 per person, €2.50-3 per child; €3-3.50 per small tent, €4-5 per large tent; €2.50-3 per car. Electricity €3.50. Cash only.) **Hotel Ionian ❷**, on the main road past the church and on the right, is a cheap in-town option. It features 16 small rooms with little more than beds, telephones, and private sinks. (☎26740 22 035. Singles €20-24; doubles €25-40. Cash only.)

Taka Taka Mam ❶, on the waterfront, combines good budget fare (gyros and salads €1.75-1.90; omelettes €3 and up) with the ultimate ocean view. (Open daily until 1am. Cash only.) **Pizza Tereza ❷**, toward the far right end (when facing inland) of the waterfront cafes, offers a little taste of Italy in very big portions. (Pizzas €5.50-7. Pasta €3.80-6.30. Cash only.) **Mermaid Restaurant ❷**, Taka's waterfront neighbor, has many vegetarian options. (Swordfish souvlaki €8.50. Grilled peppers €4.50. Cash only.)

SIGHTS AND BEACHES. A short drive or long walk from town leads to two of Sami's most popular sites, the underground caves of **Melissani** and **Drogarati.** Melissani, 2km from Sami, is part of the huge, underground Lake Karavomilos. Finding it is rather simple, though the walk will take 30-45min.; follow the beach with the water to your right until you come to a small ocean-fed "lake" with a waterwheel on the far side; turn left after the restaurant by the lake, walk inland to the road about 30m, and turn right; down this street you'll see signs to the cave. The boat tour of the cave lasts 15min., during which lake guides will row you around the two large caverns flooded with sparkling water and studded with stalactites. Because the cave has an open roof measuring 50m by 30m, you'll want to go when the sun is high in the sky. (Open daily 9am-7pm; in winter 10am-4pm. Free. Tipping the boatman is encouraged.) **Drogarati,** 5km from Sami, is a large cavern full of spectacular stalactites and stalagmites. In August an international choral society holds concerts here. To find it, head inland on the road to Argostoli and follow the signs (1hr.-1½hr.) or take the bus to Argostoli and ask to be let off at Drogarati; you'll most likely be dropped off at the fork in the road, 1.5km from the caves. (☎26740 22 950. Open until nightfall. €3, children €1.50.) **Agia Efimia,** 10km north of Sami, is a pretty harbor town that deserves a visit. Buses (10:15am, 2pm; €3) run from Sami to Agia Efimia. Ask the Fiskardo bus to let you off there (15min., €3). Isolated and alluring **Antisamos** beach is a must if you get to this side of Kephalonia. The long, white pebble beach is enclosed by rolling green hills. You can take a taxi to Antisamos (€8) or you can hike there (1¼hr.) by following the waterfront left from the plateia as you face inland; take the road between the Port Authority and Sami Travel. Since the hike is fairly long and challenging, bring plenty of water and wear good shoes.

FISKARDO Φισκαρδο ☎26740

The road north ends at must-see Fiskardo, which escaped the 1953 earthquake and is now one of few remaining examples of 18th- and 19th-century Kephalonian architecture. Fiskardo's crescent-shaped waterfront is tinged with the pastel hues of the modest buildings surrounding it. At night a romantic aura pervades the town, twinkling with the dim lights of boats resting in the water. Touristed largely by the wealthy, Fiskardo has avoided the garish trappings that sometimes mar other seaside towns; shops selling €60 strands of worry beads and cafes offering €10 cocktails subtly substitute for foam parties and winner-take-all drinking contests. A splendid walk through the woods or swim from the rocks takes you to the forested tidbit of land across the harbor, where the lighthouse and ruins of a 15th-century Venetian fortress rest. For archaeology buffs, there's an open excavation of a 2nd-century Roman graveyard near the harbor, along the water. Fiskardo's unbeatable beach lies 500m outside of town, on the hilly road back to Argostoli, in a quiet cove that has flat rocks fit for sunbathing.

TRANSPORTATION AND PRACTICAL INFORMATION. Buses for **Argostoli** leave from the parking lot next to the church, uphill from the town. Two **buses** per day run to and from **Argostoli** (1½-2hr.; 6:30am, 4:30pm; €4) and **Sami** (1hr., €3). **Ferries** go to **Nidri,** Lefkada (2hr., €5) and **Vasiliki** (1hr., €5). For transportation and lodgings questions and other helpful information, contact **Nautilus Travel Agency,** at the right end of the waterfront. (☎26740 41 440. Open daily 9am-9pm.)

ACCOMMODATIONS AND FOOD. Rooms are not cheap in Fiskardo, even in the scattered **domatia.** Early in summer, simple doubles start at €40. Although the town is full of excellent restaurants, most of them are heavily touristed and very expensive. An exception is the pink-and-blue **Lagondera ❷,** just off the waterfront, on the road to the right of Vassos Cafe. Though it lacks both attentive waitstaff and waterfront view, the food is delicious. (Salads €2.50-4. Greek entrees €3.50-6.50. Cash only.) At **Nicholas Taverna ❷,** located 200m to the right of the port (facing inland), a full-size playground and ostentatious waiters occupy the kids so couples can enjoy a romantic dinner with an extraordinary view of the water from this elevated restaurant. (☎26740 41 307. Salads €3.50. Entrees €5-13. MC/V.)

SIGHTS AND BEACHES. Venturing a few minutes away from the waterfront proves to be quite a rewarding venture. To reach the old-fashioned **lighthouse,** walk all the way around the waterfront with the sea on your right to Nicholas Taverna. A short and shaded path picks up where the road ends, and is marked with yellow circles all the way to the lighthouse. If you need to cool off and don't want to trek all the way to a big beach, you can find a smaller pebble beach very close to town. With the water on your left, head along the waterfront road for about 10min. until it turns right; the beach is on your left just past the Roman graves. Cliffs plunge into the sea along the coastal road north from Argostoli and Sami to Fiskardo. Just off this road lies one of the best beaches in Europe **Myrtos** (p. 465) which shouldn't be missed. The snowy white pebbles and clear, blue water are stunning enough, but it is perhaps the beach's location, pressed against the cliffs, that makes it so divine. The **buses** from Fiskardo to Sami and Argostoli stop at the turn-off to Myrtos, 4km from the gasp-inducing beauty of the beach—hop off there and hoof it the rest of the way. Roughly 4km up the road from the Myrtos turn-off is the equally incredible Venetian castle of **Assos,** on a steep, wooded peninsula connect to the island by a narrow isthmus. Completed in the early part of the 17th century, much of the castle and most of its houses are well preserved. The Fiskardo buses will stop at the turn-off for Assos; it's a steep downhill 4km walk to the village and another few kilometers to the castle.

ZAKYNTHOS Ζακυνθος

The varied landscapes and seascapes of Zakynthos (or Zante) comprise an exceptionally subtle palette of colors—white cliffs rise from turquoise water, sun-bleached wheat waves in the shadow of evergreens, and magenta flowers frame the twisting streets. Known as the greenest of the Ionian Islands, Zakynthos is home to thousands of plant and flower species, some of them unique to the island. The island is also home to a large population of loggerhead sea turtles, a source of pride among islanders. Still in Zakynthos Town and on its neighboring beaches, you'll encounter more sweaty tourists than nature's true beauty. Set out for the countryside to appreciate Zakynthos's natural sights—like its famous Blue Caves in the north. Smaller than Kephalonia but larger than Ithaka, its splendor can be felt many times over from any boat, beach, or bicycle. Those who venture away from shops that sell oversized, plush sea turtles will quickly come to understand why the Venetians called it Fior di Levante—the Flower of the East.

ZAKYNTHOS TOWN ☎26950

Bustling Zakynthos Town welcomes visitors with arcaded streets and white-washed buildings. After an earthquake destroyed the city in 1953, locals restored it to its former state, recreating the Venetian architecture in areas such as Plateia Solomou. The beaches just north and south of Zakynthos Town allow locals to let loose. If you have the call of the wild itching in your veins, head out to one of the more remote beaches where serene beauty pervades the countryside.

TRANSPORTATION

Flights: The **airport** (☎26950 28 322) is 6km south of town. Flights to **Athens** (45min., 2 per day, €75). The **Olympic Airways** office, Al. Roma 16 (☎26950 28 611), is 2 blocks past Il Primo and 3 blocks inland. Open M-F 8am-3:30pm.

Ferries: Ferries for **Kyllini** in the Peloponnese (1½hr.; 5 per day, M-Sa 5:30am-7:30pm, Su 8am-7:30pm; €5.10) depart from Zakynthos Town's southern dock, on the left side of the waterfront as you face inland. Tickets for Kyllini ferries can be bought at **Praktoreio Ploion** (☎26278 22 083), next to Hertz on Lomvardou past the police station with the water on your right. Open daily 8am-10pm. Skinari, north of Zakynthos Town, has ferries to **Pesada,** Kephalonia (1½hr., 1-2 per day, €5.) Be warned that both Pesada and Skinari are very small; Kephalonian buses do not go to Pesada and the town lacks accommodations and Zakynthian buses do not run to Skinari; you'll need to take a taxi (€27-35). Due to such difficulties you might save time and money by flying from the airport near Argostoli directly to Zakynthos Town. Returning to Kyllini and heading to Kephalonia by ferry is an alternative. Ferry tickets are available at the **boat agencies** along the waterfront. For more information, call the **port police** (☎26950 28 117 or 28 118).

Buses: Filita 42 (☎26950 22 255), on the corner of Pl. Eleftheriou. From Pl. Solomou, walk 6 blocks south (with the water on your left) and 1 block inland; from the police station, walk 3 blocks north (with the water on your right) and 1 block inland. Schedules can change monthly. To: **Athens** (6hr.; 5 per day, 5am-7pm; €17.50, including ferry) via **Patras** (3hr., €5.20 including ferry) and **Thessaloniki** (10hr., 7:30am, €32.80, including ferry). Schedules for local service are posted outside the bus station; a complete list is at the info window, as are flyers with bus time tables. **Local buses** run to: **Alykes** (M-F 4 per day, 6:50am-4:30pm; Sa-Su 4 per day, 7:30am-4:30pm; €1.10); **Argassi** (M-F 6 per day, 6:45am-7pm; Sa-Su 4 per day, 9:30am-3pm; €0.90); **Lagana** (M-Sa 12 per day, 7:15am-8:10pm; Su 8 per day, 7:15am-8pm; €0.75); **Kalamaki** (M-Sa 7 per day, 7:15am-6:30pm; Su 5 per day, 7:15am-5pm; €0.90); **Tsilivi** (M-Sa 10 per day, 6:20am-8:10pm; Su 4 per day, 10am-3:30pm; €0.90); **Vasilikos** (M-Sa 6:45am and 2:30pm, €1.10).

Taxis: ☎26950 48 400. On side streets off the waterfront. Available 24hr., though those seeking transportation in the early morning hours should make arrangements the day before. Taxis in Zakynthos Town are fairly expensive.

Rentals: Hertz, Lomvardou 38 (☎26950 45 706). Cars from €62 in high season, €40 per day in low season; prices include unlimited mileage, insurance, and tax. 21+. Open daily 9am-1:30pm and 5:30-9pm. **EuroSky Rentals,** A. Makri 6 (☎26950 53 117), 1 block inland on A. Makri, charges €10 per day for mopeds, €18 per day for motorcycles, and as low as €24 per day for cars. License required. 23+. Open daily 9am-9pm. **Spyros Rent a Scooter** (☎26950 23 963), toward the center of Lomvardou, also has cheap moped rates (€10 per day) though you may have to bargain with the owner. While many agencies require a 3-5 day min. on bicycle rentals, you can rent one for €5 per day at **Stamatis** (☎26950 23 963), on Karvela by Hotel Phoenix.

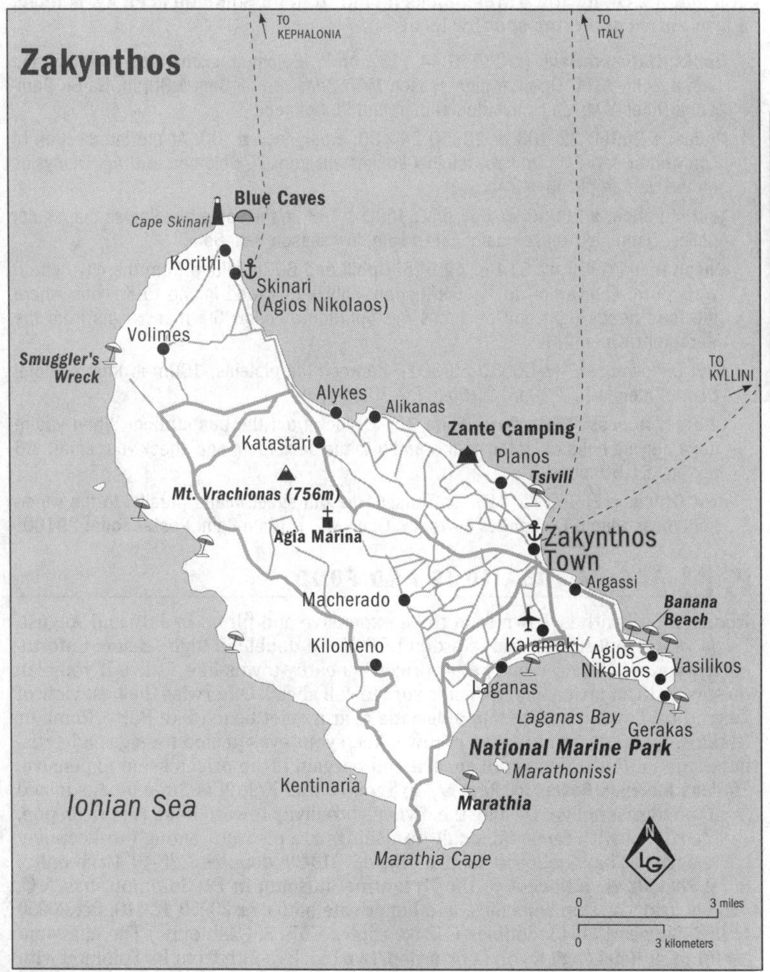

ORIENTATION AND PRACTICAL INFORMATION

The waterfront runs between **Pl. Solomou** and **Ag. Dionysios church.** Each end has a dock: Kyllini ferries usually dock at the left end (when facing inland) by Ag. Dionysios; all other boats (like daily cruises) dock at the right end by Pl. Solomou. The waterfront street, **Lomvardou,** runs between the two docks and is lined with restaurants, gift shops, car and moped rental agencies, and ferry agencies. The next street inland is **Filita,** home to the bus station, Internet cafe, and a plethora of fast-food stands; Filita becomes Klavdianou toward Pl. Solomou. Behind it are **Foskolou, Alexandrou Roma,** which is the main shopping street, and **Tertseti.** These three streets change names or end between Martinegou and Ag. Dionysios. Three blocks inland from Pl. Solomou is **Pl. Ag. Markou,** a less formal gathering spot for locals.

Banks: National Bank (☎26950 44 113), on Pl. Solomou, **exchanges currency** and has a 24hr. **ATM.** Open in high season M-Th 8am-2pm, F 8am-1:30pm, Sa-Su 9am-1pm. Other ATMs on Lomvardou and around Pl. Solomou.

Police: ☎26950 22 200 or 26950 24 480; emergency ☎100. At the intersection of Lomvardou and Fra. Tzoulati, roughly equidistant from Pl. Solomou and Ag. Dionysios on the waterfront. Open 24hr.

Tourist Police: ☎26950 27 367 or 26950 24 483. In the same building as the regular police. Open high season daily 7am-11pm, low season 8am-8pm.

Hospital: ☎26950 42 514 or 42 515. Uphill and 600m inland from the city center. Walk down Lomvardou to Ag. Eleftheriou. Follow this road inland to Kokkini, where the road heads right and becomes Ag. Spiridona. Follow the many signs from the waterfront. Open 24hr.

OTE: Dimokratias 2 (☎26950 59 301), between the plateias, 100m in front of Hotel Diana. Open M-Th 7:30am-1:30pm, F 7:30am-1pm.

Internet Access: Top's Cafe, Filita 38, 1 block from the bus station. When you're done playing billiards or foosball, wander to the back room and check your email. €6 per hr., €1.50 min.

Post Office: ☎26950 42 418. On Tertseti, the 4th street inland parallel to the waterfront, near Xenou. **Exchanges currency.** Open M-F 7:30am-8pm. **Postal code:** 29100.

ACCOMMODATIONS AND FOOD

Rooms in Zakynthos Town tend to be expensive and fill up in July and August. Large waterfront hotels charge around €80 for a double in high season; unfortunately, you won't find much better prices in nearby towns like Tsilivi. If you plan on staying in an upscale hotel, make sure to call ahead. Otherwise the best view of Zakynthos Town may be from a **domatia** near a quiet beach like Porto Roma or Geratos. If you do want to stay in town, keep your eyes peeled for signs advertising domatia. Put on your poker face and bargain if the prices seem expensive. **Athina Marouda Rooms for Rent ❷,** on Tzoulati and Koltoi, is three blocks inland from the tourist police. Despite the owner's proclivity toward loud, American pop, simple rooms with fans and small furnishings are pleasant enough to keep any backpacker at bay. (☎26950 45 194. Singles €10-20; doubles €25-40. Cash only.) **Hotel Phoenix ❸,** adjacent to the Byzantine museum in Pl. Solomou, has A/C, phones, fridges, TVs, balconies, and big private baths. (☎26950 42 419; fax 26950 45 083. Singles €30-43; doubles €42-58; triples €57-88. Cash only.) The anassuming lobby at **Hotel Aegli ❸,** on Lomvardou, two blocks south from Pl. Solomou with the water on your left, leads to immaculate, rooms with TVs, balconies, fans, and admirably large private baths. (Singles €30; doubles €45; triples €60. Cash only.) **Hotel Diana ❹,** in Pl. Ag. Markou, adjacent to the Catholic church, has fully carpeted rooms, which come with A/C, baths, TVs, and Internet access. (☎26950 28 547; fax 26950 45 047. Breakfast included. Singles €35-50; doubles €50-80. MC/V.)

Dining in Zakynthos is a pleasure. Restaurants line the waterfront and Pl. Ag. Markou; on Alex. Roma every other place is either a cafe or a candy shop. Ubiquitous fast-food joints serve staples like tiropita (€1.40). The **Coop Supermarket,** on Lomvardou, 50m to the right of the police station with your back to the water, caters to those who cater to themselves. (Open M-F 8am-10:30pm, Sa 8am-6pm.) **Il Primo ❷,** Lomvardou 22, a block and a half past Hertz with the water on your right. This unassuming restaurant dishes out filling portions of Italian cuisine that are sure to satisfy both your appetite and budget. (☎26950 77 891. Pasta €3-5. Vegetarian dishes €3-5. Pizza €3.70-7. V.) Even the tourist traffic at **House of Latas (To Spiti to Lata) ❸,** 2km above the city (follow the signs to Bohalis), near the Venetian castle, can't detract from the spectacular view of nearby Zakynthos. Occasional live local music adds to the ambiance. (☎26950 41 585. Salads €3-6. Grilled entrees €7 and up. Open daily 6pm-1am. MC/V.) **Molos Restaurant ❷,** on the waterfront, wedged between souvenir stands, exclusively serves meat from its own farm. (Chicken stuffed with corn €7. Pizza €5.60-8.80. Omelettes €2.70-3.90. English breakfast €4.50. Cash only.) **The Garden ❸,** next to Ag. Dionysios, in a quiet, spacious plateia. Duck into this floral eatery to escape the chaos of the waterfront. (☎26950 48 583. Pizza €5.60-6.60. Seafood €7.10-38. Beer €2.20-2.60. Cash only.)

SIGHTS AND HIKING

The **Church of Agios Dionysios,** named in honor of the island's patron saint has five beautifully-crafted chandeliers, under which you can peacefully meditate. In a room surrounded by golden walls, a magnificent silver chest holds some of the saint's relics. (Open 7am-1pm and 4:30-10pm. Modest dress required.) Next door is the **Ecclesiastical Museum,** with murals, vestments, and beautifully engraved Bibles on display. Make sure not to neglect the paintings by the stairs to the second floor; the one of Jesus refusing the devil's temptation is particularly intriguing. (Open daily 9am-10:30pm. €1.) In Pl. Solomou, the **Byzantine Museum** houses two floors of icons from the Ionian School, a distinctive local hybrid of Byzantine and Renaissance art styles, accompanied by elaborate iconostases, chalices, and miscellaneous church items. The 16th-century iconostasis from St. Andreas's monastery is an impressive feature, filling up the walls of an entire room. Also noteworthy is the 18th-century painting of the whale devouring the prophet Jonah. Many of these artifacts were rescued by devout locals who risked their lives to pluck them from the dusty rubble of area churches after the 1953 earthquake; poignant photos documenting the effects of the disaster are juxtaposed with many of the Byzantine artifacts. (☎26950 42 714. Open Tu-Su 8am-2:30pm. €3, students free.)

A hearty walk (or nice drive) gets you to the **Venetian Castle,** 2km above town, where Dionysios Solomos wrote the poem that became the Greek National Anthem. Take Tertseti, which becomes N. Koluva, to the edge of town or head inland from Pl. Ag. Markou and follow the signs uphill to Bohalis. Turn left after

THE HIDDEN DEAL

BICYCLE BEACH HOPPING

It can be hard to appreciate the beauty of Zakynthos (considered to be Paradise by many of the locals) when a dirty tour bus window is blocking your view of the mountains and a noisy moped is muffling the sound of crashing waves. Luckily, all hope is not lost. With only a few euros and a lot of exercise, you can experience Zakynthos the way it was meant to be.

If you're staying in Zakynthos Town, rent a bicycle and make an early morning ride to Porto Roma (18km) or Gerakas (20km), beautiful, relatively untouristed beaches on the southwestern coast of the island. When you get there, grab some water from the nearest *periptero* you see and start a full day of bicycling and beach-hopping. As you head north, you'll encounter steep climbs and easy descents, all the while surrounded by the greenest of trees. When the the greenery begins to block your view of the sea as you approach Vasilikos, simply ride down to one of the nearest beaches and unwind for a while. Areas like Banana Beach and Porto Zoro are treasured most by the locals for their miles of of turquoise waters and tourist-free sands. When you hear the road calling, mount up and continue on your way. If you like a particular place, rest assured that "Rooms to Let" signs are usually within eyesight.

Bike rentals (€5) available at Stamatis (☎26950 23 963), on Karvela by Hotel Phoenix. Less motivated riders can always catch the bus to Vasilikos (M-Sa 6:45am and 2:30pm, €1.10) and store bikes underneath.

1km, following the signs to the kastro. The journey is probably more worthwhile than the castle itself, whose walls are all that remain. If you go at night, you'll enjoy an incredible view of Zakynthos Town. (Open Tu-Su 8am-2:30pm.)

DAYTRIPS FROM ZAKYNTHOS TOWN

You can see all of Zakynthos, including the otherwise-inaccessible **western cliffs,** by boat. Shop around for a cruise on Lomvardou. Most tours leave in the morning, usually around 9am, return around 5:30 or 6pm, and prefer a reservation the day before. Don't buy from hawkers around gift shops—they'll charge a commission (€5-9) on top of the agency's fee (usually starting around €15, although competition sometimes lowers prices). Cruises go to many of the island's most spectacular sights, including the **Blue Caves** on the northeastern shore past Skinari. The azure sea reflects off the ceilings of the stalactite-filled caverns, creating a blue glow throughout. Southwest of the Blue Caves is the **Smuggler's Wreck,** a large boat skeleton whose marvel has made the area one of the most photographed beaches in the world, and Marathonissi, or **Turtle Island,** so named because of its proximity to loggerhead turtle nesting grounds and its physical resemblance to a turtle. Inquire at the tourist police or one of the agencies in town. To explore with far less hassle, get a **moped**—there are rental agencies at many beaches (€8-15). If you do decide to go solo, get several road maps (€1-5) and ask directions; the island is developing rapidly, and many new roads don't appear on old maps.

Four kilometers south of Zakynthos town is the bustling beach town of **Argassi.** Buses run to the village daily (20min.; M-F 6 per day, 6:45am-7pm; Sa-Su 4 per day, 9:30am-3pm; €0.90), but it's an easy 30-40min. walk along the main road out of town with the water on your left. Though neither quiet nor secluded, Argassi offers many of the same conveniences of Zakynthos Town with half the noise and twice the tourist to native ratio. Hotels and **domatia** line the roads off the main street. Moped and car rental agencies, plenty of restaurants, and a children-oriented go-cart race track are just a few of the town's tourist-oriented amenities. The Thai, Indian, or Chinese restaurants in town may are worth checking out if you're in the mood for something different. **Courser ❷,** off the main road to the right, in the town center, is the local favorite for Chinese cuisine. Chef Ruan Xiao serves an enormous variety of appetizers and entrees. (☎26950 42 311. Vegetarian dishes €4.35-7.70. Beef with broccoli €8. Fixed menus for 2-4 people available. Open daily 6-11:30pm; takeout until midnight. Cash only.) On the main road from Zakynthos Town, **The Mouse House** has a dozen computers with **Internet** access. (☎26950 49 510. €6 per hr., €1.50 min. Open daily 9am-midnight.) And if a 30min. of web-surfing and €4 milkshakes leave you without money for the bus, there's a 24hr. **ATM** between Courser and the main road back to town.

Wide, sandy **Tsilivi beach,** 6km up the waterfront road with the water on your right, is fairly crowded with sun-seeking foreigners. It's nearly as close as Argassi, but walking is not recommended; pedestrians are forced to share the hilly, narrow, and winding road with unyielding forces like fast motorcyclists and oblivious tour bus drivers. Fortunately, local buses run daily (30min.; M-Sa 10 per day, 6:20am-8:10pm; Su 4 per day, 10am-3:30pm; €0.90). **Planos,** the town leading to Tsilivi beach, has plenty of hotels and **domatia. Zante Camping ❶,** 3km past Planos on Ampula beach, is one of Zakynthos's only beach campsites. Its quiet location, amidst flora and sands devoid of tourist foot-prints, makes it a wonderful place to get acquainted with the island. Numerous amenities, including a cafeteria, mini-market, currency exchange, and car rental, comfort both first-time campers and lifetime backpackers. (☎26950 61 710. €4.50 per adult, €2.70 per child ages 4-10; €3.50 per small tent, €4 per large tent; €3 per car. Electricity €3.)

For those who need to escape the crowds, nearly untouched beaches carpet the peninsula that stretches out 18km from Zakynthos Town. Farthest south, 2km past Vasilikos, are the beautiful, untouched sands of **Porto Roma.** A few minutes north, just as you enter the region of Vasilikos and approach Agios Nikolaos beach, you'll find the warm-watered **Mavratzis.** And if you prefer a more authentic beach-going crowd, **Porto Zoro** and **Banana beach** are local favorites. For a truly unique experience, rent a bicycle in town and make an early morning ride to Porto Roma (or catch the early bus and store your bike down below in the bus). Then spend the day heading back to town, rewarding yourself by stopping at each beach along the way. And if a particular place strikes a chord with you, rest assured that "Rooms to Let" will not be far away. Travelers should consider that some spots on the western coast of the peninsula are protected areas that must be vacated in the evenings to accommodate the sea turtles which come ashore to nest (see below). **Buses** leave Zakynthos Town for Vasilikos (M-Sa 6:45am, 2:30pm; €1.10).

Romantic restaurants hide among tourist joints in **Alykes,** 16km from Zakynthos Town. Fringed with soft, clean, sand beaches, it can often be less crowded than its southern counterparts. In the true spirit of Greek hospitality, many hotels and pool clubs offer free lounge chairs and umbrellas. **Buses** run from Zakynthos Town to Alykes (M-F 4 per day, 6:50am-4:30pm; Sa-Su 4 per day, 7:30am-4:30pm; €1.10).

Tourists should note that they share Zakynthos's beaches with a resident population of **endangered sea turtles.** Most beachgoers are unaware that a simple stroll through the sand can destroy hundreds of turtle eggs. Zakynthos is gradually making efforts to protect the turtles and their nests, including encouraging waterfront properties to cover their lights, as freshly hatched baby turtles mistake the light for reflections off the ocean and follow the twinkling inland instead of toward the sea. Ask at tour companies which beaches are turtle territory; Gerakas, Kalamaki and Laganas have turtle populations.

SKINARI Σκιναρι ☎26950

At the extreme northern tip of Zakynthos, a breathtaking drive away from the bustle of busier beach towns, is tiny **Skinari,** locally known as **Agios Nikolaos.** Ferries to **Pesada** on Kephalonia depart from here. Bus service to town is nonexistent, so incoming ferry passengers need to arrange their own transportation to Zakynthos Town; you might require a taxi (€27-35). Skinari has no rental agencies. Above the La Grotta restaurant, 150m to the right (with your back to the water) and back toward Zakynthos Town, **Hotel La Grotta ❷** offers the only rooms in town. Each comes with A/C, balcony, and shower. (☎26950 31 224; fax 26950 31 505. Singles €20; doubles €35-40. MC/V.) Farther down the street, **La Storia Restaurant ❷** serves traditional Greek cuisine. (☎26950 31 635. Squid €6. Salads €3-6. Seafood entrees €6 and up. Non-fish entrees €6.50-8. Beer €2.50. MC/V.)

During the day, you can buy tickets on the waterfront for a fishing boat tour of the **Blue Caves** (40min., €5) or the caves and the **Smuggler's Wreck** (1¾hr., €12), accessible only by water (p. 474). These tours are smaller and shorter than those from Zakynthos Town, so if ferry schedules force you to visit, take advantage of this convenience; during high season, boats leave every 5-15min. from the dock. For more information, contact **Actipis Cruises** (☎26950 31 224). You can also rent canoes and other boats on Skinari beach.

NORTHEAST AEGEAN ISLANDS

Flung at the outskirts of Greece, closer to Turkey than to Athens, the islands of the Northeast Aegean have resisted cultural hybridity, retaining a distinct Greek local culture in spite of a long history of invasions. The islands' wooded mountains and dry, rocky hills conceal unspoiled villages next to military bunkers, both of which remind visitors of a determination to retain cultural authenticity. Deck chairs and mass hotels are rarities in this part of Greece, where vast, pristine wildernesses and charming local hospitality are the traveler's welcome and reward.

HIGHLIGHTS OF THE NORTHEAST AEGEAN

SEEK your muse on Lesvos (p. 493), inspiration to poetic minds from the ancient sensual lyricist Sappho to the Modernist Nobel laureate Odysseus Elytis.

PLUNGE into the netherworld of the vast, underground aqueduct on Samos (p. 481).

SPREAD your wings on Ikaria (p. 476), but don't fly too close to the sun like the island's mythological namesake, Icarus.

GAPE at the detailed geometric designs adorning the houses of Pyrgi on Chios (p. 492).

IKARIA Ικαρια

Ikaria is named after the reckless young Icarus, whose wax wings melted after he flew too close to the sun; a legendary rock marks the spot where he plunged to his watery demise. Ikaria's history matches the rebellious attitude of its namesake; during the Balkan Wars a revolutionary movement led to the formation of a short-lived Ikarian republic. Today the island's predominately agricultural economy remains one of the poorest in the region, without a major tourist industry. Perhaps consequently, the Communist Party (KKE) enjoys huge popularity with the island's residents; anti-NATO banners make a surprising addition amidst the otherwise peaceful, relaxed landscape. Ikaria's lush coastline is speckled by serene, largely untouristed beaches, some with natural hot springs. Looming above the sea is an enormous chain of rocky mountains that separates the north from the south. Besides providing dramatic vistas, the mountainous terrain makes transportation around the island surprisingly difficult. Visitors patient with the island's often inexplicable schedule are rewarded with an unspoiled slice of Greece, rich with the laughter of children and the crashing of waves in the black night.

AGIOS KIRYKOS Αγιος Κηρυκος ☎22750

This lovely town's shaded plateia stretches along the giant steps leading into the sea, where fishing boats dock. The plateia is nearly deserted from noon until 6pm, at which point the locals begin to circulate and sip frappés or play football by the pier. Even at 1am you'll see small children playing energetically in front of the cafes as their parents chat and gossip.

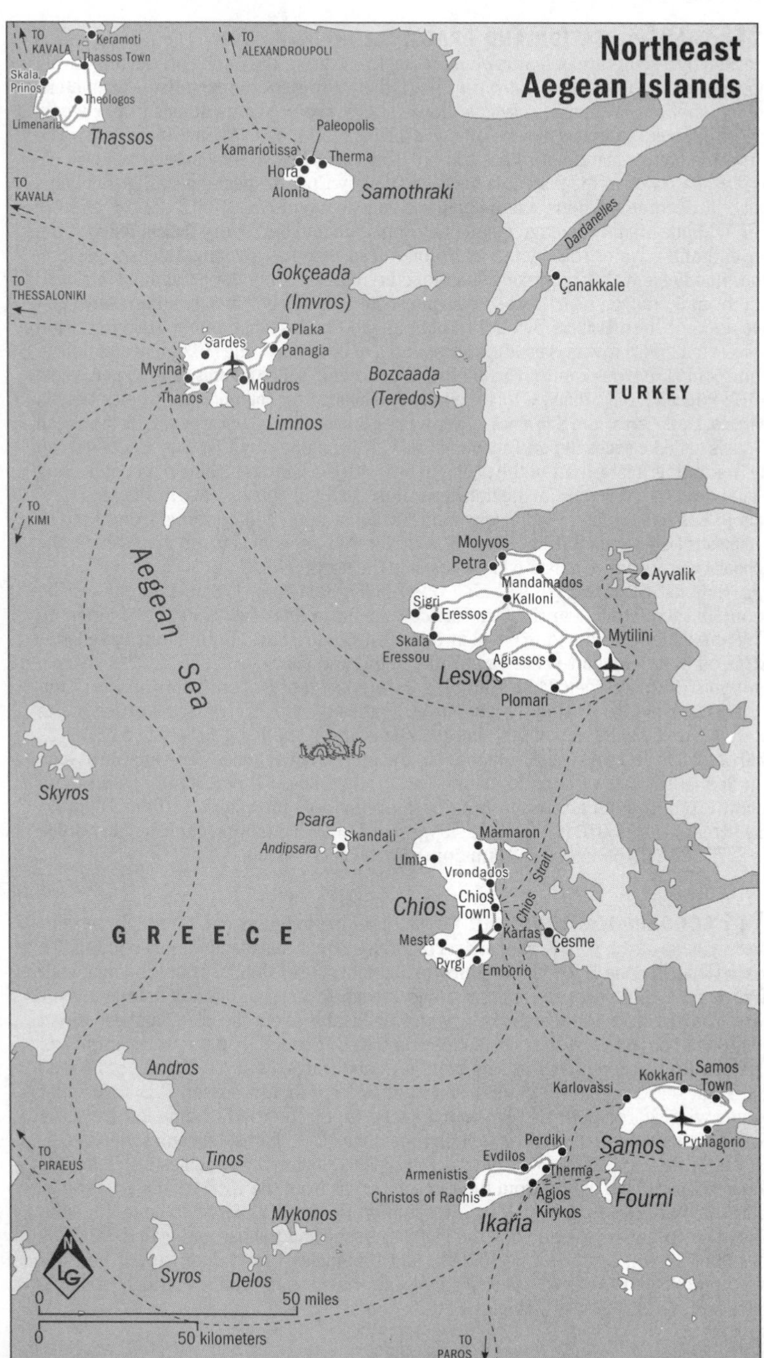
Northeast Aegean Islands
TO KAVALA
Keramoti
Thassos Town
Skala Prinos
Theologos
Limenaria
Thassos
TO ALEXANDROUPOLI
Paleopolis
Kamariotissa
Therma
Hora
Alonia
Samothraki
TO KAVALA
Dardanelles
Çanakkale
TO THESSALONIKI
Gokçeada (Imvros)
Plaka
Sardes
Panagia
Myrina
Moudros
Thanos
Limnos
Bozcaada (Teredos)
TURKEY
TO KIMI
Aegean Sea
Molyvos
Petra
Mandamados
Ayvalik
Kalloni
Sigri
Eressos
Skala Eressou
Mytilini
Agiassos
Lesvos
Plomari
Skyros
Psara
Skandali
Andipsara
Marmaron
Limia
Vrondados
Chios Strait
Chios
Chios Town
Karfas
Çesme
Mesta
Pyrgi
Emborio
GREECE
Andros
Samos Town
Kokkari
Karlovassi
Perdiki
Samos
Pythagorio
TO PIRAEUS
Tinos
Evdilos
Therma
Armenistis
Christos of Rachis
Agios Kirykos
Fourni
Ikaria
Mykonos
Syros
Delos
0
50 miles
0
50 kilometers
TO PAROS

TRANSPORTATION AND PRACTICAL INFORMATION. The town's pier is marked by a sculpture of Icarus plummeting to the ground. Coming off the ferry, walk up the pier onto the main waterfront road, then turn right to reach the town plateia, which shelters all tourist services. Ikaria's new **airport** serves **Athens** (4 per week, €46.70); contact **Olympic Airways** office (☎22750 22 214; open M-Sa 8:15am-2pm). The airport is on the island's northeastern tip, near Faros beach. **Ferry tickets** are available at **Icariada Travel,** in the plateia, where the friendly English-speaking staff gladly helps out with accommodations, excursions, and vehicle rentals. (☎22750 23 322 or 22750 22 277; ikariada@ika.forthnet.gr. Open daily 9am-2pm and 6-8:30pm.) **Dolichi Tours,** at the far end of the waterfront by the hydrofoil docks, also has a young, English-speaking staff that helps with ferry tickets and moped rentals (€12 per day). Catching ferries to and from Ikaria can be tricky as boats alternate landings between southern **Agios Kirykos** and northern **Evdilos.** Be sure to plan ahead for this since public transportation between the port towns is erratic at best and a one-way taxi ride (€20) leaves a hole in your pocket. Ferries run to: **Fourni** (1hr., 3 per week, €4.50); **Paros** (2hr., 3 per week, €16); **Piraeus** (10hr., daily, €19.40). **Flying Dolphins** go to: **Fourni** (2 per week); **Kos** via **Patmos, Lipsi, Leros,** and **Kalymnos** (2 per week); **Samos** (2hr., 3 per week, €15.45). Small vessels called **caïques** depart for **Fourni** (M,W, F 1pm; one-way €5). **Bus** schedules can be frustrating; a large part of the problem lies with the hairpin-turning road connecting Agios Kirykos with cities on the northern shore. In theory buses leave from Agios Kirykos to **Evdilos** Monday, Wednesday, and Friday at noon and continue from there to **Armenistis** (€4-5); the full trip takes at least 2hr. After school gets out in mid-June, the **schoolbus** heads twice a day to **Faros beach** in the north (€3).

A **National Bank** (☎22750 22 553; open M-Th 8am-2pm, F 8am-1:30pm) can be found in the plateia near the ferry offices. An **Alpha Bank** (☎22750 22 264; open M-Th 8am-2:30pm, F 8am-2pm) is next door to Dolichi Tours. Both banks have 24hr. **ATMs** outside. The **port police** (☎22750 22 207) and **police** (☎22750 22 222) share a building. Both are open 24 hr. Climbing the steps left of Dolichi Tours and continuing up the road, you'll find the **pharmacy,** next to the G.A. Ferry ticket office in the plateia. (☎22750 22 220. Open daily 8:30am-2pm.) The local **hospital** (☎22750 22 330 or 22 336) is two streets inland from the pier. **Internet** access is available at **Icarian Sea** to the left of Dolichi Tours. (☎22750 22 864. €2 per 20min. Open daily 10am-11pm, though afternoon hours are predictably unreliable.) About 100m up the street are the **OTE** (☎22750 22 499; open M-F 7:30am-3pm) and the **post office** (☎22750 22 413; open M-F 7:30am-2pm). **Postal code:** 83300.

ACCOMMODATIONS AND FOOD. Finding lodgings can be tough on your first night, so check your port of arrival beforehand and call ahead for reservations. To reach **Akti Pension ❷,** climb the stairs on the right side of Dolichi Tours and take your first right. A cool, quiet seaside patio and garden fosters community among guests. Greek-American owner Marsha is very knowledgeable about the island and can direct you to the hot waters in the ocean, closer and less crowded than the warm springs of Therma. Rooms come with private bath, A/C, and fridge. (☎22750 22 694 or 22750 23 905. High season singles €20; high season doubles €45, low season €25; apartment rooms with shared bath €15-20.) **Hotel Kastro ❸,** on the road leading left from the police station, offers modern, spacious rooms with TVs, baths, balconies, phones, A/Cs, and fridges. (☎22750 23 480; fax 22750 23 700. Singles €35; doubles €40.) **Pension Ikaria ❷,** one block inland from the plateia, across from the KKE headquarters, provides the perfect people-watching opportunity. Rooms are perched above the main row of coffeehouses overlooking the plateia's bustle and the harbor beyond. (☎22750 22 108 or 22 804. Doubles €30-40. Discount for singles.) Next door to Akti Pension you'll find **Hotel O'Karras ❷,** offering simple, sky-blue rooms with A/C, fridge, and spacious bath. (☎22750 22 494. Singles €20-25; doubles €30-35.)

Ag. Kirykos does not have a particularly noteworthy dining scene, mostly due to the rather surprising lack of tavernas that actually serve full meals. Taverna **Klimataria ❷**, a block inland from the plateia, is the port town's standout, serving a variety of meat and seafood dishes in the shade of a leafy arbor. (☎22750 22 686. Stuffed tomatoes €4. Entrees up to €7. Open daily 11am-midnight.) **Dedalos ❷**, in the plateia, serves up the standards for breakfast, lunch, and dinner with reasonable quality and prices. Tables next to the water facilitate boat-watching. (Omelettes €3. Greek entrees €3.50-5.)

NIGHTLIFE AND BEACHES. Remote, rocky beaches, two natural hot springs, and all the town's available nightlife are along the road heading left from the ferry dock (as you face inland) and within a 20min. walk. The stroll along the cliff road above the sea is lovely and Ikaria's low pollution means the stars are visible. Just be careful not to get sideswiped by speeding mopeds. As you walk along the road from the dock, you'll eventually come to the castle-themed bar **Camelot,** whose terrace overlooks the glistening sea below. Though the dance club below the bar is only open during the winter, **Flic Flac** (☎697 320 7115), about 10min. farther down the same road, caters to the town's clubbing needs with a fun outdoor dance floor and the occasional live DJ. (Cocktails €5-6. Open weekend nights.)

The beaches along this coast, with pearl-white pebbles and boulders set against the pure green sea, are incredible. Ask for directions for the two natural **hot springs** in the ocean. The first is just past the abandoned hotel and can only be approached via a steep, rocky dirt path, as the staircase has long since collapsed. Look for steam rising from the water and for fire-red rocks, which are covered in a medicinal mud that many bathers like to spread over their bodies. Lie back and relax; chances are you'll be the only person in sight. For the hot springs experience without the hike, head to **Therma** (Θερμα), just 2km north of Agios Kirykos on the way to the airport. A taxi ride is inexpensive; or you can walk there by taking the path beside the police station. People with ailments ranging from rheumatism to gynecological difficulties venture to the three springs of Therma, which consequently tend to attract more of an older crowd than the springs further south. Each of the springs is naturally radioactive and used for different treatments. Twenty minutes in a warm bath costs merely €1.35 so you can take your time. Farther north, close by the airport, the small town of **Faros** offers a number of pleasant pebbled beaches with three tasty fish tavernas, especially welcomed given the limited eating options in Agios Kirykos. **Grigoras ❷** (☎22750 32 208), the further right of the two tavernas facing inland, prepares a variety of fresh seafood entrees for cheap. (Entrees are €3-6. Calamari €4. Open 10am-late.) **Niki's Bar** (☎22750 32 595) provides the cocktails for after your meal. (Drinks €4-6. Open 10am-late.)

EVDILOS Ευδηλος ☎22750

Heading north from Agios Kirykos, the narrow road to red-roofed Evdilos snakes along sheer cliffs through florid hill country, providing wide coastal vistas and serious safety risks to moped drivers. The island is very green and the golden coast against the clean blue waters paint a stunning picture. From the island's eastern heights you can see Samos, Patmos, and the Fourni Archipelago. The road to Evdilos passes a few tiny villages and beaches, many of which have limited tourist accommodations. Evdilos itself is a base for many visitors, as it provides a central location for visiting the many beaches and scenic villages of the northern coast.

TRANSPORTATION AND PRACTICAL INFORMATION. Buses are difficult to catch and service tends to be spotty, but in theory regular transport to **Armenistis** does exist. Check the bulletin board on the waterfront by the taxi stand for a schedule; if nothing is posted inquire at the kiosk in the plateia. **Taxis** provide a pricier but infinitely more reliable option. (☎22750 31 275. Agios Kirykos to Evdilos €20; Agios Kirykos to Armenistis €27; Armenistis to Evdilos €9.) **Blue Nice Holidays** handles ferry and Flying Dolphin ticket sales, excursions, flights, and car rentals; it **exchanges currency** and posts a weekly schedule for **ferries** serving both **Agios Kirykos** and **Evdilos** as well as Flying Dolphins serving **Agios Kirykos.** (☎22750 31 990 or 31 428; fax 22750 31 572. Open daily 8am-2pm and 5-11pm.) A 24hr. **ATM** is found next door to Blue Nice and also at the opposite end of the harbor outside the **Alpha Bank.** (Open M-Th 8am-2pm, F 8am-1:30pm.) Facing inland, stone steps at the right end of the harbor lead uphill; take a left to find the **port police** (☎22750 31 007) and just beyond them a **pharmacy** (☎22750 41 352). In an emergency, call for **first aid** (☎22750 31 228). The **post office** sits at the top of the stairs leading up the hill. (☎22750 31 225. Open M-F 7:30am-2pm.) **Postal code:** 83302.

NORTHEAST AEGEAN

ACCOMMODATIONS AND FOOD. Satisfactory accommodations are difficult to come by here. Luckily the town has one extraordinary option. The cool, plant-lined patio of **Apostolos Stenos's Rooms to Rent ❸** leads to clean rooms with balconies overlooking the crashing waves—perfect for sunset-watching. From the port, take the winding uphill road to the top; continue straight at the small square and double back a few meters onto the coastal road. The pension is on your left—look for the red-roofed building with the pink-arched windows. Rooms come with private bath. (☎22750 31 365. Doubles €35; prices flexible.) Restaurants and *kafeneions* offering distinct flavors fill the plateia. **Cuckoo's Nest ❷,** with tables strategically surrounding the square's central monument, serves up a variety of tasty *mezedes*, mostly running €2-4. Chicken in wine sauce (€5) is also worth a try. (☎22750 31 540. Entrees €5-8. Open M-Sa 7pm-1am.) Catering to the late-night ferry arrivals with an array of sweets, coffees, and baked goods, **Ta Kimata ❶,** next to Blue Nice, is open 24hr. (☎22750 31 952. Baked goods €1.50.)

DAYTRIPS FROM EVDILOS. One of the most popular resorts in Ikaria, **Armenistis** (Αρμενιστησ; 15km west of Evdilos) boasts the beaches of **Livadi** and **Mesachti,** complemented by a variety of restaurants and bars. Though a challenge to get to, Armenistis has plenty of tourist facilities and is close to some of the best beaches and hiking routes on the island. Idle stone fountains hidden under the canopy of shady green leaves mark the entry to the town of **Christos of Rachis** (Χριστος της Ραχης), the apotheosis of a traditional Ikarian village (10km south of Armenistis). The best time to visit is after 11pm, when the locals have finished their daily farming and are ready to run their daily errands, shopping until 3 or 4am. Visit the local baker on the main road below the plateia, where the oven-baked loaves (€0.50) are left out for patrons to grab. Deposit money in the little basket on the honor system. Ikaria's best-organized hiking trails originate from here and are marked by little orange footprints. Pick up the very handy *Guide Map and Information* or the *Round of Rahes on Foot* (€4).

Five kilometers west of Armenistis, the asphalt runs out, leaving a dirt road running to **Nas,** one of the Aegean's undiscovered gems. The inspiring beach, flanked by huge rock walls, separates an aggressive sea from a serene river. Bordered by the beach, a freshwater pool is the river's final destination. A 25min. hike south takes you to the small waterfall that forms its beginning. To reach the falls, head inland past the pool. The hike is best accomplished by hugging the river, which may mean getting your feet wet. Approaching the final leg of the hike, notice the cavernous rock enclosure perched atop the eastern ledge. It's a favorite haunt for local goats. The smallish waterfall lies a few minutes beyond this point.

The **Fourni Archipelago** (Φουρνοι) makes a nice afternoon trip for venturers from Agios Kirykos in Ikaria. Most of the small population of 2700 is involved in a maritime activity of some sort; consequently enjoy some excellent fresh fish at the waterfront tavernas in **Fourni,** the sleepy and unimaginatively named port town. **Nikos Taverna** ❷ is run by a warm, affable fisherman who gladly leads you through crates of fresh seafood so you can hand-select your meal. Lobster is the house specialty. (☎22750 51 253. Lobster and fish €35 per kg and up.) The town presents a vision of Greece as it might have looked 50 years ago, before tourism began changing the local color of the islands. Most restaurants and facilities are located on either the waterfront or the main street that runs perpendicular to it. The **port police** (☎22750 51 207) and **police** (☎22750 51 222) share a white building at the end of the dock. The friendly, English-speaking staff answers questions about the island. To the right (facing inland), the bright blue and white painted **Toula Rooms** ❸ showcase studios with spotless private baths, kitchens, and fans. (☎/fax 22750 51 332. Singles €25; doubles €30-35.) Just next door **Hotel Nectaria** ❸ provides spacious rooms with baths, fridges, and A/C. (☎/fax 22750 51 365. June-July doubles €20, July-Aug. €35.) The coastal road south of the port leads to **Kambi,** which has a nice beach set against the windmill-laced hills. Weather permitting, Fourni is accessible by **caïque** from **Ikaria** (M, W, F 1pm, one-way €4.50). There is also limited **ferry** service once weekly from Fourni to **Patmos** (€6) and three times per week between Fourni and **Ikaria** (one-way €5); **hydrofoils** run twice per week to Fourni from **Patmos** (€12.18).

NORTHEAST AEGEAN

SAMOS Σαμος

Lush and lovely Samos has accommodated a more scholarly crowd over the years than some of its wilder sibling islands of the Cyclades and Dodecanese. A procession of architects, sculptors, poets, philosophers, and scientists—among them Pythagoras, Epicurus, Aesop, and Aristarchus (who discovered that the Earth revolved around the Sun 1800 years before Copernicus)—have all spent thoughtful hours on Samos's shores. Presently short-sighted tourists see the green island more as a necessary stepping stone on the way to Kuşadası and the ruins of Ephesus (p. 487) on the Turkish coast rather than a destination in its own right.

SAMOS TOWN (VATHY) Βαθυ ☎22730

A procession of waterfront tavernas unfurl along the crescent-shaped harbor of Samos Town. Inland, shady streets shelter an engaging museum and a restful public garden. The residential part of town is up the neighboring hillside, in the older, red-roofed area deemed Vathy; to clarify the two-name confusion, it's actually correct to refer to the town as a whole as either Samos Town or Vathy.

TRANSPORTATION

Flights: Olympic Airways (☎22730 27 237). Walk a couple blocks up Kanari street from the Archaeological Museum; it's on your left. To: **Athens** (1hr., 1-3 per day, €73) and **Thessaloniki** (3-5 per week, €71). Open M-F 8:10am-3:30pm. Samos's **airport** (☎22730 61 219), past Pythagorion, is only accesible by taxi (20min., €15).

Ferries: To: **Ag. Kirykos,** Ikaria (1-2 per day, €8.50); **Chios** (3 per week, €10.70); **Evdilos,** Ikaria (1-2 per day, €7.50); **Fourni** (2 per week, €6.60); **Kos** (1 per week, €14.60); **Lesvos** (1 per week, €15.40); **Mykonos** (6hr., 3 per week, €17.70); **Piraeus** (5hr., 1-2 per day, €24); **Rhodes** (1 per week, €23.10). Catamarans run to **Naxos** (6 per week, €37.10) and **Paros** (6 per week, €29.90). Daily excursion boats leave to **Kuşadası, Turkey** at 8:30am (1¼hr.; €40 round-trip, €9.13 Greek port tax); a bus ride and guided tour of nearby **Ephesus** can be included for an additional €20. Turkish entrance **visas** must be purchased at the Turkish border by Americans, Australians, British, Canadians, and Irish planning to stay for more than 1 day. A visa costs US$65.

Flying Dolphins: Leave from the port at Pythagorio (30min. bus ride from Samos Town) heading to: **Fourni** (2 per week, €13.50); **Ikaria** (2 per week, €15.50); **Kalymnos** (2 per day, €22.60); **Kos** (2 per day, €22.60); **Leros** (2 per day, €17.50); **Lipsi** (2 per day, €13.10); **Patmos** (2 per day, €12.60).

Buses: Follow the waterfront past Pl. Pythagoras, turn left onto Lekati, and continue 1 block to the **station.** To: **Chora** (6 per day); **Heraion** (5 per day); **Karlovaski** (7 per day); **Kokkari** (8 per day); **Potokaki** (3 per day); **Psili Ammos** (2 per day); **Pythagorio** (9 per day). Reduced service on weekends. Most fares €1-2. Su bus tour around the island covering major sights including the **Valley of Nightingales** leaves 8:30am.

Taxis: ☎22730 28 404. Available 24hr. in Pl. Pythagoras.

ORIENTATION AND PRACTICAL INFORMATION

The waterfront boasts most services. **Pl. Pythagoras,** identifiable by its four large palm trees, consists of cafes, a taxi stand, and a giant lion statue; it is located 250m to the right of the port when facing inland. Head past Pl. Pythagoras until you see signs pointing to the **Archaeological Museum,** about a block inland and adjacent to the **Municipal Gardens.** Many of the town's public amenities, including city hall, OTE, and the post office, are located nearby. To find the town's most densely packed pension neighborhood, head about 100m along the waterfront away from the port and walk a couple blocks inland when you see the sign for Hotel Aiolis. Three step-lined streets leading up the hillside house many good accommodations.

Tourist Office: ☎22730 28 530 or 28 582. On a side street 1 block before Pl. Pythagoras. Open July-Aug. M-Sa 7am-2:30pm.

Tourist Agencies: ITSA Travel (☎22730 25 065 or 22730 27 337; fax 22730 28 570), on the waterfront just across from the port, offers all ferry and Flying Dolphin tickets. Can also help plan excursions to Turkey. Open daily 7am-10pm and when boats arrive.

Banks: National Bank, on the waterfront just beyond Pl. Pythagoras, has a 24hr. **ATM.** Open M-Th 8am-2pm, F 8am-1:30pm.

Laundromat: ☎22730 28 833. A self-service laundromat can be found around the corner from Hotel Medusa. Purchase tokens at Mezefe Cafe next door. Wash €3.50, dry €3. Detergent €0.60. Open 8am-11pm.

Police: ☎22730 22 100. After Pl. Pythagoras on the far right of the waterfront (facing inland). Doubles as the **tourist police.** Some English spoken.

Port Police: ☎22730 27 318. A few meters to the left of the ferry docks, facing inland.

Hospital: ☎22730 83 100. 10min. to the left of the ferry dock. Open 24hr.

OTE: ☎22730 27 799. Walk down Kanari street away from the Archaeological Museum and supermarket; it's on your right, behind the big church. Open M-F 7:30am-3pm.

Internet Access: Diavos Net Cafe (☎22730 22 469), on the waterfront 200m past Pl. Pythagoras, has reasonably quick Internet connections. Scanning and printing available. €4 per hr., €1 min. Open daily 8:30am-11:30pm.

Post Office: ☎22730 28 820. Take a left at the corner with the Olympic Airways office, when walking away from the museum down Kanari. Open M-F 7:30am-2pm. **Postal code:** 83100.

ACCOMMODATIONS

The limited availability of rooms in Samos makes it advisable to call ahead during the high season. You can also get help from a travel agent. To find **Pension Trova ❷,** Kalomiris 26, head along the waterfront; when you see the sign for Hotel Ailois, take a left. Curve up the hill on Kalomiris; the pension is on your right. Large, col-

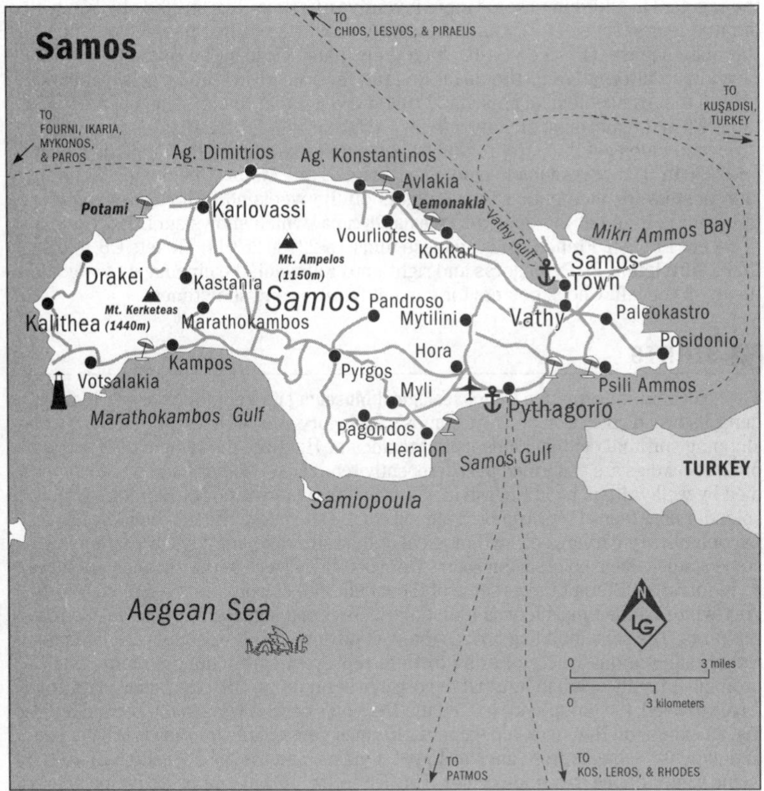

orful rooms have clean shared bathrooms. (☎22730 27 759. Doubles €20-25; studios €25-30.) Walk along the waterfront away from the docks until you reach Hotel Aiolis, take the next left onto Areos, and proceed two blocks and up the stairs to locate **Pension Avli ❷**, Areos 2. Owner Spiros maintains a laid-back environment and can offer helpful advice about the island. (☎22730 22 939. Open May-Oct. Doubles €25-30.) **Medousa Hotel ❷,** Sofouli 25, on the waterfront, about halfway between the port and Pl. Pythagoras, has rooms in a prime location with private baths, TVs, and fans. The dark lobby and lounge hide behind a cheery, brightly-lit ice cream parlor. (☎22730 23 501. Singles €20-25; doubles €25-30.)

FOOD AND NIGHTLIFE

Samos Town leaves something to be desired for notable food options, and cuisine distinguishes itself only on account of its sweet Samian wine, which is either delectable or sickeningly sweet depending on your tastes. Wine aside, the island's restaurants quickly merge into an indistinguishable waterfront blur of dull souvlaki and spaghettis. **Grigori's ❷** (☎22730 22 718), just past the post office, offers a short selection of simple but well-prepared dishes. (Entrees under €6. Open daily 8:30am-3pm and 5pm-late.) Similarly priced and more conveniently located is **Christo's ❷** (☎22730 24 792), in Pl. Nikolaos behind Pl. Pythagoras, which does up the regulars in addition to some more inventive offerings, like stuffed chicken with dill and lemon sauce (€5). Outdoor seating provides optimal people-watching in the main square. (Entrees €4-6. Open daily 10am-11pm.) The markets in Vathy provide an alternative to the usual taverna fare; head for the large **supermarket** behind the Archaeological Museum. Fruit and vegetable vendors line up in front of the OTE in the morning; pick up a fresh tomato or two for the road.

Several clubs get the party rolling on the outskirts of town; they include **Cabana** (☎22730 92 311; www.cabana-club.gr) in Kokkari and **Matrix.** Check the ubiquitous club posters for the popular theme nights on the weekends. More passive entertainment is found at the open-air **Cinema Olympia,** which shows subtitled versions of recent English, French, and Japanese films. (☎22730 25 011. Tickets €6.) To get there, turn left at Pl. Pythagoras and right onto Katavani; the cinema is two blocks down on the left. Check posters for current features and showtimes.

SIGHTS

The excellent, informative **Archaeological Museum** sits behind the municipal gardens. Its broad collection portrays Samos's past glory as a commercial and Hera-worshipping spiritual center. Finds from the ancient Heraion, the temple of Hera, and other local digs are enshrined in two recently renovated buildings and are accompanied by well-written, lucid English labels. You'll find more proof of Heraion's bygone splendor here than at the crumbled remains of the site itself. The first building houses Laconian ivory carvings of mythological and aristocratic notables, and some awesome statues like a colossal 5m **kouros** from 560 BC. Pieces of this magnificent piece were found at different times, some of them built into existing walls and cisterns; the grey-white banded marble was a distinctive regional signature of ancient Samian sculptors. The same building houses the well-preserved Genelos group, in its time a rather ostentatious votive offering to Hera representing the donors themselves, a prominent family of aristocrats. Of the original series of six life-sized sculptures, four have survived; the group once graced the Heraion's Sacred Way. In the second building, an exhibit on Hera worship parades offerings, remarkable for their workmanship and expense. Objects from ancient Egypt, Cyprus, and the Near East testify to the island's importance as a trade center. The last room, upstairs on the right, includes a case of nightmarish, gryphon-engraved **protomes** (cauldron handles) that should not be missed. (☎22730 27 469. Open Tu-Su 8:30am-3pm. €3, seniors and students €2, EU students free.) In late July and early August, Samos hosts a number of fine classical and jazz concerts featuring Greek artists as part of the **Manolis Kalomiris Festival.** Contact the tourist office for a schedule of events.

DAYTRIPS FROM SAMOS TOWN

ANCIENT PYTHAGORIO Πυθαγορειο

A bus from Vathy arrives at Pythagorio (20min., 9 per day, €1.20). A modern beach town of the same name now sits on the ruins of Ancient Pythagorio, 14km south of Vathy.

The ancient city of Pythagorio, once the island's capital, thrived as a commercial and political center during the latter half of the 6th century BC under the reign of **Polykrates the Tyrant.** Ancient historian Herodotus reports that Polykrates undertook the three most daring engineering projects in the Hellenic world, among them the **Tunnel of Eupalinus,** 1500m up the hill to the north of town. The tunnel was in fact an underground aqueduct that diverted water from a natural spring to the city below. An impressive 1.3km long, it's in remarkably good condition, although only about 200m of dank, low-ceilinged cavern are open to amaze wannabe spelunkers and to horrify their claustrophobic friends. To reach the tunnel, walk back along the road to Vathy and follow the signs. The 20min. walk to the tunnel's entrance leads past minor ancient ruins, including a Hellenistic villa and some wells; rolling hills and grazing goats fill the intervals. (Open Tu-Su 8:45am-2:45pm, last entrance 2:15pm. €4, students €2, EU students free.) You can also check out Polykrates's second feat, the 40m deep **harbor mole,** a breakwater which supports the modern pier. Blocks, columns, wall fragments, and entablatures are strewn throughout Pythagorio; random plots are fenced off to contain the ruins, which have remained relatively untended. The presentation in the tiny, unremarkable **Archaeological Museum,** located one block from the water, is no different; busts and torsos lay scattered throughout the one room collection and the sidewalk outside. (☎22730 61 400. Open Tu-Su 9am-2:30pm. Free.) On the southern side of town are the ruins of the **Castle of Lykurgus,** built during the beginning of the 19th century by Lykurgus, a native Samian and a leader in the War for Independence. The **Church of the Transfiguration** is a pale blue variation on classic Orthodox architecture.

HERAION Ηεραιον

A bus from Vathy (30min., €1.51) leaves you in Heraion Town. The temple is 1km back on the road from Vathy. ☎22730 95 277. Open Tu-Su 8:30am-3pm. €3, students €2.

Polykrates's third engineering feat, his magnum opus, is the Heraion or **Temple of Hera.** Seven centuries worth of pilgrims had worshiped Hera on Samos when Polykrates began enlarging the temple dedicated to her in the 6th century BC. At the height of its architectural grandeur, the 118-by-58m Temple of Hera was supported by 134 columns. Since fire damage in 525 BC, it has been only minimally reconstructed; today only one column remains standing of the once-majestic colonnade. After Samos's decline as a commercial power, the temple nonetheless retained its prestige; in 80 BC Cicero convinced Roman authorities to turn the building into a kind of museum for earlier votive offerings. The temple's illustrious past also made it a place of unlimited asylum under the Romans, attracting no small share of vagabonds and miscreants. With the collapse of the empire, the temple fell into decay; under the Byzantines a church was erected on the site. Today the most interesting finds from the temple can be found in the Archaeological Museum in Samos Town; the sculptures of the Genelos group appearing on the ancient **Iera Odos** (Sacred Way) from Pythagorio to the temple are casts. A walk along the beach brings you back to the temple at your own pace. If you can't enter through the beachside back gate, a path leads inland to the main road and the entrance, farther along the beach past two houses. Wrap yourself in your best toga and come prepared with a jug of libations, lest you suffer Hera's wrath.

NORTHERN AND WESTERN SAMOS

The northern coast of Samos has many crowded, sandy **beaches** and a few rarely visited pebble beaches tucked into coves. Most of the coast is easily accessible from the road to **Karlovassi.** On a peninsula 10km west of Samos Town, you'll find the village of **Kokkari,** skirted by white pebble shores and clear waters. **Lemonakia beach,** 1km west of Kokkari next to Tsamadou, and the wide white beach west of **Avlakia** are both alluring. Kokkari, Lemonakia, and Avlakia are accessible from Samos Town via the irregular KTEL **bus** service (7-9 buses per day). Infrequent buses (1-2 per day) shouldn't keep you from the splendid beaches of southwestern Samos. A few kilometers west of the red-roofed hamlet of **Marathokambos** is the spacious beach at **Votsalakia.** A bit farther is an even better beach at **Psili Ammos.**

From the village of **Agios Konstantinos,** on the northern coast of Samos, you can **hike** into the mountains through the Valley of the Nightingales, where songbirds regale the wooded valley just after midnight. The village of **Vourliotes,** 5km south of Avlakia, was a favorite of renowned Greek actress Melina Mercury, who raved about the village for years after her visit there. Several kilometers above the town, the 16th-century monastery **Moni Vrontianis** polices the populace below. (Closed for renovations for an undetermined period of time. Consult the tourist office in Vathy for info.) Two kilometers west of **Paleo** are three waterfalls in the island's northwestern corner.

NEAR SAMOS

SELÇUK, TURKEY

Selçuk serves as a base for exploring nearby Ephesus and its legendary Temple of Artemis. The House of the Virgin Mary can also be reached from Selçuk.

ORIENTATION AND PRACTICAL INFORMATION. The İzmir-Aydın road, **Atatürk,** is one of Selçuk's main drags. **Dr. Sabri Yayla,** also called **Kuşadası,** meets Atatürk from the west, and **Şahabettin Dede** meets Atatürk from the east to form the town's main crossroads. The **tourist office,** 35 Agora Çarşısı, at the intersection of Kuşadası and Atatürk, has **free maps.** (☎232 892 63 28; fax 232 892 69 45. Open M-F 8am-noon and 1-5pm; Apr.-Dec. also open Sa-Su 9am-5pm.) A **bank,** 17 Namık Kemal, **exchanges currency** and **traveler's checks** and has an **ATM.** (☎232 892 61 09 or 232 892 65 14. Open M-F 8:30am-5:30pm.) The **police** (☎232 892 60 16) have an office beside the bank and a booth by the *otogar* (bus station) on Atatürk.

For more information on travel to Turkey, see **Turkey Essentials,** p. 598. Catamarans run from Samos Town to **Kusadasi** (1¼hr.; 5 per week; US€30 1-way, €44 round-trip, €8.80 Greek port tax). From Kusadasi, buses head to **Selçuk** (30min.; every 20min. 7:30am-midnight; US$0.90) via Ephesus. Because of the instability of the Turkish lira, prices for goods and services in Turkey are listed in US$. Coverage of Selçuk and Ephesus was updated in July of 2001.

ACCOMMODATIONS AND FOOD. At **Artemis Guest House ("Jimmy's Place") ❶,** on Atatürk, guests are greeted with a refreshing drink, shown to a carpeted room cwith bath, towels, and fans, and invited to dinner (nightly, US$2.50) in the garden. (☎232 892 61 91; www.artemisguesthouse.com. Internet US$0.80 per hr. Laundry US$2.50. Breakfast US$1.60. US$5 per person.) For a truly zen-like dining experience, try **Karameşe Restaurant ❶,** Tarihi İsabey Camii Önü, beside İsa Bey Camii. (☎232 892 04 66. Open daily 9am-3am.)

SIGHTS AND MUSEUMS. The stunning Selçuk mosque **İsa Bey Camii** was built in 1375 on the order of Aydınoğlu İsa Bey. It features columns taken from Ephesus, which the Ephesians, in turn, had pilfered from Aswan, Egypt. Restored in 1975, the mosque has regained much of the simple elegance that was eroded by 600 years of wear and tear. Inside the courtyard is a collection of Ottoman and Selçuk tombstones and inscriptions. The mosque's facade features Persian-influenced geometric black and white stone inlay. A few hundred meters down Dr. Sabri Yayla, walking away from town with the tourist office on your right, are the sad remains of the **Temple of Artemis.** Once the largest temple in existence and among the Seven Wonders of the Ancient World, it now consists of a lone reconstructed column twisting upwards from a bog that approximates the area of the temple's foundation. (Open daily 8:30am-5:30pm. Free.) Directly across from the town's tourist office, Selçuk's **Efes Müzesi** (Ephesus Museum) houses a world-class collection of Hellenistic and Roman finds from Ephesus. (Open daily 8:30am-noon and 1-7pm; in winter 8:30am-noon and 1-5:30pm. US$3.)

DAYTRIP FROM SELÇUK: EPHESUS. From the starting of Greek civilization to the 6th century, Ephesus enjoyed glory and prosperity. The ruins here rank first among Turkey's ancient sites in sheer size and state of preservation; extensive marble roadways and columned avenues give an authentic impression of this ancient gateway to the eastern world. From the Selçuk otogar, take a Pamukkale-bound **dolmuş** to **Kuşadası** (5min.; Mar.-Oct. every 15min., Nov.-Apr. every 30min.; US$0.60). Ephesus is an easy **walk** (3km) from Selçuk along a fig tree-shaded path, beside Dr. Sabri Yayla Bul. Bring water and sunscreen. A good guidebook to Ephesus costs about US$2.50 in Kuşadası souvenir shops or at the entrance to the site; it provides the history of the ruins and a more lengthy explanation of the many sights. The site is open daily 8am-7pm; the best time to visit is early in the morning.

Once you reach the site, you'll see the **Vedius Gymnasium** on the left, down the road from Dr. Sabri Yayla Bul. toward the lower entrance. It was built in AD 150 to honor then-emperor Antonius Pius and **Artemis,** the city's patron goddess. Beyond the roadside vegetation, the remains of the **stadium** open up in a horseshoe. The original Greek semi-circular theater followed the land's contours to add natural emphasis to the staged dramas. Romans plunked their own stadium right on top of the Greek theater, interpreting "drama" in another way: bloody gladiator games, wild beast hunts, and public executions. Just inside the lower entrance, a dirt path leads off to the right. On the right side of the fork, you'll find the ruins of the **Church of the Seven Councils,** where the Third Ecumenical Council met in 431. Beside it lies the ruined **Archbishop's Place,** destroyed in the 6th century.

At the main entrance gate, a tree-lined path points to the **Arcadiane,** Ephesus's main thoroughfare. Buried under a dense swarm of tourists, the 30m-by-145m **Grand Theater** is a stunning, heavily restored beast; its seating area, carved into the side of Mt. Pion, seats 25,000. The **Street of Curetes** begins at a slight incline. Ruts in the road are evidence of the heavy traffic between the temple and the city, and gaps between the slabs reveal glimpses of the city's **sewer system.** At the very bottom of the Street of Curetes is the **Library of Celsus,** restored by Austrian archaeologists. The large building behind the library was probably the **Temple of Serapis,** an Egyptian god of grain. Farther up the Street of Curetes, the imposing ruins of the 118 **Temple of Hadrian** are on your left, marked by a double-layered column construction. A little farther up the hill are the ruins of the exquisite **Fountain of Trajan.**

Two pillars in the middle of the road mark the **Gate of Hercules;** farther uphill and to the left is the **Prytaneion.** Dedicated to the worship of **Vesta** (Hestia to the Greeks, and goddess of hearth and home), the Prytaneion contained an eternal flame tended by Vesta's priestesses, the **Vestal Virgins.** Vesta was vital to the Romans, and the Vestal Virgins thus gained a social standing *almost* as high as men. Immediately adjacent, the **odeon,** or *bouleterion,* remains in fine repair. The **state agora** on the right was the heart of political activity from the 1st century BC until the city's final demise. On the left lie the upper **baths.**

CHIOS Χιος

Dusty, pine-speckled hills lend a wild feel to the interior of Chios. Its port town offers a friendly welcome to visitors but the island's real charms lie in its traditional villages and on its sandy shores. The economic potential of mastic, an evergreen shrub that grows on the island's southern half, has been known by Chians since antiquity; the tree's bittersweet, gummy resin has long been used in products ranging from chewing gum to cosmetics. In addition to the creative and often tasty mastic products that visitors can sample, the island offers sweet local fruit juices, like intriguing mandarin and sour cherry, and a local fig liqueur called *suma,* which goes down surprisingly smoothly given its destructive 70% alcohol content.

CHIOS TOWN ☎22710

Chios's bustling port town has a booming pulse that doesn't relent for the wayward tourist. The waterfront shows off a number of hip cafes, where trendy young locals congregate at night over beer and billiards. The interior of the town is home to bustling fish and fruit markets, fancy shops, old tavernas, and a smattering of museums. The quieter residential section slumbers under the shadow of the castle walls, disturbed only by the occasional blare of a speeding moped.

TRANSPORTATION

Flights: Olympic Airways (☎22710 23 998), at the center of the waterfront, 2 doors past Villa Clio, sends 5 flights per day to **Athens** (€69). Open M-F 8am-4pm.

Ferries: Service to: **Ag. Kirykos,** Ikaria (1 per week, €12); **Alexandroupoli** (1 per week, €23); **Çesme, Turkey** (8:30am; round-trip €40); **Lesvos** (daily, €10.50); **Limnos** (4 per week, €18.60); **Mykonos** (1 per week, €14); **Piraeus** (2-3 per day, €20.90); **Rhodes** (2 per week, €27.70); **Samos** (2 per week, €10.70); **Syros** (2 per week, €16); **Tinos** (2 per week, €14.50). Irregular ferry service also available to **Psara.** Citizens of Australia, Canada, Ireland, the UK, and the US (among others) will have to purchase a visa (€60) if staying more than 1 day in Turkey (p. 626).

Buses: **KTEL buses** (☎22710 27 507 or 22710 24 257) leave from both sides of Pl. Vounakio, right off the municipal gardens coming from the waterfront. Intercity bus service is split between 2 lines. **Blue buses** (office ☎22710 23 08, station 22710 22 079), just up from the plateia on Dimokratias, travel short distances from Chios Town. One regular route (18 per day) travels south to **Kontari, Karfas,** and smaller towns along the way; another rolls west to **Dafnonas** (6 per day). Trips from €1; tickets available at the station, at kiosks, or on the bus. **Green buses** (☎22710 27 507; open 6am-4:30pm), on the left side of the city gardens, travel greater distances to: **Agios Georgios** (5 per day); **Mesta** (3 per day); **Nagos** (2 per day); **Pyrgi** (4 per day); **Volissos** (2 per day, M and Th only). Tickets from €2.50; last bus leaves 1:40pm.

ORIENTATION AND PRACTICAL INFORMATION

Walking left from the ferry dock along the waterfront, you'll pass many cafes and restaurants. A right on **Kanari** takes you inland to **Pl. Vounakio,** the social center of town, where most services, buses, and taxis are found on either side of the **Municipal Gardens.** Left of Vounakio lies **Aplotarias,** the market street, where groceries and bakeries are open for business. Between the ferry dock and the Municipal Gardens, fortress walls hug the predominantly residential **Old Town.**

Tourist Office: Kanari 18 (☎22710 44 344; infochio@otenet.gr). Turn off the waterfront onto Kanari, walk toward the plateia, and look for the "i" sign on your left. **Maps,** brochures, and bus schedules available; friendly staff speaks English. Open May-Oct. M-F 7am-2:30pm and 6-10pm, Sa-Su 9am-2pm and 6-10pm; Nov.-Mar. M-F 7am-2:30pm.

Tourist Agencies: Hatzelenis Tourist Agency (☎22710 26 743; mano2@otenet.gr) lies at the end of the ferry dock. The friendly staff sells ferry tickets for all lines except NEL. Open M-Sa 7am-2pm and 5:30-9pm, Su 7am-noon and 5:30-9pm. **Sunrise Tours** (☎22710 41 390, fax 22710 41 391), just doors down from the tourist office on Kanari, is open in the afternoon and is centrally located. Open M-Sa 9am-10pm. **NEL Lines** (☎22710 23 971 or 22710 40 651; fax 22710 41 319) has its own agency where Kanari meets the waterfront road. Open daily 8:30am-2pm and 5:30-10pm.

Banks: National Bank (☎22710 22 820), next to the OTE in the plateia, has a 24hr. **ATM.** Open M-Th 8am-2:30pm, F 8am-2pm.

Hospital: ☎22710 44 302. 2km north of Chios on the coastal road before Vrondados.

OTE: Kanari 1 (☎22710 40 167), up the block from the tourist office. Pay phones can be found on the waterfront. Open M-F 7am-3pm.

Internet Access: A number of cafes offering fast connections can be found on the waterfront road. **Asteras** (☎22710 41 202) has convenient hours and good prices (€4 per hr.). Open daily 10am-2am. **Enter Internet Cafe,** Aigeou 98 (☎22710 41 058; entercafe@hotmail.com), on the 2nd fl. of the waterfront building, has excellent prices (€3.60 per hr., €1.80 min.). Open daily 8:30am-2pm, M-Tu also open 6-9pm.

Post Office: ☎22710 25 668. Follow Omirou 1 block inland. Open M-F 7:30am-2pm. **Postal code:** 82100.

ACCOMMODATIONS

Most of Chios Town's accommodations are on the far end of the waterfront from the ferry dock. In high season, a tourist agency can help you find a room. Head to nearby Karfas (p. 493) if Chios Town overcrowds. **Chios Rooms ❷,** Aigeou 110, has large, breezy rooms in a converted mansion which share sparkling-clean bathrooms and a common kitchen. The owner, from New Zealand, offers advice about the island and the occasional cup of Greek coffee. (☎22710 20 198 or 6972 833 841; chiosrooms@hotmail.com. Singles €18-22; doubles €23-25, with bath €30; triples with bath €35.) **Hotel Filoxenia ❸,** just off the waterfront on Voupalou, has rather luxurious rooms with A/C, TV, private bath, fridge, and bright blue curtains. (☎22710 22 813. Breakfast included. Doubles €40-45; triples €50-55.) **Villa Clio ❷** is on the water near the Olympic Airways office. Serviceable rooms in a prime location come with A/C, TV, private bath, and the occasional balcony. (☎22710 43 755, 22710 28 0303, or 22710 41 361; vilaclio@otenet.gr. Call or inquire about rooms at the Budget Rent-A-Car office below. Doubles €30-40.)

FOOD AND NIGHTLIFE

Vendors set up shop near Pl. Vounakio. For lunch on the cheap, bite into a fresh spanakopita or tiropita available in one of the many **bakeries.** Elegant outdoor seating within the crumbling castle walls lend a graceful touch to **Ouzeri Ikobou Plita ❷,** Ag. Giorgios 20 (☎22710 23 858). Patrons hum along to the old Greek music floating across the street as they happily munch on fresh seafood *mezedes*, like sardines in oil (€3.50). To get there, walk past Hatzelenis Tours on the waterfront road and make the fourth right. Quality tavernas can be found just off the waterfront. Walking toward the Archaeological Museum from the water brings you to **Two Brothers ❷**, on M. Livanou. Greek favorites and hyped up ribs with BBQ sauce (€4.40) are served under a leafy canopy. (☎22710 21 313. Entrees €3.50-4.50.) Escape from the insanity of nearby Pl. Vounakio at **To Byzantio ❷**, around the corner from the mosque, near the Hotel Filoxenia. Select your meal from behind the counter as Greek soap operas play in the background. (☎22710 41 035. Most entrees under €5. Open M-Sa 7am-10pm.) Chios's nightlife revolves around the innumerable cafes and arcades on the waterfront. For a game of billiards (€6 per hr.) and an Amstel (€3), head to **Asteras**, which also has Internet access. (☎22710 41 202. Open daily 10am-2am.) An **open-air cinema** in the public gardens has nightly showings of foreign films (€6.50), many of which are in English.

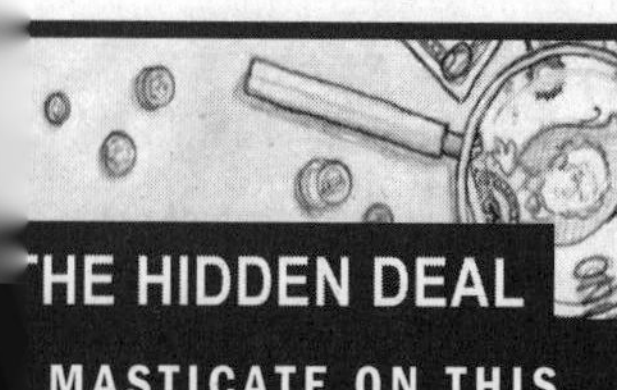

'HE HIDDEN DEAL

MASTICATE ON THIS

Mastic, a resin from the tree (*Pistacia lentiscus*) with the same common ıame, has been known to have ɔharmeceutical and cosmetic applicaions since Dioskourides, the "father ɔf the pharmacy," first sang its praises n the first century. Today an amusngly wide variety of mastic products ıre available for purchase in Chios own. If there's one location in the vorld to indulge your dental and dernatological fantasies, let it be Chios. 'he southern part of the island is the ɔnly location in the world where masic grows—some have speculated this s due to the unique soil conditions :aused by underwater volcano activty, though this has yet to be scientifi:ally confirmed.

At **Mastic Spa**, you'll find everyhing from acne gel to shaving foam ınd anti-aging cream, all containing he anti-bacterial mastic oil. Show ɔur pitiful mastic-less bath products he door with some mastic shampoo €7.10), mastic bath and shower gel €8.50), or mastic hand cream (€10.70). For a tastier experience, ıead to **Mastiha Shop**, where masticlavored Turkish delights, chewing gum, and ouzos are available. A 0.5L ɔottle of local mastic liquor runs €6-9. f all the combined candy and liquor sn't going down so easy, pop a couɔle mastic digestive capsules before ıeading to bed.

Spa: Aegou 12, along the waterfront. For more information contact ☎22710 40 223; www.uniquenastic.com. Shop: ☎22710 81 500. Also on the waterfront. Open daily 9am-10:30pm.

SIGHTS

Chios Town has lots of museums, some more compelling than others. The best in town is the **Archaeological Museum,** located inland on Michalon Porfira, which goes to the waterfront. The exhibits dissect ancient Chios's role in the Aegean, with an extensive collection of artifacts and detailed explanatory placards. (☎22710 44 239. Open Tu-Su 8am-2:45pm. €2, students €1, EU students free.) Relics of the town's past encircle Pl. Vounakio. To the right of the plateia, the walls of the **Byzantine kastro,** reconstructed by the Genovese, enclose the narrow streets of the Old Town. The castle houses a handful of well-restored 14th-century Byzantine wall paintings in the small and overpriced **Justinian Palace.** (☎22710 22 819. Open Tu-Su 8am-7pm. €3, students €2.) The mid-19th-century **Ottoman Mosque,** just across from the gardens, is undergoing heavy renovations; its courtyard and porch currently house the paltry collection of the **Byzantine Museum of Chios.** Jewish and Christian gravestones, column capitals, and Venetian brass cannons are littered throughout the small space in garage-sale fashion. (Open Tu-Su 10am-2:30pm. Free.) The **Philip Argenti Folklore Museum,** located above the **Korais Library,** next to the Mitropoli cathedral, focuses on traditional Chian embroidery and clothing, using illustrations and figurines. (☎22710 44 246. Open M-Th 8am-2pm, F 8am-2pm and 5-7:30pm, Sa 8am-12:30pm.) Battleship buffs and navy nerds will rejoice at the **Chios Maritime Museum,** in the southwestern part of town on S. Tsouri, which contains intricate wooden models and paintings of ships from a number of nations. Landlubbers may find the technical explanations of the ships more worthy of a deckside snooze. (☎22710 44 140. Open M-Sa 10am-1pm. Free.)

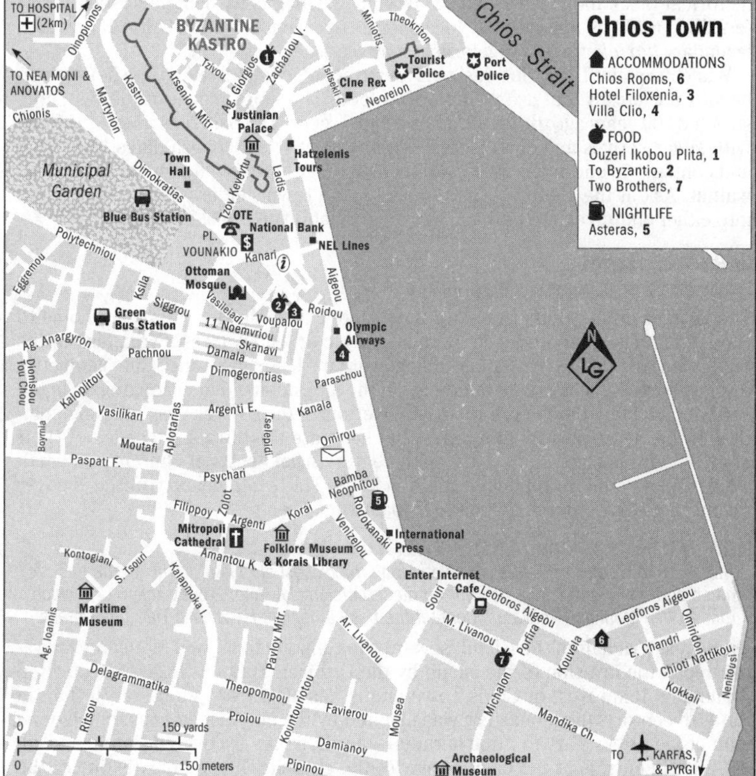

DAYTRIPS FROM CHIOS TOWN

MESTA Μεστα

Green buses run from Chios Town to Mesta M-F 3 times per day. You can also take a taxi (€25). Most travelers base from Chios Town or Karfas and visit Mesta as a daytrip, though accommodations are available in the town itself.

One of the most unique villages in southern Chios, Mesta's name comes from the Greek word *mesto* (a very well thought-out idea). The town was founded in 1038, when representatives from four neighboring towns put their heads together to solve the perennial pirate problem. Their solution was to build a town where the houses were connected to one another, forming a fortification wall like that of a castle. Today Mesta looks almost exactly as it might have during the Byzantine era; due to archaeological decree, all new houses must be built in the same original style with delightful stonework, rounded arches, and painted wooden doors. It's easy to get lost in the narrow, cobbled streets but most wind up back at the central plateia, home to the town's two tavernas and a central location for all major happenings in the life of the village. **Medieval Cafe ❶** offers local Chian juices and mastic liquors (most €1.20). The waiters speak good English and offer helpful historical facts about Mesta. (☎22710 76 050. Open daily 6am-late.) **Dionysos** ❷ (☎22710 76 400) is respected by locals for its excellent food. Chef Morias prepares legendary *hortokeftedes* (vegetarian meatballs).

While its quaint Byzantine design is an attraction within itself, Mesta houses two beautiful **churches** that are well worth a look. The more recent of the two, constructed 300 years ago, is the third largest in Greece. The pale blue interior is filled with silver votives and chandeliers. The town's original church dates from 1136 and contains an enormous *ikonostas,* which took the artist 40 years to carve from walnut. Ask at the Medieval Cafe for Elias, the town's elderly keymaster, to get into either church and to perhaps share information on the old church.

PYRGI Πυργι

Take the Pyrgi via bus from Chios (4 per day, €2.16).

The villages in the southern half of the island, called Mastichohoria, are home to Chios's famous resin produced by squat mastic or lentisk trees. Pyrgi, high in the hills 25km from Chios, is a unique village with intricate black and white geometric designs covering many of its buildings. In the afternoon old men congregate in the central plateia by the church to gossip over ouzo; their wives pass the time chatting in the rustic narrow alleyways that separate the tattooed facades of their homes. Pyrgi is also home to the 12th-century **Agioi Apostoloi** church, in a small alley off the plateia, a replica of the Nea Moni. Thirteenth-century frescoes cover the interior of the church. (Open M-F 10am-1pm. Free.)

NEA MONI Νεα Μονι AND ANAVATOS Αναβατος

There are no regular KTEL buses to Nea Moni; the closest stop is at Karies to the east. A much better bet is to take an organized bus excursion (July-Aug. 2 per week, €12), which runs to Nea Moni and Anavatos. Contact the bus stations or Hatzelenis Travel for details.

On the eastern half of the island, several sites, among them Nea Moni and Anavatos, recall the invasion of the island by the Ottoman Turks in 1822. Pine-covered mountains 16km west of Chios Town cradle **Nea Moni** (New Monastery). Built in the 11th century, the monastery was inspired by the miraculous appearance of an icon of the Virgin Mary to three hermits—the skull of one, covered in gold and silver adornments, is at the back corner of the church. The complex is one of the world's most important Byzantine monuments. Though an 1881 earthquake destroyed much of it, most structures have since been carefully restored. Before entering the main chapel, you'll pass through the inner narthex and see five 11th-century **floor mosaics,** stunning despite their age. Their artists were also responsible for the mosaics of Hagia Sophia in Istanbul. A few meters before the entrance to the complex, up a small dirt path, lies Nea Moni, where an arched crypt hosts the grisly skulls and bones of monks and villagers massacred by the Turks during the 1822 invasion. An adjoining chapel just inside the entrance to the complex also houses a **memorial** to the tragic event, when the island's southern population was literally decimated. The skeletons once belonged to 600 priests and 3500 women and children who had sought refuge from the attacks in the chapel. (Open daily 9am-1pm and 4pm-sunset. Free. Modest dress required.) An on-site **museum** displays church garments and religious items. (Open daily 8:30am-1pm. €2; free Su.)

For a memorable if somewhat haunting experience, head to **Anavatos,** an abandoned village built into the hillside, 15km west of Nea Moni. The village's women and children threw themselves from these cliffs in resistance to the 1822 invasion; today the red ruins, the pines below, and a small statuette of an angel near the village's entrance pay tribute to their heroic sacrifice. A walk among the fortifications provides amazing views of the surrounding hills. Stop by the church near the right of the site's entrance to see a folk-art rendition of the massacre of 1822. (Large parts of the ruins open to visitors daily 10am-2pm.)

SOUTHERN CHIOS

Grab a deck chair at **Karfas,** 6km south of Chios Town and home to the sandiest, most tourist-covered beach on the island. Many travelers take up temporary residence here, close to the beach and Chios Town's amenities; Karfas is also a refuge for vacationers unable to find lodgings in the capital. Blue **buses** run from Pl. Vournakio in Chios (every 30-45min., €1.20). **Karfas Rooms ❷,** right on the shore, offer conveniently located studios with large kitchens and private baths. (☎22710 31 202 or 31 902. Doubles €25-45.) **Markos's Place ❸,** up the hill at the far end of the beach (look for a blue gate), has small, monastic rooms located on a relaxed, 8000 sq. m compound. The area, adjacent to a monastery, also includes a yoga room and breakfast nook. (☎22710 31 990. Shared baths. Doubles €30. Minimum 4/5-day stay.) Near the island's southern tip lies **Emborio,** where beige cliffs contrast the black stones and blue water below. One beach is up the only road to the right (when facing the water). A smaller, less crowded shore is up the stairs to the right.

NORTHERN CHIOS

Nine kilometers north of Chios Town, you'll find the pleasant, pebbly shores of **Vrondados** and **Daskalopetra.** Blue **buses** from Pl. Vournakio in Chios Town serve both. A 2min. walk inland from the shore of Daskolopetra takes you to the **Sanctuary of Cybele.** Statues dating from the site's glory days as a center for worship can be found in the Archaeological Museum in Chios Town (p. 490). Here you can also find the **Stone of Homer,** where the poet is rumored to have held lectures. A circle of stone seats surrounds the prestigious rock which affords a magnificent view of the sea from behind a thicket of trees. After Daskalopetra ("stone teacher"), the main roads wind northwest along the coast past Marmaron to **Nagos,** with its stone beach, perhaps a popular spot to cut Homer's classes. High in the hills toward the center of the island, the village of **Volissos** is crowned by a Byzantine fort.

LESVOS Λεσβος

Escape from Lesvos's ho-hum port town as fast as you can to explore the geographically and culturally diverse interior of this vast and wonderful island. Unlike the tiny islands of the southern Aegean, Lesvos feels like its own country; the distinctiveness of its towns, not to mention the frustratingly inconvenient bus system separating them, make them feel like their own islands. Ouzo, olive groves, horse racing, remote monasteries, parched hillsides, lush green expanses, sandy beaches, art colonies, and a petrified forest demand your attention and time. Lesvos's rich cultural legacy matches the diversity of its landscape: 7th-century BC poet Sappho, fabulist Aesop, philosopher Aristotle, empiricist Epicurus, Nobel Prize-winning poet Odysseas Elytis, artist Theophilos Hadzimichali, and art critic Tériade have all called the island home. Legend has it that Lesvos's population was once entirely female. The tale may date back to the Athenian assembly's 428 BC decision to punish the unruly residents of Mytilini by executing all adult males on Lesvos. Though the assembly repealed the sentence, the idea of an Amazon island appeals to girl-power pilgrims who come to pay homage to Sappho and the etymological roots of the word "lesbian." Whether or not you number among them, arrive with an open mind and let the island's witchy ways enchant you.

MYTILINI Μυτιληνη ☎22510

Each morning, the wide harbor of the capital yawns into a modern, working city more reminiscent of Piraeus than of the tiny ports on nearby islands. Most come to Mytilini on business or en route to the rest of Lesvos; glitzy shops and bustling local markets are hence the defining features of the town. Escape the commercial beat by exploring some of the many winding side streets farther inland, where romping children and roving canines stake out territory amidst sleepy homes, small churches, and the occasional playground.

TRANSPORTATION

Flights: The **airport** (☎22510 61 590 or 61 490) is 6km south of Mytilini in the direction of Varia; take a **green bus** from the intercity bus station. **Olympic Airways,** Kavetsou 44 (☎22510 28 659 or 28 660; open 8am-3:30pm) also has an office at the airport (☎22510 61 120), as does **Aegean Airlines** (☎22510 61 801). Tickets for Olympic and Aegean flights can be purchased at nearly any travel agency in town. To: **Athens** (4 per day, €73); **Chios** (2 per week, €27.60); **Limnos** (5 per week, €35.60); **Thessaloniki** (daily, €87).

Ferries: NEL Lines, Pavlou Koundourioti 67 (☎22510 46 595 or 22510 40 802; fax 22510 40 595), on the far right side of the waterfront facing inland, before the string of cafes. Open daily 7am-10pm. Service to: **Chios** (3hr., 2 per day, €12); **Kavala** (12hr., 3 per week starting in July); **Limnos** (5hr., 6 per week, €16); **Piraeus** (12hr., 2 per day, €25.70); **Thessaloniki** (13hr., 2 per week, €30); **Aivali, Turkey** (1½hr.; 4 per week; €49, includes Greek port tax).

Intercity Buses: Intercity buses crisscross the island with Mytilini as the home base. From outlying cities, you will have to head back toward Mytilini in order to get somewhere else on the island. Other convenient transfer points are Kalloni and the fork for Eressos and Sigri. Schedules for the entire island are available at the bus station in Mytilini (☎22510 28 873) and at most information or tourist agencies throughout Lesvos. Service to: **Agiasos** (5 per day); **Mandamados** (3-4 per day); **Mistegna** (3-4 per day); **Molyvos** (2hr., 4 per day, €4.70) via **Kalloni** and **Petra; Plomari** (3-5 per day, €3.10) via **Gera; Polichnitos** (3-4 per day) via **Vatera; Sigri** (1-2 per day) via **Eressos** and **Kalloni.** Buses start running at 9am and the last usually leaves around 3pm. Reduced service Sa-Su. Prices €2-7, depending on distance.

Local Buses: ☎22570 28 873. At the northern end of the waterfront on Koundourioti. To: **Ag. Marina** (every hr., 7am-8:40pm; €0.90) via **Varia** (€0.65); **Ag. Rafael** (every 1-1½hr., 6am-9:40pm; €1.05) via **Thermi** (€0.90); **Loutra** (every hr., 6:15am-8:30pm; €0.90) via **Koundourtias** (€0.55).

Taxis: ☎22510 23 500. Line up on the corner of Ermou and Vournazon and where Pavlou Koundourioti meets Archipelagous.

Moped Rentals: N'Joy Rentals (☎22510 42 242 or 693 8779 414), on Tenedou, a small street off Koundourioti next to the NEL office. Discounts for longer rentals. €20 and up includes helmet and insurance. Open daily 8am-1:30pm and 5:30-10pm.

ORIENTATION AND PRACTICAL INFORMATION

Mytilini's harbor opens to the south. Cafes, bars, and hotels line the waterfront street **Koundourioti.** The **old market** stretches along **Ermou,** home to pharmacies, boutiques, and bakeries. Ermou becomes **Kavetsou** at its southern end where it intersects **Vournazon** one block inland on the harbor's western side. The inner harbor has a **National Bank** with a 24hr. **ATM** next to Hotel Sappho. (Open M-Th 8am-2:30pm, F 8am-2pm.) A number of ATMs are on Ermou, after Archipelagous and before the municipal gardens. Ther are **public toilets** in the park. For an **ambulance,** dial ☎166. For the **fire** department, dial ☎199. The **tourist police,** on Aristarchou near the ferry docks, provide brochures. (☎22510 22 776. Open 7am-2:30pm) The 24hr. **hospital** (☎22510 40 401) is southwest of town on P. Vostani. The **OTE** is on

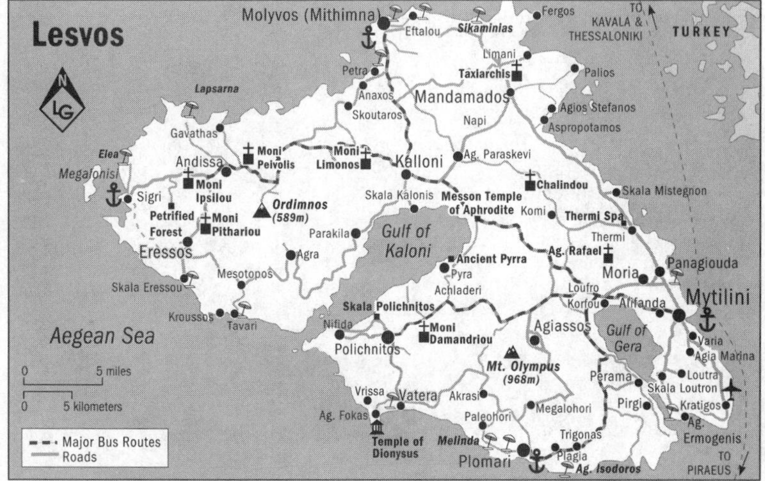

Vournazon. (☎22510 29 999. Open M-F 7:20am-1:30pm.) Find **Internet** access at the trendy cafe-bar **Super Nova,** which also features pool tables. (☎22510 23 885. €4 per hr. Open daily 9am-late.) The **post office,** next to the OTE, on Vournazon, offers **currency exchange.** (☎22510 28 836. Open M-F 7:30am-2pm.) **Postal code:** 81100.

ACCOMMODATIONS

The hotels along the waterfront tend to be elegant but quite pricey; head to Ermou to find plentiful, well advertised **domatia.** If you are met at the ferry, be sure to negotiate, and keep in mind that longer stays often result in lower rates. Doubles run €20-23 before July 15. Follow the "Rooms to Let" signs at the northern end of Ermou near Agios Theodoros church to **Antigoni Rooms ❷,** which offers spacious rooms with private baths and TVs. A quiet garden overrun by two enormous trees has a common kitchen in the back and a free phone for guests' use. (☎22510 45 749 or 6944 554 438. Doubles €15-20 in June, €25-30 July-Aug.). **Hotel Lesvion ❹,** on the waterfront south of Hotel Sappho, offers standard hotel rooms with amenities including TVs, phones, A/C, fridges, and baths. (☎22510 28 177; lesvion@otenet.gr. Breakfast €6. Check-out noon. Singles €35-40; doubles €45-55; triples available.)

FOOD AND NIGHTLIFE

The best souvlaki in town is served at **Agia Paraskevi ❶,** on Vournazon off Kavetsou, where the meat comes fresh, slow-roasted, and well-seasoned. (☎22510 46 666. Open daily 6am-2:30am.) For excellent taverna fare, head to **To Kalterimi ❷,** in the plant-lined alley Thasou off Ermou, north of the port. Try the *bekri meze* (€5.50), a hearty pork, sausage, and feta amalgamation. (☎22510 46 577. Grilled dishes €3-5. Open daily 7am-late; closed Su night.) Walking seaward on the southwestern quay brings you to Mytilini's best seafood tavernas. **O Dimitrakis ❷** has tables right by the water. Tasty grilled red mullet (€25 per kg) or octopus *stifado* (€5) complements a variety of local ouzo. Just around the corner, **O Stratos ❷** offers a similar menu of freshly-prepared fish, but with a larger, shaded seating area for big groups looking to beat the heat. (☎22510 21 739. Most entrees €4-6. Open daily 11am-late.) **Zacharoplasteio Valentino ❶,** El. Venizelou 6, has delicious

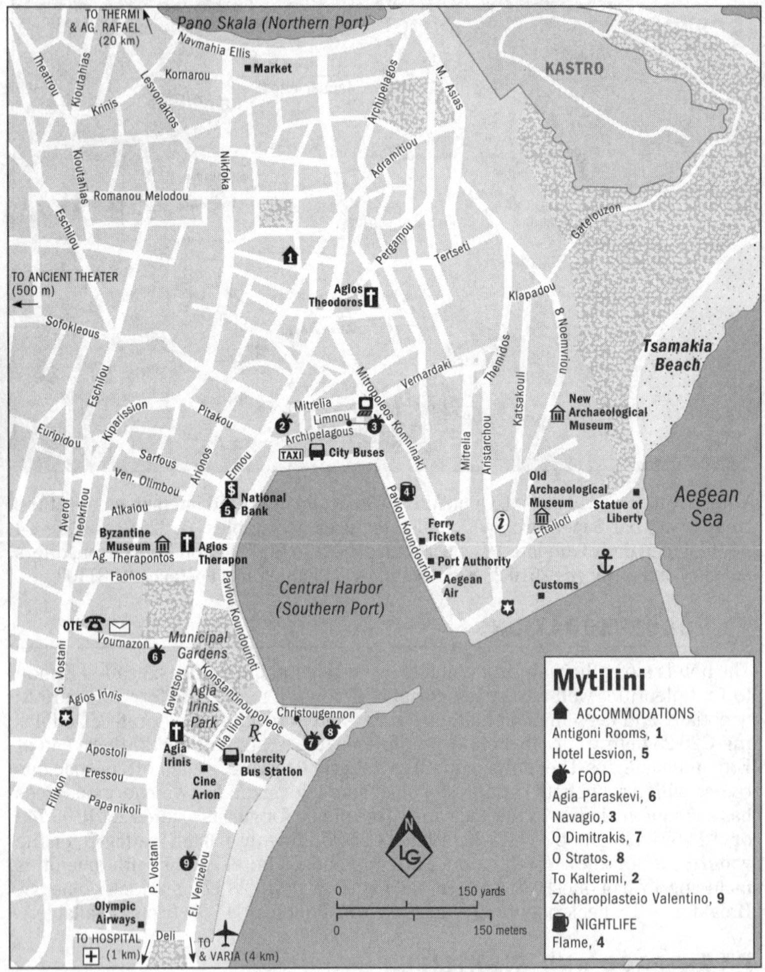

almond confections. (☎22510 23 989. Open daily 9am-8:30pm.) On the northern edge of the harbor behind the local buses, **Navagio** ❷ (☎22510 21 310) is the refuge of the moped generation and intellectual hipsters alike. Big, gooey ice cream sundaes (€4.50), cocktails (€5.90), and a variety of fancy deli sandwiches (€4.70).

Mytilini's nightlife centers on its gyrating waterfront. Head to the hypnotic colored lights of **Flame,** on the northeastern side of the waterfront, for fashionable drinks and the pulsing beats of their live DJ. To take full advantage of the experience, down a few shots (€2.30 and up) and head upstairs to Flame's trippy **neon bowling alley,** where blacklights, music videos, and glow-in-the-dark balls and pins make bowling cool again. (☎22510 46 884; fax 22510 46 886. Cocktails from €4.50. Bowling €2.50-4 per person per game, depending on time of day. Open daily 7:30am-1am.) For a more sedate evening, head to **Cine Arion** on Smyrnis across from the intercity bus station. Mostly American films play nightly on the theater's two screens. (☎22510 44 456. Weekly schedules at the ticket window. €6.50.)

SIGHTS

ARCHAEOLOGICAL MUSEUMS. Mytilini's extensive collection of archaeological relics is divided between two museums and tickets are good for both on the same day. The well-designed **new Archaeological Museum,** on 8 Noemvriou, contains finds ranging from cooking utensils dating from Lesvos's ancient Neolithic past to sculptures and busts from its days under Roman control. The clear highlights, though, are the fully-restored mosaic floors from several houses of ancient Mytilini, which are displayed in their original layout; the floors are placed under glass tiles, allowing you to walk on top. Most exhibits have English signs and the museum is handicapped-accessible. *(☎22510 40 223. Open Tu-Su 8am-3pm. €3, students €2, EU students and under 18 free. The ticket is good for the old museum as well.)* The **old Archaeological Museum,** Argiri Eftalioti 7, up the hill behind the main port, has a less inspiring collection of Lesvian artifacts, though the detailed English signs do present a thorough and informative linear history of the island. The collection focuses on earthenware jars and small figurines found during the excavations at Thermi. The smaller building hiding behind the main museum contains administrative and legal tablets written in the rare Aeolian dialect, now known to scholars primarily through the writings of Sappho. *(☎22510 28 032. Open Tu-Su 8:30am-3pm. Same ticket policy and prices as new museum.)*

OTHER SIGHTS. The sprawling Gattelusi Castle stands guard over the picturesque port from its perch on a pine-covered hill near the museums. Originally constructed by Emperor Justinian on the site of a Byzantine castle, it bears the name of Francesco Gattelusi, who received Lesvos as a dowry in 1354 after he married Justinian's daughter. Genoese, Ottomans, and Greeks have spent successive centuries maintaining the castle walls and underground tunnels. Wear good shoes for wandering the vast interior. *(☎22510 27 970. Open Tu-Su 7am-8pm. €2, EU students and children under 18 free.)* The highest point on the northern side of Mytilini is the 3rd-century BC **ancient theater,** from the Hellenistic Period, where 15,000 spectators attended performances and enjoyed near-perfect acoustics. The effect was so impressive that it inspired Pompeii to build Rome's first stone theater. *(Open Tu-Su 8:30am-7pm.)* The late 19th-century **Church of Ag. Therapon,** on the western side of the harbor and one block inland on Ermou, is impressive for its enormous size alone.

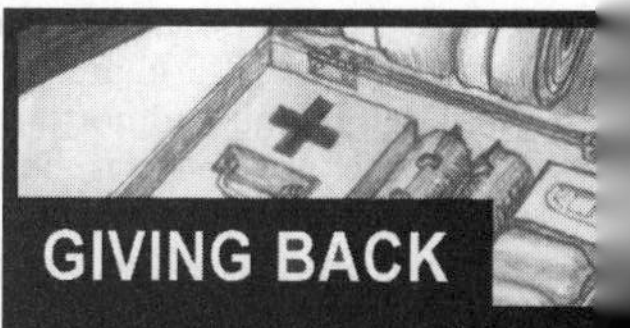

GIVING BACK

WILD THING

Lesvos is not unique among th Greek islands—and Greece as a whole—in suffering from a dir stray dog and cat problem, but th animals' predicament is perhap more troubling on an island that i home to a proliferation of uniqu wildlife.

Fortunately for Lesvos's furr and feathered residents, the Les bian Wildlife Hospital, founded i 1993 by Mrs. Ineke Peeters Lenglet and her husband, Joris strives painstakingly to provid first aid to every sick, injured, o orphaned wild animal that i brought to their attention. Tw years ago the hospital moved fro Therme to its current base of oper ations in Agia Parevski.

Though its keepers work ther full-time, the hospital is still smal and could use the help of any full or part-time volunteers, with o without prior animal care experi ence. Interns are responsible fo daily household operations of th facility, assisting in feeding an caring for the animals, and help ing construct the hospital's ne aviary. Paid opportunities are cu rently not available, though foo and accommodations can be pro vided for volunteers.

Also, for those sticking aroun Lesvos for a while, the hospita eagerly places rehabilitated an mals with people willing to tak care of them at home. The hospi tal provides assistance with an mal care to the philanthropic ne parents.

(Open 9am-7pm.) The **Byzantine Museum** is just next door. *(☎22510 28 916. Open M-Sa 9am-1pm. €2.)* The church towers over a **fish market** full of sardines, octopi, and small sharks. Inland and north of the harbor (one block off Ermou) is the impressive **Church of Ag. Theodoros,** housing the bones and skull of its patron saint. For a good gift, **Michalis Dimitrias** paints icons of the archangel Michael, on a side street at the far end of Ermou. *(☎22510 20 443. Small €1, large €7 and up.)*

VARIA. Only 4km south of Mytilini along El. Venizelou, the tiny, unassuming village of Varia (Βαρια) surprises wayfarers with the **Theophilos Museum,** featuring 86 paintings by the famous Neoprimitivist Greek artist Theophilos Hadzimichali. *(☎22510 41 644. Open Tu-Su 9am-2:30pm and 6-8pm. €2, students and children under 18 free.)* Next door the **Musée Tériade** displays an excellent collection of Picasso, Miró, Léger, Chagall, and Matisse lithographs; captions are in Greek, English, and French. Tériade, a native of Lesvos (born Stratis Eleftheriadis), was a leading 20th-century publisher of graphic art in Paris. *(☎22510 23 372. Open daily 9am-2pm and 5-8pm. €2, students and children free.)* Local **buses** to Varia leave Mytilini every hour (20min., €0.65). Tell the driver you are going to the museum.

AGIOS RAFAEL. Twenty kilometers into the hills above the capital is the **monastery** of Ag. Rafael in Thermi. The saint was particularly active in working modern-day miracles, making his chapel and grave a major place of pilgrimage. The door on the bottom level of the church, marked "Αγιασμα," leads to a source of holy water. Visitors can stay free for up to two nights; nearby **Kafe-Estiatoriou O Fotis ❷** offers "home cooking at fair prices." *(Bus from Mytilini runs every hr. for €1.)*

DAYTRIP FROM MYTILINI: VATERA

To get to Vatera (58km from Mytilini) you can take the bus (1½hr.; M-F 4 per day, Sa-Su 3 per day; €4.20). The bus enters via the main road, runs the length of the beachside road, and drops off and picks up anywhere along the beach. A one-way taxi ride runs around €40. You can also visit Vatera as a daytrip using private transportation from Plomari or Polichnitos.

With calm waters and 8km of wide, unbroken sands, Vatera is the premier beach on Lesvos. The **beach** is the only attraction in town and touristy establishments lie just across the road. The ruins of the **Temple of Dionysus** lie to the right of the beach (when facing the water) at the cape of **Agios Fokas.** Some of the column remnants at the site date to 300 BC, while others date to AD 100, when early Christian temples were built over the site. The ruins aren't hugely impressive, but great sunsets are visible from the beach on the other side of the point. The journey is a bit long by foot but makes for a pleasant bike ride. Follow the road along the beach to the right facing the water and veer left across the bridge at the sign for Villa Pouloudia. Bring water; avoid the midday heat—the latter half of the ride is hilly and taxing.

If bus schedules leave you in Vatera overnight, **Hotel Aphrodite ❹,** 800m down the road from the main intersection, on your left, has loaded rooms with A/C, TVs, fridges, kitchenettes, private baths, and even hair-dryers to tame your seawater-soaked coiffure. (☎22520 61 588. Breakfast included. High season singles €70, low season €45; doubles €85/€55.) Lavish **Camping Dionysos ❶,** 350m from the intersection and 100m from the beach, has a pantheon of perks: hot showers, bathrooms, mini-market, swimming pool, laundry, kitchen, and snack bar. (☎22520 61 710 or 61 151; fax 22520 61 155. Reception 9am-9pm. Seaside gate open 9am-9pm, main road gate open 24hr. €6 per person, children free; €6 per tent; €6 per car. Free parking outside campsite.) Two **supermarkets** are about 50m to the left of the intersection; tavernas are along the beachside road. Candlelit **Mylos Cafe,** 100m to the left of the intersection on the beach, has a chill atmosphere. (☎22520 61 161. Beer €2.30-4; cocktails €5. Open late.)

MOLYVOS Μολυβος ☎22530

Hilly and cobbled, the charming town of Molyvos (a.k.a. Mithymna) spills from the towering castle to the sea like a gingerbread village from a children's storybook. Home to an illustrious school of fine arts, a number of galleries, and a spate of artsy trinket shops, Molyvos breathes the sensibility of an artists' colony; though frequented by tourists, its atmosphere remains serene and its prices reasonable.

TRANSPORTATION AND PRACTICAL INFORMATION. The **bus** stops at the base of town on the main road. Buses run to: **Anaxos** (M-F 7 per day), via **Petra; Eftalou** (M-F 7 per day); **Mytilini** (1½hr., 5-6 per day, €4.70) via **Kalloni** and **Petra.** Ask at the tourist office for schedules and fares. To the immediate left of the National Bank, **Kosmos Rentals** rents **mopeds** (€14-24 per day) and **cars** (€35 per day and up), with prices including full insurance, tax, and unlimited mileage. (☎22530 71 710; fax 22530 71 720. Open daily 8am-1pm and 4-9:30pm.) **Taxis** (☎22530 71 480) stop at the intersection on the main road heading into town from the bus stop.

Molyvos has three main roads running along different levels of the hill. The **main road** leads from the bus station past the tourist information office and bank and runs to the port on the far side of town. Down on your left as you enter town, another road runs along the beach past hotels and restaurants. The third road veers right and uphill as you enter town and runs through the agora past shops and restaurants with views. Just into town on the left side of the main road is the **tourist information office,** where the friendly, informative staff provides **maps,** updated bus schedules, information about Molyvos, and accommodations advice. (☎22530 71 069; dimos_mithimnas@les.forthnet.gr. Open Apr.-Oct. M-F 8am-5pm, Sa-Su 10am-5pm.) The **National Bank** is next door and has a 24hr. **ATM.** (☎22530 71 210. Open M-Th 8am-2:30pm, F 8am-2pm.) The road forks just beyond the bank; head right, uphill, and left at the second fork, you'll find the local **laundry,** where €8 will get you one load of clean clothes. (☎22530 71 622. Open 9am-2:30pm and 5:30-10:30pm.) Signs will direct you to the **police station** (☎22510 71 222). To find a **pharmacy,** head along the main uphill road, just after the National Bank; one's on your right, before the road to Nassos Guest House. (☎22530 71 903. Open daily 9am-2pm and 5:30-11pm.) Continue along the road to the top of the hill and go right at the fork to find a **medical office** (☎22530 71 702). **Internet** access isn't hard to find in Molyvos. **Cinema Arion** (☎22530 71 078; sv8bsa@otenet.gr; €4.40 per hr., €1.50 min.; open in summer, daily 9am-11pm) is just up from the bus stop. Take a left at the fork in the uphill road to find **Centraal.** (☎22530 72 556. €4.50 per hr., €1.50 min.) Take a right at the fork at the top of the hill to reach the **post office.** (☎22530 71 246. Open M-F 7:30am-2pm.) **Postal code:** 81108.

ACCOMMODATIONS AND FOOD. Signs for **domatia** dot the town; the tourist office can help you find a bed. Expect to pay €25-40 for a double in high season; €15-25 low season. To find **Nassos Guest House ❷,** follow the road leading up the hill into town and head right at the first steep switchback; look for the Nassos sign. Bright, cheerful rooms have surreal views of red roofs and the harbor below. Cheerful Australian Marcia maintains a relaxed, homey atmosphere and offers helpful advice about the island. Her rooms have private balconies but share bath and kitchen. (☎22510 71 432 and 71 421; nassosguesthouse@hotmail.com. Open Apr.-Oct. Reservations recommended for Aug. stays. Doubles €22-30; triples €24-34. Discounts for longer stays.) **Evaggelia Teke ❸** (☎22530 71 158; fax 22530 71 233), on the uphill road at the corner of the port, has large rooms with fridges, clean private bathrooms, and great views. (Inquire at one of the art galleries next door if no one's around. Singles €25; doubles €40-45.) **Camping Mithimna ❶** is 1.5km out of town on the road to Eftalou. (☎22510 71 169. €5.60 per person, ages

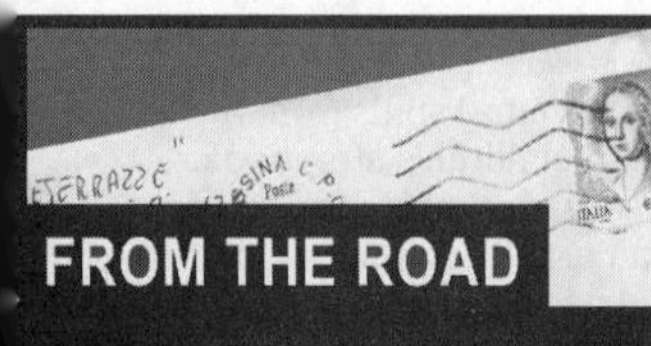

FROM THE ROAD

DEMAND LESS

Hostels are scarce in Greece, but luckily the transition to hotels in less touristed towns isn't expensive... if you know how to negotiate. Hotel price listings are set by the government, but these are "maximums," and Greek proprietors are often happy to bargain far below. There are two ways to play the act: the aggressive lodger/crooked proprietor or the poor traveler/sympathetic proprietor. I recommend the latter. Here is a simple guide:

1. Always arrive early in the day with the appearance of a light luggage load. Your apparent ability to shop around will increase your bargaining power.

2. Request to see a room before asking for the price. Besides showing that you're experienced, this puts you in control of the negotiations. Put the owner on the defensive by inquiring about something the room lacks—TV, telephone, balcony. And *always* ask if A/C is included before accepting a price. Premature acceptance often results in surcharges for the A/C remote.

3. *Now* ask for the price, which usually comes after a thoughtful pause. If it still seems high, explain that you cannot spend more than €X, but understand why the owner must charge so much for such a charming room. After checking with his or her (possibly non-existent) spouse, the proprietor will usually make you a better deal. The act may seem a bit dishonest, but it's supply *and* demand. Demand less.

—Alex Ioannidis, 2004

4-10 €3, under 4 free; €3 per small tent, €3.50 per big tent; €4 per car.)

There are several **mini-markets** on the main road. Molyvos's harbor, at the far end of the main road, is crammed with restaurants, each offering fresh seafood served to tables by the water. The stepfather of the owner of **The Captain's Table ❷** is reputedly one of the island's best fishermen. For the full experience, order the captain's platter for one (€11) or two (€20) and show up on a Wednesday evening, when *bouzouki* talent Vangelis belts out his repertoire. Complementary olives and dessert come with your meal. (☎22530 71 241. V.) **Octapus ❷** is another worthy harborside fish taverna and also one of the town's oldest. Most fish run €25 per kg. (☎22530 71 317; www.octapus-restaurant.com. Open daily 10am-late.) Restaurants on the harbor have a way of stretching the pocketbook, but don't despair; many tavernas further inland serve excellent food for friendly prices. **Taverna O Gatos ❷,** midway up the hill before the post office, has served fresh, traditional fare for over 20 years. Ask the friendly staff if you can have a rooftop seat; the view is amazing. (☎22510 71 661. Starters €3-5.50. Entrees €4-7. Open 9am-late.) Herbivores rejoice—your prayers have been answered in the form of the **Friends Gyros Stand ❶,** on the main road. The affable owner has created several meatless gyros, stuffed with cucumbers, french fries, green peppers, feta, tomatoes, and other tasty veggie products. Carnivores fear not; the standard grill options are available here as well. (☎22510 71 567. Pita €1.40-1.60. Open daily noon-late.)

SIGHTS AND ENTERTAINMENT. The dominant feature of the Molyvos skyline is the **kastro,** the medieval castle. (Open Tu-Su 8am-7pm. €2, students and children free.) The view alone is worth the climb and the castle is superbly preserved. It hosts theatrical events; ask at the tourist information office, call the town hall (☎22510 71 313 or 71 323), or keep an eye out for signs. On summer nights, head to **Conga's Beach Club,** accessible from both the beachside and main roads, where pulsing music and tropical decor (complete with hammocks) entertain a tourist crowd. (Cover €3, includes 1 beer. Beer €3-5; cocktails €7. Open daily 10am-late.) **Gatelouzoi Bar,** on the beachside road, to the right of the Olive Press Hotel facing the water, has a funky orange-cube decor and occasionally features live traditional Greek music. (Ladies Night Th. Happy Hour 10-11:30pm.)

BEACHES. A narrow, pebbly beach stretches southward toward Petra and is accessible from the first road to the left as you enter Molyvos. Beach umbrellas abound (shop around to find an agreeable rate); showers and changing rooms are available for free. More inviting shores can be found at **Eftalou,** whose beautiful black sand and pebble beaches make a pleasant daytrip from Molyvos. The bus from Molyvos drops off in the middle of the main beach. Walk about 300m to the end of road and around the rocks to find Eftalou's **thermal baths,** whose 46°C waters are medicinally potent and—for the younger and healthier—simply relaxing. (☎22530 71 245. €3.50 for pool, €5 for private bathtub. Open daily 8am-2pm and 4-8pm.) The beach continues well beyond the baths.

PETRA Πετρα ☎22530

Named for the monolithic rock in the town center, this artists' beach town suns itself on a plain 5km south of Molyvos. Petra's village ambience and long beach make it a popular daytrip from Molyvos, as well as a worthy destination in itself.

Local **buses** run to **Molyvos** in the summer (€0.90 one-way); the bus stops 200m before the central plateia. Facing inland straight ahead is **Theodokou,** hosting the **post office** (☎22530 41 230; open M-F 7:30am-2pm), which also **exchanges currency.** Parallel to the water one block inland, **Ermou** is lined with bakeries and shops. There is **no bank** in town, but there's a 24hr. **ATM** next to Supermarket Plus on Ermou. To the right on the water is **Nirvana Travel,** which has info, **currency exchange,** book exchange, and excursion bookings and helps locate accommodations or car rentals. Nirvana Travel also operates the **Lesvos Cultural Centre** upstairs, which organizes yoga, painting, and Greek dancing classes. (☎22530 41 991 or 41 977; www.nirvanatravel.gr. Open in summer daily 9am-2pm and 6-9:30pm.) Next to Nirvana Travel is a **pharmacy.** (☎22530 41 319. Open 9am-2pm and 6-9pm.) A few paces further down the same road is a **medical office,** open 24hr. (☎22530 42 205 or 6945 678 333). The **OTE** (☎22530 41 399 or 41 199; open M-F 7:30am-1:30pm) is to the left of the plateia on the road to Molyvos. **Taxis** are just a phone call away (☎22530 42 022). **Internet** access is available at **Cafe Reef** on the road to Molyvos, a full-on English pub complete with live soccer, Guinness on tap (€4), and Indian food (chicken curry €5.50) on Tuesdays. (☎22530 42 146; www.cafereef.com. €4 per hr., €2 min.) **Postal code:** 81109.

For help finding cheap lodgings, head to the **Women's Cooperative of Petra ❷,** upstairs in the central plateia (enter on Ermou), which was founded in 1983 to help local women gain some measure of financial independence by offering rooms to rent throughout town. Rooms vary in location and amenities; most come with shared bath and kitchen. Equipped studios are also available. (☎22530 41 238; fax 22530 41 309. Doubles €25 and up. Open daily 7am-midnight.) The beachfront is host to the usual slate of indistinguishable tavernas. If you're looking for a less run-of-the-mill dinner, follow Theodakou past the steps leading to the church, and continue to your left at the fork in the road. The long walk along the cobbled streets leads to **Rigas ❷,** the oldest taverna in town. (☎22530 41 405. Entrees €4-8. Open daily 7pm-late.) If you'd prefer to pick up something for a picnic on the beach, check out the **Agricultural Cooperative of Petra,** at the fork before town off from the main road, carrying locally produced wines, olive oils, and cheeses. Here you'll recapture that kid-in-a-candy-store sensation. Show up in the morning for fresh produce. (☎22530 41208. Open 8am-1pm and 7-9pm.)

At night, head to **Machine** (open 10:30pm-late), a disco/bar on the waterfront, past Nirvana Travel. If you can peel yourself off the sand, you can watch ouzo bottling at **Ouzo Petras,** Ermou 31, an ouzo store with its own equipment. (Open daily 10:30am-1:30pm and 6:30-10:30pm.) Before downing your bottle of anisette goodness, head up Theodokou past the post office to find the town's namesake, a 27m rock. The 114 steps lead to the endearing **Church of the Holy Mary with the Sweet Smile,** which grants stunning views of the village and the sea below. (Open daily

8:30am-9pm. Modest dress required.) Also in town is the **Vareltzidaina House Museum** (open in summer Tu-Su 8:30am-7pm), an opulent mansion.

SKALA ERESSOU Σκαλα Ερεσου ☎22530

Sappho's birthplace offers a seemingly endless beach, completely separated from the concrete noise of the capital city. Laid-back and welcoming, Skala Eressou attracts an eclectic group of visitors ranging from archaeologists to lesbian poets. One half of its beach remains one of the few legal nude bathing spots on Lesvos.

TRANSPORTATION AND PRACTICAL INFORMATION. An early-morning **bus** runs between Skala Eressou and **Mytilini** via the fork for **Sigri** and **Kalloni** (3hr., daily, €7.40). The bus stops in a large parking lot on the main road two blocks from the waterfront. During high season, starting in mid-July, a bus runs daily to **Sigri,** 26km to the northwest, leaving at 11am and returning at 5am (€3). There is only one **taxi** driver (☎22530 54 327) in the area, based out of Sigri.

A tree-canopied road connects Skala Eressou and **Eressos,** 4km inland to the north. The main road hits the waterfront just a few meters to the right of a short footbridge, which divides the town. Though the restaurants and cafes to the left of the bridge have a bit more soul than their brethren to the right, the entire beach strip radiates fun and relaxation. Joanna and the incredibly helpful, English-speaking team at **Sappho Travel,** one block from the bus stop before the waterfront, offer information about the town, help with accommodations, **exchange currency,** and know about gay and lesbian activities. (☎22530 52 140 or 52 130; www.lesvos.co.uk. Open May-Oct. daily 9am-11pm; Nov.-Apr. 9am-3pm.) The town's sole **doctor** commutes between the **clinic** in Skala Eressou (☎22530 53 221; open June-Sept M, W, F 9am-1pm), behind the Hotel Sappho, and his office (☎22530 52 132; open Tu-Th) in Eressos. The nearest **police** are in Eressos (☎22530 53 222). In case of **emergency,** call the **health center** (☎22530 56 440, 56 442, or 56 444), in Antissa, 11km from Skala Eressou. Though there is **no bank** in Skala Eressou, a **bank-on-a-bus** rolls through town every Tuesday and Thursday from 11am to 1pm. Though infinitely less amusing, the 24hr. **ATM** outside Sappho Travel is admittedly more convenient. **Internet** access is available at **Cybersurf Cafe,** just past the bridge on Kanari. (☎22530 52 290. €4.50 per hr., €2 min. Printing €0.45 per page. Unlimited coffee €1.50. Open 11am-10pm.) A few card **phones** are along the main road running from the bus stop to the beach; there is also one alongside Hotel Sappho. The **post office** is in Eressos. (☎22530 53 227. Open M-F 8am-2pm.) **Postal code:** 81105.

ACCOMMODATIONS. Skala Eressou generally draws visitors for weeks of stunning sunsets; many come for vacation and end up staying for good. Consequently, studios and **long-term accommodations** are plentiful, though reasonably-priced rooms for brief stays do exist as well. Sappho Travel has a separate phone number specifically for help with accommodations (☎22530 52 202). **Hotel Sappho ❸,** on the waterfront to the right (facing the water), is a women-only hotel with an open, friendly feel and original artwork decorating the walls. Basic but spacious rooms have private baths. (☎22530 53 495 or 53 233; info@sapphohotel.com. Doubles €46-58; discounts for singles.) **Pension Krinelos ❷,** just behind the bus stop, offers affordable, home-style lodgings, run by a good-humored couple. Clean rooms have private bath, A/C (additional €3), and common fridge. (☎22530 53 246; fax 22530 53 982; krinelos@otenet.gr. Singles €18-27; doubles €25-35.) Away from the waterfront, **Hotel Galini ❸** offers large, classy rooms in a quiet locale with private baths, A/C, phones, and balconies. From the waterfront, walk three blocks inland on the main road and take a right; follow the sign for the hotel down an alley to your left. (☎22530 53 138; fax 22530 53 137. Singles €29-34;

doubles €38-50.) On the beach past Hotel Sappho, to the right facing the water, is **Villa Marilena ❷**, which has sizable studios close to the beach with kitchenettes and private baths. (☎22530 53 506 or 53 156. Doubles €25-30.) **Camping on the beach** is **illegal** and the town's police have been increasingly strict about enforcing this policy.

FOOD AND ENTERTAINMENT. Food in Skala Eressou is generally very good and the town is a vegetarian paradise—at least by Greek standards. **Sappho Restaurant ❷,** at Hotel Sappho, has a spunky alternative vibe and serves a variety of delicious, healthful, meatless dishes to a soundtrack of female singer-songwriters. (☎22530 53 233. Entrees €6-8. Open daily 9am-11pm.) To the right along the waterfront, **Ouzeri Soulatso ❷** is the most legitimate Greek taverna in town and specializes in fresh fish and tidbits to accompany your ouzo. (☎22530 52 078. Grilled entrees €5; seafood prices fluctuate around the catch and season. Open daily noon-midnight.) Along the beach to the left, **Jay's Restaurant ❷** offers a diverse menu of excellent Asian and Mediterranean dishes, with a number of vegetarian- and vegan-friendly options. Friendly owners Nikki and Jay create a warm, welcoming atmosphere. (☎22530 53 624. Entrees €7-8. Open daily 1pm-midnight.)

Revelers hang at the beachfront bars and cafes that spill onto the sand. On hot summer evenings, join the crowd for a late-night plunge in the Aegean to clear your head. **The Tenth Muse** is a popular gay bar in the main plateia (☎22530 53 287. Beer €2-4.50; cocktails €5. Open 9:30am-4am.) Gay-friendly **Friends,** next to Jay's Restaurant, draws an international crowd. (☎22530 53 178; www.friends-bar.net). **Naos Music Club** (☎22530 53 787; www.naosclub.gr), at the far end of the parking lot on the main road to Eressos, keeps the local youngsters entertained until dawn.

SIGHTS. Sappho fans beware: though useless trinkets and statues of the poet are easy to find in town, actual collections of her work are not. A few photographs of the landscape that inspired her might make better souvenirs. The 5th-century mosaics once housed in the early Christian basilica of **Ag. Andreas,** three blocks north of the beach, are now in Mytilini's new Archaeological Museum. Though the church was originally named after the saint Andreas, a Cretan archbishop of the same name happened to die nearby just a couple centuries later. His grave, the **Tomb of Ag. Andreas** (open 9am-1pm) was incorporated into the site, though it supposedly only contains half of his remains, the other portion having been claimed by Crete. The river, just west of Skala's center, is home to many rare and exotic birds. Peak **bird watching** season is April to May. About 11km above Sigri on the main road is the spectacular **Ipsilou Monastery.** Situated on the peak of the Ordymnos volcanic dome, the picturesque Byzantine monastery commands an amazing view of the rugged yellow hills of northwestern Lesvos.

DAYTRIPS FROM SKALA ERESSOU. A **petrified forest** 4km from **Sigri** is one of only two such forests in the world (the other is in the southwestern United States). The remains of the fossilized trunks scattered throughout the parched hillside are around 20 million years old; the more massive remnants are over 20m in length. The trunks were preserved in amazingly precise detail during an ancient volcanic meltdown that almost instantaneously blanketed the original forest, resulting in the molecule-by-molecule replacement of the plants' organic matter with the inorganic silicon carried in the volcanic goo. Bring a hat and water, as the site is accessible only by 2.5km of walking trails and takes at least 1hr. to appreciate fully. (Open daily 8am-4pm; July-Aug. 8am-7pm. €2, children under 15 free. For more information, call the museum or the main parks office in Mytilini at ☎22510 40 132). In Sigri, the **Natural History Museum of the Lesvos Petrified Forest,** completed in 2001, has fascinating exhibits on a variety of plant fossils, both from the Lesvos site and from around the world, stretching back to the Paleozoic Era. The museum also contains exhibits on general geology and the geological history of the Aegean, both well-designed enough to turn even the biggest fossil-lunkhead into an aspiring geologist for an hour. (☎22530 54 434; www.aegean.gr/petrified_forest. Museum open M-Sa 8:30am-6pm, Su 9am-6pm; extended hours in Aug. €2, children free.) The site and museum are best accessed by private vehicle, but the road that runs directly from Eressos to Sigri is not passable. Head back toward Andissa on the main road for 10km and take a left at the fork for Sigri; on the way you'll pass the road up to Ipsilou Monastery (see above). A network of hiking **trails** connects Eressos, the petrified forest, and Sigri; obtain a detailed map of the trails from a travel agency or the museum before embarking on a hike.

Sigri, a small fishing village, is worth a look if you make the trip to the museum. Several small tavernas cluster near the main plateia on your left as you approach the harbor on the main road. **Una Fazzia, Una Razza ❷,** an Italian with welcoming owners, serves the cheapest lobster in the area (€35 per kg) as well as excellent pasta dishes. (☎22530 54 565. Entrees €5.50-8. Open Apr.-Oct. daily 9am-4pm and 6:30pm-late. MC/V.) Sandy and calm, Sigri's **beach** is protected from the northern winds by the town's 18th-century **Turkish castle.** Wander farther down the road to find less frequented beaches. Should you decide to stay longer in Sigri, Sappho Travel, in Skala Eressou, organizes accommodations.

NORTHEAST AEGEAN

PLOMARI Πλομαρι ☎22520

After arson destroyed Megalohori village in 1841, people resettled in the Turkish-inhabited region 12km south, now modern Plomari. The warmth of this crumbling fishing village has attracted an influx of tourists, some who breeze through on their way to the sandy beaches of Vatera to the west. The ouzo factories and olive groves on the outskirts of town reflect Plomari's vibrant, traditional industries.

TRANSPORTATION AND PRACTICAL INFORMATION. Plomari is a 40km **bus** ride from Mytilini (1½hr., €3.10). The **bus** stops in the main plateia, next to the **taxi** stand (☎22520 33 331) and close to the **National Bank** with a 24hr. **ATM.** (Open M-Th 8am-2:30pm, F 8am-2pm). Facing inland from the plateia, a road leads uphill to the left, past a small fountain to a square with tavernas and grocery **markets. Paper Land,** in the back of the square, sells international newspapers, magazines, and books. To the left of Paper Land, hidden behind an enormous tree, is a **pharmacy.** (☎22520 32 566. Open 8am-9pm.) Sharing a building with Hotel Oceanis, **Oceanis Rent-A-Car** (☎22520 32 498; open in summer 8am-10pm) rents mopeds (€12-20) and cars (€20-35). Reach the **police** at ☎22520 32 333 and a 24hr. **health center** at ☎22520 32 151. The **Saloon Cafe** (☎22520 32 447; www.saloon.gr), to the right from the bus stop at the end of the line of tavernas, has **Internet** access. (€4.50 per hr., €1.50 min. Open 10am-3am.) On the right side of town (facing inland) on the beachside road are the **OTE** (☎22520 31 099) and **post office** (☎22520 32 241), which **exchanges currency.** (Both open M-F 7:30am-2pm.) **Postal code:** 81200.

ACCOMMODATIONS AND FOOD. While Plomari makes a nice daytrip, it also offers accommodations for those who want to relax a bit longer. **Pension Lida ❷** is housed in two adjacent buildings, the old mansion of a Plomari manufacturer and the family home of its owner, on the hill above Platanos. Beautiful, diverse rooms are accented by Byzantine treasures tucked into walls and hardwood floors. Each comes with spotless private bath and enjoys a view of the village from either a balcony, stone terrace, or arched window. Friendly owner Yiannis Stergellis manufactures his own tasty ouzo and olive oil on the premises. (☎/fax 22520 32 507. Breakfast from €3. Singles €23; doubles €30-32; triples €36-38.) **Maki's Guest House ❷,** up the stairs to the right of Saloon Cafe (knock on the third wooden door on the left), has three pristine rooms with private baths, fridges, and common balcony overlooking the waterfront. (☎22520 32 536. Singles €15-20; doubles €20-30.) **Hotel Oceanis ❷,** the large, unadorned building that dominates the waterfront, has standard doubles with baths and balconies. A sea view comes with no extra expense. (☎22520 32 469. Singles €18-24; doubles €24-36.)

Tavernas line Platanos and the road leading to the main plateia. For great seafood, head to the two tavernas along the waterfront tucked away to the right of the main plateia, facing the water. For fresh grilled entrees, friendly owners Nikos and Nikos at **Bacchus ❷,** on the waterfront side of Hotel Oceanis, serve up celebrated meatballs with bacon (€6) and Souvlaki Bacchus (€6.50) to tables overlooking the harbor. (☎22520 31 059. Entrees €5-8. Open daily 6pm-late.)

SIGHTS AND BEACHES. Lesvos is renowned for its ouzo production, and Plomari in particular enjoys a reputation for its local brews. The **Barbayanni Ouzo Factory,** roughly 2km east on the road to Agios Isodoros from Plomari, is the modern-day production site for one of Greece's oldest and most beloved privately-owned ouzo companies. The same family has controlled the company since its founding in 1860. Today you can take a peek at 19th-century distillation devices in the adjacent **Ouzo Museum,** in addition to observing the fascinating production process in the current factory. Free samples of Barbayanni ouzo are not to be missed. (☎22520 32 741; www.barbayianni-ouzo.com. Ask at the factory for a free tour of the museum. Open M-F 7am-8pm, Sa 9am-2pm). An annual, week-long **Ouzo Festival** is held in late August and features song, dance, and—of course—free ouzo. Plomari also hosts several summertime religious celebrations and cultural events. The one-week **Festival of Benjamin,** in late June, commemorates War of Independence leader Benjamin of Lesvos with dancing and theatrical presentations. On August 15, the town celebrates the **Panagia** in time-honored style. Just 15km north of Plomari on the slopes of Lesvos's Mt. Olympus, you'll find the ceramic crafts center of **Agiassos.** In town, an Orthodox church treasures an icon of the Virgin Mary made by St. Lucas, originally destined for Constantinople in 330. When the priest transporting it heard rumors of war, he hid the icon in Agiassos's church. The village also boasts an **Ecclesiastical Museum** and a **Folk Museum.**

Beaches appear intermittently around Plomari. To reach small, rocky **Ammoudeli beach,** follow the waterfront road out of town to the right from the bus stop, facing the water. Continuing straight past the beach brings you to **Ag. Nikolaos,** a church sparkling with icons spanning 400 years. About 3km east of town, the sandy, golden expanse of **Ag. Isodoros beach** draws a large, bronzed following.

LIMNOS Λημνος

Remote and denuded, Limnos catches travelers with its uninviting austerity. But just as the dry, apparently unmanageable soil yields a surprising wealth of products to wise Limnian farmers, the solemn island reveals majestic sunsets, well-preserved wetlands, sparkling beaches, silent sand dunes, and a pack of migrating flamingoes to travelers with the patience to meet the land on its own terms.

MYRINA Μυρινα ☎22540

Myrina has a small-town feel to it, largely because of the cobbled main road, where both residents and visitors stroll in the evening to window-shop and share gossip. Two waterfronts split the town's duties admirably; one greets ferries and exhibits the fishermen's daily catch, while the other buzzes with trim waiters and idle beachgoers, as the sun evaporates behind distant Mt. Athos. The impressive, illuminated Venetian Castle dominates the evening skyline.

TRANSPORTATION. **SAOS** and **G.A. Ferries** are the two lines serving Limnos. **Ferries** run to: **Alexandroupoli** (4hr., 1 per week, €12.82); **Chios** (9-14hr., 2 per week, €18.59); **Lavrio,** near Athens (7½hr., 3 per week, €29); **Kavala** (SAOS: 4hr., 2 per week; G.A.: 4¼hr., 2 per week, €13.70); **Mytilini,** Lesvos (SAOS: 5hr., 1 per week on Sa., €16.10; G.A.: 5½hr., 4 per week, €16.40); **Piraeus** (23-25hr., 1 per week, €25.10); **Psara** (5½hr., 1 per week on Su); **Samos** (12hr., 1 per week, €23.43); **Samothraki** (2½hr.; 2 per week, Sa and Su; €10.10); **Volos** (10hr., 1 per week). Buy tickets at the **SAOS office** (☎22540 29 571; open daily 8am-1:30pm and 6-10pm), at the far end of Pl. 8 Oktovriou, where the portside road meets Kyda. Next door **Pravlis Travel** (☎22540 24 617 or 22540 22 471; open M-Sa 8:30am-6pm) sells tickets for G.A. Ferries. Airplane tickets are sold here and at the **Olympic Airways** office (☎22540 22 214 or 22 215; open M-F 8am-3:30pm), next to the post office. **Flights** to: **Athens** (2 per day, €65); **Lesvos** (daily M-Sa, €35); **Thessaloniki** (4 per week, €65). The **bus station** (☎22540 22 464 or 22540 23 196) is in Pl. El. Venizelou, the second plateia along Kyda in the far left corner between a tourist agency and a coffeeshop. Although buses serve all island villages, they are inconvenient; you run the risk of getting stranded. Many choose to rent a **bicycle** (€6), **moped** (€12-20), or **car** (€30) at one of the many harborfront agencies. On Limnos your vehicle is not the place to pinch pennies—many of the roads to the island's ecological sites are broken dirt paths that require good traction to navigate safely. **Taxis** (☎22540 23 820) are available in the main plateia.

ORIENTATION AND PRACTICAL INFORMATION. The city has two main waterfronts on opposite sides of the castle. **Turkikos,** facing Turkey, is the town's active port; Myrina's best fish tavernas and a sandy, shallow beach can be found at the far end of the harbor from the docks. To find **Romeikos,** the waterfront on the northern side of the castle, head inland up **Kyda,** past most of the town; take a left when you can spot the sea in between the buildings. The Neoclassical mansions on the strip now house hip cafes, pricey tavernas, and upscale hotels.

Kyda is the town's jubilant commercial artery; it leads inland from Pl. 8 Oktovriou to the town's central plateia, where you can find **taxis, card phones,** and the **National Bank** with a 24hr. **ATM** (☎22540 23 541; open M-Th 8am-2:30pm, F 8am-2pm). One block farther on Kyda, **Garofallidi** runs to the right; follow it to find a self-service **laundromat** on your left, in the Hotel Astron (☎22540 24 392; €6.50 for a 1-2kg load, €8 for 5-6kg; open daily 8am-2pm and 5-9pm). Farther up Garofallidi, on your right, is the **post office** (☎22540 22 462; open M-F 7:30am-2pm); two doors down is **Joy Games,** which offers cheap **Internet** access and many current video games. (☎22540 25 453; www.joyfans.gr. €3 per hr., €1 min. Open daily 9am-2pm and 5:30-10pm.) Farther down on Garofallidi is a large intersection with the 24hr. **police station** (☎22540 22 200) on the corner. Turn left and take the first right, following the signs to reach the **hospital.** (☎22540 22 222; open 24hr.) There are several **pharmacies** on Kyda. The **port police** can be found right near the docks (☎22540 22 225). In case of **fire,** call ☎22 199. **Postal code:** 81400.

ACCOMMODATIONS. There are many, generally expensive hotels in town. If you come equipped with a phone card and some patience, try the phone numbers for some of the many **domatia** advertised around town and call to compare prices. **Despina's Studios ❸** is an excellent bet for reasonably priced lodgings; delightful German-speaking owner offers clean, spacious white rooms with fridge, kitchenette, TV, A/C, and juicy plums plucked from a tree in the back. (☎22540 23 352; fax 22540 23 676. Singles €25-35; doubles €40-50; triples €60-70). **Hotel Aktaion ❷,** on the waterfront in the first plateia on the left from the ferry dock, has simple rooms with small balconies and fridges. The rooms with shared bath are a great budget deal, since prices remain constant throughout the summer. (☎22540 22 258 or 22540 23 942. Singles with shared bath €15, with private bath €20-25; doubles €20/ €25-30.) In Romeikos, the **Blue Waters Hotel ❸,** housed inside a mid-19th-century mansion, has gorgeous, crisply decorated rooms with A/C, fridges, TVs, and modern private baths; larger rooms also come with a sizable kitchen unit. Affable owners will be happy to share their knowledge of the island and its rich history. (☎22540 24 403. Doubles €45-50; quads €55-65.) **Hotel Lemnos ❸,** near the ferry dock in Turkikos, offers clean, standard hotel rooms with balconies and harbor views, as well as A/C, TVs, fridges, and phones. (☎22540 22 153 or 22540 24 023; fax 22540 23 329. Singles €30-35; doubles €40-45; triples €55.)

FOOD AND NIGHTLIFE. For the best fish in Myrina, head past the frappé- and beer-menus of the portside cafes to the *limanaki* (little port), on the marina near Pl. 8 Oktovriou. **To Limanaki ❷,** on the far end, is a safe bet for some excellent seafood. Order from the icy vats of fish near the kitchen. A heaping plate of grilled sardines (€3.82) may be enough for a cheap and satisfying seafood fix. (☎22540 23 744. Grilled entrees €4-5. Fish €27-47 per kg. Open daily 7am-late.) You'll find souvlaki and gyros (€1.40-1.50) along Kyda. The restaurants along Romeikos have menus posted along the waterfront. Seaside tables offer views of Mt. Athos.

At night, cruise the strip at Romeikos, where the young and beautiful idle away summer evenings. **Karagiozi,** past the restaurants on your left facing inland, attracts the largest, youngest, hippest crowds with three bars, colorful lighting, and mixed music. (☎22540 22 214. Beer €3.50; cocktails €5. Open daily 8am-3am.) Numerous **clubs** poster in town, advertising all-night beach parties, grand openings, and special DJ events; however, many are found at the outskirts of town, requiring some form of private transportation or a stumbling late-night trek home. Walk about 1km past Romeikos along the shore until the techno starts pounding in your chest.

SIGHTS. The **kastro,** which pierces the skyline and divides the waterfronts, also houses several dozen deer. If you don't catch sight of them, you can at least enjoy the stunning view and the ruins of the 7th-century BC fortress, reworked by Venetians in the 13th century. Many buildings are partially intact. Wear good shoes and allow 1hr. to clamber through them all. Follow signs from Myrina harbor for the easiest ascent. At the far end of Romeikos, just past Hotel Castro, the **Archaeological Museum** has a collection of artifacts with informative banners hung from the ceiling. Finds from Hephaestus, the Kabeiron, and Poliochni include an interesting collection of ceramic siren sculptures and an awesome skeleton of a sacrificed bull calf. (☎22540 22 990. Open daily 8:30am-3pm. €2, seniors and non-EU students €1, EU students and children under 18 free.)

Though most of the island's prime attractions are best reached with a car or moped, a couple travel agencies do arrange weekly bus excursions around the island. **Petrides Travel** (☎22540 22 039, 22 998, or 22540 24 787; www.petridestravel.gr), on Kida, offers a trip on Saturday that leaves at 9am and includes lunch (€15 per person). Limnos is home to a number of notable **archaeological sites,** which are all on the opposite side of the island from Myrina. **Poliochni,** on the east coast, is the oldest proto-urban settlement discovered to date in all of Europe, dating from the late Neolithic period (5000-4000 BC). It is considered to be one of the most complex fortified cities of its time and is credited with being the site of Europe's first parliament. **Ancient Hephaestia,** on the northeast coast of the island, was the location of a sanctuary to Hephaestus, the god of fire and metallurgy, who supposedly had his forge on the island (an idea which may have arisen because of Limnos's volcanic soil and the metalworking skills of its ancient inhabitants). Farther up the coast is the site of the

Kaveiron, an 8th-century BC sanctuary once used by a secret cult to worship the children of Hephaestus, the Kaveiroi. Here ceremonies were held to celebrate the birth of man and the rebirth of nature. Near the sanctuary is the cave where Philoctetes, a Greek archer in the Trojan Wars, lived after he was bitten by a snake and left by his companions; it can be explored by foot. During a full moon, islanders gather on the beach nearby for revelry with food, drink, guitars, and good spirits—all are welcome. Limnos is also home to a number of ecological sights, including the longest **sand dunes** in Europe (near Gomati beach, on the northern coast), the **waterfalls** near Kaspakas, and the **hot springs** at Therma. Ask around regarding the latter two, as the island's water supply has more than a little to do with their magnificence (or even existence). During winter and spring, the western salt plain of Lake Aliki hosts thousands of migrating flamingoes. If all the ecotourism works you up an appetite, head to one of the best (and also one of the only) eateries in the central western part of the island, **Taverna Mandela ❷** (☎22540 61 349 or 61 899), in Sares, advertised by ubiquitous signs within a 3km radius. A friendly South African expat serves up village rooster with fresh flomari pasta (€6.55) and other tasty specialties.

Most of Limnos's sandy **beaches** are found on the coast near Myrina. The most popular beach on the island is the sandy and shallow **Riha Nera,** just north of Romeikos. Farther north on the way to Kaspakas, **Avlonas** is a large, uncrowded beach with two islets of its own; continue along the steep mountain road to find **Ag. Yiannis,** another popular spot nearby. To the south from Myrina on the road to Kontias is **Nevgatis,** an accessible beach with 2km of unbroken sands.

SAMOTHRAKI Σαμοθρακη

Samothraki (also called Samothrace) was once a place of pilgrimage for Thracian settlers who worshipped the Anatolian Great Gods. When those first colonists arrived in the 10th century BC, they saw the same incredible vista you'll see when your ferry pulls into port: dry grassy fields spread outward from the base of the Aegean's tallest peak, the pine-blanketed 1670m Fengari (meaning "moon"). Remote and dominated by wilderness, Samothraki attracts visitors who prever swatting mosquitoes in a tent to clubbing until dawn. Though all kinds of people visit, there are more hiking boots than high heels, and guitars outnumber cell phones as hand-held accessories. This laid-back crowd lends the place a grungy joie de vivre—a change from the run-of-the-mill summer glitz of other islands.

KAMARIOTISSA Καμαριοτισσα ☎25510

This transportation hub is good settling place from where to explore Samothraki's charms. Even with tourist agencies along the waterfront and the comings and goings of buses and ferries, simple Kamariotissa retains a sleepy charm.

TRANSPORTATION. Ferries dock on the southern edge of town, connecting Samothraki to: **Alexandroupoli** (2½hr., 6 per week, €7.50); **Kavala** (3hr., 3 per week, €13.70); **Lavrio** via **Psara** (1 per week); **Lesvos** (1 per week); **Limnos** (2½hr.; 2 per week, Sa and Su; €10.10). **Flying Dolphins** run to **Alexandroupoli** (1hr., 1-2 per day, €15.10). For tickets and schedules, ask the port police or **Saos Tours** (☎22510 41 505 or 41 411; open daily 7:30am-2pm and 6-10:30pm). **Niki Tours** (☎25510 41 465; fax 25510 41 304; open daily 9am-2pm and 6-10pm) doesn't sell ferry tickets, but the friendly **Hatzigiannakaidis brothers** can help with accommodations, flight tickets, group excursions, and information on the island's charms. **Buses** stop on the waterfront across from Saos Tours. **Green KTEL buses** run round-trip to: **Fonias** via **Paleopolis, Kariotes,** and **Therma** (6 per day, 8:30am-10:30pm; €2.50); **Hora** (9 per day, 8am-10:30pm; €1); **Profitis Ilias** (5 per day, 6:30am-7pm; €2) via **Lakkoma. White local buses** run to **Kypos**

beach via **Paleopolis, Therma,** the **campsites,** and **Fonias;** and to **Pahia Ammo beach** via **Hora, Alonia, Lakoma,** and **Profitis Ilias.** Schedules and prices fluctuate; consult the bus drivers for more information. **Taxis** wait on the waterfront (8am-1am). Rent **mopeds** at **Pavlos Rentals** in the flag-adorned lot on the road to Hora. (☎25510 41 035 or 697 6137 888; fax 25510 41 150. Mopeds €12 per day and up. Cars €45-55. Bicycles €6 per day. Open daily 8am-2pm and 5-9pm.)

ORIENTATION AND PRACTICAL INFORMATION. Everything in Kamariotissa is close to the waterfront. The waterfront road runs out of town to the north and the road to Hora runs to the east out of town just past the bus stop (at the stop sign). Facing inland, past the waterfront docks on the left, a Greek flag marks the 24hr. **port police** (☎22510 41 305). Nearby on the waterfront is the **National Bank** with a 24hr. **ATM.** (☎22510 41 750. Open M-Th 8am-2:30pm, F 8am-2pm.) There's a **pharmacy** on the road to Hora. (☎22510 41 217 or 41 376. Open M-F 9am-2pm and 6-9pm; hours reduced Sa-Su.) The town's pharmacies rotate 24hr. duty; check the schedule posted on the door of any one for more information. **Cafe Aktaion,** on the waterfront across from the ferry docks, entertains the video game generation with 11 terminals, all with **Internet** access. (☎25510 41 056. €4 per hr., €1 min. Open daily 7am-2am.) The **OTE** (☎22510 41 299), **medical clinic** (☎22510 41 217; open 24hr.), and **police station** (☎22510 41 203; open 24hr.) are in Hora. The **post office** (☎22510 41 244) is in Kamariotissa. **Postal code:** 68002.

ACCOMMODATIONS. Samothraki's primary draw is its pristine wilderness; consequently, many travelers breeze through Kamariotissa on their way to **Therma** and the **campsites.** Some camp **illegally** in the surrounding area, but there's no reason to avoid the established campsites, which host late-night bonfires. Kamariotissa is the island's transportation hub and the only place to stay before early-morning ferries. **Domatia** signs abound along the waterfront road. **Brisko Rooms ❷,** set back off the road across from the dock, has quiet rooms off of its flower-lined terrace. Rooms come with A/C, TVs, fridges, private baths, and balconies. (☎25510 41 328. Singles €20-25; doubles €25-35; triples €30-45.) **Hotel Kyma ❷,** on the waterfront at the far end of town from the ferry docks, has clean, simple rooms close to the stone beach, with clean private baths, fridges, and A/C. (☎25510 41 263. Doubles €25-45; triples and quads also available.) **Camping Platia ❶,** 15km from Kamariotissa and 2km beyond Therma on the coast, has showers, baths, a mini-market, and card phones. (☎25510 98 244. €3 per person, €2 per child 12 and under; €2.50 per tent; €2 per car.) **Camping Varades ❶,** 5km from Therma, beyond Camping Platia on the coastal road, has similar amenities and also a cafe. (☎25510 98 291. €3 per person, €2 per child 14 and under; €2.50-3 per tent; €2 per car.)

FOOD AND NIGHTLIFE. Waterfront tavernas specialize in fresh seafood. **I Sinatisi ❷,** a few doors down from Niki Tours, draws the biggest local crowds; the menu is only in Greek, so stroll on in and simply point at your fish. Delectable seafood appetizers pave the way for perfectly grilled fresh fish. (☎25510 41 308 or 41 214. Entrees €3-10. Open daily 8am-5pm and 8pm-late.) Another excellent spot is **I Klimataria ❷,** on the left-hand side of the waterfront, where tasty home-cooked dishes wait for your selection behind a glass counter in the kitchen. Old standbys are joined by pork roasted with potatoes, yogurt, eggs, and cheese (€8), chicken fillet stuffed with tomato and feta (€8), and other unique dishes. (☎25510 41 535. Entrees €5-8. Open daily noon-5:30pm and 7pm-midnight). Goodies abound at **Cafe Moka ❶,** on the waterfront, which has a variety of pastries. (☎25510 41 093. Cream pie with powdered sugar €1.50. Frappé with Bailey's €3. Open daily 24hr.)

Nightlife in Kamariotissa is so laid-back that it's almost non-existent. Beyond a few *barakia* (little bars), the town mostly has a drink after dinner and dozes off. **Rebel,** to the right of the docks on the waterfront, is one of few dance clubs in the area. **Cafe-Bar Diva,** on the waterfront, plays an eclectic variety of music. (☎22510 41 060. Open 8am-late.) **Cafe Aktaion** keeps youngsters occupied with networked computer games, pool (€5 per hr.), foosball, and a full bar next door. Drinks at the waterfront bars are similarly priced with beer €2.50-4; cocktails €6.

BEACHES AND THE OUTDOORS. This verdant gem of an island holds a wealth of trails leading to cascading waterfalls, mountain vistas, and the summit of Fengari. Trails are generally unmarked; the best way to explore is to rent a vehicle in Kamariotissa and head to the coast or interior. Ask locals of the villages that dot the mountain's flanks for directions to nearby trails. The island's only sand beach is the soft arc of **Pahia Ammo** on the southern coast; stony beaches ring the rest. Ask a bus driver to drop you anywhere, then hunt down an isolated stretch of shore. At the end of the line along the northern coast is popular **Kypos beach.** Three **white buses** per day go to Pahia Ammo and Kypos. Schedules change frequently.

The most convenient hub for outdoor activities is the town of **Therma,** which brims with dread-locked and tie-dyed alterna-types. A multitude of mini-markets and equipment stores can outfit your camping trip. Tavernas and domatia dominate the village, making it an attractive alternative to Kamariotissa, especially for stays of multiple days. **Buses** from Kamariotissa stop at the base of town, next to the refreshing **thermal springs** that give the town its name. The trail to the **summit of Fengari** is accessible from Therma. Ask around at the base of town for the best way up. Be sure to fill up your water bottles at the **fountain** at the base of town and don't hike alone. The peak (4hr.) is usually shrouded in mist. A lovely **waterfall** is also accessible from Therma. From the bus stop, head into town and take the left fork through town. Take the first right after a mini-market and follow this road past tavernas and a bakery. When the road dead-ends, turn left and follow the road; when it meets with an asphalt paved road, turn right. The road dead-ends again at Taverna Filarakia; turn right and head up the shaded road. The dirt trail follows the stream on the right side of the road; head right 20m before the Marina Hotel.

Enchanting **Fonias** will revive any tired soul slowed by the scorching Aegean sun. The easy 2km hike meanders alongside a gurgling stream and beneath gnarled trees, where dragonflies hover languidly in shafts of light. The trail ends at a sheer cliff face at a cascading **waterfall.** Shed your clothes and jump into the pool at the waterfall's base carved out of the rock below or carefully climb up the rock face to the right of the stream for a magnificent view of the falls and the mountains. The **green bus** (8 per day, 6:45am-7pm) drops off at the trailhead's parking lot.

DAYTRIP FROM KAMARIOTISSA. **Paleopolis** and the **Sanctuary of the Great Gods,** Samothraki's premier attractions, lie 6km east of Kamariotissa. (Open daily 8:30am-8:30pm. €3 including museum admission, students €2, EU students free.) Before the island's 8th-century BC Aeolian colonization, the chief goddess worshipped here was **Axieros,** or the Great Mother. Three other gods completed the **Kaveiroi** group: Axiokersa, Axiokerson, and Kasmilos. These gods were assimilated into the Olympian Pantheon; Axieros was recast as the fertility goddess Demeter, while two of her consorts, believed to protect sailors, were associated with the twins Castor and Pollux. Disclosing initiation secrets was punishable by death, so the rituals remain shrouded in mystery. There were likely two levels of membership: the *myesis* and the higher *epopteia.* The first purification took place in the **Anaktoron,** at the lowest part of the temple complex. The second rite took place in the **Hieron,** a courtyard whose columns now form the site's central attraction. In the **palace** at the southern end, aspiring initiates donned special vestments. The palace adjoins the Anaktoron, upon which the newly inducted were presented.

The enormous cylindrical **Arsinoëin,** given to Samothraki by Queen Arsinoë of Egypt, demonstrates the importance of circles to the site. The walls (now preserved in the museum) are decorated with rosettes and heads of oxen. They once stood at the sacrificial site. The nearby **Sacred Rock** was the original center of the cult's practices. In the center, the Doric Hieron—containing pits for sacrifices, an altar for libations, and seats for the audience—saw the final stage of initiation. Confessing their worst deeds, the candidates were purified. A scrubby hillside is all that remains of an ancient **theater.** The **Winged Victory** (or **Nike**) **of Samothrace** once stood upon a marble base near the theater. It now sits as one of the greatest treasures in the Louvre in Paris, having made a side-trip to Turkey before being looted by a French consul in 1863. Above the sanctuary are the remains of the **ancient town** of Samothraki, where the apostle Paul lived for a year AD 49-50.

Beside the ruins, the **Paleopolis Museum** is somewhat underwhelming. It houses gargantuan entablatures from the **Arsinoëin** and the **Hieron,** a weathered bust of the prophet **Tiresias,** and a galling cast of the Nike of Samothrace—a "gift" to Greece, courtesy of the French. The relief of dancing girls symbolizes the marriage of Cadmus and Harmonia. The dance represented the onset of winter, a time of mourning to be followed by spring's renewal. (☎25510 41 474. Open Tu-Su 8:30am-3pm.)

THASSOS Θασος

Just 20km off the coast of Kavala (p. 308) lies Thassos, the green jewel of the North Aegean. According to legend, Thassos was founded when the devoted brother of Europa gave up pursuing his abducted sister and settled on this remote island. As an ancient exporter of gold, silver, and its famous wine, Thassos attracted the unwelcome attention of Phoenician, Athenian, and Roman conquerors. The Thassian who were not killed or sold into slavery were forced to hide, fleeing to mountain villages or caves. Along with most of northern Greece, Thassos returned to Greek rule in 1912 at the conclusion of the First Balkan War. Since then, massive forest fires have threatened the island's greenery, but the forests are slowly coming back; the northeastern regions around Thassos Town, which escaped the fires, are especially beautiful. In recent years, Thassos has become quite a tourist-oriented island, attracting throngs of Northern Europeans who seek a quiet place in the sun. Nonetheless, the "Green Island" still retains some of its original charm with cool, forested mountains, thriving beekeeping and jam-making industries, and an isolated southern coast, which is a hiker's paradise.

THASSOS TOWN ☎25930

The island's capital and tourist center is built atop the foundations of the ancient city, and ruins crowd the Old Port area. Also known as Limenas, from *limani* (harbor), Thassos Town sees the highest concentration of tourists yet maintains some of the best-priced accommodations on the island. The British and German tourists who pack the town in the summer choose it as a base for exploring the island's hundreds of secluded beaches with rented private transportation.

TRANSPORTATION

Ferries: The arrival and departure point for ferries from Kavala is not in Thassos Town, but in the village of **Skala Prinos** (18km west). In Thassos Town, the port police (at the town end of the new harbor) and ticket booth (at the far end of the new harbor opposite town) post schedules. Ferries go to **Keramoti** (30min.; 12 per day, 5:45am-9pm; €1.50). From Skala Prinos, ferries go to **Kavala** (1hr.; 10 per day, 6am-8:30pm; €3, students and children €1.50, cars €14.40) and **N. Peramus** (1¼hr.; 9am, 2pm; €2.50). Bus schedules between Prinos and Thassos Town are synchronized with the ferries. You must return to Kavala for ferry connections to other islands.

Flying Dolphins: Hydrofoils zip to **Kavala** from Thassos Town (45min.; 4 per day, 8:10am-3:45pm; €8), and from Limenaria, on Thassos's southern coast (45min.; 8:20am, 3pm; €10.27). Schedules are posted at the port police and ticket booth, and docked boats indicate departure times with signs. You can buy tickets on board.

Buses: When you arrive in Skala Prinos from Kavala, walk left to find buses for Thassos Town and Limenaria, in sync with the arrival of the ferries from Kavala. The station (☎25930 22 162) is across from the ferry landing, on the waterfront. Open daily 7:30am-8:15pm. To: **Aliki beach** (1hr.; 4 per day, 7:45am-4pm; €2.50); **Limenaria** (1hr.; 9 per day, 6:20am-7:30pm; €3) via **Skala Prinos** (20min., €1.40); **Panagia** (15min.; 12 per day, 6:30am-7:15pm; €0.90); **Skala Potamia** (30min.; 12 per day, 6:30am-7:15pm; €1.10); **Theologos** (1½hr.; 6 per day, 8:30am-4:30pm; €4); **around the island** and back to Thassos Town (3hr.; 8 per day, 6am-4pm; €7.10). Ask at the tourist police or bus office for paper schedules.

Rentals: Cars and mopeds are rented all over Thassos Town. **Budget,** Theagenus 2 (☎25930 23 150; fax 25930 22 421), rents cars (€35-50 per day including 100km and damage waiver). Open 9am-2pm and 6-10pm. **Stelios** (☎25930 22 815) is next door. Motorbikes €11. Open 8am-10:30pm.

Taxis: ☎25930 23 391. Near the ports.

Water taxis: ☎25930 22 734. Go twice daily from Thassos Town to **Golden beach** (leave 10 and 11am, return 4:15pm; €2.50 one-way) and **Makryamos** (leave 10 and 11am, return 10:20am and 5pm; €3 one-way). Schedules change frequently—call the tourist office for specific departure times.

ORIENTATION AND PRACTICAL INFORMATION

A small crossroads near the bus station and National Bank connects the waterfront road **Agousti Theologiti** and **28 Oktovriou,** a jungle of souvenir shops and souvlaki joints running parallel to the water one block inland. With your back to the water, the **Old Port,** the ancient **agora,** and the nearest beach are on the left. The small central plateia lies about two blocks farther inland.

Tourist Agencies: Thassos Tours (☎25930 22 546), under the yellow sign, on the waterfront, helps with accommodations, gives advice on island tours, and rents motorbikes (€15-22) and cars (€25-35). Open daily 8:30am-midnight. **Thassos Tourist Services** (☎25930 22 041), on 28 Oktovriou behind the row of tavernas, has **maps** of the ancient agora and **exchanges currency.** Open M-Sa 9am-1:30pm and 6-9pm.

Bank: Find **Merchant's Bank,** where 28 Oktovriou meets the waterfront, with an automated 24hr. **currency exchange,** and **Agricultural Bank** (☎25930 22 970), 1 block inland by Budget rentals. Both have **ATMs.** Both open M-Th 8am-2:30pm, F 8am-2pm.

Police: ☎25930 22 500. On the waterfront by the port police. Open 24hr. The **tourist police** (☎25930 23 111) share the building. English spoken. Open daily 8am-10pm.

Port Police: ☎25930 22 355. In the white building with the light blue roof. Enter from the backdoor on 28 Oktovriou. Open daily 6am-11pm.

Health Center: ☎25930 71 100. In Prinos. Open 24hr. There is no hospital on Thassos; the nearest is in Kavala.

OTE: On 28 Oktovriou, a block inland from Thassos Tourist Services. Open M-F 7:30am-3:10pm.

Internet Access: Millenium Net (☎25930 58 089). From the tourist office, turn left and continue walking past Hotel Xenia, 300m down on the left. 6 computers and a pool table. Internet €3 per hr. Beer €2; coffee €1.50. Also try **Corner Net Cafe** (☎25930 58 086), 2 blocks in from the police station. €3 per hr.

Post Office: ☎25930 22 114. Head inland from Thassos Tours and turn right at the 4th corner. **Poste Restante.** Open M-F 7:30am-2pm. **Postal code:** 64004.

ACCOMMODATIONS AND FOOD

There's no need to stay in a hotel on Thassos if you're traveling on a budget—the plentiful **domatia** are a much better deal. The streets behind 28 Oktovriou are crammed with rooms to let signs; most cost €18-20 per single. Hunt around for a good price, and look for screened windows, a rare but desirable amenity in Greece—the hordes of Thassian mosquitoes make them absolute necessities. **Hotel Athanassia ❷** is closer to domatia than actual hotels. Walk down the waterfront with your back to the Old Port and make a left immediately after the Hotel Xenia. On the right at the end of a narrow lane, the hotel is swallowed up by grapevines and plane trees. There are spacious rooms, some with bath, and the screened windows keep out the bugs. (☎25930 22 545. Singles €15; doubles and triples €20.) **Hotel Lido ❷,** past the post office toward the plateia, has basic rooms in the middle of town with private baths, fridges, TVs, telephones, A/C, and small balconies. (☎25930 22 929. Singles and doubles €30.)

The waterfront is packed with restaurants designed to cater to a wide range of European tastes. Multilingual menus offer "Full English Breakfasts" along with plates of schnitzel, pizza, and pasta. To hunt down a more genuinely Greek flavor, head toward the seafood tavernas along the Old Port where fresh fish and squid appetizers dominate the menus. **Simi Restaurant ❷,** in the Old Port on the waterfront, is one of the best-located and most popular spots in Thassos Town, with a laid-back atmosphere and lots of tasty fish and shellfish. (☎25930 22 517. Salads €1.50.) **Restaurant Syrtaki ❸,** past Simi and the Old Port at the end of the waterfront road, has an ocean-oriented view and menu and live Greek folk music Wednesday and Saturday nights. (☎25930 23 353. Entrees €4-10.50.)

SIGHTS AND ENTERTAINMENT

For a small town, Thassos has a huge selection of ancient sites. Maps of the **Old Town** are available at Thassos Tourist Services. Just behind the Old Port are the ruins of the ancient **agora** (open 8am-7pm). From here, or from the promontory beyond the Old Port, trails lead to the 4th-century BC **theater** (closed). Climbing past the theater a lighted trail leads to the **acropolis,** home to a **Genoese fortress.** Lights continue to the **Temple of Athena** followed by the rock-carved **Altar to Pan.** Above is the scenic peak and a **secret stairway** down. Marble **cyclopean walls,** which ringed the city, are well preserved here. Continuing down the walls is the **Gate of Parmenon,** with lintel, and eerie **Evil Eye** rock, facing downhill. Even the archaeologically drained will still enjoy a trip to the **Gate of Silenos.** A full-length excited centaur graces the side of this ancient main gate. Follow Scolis several blocks out of the town center, or turn left a block on

Scolis after re-entering town from the Gate of Parmenon on Akropoleos. Beyond Silenos the walls continue past the **Gate of Hercules** and **Gate of Zeus and Hera** both with reliefs.

Beach lovers may have a hard time choosing among Thassos's beautiful sands. Between Panagia and Potamia, the popular golden **Chrisi Ammoudia** stretches endlessly. To the south, **Aliki's** twin coves shelter slabs of bleached white rock and crevices ideal for snorkeling. More isolated spots can be found along the water in both directions from Limenaria—just rent a bike or head out on foot, and pick a cove. Ask at the bus station to find out which bus heads past a particular beach. You can find superb **hiking** in the relatively untouched interior.

For a night out, try **Zorbas** (☎25930 22 704), two blocks inland from the police station. After 2am, a tight group of five *bouzouki* players gathers here post-gig for their personal celebration of life. Down a few ouzo's and join the welcoming Greek regulars and musicians for song late into the Thassian night. Along the waterfront past the Old Harbor, find **Cafe Karnagio,** spanning the rocky promontory before the beach. Thoughtful night owls sip ouzo as they watch the stars and dark waters far from the blasting of motorbikes. (☎25930 23 170. Beer €2; specials €4.) The most popular indoor dance club in town, **Arena** (☎25930 52 683) is often hard to get into. Try your luck at the door across from much more relaxed Zorba's.

LIMENARIA Λιμεναρια ☎25930

Thriving auxiliary town Limenaria is across the island from Thassos Town on a curve of stony beach at the island's southern tip. Smaller and more relaxed than its bustling counterpart, Limenaria is a haven of unhurried calm, breeze-blown waves, and lazy sunsets. Hotels here are popular and high in quality and price. Unfortunatley Limenaria is no longer a hidden secret—that resort feel prevails.

Limenaria, like most resort towns, spreads along the waterfront. The road leading out of town **Ethn. Anastasis,** runs perpendicularly away from the shore to an intersection with **Polytechniou,** one block inland. This main intersection, or *dhiastavrosi*, has **buses** to: **Skala Prinos** (40min.; 8 per day, 6:20am-6:50pm; €1.40); **Thassos Town** (1hr.; 7 per day, 6:20am-6:50pm; €3); **Theologos** (4 per day, 9:30am-3:44pm; €1.20). Facing inland on Anastasis at the *dhiastavrosi*, the **OTE** (☎25930 51 399; open M-F 7:30am-3:10pm) is a few meters farther ahead, while an **Agricultural Bank** (☎25930 52 683; open M-Th 8am-2:30pm, F 8am-2pm) with **ATM** is a few meters to the right. Behind you is a store with bus schedules and tickets next to **Speedy Rent-a-Car.** (☎25930 52 700. Cars €35. Open 8am-2pm and 5:30-10pm.) Back at the shore, facing inland, two lanes lead right from Ethn. Anastasis while one continues left. The inland waterfront lane on the right passes the **police** (☎25930 51 111), the **post office** (☎25930 51 296; open M-F 7:30am-2pm), and finally the **National Bank** (☎25930 51 192). On the single left lane is **Blue City Tours,** which arranges excursions and has extensive information on buses, island ferries, and Kavala flights. (☎2593 052 063. Open 8:30am-1pm and 5-8:30pm.) Beyond, the road passes the hotels before turning inland past domatia. There is **no Internet** access in Limenaria; you must travel 2.6km southeast to **Potos. Postal code:** 64002.

Hotels and rented rooms abound throughout Limenaria, but budget options are uncommon. While perfect for families (usually British and German), the rooms will put a sizeable dent in a cost-conscious traveler's budget; however, there are **domatia** away from the waterfront. **Avgoustos Rented Rooms** ❷ offers standard domatia amenities, including shared kitchen, but with private baths, balconies, and A/C. Walk down Eth. Antistasis, turn right, and follow the waterfront road until it bends inland; go another block and look right. (☎25930

52 310. Doubles €33.) **Hotel Ralitsas ❸** boasts well decorated rooms overlooking the sea, balconies, baths, shared refrigerator, TVs, and sometimes A/C. (☎25930 51 578; fax 25930 52 878. Singles €25; doubles €45; triples €50.) **Hotel Molos ❷** has bright, pleasant rooms, many with balconies overlooking the water. Walk down Eth. Antistasis and turn right at the waterfront. (☎25930 51 369. Doubles €40; triples €47. MC.)

The entire waterfront in Limenaria fuses into one mega-restaurant, comprised of the town's numberless tavernas and snack bars. **Il Mare ❷,** on the right waterfront road, facing inland on Ethn. Antistasis, serves all kinds of seafood delicacies at romantic tables along the water (entrees €4-8). Much farther down the waterfront is **Restaurant Maranos ❷,** with a large wine cask teetering precariously over the entrance. It offers a shady environment, classic *rembetika*, and many fish choices (entrees €4-8). Come nightfall, the wall of waterfront restaurants becomes a single long bar. **Istos Cafe-Bar, Nile Bar,** and **Larry's Bar** are all in a row, blaring a jumbled audio mess of Greek and American favorites. (Beer €3; cocktails €5-6.) Popular, massive disco **Bolero,** 1.5km east of town on the road to Potos, booms with a different liquor promotion every night. (☎25930 52 180. Cover €3.)

DODECANESE Δωδεκανησα

Scattered along Turkey's coast, the twelve Dodecanese are the farthest Greek island group from the mainland and are in fact much closer to Asia Minor than to Athens. The history of the Dodecanese conveys successive conquests, each followed by a period of development and subsequent invasion. During the Hellenistic Period, the Dodecanese flourished culturally along with the rest of ancient Greece, only to be trumped by the Roman Empire and later by the imperial ambitions of Alexander the Great. A favorite target of proselytizing luminaries including St. Paul and St. John, the Greeks of these islands were among the first to convert to Christianity. The islands prospered in early Byzantine years before suffering from a series of pirate raids that weakened all of Byzantium. Crusaders abused the region during the 14th century, building heavily fortified castles as bases for their religious wars. The Ottomans ousted them in 1522, though the lucky Dodecanese received special concessions from the Sultan on account of their proximity to Turkey. Despite a brief period of Italian merchant rule, the Dodecanese remained largely under Turkish control until 1912 when the Italians moved in once again. Under the direction of Mussolini, the islands were developed primarily for use as naval bases. The Dodecanese ultimately joined the Greek nation in 1948.

Eclectic architecture is the most visible legacy of all these comings and goings: Greek and Roman ruins, castles built by crusaders, Ottoman mosques, and stark Italian Fascist architecture coexist, undisturbed by the bright blue and white modern homes of the locals. Travelers who venture here will find landscapes ranging from Rhodes's fertile hills to the volcanic terrain of Nisyros. Kos's hopping nightlife, the apocalyptic beauty of Patmos, the secluded beaches of Karpathos, and the hidden glory of Symi are sure to entice even the most discriminating traveler.

HIGHLIGHTS OF THE DODECANESE

THINK REVELATION when visiting Patmos (p. 541), former home of visionary gospel writer St. John.

SNIFF THE SULFUR of the smokingly active Mandraki volcano on Nisyros (p. 560).

LOSE YOURSELF in one of the many picturesque hidden coves on Symi (p. 554).

STRAIN YOUR EARS to hear the sublime whisper of millions of bright beating wings in Rhodes's Valley of Butterflies (p. 529).

CHECK THE MOVES of the peacocks in Plaka forest, then strut your own stuff on the streets of Kos Town (p. 530).

RHODES Ροδος

Rhodes has welcomed its fair share of visitors during its rowdy past, whether Roman, Byzantine, crusader, or Turk. Today, as the undisputed tourist capital of the Dodecanese, Rhodes continues to make room for all under its inviting sun. The high profile of Rhodes Town as a tourist attraction serves to shelter the centuries-old customs, natural resources, and serene escapes of the smaller coastal villages and the interior. While resort towns dominate the

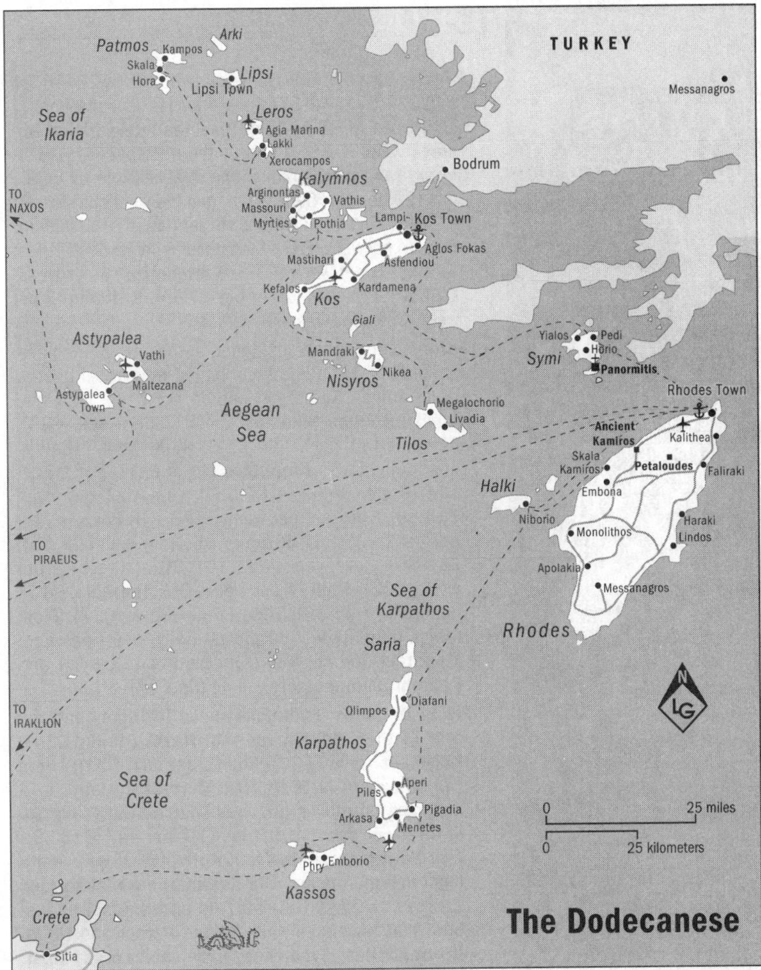

north, sandy beaches stretch along the east coast, jagged cliffs skirt the west, and green mountains freckled with villages fill the interior. Beautiful ancient artifacts, remnants from its complicated past, carpet the island. Kamiros, Ialyssos, and Lindos show the clearest evidence of Rhodes's bygone days as a Hellenic power, while the medieval fortresses slumbering in Rhodes Town and Monolithos recall a history full of conquests.

RHODES TOWN ☎22410

Go back in time as you wander through the cobblestone streets of Old Town or flash forward as you party yourself silly in the raucous bars of New Town. If the choice sounds too tough, the beach is an easy option. Rhodes Town will win you over by any means necessary. If the tourist count is any indication, it rarely fails.

N RECENT NEWS

A HOUSE DIVIDED

On April 23, 2003 the wall, which ias divided Cyprus since 1974, pened, causing an influx of visitors to he Turkish-controlled north of the sland. After the Turkish government eased the restrictions by opening the rossing points at Ledra and Pergamos, an average of 13,000 people per day excercised their newly gained reedom by crossing the border between the Greek-controlled south nd Turkish north. Greece recipricated by both reopening phone lines between the two sides and removing rade barriers on Turkish goods.

These amicable overtures spurred hopes for a reunification of the island's wo halves. Turkey's bid to join the EU s largely dependent on its fragile relaions with Greece, while many fear that when Cyprus joins the EU in 2004, if still divided, it will remain permanently ragmented. However, steps toward eunification have been plagued by setbacks and new bilateral tensions. Greek claims of airspace violations by urkey, including a June 9, 2003 incident in which Turkish F-16s harassed an Olympic Airways passenger jet, have inflamed Greece's ire, while Ankara's refusal to accept the UN blueprint for Cyprus's reunification stalled the increasingly friendly talks between the two nations.

The opening of the Cypriot border has been greeted with as much hesitaion as praise; Kofi Annan claimed the eased restrictions were not a "substiute for a comprehensive settlement." Still, the fall of the dividing wall is a giant step in the relationship between he two nations.

TRANSPORTATION

Flights: Olympic Airways, Ierou Lohou 9 (☎22410 24 571, 24 572, 42 573, or 24 574), near the central EOT. Open M-F 8am-4pm. **Diagoras International Airport** (☎22410 88 911) is on the western coast, 16km from town, near Paradisi, and is accessible by public bus (23 per day, 5am-11pm from the west bus station; €1.50). Flights to: **Athens** (5 per day, €75); **Iraklion,** Crete (4 per week, €87); **Karpathos** (6 per week, €27.50); **Kassos** (6 per week, €33); **Kastellorizo** (5 per week, €24.50); **Mykonos** (2 per week, €89); **Santorini** (2 per week, €89); **Thessaloniki** (daily, €117).

Ferries: Ferry schedules, found at the OTE, are temperamental and should be confirmed at a travel agency upon arrival. Some services do not begin until late June. To: **Agios Nikolaos,** Crete (3 per week, €23); **Astypalea** (1 per week, €22); **Halki** (daily); **Kalymnos** (daily, €18); **Karpathos** (3 per week, €15); **Kassos** (3 per week, €17.50); **Kos** (1-2 per day, €14.80); **Leros** (6 per week , €26.70); **Patmos** (1-2 per day, €28.70); **Piraeus** (4 per week, €29.70); **Samos** (1 per week, €21.10); **Sitia,** Crete (3 per week, €22); **Symi** (4 per week, €6); **Thessaloniki** (1 per week, €45.80); **Tilos** (5 per week, €27). Most ferries offer student discounts. Daily excursions from Mandraki Port to: **Kos** (round-trip €45); **Symi** and **Panormitis Monastery** (round-trip €22).

Flying Dolphins: Hydrofoils speed to Turkey and the rest of the Dodecanese. To: **Halki** (daily, €14); **Kalymnos** (daily, €30); **Kos** (2 per day, €23); **Leros** (daily, except M; €26.70); **Marmaris** (daily, €45 including port taxes); **Nisyros** (€20); **Symi** (daily Su-F, Sa 2 per day; €10); **Tilos** (1-2 per day, €18.50). Call **Zorpidis** agency (☎22410 20 625) for more hydrofoil information. The **Katamaran Dodekanissos Express** (☎22410 70 590) is an ultra-fast speedboat that travels between Kolona Harbor and **Halki, Nisyros, Tilos, Symi, Kos, Kalymnos, Leros, Lipsi,** and **Patmos** twice daily during summer months. €27 for the longest trip; no student discounts.

Buses: Stations lie on opposite sides of Papagou at Pl. Rimini. Schedules at the OTE.

East station is served by **KTEL** (☎22410 27 706 or 22410 75 134; fax 22410 24 268). Service east to: **Afandou** (13 per day, 6:45am-9:15pm; €1.60); **Archangelos** (16 per day, 5:50am-8:20pm; €2); **Faliraki** (20 per day, 6:45am-9:15pm; €1.60); **Gennadi** (9 per day, 6:45am-7:30pm; €4.30); **Haraki** (10am, 4:30pm; €2.50); **Kolymbia beach** (7 per day, 9am-7:30pm; €2.50); **Laerma** (M-F 1pm, €3.20); **Lindos** (15 per day, 6:45am-7:30pm; €3.40); **Malona** and **Massari** (4 per day, 9am-2:30pm; €2.45); **Pefki** (7 per day, 6:45am-7:30pm; €3.55).

West station is served by **RODA** (☎22410 26 300). To: **Damatria** (5 per day, 6am-9:35pm; €1.70); **Embona** (1:30, 2:45pm; €4); **Kalavarda** (7 per day, 5:40am-10:30pm; €2.20); **Kalithea, Calypso, Kastri** (19 per day, 6:45am-10:30pm; €1.55); **Kamiros** (1:30pm, €3.40); **Koskinou** (8 per day, 6:20am-9:30pm; €1.55); **Kritinia** (Su-F; 1:30pm, Sa 8am, 2:05pm; €3.55); **Monolithos** (M-F 1:30pm, €4.80); **Paradisi Airport** (21 per day, 5:55am-11:45pm; €1.55); **Pastida** and **Maritsa** (9 per day, 5:40am-9:35pm; €1.55); **Salakos** (4 per day, 6:10am-4:45pm; €2.80); **Soroni** and **Fanes** (10 per day, 5am-9:30pm; €1.70); **Theologos** (12 per day, 5am-9:35pm; €1.70).

Taxis: ☎22410 27 666. In Pl. Rimini. Radio taxis (☎22410 64 64 712, 64 734, 64 756, 64 778 or 64 790) also available 24hr.

ORIENTATION AND PRACTICAL INFORMATION

The city is composed of two districts. **New Town** spans the north and west and **Old Town** centers on **Sokratous,** a bustling, cobbled street descending from the castle to the commercial harbor; most Old Town streets branch off Sokratous. In the New Town, all international and most domestic ferries use the **Commercial Harbor** outside the Old Town. **Mandraki,** the New Town's waterfront, docks private yachts, hydrofoils, and excursion boats. Town beaches lie to the north, beyond Mandraki, and along the city's west coast. The tourist office, both bus stations, and a taxi stand are in or around **Pl. Rimini,** beneath the fortress's turrets, at the junction of the Old and New Towns. To get there from Mandraki, head a block inland with the park to your left. Tourist nightlife in the New Town converges on **Orfanidou,** dubbed **Bar Street,** while the Greek scene is largely at **Militadou** in the Old Town.

Tourist Office: EOT (☎22410 21 921 or 22410 23 655; www.ando.gr/eot), a few blocks up Papagou from Pl. Rimini, at the intersection of Makariou and Amerikis. Offers helpful advice on the essentials for your visit. **Free maps,** brochures, and accommodations advice. English spoken. Open M-F 8:30am-2pm.

Budget Travel: Castellania Travel Service (☎22410 75 860, 75 862, or 75 007; castell@otenet.gr), in Old Town's Pl. Hippocratous. Open M-F 9am-9pm, Sa-Su 9am-5pm.

Banks: Many banks spot the New Town; fewer are in the Old Town. **ATMs** are widespread throughout both. The **Eurochange** booth (☎22410 31 847), at Pl. Hippocratous in the Old Town, does **currency exchanges** and cash advances. Open daily 9am-10:30pm. The **National Bank** has an office in the Old Town at Pl. Moussiou with an ATM. Open M-Th 8am-2:30pm, F 8am-2pm. The **Commercial Bank of Emboriki** (☎22410 22 123) is just across the way, up Ipoton, and also has an ATM. Open M-F 8am-2:30pm. In the New Town, the **National Bank** in Pl. Kyprou has currency exchange.

American Express: Rhodos Tours Ltd., Amohostou 23, P.O. Box 252. Open M-F 9am-1:30pm and 5-8:30pm, Sa 7:30am-3pm.

Laundromat: Happy Wash Express Service Laundry, in the New Town at Alex. Diakou 38 (☎22410 35 693) and at Dilperaki 97(☎22410 21 546), just off Orfanidou. Wash and dry €3. Open daily 9am-11pm. **Express Laundry,** 5 Kosti Palama (☎22410 22 514), directly across from the Pl. Rimini bus station, offers full wash and dry (€3). Open daily 8am-11:30pm. In the Old Town, **Laundry Solution** (☎22410 77 731), on Lypisou by Hotel Via-Via, also does wash and dry (€4). There is also a **laundromat,** Platonos 33 (☎22410 76 047), near Yiannis Taverna. Wash and dry €4.50. Open M-Sa 8am-8pm.

Police: ☎22410 23 294. In an **emergency,** dial ☎100. On Eth. Dodekanission, 1 block behind the post office. Open 24hr. **Lost and found** open M-F 9am-noon.

Tourist Police: ☎22410 27 423. In EOT building. English spoken. Open 7:30am-9pm.

Port Authority: Central Harbor Master (☎22410 34 873), on Mandraki just left of the post office. Complete boat schedules. Open 24hr.

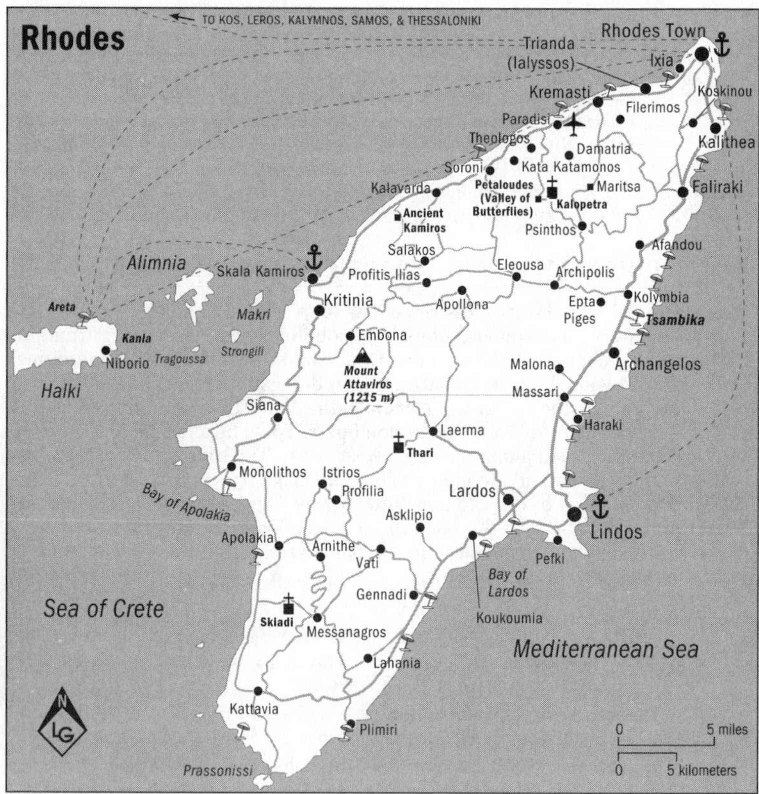

Hospital: ☎22410 80 000. On Erithrou Stavrou, off El. Venizelou. Open for emergencies 24hr. **Walk-in clinic** open noon-2pm and 5-7pm. In a **medical emergency,** dial ☎166.

OTE: Amerikis 91 (☎22410 24 599), at the corner of 25 Martiou in the New Town. Open M-Sa 7:30am-1pm.

Internet Access: Control Net Cafe, Al. Diakou 44 (☎22410 24 564; www.controlcafe.gr), just past Fanouraki in the New Town. €3 per hr. Open daily 8:30am-11pm. **Minoan Palace,** Ir. Polytechniou 13 (☎22410 20 210), at the corner of G. Efstathiou in the New Town. €3.60 per hr., €2 min. Open daily 9am-1am. In the Old Town, **Mango Bar,** Pl. Dorisos 3 (☎22410 36 957 or 22410 32 824; www.karelas.com). €4 per hr. Open M-Sa 10am-1am, Su 10am-midnight.

Post Office: Main branch (☎22410 30 290 or 22410 34 873), on Mandraki, next to the Bank of Greece, has **Poste Restante.** Open M-F 7:30am-2pm. **Postal code:** 85100.

ACCOMMODATIONS

Most pensions in the **Old Town** are scattered about the narrow pebbled paths between Sokratous and Omirou. Bargaining with pension owners will be worth your while; just allow wild shock to register on your face upon hearing the original

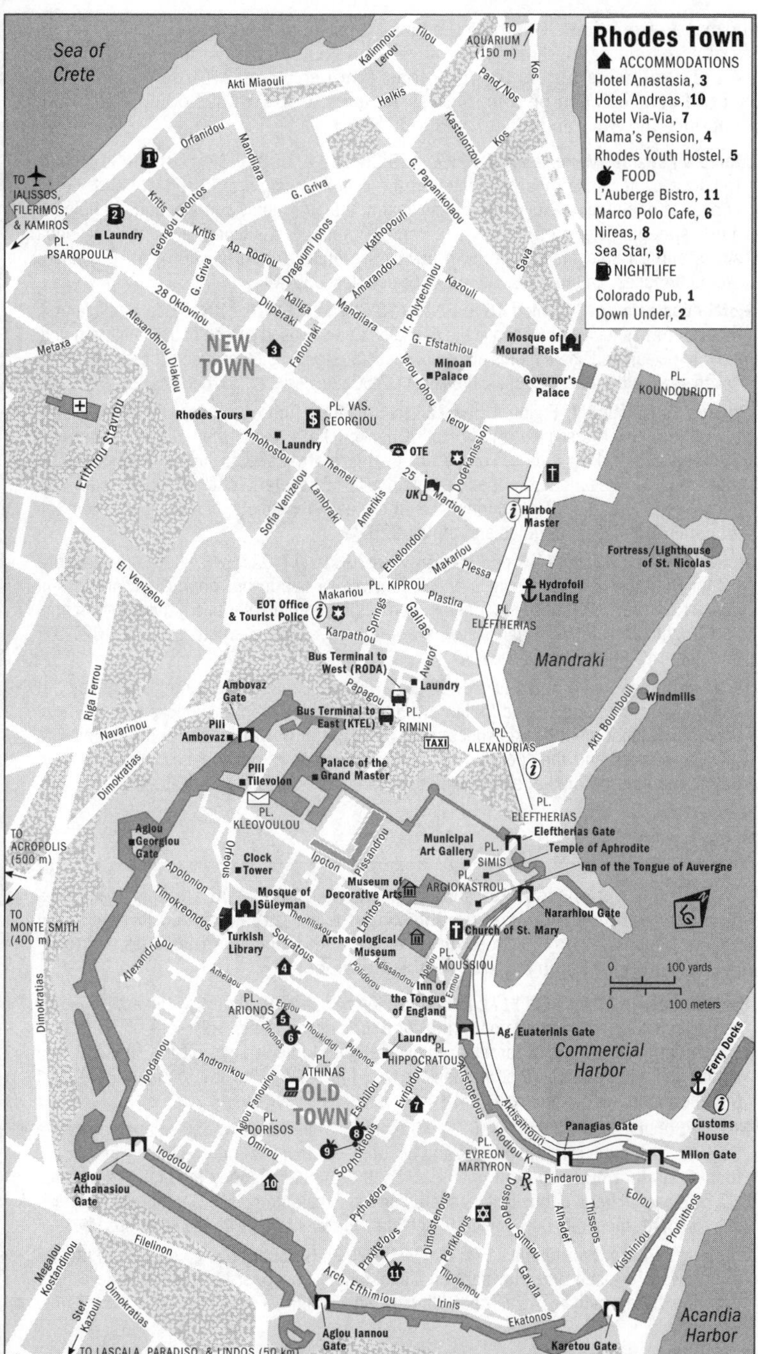
Rhodes Town
ACCOMMODATIONS
Hotel Anastasia, 3
Hotel Andreas, 10
Hotel Via-Via, 7
Mama's Pension, 4
Rhodes Youth Hostel, 5
FOOD
L'Auberge Bistro, 11
Marco Polo Cafe, 6
Nireas, 8
Sea Star, 9
NIGHTLIFE
Colorado Pub, 1
Down Under, 2
Sea of Crete
TO AQUARIUM (150 m)
TO IALISSOS, FILERIMOS, & KAMIROS
TO ACROPOLIS (500 m)
TO MONTE SMITH (400 m)
TO LASCALA, PARADISO, & LINDOS (50 km)
Akti Miaouli
Kalimnou-Lerou
Tilou
Pand/Nos
Kos
Halkis
Orfanidou
Mandilara
Kastelorizou
G. Griva
G. Papanikolaou
Kritis
Georgiou Leontos
Laundry
PL. PSAROPOULA
Ap. Rodiou
Dragoumi Ionos
Kathopouli
Sava
28 Oktovriou
Kaliga
Amarandou
Ir. Polytechniou
Kazouli
Dilperaki
Alexandrou Diakou
Fanouraki
Metaxa
NEW TOWN
G. Efstathiou
Mosque of Mourad Reis
Minoan Palace
Ierou Lohou
Governor's Palace
PL. KOUNDOURIOTI
Erithrou Stavrou
Rhodes Tours
PL. VAS. GEORGIOU
Amohostou
Ieroy
Dodekanissou
OTE
Themeli
25 Martiou
UK
Sofia Venizelou
Lambraki
Amerikis
Harbor Master
Fortress/Lighthouse of St. Nicolas
Ethelondon
Makariou
Plessa
El. Venizelou
PL. KIPROU
Plastira
Hydrofoil Landing
EOT Office & Tourist Police
Springs
Galias
PL. ELEFTHERIAS
Karpathou
Mandraki
Bus Terminal to West (RODA)
Averof
Laundry
Riga Ferrou
Ambovaz Gate
Papagou
Windmills
Bus Terminal to East (KTEL)
PL. RIMINI
Akti Boumboull
Navarinou
Pili Ambovaz
TAXI
PL. ALEXANDRIAS
Dimokratias
Pili Tilevolon
Palace of the Grand Master
PL. KLEOVOULOU
PL. ELEFTHERIAS
Agiou Georgiou Gate
Municipal Art Gallery
Eleftherias Gate
Orfeous
Clock Tower
Ipoton
Pissandrou
PL. SIMIS
Temple of Aphrodite
Apolonion
PL. ARGIOKASTROU
Inn of the Tongue of Auvergne
Museum of Decorative Arts
Timokreontos
Mosque of Süleyman
Theofiliskou
Lahitos
Nararhiou Gate
Turkish Library
Church of St. Mary
Alexandridou
Sokratous
Archaeological Museum
PL. MOUSSIOU
Arhelaou
Agissandrou
Apelou
Polidorou
Inn of the Tongue of England
Ermou
PL. ARIONOS
Ergiou
Thoukididi
Zinonos
Ag. Euaterinis Gate
Laundry
Platonos
PL. HIPPOCRATOUS
Commercial Harbor
Andronikou
PL. ATHINAS
Aristotelous
Ipodamou
Agiou Fanouriou
OLD TOWN
Eschilou
Evripidou
Ferry Docks
PL. DORISOS
Aktisantou
Omirou
Panagias Gate
Customs House
Irodotou
Sophokleous
PL. EVREON MARTYRON
Rodiou K.
Milon Gate
Agiou Athanasiou Gate
Pindarou
Eolou
Dossiadou
Pythagora
Dimostenous
Alhadef
Thisseos
Promitheos
Simiou
Periklеous
Filelinon
Praxitelous
Kisthiniou
Megalou Kostandinou
Tlipolemou
Gavala
Arch. Efthimiou
Irinis
Stef. Kazouli
Dimokratias
Ekatonos
Acandia Harbor
Agiou Iannou Gate
Karetou Gate
0 100 yards
0 100 meters

price and go from there. Combine the tacky tourism of Sokratous with the snootiness of a Versace retail outlet and you've got a good picture of **New Town.** Charmless and expensive hotels line the coast, though some affordable and even delightful pensions can be found along the narrow streets of Rodiou, Dilperaki, Kathopouli, and Amarandou.

Mama's Pension, Menekleous 28 (☎22410 25 359 or 69340 37 128), off Sokratous. Talkative owner Mike runs his hostel on the Greek principle of hospitality and hippie principles of peace and love. The rooms charm, the bathrooms sparkle, and the balcony offers sweeping views of Old Town. A comfy TV lounge, a kitchen, a one-for-one book swap, and an adjacent taverna with nightly live music (often played by Mike himself) are all bonuses. Laundry €3. Dorms €10; doubles €25. ❶

Hotel Anastasia, 28 Oktovriou 46 (☎22410 28 007; fax 22410 21 815). Take refuge from the New Town's tourist brouhaha in the peaceful, vine-enclosed garden of this family-run pension. The clean and spare rooms are simply decorated with soft lime-green sheets and walls. Ask to see the owner's pet turtles. Breakfast €3.50. Singles €21-30; doubles €24-36. V. ❷

Rhodes Youth Hostel, Ergiou 12 (☎22410 30 491). Turn onto Fanouriou from Sokratous and follow the sign for the hostel. A backpacker's hostel *par excellence,* set in a 200-year-old Turkish house. Lumpy but livable mattresses, grungy communal bathrooms, and a gregarious, happening community of travelers. Kitchen, book swap, and cheap beer. Laundry €3. No curfew. Ask at the desk for sheets, and bring your own toilet paper. Dorms €6; doubles and triples €20. ❶

Hotel Via-Via, Pythagora 45 and Lisipon 2 (☎22410 77 027; www.hotel-via-via.com). Owner Beatrice carefully designs each room with a subtle but artistic eye and a tendency towards the avant-garde. Cheery rooms open onto a colorful courtyard with plants and bright tablecloths. Binge elsewhere; this one's for the artistes. Singles €27-32; doubles €42-49; triples €62-67. ❸

Hotel Andreas, Omirou 28D (☎22410 34 156; www.hotelandreas.com). A pricey but charming option better suited for honeymooning couples than backpackers. A fully windowed breakfast room boasts spectacular views of the Old Town. Ask about rooms with private terraces and the "penthouse" suite with windows on all sides. Mostly private baths. Car and motorbike rentals available. Doubles and suites €60-75. ❹

FOOD

The best dining options in Rhodes are concentrated in the Old Town. Three types dominate: overpriced, schnitzel-touting tourist traps (concentrated largely along Sokratous), small, classy bistros run by expat chefs; and tavernas where Rhodesians might stop for lunch but stay for the afternoon.

The Sea Star (☎22410 22 117), in Sophokleous Square, right next to Nireas. Hailed by some locals as the best seafood in all of Rhodes—and deservedly so. Fish, with only lemon and olive oil added for flavor, arrives at your table straight off the charcoal. The small, delicate *petalides* (sea barnacles; €7), the smoky, flavorful octopus (€7), and the enormous, tender mussels (€5) speak for themselves. ❷

Nireas, Sophokleous 22 (☎22410 21 703). The classier, date-worthy companion to the Sea Star, has more involved recipes and beautiful outdoor seating. The quality of the seafood rivals that of its spartan neighbor. Try the pungent, gooey *fouskes* (sea snails; €7.50), a local treat, or the lightly battered and fried calamari (€6). Ordering a large fresh fish to share (most run €45 per kg) is definitely the way to go with larger groups. ❷

L'Auberge Bistro, Praxitelous 21 (☎22410 34 292). On Sokratous go past Pl. Hippocratous toward the sea and turn right on Dimostenous. Go past Klevoulinis, take a right onto the zigzag path by Agia Triada Church, and continue until you reach Praxitelous;

take a right. The covert location makes this gastronomic gem even more worthwhile. The courtyard's soft lighting and jazz floating from indoors nicely complements the light and well-balanced French dishes. Entrees €7-10. Open Tu-Su 7:30pm-midnight. ❷

Marco Polo Cafe, Ag. Fanouriou 40-42 (☎22410 37 889). Owner Spiros constantly changes the menu of creative and healthy versions of Greek classics to keep things interesting for his older, foreign clientele. The building was originally an Ottoman mansion; ask Spiros to point out the harem room, visible from the courtyard. Internet access available upon request. Entrees €6-9. Open daily 11am-midnight. ❷

SIGHTS

Few islands are known for a sight that no longer exists; Rhodes is one of them. One of the Seven Wonders of the Ancient World, the **Colossus of Rhodes,** a 35m bronze statue of sun god Helios near the harbor entrance of Mandraki, leaves no earthly trace today. Legend has it that the Colossus toppled in a 237 BC earthquake. Today two bronze deer stand on either side of the harbor entrance, marking the spots where the statue's colossal feet might once have been planted.

OLD TOWN

Scattered throughout the pebbled inclines of the medieval Old Town (constructed by the **Knights of St. John**), small bronze plaques label historical sites and museums. Upon conquering the island in AD 1309, the Knights refashioned the capital city in their image, replacing Hellenistic ruins with grandiose medieval forts and peaceful churches designed with both Gothic and Byzantine elements. Strewn amongst the many ruins of these two bygone ages, the architectural influence of the Ottomans also makes its presence felt. Though the Turkish bazaar of old has since transformed into the kitschy shopping strip of Sokratous, a beautiful mosque, library, and school still stand as reminders of the Islamic influence on this city.

PALACE OF THE GRAND MASTER. At the top of the hill, a tall, square tower marks the entrance to the Palace of the Grand Master. With moats, drawbridges, huge watchtowers, and enormous battlements, the 300-room palace survived the long Ottoman siege of 1522, though it was converted to a prison by the Turks after their victory. In 1851 an earthquake inflicted serious damage on the building, only to be followed five years later by the devastating explosion of 300-year-old ammunition in a depot across the street. The citadel was restored and embellished at the beginning of the 20th century by zealous Italians under the watchful eye of Mussolini, who had plans to use the building for his summer residence. However the interior decoration was completed only a few months before the start of WWII, and the Italians had little chance to savor the fruits of their labor. Some of the most remarkable features of the palace are the intricate **mosaics,** which the Italians brought to the citadel from Kos. *(☎22410 25 500. Open Tu-Su 8:30am-3pm. €6, students €3, EU students free.)* For an unparalleled bird's-eye view of the entire fortified city, wait for a Tuesday or Saturday and take a **walk** along the **city walls,** but come at 2:30pm sharp—there's only a 30min. window for admittance. *(Open Tu, Sa 2:30-3pm. €6, students €3.)*

PLATEIA ARGIOKASTROU. Dominating one side of the plateia with its beautiful halls and courtyards, the former **Hospital of the Knights** has been reborn as an **Archaeological Museum.** Its treasures include the exquisite marble statue from the late 4th-century BC, *Aphrodite Bathing*—also called the *Marine Venus.* Its fluid contours were partially created by centuries of erosion in the sea, into which the statue fell during an earthquake. *(☎22410 27 657. Open Tu-Su 8:30am-2:30pm. €3, students €1.50.)* The cobbled **Avenue of the Knights,** or Ipoton, sloping uphill near the museum, was the main boulevard of the city 500 years ago. The **inns** of the different divisions of knights once lined this street. The Order of the Knights of St. John of Jerusalem consisted of seven different religious orders, called "tongues" because each spoke a different language. Each order had its own inn where members would gather to eat, socialize, and share conversation in the mother tongue. The **Inn of the Tongue of England** is a 1919 copy of its 1483 predecessor, destroyed in one of many defensive battles. At the foot of Ipoton is the **Church of the Virgin of the Castle,** an 11th-century Byzantine church, which the knights gradually reworked with Gothic elements up through the 14th century. *(Open Tu-Su 8am-2:40pm.)*

PLATEIA SIMIS. To the right inside Eleftherias Gate, at the base of the Mandraki, are the **Municipal Art Gallery's** contemporary paintings by local and national artists. *(Open M-Sa 8am-2pm. Free.)* Behind the ruined **Temple of Aphrodite** (3rd century BC) in the middle of the plateia stands the 16th-century **Inn of the Tongue of Auvergne,** which features an Aegean-style staircase on the facade.

PLANE TREE WALK. Evidence of the city's Ottoman past is most evident in Pl. Kleovoulou. A walk down **Orfeous,** better known as the Plane Tree Walk, will take you past a large **clock tower,** which was part of the Byzantine walls as early as the 800s and later used to mark the wall separating the knights' quarters from the rest of the city. The tower is the highest viewpoint in the Old Town. *(€4, includes 1 drink in adjacent cafe.)* The **Mosque of Süleyman,** below the clock tower, dates back to the early 19th century, though the original was built after Sultan Süleyman the Magnificent captured Rhodes in 1522. At present the mosque is closed to visitors.

TURKISH HORA. The Hafiz Ahmed Aga Library (Turkish library), built in 1793 opposite the mosque, houses hundreds of volumes of handwritten 15th- and 16th-century Persian and Arabic manuscripts. *(Open daily 10am-1pm and 4-7pm. Donation expected.)* Other Old Town Ottoman-era buildings and monuments are in various states of decay, though the 250-year-old Turkish baths in Pl. Arionos are worth dipping into. *(Open W-F 11am-6pm, Sa 8am-6pm. €1.50.)*

JEWISH QUARTER. Pl. Evreon Martyron (Jewish Martyrs' Square) lies in the heart of the old Jewish Quarter. The Jewish community has been an integral part of Rhodes's history from its inception. Sephardic Jews arrived on the island after fleeing the Spanish Inquisition and added a distinctive Spanish flair to some of the Old Town's medieval architecture. In 1943 almost 2000 Jews were taken from this square to Nazi concentration camps. Today Pl. Evreon has been overrun by tourist cafes and shops, though a small, touching memorial in the center remains to pay tribute to the victims of the Holocaust. A few sleepy streets in the Jewish Quarter's residential area make up the loveliest and most peaceful parts of the Old Town. In this neighborhood, down Dossiadou, is the **Shalom Synagogue,** restored by the 50 Jewish men and women who survived the war. Oriental rugs cover the stone mosaic floor and "eternal lamps" hang overhead. *(Services F 5pm. Dress modestly.)*

NEW TOWN AND MANDRAKI

You'll find stately Italian architecture throughout the modern business district. The bank, town hall, post office, and National Theater are among the weighty stone buildings, inspired by the fascist aesthetic of Mussolini, presiding over wide Eleftherias. Opposite them is the majestic **Governor's Palace,** featuring a unique mix of Byzantine, medieval, and Spanish styles, and the **Church of the Annunciation,** built by the Italians in 1925 to replicate a much older cathedral destroyed in an 1856 explosion. Three defunct **windmills** stand halfway along the harbor's pier. The **Fortress of St. Nicholas,** at the end of the pier, guarded the harbor from 1464 to the end of World War II. The **Mosque of Mourad Reis,** named after the admiral under Süleyman who died trying to capture Rhodes from the Knights of St. John in 1522, recalls the importance of the past Ottoman presence. His mausoleum, the domed building inside, served as the Turkish cemetery. Turbans indicate male graves; flowers female ones. Opposite the cemetery, **Villa Kleovoulos** housed author Lawrence Durrell during his term in the Foreign Office from 1945-47. A number of Durrell's books take place in Greece, including his most celebrated *Reflections on a Marine Venus*, set in Rhodes. Rhodes Town's **aquarium,** also a marine research center, exhibits creatures of the Aegean. *(☎22410 27 308 or 22410 78 320. Open daily 9am-8:30pm. €2.50.)* Follow signs from the EOT to reach the **Acropolis of Rhodes.** The temple is a great place to watch the sunset and the ancient stadium below is a popular place to go running.

OUTSIDE THE CITY

Excursion boats trace the coast from Rhodes to Lindos. Most leave the city around 9am and return to Rhodes at 6pm, making for a great escape from the crowded beaches of the western coast. The boats make several stops, including Faliraki. Schedules and prices are posted at the dock along the lower end of Mandraki (€11 and up). Excursion boats also go to nearby islands like Symi (round-trip €22). **Waterhoppers** (☎22410 38 146) and **Dive Med Centres** (☎22410 61 115) offer **scuba diving** lessons and trips to Kalithea (lessons €45; non-diving passengers €25).

NIGHTLIFE AND ENTERTAINMENT

Nightlife in Old Town focuses around Militadou, off Apelou. Bars line the narrow street and music pours out from everywhere. By midnight, the boundaries between bars have completely disappeared, and there's not a bare spot to be found on the cushioned stone benches scattered along the street. Drink prices are comparable everywhere: wine and cocktails €5-6, beer €4. If the bartender is in a generous mood, shots may be offered to the house to down in unison—say "YAH-mas" before you throw yours back. By 2am or so, crowds tend to move to the much larger **Angel** at the head of Militadou for dancing. Quieter bars can be found in the plateias between Ag. Fanouriou and Eschilou. Nightlife in New Town is neither shy nor tame. Although popular bars and clubs are scattered throughout the New Town, crowds of travelers young and old flock to **Orfanidou,** widely known as "Bar Street." Popular places have expensive drinks; empty bars will cut deals.

For a raucous night, head to New Town. At **Down Under,** Orfanidou 37, Aussie waitresses dance on tabletops to loud 90s pop and hip hop. Lose yourself in the music or the 2-for-1 cocktails. (☎22410 32 982. Drinks from €4.50.) **Colorado Club,** Orfanidou 57, one of the few places on Orfanidou frequented by locals, features three rooms. The first has a live rock band dicing through 80s rock favorites of yore; the second offers smooth European techno; the third caters to your booty-grinding hip-hop needs. (☎22410 75 120; www.coloradoclub.gr. Cover €3. Drinks €5-7.) **La Scala,** a sprawling complex southwest of town by the beachside Rodos Palace Hotel in Ixia, is the king of Rhodes's nightclubs and has covers fit for royalty. Strap on your heels and shorten your skirt if you hope to fit in. Watch for special party nights. **Paradiso,** next to Scala, is almost as posh as its neighbor and bit wilder. Eclectic music includes house, reggae, and rave. Big-name guest DJs are known to roll by in the summertime. (☎22410 32 003. Cover €10 starting at 1am.)

St. Francis Church (☎22410 23 605), at Dimokratias and Filelinon, echoes with sublime organ recitals (every W 9pm; check at the EOT to verify schedule and time). In winter the **National Theater** (☎22410 29 678), off Mandraki next to the town hall, stages occasional productions. Nearby **Rodon** shows new flicks and subtitled classics (€4). **Folk Dance Theater,** on Andronikou, has Greek dance and song performances. (☎22410 29 085 or 22410 20 157. M, W, F 9:20pm.)

FALIRAKI Φαλιρακι ☎22410

English, German, and Austrian tourists float from ocean to bar at this packed haven. Though there's little left of Greece to be found among the Anglocentric sports and beach bars, Faliraki does succeed in providing an ideal spot for the idle.

TRANSPORTATION AND PRACTICAL INFORMATION. Faliraki is located 15km south of Rhodes City. There are two main bus stops in Faliraki; one on the Rhodes-Lindos road and one on the waterfront. **Buses** run to **Lindos** (14 per day, €2.50) from the former stop and to **Rhodes Town** (19 per day, 6:15am-8:40pm; €1.55) from the latter. Faliraki is also a base for excursion boat trips to **Lindos** (round-trip €19), **Symi** (round-trip €23), and **Turkey** (round-trip €58). Grab a **taxi** (☎22410 85 444) at the stand next to the waterfront bus stop (€10 to Rhodes Town). Ermou is the main thoroughfare connecting the beach to the Rhodes-Lindos highway. The **Lydia Travel Agency,** at the corner of Ermou and the Rhodes-Lindos road, next to the Hotel Faliro, offers **currency exchange,** international phone, fax services, excursion boat tickets, and car rental. (☎22410 85 483 or 22410 86 135; fax 22410 86 250. Open daily 9:30am-1pm and 5-10pm.) Directly opposite the waterfront bus stop, to the right of Ermou, is the **first-aid station.** (☎22410 80 000. Open 8am-6pm.) Other options for emergencies are the Faliraki 24hr. **Emergency Medical Service** (☎22410 60 260 or 22410 43 302) and the 24hr. **Medical Center** (☎22410 85 852), on the Rhodes-Lindos road. For an **ambulance,** call ☎22410 22 222. The **pharmacy** is on the main road up to the highway; look for the green cross. (☎22410 87 076. Open daily 9am-11pm.) The **Agricultural Bank,** on Ermou (open M-Th 8am-2pm, F 8am-1:30pm), has a 24hr. **ATM;** other ATMs can be found at the intersection of Ermou and the highway. **Internet** access is available at **Charlie's Easy Internet Cafe,** on a side street to your left as you walk up Ermou (€6 per hr.).

ACCOMMODATIONS AND FOOD. Lodgings are difficult to find, as most places cater to British and German package tour companies. A few are still holding out, though reserving in advance is still a must. **Hotel Faliro ❸** is inland on Ermou, directly before it joins the Rhodes-Lindos road. Rooms are spare but clean, with private baths, balconies, and pool access. (☎22410 85 483 or 22410 86 135. Singles €20-25; doubles €27-30.) **Hotel Dimitra ❸** is another fairly priced, pleasant option on Ermou, with the added bonus of A/C and fridges in every room. The lounge downstairs features a pool table, small bar, and a couple TVs. (☎22410 85 309; fax 22410 85 254. Singles €25; doubles €45.) The **Hotel Ideal ❹,** also on Ermou but closer to the sea, attracts the young and wild to its drab but clean rooms. The hotel serves tour groups but sets aside rooms for independent travelers. (☎22410 85 518; fax 22410 86 530. Breakfast included. Doubles €45.) A few signs advertising rooms to let can occasionally be seen hanging from windows off Ermou. Availability at such places is something of a crapshoot.

Dining in Faliraki often means inhaling a greasy burger or schnitzel at a fast-food joint. Ermou hosts most of these establishments, in addition to a number of sports bars advertising full English breakfasts (€4.50 at most places). The Rhodes-Lindos road offers slightly pricier variations on a similar theme plus a couple cheesy Chinese restaurants. An average meal runs €6-9. For a reprieve from the typical fast food, **Cookies Bakery ❶,** on Ermou, and **Artopoieio ❶,** on the Rhodes-Lindos road, serve up fresh fluffy loaves of bread (€0.60) and savory pies of all kinds (€1).

ENTERTAINMENT AND NIGHTLIFE. With each sunset, the sun-baked masses migrate inland from the beach toward the beer (€3-5) at jubilant bars on Ermou. **Jimmy's Pub** (☎22410 85 643), inland on Ermou, is a British bar with Guin-

DODECANESE

ness on tap and soccer and racecar viewing. For the steady of hand, Jimmy's hosts pool competitions every Saturday night at 9:30pm. For a night of oldies but goodies, head up to the free-of-cover **club** above the pub. A number of bars on Ermou also feature American movies on their TVs during the afternoons. Catch up on your cinema over a burger and beer at the **Tropical Bar** (☎22410 85 143; www.tropicalbar.gr) or **Breeze Bar** (☎22410 85 145). When the music stops at midnight, a second exodus heads toward a handful of popular dance clubs. **Chaplin's** (☎22410 85 662; www.chaplins.net), on Ermou by the beach, is one of the most popular 24hr. party spots, hosting a handful of dawn-to-dawn beach parties during the summer—look out for their posters. The most convenient option for Ermou indulgers is **Sinners,** on "Bar Street," a popular stop-over for house and techno music, with three rooms of dancing.

LINDOS Λινδος ☎22410

With whitewashed houses clustered beneath a castle-capped acropolis, Lindos is perhaps the most picturesque town on Rhodes. Vines and flowers line narrow streets and pebble mosaics carpet courtyards. The town's appeal hasn't remained a secret, however; in summer the crowds rival those in Rhodes Town. Prices rise dramatically as rooms become scarce in late July and August; visiting Lindos outside peak season is the best option.

TRANSPORTATION. Lindos is a pedestrian-only city: all traffic stops at the main road to Rhodes and Pefkos, where you'll find the **bus** and **taxi** stations. Buses to and from Lindos fill quickly, so it's best to arrive early. Buses connect Lindos to: **Faliraki** (14 per day, 6:50am-6pm; €2.50); **Kolymbia beach** (3 per day, €2.50); **Pefkos** (8 per day, €1); and **Rhodes Town** (15 per day, €3.40). Check with the tourist office for recent changes and updates to the bus schedules. **Excursion boats** from Rhodes depart at 9am and return at 5pm, hitting **Rhodes Town** and **Turkey,** among other pit stops, as they travel along the coast.

PRACTICAL INFORMATION. It's best to find your way around Lindos using landmarks, as the locals do; street signs are few and far between. From the bus station, **Acropolis** leads through town and to the acropolis; signs point to the beach after 50m or so. **Apostolou Pavlou** crosses Acropolis just past the **Church of the Assumption of Madonna.** A **tourist information booth,** located in the plateia next to the bus stop, provides bus and excursion schedules, general info on Lindos and the acropolis, and help with accommodations. It also sells stamps, postcards, and newspapers. (☎22410 31 900; fax 22410 31 288. Open daily 8:30am-8:30pm.) Next to the tourist info booth is a 24hr. **ATM. Public toilets** can be found in the plateia. **Pallas Travel,** on Acropolis, **exchanges currency,** helps with accommodations, and arranges excursions. (☎22440 31 494; fax 22440 31 595. Open 8am-10pm. Closed in winter.) Other services cluster around the intersection of Apostolou Pavlou and Acropolis. The **pharmacy** is just past Yiannis Bar. (☎22410 31 294. Open daily 9am-10pm.) Sheila Markiou, an American expat, runs the superb **Lindos Lending Library,** offering more than 7000 English, Italian, German, French, and Greek books. You can buy a book second-hand or bring an old book and trade it in. When you are standing at the base of the westernmost path leading up to the acropolis (by Il Forno), the library is just up the road on your right. (☎22410 31 443. Open M-Sa 9am-8pm.) Sheila also runs a **laundry** service out of the store, with the same hours. (Wash and dry €7.50.) The **medical clinic** is to the left before the church. (☎22410 31 224. Open M-Th 8am-2pm, F noon-2pm.) The **police** are at Apostolou Pavlou 521. (☎22410 31 223. Open M-F 8am-2pm; 24hr. for emergencies.) **Lindos Internet Cafe** (☎22440 32 100; fax 22440 32 121; lindosinternetcafe@yahoo.com), up a small path off Acropolis just past the plateia, is a comfortable place to check email over drinks and British TV. (Open daily 8am-1am.) The **post office** is uphill from the donkey stand. (☎22410 31 314. Open M-F 8am-2pm.) **Postal code:** 85107.

ACCOMMODATIONS. Package tours elbow into even the tiniest pensions, making Lindos a difficult place to spend the night. A handful of small Italian-owned pensions sometimes do have room for solo travelers. If you are facing the acropolis when standing just a few paces before Il Forno, follow the signs pointing left to the beach instead of up the hill. **Pension Lindos ❸** (☎22440 31 369) has clean and simple rooms with fan, fridge, and shared bath. (Singles €25; doubles €40.) **Pension Electra ❸,** just a block further, has clean, bright, spacious rooms, some with A/C, fridges, and bath. Common facilities include two full kitchens, a terrace for meals, and a central garden. (☎22410 31 266. Singles €20; doubles €35-45.) **Pension Katholiki ❸,** around the corner from Electra, has clean rooms centered on a quiet courtyard, with A/C, fridge, and shared bath. Access to kitchens and the rooftop view are added bonuses. It's worth inquiring about the few rooms with traditional Dodecanese loft beds. (☎22410 31 445. Singles €30-35; doubles €35-45.) Nikos Kritikis, the owner of the travel agency **Village Holidays** next to Yiannis Bar, is in the know about available accommodations; owning harbor-view rooms (usually booked) throughout Lindos, he can help you in your quest for a room. (☎22410 31 486; vi-ho@otenet.gr.) A woman named Soula also owns a few rooms (€35-50); ask for her whereabouts at the supermarket near Village Holidays.

FOOD AND NIGHTLIFE. Creperies and snack bars on Acropolis near the plateia offer the cheapest options; crepes start at €3. Grocery stores can also be found along the two main streets. **Agostino's ❷,** perched slightly above the town at the opposite end from the plateia, boasts an unbeatable view of the acropolis, the harbor, and the houses of Lindos from its rooftop terrace. Clay pot moussaka, octopus, and Italian dishes range from €7 to €10. (☎22410 31 218. Open daily 6pm-midnight.) Some *focaccia* or *panzerotti* (€2-3) at **Il Forno Bakery ❶,** around the corner from the bookstore, will help prepare for the climb up the acropolis or to refuel you upon your descent. Ingredients are imported from Italy and food is handmade by the owner. (Open daily 8am-2pm and 5-8pm.)

Lindos municipal law requires music to stop at midnight, but revelers at many bars carry on undaunted well past this deadline. Appealing open-air nightclubs line the lantern-lit streets; the action begins at **Yiannis Bar** (☎22440 31 245) on Acropolis (drinks €4-6) and continues at the newer bars further down. Catch a free late-night cab to the **amphitheater** from the plateia and dance as you overlook the acropolis and the sea. (Open daily midnight-4am.)

SIGHTS. Lindos's ancient **acropolis** stands on sheer cliffs 125m above town, caged by scaffolding and the walls of a Crusader fortress. Excavations by the Danish Archaeological School between 1902 and 1912 yielded everything from 5000-year-old Neolithic tools to a plaque inscribed by a priest of Athena in 99 BC that lists the dignitaries who visited Athena's Temple—Hercules, Helen of Troy, Menelaus, Alexander the Great, and the King of Persia. Directly before the final incline, the ancient Greek *trireme*, supposedly carved by Pythokreitos (famous for his Nike of Samothrace) is worth a look. This rectangular relief of a ship remains a symbol of Lindos's ties to the sea. Lined with staircases, the daunting 13th-century **crusader castle** marks the entrance to the site. The arcade, built around 200 BC at the height of Rhodes's glory, originally consisted of 42 Doric columns laid out in the shape of the Greek letter Π. The large stone blocks arranged against the back wall served as bases for bronze statues that have long since been removed and melted down. The remains of the **Temple of the Lindian Athena,** built by the tyrant

Kleoboulos in the 6th century BC, come into view at the top of the steps. Legend has it that this area, once a tremendously important religious site, accommodated a temple as early as 1510 BC. Kleoboulos's tomb, inscribed with Aristotle's timeless maxim, "Nothing in excess," is across the way. At the foot of the acropolis lie the remains of the **ancient ampitheatre.**

A cave called the **Voukopion,** on the north side of the rock face (visible from the path), may have been used for special sacrifices that could not be performed in the acropolis. The cave probably dates back to the 9th century BC. The Dorians later transformed it into a sanctuary for Athena. Ask for the helpful pamphlet. (☎22410 31 258. Open M 12:30-6:40pm, Tu-Su 8am-6:40pm. €6, students €3.)

DAYTRIPS ON RHODES

EPTA PIGES. Eleven kilometers south of Faliraki, just before Kolymbia, a road to the right leads 3km down to Epta Piges. Constructed by Italians seeking drinkable water for nearby Kolymbia, the aqueduct now quenches the thirst of thrill-seekers, who slide through 150m of pitch-black tunnel. Laughers and shriekers alike end up in a large, picturesque freshwater pool; if the destination sounds nicer than the journey, take the path next to the tunnel that is used to return from the pool. A decent streamside taverna (with peacocks) sits at the entrance before the tunnel. To get there, ask a Lindos/Archangelos bus driver to let you off at the tunnel. Continue inland past Epta Piges to visit the 13th- and 15th-century frescoes of the Byzantine **Church of Agios Nikolaos Fountoucli,** 3km past Eleousa. Three **buses** per day stop at Eleousa on the way to Rhodes. Villagers in **Arthipoli,** 4km away, rent **rooms.**

TSAMBIKAS MONASTERY. From the coast road, Tsambikas Monastery is marked by the restaurant that sits below it. A 1km road leads up to the restaurant; the Byzantine cloister and its panoramic views are 1km farther up a steep and poorly maintained trail. The monastery takes its name from the sparks *(tsambas)* that were reportedly seen atop the hill. Upon climbing up to investigate, locals discovered a Cypriot icon of the Virgin Mary that had mysteriously appeared here, miles from home. Angry Cypriots ordered that the icon be returned and the locals obliged—but the icon kept returning. By the third time, everyone agreed that Rhodes must be the icon's proper home. To this day some women ascend the mountain to pray to the Virgin Mary for fertility. If the prayer works, the baby should be named Tsambikos (if it's a boy) or Tsambika (if it's a girl). One bus runs to the long, flat, and sandy **Tsambika beach,** 1km south of the turn-off for the monastery (€2.20). Bus that pass the turn-off will let you off here for some rays.

KAMIROS. The smallest of the three ancient cities of Rhodes, Kamiros nonetheless surpasses Ialyssos and Rhodes in intricacy and preservation. The layout of this Hellenistic city is unique; because of the hollow in which the city was built, three levels of settlement developed: the lowest for the public, the middle sloping up, like an amphitheater, and the highest for the acropolis. The giant cistern on the north side of the temple dates from the 5th or 6th century BC, and the stone colonnade is from at least the 2nd century BC. Visit the precinct of Athena Kamiras on the acropolis to get a clear sense of the city's impressive chessboard plan. *(Buses run 2 per day, 10am and 1:30pm, from Rhodes to Kamiros. ☎22410 40 037 or 22410 75 674. Open Tu-F 8:30am-7pm. €4, students €2.)*

VALLEY OF BUTTERFLIES. Seven kilometers inland from the village of Theologos, **Petaloudes,** or the **Valley of Butterflies,** is a popular visiting spot with or without the company of its insect residents. During the summer, Jersey tiger moths flock to the valley's Styrax trees, attracted to their resin (also used in making incense) and the area's shade. While resting to live out their final days in the trees, the moths fast, living only on water and body fat to conserve energy for rigorous mating sessions. After the deed is done, they die of starvation. The valley and its many trees are worth a walk any time of year but are a particularly welcoming reprieve from the summer's sun-beaten coasts. The valley is accessible from an entrance next to an old mill or from the main entrance farther uphill. The trail winds around a blue-green stream that collects in lily-covered pools and glides under bridges. Avoid clapping and stomping to incite the moths to flight, like some foolish visitors do. *(☎22410 81 801. Open daily 8:30am-sunset. €1-3.)* Hiking up 300m from the end of the 1km trail to the **Monastery of Kalopetra,** you will encounter a restored mosaic and panoramic view of the island and perhaps enjoy fresh yogurt and honey prepared by the caretakers.

KOS Κως

Antiquity best knew Kos as the sacred land of Asclepius, god of healing, and the birthplace of Hippocrates, the father of modern medicine, who wrested the science of human health away from magicians. Today Kos attracts a young, loud, intoxicated crowd more interested in sexual healing than anything else. If you've been meaning to reduce the blood in your alcohol stream or need a primer on the anatomy of the torso or backside, the rowdy beaches of Kos Town may be just what the doctor ordered. Though the more sedate traveler can escape to the mountains of central Kos or the relatively isolated beaches of the west coast, those allergic to the party may find Kos a tough pill to swallow.

KOS TOWN ☎22420

Here you can live out your MTV Spring Break fantasies or watch skeptically as those around you do. Kos Town is the Cancun of the Mediterranean (or maybe the Mykonos of the Dodecanese) where young foreigners come to strut their stuff, blow their cash, and hopefully get some action. Many visitors extend their vacation by taking on temporary work as waiters or bartenders, giving the whole circus a temporary feeling. The tourist industry has grown exponentially in Kos Town, and the numerous five-star hotels peppering the outskirts of the town threaten to expand the generic resort-feel to the untouched beaches further southwest. Whether banishing a hangover or escaping the feeding frenzy, visitors should rent a a vehicle to explore the rest of the beautiful island during the daylight hours.

TRANSPORTATION

Flights: Olympic Airways, Vas. Pavlou 22 (reservations ☎22420 28 331 or 28 332; general information 22420 51 567), has flights to **Athens** (from €68). Ticket counter open M-F 8am-2:30pm. Olympic runs a bus (€3) to the airport from their Kos Town office 2hr. before departure. Taxis to the airport cost €25.

Ferries: To: **Kalymnos** (1hr., 3 per day, €5); **Leros** (3hr., 1-2 per day, €7); **Nisyros** (1½hr., 2 per week); **Patmos** (4hr., 1-2 per day, €10); **Piraeus** (11-15hr., 1-3 per day, €22.50); **Rhodes** (4hr., 2-3 per day, €16); **Symi** (3hr., 1 per week); **Tilos** (1 per week). Boats also run to **Bodrum, Turkey** every morning (round-trip €30-40); since travel is international, prices are not regulated by the Greek government.

Flying Dolphins: To: **Fourni** (4hr., 2 per week, €25.30); **Kalymnos** (30min., daily, €10); **Leros** (1hr., 4 per week, €14); **Lipsi** (1hr., daily, €14); **Nisyros** (45min., 6 per week, €25); **Patmos** (2hr., 3 per week, €19.50); **Rhodes** (2hr., 2 per day, €22.50); **Samos** (3½hr., daily, €25); **Symi** (1½hr., 1 per week, €17.90); **Tilos** (2hr., 1 per week).

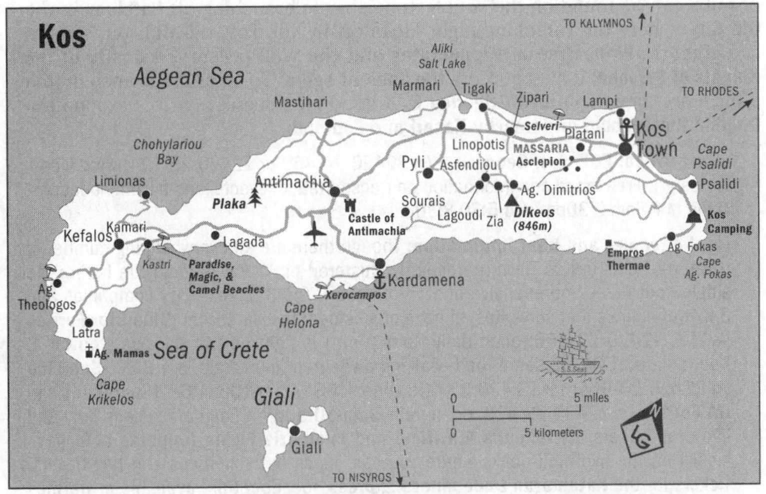

Intercity Buses: ☎22420 22 292; fax 22420 20 263. Leave from the intersection of Kleopatras, Metsovou, and Pissandrou and from the junction of V. Pavlou and A. Koundourioti at the waterfront. M-Sa with reduced service Su to: **Antimachia** (40min., 6 per day, €1.60); **Kardamena** (45min., 6 per day, €2); **Kefalos-Paradise** (1hr., 6 per day, €2.80); **Marmari** (35min., 12 per day, €1.30); **Mastihari** (35min., 5 per day, €1.90); **Pyli** (30min., 5 per day, €1.30); **Tigaki** (30min., 12 per day, €1.30). Schedule posted by the bus stop and at the EOT; buy tickets on the bus.

City Buses: Akti Koundouriotou 7 (☎22420 26 276), on the water. To: **Agios Fokas** (45 per day, 6:45am-11pm); **Lampi** (25 per day, 6:30am-11pm); **Messaria** (10 per day, 8am-8:45pm); **Platani** (15 per day, 8am-10:45pm); **Thermae** (20min., 9 per day, 9:45am-5:45pm). Fares run €0.50-1.20. Bizarre green mini-trains run from the EOT to **Asclepion** (15min.; Tu-Su 1 per hr., 9am-6pm). There are also **citywide tours** leaving every 30min. from City Hall.

Taxis: ☎22420 22 777, 22420 23 333, or 22420 23 334. Convene near the inland end of the Avenue of Palms, just after A. Koundourioti splits where the harbor curves.

Rentals: Laws restricting rentals to those with proper motorbike licenses are more strictly enforced here than on other islands. Driving behavior does not reflect this stringency, however, and drivers should exercise caution. **Mike's** (☎22420 21 729) is at the corner of Amerikis and Psaron. Mopeds €9-15 per day. Bikes €2-4 per day. Open 9am-8pm. **George,** P. Tsaldari 3 (☎22420 28 480), located near the port authority, rents mopeds from €10 per day. Bikes €1.50. Open daily 8:30am-8pm.

ORIENTATION AND PRACTICAL INFORMATION

The lamps, neon signs, and floodlit hotels that light up the coast seem to beckon ferry boats into port at night. The coastal roads (**Zouroudi** in the northwest; **Akti Koundourioti** curving around the harbor; and both **Akti Miaouli** and **Vas. Georgiou** to the southeast, past the castle) present touristic tavernas, kitschy bars, and roadside souvenir stands. **V. Pavlou,** just off A. Koundourioti, has a practical, if equally charmless, cluster of **banks,** 24hr. **ATMs,** and **travel agencies. Pl. Eleftherias,** just a bit further inland, is the center of town, and boasts the **Archaeological Museum,** a large market, and some cafes. A plethora of pubs can be found on the cobblestone streets branching off **Nafklirou** in the **Old City,** where the rollicking night kicks off in Kos Town. Nafklirou leads to the gigantic **Plane Tree of Hippocrates** and the well-preserved **Castle of the Knights of St. John;** it also borders the ancient **agora.** To scratch the ancient itch a bit more, head south to **Grigoriou E.** A good club scene revolves around the **Dolphin Roundabout** and nearby **Kanari** and **Zouroudi.**

Tourist Office: EOT, Vas. Georgiou 1 (☎22420 24 460 or 22420 28 724; www.hippocrates.gr). **Free maps** and information on transportation, events, and accommodations. Open M-F 8am-2:30pm and 5:30-8:30pm.

Travel Agencies and Boat Information: Though there are an overwhelming number of travel agencies in Kos Town, particularly clustered on V. Pavlou near the harbor, no single spot has comprehensive boat information. The 3 largest ferry companies and 3 hydrofoil lines that serve Kos all have offices near the waterfront. **Blue Star Ferries** (☎/fax 22420 22 156; open daily 7am-10pm) is right next to the bus stop on A. Koundourioti.) On the same road, walking away from the castle, are **DANE Sea Line** (☎22420 23 964; fax 22420 22 185; open M-Sa 9am-10pm, Su 10am-9pm) and **GA Ferries** (☎22420 29 920; open daily 9am-10:30pm). Each office sells ferry and hydrofoil tickets. **Kyriakoulis Maritime** and **Laoumzis Flying Dolphins** both have kiosks on the hydrofoil docks where you can check out schedules and buy tickets. Tickets for the **Katamaran Dodecanese Express** speedboat are available at **Hermes Travel Shipping Agency** (☎22420 26 607; fax 22420 26 134), on the V. Pavlou strip. Open daily 8:15am-9:30pm. **Pulia Tours** (☎/fax 22420 26 388; open daily 7am-11pm), directly opposite Hermes, is a general agency that sells tickets and offers rental assistance and **currency exchange.**

DODECANESE

Banks: You should have no trouble locating a bank on A. Koundourioti, between And. Ioannidi and Al. Diakou. Many have 24hr. **ATMs.** Typical banking hours are M-Th 8am-2pm, reduced hours on F. **Alpha Bank** is between V. Pavlou and Al. Diakou. **National Bank** (☎22420 22 167) is behind the Archaeological Museum, 1 block inland from the water, on And. Ioannidi. After banking hours, you can **exchange currency** at virtually any travel agency along the waterfront.

American Express: Full AmEx services at the **Credit Bank** (*Trapeza Pisteos;* ☎22420 28 426), Akti Koundouriotou 5, near the bus stop. Open M-Th 7:45am-2pm, F 7:45am-1:30pm.

Emergency: ☎22420 22 100. For an **ambulance,** call ☎22420 22 166.

Police: ☎22420 22 100 or 22 222. On Akti Miaouli in the big, yellow building next to the castle. Some English spoken. Open 24hr.

Tourist police: ☎22420 22 444 or 22420 26 666. In the same building as police. Open daily 7am-2pm.

Hospital: Mitropoleos 13 (☎22420 22 300), between El. Venizelou and Hippocratous. Open 24hr.

Pharmacy: Around the corner from the hospital and on the corner of Mitropoleos and El. Venizelou. Prescriptions filled 24hr. There are a number of other pharmacies in town. Open 8am-midnight.

OTE: ☎22420 23 499. At Lor. Vironos and Xanthou, around the corner from the post office. Open M-F 7am-2:30pm.

Internet Access: Del Mare Internet Cafe, Megalou Alexandrou 4A (☎22420 24 244), offers admirably fast connection speeds. €4.50 per hr. (with €2 deposit). Open daily 9am-midnight.

Post Office: ☎22420 22 250. On Vas. Pavlou. From El. Venizelou, walk 1 block inland. Open M-F 7:30am-2pm. **Postal code:** 85300.

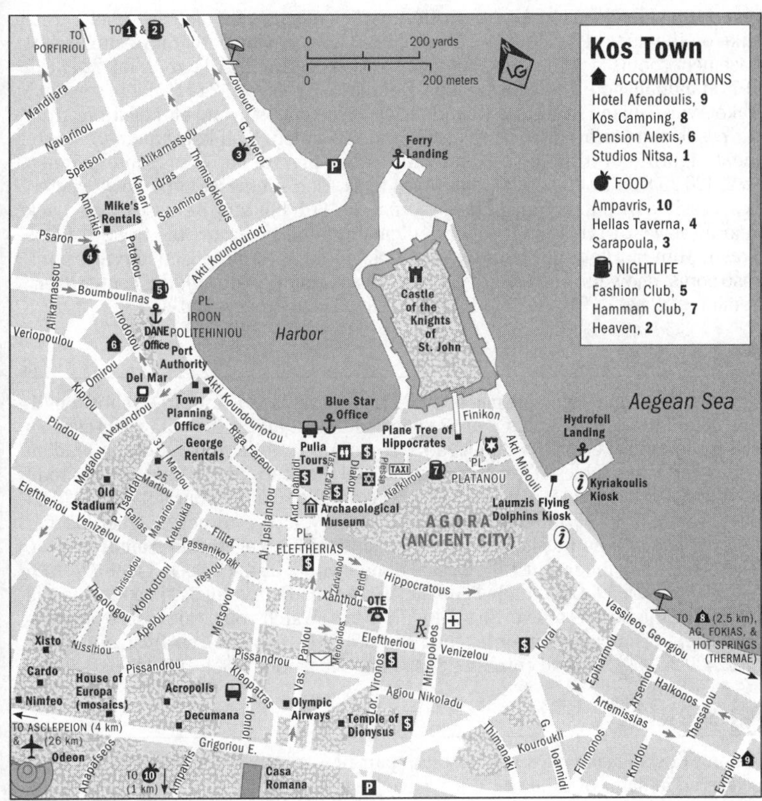

ACCOMMODATIONS

Hotel vacancies are rare in August so start searching for rooms early. Most inexpensive options are on the right side of town when facing inland. It's best to seek out your own room and avoid Kos's dock hawks as bait-and-switch is a rampant practice. If you do choose to haggle, ask for a business card, telling them you'll check out your options and come by later; if no card is produced, move on. To get to **Pension Alexis** ❷ from the port, head inland on Megalou Alexandrou; take the first right onto Irodotou and walk up one block. Kind, hospitable Sonia, sister of Alexis, presides over a beloved travel institution, offering advice about the island, help with ferry schedules, free laundry, and yummy breakfasts (€4) with equal ease. The attractive veranda is a good spot to meet the other guests or to relax with one of the magazines available free for perusal. Common baths have phenomenal showers with consistent hot water. Rooms on the upper story have breezy verandas. If full, Sonia will help arrange other accommodations or cut you a deal at her brother's elegant Hotel Afendoulis. (☎22420 28 798 or 22420 25 594. Doubles €20-22; triples €28-33.) **Hotel Afendoulis** ❷, Evripilou 1, is down Vas. Georgiou. Having left the pension largely in the hands of his sister, friendly owner Alexis now concentrates on this hotel, a classier upgrade geared more to older couples keen

DODECANESE

on privacy. Like Pension Alexis, it offers sufficient space for meeting other guests (like on the upper-level lounge). Rooms here have private bath. Surprisingly cool basement rooms lack the view, but make a good deal. (☎22420 25 321; fax 22420 25 797; afandoulishotel@kos.forthnet.gr. Doubles €24-38; €20-24 for the basement.) Take Averof inland from Akti Koundourioti at the opposite end of the harbor from the castle and **Studios Nitsa ❷,** Averof 47, is on your left. Well-kept studios, close to most nightlife destinations, come with fridge, private bath, A/C, and balcony. (☎22420 25 810. Doubles €20.) **Kos Camping ❶,** 3km southeast of the town center, is accessible by public transport (get off at the 11th bus stop). Guests come back year after year to this family-operated campground to escape the frenzy of Kos Town. Mini-market, bar, laundry facilities, cooking room, postal service, pool, restrooms, showers, and security boxes. Buses run to and from the center every 30min. (☎22420 23 910 or 23 275. €8 per tent, €10 per tent rental.)

FOOD

The large fruit and vegetable **market** in Pl. Eleftherias, inside the large yellow building, caters to tourists and is more expensive than it looks; the many **mini-markets** sell fruit at cheaper prices. At **Ampavris ❶,** on Ampavris, a father-and-son tandem cooks and waits tables. Take Grigoriou E. and then turn onto Ampavris, the road next to Casa Romana; it's about a 1km walk up the road on your left. (☎22420 25 696. Entrees €3-5.50.) **Hellas Taverna ❷,** Psaron 7, at the corner of Amerikis and Psaron, has simple but hearty Greek cuisine with a vegetarian-friendly menu. There's nothing fancy—just the basics done well. (☎22420 22 609. Lamb *kleftiko* €7. *Stifado* €6.50. Open daily 8am-late.) **Sarapoula ❷,** Averof 17, inland from the far end of the port, is a favorite spot with locals. Watch your waitress's eyes raise with skepticism when you order the *spinialo* (€6), an exotic shellfish appetizer. (☎22420 21 909. Seafood entrees €6-12. Fish €45 per kg. Open 1pm-late.)

SIGHTS

Among Kos's **Roman ruins** is a desolate pair of Corinthian columns, some of the scattered remains of what was once a lively **agora** in the 4th century BC. Today the meager field of rubble, located in the heart of the Old City, hosts little more than unruly weeds and the occasional stray tourist. Other poorly-tended ruins include the **Temple of Dionysus** and the **West Archaeological Area,** both found along Grigoriou E.; the latter does contain an excellent floor **mosaic** of Europa's abduction by Zeus in the guise of a bull. Better preserved are the 3rd-century **Odeon,** a Roman theater, and the **Casa Romana,** a villa also dating from the 3rd century that has been recently reopened after a two-year-long restoration project. Both are found on the other side of Grigoriou E. Good English labels guide you around the sculptures of the **Archaeological Museum,** with artifacts dating from Hellenistic to late Roman times. Though many of the statues are of passing aesthetic interest to any person besides a connoisseur, the northwest room contains a graceful 4th-century sculpture presumed to be of Hippocrates and the central courtyard contains an AD 2nd-century Roman mosaic depicting the arrival of Asclepius on Kos. (In Pl. Eleftherias. ☎22420 28 326. Open Tu-Su 8am-2:30pm. €3, students €2, EU students free.)

The invading Knights of St. John, never satisfied without building yet another defensive island fortification, began erecting a massive **castle** in the early 14th century. The bridge over Finikon, the street connecting Pl. Platanou to the castle, once stretched across an outer moat filled with seawater and could draw back to cut the castle off entirely from the mainland. A second phase of building in the late 15th century saw the addition of elaborate double walls and stout towers, now the most distinctive feature of the fortress. It's an unavoidable sight in Kos and one of the best preserved examples of medieval architecture in all of Greece. (Take the bridge from Pl. Platanou across Finikon. ☎22420 27 927. Ask for the helpful pamphlet available at the door. Open Tu-Su 8:30am-3pm. €3, students €2, EU students free.)

In Pl. Platanou, the **plane tree of Hippocrates,** allegedly planted by the great physician 2400 years ago, has grown to boast an enormous 12m in diameter; it's so big that metal bars now support its branches. While it is alluring to envision the ancient Hippocrates teaching and writing beneath its noble foliage, hearing the tree is only 500 years old eliminates that possibility.

NIGHTLIFE

Whether you reach Kos Town at 10am or 3am, you're bound to be greeted by a blast of hip hop or techno from a balcony full of rowdy youngsters, the open door of a bar, or a passing vehicle. Clubbing permeates the very air of Kos Town. By 11pm, watchers and the watched congregate around **Exarhia** (a.k.a. **Bar Street**), in the Old City past Pl. Platonou, and along **Porfirou,** between Averof and Zouroudi. In both areas, beers go for around €3 and cocktails for around €6. The guileful greeters standing outside the bars are armed with a cache of clever ploys to reel in the passing Anglophone. **Fashion Club,** Kanari 2, by the Dolphin Roundabout, has 20 television screens broadcast the cool demure of runway models inside this cavernous, red- and chrome-colored club. Three bars, two dance floors, and 1700-person capacity make Fashion Club Kos's biggest and most ostentatious night club. Happy Hour runs until midnight. (☎22420 22 592; fashionc@otenet.gr. Outdoor cafe no cover. Club cover €10 on weekends, includes 1 drink. Open daily 11pm-4am; cafe opens 7pm.) **Hammam Club** is inland from the Pl. Diagoras taxi station in the Old City, on Nafklirou. White chairs and cushions are arranged on the outdoor patio of this former Turkish bath. Live musicians cover cheesy songs outside, while a live DJ ushers in more interesting night activities within. (☎22420 24 938. Cocktails €6.) **Heaven** (☎22420 23 874; open Su-Th 10am-4am, F-Sa 10am-dawn), on Zouroudi opposite the beach, might not be the easiest place to locate but by day it's a frequented waterfront bar and by night a large popular disco.

DODECANESE

DAYTRIPS FROM KOS

THE ASCLEPION

About 4km southwest of Kos Town. Take a 15min. mini-train ride there in summer; by bike or moped follow the sign west off the main road and go straight; taxis €6-7. ☎22420 28 763. Open Tu-Su 8am-6:30pm. €4, students €2.

The Asclepion was an ancient sanctuary devoted to the god of healing. In the 5th century BC, **Hippocrates** founded the world's first medical school and hospital here, forever changing the course of science and man's understanding of his body. Combining early priests' techniques with his own, Hippocrates made Kos the leading medical center in ancient Greece. Present-day doctors travel here to take their Hippocratic oaths and to pay homage to the original mastermind.

Most of the ruins here date from the 2nd and 3rd centuries BC. The complex was built on three levels, called *andirons,* which were carved into a hill overlooking Kos Town, the Aegean, and the coast of Turkey. The lowest *andiron* holds a complex of 3rd-century Roman baths, complete with *natatio* (swimming pool), *tepidarium* (lukewarm pool), and *caldarium* (sauna); it was once home to the medical school and the anatomy and pathology museums. Elegant 2nd-century columns remain standing on the second level, which once contained a temple to Asclepius and a temple to Apollo. The 60-step climb to the third *andiron* leads to the forested remnants of the main **Temple of Asclepius** and a sweeping view of the site, the town below, and Asia Minor across the sea. Although the site is remarkably preserved, much of its structure is gone: it was used for raw materials by the Knights of Saint John in the building of the Kos Castle.

NORTHERN KOS

The Empros Thermae (hot springs) are east of Kos Town and along the coastal road; catch one of the regular buses at the town center (€1.20 one-way). The bus drops you off at the top of a steep cliff path; descend to the springs past impressive views of the mild green waves below. Free.

The Empros Thermae are northern Kos's ultimate attraction; once immersed in the piping hot water, marvel as your muscles melt in relaxation. For more fun on the north of the island, paved, flat roads, most of which have bike lanes, beckon the city-weary traveler eager for a taste of the pre-touristed Kos. Along the western coast, a small road suitable for biking extends parallel to the main road. Sandy **Lampi beach** lies just a few kilometers northwest of Kos Town. About 8km from town, the beautiful **Selveri beach** provides clear sand, shallow waters, and a panorama of the Turkish coast. It's possible to find along the beach rusted remains of anti-Turkish lookout and artillery posts; the tide at Selveri has been steadily encroaching on the land and has left some of these former military outposts half-submerged in the waters. It is difficult to reach the beach without private transportation or a bike; as a result it remains blissfully deserted.

CENTRAL KOS

Continuing southwest along the minor coastal road.

The tourist resort beaches of **Tigaki** (15km from Kos Town)—"Sea sports and amusement on the waves!" promises the Kos travel brochure—and **Marmari** (19km), with gargantuan new hotels, are disappointingly developed. The wise head for the deserted, beautiful middle, where casinos are replaced by a secluded nude beach. Close by, at **Aliki Salt Lake,** you may be able to spot a handful of *Caretta caretta* sea turtles, which come to the northern coastline to lay eggs in the summer. Much farther south, along the main road, lies the village of Antimachia, only an essential visit for the annual **Honey Festival** on August 17. To the south of **Antimachia** lie the serene forests of **Plaka,** just past the airport, where lush, full-feathered peacocks frolic—a truly stunning sight. Unless you happen to land there en route to or from Nisyros, avoid **Kardamena** to the east, a slightly smaller version of Kos Town with all of the tourist amenities but none of the charm.

SOUTHERN KOS

A moped allows unobstructed exploration; a taxi also does the trick. Heading south lands you at Camel; just beyond lie Paradise and Magic, with bright white sand and breathtaking views of the island's southern peninsula. The bus will let you off at any of the beaches.

Hills, ravines, and the occasional pasture roll across Southern Kos, surrounded by the island's most worthy **beaches.** A few ancient oceanside columns mark **Kefalos,** Kos's ancient capital. You probably want to trade in this crowded, bland town for its surrounding beaches. North of Kefalos, the beach of **Agios Stephanos** lies next to well-preserved ruins of a basilica. Beach bums can lie in the shade of olive trees among crumbling walls or swim to a nearby rocky islet, on top of which perches a small blue and white church. On the opposite side of the peninsula is the deserted, pebbly beach of **Agios Theologos,** where foamy green waves batter the shore. For some grub, you can hit the nearby **Theologos Sunset Wave Beach Restaurant ❷.**

NEAR KOS

BODRUM, TURKEY

For more information on travel to Turkey from Greece, see **Turkey Essentials,** p. 626. Ferries run to Bodrum from Kos every morning (round-trip €35-40). Because of the instability of the Turkish lira, prices for goods and services in Turkey are listed in US dollars. Coverage of Bodrum was updated in July of 2001.

The "Bedroom of the Mediterranean," Bodrum comes to life at night. While Bodrum's nightlife is notorious, the surrounding Acadian Peninsula is famous for its silica beaches, lush forests, secluded coves, and ancient ruins. As a multitude of visitors agree, it's easy to get sucked into Bodrum's rhythm of sun, shopping, sightseeing, and watersports—an innocent prelude to nightfall's Bacchanalian delights.

ORIENTATION AND PRACTICAL INFORMATION. Small blue signs label the streets of Bodrum; main streets radiate from the **Castle of St. Peter.** The main commercial drag, **Cumhuriyet,** runs along the beach. **Kale** runs from the left of the castle to a mosque. **Belediye Meyd,** the street to the left of the mosque, becomes **Neyzen Tevfik** along the west harbor coast. The **tourist office,** 48 Bariş Meydani, gives away free brochures and **maps** at the foot of the castle. (☎252 316 10 91; fax 316 76 94. Open Apr.-Oct. daily 8:30am-5:30pm; Nov.-Mar. M-F 8am-noon and 1-5pm.) **ATMs** pepper shopping areas. In an **emergency,** dial ☎316 12 15. The **police,** 50 Bariş Meydani, are at the foot of the castle, next to the tourist office. (☎252 316 10 04. Open 24hr.) If you need a place to sleep it off, try **Emiko Pansiyon ❶,** Atatürk, 11 Uslu Sok.; from the *otogar*, follow Cevat Çakir. toward the water, turning left onto Atatürk. After 50m, turn right down the alley marked with the pension's sign, it offers eight simple rooms with hardwood floors and bath. (☎/fax 252 316 55 60; emiko@turk.net. Breakfast US$2. Laundry US$3. Singles US$7-10; doubles US$12-16.) Another option is the **Otel Kilavus ❷,** 25 Atatürk, near the mosque on the way to the castle. A modern hotel with a pool and bar, Kilavus has 12 rooms with large baths and phones. (☎252 316 38 92. Singles US$10-13; doubles US$16-20.)

KALYMNOS Καλυμνος

Kalymnos is known throughout Greece for its fishermen's dedication to sponge diving, an activity that once defined the island's economy. In years past Kalymniot men would spend five or six months of the year diving in the Libyan Sea, often working south of Muammar Al-Qaddafi's Line of Death. Today sponges can hardly be considered the "Kalymnian gold" of days past and are of commercial value only to the extent that they can be hawked to tourists. Kalymnos has focused extensively on building up its tourism industry but efforts have not met with tremendous success. Likewise, the traveler who arrives here can take advantage of adequate tourist facilities without the corresponding mob of foreigners. The rugged central mountains of the interior cascade into wide beaches and blue-green water, offering a particularly good environment for both divers and rock-climbers.

POTHIA Ποθια ☎22430

A large and bustling port town with 11,500 residents is equipped with the goods and services of a happening metropolis. Pothia's thriving local culture has yet to feel the effects of the tourism industry. Fast, fashionable youth haplessly weave past on motorbikes along the narrow, pedestrian-unfriendly Eleftherias. During the turn-of-the-century Italian occupation, Kalymniots antagonized the Italians by painting their houses blue, the color of the Greek flag. Today only a few buildings, visible high above the harbor, retain the nationalistic shade, and the bright neon lights of the waterfront provide the bulk of the local color.

TRANSPORTATION

Flights: Olympic Airways (☎22430 29 263; fax 22430 51 800). Take the 1st left past the National Bank; it's 50m down on the right. Open Su-Tu, Th-F 9am-1:30pm and 5-9pm; W, Sa 9am-1:30pm.

Ferries: To: **Astypalea** (2½hr., 2 per week, €9.50); **Kos Town,** Kos (1hr., 2 per day, €5.50); **Leros** (1hr., 2 per day, €7); **Mastihari,** Kos (15min., 3 per day, €3); **Mykonos** (10hr., 2 per week, €18.65); **Nisyros** (3hr., 2 per week, €7); **Paros** (8hr., 2 per week, €16); **Patmos** (3hr., 2 per day, €9); **Piraeus** (12hr., 2 per day, €19.50); **Rhodes** (5hr., 2 per day, €16); **Symi** (5hr., 2 per week, €14); **Tilos** (4½hr., 2 per week, €14).

Flying Dolphins: To: **Fourni** (2 per week, €23); **Ikaria** (2 per week, €22.20); **Kos** (3-4 per day, €10); **Leros** (2 per day, €13.45); **Lipsi** (2-3 per day, €13.10); **Patmos** (2-3 per day, €17.50); **Rhodes** (1-2 per day, €30.30); **Samos** (2 per day, €22.60); **Tilos** (2 per week, €19.50).

Excursion Boats: To island beaches on **Pserimos** (€6) and **Vlichadi** (€8).

Buses: Leave 8 times per day, 6:50am-9pm to: **Hora** (10min., €0.30); **Kastel** (50min., €0.90); **Massouri** (25min.); **Myrties** (20min., €0.75); **Panormos** (15min., €0.60). 5 times a day, 7am-4pm to **Vlihadia** (€0.60). 2 times a day to **Argos** (€0.60) and **Plati Yialos** (€0.75). Buses to western towns leave from the town hall in the harbor center. Departing from the far end of the waterfront, past the town hall when walking away from the dock, find the bus to **Vathis** (M-Sa 4 per day, 6:30am-5pm; Su 3 per day; €0.90). Buy tickets before boarding at Themis mini-market, next to the town hall. Insert tickets into the automated validating box on the bus or hand them to the driver.

Taxis: ☎22430 50 300 or 50 303. Up Eleftherias in Pl. Kyprou. Available 24hr.

Rentals: Automarket Rent-A-Car/Scooteromania Rent-A-Bike (☎22430 51 780, 22430 50 193, or 697 283 4628), down a little alley off the waterfront, between the cafes (look for signs). US driver's licenses accepted. Mopeds €10 and up. Open daily 9am-1pm and 3-9pm. **AVIS Rent A Car** (☎22430 51 630) is directly behind the church by the town hall.

ORIENTATION AND PRACTICAL INFORMATION

Ferries arrive at the far left end of the port (facing inland). The road leading from the dock bends around the waterfront until it meets the large, cream-colored municipal building, a church, and the town hall. Narrow, shop-lined **Eleftherias** heads in one direction inland at this point, leading to **Pl. Kyprou,** home to the **taxi stand** and **pay phones,** and the **post office** just beyond. Continue on Eleftherias to reach **Horio, Myrties,** and **Massouri.** Follow the harbor past Eleftherias and the town hall to access the road to Vathis.

Tourist Office: ☎22430 50 879; www.kalymnos-isl.gr. In the blue hut in the middle of the harbor, opposite the Neon Internet C@fe. Though only operating sporadically, offers very helpful advice and information on accommodations, bus and boat schedules, and town events. Open July-Oct. daily 9am-11pm, though months and hours are treated rather haphazardly. A small tourist **kiosk** on the ferry dock is usually open when late boats come in and can also help with accommodations.

DODECANESE

Tourist Agencies: As each travel agency only offers tickets for the companies it represents, it's best to consult more than one to compare prices and schedules. Luckily for you they are all located in the same area. **Magos Travel** (☎22430 28 777; fax 22430 22 608), on the waterfront near the port police, sells hydrofoil tickets and offers advice with a smile. Open daily 9:30am-2pm and 5:30-9:30pm, with increased hours during the high season. Ferry tickets for **DANE Sea Lines** (☎22430 23 043 or 22430 28 200; fax 22430 29 125) can be obtained just a few doors down. Open daily 9am-2pm and 5-9pm. Just a little farther is the office for **G.A. Ferries** (☎/fax 22430 23 700). Open daily 9am-1:30pm and 5-9:30pm.

Banks: A few banks along the waterfront have full services. **National Bank** (☎22430 51 501; open M-Th 8am-2:30pm, F 8am-2pm), on the waterfront, has 24hr. **ATM** and **currency exchange.**

Police: ☎22430 22 100. Go up Eleftherias and take the left road inland from the taxi plateia. English-speaking help can be found in a blue and yellow Neoclassical building on the right. Open 24hr.

Port Authority: ☎22430 24 444 or 22430 29 304. In the yellow building at the end of the dock. Provides ferry information. Open 24hr.

Hospital: ☎22430 23 025. On the main road to Hora, 3km from Pothia. Open 24hr.

OTE: ☎22430 50 599. From the taxi stand, take the inland road on the right about 100m. Open M-F 7:30am-3:10pm.

Internet: Neon Internet C@fe (☎22430 28 343) is on the waterfront in front of the ferry deck. 3 computers, full bar, and ice cream. €5 per hr. Open daily 7am-late.

Post Office: ☎22430 28 340. Just past the police station on the right. Has **currency exchange.** Open M-F 7:30am-2pm. **Postal code:** 85200.

DODECANESE

ACCOMMODATIONS AND FOOD. Pickings are slim in Pothia when it comes to lodgings. There are better options in Myrties or neighboring Plati Yialos, though transportation there is tricky; the tourist office may help. Camping is legal on all the island's beaches but uncommon. **Greek House ❷** rents well-furnished, spacious studios accessible by narrow, treehouse-like stairs. Though A/C will cost you €5 extra, many come with separate living room, kitchen, and large balcony with harbor view; all come with private bath. Inquire at Ta Adelvia Flaskov, a cafe you'll encounter as you come from the port. (☎22430 29 559 or 22430 23 752. Singles €25; doubles €35. Some haggling permitted. Rooms for 3 or more also available.) **Hotel Therme ❷** is on the waterfront before the church (look for tiled sign hanging from balcony). Therme has the 70s motel vibe mastered, complete with retro turquoise walls, rotary phones, and shaky plastic chairs on the terrace. Rooms are clean and reasonably large, with A/C, TV, and shiny private bath. (☎22430 29 425 or 22430 28 891. Singles €20; doubles €25-30.) **Pension Niki ❷** offers clean, quiet rooms with private baths close to town. Niki's daughter Maria will be waiting at the docks if there are any vacancies. If you don't see her, take the first left after the Neon Internet C@fe, a left at the wedding store, and your first left after that. (☎22430 48 135 or 22430 28 528. Singles €15; doubles €15-25.)

You can find a couple of good dining options hidden among the standard array of waterfront tavernas and pizzerias. The food at **Xefteris ❷** will leave you craving more. Head inland on Eleftherias from the town hall; take the first street on your right and then the first left. Design your meal of piping-hot traditional Greek dishes by choosing from the many pots on the stove. (☎22430 28 642. Beef *stifado* €5. Open daily 8am-11pm.) **Mikalaras ❶** is past the church and along the waterfront; look for the sign reading "Cake shop special." This pastry connoisseur's paradise has perfected its recipes over 35 years, making five honey-drenched Greek desserts. The house specialty *galaktobouriko* (a syrupy custard and phyllo-layered dessert; €1.50) may be the sweetest, most amazing thing you've ever tasted. (☎22430 29 446. Open daily 8am-midnight.) **Navtikos Omilos Restaurant ❶,** to the left of the port police as you face inland, has good, simple food in large portions, a relaxing setting, and a view of the ocean. (☎22430 29 2339. Pork stewed in wine €5. Spaghetti Neapolitana €3. Open daily 8am-3pm and 6:30-11pm.)

NIGHTLIFE AND ENTERTAINMENT. Nightlife in Pothia is pretty tame; most folks enjoy a few drinks in the harbor bars and tavernas before heading to the clubs in Massouri. If you want to stick around Pothia, **Apothiki** is just past the town hall on the waterfront road. Though the sign reads "To Tzibaeri," locals know the place as Apothiki, Pothia's trendiest nighttime hangout. (Open daily 5pm-2am.)

For a calmer evening, catch a flick at **Cine Oasis,** at the end of a short alleyway off the waterfront, just before the church. Look for the glass displays listing show-times and current features. The building doubles as a community auditorium when it's not showing movies. (Tickets €5, children €4.)

SIGHTS AND BEACHES. The **Nautical Museum,** on the second floor of a building a few doors down from the town hall, explains the life and work of the island's sponge divers. Read plaques about the island's famous industry or ask the curator, a former diver, about the experience. (☎22430 51 361. Open M-F 8am-1:30pm, Sa-Su 10am-12:30pm. €1.50.) Follow the blue signs from Venizelou to the **Archaeological Museum of Kalymnos,** in the reconstructed former mansion of Kalymniot sponge barons of the past, Catherine and Nikolaos Vouvalis. (☎22430 23 113. Open Tu-Su 8am-2pm. Free.)

In Pothia there is a new, sandy **beach** just to the left of the port police. From the port police, take the roads to the left to reach the beach at **Therma,** only 1km out of town. Arthritic patients once came to the sanitarium to wade in its soothing **sulphur mineral baths,** but now that the springs' reputed medicinal value has diminished, a pleasant, crowded beach has replaced the baths as the main draw. A short walk around the bend leads to a quiet swimming spot. An inconvenient bus schedule keeps **Vlihadia beach,** 5km from Pothia and west of Therma, a tranquil locale. It has an organized **scuba diving** center where equipment and instruction are available and a **Sea World Museum** at the port, which has more sponge diving memorabilia and various underwater finds. (☎22430 50 662. Open daily 10am-10pm. €2.)

Grass, wildflowers, mandarins, limes, and grapes cover the **Vathis Valley** (5.5km northeast of Pothia), which begins at **Rina** village. There's no beach here, but you can swim from the pier. Within swimming range on the northern side of the inlet is **Daskalio,** a stalagmite cave. In Rina, the **Hotel Galini ❸** has decent rooms with baths and balconies. (☎22430 31 241; fax 22430 31 100. Doubles €25.)

WESTERN COAST OF KALYMNOS ☎22430

The road north from Pothia is lined with intermingling villages; **Hora**—Kalymnos's capital until the threat of piracy made seaside living too dangerous—is the first of these towns. Scattered churches line the road, including the **Church of Christ Jerusalem,** after the roundabout on the road to Argos, which was built by Byzantine emperor Arcadius after he survived a storm at sea. The half-domed stone blocks with carved inscriptions are from a 4th-century BC temple to Apollo that stood on the same site. The beachside footpath leads to a quiet **cove** with strange rock formations. Bring waterproof shoes and keep an eye out for sea urchins, often hidden on the undersides of ledges. **Rock climbing** is increasingly becoming a focal point of Kalymniot tourism efforts, especially after hosting a climbing convention in 2000. There are about 20 climbing areas located between Pothia and Emborios; the difficulty of the sectors ranges from 4c to 9a. Bring your own equipment, but be sure to contact the **Municipal Athletic Organization** (☎22430 51 601; www.kalymnos-isl.gr/climb) before heading out, as they can provide specific information on routes.

The village of **Kantouni,** home to a popular if slightly unremarkable **beach** south of Panormos, is accessible by the Plati Yialos bus from Skala. **Domus Restaurant and Bar ❷** is a nice place to sip a martini and watch the sunset. (☎22430 25 058 or 22430 47 760. Drinks €3.50. Restaurant open daily 7pm-1am; bar open 11am-4am.) Take a left from Kantouni beach and clamber over the rocks to find natural diving platforms of all heights. Another road from Panormos leads 2km to the sandy, flat, less crowded beach of **Plati Yialos. Pension Plati Yialos ❷** has rooms that overlook the coast from the cliffside. (☎22430 47 029. Doubles €25.)

The mere mention of **Massouri** lights up the faces of young Kalymniots with excitement; this beloved nighttime destination draws crowds from all over the island. With only one paved road running through Massouri, all the bars and clubs are within a 5min. walk of one another. Below and down a steep cliff stretches the quiet and serene Massouri **beach.** The last bus to Massouri is at 9pm; you can also grab a taxi (€7; €15 after midnight). **Nadir Rock Cafe** (☎697 4606 471), past the curve in the road from the bus stop, spins Greek and international hits and hosts two Happy Hours: one for draft beer (5-7pm) and one for cocktails (7-9pm). Next door is the new club **La Loca** (☎22430 47 047), which spins house and R&B within its sizzling red and orange interior. Closer to the bus stop and near the Hotel Plasa, **Lorenzo Music Cafe** is a nice place for a drink and to admire the brilliant sea. The owner runs a travel agency and knows a lot about the island. (☎697 213 4270. Open daily 9am-3am.) The cafe's terrace rather bizarrely overlooks the outdoor dance floor of **Dorian Tropical,** which is just below the cafe. (☎697 771 273. Open F-Sa.). **Cafe Del Mar** is another notable spot since it regularly features live DJs and has a dance club open on weekends. (☎22430 48018. Cafe open daily 8am-late). If you atypically arrive at Massouri during the daytime and have some emailing to do, the **Neon Internet C@fe** (☎22430 48 318) offers Internet access for €2 per 30min.

PATMOS Πατμος

Patmos has recently become a preferred destination for Greece's rich and famous, who keep mansions hidden from paparazzi among the cliffs behind Hora. The island has traditionally drawn a more pious crowd, eager to profess their devotion on this island dubbed the "Jerusalem of the Aegean" in a 5th-century inscription. Ancient Patmians worshipped the huntress goddess Artemis, said to have raised the island from the sea, but with the arrival of St. John, exiled from Ephesus in AD 95, Patmos became a center of fledgling Christianity. John purportedly wrote the Book of Revelations here, in a grotto overlooking the main town. In the 4th century, when Christianity spread with help from the Byzantine Empire, a basilica replaced the razed Temple of Artemis. In 1088 the fortified Monastery of St. John was built on a hill overlooking the entire island, and as part of the Ecumenical Patriarch of Constantinople, Patmos remains a crucial religious center today.

SKALA Σκαλα ☎22470

Built along a graceful arc of coastline, the colorful port town of Skala is mirrored in the water by a virtual city of yachts docked in the harbor. The town has been the island's main economic hub since the 16th century, and today administrative offices including the post office and customs bureau can be found here in an imposing Neoclassical building along the waterfront. Skala is the most convenient place to stay on Patmos, particularly if you plan to rely on bus transportation.

TRANSPORTATION

Ferries: Most are run by **DANE** (☎22470 31 314; fax 22470 31 685); **G.A. Ferries** (☎22470 31 217 or 22470 33 133; fax 22470 32 180); or **Blue Star** (☎22470 31 356). Tickets for all lines can be purchased at offices near the plateia; Blue Star tickets available at Apollon Travel. Ferries go to: **Agathonissi** (2hr., 3 per week, €6); **Kalymnos** (3hr., 2-3 per day, €8.70); **Kos** (4hr., 2-3 per day, €9.70); **Leros** (1hr., 2-3 per day, €5.50); **Lipsi** (1½hr., 4 per week, €4); **Mykonos** (2-3 per week, €12.50); **Nisyros** (3 per week, €10); **Piraeus** (10-12hr., daily, €16.60); **Rhodes** (8hr., daily, €10.30); **Samos** (3hr., 6 per week, €6); **Thessaloniki** (22hr., 1 per week, €37); **Tilos** (4 per week, €10.29).

Flying Dolphins: Daily to **Rhodes** (5hr., €35.67) via **Kos.** 2 per day to: **Kalymnos** (1½hr., €17.49); **Kos** (2hr., €19.51); **Leros** (50min., €11.10); **Lipsi** (20min., €8.32); **Samos** (1-2½hr., €12.60). 2 per week to: **Agathonissi** (1hr., €11.10); **Fourni** (1½hr., €12.18); **Ikaria** (1hr., €14.91).

Excursion boats: To **Lipsi, Fourni,** and **Ikaria;** prices posted by the waterfront.

Buses: Next to the Welcome Cafe at the ferry docks. To: **Grikos** (15-20min., 7 per day, €0.75); **Hora** (10min., 11 per day, €1); **Kampos** (20min., 4 per day, €0.75). Purchase tickets on bus.

Taxis: ☎22470 31 225. Congregate in main plateia 24hr. in summer, but can be difficult to catch elsewhere, especially during the post-disco flurry (3-6:30am). To Hora €3.

Car Rental: Rent A Car Patmos (☎/fax 22470 32 923 or 32 203). 2nd-fl. office can be found on the street just behind the building with the post office and police, next to the Art Cafe. Cars €35 per day and up. 10% discount when renting for a week or more. Open daily 8:30am-10pm.

Moped Rental: Widely available throughout Skala. **Express Moto** (☎22470 32 088), near Rent A Car Patmos offers new model vehicles (€6-10 per day). Open daily 8am-8pm. Bikes that can handle mountain roads are hard to come by. **Theo & Giorgio Motorbikes** (☎22470 32 066) offers a small selection, though not all are of reliable quality—be sure to check all the gears on a test run before signing any forms or heading up a mountain. Open daily 8am-7:30pm.

ORIENTATION AND PRACTICAL INFORMATION

Skala's amenities are all within a block or two of the waterfront. Excursion boats dock opposite the line of cafes and restaurants, while larger vessels park in front of the Italian-designed administrative building near the main plateia that houses the police, tourist office, and post office. Moving inland from this building, a street lined with shops and souvlaki stands leads to the OTE. Across from the Welcome Cafe by the main docks, a parallel road is lined with pensions; vehicle rental shops can also be found here. Skala is located on a narrow part of the island; you can walk from the water to Meloi beach on the opposite coast in about 15min.

Tourist Office: ☎22470 31 666. In the big Italian building across the dock. **Maps,** brochures, bus schedules, and help with accommodations. Ask for the free *Patmos Summertime Guide,* which includes maps of Skala and the island. Open daily 9am-9pm. **City Hall** (☎22470 31 235 or 31 058), in Hora, can also provide information. The **Welcome Cafe,** next to the dock, is open 24hr. and has luggage storage.

Tourist Agencies: All over the waterfront, though each offers info only for the ferry lines. Consult the tourist office or the port police for schedules, and then ask where to buy your ticket. **Apollon Travel** (☎22470 31 324 or 31 356; apollon@12net.gr) sells Flying Dolphin and Blue Star Ferry tickets, can help with accommodations and rentals, and is the local agent for **Olympic Airways.** Open daily 8am-8pm.

Banks: National Bank (☎22470 34 050 or 34 040), in the far end of the plateia. MC and V cash advances, **currency exchange,** and 24hr. **ATM.** Open M-Th 8am-2:30pm, F 8am-2pm. Currency exchange also available at **Apollon Agency.**

Police: ☎22470 31 303 or 31 571. Above the tourist office. Open 24hr.

Port Authority: ☎22470 34 131. To the left of the ferry dock, next to the snack bar. Information on ferries. Open 24hr.–knock loudly if it's late.

Hospital: ☎22470 31 211. On the main road to Hora, across from the monastery Apokalipsi (2km out of Skala). Open daily 8am-2pm. In an **emergency,** call the police–they know doctors' schedules and will contact them.

OTE: ☎22470 34 137. Follow the signs in the main plateia. Open M-F 7:30am-3:10pm.

Telephones: The **Welcome Cafe** at the ferry dock has an international phone.

Internet Access: The posh **Blue Bay Hotel,** just around the corner past the Welcome Cafe, has a sunny room with 3 terminals. €6 per hr. Open daily 8am-8pm. **Millennium Internet Cafe** (☎22470 29 300), past the OTE, has 4 terminals. €5 per hr., €2.50 min. Open daily 11am-10pm.

Post Office: ☎22470 31 316. In the main plateia, next to the police. Open M-F 8am-2pm. **Postal code:** 85500.

ACCOMMODATIONS

Domatia offered by locals who come to meet the boats will run €15-20 for singles and €20-30 for doubles. Vas. Giorgiou is lined with pensions but many nicer hotels can be found farther down the waterfront, about a 10min. walk away from the docks to the right when facing inland. **Pension Sydney ❷** is across from Pension Avgerinos, which shares management. The sparkly-eyed owner is too kind to be true. The spacious, airy rooms overlook the mountains. (☎22470 31 689. Singles €15-25; doubles €25-45.) Follow the waterfront road as it wraps along the port and up the hill to **Stefanos Flower Camping at Meloi ❶,** 1.5km northeast of Skala, 20m behind Meloi beach. Camping is to the left at the bottom—look for signs. Mini-market, snack bar, cooking and laundry facilities, clean showers, and shared fridges foster a sense of community. (☎22470 31 821 or 31 754. Scooter rental €6-15 per day. Sites €5 per person, €6 with tent.) From the docks, head along the port toward Meloi for about 10min.; past the electrical company, a sign points uphill to the left to **Pension Avgerinos ❸.** This jasmine-scented and family-run pension has clean, spacious rooms with balconies and fridges; half the rooms overlook the sea. (☎/fax 22470 32 118. Singles €18-33; doubles €20-44.) **Jason's Rooms ❸** are above Loukas Taverna, on the opposite side of the street from the OTE. Pale purple halls open onto cheery rooms. Some rooms with shared bath, most with balcony, all with fridge. (☎22470 31 832. Doubles €30-50; larger rooms available.)

FOOD

Seafood and pastries form the hallmark of Patmian cuisine and a number of excellent fish tavernas and sweet shops can be found crowded around the main plateia. Restaurants without set menus or with prices listed in pencil boast the freshest seafood. Don't settle if a plateia taverna looks suspiciously expensive; finding your

ON THE MENU

SWEET DEAL

Patmos is known for its excellent pastries, and the many sweet shops that line the main plateia in Skala are ready to prove this point with various honey-drizzled treats. While of course offering the standard favorites baklava (phyllo dough sandwiching layers of walnuts and honey), *kaitifi* (shredded wheat soaked in sweet syrup), and *galactobourico* (citrusy custard between phyllo layers), Patmian pastry chefs also bake a number of regional specialities that shouldn't be missed. *Galactobourico* reinvents itself here with a crunchier form, rolled rather than sandwiched. *Poughi* (wallets) are pockets of shortbread that are filled with almonds, walnuts, nutmeg, cinnamon, and of course honey. As the traditional cookie of Patmos, they are often wrapped in colored cellophane and delivered as gifts on weddings and christenings. *Kourabides* are made of a similar dough and come heaped with powdered sugar. Around Christmas, the cookies become ubiqutuous throughout Patmos, a popular gift, without the fruitcake stigma.

Another Patmian treat is the fried puff-pastry *diples*, a crunchy cylindrical roll that comes covered in all the usual delectable goo. Lastly, for a savory treat, try Patmos's particular take on tiropita, a tart cheese pie that contains a mixture of *misithira* (fresh goat cheese), *casseri* (a sweeter cheese), *regato* (similar to parmesan) and feta. Pastries (€0.70-1.20) are as easy on the wallet as they are on the tummy. There couldn't be a sweeter way to experience Patmos. Let the calorie counter roll.

way to a side street will more than likely reveal a similar menu with significantly lower prices. Numerous fruit markets and grocery stores satisfy hunger pains.

To Kyma (☎22470 31 192), near Meloi beach. The 2km walk from town makes for a pleasant evening stroll. Follow the waterfront road around the port and up the hill; when you start descending, look for the establishment. Persist in the same direction past a point you think reasonable; a large placard in the distance will eventually appear to vindicate your sense of navigation. Your reward is some of the freshest fish around—maybe fish you haven't even heard of. Fish €20-40 per kg. Open daily 6:30pm-2am. ❸

Koykoymabla (☎22470 32325). Walk past the Welcome Cafe; Koykoymabla is up a small street where the harbor curves. A necessary visit for coffee hounds bored by Greece's obsession with Nescafé. Escape the deleterious brew with imported Colombian, Kenyan, and Arabica roasts. A fresh sandwich of imported prosciutto, chorizo, or *manchego* (a Spanish cheese) complements your coffee. Dr. Seuss-like decor makes this a lively stopover for lunch. Double espresso €3. Open daily 8am-12:30am. ❷

Remezzo (☎22470 31 553), along the portside road to Meloi, but before the hill. Creative variations on Greek standards served on a porch overlooking the harbor. The house speciality, chicken with prunes and oranges (€8.50), and the tomatoes stuffed with cracked wheat, pine nuts, and raisins (€6) are good choices. The fluffy bread is baked on the premises. Open in high season daily noon-2am; low season 6pm-2am. ❷

Loukas Taverna (☎22470 32 515), next to Jason's Rooms and across from the OTE. The spit roaster out front cooks up gyros, chickens, and whole pigs. Pork marinated in mustard and wine sauce (€5) doesn't break the bank. Open 1:30-7pm. ❷

Yiayia (☎22470 33 226), along the waterfront past the Welcome Cafe, on the way to the Blue Bay Hotel. Noteworthy simply because it's an Indonesian restaurant in Greece. After a week of souvlaki, the beef *rendang* (€10.50) makes for a delicious treat. Elegant sandalwood decor appropriately complements the prissy English and Dutch clientele. Open M-Tu, Th-Su 7-11:30pm. ❸

ENTERTAINMENT

Perhaps in deference to the island's holy element, nightlife tends to be free of the rowdy excesses found most everywhere else. The increasing number of tourists, however, ensures a standard palette of cafes and discos. Packed in summer but pretty empty before 2am, **Koncolato** (☎22470 32 060; open daily 11:30pm-late), is popular with locals and travelers alike. Participate in the *sfinakia* (shot) tradition—line up at the bar and go bottoms up in unison. From the plateia, take the small footpath behind the post office to find **Art Cafe.** The chill downstairs bar serves respectable draft beer and spins Steely Dan. The sheltered roof garden enjoys a fantastic view of the sea. Pleasant and cozy, it caters to a slightly older crowd. (☎22470 33 092. Frappé €2; cocktails from €5. Open daily 9am-3am.) **Arion Cafe** (☎22470 31 595), on the waterfront, is an inevitable stop for the regular bar-hoppers; outdoor seating and an interior with a classic, pub feel contribute to the gregarious atmosphere. **Lampsi Club,** near Remezzo, is Patmos's best option for dancing. American faves play before 1am; Greek hits late-night. (☎22470 33 334. No cover. Drinks €5. Open daily 11pm-4am, until dawn on the weekends.)

DAYTRIP FROM SKALA: RURAL PATMOS

For the best sunset, check out **Chochlaka** at the end of the road with the Skala OTE. Follow the signs on the port side road to Meloi to get to **Aspiris Bay,** which commands fantastic views of Hora and Skala. **Meloi** itself is a pleasant 2km walk north from Skala and is the closest shore to the town. Large trees flank the back of the sandy beach making grilling in the sun optional. A bit farther north, **Agriolivado** has yet another sandy beach, an alternative to more congested **Kambos,** still a pleasant option for beach-goers traveling by bus. Its numerous hotels help pump in the tourists; the town itself has an inviting plateia and a few waterfront restaurants.

Just over the hill from Kambos, **Vagia beach** is a world apart—rocky, secluded, and serene. Go east along the road to Livadia, and follow the path down to an appealing, unmarked beach set against a small cliff. A bit farther east, cliff-lined **Livadia beach** has spectacular views of the string of islets just offshore. While bus service extends only as far as Kambos, hiking or biking to more secluded beaches provide you with solitude and peace. North of Kambos, the beach at **Lambi** is famed for its multicolored pebbles, which are rare (and growing rarer as tourists pocket them for souvenirs). The strong winds that assail this part of the island make swimming difficult.

HORA Χωρα ☎22470

The sleepy, sloping streets of Hora, lined with blinding, whitewashed walls, seem to absorb tourists without any disruption to their natural calm. Hora's streets are a maze, which hides sprawling gardens behind grand doors in the shelter of the monastery and makes precise directions impossible.

TRANSPORTATION AND PRACTICAL INFORMATION. Hora is 4km from **Skala,** a trip that you can tackle by **bus** (10min., 11 per day, €1), by **taxi** (€3), or by **foot,** although it's a steep hike. Hiking down might be a better option; it's easy to find your way by the footpaths and donkey paths which go slightly more directly than the main road does. The bus stops at the top of the hill outside the town, which is also the point of departure for buses from Hora to **Grikos.** The map of Patmos at kiosks and tourist shops comes with a questionable illustration of the town; you'll need to pick landmarks to find your way back to where you started. Take care of business before arriving, as a few card phones and a mailbox at the bottom of the hill are the only links between Hora and the outside world. From the bus and taxi station, both the monastery and main plateia can be reached by walking left and following signs.

FOOD AND NIGHTLIFE. Hora's restaurants and cafes share the spectacular view over the surrounding countryside and whitewashed town. Satiate your post-sightseeing hunger at the popular **Vangelis Restaurant** ❷ (☎22470 31 967). To reach it, follow the signs from the monastery, or ask a local to point you towards the central plateia. Tables in the back garden enjoy a fantastic view of the hills below. (☎22470 31 967. Moussaka €4. Entrees €4-6. Open daily 11am-2pm and 6-11pm.) **Cafe Stoa,** in the main plateia across from Vangelis, is the only bar in Hora proper. (Beer €3; cocktails €6. Open daily 5pm-2am.) **Pyrgos Music Bar** overlooks the harbor along the road to Skala. (Open daily noon-3am.)

SIGHTS. The turreted, 15m walls and imposing gateway of the **Monastery of St. John the Theologian** make it look more like a fortress than a place of worship. At the time of its founding by St. Christodoulos in 1088, the monastery was a constant target of pirate raids. A memorial to St. John, who visited the island in the first century AD, it was transformed into a citadel with battlements and watchtowers. The courtyard and maze-like passages are skylighted but completely closed to the outside, making them seem frozen in time. As you enter the courtyard, centered around the well of holy water, notice the 17th-century **frescoes** on the left that portray stories from *The Miracles and Travels of St. John the Evangelist*, written by John's disciple Prochoros. To the upper right, a fresco portrays St. John's duel of faith with a local priest of Apollo named Kynops; the saint threw the heathen into the water at Skala, where he froze into stone. Within its walls, the monastery holds ten chapels, which allow maximum prayer while respecting the Orthodox dictum limiting masses to one per day per altar. The **Chapel of the Virgin Mary** is covered with 12th-century frescoes, which were hidden behind the wall faces until 1956 tremors shook things up and exposed them. The excellent **treasury** museum guards numerous 12th-century icons, exemplary works of 11th-century Cretan art, a copy of St. Mark's Gospel, and a 7th-century Book of Job. Look for *Helkomenos*, an icon painted by Greek-born **El Greco,** near the end of the exhibit. (☎22470 31 223. Monastery and treasury open M, W, F-Sa 8am-1pm; Tu, T, Su 8am-1pm and 4-6pm. Treasury €6, students €3; monastery free. Modest dress required.)

Between Skala and the Monastery of St. John in Hora, the **Apocalypsis Monastery** is built on the site where St. John stayed while on Patmos. Two kilometers from both Skala and Hora, on the winding road that connects them, you'll find the large, white complex of interconnected buildings. Most people come here to see the **Sacred Grotto of the Revelation,** adjacent to the Church of St. Anne. Though the cave is natural, it is difficult even to tell that it is a cave anymore, as the chapel was built with the cave as its back wall. Silver tokens represent the prayers of supplicants. The cave is said to be where St. John dictated the Book of Revelation, the last book of the New Testament, after hearing the voice of God proclaim, "Now write what you see, what is to take place hereafter" (Rev. 1:19). Silver plating marks the spot upon which St. John is presumed to have rested his head; the crack in the wall was supposedly caused by the power of God's voice. (☎22470 31 234. Open M, W, F-Sa 8am-1pm; Tu, T, Su 8am-1pm and 4-6pm. Modest dress required.)

ASTYPALEA Αστυπαλια

Few travelers venture to butterfly-shaped Astypalea, the westernmost of the Dodecanese. Jagged hills and secluded orange and lemon groves make it a soothing place to unwind, but infrequent ferry service discourages outsiders almost as effectively as its fort once did. For those in need of tranquility, the island's undiscovered coves are worth the effort, planning, and patience required to reach them.

ASTYPALEA TOWN ☎22430

Surrounded by tawny hills, Astypalea Town is composed of Skala, also known as or Pera Yialos, by the port and Hora, at the top of the hill. This is the only major settlement on the island and all the services and amenities are found here.

TRANSPORTATION AND PRACTICAL INFORMATION. Flights from **Analypsis Airport** (☎22430 61 665) go to **Athens** (40min., €53.40.). The fickle **bus schedule** is chalked up where the waterfront meets the main road to Hora. **Buses** run as far as **Analipsi** and **Livadia** (€2.50) varying by season. **Ferries** go to: **Amorgos** (4hr., 1 per week, €9.40); **Donousa** (4hr., 1 per week, €11.40); **Kalymnos** (3hr., 2 per week, €8.50); **Kos** (3½hr., 2 per week, €10.25); **Naxos** (5½hr., 2 per week, €13.95); **Paros** (7hr., 2 per week, €18.55); **Piraeus** (10-13hr., 4 per week, €22.50); **Rhodes** (5hr., 2 per week, €16.76). The **police** are in a building just before the town beach. (☎22430 61 207. Open 8am-7pm.) The **port police** are in a white building with a Greek flag on the waterfront between the town and the port. (☎22430 61 208. Open 8am-10pm.) In an **emergency,** call ☎22430 61 544. For a **doctor,** dial ☎22430 61 222. The **National Bank** is under the Hotel Paradissos. (☎22430 61 224. Open M-Th 8am-2pm, F 8am-1:30pm.) There's a 24hr. **ATM** on the waterfront. A **tourist information center** (☎22430 61 412) operates Hora's town hall. **Astypalea Tours,** on the road to Hora, handles transportation, accommodations, and information questions, and is an **Olympic Airways** agent. (☎22430 61 571 or 61 572; fax 22430 61 328. Open daily 9am-2pm and 6-9pm.) The **OTE** is above the Maistrali Restaurant. (☎22430 61 212. Open M-F 7:30am-2pm.) Several **supermarkets** (open daily 9am-1pm and 5-9pm), and the **post office** (☎22430 61 223; open 7:30am-2pm), offering **currency exchange,** are in this part of town. **Postal code:** 85900.

ACCOMMODATIONS AND FOOD. The limited rooms on the island fill with the annual influx of summering Athenians, but vacancy is the norm the rest of the year. Bargain for rooms and **domatia** in the low season. **Mariakis Apartments ❸,** in the center of Hora, has rooms with telephones, fridges, and some TVs. (☎22430 61 413. Doubles €40.) **Camping Astypalea ❶,** 2.5km east of town, near Marmari, has similar rooms; a hip bar, self-service restaurant, mini-market, post, and exchange services are bonuses. Follow signs or take a bus toward Maltezana. (☎22430 61 338. €3.50 per person, €2.35 per tent.) A 10min. hike up the hill towards Hora will lead you to the elegant **Rooms Kaith ❹,** with balconies overlooking the azure bay. (☎22430 61 375. Doubles €45.) Restaurants cluster near the waterfront and on Hora's square. At waterside **Albatross ❷,** tapestries and a straw roof create a cozy atmosphere for a tasty assortment of Greek, Chinese, German, and Italian foods. (☎22430 61 546. *Souzoukakia* €5. Souvlaki €5.90. BBQ chicken €6.50.) With tables stunningly set on the beach below Albatross, **To Akrogiali ❹** serves a local Astypalean specialty, *astakomakaronada*, which combines fresh lobster with pasta (€44 per kg), and other daily catches from €24-35 per kg. (☎22430 61 863. Open daily 8am-2am.)

SIGHTS AND BEACHES. The **Archaeological Museum,** in Astypalea Town on the main road to Hora, just inland from the waterfront, houses a small, well-presented collection of artifacts unearthed from around the island, including stone inscriptions, early Christian sculptures, and Mycenaean grave finds. Before the castle, stop to see some of the better-preserved objects once held within the fortification. (Open M 5-7pm, Tu-Su 8am-2:30pm and 6pm-12:30am. Free.) In Hora, a striking row of windmills leads to a path up to the **kastro,** originally a line of defense built by the Knights of St. John; later, the Turks moved in, leaving the island's most significant architectural presence. Much of the structure remains intact. Exploring the chamber lets you gaze out across the island and nearby islets with a clear view. From early June through mid-September every summer, a series of multi-themed concerts is held as a part of the **Astypalea Festival** (tickets €10). Ask the tourist office for details concerning the festival, which is held at the kastro or inside the holy **Portaitissa Monastery,** to the right of the entrance to the fortress.

A 20min. hike southwest along the coast takes you to **Tzanaki beach,** an uncrowded refuge for nude bathers that's much better than **Livadia,** a beach closer to town. Four kilometers farther along a dirt path, the sand and palm trees at **Agios Konstantinos** make it the western island's best beach spot. Great beaches like **Ormos Kaminakia** and **Ormos Vatses** surround the southwestern part of the island past Tzamaki. From there, the hidden cave of **Spilia Negrou** is accessible by boat; it's worth the venture if you can convince a local fisherman to take you. A right turn after the sixth windmill in Hora begins a perilous 1hr. drive along a circuitous route leading past a military base to the monastery of **Agios Ioannis.** The monastery looks out over a small waterfall—perhaps the most charming sight on the island. Northeast of Astypalea Town, the main road leads toward the other "wing" of the butterfly-shaped island, passing the campsite and several sandy beaches.

KARPATHOS Καρπαθος

Ancient mythology claims the island of Karpathos was once home to the Titans, a clan of giants from which the complicated lineage of Greek gods originates. With one look, the gigantic, austere mountains that make up the Karpathian landscape make legend believable. Today the island is populated less by gods and more by portly, middle-class European couples who come to relax on Karpathos's stunning pale-green coastline and appreciate the slower pace of life. Indeed, tourism has been a major boon to the Karpathian economy over the last 50 years. Though many Karpathians fled to the United States after the Italian occupation during World War II destroyed many jobs, even more Greek-Americans now return during July and August to run family-owned restaurants and shops. While much of Pigadia concentrates a bit too hard on pleasing its wealthy European clientele, the rest of Karpathos has plenty to offer to the discerning backpacker with its preserved cultural traditions of the mountainous north and its hypnotically beautiful coves and beaches stretching along the southeastern part of the island. Karpathos makes the ideal one- or two-day stopover for hikers, beach bums, and anyone looking to enjoy some laid-back quality time with mother nature.

PIGADIA Πηγαδια ☎22450

The small but wealthy hub of Karpathos caters with ease to the whims of tourists and the desires of returning Greek-Americans. Stretched along a single graceful sweep of shoreline, Pigadia serves up an admirable summer night: excellent, inexpensive food, a few clubs loyally frequented by locals, and a sandy beach, perfect for the star-gazing couple, a few minutes' walk from town.

TRANSPORTATION

Ferries: To: **Kassos** (1½hr., 3 per week, €6.50); **Piraeus** (21hr., 4 per week, €28.20); **Rhodes** (5hr., 3 per week, €15.60). For other Dodecanese islands, Rhodes is the connection hub. **Chrisovalandou Lines** and **Karpathos 1** run daily excursions to **Olimpus** (leaves 8:30am, returns 6pm; €15 round-trip, €30 with guided tour). Schedules subject to significant variation; check ahead and book reservations at **Possi Travel,** or ask around near the docks.

Buses: 1 block up Dimokratias from the waterfront; across from the taxi stand and next to the supermarket. Buses don't run on a regular schedule until the end of June; check for a schedule at the bus stop. Serving most southern villages (€1-3). Tickets sold on board. No service Sundays or on local holidays. Buses to: **Aperi, Volada, Othos,** and **Piles** (3 per day); **Menetes, Arkasa,** and **Finiki** (2 per day); **Ammopi** (3 per day).

Taxis: ☎22450 22 705. Run 24hr., but are scarce from 2-7am (€5-15 to nearby villages). Government-regulated taxi prices are posted at the station on Dimokratias, across from the supermarket.

Rentals: Facing inland from the taxi stand, walk right 2 blocks to find **Moto Carpathos** (☎22450 22 382; www.motocarpathos.com). Fair and friendly service. Mopeds average €20 per day. Insurance included. International or EU driver's license required. Open 8am-1pm and 5-9pm. **Circle Rent A Car** (☎22450 22 690; fax 22450 23 289), 1 block past Moto Carpathos. Cars €35-45 per day, with 10% discount for 3 days' rental. Open 8am-12:30pm and 5-8:30pm.

ORIENTATION AND PRACTICAL INFORMATION

In Pigadia the streets have no name and are as confusing for locals as they are for tourists. Three main roads run parallel to one another. The first runs along the water and is lined with tavernas. The second extends one block up and inland from the dock, and has many shops, cafes, and rental locations. The police, post office, and some guest houses lie along the third. The taxi stand and bus station are on Dimokratias, one of the main streets that runs perpendicular to the others.

Tourist Agencies: Possi Travel and Holidays (☎22450 22 235 or 22 627; fax 22450 22 252), on the waterfront, sells ferry and plane tickets, books daily excursions, **exchanges currency,** offers bus and ferry schedules, and gives advice on accommodations and other tourist information. **Western Union** services also available here. Open M-Sa 8am-1pm and 5:30-8:30pm, Su 8-10am.

Banks: National Bank (☎22450 22 409), opposite Possi Travel, has **currency exchange** and an **ATM.** Open M-Th 8am-2:30pm, F 8am-2pm. **Agrodiki Bank,** by the police station, also has an **ATM.** Open M-Th 8am-2pm, F 8am-1:30pm.

Police: ☎22450 22 222; fax 22450 22 224. Take the 3rd street parallel to the coast, walking away from the ferry docks. Just past the post office. Open 24hr.

Port Police: ☎22450 22 227. Next to the ferry dock. Open 24hr.

Hospital: ☎22450 22 228. Take the 2nd road parallel to the waterfront straight ahead for 500m. The hospital will be on your left. English spoken. Open 24hr.

OTE: ☎22450 22 609. Uphill past the post office. Open M-F 7:30am-2:30pm.

Internet Access: Internet Cafe Potpourri (☎22450 23 709) is a short walk up the 2nd road from the seafront, at a 3-way intersection opposite Olympic Airways. Connect to the net over some crepes (€3) and Greek coffee (€1). Laid-back atmosphere replete with generic techno and hip hop. Internet €3 per hr. Open daily 7am-1am. **Enter Cafe** (☎22450 29 053), just uphill from the taxi stand. Doubles as a hip leisure lounge for younger locals, complete with pool table and coin-slot arcade games. Internet €4 per hr. Open daily 10am-2pm and 6pm-1am.

Post Office: ☎22450 22 219. Take the 3rd street from the coast uphill, away from the docks; it's on your left. Open M-F 7:30am-2pm. **Air Courier Services** available next door. **Postal code:** 85700.

ACCOMMODATIONS AND FOOD

Christina's Rooms ❷ have balconies overlooking the mountains, in addition to kitchens, TVs, and private baths. Free breakfast makes this an especially good deal. The owner occasionally cooks family-style meals for all his guests. (☎22450 22 045. Singles €15; doubles €30; triples €40.) From the bus station, walk up the stairs past the supermarket. **Elias Rooms for Rent ❸** are quiet but centrally located, with a beautiful, breezy terrace overlooking the gulf beyond. English-speaking Elias knows a lot about the island, especially about ways to save money. Ask about the traditional rooms with lofted beds. (☎22450 22 446; eliasrooms.tripod.com. Singles €20-25; doubles €25-30.) Facing inland at the bus station, turn right, and take the first left. Economical **Harry's Rooms to Rent ❷** have balconies, fridges, and shared baths. The kind owner tries to feed guests at every opportunity. (☎22450 22 188. Singles €12-16; doubles €15-20. Take a left on the stairs past Elias Rooms, then the first right to find **Rose's Studios and Rooms ❷**, which are clean but sparse and have shared bath with a simple living area. (rosesstudios@hotmail.com. Singles €15; upstairs double with great harbor view €25.)

A number of dinner options lie along the waterfront, but be sure to check out menus to avoid the ubiquitous tourist-traps. **The Life of Angels ❷**, a couple blocks past the National Bank, on the second road from the water, is one of the few restaurants in Pigadia whose culinary aesthetic has remained unaffected by the tourist hordes. Owner Zoe and her daughter serve up a mean Karpathian goat in wine sauce (€10). There's live Greek music and dancing on the weekends. (☎22450 22 984. Open daily 10am-2pm and 5pm-midnight.) **Taverna Romios ❷** is at the bend in the waterfront, near the Oxygen Club. Wreathing vines give this restaurant an earthy, natural feel. (☎22450 23 771. Stuffed souvlaki €9. Calamari €10). *Kaitifi* €2.50. Open daily 10am-1am.) **Ideal ❶**, between the waterfront National Bank and the church, has all the basics. (Gyros €1.50. Open daily 6-10:30pm.)

DODECANESE

NIGHTLIFE

Nightlife tends to pick up around 1:30am, after the waiters from the local tavernas and cafes close up shop and head to the clubs. Tropical-themed **Edem Music Cafe-Bar**, uphill from the post office, is packed by 10:30pm and spins rock, reggae, and the latest Greek hits as the background for matchmaking potential. (☎22450 23 681. Open nightly 7pm-1am.) **Oxygen Club**, on the waterfront road, hosts throngs of locals by 1am, dancing to the house and hip-hop grooves. (Cover €5, includes 1 drink. Drinks €2.50-6. Open until 3:30am on weeknights, F-Sa 6am+.) **Paradiso Club**, 2km out of town on the road heading to the airport, is *the* place to be for late-night grooving, hopping all day and night during the summer. Live music performed by Greek pop stars is an occasional treat. (☎22450 23 342. No cover. Shuttle available, call ☎22450 22 524 or 22450 23 847.)

OLIMPOS Ολυμπος ☎22450

Isolation and insularity define Olimpos, where living, centuries-old customs keep ethnographers and linguists in a tizzy. The inhabitants of two nearby villages founded Olimpos after an earthquake destroyed their homes; they chose the inaccessible location high in the mountains to avoid the raids of Arab pirates. Today visitors weave their way through tightly-packed white-and-blue houses adorned with plaster-sculpted angels, eagles, and Venetian lions. A row of 300-year-old windmills lines the mountain crest, and charming ceramic plates and hand-embroidered linens within the houses delight passersby. Though tourist interest

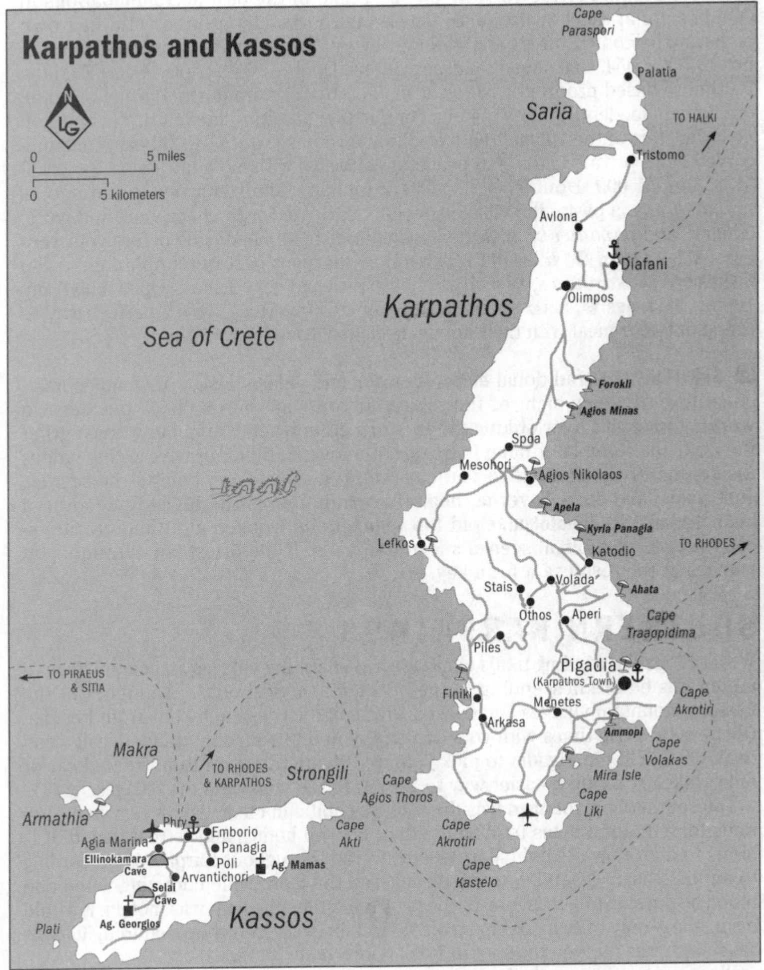

has led Olimpians to preserve and, in some cases, rekindle craft traditions, visitors should also be sensitive to the potentially disruptive effects that group tours can and do have on this close-knit community.

TRANSPORTATION AND PRACTICAL INFORMATION. Between Olimpos and **Diafani,** take a **taxi** or the small **bus** that leaves Diafani shortly after the boat from Pigadia arrives (bus fare is included in the excursion ticket). A dusty **hike** along the valley floor is another alternative if you have the time, energy, and drinking water—it's a long, hot, uphill trip. **Minas,** at the village mayor's office, is a great resource for grasping what the area has to offer. His perfect English, fascination with the Internet, and love for his hometown yield a lot of information for those interested in Olimpos or Karpathos.

ACCOMMODATIONS AND FOOD. Some of the best accommodations in Olimpos are at **Hotel Aphrodite ❸**, where big rooms, all outfitted with their own baths and balconies, offer breathtaking views of the ocean below. (☎22450 51 307; fax 22450 51 454. Call ahead for reservations. Doubles €35; triples €40.) Find the Baltimore-based proprietor Nikos at his nearby restaurant, the Parthenon Cafe; the homemade lentil soup wins big. **Pension Olympos ❷**, to the left of the bus stop near the start of the village, rents traditional rooms *(soufa)* with beautiful hand-carved beds, private baths, and peaceful balconies with mountain views. (☎22450 51 252 or 51 009. Doubles €25.) The attached, family-run restaurant serves *makarounes*, a pasta-like village specialty sprinkled with cheese, oil, and garlic (€3.50), and *papoutsaki*, a stuffed eggplant dish, all handmade before your very eyes. **Milos Tavern ❶** (☎22450 51 333; follow the signs past Hotel Aphrodite), also dishes out *makarounes*, as well as cheese pies and goat dishes. (Open daily 7am-10pm.) **Sinandes ❶**, across from Parthenonos Traverna, offers a perfect way to round out your meal with their honey-drenched, fried *loukoumades* (€3.50).

SIGHTS. The traditional culture, crafts, and village design of Olimpos itself constitute the main sight of the region. If you want more, check out the two working **windmills** overlooking the western cliffs where Olimpian women grind the flour that they later bake in huge, stone ovens. If you brave the tiny ladder inside one of the windmills, you can watch it whirl from behind the scenes. Just past Parthenos Taverna, near the windmills, is the lavishly decorated chapel **Kimisi tis Theotokou.** Gold foil blankets its wooden altar and centuries-old frescoes of biblical scenes adorn the walls. If the priest isn't around, you can ask at the restaurant for a key.

SOUTHERN KARPATHOS

West of Pigadia, winding roads climb toward charming villages and cloud-covered mountains before descending to the beach-laden west coast. A number of the island's mountain villages and coastal towns are accessible by bus from Pigadia. Check return trip times with your driver; if you find yourself stranded, call a cab (☎22450 22 705) in Pigadia to pick you up. Private transportation (rented car or motorbike) is another, easier way to get out to the coast and the villages.

The southern city of **Aperi** was the island's capital in medieval times, when Arab raids forced Karpathians to abandon their coastal homes and retreat inland. It is home to a *Panagia* (Virgin Mary) icon revered throughout Karpathos. According to an unpleasant legend, a monk discovered the icon while chopping wood and blood began spurting from one of the logs. Each time the icon was moved, it would disappear—only to reappear in an old church in Aperi. A bishop's church, **Koimisis Theotokou,** was built on the spot in 1886. (Open daily 8-11am.)

West of Aperi, a walk through **Piles,** with its enchanting narrow alleyways, leads to olive groves and charming tavernas that serve the town's famous honey. Two kilometers west of Piles, the road hits Karpathos's stunning west coast.

The wind-swept remains of five parallel Cyclopean walls mark the town of **Arkasa,** home also to the ruins of an ancient acropolis perched nearby on the cape of Paleokastro. Another noteworthy archaeological site at Arkasa, the mosaic floors of a 5th-century Christian basilica are preserved at the church of **Agia Sophia** on the shore. **Alpha Hotel ❷,** at the northern end, is one of the few hotels to accommodate solo travelers. (☎22450 61 352. Doubles €25.) South of Arkasa, campers can find shelter in a beach cove near sandy **Agios Nikolaos.**

North of Arkasa, the miniature fishing port of **Finiki** nowadays consists mostly of tourist amusements. **Dimitrios Fisherman's Taverna ❷** has earned local renown for its careful preparation of Dimitrios's daily catch. (☎22450 61 294 or 61 365.

Taverna open daily 7:30am-midnight.) The taverna also offers some of the town's few rooms. (Doubles €25. Open daily 7:30am-midnight.) Farther north the small beach town of **Lefkos** offers a gorgeous stretch of coast to those willing to trade sandy beaches for a rocky cove. Inland there is forested hiking terrain.

Karpathos is home to a number of gorgeous beaches, many of which can be found off the Pigadia Airport road. **Ammopi** is one of the finest, offering golden sands and rocky coves within minutes of each other and crystal-green waves throughout. Take a break from your beachside indolence for the rich and indulgent *dolmadazia* at **Calypso Restaurant ❶** (☎22450 81 037). At least three walking routes run from Pigadia to Ammopi; each takes about 1½hr. Head away from the ferry docks to the outskirts of Pigadia and take a left at the **7-11 Snack Bar ❶** (☎22450 22 885). A hike alongside the dusty but beautiful riverbed takes you to the main road. Take a right and walk the rest of the way to Ammopi or take a dirt road to find one of the less crowded but equally beautiful beaches. If you have transportation, the deep green-blue waves across from Mira Isle and the long coves between Cape Kastelo and Cape Akrotiri are also well worth a visit.

KASSOS Κασσος

Few landscapes better evoke Homeric times than the bare, rocky sprawl of Kassos. While the island offers little in the way of entertainment and sights, the five small villages dotting the arid countryside display peaceful charm to the wayward daytripper. A few remote beaches to the south and a couple of intriguing caves inland past Agia Marina make worthy destinations for an afternoon's hike.

PHRY Φρυ ☎22450

The small port town of Phry is a somewhat generic Greek village, but it's the biggest and best that Kassos has to offer. Because transportation to the town (and island) is difficult, it retains an untouched charm.

TRANSPORTATION. **Ferries** run to: **Agios Nikolaos,** Crete (4½hr., 3 per week, €14.20); **Karpathos** (1½hr., 3 per week, €6.50); **Piraeus** (17hr., 4 per week, €27.90); **Rhodes** (7hr., 3 per week, €18.50); **Sitia,** Crete (2½hr., 3 per week, €8.90). **Flights** go to and from **Karpathos** (6 per week, €22); **Piraeus** (6 per week, €83); **Rhodes** (5 per week, €33.50). There is **no island bus service,** so **taxis** are the most common way to get around. (☎6977 904 632 or 6945 427 308. €3-5 between villages.) **Rent A Moto,** on the main street, rents motorbikes. (☎22450 41 746. Mopeds from €12 per day. Open daily 9am-1pm and 3-8pm.)

ORIENTATION AND PRACTICAL INFORMATION. All of Kassos's tourist services are in Phry. Anglophonic Emmanuel at **Kassos Maritime and Tourist Agency** (☎22450 41 323, 41 495, or 22450 42 750; www.kassos-island.gr), behind the church in Pl. Iroön Kasou, provides maps, friendly advice, and timetables. The **Olympic Airways** office is next door. (☎22450 41 555; fax 22450 41 666. Open M-F 8am-3pm.) The **police station** is just a block inland. (☎22450 41 222. Open 24hr.) The **port police** are on the road to Emborio. (☎22450 41 288. Open 24hr.) The **Cooperative Bank of Dodecanese**, just behind O Milos taverna, offers **currency exchange** and cash withdrawal. (☎22450 42 730. Open M-F 8:30am-1:45pm). A conspicuous, blue 24hr. **ATM** sits in Pl. Iroön Kasou, just by the ferry docks. The small, two-doctor **hospital** is on Kriti, past the bus stop. (☎22450 41 333. Open M-F 8am-3pm.) The **OTE** is a few blocks inland. (Open M-F 7:30am-2:30pm.) Kassos has no public **Internet access;** try the OTE in a pinch or ask Emmanuel (see above). The **post office** is off Pl. Iroön Kasou. (☎22450 41 255. Open M-F 7:30am-2:30pm.) **Postal code:** 85800.

ACCOMMODATIONS AND FOOD. Beside in August Kassos's hotels usually have plenty of vacancies. **Anagenesis ❸**, in Pl. Iroön Kasou next to the travel agency and just to the left of the port, offers rooms with private baths, sea-view balconies, and English-speaking management; inquire at the travel agency. (☎22450 41 323, 41 495, or 22450 42 750; www.kassos-island.gr. Singles €25-32; doubles €32-42.) **Anesis ❸**, one street behind the travel agency, offers seven simple rooms with balconies and private baths; inquire at the supermarket below. (☎22450 41 234; fax 22450 41 730. Singles €25; doubles €30.) Rooms to let, advertised by signs along the main road toward Emborio and the villages, charge €15-20 for basic singles or doubles. Kassiot cuisine has received some attention for its traditional macaroni dishes, locally churned butter, and flavorful dandelion leaves *(roikio)*. During the high tourist season, George at **Zevrari ❷**, along the waterfront, cooks up the local specialities and even offers takeout if you call ahead. (☎22450 41 046. Open 9am-late.) **O Milos ❷** (☎22450 41 825) is the unavoidable restaurant/gossip hub of Phry, where fishermen gather to smoke, stare out at sea, and chomp down tasty moussaka. Ask about daily offerings. Classier **Apaggio ❷** serves up various pizzas (€6) in addition to the expected mixed seafood grill (€10-15) amid a sleek wooden decor. (☎22450 41 908. Open 8am-2pm and 6pm-2am.)

SIGHTS AND THE OUTDOORS. Leisurely excursions to the residential villages above Phry give insight into the island's agricultural life. The small cave of **Ellinokamara** makes an interesting destination for a hike through the arid countryside; start by following the road past the airport through the quaint, sleepy village of Agia Marina. Stay to your right whenever the road forks, until you eventually reach a small dirt road (stop and ask for directions along the way). After a 15min. walk you should see a small wooden gate on your left leading up the mountain; hike up between the double stone walls until you see the entrance to the cave appear over the wall on your right. Inside, mountain goats take refuge from the sun. To extend your journey, try hunting for the elusive cave of **Selai,** about 1.5km west, down the footpath beyond Ellinokamara. Wriggle on your belly to get inside and marvel at the stalactites and stalagmites of the cave's interior.

The defunct monastery of **Agios Giorgios** at Hadies commands magnificent views of the gorgeous **Helatros beach** below. The older families of the village of Phry still have cells at the monastery which they inhabit once a year for the festival of St. George; during the rest of the year visitors are welcome to spend the night.

From **Poli,** a 40min. hike to **Agios Mamas Monastery** (6km from Phry) brings you to scenic views of the southeastern coast. The boulders visible from the monastery are reputed to be the hulls of three ships, turned to stone by vengeful monks.

The tiny village of **Panagia** is notable for the showy homes left behind by Kassiot sea captains of old. Athenians and former Kassiots who summer here are gradually refurbishing these once-proud edifices.

SYMI Συμη

Pastel houses perch on the soaring hillside that overlooks Symi's main port, which has welcomed the incoming boats of sailors, fishermen, and sponge divers for thousands of years. Though Symi (like much of Greece) sank into poverty after the Italian and German occupations during World War II, spice exports and tourism have buoyed the economy. The beautiful, warm-toned colonial homes found in the three main villages of Yialos, Horio, and Pedhi, remind visitors of the island's golden years in the 18th century, when the *belles artes* flourished under special protection the ruling Ottomans granted islanders. Symi's steep, barren shores belie a healthful, buoyant quality hanging in the air, beckoning travelers looking to escape the bustle of city life. Most visitors who stop here en route from Rhodes to Kos understand why the expat population is growing—Symi's gorgeous coves and vibrant village life enchant. For the devout, Panormitis Monastery, on the southern side of the island, lingers as one of the most holy places in Greek Orthodoxy and remains an important point of pilgrimage for many residents of the Dodecanese.

SYMI TOWN ☎22460

Symi Town, the heart of the island's activity and where all public boats arrive, is divided into two sections: Yialos, the harbor area, and Horio, the charming, residential village perched on the hillside, up a daunting flight of 500 wide steps. The town was constructed in the Middle Ages as a fortification against pirate raids; trekking your way up to Horio under the hot Symian sun, you may come to appreciate the strengths of this particular urban planning tactic—luckily for you, there is an hourly bus.

TRANSPORTATION

Ferries: 2 per week to: **Astypalea** (€25); **Kalymnos** (€13); **Tilos** (€6.50). 1 per week to: **Kos** (€8.50); **Piraeus** (€33). M-Sa 1-3 per day to: **Rhodes** (€9). There are ferry ticket offices at the dock, just after the footbridge, and some on the next block; tickets are also available at the agents listed below. Updated timetables listed at www.symivisitor.com.

Hydrofoils: Daily hydrofoil to **Rhodes** (1hr., €12). The **Katamaran Dodekanissos Express** travels M and F to: **Kalymnos** (€28.80); **Kos** (€17.90); **Leros** (€34.70); and F to **Patmos.**

Excursion Boats: The boats **Poseidon** and **Triton** offer day-long round-trip tours (€28, including BBQ lunch) around the island that stop at Panormitis Monastery and a number of coves and beaches. Find them at the docks just beyond the footbridge.

Buses: A green van, aptly labelled **Symi Bus,** stops at Pl. Ikonomou, just past the traffic boom across the harbor from the ferry dock. Every hr., 8am-11pm, to: **Horio** (5min., €0.70) and **Pedhi** (10min., €0.70).

Taxis: Congregate just next to the bus stop on the eastern waterfront. The island's 6 taxis can also be reached individually; numbers available at travel agencies and posted at the taxi stand. A number of water taxis that serve the island's small beaches and coves can be found at the docks at Yialos or Pedhi.

ORIENTATION AND PRACTICAL INFORMATION

The main steps leading to Horio are tucked away behind To Vapori Bar and Kaledoukias Travel; from the ferry port, head into town over the wooden footbridge and take the last street going inland before the waterfront road curves. To reach Pedhi, a 30-40min. walk from Yialos, climb up to Horio and take the main road going down the other side.

Travel Agency: Symi Tours (☎22460 71 307 or 71 689; fax 22460 70 011; simi_tours@rho.forthnet.gr), a block inland from the gold shop on the waterfront. Sells tickets for G.A. Ferries, DANE Lines, and the Katamaran Express. Also books flights, handles **currency exchange,** and helps locate accommodations. Open 9am-1pm and 5-9pm. **Kaledoukias Travel** (☎22460 71 077; fax 22460 71 491), behind To Vapori, to the left of the steps to Horio, sells hydrofoil tickets, provides **currency exchange,** and arranges mountain walks. In emergencies, they may be able to arrange **cash advances** on credit cards. Open daily 9am-1pm and 5-9pm. **Sunny Land L.T.D.** (☎22460 71 320 or 6937 312 2447; fax 22460 71 413), to the left of the entrance steps to the church in Yialos, sells ferry tickets and provides helpful advice about the island. Open M-Sa 9am-2:30pm and 5:30-9pm, Su 10am-1pm and 6-8pm.

Banks: Alpha Bank, on the waterfront stretch as you head from the town toward the ferry docks. 24hr. **ATM,** though it may have trouble with some foreign cash cards–inquire at the bank. Open M-Th 8am-2:30pm, F 8am-2pm.

Police: ☎22460 71 111. Next to the Yialos clock tower, in a big white building on the waterfront. English spoken. Open 24hr.

Medical Center: ☎22460 71 290. To the back left of the church in Yialos, directly opposite Hotel Kokona. Open M-F 8am-1pm; after hours, call the police. The doctor in Horio can be reached at ☎22460 71 316. Urgent or life-threatening medical concerns are often handled in the hospital on Rhodes.

OTE: ☎22460 71 212. Inland along the back left side of the town square in Yialos, near the basketball court; follow signs from Neraida restaurant. Open M-F 7:30am-2pm.

Internet Access: Roloi (☎22460 71 597; roloisd@otenet.gr), over the footbridge, set back about 50m from the corner of the harbor. Electronica sets the mood for your surfing. Open daily 9am-2am. €4 per hr. **Vapori Bar** also has an Internet kiosk. €4 per hr.

Post Office: ☎22460 71 315. In the same building as the police, up the flight of stairs on the left. Open M-F 7:30am-1pm. **Postal code:** 85600.

ACCOMMODATIONS

Symi is not a cheap island—room rates reflect this reality. Accommodations tend to get classier and pricier as you ascend up toward Horio, but there are a couple more economical pensions to be found nearer the harbor. If a pension owner approaches you upon your arrival at the docks, be persistent with your haggling and marvel as prices drop as much as 50%. **Pension Agli ❸,** just past the steps to Horio, behind Symi's Burger, offers large suites, a steal for three people, with private baths, kitchenettes, and large fridges. Most suites come with shared bath and include laundry. If no one's around the owner, Chrissa, at the pharmacy. (☎22460 71 392 or 71 806. Singles €24; doubles €28-30; triples €35-45.) Manolis, the silver-haired owner of **Pension Titika ❷,** will likely meet you at the docks. Otherwise find him near the spice shop across from the footbridge; look for the "rooms to let" sign. Very small, economical rooms with private bath and A/C are the cheapest deal in town for singles. (☎2460 71 501. Singles €25; doubles €50; both prices quite negotiable.) **Hotel Kokona ❸** is over the footbridge to the left of the church tower. Light breezes blow the scent of lemons through the curtains. All rooms have baths, balconies, and A/C. (☎22460 71 549; fax 22460 72 620. Breakfast €5. Singles €30-35; doubles €35-42; triples €42-50.) **Hotel Maria ❸,** right next to Hotel Kokona, has six large doubles with private baths. Wood furniture and paintings create an intimate feel. (☎22460 71 311. Doubles €25-35.)

FOOD AND NIGHTLIFE

Like many island waterfronts, Symi's is lined with indistinguishable restaurants catering more to the tourist than the local palate. For more authentic options at reasonable prices, look in Horio and at the far ends of the waterfront along the harbor. Symian cuisine is renowned throughout the Dodecanese for its seafood preparation, particularly that of its delightful small shrimp. The smell of grilled fish is in the air at **Georgios's Taverna ❷,** at the top of the stairs to Horio, a family-owned taverna, which is one of Symi's best. (☎22460 71 984. Prawns €10. Entrees €7-11. Open daily 9am-4pm and 7pm-midnight.) Irrepressibly congenial owners preside over the Symian institution of **Meraklis Taverna ❷,** at the end of the road when walking inland from Symi Tours, which has served up delicious grilled seafood for 20 years. (☎22460 71 003. Entrees €6-10. Open daily 9am-2am.) To find

Milonos Restaurant ❷, take a left at Georgios's; it's on the road with the many parked cars. Inside an 18th-century windmill with classy terrace seating, Milonos features Mediterranean-inspired chicken and pasta dishes. (☎22460 71 871. Entrees €7-12.) Try the small Symi shrimp (€8) or the cook's specialty, stuffed vegetables if visiting **Tholos ❸,** at the far end of the small harbor to the right of the dock. (Entrees €7-12. Open 7-11:30pm.)

Nightlife in Symi tends to be bar oriented, but two clubs—the local favorite **Club Harani** and the newer **The Club**—cater to dancing impulses in July and August. **Jean and Tonic Pub,** in Horio, up the hill from Georgios's on your right, is a particularly popular hangout. Cheery expat owner Jean artfully converted the ancient walls of this 500-year-old building into a small but friendly late night hangout, where as many locals as foreigners come to sit under the pomegranate tree and enjoy polite conversation in a comfy setting. (☎22460 71 819; jeanmanship@hotmail.com. Happy Hour 9-10pm. Open 9pm-6am.) Cosmopolitan **Vapori Bar** keeps recent foreign language newspapers clothes-pinned to its blue chairs. By night, it attracts European leisure-class patrons. (☎22460 72 082; vapori@otenet.gr. Happy Hour 6:30-8:30pm. Frappé €2.50. Ouzo €2.50. Open daily 8am-late.)

SIGHTS AND BEACHES

At the top of the road to Horio, signs point toward the small **Archaeological and Folkloric Museum,** which displays labeled sculptures, relics, and icons. The folklore room holds costumes and utensils from Symi's past. The museum is housed in the **Chatziagapitos Mansion,** the former home of an old naval family, which also displays everyday objects owned by 19th- and early 20th-century Symiots. (☎22460 71 114. Open Tu-Su 8:30am-3pm. €2.) In Yialos, the **Naval Museum** floats in a yellow Neoclassical building beyond the waterfront strip. (☎22460 72 363. Open daily 10am-2:30pm. €2.) Signs also lead through a maze of streets to yet more ruins. Little remains within the walls of the **Castle of the Knights of St. John** aside from the **Church of the Virgin of the Castle.** If this isn't enough to fill your old ruins quota, follow the signs to **Pontikokastro,** a prehistoric mound near the windmills.

A number of small excursion boats function as a sort of water taxi service connecting Yialos, Pedhi, and several excellent coves and beaches. Look for signs by the small boats in the center of the Yialos harbor. **Agios Marina** is a small, charming island within swimming distance of the shore. **Agios Georgios** has deep, glassy waters and is set against a stunning 300m vertical cliff. **Agios Nikolaos,** a 30min. walk or €5 round-trip boat ride from Pedhi, is a beautiful half-sand and half-pebble beach. The tiny **Nos beach** is only a 10min. walk north along the waterfront from Yialos, past the shipyard. **Nanou** and **Marathounda** also deserve mention.

DAYTRIP FROM SYMI: PANORMITIS MONASTERY

Weekly tour boats running from Yialos include Panormitis on day-long trips around the island; daily tour boats from Rhodes stop here as well. A taxi ride costs over €20 (almost as much as the tour boat) and is only advisable for those very short on time. The steep and winding road to Panormitis has recently been resurfaced but still makes for a treacherous moped ride. By foot it's a rigorous full-day hike. Open daily 10am-3pm. Dress modestly; no bare shoulders or shorts. Free toilets are to the left of the complex. Entry to museums €2, under 12 free.

Panormitis Monastery, on the southern part of the island, is the secondmost important monastery in the Dodecanese (after the Monastery of St. John in Patmos). Dedicated to the Archangel Michael, the patron saint of sailors and travelers, Panormitis attracts hundreds of sailors throughout the islands for the feast day on November 8. Throughout the year, sailors come to the monastery to pay

HE LOCAL LEGEND

A CRUSHING DEFEAT

According to ancient mythology, he formation of Nisyros was the result of one of those heavenly skirmishes hat straddle the genres of epic and lapstick. The event supposedly took place during the momentous battle between the Olympians and the Titans, which resulted in the gods securing control of heaven over the giants. Poseidon, god of the sea, was ocked in combat with the Titan Polyvotis. After getting defeated in a hand-to-hand battle, the giant fled, racing across the Aegean looking for a place o hide. Poseidon, hot on the heels of he giant, eventually caught up with his adversary near Kos. Looking for a actic to delay his opponent, Poseidon smashed off a piece of Kos using his rident, hurling the resulting rock at Polyvotis. The giant has remained forever pinned under what we today call he island of Nisyros. The complaints of the trapped Titan explain the eruptions of the volcano—today a main crater is named after him.

One other thing the myth explains s the acute bond between Kos and Nisyros existing ever since ancient imes. Hellenistic-Era inscriptions explain how the two islands used to share a monarch, engage in joint military campaigns, and commit to the same confederations. Many Kosans ived on Nisyros and a colony of Nisyrans living on Kos went under the name "Nisyriadae." Today the island neighbors seem equally willing to share their tourists, hundreds of whom ravel the 13km from Kos to Nisyros every day to commiserate along with he giant's grumblings.

homage to the saint, and couples, hoping for child-bearing luck, come offering votives. Though the founding date of the monastery remains a mystery even to the monks, a number of the frescoes in the church date from the 1700s, when the affluent area entertained a flourishing fresco school. Other frescoes, currently being cleaned to remove centuries of oil-lamp soot, may date from much further back. The magnificent wooden altar screen was carved from a walnut tree; it displays a large image of St. Michael stepping on a dead man (which represents evil) and holding a small child in his left hand (which represents purity). The museums contain ecclesiastical relics, folk exhibits, and displays of silver tokens, beaten into shapes that represent different prayers, which were left by supplicants. If the doors are locked, head up the stairs and ask a monk if you can take a peek. The monastery will also supposedly let visitors spend the night in one of the many empty cells, if you happen to find yourself stranded without a return trip in sight.

NISYROS Νισυρος

Most visitors to Nisyros come to walk among the sulfur crystals and escaping steam of its active volcano. The year-round residents of this tiny island number only 800; the total population of the two villages perched above the volcano craters drops to about 40 in the winter. Because daytripping tourists to Nisyros move in predictable cycles from the dock of Mandraki, to the volcano to the waterfront tavernas, and back to the dock again, the rest of the island remains a quiet and peaceful place to unwind. The surreal sand and stone beaches, black with volcanic rock, is best enjoyed in relative solitude.

MANDRAKI Μανδρακι ☎22420

The calm, leisurely rhythms of life in Mandraki are hardly upset by the hordes of volcano-minded tourists who arrive on their daily voyages from Kos. Beyond the harbor the winding, stone-paved streets and handsome views make the city a pleasant stopover.

TRANSPORTATION

Ferries: DANE Sea Lines has an office at **Diakomichalis Travel,** where you can purchase ferry and hydrofoil tickets; follow the main road 50m to the right, past the bank. Open 9am-1pm and 6-8pm. To: **Kalymnos; Kas-**

tellorizo (1 per week, €9); **Kos** (4 per week, €5); **Leros** (2 per week, €10); **Patmos** (2 per week, €12.50); **Piraeus** (2 per week, €26.50); **Rhodes** (4 per week, €9.50); **Symi** (3 per week, €8); **Tilos** (3 per week, €5).

Highspeed Boats: Though there are no hydrofoils leaving from Nisyros, the high-powered boats including the **Katamaran Dodekanissos Express** run to: **Kardemena** (daily); **Kos Town** (daily); **Piraeus** (daily); **Rhodes** (3 per week, €20); **Tilos** (3 per week, €10).

Excursion Boats: Daily commercial boat to the town of **Kardamena,** Kos (7am, €6).

Buses: After school wraps up in mid-June, the school bus starts making regular rounds through the villages, leaving from Mandraki harbor 6 times a day. To: **Emporio** (20min.); **Loutra** (4min.); **Nikea** (25min.); **Pali** (10min.); the **volcano** (30min., 2 per day); **White beach** (10min.). A number of daily excursion buses to the **volcano** run when the boats from Kos arrives, usually 10am-noon. €7 round-trip, includes volcano entry. Enetikon and Nisyrian Travel both have "volcano bus" stands at the docks where you can purchase tickets.

Taxis: From Mandraki, **Babis's** (☎22420 31 460). To Loutra and the White beach €2-3; Lies beach €10; volcano €20. From Nikea, **Irini's** (☎22420 31 474).

Moped Rentals: John and John (☎22420 31 670 or 31 630). Scooters €15 per day and up.

DODECANESE

ORIENTATION AND PRACTICAL INFORMATION

The main road in Mandraki follows the waterfront (to your right as you face inland from the port) until it forks at the town's only bank. To the right, the road continues along the waterfront, leading to stairs that ascend to the monastery and beyond them a small stony beach. To the left the road takes you inland to **Pl. Ilikiomeni** ("Old Woman Square"), a cobbled plateia nearly overwhelmed by the fikas tree growing in its center.

Travel Agency: Nisyrian Travel (☎22420 31 411; fax 22420 31 610), to the left of the ferry dock. Arranges excursions, walks, accommodations, packaged "Greek Evenings" with food and dancing (€15), and special boat trips around the island (€10). Open daily 9am-9pm. **Enetikon Travel** (☎22420 31 180; fax 22420 31 168), is on the right side of the road leading into town from the docks. Tickets, hotel reservations, bus and boat tours, and **currency exchange.** Multilingual staff. Open daily 9:30am-12:30pm and 6:30-9pm.

Banks: The **Co-op Bank of the Dodecanese** (☎22420 48 900; fax 22420 48 902), located on the waterfront road; take a right from the dock. It's the only bank on the island. **Currency exchange** available M-F 9am-2pm. Cash advance MC and Visa available. Bring cash because there is **no ATM** on Nisyros.

Port Authority: ☎22420 31 222. In a white building near the dock. Open 24hr.

Police: ☎22420 31 201. In the same white building as the Port Authority. Open 24hr.

Post Office: ☎22420 31 249. In the same white building. Open M-F 7:30am-3pm. **Postal code:** 85303.

ACCOMMODATIONS AND FOOD

Rooms can be scarce in Mandraki, especially during the August 15 Festival of the Panagia, so calling ahead is advisable. The **Three Brothers Hotel ❸,** right next to the ferry dock, is one of Mandraki's best. Its breezy lounge overlooks the harbor; it's a great place to meet other guests over breakfast or hang with the charismatic brothers themselves, who can often be found there playing *tavli* in the evening. Bright, airy rooms come with clean, private bathrooms and balconies. (☎22420 31 344; fax 22420 31 640. Singles €20-30; doubles €23-36; quads with kitchens €30-

THE HIDDEN DEAL

FACTORY FOOD

If walking past the schnitzel- and ɔurger-toting cafes of Mandraki's vaterfront has you convinced your dining options couldn't look bleaker, ıead toward **I Fabrika** (the factory). 'his little gem, buried in a brightly-lit ɔasement off a side street near the vilage square, serves up tasty, cheap, ınd uncompromisingly authentic *nezedes* and features a number of dishes that are challenging to find ɪlsewhere on the island. *Boukounies* €5.50), for example, is a traditional Nisyrian dish made of pork pieces rendered delicious when cooked in their ɔwn tallow. Herbivores should fear not; young, 20-something owner Eleana is ıerself a vegetarian and spices up the nenu with a number of meatless dishes that will make accompanying neat-eaters think twice: *tiganopsomo* €4) is a fried Greek pastry that comes stuffed with feta, tomato, peppers, ınd olives. *Pitia* (€3), fried chickpea ɔalls similar to falafel, is another classic. All *mezedes* are served on their ɔwn, blessedly free from the greasy ıccompaniment of ubiquitous french ries.

Because I Fabrika stays open late, he cafe functions as much as a chill ıangout for the town's artsy/intellecual types as it does as a restaurant. 'isitors guzzle down *Mythos* beer (€3) n good Nisyrian company and enjoy he hoppin' Greek folk tunes spinning n the background.

Walk inland from the plateia; take he 1st right onto a small street. I Fabika is about 20m ahead on your right sign reads Η Φαμπρικα). ☎22420 31 552. Open 8pm-4am. ❷

60.) **Hotel Romantzo ❷,** a longstanding rival of the Three Brothers, lies just across the street. Its upstairs terrace has amazing views of the sea. Quiet rooms have private bath, fridge, and A/C (€4 extra). If you're planning a longer stay, ask about the house on the hill (€35) for two. (☎/fax 22420 31 340. Singles €15; doubles €20; triples €35; all prices rise slightly in high season.) **Volcano Studios ❷,** on the main road along the waterfront, above the Volcano Cafe, has basic rooms with fridges and private baths. (☎22420 31 680 or 31 340. Singles €15-20; doubles €20-30.)

Awesome cooks abound in Mandraki, but the tourist cafes on the waterfront are not the place to find them. Head to **I Fabrika** (see **Factory Food,** p. 560) for mouth-watering island specialities. Mandraki's best seafood may be at **Restaurant Kleanthis ❷,** far down along the waterfront, which prepares appetizing *mezedes* and shellfish entrees. (☎22420 31 484. Octopus in vinegar €4.50. Open 10am-midnight.) Check the kitchen at **Ilikomeni Irini ❶,** in the plateia, to find an array of home-cooked Greek dishes (lamb and fish are the specialities). Grab a table under the fikas tree and overhear some local gossip. (☎22420 31 365. Entrees €4-5. Open daily 9am-late.) At **Cafe Fikas ❶,** next door, enjoy a cold *soumada* (€1.20), a sweet Nisyrian drink made from almonds. (☎22420 31 215. Open daily 6am-1am.)

DAYTRIPS FROM MANDRAKI

MANDRAKI VOLCANO. Plug your nose and head into the bowels of Mandraki's enormous **Stefanos Crater,** where steam hisses from small crevices still bubbling with smoldering, viscous fluid. Yellow traces of sulfur crystals can be seen throughout the cracked, chalk-white earth. Aspiring geologists (or pyromaniacs) will want as close a look as possible, though visitors should take some caution considering the earth here is delicate and has opened underfoot before. The volcano last erupted in 1872 and is slated for another go in about eighty years. A 10min. walk along the trail behind the snack bar leads to nearby **Polyvotis and Alexandros craters,** virtually unvisited but no less spectacular. It is possible to hike back to Mandraki from here with detailed directions from someone who knows the trails; ask for information at the travel agencies. *(Entrance €1. Municipal bus from Mandraki (30min., 2 per day, €3 round-trip) stays 45min. at the sight before returning. Excursion buses also leave regularly from the harbor; €7 includes admission.)*

MONASTERY OF OUR LADY SPILLANI. At the far end of town from the docks, a twisted stone staircase leads up a cliff past tiny cells, once used to house anti-Turkish artillery, carved into the rockface. Perched at the top of the cliff is a quaint, whitewashed church dating from the 17th century, which affords sweeping views of the sea below. An altar boy recently discovered the iconographer's hidden portrait of St. Nikolaos on the rear face of the icon, which had been covered with an old cloth for over two centuries. For a closer look at the votives, check out the monastery **museum** at the bottom of the staircase. *(Monastery open 9am-3pm. Donations welcome. Museum open daily 10am-3pm. €3.)*

BEACHES. Because the stony beach in town is small, jumping from the sidewalk near where the yachts dock into the sea is a more convenient option for swimming. The black pebble beach of **Hohlaki** is a short walk from the monastery stairs along a coastal footpath. **White beach,** on the road to Pali just past Loutra, is also almost entirely black despite its name: in reality white dust from nearby pumice quarries once gave the beach a pale top layer, but now that the quarries are inactive, the beach's natural dark color has returned. **Lies beach,** 3km east of Pali, is the island's most optimal sunning spot. If there is sufficient demand, Enetikon and Nisyrian Travel run boats (€7.50 round-trip) to the beaches of **Yali,** a small island nearby. Otherwise the boat which ferries workers to Yali's quarries accepts the occasional tourist passenger. *(Leaves 7am; returns 4pm. Inquire at the tourist office.)*

DODECANESE

LEROS Λερος

Tourist brochures on Leros optimistically bill it "the best island;" whether or not you agree with that assertion, narrow, windy Leros does possess sedate charms. After Leros was reunited with the rest of Greece in 1948, the new government chose the island as a site for mental hospitals. When an exposé of the institutions' poor treatment of patients made travelers reluctant to come to the island, the hospitals were drastically reformed and improved. The silent waterfront of Agia Marina and the deserted streets of Lakki do eerily resemble a sanitarium, though the beaches of Leros thankfully emanate a more welcoming kind of hospitality. Leros is best used for a day's recovery en route to its Dodecanese neighbors.

AGIA MARINA Αγια Μαρινα ☎22470

The wind never stops blowing in Agia Marina's harbor; napkins and receipts from the colorful waterfront cafes can be seen merrily taking to the sky, floating out above the choppy, purple waves and the yellow fishing nets heaped along the docks. The stunning sea makes for a perfect venue to relax on the pebbly beach, but fighting the crashing waves for a swim might be a little rocky.

TRANSPORTATION AND PRACTICAL INFORMATION. The town supplies most administrative and commercial services, including the island's only **Flying Dolphin** service from Agia Marina to: **Kalymnos, Kos, Lipsi, Patmos, Piraeus,** and **Rhodes;** connections to **Agathonissi, Fourni, Ikaria,** and **Samos are** also available during high season. Waterfront **Kastis Travel & Shipping Agency,** near the dock, is extremely useful for **currency exchange,** organizing excursions, and ferry tickets. (☎22470 22 140 or 22470 23 500; www.kastis.gr. Open daily 8am-9pm; may be closed in the afternoon in the early summer.) An **Agricultural Bank** stands by the cafes in the port. (Open M-Th 8am-2pm, F 8am-1:30pm.) **Emboriki Trade Bank** with a 24hr. **ATM** is on the Flying Dolphin pier. The 24hr. **police station** (☎22470 22 222) and **moped rental shops** sit along the waterfront. The **OTE** (☎22470 22 899 or 22 099; fax 22470 25 549) and **post office** (☎22470 22 929) are in the same building along the road to Platanos's plateia, uphill past Kastis Travel. **Postal code:** 85400.

ACCOMMODATIONS AND FOOD. Rooms are a bit hard to find in Agia Marina, but a mere 20min. walk gets you to Panteli on the opposite coast and a 10min. walk to Platanos; the three towns form a saddle over a very narrow segment of the island. To reach **Agia Marina Rooms ❸** and its sunny, verdant courtyard, take a left at Kastis Travel and then another left after 30m; the pension is the first house on the left. The friendly owner speaks little English, but he can recommend other pensions in Agia Marina when his is full. Spacious, homey rooms include large bath, kitchen, and balcony. (☎22470 25 091. Doubles €30; price lower for longer stays.) The **pension ❷,** above Tou Kapaniri taverna, along the waterfront past the Agricultural Bank, has one wall flush with the wind-tossed sea; watching the water from the rooms' balconies is like standing on the deck of a ship. Spacious rooms have fridges and baths. (Doubles €18 and up.)

Agia Marina's numerous hip waterfront cafes provide plentiful outdoor seating, ideal for milkshake-sipping and people-watching. **O Neromilos ❸** is about 150m removed from this scene, just behind the windmill to your right as you face inland. The shallow green-blue water laps at the purple walls of its terrace, which enjoys a hypnotically serene view of the sea, Agia Marina, and the castle above. *Bekri meze* (€5.50), a traditional dish of pork pieces stewed in spicy tomato sauce, makes for an interesting meal. (Prawn house specialty €10.30. Entrees €9-15. Open 11am-midnight). The smell emanating from **Ta Kroupia ❶,** across from the taxi stand is irresistible; the souvlaki and kebabs cooked up on its open grill are delicious and cheap. (☎22470 24 204. Chicken souvlaki €1.30.)

NIGHTLIFE. When the moon rises, Agia Marina becomes suprisingly lively—bordering on naughty. **Apothiki,** the first building on the pier when coming from the hydrofoil dock, is so packed in the summer that there's barely room to move to the dance hits. (☎22470 24 654. Open daily 11pm-dawn.) **Apocalypsi,** two doors down from Kastis Travel, plays funk, soul, and jazz. (☎22470 23 506. Open daily 10pm-3am.) **Enallatiko,** right across from the dock, plays English-language hits. It's a popular early-evening hangout. **Internet** access (€3 per hr.) is available on coin-operated machines. (☎22470 25 746. Amstel €2. Open daily 8am-1:30am.)

LAKKI Λακκι ☎22470

Expressionless waterfront buildings and broad, silent avenues make the port town of Lakki an uninviting introduction to the island for those who happen to come here first. None of the residents seem quite sure what to do with the despondent, Italian Neoclassical facades that stare out at the water. The harbor is the largest in the eastern Mediterranean and may rival the actual settlement in terms of activity and interest. The closest beach to Lakki is under 1km west in **Koulouki,** which makes for a scenic coastal walk. It's a good idea to get away to more inviting destinations; a taxi (€4) can dash you to **Agia Marina.** (Lakki ☎22470 22 550; Platmos ☎22470 23 070; Agia Marina ☎22470 23 340.)

Ferries run daily to: **Kalymnos** (€6.80); **Kos** (€7.30); **Rhodes** (€16.70). Five to six per week serve **Patmos** (€5.70) and **Piraeus** (€22.90). From Kos and Patmos you can find more comprehensive ferry service. Virtually all tourist services are on or just inland from the waterfront. Walking along the waterfront from the docks brings you first to an intersection with a large abandoned building on the corner; up this street is **Rent A Car Leros** (☎22470 22 330), which rents motorbikes (€7.50 per day) and bicycles (€3). Farther along the waterfront you will meet another intersection with a cinema on the corner. A block up is a roundabout from which a major island road runs perpendicular. The **taxi stand** (☎22470 22 500) is here.

Leros Travel, on the waterfront across from the taxi stand, sells tickets for **G.A. Ferries** and the **Katamaran Dodecanese Express,** while offering helpful advice on tourism. (☎22470 24 000; fax 22470 22 154. Open daily 8:30am-1pm and 5-8:30pm.) Next door, **Kastis Travel and Shipping,** Vas. Giorgiou 9, represents the **DANE Sea Line** ferries. (☎22470 22 500 or 22 872. Open daily 8:30am-9pm.) A block inland from the cinema, **Aegean Travel** represents **Blue Star** boats. (Open daily 10am-12:30pm and 6-8:30pm.) An **Alpha Bank** with a 24hr. **ATM** sits near the taxi stand. (☎22470 26 011; fax 22470 26 014. Open M-Th 8am-2:30pm, F 8am-2pm.) A **National Bank,** back along the waterfront closer to the docks, also has an **ATM.** (Open M-Th 8am-2:30pm, F 8am-2pm.) The **police** are located next to the taxi stand. (☎22470 22 222. Open 24hr.) Back toward the docks, head inland and take your first right to find the **port police.** (☎22470 22 224. Open 24hr.) Inland another 200m is the **hospital** (☎22470 23 552). There's a **pharmacy** a couple blocks past the Hotel Miramare walking away from the docks. (☎22470 24 123. Open daily 8am-2pm and 5-9pm.) Back toward the docks is **Bilies Internet Cafe,** one of few legitimately cool places, equipped with pool tables, bar, lounge seating, **Internet** (€4 per hr.), and even Playstation 2. (☎22470 28 040. Open daily 8am-2am). The **post office** is next to Rent A Car Leros. (☎22470 22 587. Open daily 8:15am-1pm.) **Postal code:** 85400. Should ferry schedules necessitate an overnight stay, **Hotel Miramare ❷,** a block inland from the docks (look for the large sign on the balcony), has rooms with balconies, fridges, baths, and TVs. (☎22470 22 469; fax 22470 22 053. Doubles €26.)

PANDELI Πανδελι ☎22470

Pandeli, a 20min. walk or short taxi ride (€2) south of Agia Marina, is a tiny fishing village built along a gorgeous stretch of pebbled beach, where the placid green sea doesn't make waves but meditatively folds over itself. Tavernas are built just yards from the water, making an after-meal swim as easy as it is tempting. Like Agia Marina, Pandeli shares most tourist and municipal facilities with Platanos, a 10min. walk up the hill; there's nothing here but a few pensions, a sprinkling of tavernas, a mini-mart, and of course the locals' houses. **Psaropoula ❷** (☎22470 25 200), the first taverna along the water, sells excellent fresh fish and traditional favorites with a smile; tables are set up by the water in the evening. (Entrees €4-7. Open noon-late.) Pandeli is an infinitely more attractive place to stay than Lakki. If you choose to put your bags down here, **Kavos Rooms to Rent ❸,** just to the right of Savana Bar when facing the sea, has pleasant doubles overlooking the harbor, with private bath and fridge. (☎22470 23 247; fax 22470 25 020. Rooms €32-40; discount for multiple nights.) **Savana Bar,** at the far left end of the harbor as you face the sea, offers a shady, pebbled veranda and good filter coffee right by the docks. **Pandeli beach** is better for swimming than the beach in Agia Marina since the wind is much friendly on this side of the island. **Vromolithos beach,** a short walk to your right (facing the harbor), offers a golden, sandy alternative to Pandeli's pebbles.

CRETE Κρητη

Crete awes with its sheer geographic diversity, which seems to span a continent rather than a mere island of 8500 sq. km: indigenous palm tree forests collide with precipitous mountains; sheltered aquamarine coves lie alongside stepped vineyards; and windmill-strewn plains rest only minutes from dramatic gorges. Yet the diversity of the region is cultural as much it is as environmental; the circumscribing mountain ranges have preserved rural ways of life that seem utterly removed from the bustling capital cities and frenetic tourist towns that cluster along the coast. Influenced by everyone from nearby Egyptians and Phoenicians to invading Turks, Venetians, and Germans, the island is a unique fusion of Eastern, African, Mediterranean and European tastes. The island's tumultuous history is reflected in the island's conglomerate architecture: rambling remains of ancient palaces sit cheek by jowl with Ottoman Mosques and Venetian arsenals.

HIGHLIGHTS OF CRETE

DIZZY YOUR MIND by clambering through the labyrinthine leftovers at Minoan palaces at Knossos (p. 591) and Phaistos (p. 597).

OGLE endangered gryphon vultures and golden eagles as they soar above steep Samaria Gorge (p. 573).

CREEP through the rickety Venetian lighthouse to discover Hania's spectacular inner harbor shimmering on the other side (p. 565).

DANGLE YOUR TOES over the Libyan Sea from cave-riddled cliffs at Matala (p. 596).

DARE to pass through Dante's Gate to explore the ghost town of Spinalonga (p. 608), the last leper colony to close in Europe.

CRETE

The seeds of civilization sprout from the island, in the countless ruins that predate Hellenic culture and attest to the advancement of Minoan society. Records of Cretan life reach back to 6000 BC, when Neolithic inhabitants dwelled in open settlements and placed terracotta statuettes on mountaintops to honor their deities. When settlers arrived from Asia Minor around 3000 BC, they forged a civilization that would distinguish Greece, the Mediterranean, and all of Europe.

GETTING THERE. Olympic Airways (☎210 966 6666) and **Aegean/Cronus Airlines** (☎210 998 8300) run cheap, fast domestic flights from Athens to **Sitia** in the east, central **Iraklion,** and **Hania** in the west. Consult the **Practical Information** section of your destination for more information on flights. Most travelers take the **ferry** from Athens (p. 84) to Crete, landing in Iraklion, Hania, Sitia, or occasionally Rethymno or Agios Nikolaos. Boats run frequently during the summer, but often irregularly. Larger boats run more often and dependably. All prices listed are for deck-class accommodations; bring a sleeping bag to snooze on the deck.

Catastrophes—earthquakes, a tidal wave from an enormous volcanic eruption on Santorini, and Mycenaean invasions—plagued Minoan society; three times, the Minoans rebuilt from the ground up. Distinct artistic styles accompanied each rebuilding period. In the 8th century BC, the Dorians occupied the island, followed shortly by Conquering Romans, who set up camp only to find it an unstable aristocratic hangout rife with inter-city quarreling. Next Crete fell under rickety Byzantine rule, allowing for the construction of countless Byzantine churches before Arabs conquered Crete in 827. The Byzantines eventually regained the island but lost it again to Frankish crusaders in 1204. When sold to the Venetian Empire, Crete became a commercial hub. Trade developed a middle class, dominated by Venetian nobles and local merchants. From the late 17th century until Prince George's liberation of the island in 1898, Crete was Ottoman turf. After the Balkan Wars before World War I, Crete joined the Greek state. During World War II, the island combatted German occupation with strong guerrilla resistance; the period is regarded with pride.

Today Crete is divided into four main prefectures: Hania, Rethymno, Iraklion, and Lasithi. The laundry list of past invasions does little to convey the ultimate unified feel of the island. According to a Greek saying, a Cretan's first loyalty is to his island, his second to his country. The insular Cretan mentality—shaped by centuries of bitter resistance to relentless invasion—causes its people to view even their fellow Greeks as foreigners. Still, Crete is something even Kazantzakis himself, with his inspiring prose, cannot capture; the relaxed pace of island life, the strong sense of identity, the overwhelming hospitality, and the seemingly infinite diversity are only the most tangible of the island's offerings.

ON THE MENU

MUNCHING MEZEDES

Mezedes, the Greek equivalent t *tapas*, are small savory appetizers often served with alcohol such a ouzo. Cretans claim distinction in a variety of dishes and spend lon evening hours lounging over the finge foods at the town cafe or *ouzeri*. Belo is a list of important treats to recogniz on the Cretan table.

Raki: an alcohol, which is th product of wine-making and purifie with fire. It is often substituted fo ouzo on Crete. The strong-burning clear liquid is more potent than it ubiquitous licorice-laced counterpa and, Cretans contend, leaves less o a hangover in its wake.

Keftedes: small meatballs usuall made with lamb. Although enjoye throughout Greece, Cretans often us cumin in their recipes, giving them a distinctive kick.

Ntakos: dry bread sprinkled wit olive oil and smothered in gloriou heaps of tomato, feta, and oregan draws vegetarians looking to escap meat-heavy *mezedes*.

Chochlios: snails. Natives say tha the wild herbs of the mountainou island enrich the creatures' diets, mak ing Cretan snails especially tasty. *Bour bouritsi*, snails deep fried in olive oi and served with vinegar, are particularl popular.

Dolmades: vine leaves stuffed wit rice and veggies, simmered slowly ove a low flame, and served up sprinkle with lemon for a flavorful feast.

Fava: a bean puree usually pre pared with yellow split peas. It i enjoyed spread on a piece of countr bread, with fresh greens, or on its own

HANIA PREFECTURE

Gorgeous beaches, rocky gorges, and pine-covered hills dot the western tip of Crete. Because tourists flock to these natural wonders in droves, it is impressive Hania has still managed to maintain a distinct character and the prefecture's small villages and beaches off the beaten track await exploration. If you want to party in a beachside club, look no further. If you want to flee pounding techno and foam-filled orgiastic scenes, find the bus station and serenity can be yours.

HANIA Χανια ☎28210

The island's second largest city, Hania (hahn-YAH) reacts to its avalanche of summer tourists with a cosmopolitan panache typical of this port town's urban sophistication. The gritty outer streets of the city give way to pedestrian boulevards of stylish shops and cafes down by the Old Venetian Harbor. Visitors meander through winding streets, listening to folk music from streetside cafes or waiting for the setting sun to silhouette the lighthouse and nearby Ottoman domes. A day in Hania is easily spent people-watching from cafes, window-shopping, or absorbing the aura of the Old Town by casting maps aside and blazing a your own route.

TRANSPORTATION

Flights: Olympic Airways, Tzanakaki 88 (☎28210 57 701, 57 702, or 57 703), across from the public gardens. Tickets sold daily 8am-3:30pm. Phone reservations M-F 7am-6pm. Flights to **Athens** (4 per day, about €70) and **Thessaloniki** (3 per week, €120).

Buses: The **central bus station** (☎28210 93 306) fills a block within Kydonias, Zymvrakakidon, Smyrnis, and Kelaidi. Service to: **Elafonisi** (daily, €8); **Hora Sfakion** (3 per day, €5.20); **Iraklion** (17 per day, €10.50); **Kastelli** (14 per day, €3.40); **Paleohora** (4 per day, €5.30); **Platanias** (every 30min., €1.30); **Rethymno** (17 per day, €5.55); **Samaria Gorge** (4 per day, €5.20); **Sougia** (daily, €5). Schedules and fares change depending on season, so call ahead.

Taxis: ☎28210 98 700, 28210 98 701, 28210 87 700, 28210 94 300. Taxis line up on the east side of Pl. 1866. Available 24hr.

Ferries: ANEK Office, Pl. Market 2 (☎28210 27 500). Lato and Lissos go to **Piraeus** (9½hr., 9pm, €20.90). Open daily 7:30am-9pm.

Car and Moped Rental: Several agencies are on Halidon. Mopeds €18-25 per day; cars €25-35. Keep in mind that most rentals only allow for a free 100km; driving over 100km may cost from €0.06-0.16 per km.

ORIENTATION AND PRACTICAL INFORMATION

To get to the city center from the bus station, turn right onto **Kydonias,** walk one block, then turn left onto **Zymvrakakidon,** which runs along one side of a large public plaza called **Pl. 1866.** At the far end of Pl. 1866, the road becomes **Halidon** and leads to the **Old Venetian Harbor,** full of outdoor restaurants and narrow alleyways. Intersecting with Zymvrakakidon and Halidon at their meeting point is another major road, **Skalidi,** to the left (facing Halidon); to the right it becomes Chatz-

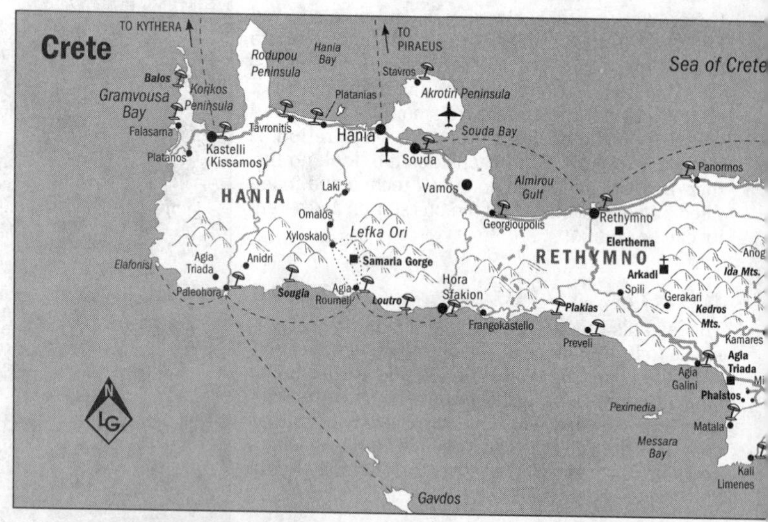

imichali and then Giannari. One hundred meters farther, Giannari forks into Tzanakaki and El. Venizelou. If you're arriving by ferry, you'll dock in the nearby port of **Souda.** Take the bus from the dock, which stops at the supermarket on Zymvrakakidon by Pl. 1866 (15min.,€1). Hania's business district is across from the **Municipal Market** near the intersection of **Gianari** and **Tzanakaki.** Its shops and restaurants cluster around the splendid Venetian Harbor. Sunbathers should head west of the harbor along the waterfront to find a long, thin stretch of well-populated sand at **Nea Hora.** A good starting point for all visitors is **Promahonas Hill,** on Baladinou just off of Halidon. Scaling the structure provides a magnificent overview of Hania and the mountains that frame it.

Tourist Office: Korkidi 16 (☎28210 36 155), just off Pl. 1866. Only worth a visit for the free, detailed **maps.** Open M-F 8am-2pm. You will have better luck at the private tourist agencies near Pl. 1866.

Banks: National Bank (☎28210 38 934), on the corner of Nikiforou, Foka, and Tzanakaki. Open M-Th 8am-2:30pm, F 8am-2pm. 24hr. **ATM.**

Luggage storage: You can leave your bags at the bus station while looking for a room. €1.50 per bag for 24hr. Open 6am-9pm.

Emergency: ☎100. **Ambulance:** ☎166.

Police: Karaiskaki 60 (☎28210 28 730). Open 7:30am-8pm. The **tourist police** (☎28210 28 708) share this office.

Hospital: ☎28210 22 000. Located in Mournies, 6km south of Hania. Open 24hr.

OTE: Tzanakaki 5 (☎28210 44 499). Open M-F 7:30am-1:30pm, Sa 7:30am-1pm.

Bookstores: Several pricey international bookstores line Halidon. **Newsstand,** Skalidi 8 (☎28210 95 888), sells guidebooks, newspapers, and a large selection of magazines in English and German. Open daily 9am-midnight. **To Pazari,** on Daskalogianni 46, has a Bostonian owner who buys and sells used books in English, French, and German. Open M-Sa 8:30am-2pm; Tu, Th-F 6-9pm.

Internet Access: Sante (☎28210 94 737), a cafe toward the western end of the harbor's waterfront, offers Internet upstairs (€4 per hr.). Drinks €2-4. Open 9:30am-1am. **Vranas Internet Cafe**(☎28210 58 618), on Agion Deka. €3 per hr. Open 9am-1am.

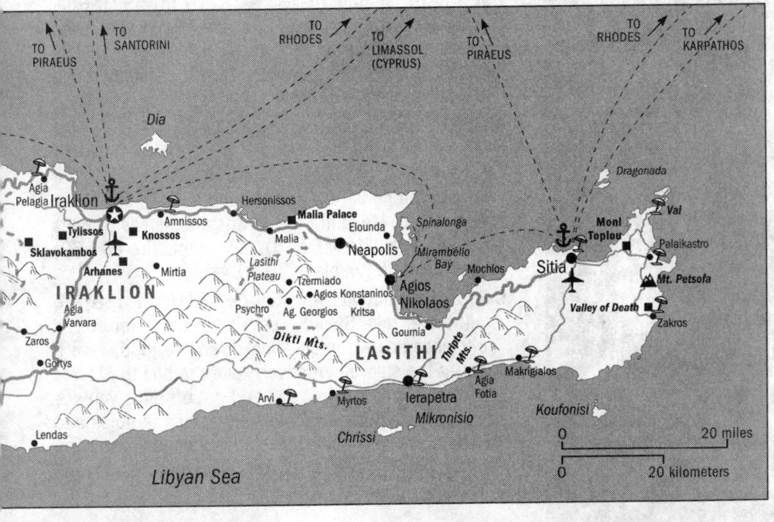

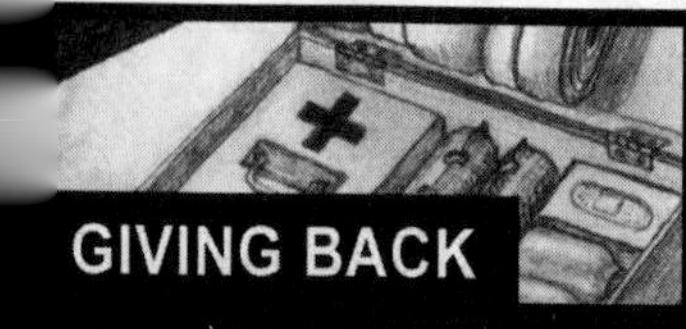

GIVING BACK

\ LITTLE LOVE FOR THE LOGGERHEADS

As most travelers to the island quickly earn, Zakynthos is home to one of the vorld's largest nesting grounds for the endangered loggerhead turtle (scientific name *Caretta caretta*). The sub-island of Marathonissi, just northeast of Marathia beach in southern Zakynthos, has even acquired the epithet "Turtle Island," for both its physical resemblance to a turtle and its unusually large nesting population. A short cruise around the island is nore than enough for most tourists, but or those travelers whose souvenir plush urtle hasn't left them satisfied, numerous non-profit organizations encourage volunteers to participate in the conservation projects to aid these animals, which, though as old as the dinosaurs, have only recently become a gravely endangered species, especially with he rise in tourism.

Perhaps the most reputable of these organizations is **ARCHELON, he Sea Turtle Protection Society of Greece.** Established over 15 years ago, this non-profit solicits volunteers or two types of work: The first consists mostly of field work, involving ong days. In the early morning, volunteers observe nesting areas to determine any changes that may have aken place over night. Afterward they ocus their efforts toward nest protection and relocation, ensuring that eggs laid in unsafe areas are removed rom the dangers of unknowing fisherman and natural predation. Finally, after the long day has worn out the novices, the most experienced volunteers return to the field to observe and tag nesting females completing a ulfilling, full day.

Post Office: Tzanakaki 3 (☎28210 28 445). Open M-F 7:30am-8pm. **Postal code:** 73100.

ACCOMMODATIONS

Inexpensive rooms are hard to come by, especially since a number of hotels and hostels have renovated their rooms and raised rates accordingly. Reasonable prices can still be found in the Old Town. New Town pensions have dazzling views of the harbor but are near noisy night spots. Small hotels sprout from the beaches to the west, but expect to pay dearly for the brown sands of Nea Kydonia and Agia Marina. The private tourist agencies around Pl. 1866 can help you find a room.

Hotel Fidias, Sarpaki 6 (☎28210 52 494). Walking toward the harbor on Halidon, turn right onto Athinagora. Half a block past the cathedral on the right, Athinagora becomes Sarpaki, and the pension is on your right. Irasmos, the philosopher/owner, provides bright, comfortable rooms with balconies as well as invaluable travel tips and life advice. Free luggage storage. Laundry downstairs €6 for wash and dry. Reception 7am-10pm. Dorms €7-13; singles €13-20; doubles €15-25; triples €25-35. ❷

Nostos Hotel, Zambeliou 42-46 (☎28210 94 743; fax 28210 94 740). Unique rooms that defy standardization with extra touches like dual level suites and perfect harbor views, all housed in an attractive building. All rooms include private bath, kitchen, A/C, TV, and breakfast.Singles €35-45; doubles €50-70; triples €60-85. AmEx/MC/V. ❹

Hotel Neli, Isodion 21-23 (☎28210 55 533). Spacious, classy rooms, with kitchenettes, fridges, and private baths, worthy of housing the Greek gods for which the rooms are named. A/C €5 per night. Doubles €35-55. ❸

Meltemi Pension, Agelou 2 (☎28210 92 802), at the western side of the harbor, next to the Maritime Museum. High ceilings, private showers, and clear views of the harbor only add to the open feel of these large rooms. Meltemi Cafe downstairs serves frappés (€2.20), breakfast (€4-6), and cocktails (€4.50) come nightfall. Doubles €30-50. ❸

Camping Hania, Ag. Apostoli (☎28210 31 138). To walk there, take Skalidi west out of town and follow as it becomes Kisamou. 4km down the road, take a right at the sign. Alternatively take the bus to Stavros (15min., every 20min., €1) and get off once you see the signs. For those who are put off by the noise and bustle of Hania proper, camping is a good alternative. With a quiet atmosphere, this site features several amenities, including laundry (€4.50), pool, restaurant (pizza €4.50; hamburger €2.30), and mini-market. Proximity to the beach is another plus. €5 per person. €4.50 per large tent, €3.50 per small tent, €8 tent rental. €3.50 car parking. 10% discount for students. ❶

FOOD

You can construct a fantasy meal from the exotic foodstuffs and affordable snacks available at the open-air **municipal market** in cleverly named Pl. Market. Wheels of cheese, fresh fish and meats (watch out for the cow's head), and homegrown vegetables accompany the many bakeries and small cafes. (Open M-W 7:30am-3pm, F-Su 8am-9pm.) Inside, **Restaurant Bonne Petite** ❷ provides freshly cooked seafood to the salivating masses. (Most fish dishes €6-8. Open daily 10am-4pm.) For other cheap options, try the well-stocked and convenient **IN.KA. Supermarket** (☎28210 90 558), in Pl. 1866, on the right coming from Halidon. (Open daily 8am-9pm.)

Anaplous (☎28210 41 320), on the right on Sifaka when headed away from the harbor. This romantic open-air bistro is set in pink stone ruins; flower vines serve as the restaurant's ceiling. Brothers Angelos and Nikos claim to offer the only *pilino* (pork and lamb cooked for 6-7hr. in fresh clay; €24.70) in Greece. Breaking the clay for this dish may also bust your wallet, but it serves 3. Traditional Hanian dishes include rabbit in white wine (€7.90) and *kreatatourta* (€8.20), a lamb, cheese pie. Anaplous moves to a Venetian house across the street during winter. Open daily 6pm-1am. AmEx/MC/V. ❷

Tamam, Zambeliou 49 (☎28210 96 080). Served up in an elegant, former Turkish bath complex, Tamam's stellar food is a secret among natives. Peek at the wine list; it's longer than the menu (wines €6-28). Many vegetarian alternatives. Stuffed peppers with cheese €4.50. Chicken in eggplant puree €7.50. Open daily 1pm-12:30am. ❷

Bougatsa Iorthanis, Apokoronou 24 (☎28210 91 345). When you walk in, the woman behind the counter will ask you "Sugar?" She needs to know how sweet you want this restaurant's sole dish *bougatsa* (goat cheese pastry; €1.95). Open daily 6am-2pm. ❶

Avgo To Kokkora (☎28210 55 776), at Sarpaki and Agion Deka, satiates vegetable-craving customers with 15 varieties of hefty-portioned salads. Eat the avocado variety (€5.50) in the loft of the chic, orange interior or take your Mexican (€6.50) out to the plateia seating. Open M-Sa 9am-1am. ❷

For those volunteers with a particular interest in turtle rehabilitation, ARCHELON offers a program in which volunteers treat injured or sickly turtles. According to the organization, daily work includes "preparation and administration of food, operation of sea water supply systems, carrying and cleaning the animals, as well as cleaning the facilities and equipment."

There are also opportunities to volunteer on Crete where merely 20 to 30 female loggerheads are believed to remain. The island, however, boasts almost 800 nests per year, primarily centered in the cities of Hania, Rethymno, and Matala. Volunteer groups in these cities live together communally on campsites where they share chores. Their daily activities include public awareness campaigns, which require slide shows and work in street-side kiosks, relocating nests to protected beach areas, and tagging turtles.

Most volunteers are needed between May 1 and October 31, during the nesting and hatching seasons. Sea Turtle Rehabilitation takes place year-round. Volunteers must be proficient in English and over 18. Paticipation requires a US$65 fee. ARCHELON requires a minimum participation duration of 28 days. All volunteers must have complete health insurance policies. High-level research opportunities are available for qualified applicants. For more information, call ☎210 523 1342 or visit www.archelon.gr.

Akrogiali, Akti Papanikoli 19 (☎28210 73 110), on the waterfront in Nea Hora, a 12min. walk westward along the water past the Maritime Museum. This modest beachfront restaurant caters to hordes of hungry Greeks. House specialties: calamari (€8) and swordfish fillet (€8.50). Open M-Sa 6pm-1am, Su 11am-1am. ❸

ENTERTAINMENT

Kick off the night by cruising the many cafes along the harbor, where young Greeks pass the time by playing *tavli* (backgammon) and talking on their cell phones. When you're ready to hit the dance floor, **Mythos,** Akti Koundourioti 52, and its fraternal twin **Street** (☎28210 78 496), next door, serve as the hip gathering places for Greeks and tourists alike, playing a rock/pop mix. (Cover €6 and €7 respectively, includes 1 drink. Drinks €3-5.) Doors open at 11pm, but the party doesn't really get started until 2am. **Mylos,** a must-see dance club for beach-party devotees, is only a €10 taxi ride away in Platanias (p. 571). **Anecdote,** Zambeliou 45 (☎28210 98 639) has a parachute covering the ceiling, orange walls, and cheap drinks. Tiny, it creates an intimate environment for a local crowd who come to listen to the ethnic, rock, and jazz mix. (Beer and wine €2; pitcher of *raki* €3. Open 9pm-2am.) For traditional music and dancing in a quiet setting, sit down and sip a drink with the older locals in **Kafe Kriti,** Kalergon 2, an outpost of Cretan culture on the east side of the harbor. Live music nightly at 8pm; ask the owner, an instructor of traditional dance, to teach you some moves, and watch for his son, a musician. (☎28210 58 661. Beer €3; bottle of *raki* €5. Open 5pm-3am.)

SIGHTS

VENETIAN INNER HARBOR. A long, hot walk to the rickety stone **Venetian lighthouse** provides a superb view of Hania from the water. This tower marks the entrance to Hania's stunning architectural relic, the Venetian Inner Harbor. The inlet has retained its original breakwater and Venetian arsenal, and the Egyptians restored the lighthouse during their occupation of Crete in the late 1830s. On the western side of the main harbor, the **Maritime Museum** describes the tumultuous (and often ferocious) 6000 years of Crete's naval and merchant history in maps and models. The second floor houses a large exhibition on Crete's remarkable expulsion of the Nazis in 1941. The Museum is currently creating a reconstruction of a 15th-century BC Minoan ship, whose inaugural voyage will be from Crete to Attica as part of the **2004 Olympic Games.** (☎28210 91 875. Open Apr.-Oct. daily 9am-4pm, Nov.-Mar. 9am-2pm. €2, students €1.) The newly renovated **Venetian Shiphouse,** at the east end of the harbor where Arholeon meets Akti Enoseos, hosts rotating exhibits, mostly architectural, in a modern building on the water. (☎28210 40 201. Open daily 10am-2pm and 6-9pm.) The melange of Ottoman and Venetian architecture in the **waterfront alleys** reflects the city's past. At the corner of Kandanoleu and Kanevaro, just north of Kanevaro on **Kastelli Hill,** lie reminders of Hania's Bronze Age prosperity, including the **Late Minoan House** (c. 1450 BC) and other fenced-off and unmarked monuments.

MUNICIPAL GARDENS. Flee the heavily touristed streets in favor of the floral shade of the **Municipal Gardens,** *Dimotikos Kypos*, to the left as you walk down Tzanakaki from the city center. Once the property of a *muezzin* (Islamic prayer caller), the garden features an open-air **movie theater** that screens international films (☎28210 41 427; €6; showtimes 8:45 and 10:45pm) and a tiny zoo housing a unique combination of goats and peacocks. UNICEF sets up an annual **International Fair** in the gardens—consult the tourist office for details.

ARCHAEOLOGICAL MUSEUM. The Archaeological Museum, on Halidon about 40m past the cathedral, features a broad collection of Cretan artifacts, from early Minoan to Hellenistic times. Once a Venetian monastery, then the mosque of Yusuf Pasha, the high-ceilinged halls are lined with clay shards, gold jewelry, and floor mosaics. The ancient coin collection includes gold tokens once placed in the mouths of the dead to pay Charon to ferry the souls of the deceased to the Underworld. (☎28210 90 334. Open Tu-Su 8:30am-3pm. €2, students €1.) You can buy a ticket at the Archaeological Museum that will also give you access to the **Byzantine Collection,** on Theotokopoulou, which charts the history of Hania from early Christian times to Ottoman rule in a variety of wall paintings, mosaics, and icons. (☎28210 96 046. Open Tu-Su 8:30am-3pm. Joint ticket €3, students €2.)

DAYTRIP FROM HANIA: PLATANIAS. Platanias (Πλατανιας), 30min. from Hania by bus (every 30min., €1.30), has long, pretty beaches and what seem to be a thousand tourists for every local. Platanias's fame sprang from a large rock island just offshore, better known as Kracken, the petrified sea monster. Perseus turned Kracken to stone with the aid of Medusa's severed head. (For a cinematic account, check out the special effects of *Clash of the Titans.*)

Present-day Platanias's most famous phenomenon, swanky rock club **Mylos,** defeats any MTV beach party in sheer numbers of gyrating bodies and hard, pumping beats. The converted bread mill draws nightly crowds of suavely dressed young Europeans from midnight until morning. Take the last bus from Hania, get off at the bus stop at Platanias Center, and continue walking away from Hania. After about 450m, a huge sign will alert you to the right-hand turn-off that leads past an enormous parking lot to Mylos and the **beach.** (☎28210 60 449. Cover €8 weekdays, €10 weekends; includes 1 drink. Beer €6; cocktails €8. Open June-Sept. nightly midnight-6am.) To get home, either take a cab (☎28210 68 423) for €10 or party until the 6:30am bus arrives the next morning.

AKROTIRI PENINSULA

Akrotiri Peninsula is most easily navigated by car. Using the bus, you will need 2 days to visit all of the sites, due to erratic bus schedules. However, it is easy to visit either the peninsula's beaches or its monasteries in a single day.

Just northeast of Hania is the sparsely populated peninsula of Akrotiri, home to herds of goats, rows of olive trees, several monasteries, and sheltered coves. At the small white sand beach of **Kalatnos,**

THE LOCAL LEGEND

ZORBA THE GREAT

Author, intellectual, essayist, phi losopher, and translator-extraordin naire, Nikos Kazantzakis (1883-1957 is the shining star of Crete. The mos established Greek author sinc Homer, he quite fittingly wrote his own *Odyssey*, intended as a sequel to the original. Most famous in the western world for *The Last Temptation of Chris* and *Zorba the Greek*, Kazantzakis's novels molded for foreigners a picture of Greece. His books, made into mov ies, fill Greek bookstores; music from the films beckons from cafes, touris agencies, and hotels.

Though educated in Athens, the author was born in Iraklion and clearl Cretans are enormously proud of thei local son: Kazantzakis's revered tomb rests regally above the capital city Networks of roads named in his hono traverse mountains and cities alike museums spotted throughout the island commemorate his life and works; Iraklion's international airport is named for none other than the famed lyric writer.

You can pay homage to this illustri ous native by visiting his grave at sur set with a copy of the renowned *Zorba* and a bottle of Cretan *raki* in hand. I you happen to be particularly familia with the hugely popular (on an interna tional scale) movie version of *Zorba* you might make a more ambitious pi grimage to the Akrotiri Peninsula (p. 571), the recognizable site of Zorba's ill-fated exploits in mining. If not, be sure to check out Anthony Quinn and Alan Bates in Michael Cacoyannis's 1964 directorial take on the nove either before or after your trip.

16km from Hania, sunbeds with umbrellas go for €5 per day. Kalatnos lies on the route of the bus to **Stavros,** another glorious beach with a handful of cafes; the view includes a mining hill you may recognize from the movie *Zorba the Greek.* Take the bus (1hr., 4 per day, €1.50) and get off at the end of the line in front of **Christiana's Restaurant ❶** (☎28210 39 152; open daily 9am-11pm), one of the few restaurants in town, which serves up hearty portions at reasonable prices with a view of the water. On the sand, rent an umbrella and a deck chair (€5 per day) or take a walk down to the rockier, though more private, end of the beach for cost-free sunbathing. Get more refreshments 100m inland at **Zorba's Original Tavern ❶** (☎28210 39 402; open daily 8am-midnight).

About 6km from Kalatnos (16.5km from Hania) is the monastery of **Agia Triada** (☎28210 63 310), which was built in 1606 near ruins of a Minoan temple and has produced traditional olive oil since 1632. Take the bus to Agia Triada (20min., 2 per day, €1.50) and enjoy a peaceful walk through the grounds and small museum, with its collection of mostly 19th-century pieces and three 17th-century Byzantine paintings. You can bottle the experience in the form of Agia Triada olive oil (€1.80 for 250mL; €2.30 for a pretty bottle). Modest dress is required. (Open 7am-2pm and 5-7pm. €1.50.) Monastery-buffs who just can't get enough may want to follow the road up a stubby knoll (complete with wild goats and narcissus flowers) 4km to **Gouverneto,** a similar but smaller monastery. (☎28210 63 319. Open 7am-2pm and 4-8pm. Free.) From the monastery, the path leading down toward the sea passes several small Venetian ruins and **Bear Cave** (600m, about 15min.). Legend has it that a monk drinking from the cave's fountains was attacked by a bear; the animal was turned into stone by a miracle, saving the monk and preserving the outline of the beast in the distinctive shape of the cave's stalagmite patterns.

BALOS Μπαλος

Be prepared for an adventure when you set out to find this little-known lagoon on the northwestern tip of Crete; it's not easy to get here, but it's worth it. Reaching Balos by car requires a harrowing drive across a Cretan mountain front. Most cars can probably handle the drive, but a 4x4 will make the experience much more pleasant. To get there, take Skalidi west out of Hania toward Kissamos. You will hit Kissamos after about 40km of beautiful countryside. Go through the town for another 2km and look for a sign for a phone on the side of the road. Make a right at the phone (you will also see signs for Kaliviani), and make an immediate left by the sign for the Balos Hotel. After about 1km, you will pass through a tiny town. Just outside of it, make a right at the small sign for Balos. After 5km on this road, you will pass a small white chapel; the parking lot lies another 3km beyond the church. When you finally arrive at the parking lot, take the sign-posted, small path and hike 30min. through goat country to the heavenly **blue lagoon.** Bright white sand and warm, shallow waters look out over an uninhabited island, which houses a fortress built by the Venetians and later used by the Turks as a prison. For those willing to see the jade-colored lagoon brim-full of other bathers, daily **boat cruises** leave from Kissamos and stop at both the island and the bay (departs 10am, returns 5:30pm; round-trip €20). Buy tickets at the Kissamos port, 3km beyond the town itself from companies like **Cretan Cruises** (☎28220 83 311; cretacru@otenet.gr). If you're feeling indulgent, continue to drive down the coast through Platanos toward Kefali and pick your spot on the breathtaking stretch of **beach.** Alternatively, take the less traveled route southward to Elafonisi to pass the late afternoon without the usual swarm of tourists.

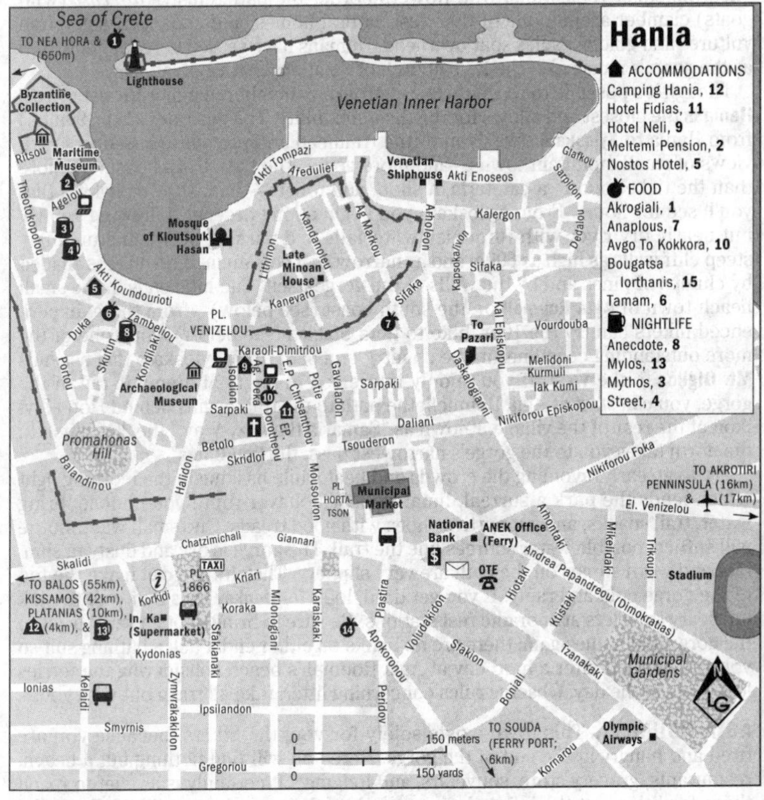

SAMARIA GORGE Φαραγγι της Σαμαριας

Buses for Omalos and Xyloskalo leave Hania (3 per day, €5.20). Early buses (6:15-8:30am) can get you to Xyloskalo in time for a dayhike; the 1:45pm bus will get you to Omalos, ready to go the next day. If you want to spend the night in Omalos, rest up at **Gigilos Hotel** ❷ on the main road. (☎28210 67 181. Singles €15-20; doubles €25.) From Rethymno, take the 6:15 or 7am buses through Hania to Omalos (€10.50). Early risers can take the 5:30am bus from Iraklion through Rethymno and Hania to Omalos (€15.50). For gorge information, call the **Hania Forest Service** (☎28210 92 287) or find info at the tourist offices in Hania, Rethymno, or Iraklion.

The most popular excursion on Crete is the spectacular 5-6hr. hike down the longest gorge in Europe, the **Samaria Gorge,** a formidable—if not inspiring—16km pass through the **White Mountains National Park.** (Open May 1-Oct. 15 6am-6pm. Admission €5, children under 15 and organized student groups free. Hang on to your ticket; you must give it back at the gorge's exit.) Sculpted by rainwater over 14 million years, the gorge retains its allure despite mobs of international visitors. The rocky trail can trip you up, but try to take a look around: epiphytes peek out from sheer rock walls, wild flowers border the path, elusive *agrimi* (wild goats) clamber around one of their last natural homes, and endangered gryphon vultures and golden eagles soar overhead. Humans have settled here for centuries, as the gorge's namesake, the 1379 church of **Saint Maria of Egypt,** attests.

Though it's possible to reach the gorge from any number of major tourist towns, **Hania** is the closest and allows for the most flexibility. The bus ride (44km, 90min.) from Hania to **Xyloskalo** takes you to the trailhead and provides passengers with views of small mountain towns—and more goats. The base town boasts no more than the ticket booth, a cafeteria, a shop, and toilets—the last of their kind that you'll see for hours. From Xyloskalo you begin a long descent, following a noisy but nearly dry river with turquoise waterfalls and passing between stunningly steep cliff walls as high as 600m and as narrow as 3.5m. Much of the hike is shaded by clumps of pines and by the walls of the gorge itself. The hike ends in the small beach town of **Agia Roumeli** on the south coast (see below)—from there, experienced hikers can try the 10hr. hike to **Hora Sfakion** (see below) along one of the more outstanding coastlines in the country or a path from Xyloskalo that ascends **Mt. Gigilos** to the west. If you're only interested in the final dramatic tail of the gorge, you can start at Agia Roumeli; the path to the trail begins behind Hotel Livikon at the rear of the village. Known as "Samaria the Lazy Way," the 2hr. climb to the north takes you to the gorge's narrowest pass: the **Iron Gates.**

Try to go early, avoiding the crowds and heat while basking in the morning light which lends the park a surreal, lunar feel. Whichever route you choose, bring water, trail snacks, and supportive shoes with good treads. One small water bottle will suffice; potable water sources line the trail. The gorge is dry and dusty in summer and worn stones on the path are very slippery. The altitude can make the top of the gorge cold and rainy. If you get tired, look for **donkey taxis** that wait to pick up weary travelers at sporadic rest stations. Be sure to bring enough **cash** to get to the gorge and home again; there are no banks on either end. Pack a bathing suit so you can cool off after a hard day at Agia Roumeli's beach considering the ferries leave late in the day. Observe rules concerning litter: take all trash out with you.

AGIA ROUMELI. This town exists solely for you, the hikers, because you are tired and hungry at the end of the gorge. Here you will find nothing but a beach, restaurants, grocery store, souvenirs, and lodgings. It certainly is a relief to reach these facilities, but the inflated prices are less than comforting. **Kri-Kri ❸,** on the street leading from the gorge, has reasonably priced but somewhat cramped rooms with A/C and fridges. (☎28250 91 089. Doubles €35; triples €40. AmEx/MC/V.) On the beach, **Hotel Agia Roumeli ❸** is a good place to chill out after a day of trekking, with easy access to the sea as well as fridges, A/C, and spacious balconies. (☎28250 91 241. Doubles 35; triples €40.) **Ferries** run from Agia Roumeli regularly April-October to **Hora Sfakion** (1¼hr., 4 per day, €4.60) and to **Paleohora** and **Sougia** (Apr.-Oct. daily, Nov.-Mar. 3 per week; €3-6.40). Call in advance for ferry times. The last **bus** from Hora Sfakion waits for the last ferry. The ferry and bus are scheduled at 6 and 7:30pm respectively, so you can make the round-trip from Hania, Rethymno, or Iraklion in one day if you leave on a morning bus (one-way from Hora Sfakion to Hania or Rethymno €5.10, to Iraklion €9.08).

HORA SFAKION Χωρα Σφακιων ☎28250

The extremely small port town of Hora Sfakion, often called simply Sfakion, lacks the intimacy of Plakias to the east or Paleohora to the west but serves as the transportation hub of the southern coast. Its quiet streets and tavernas are a necessary resting spot following the Samaria Gorge hike, and the location makes it a convenient base for daytrips to the area's smaller gorges and lovely beaches.

TRANSPORTATION AND PRACTICAL INFORMATION. The town consists of one main harborfront road, which opens off a plateia 50m uphill from the ferry dock. Four **buses** per day go to: **Hania** (2hr., last bus 7pm, €5.60); **Iraklion** (last at 7pm, €11); **Rethymno** with connections to **Vrises** (1½hr., €5.40). Buses leave Vrises for **Rethymno** and **Iraklion** every hour on the hour. If your ferry is late, don't worry—the buses wait for the boats to arrive. Boats from Hora Sfakion go to **Agia Roumeli** (1¼hr., 4 per day, €4.60). From April to October, most routes stop in **Loutro.** To get to Loutro in winter months, go by foot or fishing boat. It is a smart to check schedules with the ticket office (☎28250 91 221). **Boats** also run three days a week to **Gavdos,** a sparsely populated island that is the southernmost point in Europe (F-Su 10:30am, €9). **Caïques** to Sweetwater beach leave at 10:30am and return at 5:30pm every day (€3 one-way). In the plateia you'll find helpful travel agency **Sfakia Tours,** where you can get bus tickets and rental cars. (☎/fax 28250 91 130. Open daily 8am-10pm. Car rentals €45 per day.) There are **no police** in Hora Sfakion. The police station lies in Komitades, 4km away. The yellow building in the plateia holds the **OTE.** (☎28250 91 299. Open M-F 7:30am-3:15pm.) Next door to Sfakia Tours is the **post office.** (☎28250 91 244. Open M-F 7:30am-2pm.) **Postal code:** 73011.

ACCOMMODATIONS AND FOOD. Hotel owners in Hora Sfakion are aware that their town is a convenient rest stop after Samaria Gorge and their prices reflect this awareness. If you want to cool off on the cheap, snatch up one of the cheap air-conditioned rooms at **Hotel Samaria ❷,** one of the first buildings on the harbor road. (☎28250 91 261 or 91 071; fax 28250 91 161. Doubles €25, with breakfast €30. MC/V.) Following the right fork of the harbor road at the bakery leads to **Stavris ❷,** where the friendly owner offers clean, bargain rooms with private bath and balcony, which unfortunately lack A/C. (☎28250 91 220 or 91 201; stavris@chania-cci.gr. Singles €22; doubles €25; triples €27.) The cool, grotto-like **Hotel Xenia ❷,** on the harbor road at the far end away from the ferry landing, has pleasant and spacious rooms with refrigerators and phones. Enjoy breakfast (€3) under the flowery veranda of the waterfront deck. (☎28250 91 490; fax 28250 91 491. Doubles €30.) **Lefka Ori ❷,** on the waterfront, rents small rooms with views of the harbor. (☎28250 91 209. Doubles and triples with bath €25. AmEx/MC/V.)

The town's dining options are dominated by hotel restaurants (entrees €6-8). **Omprogialos ❷,** the first restaurant you will see as you walk to the harbor from the ferry landing, is a rare exception. An open coal oven cooks up flavorful meats. (☎28250 91 204. Entrees €4-8.) There are many **markets** in town.

PALEOHORA Παλαιοχωρα ☎28230

Once a refuge for the embattled rear guard of the 1960s counterculture, Paleohora has since retreated into a sleepier state of mind. The town, 77km south of Hania, is a peninsular retreat flanked by a rocky harbor on its eastern side and smooth beaches, set against the splendid Cretan mountains, on its western side.

TRANSPORTATION. **Ferries** leave the modest port for: **Agia Roumeli** (1½hr., 2 per day, €6.50); **Hora Skafion** (2½hr., 3 per day, €6.50); **Loutro** (2¼hr., 3 per day, €7.90); **Sougia** (45min., 2 per day, €3.80). One boat per day departs Paleohora for **Elafonisi** at 10am and returns at 4pm (1hr., €4.50 one-way). A boat goes to **Gavdos** three times per week (3½hr.; post boat: M and Th 8:30am, returns 2:30pm; tourist boat: Tu 8:30am, returns 2:30pm; one-way €9.40.) More tourist boats run in summer. For information about boats and tickets, visit the friendly people at **Notos Rentals,** to the right as you walk up Venizelou. (☎28320 42 110; fax ☎28320 41 838. Open daily 8am-1pm and 5-10:30pm.) **Syia Travel,** a left on Kentekaki past the pharmacy, is a general tourist office that is helpful for ferry information and tickets, as well as for basic information about the region. (☎28320 41 198; fax ☎28320 41 535. Open daily 9am-1:30pm and 5-9:30pm.) The **bus station** is on Venizelou on the northern edge of town. Buses run to **Hania** (2hr., 3 per day, €5.40) and **Samaria** (6:15am, €5). For a taxi, call the 24hr. **Paleohora Taxi Office** (☎28320 41 128 or 41 061). You can rent a **car** (about €30-45) or **moped** (€10-20) at any of the travel agencies in Paleohora.

ORIENTATION AND PRACTICAL INFORMATION. The restaurants and bars of Paleohora town cluster around the main thoroughfare, **Venizelou,** which runs down the center of the peninsula from north to south. Heading north on Venizelou takes you to Hania; south leads to the ruins of an old castle. Venizelou crosses **Kentekaki,** which leads west to the beach and east to the harbor. Most accommodations are located on the side streets off Venizelou.

Walking toward the center of town from the bus station, you'll find the **National Bank,** with a 24hr. **ATM** three blocks up on your right. (☎28230 41 430. Open M-Th 8am-2:30pm, F 8am-2pm.) Half a block down and also on your right is the helpful **tourist office,** which gives out **free maps** and posts updated bus and ferry schedules. (☎28320 41 507. Open M, W-Su 10am-1pm and 6-9pm.) A block and a half farther, on your right, is the **OTE.** (☎28230 41 299. Open M-F 7:30am-3pm.) The **port police** (☎28320 41 214) are three blocks farther down the main street on the right. Turning left toward the harbor at the OTE leads to the **police station** (☎28320 41 111; open 24hr.), one block down on your left. The port lies one block past the harborside police. The herculean folk at Notos Rentals (see above) on the main thoroughfare do **laundry, exchange money,** and offer **Internet** access. (Wash and dry €9. €1.50 per 15min., €4.40 per hr.) All facilities are open daily 8am-1pm and 5-10:30pm. There is a **doctor** on Venizelou, one block past the bus station on the left heading away from town. (☎28230 41 380. Open 9am-11:30pm and 5-8:30pm.) Taking a right toward the beach behind the OTE will get you to the **public health center.** (☎28230 41 211. Open M-F 8:30-2:30.) There is a **pharmacy** on Venizelou, across from the OTE. (☎28320 41 498. Open M-Sa 8:30am-2pm and 5:30-10pm.) To find the **post office,** head to the beach from the OTE and make a right when at the beach road. (☎28320 41 206. Open M-F 7:30am-2pm.) **Postal code:** 73001.

ACCOMMODATIONS. Some small hotels line the road closest to the harbor. In the middle of the harbor road stands a white building marked **Dream Rooms ❷,** run by the cordial Nikos Bubalis and his animated wife. Rooms with balconies look out onto the charming harbor and the surrounding mountains. (☎28320 41 112. Doubles €18-25; triples €32-38.) Away from the harbor, **Savas Rooms ❷** offers simple rooms with kitchenettes and private baths. To get there, walk from the bus station 150m north on Venizelou toward Hania; Savas is on your left at the edge of town. (☎28320 41 075 or 41 742. Doubles €30; triples €35.) Very warm **Villa Anna ❸** is a fine choice for families. Large apartments with private baths, a profuse garden, and children's playground provide a great alternative to Paleohora's homogenous hotels. (☎28320 46 428 or 28230 42 802. 2-bedroom apartment sleeping 4-5 €60; 1-bedroom for 2-3 €40-50.) **Camping Paleohora ❶** is a 15min. walk to the east of town. The campsite has its own **restaurant ❷** (salads €2-3; spaghetti €3; calamari €5). Across the street and within earshot of Club Paleohora, the town's popular disco, it also flaunts a beautiful **beach.** Walk north on Venizelou (away from town), turn right just after the bus station, take the second left on the last paved road before the beach, and walk 1km to the site. (☎28320 41 120. Open Apr.-Oct. €3.50 per person, €2.10 per child; €2.30 per tent, €4.50 tent rental; €2.10 per car.)

FOOD AND NIGHTLIFE. Markets and tavernas are fixtures along Venizelou and its surrounding streets; restaurants serve traditional Greek food from standard tourist menus at mid-range prices (*tzatziki* €1.50-2.50; moussaka €3-4; baklava €2-2.50). The **Third Eye Vegetarian Restaurant ❶** is one of the few remaining bastions of Paleohora's counterculture days. Asian, Greek, and European dishes—the family has a repertoire of over 80 vegetarian dishes, of which 20 are selected to be prepared each night—are created with ingredients grown on the owner's family farm. To reach the restaurant, take Kentekaki in the direction of the beach and look for the signs directing you left. (☎28320 41 234. Entrees under €4. Open Apr.-Oct. 8:30am-3pm and 5:30-11pm.) **Club Paleohora,** across from Camping Paleohora, is the town's popular open-air disco. Follow the directions to the campsite or take the minibus (every 30min., midnight-4am) that transports clients from **Skala** bar in front of the port to the disco. (☎28320 41 120. Cover F-Sa €3, includes 1 beer. Cocktails €4-6. Open Sept.-June F-Sa 11pm-5am; July-Aug. daily 11pm-5am.)

DAYTRIPS FROM PALEOHORA: **Elafonisi** is a beach across from a small uninhabited island at the southwestern corner of Crete. (Open daily 7am-sunset.) Visitors start on the mainland side of the beach and wade across the shallow 100m inlet that divides the mainland from the lovely island. Though crowded with tourists in the summer, walking away from the mainland along the island brings you to increasingly umbrella-free, pristine beaches of fine-grained sand and translucent waters speckled with small islands. Back on the mainland side are restrooms and a **taverna ❶.** (Open daily 8am-8pm. Sandwiches €2.50-3. Burgers €2.50. Beer €2.) If the sun hasn't drained all of your energy, a short walk up the road perpendicular to the beach will get you more baklava for your buck at **Panorama ❷.** (☎28220 61 548. Chicken with lemon €4.50. Swordfish €5. Open Mar.-Oct. 8am-midnight.) Panorama also has **accommodations ❷,** if you miss your boat. (Doubles €30-40.) Those tired of sun-worship can pay homage of another sort at the cliffside monastery **Chrysokalitsa,** operated by an order of nuns, built from and supported by the cliffs. Walk 5km up the road from Elafonisi to get there. The cream-colored monastery will appear on your left when you come to an unmarked but well-paved road amid a scattering of houses; turn left and make another left at the end of this road. (Open daily 8am-2pm and 5-8pm. Free. Modest dress required.) Take the ferry from Paleohora along the southern coast (leaves 10am, returns 4pm; one-way €4.50) or the bus from Hania (leaves 9:30am, returns 4pm; €8 one-way).

Escape the crowds of Paleohora's beach at nearby **Anidri beach,** accessible by car or foot. Hikers should take the road out of town past Camping Paleohora and continue 5min. until the road forks. The low road to the right (the "easy" way) takes you along a lingering but prominent road along the coast to the beach (45min.). The high road to the left (the "interesting" way) will take you through the mountains and up to the sweet village of Anidri itself. For the latter route, hike up the high road into the mountains to the village cafe (1hr.). Take a right just before the cafe (the locals can help you at this point) and onto a road with a sign pointing to a church, the gorge, and the beach. Follow this road to its end and make another right. You'll reach a stone road with a sign pointing back to the cafe; turn left and go down it to the dry riverbed. Follow the occasional sign and stone marker through the small gorge to the beach (40min. from town). The beautiful path is fairly difficult; your only company will likely be roaming goats. Wear sturdy walking shoes and bring water and trail snacks. The beaches at the bottom, especially the beach farthest to your left, are smooth, unblemished strips of pale, if somewhat rocky, sand surrounded by high cliffs and clear water. No need to weigh yourself down with a bathing suit—going nude is perfectly normal here. Most visitors leave by taking the coastal road, which will return you to the right branch of the fork near Camping Paleohora.

RETHYMNO PREFECTURE

Western Crete has struggled for years to maintain its authenticity amid surging tourism in the region. Rethymno has been greatly successful and each town in the area maintains an individual personality. Modest seaside towns fill only short sections of the shore with tavernas, leaving long stretches to the birds, waves, and hikers. The meld of Ottoman, Venetian, and Greek architecture complements the blue waters of the southwestern coast and the dark mountains of the interior.

RETHYMNO Ρεθυμνο ☎28310

The capital of the region, Rethymno is steeped in ancient folklore and spiced with urban panache. According to Greek myth, Zeus was born of Rhea to the titan Chronos in the cave of Idaion Andron outside of Rethymno. Chronos was on the verge of eating the baby to prevent Zeus's foreseen patricide, but Cretan *kourites* (spirits) danced up a storm to distract the jealous king. Once safe from Chronos, baby Zeus nursed from the goat Amaltheia and ate honey from golden bees. Crete's many conquerors—Venetians, Ottomans, and Nazis—have had a profound effect in the Rethymno of today's Old City. Arabic inscriptions on the walls, a skyline full of minarets, and the Venetian fortress unite to create a distinctive cultural atmosphere that overflows the city limits and adds an extra flavor to the Greek folk music that spills out of its cafes and garden restaurants. Even the most restless travelers may find their wanderlust inexplicably satiated as they lounge alongside contented locals, sipping *raki* into the wee hours of the morning.

CRETE

TRANSPORTATION

Flights: Olympic Airways, Koumoundorou 5 (☎28310 22 257), opposite the public gardens. Open M-Sa 8am-3:30pm.

Buses: Rethymno-Hania station (☎28310 22 212), south of the fortress on Igoumenou Gavriil. Service to: **Agia Galini** (1½hr., 3-4 per day, €4.40); **Arkadi Monastery** (45min., 2-3 per day, €2); **Hania** (1hr., 16 per day, €5.55); **Iraklion** (1½hr., 17 per day, €5.90); **Plakias** (1hr., 4-5 per day, €3.30).

Ferries: Buy tickets to **Piraeus** (8am, €24.90) at any travel office.

Taxis: ☎28310 22 316, 28310 24 316, or 28310 28 316. At Pl. Martiron 4. Available 24hr.

ORIENTATION AND PRACTICAL INFORMATION

Pl. Martiron, between Rethymno's **Old City** to the north and **New City** to the south, is about a 15min. walk from anywhere you would want to go. To get to the plateia from the bus station, climb the stairs at the back of the station's parking lot onto **Igoumenou Gavriil** and go left; Pl. Martiron is to your left just after the **public gardens.** The **waterfront** lies at the northern edge of the Old City, with a maze of ancient streets filling the space between the main thoroughfare of Igoumenou Gavriil and the water. The Venetian **Fortezza** sits at the western edge of the waterfront; the western end turns into a fine beach at the city's edge.

Tourist Office: ☎28310 29 148. By the waterfront on El. Venizelou. Pick up **free town maps,** bus and ferry schedules, info on rooms and restaurants. Open M-F 9am-2pm.

Banks: Several blocks of Koundouriotou west of the public gardens sprout more than 5 banks, several with 24hr. **ATMs.** The **National Bank** (☎28310 55 228), on Koundouriotou next to the town hall, usually has the best exchange rates. Open M-Th 8am-2:30pm, F 8am-2pm.

Bookstore: International Press, I. Petichaki 15 (☎28310 24 111), sells books, newspapers, and magazines. Open-10am-11pm. **Spontidaki Toula,** Souliou 43 (☎28310 54 307), buys and sells new and used books. Open daily 9am-11pm. **Newsstand,** in Pl. Iroön (☎28310 25 110), has a wide selection of foreign magazines and newspapers, as well as travel guides. Open daily 9am-midnight.

Laundromat: Tombazi 45 (☎28310 56 196), next to the Youth Hostel. Wash and dry €7.50. 20% discount for guests of the hostel. Open M-Sa 8am-2pm and M-F 5-9pm.

Police: ☎28310 25 247. In Pl. Iroön Polytechniou. Open 24hr. **Emergency** ☎100.

Tourist Police: Venizelou 5 (☎28310 28 156). Open daily 7:30am-2:30pm.

Port Police: ☎28310 22 276. In the Venetian Port just before the pier.

Hospital: Trandalidou 18 (☎28310 87 100), in the town's southwestern corner. From Igoumenou Gavriil at the bus station, take a right on Kriari, and turn left onto Trandalidou. Open 24hr.

Pharmacy: Moatsou 5 (☎28310 22 414), near the post office, lists the names and hours of all local pharmacies on the door. Open daily 8am-2:30pm.

OTE: Koundouriotou 23 (☎28310 59 500 or 59 345). Open M-F 7:30am-3pm.

Internet Access: Cafe E-lounge (☎28310 23 556), on Salaminos just after Ice Club, hooks you up in the sleekest of surroundings with the best deal in town at €2.50 per hr. Open daily 10am-3am. **Cafe Galero** (☎28310 54 345), at Rimondi Fountain, has Internet access for €3.50 per hr. Open daily 6am-3am. Internet also available at the **Youth Hostel** (€4 per hr.).

Post Office: Main branch, Moatsou 19 (☎28310 22 303), east of the public gardens in the New City. Open M-F 7:30am-8pm. **Postal code:** 74100.

ACCOMMODATIONS AND CAMPING

Picturesque streets near the fortress and the Venetian port are lined with ideally located but expensive hotels and **domatia.**

Elizabeth Camping (☎28310 28 694), 3km east of town on the old road to Iraklion. Take the hotel bus from Rethymno station and ask the driver to stop at the campsite (every 20min., until 9pm; €0.65). Pitch your tent under bamboo cover at this warm, family-owned campground. The owner, Elizabeth, knows the sites you'll love and how to get there. Enjoy the company of your fellow travelers at the frequent barbecues (W and Sa; complete meal €8-10) while Niko grills up

NO WORK, ALL PLAY

LOCAL LIBATIONS

With more alcohol than Oktoberfest and more class than La Rive Gauche, Rethymno's annual summer wine festival is an all-you-can-drink week-long booze-fest featuring the regional alcohol specialties of Crete. Wine-makers from the entire region transport their products in barrels and line up along the usually quiet greens of the public gardens to hand out glasses of red, white, and even bizarrely black wines.

The festival fortuitously requires no arduous picking or choosing from this panoply; with a single admission fee of a few euros, participants are invited to relish in an unlimited quantity and a (virtually) unlimited variety, ensuring that the wallet-weary need not confine themselves to a mere sporadic sampling. Tastes tend to become less discerning as the day goes on.

Upon entrance to the fair, visitors are given a small complimentary glass decorated with dancing figures, which they then use for wine tasting and keep as a token of the good times; those who prefer more robust quantities have the option to pay a few extra euros to purchase a carafe. Finally, the festivities culminate in nightly performances of traditional Cretan singing and dancing, providing a glimpse into more aspects of Cretan culture. Though the celebration lasts more than a week, locals come on the first weekend, when the wine is at its best quality and the variety at its most plentiful.

The festival takes place in Municipal Garden every summer. For more information, inquire at a city tourist office.

meat and seafood with his famous mustard sauce. Self-service taverna open 8:30am-9pm. Laundry €4. Free parking at reception. Open mid-Apr.-Oct. €6.30 per person. €4.20 per tent, tent rental €6. €5 per caravan. 10% discount with International Camping Caravan Card. ❶

Youth Hostel, Tombazi 41-45 (☎28310 22 848; www.yhrethymno.com). From the bus station, walk down Igoumenou Gavriil and take the first left at Pl. Martiron; Tombazi is the first right. The popular outdoor gardens and bar (beer and wine €1.40-1.65) bustle with friendly backpackers. Outdoor beds available in the summer. Breakfast (€1.70) available until 11:30am. Hot showers after 10am. Internet €1 per 15min. Reception 8am-noon and 5-9pm. Dorms €7. ❶

Olga's Pension, Souliou 57 (☎28310 53 206; fax 28310 29 851), off Antistassios. You'll feel like part of the family with owners George, Stella, and Yiannis. George decorates each cramped but colorful room with a collection of creative kitsch; hats carpet the hallways floor to ceiling while walls are lined with colorful dots or artistic spirals of coins. Enjoy delicious cooking from Stella's kitchen downstairs (open "early 'til late") or in the rooftop garden. All rooms with ceiling fans, some with private bath. Doubles €25, with breakfast €35; 4-person studios (available for extended visits) €600 per month. ❷

Hotel Leo, Vafe 2 (☎28310 26 197), just off of Souliou. Romantically decorated with wood floors, high windows, antique lamps, and white stucco, the rooms that line Leo's 650-year-old building also boast private bath and a quiet atmosphere in the center of town. Doubles €30-40; triples €40-45. ❷

Park Hotel, Igoumenou Gavriil 37 (☎28310 29 958). From the bus station, walk down Igoumenou Gavriil; it's on the left, across from the public gardens' entrance. Quiet rooms make you feel like you're staying at grandma's but have amenities grandma never gave you: TVs, A/C, and your own phone line. Doubles €35; triples €40. ❷

FOOD

An **open-air market,** next to the park between Moatsou and Koundouriotou, opens Thursdays at 6 or 7am and closes around 1pm; selection diminishes by 10am. Come at the end for the best deals as the vendors try to shed their final remaining products. For affordable nighttime eats, tourists and locals head to **Pl. T. Petichaki.**

Taverna Garden Ftochiko, Souliou 37 (☎28310 28 136). Sophisticated and sleek, Ftochiko provides an escape into a lemon-tree lined courtyard and garden; relax to running water while sampling any of the terrific entrees. Vineyard-style lamb €8.20. Most entrees €8. Open daily noon-midnight. ❸

Taverna Kyria Maria, Moskovitou 20 (☎28310 29 078), to the right down the small alley behind the Rimondi fountain. The eccentric interior is covered in birdcages and model big rigs. From the initial entrance into the grape-draped street seating to the complimentary *raki* and honey-drizzled cheese pie that finish off the meal, Kyria Maria provides one of the best bets in town. The octopus in wine sauce (€7) is their specialty. Open mid-Mar.-Oct. daily 11am-1am. MC/V. ❷

Katerina's, Melissinou 34 (☎28310 57 024). With seating beneath the Fortezza and flavored *raki* from Katerina herself, this establishment provides a pleasant dining experience. The fixed menus are the best bet: moussaka, Greek salad, *tzatziki,* wine, and coffee for 2 €13. Stuffed wine leaves €3. Open daily 8am-11pm. ❷

Akri, Kornarou 27 (28310 50 719). Set in a quiet side alleyway, Akri serves up solid meals with good prices and friendly service. Bask in the glow of the electric orange interior and relish the respite from the shopping bustle. Calamari €4. Moussaka €4.50. Fish €5 and up. Open daily 10am-midnight. ❷

NIGHTLIFE AND ENTERTAINMENT

The bar scene in Rethymno centers on **I. Petichaki** and **Nearchou** near the western end of the harbor. A handful of chic clubs cater predominately to locals looking to meet friends and have a drink; dancing is kept to a minimum. For a dry night, the **open-air cinema,** on Melissinou, shows Hollywood films with Greek subtitles, is a good place to unwind. (Tickets €6. Shows usually at 9, 11pm, and 1am.)

Fortezza Disco Bar, (☎28310 55 493), on Petichaki, presents a plush, sleek, and modern interior and has live DJs. Open daily midnight-late.

Ice Club, at the intersection of Salaminos and Mesologiou, is the haunt of the Rethymno elite. Beware of steep covers (up to €8) and expensive drinks (beers €6).

Rock Cafe Club, Petichaki 8, is a popular dancing location. It has less pretentious patrons than other Rethymno discos plus 3 fully stocked bars. Beers €4; cocktails €7. Open daily 10:30pm-late.

Cafe Ancora (☎28310 50 231) provides the standard plush chairs, lapping water, and strutting promenaders, that together allow for a relaxing atmosphere. Beers €3-4; cocktails €5. Open daily 9am-midnight.

Dimman Bar, on the 2nd fl. at the corner of Arkadiou and Paleologou, has a small interior covered in a collage of classic movie stars and outdated currency. The highlight is the wrap-around balcony, which serves as a perfect vantage point for watching well-dressed Greeks scamper from club to club. Open daily 10pm-3am.

SIGHTS

The sprawling **Venetian Fortezza,** a fortress built in 1580, is the highest point in the city and provides magnificent views of the coast and surrounding towns. Explore the series of caves, churches, and crumbling facades that comprise the ruins and pretend you're defending Rethymno from invaders, or just bring a picnic and dine overlooking the water. (☎28310 28 101. Open M-Th, Sa-Su 8:30am-7pm. €2.90, children €2.30.) Rethymno's **Archaeological Museum** occupies a former Ottoman prison adjacent to the fortress. In a single, large room, the collection contains an eclectic mix of knives, coins, lamps, and statues from Minoan and Classical times. The museum has enough artifacts and information to keep archaeology enthusiasts occupied for about an hour. (☎28310 54 668. Open Tu-Su 8:30am-3pm. €3, students and seniors €2, EU students and children under 12 free.) The **L. Kanakakis Center of Contemporary Art,** Himaras 5, at the corner of Salaminos, displays 19th- and 20th-century Greek paintings and hosts temporary exhibits. (☎28310 52 530; www.rca.gr. Open Tu-F 9am-1pm and 7-10pm, Sa-Su 11am-3pm. €3, students €1.50.) The **Historical and Folklore Museum,** Vernardou 28-30, showcases artifacts of Cretan social history. (☎28310 23 398. Open M-Sa 9:30am-2pm. €3, students €1.50.) Tattooed with graffiti and untamed by museum keepers, Rethymno's Ottoman monuments are in a state of forlorn disarray. Struggling for space in the modern city streets are the **Neratzes Minaret** on Antistassios; the former Franciscan church **Nerdjes Mosque,** a block away on Fragkiskou 1 (called St. Francis on many maps); the **Kara Pasha Mosque** on Arkadiou near Pl. Iroön; and the **Valides Minaret,** which presides over the gate called **Porta Megali** at Pl. Martiron. The **public gardens,** which lie at the inland end of Igoumenou, on the corner of Pl. Martiron, provide a shady retreat from the Greek sun. Romp around the playgrounds, play chess on a big board, and be nice to the sad monkey in the pen.

Rethymno's **Wine Festival,** which takes place at the end of July, is a crowded all-you-can-drink celebration, with a local dance troupe performing each evening. The city's **Renaissance Festival,** featuring theater, concerts, and exhibitions, is held in the fortress in July and August. **Carnival,** beginning on Feb. 2 in 2004, is a major event in Rethymno, as it hosts the largest celebration in Crete. Call the tourist office for festival schedules and other information.

DAYTRIP FROM RETHYMNO: ARKADI MONASTERY

Take the bus the 23km from Rethymno (40min., 2-3 per day, €2 one-way; return trips 1hr. later). ☎28310 83 076. Site open 8am-8pm. €2. Modest dress required.

The site of one of the most famous battles in the War of Independence, **Arkadi Monastery** (Μονη Αρκαδη) became a symbol to accompany the motto "Freedom or Death" (Ελευθερια η Θανατος, el-ef-theh-REE-a EE THA-na-tos). Modern Greeks refer to the event as the Holocaust of 1866. In November of that year, Greeks and Turks fought to a two-day standoff at the monastery. When Greek defenses finally gave way, the monks and *kleftes* (literally "thieves" but referring to the guerrillas fighting for freedom during the War) holding out in the monastery set off their own ammunitions supplies, sacrificing themselves to kill hundreds of Turks. The story of Arkadi inspired support for Cretan independence in Western Europe, and the original structure has since been memorialized on the now defunct 100-drachma note. Today a few monks maintain what is left of the monastery: the frame of the church and the outer complex, a roofless chamber where the ammunitions were detonated, and a small museum containing a portion of the church's original decoration, including Byzantine paintings and orthodox vestments. Despite its devastation, the church is still a stunning example of 15th-century Cretan Renaissance architecture. Stroll through the rose-lined gardens and dilapidated rooms of the remains, making sure to visit the small room, which houses the skulls of the freedom fighters, outside the monastery walls.

PLAKIAS Πλακιας ☎28320

Though it increasingly sacrifices its seclusion to tourists, Plakias remains wonderfully underdeveloped and inexpensive compared to most Cretan beach towns. Towering mountains and steep gorges shelter the palm trees, olive groves, and stunning hiking terrain that engulf the town. Most people stay on the main street that runs along the sandy beach; stepping inland you'll find yourself among palm fronds and the sound of chirping cicadas.

TRANSPORTATION AND PRACTICAL INFORMATION. You'll be able to find anything you need either on the beach road or the paths that head inland from it. From the bus stop the main road heads east toward the umbrella beach and west toward the pier. **Buses** drop off and pick up at the beach, and run to: **Preveli** (20min., daily, €1.50) and **Rethymno** (50min., 4 per day, €3.30). Find rental cars (€32-40) and mopeds (€10-20) at **Monza Travel** (☎28320 31 433; fax 28320 31 883), on the beach road east of the bus stop. (Open daily 9am-2pm and 5-9pm.) A 24hr. **ATM** is on the side of Old Alianthos Taverna. (€0.75 for 10min.) In an **emergency,** dial ☎100. **Police** (☎28320 22 027) are 20km away in Spili. Behind Monza Travel is a **pharmacy** (☎28320 31 666; open M-Sa 9:15am-1pm and 5:15-8:30pm). The **hospital** (☎28310 87 100) is in Rethymno. A **doctor's office** (☎28320 31 770 or 697 343 4934; open M-Sa 9:30am-1pm and 5-8:30pm) can be found next to the pharmacy. **Internet** access is available at Plakias Youth Hostel (€4.50 per hr.). **Forum,** across the street from the bus stop, also hooks you up. (☎28320 32 084. €4 per hr. Open daily 10am-late.) The **post office** (open M-F 7:30am-2pm) lies next to the doctor's office. **Postal code:** 74060.

ACCOMMODATIONS AND FOOD. From the bus stop, walk 50m east and turn left at Monza Travel; turn left again at the end of the road and follow the signs pointing inland to reach the **Plakias Youth Hostel ❶,** the self-proclaimed southernmost hostel in Europe. Set in an olive grove, this happening hostel goes all-out with hot showers, good music, friendly people, and cheap alcohol (beer €1.05; 0.75L wine €1.20), making it an oasis backpackers enthusiastically endorse. After one night's stay you may hear the sirens singing and never want to leave—some guests never do. (☎28320 32 118; www.yhplakias.com. Internet access €0.75 per 10min. Reception 9am-noon and 5-9pm. Open Mar.-Nov. Dorms €7.) At **Pension Kyriakos ❷,** also behind Monza Travel on your way to the youth hostel, rooms are decked out with fridges and private baths. Kyriakos insists on treating all his guests to *raki*. (☎28320 31 307. Singles €20-22; doubles €25-27; apartments for 3-4 €50.) At the far western end of town, **On The Rocks ❸** provides amazing views of the beach and surrounding cliffs. Neat rooms have fridges, kettles, private baths, and fans. (☎28320 31 023; arabatz6@otenet.gr. A/C €5 extra. Doubles €30; triples €35.) On the eastern outskirts of town, festively colored, air-conditioned **Plakias Bay Hotel ❹** sits peacefully just off the beach. To get there, walk east out of town and stay on the right branch of the fork in the road for about 400m. (☎28320 31 215; fax 28320 31 951. Breakfast included. Doubles €50-60. AmEx/MC/V.) To reach **Camping Apollonia ❶,** walk eastward from the bus stop and take the left fork in the road at the Old Alianthos Taverna. Follow this road 100m to a complex that includes a pool, basketball court, and snack bar. (☎28320 31 318. Laundry €5. Open Apr.-Oct. Reception 8am-9pm. €5 per person, €3.80 per tent, €3.40 per car.)

Quiet, little **Nikos ❷**, behind Monza Travel, serves up uncommon vegetarian dishes as well as tasty meat for the carnivorous, all for dirt cheap. (☎28320 31 921. Most dishes under €5. Open daily noon-3pm and 7pm-midnight.) The *stifado* (€5.50) and butter beans (€3.50) at the **Old Alianthos Taverna ❷**, at the eastern end of the beach road, are good choices. (☎28320 31 851. Open daily 7am-midnight. AmEx/MC/V.) Head to **Ostraco ❶**, by the harbor about 100m west of the bus stop, for light fare and drinks. (☎28320 31 710. Omelettes and sandwiches €2-3. Cocktails €5. Open 8am-1:30am. AmEx/MC/V.)

NIGHTLIFE. Quiet Plakias starts to hum come nightfall, when bars light up on the outskirts of town. Ostraco is a good place to start the night. **Meltemi,** 100m past the east end of town on the right fork, is the place to be every night until 6am for dancing. If you want to dance with the locals, don't arrive until late. (☎28320 31 305. Beers €3; cocktails €6. Open 11pm-late.) Nufaro, better known as **Joe's,** is a bar just to the east of the bus stop on the main road; look for the "Cafe/Bar" sign that hangs above the entrance. It boasts a laid-back group of regulars, occasional free movie screenings, and a small dance floor that grooves to everything from reggae to rap. (☎697 620 0979. Beer €2; cocktails €3.5-5. Open daily 9am-late).

BEACHES AND HIKING. The **Plakias beach** starts about 100m east of the bus stop and stretches the rest of the length of the town. It has fine sand and large waves; sun-worshippers are progressively less clothed as you move east. (Umbrella and chair rental €5.) If life on the beach gets dull, Plakias boasts a variety of secluded beaches and astoundingly beautiful hikes through the four gorges that run down towards the town. To reach the gorgeous **One Rock beach,** follow the left fork of the main road 1km outside of town, take a right at the signs pointing to **Damnoni beach,** walk the length of the sand and take a right on the track at the end; One Rock is the second cove on the right. Named for the small rock island in the center of the steep cove, the stunningly clear water and isolated feel make One Rock a local favorite. Look for the underwater tunnel through the cliff on the right side, which leads to **Pig's beach.** To reach the **Venetian corn mill,** follow the signs after the youth hostel down the stone path about 300m; once it becomes a dirt track, look for the stones crossing the river. Continue another 400m and when you reach the first bridge, cross it to reach the mill; you can also continue 40m straight to see the tiny church built under an overhanging cliff. To complete the fantastic (but complicated) 2hr. **hike** to **Preveli Monastery,** ask either in town or at the hostel for directions. You can also take a **bus.** (Open daily 8am-1:30pm and 3:30-8pm. Modest dress required. €2, students €1, under 14 free.) From there you can reach **Preveli beach** by walking 1km along the road to a dirt parking area; make the 1hr. hike down. Scramble up again to catch the Preveli-Plakias bus back or take the ferry to **Plakias** (€5) or **Agia Galini** (€10).

CRETE

IRAKLION PREFECTURE

Iraklion Prefecture revolves around its eponymous cosmopolitan capital. As with most of Crete, the touristed areas are pressed along the beaches in the north, while the southern half of the province and the mountains that sandwich each side host fewer visitors and sustain a more traditional lifestyle.

IRAKLION Ηρακλειο ☎2810

The fifth-largest city in Greece, Iraklion is Crete's capital and primary port. The city's size is both its greatest attraction and its main drawback; urban grit and maze-like streets make the scenery less than picturesque, but an influx of wealth has produced bustling shopping streets, posh cafes, and a chic native population with requisite urban brusqueness. While architectural aesthetes find Iraklion's unplanned jumble utterly offensive (Venetian monuments are sandwiched between both Turkish houses and two-story concrete flats), the varied buildings remind travelers of the city's impressive history. Crete's largest bus station and port are found here, making this central city a convenient base for exploring the island; in particular, the Minoan ruins that circle the outlying towns provide a pleasant respite from the frenetic pace of the city itself.

TRANSPORTATION

Flights: Olympic Airways or Aegean Airlines zip between Iraklion and other Greek destinations, with discounts for those under 25 or over 60. Planes fly to: **Athens** (45min., 13-15 per day, €85); **Rhodes** (45min., 6-7 per week, €85); **Santorini** (30min., 2 per week, €60); **Thessaloniki** (2hr., 1-2 per day, €109). To get to the city, take **bus #1**

from outside the airport parking lot to **Pl. Eleftherias** (every 10min., €0.65). Cabs to the airport cost €6-8. Inquire about flights at the **Olympic Airways** office, 25 Augustou 27 (☎2810 288 073; open M-F 8am-3:30pm), or the **Aegean/Cronus Airlines** office, Dimokratias 11 (☎2810 344 324; open M-F 8am-8:30pm, Sa 9am-2pm).

Buses: If you want to head out from the city, some planning is necessary, since there are several **KTEL** bus terminals. Be sure to match the station with your destination.

Terminal A (☎2810 245 020), between the Old City walls and the harbor near the waterfront, serves: **Agios Nikolaos** (1½hr., 20 per day, €5); **Arhanes** (30min., 20 per day, €1.30); **Hersonissos** (45min., every 30min., €2.20); **Ierapetra** (2½hr., 7 per day, €7); **Lasithi** (2hr., 2 per day, €4.20); **Malia** (1hr., every 30min., €2.70); **Sitia** (3¼hr., 4 per day, €10).

Hania/Rethymno Terminal (☎2810 221 765), opposite Terminal A, beside the ferry landing. Buy tickets in the cafe building. Service to **Hania** (3hr., 17 per day, €10.50) and **Rethymno** (1½hr., 17 per day, €5.90). From Hania and Rethymno, travelers connect to Plakias, Samaria Gorge, Hora Sfakion, and Akrotiri.

Terminal B (☎2810 255 965), outside the Hania Gate of Old City walls. Take bus #135 from Terminal A (€1) or walk 15min. down Kalokerinou from town center. Buses to: **Agia Galini** (2¼hr., 7 per day, €5.50); **Matala** (2hr., €5); **Phaistos** (1½hr., 8 per day, €4.50) via **Gortys** (€3.20).

Ferries: Boat offices line 25 Augustou; most open 9am-9pm. Ferries go to: **Mykonos** (8½hr., 5 per week, €21.50); **Naxos** (7hr., 3 per week, €18.50); **Paros** (9hr., 7 per week, €21.50); **Piraeus** (14hr., 3 per day, €29.50); **Santorini** (4hr., 2 per day, €14).

Hydrofoils: Serve same destinations as ferries but in about half the time, for twice the price. Go to www.dophins.gr or dial ☎210 419 9000 for Flying Dolphin information.

Taxis: Tariff Taxi of Iraklion (☎2810 210 102 or 210 168). Cabs often line up in Pl. Venizélou, across from the fountain and in other highly touristed areas. Available 24hr.

Car Rental: Rental car companies are scattered along 25 Augustou. Make the owners compete for your business by quoting prices from their neighbors. **Cosmos,** 25 Augustou 15 (☎2810 241 357 or 2810 346 173; fax 2810 220 379), charges €11 for a 1-day rental, plus €0.13 per km over 100km. Renting for multiple days reduces the price up to 30%. Open Apr.-Oct. daily 7:30am-9pm; Nov.-Mar. 8am-1pm and 5-9pm.

Moped Rental: Inexpensive rental agencies line Handakos, El Greco Park, and 25 Augustou. Check if quoted price includes the 20% tax and liability insurance. **Irene Rentals** (☎2810 250 268), on Kidonias next to the post office at the corner of El Greco Park, offers 1-day rentals for €20. If rentals exceed 1 day, the rate is reduced. Open daily 8am-3pm and 5-9pm.

CRETE

ORIENTATION AND PRACTICAL INFORMATION

The city has two centers. **Pl. Venizelou** (also known to tourists as **Lion Fountain** or **Four Lion Square**), home to Morosini Fountain, forms where **Handakos** meets **Dikeosinis** and **25 Augustou** in the center of town. **Pl. Eleftherias** sits at the intersection of Doukos Boufor and Dikeosinis on the east side of the Old City. Most necessities can be found in or near these two squares. Between the two centers, a maze of streets hides a seemingly endless supply of fashionable cafes. Be warned that many of the street names contain numbers, so that 25 Augustou and 1866 are street names; *Let's Go* lists the address number *after* the street name.

Tourist Offices: Info Point Europe, Xanthoudidou 1 (☎2810 228 203), across from the Archaeological Museum at Pl. Eleftherias. The English-speaking staff provides **free maps,** bus and ferry schedules, and general tourist information. Open M-F 8am-3pm.

Travel Agencies: Several agencies line 25 Augustou. **Arabatzoglou Bros. Shipping Agents Travel Bureau,** 25 Augustou 54 (☎2810 226 697 or 226 698; www.arabatzogloubros.gr), offers the standard tours and fares. Open M-Sa 8am-8:30pm.

Banks: Those on 25 Augustou have 24hr. **ATMs** and **currency exchange. National Bank,** 25 Augustou 35 (☎2810 304 850), is open M-F 8am-2pm.

Luggage Storage and Laundromat: Washsalon, Handakos 18 (☎2810 280 858). Luggage storage €1.50 per day. Wash and dry €6, including soap. Open 7:30am-10pm.

Bookstores: Planet International Bookstore, Kidonias 23 (☎2810 281 558; fax 2810 287 142), on the corner of Hortatson and Kidonias. 4 floors of books in a number of languages, with a broad selection of classics and travel literature. Some used books in the back by the stairs. Open M-Sa 8:30am-2pm; also open Tu,Th-F 5-9pm.

Library: Vikelaia Municipal Library (☎2810 399 237 or 399 249), across from Morosini Fountain. Limited selection in English, French, German, Italian, Russian, and Chinese. Most international books are philosophy, literature, classics, and history. You can peruse them in the air-conditioned reading room on the 2nd fl. Open M-F 8am-2pm; M, W also open 5-8pm.

Public Toilets: In El Greco Park, look for the underground, cage-like entrance by the swings. €0.50. Open 6am-9pm.

Road Emergency: ☎166.

Police: Pl. Venizelou 29, in a blue building among the cafes. Open 24hr. One station serves the east side of town (☎2810 284 589 or 2810 282 677); another station in the same building serves the west (☎2810 282 243). **Port Police** (☎2810 244 956 or 244 934), by the harbor.

Tourist Police: Dikeosinis 10 (☎2810 283 190), 1 block from the intersection with 25 Augustou. Also provides tourist information. Open 7am-10pm.

Hospitals: Venizelou Hospital (☎2810 368 000), on Knossou; take bus #2 from Pl. Venizelou for 20min. **Panepistimiako Hospital** (☎2810 392 111). Take a bus from Astoria Hotel in Pl. Eleftherias. The medical center, **Asklepeion of Crete,** Zografou 8 (☎2810 342 500), is on the southern side of Pl. Eleftherias. All open 24hr.

OTE: Minotavrou 10 (☎2810 395 316), on the left side of El Greco Park as you enter from 25 Augustou. Open M-F 7am-1pm.

Internet Access: Gallery Games Net, Korai 14 (☎2810 282 804), is around the corner from the cinema at Pl. Eleftherias and down 1 block on Korai. €3 per hr., €1.50 min. Open 10am-midnight. **Netc@fé,** 1878 4 (☎2810 229 569), also has a wide selection of Playstation games. Walk toward the waterfront on Handakos, turn left on Vistaki, and then right onto 1878. €3 per hr. Open M-Sa 10am-3am, Su noon-3am. **Cafe Metro,** Dimokratias 12 (☎2810 346 528), next to Aegean Airlines, offers a laid-back environment relatively free from tourists. €3 per hr. Open daily 10am-1am.

Post Office: Main office, in Pl. Daskalogianni, offers all major services. Open M-F 7:30am-8pm, Sa 7:30am-2pm. The tiny **branch** in El Greco Park offers only mailing service. Open M-F 9am-9pm. **Postal code:** 71001.

CRETE

ACCOMMODATIONS

TOOTING THEIR OWN HORN. When taking a **taxi** from the airport or port, beware of drivers who claim that the hotel you name is closed or full. It's a common scam for taxi drivers to get pay-offs from hotels for bringing customers there. Insist on your own destination and, if the cabbie won't comply, threaten to get out of the taxi.

Iraklion has many cheap hotels and hostels, most near Handakos at the center of town. Others are on Evans and 1866 near the market.

Rent a Room Hellas, Handakos 24 (☎2810 288 851), 2 blocks from El Greco Park. Simple but satisfactory, Hellas features large dorm rooms, a casual restaurant on the 4th floor, and a spectacular view of the whitewashed roofs of Iraklion from the terrace. The communal feel attracts a large portion of the backpacker set. Breakfast €2.50-4. Hot water 24hr.; free luggage storage. Dorms €9; doubles €25; triples €36. ❶

Rent Rooms Verginia, Kalimeraki 3 (☎2810 242 739), near Hotel Rea. Large windows and high ceilings distinguish Verginia's comfortable rooms. Sinks can be found in each room with a well-maintained common bath just down the hall. A small garden sitting area is the perfect place to enjoy a good book. Doubles €25; triples €35. ❷

Lato Hotel, Epimendou 15 (☎2810 228 103; www.lato.gr). Walking toward the water on 25 Augustou, make a right onto Epimendou and walk about 3 blocks. Looking out over the water, this ultra-modern building has some of the finest rooms in the city. Each room has a slightly different decorating scheme, but all have satellite TVs, A/C, and balconies. The trickling fountains and small brook in the lobby greet you with a taste of the luxury to come. Singles €88; doubles €114; triples €140. ❺

Youth Hostel, Vyronos 5 (☎2810 286 281; fax 2810 222 947). From the bus station, with the water on your right, take a left onto 25 Augustou and a right on Vyronos. Basic, blue rooms filled with beds in a family-run hostel. Curfew 12:30am. Hot water 24hr. Sheets €0.60. Luggage storage €3. Breakfast and dinner available (€3 per meal); beer €1.50. Check-out 10am. Dorms €9; singles €12; doubles €24; triples €33. ❶

Hotel Rea, Kalimeraki 1 (☎2810 223 638; fax 2810 242 189). From Pl. Venizelou, walk down Handakos and turn right after Rent a Room Hellas. The hospitable owners provide cool, airy rooms, hot showers, and free luggage storage. The bare rooms are available with common or private bath; all have fans and sinks. Breakfast €3. Singles €18, with bath €21; doubles €22/€28; triples €33/€38. ❷

 FOOD

The ritzy cafes around **Morosini Fountain,** near El Greco Park, and in Pl. Venizelou cater to tourists and other lounging sun-worshippers. Bargain seekers should take a left off 1866, one block from the plateia, to reach tiny **Theodosaki,** where 10 colorful tavernas serving big, cheap dishes (€3) are jammed side by side. Souvlaki joints abound on **25 Augustou,** and gyros are everywhere (around €2). The best show in town is the **open-air market** on 1866, starting near Pl. Venizelou. Stalls piled high with sweets, spices, produce, cheeses, meat, and Cretan muscle shirts line both sides of the narrow street. (Hours vary by stall; typically open M-Sa 8am-2pm; Tu, Th, F 5-9pm.) Located in the market about halfway down 1866, **Amaltheia,** named after the goat that nursed Zeus, has cauldrons of yogurt that eclipse the pasteurized brands found elsewhere. The store serves traditional sheep's milk yogurt and local cheeses like a Cretan gruyère. (Cheese €4-9 per kg.)

Prassein Aloga, Handakos 21 (☎2810 283 429), between Washsalon and the Planet Bookstore. Mediterranean tastes are synthesized into a diverse selection of fresh dishes served up by an English-speaking staff in a tree-lined courtyard. Risotto with seafood €8. Squid with onion €8. Open M-Sa noon-midnight. ❷

Lychnostatis, Ioannou Chronaki 8 (☎2810 242 117), 30m past El Greco Park on the same street as the OTE. Zealous locals crowd this very small, very intimate ouzeri at all hours to sample the flavorful tiropita (€3) and other specialties. Open noon-1am. ❶

Tou Terzaki, Loch. Marineli 17 (☎2810 221 444), behind Agios Dimitrios chapel, off Vyronos, 1 block from 25 Augustou. Petite portions are cooked with delectable freshness at this sophisticated ouzeri. Customers enjoy the organic ingredients at the outdoor tables or in the yellow-lit interior, serviced by a friendly waitstaff. Fried squid €5.80. Stuffed vine leaves €3.80. Open M-Sa 5pm-1am. ❷

Lukulos, Korai 5 (☎2810 224 435). From Pl. Eleftherias, walk past the cinema, and turn left onto Korai. Local, organic ingredients, good vegetarian options, and an extensive selection of Greek wines make Lukulos a delight. Although a bit touristy, the pampering waitstaff and lush patio complement gourmet Mediterranean concoctions. Lobster medallion with spaghetti €16. Veal with dried figs €18. Open noon-1am. ❹

Thraka, Platokallergon 14 (☎2810 282 355). Facing the Morosini Fountain with your back to the street, walk about 20m to the right. Popular spot for a post-party snack.

Greasy but good, this pint-sized stand serves up grilled pork gyros and souvlaki. Try the souvlaki with *thraka* bread crust (€2.20). Open M-Sa 11am-6am. ❶

Antonios Nerantzoulis, Agiou Titou 16 (☎2810 346 236), behind the Agios Titos Church. Family-run since 1900, this bakery dishes out mounds of flaky morning sweets to salivating customers. It's a great alternative to pricey cafe "tourist breakfasts." Take your steaming pastries straight from the oven in the back. Open M, W, Sa-Su 7am-3pm; Tu, Th, F 7am-3pm and 5-8pm. ❶

SIGHTS

IRAKLION ARCHAEOLOGICAL MUSEUM

Iraklion's main attraction, after Knossos (p. 591), is the superb Archaeological Museum. While most Cretan museums offer a hodgepodge of local finds strung across millennia, the Iraklion Museum presents a comprehensive and chronologically organized record of the Neolithic and Minoan stages of the island's history. A visit to Knossos or another Minoan palace around the island is incomplete without seeing the museum's inventory of artifacts excavated from the sights. Of particular interest are the original **Knossos frescoes** on display here.

ROOM 3. In Room 3 you'll find the most celebrated discovery from the palace of Phaistos (p. 597), the cryptic **Phaistos disc.** Scholars have been unable to decipher the 214 pictographs etched into the solid clay disc, but hypothesize that they represent a ritual hymn or astrological chart. The intricate impressions suggest that they were made with metal stamps, an ancient form of printing.

ROOM 4. Room 4 features three impressive diplays. Two topless **snake goddesses** (or maybe priestesses), clad in layered skirts, balance cats on their heads and support flailing serpents on each outstretched arm. Their scanty clothes are revealing in more ways than one: from the figure, scholars have deduced the look of Neolithic costumes, the Minoans' use of snake symbols for eternity, and the high status of women in the Minoan religious hierarchy. Nearby, the **bull head rhyton,** a kind of libation vase, sports a white mustache, tight curls of hair, and red eyes made of painted rock crystal. The vase is pierced by two holes, one in the skull for filling and one in the nostrils for spilling. If that sounds appetizing to you, even more enticing is the speculation that the sacred liquid used may have been blood from a sacrificial bull. Adjacent is another drinking vessel, an alabaster vase shaped like a lioness's head. Room 4 culminates in the ivory and gold **bull-leaper figurine,** featuring a contorted acrobat, probably having fun with a Minoan ritual.

MINOAN HALL OF FRESCOES. Upstairs is the Minoan Hall of Frescoes, the museum's most controversial exhibit. These are the original **wall paintings** found at Knossos—replicas adorn the reconstructed palace. The original excavator, Sir Arthur Evans, didn't spare these priceless finds from his revisionist hand; in restoring the frescoes, he added his own ideas about the original compositions. Depicting ancient Minoan life, these frescoes capture ladies offering drinks, trippy blue monkeys frolicking in palatial gardens, and Minoans in procession. Before you get too excited about the explosive colors and ancient themes, check out the restoration work up close: the frescoes were reconstructed from very small original pieces, leaving room for Evans's modern-day imagination. Subsequent study of the famous **Prince of Lilies,** for example, has revealed that the fragments actually depicted three figures: a priestess in a lily crown and two boxers flanking her.

OTHER ROOMS. Room 6 stores the **Palaikastro vase,** covered with a complex pattern of spiraling tentacles that toys with your eyes. The jumble of suction cups, seaweed, shells, and ink complements the shape of the chaotic, two-headed amphora perfectly. In Room 7 look for the intricate **bee pendant** from Chryssolakkos at Malia. The pendant is composed of two bees joined delicately at their stingers, forming a cage—the symbolic golden honeycomb of Crete. Rooms 10 and 11's collection of household charms includes the austere **Goddess of the Poppies,** who stands with raised arms and opium flowers sprouting from her head. *(Off Pl. Eleftherias. ☎2810 226 092. Illustrated guide €5-10. Open M noon-7pm, Tu-Su 8am-7pm. €6; students and EU seniors €3; classicists, fine arts students, under 18, and EU students free. Adult dual-ticket for Archaeological Museum and Knossos €10; reduced dual-ticket €5.)*

OTHER SIGHTS

KAZANTZAKIS TOMB AND MUSEUM. With views of Iraklion, the sea, and Mt. Ida to the west, the austere **Tomb of Kazantzakis** offers a peaceful break from crowded Iraklion. Because of his unorthodox beliefs, Nikos Kazantzakis, the author of *The Last Temptation of Christ* and *Zorba the Greek*, was denied a place in a Christian cemetery and was buried alone in this tomb. The grand pyramid, however, seems more fitting of an Egyptian pharaoh than a religious exile and belies the august stature of the author on his native island. The epitaph on the back of the grave, a quote from Kazantzakis's work, reads, "I hope for nothing, I fear nothing, I am free." To reach the tomb from the city center, head down Evans until you reach the Venetian walls and Agios Tou Martinengou, then turn right and walk about 100m further; the tomb is on top of the city walls, beside the football stadium. Alternatively, you can follow the crumbling outline of the city walls to the tomb.

The village of Varvari outside of Iraklion is home to the **Kazantzakis Museum,** where true devotees can see many of the author's original manuscripts, as well as photos of his theatrical productions. A slide show (in English) provides historical background. *(Take a €1.80 bus from Terminal A to Mirtia and follow the signs; make sure to check return schedules. ☎2810 741 689. Open Mar.-Oct. daily 9am-7pm; Nov.-Feb. Su 10am-3pm. €4, students and children €2.)*

CRETE

CHURCHES. Several majestic, ancient churches hide in the modern maze of Iraklion's streets. Magnificent **Agios Titos Church,** on 25 Augustou, once served as a mosque. Its architecture combines Muslim geometric designs and Christian regalia. Lit up every night, it glows a surreal green. Note the *tamata* (charm-like votives) that represent prayers. In Pl. Venizelou, **San Marco Church,** built in 1239, houses a changing exhibition space that displays everything from 14th-century monastery frescoes to modern art. *(☎2810 399 399, ext. 228. Open 9am-8pm. Free.)* Built in 1735, the **Cathedral of Agios Minas** graces Pl. Agia Ekaternis. *(☎2810 282 402. Open 7am-11pm. Free.)* **St. Catherine's Church of Sinai,** also in the plateia, served as the first Greek university after the fall of Constantinople in 1453. *(☎2810 288 825. Open M-Sa 9am-1:30pm, also open Tu, Th-F 5-7pm. Free.)* A priest gives tours of the cloistered **Armenian Church.** Head away from the town center on Kalokerinou and take a right on Lasthenous; the church is to the right of the bend. *(☎2810 244 337.)*

HISTORICAL MUSEUM. The collection at the undervisited Historical Museum includes a scale model of the city, Byzantine and medieval Cretan artwork, a folk collection, photos from the World War II Nazi invasion, displays on Kazantzakis, and perhaps the only **El Greco** painting on Crete—the unspectacular 1578 *View of Mt. Sinai and the Monastery of St. Catherine.* *(Kalokerinou 7, on the corner of Grevenon and Kalokerinou. ☎2810 283 219 or 2810 288 708; www.historical-museum.gr. Open M-F 9am-5pm, Sa 9am-2pm. €3, students €2.20, under 12 free.)*

ICON MUSEUM. St. Catherine and Ag. Minas churches share their plaza with a small church building that contains the Icon Museum. Comprised primarily of Byzantine altarpieces, the collection also features a series of six icons by the Cretan master Damaskinos, a contemporary of El Greco credited with introducing depth and perspective to Greek art. *(☎2810 288 825. Open M-F 9am-7pm, Sa 9am-1pm. €2.)*

VENETIAN IRAKLION. As you rove the city, take in the various Venetian monuments: **Morosini Fountain,** centerpiece of Pl. Venizelou, and the nearby reconstructed **Venetian Loggia,** now a town hall. The 17th-century **Venetian Arsenal,** off Sofokili Venizelou near the waterfront, and the **Koules Fortress** guard the old harbor. For an unexpected dose of peace and beauty, walk along the olive tree-lined southeastern section of the **Venetian walls.**

PANKRITIO STADIUM. Two kilometers outside Iraklion, this venue will play host to a variety of soccer matches during the **2004 Olympic Games.** Seating up to 27,000 spectators, it will also entertain some field events. To reach the stadium, follow Kalokerinou through the center of town; the stadium stands to your right.

NIGHTLIFE AND ENTERTAINMENT

Trading tourist kitsch for genuine urban energy, Iraklion outdoes nearby resort towns with its pulsing nightlife. The cafes and bars along Korai abound with a mass of under-30, sunglasses-sporting, black-clad clientele at all hours. At **Cafe Korai,** Korai 8, patrons absorb the hipness and watch the parade of well-dressed bar hoppers on an expansive deck. Inside, the loud zebra-striped decor and undulating ceiling will make you woozy if the cocktails (€6.50) haven't already done the trick. (☎2810 346 336. Frappé €2.50. Open daily 9am-3am.) A more peaceful scene can be found at **Utopia,** Handakos 5, near Rent a Room Hellas. Enveloping couches, running fountains, and complimentary multi-tiered trays of desserts make you feel like you've been transported to England for a tea-time bite with the queen mum herself. Try one of the chocolate drinks. (☎2810 341 321. Coffee drinks €4-5. Open 9am-2am.) Around 11pm, the young and the restless of all nationalities overflow onto the small streets between Pl. Venizelou and Pl. Eleftherias. Androgeou becomes a veritable river of chic, young Cretans drinking, smoking, and chatting. As the night proceeds, these activities merge with the rhythms of techno and pop along the waterfront. A walk down D. Boufor takes you to a powerful trifecta of Iraklion dance clubs with rather intimidating names: **Privilege, Envy,** and **Diamonds and Pearls.** Each has multiple bars serving pricey drinks, while Privilege and Envy both have balconies overlooking the port. The doors of Iraklion's clubs generally demand a sharp and tidy appearance (no sneakers or less-than-designer jeans) and a cover (€7), which includes one drink.

Join Greeks and tourists at sites throughout the city for Iraklion's annual **Summer Festival** (July-Aug.), with plays, concerts, theater, ballet, and folk dancing. Schedules for the **movie theaters,** including the outdoor cinemas, are posted across the parking lot from the tourist police office. (Tickets €7, reduced for students.)

DAYTRIPS FROM IRAKLION

KNOSSOS Κνωσος

From Iraklion, take bus #2 (15min., every 10min., €0.90), which stops along 25 Augustou. Buy your bus tickets at a nearby kiosk in advance. ☎*2810 231 940. Open daily 8am-7pm; low season 8am-5pm. Guides will offer you tours in English (1hr., €5-7). Make sure your guide is official and has the required papers. €6; students and seniors €3; classicists, fine arts students, and EU students free; in winter, free on Su. Adult dual-ticket for Knossos and Iraklion Archaeological Museum €10; reduced dual-ticket €5.*

Legend and fact are close cousins at the palace of Knossos, famous throughout history as the site of King Minos's machinations, the Labyrinth with its Minotaur, and the imprisonment (and winged escape) of Daedalus and Icarus. Cretans were once ridiculed for claiming Minoan roots, but Sir Arthur Evans secured for them the last laugh when his excavations confirmed the Minoans' ancient presence on the island. While other archaeological digs have unearthed similar finds in Phaistos (p. 597), Malia (p. 601), and Zakros (p. 617), at about 150 sq. m, Knossos is the largest and most intri-

THE LOCAL LEGEND

KING MINOS'S MACHINATIONS

If the labyrinthine layout of the expansive palace at Knossos seems like a maze to you, Greek myth proffers a possible explanation. Legend relates that the redundantly-named Minoan King Minos, basking in wealth and embarassed by the bestial philanderings of his wife, who bore the half-man, half-bull Minotaur, fashioned the palace as an inescapable and impenetrable hideaway. He enlisted artist Deadalus to create a maze where he could simultaneously horde his treasure and imprison his literal monster of a stepson.

To placate the beast and coerce it to guard his jewels, Minos sacrificed seven Athenian virgins to the Minotaur each year, an act which understandably inflamed the prince of Athens, Thesseus. Panicky that Thesseus would seek to solve the riddle of the labyrinth, Minos imprisoned Daedelus and his son, Icarus, in a tower, but Daedelus managed to leak the secret of the maze's construction to Thesseus, who consequently tied a string to the entrance of the labyrinth, slew the Minotaur at the center, and used the string to find his way out.

Meanwhile Daedelus, in an attempt to flee his tower, fashioned wings out of wax for himself and his son, Icarus. Icarus, however, presumptuously flew too close to the sun, melting his wings and precipitating his infamous plummet into the Aegean near the present -day island of Ikaria.

For a modern version of this mythological story, play you some *Kid Icarus* on your old skool Nintendo.

cately designed of Crete's Minoan palaces. The original palace dates back to 1700 BC, but it was partially destroyed by and subsequently forgotten because of a fire in 1350 BC. Evans, one of Heinrich Schliemann's British cronies, purchased the hill that concealed Knossos in 1900 and proceeded to spend 43 years and a fortune excavating it. Armed with the evidence he had unearthed, Evans set out to restore the palace with woeful inaccuracy. Walls, window casements, stairways, and columns were reconstructed in reinforced concrete, and some of the ruins were painted; today Evans's changes are inextricable from the original layout, a fact which only exacerbates the controversy surrounding the palace. Along with the structural alterations, copies of the magnificent frescoes have replaced the originals, which are now a must-see in **Iraklion's Archaeological Museum** (p. 589). Indeed, a visit to Knossos is incomplete without an initial excursion to the museum's collection of objects plundered from the palace. Visiting throngs and the brightly painted walls make the royal complex look like a faintly Disney-esque Minoanland, but the explanatory signs, well-preserved structure, and renowned frescoes make the palace Iraklion's premier attraction.

The gaping space in the middle of the site, the **Central Court,** was the heart of the palace and the arena for the traditional **bull-leaping.** In the back left corner of the court, a collonade hides the **Throne Room,** where the original, preserved limestone seat still sits in splendor, surrounded by paintings of gryphons. A priestess—and not King Minos—probably occupied this famous chair. Opposite the throne room, the Grand Staircase leads down to the **Royal Quarters.** Built into the landscape's rock, this sector comprises the sturdiest part of the palace. Situated two stories below the main court, it survived destructive earthquakes better than other quarters. Don't miss the **Queen's Bathroom,** where over 3000 years ago, she took milk baths while gazing up at elaborate dolphin frescoes. The king had his quarters in the attached **Hall of the Double Axes.** The tangled maze of the palace's layout and the omnipresent sacred symbol of the double axe, known as a *labyrs*, combined to form the present-day word "labyrinth." Walking north from the royal quarters, you'll stumble across the grand **pithoi**—jars so big that, according to legend, Minos's son met a Pooh Bear-esque fate by drowning in one filled with honey. The areas painted red around each window and door were originally made of wood; they cushioned the walls from frequent seismic shock but ultimately facilitated the palace's destruction by fire, following an uncertain disaster. One theory is that a tidal wave caused by a volcanic eruption on Santorini (p. 414) set in motion a chain of events that led to the devastation of Knossos.

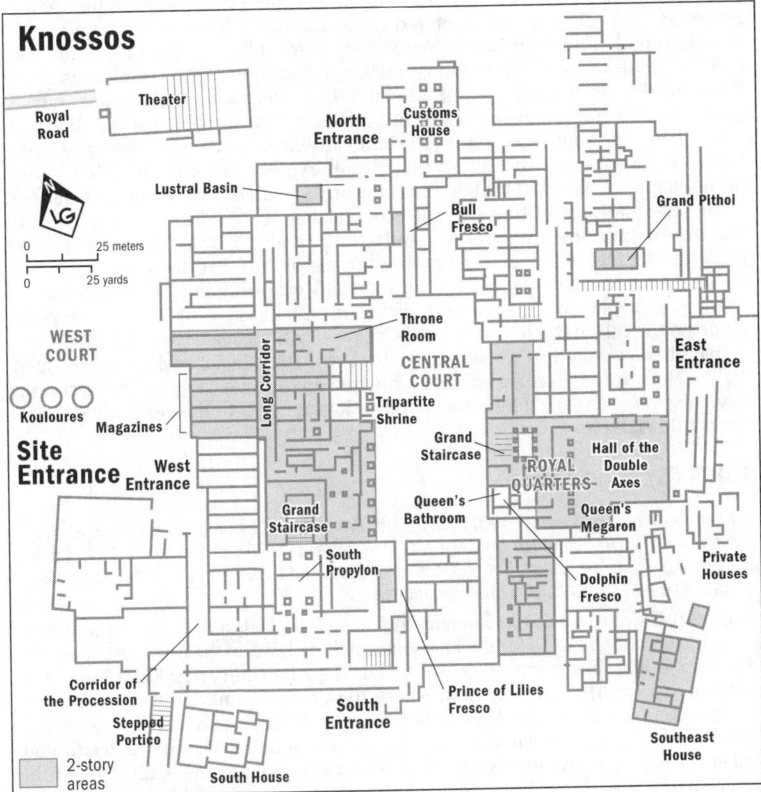

ARHANES Αρχανες

Buses run from Iraklion's Terminal A (30min., 20 per day, €1.30).

A scenic suburb of Iraklion, Arhanes once was used as burial grounds by Minoans and Mycenaeans. Modern Arhanes is characterized by neat pastel houses with clay tile roofs and a thriving grape export industry. A peaceful respite from the harrying Iraklion, Arhanes remains startlingly bereft of tourist menu billboards and harassing hosteliers. The town's official attractions are its **Archaeology Museum** and the sites where the collection originated. To reach the museum from the bus stop, head toward the center of town, keeping an eye out for the tiny sign directing you to the right, and follow the small alley 200m uphill. The one-room collection contains relics from Phourni, Anemospilia, and the Minoan cemetery at Arhanes, as well as photos of finds now in Iraklion's Archaeological Museum (p. 589). The most sensational of the Arhanes Museum's objects is the **bronze dagger** used for human sacrifice, found at the **Shrine of Anemospilia,** a 17th-century BC construction on Mt. Iouktas outside of town. The sacrifices were most likely attempts to appease the gods, perhaps to prevent the kind of earthquake that eventually destroyed the shrine. (Open M,

W 8:30am-3pm. Free.) The museum's artifacts come primarily from the *tholos* graves at the nearby **Minoan Cemetery** (2400-1200 BC), the first un-looted royal burial grounds found on Crete. Inside the stone walls, archaeologists discovered terracotta *pithoi*, sarcophagi, burial jars for babies, and skeletons from Phourni. The excavations supplied concrete evidence of the Minoans' burial practices and contained such morbid finds as a woman buried still looking in her mirror and bodies curled into fetal positions after death in order to conform to the shape of the tiny plots. If you explore the untrammeled paths between graves, you will find unassuming areas containing perfectly preserved chambers, matrices of tunnels, and stone slabs. Because the burial site itself has no explanations and retains only the crumbling graves, a visit to the museum is essential to understanding the history. To see the cemetery after checking out its artifacts, follow the signs left off of Kapetanaki and continue straight until the road becomes a dirt path; the stone walkway on the right leads up the hill to the burial grounds. (Open Tu-Su 8:30am-3pm. Free.)

Red ribbons and bright flowers adorn the town's tiny **Church of the Panagia** (open M, Tu, Th 9am-2pm), on Kapetanaki. Continue up the alleyway past the Archaeology Museum and make a left; the church is located next to the clock tower 500m farther down the large road.

GORTYS Γορτυνα

From Iraklion, take the bus to either Matala or Phaistos and ask the driver to stop at Gortyna (€3.20). You can also take the bus from Mires (€0.75). ☎ *28920 31 144. Open daily 8am-7pm; low season 8am-5pm. €4; students and EU seniors €2; under 18, classicists, fine arts students, and EU students free.*

Formerly the site of a Greco-Roman city, Gortys (or Gortyna), 45km south of Iraklion, is a stimulating stop for the historically minded. When the Romans conquered Crete in 67 BC, Gortys was made its capital. The 7th-century **Basilica of Saint Titus,** Crete's first Christian church, built where 10 saints were martyred in 250 AD, sits at the site's entrance. The Basilica's *berma* (half dome with windows) encompasses a courtyard of fallen columns. Behind the church to the right is the Roman **odeon,** where the famous **Law Code of Gortys** is lodged in the walls. Called the "Queen of Inscriptions," the code is the most important extant source of pre-Hellenistic Greek law. Across a small wooden bridge from the odeon is the **Platanos tree,** under which distinguished brothers Minos (an early Cretan ruler), Sarpidon (a Trojan warrior), and Rodaman (the family under-achiever) were born. The admission covers only these three pieces of the sprawling city; visitors are free to explore the rest of the ruins for free. After you exit this part of the site, re-enter on the other side of the entrance booth to find a small **museum** with 13 sculpted figures. To the left of the museum is a large **statue** of Roman emperor Antoninus Pius. If he appears nondescript, you're onto something—resourceful Romans used to change the statue's head every time a new emperor came to power.

The two main parts of the city lie within close walking distance. The first is an expanse of ruined structures: head 50m toward Iraklion and turn right at the small blue sign. The **Sanctuary and Sacrificial Altar of Pythian Apollo,** which lies in crumbling disarray, is the first stop on the path. To the left is the **Nymphaion,** which was the end of an aqueduct that brought spring water from Zaros. A few steps farther is Gortys's most impressive ruin, the extensive **Praetorium,** which housed the Roman administrator. Built in the 4th century BC, the innovative Praetorium had a water-heating system. The 7th-century BC **acropolis** is along another path, on the hill west of the odeon. To get there, walk 50m down the main road toward Matala from the basilica, take a right after the river, and walk 200m; when you reach the corner of the fence, hike up the road for 30min. Temple ruins and pottery dedicated to Athena Poliouchos ("guardian of the city") lie at the road's end.

ZAROS Ζαρος ☎28940

Zaros's name is known because of its spring water, which is found in supermarkets and kiosks across the country. The city's aquatic bounty is reflected in the gushing watermills, falls, fountains, and aqueducts that run along nearly every road. But the village harbors more than just the renowned spring; surrounded by smoky mountains and stunning gorges, the plethora of trails beginning outside Zaros's walls draws hikers from around the island.

TRANSPORTATION AND PRACTICAL INFORMATION. Zaros's one main road has everything but has **no bank**—you'll find one in nearby Mires. The bus stops at the downhill end of the road, near the **police station** (☎28940 31 210; open daily 8am-10pm). You can also call the **Mires police** (☎28940 22 222 or 28940 23 813). Two **buses** run daily from Zaros to **Iraklion** (1¼hr., €3.80) and **Mires** (40min., €1.20). In an **emergency,** call the hospital in Mires (☎28920 23 312; open 24hr.). Find the **pharmacy** (☎28940 31 386; open M-F 8:30am-2pm and 5-8pm) in Zaros's town center. From the police station, walking to the left at the fork in the road (near the gas station) and up the first driveway to the right gets you to the **medical center** (☎28940 31 206; open M-F 8am-2pm). The town hall (☎28940 31 331; open M-F 7:30am-3pm) is marked by a flag and stands on the right fork, which also goes up to the downtown center. The **post office** (☎28940 31 170; open M-F 7:30am-2pm) is 10m beyond the pharmacy. **Postal code:** 70002.

ACCOMMODATIONS AND FOOD. Lodgings in Zaros are a familial experience. Expect to be invited to family meals or to, at least, join in for a round (or possible four) of *raki*. **Keramos Rent Studios ❷** has a comforting, homey feel. Walk uphill and turn left before the post office; it's 20m down the road on the left. The proprietor, George, makes all the wood furniture by hand in this family-run operation. His wife, Katerina, and her two daughters tend to guests with breakfasts of fresh goat cheese from their farm and homemade Cretan delights such as *pitaraki* (Christmas pastry). Most studios have kitchenettes; all have baths and central heating in winter. (☎28940 31 352; keramos@mir.forthnet.gr. Breakfast included. Singles €25; doubles €30.) **Hariklia Rent Rooms ❷,** a cottage across from the police station, has clean, comfortable rooms with shared baths. Savor the Cretan hospitality at a table beneath the grape arbor while the owner regales you with stories of the German occupation and home photo albums. (☎28940 31 787. Breakfast €3. Singles €15; doubles €30; triples €45.) The most upscale option is **Idi Hotel ❹.** It lies on Votomos Lane, which curves to the right off the main road when walking uphill. It is about 400m up the road and well-marked. Lacking some of the local warmth, it boasts all the desirable amenities: sauna, fitness room, tennis court, indoor and outdoor pool, and A/C. (☎28940 31 301 or 31 302; fax 28940 31 511. Breakfast buffet included. Singles €30-39; doubles €45-60; triples €50-70. MC/V.)

A number of tavernas hide in Votomos's greenery. A 10min. walk from town, about 200m beyond the Idi Hotel on your right, **Petrogiannakis and Ieronimakis's ❷** is known for fish raised on the premises. Savor perfectly cooked trout (€5.50) and salmon (€25 per kg) after touring the fish farm. (☎28940 31 071 or 31 454. Open 9am-midnight.) **Papadaki Rena ❶,** 20m past Keramos Studios, sells sweets and gifts. (☎28940 31 055. *Tulta* cream cake €0.90. Baklava €0.90. Open 8am-10pm.)

SIGHTS AND HIKES. Zaros has been Crete's source of **water** since the days of ancient Gortys. At the water-bottling plant just above town, you can see the fleet of trucks loading bottles to carry to the far reaches of the island and beyond. Most years (including in June 2004), the village celebrates its export in a **water festival,** honoring St. John the Baptist. Zaros also holds an annual **summer festival** with motorcyclists, dancing, and traditional shows every August on the lake.

Hikes and walks through gorges and up to surrounding monasteries are breathtaking; check the map in front of the police station for route suggestions. At the end of the road beyond the Idi Hotel and the Votomos tavernas is the man-made **lake** of Votomos, popular with anglers. The path on the left behind the lake leads to Agios Nikolaos church and Zaros's much-revered, massive **gorge.** The climb is a satisfying daytrip (6hr. round-trip) through the dramatic scenery of the mountainside. Be warned that the way is often poorly marked and the path slippery with loose gravel. Another path up the mountains, starting at the town of Kamares 5km from Zaros, leads to the **Monastery of Vrondisi,** where you'll find impressive frescoes said to be works of El Greco. Every May the annual **festival** and bazaar take place here to commemorate St. Thomas's ascent. Trails through the hills around the monastery lead to a cliffside sanctuary dedicated to saint **Agios Euthymios.** Shepherds keep large bottles of olive oil in the sanctuary and bring hikers into the shrine's three cave chambers to meditate before frescoes of the saint. Yet another mountain road leads to the **Kamares Cave,** where Rhea hid her infant son Zeus from his father's voracious appetite. Archaeologists have made some important finds here, including ceramics and skeletons now in the Iraklion museum.

MATALA Ματαλα ☎28920

Anyone who visited Matala 20 years ago probably has only blurry memories of a hallucinogenic trip—the caves along Matala's seaside cliffs were once full of LSD-tripping psychedelic lovers listening to groovy music. Today's Matala is a far cry from that old hippie city. There's an admission fee and a fence barring access to the caves that countercultural hedonists once called home. Still, the party isn't entirely over: a short hike beyond the main drag lie magnificent beaches full of frolicking nude bathers, gorgeous reminders of those bygone days.

TRANSPORTATION AND PRACTICAL INFORMATION. Matala's single main street, where the bus stops, provides most necessities; when it hits the waterfront, the road bends and becomes a covered market with steps leading down to the waterfront. Before the covered market, a road branches to the left, eventually heading up and over the hill to Red beach. **Buses** go to: **Agia Galini** (45min., 3-6 per day, €2.30); **Iraklion** (1¾hr., 3-6 per day, €5.15); **Mires** (30min., 5-6 per day, €1.80); **Phaistos** (20min., 3-5 per day, €1.30). **Monza Travel,** in the plateia, has a 24 hr. **ATM,** rents **mopeds** (€10-15) and cars (€25-35), and helps with accommodations. (☎28920 45 732 or 45 757; fax 28920 45 763. Open daily 9am-9pm.) Several motorbike rental shops **exchange currency.** The **laundromat** (wash and dry €10) is across from Matala camping and the beach entrance. (☎69737 12 980. Open M-Sa 10am-5pm.) Free **public toilets** are across the street from the post office, on the way to the beach. In an **emergency,** call ☎28920 22 222 for police; dial ☎28920 22 225 or 28920 23 312 for a doctor. The **police, hospital,** and **pharmacy** are in Mires, 17km to the northeast. **Internet** access is available at the **Kafaneio Coffee Shop,** on the right side of the road about 100m past the bus stop. (☎28920 45 460. €3 per hr. Open daily 8am-2am.) The mini-market next to the laundromat also serves as a **post office** (☎28920 45 482; open daily 9am-1am). **Postal code:** 70200.

ACCOMMODATIONS. Though hotels in the town center tend to be pricey, don't try sleeping on the main beach or in the caves—it's illegal, and police do raid them. Instead, look off the main street for reasonable prices in a quieter setting. **Pension Matala View ❷,** 20m down the road to Red beach, offers cool rooms with private baths, balconies, fridges, and a common kitchen facility. (☎28920 45 114. Singles €15-20; doubles €20-30; triples €22-32.) Walk 200m toward Phaistos and follow the blue signs to **Dimitri's Villa ❷.** Its sharp rooms have baths, balconies, fridges, safes, and phones. A modern pool provides a chlorinated escape from the beachside crowds. (☎28920 45 002 or 45 003; www.dimitrisvilla.gr. Singles €17; doubles €19-24; triples €25-30.) **Bungalows Odysseas ❷,** just before Dimitri's, has simple two-room apartments with kitchenettes that can sleep four. (☎28920 45 777. Bungalows €55-65.) If you're set on staying in town, try **Matala Camping ❶,** just off the main road east of the post office, in a slightly wooded grove beside the beach. (☎28920 42 720. Showers available. €4 per person, €3 per small tent.)

FOOD AND ENTERTAINMENT. Only a few restaurants in town cater to budget restraints. On the western end of the beach, at the end of the main road, **Nikos at Plaka ❷** specializes in fresh seafood (☎28920 45 335. Sole with crab €7. Greek staples €3-5. Open Apr.-Oct. daily 11am-11pm. MC/V.) For good souvlaki (€2.50) and gyros (€2), head to **Notos ❶,** between the waterfront and the covered market. (☎28920 45 533. Open daily 10am-2am.) After dinner, the town offers some evening activities. Cluttered with candles and commanding a view of the main plateia, **Kantari** is a popular place to catch world music. (☎28920 45 404. Open daily 9am-late. Beer €1.80; cocktails €4.50.) At the end of the main road and up the stairs to the left, schizophrenic **Tommy's,** also known as Giorgios's, is owned and bartended by spunky bottle-wielding Tommy himself. Creative cocktails, colorful lighting, and an elevated view of the water complement the ice-cold beer. (☎28920 45 722. Open daily noon-late.) Tiny **Kahlua,** near the end of the main road, has intimate indoor seating, a mellow atmosphere, and a little deck with a view of the beach. (☎28920 45 253. Cocktails €5-6. Open daily 8pm-late.)

SIGHTS AND BEACHES. Matala attracts visitors with its three tiers of spectacular **caves** that circle the main beach. As you sit in the damp interior, reflect on the caves' previous occupants—Roman corpses, Nazis searching for British submarines, and songwriter Joni Mitchell. (☎28920 45 5342. Open June-Sept. daily 10am-7pm; Oct.-May 8:30am-3pm. €2.) Matala is blessed with some of Crete's best **beaches,** many of which are spawning grounds for endangered **sea turtles.** Environmentalists run a kiosk providing info on the turtles and their habitat; if you want to support the cause, pick up a purple **Save the Turtles t-shirt** (€10.50). The main beach, a beautiful rounded cove with yellow sand and aquamarine water, captures the "here and now" spirit of Matala with a saying that is painted in block letters on the eastern side of the beach: "Today is life, tomorrow never comes." A 35min. hike past the pension-lined street and over the steep, rough trail will bring you to a magnificent strip of sand known as **Red beach.** Bring hiking shoes, since the path is tough. Once you reach a fence, follow it to the right, and go through the goat herd gate to the shore. Cliffs surround this isolated and utterly picturesque nudist beach. Five kilometers from Matala stretches the long, pebbly **Kommos beach,** dotted with enclaves of nude bathers. The beach is free from development save one taverna. Archaeologists are currently excavating a Minoan site over the beach. To get to it, take the Matala-Iraklion **bus,** ask to be let off at Kommos (€1), and walk a dusty 500m down to the beach. Bring drinking water and an umbrella, as the beach has no shade, leading to speculation that it may take its name from the lobster skin-tone of unprepared visitors and not from its clay-colored sand.

PHAISTOS Φαιστος

Buses from Phaistos go to: Agia Galini (25min., 6 per day, €1.35); Iraklion (1½hr., 8 per day, €4.30); Matala (20min., 4 per day, €1.10); Mires (8 per day, €0.90). ☎*28920 42 315. Open 8am-1pm. €4; students and EU seniors €2; classics students, under 18, and EU students free.*

CRETE

Seated royally on a plateau with magnificent views of the mountains, the ruins of Phaistos are one of the finest reminders of the grandeur of Minoan palaces. Phaistos attracts fewer tourists and has undergone less interpretive renovation than its more famous counterpart, Knossos (p. 591). Four palaces have been discovered on the site: the first, built around 1900 BC, was destroyed by the earthquake that decimated Crete around 1700 BC. The second structure was leveled by a mysterious **cataclysm** in 1450 BC; traces of two even older palaces were detected by an excavation in 1952. Since the excavations, minor reconstruction work has been done on the walls, chambers, and cisterns. Built according to the standard Minoan blueprint, the complex included a great central court surrounded by royal quarters, servant quarters, storerooms, and chambers for state occasions.

Note that there are no explanatory signs or labels in the palace complex; pricey guidebooks are available at the giftshop for €5-6. Visitors enter Phaistos and immediately see the **West Courtyard** and **theater area** at the lower level on their right. On the left lies the intact grand staircase, the largest of its kind in Crete. The Minoans' architectural advancement is evident in the construction of the steps, which were built slightly convex to shed rainwater. Walk past the grand staircase and take the next left to reach the **main hall,** containing a central fenced-off **storeroom,** which housed the massive *pithoi*. At the top of the staircase is the propylaea, consisting of a landing, portico, central column, and well.

On the perimeter of the central court, columns and boxes mark the place where sentries used to stand guard. Beyond and in the direction of the entrance gate, sit the covered **royal apartments,** with a queen's **magaron** and a beautiful lustral basin (covered purifying pool). Just beyond in the **peristyle hall,** the remains of columns can be seen lining the walls. In the opposite direction, northeast of the central court, are the narrow halls of the palace **workshops** as well as the seven-compartmented room where the renowned **Phaistos disc,** now in the Archaeological Museum in Iraklion (p. 589), was discovered.

CRETE

AGIA GALINI Αγια Γαληνη ☎28320

A convenient hub between the east and west sides of the island, Agia Galini is the typical Cretan beach town, cluttered by picturesque strips of sand, hilly streets, and an inundation of package tourists.

TRANSPORTATION AND PRACTICAL INFORMATION. A convenient hub between the east and west sides of the island, Agia Galini is the typical Cretan beach town, cluttered by picturesque strips of sand, hilly streets, and an inundation of package tourists. The town's main street runs down a hill from the bus station to the harbor and contains all of the practical necessities. Off the main drag, more winding streets run so steep that they are often composed of steps rather than pavement; most are covered with restaurants and accommodations. Turn left from the harbor to reach the long beach, where more tavernas cater to dehydrated sunbathers. The **bus station** has service to: **Iraklion** (1½hr., 6-7 per day, €5.50); **Matala** (1hr., 2-5 per day, €2.30); **Phaistos** (30min., 5-6 per day, €1.50); **Rethymno** (1hr., 3-4 per day, €4.20). **Ferries** run to **Preveli** once a day. They leave at 10am and return at 5pm (round-trip €20). Next to the bus station is a **taxi service.** (☎28320 91 486 or 91 9091. Open 24hr.) Next door **Monza Travel** provides tourist info and rents mopeds and cars. (☎28320 91 004. Mopeds €10-20; cars €28-35. Open daily 9am-2pm and 5pm-10pm.) The street is full of **currency exchange** places. Heading downhill from the bus stop you'll pass the **police station** (☎28320 91 210; open 24hr.) and a **pharmacy** (☎28320 91 168; open M-Sa 10am-2pm and 5-9pm). There is **no doctor** in town so health needs must be addressed at the hospital in Rethymno (☎28310 87 100) or at the Spili **health center** (☎28320 22 222). The **laundromat** is around the corner to the right from the Manos Hotel as you head toward the beach. (€7 per load. Open daily 9:30am-2pm and 5-10pm.) **Internet** access is available at **Cafe Alexander,** on the eastern side of the harbor as you head toward the beach. (☎28320 91 226. €4 per hr. Open daily 8am-1am.) The **post office** (☎28320 91 393; open M-F 7:30am-2pm) can be found by the police station and pharmacy. **Postal code:** 74056.

FOOD AND ACCOMMODATIONS. Some pensions are reasonably priced and close to the beach. On the main road, **Phaistos** ❷ offers rooms with private baths. (☎28320 94 352. Doubles €30.) Next door, **Manos** ❷ has rooms with private baths and optional kitchen. (☎28320 91 394. Singles €15-20; doubles €20-30.) With a nice view of the harbor, **Hotel Acteon** ❷ has rooms with A/C and good prices attached. Walk along the harbor and turn up the street opposite a small fountain; make the first right and the hotel is at the top of the stairs. (☎28320 91 208. Singles €20; doubles €25; triples €35. Discount for students.) Large groups or beach lovers should check out **Stochos** ❹ with furnished rooms and kitchenettes, only 10m from the sand. (☎28320 91 433. Doubles and triples €50; apartments for 4-7 €60-90. Breakfast included. AmEx/MC/V.) **Camping Agia Galini No Problem** ❶ has a pool, mini-market, and **taverna** ❷, serving farm-fresh food, cooked over the embers of a traditional wood-stove (Greek salad €3. Pizzas €4. Fish €5 and up.) Call for the free minibus service or walk along the beach and take a left on the dirt path past the wooden footbridge; follow for 50m and the entrance to the campsite will be on your right. (☎28320 91 386 or 91 141; www.interkriti.org/camping/aggalini/a.htm. €4 per person, tents €3, cars €2. Laundry €5. 10% discount for *Let's Go* readers.)

If you're tired of Greek food every night, **Il Piatto** ❷, next to the bus stop provides a welcome gastronomical change of pace with simple, savory Italian dishes and fresh ingredients. (☎28320 91 497. Entrees €4-6. Open Apr.-Oct. daily 7pm-2am.) The small **bakery** ❶ (open daily 8am-9pm), next to Manos, has sweet treats for under €1.50. At night chill at a mellow waterfront bar with the inundation of Germans or check out the happening retro scene at **Juxebox,** just off the harbor across from the fountain, where the bar bridges the gap between indoors and outdoors, allowing sweat-soaked patrons to keep the libations flowing even while savoring ocean breezes. (☎28320 91 154; www.juxebox.snn-gr. Beer €2-5; cocktails €4-6; Happy Hour cocktails €2. Open daily 10pm-7am.)

HERSONISSOS Χερσονησος ☎28970

With 150 bars, discos, and nightclubs around its harbor, as well as mountain villages to the south, Hersonissos (hehr-SON-i-sos) becomes a playground for English and German youngsters every summer. Bungee-jumping, bumper cars, and waterslides clutter the beachfront; Cretan culture is preserved only in a well-polished open-air museum. You don't need to know the Greek word for gin here—your bartender won't know it either.

TRANSPORTATION

There is no **bus** station, just a kiosk at the western perimeter of the town; tickets can be purchased on the **buses,** which serve: **Agios Nikolaos** (1hr., 17-20 per day, €3); **Ierapetra** (2hr., €5); **Iraklion** (45min., 4 per hr., €2.20); **Malia** (20min., 4 per hr., €1); **Sitia** (2½hr., €7.50). A 24hr. **taxi** stand (☎28970 23 723 or 28970 22 098) is by the bus stop on El. Venizelou. There are multiple **rental agencies** on El. Venizelou. **Autotravel,** El. Venizelou 20 (☎28970 22 761), rents cars (€45-60 per day; full insurance and tax included). Motorbikes can be found on every street (€10-20 per day).

ORIENTATION AND PRACTICAL INFORMATION

Hersonissos is just 26km east of Iraklion. The lone main road, **Eleftheriou Venizelou,** has offices, markets, and discos. Perpendicular streets lead either to the beach or the hills. Turning right beyond the Hard Rock Cafe on your way to Iraklion puts you on **Dimokratias,** a less congested stretch of supermarkets and travel agencies.

Tourist Agencies: Mareland Travel has 5 branches, including one at Venizelou 141. (☎28970 24 424; fax 28970 24 150). Open 8:30am-midnight. **Zakros Tours,** Dimokratias 12 (☎28970 22 776; fax 28970 24 464), rents cars, sells boat and plane tickets, **exchanges currency,** locates rooms, and has maps. Open daily 8am-midnight.

Banks: Several on El. Venizelou **exchange currency** and have 24hr. **ATMs. National Bank,** El. Venizelou 106 (☎28970 22 377). Open M-Th 8am-2:30pm, F 8am-2pm.

Public Toilets: Across from the Zakros Tours office on El. Venizelou. Bring your own toilet paper. Free.

Police: Minos 8 (☎28970 22 100 or 22 222).

Tourist Police: Minos 8 (☎28970 21 000). Turn toward the beach before Club 99 as you walk into town from Iraklion.

Medical Services: Cretan Medicare, El. Venizelou 19 (☎28970 25 141, 25 142, or 25 143; fax 28970 21 4064), in the western outskirts of town. Open 24hr.

OTE: Eleftherias 11 (☎28970 22 299). Heading into town from Iraklion, turn right after Pelekis Jewelry and look for the sign on the opposite side of the street. Open M-F 7:30am-2:30pm.

Internet Access: Jackpot Internet Cafe, El. Venizelou 30 (☎28970 22 911), on the right heading away from Iraklion. €3.50 per hr. Open daily 9am-3am. **Net Cafe,** El. Venizelou 109 (☎28970 22 192), is both a video arcade and Internet cafe right across from the National Bank. €3.50 per hr.; printing €0.30 per page. Open daily 10am-2am.

Post Office: ☎28970 22 022. Open M-Sa 7:30am-2pm. **Postal code:** 70014.

CRETE

ACCOMMODATIONS

Hotels line El. Venizelou and offer rooms for €20-55, depending on the season. Tour companies book up most of the rooms in town for the height of the tourist season, so consider making an advance reservation if you visit in late July or August. Walking from the bus kiosk on the main road away from Iraklion, take the seventh left, just past RnB Bar, and you'll arrive at **Selena Pension ❷,** Em. Maragaki 13. Small rooms have private bath and balcony in a convenient, relatively quiet location. (☎28970 25 180. Doubles €25-50.) **Hotel Despina ❷,** Vitsentzou Kornarou 5, is slightly more upscale with a relaxed lounge area and small rooms with private baths and balconies. Some rooms have fridges. (☎28970 22 966. Singles €15-20; doubles €20-45.) To get to **Camping Caravan ❶,** in Limenas, walk or bus 1km east toward Agios Nikolaos to Lychnostatis Museum. The campsite is past the Star beach water park. (☎28970 24 718 or 28970 22 025. Restaurant, bar, and 24hr. free hot water. €4 per person, €2.50 per car. 2-person bungalow €20-35.)

FOOD

The Hersonissos waterfront sports the usual assortment of restaurants serving "traditional Greek food"—often code for inferior pre-packaged facsimiles. A number of sandwich and fast-food places line the main road. The outskirts of town contain the more peaceful and authentic eateries. **Elli Taverna ❶**, Sanoudaki 2, is just after Cretan Medicare and on your left when heading toward Iraklion. There's no menu, so lift the pot lids to choose from a rotating selection of Greek dishes, all cooked by the owner in olive oil that she produces herself. Simple, authentic, and a welcome escape from the tourist fare of the town. (☎28970 24 758. Entrees €5-7. Open noon-midnight.) To reach **Taverna Kavouri ❶**, Archeou Theatrou 9, walk toward Iraklion, turn right before the Hard Rock Cafe onto Peace and Friendship St., and then shuffle left around the bend. Kavouri's 15 outdoor tables under grapevines are a pleasant retreat from the waterfront. For dessert, the *tiganites* (€3.50), doughy fried pancakes drizzled in honey, cinnamon, and sesame seeds, with ice cream, are a tasty option. (☎28970 21 161. Lamb with garlic and lemon €9.20. Moussaka €4.60. Chicken with lemon €4.90. Open daily 5pm-midnight.) **Passage to India ❷**, on Petrakis, just off the beach road and marked by ubiquitous signs, offers traditional Indian dishes, complemented by a continuous run of eccentric Bollywood movies in the background. The spices, imported from London, make for a small, savory meal amongst the boudoir-like drapery of the interior. It's also a good pick for vegetarians. (☎28970 23 776. Chicken *tikka masala* €7.40. Most entrees €5-8. Open daily 6pm-midnight.)

NIGHTLIFE

Hersonissos's mediocre beach confirms it: you've come for the nightlife. Most venues open at dusk and close at dawn, but you'll be lonely at the clubs before 1am. You can't stray a block without encountering yet another bar or disco; they generally charge no cover and sell beers for €3 (cocktails around €6). Many clubs also have "Happy Hour All Night Long," which means with the purchase of one amazingly overpriced drink, you get your second free. **Amnesia Club**, at the western end of town is a right onto Eleftherias when walking toward Iraklion. Sophisticated with fancy light displays, it's one of the hottest clubs in town. The best dancers get a chance to strut their stuff on the elevated platforms; the masses below grind to the throbbing rhythms of the rotating DJs. (☎28970 245 490; www.amnesiaclub.gr. Opens 10pm.) **Status**, Agias Paraskevis 47, flaunts a chic decor defying the tackiness of so many of Hersonissos's clubs. The illuminated, stepped floors are justifiably crowded. (www.status-club.gr. Opens 9pm.) **Camelot Dancing Club**, across from Amnesia, bumps until the wee hours. A diverse crowd crams the dance floor and shakes to international rave. (☎28970 22 734. Open 6am-dawn.) **Tiger Bar**, on the beach road near Filoridon Zotou, has energetic bartenders and a fast spinning DJ to keep the party going. The limited dance space translates to a greater emphasis on the drinks. If you do anything incriminating, the Tiger crew will probably capture it and post your picture, preserving your drunken escapades.

MALIA Μαλια ☎28970

Mediterranean climate and nearby Minoan palace aside, Malia, with its pubs and Guinness taps, comes closer to evoking the pages of *Hello!* magazine than those of Homer or Kazantzakis. Young British tourists, booked months in advance on pre-packaged holidays, leap to Malia's beach and club-crammed streets like salmon in a mating frenzy. Locals refer to these hordes as *barbaroi* and insist that there is more to Malia than simply partying like a rock star. Many visitors only come for a daytrip to see the palace. If you're ready for the mayhem of an overnight stay, however, bring your favorite Manchester United jersey and plenty of euros.

TRANSPORTATION AND PRACTICAL INFORMATION. **Buses,** which drop off on the main road, leave from a number of stops throughout the city for: **Agios Nikolaos** (1½hr., 2 per hr., €2.70); **Iraklion** (1hr., 2-4 per hr., €2.70) via **Hersonissos** (20min., €1). **Taxis** (☎28970 31 777 or 28970 33 900) idle at the intersection of El. Venizelou and the National Bank road. (Available 24hr.) **Altino Travel Service,** across from the old church on the way to the beach, rents **cars** (€45-55) and has maps, travel advice, **currency exchange,** and airline tickets. (☎28970 29 620; fax 28970 33 659. Open daily 9am-10pm.) Walking down the road to the beach, you will stumble upon agencies that rent **motorbikes** (€12-20 per day).

The main road from Iraklion, **Eleftheriou Venizelou,** should satisfy your practical needs with its ATMs, supermarkets, and pharmacies, while the two converging paths to the beach, full of discos and watering holes, pander to the primal. The Old Village (between the main road and the inland hills) has many bars and cheaper, quieter rooms; to reach its center, turn away from the beach onto 25 Martiou, about 100m past the bus stop heading towards Agios Nikolaos. A number of banks on El. Venizelou have 24hr. **ATMs.** The **National Bank** is across from the taxi station. (☎28970 31 833 or 31 152. Open M-Th 8am-2:30pm, F 8am-2pm.) There is **no police station** in Malia; in **emergencies,** dial ☎28970 22 222. There are two 24hr. medical centers: **Medical Emergency of Kriti** (☎28970 31 594), across from the old church, and **Cretan Medicare** (☎28970 31 661). **The Internet Cafe,** Dimokratias 78, is on the right-hand side, about a 10min. walk past Altino Travel Service, on the way to the beach. (☎28970 29 563. €5 per hr.) **Zorba's Net Cafe,** on 25 Maritou, also has Internet access. (☎28970 32 958. €4 per hr.) The **OTE** is outside the Old Village; follow signs to the left 100m down 25 Martiou and continue straight about 1km outside of town. (☎28970 31 299. Open M-F 7:30am-2:30pm.) The **post office** is off El. Venizelou, behind the old church. (☎29870 31 688. Open M-F 7:30am-2pm.) **Postal code:** 70007.

CRETE

ACCOMMODATIONS AND FOOD. Finding reasonably priced rooms in Malia can be a challenge since beachside spots are either booked or pricey. The affordable housing is in the Old Village; wander around the side streets of 25 Martiou to look for a place that suits you. Walking away from the bus drop-off toward Agios Nikolaos, make a right onto 25 Martiou and then a left on Konstantinou to reach **Pension Aspasia ❷,** home to large, spartan rooms with common bath and balcony. Keep an eye out for a small sign and potted plants. (☎28970 31 290. Doubles and triples €25.) **Pension Menios ❷,** one door down from Aspasia, has similarly unadorned rooms. (☎28970 31 361. Singles €20; doubles €20-25; triples €30-35.)

The most popular dishes in Malia are the English breakfast (€2.50), the steak dinner (€7-8), and pizza (€7-8). Ironically (and perhaps fittingly), the most faithful Greek food in Malia—Greek salad (€4.20) and *stifado* (€8)—is prepared by a Dutch chef at **Petros ❷.** Follow the beach road into the Old Village; the restaurant will be on your right. (☎28970 31 887. Open daily 5-11pm.) On the main road, banana vendors sell bunches from the nearby fields (€1.50 per kg). **Milos ❷,** left off of 25 Martiou at the Kipuli Bar, serves hearty meals in a homey, orange-lit interior. (☎28970 33 150. Chicken with oregano and feta €7.80. Greek salad €3.55. Open daily 6pm-1am.)

SIGHTS. Though natives now view Malia as a British outpost incongruously transferred to the northern coast, the town was one of three great cities of Minoan Crete. Malia's **palace** lacks the labyrinthine plan of Knossos and Phaistos, but its importance as the center of Minoan power is undeniable. First built around 1900 BC, the palace was destroyed in 1650 BC, rebuilt on a larger scale, and then destroyed again (by the infamous mysterious cataclysm) around 1450 BC. The **Hall of Columns,** located on the north side of the large central courtyard, with its six columns supporting the roof is a palace highlight. The **loggia,** a raised chamber on the western side, was used for state ceremonies; west of it are the palace's living quarters and archives. Northwest of the loggia and main site is the **Hypostyle Crypt,** possibly a social center for Malia's learned. Signs mark the site well enough to allow you to find these structures. The admission fee includes entrance to a small gallery with a three-dimensional reconstruction of the site and photographs of its excavation. Follow the road to Agios Nikolaos 3km to the east and turn left toward the sea, or walk the same distance on the road that traces the coast. (☎28970 31 597. Open Tu-Su 8:30am-3pm. €4, students and seniors €2, EU students free.)

ENTERTAINMENT. The beach road is home to many of Malia's more popular dance clubs, blaring with pop, house, international, rave, and dance music. Clubs open around 9pm, get really packed by 1am, and stay that way until 4am (weekdays) or 6am (weekends). Locals would not be caught dead partying here. Instead, all venues fill with young Northern European tourists looking to fulfill their hedonistic summer vacation fantasies. Most clubs have no cover but require you to buy a drink as soon as you enter (beer and drinks €3-6). At the intersection of the beach road and the road leading from the old church, **Camelot,** with an outdoor dance floor, bar, and blaring screens, caters to those hoping to party outside in the balmy Mediterranean night. Across the street, **Havana** lets you hop the Atlantic by simply crossing the road. Streaming right out the doors and off the sidewalks, the crowd at **Malibu** blocks traffic, so you'll likely find yourself joining the party. If the club isn't loud enough for your tastes, ask the bartenders to set off some fireworks—they'll happily oblige. Farther along the beach road, the **Newcastle Bar** features a large selection of drinks and an even larger selection of British debauchery. Just beyond, in the direction of the water, **Apollo,** emphasizing trance and techno tunes, has strobe lights, smoke screens, and inebriated patrons gyrating on raised metal platforms in their own versions of a striptease.

At the bars toward the end of the beach road and in the Old Village, there's less dance and more chatter, with recent Hollywood movies and old British comedies playing all day and almost all night for free; **Zorba's Net Cafe** shows everything from music videos and nature documentaries to Woody Allen films. For a quieter night of Dionysian delight, head for the smaller spots in Old Town, where a hybrid Greek-British libation trickles down willing throats every night in open-air pubs, replete with darts and grapevines.

LASITHI PREFECTURE

Lasithi Prefecture doesn't make a great first impression—the heavily touristed towns on the western side seem only outposts of Britain incongruously placed on the coast, and all local culture is lost in a flurry of summertime hedonism and over-ripe sunburns. However, the road east from Iraklion eventually passes over these jam-packed, overpriced resort towns and transports you to the quiet, scenic inland region. The smaller villages that line the eastern edge, sustained not by tourism but by thriving local agriculture, provide welcome relief to the tired traveler, offering stretches of pristine coastline between white villages and olive plains.

AGIOS NIKOLAOS Αγιος Νικολαος ☎24810

Occupying a small peninsula on the northeast edge of Crete, Agios Nikolaos is a nouveau resort town where posh vacationers, mostly from Northern Europe, huff and puff their way up steep, boutique-lined streets, then stop in at a harborside cafe to catch their breath with a cigarette. Catering to beach-obsessed patrons, one-stop holiday-makers, and hikers on their way to more obscure destinations, the town nevertheless provides a relaxing rest stop with its meandering harbor promenades, pedestrian streets, and open-air cafes. There are few bargains in Agios Nikolaos or in its satellite beach towns, but the intense nightlife, diverse array of intriguingly glamorous tourists, and remnants of indigenous Cretan culture make for a lively combination. For release from the tourist scene, retire to the friendly former leper colony of Spinalonga, a few kilometers away by ferry.

TRANSPORTATION

Flights: Olympic Airways Office, Plastira 18 (☎28410 28 929), overlooking the lake. Open M-F 8am-3:30pm. The closest **airports** are in Iraklion and Sitia.

Buses: ☎28410 22 234. Just off Epidemou. To: **Ierapetra** (1hr., 7 per day, €2.50); **Iraklion** (1½hr., 20 per day, €5) via **Malia** and **Hersonissos; Kritsa** (15min., 11 per day, €1); **Sitia** (1½hr., 5-6 per day, €5.50). Buses to **Elounda** (20min., 14-20 per day, €1) and **Plaka** (40min., 7 per day, €1.30) leave across from the tourist office.

Ferries: Nostos Tours, R. Koundourou 30 (☎28410 22 819; fax 28410 25 336), sells tickets for departures all over Crete. Open 8am-9pm. To: **Karpathos** (7hr., 3 per week, €18.80); **Kassos** (6hr., 3 per week, €14.70); **Piraeus** (12hr., 5 per week, €26.80) via **Milos** (7hr., 3 per week, €17.60); **Rhodes** (12hr., 3 per week, €22.10); **Sitia** (1hr., 5 per week, €6.30); **Spinalonga** (2 per day, €15).

Taxis: 24hr. station (☎28410 24 000 or 24 100), at the bridge beside the tourist office. Taxis stand around the corner from the tourist office.

Car and Moped Rental: Shop around A. Koundourou. Car rentals €30-40 per day, motorbikes €15-25.

CRETE

ORIENTATION AND PRACTICAL INFORMATION

Agios Nikolaos is easy to navigate—it's set on a small peninsula, with beaches on three sides and most services, hotels, restaurants, and discos in the center. From the bus station, turn left on **Epimendou,** take the first right on **Paleologou** and follow it all the way down to the harbor. Don't confuse the nepotistic street names: **R. Koundourou, I. Koundourou, S. Koundourou.**

Tourist Office: S. Koundourou 21A (☎28410 22 357 or 28410 24 165; fax 28410 82 534). Cross the bridge at the harbor and take a right to reach the tourist office. Assists with accommodations, sells phone cards and stamps, provides transportation schedules and **maps.** Open Apr.-Nov. 8am-9:30pm.

Banks: Several on 28 Oktovriou have 24hr. **ATMs.** The **National Bank** (☎28410 28 735) on R. Koundourou has **currency exchange.** Open M-Th 8am-2:30pm, F 8am-2pm.

Police: Stavrou 25 (☎28410 22 750). To find the station, walk up E. Stavrou from the harbor, and it will be on the left. Open 24hr.

Tourist Police: Stavrou 25 (☎28410 26 900), in the same building as the police. Regulates hotels, registers complaints, and gives general info. Open 8am-2pm.

Pharmacy: Dr. Theodore Furakis (☎28410 24 011) in Pl. Venizelou. Open M, W-F 8am-2pm and 5:30-9pm.

Medical Care: The **hospital** (☎28410 25 315 or 28410 66 000), is on Paleologou, at the northern end of town. From the lake, walk up Paleologou, 1 block past the Archaeological Museum. For **emergencies,** go to **Cretan Medicare,** Paleologou 20 (☎28410 27 551, 27 552, 27 553, or 27 554; fax 28410 25 423). Open 24hr.

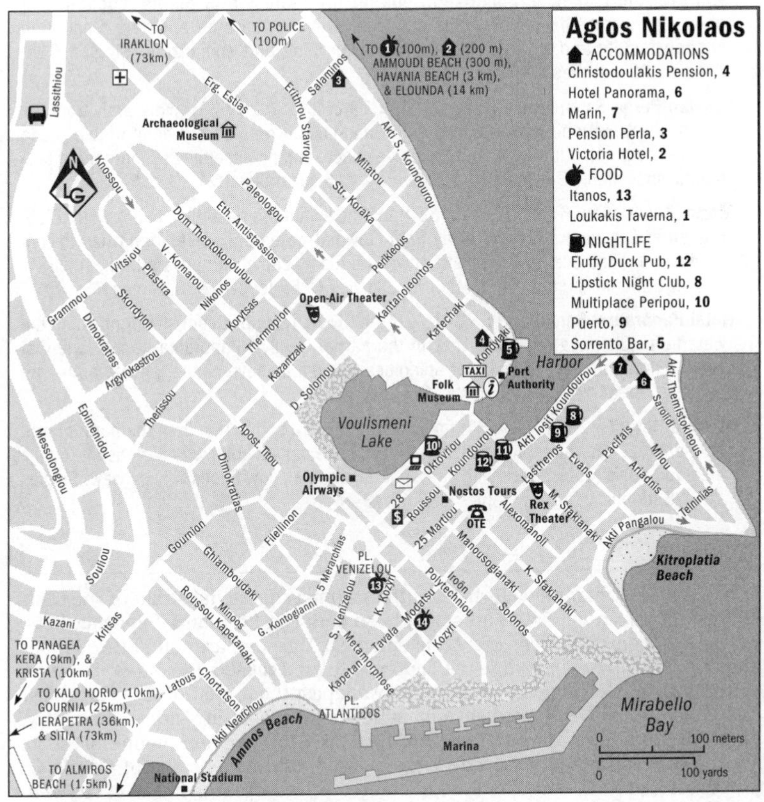

OTE: ☎28410 95 333. On the corner of 25 Martiou and K. Sfakianaki. Open M-F 7:30am-1pm.

Internet Access: Multiplace Peripou, 28 Oktovriou 25 (☎28410 24 876). €4.50 per hr. Sells CDs and books and provides funky music to accompany your web-surfing. Open daily 9:30am-2am. **Du Lac Cafe** (☎28410 26 837), near the post office on 28 Oktovriou. €4.50 per hr., €6 per 2hr. Open daily 9am-2am.

Post Office: 28 Oktovriou 9 (☎28410 22 062). Open M-F 7:30am-2pm. **Postal code:** 72100.

ACCOMMODATIONS

Many larger hotels in Agios Nikolaos fill up months in advance. There are lots of **pensions** offering clean, cheap rooms, but their rooms are also in great demand, so make a reservation. Look for cheaper accommodations inland on the eastern side of the harbor, although some pensions on the western waterfront are also affordable. The tourist office has a bulletin board with many of Agios Nikolaos's pensions and their prices. Prices are generally reduced 20-40% in the low season.

Christodoulakis Pension, Stratigou Koraka 7 (☎28410 22 525). From the tourist office, turn away from the water and turn right onto the street behind the taxi stand, then take the 2nd left onto Stratigou Koraka. The pension, the 2nd building after

CRETE

you turn the corner, is unmarked; look for the profusion of plants. Located just above the water, the bright rooms stay cool with the sea breeze. Offers a common kitchen facility and a large balcony for sunbathing and socializing. Singles €15; doubles €20; triples €30. ❷

Pension Perla, Salaminos 4 (☎28410 23 379 or 28410 26 523). Walk away from the harbor on S. Koundourou and turn onto Salaminos. Cramped but comfortable, Perla features common baths, a TV lounge, fridge space, and an unsettling assortment of taxidermic specimens. Singles €14-15; doubles €15-17; triples €21. ❷

Marin, Koundourou 6 (☎28410 23 830), on the waterfront past the Lipstick Night Club. Hidden in a garden courtyard away from crowded waterfront cafes, Marin has decent rooms in a great location at a good price. The rooms come with private bath, small TV, balcony, and ceiling fan. Open Mar.-Nov. Singles €25; doubles €30; triples €35. ❸

Hotel Panorama, Sarolidi 2 (☎28410 28 890; www.1olympus.com/panorama), on the waterfront. Claiming the "best view in the harbor, really," Panorama has a variety of small rooms with varying levels of amenities (though all have phone, private bath, and balcony). Breakfast €4. Doubles €25-50. ❸

Victoria Hotel (☎28410 22 731; fax 28410 22 266), about 1km from the harbor on S. Koundourou, near Ammoudi beach. A clean, white stucco hotel with a pleasant lounge area and basic rooms, each with bath, phone, and balcony. Prices vary by view. Singles €20-28; doubles €30-37; triples €36-45. ❸

FOOD

While Agios Nikolaos's waterfront suffers from a super-chic strain of the tourist-restaurant virus, tasty and semi-cheap eats can be found. Supermarkets, though concentrated near the Archaeological Museum, are found throughout the city. Cheap creperies line the center of town. **Loukakis Taverna ❷,** S. Koundourou 24 (☎28410 28 022), is a 10min. walk past the tourist office. The oldest taverna in Agios Nikolaos dishes up satisfying meals at low prices in an airy, unpretentious environment. (*Stifado* €6.20. Stuffed green peppers €3.20. Open daily 9am-midnight.) The vine-covered outdoor enclave of **Sarri's ❶,** Kuprou 15, provides an exuberantly colored retreat from the nearby city center. The portions are modest, but the food is flavorful. Lunch specials (€4.50) include soup, *tzatziki*, souvlaki, potatoes, and a glass of wine. To reach Sarri's, start from the harbor bridge, walk up 28 Oktovriou, and turn left onto Kuprou at Pl. Venizelou; it's on the right after one block. (☎28410 28 059. Lamb with lemon €6.50. Stuffed vine leaves €5. Open 8:30am-3pm and 6pm-midnight.) **Itanos ❷** is on Kyprou just off Pl. Venizelou. You'll find hearty food and homemade wine. Preview the day's specialties on the steamer in the back before sitting in the airy interior. (☎28410 35 340. Stuffed eggplant €4. Greek salad €2.50. Open daily 11am-11pm.)

SIGHTS AND BEACHES

Around hilly Agios Nikolaos you'll find a bathtub for goddesses, goat-inhabited archaeological sites, and a haven for cheap shopping.

MARKET. The kaleidoscopic weekly market abounds in inexpensive clothes, cracked cutlery, and sundry items like paintings, knock-off Prada bags, swimming trunks, and underwear. Pick up your picnic goods at the top of the street, where displays of watermelons, tomatoes, farm-fresh cheeses, and Cretan honey jockey for space. *(On Eth. Antistassios, next to the lake. Open W 7am-1pm.)*

MUSEUMS AND ARCHAEOLOGICAL SITES. Head away from the harbor on Paleologou to reach the **Archaeological Museum,** whose extensive collection of artifacts includes Minoan sarcophagi, a well-documented ancient coin collection, and art from the under-represented 7th-century Daedalic period. Two items not to miss: the "phallus-shaped idol" that greets you as you walk in and the strange bowl of knuckle bones in the last room. *(☎28410 24 943. Open Tu-Su 8:30am-3pm. €3; students and seniors €1.50; EU students, classicists, fine arts students, and under 18 free.)* The **Folk Museum,** next to the tourist office, displays tapestries and icons from the 16th-19th centuries. *(☎28410 25 093. Open Su-F 11am-3pm. €3, under 12 free.)* One kilometer before Kritsa on the road from Agios Nikolaos, Crete's Byzantine treasure, the tiny **Panagia Kera,** honors the Assumption of the Virgin in several narrative cycles. A crumbling patchwork of smoky 14th-century paintings adorns the central nave, while the wings bear muted 15th-century Byzantine frescoes. *(Open 8:30am-3pm. €3, students and seniors €1.50.)*

BEACHES. All of Agios Nikolaos's beaches are rated blue flag beaches by the EU, which means they're the cleanest of the clean. The constant sunshine and lack of rain makes them perfect for sunning. Three of the more mediocre beaches are a quick walk from the main harbor, but the farther you venture, the better it gets. Lazy folks sunbathe on the concrete piers that jut out from S. Koundourou, while others head to **Ammos beach** by the National Stadium, **Kitroplatia beach** between Akti Panagou and the marina, or **Ammoudi beach** farther up S. Koundourou away from town. Those with greater aspirations catch the hourly bus to Ierapetra or Sitia and get off at **Almiros beach** (1.5km east of Agios Nikolaos). With the rusting hulk of an old fishing boat adding a picturesque flair to the translucent waters and an island outcropping touting the Greek flag, Almiros is arguably the area's best beach. Just up the hill lies an EU-protected **wildlife reserve.** A river runs through the reserve and gushes water into the sea at Almiros; the hot springs mix with the cold jet for a refreshing hot/cold swim. Sandy **Kalo Horio,** 10km farther, is equally spectacular and slightly less crowded. Take either bus and tell the driver to let you off at the **Kavos Taverna.** Another beautiful, somewhat touristy spot is **Havania beach,** at the Havania stop on the Elounda bus.

NIGHTLIFE AND ENTERTAINMENT

Join the happy throng at the upscale clubs around the harbor on I. Koundourou or S. Koundourou. Or take in a movie at the **open-air theater** on Kazantzakis; from October to April, flicks are also available indoors at the **Rex** theater on Lasthenos (€6).

Puerto (puertobaragnik@hotmail.com), at the corner of A. Koundourou and Evans, caters to a sophisticated set of local hipsters. Sip your Sex on the Beach to sea breezes in the low-slung harbor seating, or retire to the plush stools of the pulsating interior. Frappé €2. Cocktails €6. Open daily 8:30pm-late.

Multiplace Peripou, 28 Oktovriou 25 (☎28410 24 876). After dinner, one-stop entertainment spot with a cafe, Internet access (€4.50 per hr.), and book and music store. From Oct.-May, the club cafe hosts live music twice a week, from Greek traditional to jazz acts. Occasional cover €5-10. Open 9:30am-2am.

Fluffy Duck Pub (☎697 626 3342), just off the harbor on 25 Maritou. Note the namesake hanging jovially from the ceiling. *The* place to party with rowdy Brits and shoot pool. Good selection of beers on tap. Beer €3-4; cocktails €6.50. Open 8pm-4am.

Sorrento Bar (☎28410 24 310), at A. Koundourou on the harbor waterfront. A good place to begin a night of debauchery with dancing bartenders, U2 look-alikes, and lots of booze. Plays a Brit pop/retro mix. Beer €2.50; cocktails €5. Open noon-4am.

Lipstick Night Club (☎28410 22 377), on A. Koundourou at the waterfront; look for a pink neon sign. Join in the frenzy with local kids. Cover €3, including 1 drink. F night free shooters with drinks. Happy Hour 8-10:30pm. Open June-Sept. daily 9pm-late.

FESTIVALS

Every other year (including 2004), the last week of June or the first of July brings **Nautical Week,** when Greek seamen race in the waters around Agios Nikolaos. There's nightly music and dancing around town. Call the tourist office (see above) for details. For more exotic entertainment, the **Feast of All Saints** during the last weekend of June gives tourists and locals alike the chance to visit the forbidden **Island of All Saints,** with its singular church and wild goats. Due to its archaeological and ecological value, visitors are normally banned from the uninhabited island, and the endangered Kri-Kri goats are granted free reign.

DAYTRIP FROM AGIOS NIKOLAOS: SPINALONGA

There are 2 ways to get to Spinalonga: Nostos Tours, in Agios Nikolaos, offers guided boat rides and walking tours of the island (€15). Note that Nostos is the only tour company that offers guided tours on the island; a number of other tour companies offer guiding only on the boat trip. Bring your bathing suit; most boats make 20min. swim stops. If you don't want a guide, you can get there more cheaply by catching one of the frequent buses to Elounda (€1) and taking a ferry from Elounda to Spinalonga (every 30min., 9am-4:30pm; €8). Once you arrive at Spinalonga, it's €2, EU students and children under 12 free.

The most touted—and most disconcerting—excursion in eastern Crete is the trip to Spinalonga Island (Σπιναλογκα). A short distance across the clear sea from Plaka, the island is painted with a dichromatic scheme: robust green brush softens the harsh lines of the orange stone fortifications. This island-wide museum's simple coloring hardly hints at the island's long and bizarre history. In 1204, after purchasing the entire island of Crete, the Venetians destroyed fortresses in Barba Rossa and Agios Nikolaos before investing 75 years building a third, almost impregnable fortress on Spinalonga. When Crete gained independence in 1898, the Greeks were determined to rid the island of all outsiders, including the Turks who had overtaken Spinalonga in 1715. In a kill-two-birds-with-one-island scheme, they established a leper colony there, simultaneously frightening away the Turks and sequestering the infected, who had previously inhabited mountain caves. On October 22, 1903, the first lepers arrived at their new home. In 1957, following the development of an effective treatment for leprosy, the colony closed, and the residents were taken to Athens and cured. Spinalonga had been the last leper colony in Europe. The island was reopened in 1970, leaving 13 years to ensure the absence of bacteria for visitors' safety. Today Spinalonga is a ghost town of crumbling stone facades and hanging door frames, a disintegrating and subtly eerie remnant of the area's madcap history.

When you arrive at the island, you will enter as the lepers did, making a grim, dark procession through **Dante's Gate** and an iron-barred tunnel. Just after the gate, the stone steps to the right lead up to the battlements of the old fortress and a spectacular view of the turquoise Mediterranean. Following the main road leads to the brightly-colored stacks of reconstructed Venetian and Turkish houses that line Agora. For the first nine years of the colony's existence, the lepers were not only poor but also exploited by their corrupt governor. It was only in 1913 that inhabitants began receiving social security payments of one drachma per day. When the government raised these payments to 20 drachmas a day, Greek citizens of the surrounding area protested: 20 drachmas was significantly more than the average worker's pay. The government, however, stood firm. Ever resourceful, Greeks began to provide goods and services to the now comparatively wealthy lepers, making Spinalonga's market street a center of local trade.

At the end of the street is the **Church of Agios Pandelemonis,** founded by the Venetians in 1709 and dedicated to the Roman doctor Pandelemon, the saint of the sick in the Greek Orthodox faith. Stairs lead from the church to the **laundry,** where water was collected into tubs, heated over fires, and used to rinse bandages. The **hospital,** halfway up the hill, is identifiable by its eight-window facade. Its lofty location theoretically allowed the wind to carry away the odor of rotting flesh. Beyond the laundry, steps lead to the sea; to the right of these are the modern concrete **apartment buildings** that housed the lepers. At the bottom of the steps is the original arched entrance to the **fortress.** In front is the **disinfecting room,** where everything from bedsheets to clothing to coins was sterilized. Continuing on the path around the rest of the island, you will find the small orange-roofed **Church of Agios George.** Built in 1661 by the Venetians, this is where lepers took communion. Past this church at the top of the ramp leading back to Dante's Gate, is the cemetery and its 44 graves, left unmarked so they could be reused.

LASITHI PLATEAU Οροπεδιο Λασιθιου

The inland route to Agios Nikolaos evades the jagged northern coastline and traverses the Lasithi Plateau, ringed by steep, crumbling mountains. This flat, fertile plain, where you might very well encounter fields overflowing with magnificent, opium-red poppies, is home to 12 whitewashed villages full of exhausted donkeys and field-tilling farmers. The residents of the region once harnessed the plain's persistent breezes with thousands of wind-powered water pumps; black-and-white pictures of their windmill-strewn fields adorn the walls of travel agencies across the northern coast. Electric pumps have taken over in recent decades, leaving the carpet of defunct mills in a state of romantic rusting decay. Much of modern life has taken the coastal road and bypassed Lasithi, preserving a rural hospitality and tranquility that seem utterly isolated from the urbanity just beyond the sequestering cliffs. All the basics can be found in Tzermiado (Dzermiado on many signs), the capital of Lasithi and the only large village in the plain.

TRANSPORTATION. It's best to visit Lasithi on wheels (with a rental **car** or **moped**). Those who use the infrequent and irregular bus service may find themselves stranded for hours in one town or limited to the few towns within walking distance. If you're coming from **Iraklion,** take the coastal road 8km past Gournes and then turn right on the road to **Kastelli** (not the one on the western coast). After about 6km, the road forks right to Kastelli; stay left, heading toward **Potamies,** pausing to ogle the giant plane tree in the center of the town: it takes 12 men to wrap arms around the trunk. Continuing on through Krassi, the main road winds around mountain ridges, cuts through the ruins of the stone windmills of the Seli Ambelou pass, and finally descends into the Lasithi Plateau. If you're heading from **Malia,** you have two options: to reach the more manageable road, head west along the coastal road and turn left about 3km outside of town at the turn-off for Mochos; this road takes you onto the road that passes through Krassi, described in the directions from Iraklion. Your second option from Malia is to take 25 Martiou out of town and follow the signs. This road is faster than the Mochos route, but it is largely unpopulated and involves even more hairpin turns. **Buses** run to **Iraklion** (2hr., daily, €5). The bus takes about 45min. to make its way around the whole plateau, so you can stop at any town that pleases you.

ORIENTATION AND PRACTICAL INFORMATION. The bus stops at the center of **Tzermiado's** main plateia in front of the Kronio Restaurant. Continuing from Tzermiado 3km around the plateau brings you to **Agios Konstantinos** and then **Agios Giorgios** 1km farther along the way. The town of **Psychro** lies across the plains, 6km from Agios Giorgios. The **Agricultural Bank** in Tzermiado has a **currency exchange** and 24hr. **ATM.** (☎28440 22 390. Open M-Th 8am-2pm, F 8am-1:30pm.) The **tourist police** for Lasithi Plateau are in Agios Nikolaos, but the regular **police station** is in Tzermiado, on the second floor a few doors down from Kronio. (☎28440 22 208. Open 24hr.) The **pharmacy** is 100m from the bus stop along the road to Agios Nikolaos. (☎28440 22 310. Open daily 8am-2pm and 5:30-10pm.) The **OTE** is past the police station. (☎28440 22 299. Open M-F 8:30am-3:10pm.) The **post office** is next door to Kronio. (☎28440 22 248. Open M-F 7:30am-2pm.) **Postal code:** 72052.

ACCOMMODATIONS AND FOOD. In **Tzermiado,** you'll find **Hotel Kourites** ❸ by following the road with the pharmacy and post office beyond the gas station. If no one is at reception, check in at the hotel's other building and taverna farther along the road. The big bedrooms come with baths, balconies, and a small breakfast. Kourites also runs a pension with shared bathrooms. (☎28440 22 194. Singles €25; doubles €40; triples €50; pension doubles €25.) In **Agios Konstantinos,** your only option is **Maria Vlassi Rent Rooms** ❶, behind Maria's embroidery shop on the road from Tzermiado. (☎28440 31 048. Doubles €15.) In **Agios Giorgios,** there are several good choices. **Hotel Maria** ❷, on the opposite side of town, offers a hipper spin on traditional style with newly remodelled rooms sparkling with cleanliness, built-in beds, and immaculate bathrooms; go to Rea Taverna on the main street to request a room. (☎28440 31 774. Singles €20; doubles €25; triples €30.) **Dias Hotel** ❶, on the main road, has limited rooms at bargain prices. With sinks and 24hr. hot water, the rooms are decorated with the friendly owner's handmade crafts. You may find her sewing when you arrive. (☎28440 31 207. Breakfast €3. Singles €10; doubles €20; triples €30. Student discount €1.50 off original price.) Just a few kilometers from Dikteon Cave, **Hotel Dionysos** ❷ has large, modern rooms with private bath and sun-drenched interiors. (☎28440 31 672. Doubles €25; triples €35.)

Most restaurants in Lasithi Plateau are linked to hotels. An exception to the rule is the family-owned **Kronio Restaurant** ❶, the oldest taverna in Lasithi, at the center of Tzermiado. There's more to this place than the hospitable atmosphere and flavorful food (moussaka €4.50; *stifado* €5; Greek salad €3). The corner by Kronio is the perfect spot to watch the bustling tourists buying embroidery and the haggling of locals settling utilities bills. (☎28440 22 375. Open daily 10am-midnight.) The **Kri Kri Taverna** ❶ offers a limited selection of tourist fare amidst the amusingly incongruous ivy-covered walls and a homey fireplace. (☎28440 22 170. Moussaka €4.80. Omelette €3. Open 9am-11pm.) The moussaka (€4.50) and Greek coffee (€0.90) at the **Dikti Taverna** ❶, on the main road in **Agios Konstantinos** is excellent. (☎28440 31 255. Open Apr.-Nov. 7am-7pm.) In **Agios Giorgios,** the only restaurants are attached to hotels. In **Psychro,** the owner of **Taverna O Stavros** ❶, a rest stop on the way to Dikteon, offers a complimentary post-meal *raki* to fortify you for the climb up the cave. (☎28440 31 453. *Tzatziki* €2; beer €2. Open 7am-1am.)

SIGHTS. Agios Giorgios is home to a **folklore museum,** located in a restored 19th-century hut. Next door is the **El. Venizelou Museum,** a hall dedicated to the great former prime minister of Greece, who was born in Hania. (Open Apr.-Oct. 10am-4pm. Admission to both museums €2.50, students €1.50, under 12 free.)

The village of **Psychro** serves as a starting point for exploring **Dikteon Cave,** 1km away. At the turn of the century, archaeologists found hundreds of Minoan artifacts crammed into the cave's ribbed stalactites; many are now at

Iraklion's Archaeological Museum. Sir Arthur Evans, who also dug up Knossos, excavated this spot and, in a blast of misguided enthusiasm, blew apart the entrance. To get there, follow signs from Ag. Giorgios. Local members of the donkey drivers will probably offer to taxi you (€10); the uphill walk is grueling, but it should take less than 1hr. Inside, the massive cave has multiple levels and irregular hanging rock formations. For good luck, throw in your addition to the coin sheets that carpet the pool where the pilgrims leave their offerings. (Open daily 7:30am-4pm. €4, students and seniors €2, EU students and children under 12 free. Parking €2.) For a nice daytrip, take the bus to Psychro, visit Dikteon Cave, and then take the 1½hr. walk across the plain to Tzermiado where you can grab a bite to eat.

The more modest **Kronion Cave,** perched above the plateau, is free from Dikteon's crowds and merits a side trip. Clear signs outside of Tzermiado will direct you toward the 1km route to the grotto, the mythical home of Zeus's parents, Chronos and Rhea. The last stretch is manageable only by foot. Stay on the people path (as opposed to the goat paths) and don't forget a flashlight to view the dripping swirls of stone. The drive to Lasithi is dotted with small, incandescent, white monastaries wedged into the cliffs; watch the sides of the road for signs. Just before the Seli Ambelou pass lies the **Monastery of the Panagia Kera.** Currently under restoration, the monastery has a small church and a magnificent view. (Open 8am-8pm. Donations requested.) Continuing along the road, you will also see a turn-off for the **Vivandi Monastery,** which has impressive ruins.

IERAPETRA Ιεραπετρα ☎28420

Ierapetra (ear-AH-peh-tra) is one of the few vacation towns on Crete that still welcomes more Greeks than foreigners. It's touted as Europe's southernmost city, but this title is difficult to confirm: after a few days in the labyrinthine streets, you won't know which way is south anyway. After centuries of foreign rule by Arabs, Venetians, and Turks, the city's architecture reflects its worldly past, but the laid-back pace of life preserves its small town atmosphere.

CRETE

TRANSPORTATION AND PRACTICAL INFORMATION. Although not a large city, Ierapetra can be difficult to navigate because of its long, maze-like streets. It has three main plateias, connected by three roads running north-south. With your back to the **bus station,** Lasthenous 41 (☎28420 28 237), **Pl. Plastira** will be on your right. Walking straight for a block on **Lasthenous,** which then turns into **Koundouriotou,** brings you to **Pl. Eleftherias,** the central square. Keep walking in the same direction for about 100m to reach another plateia: **Pl. Kanoupaki.** South of it is the Old Town district. **Buses** run to **Iraklion** (6 per day, €7.50) via **Agios Nikolaos** (€2.50) and **Sitia** (6 per day, €4.40). Pick up a **free map** of the city from one of the travel agencies along the waterfront. The **Ierapetra Express office,** Pl. El. Venizelou 25, is conveniently located. (☎28420 28 673 or 28420 22 411. Open M-F 8am-2pm and 5-9pm, Sa 8am-2pm, Su 11am-2pm.) **Radio Taxi** (☎28420 26 600 or 28420 27 350) lines up cars in Pl. Kanoupaki 24hr. **Car** and **moped rental** can be arranged at **Driver's Club,** behind Ierapetra Express. (☎28420 25 583. Cars €35. Open daily 8:30am-2pm and 5:30-9pm.) The **National Bank,** in Pl. Eleftherias next to Ierapetra Express, **exchanges currency** and has a 24hr. **ATM.** (☎28420 28 374. Open M-Th 8am-2:30pm, F 8am-2pm.) The **police station** (☎28420 22 560), in Pl. Kondouriotou, is in the big yellow building on the waterfront. (**Tourist police** in the same building. ☎28430 90 160. Both open 24hr.) The **hospital** is north of the bus station, left off Lasthenous at Kalimerake 6. (☎28420 90 222, 90 223, or 90 224. Open daily 7:30am-2:30pm; 24hr. **emergency** care.) There is a **pharmacy** in Pl. Eleftherias. (☎28420 22 236. Open M-F 8:30am-2pm, also open Tu, Th, F 5:30-9pm.) The **OTE** is at Koraka 25. (☎28420 24 199 or 28420 80 355. Open M-F 7:30am-3pm.) Chic **Polycafe Orpheas,** Koundouriotou 25, just past Pl. Plastira, offers **Internet** access at €6 per hr. (☎28420 80 462. Open M-Sa 9am-11pm.) **Netcafe,** Koundourou 16, a left off of Lasthenous as you head away from the bus station, hooks you up for €3.60 per hr. (☎28420 25 900. Open daily 9am-11pm.) The **post office** is on V. Kornarou, on the western side of the Old Town. (☎28420 22 271. Open M-F 7:30am-2pm.) **Postal code:** 72200.

ACCOMMODATIONS AND FOOD. For the most part Ierapetra makes its beds for upscale tourists, who want only the best after a day snoozing on Chrissi Island. When bargain-hunters land in town, they avoid the mainland and knock on doors in the streets surrounding the bus station. Make a sharp right out of the bus station, and you'll see signs leading to many moderately priced pensions, including sparkling **Cretan Villa ❸,** Lakerda 16. The 205-year-old building's white stucco-walled, brick-floored, high-ceilinged rooms hide a central garden. The owner, a University of Missouri alum, speaks fluent English. All rooms have very clean private baths and satellite TV. (☎28420 28 522 or 28 824; www.cretan-villa.com. A/C €6 extra per night. Singles €28-34; doubles €35-40; triples €40.) Bargains can also be found in the Old Town area. Walk past the taxis down Kyrva to the waterfront and make a right onto Ioanidou after passing the port police. To the right is **Hotel Coral ❷,** Ioanidou 18. It has standard rooms with bathtubs, fridges, televisions, and free luggage storage. (☎28420 22 846 or 28420 28 743. A/C €4 extra per night. Doubles €25; triples €35.) Outdoor enthusiasts can pitch a tent at **Koutsounari ❶,** 7km from Ierapetra on the coastal road to Sitia near the restaurant, bar, and beach. Take the bus to **Sitia** via **Makri Gialo** (20min., every 2hr., €1) and ask to be let off at the campgrounds. (☎28420 61 213. €4.80 per person, €3 per tent, €2.50 per car.)

Most of Ierapetra's waterfront restaurants are identically priced. Piled with enough pastries to make even an ascetic start salivating, **Veterano ❶,** a cafe and dessert bar on the corner of Pl. Eleftherias, also boasts a superior view of the palm-edged main plateia. Sip your cappuccino, spy on the bustling populace, and contemplate a second piece of *kalitsounia* (€0.70), an Ierapetrian sweet cheese tart. (☎28420 23 175. Open daily 7:30am-midnight.) On the waterfront near the Old Town, three restaurants stand out. **Konaki ❷,** Stratigou Samovil 32, allows you to sit on the sands of the Libyan Sea as you indulge in fresh fist. (☎28420 24 422. *Giovetsi* €6. Open 7:30am-1am. AmEx/MC/V.) **Napoleon ❷,** Stratigou Samovil 26, is the oldest restaurant in Ierapetra, open since 1955. The charismatic couple in charge cooks up seasonally priced fish, meats for €5-6, and vegetables for €3-4. (☎28420 22 410. Open M-Sa 11am-midnight. AmEx/MC/V.) The eccentric staff at **Castello ❷,** next door to Napoleon, grill fish (€7-9) and meat (€5) out in the open. The owner's mother makes the appetizers fresh every day. (☎28420 24 424. Open daily 10:30am-1am. AmEx/MC/V.)

SIGHTS. It's hard to imagine that many people come to Ierapetra for the beaches. Although they receive the highest scores for cleanliness, their gravelly texture makes for a harrowing sunbathing experience. Unfortunately Ierapetra's historical sights aren't much to look at either. In the Old Town at Tzami Square, just off Nik. Vassarmidi, a 19th-century **mosque** and a decaying **Ottoman fountain** are covered with Greek graffiti. The 13th-century restored **Venetian fortress** at the southern end of the old harbor, reputedly built by Genoese pirates, is a rather modest sight compared to some of the other fortresses in Crete. (Open Tu-Su 8:30am-3pm. Free.) The **Kyrvia Festival,** held each summer in July and August, features music, dance, and theater performances at the fortress; call the town hall (☎28420 24 115; www.ierapetra.net) for information. Ierapetra's **Archaeological Museum,** at Pl. Kanoupaki across from the taxi stand, has Minoan artifacts from the southern coast and a worthwhile collection of Greek and Roman statues. The sarcophagi in the second room, adorned by hunting scenes, are particularly well-preserved examples of Minoan painting. The collection climaxes with the town's pride and joy, the near-mint condition Persephone Statue in the third room. (☎28420 28 721. Open Tu-Sa 8:30am-3pm. €2, EU students free.)

DAYTRIP FROM IERAPETRA: CHRISSI. Ierapetra's star attraction is Chrissi Island, 15km offshore. Uninhabited and free of stores and crowds, Chrissi is completely flat, adorned by green cedars and surrounded by transparent green sea. Most beaches on the island are spread with very fine sand. Pack a lunch and bring water; there's nothing but a taverna, which tends to be pricey, near the dock. (☎28420 80 244. Stuffed tomatoes €4. Beer and soda €2. Open May-Oct. daily 7am-2am.) **Ferries** depart May through October. daily at 10:30am and 12:30pm, returning at 5 and 6pm, respectively. (€20 round-trip €5 beach chair charge.)

SITIA Σητεια ☎28430

A winding drive on coastal mountain roads from Agios Nikolaos leads to the fishing and port town of Sitia. The tourism industry has made serious inroads into Sitia, but the town maintains a grittiness that goes beyond the frippery of souvenir stands and gift shops. Travelers blend with locals at the harborside tavernas and fishing supplies mix with beach blankets at the local stores. Sitia makes a great base for your exploration of Crete's eastern coast, and it's the most convenient port for departures to Rhodes.

TRANSPORTATION

Flights: The **airport** (☎28430 24 666) connects Sitia to **Athens** (3 per week, in winter 2 per week; €66). Buy tickets at **Olympic Airways,** 4 Septembrou 4 (☎28430 22 270), just off Karamanali to the east of the main plateia. Open M-F 8am-3pm.

Ferries: Dikta Travel, Kornarou 150 (☎28430 25 080 or 25 090). Turn right off of Kapetan Sifti from the main plateia. Open daily 8am-8pm. 3 ferries per week go to: **Kassos** (4hr., €9.20); **Karpathos** (5hr., €15.80); **Rhodes** (12hr., €21.30). 5 per week go to: **Milos** (9hr., €18.80); **Piraeus** (16hr., €26.50) via **Agios Nikolaos** (1½hr., €6.30).

Buses: ☎28430 22 272. Out of town off Venizelou. To: **Agios Nikolaos** (1½hr., 4-6 per day, €5.50); **Ierapetra** (1½hr., 3-5 per day, €4.40); **Iraklion** (3¼hr., 3-5 per day, €10); **Kato Zakros** (1hr., 1-2 per day, €3.50); **Vai** (1hr., 3-5 per day, €2.10).

Taxis: ☎28430 22 700. In Pl. Venizelou. Available 24hr.

Rentals: Porto-Belis Travel, Karamanli 34 (☎28430 22 370; fax 28430 23 830), on the eastern side of the waterfront past the tourist office, rents **cars** (€25-44). Open daily 9am-9pm.

ORIENTATION AND PRACTICAL INFORMATION

Pl. Iroön Polytechniou is central and on the waterfront. With your back to the bus station, exit to the right. Make another right, then a left, and follow **Venizelou.**

Tourist Office: ☎28430 28 300. On the waterfront. From Pl. Polytechniou, head east along the water; the small white building will be on your left. **Maps, currency exchange,** and info on accommodations. Open May-Oct. M-F 9:30am-2:30pm and 5:30-8:30pm.

Banks: National Bank (☎28430 22 250 or 22 218), in Pl. Venizelou. 24hr. **ATM.** Open M-Th 8am-2:30pm, F 8am-2pm.

Tourist Police: Therissou 31 (☎28430 24 200). From the plateia, follow Kapetan Sifi 2 blocks to Mysonos; go left and continue until it becomes Therissou. Open 24hr.

Police: ☎28430 22 266 or 22 259. In same building as tourist police. Open 24hr.

Hospital: ☎28430 24 311. Past the police office off Therissou. Open 24hr.

OTE: Kapetan Sifis 22 (☎28430 28 099). From the main plateia, head inland past the National Bank for 3 blocks. Open M-Sa 7:30am-2:30pm.

Internet Access: Northnet, Venizelou 22 (☎28430 24 985). €5 per hr. Open M-F 8am-4pm and 6-10pm, Sa 9am-2pm.

Post Office: Main **branch,** Dimokritou 8 (☎28430 22 283; fax 28430 25 350). From the plateia on the waterfront, walk inland on Venizelou and go left on Dimokritou; it will be on your right. Open M-F 7:30am-2pm. **Postal code:** 72300.

ACCOMMODATIONS

Many of the hotels and pensions lie behind the western end of the waterfront on Kornarou and Kondilaki. Call ahead for reservations in August. To get to **Rooms to Let Apostolis ❸,** Kazantzakis 27 (☎28430 22 993 or 28430 28 172) from the main plateia, head inland on Kapetan Sifi and turn right onto Fountalidou, then left two blocks farther onto Kazantzakis. Bright granite stairs lead to spacious rooms with private baths and fans. Friendly owners, a basic common kitchen area, and a balconied dining area complete the welcoming atmosphere. (Doubles €27-32; triples €30-42.) To reach **Venus Rooms to Let ❷,** Kondilaki 60 (☎28430 24 307), walk uphill on Kapetan Sifi from the main plateia and make your 1st right after the OTE. Common kitchen facilities, commodious balconies, and high ceilings in a flower-lined home. (Doubles €25, with bath €30; triples €30/€36.) **Hotel Apollon ❸,** Kapetan Sifi 28, about 3 blocks back from the main plateia. Clean, modern rooms provide a variety of amenities including TV, private bath, fridge, and A/C. Lobby area has a breakfast cafe/lounge. (☎28430 22 733 or 28430 28 155; fax 28430 26 598. Breakfast €4. Singles €29-39; doubles €35-44; triples €38-47.)

FOOD

The waterfront offers typical tourist fare to light *bouzouki* strumming. You must sacrifice the water view for more local life at the tavernas on the inland streets.

Cretan House, K. Karamanli 10 (☎28430 25 133). Turn right off the main plateia as you face the water and continue past the tourist office. A relaxed seating area on the waterfront makes for a leisurely meal and an intriguing array of Cretan appetizers spices up the traditional menu. Ask for the "Cretan Viagra" to heat up your night. *Staka* €3.30. Entrees €5-8. Complimentary ouzo or *raki* at the end. Open 9am-1am. MC/V. ❷

Taverna Mixos, V. Kornarou 117 (☎28430 22 416), 1 block up from the main plateia. Dishes out diverse souvlaki, including swordfish-mushroom (€8) and calamari (€5). Another, more chic seating area on the waterfront serves drinks to coffee-sipping, card-playing Cretan youth. In winter live music F-Sa. 20% discount for students. ❷

Mike's Creperie, El. Venizelou 162 (☎28430 23 207), west of the main plateia. Piping hot and wonderfully plump, Mike's crepes defy the typical street-side fare. Go waterside after watching Mike whip up your meal. Crepes €2 and up. Open daily 7pm-2am. ❶

Taverna Kali Kardia, Fountalidou 22 (☎28430 22 249). Walk up Kapetan Sifi and turn left on Fountalidou. Decent food with more local flavor in a laid-back environment. Ask for the *escargots* (€4) and a lesson on how to eat them. Stuffed vine leaves €3. Open 8am-3:30pm and 6pm-2am. ❷

SIGHTS

The modest **fortress** presides over the town from its high hill, offering a panorama for those willing to make the short trek. (Open Tu-Su 8:30am-3pm. Free.) It hosts Sitia's **Kornareia Festival,** running from June to August, with free open-air theater and concerts of traditional and popular Greek music and dancing. Contact the tourist office for details. The **Archaeological Museum,** directly behind the bus station, displays treasures from the rich excavation sites around Sitia, where many prominent sanctuaries and villas were located in Minoan times. It also includes items from the palace complex at Kato Zakros. Be sure to note the Late Minoan Palaikastro *kouros* statuette at the entrance—a small ivory and gold masterpiece with strong Egyptian influences. (☎28430 23 917. Open Tu-Su 8:30am-3pm. €2, students and seniors €1, EU students and under 18 free.) Sitia's **Folk Art Museum** houses traditional 19th-century Cretan items, from carvings to coins, and a collection of fabrics from the early 20th century; walk up Kapetan Sifi from the main plateia and the museum is on the right past the OTE. (☎28430 22 861. Open M-Sa 9:30am-1pm. €2.) The town's long, pebbly **beach** extends 3km east toward Petra. Close to town, the beach is narrowed by a busy roadway, but the road turns inland farther down, leaving an empty expanse of sand.

NIGHTLIFE AND ENTERTAINMENT

People-watching is a favorite Sitian pastime, especially along the row of restaurants and cafes near the moonlit main plateia. A night out begins here at places like **Scala,** El. Venizelou 193 (☎28430 23 010), an ultra-modern bar with late-night DJs that draws a relaxed Greek clientele for ouzo and gossip. (Cocktails €5-6. Open 8am-2am.) Next door, **Morpheus,** El. Venizelou 192, caters to a younger crowd. (Cocktails €6. Open daily 9pm-late.) After midnight everyone heads to **Hot Summer,** on the beach 1km down the road towards Palaikastro; a swimming pool replaces the dance floor. Three fully-stocked, palm frond-capped bars provide the refreshments while the über-chic talk across the pool on their cell phones. (Cocktails €6. Open May-Oct. daily 8am-late.) Around 3am head west 2km out of town to **Planetarium Disco.** One of Crete's largest clubs, Planetarium sports multiple levels, a massive balcony, and chic decor, all overlooking the bay. (☎28430 22 504. Cover €6, includes 1 drink. Open June-Aug. 1am-dawn.)

DAYTRIP FROM SITIA: VAI Βαι

Buses from Sitia to Vai (1hr., 4-6 per day, €2.10) via Palaikastro (€1) stop in the parking lot in front of the beach. Parking: cars €2.50, motorbikes €1. Tourist information booth offers currency exchange. Pay bathrooms (€0.20; €0.50 for shower) are available in the parking lot. First aid at the back of the parking lot. In emergencies, call the police (☎28430 61 129). Chairs on the beach €3.50.

Not long ago, tourists headed east to Vai to get off the beaten path. Today several buses roll into this outpost daily, depositing tourists eager to swim at a smooth, sandy **beach** and rest under the shady fronds of Europe's only indigenous **palm tree forest.** Legend has it the forest sprouted from dropped date seeds Egyptian soldiers littered on their way to war in the 2nd century BC. In the 60s and 70s, Vai became a haven for British bands like Cream and Led Zeppelin, who would camp out, smoke up, and rock out under the palms. Nowadays camping and smoking are prohibited, but rocking out is merely frowned upon. The palm trees have been mostly fenced off except for a small patch in the area immediately next to the beach. For more secluded bathing, face the water and head up and over the hill. Those in search of a more secluded beach experience should go left along the cliff to a perfect stretch of sand. Although camping is forbidden in the park itself, many unfurl sleeping bags in this cove to the south of the palm beach. If sandy pajamas and the possibility of arrest don't appeal to you, rent a room in quiet **Palaikastro** (see below), 8km back toward Sitia. Although there is one **restaurant** and a **snack bar ❶** (small sandwiches €2) in Vai, you're better off packing a picnic or eating in Palaikastro or Sitia. A **watersports center** offers jet-skis (€35 per 15min.; reduced prices for parties of 10 or more), and the **Vai Scuba Diving Club** organizes dives at noon and 3pm. (☎28430 71 543. €50 per session.) Try a banana grown on a local plantation, or buy a bunch from the stand in the parking lot (€2 per kg).

PALAIKASTRO Παλαικαστρο ☎28340

Sitting at the crossroads between major tourist attractions, Palaikastro relishes its gatekeeper status and its role as guardian of the excellent beaches on the periphery of town. The slow pace of life serves as a pleasant contrast to a day's excitement at eastern Crete's more popular sights.

TRANSPORTATION AND PRACTICAL INFORMATION. Palaikastro is a stop on two bus routes, running from Sitia to Vai and Kato Zakros. **Buses** leave from the main plateia for: **Kato Zakros** (30min., 1-2 per day, €2.10); **Sitia** (30min., 3-4 per day, €1.50); **Vai** (15min., 3-4 per day, €0.90). Buy tickets on the bus. For **taxis,** call ☎28430 61 380 or 61 271, or inquire at the tourist office. The village has the bare necessities in its main plateia. **Lion Car Rental,** in the plateia across from the church, rents **cars** for around €25 per day. (☎28430 61 482 or 61 697; fax 28430 61 482. Open 6-9:30pm.) The extremely helpful **tourist information office,** 100m down the road to Sitia on your right, has an **ATM, currency exchange,** accommodations and restaurant info, and **maps** of local trails. (☎28430 61 546; www.photoart.gr/itanos. Open daily 9am-1pm and 6-9pm.) Across the street and a few doors down is the **police station** (☎28430 61 222), one flight upstairs in a building marked by Greek flags and open 24hr. The **pharmacy** is across the street from the tourist office. (☎28430 61 410. Open 8am-2pm and 6-9pm.) A **doctor** (☎28430 61 204) visits the village three times per week, seeing patients in the mayor's building, down the road immediately to the left of the tourist office. The **OTE** (☎28430 61 546) is in the same building as the tourist office. **Internet** access is available at the **Argo Bookstore,** opposite the church's entrance; Argo also has used English-language books. (☎28430 29 640. Internet €1.50 per 20min. Open M-Sa 9am-10pm.)

ACCOMMODATIONS AND FOOD. You can find rooms and hospitality in the home of **Yiannis Perakis ❷.** From the bus, take the right fork of the main road away from Sitia and continue for 200m to Pegasos Taverna. Take the small gravel road to the left immediately before Pegasos, and follow it around a bend to the left. Inquire for rooms at the first door to your left. (☎28430 61 310. Singles €10; doubles €15; triples €20.) On the same path as Yiannis, **Pegasos Rooms ❷,** above Pegasos Taverna, offers balconies, fridges, and private baths. (☎28430 61 479. Doubles €23.50, with A/C €29.50; triples €29.50/€32.50; quints €50.)

For the basics, visit the village's **mini-market ❶,** opposite the church entrance, and **bakery ❶,** 20m down the road to Vai. **Restaurant Mythos ❷,** in the plateia, is a local favorite with good prices. (Moussaka and *stifado* €4-6. Stuffed vine leaves

€2.60. Open daily noon-3pm and 6pm-midnight.) **Hotel Hellas ❶** serves all the standards and has the best view of the plateia. (☎28430 61 455. Greek salad €2.65. Chicken with lemon sauce €4.50. Open daily 8am-1am.) Choose your feast at **Vaios ❶,** a popular family restaurant 300m past Pegasos in the next village, Agathias. (☎28430 61 403. Entrees €2.50-5. Open Apr.-Nov. daily 6pm-midnight.)

BEACHES. If you're looking for activities outside of Palaikastro, take the bus to Kato Zakros and ask the driver to let you off at **Chochlakes.** From this village, follow signs through the valley to the secluded beach of **Karoumes.** Archaeological sights and sequestered beaches abound around Palaikastro; to reach a few of the closer sights, follow the signs along the road east from Palaikastro to the tiny village of **Agathias.** Past Agathias, the road forks: a small, well-marked dirt path to the right lead to the ruins of an ancient Minoan city at **Roussolakos;** the main road continuing to the left leads to **Hiona beach,** the area's most famous sand strip after Vai.

DAYTRIP FROM PALAIKASTRO. Surrounded by steep cliffs, cascading streams, and gushing geysers, and carpeted in wildflowers, the 4km hike through the animate—despite its morbid name—landscapes of the **Valley of Death** leads from the quiet village of **Zakros** to the beach enclave **Kato Zakros.** The ravine, also known as Death's Gorge, is named for the beehive of caves that frames the valley, in which the Minoans buried their dead. Although Samaria is larger, Death's Gorge equals it in beauty and surpasses it in tranquility. The wildlife includes the usual herds of fearless wild goats, as well a selection of snakes and scorpions. Although it's impossible to wander too far astray in a gorge, the path is poorly and sporadically marked with crude red arrows. Bring along plenty of water and trail snacks, good hiking shoes, and long pants to protect against brambles; people with bee allergies may want to proceed with caution because bees are quite common among the bright flowers on the trail. Keep an eye out for **phaskomilo,** a sweet-smelling tea plant with small, fuzzy, green leaves, and onion plants, whose purple flowers are virtually inescapable in the gorge. At the end of the gorge, turn left on the dirt path—and look for the sign that leads you to the coast and the **Minoan Palace** (☎28430 93 105) of Kato Zakros. Destroyed in 1450 BC, the royal rubble extends up a hill and is still undergoing excavation. The palace is thought to have been a center of the Minoan navy. Royalty once bathed in pools near the bottom of the hill, now home to many **turtles.** (☎28430 93 105. Open Tu-Su 8am-3pm, last entrance 2:30pm. €3, students and seniors €2, EU students free.)

Continue along the path away from the palace to Kato Zakros and its wheelchair-accessible beach. The waterfront is largely free from clutter, and the beach is pleasant, if pebbly. Restaurant **Nikos Platanias ❷** has exceptionally friendly, multilingual waiters who serve up fish fresh from the Mediterranean and vegetables from the owner's farm. (☎28430 26 887. Entrees €4-6. Open Apr.-Oct. 8am-midnight. MC/V.) For lodgings head to **George's Villa ❸,** 800m up the road, or inquire at his taverna. George treats his guests to his own good humor in bright, flower-laced villas, with private baths, shady balconies, and fridges, that overlook the sea from a hill just outside of town. (☎28430 26 883. Doubles €25-30; triples €30-35.)

Buses travel from Sitia to Kato Zakros, stopping in Palaikastro and Zakros (1hr., 2 per day, €3.75). Ask the bus driver to drop you at the gorge's entrance; look for the parking lot to your left 2km down the road from Zakros's main plateia. The 11am bus from Sitia allows enough time to hike the gorge, visit the ruins, grab a bite to eat, take a swim, and make the 4pm return bus. Zakros's bus stop is in the main plateia, which also houses a taxi service and police station (☎28430 93 323).

APPENDIX

CLIMATE

The climate varies significantly between regions of Greece, despite the country's relatively small size. Southern islands like Crete and Santorini can be exceedingly hot and dry, while the lush Ionians tend to be cooler and receive significant rainfall. Higher altitude areas (especially in the north) are cooler and snow remains on some mountain tops even in the middle of summer. For the most part, **summer** is sunny, hot, and generally dry. In **winter**, temperatures vacillate around 50°F and snow occasionally falls as far south as Athens. The rainy season spans from October to March.

Avg. Temp. (lo/hi),	JANUARY		APRIL		JULY		OCTOBER	
Precipitation	°F	in.	°F	in.	°F	in.	°F	in.
Athens	55/43	2.5	68/52	0.9	88/72	0.2	73/59	2.0
Thessaloniki	48/34	1.8	66/45	1.6	88/65	0.9	70/51	2.3
Trikala	48/32	3.4	70/46	3.2	95/66	0.8	77/54	3.2
Naxos	59/50	3.6	68/55	0.8	81/72	0.1	75/64	1.8

To convert from degrees Fahrenheit to degrees Celsius, subtract 32 and multiply by 5/9. To convert from Celsius to Fahrenheit, multiply by 9/5 and add 32.

°CELSIUS	-5	0	5	10	15	20	25	30	35	40
°FARENHEIT	23	32	41	50	59	68	77	86	95	104

METRIC CONVERSIONS

1 inch (in.) = 2.54cm	1 centimeter (cm) = 0.39 in.
1 foot (ft.) = 0.30m	1 meter (m) = 3.28 ft.
1 mile (mi.) = 1.61km	1 kilometer (km) = 0.62 mi.
1 ounce (oz.) = 28.35g	1 gram (g) = 0.035 oz.
1 pound (lb.) = 0.454kg	1 kilogram (kg) = 2.202 lb.
1 fluid ounce (fl. oz.) = 29.57ml	1 milliliter (ml) = 0.034 fl. oz.
1 gallon (gal.) = 3.785L	1 liter (L) = 0.264 gal.
1 square mile (sq. mi.) = 2.59km²	1 square kilometer (km²) = 0.386 sq. mi.

TELEPHONE CODES

See **Keeping in Touch** (p. 50) for full information and advice about telephone calls in Greece, including international access.

COUNTRY	CODES	COUNTRY	CODES	COUNTRY	CODES
Australia	61	Greece	30	South Africa	27
Canada	1	Ireland	353	Spain	34
Cyprus	357	Italy	39	Turkey	90
France	33	Japan	81	UK	44
Germany	49	New Zealand	64	US	1

GLOSSARY OF USEFUL TERMS

acropolis a fortified, sacred high place atop a city
adelfos brother
adelfi sister
afto this
aftokinito car
agape love (see *erotas*)
agora the ancient city square and marketplace
alati salt
alithea truth
ammos sand
amphora a two-handled vase for oil or wine storage
angouri cucumber
apse nook beyond the altar of a church
architrave lintel resting on columns and supporting the entablature, below a frieze
arnaki lamb
astinomia police
astra stars
Archaic Period 700-480 BC
Asia Minor Turkey, particularly its formerly Greek Aegean coast
aspro white
atrium Roman house's open interior courtyard
avga eggs
avrio tomorrow
basilica church with a saint's relic (especially holy)
bouleterion meeting place of an ancient city's legislative council
bouzouki pear-shaped stringed instrument
Byzantine Period AD 324-1453
capital decorated top of a column
cella inner sanctum of a classical temple
chrono year (or time in a grandiose sense)
chrysos gold
Classical Period 480-323 BC
Corinthian column ornate column with leaf- or flower-engraved or capital
cornice top of the entablature of a temple
Cyclopian walls massive irregularly cut Minoan and Mycenaean stone walls, so called because only a Cyclops could lift such stones
demos people, citizens
dimarchio town hall
domatia rooms to rent in private homes; rooms to let
Dorian referring to race of invaders of 1100 BC
Doric column cigar-shaped columns with wide fluted shafts, cushion tops (or capitals), and no bases
efimerevon 24hr. pharmacy
eleftheria freedom
elefthero single, free
entablature upper parts of a temple facade, atop columns
epicremeni/os upset, sad, disappointed
erotas erotic love or sex
erotevmeni/os madly in love
etos year
exoteriko international
exedra curved recess in Classical/Byzantine architecture
exonarthex outer vestibule in a Byzantine church
Faneromeni Virgin Revealer
feta soft, white, omnipresent sheep's, goat's, or cow's milk cheese
filaki (accent on la) kiss
filaki (accent on ki) jail
forum Roman marketplace
frappé whipped, frothy frozen coffee drink
frieze illustrated middle part of a temple exterior (in particular, the entablature); see *metopes* and *triglyph*
frourio medieval fortress or castle; often called a kastro
gaidouri donkey
galaktopoleio dairy shop
galaktobouriko cream and phyllo pastry
ghala milk
glika sweets
haroumeno happy
Hellenistic Period 323-46 BC
heroon shrine to a demigod
hora (chora) island capital or main town in an area
hiro carpo nuts, dried fruit
iconostasis screen that displays Byzantine icons
Ionic column slender column topped with twin scrolling spirals and with a fluted base
iperastiko long distance (phone calls, transportation)
kafeneio cafe
kaimaiki specialty ice-cream with *mastika (*gum)
kalamarakia baby squid
kasseri hard yellow cheese
kastro castle or fortifications
Katharevusa uppity, "pure" Greek literary language, taken from ancient Greek
kathemera every day
kathemerino daily
katholikon monastery's main church or chapel
kato hora the lower part of a village
kefalos head
KKE Communist Party of Greece
koini "common" Greek used before the Byzantine era
kore female statue
kotopoulo chicken
kouros male nude statue
KTEL inter-city bus service
ladthi oil
leoforos avenue
leoforeio bus
libation gift of food or liquor to a god
limani port
logariasmo check
loukoumadthes little donuts soaked in honey
magiritsa tripe soup with rice
malaka common obscenity that connotes masturbation
mastika chewing-gum or gum
mavro black
megalo big (opposite of *mikro*)
megaron large hall in a house or palace
meliztani eggplant
meltemi an unusually strong north wind in the Cyclades and Dodecanese
metopes painted or sculpted square block in a Doric frieze that contains scenes with figures; *metopes* are separated by *triglyphs*
mezedes assorted appetizers
mikro small (opposite of *megalo*)
Minoan Period 3000-1250 BC
mitera mother
moni monastery or convent
moro/moraki baby
moschari veal
moustarda mustard
Mycenean Period 1600-1100 BC
naos holy innermost part of a temple or church
narthex vestibule on the west side of a Byzantine church
nave church aisle
neh yes
Neolithic Period 3000-2000 BC
New Democracy conservative party of Greece
nomos Greek province
nosokomeio hospital
odeion semi-circular theater
odos road
ohi no
oktapodhi octopus
oikos house
omphalos belly-button
opa! much-used expression; hey!; oops!; look out!

ouzeri *ouzo* tavern serving *mezedes* and other yummy treats
ouzo high-proof Greek alcohol
omorfia beauty
ora time (hour)
OTE the Greek national telephone company
paleohora old town
palaestra classical gymnasium
Panagia the Virgin Mary
panigiri local festival, often religious
Pantokrator a mosaic or fresco of Christ in a Byzantine church dome
papaki duckling (slang for moped)
pareia a group of friends
PASOK Panhellenic Socialist Movement, liberal party in Greece
pateras father
pedthi child; "ela, pedthia" means "come on, kids"; used to call a *pareia* of any age-
pediment triangualar sculpture decorated space in an ancient temple's facade
peplos mantle worn by ancient Greek women; Athena's nightgown
periptero street kiosk
peristyle colonnade around a building
philos buddy, friend
phyllo pastry
peeima poem
piperi pepper
pithos ceramic storage jar
plateia town square
pleio ferry, ship
polis city-state
portico colonnade or *stoa*
pronaos outer column-lined temple porch
propylaion sanctuary entrance flanked by columns
prytaneion administrative building
psaras fisherman
psari fish
psomi bread
raki Cretan local liquor
retsina sharp white wine
rhyton cup shaped like an animal's head
Roman period 46 BC-AD 324
satyr horned, lascivious follower of Dionysus
simera today
skala port for an inland town
spili, spilia cave, caves
stele a stone slab that marks a tomb
stifado meat and onion stew
stoa in ancient marketplaces, an open portico lined with rows of columns
taverna restaurant or tavern
techni art
tholos Mycenean earth-covered, beehive-shaped tomb
tiri cheese
triglyph part of a Doric frieze comprised of 3 vertical grooves that alternate with *metopes*
trireme ancient ship with 3 sets of oars
tsigara cigarettes
tsipouro mainland bathtub liquor
varka boat
volta evening walk
vouno mountain
voutiro butter
yiayia grandmother
zacharoplasteio sweets shop
zachari sugar

GREEK ALPHABET

The Greek alphabet has 24 letters. In the chart below, the left column gives the name of each letter in Greek, the middle column shows lower case and capital letters, and the right column shows the pronunciation.

LETTER	SYMBOL	PRONUNCIATION	LETTER	SYMBOL	PRONUNCIATION
alpha	α Α	*a* as in father	nu	ν Ν	*n* as in net
beta	β Β	*v* as in velvet	xi	ξ Ξ	*x* as in mix
gamma	γ Γ	*y* as in yo or *g* as in go	omicron	ο Ο	*o* as in row
delta	δ Δ	*th* as in there	pi	π Π	*p* as in peace
epsilon	ε Ε	*e* as in jet	rho	ρ Ρ	*r* as in roll
zeta	ζ Ζ	*z* as in zebra	sigma	σ (ς) Σ	*s* as in sense
eta	η Η	*ee* as in queen	tau	τ Τ	*t* as in tent
theta	θ Θ	*th* as in health	upsilon	υ Υ	*ee* as in green
iota	ι Ι	*ee* as in tree	phi	φ Φ	*f* as in fog
kappa	κ Κ	*k* as in cat	chi	χ Χ	*h* as in horse
lambda	λ Λ	*l* as in land	psi	ψ Ψ	*ps* as in oops
mu	μ Μ	*m* as in moose	omega	ω Ω	*o* as in glow

Greek has a few sounds that are not intuitive for English speakers. For example **gh** marks a muted "g" sound produced from the back of your throat. **Dth** denotes a hard "th" as in thee as opposed to a soft "th" as in three. Delta is most often pronounced with a hard "th." An asterix (*) marks a syllable that can be pronounced either with a diphthong, to rhyme with "pow"—or without, to rhyme with "flow."

Below is a list of challenging double consonants and vowels that do not follow the above letter pronunciations.

SYMBOL	PRONUNCIATION	SYMBOL	PRONUNCIATION
μπ	b as in baby	τζ	j as jockey
ντ	d as in dune	ει	i as in machine
γγ	ng as in English	οι	i as in machine
γκ	g as in god	υι	i as in machine
αυ	ahf/ahv as in off/ improv	ευ	ief/ev as in effort/ever

USEFUL WORDS AND PHRASES

BASICS		
Yes	ναι	NEH
No	οχι	OH-hee
Okay	ενταξει	en-DAH-xee
Please/You're welcome	παρακαλω	pah-rah-kah-LO
Thank you (very much)	ευχαριστω (πολυ)	ef-kah-ree-STO (po-LEE)
Sorry/Pardon me	συγνομη	sigh-NO-mee
Do you speak English?	μιλατε αγγλικα;	mee-LAH-teh ahn-glee-KAH?
I don't speak Greek	Δεν μιλαω ελληνικα	DTHEN mee-LOW* eng-lee-KAH
I don't understand	δεν καταλαβαινω	DTHEN kah-tah-lah-VEH-no
How much does it cost?	ποσο κανει;	PO-so KAH-nee?
Why?	Γιατι;	yah-TEE?
Where? Who? When?	που; πιος; ποτε;	POO? PIOS? POH-teh?
Where is...?	Που ειναι;	poo EE-neh...?
Leave me alone!	ασεμε!	AH-se-me!
Help!	Βοητηεια!	vo-EE-tee-ah!
I am ill	Ειμαι αρρϖστος	EE-meh AH-rose-tose
Darling	λατρεια	lah-TREE-ah
Maybe; I'm thinking about it	το σκεπτομαι	tow SKEP-to-meh
It does (not) matter	(δεν) πειραζει	(DTHEN) peer-AH-zee
I love you	Σ'αγαπαω	sah-gah-POW*
I miss you	Μου λειπεις	moo LEE-pees
I want you	Σε θελϖ	seh THEH-lo

GREETINGS		
Good morning/Good day	καλημερα	kah-lee-MEH-rah
Good evening	καλησπερα	kah-lee-SPEH-rah
Good night	καληνυχτα	kah-lee-NEE-ktah
Hello/Goodbye (polite, plural)	γεια σας	YAH-sahs
Hello/Goodbye (familiar)	γεια σου	YAH-soo
Mr./Sir	κυριος	KEE-ree-os
Ms./Madam	κυρια	kee-REE-ah
What is your name?	Πως σε λενε;	po seh-LEH-neh?
My name is ...	Με λενε	meh LEH-neh ...

TRANSPORTATION		
Where are you going?	Που πας;	POO PAHS?
I'm going to...	Πηγαινω σε	pee-YEH-no seh...
When do we leave?	Τι ωρα φευγουμε;	tee O-rah FEV-goo-meh?
stop (as a noun)	σταση	STAH-see
I need a ticket	Χρειαζομαι εισιτηριο	kree-AH-zo-meh ee-see-TEE-ree-o
here, there	εδω, εκει	eh-DTHO, eh-KEE
left	αριστερα	ah-rees-teh-RAH
right	δεξια	dthe-XYAH
I am lost	χαθηκα	HA-thee-ka
airplane	αεροπλανο	ah-eh-ro-PLAH-no
passport	διαβατηριο	dthya-vah-TEE-rio
port	λιμανι	lee-MAH-nee
bus	λεωφορειο	leh-o-fo-REE-o
ferry	πλοιο	PLEE-o
suitcase	βαλιτσα	vah-LEE-tsah
ticket	εισιτηριο	ee-see-TEE-ree-o
train	τραινο	TREH-no
taxi	ταξι	tah-XEE
How much will the trip cost?	Ποσο θα κανει ο δρομος;	PO-so THA KAH-nee O DRO-mose?
Start the meter!	Αρχιστε το μετρητη!	ar-HEE-steh TO me-tree-TEE!

TIME		
What time is it?	Τι ωρα ειναι;	TEE O-rah EE-neh?
Monday	Δευτερα	dtheh-FTEH-ra
Tuesday	Τριτη	TREE-tee
Wednesday	Τεταπτη	TEH-tar-tee
Thursday	Πεμπτη	PEM-ptee
Friday	Παρασκευι	pah-rah-skeh-VEE
Saturday	Σαββατο	SAH-vah-to
Sunday	Κυριακη	kee-ree-ah-KEE
weekend	Σαββατοκυριακο	sah-vah-to-KEE-rya-ko
yesterday	χτες	KTAYS
today	σημερα	SEE-mer-a
tomorrow	αυριο	AV-ree-o
morning	πρωι	pro-EE
evening	βραδυ	VRAH-dthee

SIGNS		
bank	τραπεζα	TRAH-peh-zah
church	εκκλησια	eh-klee-SEE-ah
doctor	γιατρος	yah-TROSE
hospital	νοσοκομειο	no-so-ko-MEE-o
hotel	ξενοδοχειο	xhe-no-dtho-HEE-o
market	αγορα	ah-go-RAH
museum	μουσειο	moo-SEE-o

pharmacy	φαρμακειο	fahr-mah-KEE-o
police	αστυνομια	as-tee-no-MEE-a
post office	ταχυδρομειο	ta-xee-dthro-MEE-o
room	δϖματιο	dtho-MAH-tee-o
toilet	τουαλετα, λουτρο	twa-LE-ta, loo-TROW
open, closed	ανοικτο, κλειστο	ah-nee-KTO, klee-STO

COMMERCE

I need...	χρειαζομαι...	kree-AH-zo-meh...
I want...	θελω...	THEH-lo...
I would like ...	Θα ηθελα...	THAH EE-the-lah...
I will buy this one	Θα αγοραζω αυτο	THAH ah-go-RAH-zo ahf-TOE
Do you have...?	Μηπϖς εχετε...;	mee-POSE EK-he-teh...?
good	καλο	kah-LO
cheap	φτηνο	ftee-NO
expensive	ακριβο	ah-kree-VO
Can I see a room?	Μπορω να δω ενα δωματιο;	bo-ROE NAH DHO E-nah dtho-MAH-tee-o?

FOOD

restaurant	εστιατοριο	es-tee-ah-TO-ree-o
casual restaurant	ταβερνα	ta-VEHR-na
water	νερο	ne-RO
nuts	καρυδια	kah-REE-dthya
egg-lemon soup or sauce	αβγολεμονο	ahv-go-LEH-meh-no
large stuffed grape leaves (with rice and/or meat)	δολμαδες	dthol-MAH-dthes
small cold stuffed grape leaves	δολμαδακια	dthol-mah-DTHAH-kya
phyllo-cheese pie	τυροπιτα	tee-ROE-pee-tah
assorted appetizers	μεζεδες/μεζεδακια	meh-ZEH-dthes/ meh-zeh-DTHAH-kya
Greek meatballs	κεφτες	kef-TES
lasagna-like dish with egg-plant and meat	μουσακας	moo-sah-KAHS
meat (usually lamb) on a skewer	σουβλακι	soo-VLAH-kee
pita-wrapped meat sandwich	γυρο	yee-ROE
coffee with a little milk and sugar	καφες μετριος	kah-FES MET-ree-os
phyllo, custard, and honey pastry	γαλατομπουρικο	ghah-lah-to-BOO-ree-ko
ice cream	παγϖτο	pah-yo-TOE
phyllo, nut, and honey pastry	μπακλαβας	bah-klah-VAHS
Cheers!	Γεια μας!	YAH MAHS!
I am allergic to...	Ειμαι αλλεργικος σε...	EE-may ah-lehr-gee-KOS SEH...
Does this have meat?	Εχει κρεα αυτο εδω;	EK-hee KRAY-a auf-TO e-DTHO?
The bill, please	Ο λογαριασμος, παρακαλϖ	OH lo-gah-ree-yah-SMOS, pah-rah-kah-LOW

APPENDIX

NUMBERS		
zero	μηδεν	mee-DTHEN
one	ενα	Eh-nah
two	δυο	DTHEE-o
three	τρια	TREE-ah
four	τεσσερα	TES-ser-ah
five	πεντε	PEN-dheh
six	εξι	Eh-xee
seven	επτα	ep-TAH
eight	οκτω	okh-TO
nine	εννια	en-YAH
ten	δεκα	DHEH-kah
eleven	ενδεκα	EN-dheh-kah
twelve	δωδεκα	DTHO-dheh-kah
thirteen	δεκα–τρια	dthe-kah-TREE-ah
fourteen	δεκα–τεσσερα	dthe-kah-TES-ser-ah
fifteen	δεκα–πεντε	dthe-ka-PEN-dheh
sixteen	δεκα–εξι	dthe-kah-EH-xee
seventeen	δεκα–επτα	dthe-kah-ep-TAH
eighteen	δεκα–οκτω	dthe-kah-okh-TO
nineteen	δεκα–εννια	dthe-kah-en-YAH
twenty	εικοσι	EE-ko-see
thirty	τριαντα	tree-AH-ndah
forty	σαραντα	sa-RAH-ndah
fifty	πενηντα	peh-NEE-ndah
sixty	εξηντα	eh-XEE-ndah
seventy	εβδομηντα	ev-dho-MEEN-dah
eighty	ογδοντα	og-DHON-dah
ninety	ενενηντα	eh-NEE-ndah
hundred	εκατο	eh-kah-TO
thousand(s)	χιλια(δες)	hil-YAH(-dhes)
million	εκατομμυριο	eka-to-MEE-ree-o

CYPRUS ESSENTIALS

From the ancient temples and Roman mosaics scattered on its shores to the Green Line that runs through its capital city, Cyprus is an island of ancient harmonies and modern tensions. After enduring a succession of conquerors that reads like a Who's Who list of historical peoples (the Phoenicians, Greeks, Persians, Ptolemies, Romans, Arabs, Crusaders, Ottomans, and Britons have all passed through), the island now exists independently, though uneasily. Contrasting landscapes—sandy beaches, cool Troodos mountain air, developing industrial cities—mean that a change of pace is just a short bus ride away. Times are changing, too: flashy signs aimed at tourists have replaced the scrawled graffiti that once proclaimed the unification of Cyprus, yet conversations with elder Cypriots can yield nostalgic ruminations well worth a night at a small *kafeneion*. Although visiting Cyprus can be expensive, more and more tourists seem convinced that the trip is worthwhile.

PHONE HOME The country code for Cyprus is **357.** The international access code for Turkey is **011.**

GETTING THERE

Cyprus lies 64km from Turkey, 160km from Israel and Lebanon, and 480km from the nearest Greek island. **The Republic of Cyprus** (Southern Cyprus) is accessible from Greece and other European and Middle Eastern countries by airplane or ferry. There are two international airports—in **Larnaka** and **Paphos.** Cyprus is accessible by plane on **Olympic Airways** (US ☎800-223-1226; Cyprus ☎24 627 950; www.olympic-airways.gr), **Cyprus Airways** (US ☎212-714-2190; Cyprus ☎22 443 054; www.cyprusair.com.cy), and many other major airlines. Roundtrip fares from Athens to Larnaka cost about US$145 (for more information on finding flights, see **Essentials,** p. 52).

ENTRANCE REQUIREMENTS. Tourists with valid passports from Australia, Canada, Great Britain, Ireland, New Zealand, and the US do not need a **visa** to enter Southern Cyprus for stays of up to 90 days; South Africans can stay without visas for up to 30 days. Tourists wishing to stay longer should probably leave Cyprus and reenter.

TEAR DOWN THAT WALL. On April 23, 2003, Turkish officials lifted restrictions on border crossings between Northern and Southern Cyprus. People on both sides flooded the border in order to visit places off-limits to them for almost 30 years. Serious talks between the Turkish North and the Greek South have been ongoing since the country received EU approval to join with the other nine countries in 2004.

CONSULATES AND EMBASSIES

CYPRIOT EMBASSIES

Australia: 30 Beale Crs., Deakin, Canberra, ACT 2600 (☎6281 0834; fax 2810 860).

Canada: 365 Bloor St. E., Suite 1010, Box #43, Toronto, ON M4W 3L4 (☎416-944-0998; fax 944-9149).

Greece: 16 Herodotou, Athens (☎210 723 2727; fax 210 453 6373).

UK: 93 Park St., London W1k 7ET (☎020 7499 8272; fax 491 06 91).

US: 2211 R St. NW, Washington, D.C. 20008 (☎202-462-5772; fax 483-6710).

FOREIGN EMBASSIES IN CYPRUS (LEFKOSIA)

Australia: High Commission, Annis Comninis 4 (☎22 753 001; fax 22 766 486), 500m east of Pl. Eleftherias off Stasinou. Open M-F 7:30am-noon, 12:30-3:15pm.

Canada: Lambousa 1 (☎22 775 508; fax 22 779 905).

Greece: Lordou Vyronos 8 (☎22 441 880; fax 22 473 990). Open M-F 9am-noon.

UK: High Commission, P.O. Box 1978 Alexander Pallis (☎22 861 100 or 22 861 342; fax 22 861 150). Open M and W-F 7:30am-2pm, Tu 7:30am-1pm and 2-5:30pm.

US: P.O. Box 4536 Metochiou and Ploutarchou, Engomi (☎22 776 400; fax 22 720 944). Open M-F 8am-5pm, except for US and Cyprus holidays.

TURKEY ESSENTIALS

The Turkish Aegean coast is full of chill beach towns, beautiful mosques, and ancient Greek ruins. Daytrips to Turkey are cheap and easy from several Greek islands, including Samos (p. 481), Chios (p. 487), and Kos (p. 530). For a daytrip, catch a ferry to the Aegean coast from a nearby island. Not every daytrip is accessible by direct ferry, however; if your destination is Çanakkale, Eceabat, İzmir, Ephesus (Efes), or Selçuk, you'll need to head to Bodrum, Çeşme, or Kuşadası and catch a bus to your destination. For travelers headed to Istanbul or the Aegean overland, go through Alexandroupoli. For more information on transportation, accommodations, and sites, check out *Let's Go: Turkey*. Prices for goods and services in Turkey are listed throughout in US dollars, as the Turkish lira is very unstable. Information about places within Turkey was last updated in July 2001.

PRACTICAL INFORMATION

PHONE HOME The country code for Turkey is **90.** The international access code for Turkey is **011.**

Buses: Run from Alexandroupoli to **Ferres** (30min., €1.80), a €10 taxi ride to the border with Turkey, and to **Kipi** (45min.; 5 per day, 6:50am-7:30pm; €2.60), a €2 ride. Crossing on foot is not permitted. Many take taxis (US$35) to **Keşan, Turkey.** From the city's **bus station,** many buses leave for **Çanakkale, Bergama,** and **Istanbul.** From Alexandroupoli, buses also run to **Kastanies,** the northern border crossing with Turkey, from where travelers are allowed to travel on foot across the Turkish border. **Edirne, Turkey,** a large city with frequent buses running to Istanbul, is 2km from here.

Ferries: Boats run from **Samos, Chios,** and **Kos** to the Turkish Aegean coast.

Samos: From Samos Town (Vathy), 5 per week to **Kuşadası** (1¼hr.; €40 round-trip, €9.13 Greek port tax).

Chios: From Chios Town daily to **Çeşme** (8:30am, round-trip €40).

Kos: From Kos Town daily in the morning to **Bodrum** (€30-40 round-trip).

Visas: To enter Turkey, citizens of **Australia, Canada, Ireland, the UK,** and **the US** need a visa. A visa costs US$100. Citizens of **New Zealand** and **South Africa** do not need visas to enter Turkey. New Zealanders may stay for up to 3 months with a valid passport, South Africans for up to 1 month. Visas must be purchased with foreign currency. For more information consult www.turkey.org.

Tourist Offices: Offer aid with everything from directions to transportation to accommodations. **Selçuk:** 35 Agora Çarşısı (☎232 892 63 45; fax 232 892 69 45). **Bodrum:** 48 Barib Meydanı (☎252 316 10 91; fax 252 316 76 94). **Çeşme:** 8 İskele Meydanı (☎/fax 232 712 66 53; open 8:30am-5:30pm; also open in summer Sa-Su 9am-5pm). **İzmir:** 1/1D Gazi Osman Paşa (☎232 445 73 90; fax 232 489 82 84; open 8:30am-6pm).

Transportation in Turkey: Buses run up and down the Aegean coast. **Selçuk** is reachable by bus from **Bodrum** (3hr.; 1 per hr., 2am-6pm; US$8) or **İzmir** (take a Bodrum- or Kuşadası-bound bus and ask to be let off at Selçuk; 1hr., US$2). **Mini-buses** run between Kuşadası and Selçuk (20min.; every 15min. May-Sept. 6:30am-11:30pm, Oct.-Apr. 6:30am-8:30pm; US$0.80). The Selçuk *otogar* (station) is at the intersection of Şahabettin Dede and Atatürk. To get to **Ephesus** (Efes), take a taxi (US$4) or walk (3km, 25min.) from Selçuk. A bus ride there and guided tour can be included in your ferry trip from Samos for €20. **Bodrum** is very well connected to all major cities in western Turkey by bus. From Selçuk, a bus runs to **Bodrum** (3hr.; 1 per hr., 8:15am-1:15am). From İzmir, there is also a bus to **Bodrum** (4hr.; 1 per hr., 4am-7pm; US$7).

The Bodrum *otogar* is on Çevat Şakir. Buses run between **Çeşme** and **İzmir** (1½hr.; every 20min., 6am-10pm; US$2). From İzmir, you can hop a bus to wherever you want to go. The **Çeşme** *otogar* is at the corner of A. Menderes and Çevre Yolu.

SOUTHEASTERN TURKEY. The US State Department urges travelers to exercise caution in the southeastern parts of Turkey. As a result of the recent military operations in Iraq, a significant military buildup has led to tightened security and an increase in security checkpoints throughout the region. Officials also advise visitors to travel only on major highways and only during daylight hours. All travelers should be prepared to present proper identification and required passports and visas at any time.

EMERGENCY NUMBERS	Police: ☎155	Ambulance: ☎112
	Fire: ☎110	Gendarme: ☎156

INDEX

A

B

C

G

H

I

N

O

T

MAP INDEX

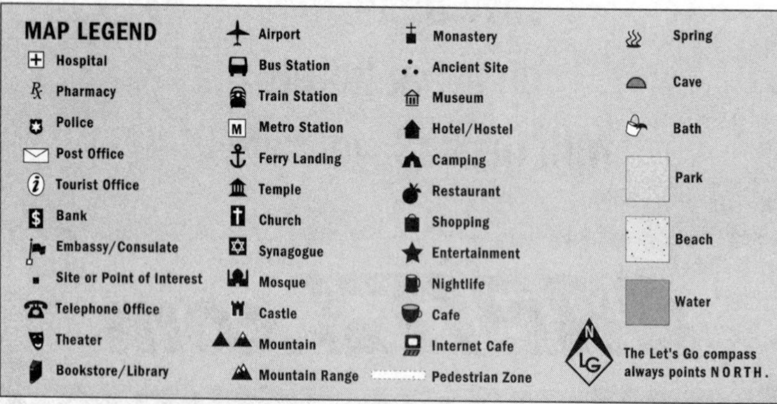

MAP LEGEND
Hospital
Pharmacy
Police
Post Office
Tourist Office
Bank
Embassy/Consulate
Site or Point of Interest
Telephone Office
Theater
Bookstore/Library
Airport
Bus Station
Train Station
Metro Station
Ferry Landing
Temple
Church
Synagogue
Mosque
Castle
Mountain
Mountain Range
Monastery
Ancient Site
Museum
Hotel/Hostel
Camping
Restaurant
Shopping
Entertainment
Nightlife
Cafe
Internet Cafe
Pedestrian Zone
Spring
Cave
Bath
Park
Beach
Water
The Let's Go compass always points NORTH.